# A BIBLIOGRA

# CRICKET

COMPILED BY

## E.W. PADWICK

SECOND EDITION
REVISED AND ENLARGED TO THE END OF 1979

THE LIBRARY ASSOCIATION
London
in association with
J.W. McKenzie (Bookseller)
on behalf of
The Cricket Society

© E.W. Padwick and The Library Association.
Published by Library Association Publishing Limited,
7 Ridgmount Street, London WC1E 7AE.

Phototypeset by Input Typesetting Ltd, London
and printed and bound in Great Britain
by Redwood Burn Ltd, Trowbridge

First published in 1977
Second edition 1984

British Library Cataloguing in Publication Data

Padwick, E. W.
A bibliography of cricket.—2nd ed.,
rev. and enl.
1. Cricket—Bibliography
I. Title    II. Library Association
016.79635'8        Z7514.c7

IBSN 0 85365 902 8

Designed by Geoff Green

FRONTISPIECE: The title-page of the first issue (1864) of "Wisden" (no. 1052)

# CONTENTS

To the memory of H. S. Altham

# PREFACE
## TO FIRST EDITION

Many people have contributed at various times to this Bibliography. The initial suggestion was embraced in 1946 by Antony Weigall, founder of The Cricket Society (then known as the Society of Cricket Statisticians), the work begun by Jim Coldham and subsequently taken over by J.P. Everitt in 1953. The great bulk of book titles was however amassed by Geoffrey Whitelock between 1955 and 1963, after which The Cricket Society approached the Library Association with a view to publication. Mr. Reynolds, then Librarian of Finchley Public Libraries, undertook to check through the accumulated material, to construct entries of an acceptable bibliographical standard and to arrange them in a logical order. With the help of the Society's Bibliographical Officer, Michael Pearce, who supplied additional references, and a number of enthusiastic librarian volunteers up and down the country who proceeded to verify the accuracy of the bibliographical information, the work went forward until Mr. Reynolds' untimely death in 1968. The Bibliography was then left in abeyance until I was asked to take up the task by the Library Association in 1970.

A decision had to be made on how comprehensive or selective the Bibliography should be. Although the initial impulse was to select, it was eventually decided to meet the wishes of The Cricket Society and make the work as comprehensive as possible. This, with some intentional omissions, I have tried to achieve, but no-one is more conscious than I am that comprehensiveness is a vain ideal. It might have been possible in A. D. Taylor's day, even though he did not have the advantage of the bibliographical apparatus now available to a compiler, but since then cricket publications have so proliferated that the time when a complete bibliography of cricket could be compiled has long since passed. Perhaps the only person who might have achieved this after Taylor was F.S. Ashley-Cooper towards the end of the 1920's, but, although his cricket writings were many and varied, he never undertook a bibliography. His wisdom in this is not to be doubted.

With certain exceptions listed in the "Explanatory Notes", the present work includes separately published books, pamphlets, brochures, yearbooks and periodicals on cricket together with entries for books known to include passages of cricket interest, culled from catalogues, bibliographies, libraries and collections in this country. I have distinguished items I have examined from those not seen, although many of the latter have been checked against catalogues and bibliographies. A minority, some with incomplete entries, stand with details as supplied by various collectors and librarians. It is hoped that readers able to complete or correct these entries will pass their information to The Cricket Society so that in the course of time the Bibliography may become more accurate and comprehensive. On the other hand, some items listed may be extant no longer; for example, a number of items to be found in Taylor's *The catalogue of cricket literature* (1906) have not come to light even after an exhaustive search.

That I have seen as many items as I have is due to the outstanding generosity and interest in the project shown by collectors and librarians. In addition to those pioneers mentioned above and their many correspondents, I must record my gratitude, in particular, to Geoffrey Copinger, who gave me complete access to his unrivalled collection involving some 23 separate visits over the course of a year or more so that I could handle and examine every item; to Alan McKay, who extended an invitation not only to examine his collection but to stay in his house until the job was completed; to Irving Rosenwater, whose library is a supreme example of a working tool and which contains much ephemeral but important material not to be found elsewhere; and to Bob Jones and Jim Coldham, for granting me access to their collections and for pointing out many matters of interest that a non-specialist would have overlooked. My thanks are also due to John Arlott, not only for allowing me to search through his books for rare items, but also for his kindness in writing the Foreword to this Bibliography.

I am also indebted to other collectors, particularly to Tony Woodhouse and Hal Cohen, who searched their extensive collections for the many items about which I needed more information; to A.M.C. Thorburn, who checked and corrected the Scottish items; to Eric Snow for Leicestershire material and to John Bromhead, D. Kelly, J.P. Sabben-Clare, Philip A. Snow, A.E. Winder and the Secretaries of numerous Cricket Clubs, who answered my queries with unfailing patience.

I have made use of many libraries and library catalogues. First and foremost I wish to thank Stephen Green, Curator of the collections at Lord's, for giving me facilities to examine the stock of the M.C.C. Library and to work through its catalogue; to Mr. Adsett, past Librarian of the Merton Public Libraries, for similar facilities at Mitcham Library; and to the Librarian of the Greenwich Libraries, for sending me a printed catalogue of the cricket books housed at the Plumstead Library and also for allowing me to check through the collection itself. I am also indebted to the Librarians of the Birmingham, Dunfermline, East Sussex, Hawick, Hove, Kensington & Chelsea, Liverpool, Perth & Kinross, Rochdale, Wandsworth and Westminster Libraries for similar assistance, and to J.W. McKenzie, bookseller, for allowing me to peruse his stock.

In particular I have been most glad of the help and advice received from Michael Pearce, who has supplied me throughout with notes on both newly published items and long-forgotten ones resurrected from the pages of old cricket periodicals, and to Irving Rosenwater for giving up so much of his time to read through the Bibliography, for correcting many errors and for his unrivalled knowledge of cricket history, so generously given.

Lastly, but by no means least, I must thank my colleagues Beryl Warren,

Peter Irving and Irene Pollock for days spent at Lord's and other libraries in seeking out new material and for veryifying the details of numerous entries, and to Mary and Veronica, my wife and daughter, for similar work in libraries, for the additional tedious work of filing, numbering and indexing the entries at home and for unselfishly easing my work over six years so that the Bibliography could reach its present form.

E.W.P.

# PREFACE
## TO SECOND EDITION

The reception given to the first edition of this Bibliography has encouraged me to extend the coverage of cricket publications to the end of 1979 and to repair omissions which a number of correspondents have kindly noted. At the same time I have taken the opportunity of correcting errors that arose either from having insufficient information at the time of publication or from the transmission of manuscript into print. It is hoped, therefore, that this second edition will prove more reliable and, with the extra coverage, more useful than the first. Of course, items that have still escaped me and errors that remain are entirely my responsibility.

The numbering of entries in the first edition has enabled a shorthand reference to be made to any recorded work and booksellers and others have found this useful as a means of quick identification. It seemed, therefore, an advantage to preserve the original numbers and to slot the new entries between them. Only in a few instances, when for example an entry was misplaced in the classification scheme, has it been necessary to renumber the original entry. Where this has occurred, a reference from the old number to the new has been given. The scheme of arrangement has been retained without alteration, except where new subjects have been introduced. For example, 'Cricketana' has been used to record the publication of auction sale-catalogues which has increased in numbers over recent years and I have had to accommodate the various international series played 1974–1979. I have also had to provide a section for World Series Cricket. As in the first edition I have distinguished between those items seen personally from those either reported to me or found recorded elsewhere.

Many friends who assisted in the compilation of the first edition continued to give their most valued support. I have again ransacked the private collection of Geoffrey Copinger, Jim Coldham and Bob Jones. Stephen Green, Curator of the M.C.C. Collections, was extremely helpful in producing for me many items from store for which, alas, no room can be found at present on the open shelves of the M.C.C. Library. Howard Milton opened the Library of The Cricket Society especially so that I could check on a number of unseen items. John McKenzie again allowed me access to the shelves of his bookshop and continued to send me copies of his excellent catalogues which most usefully from time to time record items 'not in Padwick'. Michael Pearce, Bibliographical Officer of The Cricket Society, regularly sent me titles culled from cricket periodicals, advertisements, and other varied sources.

That certain areas of the Bibliography have been considerably expanded is due almost entirely to the generous help of other enthusiasts whose interest was aroused by the appearance of the first edition. The coverage of Australian publications has been greatly improved by the tireless assistance given by Pat Mullins of Brisbane, who not only sent me a copy of his *Some the Bibliography may have Missed* but regularly over the past three years or more supplied detailed descriptions of new Australian publications and of other items acquired for his collection. Users may now feel that the inclusion of so many Queensland items is out of proportion to the coverage for the rest of Australia, but it was felt that what was known should be recorded in the hope that the compilation of some future edition or supplement will be supported by collectors and cricket enthusiasts in other parts of that country. David Frith was a great help in supplementing Pat Mullins's contributions and generously gave his time to guide me through his collection.

Three other areas which have been expanded are mentioned here to give me the opportunity of acknowledging the special help given. Timothy d'Arch Smith invited me to check through his collection of public school novels with the result that the section of boys' (and girls') school stories containing great deeds on the cricket field has been much improved. S.S. Perera, known to all followers of Sri Lankan cricket, sent me an exhaustive list of cricket publications from that country, and from Philip Snow, a considerable bibliographer in his own right, I received not only a list of books with detailed references to cricket in the various Pacific Islands, but also much encouragement. Philip Scowcroft kindly provided me with advance copies of his articles, subsequently printed in the *Journal of The Cricket Society*, on novels and detective fiction containing incidental cricket references.

I owe a great debt of gratitude to Derek Deadman who in innumerable letters over three or four years informed me of unrecorded items and who systematically searched the topographical collection of Leicester University Library for information on the formation and history of local cricket clubs. A.E. Winder in a steady stream of correspondence dating from the appearance of the first edition also kindly sent detailed descriptions of the many rare and early items in his extensive library. I have also made use of material contained in David Rayvern Allen's excellent study *a Song for Cricket* and in the *Bibliography on South African Cricket 1810–1953*, compiled by Monica A.M. Hart.

I owe a particular debt of gratitude to The Cricket Society for its continued interest in this publication through the support given both by the past Chairman, Chris Box-Grainger and the present Chairman, Nigel Haygarth. The latter has been involved in lengthy negotiations over the publication of this second edition and to him I am especially grateful. In addition to his help acknowledged above, Michael Pearce has given me much encouragement throughout and undertook the tedious task of reading the proofs. His support is much appreciated.

In addition I would like to thank those correspondents who from time to time have been interested enough to pass on information about rare and unusual books or who have corrected some of the entries in the first edition. They include Maurice B. Alexander, A.T. Barr, J.R. Batten,

Richard W. Cox, John D. Ede, Professor John Ferguson, Chris Harte of the Adelaide Branch of the Australian Cricket Society, Tony Laughton, Timothy J. McCann, Tony Mitchener, Alan Richards, P. Samara-Wick-rama, Charles Steggell (Southern Booksellers), D.G. Wayte, E.G. Willett, Martin Wood, and Peter Wynne-Thomas as well as the Librarians of the Rochdale, Johannesburg and Cape Town Libraries. To all I am grateful and if I have inadvertently omitted the name of any contributor I hope he will forgive the lapse and accept my thanks just the same.

The final appearance of this edition owes much to the support and patience shown by my wife, Mary, who has tolerated my concentration on a work which apart from a few breaks has occupied my spare-time since 1971. As with the first edition she helped specifically with the index which now provides brief author and title entries in a single alphabetical sequence for well over 10,000 cricket publications, a third more than in the previous edition.

I have written elsewhere of the need to continue a systematic bibliographical coverage of cricket publications. It is my hope that now the bulk of material published before the end of 1979 has been listed, the Bibliography will be continued by 10-yearly Supplements. One reason why December 1979 was chosen as a cut-off date for this present edition was to permit the first decennial supplement, in what I hope will be a series, to be published covering the years 1980-1989. Of course, room should also be found in the supplements for previously unrecorded items of earlier date.

E.W.P.
October, 1982

# FOREWORD

## BY JOHN ARLOTT

After many years of endeavour, hope, doubt, difficult and sheer hard work, an authoritative *Bibliography of Cricket* now appears. This is a corporate effort; launched by The Cricket Society years ago, there was never any real doubt that it would be completed; there was enough patient enthusiasm among members to ensure that. The problem was of publication; and The Library Association has solved it. Students of cricket should always be grateful to the Association for such a service to their game, as well as to the Society's original conception and prime study. The eventual extent of the work will surprise many; informed estimates when the scheme was first mooted put the number of cricket titles at a little over 7,000; the eventual 8,294 is indication of the extent of research carried out. Cricket has had nothing comparable before; there were the early efforts of A.J. Gaston, A.D. Taylor and J.W. Goldman, valuable in the absence of anything else, but essentially check-lists, not bibliographies, and based largely on individual experience.

Crucially, the *Bibliography* has been lifted above the sincere but amateur rut by the bibliographical professionalism of Tim Padwick, Deputy Librarian of the Guildhall Library, who, for five years from 1970, sought out collections, travelled, collated, became sufficiently involved with the work to carry much in his head, followed many clues and brought expert knowledge to editing, arrangement, headings and the sheer physical task of sifting and filing. This may seem like a list of polite tributes and, in fact, it is; because those responsible for this book have rendered an immense service to the entire game of cricket and those who study the social importance of sports and games in this and other countries, by providing them with an instrument of study far finer than anything available before. This is not only a fresh extension of cricket scholarship, nothing comparable exists on any other British sport or game; nor, with the possible exception of bullfighting, on any other sport in the world.

It is initially admirable in its principle, which is inclusive, not exclusive, and in its aim, which is primarily of assistance and guidance to the student, although the collector will find it valuable. One line of exclusion—that of date—was inevitable; no title has been included which was published after the end of 1973. Otherwise nothing has been excluded which might provide information. Thus, it does not include such uninformative ephemera as score cards (the details of which are available in periodical publications) or menus or school registers which include lists of elevens; (it does, though include school histories which devote space to their cricket). It takes in cyclostyled matter, even typescript and manuscript items, where their content is significant. This was undoubtedly the soundest criterion to employ if this opportunity of publication was to be taken without producing an unwieldy and extensively uninformative work.

The dedication to Harry Altham, first President of The Cricket Society, is most appropriate. His *History of Cricket* contained the best selective bibliography of the game; and he cared deeply for its scholarship.

It is primarily a work for the scholar. The layout and arrangement under subjects for the researcher into specific aspects of play or players. At the same time the collector can discover—and lament—the gaps in his shelves to an extent he never suffered before. Particularly valuable is the listing of books not obviously identifiable as of cricket interest but often containing important information about the game not available elsewhere. This field had never been adequately—nor even remotely—explored before, and the results should be of inestimable value to historians of the future.

No-one, certainly not the compilers, will claim that the *Bibliography* is either complete or flawless. There are always some who delight to discover and noise abroad errors in reference books. This one, though, rises far above such niggling criticism by virtue of the vast amount of hitherto unavailable knowledge it now puts into the hands of the student. Fortunately, too, The Cricket Society possesses, in its *Journal*, the means to publish errata; presumably, too, there will be an attempt to publish supplements—perhaps at five-yearly intervals—to keep the list up to date.

Meanwhile, it is compelling to the cricket reader or collector, simply to read through these pages; and both will be constantly amazed by the resources and sources that are available. No single person previously had full knowledge of the existence of anything approaching this list of titles. It not only dwarfs any private collection ever known, but demonstrates that it is virtually impossible that any one person will ever be able, in a single lifetime, to build one which would even approach completeness.

This, in turn, prompts the hope that somebody—M.C.C., Melbourne/ Victoria Cricket Association, some public, or university, library—might set out to build and make available to students an authoritative cricket collection, after the fashion of some American universities who have had the funds and the staff to aim at completeness. The cost would be huge; but the service to the game of cricket immense. Thus this *Bibliography*, admirable in itself, may lead to greater things, barely dreamt of by those who first conceived the idea and bent themselves so faithfully to the task, and who now are entitled to be impressed by what has been achieved.

# FOREWORD
## TO SECOND EDITION

It is disheartening—as all compilers of records of continuing events or growth sadly realize—to make a chronicle which is out of date before it even appears in print. Yet this second edition of the *Bibliography of Cricket* most rewardingly lists over 33$\frac{1}{3}$% of material not contained in the first. That includes not only fresh publications since the original edition, but a substantial filling-in of material unknown when the work was first written. Especially this is so on Australian and Sri Lankan cricket.

The Bibliography was always an item of interest and value to collectors, and to dealers, for whom it is a tool of the trade. Now, though, it has grown in stature. Many rare titles, often hitherto unknown to the chief historians of the subject, have been unearthed by diligent search and specialist research. In short, no one can hope—or should attempt—to write a history of any aspect of cricket without recourse to it.

Once again, Mr. Padwick, by his professionalism, thoroughness and unfailing enthusiasm, has rendered the game an immense service. He has completed a text of considerable scholarly significance. The aim of the editor for the Cricket Society has never been the mere collection of titles. The whole purpose—and achievement—of his Bibliography is relevance, and every cricket researcher and historian of the future must be grateful to him.

John Arlott
July, 1984

# SYNOPSIS OF CONTENTS

# CONTENTS

## GENERAL WORKS

## CRICKET IN ENGLAND AND WALES

## CRICKET IN SCOTLAND

## CRICKET IN IRELAND

## CRICKET IN AUSTRALIA

# CONTENTS

## CRICKET IN SOUTH AFRICA & ZIMBABWE RHODESIA

## CRICKET IN THE WEST INDIES

## CRICKET IN NEW ZEALAND

## CRICKET IN INDIA

## CRICKET IN PAKISTAN

## CRICKET IN SRI LANKA

# CRICKET IN NORTH AMERICA AND BERMUDA

# CRICKET IN THE REST OF THE WORLD

# INTERNATIONAL CRICKET

# ENGLAND

## CONTENTS

# SRI LANKA

# UNITED STATES AND CANADA

# TOURS OF OTHER COUNTRIES AND INTERNATIONAL TEAMS

# CRICKET IN LITERATURE

# PICTORIAL RECORDS

# CONTENTS

## SPORTS AND GAMES
### (With references to cricket)

## REMINISCENCES AND BIOGRAPHY
### (Including benefits and testimonials)

## INDEX

# The Cricketer's Almanack,

## FOR THE YEAR 1864,

BEING

### Bissextile or Leap Year, and the 28th of the Reign of

## HER MAJESTY QUEEN VICTORIA,

CONTAINING

# The Laws of Cricket,

AS REVISED BY THE MARYLEBONE CLUB;

THE FIRST APPEARANCE AT LORD'S AND NUMBER OF RUNS OBTAINED BY

## MANY CRICKETING CELEBRITIES;

SCORES OF 100 AND UPWARDS, FROM 1850 TO 1863;

# EXTRAORDINARY MATCHES;

ALL THE MATCHES PLAYED BETWEEN

# THE GENTLEMEN AND PLAYERS,

AND

# The All England and United Elevens,

With full and accurate Scores taken from authentic sources;

TOGETHER WITH

## The Dates of the University Rowing Matches,

THE WINNERS OF THE

## DERBY, OAKS, AND ST. LEGER;

RULES OF

## BOWLS, QUOITS, AND KNUR AND SPELL,

AND OTHER INTERESTING INFORMATION.

---

LONDON:

## PUBLISHED AND SOLD BY JOHN WISDEN AND CO.,

AT THEIR

CRICKETING AND BRITISH SPORTS WAREHOUSE,

2, NEW COVENTRY STREET, HAYMARKET, W.

*May be had of all respectable Booksellers in the United Kingdom, or forwarded free by the Publisher to any part of Great Britain for 13 Stamps.*

1864. [One Shilling.

W. H. CROCKFORD, GREENWICH.

# EXPLANATORY NOTES

*1. Scope.*

The aim of this Bibliography is to list in systematic order books, pamphlets, brochures, yearbooks, souvenir programmes and periodicals on cricket together with books known to contain passages of cricket interest, published before the end of 1979. Publications that appeared after 1979 are excluded. The coverage of yearbooks, annual reports, souvenir programmes, etc., is known to be incomplete but represents those seen or recorded. One purpose of the Bibliography is to present a basis for further research into cricket publications and it is hoped that omissions will be recorded in future supplements. Souvenir programmes with little or no editorial matter have been deliberately excluded, as have individual club fixture lists, score-cards and similar ephemera. School registers giving lists of scholars are also omitted, although some do contain cricket teams and names of captains. Sale catalogues, restricted to sales of named collections in the first edition, have been extended to include others of significance. Periodicals are mostly confined to cricket periodicals, but some general sports journals are listed if the amount of cricket interest seemed to warrant inclusion. Special cricket numbers are given when known. The Bibliography also includes unpublished, but nevertheless significant, manuscript material accessible to students of the game in public and private collections.

*2. Authority.*

■ against an entry indicates that the item has been seen by the compiler
□ against an entry indicates that some, but not all, editions of a work, or issues of a serial, have been seen by the compiler.

In the latter case, the dates seen are printed within oblique strokes, e.g. *1956/1959,60/* to date. Where dates are so printed, but the entry is unaccompanied by a ■ or a □, the issues for those years have been recorded but not seen by the compiler.

*3. Arrangement.*

The entries are arranged:
   (a) under their subject content except for "Cricket in Literature" (under literary form) and "Pictorial Records". Some items because of their varied contents appear under more than one subject heading.

(b) under each subject-heading alphabetically by author or title, except in a few instances, e.g. "Laws" where a chronological arrangement seemed more appropriate.

(c) under each author chronologically by date of first publication.

## 4. The entries.

The entries consist of author, editor or compiler, title, sub-title, illustrator, place of publication (London is omitted unless publication occurred simultaneously elsewhere), name of publisher (if this is not known, the printer is stated), and date. The collation consists of pagination (except when the work was published in more than one volume), illustrations, maps, match scores, statistics, glossary and bibliography. The publisher's series is stated when applicable. Editions, and for some works, separate issues, are set out below the main entry without repeating the publisher's name and the collation if these remain the same. Inferred editions and issues are printed in italic. Page measurements are not given, nor is a description of the binding except in a few exceptional instances. A fuller explanation of the application of these terms will be found below in para. 7.

## 5. Dating.

The date of publication is given as stated on the title-page or elsewhere in the preliminaries. If it is inferred the date is enclosed within "[  ]". When there is some doubt the supposed date is accompanied by a "?"

In the case of serial publications, e.g. periodicals, annuals, club handbooks, etc., inclusive dates of publication or the seasons covered are given wherever possible. The dating of serials has often proved difficult and inconclusive because complete runs of club handbooks, etc., are seldom seen. Those issues that have been seen or recorded are set between oblique strokes and the following examples show the methods adopted:

(a) *1953/1953, 55/* to date
– the run is from 1953 to 1979 at least but only the issues for 1953 and 1955 have been seen or recorded.

(b) *1954/1956. . .1969/* to date?
– various issues dated between 1956 and 1969 have been seen or recorded; it is probable that publication continued to 1979 at least, but this has not been verified.

(c) *?/1911, 20, 21/*
the date of the first issue is not known, those for 1911, 1920 and 1921 have been seen or recorded, 1921 being the last time the serial was published.

(d) *?1922–41, ?1946* to date
– the serial is thought to have been issued from 1922 to 1941 although both dates are unconfirmed; then came a break in publication followed by a second run from 1946 to 1979 at least, although again, both dates are subject to confirmation.

## 6. Index.

The index, a single arrangement by author and title, refers to entry numbers. In some instances the title has been inverted to bring key words to the fore (*see* note on p. ). The index also contains under author and title, essays, poems, articles, etc., that are mentioned in the annotations following some entries in the Bibliography.

*7. Abbreviations.*

| | |
|---|---|
| Assoc. | Association |
| bibliog. | bibliography |
| bs. | broadside |
| ch. | chapter |
| col. | coloured |
| Cttee. | Committee |
| diagr. | diagram |
| ed. | edition |
| enl. | enlarged |
| f. *or* ff. | folios or leaves |
| facsim. | facsimile |
| frontis. | frontispiece |
| illus. | illustrations other than diagrams and portraits; in items not seen by the compiler "illus" may refer to any type of illustration |
| L.P.ed. | large paper edition |
| ltd. ed. | limited edition |
| MS. | manuscript |
| *n.d.* | no date given or inferred |
| *n.p.* | no publisher given or inferred |
| p. *or* pp. | pages |
| ports. | posed portraits; action photographs of named individuals are classed as illustrations |
| rev. | revised |
| rptd. | reprinted |
| scores | full match scores (or as full as may be expected at the date of publication) |
| stats. | statistics and records of individual or team performances. |
| suppl. | supplement |
| *tog. w.* | together with |
| t.p. | title-page |
| trs. | translation |
| *v.y.* | various years |

*8. References.*

Other sources are referred to as follows:

| | |
|---|---|
| Allen, D.R. | A song for cricket (Pelham Books, 1981). |
| C.B.E.L. | Cambridge Bibliography of English Literature. |
| Eagar | Readers' guide to Hampshire cricket (No. 17). |
| Goldman. | Bibliography of cricket. (No. 20). |
| Rait Kerr. | The laws of cricket. (No. 221). |
| Taylor. | The catalogue of cricket literature (No. 39). |

Equipment: "The cricket bat maker", an engraving by William Washington (1885–1956) *photo: British Museum*

# GENERAL WORKS

## BIBLIOGRAPHIES, BOOKLISTS AND CATALOGUES

0
-1
■ **Allen, David Rayvern,** *compiler*
A catalogue of cricket catalogues, booklists, bibliographical sources and indexes, etcetera. The Author, [1980]. 24p.
*offprint of a series of 4 articles in* The Journal of the Cricket Society, *Spring, 1978 – Autumn, 1979. Limited edition of 75 copies, 60 of which were for sale*

1
■ **Arlott, [Leslie Thomas] John**
Cricket: a reader's guide. National Book League & Cambridge U.P., 1950. 20p. (The Reader's Guides)

2
■ **Arrowsmith** 1854–1954. Bristol, Arrowsmith, 1955. [vii],36p. illus.
*relations between W.G. Grace and J.W. Arrowsmith concerning the former's "Cricket", pp. 9–10, and with reference to score-card printing with facsimile, p. 22*

3
■ **Association of Cricket Umpires**
Library list. March 1957. The Association. [4]p.
——Supplementary library list. [2]p.

3
-1
■ **Australian Cricket Society**
The Dean Chamberlin Library: catalogue August 1971. [Melbourne], the Society, [1971]. [ii],16p.
*the Rev. Dean F. M. Chamberlin donated his cricket collection to the Society in 1970*

3
-2 **K. A. Auty Memorial Library of Cricket**
Catalogue. St. Catherines (Ontario), Ridley College, 1969.
*2300 books, pamphlets, papers, photographs, etc. catalogued by Messrs Aylott, Burn and Loat*

3
-3
■ **Backus, Edgar,** *bookseller*
Cricket: an important library of books relating to the game of cricket offered for sale. Leicester, E. Backus, [1934]. *typescript*
*nearly 500 items listed*

4
■ **British Council**
Some books on cricket, 1833–1953: British West Indies. British Council, 1954. 18p.
*cover-title: An exhibition of books on cricket: catalogue*

5
■ **Britton, Charles J.**
Cricket books: the 100 best (old and new) with notes, values, etc. Birmingham, Cotterell, 1929. vii,54p.
——Ltd. ed. 1929. 54f.
*3 signed copies only. Text on rectos*

6
■ **Brodribb, [Arthur] Gerald [Norcott],** *compiler*
Cricket in fiction: a bibliography. Canford, Mountjoy P., 1950. 32p.
*limited ed. of 150 signed copies*

6
-1
■ **Brown, E.K.,** *bookseller*
[Cricket books sale catalogue]. Liskeard (Corn.). *annual*
1972–1979
*generally between 200 and 300 items per catalogue; previously issued in typescript*

7
■ **Burden, J.S.,** and **Record, P.D.**
Cricket: a booklist compiled for the Library Association. Library Association, [1950]. (Book list no. 20)

8 **Sir Julien Cahn's** catalogue of cricket literature as purchased from F.S. Ashley-Cooper. 1931
*MS in Ashley-Cooper's hand in M.C.C. Library at Lord's*

9
□ **Cotterell & Co.**
A special list of cricket books & prints, etc. Birmingham, Cotterell & Co. (S.J.A. Cotterell). [c. 1929/30]. 12p.
*364 items*
A list of cricket books. [c. 1930]. 12p.
*119 items*
A special collection of cricket books only just in the market. May, 1931. 11p.
*133 items*
A special collection of cricket books. 1931. 24p.
*the F.A. Brookes collection*

A list of cricket books offered for sale.
Autumn 1931. 7p.
> *49 items*

A list of cricket books & prints . . . no. 6.
[c. 1932]. 8p.
> *352 items*

A list of cricket books. [c. 1933]. 16p.
> *102 items*
> *the majority of the above are in Mr. A.E. Winder's collection who kindly supplied the information*

**10**    **Cricket** and sporting literature. Wright.
■    *annual*
> 1893–99, 1901, 1904, 1911–12, 1914–15, 1924–30
> *formerly: List of cricket and athletic literature. See no. 26*

**11**    **The Cricket Society**
■    The library of the Cricket Society: [catalogue]. The Society, 1963. 12p.
> *typescript*
> ——*another ed. with title:* Library catalogue. December 1975. (1975). [i,90]p. *typescript*
> *Librarian: Peter Ellis*

**12**    Jubilee year 1970. Part 1: Officers and
■    members 1969/70; Part 2: The Library of the Society: [catalogue]. The Society, 1969, 52p.

**13**    ——*Northern Section*
■    A catalogue of books available for the use of members. [Leeds, the Society, 1950]. 20p. *typescript*

**14**    **The Cricket Society of Scotland**
■    Library [booklist]: [compiled by] Margaret A. Masterton. The Society, [1961]. 15p.

**15**    **The Cricketana Society**
■    Catalogue of cricket literature [incomplete]. The Society. [1934?]. [iii],110p. *typescript*
> *A to FRY, C.B. only, in one alphabetical sequence of authors, titles and subjects; issued quarterly; compiled by Dr. T.R. Hunter*

**15**    **Davies, John C. ("Not Out")**
**–1**    A bibliography of Australasian cricket. [1904 or 05]. MS. 3p.
> *in New South Wales Public Library, Sydney*

**16**    Catalogue. 32p. MS
> *in the Mitchell Library, N.S.W. Public Library, Sydney; probably his personal collection of cricket books, the latest entries being c. 1910–11*

**17**    **Eagar, Edward Desmond Russell**
■    Readers' guide to Hampshire cricket. Boscombe, Boscombe Printing Co. (1933) Ltd., 1964. [12]p.
> *limited ed. of 25 copies*

**17**    **Elkin Mathews Ltd.**, *booksellers*
**–1**    List 75. Books and pamphlets on the game of cricket. Bishops Stortford, E. Mathews, [1961]. 32p. facsims. *typescript*
> *264 entries, some from the Cahn collection*

**17**    **Epworth Secondhand Books**, *booksellers*
**–2**    Lists. 25–35 City Road, E.C.1. foolscap
> *those recorded below are in the Collection of Mr. A.E. Winder, who kindly supplied the information:*
> 1948? (List no. 3)-5pp.; 1949–8pp.; 1950–16pp.; 1952–12pp.; 1953–12 and 19pp.; 1954–18pp.; 1955–18pp.; 1957–2pp.; 1958– 28, 2 and 2 pp.; 1959–4pp.; 1960–22pp.; 1961–4pp.; 1962–38pp.; 1964–2pp.
> *stock sold in 1967 to E.K. Brown of Liskeard*

**18**    **Gaston, Alfred James**
■    Bibliography of cricket. Brighton, *privately printed*, 1895. 12p.
> *limited ed of 25 copies*
> *see also no. 1052*

**19**    Valuable cricket collection of the late T. Padwick, Esq. of Redhill to be sold. Brighton, A.J. Gaston, 1898. 20p.

**19**    Catalogue of the collection of books and
**–1**    engravings on cricket being the collection of the late Mr. A.D. Taylor. Brighton, Gaston, 1923. 7p.

**19**    Catalogue of a choice collection of books
**–2**    and engravings on cricket, including rare items from A.D. Taylor's collection. Brighton, Gaston, [1927]. 16pp.
> *probably the bulk of Taylor's collection (D.R. Allen)*

**20**    **Goldman, Joseph Wolfe**
■    Bibliography of cricket. London, the Author, 1937. 211p.
> *limited ed. of 125 copies. Serialised in* The Cricketer

**21**    Catalogue of cricket books in the
■    Goldman collection typed up to May 1956. 250p. *typescript*
> *an extended version of his "Bibliography of cricket". Only 2 copies known*

**21**    **Hart, Monica A.M.**, *compiler*
**–1**    Bibliography on South African cricket
■    1810–1953. 1954. [2], iii, 23f. *typescript*
> *original Ms. held in South African Library, Capetown*

**22**    **Hodgson & Co.**
■    A catalogue of the extensive collection of books on cricket formed by J.W. Goldman, Esq., (the first portion) . . .

November 24th, 1966. Hodgson, 1966. 26p. illus. facsims.
*lists some 300 items*
——Price list with buyers' names. 8p.

**22** **Holmes, Robert Stratten**
**–1** Catalogue of cricket books and pictures. 92p. Ms.
*a manuscript accessions-book of books and pictures acquired by Rev. R.S. Holmes from 1880's to 1933; in the collection of A.E. Winder*

**23** **Howe, Garfield**
■ Of the making of CXXV books: a publisher's bibliography. Gerald Howe, 1934. 37p.
*refers to cricket books by R.H. Lowe, J. Thorpe and H. de Selincourt*

**24** **Irish Cricket Union**
■ Catalogue of library for associate members. Dublin, Irish Cricket Union, [1956?]. 9p. *typescript*

**24** **Lewis, Guy,** *and* **Redmond, Gerald**
**–1** Sporting heritage: a guide to the halls of
■ fame, special collections and museums in the United States and Canada. South Brunswick and N.Y., Barnes; London, Yoseloff, 1974. 185p. illus. ports. maps
*includes pp. 56–7 The C. Christopher Morris Cricket Library and Collection, Haverford College, Haverford, Pa.; p. 158, The K.A. Auty Memory Library, Ridley College, St. Catherines, Ontario*

**25** **Ling, Henry**
■ List of the remaining books on cricket in my collection for sale. South Croydon, Henry Ling, [1939?]. [35]p.

**26** **List** of cricket and athletic literature.
■ Wright. *annual*
1889, 1890
*contd. as: Cricket and sporting literature.* See *no. 10*

**27** **McIlwaine, J.H. St. J.**
■ "A bibliography of Neville Cardus", in Cricket quarterly:
*Vol. 2 no. 3, July 1964, pp. 140–47*
*no. 4, Oct. 1964, pp. 251–58*
*Vol. 3 no. 1, Winter 1965, pp. 44–51*
*no. 3, Summer 1965, pp. 202–11*

**28** **McKenzie, John W.,** *bookseller*
■ Catalogue of cricket literature. West Ewell, the Compiler, [1972], iv,61,iiip. facsims.
*contains 469 entries*
[Cricket catalogues]. Ewell, Epsom (Surrey), facsims.
15. [1976]. 25p.
*645 entries*

19 *with title*: Cricket literature 1744–1796. [1976–77]. *var. pag.*
*150 bound sets of Catalogue no. 19, Pts. 1–3, containing 1703 entries with a supplement listing 69 additional items and an index*
23. [1977]. [iii],53p.
*747 entries*
26. [1978]. [iv],52p. incl. covers
*1170 entries*
28. [1978]. [ii],38p.
*609 entries*
30. [1978]. [ii],43p.
*807 entries*
32. [1978]. [ii],55p.
*826 entries*
35. [1979]. [iii],65p.
*1163 entries*
38. [1979]. [i],28p.
*567 entries*

**29** **Madras Cricket Association**
■ Dr. P. Subbarayan Memorial Library; gifted by General P.P. Kumaramangalam [and others] to the Madras Cricket Association . . . 1968: [catalogue of books]. Madras, the Assoc., 1968. [iii],26p. port.

**29** **Maurice, A., & Co.,** *booksellers*
**–1** Catalogue of a choice collection of books and engravings on cricket (Catalogue 93: new series). A. Maurice & Co., 1909. 12p.
*a list of 384 items*

**30** **[C.C. Morris Cricket Library**
■ **Association]**
The C. Christopher Morris Cricket Library and collection at the Haverford College Library, Haverford, Pa. Haverford, the Assoc., [1968]. [14]p. illus. port. plan

**30** **The C.C. Morris Cricket Library**
**–1** **Association**
■ Newsletter. Haverford, the Association. *typescript. quarterly*
*No. 1 June 1971 to date*

**30** The C.C. Morris Cricket Library Associ-
**–2** ation, Haverford College Library, Haver-
■ ford, Pa., 19041, USA: membership list 1979. 16p.

**30** **Mullins, Patrick J.,** *compiler*
**–3** A catalogue of the cricket and sporting
□ collection of P. J. Mullins. Coorparoo (Qld.), August, 1973. *typescript*
*12 copies only*
——rev. ed. March, 1978. 95f. *typescript*

**30** Some the Bibliography may have missed.
**–4** December, 1977. The Compiler. [28]f.
■ *typescript*
——Supplement no. 1. 1978. 6f. *typescript*

Boston Cricket Club. Members only. Boston. 1809.

[Of value on account of its antiquity, but of no real interest.]

Bowen (C. P.) English Cricketers in the West Indies. R. Slade Lucas's XI. *Herald* Office, Barbados. 1895.

[This book is somewhat difficult to obtain in England, but probably easily met with in Barbados. Worth from six to eight shillings.]

Bowen (E. E.) Willow the King. Harrow School Song. Music by John Farmer. Dedicated to the Hon. R. Grimston and the Hon. F. Ponsonby. Duke and Son, Penshurst. Gratis.

Box (Charles). The Cricketers' Manual. 1s. Joseph Myers and Co., London. There were eight editions of this little book, the first appearing in 1848 and the eighth in 1851.

[The first edition being somewhat rare, is probably worth half-a-guinea; the other editions from 5s. to 7s. 6d. a copy.]

Box (Charles). The English Game of Cricket. Comprising a digest of its Origin, Character, History and Progress; together with an exposition of its laws and languages. Illustrated. *Field* Office, London.

[One of the finest books ever published in connection with the game. May still be obtained for half-a-guinea from Horace Cox, publisher, London.

Box (Charles). The Theory and Practice of Cricket. From its origin to the present time. 1s. and 2s. 6d. Frederick Warne & Co., London. Two editions. 1868.

[Copies may occasionally be met with at second-hand bookstalls. Value 8s.]

Boxall (T.) Rules and Instructions for playing at the Game of Cricket, as practised by the most eminent players. To which is subjoined the Laws and Regulations of cricketters (*sic*). Folding plate repre-

Bibliographies: A page from Alfred D. Taylor's "The Catalogue of Cricket Literature" (no. 39)

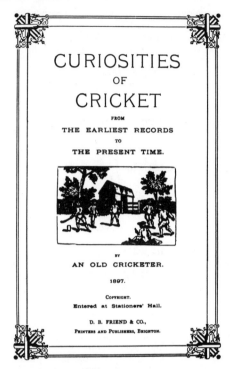

CURIOSITIES
OF
CRICKET
FROM
THE EARLIEST RECORDS
TO
THE PRESENT TIME.

BY
AN OLD CRICKETER.
1897.

COPYRIGHT.
Entered at Stationers' Hall.

D. B. FRIEND & CO.,
PRINTERS AND PUBLISHERS, BRIGHTON.

Records and statistics: The title-page of no. 108. The author has been identified as A. L. Ford *photo: M.C.C.*

The LAWS of the NOBLE GAME of CRICKET,
as Established at the Star and Garter Pall-Mall by a Committee of Noblemen & Gentlemen

The Laws: The first broadsheet edition of the Laws published September 1st, 1785 (no. 155). The copper engraving is based on Francis Hayman's painting "Cricket in Marylebone Fields" (1748) although according to Robin Simon and Alastair Smart *The Art of Cricket* (1983) p. 9, the venue is doubtful *photo: M.C.C.*

"Cricket in the Artillery Ground, Finsbury after an engraving, published 1743 by C. Benoist from a painting traditionally attributed to Francis Hayman but dismissed as "impossible" by Robin Simon and Alastair Smart in their *The Art of Cricket* (1983). The venue is also considered doubtful
photo: M.C.C.

WICKET KEEPER.
42 – If the wicket-
keeper incommode
the striker by any
noise or commotion
the striker shall not
be put out.
*Copyright of "Perrier" Water.*

The Laws: Law 42 as depicted by Charles E. Crombie in the 'Perrier' Water "Laws of Cricket"
(no. 7012)

——Supplement no. 2. 1978. 10f. *typescript*
*items in the Mullins collection most of which were not included in the first edition of this work*

**31** **National Book League**
■ Cricket: a catalogue of an exhibition of books, manuscripts and pictorial records presented by the National Book League with the co-operation of the Marylebone Cricket Club; arranged by Diana Rait Kerr. Cambridge Univ. P., 1950. 120p. illus. port

**32** The Festival of Britain: exhibition of
■ books. Cambridge Univ. P. for N.B.L., 1951. 224p.
*cricket books pp. 42–44*

**33** Cricket: an annotated book list. N.B.L.,
□ 1964.
*published on the occasion of the 18th annual (World Book Fair) cricket match*
——1968. N.B.L., 1968. 11p.
*contains 60 items in print, selected on the occasion of the 20th cricket match between The Authors and the N.B.L.*

**34** ——*Touring Exhibition*
■ Cricket books: books in print June 1956, selected by E.W. Swanton. The League, [1956]. 3p.

**35** **Nederlandse Cricketbond**
■ Bibliotheek Nederlandse Cricketbond, Koninklijke Bibliotheek, Den Haag: [catalogue of books]. [den Haag, N.C.-B., 1957]. 14p.
*compiled by F. Ruychaver, B. Kleefstra, R.G. Ingelse and E.J.A. Schill. Contains inter alia 43 Dutch cricket books*

**36** **Nottingham Public Libraries**
■ Cricket: reader's guide and booklist; compiled by Violet Walker and Margery Northrop. Nottingham Public Libraries, 1934, pp. 45–52. illus. (Bulletin. No. 303)

**37** **Nottinghamshire County Cricket Club**
■ Catalogue of books in the cricket Library at the Trent Bridge Cricket Ground; [compiled by Miss D. Bradbury]. Nottingham, the Club, 1950. [iii],33p. *typescript*

**37** **Rosenwater, Irving**
**–1** Cricket books: great collectors of the past.
■ *Privately printed*: distributed by the Cricketer, 1976. [iii],40p. ports.
*A.L. Ford, Thomas Padwick, Charles Pratt Green, Rev. R.S. Holmes, Alfred D. Taylor, F.S. Ashley-Cooper, Sir Julien Cahn, C.J. Britton and E.R. Wilson*
*limited ed. of 200 copies numbered and signed (190 for sale)*

**37** **Sotheby, Wilkinson** *and* **Hodge,**
**–2** *auctioneers*
Catalogue of books & manuscripts, including the library of the late Rev. C. Perring . . . and the library of Fredk. Gale, Esq., comprising many works on cricketing . . . which will be sold by auction by Messrs. Sotheby, Wilkinson & Hodge . . . on Monday 20th July 1891, and three following days. 98p.

**38** **South Australia State Library.** *Research Service*
Cricket: a list of books about cricket in the State Library of South Australia; compiled by K. J. Polden. Adelaide, the Library, 1967. 31p.

**38** **Taylor, Alfred Daniel**
**–1** [A catalogue of books for sale]. For sale. Having recently purchased a quantity of books on cricket and football, they are offered for sale at very moderate charges by Alfred D. Taylor. Brighton, [Taylor, c. 1900]. [4]p.
*includes 142 cricket items*

**39** The catalogue of cricket literature.
■ Merritt & Hatcher, 1906. [v],115p., *interleaved*
*serialized in "Cricket", 1906; limited ed. of 50 copies only; no title-page, cover-title only*
——*rptd.* Wakefield, S.R. Publishers, 1972. vii, 115p.

**40** **Waghorn, Henry Thomas,** *compiler*
■ The dawn of cricket; edited by Lord Harris. M.C.C., 1906. v,204p. scores. bibliog.
*bibliography "evidently a list of cricketical items to be found in the B.M." (Ashley-Cooper)*

**41** **Weston, George Neville**
■ "My cricket collection" and "Cricket literature": a guide to books and articles on the bibliography of cricket. 2 pts. Kidderminster, the Author, [1929]. 47p. frontis.
*1st issue of 12 copies; 2nd issue of 6 copies, all signed and numbered 1–18*
——3rd ed. [i.e. 2nd ed.]. [1974]. [v],viii, [2],52p.
*limited ed. of 50 copies numbered and signed*

**42** Bibliography of the cricket works of the
■ late F.S. Ashley-Cooper. *Privately printed*, 1933. [19]p., *interleaved*. port.
*limited ed. of 100 copies*

**43** "Nyren": a short bibliography. W. H. Smith, Arden P., 1933. 29p. facsims.
*limited ed. of 20 copies*

44   The cricketers' manual by "Bàt" (Charles
■   Box): a short bibliography. [W.H. Smith],
  1936. 32p. facsims.
    *limited ed. of 20 copies numbered and*
*signed*

44   **Whitelock, Geoffrey K.**
–1   "Bibliography of the writings of John
■   Arlott'. 4 parts. *In The Journal of the Cricket*
  *Society*
    Vol. 8, no. 2. Spring 1977. pp. 17–21
          no. 4. Spring 1978. pp. 46–54
    Vol. 9, no. 2. Spring 1979. pp. 62–65
          no. 4. Spring 1980. pp. 44–45

45   **Wisden Cricketers' Almanack**
■   Wisden's list of books on cricket, 1950.
  W.H. Smith, [1950]. 14p.
    *crickets books in print at end of 1949, off-*
*printed from list given in Wisden (1950)*

## CRICKETANA

(See also under Pictorial Records)

45   **Catalogue** of great cricket charity auction
–1   sale (on behalf of St. Dunstan's Hostel)
  on Lord's Cricket Ground, July 14th 1917.
  Auctioneer: George Robey, Esq. Auction
  clerk: Mr. J. Cannon. On the occasion
  of the military charity match, an English
  Army XI v. an Australian Imperial Force
  XI. *Printed by* the "Sporting Life", 1917.
  4p.
    *an auction of bats, balls, engravings, photo-*
*graphs, etc.*

45   **Harry Langton's** cricketana: second exhi-
–2   bition of cricketana. April 3 to April 7,
  1979. Islington Green, Langton, [1979].
  7p.
    *a sale catalogue*

45   **Northern Cricket Society**
–3   Auction of cricketana at the Guildford
■   Hotel, Leeds, Monday, November 26th.
  Leeds, the Society, [1973]. [7]p. *typescript*

45   **The S.C. Packer** collection "Cricketana".
–4   Auction sale, 12th September, 1961, the
■   Auction Mart, Halford St., Leicester.
  Leicester, Warner, Sheppard & Wade
  Auctioneers, [1961]. 8p.
    *S.C. Packer was former secretary of*
*Leicestershire C.C.C.; 93 cricket lots*

45   **Phillips, Son** *and* **Neale**, *auctioneers*
–5   English, continental and oriental ceramics
■   and glass to be sold by auction on
  Wednesday, May 22nd 1974. Phillips,
  Son and Neale, [1974]. 43p. illus.
    *cricket lots included*

45   Oil paintings, English and continental
–6   schools; cricketana, including pictures,
■   books and ephemera, the property of
  Anthony Baer, Esq., H.M. Cohen, Esq.,
  and others. To be sold by auction
  Monday, September 18th, 1978. Sale no.
  21,905. Phillips, Son & Neale, [1978]. 37p.
  illus.
    *120 cricket lots nos. 110–229*

45   Cricketana, to be sold by auction on
–7   Wednesday, 4th April, 1979. Phillips, Son
■   and Neale, [1979]. 47p. illus.
    *316 cricket lots; with prices realised at sale*
*18th Sept. 1978*

45   **Sporting memorabilia**, including items
–8   related to cricket, golf, tennis, to be sold
■   by auction on Wednesday 26th
  September 1979. Phillips, Son and Neale,
  [1979]. 36p. illus. team port.
    *209 cricket lots; with prices realised at the*
*sale of cricketana on 4th April, 1979*

45   **Sport Design International Ltd.**
–9   First cricket exhibition June 1975. Sports
■   Design, 1975. 5f. illus. *typescript*
    *prints, cigarette cards, pottery, etc.*

45   **Sussex County Cricket Club**
–10   A descriptive catalogue of the unique
■   collection of cricket trophies, curios,
  historic bats, balls, early cricket pictures,
  engravings and prints; arranged by W.L.
  Murdoch, Esq., & Mr. Alfred J. Gaston.
  Exhibited in aid of the funds of the Sussex
  C.C.C. Brighton, Southern Publishing
  Co., [1894]. 16p. 1 illus. on cover

45   **Worcestershire County Cricket Club**
–11   Descriptive catalogue of the unique
■   collection of cricket trophies, historic
  bats, balls &c. organised by Mr. C.P.
  Green, and exhibited in aid of the Worcestershire County Cricket Club bazaar.
  Worcester, Baylis, Lewis, 1903. 15p. illus.

## ENCYCLOPAEDIAS

46   **Golesworthy, Maurice**, *compiler*
■   The encyclopaedia of cricket. Hale, 1962.
  224p. illus. ports. diagr. stats. bibliog.
  ——New and revised ed. 1964. 224p.
  ——3rd ed. 1966. 224p.
  ——4th ed. 1972. 224p.
  ——5th ed. 1974. 224p.
  ——6th ed. 1977. 222p.

47   **The world** of cricket; general editor E.W.
■   Swanton, associate editor Michael
  Melford, assistant editors Irving Rosenwater and A.S.R. Winlaw. M. Joseph,
  1966. 1165p. illus. (some col.), ports.
  diagrs. stats. bibliog.

## DICTIONARIES AND CRICKET TERMS

48 **Avis, Frederick Compton**
■ The sportsman's glossary. Souvenir P.,
1961. 301p. diagrs.
*cricket pp. 109–142*

48 **Baker, Sidney John**
–1 The Australian language. [2nd ed].
Sydney, Currawong Publishing Co. Pty.
Ltd.; London, Angus & Robertson, 1966.
517p.
——*another ed.* Melbourne, Sun Books,
1977
*cricket pp. 247–9*

49 **Brown, Ivor [John Carnegie]**
■ Chosen words. Cape, 1955. 304p.
*"Umper" pp. 278–9*

50 **Burgschmidt, Ernst**
■ Studien zum Verbum in englischen Fach-
sprachen (Cricket): Inauguraldissertation
der Philosophischen Fakultät der Fried-
rich-Alexander-Universität Erlangen-
Nürnberg. Ulm, Donau, 1970. vi,517p.
bibliog. diagrs.
*limited ed. of 240 copies*
——rptd. 1977

50 **Cillié, Christoffel,** *and* **Jordan, J.H.**
–1 Krieketterme: 2217 terme; kommentaar
gelewer deur D. Dykman . . . [*et. al.*]
[Aucklandpark, Johannesburg, Federasie
van Afrikaanse Kultuurvereniginge, 1977
d.i. 1979]. 31p. illus. (Nuwe handhaaf en
boureeks: no. 3)
*in Afrikaans*

51 **Cricket** reference dictionary. F.C. Avis,
■ [1954]. 128p. diagr.

52 **Federasie van Afrikaanse**
■ **Kultuurvereniginge**
Engels-Afrikaanse woordelys van a) Krie-
ket-b) Skyfskiet- en c) Brugspelterme.
Bloemfontein, Nasionale Pers, Bpk., 1935
*English-Afrikaans glossary of cricket, etc.*

53 **Lang, Andrew**
■ "Yorker". [c. 1892–4] MS. *typescript.* 6f.
*in M.C.C. Library Lord's. On the deriva-
tion of the term*

54 **Lewis, W.J.**
■ The language of cricket; with illustrative
extracts from the literature of the game.
Oxford Univ. P., 1934. viii,317p. bibliog.
—*another edition.* 1938. (Oxford Bookshelf)
*a supplement by G.B. Buckley appeared in*
Cricket Quarterly, vol. 1. [1963], p. 17–29

55 **Macleod, John**
■ The cricketer's dictionery [sic]. Sydney,

Dunvegan Publications, [1946?]. [112]p.
illus.
*humorous definitions*

## GENERAL BOOKS AND HISTORY

For early references to the game, *see*: CRICKET
IN ENGLAND AND WALES: BEFORE 1725; for
national cricket *see under* names of individual
countries.

56 **Alcock, Charles Williams,** *editor*
■ Famous cricketers and cricket grounds,
1895. Hudson & Kearns; "News of the
World", 1895. 292p. illus. ports.
*originally published in 18 weekly parts by*
News of the World

57 **Altham, Harry Surtees**
■ A history of cricket. Allen & Unwin, 1926.
391p. illus. ports. bibliog.
*previously serialised in* The Cricketer
——2nd ed. by H.S. Altham and E.W.
Swanton. 1938. 450p. [bibliog. omitted]
——3rd ed. (with a new postcript). 1947.
476p. [bibliog. omitted]
——4th ed. 1948. 480p. [bibliog. omitted]
——5th ed. 2 vols. 1962
*Vol 1: From the beginnings to the First
World War, by H.S. Altham. 323p. illus.
ports. starts. bibliog.*
*Vol. 2: From the First World War to the
present day, by E.W. Swanton. 334p. illus.
ports. bibliog.*

58 **Arlott, [Leslie Thomas] John**
■ Rothmans jubilee history of cricket,
1890–1965. Barker, 1965. 212p. illus.
ports.

58 ———, *and* **Trueman, Frederick**
–1 **Sewards**
■ Arlott and Trueman on cricket; edited by
Gilbert Phelps. B.B.C., 1977. 280p.
illus. & ports. (some col.), facsims. score,
stats.
*accompanied the B.B.C. Further Education
Television programmes of the same title first
shown on BBC 2 starting 11 April, 1977.
Includes an anthology of cricket literature*

59 **Ashley-Cooper, Frederick Samuel**
■ Cricket and cricketers. Philadelphia, The
American Cricketer, 1907. 102p. illus.
ports. diagr. score

60 **Cricket** highways and byways. Allen &
■ Unwin, 1927. 288p. illus. ports. scores

60 **Bailey, Trevor**
–1 A history of cricket; with . . . records
■ compiled by Bill Frindall. Allen & Unwin,
1979. 192p. illus.(some col.), ports.
facsims. stats.

**61** **Birkett, William Norman**, *1st baron Birkett*
■ *of Ulverston*
The game of cricket: illustrated by a series of pictures in the museum of the Marylebone Cricket Club, principally from the collection of the late Sir Jeremiah Colman; with an introductory essay by Sir Norman Birkett and notes on the illustrations by Diana Rait Kerr. Batsford, 1955. 144p. illus. & ports. (some col.)

**61** **Birley, Derek**
**–1** The willow wand: some cricket myths
■ explored. Queen Anne P., 1979. [vii], 214p. illus. ports. bibliog. (Wisden Cricket Library)
*includes an examination of amateurism, W.G. Grace, the M.C.C., Sir Pelham Warner, riots in the West Indies, the d'Oliviera affair and the advent of Kerry Packer*

**62** **Bowen, Rowland**
■ Cricket: a history of its growth and development throughout the world. Eyre & Spottiswoode, 1970. 421p. illus. ports. map, bibliog.

**62** **Boys' Magazine**
**–1** Cricket hints and information.
■ Manchester, Allied Newspapers Ltd., [1932]. 28p. incl. covers. illus. diagrs. (Boys' Magazine Wonder Book. New Series no. 7)

**62** **The British** Empire. B.B.C. TV/Time-Life
**–2** Books, 1973. illus. & ports. (some col.)
■ *Part no. 94 (pp. 2605–26). "The presence that changed the world".*
*pp. 2611–15 "Bowled over" – on the export of cricket from the British Isles*

**63** **Butler, S.H.**
■ A concise history of cricket. Hunstanton, Cricket Book Society, [1946]. 32p. (Publications. Ser. 1, no. 1)
——*re-issued in* Webber. Roy, *ed.* Cricket omnibus. 1946. *See no.* 982

**64** **Cardus** *Sir* **Neville**
■ Cricket. Longmans, Green, 1930. ix,177p. (The English Heritage Series)
——*rptd.* 1949. (Clifford Library)

**65** **Cavalcade** of cricket, 1748–1937. Gradidges Ltd., [1937]. [8]p. illus.
■

**65** **Clarke, P.D.**
**–1** Cricket from the inside. 1961. 190p. &
■ index. col. illus.
*MS on miscellaneous cricket topics by a prisoner at Wandsworth & Camp Hill: in the Cricket Society's Library*

**66** **Constantine, Learie Nicholas,** *Lord*
■ *Constantine, and* **Batchelor, Denzil**
The changing face of cricket. Eyre & Spottiswoode, 1966. xii,178p. illus. ports. diagr.

**67** **Cross, Jack,** *compiler*
■ Cricket. Jackdaw Publications, [1971]. illus. facsims. ports. (Jackdaw, no. 101)
*portfolio containing 8p. booklet, 7 reproductions of contemporary documents, 7 explanatory broadsheets, illustration sheet & field-placing card*

**67** The Dunlop Cricketer's companion.
**–1** Lavenham, Eastland P., 1976. 128p. illus.
■ facsims. ports. bibliog.

**67** **Dugan, Michael**
**–2** Cricket. Melbourne, Macmillan, 1979. 23p. illus. ports. diagrs. (Australian Fact Finders)
*for children*

**67** **Farmer, Bob**
**–3** Cricket guide; with additional records by
■ Ron Wills. Hamlyn, 1975. 96p. illus. stats. (Hamlyn Pocketbooks)

**67** **Frith, David Edward John**
**–4** The golden age of cricket 1890–1914.
■ Guildford, Lutterworth P., 1978. 192p. illus. & ports. (some col.), facsims.

**68** **Garnsey, George Leonard,** *compiler*
■ Cricket: its origin and development. Sydney, Australian Broadcasting Commission, 1935. 48p. illus. ports. diagrs. bibliog.

**69** **Gordon,** *Sir* **Home Seton Charles**
■ **Montagu,** *bart.*
Background of cricket. Barker, 1939. 348p. illus. ports.

**69** **Greig, Anthony William ("Tony")**
**–1** Cricket: the men and the game; as told to
■ David Lord. London, Hamlyn; Sydney, Ure Smith, 1976. 128p. illus. & ports. (some col.)
——rev. ed. Hamlyn, 1977. 136p.

**70** **Harris, Bruce**
■ The true book about cricket; illustrated by Leonard Hagety. Muller, 1958. 144p. illus. (True Books)

**71** **Hill, Barrington Julian Warren**
■ Cricket. Oxford, Blackwell, 1960. [vii], 109p. illus. ports. (Pocket histories)

**72** **Hutchinson, Horace Gordon,** *editor*
■ Cricket. Country Life, 1903. xxii,454p. illus. ports. (Country Life Library of Sport)

73 ■ **Johnston, Brian Alexander**
All about cricket. W.H. Allen, 1972. 170p.
illus. ports. diagrs. scores, stats. glossary
——[2nd ed.] Carousel Books, 1974.
206p. pbk.
——3rd ed. Carousel Books, 1978. 223p.
pbk.
*updated to end of 1977 season*

73 **M.C.C. Company Ltd**
–1 A short history of cricket. Bedford, the
■ Company, [193–?]. [6]p. fold. illus.

73 **Marlar, Robin**
–2 The story of cricket; edited by Susan Hill
■ . . . tables and statistics compiled by C.J.
Bartlett. Marshall Cavendish, 1979. 216p.
illus. & ports. (some col.), stats.

73 **Merchant, Vijay**
–3 Cricket. New Delhi, National Book Trust,
■ 1975. 64p. illus. ports. facsims, diagrs.
(Nehru Library for Children)

74 **Parker, Eric**
■ The history of cricket. Seeley Service,
[1950]. 672p. col. frontis. illus. ports.
scores, stats. (The Lonsdale Library of
Sports, Games & Pastimes)

75 **Pollard, Jack**
■ Bumpers, boseys and brickbats.
Sydney & Melbourne, Murray. [1971].
192p. illus. ports. diagrs. score, bibliog.
*accounts of controversial events, mostly in
Test cricket*

76 **Ross, Gordon**
■ A history of cricket. Barker. 1972. [viii],
192p. illus. ports.

76 **Sheppard, John**, *editor*
–1 Cricket: more than a game. Angus &
■ Robertson, 1975. viii, 256p. illus. & ports.
(some col.), stats.
*contributions by Arlott, Benaud, Cozier,
Duffus, Fingleton, etc*

76 **Smith, Peter**
–2 The observer's book of cricket. Warne,
■ 1973. viii, 182p. illus. (some col.), diagrs.
on end-papers, stats. (The Observer's
Pocket Series)
——revd. ed. by Reg Hayter. 1976. viii,
184p
——2nd revd. ed. by Reg Hayter. 1979.
190p.

77 **Southgate, Vera**
■ The story of cricket: with illustrations by
Jack Matthew. Loughborough, Wills &
Hepworth, 1964. 52p. col. illus. (Ladybird
"Easy Reading" Books)

78 **Sparks, Victor G.**
■ The cricketers' compendium: or, Cricket
from the country angle: being a complete
history of cricket and other items on the
good old game—how to play
successfully. etc. Natal, Besters, the
Author, [1948]. 124p. illus. diagrs. scores,
stats.

79 **[Symond, Ronald T.]**
■ Homage to cricket, by "Gryllus". Harmsworth, 1933. xi,156p.

80 **Thomson, Arthur Alexander**
■ Cricket; the golden ages. S. Paul, 1961.
224p. illus. ports. scores, stats.
——*another ed.* Sportsmans Book Club,
1962

81 **Warner, *Sir* Pelham Francis**
■ Cricket: a new edition, with contributions
by the Hon. R.H. Lyttelton, G.L. Jessop,
D.J. Knight, J. Shuter, E.R. Wilson. Longmans, Green, 1920. xii,348p. illus. ports.
stats. (The Badminton Library of Sports
and Pastimes)
*a new edition of no. 473*

82 Cricket between two wars. Chatto &
■ Windus, 1942. [vi],288p. illus. ports.
scores

83 ————, *editor*
■ Imperial cricket. London & Counties
Press Association, 1912. xxi, 503p. illus.
(some col.), ports. scores
——*subscribers' edition*, 1912

84 **Webber, Roy**
■ The Phoenix history of cricket. Phoenix
House, 1960. 264p. illus. ports. (Sports
Books)
——*another ed.* Sportsman's Book Club,
1961

85 **Whitbread and Co., Ltd.**
■ Catalogue of the collection of pictures and
other items illustrating the history of
cricket at "The Yorker"; with an introduction and an anthology of quotations on
cricket by A. Lloyd-Taylor, Whitbread,
[1954]. 76p. illus. ports.
——*abridged ed.* Cranbourne P., *n.d.* 15p.
*a list of items in the full Catalogue without
the illustrations, introductory matter and
selection of writings on cricket*

86 **Zulfiqar Ahmed**
■ [Cricket–history, how to play and
records]. Lahore, Nawa-i-Waqt Book
Depot, 1955. 120p. illus.
*in Urdu*

# MEMORABLE MATCHES

**86** **Arlott, [Leslie Thomas] John**
**–1** British sporting stories. News of the World, 1953. xi,223p.
*includes, pp. 154–61. "The greatest Test match" by Neville Cardus from his A cricketer's book*

**87** **Batchelor, Denzil Stanley**, *editor*
■ The match I remember. Laurie, 1950. 208p. illus. ports. scores
*accounts by eleven players*

**88** **Buchan, John**, *1st baron Tweedsmuir*, *compiler*
Great hours in sport. Nelson, 1921. 288p. illus.
*includes "The finest match I ever played in", by P.F. Warner*

**89** **Buchanan, Edward Handasyde**, *compiler*
■ Great cricket matches. Eyre & Spottiswoode, 1962. 408p. scores
*an anthology*

**90** **Buchanan, John**, *editor*
■ Cricket's greatest headlines. Lane Cove (N.S.W.), Project Publishing Pty, [1973]. 114p. illus. ports. scores
——2nd rev. printing. 1977
*accounts of memorable Test matches*

**90** Great moments in England v. Australia
**–1** Test cricket. Lane Cove, (N.S.W.), Project
■ Publishing Pty., [1975?]. 100p. incl. covers. illus. ports. stats.
*mostly from 1932–33 to 1974–75*

**91** **The Field**
One crowded hour. The Field, [1935]. 122p.
*includes "The best innings I ever played", by Lord Tennyson*

**92** **Fisher, Norman**
■ Great days in sport. Mitre P., [1943], 95p.
*cricket pp. 20–24, 45–46, 68–71, 78–81*

**93** **Graydon, John Allen**
■ Never-to-be-forgotten sports thrills. Findon Publications, [1946]. 64p. illus.
*cricket, pp. 15–17, 25–27, 31–33*

**93** More never-to-be-forgotten sports thrills.
**–1** Findon Publications, [1946]. 64p. illus.
*cricket chs. 2, 10*

**94** Still more never-to-be-forgotten sports
■ thrills. Findon Publications, [c. 1947]. 62p. illus. ports.
*cricket chs. 3, 10 and 15*

**95** **"I was there"**: twenty exciting sporting
■ events by sports writers of the "Daily Telegraph" and "Sunday Telegraph". Collins, 1966. viii,152p. illus. scores
*includes accounts of England v. Australia at Lord's, 1930, by E. W. Swanton pp. 52–62; and England v. West Indies at Lord's, 1963, by Alan Gibson, pp. 113–120*

**96** **Ledbrooke, Archibald William**
Great moments in sport; illustrated by Edmund Blandford. Phoenix House, 1956. 128p. illus.

**96** **McWhirter, Ross,** *and* **Norris**
**–1** Great moments in sport: a pictorial record of events that made headlines. Liverpool, Vernon Pools, 1962. 128p. illus. pbk.
*cricket pp. 12–13 "The fantastic Test at Brisbane" by E.M. Wellings*

**97** **Nickalls, Guy Oliver,** *editor*
■ With the skin of their teeth: memories of great sporting finishes in golf, cricket, . . . . Country Life, 1951. 168p. illus.
*cricket section pp. 28–47, by Herbert Sutcliffe, contains accounts of England v. Australia Tests at Adelaide, 1924–5; at the Oval, 1926; and at Melbourne, 1928–9*

**97** **Ross, Gordon,** *editor*
**–1** Great moments in cricket: a *Cricketer*
■ special. Ashurst, Tunbridge Wells, The Cricketer, 1975. 48p. illus. ports. facsims. of scores
*recalls 13 historic cricket matches*

**97** **Sport's** greatest headlines. Sydney,
**–2** Project Publishing Pty., 1974. illus.
*includes the Australia v. West Indies tied Test at Brisbane, 1960–61 series*

**97** **Thomas, Andrew,** *and* **Harris, Norman**
**–3** Great moments in cricket. Queen Anne
■ P., 1976. 143p. illus. ports.
*mostly Test match cricket from 1894; a collection of 20 pieces*

**98** **Tomkinson,** *Sir* **Geoffrey Stewart**
■ Memorable cricket matches. Kidderminster, G.T. Cheshire, 1958. 129p. col. port. scores
*limited ed. of 500 signed and numbered copies.*

# RECORDS AND STATISTICS

(Only general cricket records are listed here: for Test match records *see* INTERNATIONAL CRICKET: Test match cricket: England v. Australia, etc.; for records relating to English cricket *see* CRICKET IN ENGLAND AND WALES: History (and its subdivisions)

99 **Ashley-Cooper, Frederick Samuel**
■ Curiosities of first-class cricket [1730–1901]. Edmund Seale, 1901. viii,126p.
——*another ed.* 1901
*limited to 100 copies signed and interleaved*

100 Cricket veterans: [a Christmas card].
■ Milford, the Author, 1928. 7p.
*records examples of oldest playing cricketers*

101 **Association of Cricket Statisticians**
■ Unpublished scores 1. The Assoc., [197–]
*a series of 53 score cards of selected matches*

102 **Birch, John**
■ Cricket facts and figures. Drane, 1907. 118p. stats.

103 **Bland, Ernest A.**, *editor*
■ Fifty years of sport: records of sporting events from 1896 compiled by experts. "Daily Mail", [1947]. [v],576p. diagrs. stats.
*cricket pp. 132–160 by Ronald Symond*
——Fifty-two years of sport: . . . 1896 to 1949. [1949]. vi,637p. illus. diagrs. stats.
*cricket pp. 194–218*

104 **Brodribb, [Arthur] Gerald [Norcott]**
■ Champions of cricket: a new book of cricket records . . . Hunstanton (Norfolk), Cricket Book Society, 1947. 94p. stats.
——ltd. ed. 1947
*limited to 40 copies*
*covers all first-class cricket played May 1864–April 1947*

105 All round the wicket: a miscellany of facts
■ and fancies of first-class cricket. Sporting Handbooks, 1951. 215p. plan, stats.
*includes a list of cricket in fiction*

106 **Coxhead, A.C.**
■ Cricket records, with a commentary. Lawrence & Bullen, 1899. vii,91p. stats.

107 **Dale, Bernard**
■ Some statistics of cricket; or, The influence of the weather on the wicket, with a method for its elimination in the comparison of averages. Berridge, 1891. 31p.

107 **Desai, Kumarpal**
–1 Cricket world records; artist Rajnee Vyas.
■ Ahmedabad and Bombay, A.R. Sheth, [197–?]. 20p. col. illus.
*pen-pictures of selected record holders*

108 **[Ford, Alfred Lawson]**
■ Curiosities of cricket from the earliest records to the present time, by An Old Cricketer. Brighton, D.B. Friend, 1897. [39]p.
*25 copies only for private circulation*
——facsim. ed. with introduction by Irving Rosenwater. Ewell, Epsom (Surrey), J.W. McKenzie, 1978. 48p.
*limited to 150 copies*

109 **Frindall, William H.**, *compiler*
■ The Kaye book of cricket records. Kaye & Ward, 1968. xix,534p. stats.
——*supplement.* 1970. 62p. stats.

110 **Gordon**, *Sir* **Home Seton Charles**
■ **Montagu**, *12th bart., compiler*
Cricket form at a glance, showing the batting and bowling of every cricketer who has played in first class matches in any two seasons between 1878–1902, with every run scored for or against the Australians in England, the elevens they met, the results; and that of every county match. Constable, 1902. xv,314p. stats.

111 Cricket form at a glance in this century:
■ showing the batting and bowling of every cricketer who has played in first class matches in any two seasons between 1901 and 1923, with Test match averages, aggregates and out and home aggregates in the county championship, complete record of results and aggregates of results of all first class matches, charts of captains and teams and the Role of Honour of cricketers. Duckworth, 1924. xiv,278p. stats.

112 Cricket form at a glance for sixty years
■ 1878–1937. Barker, [1938], 423p. stats.

113 **The Guinness** book of records. Guinness
□ Superlatives. *annual.* illus. & ports. (some col.), diagrs. stats.
26th ed. edited and compiled by Norris McWhirter; sports editor Stan Greenberg. 1979. 352p. incl. covers
*1st publd. 1955; 4th ed. 1960; following ed. published as 10th ed. 1962*
*with cricket section*

114 **Hay & Son**
■ Cricket records compiled from Wisden's cricketers' almanack. Hove, Combridges, 1926. 74p. stats. (Hay's Sports and Games Series)
*rptd. from Wisden for 1926*

115 **Ironside, Frederick James**
■ The world's cricket record chart. Sydney, Hordern, 1900. bs.
——*another ed.* 1903. bs.
——*another ed. with title:* World's cricket records. 1912. bs.

116 **Jeffery, Gordon**, *editor*
The Armada book of sporting records. Collins, 1973. stats.
*cricket, pp. 59–76*

116 **Kathirgamathesan, C.**
-1 All time all world records, Ceylon – M.C.C. (1970): match souvenir. Jaffna, Rangi Publication, [1970]
*sponsored by Jolly Rogers Sports Club*

117 **Lester, John Henry**, *compiler*
Scores of fifty runs and upwards made by leading cricketers in matches played since 1864. 1899. 632p. *MS*
*in M.C.C. Library, Lord's*

118 Bat v. ball: the book of individual cricket
■ records, &c., 1864–1900. Nottingham, Boots: London, Simpkin, Marshall, [1900]. l,366p. stats.
*also paper and de luxe eds. Contains a chapter by A.J. Gaston on 'Cricket curiosities'*

118 **The Lonsdale** book of sporting records.
-1 Seeley Service, 1937. xvi,458p. illus. ports. diagrs. (Lonsdale Library)
*contains pp. 93–9 "The cricket season 1936" by D.R. Jardine*

119 **Morgan-Browne, Hubert**
■ Sporting and athletic records. Methuen, 1897. xx,[ii],366p. stats.
*cricket pp. 31–70*

120 **Moti Nandy**
■ Cricket records (from 1876 to September 1966). Calcutta, Subarnarekha, 1966. x,144p. illus. stats.

121 **Pogson, Norman J.**
■ International wicket-keepers of three countries. Lincoln Williams, 1932. 88p stats.
*a statistical record of all Australian, English and South African Test wicket-keepers, 1877–1931*

122 **Prudential Assurance Co.**
■ Sports records. The Company, 1928. xii,248p. illus. stats
*cricket statistics pp. 49–70*

123 **Roberts, Edward Lamplough**, *compiler*
■ Batsmen and bowlers 1900–1934. Purley, A. Robertson, [1934]. 64p. stats.

124 Cricket careers at a glance. Horbury
■ (Yorks.), Sykes, [1934]. 32p. incl. adverts. stats.
*statistics of leading players*

125 Cricket facts and figures, *annual*
■ 1934. Purley, Robertson, 1934. 40p.
1935. Croydon, Roffey, 1935. 44p.
1936. Birmingham, Hudson, 1936. 22p.
[1937]. n.p., [1938]. 48p. + folding suppl.
*illus. ports. stats. bibliog.*
*stats. to end of 1937 season and suppl. of England v. Australia 1877–1937*

126 Cricket records, stats.
□ 1935. Purley, Robertson, 1935. 32p.
1936. The Author, 1936. 32p.
1938. Nottingham, Notts. C.C.C., 1938. 32p.
——Leeds, Yorks. C.C.C., 1938, 32p.
1939. The Author, for Yorks. C.C.C., 1939. 32p.
1940. Birmingham, Hudson, 1940. 32p.
1946.      ,,           ,, 1946, 32p.
1948.      ,,           ,, 1948. 34p.
1949.      ,,           ,, 1949. 32p.
1951.      ,,           ,, 1951. 34p.
*frontis.*

127 Cricket odds and ends 1936. Nottingham,
■ Gunn & Moore, [1936]. 22p. stats.

128 Giant killers: (a record of some unex-
■ pected cricket). Nottingham, Gunn & Moore, [1939?]. 32p. score.

129 **Royal Insurance Company**
Record of sports. Liverpool, the Company. *annual. stats.*
*for 1904 [no edition given]. cricket pp. 12–23*
1905 [no edition given]. cricket pp. 16–33
1906 4th ed. cricket pp. 26–45
1907 5th ed.      ,, pp. 35–56
1908 6th ed.      ,, pp. 34–55
1909 7th ed.      ,, pp. 52–73
1911 8th ed.      ,, pp. 86–107
1914 9th ed.      ,, pp. 75–91

130 **Somerset, A.F.**, *compiler*
The "Somerset" cricket scorebook; introduction and curiosities by A.F. Somerset compiled with assistance of A.L. Ford and A.J. Gaston. Brighton, Southern Publishing Co., 1912. 170p.

131 **Taylor, Alfred Daniel**
■ Cricket extraordinary; reprinted from "Hove Gazette". Hove, Emery, 1903. 22p.

132 **[Tufnell, Carleton F.]**
■ The cricketer's "form at a glance": an explanatory key to Tufnell's individual player's batting and bowling charts. Cricket Office, [1889]. 4p. with 5 folding charts

133 **Webber, Roy**, *compiler*
■ Cricket records, 1947. Hunstanton, Cricket Book Society, [1947]. 28p.

134 ■ The Playfair book of cricket records. Playfair Books, 1951. 320p. stats.
——completely revised and reset ed. *with title:* The book of cricket records. Phoenix House, 1961. 480p. stats.
——*another ed.* Sportsmans Book Club, 1962
——*concise ed.* Phoenix House, 1963. 128p. stats.
——*re-issued.* 1965. pbk.

# QUIZ BOOKS

135 **Bell, W.,** *compiler*
The sporting what do you know: 1,500 questions and answers to things not generally known in the realms of sport. W. Foulsham, [1937]. 190p. (Knowledge Library)
*cricket pp. 76–86*

136 **"Big Chief I-Spy",** *pseud.*
■ I-spy cricket. Dickens P., 1970. 48p. illus. ports.

136 **Boycott, Geoffrey**
–1 Geoff Boycott's cricket quiz book; edited
■ by Barrie J. Tomlinson. Mirror Books, 1979. 159p. illus. diagrs.

137 **Carpenter, Peter**
Sport for fun: a quiz book. Hutchinson, 1959. 165p.
*includes cricket*

138 **Cleaver, Hylton**
■ Sport problems, can you solve them?: one hundred and fifty intricate sports questions and authoritative rulings. Warne, 1937
*includes application of cricket laws*

138 **Coley, Chris**
–1 Chris Coley's sportsquiz book. [Gloucestershire C.C.C., 1979?] 44p. illus. ports.
■ *includes cricket questions and answers*

138 **Culverhouse, Jonathan,** *compiler*
–2 Cricket quiz book. Marshall Cavendish
■ Books, 1979. 96p. illus. ports. (some col.), diagrs.

138 **Frindall, William H.**
–3 Playfair cricket quiz book. Queen Anne
■ P., 1976. 120p. illus. maps.

138 **Goodchild, R.A.**
–4 Cricket quiz book. Number one. Wend-
■ over (Bucks.), John Goodchild, 1978. 47p. illus.

139 **Hoyle, Fred**
■ The nature of the universe: a series of broadcast lectures. Oxford, Blackwell, 1950. v,121p. illus.

*obviously not a 'quiz book', but it contains, pp. 22–24, a mathematical problem first set by Sir Arthur Eddington in* The New Statesman, 1938, *which consists of reconstructing the whole innings in a cricket match from the score-card and one or two additional facts.*

139 **Jeffery, Gordon**
–1 The Armada cricket quiz book. Collins,
■ 1975. 128p. illus. diagrs. maps. score, stats. (Armada Paperbacks)
*with answers*

140 **Kosky, Jack,** *compiler*
■ Sports quiz book. Godwin, 1963. 96p. illus.
*includes cricket*

141 **Langley, Brian,** *compiler*
■ Cricket quiz: over 500 questions and answers about the "King of games". Danceland Publications, 1945. 25p.
*errata slip bearing name of author pasted over that of Robert Tearle*

141 **Lewthwaite, Hazel,** *and* **Barnes, David,**
–1 *compilers*
■ A question of sport. B.B.C., 1976. 127p. illus. ports. pbk.
*based on B.B.C.1 television series of same name; with answers. Includes cricket*

142 **McMahon, J.K.**
■ First class cricket quiz: Test match features 1880 to 1948. Belfast, Macgowan, 1948. 70p. illus. scores. stats.
*includes scores and statistics of England v. Australia, 1948.*

143 **Norrie, Ian,** *and* **Jones, Maurice,** *compilers*
■ Cricket quiz: 308 questions and answers about cricketers, cricket records and the laws of the game. Joiner & Steele, 1955. 44p.
——*2nd ed. with title:* Test your cricket: nearly 400 questions and answers on all aspects of cricket. Constable, 1960. 45p.

143 **Puri, Narottam**
–1 Cricket quiz. New Delhi, etc., Vikas Publishing House PVT Ltd., 1977. xii,125p. illus. ports. pbk. (Bell Books)

144 **Rae, Victor**
■ Cricket quiz and score book. West Ealing, the Author. [1954]. 9p. + 23p. of score sheets

145 **Roberts, Edward Lamplough**
■ Cricketers' quiz and a list of books on cricket and cricketers. Birmingham, Hudson, [1941]. 32p. incl. adverts.

145 **Rosenwater, Irving,** *compiler*
–1 The Cricketer's book of crossword
■ puzzles. New English Library, 1975.
128p.

*"presented by The Cricket Society";*
*consists of 56 puzzles originally compiled for*
*The Cricketer*

# THE CONDUCT OF THE GAME

## ADMINISTRATION

*(see also:* CRICKET IN ENGLAND AND WALES:
ADMINISTRATION)

146 **Imperial Cricket Conference**
■ Rules. The Conference.
1950
*amended 1953, 1958, 1959, 1960, 1961*
*contd. as: International Cricket Conference.*
*Rules*

147 **International Cricket Conference**
■ Rules. The Conference. *annual*
1965 to date
*formerly: Imperial Cricket Conference.*
*Rules*

## LAWS

(arranged in order of first publication)

148 **Articles** of agreement by and between his
Grace the Duke of Richmond and Mr
Brodrick (for two cricket matches)
concluded the eleventh of July, 1727. *Ms.*
signed Richmond and A. Broderick
n.b. *The 14th article: The Batt Men for*
*every one they count are to touch the Umpire's*
*stick*
see *National Book League. Cricket: a cata-*
*logue of an exhibition . . . 1950*

148 **250th anniversary** cricket match in the
–1 dress and under the laws of 1727, The
■ Duke of Richmond's XII v. The
Gentlemen of Pepperharrowe, the cricket
ground, Goodwood, Sussex, Sunday July
10, 1977: souvenir scorecard. Illustrated
London News, 1977. 12p. incl. covers &
adverts. illus. ports. facsim.
*explanatory article by Timothy J. McCann*
*and a facsimile of the Articles of Agreement*
*signed on July 11, 1727 by the 2nd Duke of*
*Richmond and the Captain of Peper Harow,*
*Mr. A. Brodrick*

149 **The Laws** of the game of cricket. Cray-
ford, J. Ware
*a print on linen: the cricket scene is an*
*adaptation of Hayman's picture "Cricket in*
*Marylebone Fields" and the Laws (1744*
*Code) are printed as a border. (D. Rait Kerr).*
*Almost certainly before 1752*

150 **The new** universal magazine: or,
■ Gentleman and lady's polite instructor.
M. Cooper
*Vol. II, Nov. 1752, pp. 581–2 contains first*
*known publication of the earliest Code of Laws*
*which had been drawn up in 1744. They*
*appear under the heading "The game at*
*cricket, as settled by the Cricket Club in 1744,*
*and play'd at the Artillery-Ground, London"*

151 **The game** of cricket, as settled by the
□ several cricket-clubs, particularly that of
the Star and Garter in Pall-Mall. Printed
for M. Read and sold by W. Reeve in Fleet
Street, 1755. 19p. folding frontis.
*the first publication of the Laws in booklet*
*form*
——*another issue. 1757*
——*rptd. in* The Daily Journal. R.
Baldwin, 1764, pp. 89–91 *under title:* Articles of the game of cricket . . .
——*another ed. with title:* Articles of the
game of cricket. . . . J. Williams, 1774.
16p. folding frontis.

152 **The Laws** of cricket, revised at the Star
■ and Garter, Pall-Mall, February 25, 1774,
by a Committee of Noblemen and
Gentlemen of Kent, Hampshire, Surry
[sic], Sussex, Middlesex, London. Printed
for J. Ridley, St. James's Street, by order
of the Committee. [1774]. 18p.
——*another ed.* Sevenoaks, T. Clout, Jun.,
[177–]. 16p.

153 **Hoyle, Edmund**
■ Hoyle's games improved; revised and
corrected by Charles Jones, esq. J.
Rivington & J. Wilkie, [etc], 1775.
xii,228p.
*contains "The laws of cricket revised at the*
*Star and Garter, Pall-Mall, February 25,*
*1774, pp. 210–14*
——*another ed.* W. Wood, 1778. xi,216p.
*"The Laws of cricket" pp. 198–201*

154 **New** articles of the game of cricket, as
■ settled and revised at the Star and Garter,
Pallmall, February the 25th 1774; by a
Committee of Noblemen and Gentlemen
of Kent, &c. To which is added the old
laws as settled by the several cricket-
clubs. J. Williams, 1775. 16p. folding
frontis.

154 **The Laws** of cricket, revised at the Star
–1 and Garter, Pall-Mall, Feb. 25th 1784, by
■ a Committee of Noblemen and
Gentlemen of Kent, Hampshire, Surrey,
Sussex, Middlesex, and London. H.
Reynell, No. 2 Piccadilly, near the Hay-
Market. bs.
*the only copy known is in the Finch MSS
(ref. no. DG7/3/141) held at the Leicestershire
Records Office, Leicester: refers to a 6-ball over*

155 **The Laws** of the noble game of cricket as
■ established at the Star and Garter, Pall
Mall by a Committee of Noblemen and
Gentlemen. J. Wallis, 1785. bs. 1 illus.
*reliable ed.*

156 **New** articles of the game of cricket, as
■ settled and revised at the Star and Garter,
Pall Mall, February the 25th, 1774, by a
Committee of Noblemen and Gentlemen
of Kent, &c. Maidstone, printed and sold
by J. Blake, [c. 1786]. 12p. folding frontis
——*reprint. Printed by Ford, Shapland and
Co. for Ernest A. Watkins, [c. 1956]*

157 **New** articles of the game of cricket, as
■ settled and revised at the Star and Garter,
Pall Mall, February, 1786; by a Committee
of Noblemen and Gentlemen of Kent &c.
To which is added the old laws as settled
by the several cricket-clubs. H. Turpin,
1786. 21p. folding frontis.

158 **The new** universal magazine, July, 1787.
■ *pp. 38–40 contains "The laws of the noble
game of cricket, as established at the Star and
Garter, Pall-Mall, by a Committee of
Noblemen and Gentlemen." 1 illus.*

159 **Hoyle, Edmund**
■ New Hoyle, or the general repository of
games; containing rules and instructions
for playing . . ., from the manuscript of
the late Charles Pigott, Esq. 2nd ed.
James Ridgway, [179–?]. x,238p.
*rules of cricket pp. 210–14*

160 **The sporting** magazine, or monthly
calendar of the transactions of the turf,
the chace, and every other diversion
interesting to the man of pleasure and
enterprise. Vol. 2. Printed for the proprietors and sold by J. Wheble, 1793
*the issue for June contains "The Laws of
cricket, as revised by the Cricket Club at St.
Mary-le-bone"*

161 **Britcher, Samuel**
A complete list of all the grand matches.
1796. Printed by T. Craft, 1796. 40p.
*this issue contains the 1788 revision of the
Laws by the M.C.C. "Reasonable to suppose
an authoritative edition" (D. Rait Kerr)*

162 **Notes** on the laws of cricket. Heckmondwike, C. Ward. [c. 1800]. 8p.

163 **Laws** of the manly game of cricket.
■ Gravesend, *printed by* R. Pocock, 1803.
10p.

164 **Boxall, Thomas**
■ Rules and instructions for playing at the
game of cricket, as practised by the most
eminent players, to which is subjoined
the laws and regulations of cricketters
[sic], as revised by the Cricket Club at
Mary-le-bone. Printed by Harrild and
Billing
——3rd ed. 1804. 80p. frontis.
*the 3rd ed. printed the current laws; for
fuller entry see no. 373*

165 **Laws** of cricket. Boston. 1806
*in Taylor*

166 **Hoyle, Edmond**
■ The new pocket Hoyle. Part II consisting
of gentleman's games . . . accurately
displaying the rules and practice . . . with
a variety of new improvements by
Charles Jackson. R. Scholey, [etc.], 1808.
[i],371p. illus.
*issued in slip-case. Laws of cricket
pp. 36–41*

167 **Laws** of the noble game of cricket, as
revised by the Club at St. Mary-le-Bone,
to this present day. J. Bailey, [1809?]. 12p.
folding frontis.

168 **The Laws** of the noble game of cricket as
revised by the Club at St. Mary-le-Bone.
John Wallis, 1809. bs. 1 illus.

169 **Laws** of the noble game of cricket.
■ Corrected to the present time, according
to the rules of the St. Mary-le-bone Club.
Lewes, J. Baxter, 1809. 12p.

170 **The Laws** of cricket, as revised by the St
■ Mary-le-bone Club, 1809. Printed for the
use of the L[iverpool] C.C., established
May, 1811. Liverpool, printed by Harris
Bros., 1811

171 **The Laws** of cricket, as revised by the
■ Cricket Club, at St. Mary-le-bone, 1816.
T. Craft. bs.
——*another ed. [with laws revised to
1820]. 1820*
*reliable versions (Rait Kerr)*

172 **The Laws** of cricket, revised by the Mary-
■ lebone Club in the year 1823. Carpenter
and Son, 1823. bs.
*reliable version (Rait Kerr)*

173 **Rules** of the game of cricket, as revised
■ by the Cricket Club at St. Mary-le-bone,
1819. Farnham, C. Clapshaw, 1823. 12p.
——*another ed. with title: The laws . . . as
revised . . . 1825,* 1825. 12p.
*unreliable versions (Rait Kerr)*

174 **The Laws** of Cricket, as approved by the
■ Mary-le-bone Club, and appeared in
Bell's Life in London, June 15th, 1828.
Ripon, T. Langdale, 1828. 16p.

175 **The sporting** magazine
*issue for June, 1828. This ed. of the rules
was reprinted by Haygarth in Scores and biographies, vol. II*

176 **The Laws** of cricket revised by the Mary-
■ lebone Club in the year 1830. B. Dark,
1830. bs.
——*another ed.* Traveller, [1830]. bs.
*both reliable versions (Rait Kerr)*

177 **Laws** of the manly and noble game of
■ cricket, as revised by the Mary-le-bone
Club. *Printed by* Lewis & Co. [1830]. 14p.
*probably reprint of the Farnham editions of
1823 and 1825 with a few alterations. Unreliable. (Rait Kerr)*

178 **The Laws** of cricket, revised by the Marylebone Club in the year 1835. J.H. Dark,
1835. bs.

179 **New** laws of the game of cricket, 1835. E.
Wallis, [1835]. bs.
——*another issue.* n.d.
*unreliable . . . apart from one or two correc-
tions, they have been lifted from the 20th
edition of Lambert's Guide (Rait Kerr)*

180 **The oracle** of rural life and sportsman's
■ almanac 1840. Baily, 1840. 96p. illus.
*includes the laws of cricket pp. 87–9*

181 **The Laws** of cricket as revised and
amended by the Mary-le-bonne Club,
2nd June, 1845, with notes explanatory of
the usages of the game and practical hints
to the young cricketer, by a Member of
the Toronto Club, 1845. Toronto, Toronto
C.C., 1845. 29p.

182 **The Laws** of cricket by authority of the
Marylebone Club as altered and revised,
2nd June, 1845. Ongar, T.S. Richardson,
1845

183 **The Laws** of cricket. J.D. Mills, 1848

184 **Burden, James W.**
■ The illustrated laws of cricket, as revised
by The Marylebone Club, 1849, with
copious explanatory remarks . . . to
which is added an essay On cricket, by

Ned Rub [pseud. of Burden], with the
alteration of the laws, and an abstract of
the averages of 1848. W. Gibbs, 1849. 30p.
illus. stats.

185 **The Laws** of cricket, dedicated to the
members of the Langley Club. *Printed by*
L. Bradley, 1850. 16p.
*in Goldman*

186 **Burden, James W.,** *compiler*
The cricketers' chronicle, containing the
laws of cricket, as revised by the Marylebone Club, 1852, with copious explanatory remarks; to which is added an
abstract of the averages of 1851 . . . and
other . . . information. G. Vickers, [1852].
31p.

186 **Mills, J.D.**
–1 Mills's unique pocket edition of the laws
of cricket. Wandsworth, J.D. Mills,
[1852?]

187 **Lillywhite's** pocket book of the laws of
■ cricket, as revised by the Marylebone
Cricket Club, May 15, 1854. 2nd ed. [F.
Lillywhite, 1854?] 16p.
*reprint of the laws in Lillywhite's Guide.
7th ed. (see no. 1086), except that amendments listed on p. 101 of the Guide and
adopted by the M.C.C. on 15th May, 1854,
are included. Many editions, e.g. 60th ed.
[c. 1875], 16p.*

188 **The Laws** of cricket, as arranged by the
Marylebone Club, London, for the season
1856 . . . republished in Victoria for the
use of the clubs. Melbourne, Wilson,
Mackinnon & Fairfax, [1856]. 8p.
——*another ed.* 1862. 8p.

189 **The Laws** of cricket, as revised by the
Marylebone Club and adopted by the
Worcester Cricket Club. Worcester,
*printed by* Edward R. Risk, 1857. 20p.

190 **The Laws** of cricket for single and double
wicket at adopted by the Marylebone
Club, London, England. Toronto, Henry
Rowsell, 1857. 12p.
*amendment slip issued 1858 giving altera-
tion to Law 10 by M.C.C. May 1858*

191 **The Laws** of cricket as revised by the
■ Marylebone Cricket Club, in 1860. Chesterfield, *printed by* J. Walton, [1860]. 8p.

192 **Ironside, Frederick James**
■ The laws of cricket as revised by the
Marylebone Club with explanatory notes;
together with the scores of all the intercolonial matches, Victoria v. N. S. Wales
. . . 1856 up to 1875. Sydney, Gibbs, Shallard, 1875. viii,63p. scores. stats.

193 **Cricket:** its rules, laws and regulations. Adelaide, Frearson, 1876. 52p. illus.
*cover-title: Frearson's cricketers' guide and annual for season 1876–77*

194 **Laws** of cricket. Sheffield, Hurst, 1877

195 □ **The Laws** of cricket as revised by the Marylebone Cricket Club in 1884: together with instructions and diagrams showing how to place a team in the field for fast, medium, or slow bowling. Wright, [1884]. [2],xviiip. incl. adverts. diagrs.
*numerous eds. with varying titles published by Wright & Co. and the "Cricket Press", 1884–1931. The majority include "Short hints to young players" by W.W. Read*

196 **The Laws** of cricket, as revised by the Marylebone Club. Sheffield, Hurst, [1885]. 14p.

196 –1 **The Laws** of cricket, lawn tennis, badminton, croquet, archery, bowls, etc., etc. Mead & Deverell, [c. 1885]. 28p.

196 –2 **Nederlandsche Cricket Bond**
Regels van het cricketspel; uitgegaven en herzien door het hoofdbestuur van den Nederlandsche Cricket Bond benevens wenken voor de beoefening. Hague, Moulton, 1886
——3rd ed. 1891
*rules of cricket; Dutch text*

197 **The Laws** of cricket. Cricket Field, [c. 1892]. 25p.

198 **Laws** of cricket. Horace Cox.
*"several issues, 1892–95". (Taylor)*

199 ■ **The amended** laws of cricket, as adopted at a special general meeting of the Marylebone Club, 1st May. 1889. Bury, Fletcher and Speight, 1894. [12]p.

200 **Pentelow, John Nix**
Proposed revision of the laws of the game. Wright & Co, 1894

201 **The Laws** of cricket, with list of fixtures and memoranda. "Cricket" Office, 1899. 48p.

202 **Laws** of cricket. Edinburgh, Stewart, 1900

203 **Amended** laws of cricket. Benetfink & Co., 1901
*in Taylor*

204 **Laws** of cricket, as revised by the M.C.C., 1884, 1889, 1900 and 1902. *Printed by* Morton and Burt, [1902?]. bs.

205 □ **Marylebone Cricket Club**
The laws of cricket: rules of county cricket and instructions to umpires with decisions and interpretations authorized by the M.C.C. London, the Club, 1902. 23p.
——2nd ed. 1904
——3rd ed. 1906. 24p.
——4th ed. 1908. 25p.
——5th ed. 1909?
——6th ed. 1910. 25p.
——7th ed. 1911. 26p.
——8th ed. 1913. 26p.
——9th ed. 1914. 26p.
——10th ed. 1918. 26p.
——11th ed. 1920. 26p.
——12th ed. 1920. 27p.
——14th ed. 1923. 27p.
——15th ed. 1932. 28p. with insert "Alterations and additions to the laws of cricket for matches overseas"
——16th ed. *with title* The laws of cricket, with decisions and interpretations authorized by the M.C.C. together with rules of the following bodies: Imperial Cricket Conference, Board of Control of Test Matches at Home, Advisory County Cricket Committee, Minor Counties' Cricket Association. 1939. 39p.
——re-issue. 1945

205 –1 **New South Wales Cricket Association**
Laws of cricket, instructions to umpires (amended to 1902). Sydney, the Assoc., 1902

206 ■ **[The Laws** of cricket as revised by the Marylebone Cricket Club, London], Surat, Airish Mission Printing P., 1903. 16p. diagr.
*Gujarati text*

207 ■ **Dansk Boldspil-Union**
Love for kricket med Marylebone Klubbens decisioner og forklaringer. 4de oplag. Autoiseret udgave. Kobenhavn, H. Hagerups, 1906. 58p. diagr.
*the laws of cricket in Danish*
——Fjerde udgave. Dansk Cricket Forbund, 1965. 52p. diagrs.

208 ■ **Deutscher Cricket-Bund**
Cricket-regeln. Berlin, the Bund, [1913?] 22p. diagrs.
*the laws of cricket in German*

209 ■ **Polishwalla, Ponchaji Nussarwanji**
Cricket law points, *n.p. or d.* [192–]. 4p.
*loose leaf oblong*

210 ■ **Thomas, Percy Francis, "H.P.-T.",** *pseud.*
Old-time cricket: the oldest laws of the game; with their orthographic and dimensional analysis; and a review of the conditions under which they were

collected. Nottingham, Richards, 1924. 80p. illus.

**211 Nederlandsche Cricket Bond**
■ De regels van het cricketspel en wenken voor scheidsrechters met beslissingen en uitleggingen vastgesteld door de Marylebone Cricket Club. N.C.B., [1925], 24p.
*the laws and notes for umpires with decisions established by the M.C.C. translated into Dutch*

**212 Illinois Cricket Association**
■ A brief explanation of the game of "cricket", by K.A. A[uty]. Chicago, the Assoc., [193–]. [6]p. folded. diagr.

**213 'Barrier' book of rules: cricket. Bedford,**
□ M.C.C. Co., [1931]. 48p. diagr.
——*another ed.* 1935. 64p.

**214 Bett, H. Drysdale,** *editor*
■ The key to the laws of cricket. Melbourne, Australian Cricketer, 1932. 36p.
——2nd ed. 1933
*both issued as supplement to the Australian Cricketer*
*later copies have 1 leaf insert of amendments (supplement for 1933–34)*

**215 Watson, C.S.,** *editor*
■ The comprehensive index to the laws of cricket and their interpretation. Sydney (N.S.W.), Metropolitan Business College, 1923. diagrs.
——rev. ed. Sydney, N.S.W. Junior Cricket Union, 1942. 79,24p. diagrs.
——rev. ed. *with title*: Watson's index to the laws. 1950. 128p. diagrs.

**215 Women's Cricket Association**
**–1** Notes on the laws of cricket for umpires, scorers and players. The Assoc., 1933. 28p.

**216 A handbook on women's cricket**
■ including the laws of cricket and notes for players, umpires and scorers. The Assoc. [c. 1935]. 47p. diagrs.

**217 Parthasarthy, C.D.**
Laws of cricket as laid down by the Marylebone Cricket Club, England, and umpire's chart. Madras, P.V.K. Moorthy, 1946. 36p. illus.

**218 Marylebone Cricket Club**
■ The laws of cricket: 1947 code. London, the Club, 1947. 30p.
——2nd ed. 1952. [i],30p.
——3rd ed. 1962. [i],36p.
*2nd issue.* [1962]. 36p.
——4th ed. 1968. 38p.
——5th ed. 1973. 41p.

**219 Sports** and games: official rules. N. Kaye,
□ 1949. 488p. illus. diagrs.
——*subsequently issued with title*: Official rules of sports and games
——2nd ed. 1950–51. 1950. 500p.
——3rd ed. 1954–55. 1954. 539p.
——4th ed. 1957–58. 1957. 554p.
*rptd.* Sportman's Book Club, 1958
——5th ed. 1961–62. 1961. 596p.
——6th ed. 1964–65. 1964. 682p.
——7th ed. 1966–67. 1966. 675p.
——8th ed. 1968–69. 1968. 716p.
——9th ed. 1970–71. 1970. 778p.
——10th ed. 1972–73. 1972. 801p.
——[11th ed.] 1974–75. 1974. 806p.
——[12th ed.] 1976–77. 1976. 862p.
——[13th ed.] 1978–79. 1978. 870p.
*includes the laws of cricket*

**220 Tate, Maurice William,** *and* **Goodall, Roy**
Vexed points in the laws of cricket and football, with some talk about beer, *n.p.,* [195–?]
*section on football by R.G.*

**221 Rait Kerr, Rowan Scrope**
■ The laws of cricket: their history and growth. Longmans, Green, 1950. xvi, 127p. illus. bibliog.
*contains "In certamen pilae", 1706, with Perry's translation, 1922. See no. 855*

**222 Marylebone Cricket Club**
□ The laws of cricket. Educational Productions, for the M.C.C., 1951. 48p. illus. & diagrs. (some col). ("Know the Game" Series)
——2nd ed. corrected to 1952. [1952]
*2nd issue* corrected to 1953. 1953
*3rd issue* corrected to 1954. 1954
*4th issue* corrected to 1955. 1955
*5th issue* corrected to 1956. 1956
*6th issue* corrected to 1957. 1957
*7th issue* corrected to 1958. 1958
——3rd ed. 1962
*2nd issue* with amendments incorporated for 1967 season. [1967]
*3rd issue* with amendments. 1969
*4th issue* with amendments. 1970
*5th issue* with amendments. 1971
*6th issue* with amendments. 1973
*7th issue* with amendments. 1974
*8th issue* with amendments. 1975
——9th ed. [sic] *with title*: Cricket. Wakefield, EP Publishing [for] the M.C.C., 1976. 48p. illus. (some col.). ("Know the Game" Series)
*cover title*: The Laws of Cricket
*rpdt. 1977, 1978*

■ ——*Dutch ed. with title*: Cricket; Nederlandse bewerking by R.G. Ingelse. Amsterdam, Duwaer & Zonen, *n.d.* 48p. illus. diagrs. (Ken uw sport)

223 **Brodribb, [Arthur] Gerald [Norcott]**
■ Next man in: a survey of cricket laws and
customs. Putnam, 1952. 248p. illus.
diagrs. stats.
——*another ed.* Sportsman's Book Club,
1953

224 **Marylebone Cricket Club**
[The laws of cricket] Die krieketreëls
(kode vir 1947-2de uitgawe 1952). South
African C.A., [195?]. 13p.
*a translation into Afrikaans of the M.C.C.
Laws of cricket 1947 code. 2nd ed. 1952*

225 **Laws** of cricket as revised by Marylebone
□ Cricket Club. (Corrected to 1954). W.B.
Tattersall Sports Press, [1955?]. 22p.
——*another issue with cover-title over
printed* (Corrected to 1955). [1955?]
——*another issue with title:* Cricket laws
(Corrected to 1960). [1960?]
——*another issue with cover-title overprinted*
(Corrected to 1961). [1961?]. 23p.

226 **Nederlandse Cricket Bond**
■ De regels van het cricketspel: with foreword by W.F. Bok. [Haarlem, Propaganda Commissie van de Nederlandse
Cricket Bond], 1956. 43p. illus. diagrs.

227 **Laws** of cricket. New Delhi, 1964. 48p.
illus.

228 **Glen of Michigan Cricket Club**
■ The laws of cricket as edited by the Glen
of Michigan Cricket Club. New York, the
Club, 1965. [24]p. illus.
*an advertisement & price list for ladies'
fashions. Includes a reprint of the Laws*

229 **Cooke, James Gerard**
Krieketreg: goedgekeur deur die Suid-
Afrikaanse Krieketraad en met verlof van
de M.C.C. uitgegee. Johannesburg, Voor-
trekkerpers, 1966. 200p. illus.
*Afrikaans text: Cricket laws: approved by
the S.A. Cricket Board and published with
permission of the M.C.C.*

230 **National Cricket Association**
■ Experimental laws and conditions. The
Association. *annual.* diagr.
*1969 to date*

230 **Wright, Billy,** *editor*
–1 Rules of the game. S. Paul, 1971. 285p.
■ diagrs.
*published in association with an ATV tele-
vision series; cricket pp. 79–97, an explanation of the laws with a glossary of terms*

230 **Banerjee, S.K.**
–2 The laws of cricket & umpiring. West
Bengal, J. Banerjee, 1973. 92p. illus.

230 **Rules** of the game: the complete illus-
–3 trated encyclopedia of all the sports of the
■ world; by the Diagram Group. N.Y. &
London, Paddington P., [1974]. 320p.
illus. col. diagrs.
——rptd. Bantam Books, 1976
*cricket pp. 174–7*

## Brighter Cricket

231 **Gamage, A.W., Ltd**
Gamage's rules for brighter cricket; illustrated by Rip! A.W. Gamage, Ltd., 1919.
16p. illus.

232 **Meyers, Edward**
■ Improvement of cricket by enforced retir-
ements. Melbourne, [the Author], 1926.
16p.

233 **Young, Richard A.**
■ A time of experiment: a suggested
solution of the cricket controversy. Eton,
Spottiswoode, Ballantyne & Co., Eton
College, 1935. iii,31p.
*proposals for overcoming the slow rate of
the fall of wickets*

## L.B.W.

234 **Ahern, W. T.**
■ LBW round the wicket. Melbourne, *privately printed by* Ford & Sons, [1906?]. 8p.
diagrs.

235 **Bligh,** *the Hon* **Edward Vesey**
■ "L.B.W." and cricket reform: a series of
articles which have appeared in "Baily's
Magazine". Vinton, 1907. 31p. diagrs.
*the articles appeared 1898–1907*

236 **Denison, William Evelyn**
■ Observations on the proposed alteration
of the law of l.b.w. Newark, S. Whiles *for
private circulation*, 1900. 7p.

237 **Lyttelton,** *the Hon.* **Robert Henry**
■ The crisis in cricket and the "Leg before"
rule. Longmans, Green, 1928. ix,83p.
illus.

237 **MacCanlis, K.**
–1 Cricket diagram of L.B.W. law. BCM/
Scoring, [1948]. bs. folded (wallchart)

238 **Martin, Leonard W.K.**
■ A look at the leg before wicket law.
Eastbourne, the Author, 1969. 30p.
diagrs.

239 Cricket umpiring: technique and evolu-
■ tion of the L.B.W. law. Eastbourne, the
Author, [1972]. [27]p.

239 Another look at the Leg Before Wicket
-1 law. Eastbourne, the Author, [1979?]
■ [39]p. diagrs.

### No Balls

240 **Milne, Alan Alexander**
■ Suggestion for the amendment of Law 26,
governing no balls. 1949. 6p.
*MS. in the M.C.C. Library at Lord's*

### Substitutes

241 **Roylance, David**
■ Substitutes. [The Author, 1973]. 3–13p.
bibliog.
*limited ed. of 75 copies numbered and
signed*

### Throwing

242 **Marylebone Cricket Club.** *Throwing Sub-*
■ *Committee*
Report. M.C.C., 1966. 6p.
*Chairman: F.G. Mann*

243 **Peebles, Ian**
■ Straight from the shoulder: 'throwing' –
its history and cure. The Cricketer;
Hutchinson, 1968. xx,131p. illus. ports.
*—another ed.* Sportsman's Book Club,
1969

# UMPIRING

244 **Association of Cricket Umpires**
□ How's that?: the official organ of the
Association of Cricket Umpires. New
Malden, the Association. *irregular*
*1953/1953 . . . 1960/to date*

245 Rules. New Malden, the Association,
■ [1955]. 6p.

246 Handbook. [New Malden], the Associ-
■ ation. *biennial*
*1961, 1964, 1966, 1968, 1970, 1972, 1974,
1976, 1978*

247 The Association of Cricket Umpires.
■ [New Malden, the Assoc.], [c. 1971]. [7]p.
*—2nd issue.* [c. 1973]. [7]p.
*a descriptive brochure of aims and objects*

248 Membership directory 1973; compiled by
■ E. Johnston. [New Malden], the Assoc.,
[1973]. 104p.
*—1977.* [1977]. 114p. incl. adverts.

248 **Association of Cricket Umpires, Ceylon**
-1 Silver jubilee souvenir; compiled by
J.M.C. Jayasinghe. The Assoc., 1969

249 **Association of Cricket Umpires [Sri**
■ **Lanka]**
Official handbook with the laws of cricket
1972/73. Colombo, the Association, 1972.
48p.
*——4th ed.* supplement: Additions,
amendments and comments on the laws
of cricket. 1979.
*see also: no. 278–2*

250 **Australian Capital Territory Umpires**
**Association**
Newsletter. Canberra, the Association
*No. 1. Sept. 1970–*

250 **Banerjee, S.K.**
-1 The laws of cricket & umpiring. West
Bengal, J. Banerjee, 1973. 92p. illus.

251 **Board of Control for Cricket in India**
Umpires handbook; edited by H.N.
Contractor. Delhi, the Board, 1945. 41p.

252 All-India umpires' examination. The
□ Board. *annual?*
*?/1973–.*
*examination questions*

253 **Bok, Willem Feye**
■ Het scheidsrechteren. Propaganda
Commissie van der Nederlandschen
Cricket Bond. [1939]. 94p. (De Groene
Krekelserie]
*umpiring*

254 **Bristol and District Cricket Umpires'**
**Association**
Year book. Bristol, the Association
*?/1970 to date?*

254 The appeal: the newsheet of the . . .
-1 Association. Bristol, the Assoc.
*?/1978/to date*

254 **The Buckinghamshire Association of**
-2 **Cricket Umpires**
□ Handbook. The Assoc. *annual*
*?/1977,79/to date*
*founded 1963*

254 **Ceylon Cricket Association**
-3 Hints to umpires, No. 1. [Colombo], the
Assoc., 1922.

255 **Chester, Frank**
■ How's that! Hutchinson, 1956. 208p.
illus. ports.

256 **Cricket** umpiring. Training and Educa-
■ tion Associates Ltd., 1973. [iv], 44p. illus.
pbk. (National Westminster Bank Sport
Coaching Series)

Umpiring: Bill Alley at an England v. West Indies test
match at Leeds *photo: Patrick Eagar*

Scoring: William Davies, scorer to Lewes Priory C.C.,
painted by Thomas Henwood in 1842 *photo: M.C.C.*

Care of grounds: Mowing the outfield, Karachi, 1978
*photo: Patrick Eagar*

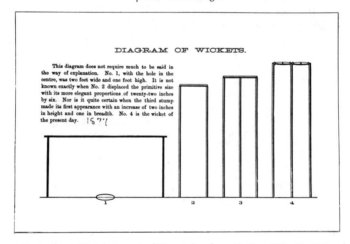

Equipment: Development of the wicket from C. Box "The English
game of cricket" (no. 799) *photo: M.C.C.*

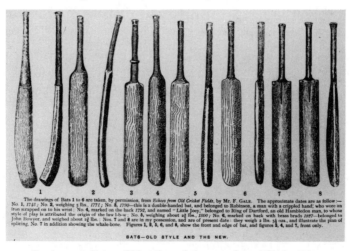

Equipment: Bats – Old style and the new from "Cricket" by
W. G. Grace (no. 433) *photo: BBC Hulton Picture Library*

257
■ **Dominica Cricket Umpires Association**
How's that. 8th anniversary magazine 1965–1973. Dominica, the Association, [1973]. 33p. illus. diagrs.

257
−1 **Durban and District Cricket Umpires' Association**
Hints on the laws of the game. [Durban, the Assoc., 195–?]. 8p. *typescript*

257
−2
□ **Federation of Australian Cricket Umpires**
Over: [official magazine]. Quinns Rocks [W. Aust.], the Federation. *3 times a year [Sept., Dec., Mar.). typescript*
*Sept. 1978 to date*

258
■ **Ganguli, Santosh,** *and* **Banerjee, Sunil**
The cricket umpire's manual (questions & answers on M.C.C. laws). P.O. Ariadaha, 24, Parganas, West Bengal, S.K. Banerjee, 1955. xxiii,63p.

259 **Harvey, J.H.**
How's that?: suggestions to young cricketers on umpiring. Auckland, the Author, 1938. 32p.
*originally appeared in sports ed. of "Auckland Star", 6th & 13th Dec., 1930.*

260
■ **Haydon, Herbert W.,** *compiler*
How's that?: the cricket umpires' test questionnaire. Weston-super-Mare, the Compiler, [1957?]. 8p.

260
−1 **Hints** for cricketers and umpires. Surridge, 1957

260
−2 **How zat**; presented by Lylie Goodridge in aid of the Umpires Association of Ceylon. Cricket, 7th September 1963 [Colombo?]

261 **Jog P.B.**
Cricket umpires and umpiring in India. Poona, the Author, 1951. 10p.

262
■ I challenge: open challenge to Messers [sic] B.J. Mohoni, A.R. Joshi and M.G. Bhave. Umpires & cricket. Poona, the Author, [1957]. 4p.

263
■ Maharashtra Cricket Association: a huge fraud. [Poona], The Author, 1960. 40p.

264
■ Hunger strike at the time of the Test Match. M.C.C. vs. India. Poona, the Author, 1963. 4p.

265
■ How's that? "Board of Control" out. Poona, the Author, [1964]. 39p.
*the above four publications support the Author's attempt to assert his umpiring rights*

266
■ **Lee, Frank Stanley**
The umpire's decision. Phoenix House, 1955. 64p. illus. diagrs. (Sports Books)

267
■ **Lee, Harry William**
"How's that?"; every cricketer's guide to umpiring. Lantern Publishing Co., [1947]. 40p.
——*2nd ed.* Clerke & Cockeran, 1948. 48p. illus.

268 **Leicestershire Cricket Umpires' Association**
How's that: a news review edited by S.J.K. Hudson. The Assoc., 1951. *typescript*
*4 issues—June, July, Oct. & Nov., 1951*

269
□ **Madras Cricket Association**
Cricket umpires' examination. Madras, the Association. *annual*
*season ?/1963–64 to 1967–68/1969–70?*
*examination questions: for later issues see no. 279*

270
■ **Martin, Leonard W.K.**
Cricket umpiring: technique and evolution of the L.B.W. law. Eastbourne, the Author, [1972]. [27]p.

271 **Natal Cricket Association**
Cricket teasers for junior umpires (with separate answers). Durban, the Association, *n.d.* 20p. illus.

271
−1
□ **New South Wales Cricket Umpires' Association**
Annual report and financial statement. Sydney, the Assoc. *typescript*
*season 1914–15/1978–79/ to date*
*founded 1913*

272
■ Golden jubilee report and official history. Sydney, the Assoc., 1963. 48p. ports.
*Special issue of no. 271–1 for the season 1963–64*

273 **N.E. Transvaal Cricket Umpires' Association**
A cricketer's guide. The Assoc., 1950. 56p. illus.

273
−1
■ **Northern** Cricket Umpires' Association [1954–79]. Trinidad & Tobago, the Assoc., [1979]. 52p. incl. adverts. illus. ports.

274
□ **Oxfordshire Cricket Umpires' Association**
Handbook. Oxford, the Association, *annual*
*1954/1954, 1955/to date?*

275
■ **Polishwalla, Ponchaji Nussarwanji**
All about umpiring: decisions and interpretations of cricket rules. Bombay, the Author, 1918. 82p. illus. diagrs.

276 Umpire's guide: decisions and interpreta-
■ tions of cricket rules. Bombay, the
Author, 1929. 64p. port. diagrs.

277 **Rait Kerr, Rowan Scrope**
■ Cricket umpiring and scoring: a text-book
for umpires and scorers compiled for the
Association of Cricket Umpires. Phoenix
House, 1957. 120p. illus. diagrs. (Sports
Books)
——revised to 1961. 1961
——*2nd ed.* revised to 1962. 1963
——*3rd ed.* revised to 1969 by T.E. Smith,
Dent. 1969. 118p.

277 **Rhodesia Cricket Umpires' Association**
–1 Newsheet. Salisbury, the Assoc. *irregular*
*1971–?*

278 **Skelding, Alec**
Duties, trials and troubles of a county
cricket umpire.
*unpublished typescript in M.C.C. Library
at Lord's*

278 **Southern Districts Umpires League**
–1 Annual report. Liverpool (N.S.W.), the
□ League. *typescript*
*?/season 1976–77/to date*

278 **Sri Lanka** Cricket Umpires Association.
–2 Colombo, the Assoc. *Quarterly*
*1st issue Jan/April 1979*
*see also: no. 249*

278 **Strang, Herbert**, *editor*
–3 The crimson book for boys. Oxford Univ.
P., [c. 1918]. 304p. illus.
*contains pp. 94–100 "Umpires I have
met", by Walter Rhoades*

279 **Tamil Nadu Cricket Association**
□ Cricket umpires' examination. Madras,
the Association. *annual*
*season 1970–71 to 1972–73/to date?*
*for earlier issues see no. 269*

280 **Wallach, Benjamin**
How's that? Johannesburg, Salker &
Snashall, 1924. 36p. illus.

281 **West Indies Cricket Board of Control**
■ First umpires' convention 12–16 June
1962. Trinidad, W.I.: [proceedings]. The
Board, [1962]. 28p. variously numbered.
*typescript*

281 **West Indies Cricket Umpires Association**
–1 Ninth biennial convention May 7th–11th,
■ 1979: convention reports. Christchurch,
the Assoc., [1979]. 17p. *typescript*
*the latest convention, first held 1962. See
no 281*

281 **Whiley, David**
–2 The art and technique of cricket umpi-
■ ring. Ashurst (Kent), The Cricketer, 1976.
92p. illus. diagrs.

282 **Yorkshire Federation of Cricket Umpires**
□ Handbook and simple explanation of the
M.C.C. Laws of cricket. Leeds, the Federation, 1949. 10p.
——*2nd ed.* 1950. 10p.

# SCORING

283 **All** England cricket match scoring book.
Simpkin, 1852

284 **Arrowsmith, James W.**
Arrowsmith's cricket scoring book.
Bristol. Arrowsmith, 1896.
*contains "Hints on cricket", by Richard
Daft. See no. 425*

285 **Cricket** scoring book. **Simpkin**, 1878

286 **Cricketers'** own register: score sheets and
instructions . . . for thirty matches. F.
Lillywhite & Ward, [1865].

287 **Cricketers'** scoring book. Whittaker, 1861

288 **Individual** batting analysis for cricket.
Yeovil. Western Gazette, 1912. (Thick's
copyright form)

289 **Polishwalla, Ponchaji Nussarwanji**
■ Polishwalla's score book. Bombay.
Nadkarni, 1924. [i],4p. of text, score
pages for 25 innings
——*another issue* with score pages for 50
innings

290 **Rait Kerr, Rowan Scrope**
■ Cricket umpiring and scoring: a textbook
for umpires and scorers compiled for the
Association of Cricket Umpires. Phoenix
House, 1957. 120p. illus. diagrs. (Sports
Books)
——revised to 1961. 1961
——*2nd ed.* revised to 1962. 1963
——*3rd ed.* revised to 1969 by T.E. Smith.
Dent, 1969. 118p.

290 **Sportsman's** record: [cricket diary].
–1 Redruth, Cramp Retail Ltd., *n.d.* [126]p.
■ *diary of blank ruled forms on which to
record club or team's results throughout a
season*

290 **Spurdle, A.T.**
–2 Cricket scoring for club and school: a
■ handbook for players prepared for the
Auckland Cricket Association. [Auck-
land, the Author], 1975. [ii],27,11p.
scoresheets & diagrs. *typescript*

291 **[Tomkinson, Sir Geoffrey Stewart]**
■ The cricketer's record book, [by] G.S.T. Kidderminster, G.T. Cheshire, 1930. [64]p. stats.
*for keeping personal cricket records*

## CARE OF GROUNDS

291 **Auckland Cricket Assocation**
–1 The development, preparation and maintenance of cricket pitches. Auckland, the Assoc., 1970. 23p. diagrs.

291 **Beale, Reginald**
–2 Lawns for sports: their construction and upkeep. Simpson & Marshall, 1924. x, 276p. illus. (some col.), port.
——Supplement . . . materials, tools and fittings. *Printed by* W. H. Smith & Son, [1924]. 67p. illus.

292 Cricket squares. Raynes Park, Carters Tested Seeds, [1935?] 16p.
——another ed. [1969?]

293 **Carter, James & Co.**
Cricket grounds: how to make and repair them. Carter, *n.d.*

294 Lawns, lawn tennis and cricket grounds: their formation and after-management. [Carter, *n.d.*]. illus.

295 **Carters Tested Seeds Ltd**
□ Treatment of golf courses and sports grounds. Carters. *annual. illus.*
*1950–1958?*
*includes cricket grounds*

296 **Cement & Concrete Association**
All-weather tennis courts and cricket pitches. The Association, *n.d.*
——2nd ed. *n.d.* 12p. illus.

297 Concrete cricket pitches. Cement & Concrete Assoc., 1948. [6]p. illus.
■ ——revised ed. 1957. [8]p.

298 **Clouston, David**
The establishment and care of fine turf for lawns and sports grounds. Aberdeen, D. Wyllie & Son, [1937]. 121p. illus. col. diagr.

299 **Concrete Association (Bombay)**
Concrete tennis courts and cricket pitches. Bombay, Concrete Association, 1953. 20p. illus.

299 **Escritt, John Robert**
–1 ABC of turf culture. Kaye & Ward, 1978.
■ vii,248p. illus.
*cricket tables and outfields pp. 23–32*

300 **Gibbs, Joseph Arthur**
■ The improvement of cricket grounds on economical principles. Cox, 1895. ix,42p.

301 **Harris, J.R.**
■ The crumbling of cricket pitches. Adelaide. Commonwealth Scientific and Industrial Research Organisation, Division of Soils, 1961. 6f. illus.
rptd. *from* The Australian Scientist, *Vol. 1, no. 3, pp. 173–8, Apr. 1961*

302 ——, *and* **Bond, R.D.**
■ The problem of soil salinity in turf wicket management. Adelaide, Commonwealth Scientific and Industrial Research Organisation, Division of Soils, 1960. [i],22p. bibliog. (Divisional Report 3/60)

302 **Hope, Frank**
–1 Turf culture: a complete manual for the
■ groundsman. Poole, Blandford P., 1978. [x],294p. illus. diagrs.
*cricket squares and wickets pp. 205, 217–20, 262, 263*

303 **Hough, Gerald de Lisle**
■ Coaching and pitches; prepared by the Kent County Cricket Club. [Canterbury, Kent C.C.C.], 1950. 20p. illus. diagrs.

304 **Lock, Herbert Christmas, ("Bert")**
■ Cricket ground maintenance. [The Oval], Surrey Junior Cricket Committee, 1957. 44p. illus. diagrs.

305 Lawn and turf culture for gardens and
□ grounds. [The Oval], Surrey C.C.C., 1957
——rev. ed. 1963. 56p. illus. diagrs.

306 Cricket—take care of your square. EP
■ Publishing Ltd. in collaboration with the National Cricket Association and supported by The Wrigley Cricket Foundation, 1972. 33p. illus. diagrs.

307 **Macdonald, James**
Lawns, links and sportsfields. Country Life, 1923. ix,78p. illus.
*ch. xii "Cricket grounds"*

307 **Macself, Albert James**
–1 Lawns and sports greens. Collingridge, [1932]. x,134p. illus. diagrs.
*cricket squares pp. 89–94*
——revd. and enl. ed. [1947]. 103p.

308 **Middlesex C.C.C.** *Junior Cricket Committee*
□ Instructions and advice upon the preparation of cricket pitches and the maintenance of playing fields. The Committee, [1956]. [ii],17p. illus. diagrs.
——another ed. 1963.

309
■ **National Cricket Association**
Non-turf pitches: an assessment. The Assoc., supported by the Wrigley Cricket Foundation, 1972. 12p. diagr. (Bulletin no. 1.)

309
–1 **National Playing Fields Association**
Sports ground maintenance: an elementary guide to club committees. N.P.F.A., [1978]. 31p. illus.

310
■ ———, *and* **Marylebone Cricket Club**
*Standing Joint Committee on Non-Turf Cricket Pitches*
First report: On artificial cricket pitches. N.P.F.A. & M.C.C., 1951. 25p. diagrs.
Second report: cricket on non-turf pitches indoor & outdoor. N.P.F.A. & M.C.C., 1954. 40p. diagrs.
———4th impr. revised. 1959. 43p. diagrs.
Third report: Cricket on non-turf pitches, indoor & outdoor. N.P.F.A. & M.C.C. 1966. 41p. illus. diagrs.

310
–1 **New Zealand Cricket Council**
Preparation and maintenance of cricket grounds and wickets in New Zealand, compiled for the New Zealand Cricket Council. Christchurch, Wyatt & Wilson, [1930?]. 28p.

310
–2 **Nottinghamshire County Council.**
*County Playing Fields Service*
■ Cricket pitch research. West Bridgford, Nottingham, the Service, 1978. 16p. illus. diagrs.
*includes 3 papers by Peter Dury, the County Playing Fields Officer*

311
■ **Ruberoid Co. Ltd.**
The Ruberoid all-weather wicket. The Co., 1966. [4]p. illus. diagrs.
*an advertisement leaflet*

311
–1 **The Sports Council**
■ Provision for sport. Volume II. Specialist facilities: a document for consultation based on the returns of the national governing bodies of sport. The Sports Council, 1973. 55p.
*pp. 33–4. National Cricket Association. List of requirements of indoor cricket pitches*

312 **Sutton and Sons Ltd**
Garden lawns; tennis lawns; bowling greens; croquet lawns; putting greens; cricket grounds. Reading, Sutton & Sons, 1906. [iv],50p. illus. diagrs.

313
■ Sutton's grass seeds, turf dressings, equipment, etc. Sutton & Sons Ltd., 1955. 16p. illus.
*with hints on maintenance*

314
■ **Tressider, J.O.**
Specification for construction of an artificial cricket pitch, prepared by J.O. Tressider in consultation with J.N. Gell, after the method used by B.A.O.R. [The Author, 1949]. 5p. diagrs. *typescript*

314
–1 **Trumble, Hugh Christian**
Blades of grass. Melbourne, Georgian House, [c. 1946]. xii,294p. illus.
*cricket pp. 1–10, 12*

314
–2 **Watt, W.B.**
Turf wickets, their overhaul, preparation and repair. Melbourne, Contractors Record Ltd., [1955]. 9p. diagr. *typescript*
*author was Curator, Melbourne Cricket Ground*

315 **Webster, Frederick Annesley Michael**
Sports grounds and buildings: making, management, maintenance and equipment. Pitmans, 1940. xviii,305p. illus. plans

316
■ **Wesley, Reginald**
Artificial cricket pitches. Contractor's Record in association with Journal of Park Administration, 1955. 70p. illus. diagrs.

317 **White, Lawrence Walter,** *and* **Bowles, William Henry George**
Practical groundsmanship. English Universities P., 1952. xiii,258p. illus. diagrs.
*Chap. 1. "Cricket" pp. 3–32*

# EQUIPMENT

318
■ **Adburgham, Alison**
Lillywhites centenary book. Lillywhites Ltd., 1963. [21]p. illus. ports.

318
–1 **Benetfink & Co.**
■ Sports, games & athletic outfitting catalogue. Benetfink & Co., 1897. 106(?)p. illus.
*cricket equipment pp. 13–20, 38, 39, 50, 51, 58*

318
–2 **Birmingham and Midland Institute**
■ Conversazione (a festival of the arts and sciences) January 13, 14, 15, 16, 1953: programme. [Birmingham], the Institute, [1953]. 40p.
*pp. 25–26 describes cricket items exhibited, including the making of cricket bats and balls*

319
■ **The Book** of public school old boys, university, Navy, Army, Air Force & club ties; introduced by James Laver. Seeley Service, 1968. 96p. col. illus.
———rptd. 1974
*plate 25 "Cricket–first class counties and some clubs"*

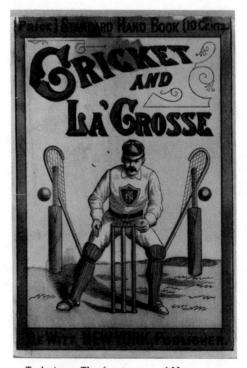

Technique: The title-page of the first
edition of John Nyren's "The Young
Cricketer's Tutor" (no. 390) *photo: M.C.C.*

Technique: The front cover of Henry
Chadwick's "Cricket and La 'Crosse" (no. 412)

Injuries: "The play ground described"
engraved by S. Bellin from a drawing by
R. Seymour *photo: BBC Hulton Picture Library*

Technique: "The cross bat illustrated by a cross
boy" from Jones Wister's "A 'Bawl' for
American cricket" (no. 483)

Coaching: Cricket coaching classes at Lord's
with Bill Voce bowling *photo: Patrick Eagar*

320 **Cunnington, Phillis,** *and* **Mansfield,**
■ **Alan**
English costume for sports and outdoor
recreation from the sixteenth to the nineteenth centuries. Black, 1969. 388p. col.
frontis. illus. bibliog.
*cricket, including women cricketers,*
*pp. 13–46*

321 **En-Tout-Cas Co. Ltd**
□ Price list. Syston, Leicester, En-Tout-Cas.
*annual?* illus.
?/1960 . . . 63/to date
*includes cricket equipment*

322 **Eurosport**
■ "First class in cricket material". Eurosport, Meerle (Belgium), [197–]. 7 loose
leaves in folder. port.
*advertisement brochure with batting aver-*
*ages of Dutch cricketers and portrait of Gary*
*Sobers*

323 **Frank Bryan Ltd**
■ Cricket equipment. F. Bryan Ltd., [1958].
[6]p. fold. illus.
*advertising brochure*

323 **Frank Sugg Ltd.**
–1 Cricket catalogue. Catalogue no. 49.
Liverpool, Frank Sugg Ltd., [1909]. 48p.
illus.

324 **Goodman, Malcolm R.V.**
■ The cricket bat and ball industries: a
glance at some economic aspects. 42p.
diagrs. bibliog. *typescript*
*academic thesis; copy at M.C.C. Library,*
*Lord's*

325 **Gunn & Moore Ltd**
■ [Trade catalogue of cricket equipment].
[Nottingham]. Gunn & Moore, [c. 1971].
8p. illus. port.

325 The story of Gunn & Moore. Nottingham,
–1 Gunn & Moore, 1978. [16]p. incl. covers.
■ illus. ports.

326 **Hadfield, John Charles Heywood**
■ A Wisden century, 1850–1950. Sporting
Handbooks for John Wisden & Co. Ltd.,
1950. 77p. illus. ports. bibliog.

326 **Jack Hobbs Ltd.**
–1 [Catalogue of sports wear and equip-
ment]. 59, Fleet Street, Jack Hobbs Ltd.,
[c.1922]. 28p. illus. port.

327 [Sales catalogue]. 59, Fleet St., E.C.4.
■ 1931. 32p. illus. port.

328 **John Wisden & Co.**
John Wisden & Co., cricketing, football
and lawn tennis outfitters: revised illus-

trated list of prices for 1882. J. Wisden,
[1882]. 20p. illus.

329 The past and present of Wisden's, with
■ some interesting cricket notabilia. J.
Wisden, 1917. 72p. incl. adverts. illus.
ports.
——another ed. 1922. 36p. illus. ports.
——another ed. 1850–1931. [1931]. 96p.
incl. adverts. illus. ports.
*includes articles on Widen's cricket bat*
*museum, with illus. of 106 bats held there;*
*bat-making, ball making, etc.*

329 A book of sense and nonsense. John
–1 Wisden, [1928]. 15p. incl. adverts.
■ *an advertising 'magazine'*

329 One hundred not out 1850–1950: a
–2 luncheon to mark the first centenary of
John Wisden & Co. Ltd. . . . Café Royal,
London, 18 May 1950. Penshurst,
Wisden, [1950]. [8]p. incl. covers. 1 port.
*with historical notes on the Company and*
*on the Almanack*

330 **Kent, Richard**
■ The story of Gunn & Moore. Nottingham,
Gunn & Moore, [196–]. [6]p. illus.

331 **Lillywhites**
□ Summer equipment catalogue. Lillywhites. *annual?* illus.
?/1961 . . . 68/–?

332 **Luscombe, William**
■ The care and maintenance of sports
equipment. Arlington Books, 1962.
[v],53p. incl. adverts.
*cricket equipment, pp. 16–19*

333 **Martineau, Gerard Durani**
■ Bat, ball, wicket and all: an account of the
origin and development of the imple-
ments, dress and appurtenances of the
national game. Sporting Handbooks,
1950. [iv],128p. illus. ports. bibliog.
——another ed. with combined title: The
field is full of shades, and, Bat, ball,
wicket and all. Sportsman's Book Club,
1954

334 [See no. 45–3]

335 [See no. 45–4]

336 **Peabody Institute Library,** *Baltimore*
■ Play ball: books, pictures and relics of ball
games of many kinds: exhibition at The
Peabody Institute Library, Baltimore,
Maryland, March 20–May 20, 1963. [27]p.
*cricket items nos. 114–66, 176*

337 **Reading University.** *Museum of English*
■ *Rural Life*
The rural game of cricket: a loan exhibition illustrating scenes, personalities, and the making of the bat and ball. Reading, Univ. of Reading, [1957]. 9p.

338 **The Saturday** book. Ninth year; edited by
■ Leonard Russell. Hutchinson, 1949. 288p. illus. & ports. (some col.)
*includes "Cricket gadgets" by John Arlott, pp. 275–280*

339 **Slazengers, Sykes, Gradidge, Ayres**
Eighteen-hundred-and-ten to nineteen-forty-six: a record of constant progress. Slazengers, *etc.*, [1946]. 56p. illus. map

340 **Slazengers Ltd**
Cricket '70. Slazengers, [1970]. 8p. illus.
*catalogue of cricket equipment with illus. of Sobers, Cowdrey & Knott*

340 **A.G. Spalding & Bros.** .
–1 1909 cricket: [trade catalogue]. Spalding &
■ Bros., [1909]. 24p. illus. team port.
*trade catalogue of cricket equipment. Includes portrait of the Yorkshire team, 1908, and a page of wicket-keeping, bowling and fielding actions*

341 [See no.45–10]

341 **3-D Sports (Wholesale)**
–1 Specialist cricket catalogue. Cheltenham,
■ 3-D Sports, 1977. 36p. incl. covers. illus. ports.
*mail order catalogue of cricket equipment and clothing*

342 **Universal Mat Co. Ltd**
■ How's that?: Universal cricket mats . . . The Co., [1969]. [4]p. illus.
*an advertisement leaflet*

342 **Woodcroft, Bennet**
–1 Patents for inventions: toys, games & exercises 1672–1866. Eyre & Spottiswoode, 1871. [xvi],201p.
*includes cricket items*

343 [See no. 45–11]
■

344 **Wymer, Norman George**
English country crafts: a survey of their development from early times to present day. Batsford, 1946. xi,116p. illus.
*references to manufacture of bats and balls pp. 81, 91–3, 127–31*

345 English town crafts: a survey of their development from early times to present day. Batsford. 1949. viii,128p. illus.
*reference to manufacture of cricket bats and balls pp. 111, 116–9, 123–6*

**Bats**

345 **Barty-King, Hugh**
–1 Quilt winders and pod shavers: the
■ history of cricket bat and ball manufacture. Macdonald & Jane's, 1979. 208p. illus. ports. plans, facsims. bibliog.

346 **Bean, William Jackson**
■ "The cricket bat willow". *In* Royal Botanic Gardens. Bulletin of miscellaneous information (*now* "Kew bulletin"). 1907. no.8. pp. 311–316. illus.

347 **Brighten, Claude W.**
■ Cricket bat willow culture. Reprinted from the *Quarterly Journal of Forestry*, January 1951. 9p. with 2p. insert. illus.

348 **British Association for the Advancement**
■ **of Science**
Report of the annual meeting, 1935, Norwich, Sept. 4–11. The Assoc., 1935. xlviii,500,139p.
*contains precis of paper by W.J. Dowson. The watermark disease of cricket bat willow, p. 445*

348 **Britton, Poole & Burns,** *auctioneers*
–1 [By order of B. Warsop & Sons] 127a Park
■ Road N.W.8 a cricket bat manufacturers' premises . . . to be sold by an auction . . . 21st November, 1973. [8]p. incl. covers. 2 plans (1 col.)

349 **Browning, John**
Provisional specification: triangular bats for cricket and other out door games. AD 1887, 31st January, no. 1484. H.M.S.O., 1887. 3f.illus.
*see also advertisement at end of Wisden 1894*

350 **Bussey, George C.**
□ The bat of the Victorian era; or, The evolution of the "Demon Driver"; a popular treatise. Bussey, 1897. 32p. illus
——2nd ed. 1898
——3rd ed. *with title:* The evolution of the "Demon-Driver". Bussey, 1899. 32p. illus.
——4th ed. *with title:* The evolution of a cricket bat. Bussey, 1907. [ii],32p. illus.
——9th ed. 1924

351 **Church, Richard**
■ Kent. Hale, 1948. xii,289p. illus. map. (County Books Series)
*reference to cricket bat industry, p. 83*

351 **Claxton, William J.**
–1 Journeys in industrial England. Harrap,
* 1914. 192p. illus.
*ch. xvii. "How cricket bats are made", pp. 118–24. Written for children*

**352** ■ **Department of Scientific and Industrial Research.** *Forest Products Research Laboratory*
Timbers used in the sports goods industry: a survey by F.G.O. Pearson and Constance Webster. Aylesbury, F.P.R.L., 1957. [iii],40p.
*cricket pp.2–6*

**353** ■ **Forestry Commission**
Cultivation of the cricket bat willow. H.M.S.O., 1936. 48p. illus. diagrs. bibliog. (Bulletin no. 17)
——2nd ed. 1958. vi,33p.
——3rd ed. 1968. [v],35p.

**354** ■ **Gradidge and Sons**
How to make 1,000 runs in May! Gradidge, [1933]. 12p. col. illus.

**355** ■ How they made 1,000 runs in May! Gradidge, [1934]. [12]p. col. illus.
*advertising brochures*

**356** ■ **Gunn & Moore Ltd.**
Souvenir, British Empire Exhibition, Wembley: part & present of a world-famous cricket bat firm. Nottingham, Gunn & Moore, [1924]. 8p. illus.
*an account of Gunn & Moore, cricket bat manufacturers: rptd. from* The Sports Trader *Feb., 1924*

**357** ■ **Hogg, Garry**
Country crafts and craftsmen. Hutchinson, 1959. 152p. *illus.*
*cricket bat making, pp. 20–23, 32, 114*

**357** **India. Central Small Industries**
**–1** **Organization**
Cricket bats. Delhi, Manager of Publications, 1963. 8p. (Small Industry Impact Scheme, no. 55)

**358** ■ **M.C.C. Company, Ltd**
The whole world contributes to make the Barrier bat. M.C.C. Co., [19–]. [16]p. illus. diagrs.
*advertisement brochure*

**359** ■ **Pentelow, John Nix**
Historic bats: bibliographical catalogue of the unique collection, 149 in number, formed by Mr. Charles Pratt Green, of Malvern. *Printed by* Warwick P., [1931]. 43p. stats.
*the collection was acquired by Sir Julien Cahn*

**359** **Preece, Thomas Francis**
**–1** Watermark disease of the cricket bat willow. 3rd ed. H.M.S.O., 1977. 9,[1]p. illus. [some col.]. (Forestry Commission Leaflets 20)

**360** ■ **Redmayne and Todd, Ltd**
A collection of historic bats offered [for sale] by Redmayne & Todd . . . for the Nottinghamshire C.C.C. Nottingham, Redmayne & Todd, [c.1938]. 6p.

**361** **Stuart Surridge & Co. Ltd**
From willow to wicket: the making of the bat. Stuart Surridge & Co. Ltd., 1911
rptd. *from* The Sportsman

**362** ■ Cricket history made by "Perfect" and "Herbert Sutcliffe" cricket bats. Stuart Surridge & Co. Ltd., *n.d.* [6]p. fold. illus.
*advertisement brochure with accounts of innings played by Sutcliffe and Hammond using "Herbert Sutcliffe" and "Perfect" bats*

**363** ■ **Vesey-Fitzgerald, Brian**
The Ladybird book of trees; illustrated by S.R. Badmin. Loughborough, Wills & Hepworth, 1963. 52p. col. illus. (Ladybird Nature Book)
*pp. 16–17 The cricket bat willow, with illus.*

**363** **The world** of manufacture: E.J. Page &
**–1** Co., London. 8p. incl. covers. illus.
*offprint from* The Sports Trades Journal, *January, 1904: cricket-bat makers*

## Balls

**364** **An ancient** Kentish industry. *n.p.*, [193–]. [4]p.

**364** **Barbour, B. M'Call,** *editor*
**–1** Bits for our boys. Edinburgh, The Boys' Purity Band. illus.
*vol. vi, pp. 33–4 "Cricket balls"*
*a description, with religious inferences, of how cricket balls are made; pictorial front cover with boy leaning on wall with cricket bat over his shoulder*

**364** **Barty-King, Hugh**
**–2** Quilt winders and pod shavers: the
■ history of cricket bat and ball manufacture. Macdonald & Jane's, 1979. 208p. illus. ports. plans, facsims, bibliog.

**365** **Craig, Albert**
About a cricket ball. All England Publishing Co., 1899. 4p.

**366** **Crawley, Alfred Ernest**
■ The book of the ball. Methuen, 1913. x,220p. illus. diagrs.
*4pp. on cricket with other refs.*

**367** ■ **Duke and Son**
Cricket balls in court. High Court of Justice, Queen's Bench Division. Before the Lord Chief Justice of England and a Special Jury: Duke & Son v. John Wisden & Co. Verbatim report. February 7th, 1898. 8p.

368 Cricket ball makers for 200 years,
■ 1760–1960: a bicentenary souvenir.
Penshurst (Kent), Wisden, [1960]. [5]p.
illus.

369 **Gale, Frederick**, *'A Wykehamist', pseud.*
■ About an old cricket ball. Penshurst,
Duke & Son, 1882. 10p.
*rptd. from* Baily's Magazine, *Nov. 1882,
pp. 389–394; a fanciful account of a visit to
Duke's cricket ball factory*

369 **Severn, Joan**
–1 The Teston story: Kent village life

through the age. Teston, Rufus Fay Publications, 1975. 76p. illus.
*contains pp. 6, 62, 66–7, notes on Alfred
Reader & Co., cricket ball makers*

370 **[Wright, W.R.]**, *compiler*
■ Between the innings: cricket items—old
and new: collected by W.R. Weir. Wright,
1913. 30p. illus.
——2nd ed., *i.e. reprint*. 1913. *with errata
slip*
*contains "The cricket ball: something about
its evolution" first published in* American
cricketer. *March 1906*

# THE TECHNIQUE OF THE GAME
## (*See also:* Coaching)

## TECHNIQUE BEFORE 1865

371 **"An Amateur"**, *pseud.*
■ Familiar instructions for playing the noble
game of cricket, according to the rules &
regulations practised by the most
scientific players of this delightful game
and healthy exercise; with the laws of the
game . . . J. Limbird, [1836]. 40p. frontis.
——*another issue*. Henry Lea, *n.d.* 32p.

372 **"A Batsman"**, *pseud.*
Cricketers' pocket companion. W. Cole,
1826. 60p. illus.

373 **Boxall, Thomas**
■ Rules & instructions for playing at the
game of cricket, as practised by the most
eminent players; to which is subjoined
the laws and regulations of cricketters
[sic], as revised by the Cricket Club at
Mary-le-Bone. *Printed by* Harrild and
Billing, [c.1801]. [i],92p.
——2nd ed. [c.1802]. [i],92p. frontis
———2nd issue. [c.1802]. vi,[ii],7–92p.
frontis.
*has leaf "A part of the subscribers" inserted
between pp.vi and 7*
——3rd ed. Printed by E. Billing, 1804.
80p. frontis.
*A3 inserted before A2*
———2nd issue. 1804
*A2 and A3 in correct order; 'as revised' on
t.p. now reads 'and revised'*
———3rd issue. 1804
*t.p. still reads 'and revised' but on p. 15
'cricketters' printed in earlier issues corrected
to 'cricketers'*

374 **Chadwick, Henry**
Beadle's dime book of cricket: a desirable
cricketer's companion, containing

complete instructions in the elements of
bowling, batting and fielding: also the
revised laws of the game, remarks on the
duties of umpires, etc., etc. N.Y., Beadle,
[1860]. 40p.

374 Clark's Companion to cricket. Clark,
–1 1844. bs.
*reported in Bell's Life, May 19th, 1844*

375 **Cricket** made easy: the standard
authority, giving plain and perfect directions both of the theory and practice of
this noble outdoor sport: so that it can be
perfectly learned without a master. New
York, Advance Publishing Co., [1857?].
64p. illus. diagrs.
——*another ed.* [187–?]

376 **The cricketer's** guide: a complete manual
□ of the game of cricket. Manchester, John
Heywood, [1863]. 36p. illus. diagrs.
*excludes 1864 revision to law 10 and refers
in a note to "this year, 1863."*
——rev. ed. 1873
——new ed. 1879. 30p. illus. diagrs.
——new ed. 1882. 32p. incl. adverts.
illus. diagrs.
——*another ed.* revised in accordance with
the new rules passed by the M.C.C. 1st
May, 1889. [1889?]. [iv],24p. illus. diagrs.
——*another issue.* [1890?]. *with different
illus.*
——*another ed.* 1893
——*another ed.* revised in accordance with
the new rules passed by the M.C.C. [post
1894]. [iv],24p. illus.
——*another ed.* 1896

□ **The cricketer's** guide: a complete manual
. . . . Heckmondwike, Ward, 1877
——new ed. [1883]. 16p. illus. diagrs.

——*another issue* together with "An essay on cricket"; *also* "Reverie on cricket"; *and* "Cricket practice and club management". 1884. 16 + [5] + [1] + [1]

□ **The cricketer's** guide: being a complete manual . . . . F. Bryan. [c.1884]. 20p.
*contains laws passed 21 April, 1884*
——*another ed.* rev. in accordance with the new rules passed by the M.C.C. [post 1894]. 24p. diagrs.

377 **The cricketer's** hand-book: containing the
■ origin of the game, remarks on recent alterations, directions for bowling, striking and placing the players, and the laws as altered by the Marylebone Cricket Club. London, R. Tyas; Edinburgh, J. Menzies, 1838. [vi],37p. frontis
——new ed. R. Tyas, 1841. [vii],48p. frontis
——1st American ed. Boston, Saxton, Peirce & Co.; N.Y., Saxton & Miles, 1844. vi,48p. frontis.

378 **The cricketer's** handbook, in three parts:
□ 1—History and chronology of cricket. II—Instructions for the game. III—The revised laws. By the Author of "Training for pedestrianism and wrestling, etc." W.M. Clark, [c.1845]. 56p. frontis. scores. (Clark's Sporting Handbooks)
*contains Laws 1844 and scores of matches played in 1843*
later eds. with title: "*Clark's cricketer's handbook, by a Member of the Marylebone Cricket Club*". The editions recorded:
——10th ed. [c.1849]. frontis. 54p. scores
*contains the Laws of 1845, but omits amendment to Law 7, 1849*
——14th ed. [1858]
*in B.M. Catalogue*
——15th ed. [c.1859]. *frontis. 50p. score contains Law 10 made in 1858 and score of match played May 1858*

379 **The cricketer's** manual: containing the
■ rules of the Marylebone Club. Dipple, [c.1850]. 16p. diagr. (Dipple's Handbooks, no.25)

380 **[Gale, Frederick)**
■ Practical hints on cricket, for the direction and guidance of beginners, by a Wykehamist. Cheltenham, Davies, 1843. vii,43p. col. illus.
——2nd ed. Cheltenham, Davies: London, Orr, 1848. 60p. col. frontis. illus.
*has frontis. lithographed by G. Rowe, similar to but not identical with that in 1st ed.*
——2nd issue? 1848
*frontis. is lithographed by Day & Son*

381 **How to** play cricket. Stevens, [1859?].
□ 39p. diagr. (Family Herald Handy Books)
*includes Law 10, pre 1864 but post 1858. and Law 7. pre 1860 but post 1849*
——*another ed. with title:* How to play cricket and football. [1864]. 59p. diagrs.
——*another ed.* (... and football). [c.1880]. iv,64p. diagrs.

382 **Instructions** for playing the game of
■ cricket: with revised laws, as adopted by the principal clubs in the Kingdom. *n.p.,* [c.1838]. 16p. illus.
*changes in Laws 1 & 3 which took place in 1838 included, but not those in Laws 14 and 29: amendments of May 1839 not included. (Lord's catalogue)*

383 **Lambert, William**
□ Instructions and rules for playing the noble game of cricket, as practised by the most eminent players: containing a variety of directions little known to players in general ...: to which are subjoined the laws of the game, with additions and corrections. Lewes, J. Baxter, Sussex P., 1816. 55p. frontis.
——2nd issue [1816]
——2nd ed. Lewes, J. Baxter, Sussex P.; London, R. Harrild. etc. [1816?].55p.
——3rd ed. with considerable additions and corrections, *with title:* The cricketers' guide; or a concise treatise on the noble game of cricket, as practised ... directions not generally known; to which is added a plan of a new single wicket game on an improved principle; with other interesting matter ..., to which are subjoined the laws of the game, with notes. Lewes, J. Baxter, Sussex P.; London, Langley, [etc.] [1817?]. 62p. frontis. diagr.
——4th ed. with considerable additions and corrections. [1818?]
——5th ed. with considerable additions and corrections. Lewes. J. Baxter, Sussex P.; Derby, Mozley; London, Langley, [etc.] [1819?]
——*another issue.* Lewes. J. Baxter, Sussex P.: London, Baldwin [etc.], [1819?]
*labelled 4th ed. on cover*
——6th ed. [1820?]
——7th ed. [1821?]. 61p.
——8th ed. corrected to the present time. Lewes, J. Baxter, Sussex P.: London, Baldwin, etc.; Derby, Mozley, [1822?]. 62p.
——9th ed. *with title* Lambert's cricketer's guide, or instructions and rules for playing the noble game of cricket with its laws corrected. [1823?]. 48p.
——10th ed. [1825?]. 48p.
——11th ed. [1828]
——20th ed. [sic]. Lewes, J. Baxter; London, Joy, [etc.]. [1829?]. 47p.

——12th ed. Lewes. J. Baxter; London, Simpkin, Marshall, [between 1830 and 1832].

*probably the last edition*

——13th-19th eds. have not been traced and probably were never published

see *G.B. Buckley in* The Cricketer, Spring annual, 1942, *and Col. R.S. Rait Kerr in* The Cricketer, Spring annual, 1949

384 **Lillywhite, Frederick**
■ Cricket: with full instructions how to learn and how to play. W. Twedie, 1862, 32p. illus. diagr. (Young England's Cricket)

385 ——, *editor*
■ The young cricketer's guide, containing full directions for playing the noble and manly game of cricket, by William Lillywhite. To which is added the Laws of the game, with the latest alterations and some brief remarks upon fifty of the most celebrated gentlemen and players in England. The whole collected and edited by Frederick Lillywhite, Junr. F. Lillywhite [1849]. 32p.

——2nd ed., *i.e.* issue with inserted slip "Alteration of Law VII". [1849]

*a manual of the game; subsequently publd. annually under title: The guide to cricketers. For full entry see no. 1086*

386 **[Lillywhite, Frederick William]**, *editor*
■ Lillywhite's illustrated hand-book of cricket; containing portraits of Pilch, Box, A. Mann, C. Taylor, Lillywhite, Cobbett, G.H. Langdon, R. Kynaston, also the laws of cricket . . . edited by 'A Cantab'. London, Ackermann;. Brighton, Mason, 1844. 22p. ports

——2nd ed. 1844. 22p. ports

*both editions were also issued with 1 portrait (Lillywhite) or with 4 portraits of the Players only*

——*facsimile reprint in:* Chronicles of cricket, 1888. *See* no. 873

386 **A manual** of cricket and baseball; contai-
-1 ning plans for laying out the grounds, plans for forming clubs etc., to which are added rules and regulations for cricket adopted by the Marylebone Cricket Club; also rules and regulations which govern several celebrated baseball clubs. Boston, Mayhew and Baker, 1858. 24p. illus.

——2nd ed. *with title* The cricket player's pocket companion. 1859. 32p. illus.

*the second ed. contains only the matter relating to cricket, baseball being treated in another book under the title of "The base-ball player's pocket companion"*

387 **"A Member of the Mary-le-Bone Club,"**
■ pseud.
The cricketers' guide: containing complete instructions to persons of all ages, now playing at this healthful and manly exercise, and for the choice of the bat, ball & wickets: with the laws of the game. Dean, [c.1836]. iii-vi,7–62p. folding frontis. illus. diagr.

——2nd ed. Dean and Munday, [1840]. [ii],ii,7–62p.

388 **"A Member of the M.C.C."**, *pseud.*
Cricketers' handbook: a complete guide to field sports in general. W. G. Kerton, 1852. 16p.

389 **Mitford, John**
■ The Rev. John Mitford on cricket; with a biographical note by F.S. Ashley-Cooper. Nottingham, Richards, 1921. 24p.

*reprints of articles reviewing Nyren's Young Cricketer's Tutor published in Gentleman's Magazine vol. CIII, pt. 11, 1833, pp. 41–46, 235–40; also rptd. in no. 794*

390 **Nyren, John**
■ The young cricketer's tutor: comprising full directions for playing the elegant and manly game of cricket; with a complete version of its laws and regulations: to which is added "The cricketers of my time," or, Recollections of the most famous old players: by the same author. The whole collected and edited by Charles Cowden Clarke. Effingham Wilson, 1833. 126p. frontis. score.

*2nd to 11th eds. with title: Nyren's Cricketers guide:—*

——2nd ed., *corrected and improved*. Edinburgh, T.P. Caldwell. 1840. xviii,101p. frontis. [differs from that in 1st ed.] scores

——3rd ed.——. H. Washbourne, 1845. xviii,101p. frontis. scores

——4th ed.——by the latest authorized laws. [1846]. xviii,101p.

*issued with frontis. Variant bindings with lettering "corrected to 1846 (1847)"*

——5th ed.—— ——. [1848 on binding] vi,101p.

——6th ed.—— ——. [1848 on binding]

——7th ed.—— ——. [1849, (1850), (1851) on variant bindings]

——8th ed.—— ——. [1851, (1853) on variant bindings]

——9th ed.—— ——. [1854 on binding]

——10th ed.—— ——. [1854, (1855), (1856) on variant bindings]

——11th ed.—— —— [1855, (1857), (1858) on variant bindings]

*there have been seven modern reprints to 1979:*

1) Chronicles of cricket: facsimile reprints of Nyren's "Cricketer's guide", Lillywhite's "Handbook of cricket", Denison's

"Sketches of the players". Swann Sonnenschein, 1888. iv,[6],101:30: viii,76p. illus. ports. scores
——*another issue.* Maurice, *n.d.*
2) The young cricketer's tutor: new ed., with an introduction by Charles Whibley. Nutt, 1893. xxxiii,140p. frontis. (The Classics of Cricket)
*some copies issued without facsimile of 1833 title-page, the Dedication by John Nyren and the original introduction by C.C.C. (pp.1–10)*
——L.P. ed. 1893. Limited to 100 copies
3)——; ed. with an introduction, by F.S. Ashley-Cooper. Gay & Bird, 1902. xix, 183p. illus. port. diagr. (The Sportsman's Classics)
4) The Hambledon men: being a new edition by E.V. Lucas of John Nyren's 'Young cricketer's tutor'. . . .Frowde, 1907. xxviii,252p. illus. ports. scores.
——*rptd.* Sportsman's Book Club, 1952.
——*another ed.* Phoenix House, 1954. xxvii,252p.
5) From Hambledon to Lord's: the classics of cricket: John Nyren, Charles Cowden Clarke, the Rev. James Pycroft, the Rev. John Mitford; edited by John Arlott. Johnson, 1948. 143p. illus. ports. scores
6) The young cricketer's tutor. . . . by John Nyren and originally published in 1833 and now reprinted; illustrated with wood engravings by John O'Connor, with an introduction by Neville Cardus. Dropmore P., 1948. [3],xii,94p. illus. scores
*limited ed. of 750 copies, 50 specially bound in buckram*
7) The young cricketer's tutor. . .; with an introductory essay by John Arlott. Davis-Poynter, 1974. 100p. illus. diagr. score, bibliog.
*reprint of 1st ed.*
See also *no. 1205–2*

391 **"An Old Batsman"**, *pseud.*
The cricketer. J. Neal, [c.1844]. 31p.
*with cover-title:* The whole game of cricket
——*another ed.* Newcastle, Bowman, [c.1844]. 31p.
with half-title: *Cricket*

392 **Paterson, Alexander D.**
■ The manual of cricket . . . to which is added the body and all that is important of "Felix on the bat". New York, Berford, 1847. 163p. illus. diagrs.

393 **Penny** illustrated guide to the cricket
■ field. Maddick & Pottage, [1863]. [16]p. illus. diagrs. score

394 **Pycroft, James**
■ The cricket field; or The history and the

science of cricket. By the author of "The principles of scientific batting" . . . Longman, Brown, Green, and Longmans, 1851. xvi,242p. port. diagrs. score
——2nd ed. 1854. xvi,267p. ports. diagrs. score
——3rd ed. *with title:* The cricket-field. . . . 1859, xx,269p. ports. diagrs. score
——4th ed. by The Rev James Pycroft, B.A. Longman, Green, Longman, and Roberts, 1862. xix,281p. ports. diagrs. score
——5th ed. . . . or, The history and the science of the game of cricket. Longman, Green, Longman, Roberts and Green, 1865. xx,344p. ports. diagrs. score
—— ——*another issue.* Longmans, Green, Reader, and Dyer, 1868. xvii,344p. ports. diagrs. score
——6th ed. rev. *with title:* The cricket-field. Virtue, 1873. vi,344p. mounted frontis. diagrs. score
——7th ed. rev. Cricket P., 1882.vi,370p. diagrs. score
——8th ed. rev. Cricket P., 1884. vii,374p. diagrs. scores
——9th ed. rev. Cricket P., 1887. v,380p. diagrs. scores
——*American ed. with title:* The cricket-field, or, The history and science of cricket. By the author of "The principles of scientific batting . . . Boston, Mayhew and Baker, 1859. 238p. port, diagrs. score
——The cricket-field with some notes by H.H. Stephenson: edited with an introduction, by F.S. Ashley-Cooper. St James's P., 1922. xxiii,318p. illus. ports. scores, stats. bibliog.
—— ——Subscribers' ed. 1922
*limited to 100 copies*
*for more details see L.E.S. Gutteridge in Cricket Society. News letter, no. 35 (1954)*
*see also nos. 794*

395 The cricket tutor, by the author of The
■ cricket field. Longman, Green, Longman and Roberts, 1862. viii,85p. illus.
——2nd ed. 1862. x,85p. illus.

396 **Routledge, Edmund**
■ The handbook of cricket. Routledge, 1862. 64p. illus. diagrs. (Routledge's Sixpenny Handbooks)
——2nd ed. 1862
——3rd ed. 1862
——*another ed.* 1866
——*another ed.* [c.1866]
——*another ed.* [c.1869]
——*another ed.* [c.1869]
*for Dutch translation see no. 426*

396 **Take** my advice on games and how to
–1 play them. J. Blackwood, [c.1853]. diagrs. 56p.
*includes cricket with Laws*

397 **[Wanostrocht, Nicholas]**
■ Felix on the bat: being a scientific inquiry into the use of the cricket bat; together with the history and use of the catapulta. Also, the laws of cricket, as revised by the Marylebone Club, 1845. Baily Bros., 1845. 40p. illus. (some col.), diagrs.
——2nd ed. 1850. xii,58p.
——3rd ed. 1855. x,74p.
see also *no. 688*

398 The cricket bat; and how to use it: a treatise on the game of cricket. With practical and scientific instructions in batting, bowling, and fielding: the laws of cricket, match-playing, single-wicket, &c. By an Old Cricketer. Baily Bros., 1861. [iv],96p. (Handbooks of field-sports)
*some copies have variant t.p. dated 1860*
——*new issue.* Houlston & Wright, 1863. [iv],96p.
——*2nd ed.* Houlston & Wright, 1865. viii,96p. (Handbooks of Field & River Sports)

399 **The whole** art of cricket and how to play it; including batting, bowling, fielding, wicket-keeping; laws of double wicket . . . Bishop, [c. 1840]. 12p.

# TECHNIQUE 1865–1919

400 **Abel, Robert**
■ Cricket and how to play it, with the rules of the Marylebone Club. Dean. 1894. 56p. illus. ports. diagrs.
——New and rev. ed. 1894. 56p.
——*another ed.* 1895. 62p.
*for earlier eds. see no. 482*

401 **Ayres, F.H.**
■ The manual of cricket. Ayres, [1895]. 57p. illus. diagrs.

402 **Barlow, Richard Gorton**
■ Batting and bowling, with hints on fielding and wicket-keeping. G. Bussey, [1882]. 31p. illus. diagrs.
*includes "Wicket-keeping" by Richard Pilling*

403 **Beldam, George William**
■ Cricket illustrated: sixty photographs by G.W. Beldam of famous cricketers engaged in actual play with notes by the author. Gowans & Gray, 1908. 78p. illus. (Gowan's Practical Picture Books)

404 **Benson, Claude Ernest**
■ Cricket for beginners: rewritten from the volume by A.C. MacLaren. Routledge, 1913. 87p. illus. diagr. (Oval Series of Sports and Pastimes)
*see no. 452*

405 **Benson, Edward Frederic,** *and* **Miles,**
■ **Eustace Hamilton,** *editors*
The cricket of Abel, Hirst and Shrewsbury. Hurst & Blackett, 1903. xx,287p. illus. (Athletic library)

406 **Bonner, H.**
■ Cricket for boys, with hints on how to play the game. Camden P., [c.1916]. 8p. diagrs.

407 **[Box, Charles]**
■ The theory and practice of cricket from its origin to the present time; with critical & explanatory notes upon the laws of the game, by "Bat". Warne, 1868. ix,165p.
——*another issue with title:* Cricket, its theory and practice. 1868

408 **The "Boy's Realm"** cricket book (1909):
■ being the only cricket handbook for junior players. Amalgamated P., [1909]. 40p. illus. ports. diagrs.

409 **Brett, Edwin John**
■ "Boys of England" cricket guide. "Boys of England" Office, [1867?]. 32p. illus. diagrs.
*date as given in B.M. catalogue, but laws and instructions on bowling are pre-1864 (Lord's catalogue)*
——new and revised ed. [186–]. 32p. illus. diagrs.
——— with portraits. [186–]. 32p. illus. ports. diagrs.
——*with title:* Young men of Great Britain cricket guide. New & revised ed. with portraits. [186–]. 32p. illus. ports. diagrs.

410 **Carlsruhe Cricket Club**
Cricket. Carlsruhe. [the Club], 1874. 12p. diagrs.
*in German*

411 **Chadwick, Henry**
■ Chadwick's American cricket manual, containing the revised laws of the game, with an explanatory appendix to each rule, instructions in bowling, batting, and fielding. New York, de Witt, 1873. 128p. illus. scores
——*another ed. with title:* De Witt's cricket guide containing very full and accurate information as to the best manner of bowling, batting and fielding . . . New York, de Witt, 1879. 105p. illus. diagrs.
*includes an account, with scores, of the international matches played in the U.S. 1859, 1868 and 1872*

412 Cricket: rules and requisites of the great
■ national game of England; also La crosse. New York, de Witt. [c.1880]. 48p. illus. diagrs. [De Witt's Standard Handbook Series)

——*another ed. with title:* Wehman's book of cricket and la crosse. N.Y., Wehman, [c.1880]

413 ——, *editor*
Beadle's dime book of cricket and football, being a complete guide to players, and containing all the rules and laws of the ground -and games. N.Y., Beadle, [1866]. [vii],50p.

414 **The champion** cricketers' guide and
■ companion: the whole art of cricket. R. March, [c.1865]. 32p. diagr.
*several issues*

415 **Collings, Thomas Chapman**
■ Cricket: with contributions by T.A. Hearne, Albert Ward, M.A. Noble, P.F. Warner, Lord Harris, C.W. Alcock, F.G. Bull, and others. T. Fisher Unwin, 1900. xv,176p. illus. ports. (Sports Library)

416 **Crawford, John Neville**
■ The practical cricketer. Health & Strength Ltd. 1909. 93p. illus. port.

417 **Cricket.** J & R Maxwell, [1882?]. 32p.
■ illus. diagrs. (British Standard Handbooks of Sports and Pastimes)
——*another issue.* Griffith, Farran, [1882?]
——*another issue.* Blackett, [1882?]

418 **Cricket:** containing hints on bowling,
■ batting, fielding and captaincy. Ward, Lock, [1898?]. 86p. illus. (New Penny Handbooks)
——*several issues*, at least one dated 1898 and one published by Ingram Clark. Bristol

419 **Cricket:** its theory and practice. Heck-
□ mondwike, C. Ward, 1870. 22p. diagrs.
——*another ed.* [c.1885]. 29p. illus. diagrs.

420 **Cricket** and how to play it. London &
■ Otley, W. Walker, [c.1885]. 16p. illus.

421 **Cricket** tips: helpful hints on the great game. London, *n.d.*
*in Taylor*

422 **The cricketer:** a handbook on the game. London, *n.p.,* [c.1869]
*in Taylor*

423 **The cricketers'** pocket companion,
■ containing character & history of cricket, hints on batting, bowling and fielding. M.C.C.'s revised rules, notabilities of cricket, original and other songs. J. Vincent, [c.1883]. 32p.

424 **D., A. O.**
■ Cricket drill and training, by A.O.D. Long, 1904. 68p. illus. diagrs.
*by Augustine O'Dormey?*

425 **Daft, Richard**
■ Hints on cricket. Bristol, Arrowsmith; London, Simpkin, Marshall, [1893]. 52p. illus. port.
——*another ed. In:* Arrowsmith, James W. Arrowsmith's cricket scoring book. [1896]. *See* no. 284

426 **Dekker, L.**
■ Handleiding tot het cricketspel naar het Engelsch. Haarlem, Bohn, 1881. 75p. illus. diagrs.
*a translation into Dutch of Edmund Routledge's "Handbook of cricket" See no. 396*

427 **An essay** on cricket. Heckmondwike, C.
■ Ward, [1884?] [5]p.
*see also no. 376*
——*another issue together with* "School cricket hints", "Cricketers progress" "Reverie on cricket", etc. Heckmondwike, C. Ward, [c.1884]. 32p. illus.

427 **"An Etonian",** *pseud.*
–1 A few hints on cricket. Eton, E.P. Williams, [1871?]. 8p.
*possibly the first edition of no. 455?*

428 **"Ex-Captain",** *pseud.*
■ Cricket as it should be played, with the rules of the Marylebone Club, and practical directions for amateurs. Ward Lock, [1878?]. 93p. illus. diagrs. (Ward & Lock's Sixpenny Handbooks]
*Several editions – 1894. Contents almost identical with cricket section in no. 466*

429 **[Farmer, James Herbert]**
□ Cricket hints for youngsters and others by an Old Harrovian Member of the M.C.C. Solicitors' Law Stationery Society, 1910, 8p.
——*2nd ed.* 1910, 8p.
——*3rd ed.* Privately published, 1911. 12p.
——*4th ed.* 1913. 12p.
——*5th ed.* Spalding. [c.1924]. 16p.

430 **Ford, William Justice,** *and others*
■ Cricket: with contributions by F.G.J. Ford, Tom Richardson and M.C. Kemp. Lawrence & Bullen, 1897. 94p. illus. diagrs. (Suffolk sporting series)
*rpts. with slight alterations from "The encyclopaedia of sport", part 4, by H.C. Howard, earl of Suffolk & Berkshire, and others, See no. 7049*

431 **Fry, Charles Burgess,** *and others*
■ Cricket, by C.B. Fry, K.S. Ranjitsinhji,

G.L. Jessop, C.L. Townsend, G. Brann; edited by G.L. Jessop. A. Pearson, 1903. 123p.

432 ■ **The game** of cricket. Cassell, [1866]. 59p. illus. diagr. (Cassell's Sixpenny Handbooks)

433 ■ **Grace, William Gilbert**
Cricket. Bristol, Arrowsmith: London, Simpkin, Marshall, 1891. viii,489p. illus. ports. scores. stats.
——L.P. ed. 1891. xii,512p.
*limited to 635 copies and 10 presentation copies*
——*another ed.* Leipzig, Heinemann and Balestier, 1892. [vii],350p. (The English Library)

434 ■ Batting, bowling and fielding. Bristol, Arrowsmith; London, Simpkin, Marshall, [1892]. 3–95p. frontis. (port.)
*rptd. from Grace, W.G. Cricket. 1891*

435 ■ ——, *and others*
Cricket: a handbook of the game, by Dr. W.G. Grace, A.C. MacLaren, A.E. Trott, and others. Greening, 1907. 126p. ports. (Greening's Useful Handbooks)

436 ■ **Harris, George Robert Canning Harris,** *4th baron*
Hints to young cricketers: also the laws of cricket, and other useful matter connected with the game. London, Wisden: Maidstone, Burgiss-Brown, 1896. 19p. diagr.

437 ■ **Hayward, Thomas Walter**
Cricket. British Sports Publishing Co., 1907. 132p. illus. port. (Spalding's Athletic Library)

438 ■ **Heineken, Philipp**
Das Cricket-spiel nach den neuesten vom englischen Marylebone Cricket Club herausgegebenen Regeln, bearbeitest von Ph. Heineken. Stuttgart, Weise, 1893. [viii],21p. illus. diagrs.
*consists of pp. 123–44 from his "Beliebtesten Rasenspiele", 1893. See no. 7048*

439 ■ **Holland, Frederick, C.**
Cricket. G. Bell, 1904. [viii],115p. illus. (All-England Series)

440 **How** to play cricket. Manchester, J. Heywood, 1892
*in Taylor*

441 ■ **Hutchinson, Horace Gordon,** *editor*
Cricket. Country Life, 1903. xxii,454p. illus. ports. (Country Life Library of Sport)

442 ■ **Hutchison, George Andrew,** *editor*
Cricket: a popular handbook on the game, by Dr. W.G. Grace, Rev. J. Pycroft, Lord Charles Russell, Frederick Gale and other well-known veteran authorities. Religious Tract Society, [1887]. xii,244p. illus. ports. diagrs. (Boy's Own Bookshelf III)
*contains a chapter on "How to make a cricket bat" by W.G. Grace*

443 ■ **Ireland, Arthur J.**
The complete cricketer. J. Dicks, [1905]. 79p. illus.
*cover-title: Dick's cricket*

444 ■ **Jessop, Gilbert Laird**
Cricket notes; with chapters by A.O. Jones and C.L. Townsend. Bristol, Arrowsmith; London, Simpkin, Marshall, [1903]. 189p. illus. port.
*1st published serially and now revised*

445 □ **Den Kjøbenhavnske Boldspilklub**
Haandbog i cricket og langbold. Kjøbenhavn, C.C. Lose, 1866. [iii],50p. illus. diagrs.
*cricket pp. 1–38*
——*3rd ed. with title:* Haandbog i cricket, langbold og fodbold. Kjøbenhavn, Pio, 1895. 62p. illus. diagrs.
*Danish text: trs. "Handbook to cricket . . .*

446 ■ **Knight, Albert E.**
The complete cricketer. Methuen, 1906. xi,368p. illus. ports. diagrs. glossary
——*2nd ed.* 1911. (Methuen's Colonial Library)

446 -1 **L., A.J.H.**
Cricket notes for boys. Rugby, G.E. Over, [1913]. 8p.

447 **The Ladies'** guide to cricket, by a Lover of Both, with a glossary of technical terms and cricket slang and the laws of cricket. Auckland, Freeman's Journal Office, 1883. 41p. diagrs. score

448 ■ **Lyttelton,** *the Hon.* **Edward**
Cricket. London, Bell: New York, Stokes, 1890. [viii],104p. illus. diagrs. (All England Series)
——2nd ed. Bell, 1890
——new [3rd] ed. 1894
——4th ed. 1898
——5th ed. 1919
——6th ed. 1910
——another ed. 1922
*the order of the 5th and 6th eds. has not been verified; dates as given on title-page*

449 ■ International cricket guide; containing the latest rules and regulations for this popular game. New York, Street & Smith,

1891. 63p illus. diagrs. (Manual Library—no. 31)
*a revised ed. of "Cricket", by the same author*

450 **Lyttelton, the Hon. Robert Henry**
■ Cricket. Duckworth, 1898. 124p.

451 Outdoor games: cricket and golf. Dent,
■ 1901. vii,252p. col. ports. (The Haddon Hall Library)
——L.P. ed. 1901
*limited to 150 copies*

452 **Maclaren, Archibald Campbell**
■ Cricket for beginners. Routledge, 1896. 77p. illus. (The "Oval" Series of Games)
*for revised ed. see no. 404*

453 Cricket. Treherne, 1906. 95p. ports.
■ ——2nd ed. 1909. 64p. frontis. (port.)

454 **"A Member of the Marylebone Club",** *pseud.*
Cricket and how to play it. Dean, [c.1869]. 59p. illus. diagrs.
*date of publication inferred from Laws 9 and 10, which are post 1864 and pre 1870 (Lord's catalogue)*

455 **Mitchell, Richard Arthur Henry**
■ A few hints on cricket. Eton, R. Ingalton Drake, 1882. 16p.
——2nd ed. 1887. 16p.
see also: no. 427–1

456 **Mohummud Abdullah Khan**
■ The cricket guide intended for the use of young players, containing a short but comprehensive account of the game, embracing all the important rules and directions nicely arranged in due succession. Lucknow, Royal Printing Press, 1891. ii,28p. diagr.

457 **Mulier, W.**
■ Cricket; geillustreerd door den schrijver Haarlem, Loosjes, 1897. xii,247p. illus. ports. diagrs. score. stats.
*Dutch text*

458 **Murdoch, William Lloyd**
■ Cricket. Routledge, 1893. 95p. illus. ports. (The "Oval Series of Games")
——2nd ed. 1894
——another ed. 1902. 94p.

459 **Newhall, George Morgan,** *editor*
■ How to play cricket: a manual for American cricketers. Philadelphia, T.S. Dando, 1881. 74p. diagrs.
*cover-title: American cricketers' manual*

460 **"An Old Stump,"** *pseud.*
■ La clef du cricket; ou, courte explication

de la marche et des principales règles de ce jeu, par An Old Stump, M.P.C.C. [Paris, privately printed, 1864?]. 23p.
*French text; with rules of the Paris C.C., pp. 21–23*

461 **[Pardon, George Frederick]**
□ Cricket: it's [sic] theory and practice, by Capt. Crawley. Chambers, [1865]. viii,72p. illus. diagrs. stats. (Chambers's Useful Handbooks)
*numerous eds.-1889*

462 **Pavri, Mahrvanji Erachji**
■ Parsi cricket, with hints on bowling, batting, fielding, captaincy, explanation of laws of cricket &c. &c. Bombay, J.B. Marzban, 1901. xvi,196p. ports. diagrs. score. stats.

463 **Pelham, Thomas Henry William**
■ Cricket notes. Wyman, [1886?] 16p.
*dated 1880 in B.M. Catalogue*

464 **Pickering, William Percival**
■ Cricket "wrinkles". Vancouver, B.C., Trythall, *for private circulation*, 1900. 12p.
——2nd ed. 1902

465 **Pilch, Fuller**
■ Whole art of cricket, containing instructions to batter, bowler, wicket-keeping . . . . W.S. Forty, [c.1870]. 8p. diagr.
——another ed.——, with instructions how to bat and bowl . . . Ingram, [c. 1875]. 8p. diagrs.

466 **Planché, Frederick d'Arros**
■ Cricket as now played; and Baseball and rounders by Captain Crawley. Ward Lock, 1877. viii,120p. illus. diagrs. (Captain Crawley's Handbooks of Outdoor Games)
*contents of cricket section almost identical with no. 428*
——another issue. c.1892. viii[4],120p.
*identical with above except for rearrangement of prelims and insertion of 4p. on parks and open spaces available for cricket in the vicinity of London*

467 **Ranjitsinhji, Kumar Shri**
■ The jubilee book of cricket. Edinburgh & London, Blackwood, 1897. xvi,465p. illus. ports, plans, stats.
*with chs. on public school and Cambridge University cricket by W.J. Ford, Oxford University by Thomas Case and County cricket by various writers*
*six "editions" 1897–98; also:*
——L.P. ed. 1897. xvi,474p.
——limited ed. of 350 copies. 1897. xvi,474p. *with additional plates*
——pbk. ed. 1901. 160p.
——cheap ed. Nelson, [c.1904]. 382p.

——*rptd.* [1912?]. 382p. (Nelson's Shilling Library)

468 Cricket guide and how to play cricket.
■ British Sports Publishing Co. 1906. 117p. illus. port (Spalding's Athletic Library)
——*another ed.* 1906 [i.e. 1907]. 125p. illus. port. [Spalding's Athletic Library]

469 **Read, Walter William**
☐ Short hints on cricket. W.H. Cook, [c.1885]. [18p].
——*2nd ed.* Wright, *n.d.*

470 **Selkirk, George H.**
■ Guide to the cricket ground. Macmillan, 1867. vii,131p. illus. diagrs.

471 **Sewell, Edward Humphrey Dalrymple**
■ Cricket points for the county, 'varsity, public school, and club cricketer. "Sporting Life", [1911]. 64p.

472 **Smink, Pieter Johannes**
Volledige handleiding bij het cricketspel. Baarn, J.F. van de Ven, [1908?]. 32p. illus.
——*2nd ed.* [1912?]. (Bibliotheek voor Sport en Spel)
*in Dutch: trs. "Complete instructions for playing cricket"*

473 **Steel, Allan Gibson,** *and* **Lyttelton,** *Hon.*
■ **Robert Henry**
Cricket: with contributions by A. Lang, W.G. Grace, R.A.H. Mitchell, and F. Gale. Longmans, 1888. xiii,429p. illus. diagrs. (The Badminton Library of Sports and Pastimes)
——*L.P. ed.* 1888. xv,465p.
——*2nd ed.* 1888. xiii,429p.
——*3rd ed.* 1889. xiii,429p.
——*4th ed.* 1890. xiii,429p.
——*5th ed. rev.* 1893. xiii,420p.
——*6th ed. thoroughly rev.* 1898. xiii,408p.
——*7th ed. thoroughly rev.* 1904. xiii,408p.
*for 1920 ed. see no. 480*

474 **Strickland, W. Poole**
■ Present-day cricket for youths and amateurs; edited by L.G. Brown; illustrated by R. Wallace Coop. Lund, Humphries, 1902. 137p. illus. diagrs.

475 **Thomas, Isaiah**
■ A concise hint and guide to cricket. [Belize, British Honduras, *privately printed*, 1908]. [4]p.

476 **[Thomas, Herbert Preston,** *and*
■ **Ponsonby, J. H.]**
Cricketers in council, by Thomsonby. Bell & Daldy, 1871. viii,114p.

476 **Van Booven, Henri C.A.**
–1 Cricket-spel. Dordrecht, Morks, 1917. 80p. frontis. (Natuur en Sport)
*Dutch text; mostly on technique and the Laws, but includes a brief history of the game in England and Holland*

477 **[Vasey, P.W.,** *and* **Vasey, G.H.]**
■ Hints and suggestions to school cricketers. Watford, *printed by* H.E.R. Dorant, 1913. 48p.

478 **Von Rauch**
Anleitung für des Lawn Tennis, Cricket, usw. 1905
*in German: An introduction to . . . cricket, etc.*

479 **Warner,** *Sir* **Pelham Francis**
■ The book of cricket. Dent, 1911. xii,253p. illus. ports. diagrs.
——*revised ed.* 1922. xx,234p.
——*3rd ed. revised and reset.* 1934. xii,233p.
——*new ed. with an additional chapter.* Sporting Handbooks, 1943. 212p.
——*4th ed. revised and reset.* Sporting Handbooks, 1945. viii,296p.

480 Cricket: a new edition, with contributions
■ by the Hon. R.H. Lyttelton, G.L. Jessop. D.J. Knight. J. Shuter, E.R. Wilson. Longmans, Green, 1920. xii,348p. illus. ports. stats. (The Badminton Library of Sports and Pastimes)
*a new edition of the work by A.G. Steel and the Hon. R.H. Lyttelton, see no. 473*

481 **Williams, J.W.**
■ La tranca: juego atletico. Buenos Aires, Las Librerias Inglesas, 1881. 17p. frontis. diagrs.
*In Spanish; trs. "The bat: athletic games"*

482 **Wisden, John**
■ Cricket, and how to play it; with the rules of the Marylebone Club. Darton and Hodge, [1866?]. 62p. illus. diagrs. (The Champion Handbooks)
——*another ed.* Henry Lea, [1868?]. 62[4]p.
——*New and revised ed.* Graphotyping Co., & Simpkin, Marshall, [1873]
——*New and revised ed.* Dean & Son, [1880?]
*for later eds. see no. 400*

483 **Wister, Jones**
■ A "Bawl" for American cricket, dedicated to American youth. Philadelphia, Pa., [the Author?], 1893. 62p. illus. diagr.
——*pbk. ed.* 1893

484 **Wood, Frederick**
■ Beeton's cricket book: with "A match I

was in", by the author of "The cricket field", [J. Pycroft]. Warne, [c. 1866]. iii,86p. illus. diagr.
——2nd ed. S.O. Beeton, [c. 1869]. iv,116p. illus. diagrs.

485 Cricket, by Frederic [sic] Wood. Warne,
■ [1866]. 96p. col. frontis. illus. diagrs. (Warne's Bijou Books)
——another ed. 1868. 96p. (The Bijou Book of Out-door Amusements)

486 **Wright, George**
Cricket guide. Boston, (Mass.), Wright & Ditson, 1892
*in Taylor*
——another ed. Cricket guide: how to bat, how to bowl, how to field, diagrams how to place a field, valuable hints to players, and other valuable information. Rules of the game. [New York], American Sports Publishing Co., [1894]. 57p. illus. cover-title: *"Spalding's Athletic Library"*

487 **The young** cricketer's companion. R. March. [c.1870]. 19p. illus.

## TECHNIQUE 1920–1945

488 **Altham, Harry Surtees**
■ Some cricket principles. *Privately printed,* [c.1920]. 4p.

489 **Armstrong, Warwick Windridge**
■ The art of cricket. Methuen, 1922. vii,149p. illus.
*contains chapter of the Australian team in England, 1921 and a note on W.W. Armstrong by A.C. MacLaren*
——2nd ed. 1923
——3rd ed. 1924

490 **Barbour, Eric Pitty**
■ The making of a cricketer: a handbook for the young player with ambition to improve. Sydney, Sydney & Melbourne Publishing Co. 1926. 232p. illus. diagrs.
——2nd ed. 1933. 219p.

491 **Beus, Anthony Marius Justus de,** *and*
■ **Feith, Jan**
Jongens! wat is cricket? Amsterdam, Jacob van Campen, 1928. 174p. illus. port.
*A book of instruction in Dutch*

492 **Bradman,** *Sir* **Donald George**
□ How to play cricket. Associated Newspapers, 1935. 95p. illus. diagr.
——Revised ed. Daily Mail Publications, 1948. 95p. illus. diagr. (Daily Mail educational series)
——Revised ed. Daily Mail, 1949. 96p. illus. diagr.

*another ed.* Hodder & Stoughton, 1953. 94p. frontis. (port.), illus. diagr.
——revised and updated ed. *with title:* Cricket; photographs by Patrick Eagar; drawings by Reg Cartwright. Leicester, Knight Books for Hodder & Stoughton, 1977. 96p. illus. (some col.), facsim. diagr. (Illustrated Teach Yourself)
——*1st Australian ed.* Melbourne, Georgian House, 1945. 96p. illus. diagr.
——*2nd ed.* 1948. 87p. illus. diagr.
——Revised ed. London, Angus & Robertson: Adelaide, Rigby, 1963. 79p. illus. diagr. stats.

493 **Brincker, R.E.**
Vejledning i cricket. Vejle (Denmark), Eget Forlag, 1921. 80p. illus. diagr.
*in Danish: trs. "Instruction in cricket"*

494 **Burton, David Cecil Fowler**
■ Don'ts for young cricketers. London & Keighley. The Cricket P., & The Keighley Printers, [1921?]. 15p.

495 **[Cardus,** *Sir* **Neville]**
■ The club cricketer: hints by "Cricketer" of the Manchester Guardian. Manchester, Manchester Guardian, 1922. 54p. diagrs.

496 **Chapman, Arthur Percy Frank,** *and others*
■ The game of cricket, by A.P.F. Chapman, P.G.H. Fender, W.B. Franklin, D.R. Jardine, D.J. Knight, H.D.G. Leveson-Gower, E.G. Martin, R.C. Robertson-Glasgow, H. Strudwick, E.A.C. Thomson, & H.E. White. Seeley, Service, 1930. 255p. illus. ports. diagrs. (The Lonsdale Library)

497 **Clarke, Basil**
■ Cricket at preparatory schools: a few hints for the young cricketer. Winchester, Warren, [1930]. 31p.

498 **Currie, F. Davison**
■ The cricketer's companion; or, The secrets of cricket. London, Routledge: N.Y., Dutton, [1917?] 95p. illus.

499 **De Selincourt, Hugh**
■ 'Over!': some personal remarks on the game of cricket: with 35 illustrations by J.H. Thorpe. Howe, 1932. 223p. illus.
——*another ed.* 1934

500 **Dipper, Alfred Ernest**
■ Cricket hints. Athletic Publications, [c. 1926]. 79p. illus. port.

501 **Ducat, Andrew**
■ Cricket. Hutchinson, [1933]. 159p. illus. port.

502 **Fender, Percy George Herbert**
■ An ABC of cricket. A Barker, 1937. 172p.
illus. diagr.

503 **Fenn, Eric Alfred Humphrey**
■ Cricket for young boys. Glasgow, James
Brown, 1921. 51p. illus.

503 **"The Globe"** cricket hints by Don
–1 Bradman, W.A. Oldfield, Arthur Mailey,
■ A.G. Moyes. Sydney, Sun Newspapers
Ltd., 1934. 40p. illus. diagrs. stats.
*results and stats. of 1934 Australian tour
of England on back cover*

504 **Gold, Jørgen**
Cricket. Odense, Forlaget Arnkrane, 1945
*in Danish*

505 **[Haydon, Arthur Lincoln]**
■ Cricket, by "Cover Point". Warne, 1928.
64p. diagrs. (Warne's "Recreation"
Books)
——*another ed.* 1931

506 **Hendren, "Patsy",** *i.e.* **Elias Henry**
■ **Hendren**
The complete cricketer. Hutchinson,
[1933]. 127p. illus. diagrs.

507 **Henley, Francis Anthony Hoste**
■ The boys' book of cricket. Bell, 1924.
xii,147p. illus.
——*new ed.* 1928

508 **Herman, Herbert Maurice**
■ How's that?: a little book on cricket for
boys and beginners. Hutchinson, [1937].
159p. illus. diagrs.

509 **Hobbs,** *Sir* **John Berry**
■ Cricket for beginners. Pearson, 1922.
121p. illus. diagrs.
——*rptd.* 1924, 1932, 1936

510 ————, *and others*
■ The game of cricket as it should be
played, by Sir J.B. Hobbs, Maurice Tate
and Herbert Strudwick. Foulsham,
[1926]. 88p. illus. ports. diagrs. (Foulsham's Outdoor Library)
——Revised ed. [1948]. 92p.
*for later eds.* see nos. 571, 570

511 **Hone, Brian William**
■ Cricket practice and tactics. E. Arnold,
1937. 120p. illus. diagrs. bibliog.
——*rptd.* 1946, 1948

512 **Howell, R.G.D.**
■ Hints on cricket. W.H. Hillman, [1931].
23p.

513 **Hubble, Jack Charlton**
■ Hints on cricket, Maidstone, the Author,
[1935?]. 14p. 1 port.
*cover-title:* All round hints on cricket

514 **Jardine, Douglas Robert**
■ Cricket. Dent, 1936. xi,224p. illus. ports.
diagrs. (Modern Sports)
——*revised ed.* 1945. xiii,240p. illus. ports.
diagrs.
——*rptd.* (with additional illustrations).
1949

515 Cricket: how to succeed; with a chapter
■ on women's cricket by Marjorie Pollard.
Evans, for the National Union of Teachers,
[1936]. 32p. illus. diagr.

516 **Jessop, Gilbert Laird**
■ Cricket and how to play it. Harrap, 1925.
128p. illus. diagrs. (Masters of Sports)

517 **Jordan, B.**
■ Cricket: a concise guide for enthusiast
and novice. Universal Publications, [1939].
89p. illus.

518 **Jørgensen, Poul**
Kricket: en laerebog for begyndere. Copenhagen, H. Hagerups, 1933. 79p. illus.
*a manual in Danish*

519 **Kemp, Percival Hepworth**
■ Cricket for schools: its organisation and
practice. H. Russell, [1932]. vi,54p. illus.
diagrs.

520 Cricket practice for boys. H Russell,
■ [c.1935]. [iii],43p. illus. diagrs.

521 **Kippax, Alan Falconer**
■ Cricket as demonstrated by Australia's
greatest stroke maker. Kellogg (Aust) Pty.
Ltd., [1939?]. [16]p. illus. port. diagrs.
stats.

522 **Knight, Donald John**
■ The more compleat cricketer. Country
Life, 1925. xi,58p. illus.

523 **Lucas, Richard Macdonald**
■ Le cricket pour les sportsmen français: les
principes du jeu avec le code officiel du
Marylebone Cricket Club (Le "M.C.C.")
et un vocabulaire du sport. Saint-Cloud,
Goupy, [1927]. 48p. diagrs.

524 **Lyon, Malcolm Douglas**
■ Cricket. Eyre & Spottiswoode, 1932.
197p. illus. ports. diagrs. (The Aldin
Series)
——*revised ed.* 1938. 191p.

43

525 **MacCuaig, Donald**
■ Stepping stones to cricket, football and hockey for school use. Longmans, 1927. xv,53p. illus.
*cricket pp. 1–24*

526 **Maclaren, Archibald Campbell**
■ Cricket old and new: a straight talk to young players. Longmans, Green, 1924. xii,211p. illus. ports., diagrs.
——*rptd.* 1930

527 **The making** of a cricketer. The Times, ■ [1919]. 15p.
*rptd. from "The Times", April 25, 26, 28, 29, 1919. The introduction is by R.H. Lyttelton*

527 **Nederlandsche Cricket Bond**
–1 Cricketlessen, beknopte. Hague, Propaganda Commissie van de N.C.B., 1941. 28p. (De Groene Krekelserie no. 5)
*Dutch text, trs.: "Concise cricket lessons"*

528 **Noble, Montague Alfred**
■ The game's the thing: a record of cricket experience; with special chapters on the genius of Victor Trumper. Cassell, 1926. xv,248p. ports. diagrs.

529 **Overend, J.W.**
Cricket for boys and how to play the game. [c.1917].

530 **Pollard, Marjorie**
■ Cricket for women and girls. Hutchinson, [1934]. 158p. illus. ports. scores
——*another ed.* 1935

531 **[Protheroe, Ernest]**
■ A book about cricket, by 'An Old Hand'. Epworth P., 1924. 120p. ports.

532 **Rathbone, W.**
■ A chat on cricket . . . in a recent address to the St. Helen's and District Cricket League. St. Helen's, St. Helen's & Prescot Reporter, 1926. [18]p.
*rptd. from St. Helen's and Prescot Reporter 28th May, 4th & 11th June, 1926*

533 **Rosenkrantz,** *Baron* **H.**
■ Cricket, udarbejdet efter forskellige engelske fagskrifter og blade samt bearbejdet for Danske forhold. Aarhus, *privately printed*, [1926]. 118p. illus. diagrs.
*in Danish, with glossary of English terms explained in Danish; trs. "Cricket, compiled from various English authorities and books and adapted for Danish conditions"*

534 **[Rudd, Cecil Thomas,** *and* **Witham,** ■ **Edgar Murray]**
Cricket for boys, by two Wellingborough

masters. Nisbet, [1937]. 64p. illus. diagrs.
——*revised ed.* [1950]

535 **Russell, A.C.,** *and* **Stevens, W.N.**
■ The budding cricketer: general hints to the aspirant and young club cricketer. Edinburgh, Chambers, 1926. 60p. illus.

536 **[Sellers, Arthur]**
■ Hints to young cricketers. [York, the Author, 1929]. 3p.
*based on a work by S.M. Toyne of St. Peter's, York (Ashley-Cooper). See no. 546–1*

537 **Sewell, Edward Humphrey Dalrymple**
■ Cricket and how to play it. Bombay, Times of India, 1929. vii,79p. illus. diagrs.

538 First principles of cricket, etc. "The Boys ■ Own Paper" Office, [1935]. 86p. illus. ports.

539 **Shirley, William**
■ How to play cricket, with notes by A.C. MacLaren. Williams & Norgate, [1925]. xxiv,72p.
——*2nd ed.* [1926]
——*3rd ed.* [1926]

540 **Stevens, Greville Thomas Scott,** *and* ■ **Bruce-Kerr, J.**
Cricket guide, and how to play cricket. Otley, Renwick, 1924. 110p. illus. stats. (Spalding's Athletic Library)
*the illus. are rptd. from "Cricket", by T.W. Hayward. See no. 437*

541 **The Sun**
Sun cricket hints. Sydney, Sun Newspapers, 1934. 40p. illus. stats.
*articles by Sir Donald Bradman, W.A. Oldfield, A.A. Mailey and A.G. Moyes.*
*includes stats. of 1934 Australian tour of England*

542 **Sutcliffe, Herbert**
■ Cricket memoirs and records, with advice to youths and others. Leeds, Storey Evans, [1928?]. 32p. illus. port. stats.

543 **[Symond, Ronald T.]**
■ Homage to cricket, by "Gryllus". Harmsworth, 1933. xi,156p.

544 **Taylor, Claude Hilary,** *and* **Macindoe,** ■ **David Henry**
Cricket dialogue. Collins, 1949. 143p. diagrs.

545 **Taylor, Herbert Wilfred**
■ Cricket: how to play correctly: tips for young and old. Johannesburg, Argus Publ. Co., [1924]. 64p. illus. diagr.

546 Cricket for young and old (not forgetting
■ father). Maitland, S. Africa, the Author,
[1945]. 20p. illus. diagrs.

546 **Toyne, Sam M.**
–1 Cricket maxims for Peterite cricketers and
any others who are old enough to learn,
by S.M.T. York, Yorkshire Herald,
[192–?]. [4]p.

547 **Treadgold, Geoffrey William Robbs**
■ Junior cricket. Dent, 1926. xvi,79p. illus.
port. diagrs.

548 **Veerasawmy, J.A.**
■ Cricket: how to become a great batsman
and a great bowler. Georgetown, British
Guiana, the Author, 1936. 103p. port.
——2nd ed. 1945. 125p. illus. ports.
diagrs.

549 **Warden, Jehangir Sorabji**
■ Knotty cricket problems solved. Bombay,
the Author, [1923]. xiv,258p. diagrs.

550 **Weigall, Gerald John Villiers**
■ Cricket: the art of "playing the game".
Cricket P., [1922]. 45p.

551 **Wilson, Benjamin B.**
■ Hints to young cricketers. Leeds, Arthur
Wigley, the Waverley P., [1929]. 72p.
illus. diagrs.

552 **Woodfull, William Maldon**
■ Cricket. Pitman, 1936. x,154p. illus. diagrs.
(Games and Recreations Series)

553 **Wyatt, Robert Elliott Storey**
■ The ins and outs of cricket. Bell, 1936.
xi,298p. illus. diagrs.
——cheap ed. 1939. x,302p. diagrs.

## TECHNIQUE 1946–1979

554 **Agravāl, P.N.**
Cricket. Delhi, Narayandatta Sahgal &
Sons, 1958. 68p. diagrs.
*in Hindi*

554 **Andrew, Keith,** *and others*
–1 Cricket, by Keith Andrew, Bob Carter
■ and Les Lenham. Wakefield, EP Publishing, 1978. 116p. illus. diagrs. (EP Sport
Series)
*cover-title*: Cricket: the techniques of the
game
*an official National Cricket Assoc. publi-
cation*

555 **Bailey, Trevor Edward**
■ Cricket. Eyre & Spottiswoode, 1956.
189p. illus. diagrs.

——another ed. Sportsman's Book Club,
1957

556 Improve your cricket. Harmondsworth,
■ Penguin, 1963. 160p. illus. diagrs. (Penguin Handbooks)

557 ————, and **Wilcox, Denys Robert**
■ Cricketers in the making. Hutchinson,
[1950.] 131p. illus. diagrs. (Library of
Sports and Pastimes)
*for boys*

558 **Benaud, Lou,** *i.e.* **Louis Richard Benaud**
■ The young cricketer; with foreword and
photo demonstration by Richie Benaud.
Sydney & London, Angus & Robertson,
1964. 87p. illus. diagrs.
——rev. ed. 1976. 87p. illus. diagrs.

559 **Benaud, Richie**
■ Way of cricket. Hodder & Stoughton,
1961. 247p. illus. ports. scores

560 **Betham, Geoffrey Robert Keyes**
■ Bat v. ball: a small book about cricket for
young players; photographs by E.A.
Harle. Newport, Johns, [1951]. 107p.
illus. diagrs. bibliog.

560 **Bhattacharya, Rakhal,** *editor*
–1 Cricket the Indian way. Calcutta, Rupa,
■ 1976. [vii],iv,128p. illus. port. diagr. stats.
*an anthology of articles by Indian cricketers
and officials*

561 **The Birmingham Mail Sports Final**
■ Learn cricket with the champions: illustrated lessons by members of Warwickshire County Cricket Club, winners of the
1951 County Cricket Championship.
Birmingham, The Birmingham Mail,
[1951]. 32p. illus. ports. diagr.

562 **Bland, Colin**
■ Dynamic cricket: a new approach. Salisbury (Rhodesia), The College P., 1969.
[ix],116p. illus. diagrs.

563 **Board, John**
■ The right way to become a cricketer (illustrated). Kingswood (Sy.), Elliot, [1950].
158p. illus. diagrs. (Right Way Books)

563 **Boycott, Geoffrey**
–1 Geoff Boycott's book for young cricketers.
■ S. Paul, 1976. 64p. illus. diagrs.
——pbk. ed. 1976

564 **Bradman, Sir Donald George**
■ The art of cricket. Hodder & Stoughton,
1958. 239p. illus. ports. diagrs.
——5th impression revised. 1969

**564** **Brayshaw, Ian**
**-1** The elements of cricket. Sydney, etc., Methuen of Australia, 1978. 144p. illus. ports. pbk.

**564** **Carmody, Keith**
**-2** Keith Carmody on cricket. Perth, *n.p.*, 1948
——2nd ed. revd. & enl. 1948. 63p. illus. ports. diagrs.

**564** **Chappell, Gregory Stephen,** *and others*
**-3** Successful cricket, from beginner to
■ expert in forty lessons, with Dennis Lillee, Ashley Mallett, Paul Sheahan, Brian Taber. Melbourne, Nelson (Australia), 1974; London, Pelham Books, 1975. 81p. illus. diagrs.

**565** **Close, Brian,** *i.e.* **Dennis Brian Close**
■ Close on cricket. S. Paul, 1966. 119p. illus. diagrs.
——*another ed.* Sportsman's Book Club, 1967

**566** **Constantine, Learie Nicholas,** *Lord Constantine*
■ Cricketers' cricket. Eyre & Spottiswoode, 1949. 269p. illus.
——*re-issued with title:* How to play cricket. 1951

**567** The young cricketer's companion: the
■ theory and practice of joyful cricket. Souvenir P., 1964. 207p. illus.
——*another ed.* Sportsman's Book Club, 1966
'*replaces* Cricketers' cricket, *later renamed* How to play cricket'—*preface*

**568** **Cowdrey, Michael Colin**
■ Tackle cricket this way. S. Paul, 1964. 128p. illus. ports. diagrs. (Tackle Series)
——*new ed.* 1969
——*new ed.* 1974
*with some new illus.*

**569** **Creek, Frederick Norman Smith**
■ Teach yourself cricket. English Universities P., 1950. 182p. illus. diagrs. (Teach Yourself Books)
——*rptd.* 1958
——2nd ed. 1973. 192p. pbk.
——*Hindi ed. with title:* Kriket kaisē karem; translated from English by Avināsacandra Māthur. Calcutta, Orient Longmans, 1963. vi,218p.

**570** **Cricket.** Foulsham, 1961. 96p. illus. ports.
■ diagrs. (New Sports Library)
contents: *Batting, by Sir Leonard Hutton; Bowling, by Alec Bedser; Wicketkeeping, by Godfrey Evans; Fielding, by J.T. Ikin.*
——*new ed.* Slough, Foulsham, 1969. 96p.

illus. ports. diagrs. (Pocket Sports Books)
*for previous eds. see nos. 510, 571*

**571** **Cricket** as it should be played. Foulsham,
■ 1952. 94p. illus. diagrs. (Foulsham's Sports Library)
contains—*Batting, by Len Hutton; Bowling, by Alec Bedser; Wicket-keeping, by Godfrey Evans; Fielding and field placing, by J.T. Ikin*
*for later eds. see no. 570*

**572** **Cross, Jack,** *compiler*
■ Cricket. Jackdaw Publications, [1971]. illus. facsims. ports. (Jackdaw, no. 101)
*portfolio containing 8p. booklet, 7 reproductions of contemporary documents, 7 explanatory broadsheets, illustration sheet & field-placing card*

**573** **Dansk Cricket Forbund**
■ Cricket—hvordan det skal spilles. København, D.C.F., 1968. 95p. diagrs.
*a translation into Danish of M.C.C. Cricket—how to play. See no. 595*

**573** **Davidson, Alan Keith**
**-1** Alan Davidson's cricket book; edited by Phil Tresidder. Sydney, Shakespeare Head P., 1965. 104p. illus. ports.

**573** **Dodds, Thomas Carter, ("Dickie")**
**-2** Cricket from father to son; illustrations by
■ Bob Bond. Kaye & Ward, 1979. 95p. illus. port. diagrs.
——*another ed.* pbk. 1979

**573** **Duff, Alan,** *and* **Chesterton, George**
**-3** Your book of cricket. Faber, 1974. 62p.
■ illus. diagrs. (The 'Your Book' Series)
*for children*

**573** **Dugan, Michael**
**-4** Cricket. Melbourne, Macmillan, 1979. 23p. illus. ports. diagrs. (Australian Fact Finders)
*for children*

**573** **Dunn, John,** *editor*
**-5** How to play cricket Australian style.
■ Adelaide, etc., Rigby, 1974; London, Souvenir P., 1975. [vi],121p. illus. ports. diagrs. stats.

**574** **Fairfax, Alan George**
■ The science of cricket: how to improve your play. Odhams P., [1952]. 65p. illus. diagrs.

**575** **Faragher, Harold Alker**
■ "Let's play cricket:" a practical manual for the learner, player & coach. Ilford, South Essex Recorders, Ltd., [1952]. 32p. illus. diagrs.

575 **Farmer, Bob**
-1 How to play cricket. Hamlyn, 1979. 3–61p. illus. ports.

575 **Fogg, John**
-2 Play better cricket; illustrated by Elmo
■ Eustace. Bridlington, Wolfe Publishing Ltd. for the Dairy Industry, 1970. 64p. illus. diagrs. (Project Book 172)
*for children*

576 **Foster, Denis**
■ Improve your cricket: with cine-camera instructional photographs specially posed by Jack Robertson. Findon Publications, [1948]. 128p. illus. diagrs.

577 **Fowler, Archibald J.B. ("Archie"), and**
■ **Bannister, Alexander James ("Alex")**
Hints on cricket. Daily Mail School-Aid Dept., [1946]. [i],11p. (Visual Education Film Strip)
*commentary to accompany film strip*

577 **Goldman, Arthur**
-1 What is cricket – rugby? illustrations by Lennie Sak. Johannesburg, South African Maccabi Council, [1969]. vii,132p. illus.

578 **Gover, Alfred Richard**
■ Cricket; with chapters by Herbert Strudwick and Frank Chester. Pitman, 1949. x,118p. illus. diagrs. (Games and Recreations Series)

579 How to play cricket; illustrated by Leon-
■ ard Hagerty. Harmondsworth, Penguin Books, 1957. 32p. illus. (some col.) diagrs. (Puffin Picture Books)

580 **Graveney, Tom,** *i.e.* **Thomas William**
■ **Graveney,** *and* **Statham, [John] Brian**
Instructions to young cricketers. Museum P., 1955. 109p. illus. diagrs. (Brompton Library)
——*revised and rptd. ed.* 1961

580 **Greig, Anthony William ("Tony")**
-1 Greig on cricket [by] Tony Greig with
■ Peter Smith. S. Paul, 1974. 79p. illus.
——*another ed.* 1974. pbk.

581 **Grimmett, Clarence Victor**
■ Grimmett on cricket: a practical guide. Nelson, [1952]. xii,131p. illus. port.

582 **Guise, John Lindsay**
■ Successful cricket. Barker, 1951. 124p. illus. ports. diagrs.

583 Talking of cricket: the book of the broad-
■ casts "Cricket for all." Methuen, 1952. ix,117p. illus. port.

584 **Gunasekara, C.H.**
■ What every young cricketer should know. Bombay, Thacker, 1953. xii,108p. illus. diagrs.

584 **Hall, Wesley Winfield ("Wes")**
-1 Secrets of good cricket. Sydney, Esso Standard Oil (Australia) Pty. Ltd., [1962?]. 12p. illus.

585 **Hammond, Walter Reginald**
■ Cricketers' school. S. Paul, [1950]. 231p. illus.

586 **Hassett, Lindsay,** *and* **Johnson, Ian**
■ Better cricket. Melbourne, Robertson and Mullens, [1951]. v,83p. illus. diagrs.

587 **Hinchcliffe, H.B.**
Cricket for beginners. *n.p.,* [1966?]. 28p.

587 **Hints** for cricketers and umpires. Sur-
-1 ridge, 1957

588 **Illingworth, Ray**
■ The young cricketer. S. Paul, 1972. 112p. illus.

588 **Jackman, Robin**
-1 Know your game and win. [Salisbury?]
■ Dairibord, [1976]. illus. port. diagrs.
*folder with 6 cards: field placings; running between wickets and calling; captaincy; batting; bowling; fielding and wicket keeping. Aimed at junior schools cricket with insert calendar of Rhodesia C.U. season 1976–7*

589 **Jagat Singh Bright**
Right way to play cricket. Delhi, Universal Publications, 1966. 144p. illus.

590 **Johnston, Brian Alexander**
■ All about cricket. W.H. Allen, 1972. 170p. illus. ports. diagrs. scores, stats. glossary

590 **Jones, Ronald**
-1 Cricket. Nelson, 1974. 56p. illus. (Sports for the Caribbean: Book 2)

591 **Kriket** ramatām sīkho. Surat, Sahita sangam, [1971]. 159p. illus.
*in Gujarati; trs. "Learn to play cricket"*

592 **McCool, Colin [Leslie]**
■ The best way to play cricket. Daily Mirror, 1961. 127p. illus. diagrs. (Young Sportsman's Books)

592 **Maine, Jim**
-1 How to play cricket Australian style. Melbourne, 1974
——*2nd ed.* Melbourne, Lloyd O'Neil, 1978. 134p. illus. (some col.) diagrs.

592 **Mankad, Vinoo**
-2 How to play cricket. Calcutta, Rupa in
■ collaboration with Sportsweek, 1976.
[vi],94p. illus. pbk.

593 **Mantri, Mādhav Krsnāji**
Kriket Ramvani kala. Bombay, Parichay
Trust, 1962. ii,30p.
*in Gujarati; trs. "The art of playing cricket"*

594 **Marylebone Cricket Club**
■ Cricket. Educational Productions,
[1950?]. 48p. illus. diagrs.

595 Cricket—how to play. Educational
■ Production for the M.C.C., 1955. 94p.
illus. diagrs. ("Play the Game" Series)
——*2nd ed.* 1957
——*3rd ed.* 1969
——*3rd ed. revised.* Wakefield, EP Publishing, [1976]. 94p. illus. (some col.).
("Play the Game" Series)

596 [Cricket—how to play] Krieket—hoe om
■ te speel; in Afrikaans verwerk deur Victor
Holloway en uitgegee vir die M.C.C.
Elsiesrivier, Nasionale Handelsdrukkery
Beperk, [1959]. 99p. illus. diagrs.
*in Afrikaans*

597 M.C.C. guide to better cricket. Niblick
■ Publishing Co. for Educational Publications, 1960. 16p. illus.
——*another issue,* sponsored by
Cadburys. 1960. 17p. col. illus.

597 **Merchant, Vijay**
-1 Cricket. New Delhi, National Book Trust,
■ 1975. 64p. illus. ports. facsims. diagrs.
(Nehru Library for Children)

598 **Merwe, Peter Laurence van der**
Wenkrieket; so word dit gespeel, deur
Peter van der Merwe in samewerking met
Fritz Joubert. Cape Town, Nasionale
Boekhandel, [1967]. [x],100p. illus.
diagrs.
*in Afrikaans; trs. "Winning-cricket"*

599 **Miller, Keith,** *and* **Pollard, Jack**
■ Keith Miller on cricket, in association
with Jack Pollard: drawings by Peter
Harrigan. Pelham, 1965. 128p. illus.
ports. diagrs.

599 Murray's guide to cricket: a how-to-play
-1 book of the game. Covers history, gear
needed, positional play, do-it-yourself
learning the game—for beginners and
players. Ultimo, (N.S.W.), Murray Book
Distributors, 1978. 119p. illus. ports.
diagrs. (How-to-play Books)

600 **Nazir Hussain,** *translator*
[Cricket]. Lahore, Naobahar Book Depot,
1962. 208p.
*in Urdu*

601 **O'Connor, Jack**
■ The young cricketer's manual. Thorsons,
1948. 124p. illus. diagr. (Let's Talk It
Over)

602 **Parker, Michael**
■ Your book of cricket. Faber, 1957. 71p.
illus. diagrs.
*for boys*

603 **Philpott, Peter**
■ How to play cricket, with special advice
for cricket coaches. North Sydney, Jack
Pollard Pty Ltd., 1973. 159p. illus. (some
col.), diagrs. (Sportsmaster Series)

603 Cricket fundamentals. Rev. ed.
-1 Wellington (N.Z.), A.H. & A.W. Reed,
1978. 111p.

604 **Pollard, Jack,** *editor*
■ Cricket: the Australian way. Melbourne,
Lansdowne P.: London, Kaye, 1961.
127p. illus. ports.
——*another ed.* Feltham, Newnes, 1968.
[xii],197p. illus. ports. diagrs.

605 **Rawal, D.S.**
■ Cricket and its technique. Porbandar
(India), the Author, 1961. 30p.

605 **Reddick, Tom**
-1 Play cricket the right way. Cape Town,
Seven Seas Publications, [1976?]. 70p.
illus. ports.
——*Afrikaans ed. with title:* Speel krieket
op die regte manier

606 **Richards, Barry**
■ Barry Richards on cricket: attack to win.
Pelham, 1973. 127p. illus. diagrs.

606 Cricket. Pelham Books, 1975. 61p. illus.
-1 diagrs. (Pelham Pictorial Sports Instruc-
■ tion Series)
*for schoolboys*

607 **Richardson, Peter**
■ Tackle cricket this way. S. Paul, 1958.
128p. illus. diagrs.

608 **Ross, Gordon,** *editor*
■ The Gillette book of cricket and football.
Muller, by arrangement with the Gillette
Safety Razor Co., 1963. 207p. illus. stats.
*cricket pp. 17–108*
——*pbk. ed.* 1963. 196p.

608 **Rothmans Ltd**
-1 The Rothmans guide to cricket, produced

■ in association with the New Zealand Cricket Council and the Auckland Cricket Association. Auckland, the Assoc., 1963. 24p. illus.

609 **St. John, John,** *editor*
■ The young cricketer; compiled with the assistance of the Cricket Enquiry and approved by the M.C.C. Naldrett P., 1950. 192p. illus. (some col.), diagrs. bibliog.
——*re-issued with title:* The M.C.C. book for the young cricketer, 1951 and 1953
*each re-issue contains articles by different contributors*

610 **Sandham, Andrew**
■ Cricket: with photographs by Photo-Records. Foyle, 1950. 90p. illus. diagrs. (Foyle's Handbook Series)
——*S. African ed. with title:* Krieket; vertaal deur D. Niehaus. Johannesburg, Super Krag, 1950. 74p. illus. diagrs. (Foyle Handboeke)
——2nd ed. 1952

611 **Sharpe, Philip**
■ Cricket for schoolboys, Pelham, 1965. 136p. illus. ports. diagrs. (Schools Library)

612 **Silk, Dennis [Raoul Whitehall]**
■ Cricket. Weidenfeld & Nicolson, 1964. 76p. illus. port. diagr. (Sports for Schools Series)

613 **Simpson, Reginald Thomas**
■ Cricket. N. Kaye, 1952. 122p. illus. diagrs.

614 **Smith, Mike,** *i.e.* **Michael John Knight**
■ **Smith**
Better cricket for boys. Kaye, 1965. [v],90p. illus. diagrs.
——rptd. with corrections. Kaye & Ward, 1972.
——rev. ed. Kaye & Ward in assoc. with Methuen of Australia and Hicks, Smith and Sons, New Zealand, 1977. 80p. illus. diagrs.

614 **Snow, John**
–1 Cricket: how to become a champion;
■ edited by Martin Tyler. Luscombe (in assoc. with Mitchell Beazley), 1975. 118p. illus. diagrs. (The 'Challenge' Series)
——*another ed.* 1975. pbk.

615 **Sobers, Gary,** *i.e.* **Sir Garfield St.Aubrun**
■ **Sobers**
Cricket, advance! Pelham, 1965. 109p. illus. ports.

616 **Sparks, Victor G.**
■ The cricketers' compendium; or, Cricket

from the country angle: being a complete history of cricket and other items on the good old game—how to play successfully, etc. Natal, Besters, the Author, [1948]. 124p. illus. diagrs. scores, stats.

617 **Strutt, Rayleigh Gordon**
■ Schoolboy cricket: the boys' and masters' guide. Hutchinson, [1950]. 128p. illus. diagrs. (Library of Sports and Pastimes)
——*2nd ed.* 1952
——*3rd ed.* S. Paul, 1958. 128p. illus. port. diagrs.

617 **Sutcliffe, Peter**
–1 Teach your child cricket. Lepus Books,
■ 1977. 112p. illus. diagrs.
*issued in cased and limp bindings*

618 **Taiwan University Cricket Group**
■ [Instructional booklet on cricket produced to aid cricket in Formosa]. The Group, [1961]. 23p. illus. diagrs.
*Chinese text*

619 **Taylor, Herbert Wilfred ("Herby")**
■ Hints on cricket. Cape Town, Western Province C.U., [1968]. folded bs. illus.

620 **Townsend, L.F.**
How to improve your cricket. Auckland, Auckland C.A., *n.d.* 12p. illus. ports.

621 **[Tribe, George]**
■ Playing the game: the George Tribe testimonial book. Kettering, *printed by* Dalkeith P., 1956. 16p. 1 illus. diagrs.
*with articles by Dennis Brookes and F.R. Brown*

622 **Trueman, Freddie,** *i.e.* **Frederick Seward**
■ **Trueman**
Cricket. Pelham, 1963. 120p. illus. ports. (Practical Books)

623 **Vajiphdar, Homi J.**
How to play good cricket, or cricket step by step. Bombay, Norman Bros., 1963. vi,165p.

624 **Walker, Peter Michael**
■ Winning cricket. Collins, 1965. 128p. illus. diagrs. (Nutshell books)

624 The all-rounder. Pelham Books, 1979.
–1 120p. illus. diagrs. (Sporting Skills Series)
■ *includes one ch. on great all-rounders*

625 **Wheatley, Garth Angus,** *and* **Parry,**
■ **Raymond Howard**
Cricket . . . do it this way; with photographs by John Barlee. Murray, 1948. 80p. illus.
——2nd ed. 1959. 79p. illus.

625 **Wright, Douglas Vivian Parson**
-1 **("Doug")**
■ Cricket skills and techniques: a comprehensive guide to coaching and playing. Barker, 1971. 121p. illus. diagrs.
——5th ed. Delhi, Vikas, 1975. (Bell Books). pbk.

626 **Young, Robert S.**
■ Cricket on the green for club and village cricketers and for boys. Prologue and epilogue by C.B. Fry; illustrations by Webster Murray. Hollis & Carter, 1947. xi,140p. illus.
——*revised ed.* 1949. xi,133p.

627 **Zulfiqar Ahmed**
[Cricket—history, how to play and records]. Lahore, Nawa-i-Waqt Book Depot, 1955. 120p. illus.
*in Urdu*

## SPORTSMANSHIP

627 **Atyeo, Don**
-1 Blood & guts: violence in sports. N.Y. &
■ London, Paddington, P.,1979. 384p. illus. bibliog.
*cricket pp. 293–5*

628 **Burlton, Bobbie,** *i.e.* **Arthur Temple**
■ **Burlton**
Cricketing courtesy. Bromsgrove, Messenger & Co., 1954. 81p. diagrs.
——*2nd ed.* Privately publd., 1955. [v],81p.
——*3rd ed.* [Catterick Camp, the Author], 1956. [v],81p. diagrs.

629 **Cook,** *Sir* **Theodore**
■ Character and sportsmanship. Williams & Norgate, 1927. xxvii,350p. illus. ports.
*reference to George Osbaldeston, pp. 265–66, and to Eton & Harrow match, pp. 318–21*

630 **French,** *Hon.* **Edward Gerald**
■ It's not cricket: an analysis of the game's unwritten laws, its moral code, customs and etiquette. Glasgow, MacLellan, 1960. 77p. front. (port.)

631 **[Gale, Frederick]**
Twenty golden rules for young cricketers, by A. Wykehamist. *Privately printed*, 1869. 7p.

631 **Goulden, Mark**
-1 Mark my words! W.H. Allen, 1978.
■ vii,256p. illus. ports. facsims.
*cricket pp. 162, 250 concerning shining the ball*

632 **McDonell, H.C.**
What is cricket? The Author, [1942]. 4p.
*discusses fair and unfair tactics*

632 **Scholtz, Gest Johannes Lindeque**
-1 Kompetisie en aggressie in spel en sport. Potchefstroom, Pro Rege-pers, 1977. vii,338p. bibliog.
*in Afrikans: trs. "Competition and aggression in games and sport"*

## FITNESS

633 **Bjerregaard, Aksel**
■ Lidt om konditionstraening for cricketspillere. Aalborg, Dansk Cricket-Forbund, 1955. 17p. illus.
*in Danish; trs. "A little on fitness-training for cricketers"*

634 **Fallon, Michael**
Weight-training for sport and fitness. N. Kaye, 1957. 125p. illus. diagrs.

635 **Fry, Charles Burgess**
■ Diet and exercise for training. [The Author], 1902. 59p.

636 **Miles, Eustace Hamilton,** *editor*
Alphabet of athletics. Routledge, 1904. 108p. diagrs. (The Fitness Series)
*the mechanics of the body in relation to various games including cricket*

637 Fitness for play and work. T. Murby, 1912. xiv,110p.

638 **Stanton, Victor E.**
■ 'I must be fit': for the student. Sydney, N.S.W. Band of Hope Union & Young People's Temperance Educational Council, [192–]. 32p. illus. ports.
*advocates health through fitness and temperance, with a foreword by W.M. Woodfull and quotes by Hedley Verity, Don Bradman and Ernest Tyldesley*

## INJURIES; WELFARE

639 **Campbell, R.H.**
Some statistics concerning cricket casualties. Melbourne, A.B.C., 1933. 28p.

640 **Colson, John H.C.,** *and* **Armour, William**
■ **J.**
Sports injuries and their treatment. S. Paul, 1961. 224p. illus. diagrs.
*cricket injuries, pp. 59, 201*

641 **Cricketers' Fund Friendly Society**
■ Rules. The Society, 1934. 16p.

642 **Featherstone, Donald F.**
Sports injuries. Bristol, Wright, 1957. 195p. illus.

643
■
**The Hornsby Professional Cricketers'
Fund Charity**
Scheme. 1926. [i],8p.

643
–1
■
**Tucker, William Eldon,** *and* **Castle,
Molly**
Sportsmen and their injuries: fitness,
first-aid, treatment and rehabilitation.
Pelham Books, 1978. 236p. illus. diagrs.
bibliog.
*cricket injuries, pp. 57–60, 168; posture p.
23*

644
**Woodard, Christopher**
Sports injuries: prevention and active
treatment. Max Parrish, 1954. 128p. illus.

# COACHING

(*See also:* Technique)

645
**Altham, Harry Surtees,** *compiler*
Cricket coaching. Southampton,
Hampshire Youth Cricket Council,
[1954]. 11p.
——reissued 1959

645
–1
□
**Association of Cricket Coaches**
Cricket coach: the journal of the Association of Cricket Coaches. *irregular.* illus.
port. diagrs.
*No. 1 Oct. 1975/1975–77/to date?*

646
■
**Broughton, J.J.**
The cricket coach in brief. Wigan, the
Author, [c.1930]. [6]p. folded

647
■
**Canterbury Cricket Association**
National cricket: [coaching manual].
Christchurch (N.Z.), the Assoc., [c.1947].
60p. illus. ports.

648
■
**Central Council of Physical Education**
Lectures and demonstrations arranged
. . . in co-operation with the Middlesex
Junior Cricket Committee: [programme]
[The Council, 1961]. [9]p.

648
–1
□
**Central London Cricket School & Sports
Club Ltd.**
Fixture bureau and sports gossip; edited
by Peter F. Judge. The School. *weekly.*
illus. ports.
*1935/vol. 1, no.1. July 6th; vol. 1, no. 18.
Apr. 4th, 1936/–?*

648
–2
■
**Chappell, Ian Michael,** *and others*
Ian Chappell's cricket coaching book;
assisted by Greg Chappell, Dennis
Lillee & Rod Marsh. B.P. Sports
Australia, [1975?] 24p. illus. diagrs.

649
■
**Connelly, George F.,** *compiler*
Thinking cricket? Canberra, [the Author].
1972. 58p. diagrs.

650
□
**Crabtree, Harold P.**
Group coaching. Lancashire Youth
Cricket Council, [c.1952]. 12p. diagr.
——*another issue.* Birmingham, The
Warwickshire Youth Cricket Council, *n.d.*
12p. diagr.
——*another issue.* Chelmsford, Essex
Youth Cricket Council, *n.d.* 12p. diagr.
——*another issue.* Taunton, Somerset
Youth Cricket Council, [1958]. 15p. diagr.
——*another issue.* Surrey Junior Cricket
Cttee., 1952. [11]p. diagr.
——*another issue.* Worcester, Worcestershire Youth Cricket Council, *n.d.* [11]p.
diagr.
——*another issue with title:* Group
coaching in cricket. Salisbury, Rhodesia
Cricket Union. *n.d.* 16p. diagr.

651
■
**Cricket.** Bombay, Sadbhakti Publications,
1948. [iii],50p. illus. port. diagrs.
*contains speeches by H.H. The Maharaja of
Porbander and Maharaj Shri Duleepsinhji at
the opening of the Duleep School of Cricket,
and the Vijay Pavilion at Porbander on 7th
June, 1947, together with description of the
school and pavilion*

652
**Datta, P.D.**
Cricket coaching made easy. Calcutta,
Badu Mitra, 1965. xx,73p.

653
■
**Faulkner, George Aubrey**
Cricket, can it be taught? Chapman &
Hall, 1926. xiii,99p. illus.

654
■
**The Faulkner School of Cricket Ltd.**
Provisional prospectus last February
1926. The School, [1926]. [10]p. stats.
*with statistics of G.A. Faulkner's career*

655
**Goodwin, Christopher John**
Coming in to bat: a handbook for those
who coach and play cricket. Melbourne,
Hill of Content Publishing Co.; London,
Pelham, 1967. viii,61p. illus. diagrs.
*for school cricket coaches*

655
–1
**Gordon, Norman,** *and* **Gordon, H.**
Basic cricket for South African schools;
illustrations by H.E. Winder, etc. [Johan-
nesburg], Central News Agency, [1955].
[16]p. illus.

656
■
**Gover, Alfred Richard**
How I teach better cricket; batting and
bowling actions demonstrated by Don
Bennett. Muller, 1954. 96p. illus. ("Play
Better" Books Series)

656 **Hampshire Youth Cricket Council**
–1 Cricket coaching: group practice and
conduct of a net. The Council, 1959
——enl. ed. 1959. 12p.

657 **Hankinson, John Trevor**
■ Cricket for schools. Allen & Unwin, 1946.
xii,124p. illus. diagrs.

657 **Horton, Martin,** *and* **Sutcliffe, Bert**
–1 Cricket: a guide book for teachers,
■ coaches and players. N.Z. Dept. of
Education. Physical Education Branch,
1975. 40p. illus. diagrs. (Sports Instruction Series)

658 **Hough, Gerald de Lisle**
■ Coaching and pitches: prepared by the
Kent County Cricket Club. [Canterbury,
Kent C.C.C.], 1950. 20p. illus. diagrs.

659 **Kent County Cricket Club**
■ Notes on cricket, [by Gerald de Lisle
Hough]. Canterbury, [the Club, 1938].
8p.

660 **Lacey,** *Sir* **Francis Eden**
□ Instructions to cricket coaches at Lord's
cricket ground. Marylebone C.C., 1909.
12p.
*includes "Advice to young players" by C.B.*
*Fry and "Hints on fielding" by E.G.*
*Wynyard*
——*6th ed. 1923. 18p.*

661 **The Lancashire Youth Cricket Council.**
*Sub-Committee*
Cricket coaching in Lancashire: a Sub-
Committee consideration for submission
to The . . . Council, 5th December, 1970.
The Sub-Cttee., [1970]. [i],8p. *typescript.*
diagrs.

661 **Le Mesurier, Peter Neil,** *compiler*
–1 Cricket sense: a series of notes for all
young students of the game and for those
who coach them. Cape Town, Ronde-
bosch, Diocesan College Preparatory
School, [1962?]. [i],7p.

662 **Lovatt, Kenneth John,** *and others*
Start the right way: cricket and rugby
football for the junior boy and his coach,
by K.J. Lovatt, W.M. Russell and T.
McMurray. [Belfast, W.M. Russell], 1951.
80p. illus. diagrs.
*cricket pp. 9–40*

663 **Madras Cricket Association**
■ Coaching and training course under Mr.
C. Subramaniam Coaching Scheme at . . .
Chepauk: rules, instructions and pass.
Madras, the Assoc., [195–]. 8p.

664 **Marylebone Cricket Club**
■ The M.C.C. dumb cricket tutor (as used
at the Lord's cricket classes). M.C.C.,
[1921]. 4p. diagr.

665 Suggestions for cricket coaches and
pupils. [M.C.C., c.1932]. bs.

666 The M.C.C. cricket coaching book. Nald-
■ rett P. in assoc. with The World's Work
for the M.C.C., 1952. 155p. illus. diagrs.
——rev. ed. 1955. 155p. illus. diagrs.
——3rd ed. Heinemann for the M.C.C.,
1962. viii,152p. illus. ports. diagrs.
——4th ed. 1976. x,175p. illus. diagrs.

666 ——. *Indoor School*
–1 Newsletter. M.C.C. *typescript*
□ *no. 1. April 1978 to date*
*manager A.W.P. Fleming; chief coach Don*
*Wilson*

667 **Massie, R.J.A.**
■ Bowling: a few hints to assist coaches in
the work of instructing schoolboys.
[Sydney], New South Wales C.A., [1926].
34p. illus.

668 **Middlesex County Cricket School**
■ [Prospectus]. Alexandra Palace, N.22,
[The School, 1952]. [4]p.
——*another issue.* Finchley, N.3 [The
School, 1956]. [4]p. map

669 **National Cricket Association**
■ Development of the coaching scheme.
The Assoc., 1971. [9]p.

670 'Test' cricket. The Association, [197–] 12p.
■ diagrs.
*the 'Proficiency Awards Scheme' of the*
*Association to encourage boys & girls to learn*
*and enjoy the skills of cricket*

670 'Test' cricket in clubs and schools . . .
–1 featuring the Proficiency Award Scheme.
■ The Assoc., [1977]. 28p. illus. diagrs.
*sponsored by the Wrigley Cricket*
*Foundation*

671 **New South Wales Cricket Association**
□ Coaching magazine for the benefit of
sportsmasters and coaches; edited by
G.L. Garnsey. Sydney, the Association.
*monthly.* illus. diagrs.
*Aug. 1930/Aug. 1930 . . . Dec. 1931/–?*

672 Calling all cricketers: a cricket coaching
■ manual. Sydney, the Assoc., 1955.
viii,191p. illus. diagrs.
——new and revised ed. 1964. 276p. illus.
diagrs.

673 **New Zealand. Department of Education**
■ Cricket: a guide book for teachers,

coaches and players; prepared by the Physical Education Branch of the Department of Education. Wellington (N.Z.), R.E. Owen, Government Printer, 1957. 40p. illus. diagrs. (Special Series of Sports Instruction Publications—No.6)
——rev. ed. 1966
——rev. ed. 1970
——rev. ed. 1975. 40p.

674 **Peerbhai, Adam**
■ Cricket coach. Durban, [the Author, c.1955]. 60p. illus. ports.

675 **Phebey, Arthur,** *and others*
■ The Arthur Phebey benefit and coaching book. [Canterbury], *printed by* "Kentish Gazette", [1960]. 32p. illus. ports.

676 **Philpott, Peter**
■ How to play cricket, with special advice for cricket coaches. North Sydney, Jack Pollard Pty Ltd., 1973. 159p. illus. (some col.). diagrs. (Sportsmaster Series)

677 **Poidevin, L.O.S.**
Cricket tuition. 1922.

677 **Poore, Robert Montagu**
–1 Notes on cricket coaching. [Wimborne, the Author], 1928. 24p. *typescript*

678 **Queensland. Department of Public**
■ **Instruction.** *Physical Education Branch, and* **Queensland Cricket Association,** *compilers*
Cricket syllabus. Brisbane, Dept. of Public Instruction, [1949]. 48p. illus. ports. diagrs.

679 **Richardson, Arthur J.**
Cricket coaching manual. [Adelaide], South Australian C.A., 1947. 21p. illus.

679 **Ross, Gordon,** *editor*
–1 Cricket under cover: to commemorate the
■ opening of the M.C.C. Indoor School. M.C.C., [1977]. 40p. incl. adverts. illus. ports. stats.

679 **Silk, Dennis [Raoul Whitehall]**
–2 Attacking cricket: a coaching manual.
■ Pelham Books, 1965. 117p. illus.

679 **Sutcliffe, Peter**
–3 Teaching cricket simply. Lepus Books,
■ 1975. [ix],144p. illus. diagrs.
*aimed at primary school teachers*

679 **Suttle, Charles Richard William**
–4 Stimulating the CADA in cricket. Chesterfield, the Author, [1977]. 68p. illus. ports.

*concerned chiefly with junior cricket in Derbyshire. CADA = concentration, dedication and ability*

679 **Taber, H. Brian**
–5 National Cricket coaching plan. Sydney, Rothmans National Sports Foundation, 1973. 221p. illus. diagrs. *typescript*

680 **[Tindall, Mark,** *and* **Webster, John]**
■ Cricket coaching and practice. Harrow-on-the-Hill, [*priv. publd.* Harrow School], 1947. xi,50p. illus. port. diagrs.

681 **Townsend, David**
■ The Oxford pocket book of cricket coaching. Oxford Univ. P., 1953. 90p. illus.

681 **Tyson, Frank Holmes**
–1 Complete cricket coaching illustrated.
■ Melbourne, Nelson (Australia), 1976; London, Pelham Books, 1977. viii,152p. illus. diagrs.
——*another ed.* 1977. pbk.

681 **UTAH – QCA** coaching manual for the
–2 UTAH coaching plan. Brisbane, [UTAH?], 1978. 13p. illus. diagrs.

681 **Victorian Cricket Association**
–3 Packaged coaching. Jolimont, the Assoc.,
■ 1977. [4]p. fold
*system of coaching organised by V.C.A. to all zones, associations, clubs, schools and other organisations within Victoria*

681 Coaching plan. [Melbourne, the Assoc.],
–4 *n.d.* [4]p.
■

682 **Women's Cricket Association**
■ Mini-cricket for girls & boys. The Association, 1970. 20p. diagrs.
*coaching for the middle school*

683 ————. *Umpires Sub-Committee*
■ Coaching cricket: suggestions for players, umpires and scorers; compiled by the Umpires Sub-Committee on behalf of the Women's Cricket Association. W.C.A., 1934. 16p.

684 **Wormald, Alec**
How to play cricket. Leeds, Yorkshire Evening Post, *n.d.* 16p.
cover-title: *Manual for schools' cricket*

684 **Wright, Douglas Vivian Parson**
–1 **("Doug")**
■ Cricket skills and techniques: a comprehensive guide to coaching and playing. Barker, 1971. 121p. illus. diagrs.
——5th ed. Delhi, Vikas, 1975. (Bell Books). pbk.

## BATTING

685 **Amphlett, Edgar Montague**
■ How to bat: an analysis of the principal strokes for the use of young cricketers. Treherne, 1902. 78p. illus. diagrs.

686 **Batting** at a glance. [1923]. 8p. illus.
■ *no author, publisher or printer named*

687 **Beldam, George William,** *and* **Fry,**
■ **Charles Burgess**
Great batsmen: their methods at a glance; illustrated by 600 action-photographs. Macmillan, 1905. xiv,716p. illus. (1 col.)
——*re-issue.* 1907

688 **Brodribb, [Arthur] Gerald [Norcott]**
■ Felix on the bat: being a memoir of Nicholas Felix, together with the full text of the 2nd ed. of 'Felix on the bat'. Eyre & Spottiswoode, 1962. xiv,145; [4], viii,58p. illus. (1 col.), ports. diagrs.
*see no. 397*

689 **Craig, Albert**
■ A few words to willow wielders. All England Athletic Publishing Co., [c.1900]. 3p.

690 **Cricket** batting. Training and Education
■ Associates Ltd., 1973. [iv],32p. illus. pbk. (National Westminster Bank Sport Coaching Series)

691 **[Davies, D.H.]**
■ How to score a century; illustrations by Eustace Nash. Thorson, 1949. 191p. illus. diagrs.

692 **Davis, D.S.**
■ Great batsmen photo-analysed: W.J. Edrich. Photo Instruction Books, [1949]. [31]p. illus. ports.

693 **Flicker Productions Ltd**
□ Cricket: Don Bradman. Flicker Productions, [1930]. (Flickers Sports Series)
*No. 1. On drive and off drive*
*2. Square cut and late cut*
*3. Leg glance and pull*
*cine-photographs in the form of a 'flicker-book'*

694 Cricket: Frank Woolley: square cut and
■ walking shot. Flicker Productions, [c.1936] illus.
——: ——: pull to leg and forcing shot, off the back foot, to the off. [c.1936]. illus.
*both are overprinted with "Frank Woolley's Cricket School"*

695 **Fort, James Alfred**
Some remarks about batting. Winchester, Wells, 1902. 12p.

696 **Fry, Charles Burgess**
■ Cricket (batmanship); with thirty-two action photographs. Nash, 1912. 253p. illus. (National Library of Sports and Pastimes)
——popular ed. 1914
——*another ed.* 1920
——*another ed.* 1932

696 **The Guardian**
–1 The bedside 'Guardian' 28: a selection
■ from The 'Guardian' 1978–79; edited by W.L. Webb. Collins, 1979. 251p. illus.
*includes pp. 207–10 "Caught in the middle", by Ian Peebles [on batsmen being run-out]*

697 **Hobbs,** *Sir* **John Berry**
■ How to make a century: containing twelve full-page illustrations from action photographs. Black, 1913. 87p. illus.

698 **Ingelse, R.G.**
■ Het batten. [The Hague]. Propaganda-Commissie van den Nederlandschen Cricket Bond, 1940. 68p. illus. diagrs. (De Groene Krekelserie)
——2nd ed. 1952. 62p.
*in Dutch: trs. "Batting"*

699 **Insole, Douglas John**
■ Batting: the young cricketer talks to D.J. Insole; illustrated by Calton Younger. Phoenix House, 1961. 64p. illus. (Young Sportsman Series)

700 **Knight, Donald John**
■ First steps to batting; with 72 illustrations from photographs taken . . . [by] E.H.D. Sewell. Mills & Boon, 1922. 158p. illus. diagrs.

701 **Lee, E.C.**
Fundamental points: batting and fielding. Petersfield, the Author

702 **Liddell, Laurence Ernest**
■ Batsmanship today & tomorrow: aspects of contemporary cricket, experiments in stroke production, and suggestions for progressive match play practice. Newcastle-upon-Tyne, King's College Dept. of Education, 1958. 42p. illus. diagrs.

703 **Maclaren, Archibald Campbell**
■ The perfect batsman: J.B. Hobbs in action; with 98 cinema-photographs of J.B. Hobbs at the wicket. Cassell, 1926. [viii],138p. illus.

704 **Payne, C.A.L.**
■ What matters in batsmanship. Vancouver, Canada, North Shore P., [1939]. [27]p. illus.

**704** **Procter, Michael John**
**-1** Batting hints. [Salisbury, Caltex Oil Rhodesia, 1972]. [6]p. folded. illus. diagrs.

**705** **[Pycroft, James]**
■ The principles of scientific batting, or Plain rules, founded on the practice of the first professors and amateurs, for the noble game of cricket, by a Gentleman; revised by J.H. Dark. Oxford, H. Slatter, 1835. 44p.
*cover-title: The cricketer's new guide to scientific batting*
——new ed., containing the laws of cricket revised . . . 3rd June, 1844. [1844?] 48p.
——3rd ed., containing the laws of cricket revised . . . 2nd June, 1845. [1845?] 48p.

**706** **Realist Film Unit**
■ Batting strokes demonstrated by Len Hutton; coaching by H.P. Crabtree: the book of the Visual Unit "Cricket batting strokes" made in co-operation with the N.C.V.A.E. by Realist Film Unit, Methuen, 1950. 32p. illus.

**707** **Quaife, William George**
■ Strokes and style in cricket. Benn, 1929. 32p. illus. port.

**708** **[Rudd, Cecil Thomas, and Witham,**
■ **Edgar Murray]**
Batting for boys: strokes and how to play them concisely explained with action photographs; by Two Wellingborough Masters. [The Authors], 1937. 35p. illus.

**708** **Shell Company of South Africa Ltd.**
**-1** Batting strokes with Jackie McGlew. [Capetown], the Co., [1960?]. 6p. (Shell Educational Filmstrip no.16)
*text to accompany filmstrip*

**708** **Sporting Flicks** Productions presents
**-2** Lindsay Hassett (Vice-Captain, Australian XI) demonstrating 1. The pull shot. 2. The off-drive. Sporting Flicks Productions, [194-]. illus.
*flicker illus. of Hassett's strokes*

**709** **Sugden, Joseph**
■ Hints on batting; with an introduction (on fielding) by J.E. Raphael. Croydon, Smith, Crotch, [1909]. 18p. port.

**710** **Sutcliffe, Herbert**
■ Batting. Blackie, 1937. 88p. illus. diagrs. (Blackie's Sports Series)
*flicker illus. of Sutcliffe's batting strokes*

**711** How to become a first class batsman.
■ Leeds, H. Sutcliffe Ltd., 1949. 64p. illus. port. diagrs. stats.

**712** **[Wanostrocht, Nicholas]**
■ How to play Clarke, being an attempt to unravel the mysteries of the ball, and to show what defence and hitting are to be employed against this celebrated bowler; by the author of "Felix on the bat". Baily Bros., 1852. 16p. illus.
——reprint; edited with an introduction by F.S. Ashley-Cooper. Nottingham, Richards, 1922. iv,[i],10p. illus.

## Batsmen

**713** **Arlott, [Leslie Thomas] John,** *general*
■ *editor*
Cricket: the great ones: studies of the eight finest batsmen of cricket history. Pelham, 1967. 188p. ports. stats.
——rptd. Sportsman's Book Club, 1968.
*W.G. Grace, Victor Trumper, Jack Hobbs, Walter Hammond, Don Bradman, George Headley, Len Hutton, Denis Compton*

**714** **Cricket:** the great all-rounders: studies of
■ ten of the finest all-rounders of cricket history. Pelham, 1969. 184p. ports. stats.
——rptd. Sportsman's Book Club, 1971
*George Hirst, Wilfred Rhodes, Warwick Armstrong, Frank Woolley, Sir Learie Constantine, Keith Miller, Trevor Bailey, Trevor Goddard, Richie Benaud, Garfield Sobers*

**715** **Barker, Ralph**
■ Ten great innings. Chatto & Windus, 1964. x,230p. illus. ports. scores.
——rptd. Sportsman's Book Club, 1965
*Jack Hobbs, Learie Constantine, Stan McCabe, Don Bradman, Harold Gimblett, Len Hutton, Bill Edrich, Denis Compton, Russell Endean, Cyril Washbrook*

**716** **Brodribb, [Arthur] Gerald [Norcott]**
■ Some memorable innings. Hunstanton, Cricket Book Society, 1946. 32p. scores. (Publications. Ser. 1, no. 3)
——re-issued in "Cricket omnibus 1946", edited by Roy Webber. *See* no. 982

**717** Hit for six: a survey of the great blows of
■ cricket and of those who struck them. Heinemann, 1960. 224p. ports. stats.
——another ed. Sportsman's Book Club, 1961
*a history of big hitting in first-class cricket*

**717** **Morawalla, Mahiyar Dara**
**-1** Cricket cavalcade. Bombay, Jaico, 1976.
■ xiii,167p. pbk.
*studies of great batsmen*

**718** **Moyes, Alban George**
■ Australian batsmen from Charles Bannerman to Neil Harvey. London,

Batting: "Forward". One of a series of lithographs depicting cricket strokes drawn by G. F. Watts from "Felix on the bat" (no. 397). Felix (Nicholas Wanostrocht) himself was the model *photo: M.C.C.*

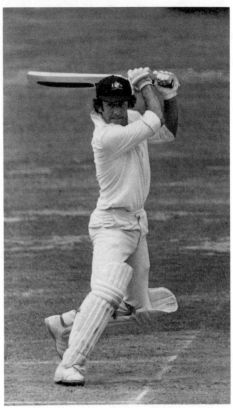

Batting: Ian Chappell, Lord's 1975 *photo: Patrick Eagar*

Bowling: "The Bowler". One of a series of lithographs drawn by John Corbet Anderson, published by Fred Lillywhite, 1860 *photo: BBC Hulton Picture Library*

Bowling: Dennis Lillee, England v. Australia, Trent Bridge, 1972 *photo: Patrick Eagar*

Fielding: O'Keefe, caught Brearley, bowled Underwood, during the Centenary Test, Melbourne, 1977 *photo: Patrick Eagar*

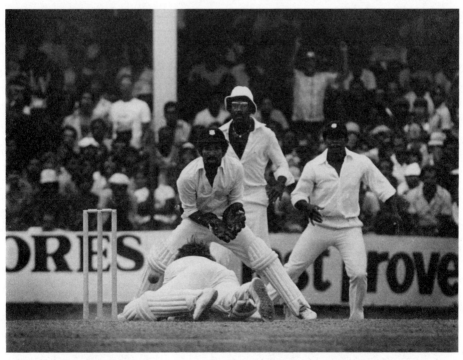

Wicket-keeping: Deryck Murray in position while Gary Cosier dives for the crease during West Indies v. Australia, Port of Spain, Trinidad, 1978 *photo: Patrick Eagar*

Harrap; Sydney, Angus and Robertson, 1954. 203p. ports. stats.

718 **Parker, John**
-1 Cricket styles and stylists. London &
■ Sydney, Angus & Robertson, 1979. 160p. illus. ports.

718 **Varma, Arvind**
-2 Eminent cricket left handers. Bombay,
■ Jaico, 1972. x,128p. ports. stats.

719 **Wakley, Bertram Joseph**
■ Classic centuries in the Test matches between England and Australia. Kaye, 1964. xxi,345p. stats.
——*another ed.* Sportsman's Book Club, 1965
*largely statistical*

# BOWLING

720 **Bedser, Alec Victor**
■ Bowling; with action pictures . . . by Hubert Davey. Hodder & Stoughton, 1952. 96p. illus. port. diagrs. stats.

721 **Beldam, George William**, *and* **Fry,**
■ **Charles Burgess**
Great bowlers and fielders: their methods at a glance; illustrated by 464 action-photographs. Macmillan, 1906. xv,547p. illus. (1 col.)
——*re-issue.* 1907
*contains chapter on "Bowling" by F.R. Spofforth and one on "Fielding" by G.L. Jessop*

722 Cricket–bowling. Training and Education
■ Associates Ltd., 1973. [iv],46p. illus. pbk. (National Westminster Bank Sport Coaching Series)
——*rptd.* 1974

723 **Daurh,** jhamp-o-nikshep. 2nd ed. Dacca, Sports Publications, 1964
*Part I. iii,21,xi,p. illus.*
*in Bengali; trs. "Running and Bowling"*

724 [**Davies, D.H.**]
■ How to bowl them out: a handbook for young cricketers, by Christopher Sly. Thorsons, 1948. 192p. illus. diagrs.

725 **Fairservice, William John**
■ Hints on bowling. Tonbridge, Tonbridge Free P., [1922]. 29p. diagrs.

726 **Flicker Productions Ltd**
Cricket: C.V. Grimmett. Flicker Productions, [1930]. (Flickers Sports Series). illus.

*No. 4. Leg break delivery and leg break finger spin*
*5. Googley delivery and off break finger spin*
*6. Overspin delivery and finger spin*
*cine-photographs in the form of a 'flicker-book'*

727 **Goonesena, Gamini**
■ Spin bowling: the young cricketer talks to G. Goonesena; illustrated by Calton Younger. Phoenix House, 1959. 62p. illus. diagrs. (Young Sportsman Series)

728 **Grimmett, Clarence Victor**
■ Getting wickets. Hodder & Stoughton, 1930. 120p. illus. ports.

729 Tricking the batsman. Hodder &
■ Stoughton, 1934. 157p. illus. port.

729 **The Guardian**
-1 The bedside 'Guardian' 17: a selection
■ from The Guardian 1967–68; edited by W.L. Webb. Collins, 1968. 254p. illus.
*includes pp. 93–96, "An obsession with the new ball", by Neville Cardus*

729 The bedside 'Guardian' 24: a selection
-2 from The Guardian 1974–75; edited by
■ W.L. Webb. Collins, 1975. 263p. illus.
*includes pp. 212–5, "Latest rice-pudding man" by Neville Cardus [on bouncers]*

729 **Illingworth, Ray**
-3 Spin bowling [by] Ray Illingworth with
■ the assistance of Ralph Ellis. Pelham Books, 1979. 119p. illus. (Sporting Skills Series)

730 **The illustrated** Australian magazine. Melbourne, Thomas Ham
*Vol. III. No. 13. July 1851 contains an article on Chess, Cricket-balls and Theatres, written in the form of a dialogue and includes a discussion of the comparative merits of fast and slow bowling*

730 **Knox, Nevill A.**
-1 On fast bowling; reprinted by kind per-
■ mission of Editor of Daily Mail. [Cantrell & Cochrane, 1907]. [4]p.
*Cantrell & Cochrane were manufacturers of ginger ale which is recommended, though not by name, by Knox, but is praised in letters printed on the inside back cover from C.B Fry and T. Hayward*

730 **Lillee, Dennis Keith**
-2 The art of fast bowling [with Ian Bray-
■ shaw]. London, Lutterworth P., Richard Smart Publishing; Sydney & Auckland, Collins, 1978. 160p. illus. ports. diagrs. stats.

730 Bowled out. [Sydney], T. & G. Insurance,
–3 *n.d.* [20]p. incl. covers. illus. ports.
■ diagrs.

731 **Lyttleton, Raymond Arthur**
■ "The swing of a cricket ball". In: *Discovery*, vol. 18, no. 5, May, 1957. pp. 186–91

732 **Marriott, Charles Stowell**
■ The complete leg-break bowler; introduction by Ian Peebles, postscript by Richie
Benaud. Eyre & Spottiswoode, 1968.
176p. frontis. diagrs.

733 **Marylebone Cricket Club**
■ Notes on bowling instruction for young
cricketers. M.C.C., 1939. [10]p. illus.
diagr.

734 **Massie, R.J.A.**
■ Bowling: a few hints to assist coaches in
the work of instructing schoolboys.
[Sydney], New South Wales C.A., [1926].
34p. illus.

735 **Melville, J.H.**
■ How to bowl. Gloriana P., [1938?]. 58p.
illus. diagr.
cover-title: *A few hints on how to bowl at
good batsmen*
——*revised ed.* Aylesbury, *printed by* F.
Samuels, [1939]. illus. port. diagr.

736 **Nichols, Morris Stanley**
■ Bowling. Blackie, 1937. [vii],88p. illus.
(Blackie's Sports Series)
*the illus. are a series of flicker film-strips*

737 **Peebles, Ian [Alexander Ross]**
■ How to bowl. Chapman & Hall, 1934.
vii,97p. illus. diagrs.

738 **Pocock, Pat**
■ Bowling. Batsford, 1969. 111p. illus.
ports. diagrs. (Batsford Sports Books)

738 **Procter, Michael John**
–1 Bowling hints. [Salisbury, Caltex Oil
Rhodesia, 1972]. 6p. folded. illus. diagrs.

739 **Realist Film Unit**
■ Bowling: made by Realist Film Unit with
Ray Smith and Peter Smith, supervised
and approved by the M.C.C. Cricket
Enquiry Committee. Methuen, 1952. 48p.
illus. diagrs.
*contains articles by G.O. Allen, H.S.
Altham, H.P. Crabtree and R.W.V. Robins*

740 **Rege, Madhukar Ramcandra**
Khubīdār, golandājī. Poona, Iramdar
Bandhu, 1970. 133p. illus.
*in Marathi; trs. "The artful bowler"*

741 **The Saturday** book: eleventh year; edited
by Leonard Russell. Hutchinson, 1951.
280p. illus. & ports. (some col.)
*contains "The bowling called bodyline" by
John Arlott with illus.*

742 **Shaw, Alfred**
Jottings on bowling. Shaw and Shrewsbury, 1883.

743 **Snow, John**
■ The art of bowling, by John Snow (as told
to Kenneth Wheeler). S. Paul, 1968. 120p.
illus. ports. stats.

744 **Sodderland, L.J.**
■ Het bowlen. [The Hague], Propaganda-
Commissie van de Nederlandse Cricket
Bond, [1941]. 92p. (De Groene
Krekelserie)
*in Dutch; trs. 'Bowling'*

745 **Turner, Charles Thomas Biass**
■ The quest for bowlers. Sydney, Cornstalk
Publishing Co., 1926. 54p. illus. port.
stats.
*publd. in the aftermath of the 1926 Austra-
lian tour of England*

746 **Vaile, Philip A.**
■ Swerve on the flight of the ball. J.
Tamblyn, 1905. 83p. illus. port. diagrs.

746 **Verity, Hedley**
–1 Bowling 'em out. Hutchinson, [1936].
■ 159p. illus. port.

747 **Warr, John James**
■ Pace bowling: the young cricketer talks to
J.J. Warr; illustrated by Calton Younger.
Phoenix House, 1959. 59p. illus. diagrs.
(Young Sportsman Series)

747 **Willis, Robert George Dylan ("Bob")**
–1 Pace bowling, by Bob Willis with assist-
■ ance of Patrick Murphy. Pelham Books,
1978. 116p. illus. (Sporting Skills Series)

## Bowlers

748 **Arlott, [Leslie Thomas] John,** *general
■ editor*
Cricket: the great bowlers: studies of ten
great bowlers of cricket history. Pelham,
1968. 190p. illus. stats.
*S.F. Barnes; Maurice Tate; Harold
Larwood; Grimmett & O'Reilly; Ray Lindwall; Alec Bedser; Jim Laker; Trueman &
Statham*
——*another ed.* Sportsman's Book Club,
1970

749 Cricket: the great all-rounders: studies of
■ ten of the finest all-rounders of cricket
history. Pelham, 1969. 184p. ports. stats.

*George Hirst, Wilfred Rhodes, Warwick Armstrong, Frank Woolley, Sir Learie Constantine, Keith Miller, Trevor Bailey, Trevor Goddard, Richie Benaud, Garfield Sobers*
——*another ed.* Sportsman's Book Club, 1971

750 **Barker, Ralph**
■ Ten great bowlers. Chatto & Windus, 1967. x,278p. illus. ports. diagr.
*F.R. Spofforth: George Lohmann; W.H. Lockwood; Tom Richardson; J. Barton King; S.F. Barnes; Maurice Tate; C.V. Grimmett; Hedley Verity; W.J. O'Reilly*

751 **Brodribb, [Arthur] Gerald [Norcott]**
■ Some memorable bowling. Hunstanton, Cricket Book Society, 1947. 32p. scores, stats. (Publications. Ser. 2, no. 1)
*re-issued in "Cricket omnibus 1947", edited by Roy Webber. See no. 982*

751 **Frith, David Edward John**
–1 The fast men: a 200-year cavalcade of
■ speed bowlers. Wokingham, Van Nostrand Reinhold, 1975. 168p. illus. ports. bibliog.
——*another ed.* Newton Abbot, Readers Union, 1976
——rev. and up-dated ed. Corgi Books, 1977. 221p. pbk.

752 **Moyes, Alban George**
■ Australian bowlers from Spofforth to Lindwall. London, Harrap; Sydney, Angus & Robertson, 1953. 192p. ports. stats.

# FIELDING

753 **Bashir, S.M.**
■ The forgotten factor. Kanpur, [the Author, 1972]. 8p. illus. on covers
*on fielding: an offprint of an article specially contributed for* The glory of Indian cricket, *edited by W.D. Begg*

753 **Beldam, George William,** *and* **Fry,**
–1 **Charles Burgess**
■ Great bowlers and fielders: their methods at a glance; illustrated by 464 action-photographs. Macmillan, 1906. xv,547p. illus. (1 col.)
——re-issue. 1907.
*contains chapter on "Bowling" by F.R. Spofforth and one on "Fielding" by G.L. Jessop*

754 **Cricket** field placement chart. W.S. Surridge. *annual*
*?/1954/–?*

755 **Fenton S.J.**
■ Cricket fielding diagrams for right and

left hand, fast, medium, slow and spin bowling. Halifax, E. Mortimer, [1947]. 16p. diagrs.

756 **Ingelse, R.G.**
■ Fielden. [Den Haag], Nederlandsche Cricket Bond, Propaganda-Commissie, [1952?]. 32p. illus. diagr. (De Groene Krekelserie)
*in Dutch: trs. "Fielding"*

757 **Lee, E.C.**
Fundamental points: batting and fielding. Petersfield, the Author

757 **Procter, Michael John**
–1 Fielding hints. [Salisbury, Caltex Oil Rhodesia, 1972]. 6p folded. illus. diagrs.

758 **Stewart, Michael James**
■ Fielding; the young cricketer talks to M.J. Stewart; illustrated by Calton Younger. Phoenix, 1961. 59p. illus. diagrs. (Young Sportsman Series)

758 **Van Booven, Henri C.A.**
–1 Het fielden. Hague, Propaganda
■ Commissie van de Nederlandsche Cricket Bond, 1941. 22p. (De Groene Krekelserie no. 1)
*Dutch text*

758 **Van Manen, H.**
–2 Veld-uitzetten. Hague, Propaganda
■ Commissie van de Nederlandsche Cricket Bond, 1941. 85p. diagrs. (De Groene Krekelserie)
*Dutch text; trs. "Field-placing"*

# WICKET-KEEPING

759 **Beus, Anthony Marius Justus de**
■ Het wicketkeepen. [Den Haag], Nederlandsche Cricket Bond, Propaganda-Commissie, [1937]. 35p. illus. (De Groene Krekelserie)
*in Dutch; trs. "Wicket-keeping"*

760 **Ingelse, D.L.**
■ Wicketkeepen. [Den Haag] Nederlandse Cricketbond, Propaganda-Commissie, [1952?]. 53p. illus.
*in Dutch; trs. "Wicket-keeping"*

760 **Knott, Alan**
–1 Alan Knott on wicket-keeping. S. Paul,
■ 1977. 64p. illus. diagrs.
——pbk. ed. 1977

760 **Oldfield, William Albert (Bert)**
–2 Some practical and valuable advice to
■ enthusiastic wicketkeepers, by the world's master 'keeper. Sydney, W.A.

(Bert) Oldfield's Sports Store, [196–?].
[16]p. incl. adverts. illus. ports. diagr.
stats.

761 **Stanyforth, Ronald Thomas**
■ Wicket-keeping. Aldershot, Gale &
Polden, 1935. [vii],56p. illus. diagr. stats.

761 **Taylor, Robert William**
–1 Wicketkeeping [by] Bob Taylor, with the
■ assistance of Patrick Murphy. Pelham
Books, 1979. 120p. illus. (Sporting Skills)
*includes chs. on 'The Great Wicketkeepers'
and 'The Great Batsmen'*

## Wicket-keepers

762 **Martineau, Gerard Durani**
■ The valiant stumper: a history of wicket-
keeping. S. Paul, 1957. 176p. illus. ports.
bibliog.

763 **Pogson, Norman J.**
■ International wicket-keepers of three
countries. Lincoln Williams, 1932. 88p.
stats.
*a statistical record of all Australian,
English and South African Test wicket-
keepers, 1877–1931*

# CAPTAINCY

764 **Benaud, Richie**
■ A tale of two Tests: with some thoughts
on captaincy. Hodder & Stoughton, 1962.
125p. illus. ports.

765 **Dollery, Horace Edgar (Tom)**
■ Professional captain. S. Paul, 1952. 192p.
illus. port. diagrs.
*contains advice on captaincy*

766 **Thomas, Robert Cyril Wolferston**
■ Cricket captaincy: 101 hints on the art of
captaincy for club and school cricketers.
[Ashford (Kent), Geering, 1950]. 16p.

## Captains

767 **Arlott, [Leslie Thomas] John,** *editor*
■ Cricket: the great captains: studies of
eight great captains of cricket history.
Pelham Books, 1971. 152p. illus. ports.
——*another ed.* Sportsman's Book Club,
1972
*A.C. MacLaren, Sir Pelham Warner, D.R.
Jardine, Brian Sellers, Wilfred Wooller,
Stuart Surridge, Jack Cheetham, Sir Frank
Worrell*

767 **Gibson, Alan**
–1 The cricket captains of England: a survey.
■ Cassell, 1979. [xi],235p. illus. ports. stats.
——*another ed.* Sportsmans Book Club,
1979

767 **Puri, Narottam**
–2 Portrait of Indian captains. Calcutta,
■ [etc.], Rupa, 1978. [xiv],193p. illus. ports.
stats. pbk.

767 **Robinson, Ray**
–3 On top down under: Australia's cricket
■ captains. Stanmore (N.S.W.) Cassell
Australia, 1975. [xii],320p. illus. ports.
bibliog.
*the careers of 34 Australian captains from
1877 to 1975*
——*another ed.* 1976. xiv,336p. illus. ports.
pbk.
*updated to include Greg Chappell*

768 **Thomson, Arthur Alexander**
■ Cricket: the great captains. S. Paul, 1965.
208p. ports. bibliog.
——*another ed.* Sportsman's Book Club,
1967

769 **Webber, Roy**
■ Test match captains, 1876–1939.
Hunstanton, Cricket Book Society, 1947.
32p. stats. (Publications, Series 1, no. 6)
*a statistical record
re-issued in "Cricket omnibus, 1946"
edited by Roy Webber. See no. 982*

# WATCHING CRICKET

770 **Alston, Rex,** *i.e.* **Arthur Reginald Alston**
■ Watching cricket: an aid to the appreciation of first-class cricket, and a guide
to the laws. Phoenix House, 1962. 115p.
diagrs. glossary. (Sports Books)

771 **Arlott, [Leslie Thomas] John**
■ How to watch cricket. Sporting Handbooks, 1948. 86p. diagrs.
—— *2nd ed.* 1949. 90p.

772 **Bailey, Trevor Edward**
■ Hints on watching cricket. Chelmsford,
[Essex C.C.C., 1950]. [4]p. *folded card*

773 **Basu, Ajay**
■ Ākāse kriket bani. Calcutta, Phalguni,
[1965/6?]. iv,134p. illus.
*in Bengali; trs. "Cricket broadcasting"*

774 **Dimmock, Peter,** *editor*
■ Sports in view. Faber & Faber, 1964. 189p.
illus. diagrs.
*"Cricket" by Brian Johnston, pp. 39–58*

774 **The Guardian**
–1 The bedside 'Guardian' 17: a selection
■ from The Guardian 1967–68; edited by
W.L. Webb. Collins, 1968. 254p. illus.
*includes pp. 96–8 "Batting for posterity",
by Geoffrey Moorhouse on cricket films*

775 Johnston, Brian Alexander *and* Webber,
■ Roy
Armchair cricket. B.B.C., 1956. 78p. illus.
ports. diagrs. plans, stats. glossary
——*reissued* 1957 with leaf inserted in
pocket "Experimental changes for trial in
1957"
——*rev. and enl. ed.* by Brian Johnston.
B.B.C., 1966. 128p.
——*another ed.* 1968. 142p.
——*4th ed.* by Brian Johnston. 1975. 224p.
pbk.

776 Labuschagne, Awie, *and* Ettlinger,
■ Duggie
Krieket vir die Tuisblyer: 'n handleiding
vir radioluisteraars. Johannesburg, Suid-
Afrikaanse Uitsaaikorporasie, [1966]. 42p.
illus. diagrs.
*an explanation of cricket for radio listeners*

777 Willock, Colin, *editor*
■ The man's book. Hulton, 1958. vii,345p.
illus. diagrs. map
*contains "An eye for cricket" by John Arlott*

Watching cricket: A section of the 77,000 spectators at the Third Test, Australia v. England on
Boxing Day, 1974, at Melbourne *photo: Patrick Eagar*

English cricket: W. G. Grace at the Gentlemen v. Players match at Lord's,
1891 *photo: BBC Hulton Picture Library*

# CRICKET IN ENGLAND AND WALES

## ADMINISTRATION

**778**    **Advisory County Cricket Committee**
☐    Rules. The Committee. *annual*
?/1965 . . .1968/
*formed 1904*
contd. as: *Test and County Cricket Board.*
*Rules.* See *no. 792*

**779**    Interim report of a Sub-Committee appo-
■    inted by the Advisory County Cricket
Committee under the chairmanship of
Col. R.S. Rait Kerr to investigate the
proposal for a cricket knock-out competition. 1945. 9p. *typescript*
——second report. 1966. 13p. *typescript*

**780**    **Board of Control for Test Matches in**
☐    **England**
Rules. The Board. *annual*
?/1965–1968/
contd. as: *Test and County Cricket Board.*
*Rules.* See *no. 792*

**781**    **Cricket Society**
■    Evidence prepared by the Cricket Society
for presentation to the Marylebone
Cricket Club April 1961. [Cricket Society,
1961]. 32p.
*2 issues, 1 with name and address of the*
*Society on page 1, and 1 without*

**782**    **Marylebone Cricket Club**
☐    Playing conditions for first class matches,
including Test matches and tourist
matches against counties. M.C.C. *annual*
?/1968/
contd. as: *Test and Country Cricket Board.*
*Playing conditions . . .* See *no. 793*

**783**    Report of the Commission appointed by
the M.C.C. at the request of the Advisory
County Cricket Committee to investigate
the problems confronting the counties
taking part in the first class county cricket
championship. M.C.C., 1937. 23p.
*Commissioner: W. Findlay*

**784**    The case for relieving cricket and other
similarly placed games and pastimes from
Entertainments Duty, submitted by the
M.C.C. for the consideration of the Chan-
cellor of the Exchequer. M.C.C., 1944.
*typescript*

**785**    ——.*Cricket Enquiry Committee*
■    Report of the Cricket Enquiry Committee
appointed by the Marylebone Cricket
Club at the request of the Advisory
County Cricket Committee. [M.C.C.],
1950. 44p.
——Summary. 4p.
*chairman: H.S. Altham*

**786**    ——. *Select Committee*
■    Report of the Select Committee appointed
by the Marylebone Cricket Club at the
request of the Advisory County Cricket
Committee to investigate the problems
confronting county cricket after the cessation of hostilities. M.C.C., 1944. 24p.
*Chairman: Sir Stanley Jackson*

**787**    ——. *Special Committee*
■    Report of the Special Committee appo-
inted by the M.C.C. to consider the
future welfare of first-class cricket, 1957.
M.C.C., 1957. 8p.
*Chairman: H.S. Altham*

**778**    ——. *Youth Cricket Association*
**–1**    Report of progress from Jan. 1952 to June
■    1955. [M.C.C.], 1955. 8p.
*Chairman: H.S. Altham*

**788**    **Marylebone Cricket Club National**
■    **Cricket Association**
The future of the game: report of the
regional cricket conference held at Bury
St. Edmunds, April, 1968. Arranged by
the Central Council of Physical Recreation (Eastern Region). [M.C.C.N.C.A.,
1968]. 18p. *typescript*

**789**    **National Association of Young**
☐    **Cricketers**
Year book. The Association. team illus.
ports. map. scores. stats. *in v.y.*
?/1970–8/to date

**790**    **The National** Cricket Association. [The
■    Association], 1969. [3]p.
*a descriptive folder*
——2nd ed. 1970. [3]p.

791  **National Cricket Association**
■  Regulations for junior cricket. The Assoc., 1971. [8]p. diagr.

791  Handbook. The Assoc. illus. ports. *annual*
-1  *1974 to date*
□

791  ——, *and* **The Wrigley Cricket**
-2  **Foundation**
■  A report on school and youth cricket in the seventies. The Association, 1971. ii,19,8,5f. *typescript*

792  **Test and County Cricket Board**
■  Rules. The Board, [1969]. 3p. *typescript*
——Appendices 'A'—'J'. 1970 *to date. loose leaf*
*App. 'A'. Rules governing the receipt and distribution of moneys*
*'B'. Rules governing the registration and qualification of cricketers in county cricket*

*'C'. Regulations for Test matches in the United Kingdom*
*'D'. Regulations for county cricket*
*'E'. Playing conditions for first class matches and one-day international matches*
*'F'.(i) Rules of Gillette Cup*
*(ii) Rules of John Player League*
*(iii) Rules of Benson & Hedges Cup*
*'G'. Rules of First-Class counties 2nd eleven championship*
*'H'. Rules of Under-25 county cricket competition*
*'I' Minor Counties competition*
*'J'. Regulations for Discipline Sub-Committee*
formerly: *Advisory County Cricket Committee. Rules. See no. 778, and Board of Control for Test Matches in England. Rules. See no. 780*

793  Playing conditions for first class matches
□  . . . The Board. *annual*
*1969/1969 to date*
formerly: *Marylebone C.C. Playing conditions . . . See no. 782*

# HISTORY

794  **Arlott, [Leslie Thomas] John,** *editor*
■  From Hambledon to Lord's: the classics of cricket: John Nyren, Charles Cowden Clarke, the Rev. James Pycroft, the Rev. John Mitford. Johnson, 1948. 143p. illus. ports. scores
——new ed. Winchester, Barry Shurlock and Co. (Publishers) Ltd., 1975. 141p. illus. ports. scores

795  The middle ages of cricket: being "Sketches of the players" by William Denison; "Cricket recollections" from "Oxford memories" by James Pycroft; the whole assembled, edited and discussed by John Arlott. C. Johnson, [1949]. 187p. illus. ports.

796  ——, *and* **Daley, Arthur**
■  Pageantry of sport from the age of chivalry to the age of Victoria; with selections from the writings of William Hazlitt and many others. Elek, 1968. [i],129p. illus. (some col.)
*cricket pp. 72–8*

797  **Ashley-Cooper, Frederick Samuel**
■  Curiosities of first-class cricket [1730–1901]. Edmund Seale, 1901. viii,126p.
——*another ed.* 1901
*limited to 100 copies signed and interleaved*

797  **Association of Cricket Statisticians,**
-1  *compilers*
■  A guide to first class cricket matches

played in the British Isles. Hampton in Arden (Warks.), the Assoc., 1976. 40p. scores
*"matches played 1864–1946 not automatically regarded as first-class, but which appear to deserve that ranking" (Wisden)*

798  **[Box, Charles]**
□  The cricketers' manual, for 1848, containing a brief review of the character, rise, and progress of the manly and noble game of cricket and the laws . . . by "Bat." Brittain, 1948. 39p. stats.
*p. 39 carries an apology for inaccuracies*
——*2nd issue.* 1848. 38p. stats.
*p. [39] blank; corrections made to averages on p. 15*
——, for 1849, containing a brief review of the rise and progress of cricket, and the laws appertaining to the game; the averages of the principal amateur & professional players . . ., by "Bat." Baily Brothers, [1849], [iv],48p. stats.
*some copies contain erratum slip referring to changes in Laws 7 and 29 made on 3rd May, 1849*
——[for 1850], containing a brief review of the character, history & elements of cricket, with the Laws . . ., by "Bat." Baily Brothers, 1850. 102p. stats.
*"Opinions of the press" printed on verso of "Contents"*
——*2nd issue.* 1850. 102p. stats.
*"Erratum" printed on verso of "Contents"*
——*5th ed.* 1851. viii,9–110,[i]p.
*in his 'Preface to the fifth edition', p.[vii],*

*author refers to four previous editions. Only three known. "Contents" includes 'Curiosities of cricket' p. 70; 'Recitation' is listed incorrectly as p. 102; 'The Character of Cricket' has no page ref.; 'of' dropped from line 4, p. 8.*

——*2nd? issue.* viii, 9–110, [i]p.

*"Contents" does not include 'Curiosities of cricket'; 'Recitation' corrected to p. 109; 'List of principal players' listed out of order and its page reference has last two digits dropped; 'of' inserted line 4, p. 8*

——*3rd? issue.* viii, 9–110[i]p.

*"Contents" has 'List of principal players' correctly numbered p. 91*

——*4th issue.* Joseph Myers, 1851. viii,9–110p.

*"Contents" as in 1st issue but with page '9' added against 'The Character of Cricket'*

*for further details see Weston, G.N. The cricketers' manual by "Bat"*

799 ■ The English game of cricket: comprising a digest of its origin, character, history, and progress, together with an exposition of its laws and language, by "Bat". "The Field" Office, 1877. x,496p. illus. diagrs. glossary, scores, stats.

799 **Brookes, Christopher**
–1 English cricket: the game and its players
■ through the ages. Weidenfeld and Nicolson, 1978. [xiii],210p. illus. ports. bibliog.

——*another ed.* Newton Abbot, Readers Union, 1978

799 **Bryant,** *Sir* **Arthur**
–2 Protestant island. Collins, 1967. 359p.
■ (English Social History)
*cricket pp. 99–101, 103, 124, 148, 159–60, 225, 271, 279, 297, 327*

800 **Buckley, George Bent,** *compiler*
Cricket notices. *MS typescripts*
——1681–1854. 373p.
——1744–1845. 472p.
*press notices. In M.C.C. Library, Lord's*

801 Fresh light on 18th century cricket: a
■ collection of 1,000 new cricket notices from 1697 to 1800 A.D. arranged in chronological order. Birmingham, Cotterell, 1935. x,261p. scores
*some copies lettered on spine "Fresh light on cricket from 1697 to 1800"*

802 Historical gleanings. 1954. *MS. typescript.*
■ [iii],79f.
*in M.C.C. Library, Lord's*

803 More historical gleanings. 1956. *MS. type-*
■ *script.* [iii], 105f.
*in M.C.C. Library, Lord's*

804 **Cardus,** *Sir* **Neville**
■ English cricket. Collins, 1945. 48p. illus. (some col.), ports. (Britain in Pictures)

805 **Cricket** scores and biographies of
■ celebrated cricketers. 15 vols.
*vols. 1–4 with title Frederick Lillywhite's cricket scores . . . 1746 to 1854. The Oval, Kennington, Lillywhite, 1862–63 (vol. 4 publd. jointly with Kent of Paternoster Row, London)*
*vols. 5–6 with title Arthur Haygarth's cricket scores . . . 1855 to 1860. Longmans, at the expense of the M.C.C., 1876*
*vols. 7–14 with title Marylebone Club cricket scores . . . 1861 to 1878. Longmans, at the expense of the M.C.C., 1877–1895.*
*vol. 15 with title M.C.C. cricket scores . . . (Based on notes by the late Arthur Haygarth to the end of 1898 and the records brought up to date by F.S. Ashley-Cooper). Longmans, 1925*
*final vol. composed solely of notices of cricketers*
——Index. Vols. 1–13; compiled by A.L. Ford. Cricket Office, 1885. 19p.
——Index. Vol. 14; compiled by A.L. Ford. 27p. *MS typescript*
——A list of matches to be published in F. Lillywhite's large work of cricket scores from 1746 to 1856, inclusive. Greenwich, *printed by* W.H. Crockford, 1857
——Index to all first-class matches in "Scores and biographies", vols. 1–XIV, 1746–1878; compiled by J.B. Payne. Harrogate, the Compiler, 1903. [iv],36p. scores
*limited to 100 copies*
——An index of minor matches . . . up to 1878; compiled by G.B. Buckley 1957. MS *typescript.* [v],136p.
*in M.C.C. Library, Lord's*

806 **The cricketer's** handbook, in three parts:
□ I—History and chronology of cricket. II—Instructions for the game. III—The revised laws. By the Author of "Training for pedestrianism and wrestling, etc." W.M. Clark, [c.1845]. 56p. frontis. scores. (Clark's Sporting Handbooks)
*later eds. with title: "Clark's cricketer's handbook, by a Member of the Marylebone Cricket Club", e.g. 10th ed. [c.1849]; 14th ed. [1858]; 15th ed. [c.1859]*
*for full entry see no. 378*

807 **The "Daily Graphic"**
■ Cricket number. Daily Graphic, 1914. 40p. incl. adverts. illus. ports. stats.

808 **Ford, John**
■ Cricket: a social history 1700–1835. Newton Abbot, David & Charles, 1972. 179p. illus. ports. bibliog.

808 This sporting land, by John Ford in
-1 association with Thames Television. New
■ English Library/Times Mirror, 1977. 256p.
illus. ports.
——pbk. ed. 1977
*historical account of English sports
including cricket*

809 **Gale, Frederick**
■ Echoes from old cricket fields; or, Sketches of cricket and cricketers from the
earliest history of the game to the present
time. Simpkin Marshall, 1871. xii,112p.
frontis.
——new and revised ed. Nutt, 1896. 96p.
frontis.
——reprint of 1st ed. with a new foreword by John Arlott. Wakefield, S.R.
Publishers, 1972. vii,xii,112p. frontis.

810 **Grace, William Gilbert**
■ Cricket. Bristol, Arrowsmith; London,
Simpkin Marshall, 1891. viii,489p. illus.
ports. scores, stats.
——L.P. ed. 1891. xii,512p.
*limited to 635 copies and 10 presentation
copies*
see also *nos. 2, 818*
——*another ed.* Leipzig, Heinemann and
Balestier, 1892. [vii],350p. (The English
Library)

810 **Harris, Harold Arthur**
-1 Sport in Britain: its origins and develop-
■ ment. S. Paul, 1975. 224p. illus. ports.
facsims.
*cricket pp. 35–78, 192, 195–6, 198ff.*

811 **Hole, Christina**
■ English sports and pastimes. Batsford,
1949. viii,183p. illus. (1 col.)
*cricket references and illus. including
coloured frontis.*

812 **Hutchison, George Andrew,** *editor*
■ Cricket: a popular handbook on the
game, by Dr. W.G. Grace, Rev. J. Pycroft,
Lord Charles Russell, Frederick Gale and
other well-known veteran authorities.
Religious Tract Society, [1887]. xii,244p.
illus. ports. diagrs. (Boy's Own
Bookshelf)
*contains a chapter on "How to make a
cricket bat" by W.G. Grace*

813 **Labour** history: journal of the Australian
■ Society for the Study of Labour History.
Canberra City. Twice yearly, May &
November. No. 23, Nov. 1972; ed. by Jill
Waterhouse
*contains "The professional cricketer in
England in the nineteenth century", by W.F.
Mandle, pp. 1–16
a study of salaries and benefits*

814 **Lyttelton,** *the Hon.* **Robert Henry**
■ Outdoor games: cricket and golf. Dent,
1901. vii,252p. col. ports. (The Haddon
Hall Library)
——L.P. ed. 1901
*limited to 150 copies*

815 **Martineau, Gerard Durani**
■ The field is full of shades: historical
portraits of men who helped to make the
national game. Sporting Handbooks,
1946. 111p.
——*another ed.* Sportsman's Book Club,
1954
*printed with 'Bat, ball, wicket and all'*

816 They made cricket. Museum P., 1956.
■ 232p. illus. ports. bibliog.
——*another ed.* Sportsman's Book Club,
1957

817 **Montgomery, Henry Hutchinson**
■ Old cricket and cricketers. H. Stacey
Gold; Wright, 1890. [xiii],77p. illus. ports.
scores
*a reprint of the chs. on cricket in Author's
"The history of Kennington"*

818 **Press** critiques: Cricket: past, present,
■ and future, by W.G. Grace, with
complete laws of cricket; also, Kings of
cricket, by Richard Daft, Nottingham,
Howe, [c.1893]. 32p. port.

819 **[Pycroft, James)**
■ The cricket field; or, The History and the
science of cricket, by the author of "The
principles of scientific batting". Longmans, etc., 1851. xvi,242p. ports. diagrs.
score
*for full entry see no. 394*

820 **Roberts, Edward Lamplough,** *compiler*
■ All-rounders in English cricket.
Birmingham, Hudson, [1947]. 32p. incl.
adverts. stats.
*a statistical record*

821 **Trevelyan, George Macaulay**
■ English social history: a survey of six
centuries, Chaucer to Queen Victoria.
Longmans, 1942. xii,628p.
*cricket pp. 316, 317, 407, 408, 549*

822 **[Warner,** *Sir* **Pelham Francis],** *editor*
□ British sports and sportsmen past and
present; compiled and edited by "The
Sportsman". British Sports and
Sportsmen, [1908–1936?]. 16 vols. illus.
ports.
*Vol. 5. Cricket and football, 1917. xiii,
597p.
limited to 1000 copies; cricket pp. 1–211*
——*another ed.* Sports & Sportsman Ltd.
[c.1934]. 485p. illus. ports.
*limited to 1000 numbered copies*

823 **[Entry cancelled]**

824 **Watson, James**
Some historical and literary references to English games. Folkestone, The Author, 1907. 123p.
*cricket pp. 72–78*

825 **Wymer, Norman George**
■ Sport in England: a history of two thousand years of games and pastimes. Harrap, 1949. 271p. illus. bibliog.
*has ch. on cricket*

# BEFORE 1726

(Includes early references to the game played elsewhere)

825 **Aspin, Jehoshaphat**
–1 A picture of the manners, customs, sports and pastimes, of the inhabitants of England ... down to the eighteenth century, selected from the ancient chronicles, and rendered into modern phraseology. J. Harris, 1825. iv,296p. illus.
*cricket pp. 246–9; based on Strutt's "Manners & customs". For children*

826 **Bartlett, Vernon**
■ The past of pastimes. Chatto & Windus, 1969. 160p. illus.
*ch. 4 "From Pall Mall to the cricket pitch", pp. 42–55*

827 **Brailsford, Dennis**
■ Sport and society: Elizabeth to Anne. London, Routledge & Kegan Paul; Toronto, Univ. of Toronto P., 1969. vii,279p. bibliog.
*cricket pp. 82, 115–16, 209–10, 213, 230, 239–40, 253–54*

828 **Brasch, R.**
■ How did sports begin?: a look into the origins of man at play. Longman, 1972. xii,279p. illus. ports.
*cricket pp. 49–53*

829 **Ditchfield, Peter Hampson**
■ Old English sports, pastimes and customs. Methuen, 1891. xii,132p. illus.
*cricket pp. 38,61–65*

830 **Hackwood, F.W.**
Old English sports; with six coloured and thirty-two half-tone plates from old prints. Unwin, 1907. xvi,361p. illus.

831 **Henderson, Robert William**
Ball, bat and bishop: the origin of ball games. N.Y., Rockport P., 1947. xx,220p. illus.
*cricket pp. 128–31*

832 **MacGregor, Robert**
■ Pastimes and players. Chatto & Windus, 1881. [ix],203p. (The Mayfair Library)
*ch. 1 "Early forms of cricket"; ch. 11 "Cricketana", pp. 1–24*

833 **Mathys, Friedrich Karl**
Ballspiele und ihre historische Entwicklung. Schorndorf bei Stuttgart, Karl Hofmann, 1956. illus. bibliog.
*in German; includes the origins of cricket*

834 **Monckton, O. Paul**
Pastimes in times past. West Strand Publishing Co., 1913., 256p. illus.
*ch. vii "Cricket or stool-ball"*

835 **Stokes, Adrian**
■ A game that must be lost: collected papers. Carcanet P., 1973. iv,160p. port.
*includes "Psycho-analytic reflections on the development of ball games, particularly cricket", pp. 38–52*

836 **Strutt, Joseph**
□ Glig-gamena angel deod; or, The Sports and pastimes of the people of England. T. Bensley for J. White, 1801. [2],lvi,301p. illus.
*cricket pp. 83–84*
——2nd ed. 1810, lvi,357p. col. illus.
*cricket pp. 97–99; many later eds. including:*
——new ed. by William Hone *with title*: The sports and pastimes of the people of England; including the rural and domestic recreations . . . from the earliest period to the present time. Tegg, 1831. lxvii,420p. illus.
*cricket pp. 106–107*
——much enlarged & corrected new edition by J. Charles Cox. Methuen, 1903. 377p. illus.
——*rptd.* Detroit, Singing Tree P., 1968

837 **[Thomas Percy Francis]**
■ Old English cricket: a collection of evidence concerning the game prior to the days of Hambledon, by H.P.-T. Nottingham, Richards, 1923–29
*a set of 6 pamphlets:*
[1]. Cricket's cradle: the pedigree, transformation, and discovery of the game. 1923. 48p. illus.
[2]. Early cricket: a description of the first known match; and some comments on creag', criquet, cricce, and Shakespeare's clue. 1923. 51p. illus.
[3]. Old-time cricket: the oldest laws of the game; with their orthographic and dimensional analysis; and a review of the conditions under which they were collected. 1924. 80p. illus.
[4]. Cricket's prime: history before the days of Hambledon. 52p. map

102

# MUSÆ
# JUVENILES.

Per *Gulielmum Goldwin*, A. B.
Collegii Regalis Socium.

—— *Studiis florentem ignobilis oti,*
*Carmina qui lusi.* —— Virg. Georgic. Lib. 4.

*LONDINI,*
Proftant Venales apud *A. Baldwin,* in Vico
Vulgo dicto *Warwick-lane,* 1706.
29. *March*:

English cricket: The title-page of William Goldwin's "Musae Juveniles" which
contains the earliest description of a cricket match (no. 855)

English cricket: Cricket at the White Conduit Fields, 1787 *photo: BBC Hulton Picture Library*

English cricket: cricket in 1832 *photo: BBC Hulton Picture Library*

[5] More old time cricket: treating of the game in the public schools, on the stage, in the directory, etc.; with an appendix of footnotes to the previous parts. 1926, *i.e.* 1927. 72p. 1 illus.

[6]. Cricket in the Weald; with final footnotes to the previous issues of this series. 1928 *i.e.* 1929. 128p. 1 illus.

*contains 23p. index to the six pamphlets*

837 **Toyne, S.M.**
–1 "The early history of cricket". *In* History
■ today; edited by Peter Quennell and Alan Hodge. June, 1955. pp. 357–65. illus.

838 **Waghorn, Henry Thomas,** *compiler*
■ The dawn of cricket; edited by Lord Harris. M.C.C., 1906. v,204p. scores, bibliog.
*bibliography "evidently a list of cricketical items to be found in the B.M." (Ashley-Cooper)*

## Early references (In chronological order)

See also *"References to cricket pre-1700"* compiled by Stephen Green, *in* The Journal of The Cricket Society, vol. 10, no. 3, Autumn 1981.

839 **Hector, Leonard**
■ The ghost of cricket walks the archives. *Offprint* of the Journal of the Society of Archivists, Vol. 4, no. 7 (April 1973), pp. 579–80. facsim.
*examination of Register of "Lettres de remission', Archives Nationales, Paris (JJ205,f.103ᵛᵒ) for the year 1478, 11.1–8, disproving supposed use of the word 'criquet'*

840 **Guildford** book of court. 1598
■ M.S. The proceedings for January 16th give earliest specific reference to cricket in English. John Derrick, witness concerning a disputed piece of land, "being of the age of fyfty and nyne yeeres or thereaboutes", stated that he and other scholars of the Free School "did runne and play there at Creckett and other Plaies".
——facsimile reproduction with title: Cricket—the first time in English. [Guildford, Guildford Museum and Muniment Room, 1969?] bs.

841 **Florio, John,** *compiler*
■ A worlde of wordes, or most copious, and exact dictionarie in Italian and English. Printed at London, by Arnold Hatfield for Edw Blount, 1598. [xiv],461p.
*on p. 370, "Sgrillare", to make a noise as a cricket, to play cricket-a-wicket, and be merry*

842 **Kent Archaeological Society**
■ Archaeologia Cantiana, vol. LXIII for 1950. The Society, 1951. illus.
*includes "A note on early Kent cricket" by L.R.A. Grove, which refers to records of cricket in Kent in the 17th century from c.1610*

843 **Cotgrave, Randle**
A dictionarie of the French and English tongues. Printed by Adam Islip, 1611
*The French word "crosse" is translated as "a crosier, or Bishops staffe; also, a Cricket-staffe; or, the crooked staffe wherewith boyes play at cricket"*

844 **Sussex Archaeological Society**
■ Sussex notes and queries. Vol. 12. 1948–49. Lewes, the Society, 1950
*references pp. 42 and 65 to the use of the words 'cricket bat'. The first quotes the records of the Quarter Sessions held for West Sussex at Arundel 1647–48: Margaret Brand stated on oath . . . that her brother, Henry Brand of Selsey, had told her that he had recently received a wound in the head "given him by one Thomas Hatter of the sayd parish with a cricket bat". Henry died a month later. The second quotes from the Easter bills of presentment from Boxgrove for 1622 when on Sunday 5th May certain persons who played cricket in the churchyard were presented not only as Sabbath-breakers, but because "they use to breake the church windowes with the ball" and "a little childe had like to have her braynes beaten out with a crickett bat". This latter reference was first noted in Sussex Records Society. Vol. XLIX for the years 1947–48, under "Churchwardens' presentments (17th century). Part I: Archdeaconry of Chichester, ed. by Hilda Johnstone*

844 **McCann, Timothy J.,** *and* **Wilkinson,**
–1 **Peter M.**
■ "The cricket match at Boxgrove in 1622". *In* Sussex Archaeological Collections, vol. 110. 1972. pp. 118–22
*25 offprints were printed. "The earliest recorded instance so far discovered of a game of cricket played by several named players"*

845 **Olearius, Adam**
The voyages and travels of the ambassadors sent by Frederick Duke of Holstein, to the Great Duke of Muscovy, and the King of Persia . . . begun in the year 1633, and finished in 1639 . . . Faithfully rendred into English, by J. Davies. 2pts. 1662.
*cricket reference p. 297 in a description of the exercises indulged in by the Persian grandees in 1637 a statement is made that "They play there also at a certain Game, which the Persians call Kruitskaukan, which is a kind of Mall, or Cricket."*

846 **A wager** on a game of cricket. [16—]. MS.
*undated, now in a custody of Corporation of Maidstone. Nicholas Hunt sues William Wood for 12 candles wagered on a game of cricket played at Coxheath on 28th May, 1646*

847 **Rabelais, François**
The first [and second] book of the works of Mr. Francis Rabelais, Doctor in Physick: containing . . . the lives, heroick deeds, and sayings of Gargantua and his sonne Pantagruel . . . Translated into English by S.T.U.C. [i.e. Sir Thomas Urquhart]. 2 pts. R. Baddeley, 1653
*pt. 1. ch.xxii,p.97; mention of cricket in "The games of Gargantua"*

848 **[Phillips, Edward]**
The mysteries of love and eloquence, or, the arts of wooing and complementing; as they are manag'd in the Spring Garden, Hide Park, the New Exchange, and other eminent places. 2 parts. Printed for N. Brooks, at the Angel in Cornhill, 1658
*contains following passage: "Aye, but Richard will you think so hereafter? Will you not when you have me throw stools at my head; and cry, 'Would my eyes had been beat out of my head with a cricket-ball, the day before I saw thee' "*

848 **Royal Commission** on Historical Manus-
–1 cripts (England)
■     Sixth report. Part 1. Report and appendix. The Commission, 1877.
*The appendix p. 365 contains a letter dated 1666, May 29th from Sir Robert Paston (later Earl of Yarmouth) of Oxnead, Norfolk to his wife which includes "Post now comes in the Squire of the Body who says he saw your son very well engaged in a game at cricquett on Richmond Green".*

849 **[Swinnock, George]**
■ The life and death of Mr. Tho. Wilson, Minister of Maidstone, in the county of Kent. M.A. Printed in the year 1672. [xi],99p.
*Ch.xviii,p.40: "Maidstone was formerly a very prophane Town, insomuch that I have seen Morrice dancing, cudgel playing, stool-ball, crickets, and many other sports openly and publickly on the Lords Day . . ."*

850 **Wit** at a venture; or, Clio's privy-garden,
■ containing songs and poems on several occasions never before in print. Printed for Jonathan Edwin at the three Roses in Ludgate Street, 1674
*one poem "The virtue of a hot-house" contains the lines:*
*"Cricket or Gauff, which to some men is As pretty a sport as Trap or Tennis"*
*the Epistle dedicatory is signed C.F. but "at least three hands in this". (C.B.E.L.)*

851 **Teonge, Henry**
■ The diary of Henry Teonge, Chaplain on board His Majesty's ships Assistance, Bristol, and Royal Oak, anno 1675 to 1679. Now first published from the original MS. with biographical and histor-ical notes. Printed for Charles Knight, Pall Mall East, 1825. xviii,327p. facsim.
——*another edition;* edited by G.W. Main-waring. Routledge, 1927. x,318p. illus. (Broadway Travellers)
*entry for 6th May, 1676 "This morning early (as it is the custom all summer longe) at least 40 of the English, with his worship the Consull, rod out of the cytty [Aleppo] about 4 miles to the Greene Platt, a fine vally by a river syde, to recreate them selves. Where a princely tent was pitched; and wee had severall pastimes and sports, as duck-hunting, fishing, shooting, handball, krickett, scrofilo; and then a noble dinner brought thither, with greate plenty of all sorts of wines, punch and lemonads; and at 6 wee returne all home in good order, but soundly tyred and weary"*

851 **Barrett-Lennard,** *Sir* **Thomas**
–1 An account of the families of Lennard and Barrett; compiled largely from original documents. [The Author], 1908.
*p. 317 (1677–8): p^d to my Lord when his Lord^p went to the crekitt match at ye Dick^er [Dicker Common] 03 . . 00 . . 00*

851 **Miege, Guy,** *compiler*
–2 The great French dictionary. Printed by J. Redmayne for Tho. Basset at the George near St. Dunstan's Church in Fleet Street, 1688. *unpaginated*
*contains entry: 'cricket: sorte de jeu Anglon aved une bale qu'on ponsse avec une crosse'*

852 **D'Urfey, Thomas**
■ The Richmond heiress; or, A woman once in the right: a comedy, acted at the Theatre Roayl [sic], by their Majesties servants. Printed for Samuel Briscoe, over-against Will's Coffee-House in Covent Garden, 1693. [vi],64p.
——*re-issued with corrected t.p., 1693*
*reference to cricket in Shinken's 'Song of the Harp', Act. IV*
*"Hur was the prettiest Fellows, trum, trum, etc.*
*At Bandy once and Cricket, trum, etc."*

852 **Kennet, White**
–1 Parochial antiquities attempted in the history of Ambrosden, Burcester and other adjacent parts of the Counties of Oxford and Bucks. Oxford, printed at the Theatre, 1695. [xvi], 703, [152], illus.
*Glossary:* Salicetum: *An osier-bed. . . .The* wicket *or cross stick to be thrown down by the ball at the game call'd* Crickets

853 **D'Urfey, Thomas**
□ Wit and mirth; or, Pills to purge melancholy: being a collection of the best merry ballads and songs, old and new. . . 1699
*p. 311, "A song", verse 3:*
*"Her was the prettiest Fellow*
*At Foot-ball, or at Cricket:*
*At Hunting Chace, or nimble Race,*
*Cots-plut how Her cou'd prick it"*
——another *ed.* 6 vols. Printed by W. Pearson, for J. Tonson, 1719–20
*vols. I, III, IV and V have a second t.p.*
*"Songs compleat, pleasant and divertive"*
*reference appears vol. II, p. 172*

854 **[Ward, Edward]**
The world bewitched: a dialogue between two astrologers [viz. P—r. i.e. George Parker and P—dge. i.e. John Partridge,] and the author. With infallible predictions of what will happen in this present year, 1699. . . .1699. 32p.
*p. 22 on the approach of summer. "Quoits, Cricket, Nine-Pins, and Trap-Ball will be very much in fashion and more Tradesmen may be seen Playing in the Fields than working in their shops."*

854 **A rod for Tunbridge Beaus,** bundl'd up
–1 at the request of the Tunbridge ladies, to jirk fools into more wit, and clowns into more manners. A burlesque poem. To be publish'd every summer, as long as the rakes continue their rudeness, and the gentry their vertue. London, Printed, and are to be sold by the booksellers of London and Westminster, 1701. [ii],30p.
——another *ed.* 1705
*reference on p. 6*
*"Its true he can at Cricket play, With any living at this day;"*

855 **Goldwin, William**
■ Musae juveniles. A. Baldwin, 1706. [i], 28p.
*Latin verses including pp. 9–12, "In certamen pilae" which describes a game of cricket conforming almost entirely with the Code of Laws laid down in 1744. The earliest description of a match. A translation by Harold Perry appeared in Etoniana No. 31, Dec. 1922, and in The Cricketer, Feb. 1923, and is rptd. in "The laws of cricket" by R.S. Rait Kerr. See no. 221*

855 **Phillips, Edward,** *compiler*
–1 The new world of words; or, Universal English dictionary. . . .Revised. . . .with the addition of near twenty thousand words by J.K. [John Kersey]. Printed for J. Phillips, [etc.], 1706. [711]p.
*"Bat: A kind of Club to strike a Ball with, at the Play call'd Cricket"*

856 **Chamberlayne, Edward**
■ Angliae notitia: or, The present state of England: together with divers reflections upon the antient state thereof, by Edward Chamberlayne and continu'd by his son John Chamberlayne. 22nd ed. In three parts. Printed for S. Smith and B. Walford, etc., 1707. xix,704p.
*1st ed. published 1669; cricket first mentioned in list of recreations in this ed. p. 313*

857 **Byrd, William**
The secret diary of William Byrd of Westover 1709–1712; edited by Louis B. Wright and Marion Tinling. Richmond (Va), The Dietz P., 1941. xxviii,622p. facsims.
*references to early cricket in Virginia, 1709–10*

858 **[Arbuthnot, John]**
■ Lewis Baboon turned honest, and John Bull, politician: being the fourth part of "Law is a bottomless pit". Printed from a manuscript found in the cabinet of the famous Sir Humphrey Polesworth and published by the Author of The New Atlantis. John Morphew, 1712. [viii],37p.
*reference to a match at cricket, p. 18*

859 **The Devil** and the peers; or, The princely way of Sabbath breaking. J. Barker, Paternoster Row, 1712. bs.

860 **The Sabbath-breakers,** or a young man's
■ dreadful warning-piece. E. Midwinter, 1712. 20p. 1 illus.
*sermons, one of which records what befell four young men who played cricket on Sunday, 6th July, 1712, the sub-title reading: "being a very dismal Account of four Young-Men, who made a Match to Play at Cricket, on Sunday, the 6th of this Instant July 1712 in a Meadow near Maiden Head- Thicket; and as they were at Play, there rose out of the Ground, a Man in Black with a Cloven-Foot, which put them in a great Consternation; but as they stood in this Frighted Condition, the Devil flew up in the Air, in a Dark Cloud with Flashes of Fire, and in his Room he left a very Beautiful Woman, and Robert Yates and Richard Moore hastily stepping up to her, being Charm'd with her Beauty went to kiss her, but in the Attempt they instantly fell down Dead . . .*

860 **Lucas, Theophilus**
–1 Memoirs of the lives, intrigues and comical adventures of the most famous gamesters and celebrated sharpers. Printed for J. Brown, etc., 1714. xxiv,285p. frontis.
——rptd. *in* Games and gamesters of the Restoration: The compleat gamester, by

Charles Cotton, 1674, and Lives of the gamesters, by Theophilus Lucas, 1714; with an introduction by Cyril Hughes Hartmann. Routledge, 1930. xxx,281p. illus. (English Library)

*contains an account of Patrick Hurley "very expert beyond the rest of his companions; as [sic] tipcat, cricket, skittles . . ."*

861 **Stow, John**
■ A survey of the cities of London and Westminster . . . corrected . . . and brought down from . . . 1633 . . . to the present; by John Strype. . . .Churchill, 1720. 2 vols. illus. maps.

*vol. 1, book 1, p. 257 in speaking of the recreations of the citizens, "The more common sort divert themselves at Football, Wrestling, Cudgels, Ninepins, Shovel-board, Cricket. . . ." The reference first appears in this ed.*

862 **Bailey, Nathan**
An universal etymological English dictionary. . . .Printed for E. Bell [and others], 1721. [964]p.

*cricket defined as 'sort of play with a ball'. In 1733 the 6th ed. added 'and bats'; many later eds.*

863 **Downing, Clement**
A compendious history of the Indian wars. . . .Printed for T. Cooper, 1737. iv,238p.

——*another ed. with title:*
A history of the Indian wars; edited by William Foster, Oxford Univ. P., 1924. xxxii,206p. port. maps

*reference to mariners of the East India Company playing cricket at Cambay, India in 1721, pp. 228–29 (1737 ed.); pp. 188–89 (1924 ed.)*

863 **Historical Manuscripts Commission**
–1 Report on the manuscripts of his Grace the Duke of Portland, K.G., preserved at Welbeck Abbey. H.M.S.O.

*vol. vi (1901) contains* Journeys in England, *by Lord Harley, afterwards the 2nd earl of Oxford, which describes a journey through Kent in 1723 and notes: ". . . upon the heath as we came out of the town [Dartford] the men of Tunbridge and the Dartford men were warmly engaged at the sport of cricket, which of all the people of England the Kentish folk are most renowned for, and of all the Kentish men the men of Dartford lay claim to the greatest excellence."*

863 **Cheyne, George**
–2 An essay of health and long life. 3rd ed.
■ Printed for George Strahan . . . and J. Leake, 1725. [4], xx,[24],232p.

*pp.97–98 Cheyne recommends "To those that have Rheumatick Pains, to play Billiards,*

*Tennis or Cricket till they* sweat *plentifully . . .", 1st publd. 1724*

# 1726–1845

863 **An adieu** to the turf: a poetical epistle
–3 from the E–L of A–N to his Grace the A–P of Y–K. 2nd ed. London, printed for M. Smith, 1778. [4], vii,24p.

*stanza on p. 3 reads:*
*Scarce fourteen years had pass'd away*
*When first I thought of am'rous play*
*Of women not afraid:*
*For then I left more childish cricket;*
*I only strove to hit their wicket,*
*And put out every maid*

864 **Arnold, Ralph Crispian Marshall**
■ A yeoman of Kent: an account of Richard Hayes, 1725–1790, and of the village of Cobham in which he lived and farmed. Constable, 1949. xii,203p. illus. (1 col.) score

*includes a history of Cobham cricket and an account of England v. Hampshire at Sevenoaks Vine 1776*

865 **Ashley-Cooper, Frederick Samuel**
■ Cricket 1742–1751. Merritt & Hatcher, [1900]. x,74p.

*private circulation; limited ed. of 15 copies*

866 **Ashton, John**
■ Men, maidens and manners a hundred years ago. Field & Tuer, 1888. 124p. illus.

*cricket in 1787 pp. 76–78 with 1 illus.*

867 **Bolland, William**
■ Cricket notes; with a letter containing practical hints, by W. Clark. Trelawney Saunders, 1851. iv,155p.

*historical essays, reminiscences and commentary*

868 **Branch-Johnson, William**
The Carrington diary (1797–1810). C. Johnson, 1956. 184p. illus. diagr.

*contains scattered references to single wicket matches at Bramfield, Hertfordshire*

868 "Memorandums for . . .": the diary
–1 between 1798 and 1810 of John Carrington. Phillimore, 1973. xiii,200p. illus.

869 **Britcher, Samuel**
□ List of all the principal matches of cricket that have been played in the year [1790–1805]. With a correct state of each innings.

*1790. Maidstone, printed by D. Chalmers, 1791. 16p.*
*1791. Maidstone, printed by D. Chalmers, 1792. 28p.*

1792. with title: *A complete list of all the grand matches . . . .* printed by *Cane & Glindon, 1793. 28p.*

1793. printed by *Cane & Glindon, 1793. 28p.*

1794. *[London]; n.p. 1794. 30p.*

1795. *[London]; n.p. 1795. 36p.*

1796. printed by *T. Craft, 1796. 40p.*

1797. printed by *T. Craft, 1797. 36p.*

1798. printed by *T. Craft, 1798. 48p.*

1799. printed by *W. Blake, 1799. 32p.*

1800. printed by *W. Blake, 1800, 44p.*

1801. printed by *W. Calvert, 1801. 48p.*

1802. printed by *W. Calvert, 1802. 32p.*

1803. printed by *G.G. Hayden, 1803. 35p.*

1804–5. *Stanhope & Graham,* printed by *G.G. Hayden, 1806. 30p.*

870 **Buckley, George Bent,** *compiler*
■ Fresh light on pre-Victorian cricket: a collection of new cricket notices from 1709 to 1837 arranged in chronological order. Birmingham, Cotterell, 1937. x,250p. scores

871 **Burney, Frances,** *afterwards* **Mrs. D'Arblay**
The early diary . . . 1768–1778; with a selection from her correspondence, and from the journals of her sisters Susan and Charlotte Burney; edited by Annie Raine Ellis. 2 vols. Bell, 1889
*quotes a letter (in vol. 1) from Mrs. Rishton, dated 1773, requesting Miss Burney to obtain two cricket balls made by Pett of Sevenoaks*

872 **Chesterfield, Philip Dormer Stanhope,**
■ *4th earl of*
Letters . . . to his son, Philip Stanhope . . . 11th ed. J. Nichols [and others], 1800. 4 vols.
*letter no. LXXI, dated Tuesday (May, 1741), first printed in this edition, urges his son 'to excell all boys of your age, at cricket . . .'*

873 **Chronicles** of cricket: facsimile reprints of
■ Nyren's "Cricketer's guide", Lillywhite's "Handbook of cricket", Denison's "Sketches of the players"; with facsimile illustrations. Swan Sonnenschein, Lowrey, 1888. iv,[7],101; 30; viii,76p. illus. ports. scores
——another issue. Maurice, n.d.
*the same as above but lacks a general t.p.; name of publisher lettered on spine*
——2nd ed. Swan, Sonnenschein, [1888?]
——facsim. rpt. of 1st ed. Wakefield, EP Publishing, 1975. 102; 30,76p.
*reprints of 7th ed. of Nyren; 1844 ed. of Lillywhite; 1846 ed. of Denison*

874 **Colman, George,** *the younger*
The heir-at-law: a comedy in five acts, as performed at The Theatres-Royal in London and Dublin. Dublin, P. Byrne, 1797
——2nd ed. 1800. 66p.
*"recognition of the penetration of the game into the lives of every class of society" ("Cricket". National Book League. p. 20)*

875 **The connoisseur.** By Mr Town, critic, and
■ censor-general. Printed for R. Baldwin, at the Rose in Pater-noster-Row. No. CXXXII. Thursday Aug. 5, 1756
*pp. 795–8 contains an account of a gentleman who kept low company . . . "but his greatest excellence is cricket-playing, in which he is reckoned as good a bat as either of the Bennets: and is at length arrived at the supreme dignity of being distinguished among his brethren of the wicket by the title of Long Robin"*

876 **Denison, William**
■ Cricket: sketches of the players. Simpkin, Marshall, [etc.], 1846. viii,76p. scores
*rptd. in nos 795, 873*

876 **Disney, John**
–1 The laws of gaming, wagers, horse-racing, and gaming-houses. London, J. Butterworth; Dublin, J. Cooke, 1816. xiii,132p.
*cricket pp. 61, 85*

877 **Epps, W.**
■ Cricket: a collection of all the grand matches of cricket, played in England, within twenty years; viz. from 1771 to 1791, never before published. Troy-Town Rochester, W. Epps, 1799. 104p. scores

877 **Geere, John**
–1 Serious considerations on plays, games,
■ and other fashionable diversions. Shewing the sinfulness, and dangerous tendency thereof. Guildford, printed for the Author, by Charles Martin . . ., 1763. 47p.
*cricket reference p. 24*

878 **Guest,** *Lady* **Charlotte Elizabeth**
■ Lady Charlotte Guest: extracts from her journal, 1833–1852; edited by the Earl of Bessborough. Murray, 1950. x,309p. illus. ports.
*cricket references*

878 **Hickey, William**
–1 Memoirs of William Hickey; edited by
■ Alfred Spencer. 4 vols. Hurst & Blackett, 1913–25. illus. ports.
*vol. 1 [1749–1775], pp. 99–106 includes an account of his arrangements to play for Eleven Gentlemen who had been educated at Westminster v. Eleven of Eton on Moulsey Hurst in 1768*

**879 Hurn, William**
Heath-Hill: a descriptive poem, in four
cantos. Printed for the author and sold by
W. Keymer, Colchester and G. Robinson,
London, 1777. [i],48p.
*five lines referring to cricketers, pp. 30–31*

**880 Jenyns, Soame**
■ The works . . . including . . . short
sketches . . . of the author's family, and
. . . his life, by Charles Nalson Cole.
Cadell, 1790. 4 vols. port.
*vol. 1 includes "The first epistle of the
second book of Horace, imitated . . . written
in the year 1748," which contains following
extract on p. 93*
*"England, when once of peace and wealth
possest*
*Began to think frugality a jest,*
*So grew polite: hence all her well-bred heirs*
*Gamesters and jockies turn'd, and cricket-
play'rs"*

**880 Johnson, Samuel**
**–1** The rambler. No. 30. Saturday June 30,
■ 1750
*". . . though as much as I delight in the
honest country folks, they do now and then
throw a pot of ale at my head, and sometimes
an unlucky boy will drive his cricket-ball full
in my face"*

**881 The microcosm;** edited by Gregory
■ Griffin [George Canning]
*6th Nov. 1786–30th July, 1787.*
*No. XXXIII, Monday 2nd July, 1787
contains article referring to cricket written by
Robert Smith, who signed himself "C".*

**882 Morrah, Patrick**
■ Alfred Mynn and the cricketers of his
time. Eyre & Spottiswoode, 1963. 224p.
illus. ports, scores, stats. bibliog.
——another ed. Sportsman's Book Club,
1965

**883 Nyren, John**
■ The young cricketer's tutor; comprising
full directions for playing . . . cricket; . . .
to which is added "The cricketers of my
time," or, Recollections of the most
famous, old players. The whole collected
and edited by Charles Cowden Clarke.
Effingham Wilson, 1833. 126p. frontis.
*for full entry and later eds. see no. 390*

**884 [Pope, Alexander]**
The Dunciad in four books, printed according to the complete copy found in the
year 1742. Printed for M. Cooper at the
Globe in Pater-noster-row, 1743
*book iv, lines 591–592 a derisive reference
to cricket "The Senator at cricket urge the
ball"*

**885 Priestcraft**, or the way to promotion: a
poem addressed to the inferior clergy of
England. Being wholesome advice, how
to behave at the approaching election.
Printed for J. Wilford, 1734. 10p.
*reference to cricket at Eton on p. 8*

**886 Pycroft, James**
■ Cricket: reminiscences of the old players
and observations on the young ones, by
the author of 'The cricket field'. [n.p.],
[1868]. 22p. port.

**887 Reeves, Boleyne,** *editor*
Colburn's kalendar of amusements in
town and country for 1840. H. Colburn,
1840. iv,356p. illus.
*scattered cricket references*

**888 Richardson,** *Sir* **Albert Edward**
■ Georgian England: a survey of social life,
trades, industries & art from 1700 to 1820.
Batsford, 1931. viii,202p. illus. (1 col.)
*cricket pp. 86–87 with illus.*

**889 Rosenwater, Irving**
■ The story of a cricket playbill. The
Author, 1968. [4]p. facsim.
*limited ed. of 25 copies only; refers to a
playbill "At the Theatre, Leeds, 12th June,
1780" which contained an allusion to the game
of cricket being played at that time in
Yorkshire*

**890 Sussex Archaeological Society**
■ Sussex archaeological collections, relating
to the history and antiquities of the
county: Vol. 28. Lewes, the Society, 1878
*"On the archaeology of Sussex cricket", by
the editor [Charles Francis Trower], pp.
59–82, with a lithograph of cottage at
Westhampnett where Lillywhite was born.*
——: Vol. 52. 1909
*"Extracts from John Baker's Horsham
diary", by Wilfrid Scawen Blunt, pp. 38–82
includes references to cricket c.1772–76*
——: Vol. 114. 1976
*"Cricket and the Sussex County by-election of
1741", by Timothy J. McCann, pp. 121–5*

**891 Sussex** notes and queries. Vol. 11.
■ 1946–47. Lewes, the Society, 1948
*p. 133 a note by H.J. Glover on the burial
at Chailey, in 1737, of one John Boots "killed
at Newick by running against another man in
crossing the wickets".*

**892 Taylor, Alfred Daniel**
■ Ireland's Gardens and its cricket associations. *Privately printed*, 1899. 36p. scores
*limited to 50 uncorrected proof copies*

**892 The torpedo,** a poem to the electrical eel.
**–1** Addressed to Mr John Hunter, surgeon:
and dedicated to the Right Honourable

"The Critics" by Lucien Davis from "Cricket" by A. G. Steel and the Hon.
R. H. Lyttelton (no. 473) *photo: M.C.C.*

Cricket grounds: Trent Bridge, Nottingham *photo: Keystone Press*

Cricket grounds: Fenner's, Cambridge, 1965 *photo: Patrick Eagar*

Lord Cholmondeley. Printed for Fielding and Walker, No. 20, Pater-Noster-Row, 1777. iv,17p.

*reference p. 14 to the Duke of Dorset, with footnote: "Every one knows the attachment of the Duke of D-rs-t to Cricket: the Following anecdote will prove it. Two Clergymen were candidates for a living in hs Grace's presentation, which he bestowed on the best Batsman."*

**892** **The town** and country magazine; or,
**–2** Universal repository of knowledge, instruction and entertainment. A. Hamilton

*vol. 8. Oct. 1776. p.513 "Histories of the Tête-à-Tête annexed, or Memoirs of the Noble Cricketer". Refers to John Frederick Sackville, 3rd Duke of Dorset*

**893** **Tuer, Andrew White,** *and* **Fagan, Charles Edward**
The first year of a silken reign (1837–8). Field & Tuer, 1887. xi,283p. illus. ports.

*cricket pp. 84, 173–75*

**894** **Turner, Thomas**
■ The diary of Thomas Turner of East Hoathly (1754–1765); edited by Florence Maris Turner (Mrs. Charles Lamb); with an introduction by J.B. Priestley. Lane, 1925. xxxi,112p.

*references to cricket in 1763 and 1764, pp. 77, 85*

——2nd ed. *with title:* The diary of a Georgian shopkeeper; a selection by R.W. Blencowe and W.A. Lower; edited with a new introduction by G.H. Jennings. O.U.P., 1979. 32;95p. 1 illus.

**895** **Waghorn, Henry Thomas,** *compiler*
■ Cricket scores, notes, &c., from 1730–1773 written as reported in the different newspapers; to which are added two poems, with remarks, published in 1773, on Kent v. Surrey, also rules of the game when betting was permitted. Edinburgh & London, Blackwood, 1899. xiv,126p. scores

**896** The dawn of cricket; edited by Lord
■ Harris. M.C.C., 1906. v,204p. scores, bibliog.

*bibliography "evidently a list of cricketical items to be found in the B.M." (Ashley-Cooper)*

**897** **[Wheeler, C.A.],** *editor*
■ Sportascrapiana: cricket and shooting . . . by celebrated sportsmen; with hitherto unpublished anecdotes of the nineteenth century . . . ; edited by Caw. Simpkin, Marshall, 1867. xvi,328p.

——2nd ed. *with title:* Sportascrapiana: facts in athletics. 1868. xvi,301p.

*reminiscences of E.H. Budd*

**898** **Wilson, George**
Reports of cases argued and adjudged in the King's Courts at Westminster. Vol. 1. Printed by A. Strahan for E. and R. Brooke, etc., 1799

*p. 220 in the case of Jeffreys v. Walter, 1748, judgement was given that cricket was a game within the meaning of the Act of 9 Anne and that a bond given as a collateral security for money won at it was void. (National Book League. Cricket: a catalogue of an exhibition)*

**898** **Wraxall,** *Sir* **Nathaniel William**
**–1** Historical memoirs of my own time . . . from 1772 . . . to 1784. 2 vols. T. Cadell & W. Davies. 1815

*vol. 1, p. 417: "The Prince [Frederick, Prince of Wales, son of George II] expired suddenly in the beginning of 1751 . . . His end was ultimately caused by an internal abscess, that had long been forming, in consequence of a blow which he received in the side from a cricket-ball, while he was engaged in playing at that game on the lawn at Cliefden House in Buckinghamshire . . ."*

**899** **[Wright, W.R.]**
■ A peep into the past, [by] W.R. Weir. Ayres, 1902. 3–23p. illus.

**900** ——, *and* **Craig, Albert**
■ The cradle of cricket: a Hambledon souvenir. Wright, [1908]. 15p. illus. port.
——2nd ed. 1909. with additional illus.

# 1846–1894

**900** **Association of Cricket Statisticians,**
**–1** *compilers*
■ First class cricket matches 1864–1866. Haughton Mill (Notts.), the Assoc., 1979. 159p. scores

*the first of a series which aims to publish the scores of every first class match before 1900*

**901** **Athlete's** diary for 1883: directory of athletic sports and pastimes. 1883. 204p. stats.

*cricket records pp. 23–86*

**901** **Bailey, Peter**
**–1** Leisure and class in Victorian England:
■ rational recreation and the contest for control 1830–1885. London, Routledge & Kegan Paul; Toronto & Buffalo, Univ. of Toronto P., 1978. x,260p.

*cricket pp. 128–9, 137, 144–5, 199n. 12, 215n. 18, 19*

*note 19 on p. 215 reads: "The claims made for cricket were many and remarkable, but one in particular I find irresistable; it comes from Thomas Hughes, reporting a letter from an officer in the engineers before Sebastopol: 'The round shot which were ever coming at him*

*were very much like cricket balls from a moder-
ately swift bowler; he could judge them quite
accurately, and by just turning round when
the gun which bore on him was fired, and
marking the first pitch of the shot, he could
tell whether to move or not, and so got on
with his work very comfortably' ".* This first
appeared in Physical education, Working
Men's College magazine, *May 1859*

901   **Bax, Clifford**
–2    Members only. 8p.
■     *offprint from The New English Review,
      Sept. 1946, pp. 283–90; cricket in England
      1884 including the visit of the Australians*

902   **Bayly, W.**
■     The cricket chronicle for the season 1863:
      a record of matches played in 1863. A.H.
      Bailey, 1863. v,513p. scores
      *the only issue although covers are variously
      dated 1863 and 1864*

903   **Daft, Richard**
■     Kings of cricket: reminiscences and anec-
      dotes with hints on the game. Bristol,
      Arrowsmith; London, Simpkin, Marshall,
      [1893]. xiv,274p. illus. ports. scores
      ——subscribers' ed. of 150 copies. Bolton,
      Tillotson, 1893. xiv,274p.
      see also *no. 818*

904   **Gibson, Alfred**
■     County cricket championship, with an
      appendix on the selection of an England
      eleven by "Rover" (Alfred Gibson).
      Mentz, Kenner & Gelberg, 1895. xi,148p.
      stats.
      *covers 1873–94*
      ——*2nd ed. 1896*

905   **Glover, William**
■     The memoirs of a Cambridge chorister. 2
      vols. Hurst & Blackett, 1885
      *references to mid-19th century cricket in
      chs. xxvii-xxix, pp. 150–171*

906   Reminiscences   of   half   a   century.
■     Reminton, 1889. [2], xvi,360p.
      *contains recollections of mid-19th century
      cricket*

906   **Haley, Bruce**
–1    The healthy body and Victorian culture.
■     Cambridge (Mass.); London, Harvard
      Univ. P., 1978. ix,296p.
      *cricket pp. 124, 125–7, 132, 157, 161–79,
      209, 210, 220–3, 228, 229, 230, 237, 238,
      244, 257–9*

907   **Holmes, Robert Stratten**
■     The county cricket championship, 1873 to
      1896. Bristol, Arrowsmith, [1897]. 168p.
      stats. (Arrowsmith's Bristol Library)

907   **Kellett, Ernest Edward**
–1    As I remember. Gollancz, 1936. 400p.
■     illus. port.
      *cricket pp. 272, 273, 297; 298–9, 301, 302,
      303–6*

907   **Mandle, William Frederick**
–2    Games people played: cricket and football
      in England and Victoria in the late nine-
      teenth century. Melbourne, Univ. of
      Melbourne P., [1973?]. [28]p.
      *off-print from Historical Studies, vol. 15,
      no. 60, April, 1973, pp. 511–38*

908   **Payne, John Bertram,** *compiler*
■     Scores and analyses 1864–1881: a collec-
      tion. Harrogate, J. Hodgson, 1904. iii,64p.
      scores
      *limited to 100 copies. Contains 60 matches
      not recorded in Wisden*

908   **Phillips, Janet,** *and* **Peter**
–1    Victorians home and away. Croom Helm,
■     1978. [ii],220p. illus. ports.
      *cricket pp. 123–4, 151, 174, 192*

909   **[Pycroft, James]**
■     Cricketana. By the author of "The cricket
      field". Longmans, 1865. vi,238p. ports.
      ——*reissue. 1865*
      *originally publd. as series of papers to
      "London Society" 1863–4*

910   **Ranjitsinhji, Kumar Shri**
■     The jubilee book of cricket. Edinburgh &
      London, Blackwood, 1897. xvi,465p. illus.
      ports. plans, stats.
      *for full entry see no. 467*

911   **Read, Walter William**
■     Annals of cricket: a record of the game
      compiled from authentic sources and my
      own experiences during the last twenty-
      three years. S. Low, 1896. 268p. illus.
      port. map, scores, stats.
      ——de luxe ed. of 250 copies signed and
      numbered. 1896
      ——*2nd ed. 1896. 280p.*
      ——*3rd ed. 1897. [ii],284p.*

912   **"A Spectator Esq.",** *pseud.*
■     A digest of cricketing facts and feats
      appertaining to the year 1862, to which
      are added two new songs from the note-
      book of "Bat", also the laws of cricket as
      recently revised by the Marylebone Club.
      F. Platts, 1863. [iv],62p. frontis. scores,
      stats.

913   **Steel, Allan Gibson,** *and* **Lyttelton,** *Hon.*
■     **Robert Henry**
      Cricket; with contributions by A. Lang,
      W.G. Grace, R.A.H. Mitchell, and F.
      Gale. Longmans, 1888. xiii,429p. illus.

diagrs. (The Badminton Library of Sports and Pastimes)
*for full entry see no. 473*

**914** **Thorp, Richard Clarke,** *compiler*
■ Cricket: the full scores of all the All-England, United, county, and first-class eleven a side matches played in the season 1862. Barnsley, T. Lingard, 1862. 88p. scores

**915** **Walmsley, E.**
■ Cricket celebrities of 1890 with a complete resumé of the season's doings. Manchester & London, Heywood, 1890. xvii,76p. ports. stats.

**916** **[Wanostrocht, Nicholas]?**
A succinct account of the Eleven of England, selected to contend in the great cricket matches of the north, for the year 1847. [Baily, 1847]. bs.

**917** **[Wanostrocht, Nicholas]**
The doings of the eleven, being a true full and particular account of the campaigne of 1851 and 1852. Wherein will be found an enigmatical chart of the Gentlemen and Players thereto attached; a geographical account of the places wherein the cricketing battles were fought; and a topographical account of those very same battles. The whole interspersed with anecdotes gleaned by the way side: incursions, excursions, accidents and offences. London: Published by Much Loss & Co. Read by Many Less & Co. Bailey Brothers, Cornhill.
*scrapbook and MS in 2 vols. in M.C.C. Library at Lord's*

**918** **Watson, Alfred Edward Thomas,** *editor*
■ The year's sport: a review of British sports and pastimes for the year 1885. Longmans, Green, 1886. vii,549p. scores, stats.
*"Cricket" by F. Gale, pp. 113–199*

**918** **Young, George Malcolm,** *editor*
**–1** Early Victorian England 1830–1865. 2
■ vols. Oxford Univ. P., 1934. illus. facsims.
*cricket vol. 1. pp. 46, 237–8, 266–7, 269, 273–9, and errata slip*

## 1895–1919

**919** **Aflalo, Frederick George,** *editor*
■ The cost of sport, by the Earl of Coventry, [and others]. Murray, 1899. xiv,364p.
*cricket by W.J. Ford, pp. 271–277*

**920** **Ashley-Cooper, Frederick Samuel**
■ Feats, facts and figures. Merritt & Hatcher, *for private circulation.* stats.

——of 1899. [1899]. 51p. 20 copies only
——of 1901. 1902. [vi],60p. 30 copies only
——of 1902. [1903]. [viii],52p. 30 copies only
——of 1903. 1904. [v],51p. 30 copies only
——of 1904. 1905. [v],63p. 30 copies only
——of 1906. 1906. [vi],76p. 30 copies only
*reprinted from "Cricket"*
——of 1912, 1913, 1914—unpublished MSS at M.C.C. Library, Lord's

**921** Noteworthy events of 1905. Merritt & Hatcher, *for private circulation,* 1906. [v],36p. stats.
*limited ed. of 30 copies*

**921** **The Cricket Society**
**–1** First class matches outside the Championship (1895–1914). The Society, [c.1955]. 11p. *typescript*
*list of matches alphabetically by name of team*

**921** **The Daily News**
**–2** The wonderful year 1909: an illustrated record of notable achievements and events. London & Manchester, The Daily News, 1909. 174p. illus. ports.
*cricket pp. 118–25, including portraits of the Australian team in England and Kent the champion county*

**922** **Dobbs, Brian**
■ Edwardians at play: sport 1890–1914. Pelham Books, 1973. 186p. illus. ports.
*ch. 4—"The golden age of cricket?"*

**923** **English** cricket records [of 1912]. Mansfield & Co., [1913]. 31p. stats.
*17 parts: 1. Marylebone. 2. Yorkshire. 3. Northamptonshire. 4. Kent. 5. Lancashire. 6. Middlesex. 7. Hampshire. 8. Surrey. 9. Nottinghamshire. 10. Warwickshire. 11. Sussex. 12. Gloucestershire. 13. Derbyshire. 14. Leicestershire. 15. Somersetshire. 16. Essex. 17. Worcestershire*

**924** **[Entry cancelled]**

**925** **Lyttelton,** *Hon.* **Robert Henry**
■ Cricket. Duckworth, 1898. 124p.

**925** **Macqueen-Pope, Walter James**
**–1** Twenty shillings in the pound. Hutchinson, 1948. 414p. illus. ports.
*on English life 1890–1914; cricket pp. 67, 68, 281, 289–93 with portraits of W.G. Grace & Tom Hayward, f.p. 142, Lord Hawke f.p. 143*

**926** **Morgan, William Alphonse,** *compiler &*
■ *editor*
The "House" on sport, by members of the London Stock Exchange. 2 vols.

Aldershot, Gale & Polden, 1898–99. illus. ports.

> *vol. 1 includes 'Cricket in 1898' by Gregor MacGregor, and 'Cricket' by Charlie C. Clarke, pp. 89–107.*
>
> *vol. 2 includes 'Cricket, 1899' by C.J. Burnup, pp. 113–26*

927 **Morrah, Patrick**
■ The golden age of cricket. Eyre & Spottiswoode, 1967. 3–270p. illus. ports. scores, stats.
> *covers period 1895–1914*

928 **Nowell-Smith, Simon,** *editor*
■ Edwardian England 1901–1914. O.U.P., 1964. xxv,619p. illus. ports. facsims.
> *includes "Sport" by John Arlott, pp. 447–486*

929 **Roberts, Edward Lamplough**
■ Cricket in England, 1894–1939. E. Arnold, 1946. 248p. ports. stats.
> *a statistical record*

930 **Santall, Sydney,** *compiler*
■ Ten years of first class cricket in England (1894–1903): a complete record of batting, bowling, fielding, and wicket keeping during the last 10 years. Birmingham, White & Pike, 1904. 90p. illus. ports. stats.

931 **Standing, Percy Cross**
■ Cricket of to-day and yesterday. 2 vols. Edinburgh, Jack, 1902. illus. & ports. (some col.), scores, stats.
> *originally issued in 12 fortnightly parts; covers events in 1902 season*
——Subscription illustrated ed. with [additional] special articles by famous cricketers, including K.S. Ranjitsinhji, P.F. Warner, D.L.A. Jephson, Robert Abel and Wilfred Rhodes. 2 vols. Blackwood, Le Bas. [1902]
——*2nd issue.* 2 vols. Caxton Publishing Co. [1904]
> *contains the additional contributions as above with 16p. insert between pp. 180 and 181 of vol. II on County cricket in 1903 and on the M.C.C. team in Australia 1903–04*

932 **Swinstead, George Hillyard**
■ The new cricket: or, What's up with the game. [Daily News, 1914]. 16p. illus. port.

933 **"Tit-Bits"**
■ Monster cricket book about play and players, batting and bowling averages, fixtures, etc. Newnes, [1899]. 80p. ports. scores, stats.
> *account of 1898 season and fixtures for 1899*

934 **Trevor, Philip Christian William**
■ The problems of cricket. Sampson Low, 1907. vii,253p.
——cheap ed. 1908

935 **The year** 1912 illustrated. Headley Bros., 1913. 184p. illus.
> *"The cricket season and the Triangular Tests", pp. 155–162*

## 1920–1945

936 **Arlott, [Leslie Thomas] John,** *and others*
■ Wickets, tries and goals; reviews of play and players in modern cricket, rugby and soccer, by John Arlott, Wilfred Wooller and Maurice Edelston. Sampson Low, Marston, 1949. x,236p.
> *contains J. Arlott, "Wickets: great cricket and cricketers of two decades" [1926–1948], pp. 1–70. illus. ports.*

937 **Bird, K.G.**
■ West of England cricket: (a history of the wartime West of England XI and their record for the season of 1944). Gloucester, Minchin & Gibbs, [1945]. 40p. ports. stats.

938 **British Field Sports Society**
■ Athletic sports, games, etc.: principal results 1919–1939. Petworth, the Society, [1942]. 32p. (Prisoners of War Booklet no.3)
> *cricket p. 13*

938 **Chisholm, Alexander Hugh**
–1 The incredible year: an Australian sees Europe in "Adolf Hitler weather". Sydney, London, Angus & Robertson, 1944. xiii,239p. illus.
> *cricket in the year 1938, pp. 42–3, 48–9*

938 **The Cricket Society**
–2 Statistics 1919–1939: Derbyshire, Essex, Gloucestershire, Middlesex, Northamptonshire, Sussex, Yorkshire, New Zealanders. The Society, [c.1955]. [16]p.
■ typescript
> *batting and bowling averages*

939 ——————*Statistical Sub-Committee*
■ 1920— a season in statistical analysis. The Society, [1966]. [ii],42p. team port. stats.

940 **Hammond, Walter Reginald**
■ Cricket's secret history. S. Paul, [1952]. 191p. illus. ports.

941 **Hoskin, E.**
■ Shadows over the wicket: with the British Empire XI seasons 1940 to 1945. Gloucester, Jennings, 1946. 76p. illus. ports. stats.
> *all matches played in England*

942 **Inland Revenue.** *Board of*
■ Reports of tax cases. Volume XI, 1926–27.
H.M.S.O., 1928. v,840p.
  *pt. viii, pp. 625–56, no. 617—High Court*
  *of Justice (King's Bench Division) 4th March,*
  *1926: Court of Appeal—12th and 13th May,*
  *1926: House of Lords—4.5, 24th May, 1927.*
  *"Reed (H.M. Inspector of Taxes) v. Seymour"*
  *ruling on whether proceeds of a benefit*
  *match [to James Seymour, Kent C.C.C.] was*
  *assessable to Income Tax. Final ruling by*
  *House of Lords was that the proceeds were in*
  *the nature of a gift and not taxable*

942 **Jenkins, Alan C.**
–1 The Thirties. Heinemann, 1976. 240p.
■ illus. & ports. (some col.). bibliog.
  *cricket pp. 14, 144–6*

943 **Langford, Arthur William T.,** *and*
■ **Roberts, Edward Lamplough,** *compilers*
Who's who in county cricket 1937.
Birmingham, Hudson, [1937]. 37p. stats.
  *a statistical record*

943 **Laver, James,** *compiler*
–1 Between the wars. Vista Books, 1961.
240p. illus. & ports. (some col.), bibliog.
  *cricket pp.32–9*

943 **The Lonsdale** book of sporting records.
–2 Seeley Service, 1937. xvi,458p. illus.
ports. diagrs. (Lonsdale Library)
  *contains pp. 93–9 "The cricket season*
  *1936" by D.R. Jardine*

944 **MacColl, René Marie**
A flying start: a memory of the nineteen
twenties. Cape, 1939. 304p.
  *ch. vi, "Our great national game"*

945 **Montgomery, John**
The twenties: an informal social history.
Allen & Unwin, 1957. 336p. illus. bibliog.
  *cricket pp.245–8*

946 **Powell, W.A.**
The future of cricket: the cause of its
decline. A suggested remedy. Romsey,
[the Author], 1937. 8p.

946 **Rayner, G.H.**
–1 After the golden age: some thoughts on
■ 60 years of cricket – especially Yorkshire
cricket – since 1919. [The Author], 1979.
[viii],63p. illus. ports.

947 **Roberts, Edward Lamplough**
■ Cricket in England, 1894–1939. E. Arnold,
1946. 248p. ports. stats.
  *a statistical record*

948 **Robertson-Glasgow, Raymond Charles**
■ Cricket prints: some batsmen and

bowlers, 1920–1940. Laurie, 1943. 192p.
frontis. (port.)
  ——*another ed.* Sportsman's Book Club,
  1951

949 More cricket prints: some batsmen and
■ bowlers, 1920–1945. Laurie, 1948. 143p.
frontis.

949 **The Saturday** book. 12th year; edited by
–1 John Hadfield. Hutchinson, 1952. 296p.
illus. & ports. (some col.)
  *includes pp. 247–57 "The Twenties – the*
  *golden age of sport" by Howard Marshall*

950 **[Sewell, Edward Humphrey Dalrymple]**
■ A searchlight on English cricket. Holden,
1926. 214p.
  *the game in 1926*

951 **Warner,** *Sir* **Pelham Francis**
■ Cricket reminiscences with some review
of the 1919 season. G. Richards, 1920.
239p. illus. ports. scores

952 Cricket between two wars. Chatto &
■ Windus, 1942. [vi],288p. illus. ports.
scores

# 1946–1979

953 **Andrews, Eamonn,** *and* **Mackay, Angus,**
■ *editors*
Sports report. Heinemann, 1954. 200p.
illus. ports.
  ——*another ed.* Sportsman's Book Club,
  1955
  *includes "Cricket across the world", by*
  *Crawford White, and "The cricket scene*
  *1948–53" by John Arlott*
  ——Sports report no. 2. Heinemann,
  1954. 192p. illus. ports.
  *includes "Roll on, Australia", by Alec*
  *Bedser, and "The British approach to sport"*
  *by John Arlott*

954 **Arlott, [Leslie Thomas] John**
■ Gone to the cricket. Longmans, Green,
1948. 206p. illus. ports. scores. stats.
  *1947 season including account of South*
  *Africans' tour*

955 Cricket journal. Heinemann, 1958. 255p.
■ illus. ports. scores
  *1958 season, including account of N.Z.*
  *tour*

956 Cricket journal—2. Heinemann, 1959.
■ 260p. illus. ports. scores, stats.
  *1959 season, including account of Indian*
  *tour*

957 Cricket journal—3: Cricket on trial.
■ Heinemann, 1960. 256p. illus. ports.
scores, stats.
*1960 season, including account of S.A. tour*

957 Cricket journal—4: The Australian chal-
–1 lenge. Heinemann, 1961. 238p. illus.
ports. scores
——*another ed.* Sportsman's Book Club,
1963
*includes 1961 season*

958 Vintage summer: 1947. Eyre & Spottis-
■ woode, 1967. 190p. illus. ports. scores,
stats.
——*another ed.* Sportsman's Book Club,
1968
*includes account of the South African v.
England Tests*

959 ————, *editor*
■ Cricket in the counties: studies of the
first-class counties in action. Saturn P.,
1950. 272p. ports. scores
*1949 season*

960 **Bailey, Trevor Edward**
■ Championship cricket: a review of county
cricket since 1945. Muller, 1961. 216p.
illus. ports.
——*another ed.* Sportsman's Book Club,
1962

961 **Batchelor, Denzil Stanley,** *and* **Surridge,**
■ **Stuart**
Denzil Batchelor discusses the future of
county cricket with Stuart Surridge.
Newman Neame, [1957]. 16p. illus. ports.
(Newman Neame Take Home Books)

962 **Burk, Frank**
New cricket. 1952
*unpublished MS in M.C.C. Library at
Lord's*

963 **Central Office of Information.** *Reference*
■ *Division*
Sport in Britain. H.M.S.O., 1972. [iv],
32p. illus. bibliog. (C.O.I. Reference
Pamphlet)
——*2nd ed. with title:* Sport and recreation in Britain. 1976. [iii],43p. illus. port.
bibliog.

964 **Cowdrey, Michael Colin**
■ Cricket today. Barker, 1961. 127p. illus.
port.

965 **Craven, Nico**
■ 9, 10, joker: a tale of cricket in 1972. West
Cumberland, the Author, 1973. 47p.
*a personal account of cricket in 1972*

966 A summer affair: 5th annual report from
■ 'Our man in Duckland' to vintage Gloucestershire ('73 was a good year!). The
Author, 1973. 43p. scores
*personal thoughts on the 1973 season*

966 The merry months: a game for all
–1 seasons. Seascale, [the Author, 1974].
■ 43p.
*sub-title on cover:* Who's for cricket 1974

966 The festive season: 'happy hours'. Seas-
–2 cale, the Author, [1976?]. 23p.
■ *subtitle on cover:* the year of the bat 1975

966 Best out of five: cricket with a chuckle.
–3 [Seascale, the Author, 1976]. 165p. 1 col.
■ illus.
*subtitle on cover:* game and match
1970–1974
*limited ed. of 500 copies. A selection from
his five diaries*

967 **Cricket Book Society**
■ The cricket season 1946: a statistical
review. Hunstanton, C.B.S., 1947. 48p.
scores, stats. (Publications. Ser. 1. no. 7)
*reissued in "Cricket omnibus 1946", edited
by Roy Webber. See no. 982*

968 The counties 1947. Hunstanton, C.B.S.,
■ 1947. 24p. stats. (Publications. Ser. 2. no.
7).
*reissued in "Cricket omnibus 1947", edited
by Roy Webber. See no. 982*

969 The 1947 cricket season. Hunstanton,
■ C.B.S., 1947. 36p. stats. (Publications,
Ser. 2, no. 8)
*reissued in "Cricket omnibus 1947", edited
by Roy Webber. See no. 982*

970 **Cricket 64:** Australian tour complete
■ report. A Flamingo Production, [1964].
[40]p. illus. stats.
*a record of the English season including the
Australian tour*

970 **The Cricketer**
–1 National census of English cricket. "The
Cricketer" Ltd., 1973. 29p. *typescript*

971 **Insole, Douglas John**
■ Cricket from the middle. Heinemann,
1960. x,190p. illus. ports.
——*another ed.* Sportsman's Book Club,
1961

972 **Johnston, Brian,** *and* **Shepherd, Bill,**
■ *compilers*
Cricket glossary '69: a comprehensive
guide to the cricket scene in 1969. Test &
County Cricket Board, 1969. diagrs. stats.
*averages for 1968, fixtures for 1969, with
laws and playing conditions for the County
Championship, the Gillette Cup, the Sunday
League and the Bass-Charrington trophy*

Cricket Grounds: Lord's, 18th July 1842 when "the relative merits of the fast and slow systems of bowling were tried by eight gentlemen and players with three bowlers on the new system and the same number with three slow bowlers". (Illustrated London News, 23/7/1842) *photo: BBC Hulton Picture Library*

Cricket grounds: the Oval in 1846, shortly following its completion, an engraving after the original oil painting by C. Rosenburg, Junr. *photo: BBC Hulton Picture Library*

# THE . . .
# CRICKETER

Edited by P. F. WARNER.

Published Weekly.

Vol. I. No. 1.    SATURDAY, APRIL 30th, 1921.    Price 6d.

## AN EDITORIAL FOREWORD.

The popularity of, and interest in, cricket, not only here, but in every part of the world where Englishmen are gathered together, was never greater than at the present time. Cricket, indeed, as Tom Brown has told us in the best of all school stories, is an institution and the *habeas corpus* of every boy of British birth, for it is a typically British game.

The Editor believes that there is room for such a paper as THE CRICKETER, which will endeavour to criticise justly and to comment fairly and accurately not only on first-class cricket, which, after all, is but a small part of our national game, but on Club, Services, and School cricket as well. The very essence of cricket is camaraderie and good sportsmanship, and the contributors to THE CRICKETER will strive to write in such a spirit, hoping thereby to spread an even greater love of cricket than exists at present, and, at the same time, to educate the general public in the finer points of the game.

THE CRICKETER will not confine itself entirely to English cricket, it is catholic in its aims and objects, and will deal with the game in our Overseas dominions; in fact, in every country where cricket is played. News from the outposts of the Empire will be specially welcomed, for it is hoped that the paper will become the recognised medium whereby all players and followers of the game may keep in touch with one another.

THE CRICKETER makes a special appeal to the boys who are now learning to play the game, in every sense of the phrase. Within its covers will be found instructive articles by famous cricketers whose names are household words, and who from their vast experience will impart knowledge that can be gained from no other source. Young batsmen, bowlers, and fieldsmen will all be considered, and it is hoped that the hints given in these pages will form a valuable adjunct to the general school coaching.

The Editor invites correspondence on any subject connected with cricket, and will gladly do his best to answer questions or to give advice on the game. He is naturally dependent for much information on the goodwill of club secretaries and other enthusiasts, and will always gladly receive suggestions for the benefit of either cricket or THE

CRICKETER. He feels that the first number of the paper has scarcely realised his ideal, but he hopes to do better in the future, confident that he will receive the help and sympathy of all lovers of the greatest of English games.

The contributors require but little introduction. Mr. MacLaren, who will make a special feature of School Cricket, is one of the greatest batsmen that ever lived. He captained England in no less than twenty-two Test matches, and his record in these great contests has been surpassed by few. He was also a most able captain, with a genius for placing the field and getting the best out of his bowlers. In any history of international cricket Mr. MacLaren will always have a foremost place.

Mr. Jessop was, in some sense, the greatest genius that cricket has produced, and of him it may well be said that he reduced rustic cricket to a science. He was the idol of every cricket ground, and many of his innings are historic. As a fieldsman at cover point he has had few, if any, equals.

Mr. Knight is one of the younger generation, but his batting in 1919 stamped him as a player of rare distinction and class, and as his chapter on batsmanship in the "Badminton Cricket" proved, he has the power of expressing his ideas on batting with no mean ability.

Mr. Altham, who was in the Repton, Oxford, and Hampshire XI.'s, has long been recognised as one of the greatest authorities on School Cricket, and his style of writing should satisfy even the most critical expert.

Mr. G. N. Foster, a fine batsman and a brilliant field, is one of the famous cricketing family, and Mr. F. B. Wilson, a former captain of the Cambridge XI., has a sound knowledge of the game, and a keen sense of humour with which to express his opinions.

The Editor considers himself fortunate in enlisting the co-operation of Mr. Charles Grave, the famous cartoonist, who makes such a speciality of sporting subjects. In each future number Mr. Grave will produce a full page cartoon of a famous cricketer, together with other sketches, and will also have the assistance of other well-known artists. No cricket paper would be complete without photographs, and each issue will be considerably indebted to the work of the camera.

The scores of the Test matches in Australia during the past winter, with critical comments on each, are included from the point of view of statistical record.

Cricket periodicals: the first page of the first issue of "The Cricketer" (no. 1199) *photo: M.C.C.*

973 **Kay, John**
■ Cuts and glances. Altrincham, Sherratt, 1948. 144p. illus. ports. scores, stats.
*account of 1947 season*

974 Ducks and hundreds. Altrincham, Sher-
■ ratt, 1949. ix,180p. illus. ports. scores, stats.
*account of 1948 season*

974 **Lewis, Tony (***i.e.* **Anthony Robert Lewis)**
–1 A summer of cricket. Pelham Books,
■ 1976. 179p. illus. scores
——*another ed.* Newton Abbot, Readers Union, 1976
*the 1975 English cricket season; includes Prudential Cup matches and the short Test series with the Australians*

974 **The Limited Overs Cricket Information**
–2 **Group**
■ A statistical survey of the 1979 cricket season. Sheffield, The Group, [1979?] [i],23p. stats.

974 **Moorhouse, Geoffrey**
–3 The best loved game: one summer of
■ English cricket. Hodder & Stoughton, 1979. 188p. scores
——*another ed.* Newton Abbot, Readers Union, 1979
*the 1978 season with accounts of games from many sections of English cricket*

975 **Nicholson, Geoffrey**
■ The professionals. Deutsch, 1964. 224p. illus. ports.
*chapter on cricket pp. 42–52*

976 **Oliver, Charles Morley,** *compiler*
■ English cricket form 1948: the complete record in first-class cricket of all players appearing in the 1948 season. Hunstanton, Cricket Book Society, 1949. 16p. stats. (Pamphlet no. 1)

977 **Political and Economic Planning**
■ The cricket industry. P.E.P., 1956. 14p.
*Vol. XXII, no. 401. Planning. 13th Aug., 1956, pp. 158–71*

977 **Rayner, G.H.**
–1 After the golden age: some thoughts on
■ 60 years of cricket–especially Yorkshire cricket—since 1919. [The Author], 1979. [viii],63p. illus. ports

978 **River, James,** *compiler and editor*
■ The sports book. Macdonald, 1946. 288p. illus.
*cricket section by Frank Chester, pp. 67–81*
——*2: Britain's prospects in the Olympic Games and in sport generally. Macdonald, 1948. 270p. illus.
*cricket section by W.E. Bowes, pp. 141–57*

——*3. Macdonald, 1949. 224p. illus.
*cricket section by D.R. Jardine, pp. 43–50*

979 **Swanton, Ernest William**
■ Cricket and the clock: a post-war commentary. Hodder and Stoughton, 1952. 256p. illus. scores
*covers 1946–51*

980 **Sutcliffe, Herbert**
■ English cricket—what's wrong and why! Harrow, Banks, 1951. 16p. port.

981 **The Times**
■ Cricket: a special report. The Times [Supplement]. June 21, 1973. 8p. incl. adverts. illus.

982 **Webber, Roy,** *editor*
■ Cricket omnibus. Hunstanton (Norfolk), Cricket Book Society.
*1946. 1946. various paging. scores, stats.
*a composite volume of five C.B.S. pamphlets*
*1947. [1948]. various paging. scores, stats.
*a composite volume of six C.B.S. pamphlets*

982 **Willis, Robert George Dylan ("Bob")**
–1 Diary of a cricket season. Pelham Books,
■ 1979. 157p. illus. team ports.
*the 1978 season*

983 **Wolfenden Committee on Sport**
■ Sport & the community: the report of the Wolfenden Committee on Sport. Central Council of Physical Recreation, 1960. vi,135p.
*scattered cricket references*

# CRICKET GROUNDS

984 **Meynell, Laurence Walter**
■ Famous cricket grounds: a brief history of some of the famous grounds in England; together with an account of their more notable games and incidents; & the celebrated personalities connected with them. Phoenix House, 1951. 255p. illus. ports. bibliog.

985 **Peebles, Ian [Alexander Ross]**
■ The Watney book of Test match grounds. Queen Anne P., 1967. 110p.
*in England*

986 **Yardley, Norman [Walter Dransfield],**
■ *and* **Kilburn, James Maurice**
Homes of sport: cricket. Garnett, 1952. xiv,193p. illus. map, plans (Homes of Sport)

## Birmingham: Edgbaston

987 **Birmingham Post**
■ Supplement in commemoration of

Edgbaston Test match. Birmingham, Birmingham Post, 30th May, 1957. viiip. illus. ports.

*issued in commemoration of the return of Test cricket to Edgbaston after 28 years (England v. West Indies)*

## Brighton: Ireland's Gardens

988 **Taylor, Alfred Daniel**
■ Ireland's Gardens and its cricket associations. *Privately printed*, 1899. 36p. scores
*limited to 50 uncorrected proof copies*

## Cambridge: Fenner's

989 **Cambridge School of Art**
■ Green and white—Fenner's observed; drawings and photographs of Fenner's, Cambridge, Cambridge School of Art, 1962. [32]p. illus.

## Chelmsford: The County Ground

990 **Craig, Albert**
■ The Essex County Ground. [All England Athletic Publishing Co.], 1899. 4p. illus.

## Hastings: Central Cricket Ground

991 **Ransom, W.J.**
■ Central Cricket Ground, Hastings: an address . . . at the Rotary Club, 12th May, 1933. [The Author, 1933]. 8p.

## Hove

991 **Hove 1938–39.** (In praise of Hove, by E.V.
–1 Lucas – Facts and figures, compiled by C.G. Browne). Hove, Hove Corporation, [1938]. 100p. plan
*cricket pp. 25–9*

992 **Sussex County Cricket Club**
■ Hove 1872–1972. Hove, the Club, 1972. 49p. illus. ports. scores. stats.
*issued to celebrate the centenary of the Hove cricket ground*

## Leeds: Headingley

992 **Dalby, Ken**
–1 Headingley Test cricket, 1899–1975.
■ Otley, Olicana Books, 1976. xi,158p. illus. ports. facsims. scores. stats.
*with full scores of all the Headingley Test matches*

993 **Marshall, John**
■ Headingley. Pelham Books, 1970, [x]. 145p. illus. ports. bibliog.
——*another ed.* Sportsman's Book Club, 1972

## London: Lords'
(*see also:* **M.C.C.**)

994 **Altham, Harry Surtees**
■ Lord's: speech delivered at the M.C.C. anniversary dinner, Wednesday, 6th May, 1964. 5p. *typescript*
*unpublished MS in M.C.C. Library at Lord's*

995 ——, *and* **Arlott, [Leslie Thomas]**
■ **John**
The pictorial history of Lord's and the M.C.C. Pitkin Pictorials Ltd., 1967. 24p. illus. ports. plans. (Pride of Britain)

996 **Benguria, Guillermo**
■ "Recalando en Londres". Buenos Aires, the Author, 1971. 99p. illus.
*"El cricket en Lord's," pp. 63–66*

997 **Dickens, William F.**
The origin and early history of the Philanthropic Institution. Marylebone Record, 1925. 12p. illus.
*reprinted from the Marylebone Record, 4th May, 1925. Contains references to Lord's, pp. 7–8*

998 **Douglas, James**
■ Adventures in London. Cassell, 1909 xv,415p. port.
*includes "Bushido at Lord's"*

999 **Doyle, Richard,** *illustrator*
■ Manners & customs of ye Englyshe, drawn from ye quick, by Richard Doyle; with extracts from Mr. Pips his diary by Percival Leigh. Bradbury, 1850. 98p. illus.
——*rptd.* London & Edinburgh, Foulis, 1911. viii,98p. illus. (The Cities Series)
*includes "A view of Mr. Lorde hys cryket grounde" pp. 35–36*

1000 **Eyre, Alan Montgomery**
St. John's Wood: its history, its houses, its haunts and its celebrities. Chapman & Hall, 1913. xii,312p. illus. ports. plans
*references to Lord's, pp. 94–106, and to Thomas Lord's house overlooking the ground, pp. 126, 129*

1001 **Fixtures** at Lord's. Motler Red Cap, 1955. 4p.

1002 **Gorham, Maurice Anthony Convens**
■ Londoners; with illustrations by Edward Ardizzone. Percival Marshall, 1951. vii, 158p. illus.
"Lord's", pp. 63–67

1002 **The Guardian**
–1 The bedside 'Guardian' 28: a selection
■ from The Guardian 1978–79; edited by W.L. Webb. Collins, 1979. 251p. illus.
*includes pp. 121–3 "Hot dog days at the Nursery End", by Frank Keating*

1003 **Harris, George Robert Canning Harris,**
■ *4th baron, and* **Ashley-Cooper, Frederick**
**Samuel**
Lord's and the M.C.C.: a cricket chronicle
of 137 years, based on official documents,
and published with the knowledge and
sanction of the Marylebone Cricket Club,
to commemorate the centenary of their
present ground. London & Counties
Press Association, 1914. xvi,314p. illus.
ports. plans, stats.
——*rptd*. H. Jenkins, 1920

1004 **Jones, James A.**
■ Wonderful London to-day. Long, 1934.
352p. illus.
*"A day at Lord's" pp. 90–96*

1005 **[Entry cancelled]**

1006 **[Lacey,** *Sir* **Francis Eden]**
■ Centenary of Lord's cricket ground,
1814–1914. M.C.C., [1914]. 40p. illus.
ports. scores

1007 **Lord's** Cricket Ground almanack. J. Day.
bs. *annual*
*?/1870,75/–?*
*compiler W. H. Knight*

1008 **Lucas, Edward Verrall**
■ London revisited; with . . . drawings . . .
by H.M. Livens. . . . Methuen, 1916.
xi,285p. illus. (some col.)
*ch. XI "The Oval", pp. 130–141; ch. XXI*
*"Lords", pp. 245–255*
——6th ed. rev. 1926. xi,247p.
*ch. XIII "Two cricket grounds", pp.*
*173–190*

1009 **Lynd, Robert**
It's a fine world: [essays]. Methuen, 1930.
viii,213p.
*includes "At Lord's"*

1010 **Mackenzie, Gordon**
■ Marylebone: great city north of Oxford
Street. Macmillan, 1972. 320p. illus.
maps, ports. bibliog.
*references to Lord's pp. 15, 18, 70, 141,*
*152, 156, 157, 298*

1011 **Marshall, John**
■ Lord's. Pelham, 1969. x,182p. illus. ports.
——*another ed*. Sportsman's Book Club,
1970

1012 **Marylebone Cricket Club**
■ Imperial cricket memorial at Lord's: an
appeal addressed to Members of the
M.C.C. [M.C.C.], 1952. 6p. illus. on cover
*appeal signed by W. Findlay, President,*
*and H.S. Altham, Treasurer*

1012 Lord's cricket ground – 1814–1964: fixture
–1 list and souvenir to commemorate the
■ one hundred and fiftieth anniversary of
the present ground. M.C.C., [1964]. [4]p.
fold. 1 col. illus.
*includes a list of matches played at Lord's*
*in 1814*

1013 Lord's Cricket Ground redevelopment
■ scheme. M.C.C., 1965. [ii],5p. 1 illus.
plan

1014 History of Lord's and the M.C.C. The
■ Club, 1961. [8]p. plan
——*another ed*. 1968

1015 **Nickolls, Louis Albert**
■ The crowning of Elizabeth II: a diary of
coronation year. Macdonald, 1953. 127p.
illus. ports.
*refers to Duke of Edinburgh's visit to East*
*Moseley C.C. and to Lord's to open the*
*Imperial Cricket Memorial Gallery*

1015 **Peebles, Ian Alexander Ross**
–1 Lord's, headquarters of cricket and of
■ M.C.C. Derby, English Life Publications,
1979. 24p. illus. (1 col.), ports. plan
——*cover-title*: Lord's: the official pictorial
souvenir

1016 **Rait Kerr, Diana Mary** *and* **Peebles, Ian**
■ Lord's 1946–1970. Harrap, 1971. 349p.
illus. ports. stats.

1017 **St. Marylebone Public Libraries**
■ **Committee**
Handlist to the Ashbridge Collection on
the history and topography of St. Maryle-
bone; compiled by Ann Cox-Johnson.
The Committee, 1959. [i],215p. *typescript*
*Items relating to Lord's and the M.C.C.*
*listed pp. 130–133*

1018 **Short, Ernest**
Back to the pavilion: recollections of
Lord's. *MS typescript*
*in the M.C.C. Library at Lord's*

1019 **Slatter, William H.**
■ Recollections of Lord's and the Marylebone Cricket Club, 1914. [The Author],
*n.d*. 32p. plan mounted on half-title

1020 **Taylor, Alfred Daniel**
■ Annals of Lord's and history of the
M.C.C. Bristol, Arrowsmith; London,
Simpkin, Marshall, [1903]. [vi],300p.
illus. ports. scores, stats.
——L.P. ed. 1903

1021 **Warner,** *Sir* **Pelham Francis**
■ Lord's, 1787–1945. Harrap, 1946. 324p.
illus. ports. scores. stats. bibliog.

——limited ed. of 150 numbered and signed copies. 1947
——L.P. ed. 1947
——*another ed.* Sportsman's Book Club, 1951
——rptd. White Lion Publishers, 1974

## London: Oval

1022 **Christian, Edmund Brown Viney**
■ The epic of the Oval. *Privately printed,* 1930. 36p.

1022 **[Knight, W.H.],** *compiler*
–1 Scraps of bygone cricket on the Oval; compiled by W.H.K. London, [1872]. single sheet folded

1023 **Lucas, Edward Verrall**
■ London revisited; with . . . drawings . . . by H.M. Livens . . . Methuen, 1916. xi,285p. illus. (some col.)
  *ch. XI "The Oval", pp. 130–141; ch. XXI "Lords", pp. 245–255*
——6th ed. rev. 1926. xi,247p.
  *ch. XIII "Two cricket grounds", pp. 173–190*

1024 **Palgrave, Louis**
■ The story of the Oval and the history of Surrey cricket 1902 to 1948. Birmingham, Cornish, 1949. [viii],215p. illus. ports. scores

## Manchester: Old Trafford

1025 **Lancashire County Cricket Club**
■ One hundred years of Old Trafford, 1857–1957. Manchester, the Club, 1957. 32p. illus.

1026 **Marshall, John**
■ Old Trafford. Pelham Books, 1971. 170p. illus. ports.
——*another ed.* Sportsman's Book Club, 1973

## Nottingham: Trent Bridge

1027 **Lucas, Edward Verrall,** *editor*
■ A hundred years of Trent Bridge.

Nottingham, *privately printed* for Sir Julien Cahn, 1938. xi,80p. illus. (1 col.), ports.

1027 **Mellors, Robert**
–1 West Bridgford: then and now, including Trent Bridge, the cricket ground, &c. Nottingham, J. & H. Bell, 1914. 66p. illus. ("Then and Now")

1027 **Nottinghamshire County Cricket Club**
–2 A Silver Jubilee tribute to Her Majesty the Queen marking the Queen's visit to Trent Bridge, July 28, 1977. Nottingham, the Club, 1977. 28p. incl. adverts. illus. scores

1027 **Trent Bridge** journal. Nottingham,
–3 printed by R. Milward & Sons
   No. 1. June 1963. 12p. illus. scores (of matches played in May)
   No. 2. Nov.? 1963. 10p. *typescript.* (news items only)
   *no more issued?*

1027 **Trent Bridge** monthly. Nottingham,
–4 Lawson & Bowles/Notts. C.C.C. *tabloid format*
   1979 *to date;* published in May, June, July, August

## Richmond: Old Deer Park

1028 **Old Deer Park**: [being a history of the
■ royal and ancient park, and of the well-known sporting clubs associated with it]. Richmond, Richmond C.C., [1951]. 47p. illus. ports. map

## Sheffield: Bramall Lane

1029 **Farnsworth, Keith**
■ The story of cricket at Bramall Lane: end of an era 1855–1973. [Leeds, Yorkshire C.C.C.], 1973. 60p. illus. ports. scores, stats.

1030 **Marston, Charles Montague**
■ Bramall Lane 1855 to 1955. Sheffield, Sheffield United C.C., 1955. 49p. illus. ports. scores

# ANNUALS AND PERIODICALS

## ANNUALS

1031 **Almanack** of sport. Low, Marston;
■ Purnell
   *1966; ed. by Charles Harvey. [xvi],*
*A128,624p. illus. ports. map, plans. stats.*
   *contains calendar of sporting events for*
*1966, brief biographies of great cricketers,*
*records, etc.; the only issue*

1032 **Angus, J. Keith,** *editor*
■ The sportsman's year-book for 1880:
containing a digest of information relating to the origin and present position of
British sports, games and pastimes.
Cassell, Petter, Galpin, [1880]. 272p.
   *cricket pp. 143–69; the only issue*

1033 **"The athlete".** An almanack and record
□ of all athletic sports; edited by H.F. Wilkinson. Virtue & Co.
   *cover-title:* "The athlete" and athletic
almanack
   *?/1869, 1871/–?*
   *not published 1870. 1871 issue with*
*x,240p.*
   *record of athletic meetings of various clubs*
*including cricket clubs; most meetings include*
*'Throwing the cricket ball'*

1034 **The athletic news**
■ Cricket annual. London & Manchester,
Athletic News. ports. (in v.y.) scores,
stats.
   *1888–1902*
   *1903–14, 1919–24; ed. by "Tityrus", [i.e.*
*J.A.H. Catton]*
   *1925–39, 1946; ed. by Ivan Sharpe*
   *1946 with title: Cricket and golf annual.*
*illus. ports.*
   *contd. as: Sunday Chronicle cricket and*
*golf annual*

1035 **Ayres'** cricket companion: how to bat,
■ bowl and field. F.H. Ayres. *annual.* illus.
ports. scores. stats.
   *1902–27; ed. by W.R. Weir*
   *1928–31; ed. by J.N. Pentelow*
   *without sub-title 1903–*
   *See article by E.D.R. Eagar in The crick-*
*eter annual 1960–61, p. 487*

1036 **Banks, James,** *compiler and editor*
■ Cricketers' handbook. Manchester, John
Heywood, 1865. xvi,45p. stats.
   ——— . . . for 1866. Manchester, "Cricketers News" Office, 1866. 184p. stats.
   *contain lists of all principal clubs in*
*England, Ireland & Scotland and record of*
*1864 and 1865 seasons*

1037 **Bristol Evening World**
■ Cricket annual. Bristol, Bristol Evening
World. illus. scores, stats. ports.
   *1947, 1948*
   *cover-title:* Pink 'Un cricket annual

1038 **Bussey's** cricketer's diary and
□ companion. G.G. Bussey. *annual.* stats.
   *1892–1916; 1923–31*

1039 **The cricket** annual 1892: edited by
■ William Dewar. Driffield, Fawcett;
London, Simpkin Marshall, [1892].
xv,310p. illus.
   *only issue; contains "Cricket as a sport" by*
*W.G. Grace*

1040 **The cricket** annual: by Roy Webber.
■ Dickens P., 192p. stats.
   *1961. [1961]*
   *1962. [1962]*
   *formerly: News Chronicle cricket annual;*
*contd. as: Playfair cricket annual*

1041 **The cricket** annual and calendar; edited
■ by H.V. Dorey. Cricket & Sports Publishers. stats.
   *1909, 1910*

1042 **The Cricket Book Society**
■ Cricket annual 1948. Hunstanton, C.B.S.,
1948. 96p. scores, stats.
   *only issue*

1043 **Cricket** chat: gleanings from "Cricket"
■ . . . : portraits and biographies of
eminent cricketers. "Cricket" Office.
ports. *annual*
   *1884–92, 1914 (2 issues by Archibald*
*Sinclair, May and July)*

1043 **Cricket** directory giving the names and
–1 addresses of secretaries of the counties,
the universities, the public schools, and
the principal clubs, leagues, and associations. Cricket P. *annual*
   *1889–1914*
   *1st publd. with title: The cricket and lawn*
*tennis clubs directory*

1044 **The cricket** handbook [edited by J.B.
■ Payne]. "Cricket Field" Office. *annual.*
ports. stats. (Pastime series)
   *3 issues 1893–95*

1045 **The cricket** handbook: facts, figures and
■ fun. John Leng. *annual.* illus. scores,
stats.
   *1902–12; from 1906 known as* Leng's
Cricket handbook

1046 **1973 cricket** handbook: the East Midlands
■ guide to county, club., junior & women's
cricket: edited by T. Frecknall.
Nottingham, T. Bailey Forman Ltd.,
[1973]. 176p. illus. ports. stats.
*covers Derbyshire, Leicestershire,
Lincolnshire, Notts. & Yorkshire*
*1974 with title: 'Evening Post' cricket
handbook*
*later issues?*

1047 **The cricket** spectator, including the up-
■ to-date edition of 'Our leading cricketers',
giving all their batting, bowling and
fielding averages for the past five years;
edited by P.F. Thomas. Walter Jenn.
*annual. illus. stats.*
*1927–31*
*a Ms. summary and index has been
compiled by Charles J. Britton*

1048 **Cricket** spotlight. Findon Publications.
■ *annual. illus. ports. scores, stats.*
*1948. [1948]. 64p.*
*1949. [1949]. 64p.*
*in 1950 incorporated with Findon's cricket
annual*

1049 **Cricket** spotlight; edited by Robert Baker.
■ *annual. illus. ports. scores, stats.*
*1957–71. Northampton, the Editor for the
English Schools Cricket Association*
*1972–76. Leicester, the Editor for the affili-
ated Counties and Youth Cricket Associations
and the English Schools' Cricket Association.
Final issue (20th) published at Market
Harborough, by Editor. 52p. incl. covers &
adverts. team ports. stats.*
*see also no. 1112–1*

1050 **Cricket** world; edited by Bill Frindall.
■ Gresham Publishing Group. *annual. illus.
(some col.), ports. stats.*
*1972, 1973, 1974*

1051 **The cricket** year book: for general refer-
■ ence in all matters relating to the game
for the year. *annual. ports. scores, stats.*
*1886 (two issues)–88 Manchester,
Heywood; London, C. Lillywhite*
*1889. Manchester, Heywood; London,
Wright & Co.*

1051 **The cricketer**
–1 Spring and winter annual. 1921–22 *to date*
■ *See no. 1199; from May 1974 with title*
The Cricketer International

1052 **The cricketer's** almanack, for the year
■ 1864, being bissextile or leap year, and
the 28th of the reign of Her Majesty
Queen Victoria, containing the laws of
cricket, as revised by the Marylebone
Club; the first appearance at Lord's and
number of runs obtained by many cricke-

ting celebrities; scores of 100 and
upwards, from 1850 to 1863; extraordinary matches; all the matches played
between the Gentlemen and Players, and
the All England and United Elevens, with
full and accurate scores taken from
authentic sources; etc., etc. John Wisden,
1864. scores, stats.
*1864 to date. (2 issues appeared during the
years 1889–95, 1897–99, 1901–02)*
*1864–1878 rptd. facsimile, 1961*
*1870–1937 with title: John Wisden's crick-
eters' almanack*
*1938 to date with title: Wisden cricketers'
almanack*
*Publishers: 1864–67 John Wisden & Co.*
*1868 Wisden and Maynard*
*1869–1914 John Wisden & Co.*
*1915–37 John Wisden & Co. Ltd.*
*1938–43 J. Whitaker & Sons Ltd. for John
Wisden & Co. Ltd.*
*1944–78 Sporting Handbooks Ltd. for John
Wisden & Co. Ltd.*
*1979 Macdonald and Jane's for John
Wisden & Co. Ltd.*
*Editors: 1864–69 W.H. Crockford (?) &
W.H. Knight(?)*
*1870–79 W.H. Knight*
*1880–86 George H. West*
*1887–90 C.F. Pardon*
*1891–1925 S.H. Pardon*
*1926–33 C.S. Caine*
*1934–35 S.J. Southerton*
*1936–39 W.H. Brookes*
*1940–43 Haddon Whitaker*
*1944–51 Hubert Preston*
*1952 to date Norman Preston*
*Bibliography: "The bibliography of cricket"
by Alfred J. Gaston appeared in the issues of
1892, 1894, 1900 and 1923. A list of cricket
books in print appeared 1938–42 and again in
1950 with an additional list of titles to be
published during the year. From 1950–78 John
Arlott reviewed books published during the
previous year. 1979 carried a highly selective
review section.*
*for further details see article by L.E.S.
Gutteridge in Wisden 1963*

1053 ——**An index** to Wisden Cricketers'
■ Almanack 1864–1943, containing references to special articles, obituaries, tours,
etc., that cannot otherwise readily be
identified with any particular issue;
compiled by Rex Pogson. Sporting Handbooks, 1944. [vi],101p.

1054 ——**One hundred** not out 1850–1950: a
luncheon to mark the first centenary of
John Wisden & Co. Ltd . . . Cafe Royal,
London, 18 May 1950. Penshurst,
Wisden, [1950]. [8]p. incl. covers. 1 port.
*with historical notes on the Company and
on the Almanack*

1054 ——**Wisden** anthology 1864–1900; edited
-1 by Benny Green. Queen Anne's P.,
Macdonald and Jane's, 1979. [viii],975p.
scores, stats. (Wisden Cricket Library)

1055 [See no. 1126]

1056 **The cricketer's** handbook 1913. Hoare &
■ Son, [1913]. 16p. stats. (Cricket Press
Series)
*record of 1912 season & fixtures for 1913*

1057 **The cricketers'** register for 1833. No.
■ XXVIII. Vol. V. 32p. scores

1058 **"Cricket's"** year book. Cricket Office.
■ *annual. illus. ports. stats.*
*1897–1911*

1058 **The Critic** cricket guide. Hull, Critic P.,
-1 1892
*the only issue?*

1059 **Daily Chronicle**
■ Cricket guide: compiled by "Linesman".
Daily Chronicle, 1905. 99p. illus. ports.
stats.
*only issue, containing record of 1904 and
fixtures for 1905*

1060 **Daily Express**
■ Cricket annual. Daily Express, scores,
stats.
*1929*
*1930*
*records of 1928–29 with fixtures for
1929–30*

1061 **Daily Mail**
■ Cricket annual for 1908; compiled by
"Bluemantle"; illustrated by "Rip".
Amalgamated P., 1908. 112p. illus.
scores, stats.
*only issue*

1062 Cricket guide; edited by Alex Bannister.
■ Associated Newspapers. *annual.* scores,
stats.
*1958. [1958]. 48p.*
*1959. [1959]. 56p.*

1063 **Daily News**
■ Cricket and tennis annual; edited by
Frank Thorogood. The Daily News Ltd.
scores, stats.
*1921–26*
*formerly: The Daily News and Leader
cricket annual; cont. as: Daily News cricket
annual*

1064 Cricket annual; edited by Frank Thoro-
■ good. Daily News. *annual.* scores, stats.
*1927–30*
*formerly: Daily News cricket and tennis
annual; contd. as: News Chronicle cricket
annual*

1065 **The Daily News and Leader**
■ Cricket annual; edited by Alfred Gibson.
The Daily News and Leader. *annual.*
ports. stats.
*1912–14*
*formerly: Morning Leader cricket annual;
cont. as: Daily News cricket and tennis
annual*

1066 **Daily Worker**
■ Cricket handbook; edited by A.A.
Thomas. Peoples Press Printing Society.
*annual. illus. ports. scores, stats.*
*3 issues 1948–50*

1067 **Day, Cedric,** *and* **Mason, Michael,** *editors*
■ The Day and Mason cricket annual. illus.
ports. stats.
*1949–50. Windsor, Day & Mason*
*1951–53. Windsor, Day, Mason & Ford*

1068 **Denison, William**
■ The cricketer's companion, containing
the scores of all the grand and principal
matches of cricket, played at Lord's and
other grounds in the season 1843. W.
Clement, [1844]. [2],iv,54p. illus. scores,
stats.
——2nd ed., *i.e. 2nd issue with laws as
altered 3rd June, 1844.* Clement, [1844].
[2],iv,62p.
——[Season 1844]. Sherwood, [1845].
xii,124p. (p. 124 misnumbered p. 133]
—— ——*2nd issue with laws as altered
2nd June, 1845.* Sherwood, [1845].
xii,124p.
——[Season 1845]. Simpkin, Marshall,
[1846]. xvi,100p.
——[Season 1846]. Simpkin, Marshall,
[1847]. xxviii,108p.
*for more detailed bibliographical details see
Cricket Quarterly, vol. 1, no. 4, Oct., 1963,
pp. 190–91*

1069 **The Empire** cricket annual: cricket
stories, sketches, fixtures and records;
[compiled by Rip!]. Gee, on behalf of St.
Dunstan's Cricketers' Fund, 1924. 80p.
illus.

1070 **Evening News**
■ Cricket annual; compiled by "Umpire",
with sketches by Rip! Associated Newspapers. illus. stats.
*1897–1907*
*1897 issue has "Cricket" on cover,
"Kricket" on title-page*
*1900–1907 no mention of "Umpire"*
*1906, 1907 with title: Cricket and sporting
annual*

1071 Summer sports annual for 1922; compiled
■ by "The Twelfth Man" (of Sports Gossip).
Associated Newspapers, [1922]. 96p. incl.
adverts. ports. stats.

cricket pp. 13–28 (fixtures for 1922, leading averages for 1921)

1072 ■ **Feltham's** cricket directory for 1883; compiled by W. Feltham. Griffith & Farran, [1883]. 175p. scores, stats.
*only issue; contains addresses of clubs & records for 1882*

1073 ■ **Feltham's** cricketer; edited by George West. Virtue and Feltham. *annual.* frontis. scores
*1877, 1878*
*accounts of 1876 & 1877 seasons and fixtures*

1074 ■ **Findon's** cricket annual; compiled and edited by Matty Watson. Findon Publications. illus. ports. scores, stats.
*1947–50, post season*
*1950 with title: Cricket annual and spotlight*

1075 **Fitzgibbon's** sporting almanack: a comprehensive epitome of all sports. Fitzgibbon
*for 1900. 1900. 434p.*
*the only issue?*

1076 ■ **Five** years' averages of our leading cricketers: a comparison of the batting, bowling & fielding performances of all the foremost county cricketers since the war; compiled by "H.P.-T." [P.F. Thomas]. Walter Jenn. stats.
*(1919–23). 1924. 15p.*
*(1920–24). 1925. 15p.*
*(1921–25). 1926 with title: Our leading cricketers. 22p.*
*contd. as: The cricket spectator*

1077 ■ **"Flagstaff"** cricket annual; edited by Roy Lester. Flagstaff P. illus. ports. stats.
*1954–69*

1077 –1 **Gale, B.T.**
Gale's almanac for licensed victuallers and sporting men. Printed by Robson & Sons Ltd., 1892. 224p. incl. adverts. ports.
*cricket p. 148, 150–62; the only issue?*

1078 **Gauntlet's** cricketers' record, containing the full scores of all the great matches played during the season; with the averages of the players, together with a list of batsmen who have obtained 100 runs and over. Sevenoaks, Gauntlet. *annual.* scores, stats.
*season 1859, 1860*

1079 **Glance** guide to first class county cricket. Taunton, Barmcoat and Pearce. *annual*
*1892–4*
*a pennycard for recording results of first class county cricket*

1080 ■ **The Golden Penny**
Cricket album 1902: special photographic groups of the Australians and all the first-class counties: the story of each club illustrated. Golden Penny, [1902]. 28p. illus. ports.
——1903. [1903]. 28p. illus. ports.

1080 –1 ■ **Guardian** cricket annual. London and Essex Guardian Newspapers Ltd. stats.
*1948/1949/–?*
*2 issues only?*

1080 –2 □ **The Haig** village cricket annual. The Cricketer for John Haig & Co. illus. ports. scores, stats.
*1974–79*
*largely devoted to The Haig National Village Cricket Championship; 1974 issue edited by Tom Scanlan, 1975 onwards by Findlay Rae*

1081 ■ **The International** Cavaliers' cricket book; ed. by Ian Wooldridge, Purnell, 1969. 157p. illus. ports.
——1970 *with title:* The International Cavaliers' world of cricket; ed. by Ian Wooldridge and Ted Dexter. 1970. 142p. illus. ports. (World of Sport Library)
——1971:——; ed. by Ian Wooldridge. 93p. illus. ports. (World of Sport Library)

1081 –1 **Invincible** cricket guide. Swansea, 1895
*the only issue?*

1082 ■ **John Player** cricket yearbook; edited by Trevor Bailey. Queen Anne P. illus & ports. (some col.). scores, stats.
*1973–76*
*contd. as: World of cricket*

1083 **The John Player** Sunday League annual; edited by Terry Harris, statistics by Bill Frindall. illus. ports. scores.
*1971. Wigston, Leicester, East Midland Press Services, [1971]*
*1972. Sales Link Ltd., [1972]*
*1973. Sales Link Ltd., [1973]*

1084 ■ **John Wisden's** cricketers' note book; edited by F.S. Ashley-Cooper. Wisden. *annual.*
*1900–13*
*a diary, with the Laws of cricket and miscellaneous records*

1085 **Kay's** cricket guide. Bradford, John A. Kay. *annual*
*1894. 128p.*
*1895. 128p.*
*1896. 64p.*

1086 □ **Lillywhite, Frederick,** *editor*
The young cricketer's guide, containing full directions for playing the noble and

manly game of cricket by William Lilly-white. To which is added the Laws of the game, with the latest alterations, and some brief remarks upon fifty of the most celebrated gentlemen and players in England. The whole collected and edited by Frederick Lillywhite, Junr. F. Lilly-white, [1849]. 32p.

——2nd ed., *i.e.* issue with inserted slip "Alteration of Law VII". [1849]

——3rd ed. [sic] *with title:* The guide to cricketers . . . by William and Frederick Lillywhite. W.&T. Piper, 1850. 72p. incl. adverts.

——4th ed. 1851. 84p. incl. adverts.

——5th ed. [1852]. 104p. incl. adverts. stats.

——6th ed. [1853]. 104p. incl. adverts. stats.

——7th ed. [1854]. Piper, Spence and Stephenson, 1854. 104p. incl. adverts.

——8th ed. Frederick Lillywhite. [1855]. 112p. incl. adverts. port. stats.

——9th ed. Lillywhite and Wisden, [1856]. 108p. incl. adverts. port. stats.

——10th ed. [1857]. 96p. incl. adverts. port. stats.

——11th ed. [1858]. 112p. incl. adverts. stats.

——12th ed. Fred. Lillywhite, [1859]. 120p. incl. adverts. stats.

——13th ed. [1860]. 120p. incl. adverts. stats.

——14th ed. [1860]. 116p. incl. adverts. stats.

—— ——*2nd issue* with an appendix for the Spring edition. [1861]. 124p. stats.

——16th ed. *i.e.* 15th ed. [1861]. 104p. stats.

*'Winter edition' on cover*

——16th ed. [1862]. 132p. incl. adverts. stats.

*'Spring edition' on cover*

——17th ed. [1862]. 128p. incl. adverts. stats.

*'Winter edition' on cover*

——18th ed. [1863]. 152p. incl. adverts. stats.

*'Spring edition' on cover*

——19th ed. [1864]. 104p. incl. adverts. stats.

——20th ed. W. Kent; Fred. Lillywhite, [1865]. [iv],124p. incl. adverts. stats.

——21st ed. Fred Lillywhite; W. Kent, 1865. 172p. incl. adverts. stats.

—— ——*2nd issue.* 1866. 172p. incl. adverts. stats.

——22nd ed. Fred. Lillywhite, 1866. 184p. incl. adverts. stats.

*all editions were edited by Frederick Lilly-white, junior; the work was subsequently incorporated with John Lillywhite's "Cricke-ter's companion", the 3rd issue of which, appearing 1867, is called 23rd ed.*

1087 **Lillywhite, James,** *publisher*
■ Cricketers' annual; edited by Charles W. Alcock. Lillywhite, Frowde. illus. ports. diagrs. scores. stats.
*1872–1900 (2 issues of 1872 vol.)*
*the 'Red Lillywhite'. From 1885 onwards incorporates John Lillywhite's Cricketer's companion*

1088 **Lillywhite, John,** *publisher*
■ Cricketer's companion. Lillywhite. scores, stats. *annual*
*1865–1885*
*the 3rd issue is called "Twenty-third edition" owing to its incorporation with "The young cricketer's guide".*
*1865–1879 publd. by John Lillywhite*
*1880–1882 by John and James Lillywhite*
*1883–1885 by James Lillywhite*
*titles vary slightly; The "Green Lilly-white"; after 1885 incorporated with James Lillywhite's Cricketers' annual*

1089 **The Lord's** and Oval annual; edited by
■ Robin Baily. John Smith, Lord's Book-stall, 1929. 16p. ports. stats.
——England v. Australia: special Test match edition. 1930. 16p. ports. scores

1089 **Moffatt, William,** *publisher*
–1 Moffatt's handbook and guide to football (association) and cricket, 1894–95. Moffatt & Paige, [1894]. 48p.

1090 **Morning Leader**
■ Cricket annual; edited by Alfred Gibson ("Rover"). Morning Leader. illus. ports. stats.
*1900–08*
*1909–11 with title:* Cricket and sports annual, edited by "Rover" and Captain Coe
*formerly: The Star and Leader cricket annual;* contd. as: *The Daily News and Leader cricket annual*

1091 **Myers, Arthur Wallis,** *editor*
The sportsman's year book. Newnes, 1904. 354p.
*only issue*

1092 **News Chronicle**
■ Cricket annual. News Chronicle. scores, stats.
*1931–39 ed. by Frank Thorogood*
*1946 ed. by Percy Rudd*
*1947–56 ed. by Crawford White*
*1957–60 ed. by Crawford White and Roy Webber*
*formerly: Daily News cricket annual;* contd. as: *The cricket annual compiled by Roy Webber*

1093 The 1948 cricket almanack; compiled by
■ Richard Edmonds. Douglas Beaton
[1948]. [32]p. scores, stats.
*1947 season and fixtures for 1948; the only
issue*

1094 Northern Daily Telegraph
□ Cricket annual. Blackburn, Northern
Daily Telegraph. ports. scores, stats.
*1906–15*

1095 Northern Echo
Cricket annual for 1905. Darlington,
Northern Echo, 1905. 116p. ports.
*only issue?*

1095 Peacock's polite repository, or pocket
–1 companion: containing an almanack . . .
■ and various other articles of useful information. London, printed for Peacock and
Bampten. illus. *annual*
*1812–73*
*issue for 1826, 120p., contains facing p.3
engraving of a cricket match and a reference
on p. 9.*

1095 Pelham cricket year: a chronological
–2 record of first-class cricket throughout the
■ world; edited by David Lemmon. Pelham
Books. illus. ports. scores, stats.
Oct. 1978 to Sept. 1979. 1979.

1096 The 1d cricket annual and calendar.
London, [1910]
*only issue*

1097 Personna year book of sports. Pelham
Books. illus. ports.
*No. 1, written & compiled by Robert
Martin. 1969
the only issue?*

1098 Playfair cricket annual
■ *1948–53; edited by Peter West. Playfair
Books. illus. ports. scores, stats.
1954–62; edited by Gordon Ross. Playfair
Books. illus. ports. scores, stats.
1963–73; edited by Gordon Ross. Dickens
P. illus. scores, stats.
1974 to date; edited by Gordon Ross.
Queen Anne P. stats.
formerly: The Cricket annual*

1098 Punch
–1 Punch's pocket book for 1869 . . . an
■ almanack . . . in two parts. Punch Office,
[1869]. [i], 1–140[i]141–192. folding col.
frontis. illus.
*frontis. is of a ladies' cricket match; pp.
141–3 "The ladies' cricket ground"*

1099 The Reporter
■ Cricket annual for 1910; edited by Olym-
pian. Ashton-under-Lyne, Reporter
Office, [1910]. [172]p. ports. stats.

*records of 1909, fixtures for 1910; the only
issue*

1100 Routledge's sporting annual; edited by
W. Sapte, junior. Routledge
*1882. 1881
1883. 1882*

1100 Saunders, Albert, *compiler and editor*
–1 The athletes' directory and handbook for
■ 1892. Saunders, 268p.
*cricket pp. 89–122; the only issue*

1101 Sheffield Telegraph
■ Cricket guide and annual: a club and
county chronicle: edited by "Looker-On".
Sheffield, Sheffield Telegraph. illus.
ports. stats.
*1904–06
includes all English first-class cricket
results*

1102 Spalding's cricket annual; edited by
■ "McW" [J.A. McWeeney]. British Sports
Publishing Co., ports. scores, stats. (Spalding's Athletic Library)
*5 issues 1907–1911; record of previous
season*

1103 [Entry cancelled]

1104 Sporting and athletic register 1908;
■ including the results for the year 1907 . . .
Chapman & Hall, [1908]. xvi,432,xii,212p.
*cricket pp. 87–149,432. scores, stats.*
——*second issue with title:* Sport and athletics in 1908: an annual register. 1908.
xviii,458,160p.
*cricket pp.104–68. scores, stats.*

1105 The sporting annual, or, The sportsman's
■ guide and athlete's companion for
1878–79; edited by R. Watson. Etherington, 1879. 150p. incl. adverts.
*sporting events of 1878: cricket pp. 48–58;
the only issue*

1105 The Sporting Chronicle annual: a book
–1 of records in every branch of sport.
"Sporting·Chronicle". illus. stats.
*1877–1896?
includes cricket*

1106 Sporting News
Annual 1956–57. W. Hill (Football) Ltd.,
1956. 128p. illus. ports.
*cricket by A. Smith and Peter May, pp.
50–53; the only issue?*

1107 Sporting Record
Sports handbook, 1949–50. Sporting
Record, 1949
*only issue?*

1108 ■ **Sports:** cricket, cycling, football; contributors: W. Brockwell, F.W. Shorland, "Forward", &c. Port Sunlight, Lever Brothers, [1895]. 156p. scores, stats. ("Sunlight" year books. 1895)
*cricket—"The game and how to play it" by William Brockwell, with records for 1894, pp. 11–87; the only issue*

1109 ■ **The Sports Argus**
Cricket annual. Birmingham, Birmingham Gazette Ltd. illus. ports. scores, stats. (of prev. yr.)
*1949 ed. by Lloyd Roberts*
*1950–67 ed. by R. Haynes*
*1968 ed. by Barry James*
*replaced in 1969 by "Cricket guide" issued as supplement to "The Sports Argus" of 19th April.*
*1973 with title: Cricket annual and summer sports special*

1109 **Sports form** guide. Macmillan.
-1 78; edited by Peter Grove. 1978. 240p.
■ illus. ports. stats.
*cricket pp. 37–43. 'Forecasts' of ten sports for 1978 & résumés of results since 1974*
*not published 1979*

1110 **Sports** review, by Louis T. Stanley. Macdonald. illus.
*1951. 191p.*
*month by month record of sport Sept. 1950–Aug. 1951*
*1952. 208p.*
*Sept. 1951–Aug. 1952*

1111 **The sportsman's** pocket book. Sportsman
□ Office. *annual*
*1876/1878, 1879, 1883/–?*

1112 **The sportsman's** year-book; edited by
■ C.S. Colman and A.H. Windsor. Lawrence & Bullen, 1899. 512p. scores, stats.
*review of 1898 season: cricket section by W.J. Ford. pp. 131–62; the only issue*

1112 **Spotlight** extra; edited by Robert Baker.
-1 Market Harborough, R. Baker, 1974.
■ ports. stats.
*review of 1973–74 tour of West Indies, biographies of 1974 Indian team; "career best" figures of county players in the three one-day competitions; one-day fixtures for 1974.*
*the only issue?; see also no. 1049*

1113 **The Staffordshire Sentinel**
□ Cricket annual. Hanley, Staffordshire Sentinel. ports. stats.
*1907–14; 1922–24*

1114 **Star and Leader**
■ Cricket manual; edited by Alfred Gibson.

Star and Morning Leader. *annual.* stats.
*1895–99*
contd. as: *Morning Leader. Cricket annual. 1900–08*
*Morning Leader. Cricket and sports annual 1909–11*
*Daily News and Leader. Cricket annual 1912–14*
*Daily News. Cricket and tennis annual 1921–26*
*Daily News. Cricket annual 1927–30*
*News Chronicle. Cricket annual 1931–39, 1946–60*
*The Cricket annual 1961–62*
*Playfair Cricket annual 1963–*

1115 **Sugg's** pocket cricket annual and advice
□ to young cricketers; edited by Frank & Walter Sugg. Liverpool, F. Sugg. ports. diagr. stats.
*1894–1905; titles vary*

1116 **The Sun**
□ The Sun's cricket comic. W.C. Hall, the Sun Office. *annual. illus.*
*1901: peing der remarks off Herr Teufels on der kame mit many funny drawings py Sol. 32p.*
*1902: with drawings by Sol and J.J. Proctor*

1117 **Sunday Chronicle**
■ Cricket and golf annual; edited by Ivan Sharpe. Manchester, Kemsley Newspapers. illus. ports.
*1947–54*
*1955, with title: Sunday Chronicle cricket annual. illus.*
*formerly: The Athletic News cricket and golf annual*

1118 **Sunday Pictorial**
■ Sports parade; edited by George Casey. Sunday Pictorial, [1950]. 160p. illus. ports.
*includes "Cricket cavalcade" by E.L. Roberts, and "These pampered batsmen" by C.F. Root: the only issue*

1119 **Sutcliffe, Herbert**
■ Herbert Sutcliffe's cricket annual 1947. Programme Publications Ltd., [1947]. 112p. illus. ports. scores, stats.
*only issue*

1120 **Test and County Cricket Board**
□ Cricket. The Board. illus. & ports. (some col.), stats.
*'72 to date*
*'72–'74 edited by J.A. Bailey and R.J. Roe*
*'75 to date edited by R.J. Roe*
*contains review of previous season*

1121 **The Topical Times**
□ Sporting annual. Topical Times. stats.
*?/1932–33 to 1939–40/*

1122 **[Trowsdale, T. Broadbent]**
■ Coverpoint's cricket annual: fact, fun and fiction from the cricket field, by the author of "The History of the Test matches", etc. Everett, 1905. 106p.
*only issue*

1123 **The Umpire**
■ Cricket companion. Manchester, the Umpire Publ. Co. *annual.* ports. stats.
*1906–14*

1124 **Vernon's** handbook, 1936–7. Liverpool, C. Tinling, 1936. 128p. illus.
*cricket pp. 101–105*

1125 **Washbrook, Cyril**
■ Cyril Washbrook's cricket annual 1949. Sportsguide Publications, [1949]. 145p. illus. ports. scores, stats.
*only issue*

1126 **Watson's** cricket diary and record. 1891
*in Taylor; the only issue?*

1127 **Webber, Roy,** *compiler*
■ Webber's cricket year book.
*1946–47. Hunstanton, R. Webber, [1947]. [132]p. scores, stats.*
*limited ed. of 100 copies*
*1947–48. Hunstanton, Cricket Book Society, 1949. 244p. scores, stats.*
*limted ed. of 250 copies*

1128 **The Weekly Dispatch**
■ Cricket annual 1904; illustrated by "Rip!" Manchester, Weekly Dispatch, [1904]. 101p. illus. scores, stats.
*only issue?*

1129 **Wm. Whittam's** modern cricket and other
■ sports; edited by G.T. Groves. Sheffield. scores, stats. *annual*
*1883–5. publd. by Whittam*
*1886. publd. by Groves & Son*
*contd. as: Cricket! W. Whittam's list of matches*

1130 **Whittam, William M.,** *compiler*
■ Cricket!: W. Whittam's list of matches. Sheffield, J. Whittam; Manchester, W. Whittam. scores, stats. *annual*
*1886–1898*
*formerly Wm. Whittam's modern cricket and other sports*

1131 **Windsors** cricket annual. Leeds, Wind-
■ sors (Sporting Investments) Ltd. ports. stats.
*1963*
*1964; edited by Ken J. Adams*

1131 **World of cricket**; edited by Trevor Bailey;
–1 compiled by Bill Frindall.
■ *1977. Queen Anne P. 222p. illus. ports.*

*1978. Macdonald & Jane's. 256p. illus. ports. scores, stats.*
*1979. Macdonald & Jane's. 255p. illus. ports. scores, stats.*
*formerly: John Player cricket yearbook (no. 1082)*

1132 **Yorkshire Post and Evening Post**
■ Cricket annual; edited by "Old Ebor". Leeds, Yorkshire Conservative Newspapers, 1906. 128p. team port. stats.
*only issue*

# JUNIOR ANNUALS AND ALBUMS

(*See also:* Sports for children)

1132 **Boycott, Geoffrey**
–1 Geoff Boycott cricket annual. IPC
■ Magazines
*1980. publd. 1979. 96p. incl. covers. illus. & ports. (some col.), diagrs. (A Fleetway Annual)*

1133 **The boy's** book of cricket; edited by
■ Patrick Pringle. Evans Bros. *annual.* col. frontis. illus. ports. scores
*1949–1954*

1133 **Boy's Own Paper**
–1 Boy's own companion; edited by Jack Cox. Lutterworth P. illus.
*No. 3. 1961. 192p.*
*pp. 44–5 "Goodnight sweet prince! being a soliloquy by Hamlet being given out LBW when playing for Denmark against a neighbouring state" by Robert Benson*
*Other vols. of this series which ran 1959–1966 and subsequently as Boy's own annual until 1971 also contain cricket articles*

1132 **The bumper** book for boys. Children's P.,
–2 [193–?]. [88]p. illus.
*contains [4]pp. "Getting the best out of cricket" by Norman Clark*

1133 **The Champion** annual for boys. Cham-
–3 pion (The Amalgamated Press Ltd.), 1947. 192p. illus.
*contains pp. 19–30 "His Highness Jimmy Smith", by Hugh Tempest*
*——1948. 1948. 192p. illus.*
*contains pp. 32–42 "Yorker sent down smashers" by Reg Wilson*

1134 **Compton, Denis Charles Scott,** *editor*
■ Every boy's book of sport for 1951. Clarke & Cockeran, 1950. 160p. illus. (some col.)

1135 **The Denis Compton** annual. illus. ports.
■ scores
*1951; edited by Leslie Compton. Mandeville Publications, 1950*

*1952–56; edited by Denis Compton.*
*S.Paul, [1951]*
*1957; edited by Denis Compton. Evans,*
*[1956]*

1136 **Dexter, Ted., i.e. Edward Ralph Dexter**
■ Tex Dexter's cricket book. Barker, 1963.
128p. illus.

1137 **Every** boy's book of sport for 1955. Guildford P., 1954. 152p. illus.
  *with six articles on cricket*

1138 **Glendenning, Raymond,** *compiler*
Raymond Glendenning's book of sport
for boys. *annual.* illus. ports.
——. Sportsguide Publications. 1949,
1950·
——, 1952–54. Sportsguide Publications,
1951–53
——, 1955–60. Dakers, [1954–59]
——, 1961. Spring Books, [1960]
——, 1962. Vernon Holding & Partners
[1962]

1139 **May, Peter [Barker Howard]**
■ Peter May's book of cricket. Cassell, 1956.
viii,119p. illus. ports. diagr.

1140 **News Chronicle**
Boys' book of all sports; edited by W.J.
Hicks. News Chronicle. illus. ports.
*annual*
  *1950–61*

1141 **Schools** summer sports annual 1951;
■ edited by Lionel Johnson. News Chronicle, [1951]. 104p. illus. diagrs. scores
  *only issue; cricket pp.59–104 by Charles*
  *Smeathers*

1142 **Parks, Jim,** *editor*
■ The book of cricket. S. Paul, 1962. 128p.
illus. ports.

1143 The Commonwealth book of cricket. S.
■ Paul, 1963. 128p. illus. ports. stats.
——No. 2. 1964. 128p. illus. ports. diagrs.
stats.
——No. 3. 1965. 128p. illus. ports.
  *contains an illustrated article on the Baer*
  *Collection of cricketana*

1144 **Routledge's** every boy's annual; edited
by E. Routledge. Routledge, 1863. 704p.
illus.
  *cricket pp. 251–6, 305–14, 371–8, 468–75,*
  *being "Hints on cricket" by the author of The*
  *Cricket Field, J. Pycroft*
——1867. 772p. illus.
  *includes "Notes on cricket", by An Old*
  *Boy, pp. 353–8, 427–32, 507–12; also serial-*
  *ised "Barford Bridge", by H.C. Adams*
——1868

1145 **Schoolboys'** album 1951. Swan, 1950.
128p. illus.

1146 **Sporting Record**
Sports thrills: Sporting Record junior
annual. Country and Sporting Publications, 1950. 96p. illus.
  *only issue?*

1146 **Strang, Herbert,** *editor*
–1 Herbert Strang's annual. Humphrey
Milford, Oxford Univ. P., illus. (some
col.)
  *1908–40*
  *in early 1920's changed title to:* The
  Oxford annual for boys. *Many issues*
  *contain cricket material e.g.*
  23rd year. [1930?]. 240p.
  *contains "Spikey's wicket", by J.C. Bristow*
  *Noble*
  26th year. [1933?]. 256p.
  *pp. 122–8 "Building the cricketer" by R.M.*
  *Lloyd*

1146 The crimson book for boys. Oxford Univ.
–2 P., [c.1918]. 304p. illus.
  *contains pp. 94–100 "Umpires I have met",*
  *by Walter Rhoades*

1147 **Trueman, Freddie, i.e. Frederick**
■ **Sewards Trueman**
Book of cricket. Pelham, 1964. 112p. illus.
ports.

# FIXTURES

1148 **Advisory County Cricket Committee**
□ Fixtures. Rothmans, for the Committee.
*annual*
  *?/1964–1968/*
  *contd. as: Test and County Cricket Board.*
  *Fixtures*

1149 **Aertex Ltd.**
□ Cricket fixtures. Aertex Ltd. [4]p. folded
card. *annual*
*?/1954,56/–?*

1149 **Arrowsmith's** cricket calendar. Bristol,
–1 Arrowsmith.
  *1887*
  *the only issue? Contains lists of fixtures*
  *in Bristol & neighbourhood, county teams,*
  *Challenge Cup rules, etc.*

1150 **Bailey, Thomas**
■ First-class cricket fixtures, 1908. Bailey,
[1908]. [8]p.

1151 **Billingham, Sidney,** *compiler*
■ A cricket handbook, containing a
programme for 1901; under each fixture
details of last year's match are given.

Remarkable performances are also included. Sun Office, 1901. 62p.
*varying cover titles*

1152 **The Bristol United Breweries,** *and* **The**
■ **Oakhill Brewery Co. Ltd.**
Fixtures 1950 and a few records: Gloucester, Somerset, West Indies. Bristol, The Bristol United Breweries & The Oakhill Brewery Co. Ltd., [1950]. [12]p.
see also *no. 1169*

1153 **Carreras**
■ Cricket notes. Carreras, 1900. 32p. incl. adverts. stats.
*fixtures for 1900, statistics for 1899*

1154 **County** (first class) cricket diary. Liverpool, Capleton. *annual*
*1892, 1893*

1155 **The cricket** calendar: a pocket annual
□ containing all the cricket fixtures for the ensuing season. Thomas Murby
*46 vols. 1869–1914*
*compilers: early issues, G. Kelly King*
*1879 C.W. Alcock*
*1891, 1892 P. Cross Standing*
*1893, 1894 (Anon.)*
*1895 Charles Plairre*
*1896 (Anon)*
*1897, 1898 H.L. Bourke*
*1899 J.N. Pentelow*
*1900, 1901 Sidney Billingham*
*1902 (Anon.)*
*1903, 1905, 1906 A. Sinclair*
*1907 (Anon.)*
*1908 "Penrunnon"*
*1909, 1910, 1911, 1912 (Anon.)*
*1913, 1914 A. Sinclair*

1156 **Cricket** fixture list, hints for cricketers and fielding chart. Surridge, 1957

1157 **The cricketers'** handy book: rules,
■ fixtures, &c. *Printed by* Cricket Press
*1912, 1913, 1920, 1922, published by Benetfink & Co. Ltd.*
*1914, 1919, 1921, published by Gamages*

1158 **The cricketers'** vade mecum for 1881.
■ Spalding (Lincs.), J.H. Saul; London, F. Southwell, [1881]. score
*fixtures and diary for 1881*

1159 **Dunn's**
Cricket fixtures. Sheffield, Dunn's Famous Hat Stores, 1895. 6p.

1160 **Elliman Sons**
■ Cricket fixtures for 1948: 1st class county, minor counties, public schools. Elliman Sons, 1948. 32p.

1161 **First** class fixture list. The Cricket P., 1934

1162 **Gillette Industries Ltd.**
■ India tour and first-class county cricket fixtures for 1946. Gillette Industries, [1946]. [26]p.

1163 Cricket fixtures 1947: South African tour,
■ first class & public schools. Gillette Industries, 1947. [48]p.

1164 **Imperial Tobacco Co.**
Cricket fixtures. Imperial Tobacco Co. *annual*
*?/1935–39/–?*

1165 **Marylebone Cricket Club**
The M.C.C. diary 1907. E.T.W. Dennis, by the authority of the M.C.C., 1907
*issued in cloth and leather*

1166 Matches at Lord's [and] Out matches.
□ M.C.C. *annual*
*1887?/1928 to date/*

1167 M.C.C. cricket diary. M.C.C. *annual*.
□ stats. diagr.
*1951–54. Naldrett P.*
*1955. Heinemann*
*1956–62. Playfair Books*
*1963 to date Collins*

1168 **M.C.C. Co. Ltd.**
Cricket fixtures. Bedford, M.C.C. Co. Ltd. *annual*
*?/1930–35/–?*

1169 **Oakhill Brewery Co. Ltd.**
■ Fixtures 1934: Somerset, Gloucestershire, Australia; laws of cricket and a few records. Oakhill (Som.), Oakhill Brewery Co. Ltd., [1934]. [16]p. inc. adverts.
see also *no. 1152*

1170 **Pioneer Catering Co.**
Cricket fixtures 1939. Pioneer Catering Co., 1939
*only issue?*

1170 **Smith & Sons (Tailors)**
–1 First class cricket fixtures, 1908. Smith &
■ Sons, [1908]. [8]p. illus. on covers.

1171 **Smith Meters Ltd.**
■ Cricket fixtures 1947: county and Test matches. [12]p. col. illus.
*only issue?*

1172 **Spalding**
List of cricket fixtures 1907. Spalding, [1907]
*only issue?*

1173 **The Sun**
■ County, &c., cricket fixtures. The Sun, [1897]. [4]p. folded card

*together with* Race fixtures *for 1897*
*only issue?*

1174 **Terry, Frederick, & Co.**
■ Cricket fixtures, 1910. Terry, [1910]. 8p.
*only issue?*

1175 **Test and County Cricket Board**
□ Fixtures. Rothmans, for the Board. *annual*
1969–1973
1974–1977 *with title* Test and county
cricket. John Player, for the Board
1978, 1979 *with title* Complete fixture
list for Test and county cricket. Cornhill
Insurance Group, for the Board.
*formerly:* Advisory County Cricket
Committee. Fixtures

1176 **The Times**
□ Cricket fixtures: first class and minor
counties from "The Times". "The Times"
Publishing Co. *annual*. stats.
*1951–1969?*

1177 **Wisden and Co. Ltd.**
■ Cricket fixtures for 1931. Wisden, 1931.
24p. incl. adverts. illus.
*only issue?*

## PERIODICALS

1178 **All England** cricket and football journal
■ and athletic review. Sheffield, M. Hurst;
London, A. Heywood. *monthly*. illus.
ports. scores, stats.
*29 issues April, 1877—Oct., 1879*

1179 **The Annals** of sporting and fancy gazette:
■ a magazine entirely appropriated to sporting subjects and fancy pursuits. Sherwood, Neely & Jones. *monthly*. illus.
(some col.), scores
*13 bi-annual vols. 1822–28. Vol. 1. no. 1.
1st Jan., 1822*

1179 **Arena**: incorporating university and
–1 public school life and amateur sport.
*monthly*
*19 issues Mar. 1912 – Sept. 1913*

1180 **Baily's** monthly magazine of sport and
□ pastimes
*vol. 1–50, 1860–88*
contd. as: Baily's magazine
*vol. 51–125 (no. 796), 1889–June, 1926*

1181 **Bat** and ball: a weekly journal.
Manchester
*5 issues 13th Sept. to 11th Oct., 1882*

1182 **Bat**, ball and wheel: a weekly journal
chiefly devoted to cricket. The Sportsman
*52 issues 5th May, 1898 to 27th Apr., 1899*

1182 **Boy's own paper**
–1 The best of British pluck: the Boy's Own
■ Paper revisited by Philip Warner.
Macdonald & Jane's, 1976. [vi],202p.
illus. ports.
*articles and illustrations from mainly pre-
1914 B.O.P. with linking chs. Cricket pp. 8,
9, 43–5, 94–5, 123–4, 141–2, 155–6, 158,
164*

1182 **The captain**: a magazine for boys and
–2 "old boys"; edited by The Old Fag.
□ Newnes. *monthly*. illus. & ports. (some
col.)
*50 vols. Vol. 1 Apl-Sept 1899–1924
includes cricket articles*

1182 **Chums**
–3 The best of Chums; edited by Philip
■ Warner. Cassell, 1978. 192p. illus. ports.
diagrs.
*a selection from "Chums" magazine.
Cricket excerpts pp. 146–60 "Between the
wickets", by Jack Hobbs; pp. 159–62 "Play
the game!" by J.W. Hearne; pp. 181–3 "The
final Test" by "Patsy" Hendren*

1183 **Cricket**: a weekly record of the game.
■ *weekly, Apr.-Sept., monthly, Oct.-Mar.*
*949 issues in 32 vols. (vols. 1–30; new
series, vols. 1–2); vol. 1, no. 1. 10th May,
1882 to 17th Dec., 1913; from 7 Oct.–23 Dec.
1911 the title changed to* Rugby Football and
Cricket
*editors: 1882–1907 C.W. Alcock
1907–1911 F.S. Ashley-Cooper
1911–1913 J.N. Pentelow
publishers: 1882–1894 W.R. Wright
1894–1912 Merritt & Hatcher
1912–1913 Cricket & Sports Publishers*
contd. as: The world of cricket. See no.
1215
——Index to the matches, 1905–11. 2
vols. Ms. compiled by F.S. Ashley-
Cooper

1184 **The cricket** and athletic gazette: a
monthly magazine devoted to the interests of cricket and other sports.
Feltham & Co.
*only one issue, May 1875. 24p.*

1185 **Cricket** and football field and sports telegram. Bolton
*Jan. 1888–1st May, 1915*
formerly: Football field and sports telegram
*20th Sept., 1884-Dec. 1887*

1186 **Cricket and football times.** Vols. I-IV,
1878–1881. *weekly*
*vol. 1. 27 issues 2nd May to 31st Oct.,
1878, 316p.
vol. II. 24 issues 7th Nov., 1878 to 17th
Apr., 1879. 247p.*

*vol. III. 26 issues 24th April to 16th Oct., 1879. 312p.*

*vol. IV, 26 issues 23rd Oct., 1879 to 15th Apr., 1880. 324p.*

*vol. V. 27 issues 22nd Apr. to 21st Oct., 1880. 324p.*

*vol. VI. 21 issues 28th Oct., 1880 to 17th Mar., 1881. 252p.*

*cricket statistics by H.V.L. Stanton*

1187 **Cricket** and football times. New series. Bolton, Tillotson. *weekly*
*1888–1905*
*in Taylor: formerly: Football times. 1884–1888*

1188 **Cricket** argus. Bradford
*no. 1, May 1909–21st Aug., 1926 (no. 647)*

1189 **Cricket** chronicle and herald. Bath
*no. 1–500, 9th May, 1925–19th Aug., 1939*

1190 **Cricket,** cycling and football chronicle. Grantham
*13th Aug.–5th Nov., 1895*
*formerly: Football chronicle, 2nd Sept., 1890–Dec. 1894*

1191 **The cricket** enthusiast: a friendly satire. Cricket Enthusiast. *weekly.* illus.
*7 issues 13th May to 24th June, 1922*

1192 **Cricket** extra: a weekly cricket magazine
■ available only through the County Clubs; edited by Bryan Ghent. Manchester, Sport & County Publications Ltd. *weekly during season.* illus. ports. stats.
*vol. 1, nos. 1–[15], 1966*
*no more published?*

1193 **The cricket** field: an illustrated record and
■ review; edited by A.W. Browne. *weekly in summer, monthly in winter.* illus. ports. scores, stats.
*4 vols. 7th May, 1892 to 21st Sept., 1895*
*publishers: May 1892–Sept. 1894. Pastime Office*
*Nov. 1894–Sept. 1895. Field Office*
*no issue for Oct. 1894*

1194 **Cricket** magazine; edited by M. Shuker
□ and R.N. Baker
*June 1968*
*July 1968. 20f. diagr. stats. typescript*
*for young readers, published in Hampshire?*

1194 **Cricket news:** a weekly review of the
–1 game; executive editor Peter Wynne-
■ Thomas; general editor Robert W. Brooke. Retford (Notts.), Cricket News. illus. ports. scores, stats. *weekly in summer, monthly in winter*
*Vol. 1, no. 1. Apr. 30, 1977 weekly to no.*

*20, Sept. 17, 1977; monthly no. 21, Oct. 1977 to no. 26, Mar. (Apr.) 1978, and Index to vol. 1, including errata and additional scores*
*Vol. 2, no. 1. Apr. 29, 1978 weekly to no. 20, Sept. 16, 1978; monthly no. 21, Oct. to no. 26, Mar. (Apr.) 1979, and index to vol. 2*
*Vol. 3, no. 1. Apr. 30, 1979 weekly to no. 4, May 29, 1979 (no issue May 22)*

1195 **The cricket** quarterly: a journal devoted
■ to the noble game of cricket; edited by Rowland Bowen. Eastbourne; [and from vol. VII] Mullion. illus. (some col.), ports. scores, stats.
*vols. I–VIII, 1963–70*
——Index, compiled by Michael Fordham. 11p. *typescript*

1196 **Cricket Society**
■ Journal. The Society. ½ *yearly.* illus. ports. scores, stats.
*Vol. 1, no. 1, Apr. 1961 to date*
*editors: Vol. I, no. 1 to Vol. II, no. 4, Irving Rosenwater (1961–65)*
*Vol. III, no. 1 to Vol. IV, no. 4, Cdr. H. Emmet (1965–70)*
*Vol. V, no. 1 to date, J.D. Coldham (1970–)*

1197 **The cricket** world: a weekly journal for cricketers. Premier Press
*10 issues, 20th May–22nd July, 1899*

1198 **The cricketer:** a weekly journal for the publication of cricket intelligence and other athletic sports; edited by G.M. White. Maurice Udloff
*only one issue 31st Dec., 1869*

1199 **The cricketer**
■ *Vol. 1, no. 1, April 30, 1921 to April, 1974*
*Vol. I weekly 30.4.21–24.9.21 and winter annual 1921–22*
*Vol. II weekly 6.5.22–23.9.22, Oct.*
*Vol. III annual 1922–23, monthly Dec.–Apr. 1923*
*Vol. IV weekly 12.5.23–8.9.23, Oct., annual 1923–24, monthly Dec.–Apr. 1924*
*Vol. V weekly 3.5.24–6.9.24, Oct., annual 1924–25, monthly Dec.–Apr. 1925*
*Vol. VI weekly 9.5.25–12.9.26, annual 1925–6*
*Vol. VII-XXII (1941) weekly May–Sept., spring & winter annuals*
*Vol. XXIII-XLIII (1962) fortnightly May–Sept., spring & winter annuals*
*(n.b. Vol. XL comprised only 8 'fortnightly' issues instead of 10 as owing to a general printing strike issues 6, 7 & 8 were merged into one issue, Aug. 22, 1959)*
*Vol. 44 monthly Feb.–Apr., spring ed., fortnightly May–Sept., Nov., winter ed., Jan. (1964)*

English Clubs: "A view of the Mary-le-Bone Club's cricket ground", published as the frontispiece to Nyren (no. 390) *photo: M.C.C.*

English Clubs: The founders of I Zingari (Sir Spencer Ponsonby-Fane, J. L. Baldwin and the Hon. F. Ponsonby, later Lord Bessborough) *photo: M.C.C.*

English clubs: Allahakbarries C.C. "An indispensable part of their luggage" drawn by E. T. Reed (no. 1296)

School cricket: A view of Harrow School with a game of cricket in progress, 1802 *photo: BBC Hulton Picture Library*

*Vol. 45 monthly Feb.–Apr., spring ed., fortnightly May–Sept., monthly Oct.–Dec.*

*Vol. 46 monthly Jan.–Apr., fortnightly May-Sept., monthly Oct.–Dec.*

*Vol. 47–50 (1969) spring annual, fortnightly May–Sept., annual 1967–68 (–1969–70)*

*Vol. 51 monthly Feb.–Nov. (annual), Dec.*

*Vol. 52 monthly Jan.–Dec. (Apr. Jubilee no. 1921–1971, Nov. winter annual)*

*Vol. 53–54 monthly Jan.–Dec. (Apr. spring annual, Nov. winter annual)*

*Vol. 55 monthly Jan.–Apr. (Apr. spring annual, 1974)*

*contd. as:* **The cricketer international**
*Vol. 55, no. 5 (May 1974) to date*
*editors: 1921–1962 (Vol. I, no. 1—Vol. XLIII, no. 10) P.F. Warner*
*1963–1964 (XLIII, no. 11—Vol. 45, no. 1) J. Warner, managing editor, P. Morris, editor*
*1964–1966 (Vol. 45, no. 2—Vol. 47, no. 14) J. Warner, business manager, A.W.T. Langford, editor*
*1967 to date (Vol. 47, no. 15—) E.W. Swanton, editorial director, with various assistant editors and from 1973 (vol. 54, no. 3) to July 1978 (Vol. 59, no. 7) D. Frith, editor Aug. 1978 to date, R.J. Hayter, editor.*
*from Vol. 54, no. 5, May 1973 incorporated "Playfair cricket monthly" and Gordon Ross appointed executive editor*
see also *no. 1206*

——Index to 'The cricketer" 1921–1960; compiled by H.A. Cohen. *In* The Journal of the Cricket Society

*Vol. 1, no. 1. pp. 53–64; no. 2. pp. 56–60*
*no. 3. pp. 57–64; no. 4. pp. 58–64*
*Vol. 2, no. 1. pp. 57–64; no. 2. pp. 61–72*
*no. 3. pp. 53–64; no. 4. pp. 62–64*
*Vol. 3, no. 2. pp. 63–64; no. 3. pp. 59–63*
*no. 4. pp. 61–64*
*Vol. 5, no. 2. 8pp.; no. 3. 8pp.; no. 4. 8pp.*
*Vol. 6, no. 1. 4pp.*

1200 **The cricketer** and football player: a
■ weekly journal of summer sports and winter pastimes. "The Sporting Life", *weekly.* illus. ports. scores, stats.
*June 7, 1906–Sept. 13, 1906*
contd. as: *The cricketer and hockey and football player. weekly*
*Sept. 20, 1906–Mar. 28, 1907*
and as: *The cricketer and hockey player. weekly*
*Apr. 4, 1907–Sept. 12, 1907*

1200 **The cricketer quarterly** facts and figures;
–1 edited by Gordon Ross. Ashurst,
□ Tunbridge Wells, The Cricketer Ltd. illus. ports. scores, stats.
*Vol. 1, no. 1. Summer 1973 – no. 4. Spring 1974*
*with title:* The cricketer international quarterly facts and figures

*Vol. 2, no. 1. Summer 1974 to date*
*Autumn 1979 was Vol. 7, no. 2*

1201 **The cricketers'** athletic news
*?/2 June, 1874 (no. 307)/–?*

1202 **The cricketer's** herald, athletic and football times. Manchester. *weekly*
*Nos. 1–245. 1884–Jan. 8, 1889*
contd. as: *British sport. Jan. 15, 1889-Mar. 26, 1895*
and as: *Cycler's news. Apr. 2, 1895-May 5, 1903*

1203 **The Eichstätt** cricketer; edited by L.H.
■ Garrett. MS.
*June–August 1943 with a Christmas supplement*
*a magazine in manuscript circulated amongst prisoners-of-war at Eichstätt, Germany. In M.C.C. Library, Lord's*

1204 **Football** and cricket world. Sheffield.
*weekly*
*Nos. 1–85, Sept. 9, 1895–Apr. 26, 1897*

1205 **C.B. Fry's** magazine of sports and
■ outdoor life. Newnes. illus. ports. (some col.). *monthly*
*14 vols. Apr. 1904–Mar. 1911; edited by C.B. Fry*
*Vol. III with title: C.B. Fry's magazine*
*Vol. IV-VIII with title: C.B. Fry's the outdoor magazine*
*IX-XIV with title: Fry's the illustrated magazine of sport, travel and outdoor life*
*(n.b. apart from a quote from Hon. Sir Neville Lyttelton, final vol. contains no cricket references)*

1205 **Guardian**
–1 Ayerst, David. Biography of a news-
■ paper. Collins, 1971. 702p. illus. ports. facsims. bibliog.
*cricket: minor references, pp. 262, 307, 447, 479, 531, 584*

1205 **London** journal; edited by Leigh Hunt
–2 *issue no. 8, May 21, 1834*
■ *p. 57 "Cricket, and exercise in general"; pp. 58–9 "Fourth week in May. Recollections of cricket." [review with extensive extracts from Nyren's The Young cricketer's tutor]*

1206 **The Mercury House Group.** *Research*
■ *Dept.*
A survey conducted on "The Cricketer" to evaluate the readership and editorial content. The Group, [1970]. [iv],16f. *typescript*
See *no. 1199*

1207 **Playfair** cricket monthly. Playfair Books.
■ illus. ports. scores, stats.

*Vol. 1, no. 1. May 1960–Apr. 1973*
*editors: May 1960–Nov. 1962 Gordon Ross & Roy Webber*
*Dec. 1962–Apr. 1973 Gordon Ross*
*——index prepared by Howard Milton. Ms.*

1208 **Rugby** and cricket news; edited by Charles Burton. Rugby and Cricket News. *weekly. illus.*
*four issues, 30th Nov., 7th, 14th and 21st Dec., 1957*

1209 **South Wales** cricketers' magazine. Newport, R.H. Jones. ports. scores, stats.
*Vol. I. 1948, 3 issues: July, Sept., and annual*
*Vol. II. 1949, 6 issues: May, June, July, Aug., Sept., Nov.*
*Vol. III. 1950, 6 issues: May, June, July, Aug., Sept., and annual*
*Vol. IV. 1951, 7 issues: May, June, July, Aug., Sept., Oct., and annual*
*Vol. V. 1952, 5 issues: May, June, July, Aug., Sept.*
*Vol. VI. 1953, 1 issue: Apr.–May*
*in July 1950 (Vol. III, no. 2) title changed to* The cricketers magazine
*editors: 1948–51 Harold H. Jarrett; 1952 J.W. Speight; 1953 Tim Saunders*

1209 **Sport pictures**. Webster's Publications
-1 Ltd. weekly. illus. ports. diagrs.
□ *no. 1–177, 28 Mar. 1919–19 Aug. 1922 contd. as:*
**Sports pictures**
*no. 178–282, 26 Aug. 1922–23 Aug. 1924 contd. as:*
**Sports pictures** and football mirror
*no. 283–567 30 Aug. 1924–29 Feb. 1930 contd. as:*
**Greyhound** outlook & sports pictures
*no. 568–1064 1 Mar. 1930–2 Sept. 1939*
*general sports but good cricket coverage in earlier years*

1210 **The sporting** magazine. *monthly in bi-*
□ *annual vols.* illus. scores
*156 vols. 1792–1870 in 3 series:*
*1 (vols. 1–50), 1792–1817*
*2 (vols. 51–100), 1817–42*
*3 (vols. 1–56, new series), 1843–70*
*publishers: 1793–1817 J. Wheble*
*1817–1821 J. Wheble and I. Pitman*
*1821–1845 I. Pitman*
*1846–1870 Rogerson*
*cricket extracts 1793–1842 gathered in 2 vols. in M.C.C. Library at Lord's*

1211 **The sporting** mirror, celebrities, votaries,
□ portraits, biographies, doings; edited by "Diomed". Etherington. *monthly. illus.* ports.
*Vol. 1, no. 1 Jan. 1881–Nov. 1885*
*contains cricket articles, portraits and biographies*

1211 **The sporting** review. London. illus.
-1 ports. *monthly*
*Vols. 1–64 (1839–70)*
*scattered cricket references and reports of matches*

1211 **Sports quarterly** magazine; edited by
-2 John Goulstone. Bexleyheath, the Editor.
□ *quarterly. typescript*
*No. 1. Spring 1977 to date*
*includes cricket*

1211 **Sportsman's** magazine. Hodgson & Co.
-3 illus. ports.
*3 vols. 1823–25*
*includes cricket; e.g. vol. II (Feb–July 1824) pp. 277–8, 272–4*

1212 **The sun:** issue for May 11th, 1903
*consisted mainly of cricket articles edited by K.S. Ranjitsinhji*

1213 **Umpire** and notcher: a journal devoted to East Scotland cricket; edited by M. Patterson and J.S. Cochrane. Edinburgh.
*weekly*
*3 issues only c.1866*

1213 **Wisden** cricket monthly; edited by David
-1 Frith. Wisden Cricket Magazines Ltd.
□ illus. & ports. (some col.), scores, stats.
*No. 1. June 1979 to date*

1214 **Women's** cricket: the official organ of the
■ Women's Cricket Association. *monthly.* illus. ports. scores. stats.
*May, 1930–Dec. 1967*
*editors: Majorie Pollard, May 1930–Sept. 1949*
*Netta Rheinberg & Nancy Joy, April 1950–Oct. 1951*
*N.R., N.J. and Helen Sharpe, Apr. 1952–Oct. 1954*
*N.R. & H.S. Apr. 1955–Dec. 1961*
*N.R., M. Shimeild & H.S. Jan. 1962*
*N.R. Feb. 1962–Dec. 1967*

1215 **The world** of cricket; edited by A.C.
■ Maclaren and J.N. Pentelow. illus. ports. scores, stats.
*23 issues, 31st Jan. to 14th Nov. 1914. The successor to "Cricket", no. 1183*
*monthly Jan.–Apr., weekly 2 May–15 Aug., monthly Sept.–Nov.*

1216 **The Yorkshire** cricket chronicle.
■ Sheffield, J.W. Northend by the authority of the Yorkshire C.C.C. *irregularly.* ports. stats.
*15 issues 4th May to 17th Aug. 1903*

1217 **The Yorkshire Post** cricket record. Leeds, Yorkshire Post Office. *monthly.* scores
*4 issues only, June-Sept., 1886*
*mostly Yorkshire cricket*

1217  **The young** cricketer. Ashurst, Tunbridge
–1    Wells, The Cricketer Ltd. illus. & ports.
■     (some col.), stats.
      *no. 1. 1978; edited by Roger Truelove*

*only issue apart from supplement which
appeared in Winter annual (Nov. 1978) of
The Cricketer International*

# ENGLISH CLUBS

1217  **Darwin, Bernard**
–2    British clubs. Collins, 1943. 47p. illus.
■     (some col.) (Britain in Pictures)
      *cricket pp. 37–41, 45–47*

1218  **French,** *Hon.* **Edward Gerald Fleming**
■     The cornerstone of English cricket.
      Hutchinson, [1948]. 167p. illus. ports. (1
      col.), scores
      *Wandering clubs, Home clubs, University,
      Public School and Associate County clubs,
      Service cricket, Civil Service, Church and
      stage cricket, Country house cricket, Tours,
      M.C.C. Out-matches, League cricket, Uses
      and abuses*

## MARYLEBONE C.C.

1219  **Altham, Harry Surtees,** *and* **Arlott,**
■     **[Leslie Thomas] John**
      The pictorial history of Lord's and the
      M.C.C. Pitkin Pictorials Ltd., 1967. 24p.
      illus. ports. plans. (Pride of Britain)

1220  **Ashley-Cooper, Frederick Samuel**
■     M.C.C. match list: a summary of 8642
      matches played in the United Kingdom
      by the Marylebone Cricket Club since its
      formation in 1787. M.C.C., 1930. 24p.

1221  **Bentley, Henry**
■     A correct account of all the cricket
      matches which have been played by the
      Mary-le-bone Club, and all other prin-
      cipal matches, from the year 1786 to 1822
      inclusive. Printed by T. Traveller, 1823.
      [374]p. scores
      ——An account of the principal matches
      played in the year 1823 with particulars
      of each innings. H. Bentley, 1823. [20]p.
      scores
      ——A correct account of the principal
      matches, in the years 1824 and 1825;
      being an Appendix to the book printed in
      1823 . . . which . . . may be had of H.
      Bentley. 1826. [42]p. scores

1222  **[Entry cancelled]**

1223  **Harris, George Robert Canning Harris,**
■     *4th baron, and* **Ashley-Cooper, Frederick**
      **Samuel**
      Lord's and the M.C.C.: a cricket chronicle
      of 137 years, based on official documents,
      and published with the knowledge and
      sanction of the Marylebone Cricket Club,

to commemorate the centenary of their
present ground. London & Counties
Press Association, 1914. xvi,314p. illus.
ports. plans, stats.
——*rptd.* H. Jenkins, 1920

1224  **Marylebone Cricket Club**
□     Annual report. M.C.C.
      *1788* to date
      *formed 1787; no reports prior to 1845
      survive; 1825–44 they are in manuscript and
      pasted into Minute Book; 1845 to date issued
      in printed form*

1225  Accounts. The Club. *annual*
□     *?/1867–1952*
      *subsequently incorporated in Annual report*

1226  Extracts from the minutes of the
■     Committee 1826–1867; compiled and
      arranged by the Hon. Secretary [R.A.
      Fitzgerald]. Harrison, 1867. 38p.
      *private circulation*

1227  Pavilion and ground regulations, list of
■     members, &c. M.C.C., *annual or biennial*
      *70 vols. 1871 to 1959–60*
      *issues before 1882 with title: "Members of
      the M.C.C."; after 1961 the 'List of members'
      was discontinued, but 'Pavilion and ground
      regulations' appeared under title "Regulations
      of M.C.C." See no. 1234*

1228  Matches for the season, with full scores
□     and batting averages. M.C.C. *annual.*
      scores. stats.
      *season 1886 to 1948–49
      annually to 1943, then biennial volumes,
      1944–45, 1946–47, 1948–49*

1229  The centenary of the Marylebone Cricket
■     Club: a short summary of the history of
      the Club, the names of those present at
      the Centenary Dinner, and a resumé of
      the speeches delivered threat; [compiled
      by Henry Perkins]. M.C.C., 1887. 27p.
      frontis. scores

1230  Rules. The Club, 1936. 7p.
□     ——*rptd.* with amendments *to date*

1231  Speeches made at the 150th anniversary
■     dinner of the Marylebone Cricket Club
      held on Thursday, 15th July, 1937 at the
      Savoy Hotel, London. [M.C.C., 1937].
      14p. *typescript*

1232 M.C.C. cricket diary. M.C.C. *annual*.
☐ stats. diagr.
1951–54. Naldrett P.
1955. Heinemann
1956–62. Playfair Books
1963 *to date* Collins

1233 M.C.C. and the organization of cricket.
■ M.C.C., 1962. 7p. diagr.

1234 Regulations. M.C.C. *annual*
☐ *?/1966, 1970, Jan. 1972, Dec. 1972, 1973/*
to date
*contain 'Pavilion and ground regulations'*
*which were formerly published separately with*
*'List of members'. See no. 1227*

1235 History of Lord's and the M.C.C. The
■ Club, 1968. [8]p. plan

1235 Match manager's handbook. *annual*
–1 *?/1973/to date?*
■ *lists of Probationers who complete their*
*matches in the year and of Members who*
*participate in M.C.C. Out-matches*

1236 ———. *Imperial Cricket Memorial Gallery*
■ Temporary catalogue. M.C.C., 1953. 9p.
*typescript*

1236 ———. *Indoor School*
–1 Newsletter. M.C.C. *typescript. annual*
☐ *no. 1. April 1978* to date
*manager A.W.P. Fleming; chief coach Don*
*Wilson*

1237 **Moon, Arthur Reginald,** *and* **McKay,**
**George Harry,** *editors*
Leaders and pages. Longmans, 1938, [*i.e.*
1939], xvi,272p. (Heritage of Literature
Series)
*includes "150 years of M.C.C. cricket" by*
*Howard Marshall*

1237 **Ross, Gordon,** *editor*
–1 Cricket under cover: to commemorate the
■ opening of the M.C.C. Indoor School.
M.C.C., [1977]. 40p. incl. adverts. illus.
ports. stats.

1238 **Slatter, William H.**
■ Recollections of Lord's and the Marylebone Cricket Club, 1914. [The Author],
*n.d.* 32p. plan mounted on half-title.

1239 **Taylor, Alfred Daniel**
■ Annals of Lord's and history of the
M.C.C. Bristol, Arrowsmith; London,
Simpkin, Marshall, [1903]. [vi],300p.
illus. ports. scores. stats.
———L.P. ed. 1903

1239 **The Times**
–1 M.C.C. number, Tuesday, May 25, 1937.
The Times, 1937. 24p. illus. ports.

*includes 'Lord's and its founder' by R.S.*
*Rait Kerr, 'The cradle of cricket [Hambledon]*
*by John C. Squire and contributions by*
*P.G.H. Fender, Lord Hawke, H.S. Altham*
*and Sir Home Gordon*

1240 The M.C.C. 1787–1937; reprinted from
■ the Times M.C.C. number 25th May,
1937. The Times Publishing Co., 1937.
[viii],134p. illus. ports. map

# WANDERING CLUBS

1241 **Powell-Jones, Henry Ellis**
■ Famous cricket clubs. H.F.W. Deane,
[1929]. 87p. illus. ports.

## Band of Brothers

1242 **Band of Brothers Cricket Club**
☐ The mystery of B.B. The Club. *annual*
*?/1920 . . . 1971/to date*
*formed 1858*

1243 Averages and results. The Club. *annual*
☐ *?/1967 . . . 1970/to date*

1244 **Tassell, Bryan**
■ Band of Brothers 1858–1958. Chatham,
*privately printed by* W. & J. Mackay, 1958.
[ii],20p. illus. ports. facsim.

## Buccaneers

1245 **Bax, Clifford**
■ The Buccaneers Cricket Club 1930–1951.
Kingston-on-Thames, Stringer, Briggs &
Stockley, 1956. 80p. scores, stats.

1246 **Buccaneers Cricket Club**
☐ Fixtures and list of members. The Club.
*annual*
*?/1971–73/to date*
*formed 1930*

1247 Buccaneers' tour in France: Buccaneers v.
Afcent C.C. at Fontainebleau; Buccaneers
v. Combined Shape/Afcent XI at
Versailles, June 13–14, 1964. The Club,
[1964]. *typescript*

## Cardinal

1248 **Cardinal Cricket Club**
Cardinal jottings and tottings: an account
of two matches played by the Cardinal
C.C. Whitchurch, Marbary, 1865. 50p.
*matches played in August 1865 against*
*Cheshire and Cheshire Colts*

## Cornish Choughs

1248 **Prothero, John E.**
–1 The Cornish Choughs Cricket Club

■ 1906–1976. [Truro, the Author, 1976]. [16]p.
 *limited ed. of 300 copies*

## Crofton Wanderers

1249 **Fernandes, C.W.L.,** *compiler*
■ The Crofton Wanderers' cricket tours 1883–1893. Leeds, Beck & Inchbold, 1893. 90p. scores, stats.

1250 **[Entry cancelled]**

1251 **[See no. 1647–1]**

## Devon Dumplings

1252 **Elwin, Malcolm,** *editor*
■ Devon Dumplings Cricket Club jubilee book, 1902–1952. *Privately printed* for the Club, (1952). 120p. ports.

## Druids

1253 **Argentine Cricket Association**
The Druids tour January 1966: official programme. [Buenos Aires, the Assoc., 1966?]. 20p. illus. ports.

1254 **Druids Cricket Club**
■ Records of the cricket matches played at Skegness by the Druids, years 1891 to 1911. G. Street, 1912. [iii],152p. scores

## Early Birds

1255 **[Reid, George K.]**
■ A brief history of the Early Birds Cricket Club. [The Club], 1963. 5p. *typescript*. score
——*revd. ed.* 1964. 10p. *typescript*. score

## Emeriti

1256 **The Emeriti Cricket Club**
□ Report. The Club. *annual.* stats.
 *1873/1877–80, 1882–93, 1896–1905, 1925–26,1931/–?*

1257 **Welman, C.,** *and* **Wheeler, L.**
■ The song of the Emeriti; song by Capt. C. Welman, music composed by L. Wheeler. Francis Bros. and Day, [1878]. 5p

## Forty Club

1258 **The Forty Club**
□ Fixture list. The Club. *annual.* scores (prev. yr.)
 *1937?/1939,45 . . . 66/*
 *contd. as:* Handbook 1967 *to date*
 *contains list of members; report of previous year, the early years without scores*
 *formed 1936*

## Free Foresters

1259 **Bedford,** *Mrs.* **Charles**
■ What came of wearing the Free Foresters' ribbon. Lichfield, *printed by* Lomax, [18—]. 17p.

1260 **Bedford, William Kirkpatrick Riland**
■ The chronicles of the United Though Untied F.F. [Pt I]. Birmingham, Benjamin Hall, 1863. 47p. scores, stats.
——Pt. II. 1867. 46p. scores

1261 ————*, and others*
■ Annals of the Free Foresters from 1856 to the present day. Edinburgh & London, Blackwood, 1895. xiv,401p. illus. ports. scores, stats.

1262 **The Free Foresters Cricket Club**
□ List of members. The Club
 *1922, 1926, 1935, 1939, 1951, 1954, 1957, 1960, 1963, 1966, 1969, 1972, 1975, 1978*
 ——Amendments to the list of members 1951 onwards were published 1952 onwards
 ——and amendments [to the above two lists] 1952 onwards were published 1953 onwards
 ——New members list
 *?/1963 . . . 71/to date?*

1263 **De Flamingo's Cricket Club**
Twenty five tours with Free Foresters in Holland 1921–1954. Presented by Flamingo's to Free Foresters during their 25th tour to Holland, 11th Aug., 1954. [The Club, 1954]. 12p.

## Frogs

1264 **Prain, Ronald L.**
■ The Devon tour 1907–1950: a short history. Nottingham, *printed by* D.H. Vaulkhard, 1951. 60p. ports. scores

1265 **Tregoning, E.A.**
■ History of the Frogs Cricket Club 1903–1953. Dorchester, Friary P., 1954. 68p. illus. ports. stats.

## Googlies

1266 **The "Googlies" Cricket Club**
□ List of members. The Club. *irregular?*
 *?/1928 . . .1939/–?*

## Grasshoppers

1267 **Parker, Eric**
■ Surrey. Hale, 1947. viii,256p. illus. map. (The County Books Series)
 *school cricket in Surrey and the Grasshoppers C.C., pp.245–51*

## Hampshire Hogs

**1268  Hampshire Hogs Cricket Club**
□     Year book. The Club. stats.
      ?/1964 . . . 1975/to date
      *officers, members, review of past season*

## Hawks

**1269  Hawks Cricket Club**
□     [Handbook]. The Club. *annual*
      ?/1958/to date?
      *fixtures, rules, members*

## I Zingari

**1270  I Zingari**
■     Full play members: names, addresses,
      qualifications. The Club, 1956. 18p.
      *typescript*
      *playing members qualifications, e.g.*
      *batsman, bowler, etc. with year of birth*

**1271  I Zingari** Club. Harrison, *printers*, 1857.
■     16p.
      later issues with title: *I Zingari: origin,*
      *rise, progress, results, 1862, 1865, 1866,*
      *1869, 1872, 1876, 1880, 1883, 1886, 1889,*
      *1892, 1895, 1898, 1900, 1904, 1906, 1907,*
      *1909, 1911, 1914, 1920, 1924, 1929, 1935,*
      *1950, 1956, 1961, 1966, 1971–?*
      *the 1895 issue was a jubilee number with*
      *sub-title: "origin, rise, progress, present*
      *position"*

**1272  Perkins, Theron D.,** *composer*
■     "Zingari" march: two step. Boston
      (Mass.), Jean White, 1897. 6p. incl. covers
      *piano score*

**1273  Trevor, Harry,** *and* **Trevor, Leo.**
■     "Cricket"; words by Harry & Leo. Trevor;
      music by Alfred Scott-Gatty. Boosey,
      1898. 9p. (Country House Ditties, no. 1)
      *dedicated to I Zingari*

## Incapables

**1274  Cricket** matches, played by the Incapa-
■     bles, 1872–1887. Odiham, Hants, *printed*
      *by* A. Gotelee, [1888]. 80p. scores. stats.

## Incogniti

**1275  Collins, Philip,** *and* **Falcon, Michael**
■     Incogniti Cricket Club: an account of the
      American tour, 1913. Beckenham, T.W.
      Thornton, [1914]. 47p. illus. ports. scores,
      stats.

**1276  England's** Incogniti XI v. All New York,
■     Sept. 22, 23, 1920: souvenir programme.
      New York, Livingston, [1920]. 8p.

**1277  Incogniti Cricket Club**
□     Scores of the "Incogniti" Cricket Club
      1861 to 1870; [compiled by Sir Augustus
      William Lawson Hemming]. *Printed by*
      James Wakeham, 1871. 148p. scores,
      stats.
      ——Scores and averages, 1871 to 1884.
      [The Club, 1885]. 300p. scores, stats.
      ——*annual issues?* 1885?–1914, 1919–39?
      1946?– season 1972. scores, stats. of same
      season
      ——season 1973 *to date with title:* Annual
      report. stats.

**1277  Souvenir** of the Incogniti Cricket Club
**–1**   jubilee anniversary dinner held at the
      Hotel Russell London on Thursday 15th
      February 1912. 17p.
      *with details of all the matches played in the*
      *first 50 years*

**1278  Rules** and list of members. The Club.
□     *annual*
      ?/1968–1970/
      *1971 to date?: Rules [only]*

## Ishmaelites

**1279  [Gaddum, F.D.]**
■     The Ishmaelites' tours, 1882–91. *Privately*
      *printed*, 1892. 86p. scores, stats.

## Jesters

**1279  Meyer, Michael,** *editor*
**–1**   A history of the Jesters Cricket Club.
■     [London, the Editor, 1976]. [vi],123p.
      ports. facsim.
      *covers 1928–1975. Founded 1927 by J.R.*
      *Burnet for his fellow Paulines and their friends*
      *from other schools*

## Midland Rangers

**1280  "Senex",** *pseud.*
      The Midland Rangers tour, August 1st-
      12th, 1882. *Privately printed.* [1882]. 38p.
      *account of tour of West Country in doggerel*
      *verse*

## The Musketeers

**1281  The Musketeers Cricket Club**
□     List of members and fixtures. The Club.
      *annual?*
      /1970/to date?

## Nondescripts

**1282  Nondescripts Cricket Club**
■     The fiftieth anniversary dinner of the
      Nondescripts Cricket Club held at the
      Cafe Monico 27th January, 1926: menu
      card. [Nondescripts C.C., 1926]. 8p. illus.
      ports.

## Northern Nomads

1283 **Northern Nomads Cricket Club**
□ [Handbook]. Liverpool, the Club. *annual.*
scores
*?/1899–1914, 1926–38, 1946/–?*
*with lists of members*

## Reptiles

1284 **Thomas, Basil**
■ The history of the Reptiles. [The Author],
[1953]. 28p. stats. *typescript*

## Romany (London)

1285 **The Romany Cricket Club**
□ [Handbook]. The Club. *annual*
*?/1967, 1971/to date?*
*formed 1929*

1285 The Romany globetrotter. South
–1 Croydon, The Club. December 29, 1977.
■ [4]p. incl. adverts. ports.
*newspaper format issued on the occasion of*
*the Club leaving for a tour of Sri Lanka*

## Romany (Yorkshire)

1285 **Howgate, John V.**
–2 The Romany Cricket Club 1902–1975.
■ [The Club, 1976]. 58f. illus. stats.
*typescript*

## South Oxfordshire Amateurs

1286 **South Oxfordshire Amateurs**
■ Report for season. The Club
*1934 and 1935. [1935]*
*1936, 1937, 1938*
*1939–47. [1948]*
*1948–1952. [1953]*
*1960–71 with title "History of the years*
*1960 to 1971," by Peter Frankenburg. [1972].*
*[iii],244p.*
*the years 1953–59 not published*

## Sou'westers

1286 **The Sou'westers' Cricket Club**
–1 Year book. The Club. stats.
□ *-/1956/to date?*
*results and averages of previous year;*
*founded 1930*

## Spar Ramblers

1286 **Gowing, Sidney,** *and others*
–2 History of Spar Ramblers Cricket Club
■ 1925–1975. [The Club], 1976. [60]p. ports.
facsims. scores, stats.

## Sussex Martlets

1287 **[Bolton, Geoffrey]**
■ Sussex Martlets, 1905–1955, by The President. *Privately published*, 1955. 16p.

1288 **The Sussex Martlets**
□ Secretary's report. Hove, the Club.
*annual.* stats.
*?/1973/to date*

## Wanderers

1289 **The Wanderers Cricket Club**
■ Rules and list of members, with
addresses. The Club. *annual*
*?/1903–31/–1977?*
*formed 1873 as 'The Grafton', subsequently*
*changed to 'Clapham' then 'Clapham Wand-*
*erers', and in 1893 to 'The Wanderers'*

1290 Centenary year 1873–1973; [compiled by
■ Peter J. Marsh]. [The Club, 1973]. 8p.
port. score

1290 Newsletter. The Club. *typescript*
–1 *?/end of 1973 season/to date?*
□

1290 South Africa 1978. The Club, [1978]. 24p.
–2 incl. adverts. ports.
■ *pre-tour; includes a history of the Club*
*1873–1978*

## Wayfarers

1291 **Wayfarers Cricket Club**
■ The way of the Wayfarers: an account of
the . . . cricket tour of the Wayfarers (a
band of strolling cricketers). Dudley, [the
Club]. *annual.* illus. ports. scores, stats.
*in v.y.*
*1913, 1914, 1920–21; ed. by Cover-Point,*
*i.e. Joseph Lewis*
*1922–23; ed. by J. Lewis & J.E. Cartwright*
*1924–39; ed. by J.E. Cartwright*
*1947; ed. by H. Mayhew*

1292 **[See no. 1313–1]**

## Yellowhammers

1293 **Langdale, Simon**
■ A history of the Yellowhammers Cricket
Club, 1909–1964. [The Author], 1964.
[i],28p.
*limited ed.*

## Yorkshire Wanderers

1293 **The Yorkshire** Wanderers Dutch tour
–1 August 1893. 29p. stats. MS.
*post-tour; in A.E. Winder's collection*

# PRIVATE CLUBS

## Allahakbarries

1294 **Adlard, Eleanor,** *editor*
■ Dear Turley, contributed by Fougasse, [and others]. Muller, 1942. 136p. illus. ports.
*includes account of The Allahakbarries, by Cynthia Asquith*

1295 **[Barrie,** *Sir* **James Matthew]**
■ Allahakbarries C.C. *Privately printed,* 1893. 9p.

1296 The Allahakbarrie book of Broadway
■ cricket for 1899. *Privately printed,* [1899]. 33p. illus. ports.
——*rptd. as* J.M. Barrie's Allahakbarries C.C. 1899. Barrie, 1950. 40p. illus. ports.

1297 The greenwood hat, being a memoir of
■ James Anon 1885–1887. *Privately printed,* 1930
*limited ed. of 50 copies*
——reset. P. Davies, 1937, xi,285p. illus. ports.
*describes in ch. 8 the formation of The Alla-hakbarries and their matches at Broadway*

1298 **De Navarro, Mary Anderson**
■ A few more memories. Hutchinson, 1936. 286p. illus. ports.
*chap. ix "Early days at Broadway—Barrie and cricket", pp. 69–78*

1299 **Mackail, Denis George**
■ The story of J.M.B.: a biography. P. Davies, 1941. [v],736p. port.
*numerous cricket references*

## Sir Julien Cahn's XI
(for the tours *see under* International cricket: English tours)

1300 **Snow, Edward Eric**
■ Sir Julien Cahn's XI. Evington (Leics.), the Author, 1964. 60p. illus. ports. stats.
*most of this book first appeared in "The Cricket Quarterly"*

## Chinghoppers

1301 **Chinghoppers** cricket club 1932–1953.
■ The Club, [1953]. 24p. illus. ports. score, stats.
*formed by F.G. Cheeswright of Chingford C.C. to raise occasional elevens for Sunday games against local teams*

## Corinthians

1301 **Corbett, Bertie Oswald,** *editor*
–1 Annals of the Corinthian Football Club. Longmans, Green, 1906. xiii,254p. illus.
*contains notes and scores of cricket matches played by the Club on their overseas tours, viz. p. 61 (S. Africa, 1897); p. 81 (S. Africa, 1903); pp. 128–9 (Canada, 1906); pp. 145–6 (United States 1906); p. 148 (v. Mr. St. John Walker's Cricket XI, U.S.A., 1906)*

## Cross Arrows

1302 **Cross Arrows Cricket Club**
■ Rules. The Club, 1954. [4]p. folded card

1302 **Gaby, Richard T.**
–1 The history of the Cross Arrows Cricket
■ Club 1880–1980. The Club, 1979. 16p.

## Cyphers

1302 **The Cyphers Club**
–2 Official opening of the Cyphers Club new
■ pavilion by Sir Edward T. Campbell, M.P., on Saturday, May 30, 1936 . . . [The Club, 1936]. [4]p. illus. port.

## Heartaches

1302 **Rice, Tim,** *editor*
–3 Heartaches cricketers' almanack by Clava
■ Recta. The Editor. illus. ports. scores, stats. *annual*
*for 1975 to date. published 1974 to date*
*1975, 1977, 1978* limited to 50 copies
1976 to 250 copies
1979 to 100 copies

## Invalids

1303 **Macdonell, Archibald Gordon**
■ The village cricket match. St. Hugh's P., [1950]. 56p.
*reprinted from "England, their England"* Description based on The Invalids

1304 **Squire,** *Sir* **John Collings**
■ The Invalids: a chronicle. *Privately printed,* Westminster P., 1923. 35p. illus. ports. scores
*limited to 125 copies*

## Jack Frost XI

1305 **Jack Frost XI:** history and statistics,
■ 1961–1970. [The Club, 1970?] 34f. port. stats. *typescript*

1305 **Greenwood, Richard G.,** *editor*
–1 Jack Frost XI California 1975. The Tour
■ Cttee., [1975]. 32p. incl. adverts. illus. ports.

## Lords and Commons

1306 **Bullus, Eric Edward**
■ A history of Lords and Commons cricket. *Printed by* Blades, East and Blades, [1959]. iii,21p. illus. ports. stats.

1307 **Ebbisham, Rowland Blades,** *1st baron*
■ Speeches made at a dinner given by Lord Ebbisham to the members of the Lords and Commons cricket team on the occasion of the presentation by Rt. Hon. Stanley Baldwin, M.P., to Sir Edward T. Campbell at the House of Commons on 21 March, 1934. *Privately printed,* [1934]. 19p.

## Old Broughtonians

1308 **[Bax, Clifford],** *editor*
■ The Old Broughtonians cricket weeks. 6 vols. Favill P., 1921–1938. ports. scores, stats.

1308 **Waugh, Arthur**
–1 Old Broughtonians: [a poem]. [*Privately printed*], 1928. fold (2p. of text)

## Lord Sheffield

1309 **[Golding, Edwin J.]**
The log of a trip in Lord Sheffield's yacht "Heloise" to Boulogne and back, by "One of the team". Haywards Heath, *printed by* C. Clarke, 1890. 12p. scores
*with scores of matches played at Newhaven and Boulogne in July 1890*

1310 ————, *and* **M.,W.**
■ The log of a trip in the Earl of Sheffield's yacht "Heloise" to Torquay and back, by "E.J.G." and "W.M." Haywards Heath, *printed by* C. Clarke, [1890]. [14]p.

## The Swallows

1310 **The Swallows:** Southern Africa tour 1976.
–1 [The Club, 1976?]. 16p. incl. adverts. 1
■ illus. ports.
*the Club was formed specifically for touring Southern Africa. One previous tour in 1971*

## Twenty-Five Club

1311 **The Twenty-Five Club**
■ Rules and list of members. [The Club, 1968]. [4]p.

## Vic Lewis C.C.

1311 **Lewis, Vic**
–1 Vic Lewis Cricket Club. Theatregraphics,
■ [1974]. [20]p. incl. adverts. illus. ports. scores

## Water Martins

1312 **Martineau, Hubert M.**
■ My life in sport. *Privately printed*, The Water Martin P., 1970. viii, 349p. illus. & ports. (some col.). scores
*ch. 2 "Cricket story", pp. 25–206*

1313 **The Water Martins C.C.:** [rules, members
■ list, fixtures]. [Privately publd. for H.M. Martineau]. *annual*
*5 issues 1930?–1934: all undated except the latest(?) which contains fixtures for 1934*

## West Kent Wanderers

1313 **Fear, Herbert**
–1 "The W.K.W.C.C." [West Kent Wand-
■ erers C.C., 1856–1955: souvenir history of the Club]. Blackheath, [the Club, 1955]. 34p. scores. stats.

## Wingers

1314 **The Fieldsman:** the journal of the
·□ Wingers C.C. The Club. *typescript.* stats.
*2 issues only, June and August(?) 1956*

# COUNTRY HOUSE CRICKET

## Althorp

1314 **Northamptonshire** past and present: the
–1 journal of the Northamptonshire Record
■ Society
*Vol. iv, no. 5*
*pp. 312–3 "Cricket at Althorp, 1867", by Stephen Green. ports. score*

## Ampthill House

1314 **Cooper, Charles W.**
–2 Town and county; or, Forty years in
■ private service with the aristocracy; illustrated by J.S. Goodall. Lovat Dickson, 1937. xiii,209p. illus.
*cricket pp. 17, 42, 51, 89, 92, 104, 105, 106, 107, 147, 181*

## Audley End

1315 **Audley End** cricket book: being the scores
■ of matches played on the lawn in front of the house from the 1st May, 1842 to the 31st August, 1844. Saffron Walden, *privately printed*, G. Youngman, 1844. 40p. scores

## Backwell House

1316 **Backwell** House cricket matches: a record
■ of the matches played by the Robinson

family of Gloucestershire 1878–1914. [1914?]. 150p. *typescript*
*Taylor mentions an earlier publication "Robinson family matches"—"A book, which I have never seen, was issued for private circulation a few years back. . . ."*

## Broughton-Gifford

1317 **The Broughton-Gifford** Manor House
■ cricket weeks. *n.p.,* [1913]. [i],60p. scores. stats.
*covers seasons 1911–1913; rptd. in "The Old Broughtonians cricket weeks", edited by Clifford Bax*

## High Elms

1317 **Gale, Frederick,** *compiler*
–1 Sports at High Elms 1859–1875. *n.p., n.d.* 86p.
*includes pp. 58–9 an account of a cricket match, July 28, 1866, High Elms v. The World. High Elms was a country house near Farnborough, Kent, owned by the Lubbock family*

## Lee-Odds

1318 **Ye Lee** week: a chronicle of merrie
■ makings holden by youths and maidens on ye Chiltern Hills in ye month of August, 1905. *n.p.,* [1905]. 23p. illus. scores
*humorous account and drawings of cricket and tennis matches played by the Lee-Odds against Braziers Ends and Chartridge Chips*

## Marchwiel

1319 **A.J. McAlpine's XI** tour of South Africa
■ and Rhodesia, 1969. Ellesmere Port, Cheshire, Sir Alfred McAlpine & Son Ltd., [1969]. 8p. 1 col. illus. on cover
*touring side based on those who have played in the Marchwiel Cricket Week—a country house cricket festival*

## Porter's Park

1319 **Porter's Park Cricket Club**
–1 Cricket scores. [July 1906–Sept. 1910]. Ms.
*presented to C.F. Raphael, March 2nd 1910, by his cricket employees*

## Stede Hill

1320 **Goodsall, Robert Harold**
■ Stede Hill: the annals of a Kentish home. Headley Bros., 1949. xii,212p. illus. map
*Edwyn Stede's cricket team pp.126–8*

# CLUBS OF FIRMS, PROFESSIONS, etc.

## Barclays Bank

1321 **Barclays Bank Cricket Club**
News letter. The Club. *monthly during season?*
*?/1960, 61/to date?*

1321 **Marriott, John**
–1 Barclays Bank Cricket Club: a brief history
■ 1918–1976. [The Club, 1976?]. [ii],18p. facsims. *typescript*

## British Steel Corporation

1321 **Purday, Richard**
–2 One hundred years of the Phoenix, the
■ story of the Panteg Cricket Club 1876–1976. Griffithstown (Gwent), [the Club, 1976?] 96p. illus. ports. stats.

## Civil Service

1322 **Civil Service Cricket Club**
■ The rules and list of members . . . with scores of matches played from 1861 to 1864 inclusive. W. Blanchard, 1865. 69p.

## Coutts

1323 **Coutts'** Cricket Club 1860–1960; compiled
■ by Malcolm Dawkins. [The Club, 1960]. [i],68p. illus. port. scores, stats. *typescript*
*the illustrations are mounted photographs; limited ed. of 100 copies only*

## Fatstock Marketing Corporation

1324 **[Fatstock Marketing Corporation]**
■ F.M.C. XI versus the Lord's Taverners at the Marsh and Baxter Sports Ground on Sunday, 18th May, 1969: [souvenir scorebook]. [F.M.C., 1969]. 12p. ports.

## Gas, Light and Coke Co.

1325 **Gas, Light and Coke Co. Cricket League**
Handbook. The League
*1908; edited by W.H. Kirrage. 24p.*
*possibly other issues*

## The Guardian

1325 **The Guardian**
–1 The bedside 'Guardian' 23: a selection
■ from The Guardian 1973–74; edited by W.L. Webb. Collins, 1974. 255p. illus.
*includes pp. 126–9 "Bombay ducks" by Derek Malcolm [on The Guardian Cricket Club's tour of India]*

## Lloyd's

1325 **Lloyd's Cricket Club**
-2 Hong Kong tour 1978. The Club, [1978].
■ 24p. illus. ports.
*pre-tour*

## Lloyds Bank

1325 **Penn, H. Frank,** *and* **Laudy, David G.,**
-3 *compilers*
■ A history of Lloyds Bank Cricket Club
1875–1975. [The Club, 1975]. [ii],56p.
illus. team ports. scores, stats.

## Lloyd's Register

1326 **[Kidd, Denis H.G.]**
■ Lloyd's Register Cricket Club 1882–1956.
[The Club, private circulation only, 1957].
[viii], 100p. illus. ports. score, stats.

1327 **Lloyd's Register Cricket Club**
■ Report of the proceedings at the first
outport match and reunion which took
place at Tynemouth on Monday 1st
August, 1892. The Club, 1892. 16p. score

## Midland Bank

1328 **Roberts, David**
■ Midland Bank Cricket Club: a centenary
history. Batsford, *private circulation*, 1970.
160p. illus. ports. stats.
——*supplement containing items of statistical
interest in the seasons since 1920*. [1970].
[32]p. *stats. typescript*

## National Provincial Bank

1329 **The First** hundred years 1866–1966:
■ National Provincial Bank Cricket Club.
[The Club, 1966]. [12]p. illus. ports. score

## Prudential Assurance Co. (Ibis)

1330 **Watson, Tom**
■ Ibis cricket, 1870–1949. [Prudential Assurance Co., 1950?]. 226p. scores, stats.

## Shell

1330 **Lensbury Cricket Club**
-1 Jubilee booklet 1969. Teddington, the
■ Club, [1969]. 50p. 1 illus. 1 port. stats.
*contains short history of the club pp. 4–16*

## Tate and Lyle

1331 **A grand** charity cricket match in aid of
■ The Royal London Society for the Blind:
Tate & Lyle v. West Indies, Sunday, 3
July, 1955 at the Tate & Lyle Sports
Ground, Manorway, East Ham: souvenir
programme. Tate & Lyle C.Cs., [1955].
24p. incl. covers & adverts.

## Thanet Works Cricket League

1331 **Thanet Works Cricket League**
-1 Handbook. The League. *annual*
□ 1969 season *to date*; edited by John
Websper
*founded 1968; includes rules, fixtures*

## United London Banks

1332 **United London Banks Cricket
Association**
Rules, 1951. The Assoc., [1951]. 8p.

1332 Silver jubilee 1974. [The Assoc., 1974].
-1 [16]p. stats.
■

# SCHOOL CRICKET

1333 **The Esso** colts cricket trophy for schools:
■ under-15 final at the Oval . . . July 11,
1972: souvenir scorecard. Esso, [1972].
[4]p. fold. 1 illus.
——National final, the Oval, 13th
July, 1973: souvenir scorecard. Esso,
[1973]. [8]p. ports.

1334 **The Esso** colts cricket trophy for schools:
■ rules [and] playing regulations. Esso,
[1973]. [4]p. fold. illus.
*with inset of results cards*

1334 **Lamb, Geoffrey Frederick**
-1 The happiest days. M. Joseph, 1959.
■ 252p. illus. ports. bibliog.
*cricket pp. 220–1, 228–9, 236*

1335 **Marylebone Cricket Club**
M.C.C. schools tour South Africa,
1965–1966: itinerary, match programme
. . . [M.C.C., 1965]

1336 **National Cricket Association,** *and* **The**
■ **Wrigley Cricket Foundation**
A report on school and youth cricket in
the seventies. The Association, 1971.
ii,19,8,5f. *typescript*

1337 **News Chronicle**
■ Schools summer sports annual 1951;
edited by Lionel Jackson. News Chronicle, [1951]. 104p. illus. diagrs. scores
*the only issue; cricket pp. 59–104 by
Charles Smeathers*

## English Schools Cricket Association

1338 **Board of Control for Cricket in India**
■ English Schoolboys cricket tour of India
1970–71: official souvenir. New Delhi, the
Board, [1970]. [36]p. incl. adverts. ports.
*cover-title:* English Schoolboys cricket
team vs. All India Schools team

1339 **English Schools Cricket Association**
☐ Handbook. The Association. *annual. illus.
ports. stats.* [in later issues]
*1949/1949 . . . 75/*to date
*gives results of matches of previous season
and fixtures; 1952 typescript; 1969 commemorates 21st anniversary and contains a
concise history of the Association*

1340 North of England v. South of England at
■ The Pollards, Oldham, Lancs., 28th July,
1956: programme and scorecard. The
Assoc., [1956]. 24p.

1341 The match of the year at the County
Ground, Northampton. Northampton-
shire v. Lancashire. Northampton,
Mercury P., 1958. [4]p. illus.

1342 Lincoln festival, July 21st to 25th, 1969:
programme. The Assoc., [1969]. 8p.
*with short history of the Association*

1342 Northumberland – the Under 15 Cricket
–1 Festival July 21st-28th, 1974. The Assoc.,
■ [1974]. [12]p. incl. covers
*the 5th successive E.S.C.A. Junior Festival
with articles on Northumberland cricket and
Northumberland Schools' C.A.*

1342 English Schools cricket festival 1976,
–2 Bradford 25–30 July, organised by York-
■ shire Schools Cricket Association:
souvenir brochure. Bradford, the Assoc.,
[1976]. 32p. incl. adverts. illus. ports.

# PUBLIC AND INDEPENDENT SCHOOLS

**N.B. School registers, which frequently contain
lists of cricket elevens, captains, and results of
matches, have been omitted**

1342 **Arena**: incorporating university and
–3 public school life and amateur sport.
*monthly*
*19 issues Mar. 1912-Sept. 1913*

1343 **Ayres'** (public schools) cricket companion
■ 1932; edited by John Slee. F.H. Ayres,
[1932]. 338p. illus. ports. scores. stats.
*only issue*

1343 **Darwin, Bernard Richard Meirion**
–1 The English public school. Longmans,
Green, 1929. xv,175p. (The English Heritage Series)
*cricket in ch. vi, "Games", pp. 62–83*

1344 **Fifty** years of sport at Oxford, Cambridge
■ and the great public schools; arranged by
the Right Hon. Lord Desborough of
Taplow, K.C.V.O. 3 vols.
*Vol. III. Eton, Harrow and Winchester;
edited by Hon. R.H. Lyttelton, Arthur Page
and Evan B. Noel. Southwood, 1922. ports.
scores
Eton v. Harrow, pp.132–230; Eton v.
Winchester, 266–321; Harrow Wanderers,
231–235*

1345 **[Gale, Frederick]**
■ The public school matches, and those we
meet there. By a Wykehamist. Chapman,
1853. 65p. illus.
——*Together with:* Ups and Downs of a
public school. Routledge, 1867. [ii],153p.
illus.
——2nd ed. *with title:* The public school
cricket matches of forty years ago. Nutt,
1896. 71p. illus.

1346 In memoriam gloriosam ludorum Etoni-
■ ensium, Harroviensium, Wykehamico-
rumque, nuper intermissorum anno 1854.
*Privately printed,* [1854]. 11p.
*Latin text; a skit, projected to 10th Dec.,
1957. The Lord's copy has a 2p. translation
bound in*

1347 **Great** public schools — Eton — Harrow
☐ — Charterhouse — Cheltenham — Rugby
— Clifton — Westminster — Marlborough — Haileybury — Winchester, by
various authors. E. Arnold, [1893]. vi,
344p. illus.
*rptd. from* English Illustrated Magazine
——new ed. 1896. 252p.
*scattered cricket references*

1348 **[Haygarth, Arthur],** *compiler*
☐ The public school matches: a correct
account of all the matches of which the
scores are in existence, played between
the schools of Eton, Harrow and
Winchester from 1805 to 1852 (–1868)
inclusive. F. Lillywhite, 1853 (–1869).
scores
*9 editions published 1853, 54, 55, 56, 61,
64, 67, 68, 69
1869 edition with title: John Lillywhite's
public school matches*

1349 An account of all the cricket matches
■ played between Eton and Winchester;
Westminster and Charterhouse; Rugby
and Marlborough; and Marlborough and
Cheltenham. By the Compiler of the
Harrow, Eton and Winchester school
matches from 1805. Lillywhite and
Wisden, 1857. 16p.

1350 **[Kidd, Abel]**
■ Ode to the light and dark blue, or Oxford and Cambridge, Rugby and Marlborough, Eton and Harrow, at Lord's 1871 with a prophecy, by An Old Stump. Published & sold by the kind permission of the Marylebone Club for the benefit of the Author, [1871]. [3]p.

1351 The battles of the blues: Oxford and
■ Cambridge . . . Eton and Winchester . . . Harrow and Eton . . . [1873]. Published and sold by kind permission of the Marylebone Cricket Club, for the benefit of the Author, [1873]. [3]p.

1352 **Lambton, Arthur**
■ The galanty show. Hurst & Blackett, 1933. 288p. frontis.
    *references to public school cricket pp.33–83*

1353 **Lane-Joynt, A.W.,** *editor*
■ The public school cricket year book 1914. Hammond, 1914. 141p. ports. scores, stats.
    *the only issue; record of 1913 season*

1354 **Lyon, W.R.,** *editor*
■ The elevens of three great schools, 1805–1929: being all recorded scores of cricket matches played between Winchester, Eton and Harrow, with memoirs and biographies of the players. Eton, Spottiswoode, Ballantyne, 1930. vi,524p. scores

1354 **Minchin, James George Cotton**
–1 Our public schools: their influence on English history. Charterhouse, Eton, Harrow, Merchant Taylors', Rugby, St. Paul's, Westminster, Winchester. Swan, Sonnenschein, 1901. xii,462p.
    *scattered cricket references*

1355 **Pardon, Sydney Herbert,** *editor*
■ John Wisden's public school matches: a correct record of the matches played between Eton, Harrow and Winchester. Wisden, 1898. xxvi,170p. scores

1356 **Parker, Eric**
■ Surrey. Hale, 1947. viii,256p. illus. map. (The County Books Series)
    *school cricket in Surrey and the Grasshoppers C.C., pp. 245–51*

1357 **Public** school athletics; edited by three
☐ public schoolmen—Eton, Harrow, Winchester. Swan Sonnenschein. *annual.* scores, stats.
    *season 1889–90/1891–92/–?*
    *includes c. 60pp. of cricket*

1358 **Roe, W. Nichols,** *editor*
■ Public schools cricket, 1901–1950. Parrish, 1951. 247p. scores

1359 **School** and college cricket scheme: report on the first year, 1922. 1923. bs.

1360 **Staunton, Howard**
■ The great schools of England. Sampson Low, 1865. lvi,517p. illus.
——2nd ed. 1869
    *scattered cricket references*

1361 **Teams** of the universities and public schools. J. Cornish & Sons, 1882
    *in Taylor*

1361 **Warner, Rex**
–1 English public schools. Collins, 1945. 46p. illus. (some col.) (Britain in Pictures)
    *cricket pp. 30, 31, 33, 36, 40*

1362 **Webster, Frederick Annesley Michael**
■ Our great public schools: their traditions, customs and games. Ward, Lock, 1937. 383p. illus.
    *scattered cricket references*

1362 **The world** of the public school, intro-
–1 duced by George Macdonald Fraser.
■ Weidenfeld & Nicolson, 1977. [vii],210p. illus. ports.
    *cricket in ch. 9 "The shadow of Tom Brown" by Richard Usborne, and ch. 10 "Breathless hush in the close" by Gordon Ross*

## Ackworth

1363 **Atkinson, Sam,** *compiler and editor*
■ Ackworth games, and the men who made them. The Author, 1917. vii,79p. illus. ports.
    *cricket chapters by A.G. Linney and Osgold Cross; limited ed. of 600 copies*

## Aldenham

1364 **Beevor, Edmund,** *and others, compilers*
■ The history and register of Aldenham School. 7th edition. Worcester & London, E. Baylis, 1938. xcv,373p. illus.
    *cricket XIs & matches pp. 316–323*

## Ardingly College

1365 **Ardingly School**
■ The Ardingly annals. Vol. xvii, no. 100, May 1903.
    *contains: "Some reminiscences of Ardingly cricketers", by W.A. Bettesworth, pp. 62–72*

1366 **Perry, Reginald**
■ Ardingly 1858–1946: a history of the
school. Old Ardinians Society, 1951.
xv,285p. illus. ports.
*scattered cricket references*

## Bancroft's

1367 **Francombe, Donald Courtney Ridsdale,**
■ *and* **Coult, D.E.,** *editors*
Bancroft's School 1737–1937. Woodford,
the School, *published privately*, 1937.
xv,198p. illus. ports. maps
——2nd imp. (with minor corrections).
1973
*cricket pp. 41–2, 77, 78, 87, 88, 90, 116,
120, 139, 194–5; includes a poem "Cricket
group, 1913" by D.C.R. Francombe*

## Beaumont College

1368 **[Bowring, Wilfrid J.]**
■ Beaumont v. Oratory, 1867–1925, by
"Ignotus". Windsor, Brodie, 1926. 51p.
scores, stats.

1369 Some Beaumont scores, 1872–1891; by
■ "Ignotus". Slough, Brodie, [1934]. 79p.
scores, stats.

1369 **The history** of St. Stanislaus' College
–1 Beaumont: a record of fifty years,
1861–1911. Beaumont, Old Windsor,
"The Beaumont Review" Office, 1911.
169p. illus.
*cricket pp. 114–116 with team port. of 1889*

1370 **Levi, Peter** *S.J.*
■ Beaumont 1861–1961. Deutsch, 1961. 76p.
illus.
*several pp. on cricket including illus. of
cricket ground and reference on p. 33 to first
coloured boy to play at Lord's*

## Bedford

1370 **Sargeaunt, John**
–1 A history of Bedford School; edited and
completed by Ernest Hockliffe. Bedford,
F.R. Hockliffe; London, T. Fisher Unwin,
1925. xii,260p. illus. ports. plan
*cricket pp. 138–9*

## Bishop's Stortford College

1371 **Ferguson, John**
■ Cricket at Bishop's Stortford College,
1868–1968. [Bishop's Stortford, the
College, 1970]. [ii],19p. illus. ports.

## Bishop's Stortford Grammar School

1372 **Porter, G.**
■ The Grammar School, Bishop's Stortford:
register of the cricket and football

matches and athletic games for the year.
Bishop's Stortford, *printed by* H. Collings.
scores
*8 annual issues 1870–77 published
1871–77, subsequently issued in one volume
in 1878*

1373 **[Entry cancelled]**

## Bootham

1374 **Pollard, Francis Edward,** *editor*
■ Bootham School, 1823–1923. Dent, 1926.
xix,207p. illus. ports.
*scattered references to cricket and two plates*

## Bradfield College

1375 **Bradfield** v. Radley cricket
■ *1853–1898. [1899?]. 46p.
1853–1911. [1912?]. 84p.
1853–1920; with a supplement giving our
matches with other schools; compiled by T.
Steele. Reading, Blackwell, 1921. 108p. scores*

1376 **Leach, Arthur Francis,** *editor*
■ A history of Bradfield College, by Old
Bradfield Boys. H. Frowde, 1900.
xii,253p. illus. ports. score
*cricket pp. 205–19, etc.*

## Brighton College

1377 **Burstow, George Philip**
■ Cricket reminiscences 1923–1966;
extracted from his diaries and journal.
Brighton, Brighton College, the Author,
1966. [iii],59p. *typescript*

1378 ———, *and* **Whittaker, Mark Barry,**
*compilers*
A history of Brighton College; edited by
S.C. Roberts. Brighton, Brighton College,
1957. [viii],150p. illus. bibliog.

## Bristol Grammar

1378 **Hill, Charles Peter**
–1 The history of Bristol Grammar School.
Pitman & Sons, 1951. xvi,256p. illus.
• ports. bibliog.
*cricket pp. 92, 134–5, 153–6, 171–2,
180–2, 206, 211*

## Bromsgrove

1379 **Leigh,** *Hon.* **James Wentworth**
Other days. T. Fisher Unwin, 1921. 255p.
illus. ports.
*references to Bromsgrove cricket*

1380 **"An Old Pupil",** *pseud.*
Nugae scholasticae. A. Hall Virtue, 1858.
81p.

*"A Bromsgrove match"*, pp. 35–59; an account of the match between King Edward's, Birmingham and Bromsgrove

## Charterhouse

1380  **Charterhouse** [and] Westminster tour of
–1    New Zealand December, 1976 – January,
■     1977. *n.p.*, [1976]. 36p. incl. adverts. illus.
      on covers
      *pre-tour*

1381  **Eardley-Wilmot, Edward Parry,** *and*
■     **Streatfield, Edmund Champion**
      Charterhouse old and new. Nimmo,
      1895. xii,295p. illus. plan
      *chap. vi "Cricket quarter", pp. 110–127*

1382  **Ellis, Bernard,** *editor*
■     A complete record of scores with bowling
      analyses of all cricket matches, and full
      particulars of all football matches and rifle
      contests between Charterhouse and other
      public schools from 1850 to 1890. Wright,
      [1891]. v,103p. scores
      *cricket pp. 7–54*

1383  **Jameson, Edward Mellor**
■     Charterhouse. Blackie, 1937. [ix],196p.
      illus.
      *Cricket pp. 102, 119–122, 154–5*

1384  **Radclyffe, Charles Walter,** *artist*
■     Memorials of Charterhouse: a series of
      original views . . . drawn on stone. Nutt,
      1844. illus.
      *includes one plate of cricket in the Charter-
      house Fields*

1385  **Sammes, John**
      Charterhouse cricket, June 1942: [A
      poem]. Reigate, the Author, [1942]. 4p.

1386  **Tod, Alexander Hay**
■     Charterhouse. Bell, 1900. xxii,241p. illus.
      (Handbooks to the Great Public Schools)
      *cricket, pp. 140–154*
      ——2nd ed. rev. 1919. xii,258p.

1386  **Veale, W.**
–1    From a new angle: [reminiscences of
      Charterhouse 1880–1945]. Winchester,
      Wells, 1957. 75p. 1 port.
      *cricket pp. 22–25*

## Cheam

1386  **Peel, Edward**
–2    Cheam School from 1645. Thornhill P.,
      1974. 330p. illus. (some col.)
      *includes section on sport containing cricket;
      mentions all first class cricketers educated at
      Cheam*

## Cheltenham College

1387  **Hunter, Andrew Alexander,** *editor*
■     Records of the Cheltenham College
      cricket, boating, rifle, and racquet
      matches against public schools,
      1856–1883. Wright, [1884]. 128p.
      ——*2nd ed. with title:* Records of Chel-
      tenham College matches against public
      schools, 1856–1900. Cheltenham, J.
      Darter, 1901. 227p. scores
      *cricket pp. 9–97*

1388  **[James, Henry,** *baron James of Hereford*],
■     *editor*
      Scores of the principal cricket matches
      played by Cheltenham College; edited by
      An Old Collegian. Cheltenham, Darter,
      1868. 95p. scores

1389  **Morgan, Michael Croke**
■     Cheltenham College: the first hundred
      years. Chalfont St. Giles, Sadler for the
      Cheltonian Society, 1968. x,246p. illus.
      ports. bibliog.
      *cricket pp. 18, 22, 50, 186–8*

1390  **Turnbull, R.W.**
      Cheltenham College cricket, 1855–1900.
      Cheltenham, Shenton, 1900. 48p. illus.
      *title as given in Taylor*

1391  **[Ward, Paul]**
      Reminiscences of Cheltenham College,
      by an Old Cheltonian. Bemrose, 1868.
      vii,167p.
      *cricket, ch. vii, pp. 58–81*

## Chigwell

1392  **Stott, Godfrey**
■     A history of Chigwell School. Ipswich,
      Cowell, 1960. 268p. illus. ports. diagr.
      plans
      *cricket pp. 117, 131 and 215 incl. portrait
      of J.A. Dixon, later Capt. of Notts C.C.C.*

## Christ College, Brecon

1392  **Smith, David T.,** *and* **Jonathan B.**
–1    First-class cricketers from Christ College,
■     Brecon. [Corsham (Wilts), D. Smith],
      1979. 43p. ports. diagr. stats.
      *limited to 100 numbered copies*

## Clifton College

1393  **Christie, Octavius Francis**
■     Clifton School days (1879–1885). Shaylor,
      1930. xiii,144p. ports. bibliog.
      *cricket pp. 68–73*

1394  A history of Clifton College, 1860–1934.
■     Bristol, Arrowsmith, 1935. 384p. illus.
      ports. plans on end-papers
      *cricket pp. 254–271*

1395 **Fox, Ernest L.**
Clifton College cricket records, 1863–1891. Bristol, Arrowsmith, 1892. 80p.

1396 **Hammond, Nicholas Geoffrey Lemprière,** *editor*
Centenary essays on Clifton College. Bristol, Arrowsmith, for the Council of Clifton College, 1962. ix,217p. illus.

1397 **[Newbolt, *Sir* Francis George]**
■ Clifton College twenty-five years ago: the diary of a fag. F.E. Robinson, 1904. [iii],192p. frontis.

1398 Clifton College, forty years ago: the diary
■ of a praeposter. P. Allan, 1927. vi,176p. illus. ports.
*cricket pp.110–146 etc.*

## Denstone College

1399 **Adamson, John Alfred**
■ Denstone cricket, 1874–1952. Shrewsbury, Wilding, [1954]. 173p. ports. stats.

## Downside

1400 **Birt, Henry Norbert**
■ Downside: the history of St. Gregory's School from its commencement at Douay to the present time. Kegan Paul, 1902. xv,359p. illus. ports.
*cricket, with illus. pp.300–04, and other references*

1401 **Snow, Terence Benedict**
■ Sketches of old Downside. Sands, 1903. [ix],347p. port. scores
*cricket pp. 172–186, 329–334*

1402 **Van Zeller, Claude Hubert**
■ Willingly to school: a study in unceremonial practice. Sheed & Ward, 1952. x,262p. illus.
*memoirs of cricket at Downside, particularly of Maurice Turnbull*

## Dulwich College

1402 **Dulwich College** cricket, hockey and
–1 rugby tour to Sri Lanka, and Thailand 1978. [Dulwich College Tour Party, 1978]. 32p. incl. adverts. tour port.
*includes "Cricket: the rich Alleynian contribution" by E.W. Swanton*

1403 **Leake, William Ralph Martin**
■ Gilkes and Dulwich 1885–1914: a study of a great headmaster. Dulwich, the Alleyn Club, [1929?]. xxxii,278p. port.
*scattered cricket references*

1404 **Old Alleynians**
■ Memories of Dulwich College in the 'sixties and the 'seventies. Dulwich, the College on the tercentenary (1619–1919), 1919. 125p.
*cricket references pp. 15, 16, 23, 29–30, 33, 36, 55, 56, 66, 78–79, 81, 103, 107*

## Edward Worlledge

1404 **The Edward Worlledge** School, Great
–1 Yarmouth. Great Yarmouth, Old Worlledgers' Assoc., 1952. 84p. illus.
*cricket pp. 40–4*

## Emanuel

1405 **Scott-Giles, Charles**
■ The history of Emanuel School. London, The Portcullis; Wandsworth, Emanuel School, 1935. xv,313p. illus. ports.
*cricket, pp. 132, 172–4, 206, 230, 232, 241*

## Eton College

1406 **Ainger, Arthur Campbell**
■ Memories of Eton sixty years ago . . . with contributions by N.G. Lyttelton and John Murray. Murray, 1917. xvii,353p. illus. ports.
*chapter on cricket by N.G. Lyttelton, pp. 147–157*

1407 **Arkwright, J.S.,** *compiler*
■ Keate's Lane papers: an Eton miscellany, by J.K.S., J.R.C.R., H.J.S., K.E.C., W.F.S.D. and J.S.A. Eton, New, 1891. [viii],36p.
*cricket verses pp. 1 & 19*

1407 **Austen-Leigh, Richard Arthur**
–1 Eton records. Eton, Spottiswoode, 1903. viii,96p.
*cricket XIs. 1805–1902, pp. 24–37*

1408 **[Blake, Henry John Crickitt]**
Reminiscences of Eton, by an Etonian. Chichester, the Author, 1831. 152p.
*cricket, pp. 47–53*

1409 **Brinsley-Richards, James**
■ Seven years at Eton, 1857–1864. Bentley, 1883. viii,447p.
*cricket pp. 218–226*
——2nd ed. 1885

1410 **Bryne, Lionel Stanley Rice,** *and*
■ **Churchill, Ernest Lee**
Changing Eton: a survey of conditions based on the history of Eton since the Royal Commission of 1862–64. Cape, 1937. ix,278p. frontis. maps
*cricket pp. 229–236*

1411 **Clutton-Brock, Arthur**
■ Eton. Bell, 1900. xii,246p. illus. map.
(Handbooks to the Great Public Schools)
*cricket pp. 82–3, 213–19*

1412 **[Coleridge, Arthur Duke]**
■ Eton in the forties, by An Old Colleger.
Bentley, 1896. 404p. illus.
——2nd ed. rev. & enl; with new illustrations by F. Tarver. Bentley, 1898. xi,458p.
illus. ports. score
*cricket in chaps. vii and x*

1413 **Coleridge, Gilbert James Duke**
■ Eton in the 'seventies. Smith, Elder, 1912.
xiii,293p. ports.
*cricket pp. 168–185*

1414 **Collins, William Lucas**
Etoniana, ancient and modern: being
notes of the history and traditions of Eton
College, republished from 'Blackwood's
Magazine', with additions. Edinburgh
and London, Blackwood, 1865. viii,238p.
*cricket refs., especially in chapter 12*

1415 **Cust,** *Sir* **Lionel Henry**
A history of Eton College. Duckworth,
1899. xvi,318p. ports. (English Public
Schools)
——new and cheaper ed. 1909
*Ch. xi "Sports and pastimes"*

1415 **Devereux, Ernest Cecil**
–1 Life's memories of Eton, and Eton
■ colours. Eton, the Author, 1936. 140p.
col. illus.
*cricket ch. 8, pp. 28–31 and colours of
College cricket, Eton Ramblers, Lazaroni, etc.*

1416 **Eton** register boating, cricketing and rifle
corps for 1862. Eton, Ingalton & Drake,
1862. 39p.
——*another issue* 1863

1417 **Eton** School songs. 2 series. Novello,
■ [c.1878]
*First series, no. 4: Cricket song: [words by]
A.C. Ainger, composed by J. Barnby.* [4]p.
——*with title:* Eton songs, written by
Arthur Campbell Ainger, set to music by
Joseph Barnby; illustrated by W.
Marshall. First series. Novello, [c.1891].
[4]p. illus.
*includes "Cricket is king"*

1418 **Gambier-Parry, Ernest**
■ Annals of an Eton House, with some
notes on the Evans family. Murray, 1907.
xv,472p. illus. ports. scores
*ch. x 'The revival of cricket at Eton; the
House Cricket Cup, 1860–71', pp. 143–53
and numerous other references*

1419 **Hill, Barrington Julian Warren**
■ Eton medley. Winchester Publications,
1948. x,246p. illus. (1 col.). maps on
endpapers. bibliog. (The English Public
Schools)
*cricket pp. 150–7, with illus.*

1419 **Windsor** and Eton. Batsford, 1957. 199p.
–1 illus. bibliog. (British cities & towns
series)
*cricket at Eton, pp. 131, 181, 182*

1420 **Junior** cricket matches. Eton, the College
□ P. *scores*
*1902.* [1902]. [ii],33p.
*1903.*

1421 **Lubbock, Alfred**
■ Memories of Eton and Etonians;
including my life at Eton, 1854–1863 and
some reminiscences of some subsequent
cricket, 1864–1874. Murray, 1899.
xvi,320p. illus. ports.

1422 **Lubbock, Percy**
Shades of Eton. Cape, 1929. 224p.
*scattered cricket references*

1423 **Lyte,** *Sir* **Henry Churchill Maxwell**
□ A history of Eton College, 1440–1875;
with illustrations by P.H. Delamotte.
Macmillan, 1875. 527p. illus. ports. plans
—— . . . 1440–1884. New ed. enlarged.
1889. xxiii,543p.
—— . . . 1440–1898. 3rd ed. rev.
xxvii,640p.
—— . . . 1440–1910. 4th ed. rev.
xxiv,627p.
*scattered cricket references*

1424 **[Malden, Charles Horace]**
■ Recollections of an Eton Colleger
1898–1902, by C.H.M. [Eton], Eton
College, Spottiswoode, 1905. vii,245p.
map.
*cricket pp. 159–170*

1425 **Mitchell, Richard Arthur Henry**
■ Eton cricket. Eton, Eton College P., R.
Ingalton Drake, 1892. 22p.

1426 **[Morton, Arthur Henry Aylmer]**
The miseries of Etonians, by One of
Themselves. Eton, *printed by* E.P.
Williams, 1854. 36p.
*chapter ii "The miseries of cricketers"*

1427 **Nevill, Ralph Henry**
■ Floreat Etona: anecdotes and memories of
Eton College. Macmillan, 1911. xii,336p.
illus. (some col.). ports.
*cricket pp. 271–281*

1428  **Parker, Eric,** *compiler*
■  Floreat: an Eton anthology. Nisbet, 1923.
xxi,333p.
*cricket pp. 124–48*

1429  College at Eton. Macmillan, 1933. x,272p.
■  frontis.
*cricket pp. 167–84*

1430  **Priestcraft:** or, The way to promotion: a
poem addressed to the inferior clergy of
England. Being wholesome advice, how
to behave at the approaching election.
Printed for J. Walford, 1734. 10p.
*reference to cricket at Eton on p. 8*

1431  **Selwyn, Thomas Kynaston**
Eton in 1829–1830: a diary of boating and
other events written in Greek; edited with
translation and notes by E. Warre.
Murray, 1903. xl,312p. illus.

1432  **Stone, Christopher Reynolds**
Eton; painted by E.D. Brinton, described
by Christopher Stone. Black, 1909.
xi,174p. illus.

1433  **Sterry,** *Sir* **Wasey**
■  Annals of the King's College of Our Lady
of Eton beside Windsor. Methuen, 1898.
xii,362p. illus. ports.
*cricket pp. 321–5, etc.*

1434  **[Tucker, William Hill]**
■  Eton of old; or, Eighty years since
1811–1822, by An Old Colleger. Griffith
Farran, 1892. x,244p. illus.
*cricket pp. 107–115, 188–190*

1435  Eton memories, by an Old Etonian. Long,
1909; xi.336p. illus.
*scattered cricket refs.*

1436  **Wilkinson, Charles Allix**
Reminiscences of Eton (Keate's time).
Hurst & Blackett, 1887. xvi,340p. port.
——re-issued 1888

## Eton v. Harrow Matches

1437  **Ashley-Cooper, Frederick Samuel**
■  Eton v. Harrow at the wicket; with some
biographical notes, poems and genealogical tables. St. James's P., 1922. 155p.
illus. scores
——*de luxe ed.* of 100 signed copies. 1922

1438  **Brook, Franklyn,** *editor*
■  Scores of the cricket matches between
Eton and Harrow from the beginning up
to date. Robinson, 1900. 85p. scores
——*subsequently issued 1901?–1905? with
additional leaves tipped-in with match scores
for 1900 (p. 75), 1901 (p. 76), 1902 (p. 77),*

*1903 (p. 78), 1904 [p. 79], 1905 [p. 80] – the
last two pages unnumbered and in larger type*

1438  **Cheetham, Anthony,** *and* **Parfit, Derek,**
–1  *compilers*
Eton microcosm; illustrations by Edward
Pagram. Sidgwick & Jackson, 1964. 198p.
illus.
*pp. 94–5 "Byron at Lord's"*

1439  **The cricket** matches between Harrow and
Eton and Harrow and Winchester from
1818–1852. *Privately printed,* [c.1853].
[53]p.

1440  **Cricket** song: Eton v. Harrow. Swain,
1864
*in Taylor*

1441  **Eggar, William Douglas**
■  A song of Lord's and poems for the mag.
Eton College, Spottiswoode, Ballantyne,
1942. 51p. score
*includes "A song of Lord's, July 8, 9,
1910" and the full score of Fowler's match
(Eton v. Harrow)*

1442  **Eton** v. Harrow 1805 to 1883. Harrow,
W.R. Wright for J.C. Wilbee, 1883. 8p.
scores, stats.
*a special supplement to "Harrow notes",
Friday, July 13, 1883*

1443  **Gordon,** *Sir* **Home Seton Charles**
■  **Montagu,** *bart., editor*
Eton v. Harrow at Lord's; the story of the
matches by Bernard Darwin and reminiscences of every match since 1861 by an
actual player in each game. Williams &
Norgate, 1926. xv,319p.
*limited to 650 copies: 325 Eton ed., 325
Harrow ed.*

1444  **Jeff, Wilfrid Wykeham**
Sport in silhouette; illustrated by Gilbert
Holiday. Country Life, 1933. 128p. illus.
*essays mostly reprinted from the* Morning
Post; *includes the Eton and Harrow match*

1444  **[Johnstone, Charles Frederick]**
–1  Recollections of Eton, by an Etonian; with
■  illustrations by Sydney P. Hall.
Chapman & Hall, 1870. iv,362p. illus.
*contains an imaginary account of an Eton
and Harrow match, pp. 313–332*

1445  **[Kidd, Abel]**
■  Ode to Harrow with a prophecy, by An
Old Stump: grand match at Lord's on
Friday & Saturday, July 8th & 9th
between Eton and Harrow. Published
and sold by kind permission of the Marylebone Club for the benefit of the Author,
[1870]. [3]p.

School cricket: The Eton v. Winchester match at Eton, 1902 *photo: P. S. H. Lawrence*

University cricket: Cricket at Parker's Piece, Cambridge, c. 1861, probably between the University and the Town with the University fielding *photo: M.C.C.*

Village cricket: Haig village cricket match in progress at Welford Park (Berks) *photo: Patrick Eagar*

Minor Counties: A match at South Hill Park (Berks) *photo: Patrick Eagar*

**1446** A cricket carnival at Lord's ground, July 14th & 15th, 1871: ode to Old Harrow, with a prophecy, by An Old Stump. Published & sold by the kind permission of the Marylebone Club for the benefit of the author, [1871]. [3]p.
——: ode to Eton. [1871]. 3p.

**1447** **Liddell, Adolphus George Charles**
Notes from the life of an ordinary mortal, being things done, seen and heard at school, college and in the world in the latter half of the nineteenth century. Murray, 1911. xiii,370p.
——2nd ed. 1911
*includes "Eton and Harrow"*

**1448** **Lord's,** July 13th and 14th, 1906. Eton v. Harrow: souvenir. Souvenir Publishing Syndicate, [1906]. 52p. ports.

**1449** **Morton, Henry Vollam**
The London year: a book of many moods; decorated from 'A London sketch book' by A.E. Horne. Methuen, 1926. xii,211p. illus.
——2nd ed. rev. 1933. xiii,213p.
*Eton v. Harrow, pp.134–137*

**1450** **"O[ld] E[tonian]," pseud.**
Floreat Etona: Lord's 1910, by O.E. Windsor, *printed by* Oxley & Sons, 1910. [4]p.
*a poem*

**1451** **Parker, Eric**
Eton in the 'eighties. Smith, Elder, 1914. ix,331p. illus.
*ch. vii "Lord's" pp. 102–113*

**1452** **"Present Etonians", editors**
This wicket world. No. 1. 14th July, 1922; contributions by E.V. Lucas, Eric Parker, Canon Hall-Hall, etc.-etc. Eton, Spottis-woode, Ballantyne & Co., [1922]. 30p.
*issued on the occasion of Eton v. Harrow match, Lord's, July 14 & 15, 1922*

**1453** **Russell, George William Erskine**
A pocketful of sixpences. Richards, 1907. viii,344p.
——*another ed.* Nelson, [1911]. 371p. port. (Nelson's Shilling Library)
*includes essay on Lord's on the occasion of an Eton v. Harrow match*

**1454** **Salt, Henry Stephens**
Memories of bygone Eton. Hutchinson, [1928]. 263p. illus. ports.
*chap. ix "Lord's in the sixties" rptd. from The Observer, 19th June, 1927*

## Eton v. Winchester matches

**1455** **Austen-Leigh, Richard Arthur**
Eton v. Winchester 1826–1902. Eton, Spottiswoode (Eton College P.), 1903. 80p. scores
——1826–1904. 1905. 78p. scores

**1456** **Warner, Robert Townsend**
Eton and Winchester: a song of the Eton & Winchester match; words by R.T. Warner, music by F.S. Kelly. Eton, College P., 1903. [i],7p.

## The Eton Mission

**1457** **Pilkington, Ernest Milbourne Swinnerton**
An Eton playing field: reminiscences of happy days spent at the Eton Mission. E. Arnold, 1896. 128p.

## Felsted

**1458** **Craze, Michael**
A history of Felsted School, 1564–1947. Ipswich, Cowell, 1955. 360p. illus. ports. plans
*references to J.W.H.T. Douglas, pp. 233, 235, 238–9, 240, 271, 275, 283, 289*

## Framlingham College

**1459** **Booth, John**
Framlingham College: the first sixty years. [Framlingham], Society of Old Framlinghamians, 1925. 192p. illus. ports.
*cricket pp. 166–172*

## Giggleswick

**1460** **Bell, Edward Allen**
History of Giggleswick School from its foundation 1499 to 1912. Leeds, R. Jackson, 1912. 294p. illus. ports.

## Haileybury College

*(see also* Imperial Service College; both schools were combined in 1942)

**1461** **Danvers, Frederick Charles, and others**
Memorials of Old Haileybury College. Constable, 1894. xxvii,668p. illus. ports. plans, map.
*cricket, pp. 77–78*

**1461
–1** **Haileybury** verses. Hertford, Stephen Austin, 1882. viii,64p.
*pp. 51–60 "Ye anciente cricket match"*

**1462** **Matches** played by the Haileybury Cricket Club 1840–51. Hertford, *printed by* G. & S.E. Simson, [1852]. [82]p. scores

**1463 Milford, Lionel Sumner**
■ Haileybury College, past and present. Unwin, 1909. 336p. illus. ports.
*cricket pp. 149–161 with illus.*


## Harrow

**1464 Bowen, Edward Ernest**
■ Harrow songs, and other verses. Longmans, 1886. viii,80p.
*includes "Willow the king", "Lord's 1873", "Lord's 1878", "Giants", "R.G.", and "F.P."*

**1465** Willow the king: Harrow cricket song:
■ words by E.E. Bowen, music by John Farmer. Penshurst, Duke & Sons, [189–]. 4p. (Harrow School Song, no. 7)

**1466 Bryant, Philip Henry Morgan**
■ Harrow. Blackie, 1936. [xi],170p. illus. ports. map
*many cricket references*

**1467 Byron, George Gordon Noel,** *6th baron Byron*
Hours of idleness, a series of poems, original and translated. Newark, S. & J. Ridge, 1807. xiii,187p.
*includes "Memories of Harrow"*

——

**1468 Characters** of the Harrow XI, 1853. *Privately printed* by S.R. Chichester, [1959]. [4]p. folded card
*rptd. from Lillywhite's "Guide to cricketers" for 1854*

**1469 The cricket** matches between Harrow and Eton and Harrow and Winchester from 1818–1852. *Privately printed*, [c.1853]. [53]p.

**1470 Daryl, Sidney**
Harrow recollections, by an Old Harrovian (S. Daryl). Routledge, 1867. viii,124p.
——*reissue with additional t.p.* "Schooldays at Harrow". Routledge, 1868

**1471 Fox, Archibald Douglas**
Follow up! The story of a commonplace Harrovian. Brown, Langham, 1908. 320p.
——*another ed. with title:* Follow up! The story of Harrow School; illustrated by J.E. Sutcliffe. Partridge [c.1920]. 320p. illus.
*a boy's story; a ch. on "The School v. Eton"*

**1472** Harrow; edited and specially illustrated
■ by the Sport and General Press Agency. Pitman, 1911. [xii],119p. illus. ports. (Public School Life)
*cricket pp. 38–48*

**1473** **Harrow** Association record and list of members. Harrow, the Association. *annual*
*23 issues 1907–08 to 1929–30*

**1473 Harrow Colts Cricket Club**
**–1** The rules of the Colts Club and the Declaration of cricket principle. The Club. bs. card
*formed in 1876*

**1474 [Harrow School]**
■ House matches and lists of prizemen of Rev. Dr. Vaughan's House 1845–1859; and of Rev. Dr. Butler's 1860–1864. Harrow, *printed by* Crossley & Clarke, 1865. [iii],172p. scores
*not only cricket*

**1474 Harrow School**
**–1** Churchill centenary songs. 30th October,
■ 1974, Royal Albert Hall. The School, [1974]. 24p. incl. covers
*includes p. 11 by E.E. Bowen, "Giants" and "A gentleman's a-bowling," dedicated to F.S. Jackson, Lord's 1888*

**1474 Harrow School** 1st XI tour of Barbados
**–2** July 21st – August 12th, 1979. [The
■ School, 1979]. 72p. incl. adverts. illus. ports.

**1475 Harrow** School songs; edited by John
□ Farmer. London, Novello; Harrow, J.C. Wilbee, *n.d.* 147p.
*includes p. 16 "Willow the king", and p. 62 "Giants"*
——New series; edited by Eaton Faning. London, Novello; Harrow, J.C. Wilbee, *n.d.*
——No. 2. The niner: a cricket song. Words by E.E.B. [Edward Ernest Bowen]; music by E.F. [Eaton Faning]. 3p.
*1st publd. 1887*
——No. 6. A gentleman's a-bowling. Words by E.E.B.; music by E.F. 3p.
*1st publd. 1888 to mark the Eton v. Harrow match of that year*
——No. 11. If time is up. Words by E.E.B.; music by E.F. 3p.
*1st publd. 1895*

**1476 Haygarth, Arthur**
The cricket matches played by the Harrovians in 1842 and 1843. 1844

**1477** Harrow School cricket matches: a register of the principal matches played at Harrow and Lord's during the season of 1854, with the averages of the Harrow XI. Harrow, W. Winkley, 1854. stats.

**1478 Howson, Edmund Whytehead,** *and*
■ **Townsend-Warner, George,** *editors*
Harrow School; illustrated by Herbert M.

Marshall. E. Arnold, 1898. xvii,291p. illus. ports.

> chap. xx "Cricket at Harrow", by Spencer W. Gore; chap. xxi "The Eton and Harrow match", by Walter H. Long; chap. xxii "Ponsonby and Grimston" by Hon. E. Chandos Leigh

**1479** **Laborde, Edward Dalrymple**
■ Harrow School yesterday and today. Winchester Publications, 1948. 256p. illus. ports. maps. diagrs. bibliog. (English Public Schools)
> cricket with illus. pp. 25, 42, 44, 55, 73, 165, 174, 192–96, 212–13

**1479** **Lunn, Harold**
**–1** The Harrovians. Methuen, 1919. 312p.
> cricket pp. 109–16

**1480** **Mayo, Charles Harry Powell**
Reminiscences of a Harrow master. Rivington, 1928. xii,230p. illus.

**1481** **Minchin, James George Cotton**
■ Old Harrow days; with original sketches by Miss F. Holms. Methuen, 1898. [viii],331p. illus.
> chap. 4 "Cricket at Harrow", pp. 144–185 with plate and results of Eton & Harrow matches, pp. 312–318

**1482** [Entry cancelled]

**1483** **Savillon's** elegies or poems, written by a gentleman, A.B. late of the University of Cambridge. T. Rickaby for Hookham and Carpenter, 1795. 155p. frontis.
> engraved frontis. by B. Reading after T. Cruikshank shows Harrow School with cricket in progress

**1484** **Storr, Francis,** editor
Life and remains of the Rev. R.H. Quick. Clay, 1899. 550p.
> references to cricket at Harrow

**1485** **Thornton, Percy Melville**
■ Harrow School and its surroundings. W.H. Allen, 1885. xii,482p. illus. maps
> chap. xiv "Harrow cricket", pp. 317–349

**1486** **Torre, Henry John**
■ Recollections of school days at Harrow more than fifty years ago. Manchester, printed by C. Simms, 1890. 127p. ports. scores
> cricket pp. 109–126

**1486** **Views** and scenery of Harrow. J.E. Kay,
**–1** 1871?
> 12 topographical prints including one of "The cricket ground, Harrow, 11th September 1860"

**1486** **Warner, George Townsend,** editor
**–2** Harrow in prose and verse. Hodder & Stoughton, [1913]. vi,207p. illus. & ports. in col.

**1486** **Williams,** Sir **John Fischer**
**–3** Harrow. Bell, 1901. xiv,226p. illus. map. (Handbooks to the Great Public Schools)
> cricket pp. 163–175

## Harvey Grammar

**1486** **Brown, J. Howard**
**–4** A history of the Harvey Grammar School. Folkstone, Old Harveians Assoc., 1962. 240p. illus.
> cricket pp. 93, 116–7, 139, 154, 160, 174, 176, 191, 212–3

## Hastings Grammar

**1486** **Baines, J. Manwaring, Conisbee, J.R.,**
**–5** and **Bygate, N.**
The history of Hastings Grammar School 1619–1966. Hastings, the School, 1966
——revd. ed. 1967. xi,324p.
> cricket pp. 160–7, 271–3

## Hereford

**1486** **Ruscoe, Reginald Guy,** compiler and editor
**–6** Hereford High School for Boys: an account of its first fifty years 1912–1962. Hereford, [the School?], 1962. xi,140p. frontis.
> cricket pp. 92–5

## Huddersfield College

**1486** **Huddersfield College** cricket matches
**–7** past and present 1873–1893. Huddersfield, the College, [1893]. 56p. typescript

## Hurstpierpoint College

**1486** **Hurstpierpoint College**
**–8** Cricket tour of India Dec. 1977-Jan. 1978:
■ souvenir brochure. Hurstpierpoint, the College, [1977]. [20]p. incl. adverts. illus. ports.
> pre-tour

## Imperial Service College
## (see also Haileybury College)

**1487** **Beckwith, Edward George Ambrose**
■ Imperial Service College 1912–1933: a short history. Windsor, Duff, [c.1934]. [vi],70p. port.
> scattered cricket references with memorial list of the cricket XI killed in World War I

## Ipswich

**1488** **Gray, Irvine Egerton,** *and* **Potter, William**
■ **Edward**
Ipswich School 1400–1950. Ipswich, Harrison, 1950. x,180p. illus. ports. plans (on end papers)
*scattered references in text with captains of cricket 1849–1949, pp. 170–73, and results up to 1947, p. 175*

## King's School, Canterbury

**1489** **Baldock, E.L.**
■ Thirty five seasons. Canterbury, O.K.S. Association, [c.1971]. [20]p.
*author was head gardener at The King's School Canterbury; cricket references*

**1490** **Edwards, David Lawrence**
■ A history of the King's School Canterbury. Faber and Faber, 1957. 224p. illus. ports.
*cricket pp. 140, 151, 153, 157, 189, 196*

**1490** **Pater, Walter Horatio**
**–1** Emerald Uthwart. [Canterbury?], *privately printed* for the King's School, 1905. 47p.
*short novel with brief references to cricket; originally printed in the New Review, June & July 1892 and reissued for the first time in book form in 'Miscellaneous Studies', 1895*

**1491** **Woodruff, Charles Eveleigh,** *and* **Cape,**
■ **Henry James**
Schola regia Cantuariensis: a history of Canterbury School commonly called the King's School. Mitchell, Hughes & Clarke, 1908. xvi, 368p. illus. ports. plan, stats.
*cricket pp. 233, 284–295 with 2 team portraits*

## Lancing College

**1492** **Handford, B.W.T.**
■ Lancing: a history of SS. Mary and Nicolas College, Lancing 1848–1930. Oxford, Blackwell, 1933. xx,417p. illus. ports. stats.
*ch. xv, 'Cricket' by A.L. Hilder, pp. 316–334*

## Liverpool College

**1492** **Wainwright, David**
**–1** Liverpool gentlemen: a history of Liverpool College, an independent day school, from 1840. Faber & Faber, 1960. 342p. illus.
*cricket pp. 273–7, 285–6*

## Liverpool Institute

**1492** **Tiffen, Herbert Joseph**
**–2** A history of the Liverpool Institute Schools 1825 to 1935. Liverpool, The Liverpool Institute Old Boys' Assoc., 1935. 190p. illus.
*cricket pp. 87–8, 95, 101, 131, 134–5, 169*

## Lord Weymouth

**1493** **Hope, Robert**
History of the Lord Weymouth School, Warminster. Bradford, Broadacre Books, 1961. 134p. illus. ports.
*many references to cricket*

## Loughborough Grammar

**1493** **Loughborough Grammar School**
**–1** Rugby tour of Sri Lanka, November-December 1978.
*20p. of cricket*

## Louth Grammar School

**1494** **Louth Grammar School Cricket Club**
Rules and regulations. Louth, [the School, c.1833]
*Lord's copy has names of officers added in MS*

## Magdalen College School

**1495** **Stanier, R.S.**
■ Magdalen School; a history of Magdalen College School, Oxford. 2nd ed. Oxford, Blackwell, 1958. xv,251p. illus. ports. map. diagr.
*scattered references*

## Magnus Grammar, Newark

**1495** **Jackson, Noel George**
**–1** Newark Magnus: the story of a gift. Nottingham, J. & H. Bell Ltd., 1964. 298p. illus. ports.
*cricket pp. 146, 161, 162, 189, 190, 222, 233, 239*

## Malvern College

**1496** **Blumenau, Ralph**
■ A history of Malvern College 1865 to 1965. Macmillan, 1965. xiv,194p. illus. ports. bibliog.
*scattered references*

## Marlborough College

**1497** **Andrew, Edwyn Silverlock**
■ Scores of the cricket matches between Rugby & Marlborough from the commencement up to date. Hurst & Blackett, 1904. 61p. scores
——2nd ed. 1906. [iv],71p. scores, stats.

1498 **Bradley, Arthur Granville,** *and others*
■ History of Marlborough College during fifty years from its foundation to the present time, by A.G. Bradley, A.C. Champneys and J.W. Baines. Murray, 1893. xxx,323p. illus.
——Now revised and continued by J.R. Taylor, H.C. Brentnall and G.C. Turner. Murray, 1923. xi,331p. illus.
*cricket in chaps. xxiii and xxiv*

1499 **Marlborough** College cricket elevens, etc. up to Christmas 1880. Marlborough, W. Gale, 1880. 19p.

1500 **Sketches** from Marlborough. Marlborough, Chas. Perkins, Times Office, 1888. 105p.
——2nd ed. 1905. 100p.
*cricket in chaps. vi & vii*

## Merchant Taylors'

1501 **Draper, Frederick William Marsden**
■ Four centuries of Merchant Taylors' School, 1561–1961. Oxford U.P., 1962. viii,260p. illus. ports.
*cricket pp. 101 (James Love). 166–70, 177, 179, 237*

## Merchant Taylors' School, Crosby

1501 **Luft, Hyam Mark**
-1 A history of Merchant Taylors' School, Crosby, 1620–1970. Liverpool, Liverpool Univ. P., 1970. xiv,338p. illus. ports. facsims. plan
*cricket pp. 172, 217–8, 225, 257–8*

## Mill Hill

1502 **Brett-James, Norman George**
■ The history of Mill Hill School 1807–1907. Melrose, [1909]. xii,415p. illus. ports. map, plans
*scattered references*

## Monkton Combe

1502 **Lace, Arthur Frederick**
-1 A goodly heritage: a history of Monkton
■ Combe School . . . 1868 to 1967. Bath, Pitman for the School, 1968. xiii,298p. illus. ports. map
*cricket pp. 32–4, 54, 61, 79, 101, 125–7, 143, 154, 168, 185–6, 213, 225, 260*

## Newport

1502 **Glover, E.P.**
-2 The first sixty years 1896–1956: the Newport High School for Boys. Newport, *printed by* R.H. Johns, 1957. 168p. frontis.
*cricket pp. 107–9*

## Nottingham

1502 **Widdowson, Vic C.,** *and* **Peel, N.**
-3 **Jonathan**
■ Nottingham High School: a century of cricket 1871–1970. [Nottingham, the School, 1970?]. 103p. stats. *typescript*

## Oratory

1503 **[Bowring, Wilfrid J.]**
■ Beaumont v. Oratory, 1867–1925, by "Ignotus". Windsor, Brodie, 1926. 51p. scores, stats.

## Oundle

1504 **Walker, William George**
■ A history of the Oundle Schools. The Grocer's Company, 1956. xviii,748p. illus. ports. plans, diagrs.
*p. 514—account of the visits of W.G. Grace between 1897 and 1902 to play for the Masters XI, his son, W.G. jnr. being a master at the school*

## Perse School

1504 **Gray, J.M.**
-1 A history of Perse School, Cambridge. Cambridge, Bowes and Bowes, 1921. 161p. illus.
*cricket pp. 131–2*

## Price's College

1504 **Tuck, Charles,** *compiler*
-2 Price's College Cricket Club . . . tour of
■ the West Indies, March–April 1975. Fareham, the College C.C., [1975]. 56p. incl. adverts. illus. ports.
*souvenir issued to raise funds for a tour of St. Lucia and Trinidad*

## Radley College

1505 **Boyd, Alfred Kenneth**
■ The history of Radley College 1847–1947. Oxford, Blackwell, 1948. xv,464p. illus. (1 col.), ports.
*cricket pp. 405–428 with illus. and account of Radley Rangers C.C.*

1506 **Bradfield** *v.* Radley cricket
■ *1853–1898 [1899?]. 46p.*
*1853–1911. [1912?]. 84p.*
*1853–1920; with a supplement giving our matches with other schools; compiled by T. Steele. Reading, Blackwell, 1921. 108p. scores*

1507 **Sicut** Columbae: fifty years of S. Peter's
■ College, Radley, by T.D. Raikes, and other Old Radleians. Oxford & London, Parker, 1897. xiii,320p. illus. ports.

*ch. x "Cricket" by T.F. Hobson, pp. 239–70, and other refs.*
——: a history of S. Peter's College, Radley, 1847–1924: being a continuation . . . by Ernest Bryans, Oxford, Blackwell, 1925. xvii,317p. illus. port.
*cricket pp. 39, 151, 249–73*

## Repton

1508 **Bradstreet, John**
■ Repton sketches; with illustrations from drawings by Arthur Norris. Benn, 1928 [viii],87p. illus.
*"School matches" pp. 61–67*

1509 **Cochrane, Alfred John Henry**
■ Reptonian reprints: verses reprinted from "The Reptonian", 1883–1907. Repton, A.J. Lawrence, 1907. vii,63p.
*includes several of cricket interest*

1510 Repton cricket (1865–1905). Repton, A.J.
■ Lawrence, 1908. viii,217p. ports. plans. scores, stats.

1511 **Macdonald, Alec**
■ A short history of Repton. Benn, 1929. 256p. illus. ports. plans, bibliog.
*cricket pp. 162–64, 179–83, 207–10, 226–27*

1512 **Messiter, George Stephen,** *editor*
■ Records and reminiscences of Repton. Repton, A.J. Lawrence for private circulation, 1907. [vii],116p. score
*cricket pp. 48–51*

1513 **Monro, Frederick Robert D'Oyley**
■ Repton cricket (1901–1951). Rugby, George Over, 1953. [x],80p. illus. ports. stats.

1514 **Thomas, Bernard,** *editor*
■ Repton 1557 to 1957. Batsford, 1957. xii,219p. illus. ports.
*chap. v "Repton cricket" pp. 136–59*

## Rossall

1515 **Furness, William,** *editor*
■ The centenary history of Rossall School. Aldershot, Gale & Polden, 1945. xvi,387p. illus. ports.
*cricket pp. 277–287, etc.*

1515 **Memorial** of the jubilee of Rossall School,
–1 June 21,22,23,1894. Manchester, Geo. Falkner & Sons, 1894. viii,67p. illus.
*cricket pp. 58–61*

1516 **Rowbotham, John Frederick**
■ The history of Rossall School. Manchester, Heywood, [1894]. x,447p. illus. ports.

——2nd ed. enlarged. 1901. x,469p. illus. ports.
*chap. x "Rossall cricket"*

## Rugby

1517 **Ackermann, Rudolph**
The history of Rugby School. R. Ackermann, 1816. illus.
*includes aquatint by J. Stadler after W. Westall of view of the Southern School and dormitories of Rugby School with cricket being played*

1518 **Andrew, Edwyn Silverlock**
■ Scores of the cricket matches between Rugby & Marlborough from the commencement up to date. Hurst & Blackett, 1904. 61p. scores
——2nd ed. 1906 [iv],71p. scores, stats.

1519 **Bradby, Henry Christopher**
■ Rugby. Bell, 1900. xii,231p. illus. ports. map. (Handbooks to the Great Public Schools)
*cricket pp. 201–208*

1520 **Chatwin, G.A.F.M.**
Rugby School cricket teams from 1831 and football teams from 1867. Rugby, George Over, 1938. 184p.

1521 **Guillemard, Arthur George**
■ Rugby School cricket scores (Foreign and Bigside matches) 1831–1893, with a few tables of statistics; compiled under the revision of the Old Rugbeian Society. Rugby, Lawrence; London, Whittaker, 1894. viii,679p. scores, stats.

1522 **Hardy, Henry Harrison**
■ Rugby; edited and specially illustrated by the Sport and General Press Agency. Pitman, 1911. [x],128p. illus. (Public School Life)
*cricket pp. 80–84*

1523 **[Hughes, Thomas]**
Tom Brown's school days, by an Old Boy. Cambridge, Macmillan, 1857. viii,420p.
*numerous subsequent editions; ch. viii, "Tom Brown's last match"*

1524 **[Entry cancelled]**

1525 **[Newmarch, Charles Henry]**
■ Recollections of Rugby, by an Old Rugbaean. Hamilton & Adams, 1848. 180p.

1526 **Radclyffe, Charles Walter,** *artist*
■ Memorials of Rugby, from drawings by C.R. [sic] Radclyffe. Rugby, Crossley, 1841–2. illus.
*6 parts in 1. A series of lithographs*

including in pt. 5 "The school, from the close", showing cricket being played in the foreground.

1527 **Rouse, William Henry Denham**
■ A history of Rugby School. Duckworth, 1898. xvi,420p. illus. ports. plan. (English Public Schools)
*cricket pp. 170–71, 262, 283, 287, 326–29*

1528 **The scores** of the cricket matches played
□ by Rugby School from the year MDCCCXXXI. Rugby, J.S. Crossley, [1842]. [i],69p. scores
*covers the years 1831–1842*
——*another ed. with title:* The scores . . . played at Rugby School from the year 1845. Rugby, Crossley & Billington, [1852]. 109p. scores
*covers the years 1845–51*
——*another ed.*—— ——, [1859]. 135p. scores
*covers the years 1845–58*
——*another ed. with title:* The scores . . . played by Rugby School from the year 1859 to 1864 inclusive. 1864. [ii],122p. scores

1529 **Simpson, J.B. Hope**
■ Rugby since Arnold: a history of Rugby School from 1842. Macmillan, 1967. xii,316p. illus. ports. maps, bibliog.
*cricket pp. 64, 255–73*

### Rutherford Grammar, Newcastle

1529 **Maw, William**
–1 The story of Rutherford Grammar School (formerly Rutherford College, Newcastle-upon-Tyne). Gateshead, Northumberland P., 1964. 260p. illus.
*cricket pp. 174–83*

### Rydal

1530 **Rydal** School 1885–1935. Colwyn Bay,
■ Rydal P., [1936]. 240p. illus. ports.
*cricket pp. 64–74*

### S. Anselm's School, Bakewell

1530 **Piper, Geoffrey**
–1 A history of S. Anselm's cricket
■ 1888–1975. Bakewell, [S. Anselm's School], 1975. 44p. 1 illus. ports, stats.

### St. Edward's School, Oxford

1531 **Hill, R.D.**
■ A history of St. Edward's School, 1863–1963. [Oxford], St. Edward's School Society, 1962. xvi,408p. illus. ports.
*Appendix C. Cricket pp. 374–396*

### St. Peter's School, York

1532 **Raine, Angelo**
■ History of St. Peter's School: York, A.D. 627 to the present day. Bell, 1926. xii,212p. illus. ports.

1532 **Wiseman, Francis Jowett**
–1 The recent history of St. Peter's School. York, York Herald Printers, [1969]. illus. (1 col.), ports. 173p.
*cricket pp. 143–8*

### Sedbergh

1533 **Ainslie, Ralph St. John**
■ Sedbergh School songs, written and illustrated by R. St. J. Ainslie. Leeds, Jackson, 1896. 102p. illus.
*includes "A cricket song"*

1533 **Sedbergh School Cricket Club**
–1 Caribbean cricket tour March – April
■ 1979: [souvenir brochure]. [The Club, 1979]. 24p. illus. ports.
*cover title:* Sedbergh School centenary cricket tour to the West Indies April 1979

### Sherborne

1534 **Gourlay, Arthur Bellyse**
■ A history of Sherborne School. Winchester, Warren, 1951. xii,291p. illus. ports. plan, bibliog.
*cricket pp. 211–215 and scattered references*
——*2nd ed.* Sherborne, Sawtells, 1971 [xvi],335p.
*cricket pp. 107, 140, 196–7, 242–7*

1535 **Photographs** of the teams who have represented Sherborne School at football and cricket 1901–1915. Sherborne, F. Bennett, 1915. ports.

### Shrewsbury

1536 **Fisher, George William**
■ Annals of Shrewsbury School; revised by J. Spencer Hill. Methuen, 1899. xv,508p. illus. ports.
*cricket pp. 407–11*

1537 **Oldham, J. Basil**
■ A history of Shrewsbury School 1552–1952. Oxford, Blackwell, 1952. xii,323p. illus. ports. map, plans
*cricket pp. 238–40*

1538 **Pendlebury, William John,** *and* **West,**
■ **John Milns**
Shrewsbury School: the last fifty years. Shrewsbury, Wilding, 1932. 94p. illus. ports, plans

1539 **West, John Milns**
Shrewsbury. Blackie, 1937. vii,156p. illus.

## Sidcot

1540 **Knight, Francis, A.**
■ A history of Sidcot School: a hundred years of west country Quaker education, 1808–1908. Dent, 1908. viii,346p. illus. (1 col.). ports. plans.
*cricket pp. 65, 93, 124, 144, 191–93, 210, 214, 219, 220, 237, 269, 321*

## Stonyhurst College

1541 **Gerard, John**
Stonyhurst College: its life beyond the seas, 1592–1794, and on English soil 1794–1894 (centenary record.). Belfast, Marcus Ward, 1894. xiv,316p.

1542 **Gruggen, George,** *and* **Keating, Joseph**
Stonyhurst: its past history and life in the present. Kegan, Paul, Trench, Trübner, 1901. 280p. illus.
*includes account of Stonyhurst cricket with illus.*

## Taunton

1542 **Record, S.P.**
–1 Proud century: the first hundred years of Taunton School. Taunton, E. Goodman, 1948. 307p. illus.
*cricket pp. 245–6, 249–52*

## Tonbridge

1542 **Hodge, Hugh S. Vere**
–2 Five overs & 2 wides; with illustrations
■ by Phillida Gili. *Privately printed*, 1975. xvii,72p.
*limited ed. of 500 copies*

1543 **Rivington, Septimus**
The history of Tonbridge School from its foundation in 1553 to the present date. Rivingtons, 1870. illus.
——2nd ed. rev. & enlarged. 1898. xiv,368,lxiiip.
——3rd ed. rev. & enlarged. 1910. xv,432,lxiiip.
——4th ed. rev. 1925,xi,372p.

1544 **Somervell, David Churchill**
■ A history of Tonbridge School. Faber, 1947. 150p. illus. ports.
*cricket pp. 50, 64, 105, 115 and frontis.*

1544 **Views** of Tonbridge School. Rock & Co.,
–1 1865.
*six topographical prints, including one of the cricket ground*

## Twyford

1545 **Wickham, Charles Townshend**
■ The story of Twyford School from 1809 to 1909. Winchester, Warren, 1909. xi,215p. illus. port. scores
*cricket pp. 72–73 and illus.*

## Uppingham

1546 **Bennet, Norman**
■ Our cricket match. Cambridge, Gray; Brighton, Friend; London, Simpkin, Marshall, [1893]. 16p.

1547 **Graham, John Parkhurst**
■ Forty years of Uppingham: memories and sketches. Macmillan, 1932. xiv,173p. illus.

1547 **Hornung, Ernest William**
–1 Fathers of men. Smith, Elder, 1912.
■ vi,371p.
*a school story. "It was not always intended that the school in this story should be expressly identified with Uppingham. To Uppingham men, indeed, the scenes and customs described were meant to be unmistakeable; . . .'* (Preface)

1548 **"An Old Boy",** *pseud.*
■ Early days at Uppingham under Edward Thring. Macmillan, 1904. x,163p.
*cricket pp. 98–102*

1549 **Patterson, William Seeds**
■ Sixty years of Uppingham cricket. Longmans, Green, 1909. xv,316p. ports. scores

1550 **Public** school matches, 1865–1886. Uppingham, [the School?], 1887. 32p.
*Uppingham v. Repton and Haileybury*

1551 **Thring, Edward**
■ Uppingham School songs and Borth lyrics. T. Fisher Unwin, 1887. [v],79p.
*includes "Uppingham cricket song, 1856", and "The Old Boys' Match", pp. 21–27*

## Warwick

1552 **Leach, Arthur Francis**
■ History of Warwick School. . . . Constable, 1906. xvi,262p. illus. ports.
*cricket pp. 237–241*

## Wellington College

1553 **Berkeley, George Fitz-Hardinge**
■ My recollections of Wellington College. Newport, R.H. Johns, 1946. 168p. ports. plan, stats.
*cricket—chs. 4, 8 and 10*

**1554 Newsome, David**
■ A history of Wellington College 1859–1959. John Murray, 1959. xii,414p. illus. ports.
*cricket pp. 162, 221, 223–4, 263, 343–4*

## Westminster

**1555 Carleton, John Dudley**
■ Westminster School: a history. Rev. ed. Hart-Davis, 1965. x,182p. illus. (1 col.), ports.
*cricket pp. 135–36, 138–39*

**1555 Charterhouse** [and] Westminster tour of
**–1** New Zealand December, 1976—January,
■ 1977. *n.p.*, [1976]. 36p. incl. adverts. illus. on covers
*pre-tour*

**1556 Forshall, Frederick H.**
■ Westminster School past and present. Wyman, 1884. xvi,607p. illus.
*cricket pp. 566–570*

**1557 Markham, Francis**
■ Recollections of a town boy at Westminster, 1849–55. E. Arnold, 1903. xv,232p. illus. port.
*cricket pp. 148–52*

**1558 Sargeaunt, John**
■ Annals of Westminster School. Methuen, 1898. xi,303p. illus. ports
*cricket pp. 186–87, 205, 227, 237–38, 261*

**1559 Shore, William Teignmouth**
■ Public school life: Westminster. Pitman, 1910. 126p. illus.
*cricket pp. 63–65 with illus.*

**1560 Tanner, Lawrence Edward**
■ Westminster School: a history. Country Life, 1934. x,132p. illus. ports.
——2nd ed. 1951. 144p. illus. ports.
*cricket pp.111, 122–3*

## Whitgift Grammar

**1560 History** of the Whitgift Grammar School
**–1** with a register of all Whitgiftians from 1871 to 1892. Croydon, W.D. Hayward, 1892. xv,509p. illus. ports. plan, score, stats.
*Cricket pp. 180–214*

## William Ellis

**1561 Wickenden, Thomas Douglas**
■ William Ellis School 1862–1962; the history of a school and those who made it. The School, 1961. [xiii],305p. illus. ports.
*scattered references to school cricket and to the Old Elysians' C.C.*

## William Hulme's Grammar

**1561 William Hulme's Grammar School,**
**–1** *Manchester*
■ Caribbean cricket tour March–April 1978: souvenir brochure. [Manchester, the School, 1978]. 52p. incl. adverts. illus. ports. map
*pre-tour*

## Winchester College

**1562 Adams, Henry Cadwallader**
Wykehamica: a history of Winchester College and Commoners, from the foundation to the present day. Oxford & London, James Parker; Winchester, Wells, 1878. x,496p. illus. plan
*cricket pp. 365ff.*

**1563 [Blore, George Henry]**
College in the Eighties, by An Old Wykehamist. Winchester, Warren *for private publication*, [c.1935]. 55p. illus.

**1564 Cook, Arthur Kemball**
■ About Winchester College: to which is prefixed, De Collegio Wintoniensi, by Robert Mathew. Macmillan, 1917. xvii,583p. illus. plan
*cricket pp. 129–30, 132, 356, 359, 429*

**1565 [Cowburn, Allen)**
□ Wykehamical scores from the year 1825. Winchester, Robbins & Wheeler, 1838. 80p. scores
——*another ed.* [1840]
——*another ed.* [1841]
——*another ed.* [1843]
——*another ed.* [1850]. 152p.
——*another ed.* [1851]. 164p.
*the later eds. contain additional scores, but all retain the original title-page dated 1838*

**1566 The cricket** matches between Harrow and Eton and Harrow and Winchester from 1818–1852. *Privately printed*, [c.1851]

**1567 Fellowes, Edmund Horace**
■ A history of Winchester cricket. Winchester, Wells, 1930. xii,203p. scores. stats. bibliog.
——Supplement 1930–1941. Wells, 1942. 68p. scores, stats.
——Second supplement 1942–1951. Wells, 1951. 47p. scores

**1568 Firth, John d'Ewes Evelyn**
■ Winchester. Blackie, 1936. [xi],184p. illus. (English Public Schools)
*cricket pp. 118–124, etc.*
——revised ed. *with title:* Winchester College. Winchester Publications Ltd., 1949. 256p. illus.
*cricket pp. 111–13, 135–40, etc.*

1569 **Irvine, Andrew** Leicester
College in the Nineties. Winchester, Warren, 1947. 62p.
*cricket pp. 46–50*

1570 **Leach, Arthur Francis**
■ A history of Winchester College. Duckworth, 1899. xiv,564p. illus.
*cricket pp. 440–5, 463, 503–8, 532–3*

1571 **[Mansfield, Robert Blachford]**
■ School life at Winchester College; or, The reminiscences of a Winchester Junior . . . by the author of "The log of the Water-Lily". Hotten, 1866. 243p. illus. plan, glossary
——2nd ed. 1870
——3rd ed. 1893
*ch. x, pp. 128–36 includes cricket reminiscences; glossary defines "watching out" as "fielding at cricket. When a Junior made a catch, he was let off for the rest of the day"*

1572 **Mason, C.E.S.,** *compiler*
□ Winchester College matches, 1825–1890. Winchester, Wells; London, Wright, 1891. 52p. scores
——2nd ed. 1893. [v],97p. scores
——3rd ed. 1902. 106p. scores

1573 **Noel, Evan Baillie**
■ Winchester College cricket; with contributions by . . . J.A. Fort [and others]. Williams & Norgate, 1926. xi,250p. frontis. scores
——L.P. ed., 100 copies, signed. 1926

1574 **Old Wykehamists**
■ Winchester College 1393–1893; illustrated by Herbert Marshall. E. Arnold, 1893. ix,187p. illus.
*cricket, pp. 129–135 with 5 plates*

1575 **Palmer, Arnold Nottage**
Winchester 1900–1950. Winchester, Wells, 1954. 47p.
*cricket pp. 28–29*

1576 **[Rich, Edward John George Henry]**
Recollections of the two St. Mary Winton colleges (Winchester—New College). By an Old Wykehamist. Walsall, W. Henry; London, Simpkin Marshall, 1883. viii,199p. illus.

1577 **Tuckwell, William**
The ancient ways: Winchester fifty years ago. Macmillan, 1893. xii,171p.
*cricket pp. 32, 126, 129*

1578 **Warner, Robert Townsend**
Winchester. Bell, 1900. xvi,216p. illus. (Handbooks to the Great Public Schools)
*cricket pp. 50–54*

1579 **Winchester College**
Cricket regulations. Winchester, the College, [1937]

1580 **The Winchester** register of athletic sports,
□ cricket, football and rifle shooting. Winchester, Nutt. *annual.* scores
*1858–1866*
*later publishers: Nutt and Wells; Wells; Oxford, J. Vincent*

# OTHER SCHOOLS

## Brent Schools

1581 **Brent Schools' Cricket Association**
□ Annual general meeting & fixtures list. The Association. *typescript*
*/1965, 66/-?*

## Croydon Schools

1582 **Croydon Schools Cricket Association**
□ How's that?: the handbook of the . . . Association. Croydon, the Association. *annual.* illus. team ports. diagrs. stats.
*/1949–57/ to date*

## Cumberland Schools
(*see also:* **Lancashire Schools**)

1583 **Cumberland Schools Cricket Association**
Cumberland Boys versus Lancashire Boys on the Cricket Field, Workington, 1953: official programme and score card

## Lancashire Schools
(*see also:* **Manchester Schools**)

1584 **Lancashire County Elementary Schools' Cricket Association**
Cricket handbook. Manchester, the Association. *annual?*
*?/1944, 1946/–?*
*formed 1922*

1585 **Lancashire Schools Cricket Association**
□ Cricket handbook. Manchester, the Association. *annual.* illus. ports. diagrs. scores
*1925 to date*

1586 **Thomas, Herbert F.B.,** *compiler*
■ Schoolboy cricket in Lancashire: short history of the Lancashire Schools' Cricket Association. [Manchester, the Assoc., 1957]. 32p. port.

*v. Cumberland*

1587 **Lancashire Schools Cricket Association**
Lancashire schools. v. Cumberland schools. Nelson, Coulton, 1952. [4]p.

1588　**Lancashire and Manchester Schools'**
■　**Cricket Associations**
Lancashire Boys v. Cumberland Boys, Old Trafford, 19th July, 1958: official programme and score card. [Manchester], the Assocs., [1958]. 16p. incl. adverts. illus. ports.

*v. Derbyshire*

1589　**Lancashire Schools Cricket Association**
Lancashire Boys v. Derbyshire Boys, County Cricket Ground, Old Trafford, Manchester, 4th July, 1953: official programme and score card. Manchester, the Assoc., [1953]. ports.

*v. Durham*

1590　**Lancashire Schools' Cricket Association,**
*and* **Rochdale Schools' Sports and Games Association**
Schoolboys' county cricket: Lancashire v. County Durham at . . . Rochdale . . . 27 June, 1953: souvenir pamphlet. [The Associations, 1953]

1591　**Lancashire Schools Cricket Association**
□　Lancashire Boys v. Durham Boys, Old Trafford: official programme and score-card. [Manchester], the Association 1957. 16p. illus. ports.
1961. 16p. illus.

*v. Hampshire*

1592　Lancashire Boys v. Hampshire Boys, Old Trafford, Saturday, July 10, 1965: official programme and scorecard. Manchester, the Assoc., [1965]. 20p. ports.

*v. London and Home Counties*

1593　Cricket match on the Pollards . . .
□　Oldham, Tuesday July 29, 1947: Lancashire Schools Cricket Association and London and Home Counties Schools' Cricket Association: official programme. [Manchester, the Assoc., 1947]
——[1952]. 12p.

*v. Warwickshire*

1594　Lancashire Boys v. Warwickshire Boys,
■　Old Trafford, July 27, 1963: official programme and score card. [Manchester]. The Assoc., [1963]. [16]p. incl. adverts. illus. ports.

*v. Yorkshire*

1595　Lancashire Boys v. Yorkshire Boys.
□　Manchester, the Association. illus.
?/1930, 1932–35, 1937/1946? to date?

*Merseyside Boys v. Isle of Man Boys*

1596　Schoolboys' cricket, organised by the Liverpool, Prescot and Birkenhead Associations (affiliated to the Lancashire Schools Cricket Association): Merseyside Boys' XI v. Isle of Man Boys' XI at Aigburgh . . . 15th July, 1952; at Huyton . . . 17th July, 1952, at Birkenhead . . . 19th July, 1952: souvenir programme. [The Assoc., 1952]

*North v. South Lancashire*

1597　North Lancashire Boys v. South Lanca-
□　shire Boys, Old Trafford: official programme and score card. ports. *annual* ?/1950 . . . 79/to date

## Leeds Schools

1598　**Leeds Schools Cricket Association**
□　Handbook. Leeds, the Association. stats. *season?/1956/*to date?

## Leicestershire Schools

1598　**The Leicester** and Leicestershire school
–1　boys' cricket handbook. Leicester, Leicester School Boys' Association. *annual.* diagr. stats.
*1955* to date?

## London Schools
## (*see also:* **Brent Schools, Croydon Schools**)

1599　**London Schools Cricket Association**
Handbook. The Association. *annual*
*10 issues 1927–36*
contd, as: *The Schoolboy cricketer; edited by A.J. Drakes.* annual. team ports. diagrs. stats.
*6 issues 1937–39; 1948–50*

1599　Annual report. The Schools. *typescript.*
–1　*1966?* to date
□

1599　Jubilee souvenir 1925–1975. The Assoc.,
–2　[1975]. 17p. incl. adverts. ports.
■　*contains "The story of L.S.C.A." (based on an early account by J.H. Brown)*

*1965–66 tour to India and Ceylon*

1600　**Board of Control for Cricket in India**
■　Official souvenir of London School Boys cricket tour of India 1965–66. New Delhi, the Board, [1965]. [32]p. incl. adverts. ports.
*pre-tour*

1601　**Ceylon Schools Cricket Association**
■　London Schools vs. Ceylon Schools, the Oval [Colombo], January 18th and 19th

136

1966. Colombo, the Assoc., [1966]. [28]p. ports.
*pre-match*

1602 **Kerala Cricket Association**
■ London Schoolboys cricket team's visit to India, Jan. 11, 12. [1966] playing against the South Zone schools. Ernakulam, the Assoc., [1966?]. illus. ports.
*pre-visit*

1603 **London** Schools—Indian Schools Test
■ cricket matches 1965–66, Jan. 1, 2 & 3, 1966, Eden Gardens, Calcutta. Calcutta, Samira Biswas, [1965]. 68p. incl. adverts. ports.
*pre-matches*

1604 **London Schools' Cricket Association**
■ Report of 1st XI tour of India and Ceylon, December 1st–January 23rd, 1965–6. The Assoc., [1966]. 19f. stats.
*post-tour*

*1969 Colts' tour to Zambia and East Africa*

1605 **London Schools' Cricket Association**
London Schools' Cricket Association tour of Zambia & East Africa: official souvenir. The Assoc., [1969]. 12p. ports.
cover-title: *Colts' tour 1969*
*pre-tour*

1606 Report of the colts' tour 1969. The Assoc.,
■ [1969]. 18f. team port. stats.
*post-tour*

**Manchester Schools**

1607 **Manchester and District Schools' Athletic Association**
Cricket handbook, 1924. Manchester, the Assoc., 1924. 24p.

1608 **Manchester Schools Cricket Association**
□ Handbook. Manchester, the Association. *annual*. illus. ports. diagrs.
*1920 to date*

1609 **Thomas, Herbert F.B.,** *compiler*
■ Schoolboy cricket in Manchester: short history of the Manchester Schools' Cricket Association (from 1919 to 1947). [Manchester, the Assoc., 1948?]. 16p. port.

**Nottingham Schools**

1610 **City of Nottingham Schools Cricket Association**
The schoolboys' cricket handbook. Nottingham, the Assoc., 1955

**Oxford Schools**

1611 **Cricket** scheme for Oxford Elementary Schools; edited by J.R.F. Turner. Cowley and London, C.A. Press. *annual*
*1921–30*

**Wallasey Schools**

1612 **Wallasey Elementary Schools Sports Association**
School sports handbook. [Wallasey], the Association. *annual*. team ports.
*/1904–5 to 1907–8/–?*
*1907–8 contains articles by Gilbert L. Jessop and Frank Sugg*

**Welsh Schools**

1613 **Wales Secondary Schools' Cricket**
■ **Association**
Wales v. England, St. Helen's Ground, Swansea, Wednesday and Thursday, August 6 and 7, 1952: souvenir programme. The Assoc., [1952]. [12]p. incl. adverts.
*pre-match*

1614 Wales v. England, Rhos-on-Sea Ground, Colwyn Bay, Aug. 24, 25, 1959: souvenir programme. The Assoc., [1959]
*pre-match*

**Worcestershire Schools**

1615 **Worcestershire Schools Cricket**
□ **Association**
Hon. Secretary's report. Stourbridge, the Assoc. *annual*. scores, stats. *typescript*
*season/1947 . . . 56/to date?*

**Yorkshire Schools**
(*see also:* **Lancashire Schools; Leeds Schools**)

1616 **Yorkshire Schools' Cricket Association**
Yorkshire Boys v. Lancashire Boys at Headingley, Leeds . . . , 27 & 28 May, 1953: souvenir programme. [Leeds, the Assoc., 1953]. ports.

1616 [Golden jubilee] 1973. The Assoc., 1973.
–1 16p.
■ *includes brief history of the Association and Festival programme of matches with other County School Associations*

1617 **Yorkshire Youth Council.** *Cricket Advisory Committee*
The first report. The Cttee. 1953. illus.

137

# UNIVERSITY AND COLLEGE CRICKET

1617 **British Colleges Sports Association**
-1 Cricket tour of the West Indies
■ March–April 1978: souvenir brochure;
edited by David Gaunt. The Assoc.,
[1978]. 32p. incl. adverts. team port.
*pre-tour; sponsored by Agatha Christie Ltd.*

1617 West Indies tour 1979, 29 March to 19
-2 April. The Assoc., 1979. 20p. incl.
■ adverts. illus. ports.
*pre-tour; sponsored by Agatha Christie Ltd.*

1618 **The British Universities Sports**
■ **Federation**
First British Universities cricket tourna-
ment (for the Courtauld Trophy) to be
held on 19th July to 23rd July, 1971. The
Federation, [1971]. [10]p. map insert
——Second . . . tournament . . . to be
held 5–7th July, 1972: programme. The
Federation, [1972]. [11]p. *typescript*

1618 **Oxford** and Cambridge Universities
-1 cricket tour of Australia, December 1979
■ – January 1980. The Tour Management,
[1979]. [24]p. incl. adverts. ports.
*pre-tour itinerary with pen-portraits of
team*

1619 **Players** in inter-university cricket
■ matches from 1827 to 1877. Tiverton,
Devon, "Gazette" Printing Works, 1877.
14p.

1620 **Teams** of the universities and public
schools. J. Cornish & Sons, 1882
*in Taylor*

1621 **Universities Athletic Union**
■ "50 years of university sport": 1919–1969.
[The Union, 1969]. 32p.

1622 **Wordsworth, Christopher,** *compiler*
Social life at the English universities in
the eighteenth century. Cambridge, Bell,
1874. 728p.
*cricket pp. 178–80, 666–7*

## Cambridge

1623 **Cambridge School of Art**
■ Green and white—Fenner's observed:
drawings and photographs of Fenner's.
Cambridge, Cambridge School of Art,
1962. [32]p. illus.

1624 **Cambridge University**
■ Almanac and sports register. Cambridge,
H. Wallis; London, W.B. Clive. *annual*
scores, stats.
*1853–1894*

1625 **The Cambridge** University cricket
■ calendar; [edited by G.J. Gray].
Cambridge, *printed by* Metcalf
*1890. 1891. 119p. scores, stats. [season 1890]*
*1892. 1892. 108p. scores, stats. [Season 1891]*

1626 **Fifty** years of sport at Oxford, Cambridge
■ and the great public schools; arranged by
The Right Hon. Lord Desborough of
Taplow, K.C.V.O. 3 vols.
*Vols. I and II. Oxford and Cambridge;
edited by A.C.M. Croome. Southwood, 1913.
ports. scores
cricket in vol I, pp. 83–189*

1627 **Ford, William Justice**
■ A History of the Cambridge University
Cricket Club 1820–1901. Blackwood, 1902.
xv,561pp. illus. scores, stats.

1628 **Piggott, Percy**
■ Incidents in fifty years of Cambridge
University Cricket. Cambridge, F. & P.
Piggott, [1936]. 38p.
——*2nd ed. with title:* Fenner's: reminiscences of Cambridge University cricket.
[1948]. 39p.

1628 **Reeve, Frank Albert**
-1 Cambridge. Batsford, 1976. 184p. illus.
port. maps, bibliog.
*University cricket pp. 102–3*

## Cambridge: Cambridge University Vandals

1629 **[Illinois Cricket Association]**
■ The Cambridge University Vandals
Cricket and Rugby Football Club of
England on tour U.S.A. and Canada.
Season 1933. Chicago, the Assoc., [1933].
[4]p. folded card

## Cambridge: Crusaders' Cricket Club

1630 **Crusaders' Cricket Club**
Rules. Revised ed. Cambridge, the Club,
1928. 4p.

## Cambridge: Jesus College

1631 **Gray, Arthur,** *and* **Brittain, Frederick**
■ A history of Jesus College Cambridge.
Heinemann, 1960. ix,221p. illus. ports.
plan
*cricket pp. 108n, 167, 172, 178, 180,
187–88*

## Durham

1632 **Fowler, J.T.**
Durham University: earlier foundations and present colleges. F.E. Robinson, 1904. xii,312p.

## London: Goldsmiths' Institute

1633 **Joanes, H.**
■ Some cricket outings of the Goldsmiths' Institute Cricket Club in 1892–1898, by their Hon. Secretary. *Private circulation*, 1898. vi,92p. illus. port. scores
——2nd series, *with title:* Cricket tours of the Goldsmiths' Institute Cricket Club. 1904

## London: Polytechnic C.C.

1634 **The Polytechnic Cricket Club**
□ Hon. Secretary's report. The Club. stats. *typescript*
*?/1954 . . . 1964–65/ to date?*

## Oxford

1635 **Bolton, Geoffrey**
■ History of the O.U.C.C. Oxford, Holywell P., 1962. xix,374p. illus. ports. scores, bibliog.

1636 **Fifty** years of sport at Oxford, Cambridge
■ and the great public schools; arranged by the Right Hon. Lord Desborough of Taplow, K.C.V.O. 3 vols.
*Vols I and II. Oxford and Cambridge; edited by A.C.M. Croome. Southwood, 1913. ports. scores*
*cricket in vol. I, pp. 83–189*

1637 **Dodgson, Charles Lutwidge**
Notes by an Oxford Chiel. Oxford, Parker, 1865–1874.
*6 pamphlets by "Lewis Carroll"; includes in verse form "The deserted parks" in which he deplores the reservation of the Parks for cricket*

1637 The complete works . . . with an intro-
–1 duction by Alexander Woollcott and the
■ illustrations by John Tenniel. The Nonesuch P., 1939. xv,1165p. illus.
*includes pp.823–5 "The deserted parks"*

1638 **Foster, Joseph**
Oxford men and their colleges; illustrated with portraits and views (from Loggan, Hearne, Skelton, Ackerman & others). 2 vols. Oxford, Parker, 1893. illus. ports.

1639 **Masterman,** *Sir* **John Cecil**
To teach the senators wisdom; or, An Oxford guide-book. Hodder & Stoughton, 1952. 283p. illus.
*cricket pp. 133–6*

1640 **Pycroft, James**
■ Oxford memories: a retrospect after fifty years. Bentley, 1886. 2 vols.
*cricket in vol. 2 only; includes early history of Oxford University cricket; see also no. 795*

## Oxford: Authentics

1641 **Crawfurd, John William Frederick**
■ **Arthur**
The Oxford colleges and the Oxford Authentics no. 4. St. John's College *[priv. publd.]*, 1929. 48p.

1642 **Headlam, Cecil**
■ Ten thousand miles through India and Burma: an account of the Oxford University Authentics' cricket tour with Mr. K.J. Key in the year of the Coronation Durbar. Dent, 1903. xii,297p. illus. ports. scores

1643 **Lake, Harold W.**
■ The Oxford colleges and the Oxford Authentics. No. 2. Oriel. *[Priv. publd.]*, 1927. 28p.

1644 **Oxford University Authentics**
■ The names of the Oxford University Authentics who died during the years 1914–1918. [O.U.A., *n.d.*]. 26p. port.

1645 **Handbook.** [Oxford, the Club]. *annual?*
□ scores, stats.
*season 1884?/1892, 1909, 1911, 1950, 1957/ to date?*

1646 **Stallybrass, W.T.S.**
The Oxford Authentics and the Oxford Colleges. No. 1. B.N.C. *priv. publd.*, 1926. 32p.

## Oxford: Brasenose College

1647 **Buchan, John,** *1st baron Tweedsmuir*
■ Brasenose College. Robinson, 1898. xi,202p. illus. (University of Oxford College Histories)
*cricket pp. 115–17*

## Oxford: Cryptics

1647 **Cryptics Cricket Club**
–1 [Report and members' addresses, etc.] [Oxford], The Club. *annual*
*?/1968 . . . 1977/to date*

1647 Cryptics Cricket Club 1910–1960:
–2 programme of the Golden Jubilee celebra-
■ tions at St. Edward's Oxford on 9, 10, 11 September 1960. [Oxford, the Club, 1960]. [8]p. plan

## Oxford: Emeriti

1648 **Nugee, F.J.** *editor*
■ The records of the Oxford University Emeriti Cricket Club. Farnborough, printed by Marlborough P., 1922 *i.e.* [1932?]. 117p. scores, stats.
*formed 1910: preface signed 1922 but matches recorded 1910–1930*

## Oxford: Magdalen College

1649 **Magdalen College [Cricket Club]**
■ Report of the Committee. Oxford, the Club, [c.1860]. [4]p. fold
*with rules of the Club*

## Oxford v. Cambridge Matches

1650 **Abrahams, Harold Maurice,** *and* **Bruce-**
■ **Kerr, John C.**
Oxford versus Cambridge: a record of inter-university contests from 1827–1930. Faber, 1931. 620p. scores
*cricket p. 163–264*
——Supplement. 1932. 24p. scores

1651 **Betham, John Dover**
■ Oxford and Cambridge scores and biographies. London, Simpkin Marshall; Sedbergh, Jackson, 1905. 286p. scores.
*covers 1827–1904*

1652 **Casson, Thomas Edmund**
A century of roundels: for the centenary of the Oxford and Cambridge cricket match, 1927. Ulverston, James Atkinson, 1927. 36p.

1653 **French,** *Hon.* **Edward George**
■ Oxford v. Cambridge 1870: centenary of Cobden's sensational hat-trick. Hove, Hove Shirley P., 1970. 10p. port. score

1654 **[Kidd, Abel]**
■ The Oxford & Cambridge match reviewed by "Old Stump", with notes on Rugby and Marlborough, M.C.C. and Cheltenham. [The Author, 1870]. bs.

1655 Ode to the light and dark blue, or Oxford
■ and Cambridge, Rugby and Marlborough, Eton and Harrow, at Lord's 1871 with a prophecy, by An Old Stump. Published & sold by the kind permission of the Marylebone Club for the benefit of the Author, [1871]. [3]p.

1656 The battles of the blues: Oxford and
■ Cambridge . . . Eton and Winchester . . . Harrow and Eton . . . [1873]. Published and sold by kind permission of the Marylebone Cricket Club, for the benefit of the Author, [1873]. [3]p.

1657 **Mudge, C.A.,** *compiler*
■ Inter-university records: full particulars of all competitions between Oxford and Cambridge 1827–1887. Wright, 1887. iii,144p. scores
*cricket pp. 32–80*

1658 **[Pentelow, John Nix],** *editor*
■ The Blues and their battles, with scores of all cricket matches played between the universities from 1827 to 1892. Wright & Co., [1893]. xxi,98p. scores
——2nd ed. [1894]. xxi,100p. scores

1659 **Perkins, Henry**
■ Scores of the cricket matches between Oxford and Cambridge from the commencement up to date. Virtue, 1887. [iv],94p. scores
——2nd ed. Virtue, 1890. [iv],102p.
——3rd ed. F.E. Robinson, 1898. 77p.
——4th ed. F.E. Robinson, 1900. 79p.
——5th ed. F.E. Robinson, [1904]. 82p.
*a re-issue of 1898 ed. with additional scores to 1904 match inclusive.*
——6th ed. Hutchinson, 1906
*the same as 5th ed. but with score of 1905 match added*

1660 **Rysden, Ogier,** *editor*
■ The book of Blues: being a record of all matches between the universities of Oxford and Cambridge in every department of sport. 2 vols. F.E. Robinson, 1900–1
*Vol. I. xv,267, xvii–lvip. scores*
*Vol II.*——*from the year 1900. [ii],14p. score*

1660 **Sassoon, Siegfried**
–1 Collected poems 1908–1956. Faber, 1961.
■ xix,317p.
*includes pp. 138–9 "The Blues at Lords's"*

1661 **Warner,** *Sir* **Pelham Francis,** *and* **Ashley-**
■ **Cooper, Frederick Samuel**
Oxford v. Cambridge at the wicket. Allen & Unwin, 1926. 208p. scores

1662 **Wisden, John,** *publisher*
■ Cricket: Oxford v. Cambridge: full scores &c. of all matches played from 1827 to 1876. Wisden, 1877. iv,115p. scores, stats.

# EX–UNIVERSITY AND OLD SCHOOL CLUBS

## Bradfield Waifs

1662 **Moulsdale, John R.B.**
–1 Bradfield Waifs Cricket Club: a history
■ 1877–1977. [The Author, 1977]. 11p.

## Butterflies

1663 **Arrowsmith, R.L.,** *and others*
■ Butterflies Cricket Club, 1862–1962; by
R.L. Arrowsmith, J.G. Dunbar and
J.N.A. Armitage-Smith. [The Club, 1962]
[i],27p. ports. scores, stats.
*limited ed. of 250 copies*

1664 **The Butterflies Cricket Club**
■ Laws and list of members. [The Club],
1935. 46p.
——1953. 38p.

## Eton Ramblers

1665 **Eton Ramblers**
List of members. Eton, [the Club], 1890.
78p.
——(Active list). 1912. 35p.
——1919. 46p.
——1920. 109p.
——1925. 123p.

1666 **The Eton Ramblers' Cricket Club**
■ [Vol. 1]: from its foundation in 1862 until
1880, by Philip Norman. Longmans,
Green, 1928, xiv,195p. illus. ports. scores
——Additions and corrections. Spottis-
woode, Ballantyne, 1930. 8p.
Vol. 2: a history of its activities from 1881
until 1914, by G.A. Foljambe. George
Burge, 1937. [x],436p. illus. ports. scores,
stats.

1667 **Eton Ramblers' Cricket Club**
□ [Results and averages]. Eton, the Club.
*annual.* stats.
*1893–1913, 1919–1939, 1946 to date*

1668 [Rules and list of members] 1957. The
■ Club, [1957]. 132p.

1669 Notice [by President]. Eton, the Club.
□ *annual*
*?/1967/to date*

## Harlequins

1670 **Cochrane, Alfred John Henry**
■ Records of the Harlequin Cricket Club,
1852–1926. Eyre & Spottiswoode, 1930.
xii,238p. frontis. (col.), illus. ports. scores

## Harrow Wanderers

1671 **B., H.J.**
Forsan et haec. H. Reiach, 1922. 10p.
illus.
*history of the Harrow Wanderers*

1672 **Harrow Wanderers Cricket Club**
□ Rules and list of members. The Club.
*occasional?*
*?/1961/to date?*
with annual Addenda and Corrigenda
*?/1962–64/to date?*

## Lancing Rovers

1673 **Lancing Rovers Cricket Club**
■ Year book. The Club. scores, stats.
*1929–39, 1947–60, 1963–4, 1965–72,
1973–74 (typescript)*
*no issues for 1961, 1962; 1963–4 and
1973–4 combined issues*
*formed 1928*

## Old Askeans

1673 **Alexander, Maurice Benjamin**
–1 A history of The Old Askean Club
■ 1879–1979. The Old Askean Assoc., 1979.
86p. illus. ports. facsims.
*includes an account of the Cricket Club*

## Old Carthusians

1674 **Old Carthusian** Cricket and Football
Club, founded with the title of Greyfriar
Cricket Club, 1874 . . . : rules, list of
members, result of matches, etc. Godalming, [the Club], 1921. 206p.

## Old Cheltonians

1675 **Old Cheltonian** Cricket Club (1921–1935).
■ The Club, 1936. 12p.

## Old Dartfordians

1675 **Hudson, Ronald L.**
–1 History of Dartford Grammar School.
Dartford, [the School(?)], 1966. 88p. illus.
*pp. 80–1 The Old Dartfordian's Cricket
Club*

## Old Dorkinians

1676 **Old Dorkinians Cricket Club**
■ Annual magazine. Dorking, the Club.
team port. stats. *typescript*
*1949 to date; edited by W.J. Bonner to
1976, and since then by I.H. Rutter*

## Old Gaytonians

1677 **Old Gaytonians' Cricket Club**
□ Report on the . . . season. The Club. *annual. typescript*
*?/1968/*to date?

## Old Haberdashers

1678 **Old Haberdashers' Association**
□ [Handbook]. Boreham Wood, the Association. 2x yearly. team ports. stats. in autumn or winter issue
*?/1962 to 1969–70/*to date?

## Old Harrovians

1678 **Old Harrovian Field House Cricket Club**
–1 Rules drawn up Jan. 1898. The Club, 8p.

## Old Parkonians

1678 **Kesby, D.J.**
–2 The Old Parkonians Cricket Club: the
■ Club in the war years (1939–1945). [Ilford], the Club, [1947?] 32p. stats.

## Old Rossallians

1679 **The Old Rossallian** tour of 1911, with a
■ brief note about former tours. [Old Rossallian C.C.), 1911, 16p. frontis. scores, stats.
*reprinted from "Cricket"*

## Old Westminster

1680 **Old Westminster Cricket Club**
■ Rules of the Old Westminster Cricket Club, 1828. Westminster, [the Club, 1828]. [4]p. fold

## Old Whitgiftians

1680 **Horn, Robert M.**, *editor*
–1 The centenary history of the Old Whitgiftians Cricket Club 1878–1978. Croydon,
■ the Club, [1978]. 28p. incl. covers. illus. ports.

## Old Wykehamist

1681 **Old Wykehamist Cricket Club**
List of members. The Club. *occasional?*
*?/1971/–?*

## Old Yverdonian

1682 **Old Yverdonian Club**
□ Rules, list of members, report &c. of the

Old Yverdonian Club: being the year-book. [The Club]
*/1894–1903/–?*
*formed 1890; in 1893 fixture card only issued*

## Quidnuncs

1683 **Quidnunc Cricket Club**
List of members of the Cambridge University Quidnunc Cricket Club. Cambridge, the Club, 1853. 16p.

1684 [Rules, officers, and list of members].
■ [Cambridge, the Club], 1884. 24p.

1685 **Quidnunc** Cricket Club. W.H. Smith, 1895. 27p.

## St. Peter's Old Boys

1685 **Knox-Shaw, P.**, *and others*
–1 "Ourselves": 1927–1930. *Privately printed,* [1930]. [40]p. scores, stats.
*the record of O.P. XI matches – St. Peter's Old Boys, St. Peter's Preparatory School, Seaford, Sussex*

## Sherborne Pilgrims

1686 **Sherborne Pilgrims**
□ Members' handbook (incorporating the annual report). The Club, *annual*
*?/1963/*to date?

## Stoics

1686 **Mendelsohn, Martin**
–1 Stoics Cricket Club 1877–1977: centenary
■ booklet. [The Club, 1977]. [36]p. scores, stats.

1686 **The Stoics Cricket Club**
–2 75th anniversary dinner, Friday, 14
■ November 1952, Simpsons Restaurant, Strand, London, W.C.2. [The Club, 1952]. [12]p. ports. facsims.
*includes brief history of the Club*

## Uppingham Rovers

1687 **Uppingham Rovers Cricket Club**
□ List of members. Uppingham, the Club. *annual. stats.*
*?/1921, 1929–40/–?*
*formed 1863; from 1929–40 contained rules, fixtures, etc. (no fixtures in 1940)*

# SERVICES CRICKET

1688 **Army Sport Control Board**
□ Games and sports in the Army. The Board. *irregularly*. illus. ports. diagrs.
*1931–32, 1932–33, 1934–35, 1935–36, 1937–38, 1939–40, 1942–43, 1943–44, 1950–51, 1952–53, 1953–54, 1955–56, 1957–58, 1959–60, 1962–63, 1966–67*
*contains section on Army Cricket Association*

## Coldstream Guards

1688 **Second** Battalion Coldstream Guards
–1 cricket matches 1856–1878. Windsor, *printed by* R. Oxley & Son, 1879. 82p. scores

## The Green Jackets

1689 **The Green Jackets Club**
■ Rules and roll of members 1966. Winchester, the Club, [1966]
*formed 1884 and now comprises serving officers & officers who have served in Royal Green Jackets, the 43rd and 52nd., the King's Royal Rifle Corps, the Rifle Brigade and their Territorial regiments*

## Honourable Artillery Company

1690 **Raikes, George Alfred**
■ The history of the Honourable Artillery Company. 2 vols. Bentley, 1878–9. col. frontis. illus. ports. maps
*cricket vol. 1, p. 272; vol. 2, pp. 29, 304, 305, 328, 338–40, 369*

1691 **Walker, George Goold**
■ The Honourable Artillery Company, 1537–1926. J. Lane, Bodley Head, 1926. xv,298p. illus.
*cricket pp. 145–48; limited to 250 numbered copies*
——*2nd ed.* ——,1537–1947. 1954. xiii,380p. illus. (some col.), ports. maps
*cricket pp. 132–34*

## Royal Engineers

1692 **Rait Kerr, Rowan Scrope**
■ A history of Royal Engineers cricket 1862–1924. Chatham, Institution of Royal Engineers, 1925. 96p. illus. ports. score, stats.

## Royal Military Academy

1693 **Guggisberg,** *Sir* **Frederick Gordon**
■ "The Shop"; the story of the R.M.A. Cassell, 1900. ii,276p. illus. (some col.) ports. plans
*cricket pp. 215–251*

## Royal Military College

1694 **Mockler-Ferryman, Augustus Ferryman**
■ Annals of Sandhurst: a chronicle of the Royal Military College from its foundation to the present day. Heinemann, 1900. vii,318p. illus. scores, stats.
*cricket pp. 97–154*

## Royal Navy and Royal Marines

1695 **Royal Navy and Royal Marines.** *Sports*
□ *Control Board*
Sports handbook. The Board. *annual 1922?/1932,35/–?*
*1935 issue was no. 14. Includes cricket section*

1696 Sports and recreation in the Royal Navy.
□ The Board. *annual*. port, diagrs.
*?/1950, 1953–54 to 1962–63/*
——*with title:* Sports handbook. port. diagrs.
*1963–64, 1966–67*
*contains cricket section*

1696 **S[tevens], H[arold] E.,** *editor*
–1 H.M.S. "Enterprise": story of the first
■ commission April 7th, 1926, to December 19th, 1928. Aldershot, Gale & Polden, [1929]. xi,193p. illus. ports. map
*pp. 149–51 gives an account of the cricket matches played with summary scores and team portrait*

## 7th (Q.O.) Hussars

1697 **Ridley, H.M.,** *compiler*
■ 7th (Q.O.) Hussars cricket matches played from 1873 to 1888. Wincanton, [the Compiler], 1889. iii,127p. scores

# LEAGUE, CLUB AND VILLAGE CRICKET

## LEAGUE CRICKET
### (For individual leagues see under names of counties, towns, etc.)

1697 **Central Cricket League**
-1 [Handbook]. The League. *annual*
□ ?/1975,76/to date
*founded 1972*

1698 **Genders, Roy**
■ League cricket in England. Laurie, 1952.
188p. illus. ports.

1698 **John Hampshire** benefit brochure and
-1 Tribute to the Leagues. [Benefit Cttee.,
■ 1976]. 48p. illus. ports.
*contains "A tribute to the leagues" by Keith Farnsworth*

1699 **Kay, John**
■ Cricket in the leagues. Eyre & Spottiswoode, 1970. 208p. illus. ports.

## CLUB CRICKET
### (For individual clubs see under names of counties, towns, etc.)

1700 **Bennett, Alfred Charles Leopold**
■ The week-end cricketer. Hutchinson,
1951. 287p. illus. ports. (Library of Sports
and Pastimes)

1701 **The club** cricket book. H. Grant,
■ *2 issues 1901–02*
*a score book with names and addresses of clubs' secretaries*

1702 **Club** cricket review; edited by Beaumont
■ Bissell. *monthly during summer*
*12 issues: Vol. 1, no. 1. May 1956—Vol.
3, No. 2 June/July 1958*

1703 **The club** cricket yearbook. West Country
■ edition. Bristol
*1950–51; ed. by J.L. Taylor. [1951]
1951–52, 1952–53; ed. by J.L. Taylor &
J.H.C. Cowgill. [1952–53]*

1704 **The club** cricketer's companion 1914:
■ records, fixtures, etc. Hoare, [1914]. 16p.

1705 **Goulstone, John**
■ Early club & village cricket. *Privately published,* 1972. [126]p.
*limited ed. of 100 copies. Entries for
approx. 1100 towns & villages in England &
Wales up to c.1830*

1706 **The Mac** team selection book. Gamage,
1907

*contains club rules and other information
for cricket club secretaries*

1707 **Midland** cricketer's handbook. Bury,
□ Fletcher & Speight, *annual*. stats.
*1885–1900*

1708 **National Club Cricket Association**
■ Rules. Eastbourne, [the Association,
1947]. 8p.

1709 **National Cricket Association**
■ An interim report of the national census
of cricket clubs, September 1970. The
Assoc. in conjunction with "The Cricketer", [1970]. 51f. *typescript*
——A summary of certain results from
the interim report . . . The Assoc.,
[1970?]. 4f. *typescript*

1710 **Stocken, A.R.**
Cricket club directory. Knightsbridge,
May, 1888
*place of publication given as Wembly [sic]
in Taylor*

1711 **[Turner, Henry]**
■ Memories of club cricket, by a
Nottingham Secretary. Nottingham, [the
Author], 1890. 27p.
*an account of running a cricket club*

1711 **Who's who** in club cricket. Cricket Publi-
-1 shing Co., [1909?]
*noted in* Cricket who's who, *1909, no.
7194*

## Club Cricket Conference

1712 **Club Cricket Conference**
□ Annual report. The Conference
*season 1915/1957–69/to date*

1713 Handbook. The Conference
■ *annual issues 1928 to date. illus. ports.
in v.y.
1928–40; ed. by E.A.C. Thompson
1941; ed. by E.A.C. Thompson and Joan
Chamley
1942–45; ed. by Joan Chamley
1946–52; ed. by H.A.E. Scheele
1953–; [no editor given]
formerly London and Southern Counties
Cricket Conference. Cricket clubs' annual*

1714 What it is and what it does. The Confer-
■ ence, [195–?]. 3p.

1715 **The Club Cricketers Charity Fund**
■ Official handbook; compiled and edited
by E.A.C. Thomson and W.H. Long.
Simpkin, Marshall. *annual*. ports. stats.
*1911–14*

1716 **London and Southern Counties**
■ **Conference**
Cricket annual handbook and directory;
edited by E.A.C. Thomson
*2 issues, 1920, 1921*
contd. as: *"London and Southern Counties
Cricket Conference. Cricket clubs' annual"*

1717 **London and Southern Counties Cricket**
■ **Conference**
Cricket clubs' annual and English secreta-
rial directory; compiled by E.A.C.
Thomson. *annual*. ports. stats.
*1922–27*
contd. as: *"The Club Cricket Conference
handbook"*

1718 **London Club Cricket Conference**
■ Official booklet 1919. The Conference,
[1919]. 11p.
*the only issue; contd. as: "London and
Southern Counties Conference. Cricket
annual"*

*1971 Tour to Australia*

1719 **Club Cricket Conference**
■ 1971 Australian tour: programme. The
Conference, [1971]. [28]p. incl. adverts.
port.
——[Results]. [1971]. bs.

1720 **[Speakman, Arthur]**
■ The Club Cricket Conference tour of
Australia, Jan. 1st to Feb. 7th, 1971 as
seen, heard, and enjoyed by one of the
party. The Author, [1971]. [iii],12p.
*typescript*

*1975 Tour to Australia*

1720 **Club Cricket Conference**
–1 Australian tour 75. The Conference,
■ [1975]. [48]p. incl. adverts. 1 illus. ports.
*pre-tour*

*1979 Tour to Australasia*

1720 **The Club Cricket Conference**
–2 Tour to Australasia 1979. The Confer-
■ ence, [1978]. [52]p. incl. adverts. 1 illus.
ports.
*pre-tour. Inclues "A brief history of The
Club Cricket Conference" by G.A. Copinger*

1720 Tour of Australasia – Jan/Feb. 1979. The
–3 Conference, [1979]. [44]f., facsims. scores
■ *post-tour*

**Midlands Club Cricket Conference**

1721 **The Midlands Club Cricket Conference**
■ Yearbook. Birmingham, Midlands C.C.C.
illus. ports. scores, stats.
*1948 to date.*

*1976 contains a history of the Conference
by Norman Sharp*

*1973 Tour to Australia and Far East*

1722 Australia and Far East tour, 1973. Allen
■ Stanley Advertising Ltd., [1973]. [20]p.
incl. adverts. ports.
*pre-tour*

*1977 Tour to Australasia*

1722 **Midlands Club Cricket Conference**
–1 1977 Australasian tour. The Conference,
■ [1976]. 32p. incl. adverts. ports.
*pre-tour; pen-pictures by Barry Bowker*

# VILLAGE CRICKET
(see also: Cricket as part of the English scene)

1723 **Blunden, Edmund Charles**
English villages. Collins, 1941. 48p. illus.
(some col.). (Britain in Pictures)
*references to cricket and reproduction of
"The cricketers" by Peter de Wint*

1724 **Forrest, Alec John**
■ Village cricket. Hale, 1957. 192p. illus.
(Champion Sports Books)
——*another ed.* Sportsman's Book Club,
1959

1725 **Goulstone, John**
■ Early club & village cricket. *Privately published, 1972*. [126]p.
*limited ed. of 100 copies. Entries for
approx. 1100 towns & villages in England &
Wales up to c.1830*

1726 **Hughes, Arthur George,** *and* **Parker,**
**Ernest Walter,** *compilers*
Adventurers all. Longmans, 1947. 288p.
illus.
*"Village cricket" by Richard Binns, pp.
254–261*

1727 **Mais, Stuart Petre Brodie**
Village cricket; the path to the heart of
England. [1935?] 4p.

1728 **Poole, F.F.**
■ Village cricket: hints on the running of
the smaller cricket club. Sandbach, the
Author, 1938. 55p. diagrs.
——*rptd.* [1949]

**Haig National Village Cricket**
**Championship**

1729 **Fogg, John**
■ The Haig book of village cricket. Pelham
Books, 1972. 232p. illus. ports. scores
*account of the Haig National Village
Cricket Championship, 1972*

1730 **Haig National Village Cricket**
■ **Championship**
Rules, etc. [The Cttee. of the Championship], 1971. [4]p. illus. on cover
*organised by "The Cricketer" in conjunction with John Haig & Co. Ltd., and the N.C.A.*
——Rules & conditions 1972 (amended). [The Cttee. of the Championship 1972]. [4]p. with tear-off insets

1730 **The Haig** village cricket annual. The
–1 Cricketer for John Haig & Co. illus. ports.
☐ score, stats.
*1974–78*
*largely devoted to The Haig National Village Cricket Championship; 1974 issue edited by Tom Scanlan, 1975 onwards by Findlay Rae*

1731 **Hughes, Simon**
■ Kings of village cricket: the Troon story—from the beginning to their first trip to Lord's. Troon (Cornwall), Troon C.C., 1973. 24p. team ports.
*Troon were winners of The Haig National Village Cricket Championship, 1972*

1731 **The village** cricket championship 1978
–1 organised by The Cricketer. Ashurst
■ (Kent), The Cricketer, [1978]. [16]p. score, stats.
——The Samuel Whitbread village cricket championship 1979 . . . [1979]. 20p. ports. score, stats.
*in 1979 Samuel Whitbread Ltd. took over the sponsorship from John Haig & Co.*

## COUNTY CRICKET

1732 **Arlott, [Leslie Thomas] John**
■ County cricket 1873–1973: British Post Office mint stamps [presentation pack]. British Post Office, 1973. *folded card.* illus. port. diagr.
*contains 3 Grace stamps 3p., 7½p., 9p. in value*

1733 A hundred years of county cricket: a
■ souvenir containing three commemorative stamps from the British Post Office. British Post Office, 1973. [24p.] illus & ports. (some col.)

1734 ————, *editor*
■ Cricket in the counties: studies of the first-class counties in action. Saturn P., 1950. 272p. ports. scores
*1949 season*

1735 **Bailey, Trevor Edward**
■ Championship cricket: a review of county cricket since 1945. Muller, 1961. 216p. illus. ports.

——*another ed.* Sportsman's Book Club, 1962

1736 **Batchelor, Denzil Stanley,** *and* **Surridge, Stuart**
Denzil Batchelor discusses the future of county cricket with Stuart Surridge. Newman Neame, [1957]. 16p. illus. ports. (Newman Neame Take Home Books)

1737 **Carew, Dudley Charles Hemington**
■ To the wicket. Chapman & Hall, 1946. 191p.
——revised ed. 1947. 215p.

1738 **Daft, Richard**
Daft's guide to county cricket. Nottingham, *n.d.*
*in Taylor*

1739 **Dowsett's** guide to county cricket. Hastings, Dowsett, 1902

1739 **First** class counties second eleven cham-
–1 pionship: rules of competition and
■ instructions to umpires. Second Eleven Championship, 1961. 10p.

1740 **The Fixord** county cricket championship. Watford, E.B. Hanson, 1930. bs.

1741 **Gibson, Alfred**
■ County cricket championship, with an appendix on the selection of an England eleven by "Rover" (Alfred Gibson). Mentz, Kenner & Gelberg, 1895. xi,148p. stats.
*covers 1873–94*
——2nd ed. 1896

1741 **The Guardian**
–1 The bedside 'Guardian' 23: a selection
■ from The Guardian 1973–74; edited by W.L. Webb. Collins, 1974. 255p. illus.
*includes pp. 230–45 "Queering the pitch" by Stanley Reynolds (A Northern view of Southern cricket)*

1742 **Holmes, Robert Stratten**
■ The county cricket championship, 1873 to 1896. Bristol, Arrowsmith, [1897]. 168p. stats. (Arrowsmith's Bristol Library)

1743 **Marylebone Cricket Club**
Report of the Commission appointed by the M.C.C. at the request of the Advisory County Cricket Committee to investigate the problems confronting the counties taking part in the first class county cricket championship. M.C.C., 1937. 23p.
*Commissioner: W. Findlay*

1744 ————. *Select Committee*
■ Report of the Select Committee appointed by the Marylebone Cricket Club at the

request of the Advisory County Cricket Committee to investigate the problems confronting county cricket after the cessation of hostilities. M.C.C., 1944. 24p.
*Chairman: Sir Stanley Jackson*

1745 ———. *Special Committee*
■ Report of the Special Committee appointed by the M.C.C. to consider the future welfare of first-class cricket, 1957. M.C.C., 1957. 8p.
*Chairman: H.S. Altham*

1746 **National Opinion Polls**
Major county cricket: survey. N.O.P., [c.1966]. 13p. + 37 tables + 2 appendices

1747 **Ryder, R.V.**
Trials of a county secretary. Wisden, 1936. 6p.

1748 **Shrewsbury, Arthur**
■ County cricket: a new and rational method for arriving at the order of merit between the county teams of Nott's., Surrey, Lanc's., York's., Middlesex, Glo'ster, Kent, Sussex, Derby. J. Heywood, 1887. 15p. stats.

1749 **Texaco**
■ Grandstand. Vol. 3: First class cricket. S. Painter Ltd. for Texaco, 1971. 52p. col. illus. ports. and maps
*a guide to country cricket with fixtures for 1971*

1750 **Thomson, Arthur Alexander**
■ Cricket bouquet: comedy and character in the counties. Museum P., 1961. 207p. ports. bibliog.

1751 Vintage elevens; [completed by Denzil
■ Batchelor]. Pelham, 1969. 128p. illus. ports. stats.

1752 **Turner's** guide to county cricket. Oxford, Turner, *n.d.*
*in Taylor*

1753 **[See no. 1754-1]**

1754 **Warwickshire County Cricket Club**
Explanation of points scoring system in operation in the County Cricket Championship in 1968. Edgbaston, the Club, 1968. [4]p. fold

1754 The Warwick Pool Under-25 county
–1 cricket competition: rules of competition
□ and fixtures. Birmingham, Warwickshire C.C.C. *annual*
*1972?/1973 . . . 1978/* to date

*1973* with title: *Under 25 county cricket competition*

1755 **Webber, Roy**
■ The county cricket championship: a history of the competition from 1873 to the present day, with each season's final placings in full, team and individual playing records, etc. Phoenix House, 1957. 144p. illus. ports. stats.
——Appendix B. [1957]. pp. 145–51 *covers 1957 season*
——*another ed.* Sportsman's Book Club, 1958

# MINOR COUNTIES

1756 **Burrell, J.F.,** *compiler*
□ Who's who in the Minor Counties. Bristol, the Compiler, [1960]. *typescript.* stats.
*Pt. 1. Southern counties. [11]f.*
*Pt. 2. Northern counties plus Berkshire and Hertfordshire. [8]f.*
——*annual.* [Covering all Minor Counties]. *typescript.* stats.
*1961–76*
from 1962 with title: *Minor Counties who's who*
*1976 issue published by Association of Cricket Statisticians; ed. by R.W. Brooke*
*contd. as:-*
Minor Counties who's who & annual 1977; compiled by Brian Hunt, Jack Burrell and Robert Brooke. Hampton-in-Arden, Assoc of Cricket Statisticians. stats.
*contd. as:-*
Minor Counties annual. Assoc. of Cricket Statisticians. stats. *1978 to date*
*editors: 1978–J.R. Burrell, B. Hunt, R.W. Brooke, P. Wynne-Thomas*
*1979–R.W. Brooke, P. Wynne-Thomas*

1757 **The cricketers'** manual for the border counties. Oswestry, Roberts, Woodall & Venables, 1869. 72p.

1758 **Minor Counties Cricket Assocation**
■ [Handbook]. The Association.
*1905–14, 1920–39, 1946 to date*
*cover-title from 1929* Official handbook
*1977 to date published in smaller format*

1758 **Minor Counties** Cricket Association on
–1 tour in Kenya, January 10 to 29, 1978.
■ [The Assoc., 1977?] [8]p. incl. covers.
*pre-tour itinerary*

1759 **Norman, James Earl,** *compiler*
■ The Minor Counties roll of honour 1914–1920. St. Alban's, Minor Counties C.A., 1921. [9]p.

# CRICKET IN THE COUNTIES

## BEDFORDSHIRE

1760 **Meynell, Laurence Walter**
Bedfordshire. Hale, 1950. xv,366p. illus.
map. (County Books)
*cricket pp. 71–4*

1761 **Russell, Charles James Fox,** *Lord*
■ Woburn echoes. Woburn, H.G. Fisher,
1881. 262p.
*essays, including Bedfordshire cricket pp.
182–191*

1762 **The Victoria** history of the counties of
■ England: Bedfordshire; edited by William
Page. Vol. 2. Constable, 1908
*cricket p. 199*

### Bedford

1762 **Hamson, John**
–1 Bedford town and townsmen
[1845–1895]. Bedford, Bedfordshire Times
Office, 1896. 168p.
*cricket p. 117 – formation of Town and
County Cricket Club in 1870*

### Flitwick

1763 **Russell, Charles James Fox,** *Lord*
■ Opening of the Flitwick Recreation
Ground, 15th July 1889: [address]; *together
with* Written for the Flitwick Cricket Club
1889. Woburn, *priv. printed by* Fisher,
1889. 9;6p.
*no title-page—cover title: Cricket,
1757–1889. Limited ed. of 12 copies*

### Woburn

1763 **Woburn** cricket scores 1833–1849. Ms.
–1 *bound with* 8 annual reports 1839–57. 47p.
*in the collection of A.E. Winder*

## BEDFORDSHIRE C.C.C.

1764 **Bedfordshire County Cricket Club**
□ Annual report. Bedford, the Club. stats.
*?/1929–39, 1946–68, 1973/to date*

1765 Cricket week: programming and
■ souvenir; compiled by Percy Burke.
Bedford, the Club.
*1923. [1923]. 20p. scores, stats.
1924. [1924]. 40p. ports. stats.*

1766 **The Bedfordshire** cricketer: the official
□ newsletter issued by The Bedfordshire
Association of Cricket Clubs. *six monthly?
Spring 1969–?*

1767 **Bedfordshire** v. Hertfordshire at Southill
■ Park, Bedfordshire, Sat. & Sun., 22–23
July, 1972: souvenir. *n.p.,* [1972]. 36p.
incl. adverts. illus. ports.
*includes brief history of Bedfordshire cricket*

## BERKSHIRE

1768 **Jones, Peter K.**
Cricket in Berkshire: the story of the
beginnings of cricket in the county of
Berkshire. iv,50p. *MS typescript
in M.C.C. Library, Lord's*

1769 **The Victoria** history of the counties of
■ England: Berkshire; edited by P.H.
Ditchfield and William Page. Vol. 2.
Constable, 1907
*cricket pp. 317–27*

### Ascot

1769 **Searle, C.W.**
–1 The origin and development of
Sunninghill and Ascot. Chertsey, T.E.
Stevens & Son, 1937. 142p. illus.
*pp. 89–91 the history of the Royal Ascot
C.C., and pp. 91–92 Silwood Park C.C.*

1770 **T., F.B.**
■ Royal Ascot Cricket Club 1883–1933. *n.p.,*
[1933?]. 8p.

### Maidenhead

1771 **Maidenhead and Bray Sports Club**
■ M.C.C. 1798–1948; souvenir of the 150th
anniversary of the foundation of the
Maidenhead Cricket Club. Maidenhead,
the Club, 1948. 18p. illus. scores

1772 Maidenhead and Bray Cricket Club v.
Middlesex C.C.C., Bray, 28 May 1969.
Maidenhead, the Club, [1969]. 12p. incl.
adverts. 1 illus. ports.

1772 Maidenhead & Bray Cricket Club v. York-
–1 shire C.C.C. at Bray on Thames, Berk-
■ shire, 10 June. Maidenhead, the Club,
[1979]. 70p. incl. adverts. ports.

1772 **Walker, John Wesley**
–2 A history of Maidenhead. Hunter &
■ Longhurst, 1909. xvi, 238p. frontis.
*cricket pp.164–7*
——2nd ed. (enlarged). St. Catherine P.,
1931. 236p. illus.
*cricket pp. 159–61*
——rptd. with new introduction.
Maidenhead, Thames Valley P., 1971.
xxii,236p. illus.

## Reading

1772 **Jones, John B.**
-3 Sketches of Reading, historical, archaeo-
■ logical and descriptive. Reading,
Lovejoy, Southern Counties Library,
1870. [iv],80p.
*cricket pp. 34–5*

1773 **The Reading** and district cricketers'
□ annual companion; edited by W. Crit-
chley. Reading, Farrer & Sons
*?/1892–95*
*1894, 1895 with title: The Reading and
district cricket, cycling & athletic handbook*

1774 **Reading Cricket Club**
■ Centenary 1859–1959. [Reading, the
Club, 1959]. 40p. illus. ports.

### Windsor and Eton

1775 **Windsor and Eton Cricket Club**
■ "The first century"; [1867–1967]. E.
Finchley, Edgar Pub. Co., [1967]. 56p.
ports.

## BERKSHIRE C.C.C.

1776 **Berkshire County Cricket Club**
■ [Annual].: Officers . . ., affiliated clubs,
rules (Berks. C.C.C.), rules (Berkshire
Gentlemen C.C.), statements of accounts,
list of members. Reading, the Club. stats.
[in later yrs]
*1945 to date*
*includes report of Berkshire Gentlemen
C.C.*

## BUCKINGHAMSHIRE

1776 **Buckinghamshire Women's Cricket**
-1 **Association**
Women's cricket notes. The Assoc.
*typescript*
*?/May 1950/–?*
*the May 1950 issue consisted of 12pp.*

1777 **The Victoria** history of the counties of
■ England: Buckinghamshire; edited by
William Page. Vol. 2. Constable, 1908
*cricket p. 239*

### Amersham

1777 **Quin, Gilbert**
-1 Cricket in the meadow: a short history of
■ the Amersham Cricket Club, 1856–1955.
[Amersham, the Club, 1956]. 90p. port.
scores

## Beaconsfield

1777 **Naish, Howard,** *compiler*
-2 Beaconsfield Cricket Club 150 not out: a
■ short history of cricket at Beaconsfield
since 1825. Beaconsfield, the Club,
[1975?]. 52p. incl. adverts. ports. facsims.
scores

### Datchet

1778 **Datchet** Cricket Club 1869–1969. Datchet,
■ the Club, [1969]. 24p. illus. ports. score

### Marlow

1779 **Marlow** Cricket Club: a short history
■ (1829–1959); compiled from minutes and
scorebooks . . . reports from local newspapers . . . [Marlow, the Club, 1959]. 4p.
*typescript*

### Milton Keynes

1779 **Markham,** *Sir* **Frank**
-1 A history of Milton Keynes and District.
Volume II—from about 1800 to about
1950. Luton, White Crescent P., 1975.
x,330p. illus. ports. map, plan
*cricket pp. 228–9*

### Slough

1780 **Slough Cricket and Bowls Club**
□ Handbook and fixtures lists. Slough, the
Club. *annual*
*1952/1956–58/–?*
*formed pre-1899; now Slough Sports Club*
*?/1973 . . . 1977/to date*

### Taplow

1781 **Wilson, Peter**
■ Taplow Cricket Club presents 100 years
on the hill, 1850–1950: an illustrated
record. Taplow, the Club, [1950]. 32p.
incl. adverts. illus. ports. score

## BUCKINGHAMSHIRE C.C.C.

1782 **Buckinghamshire County Cricket Club**
Bazaar manual 1895. Aylesbury, the
Club, 1895

1783 Handbook for 1905. Aylesbury, the Club,
1905. 24p.

1784 [Handbook]. Aylesbury, the Club.
■ *annual.* illus. ports. scores, stats.
*1932–39, 1946 to date*

1785 Buckinghamshire v. Bedfordshire,
Sunday 25 Aug., Monday 26 Aug., 1969:
souvenir programme. The Club, [1969]

# CAMBRIDGESHIRE

1786 **Cambridgeshire Cricket Association**
□ Official handbook. Cambridge, the Association. *annual*
*?1889–1913, ?1920–39, 1947* to date

1787 1889–1949 diamond jubilee celebration, Sept. 30th 1949. Cambridge, [the Assoc., 1949]. 8p. illus. ports.

1788 **The Victoria** history of the counties of
■ England: Cambridgeshire and the Isle of Ely; ed. by C.R. Elrington. Vol. 5. O.U.P., 1973
*cricket pp. 294–96 with illus.*

## Papworth

1789 **Papworth Cricket Club**
□ Annual report. Papworth, the Club. stats.
*?/1968/–?*

## Wisbech

1790 **Wisbech and District Cricket League**
Official handbook. Wisbech, the League. *annual*
*?/1921* to date

# CHESHIRE

1791 **Cheshire Cricket Association**
□ [Handbook]. The Association. *annual*
*season 1957?/1966* to date/
*rules, fixtures, final tables of previous season*

1792 **Derbyshire and Cheshire Cricket League**
□ Annual report. The League. stats (for same year)
*1952/1956 . . . 72/*to date

1793 **Lancashire and Cheshire Cricket League**
□ [Handbook]. Manchester, the League. *annual*. stats.
*season 1919/1956 . . . 74/*to date
*formed 1915*

1794 Hon. Secretary's report. Manchester, the
□ League. *annual*. stats. *typescript*
*1953* to date

1795 **North Staffordshire and South Cheshire**
□ **Cricket League**
Annual report. The League. stats. (for same yr.)
*1963, 1964*
*1965* to date with title: *Official report*

1796 Official handbook. The League
□ *1963* to date

1796 **South Cheshire Cricket Alliance**
–1 The official handbook. The Alliance.
■ *annual*
*1977* to date
*edited by Rupert Rigby; the Alliance was formed in 1976*

## Birkenhead

1797 **L[iverpool] C.C.** public school tour, 1866
■ to 1896; also Birkenhead Park 1865 to 1896. *n.p.*, [1896]. 142p. scores
*no title-page. Preface signed T.O.P.[otter]*

1797 **Neilson, Harry Bingham**
–1 Auld-Lang-Syne. Recollections and rural
■ records of Old Claughton, Birkenhead and Bidston with other reminiscences. Birkenhead, Willmer Brothers & Co., 1935. [xvii],296p. illus. ports. score
*cricket pp. 110–4 "The historic cricket match played at Birkenhead Park, June, 1869. (i.e. Birkenhead Park C.C. and the All England Eleven)*

1797 **Rock Ferry Cricket Club**
–2 [Annual report]. Birkenhead, the Club. stats.
*?/1911,12,13/–?*
*officers of the Club, statement of accounts and results for past season*

## Boughton Hall

1797 **Robinson, Alan**
–3 A century at Boughton Hall: a history of
■ Chester Boughton Hall Cricket Club 1873–1973. Boughton Hall, the Club, [1973]. [ii],38p. illus. ports. map, scores, stats.

## Bowdon

1798 **[Jackson, F.M., and Longson, E.H.]**
■ A fifty years' record of the Bowdon Cricket Club. [E.H. Longson], 1906. 60p. illus. scores

## Cheadle Hulme

1798 **Cheadle Hulme Cricket, Bowling and**
–1 **Tennis Club**
■ Bazaar handbook, including a short history of the Club over the past fifty-five years . . . 1936. [Cheadle Hulme, the Club, 1936]. 36p. incl. adverts
*founded 1881*

## Compstall

1799 **Compstall Cricket Club**
■ Centenary 1870–1970. [Compstall], the Club, [1970]. [4]p.

## Dukinfield

1800 **Dukinfield Cricket Club**
Centenary book. Dukinfield, the Club,
[1969?]

## Elworth

1801 **Elworth Cricket Club**
■ New pavilion scheme. Elworth, the Club,
1970. 5p. illus. (on cover), plan
*with brief history of club*

## Hale Barns

1802 **Hale Barns Cricket Club**
■ Twenty-fifth anniversary: souvenir
brochure. Hale Barns, the Club, [1972].
[68]p. incl. covers & adverts. illus. ports.
stats.

1802 Scoreboard: [newsletter]. Hale Barns, the
–1 Club
*?/25th issue, June 1979/to date*

## Hyde

1802 **Middleton, Thomas**
–2 The history of Hyde and its neighbourhood. Hyde, the Higham P., 1932.
xxxiv,579p. illus. ports.
*cricket p. 550 "Notable cricket clubs and
cricketers"*

## Lyme Park

1802 **Laurie, Kedrun,** *editor*
–3 Cricketer preferred: estate workers at
Lyme Park 1898–1946. Lyme Park Joint
Committee, 1979. 39p. illus.
*cricket p. 33 with illus.*

## Macclesfield

1802 **Davies, Clarice Stella,** *editor*
–4 A history of Macclesfield. Manchester,
■ Manchester Univ. P., 1961. xiv,404p.
illus. (some col.), bibliog.
*cricket pp. 366–7*

## Mellor

1803 **Mellor Cricket and Sports Club**
■ Souvenir score card: opening of the
Cricket Ground, Saturday, April 21, 1956:
President's XI v. Mellor. Mellor, the Club,
1956. 4p.

## Nantwich

1804 **Cricket** sketches. Nantwich. 1929.
■ Reprinted from The Crewe and Nantwich
Observer. Nantwich C.C., 1929. 15p.
frontis.
*verses on members of Nantwich C.C. team*

## Neston

1805 **Gilling, J.H.**
■ Fifty years of Neston cricket. [The
Author?, c.1947]. 72p. illus. ports. scores,
stats.

## Oxton

1805 **Oxton** Cricket Club 1875–1975. Oxton,
–1 the Club, 1975. 20p.

## Stockport

1806 **Stockport and District Cricket League**
[Handbook]. Stockport, the League.
*annual*
*?/1956–8/to date?*

1806 **Stockport Cricket Club**
–1 Minutes 1837–38. Stockport, the Club.
MS.
*from 9 March 1837 to 13 November 1838;*
see: *entry no. 131 in* Cricket: a catalogue
of an exhibition . . . by the National Book
League

## Tattenhall

1806 **Latham, Frank Alexander,** *editor*
–2 Tattenhall: the history of a Cheshire
■ village. Local History Group, 1977. 106p.
illus. maps on end-papers, bibliog.
*cricket p. 78*

## Timperley

1807 **Timperley** Cricket, Hockey and Lawn
■ Tennis Club 1877–1952: 75th season
official brochure and programme.
[Timperley, the Club], [1952]. [16]p. incl.
adverts. illus. ports.

## Wallasey

1808 **Wolfe, H.A.**
■ Wallasey Cricket Club 1864–1964;
centenary souvenir brochure. Wallasey,
the Club, [1964]. 32p. incl. adverts. illus.
ports. stats.

1808 **Woods, Edward Cuthbert,** *and* **Brown,**
–1 **Percy Culverwell**
■ The rise and progress of Wallasey. 2nd
ed. Wallasey Corporation, 1960.
[xiv],412p. col. frontis. illus. maps, plans
*pp. 309–10 New Brighton Cricket and
Bowling Club; pp. 310–2 Wallasey C.C.; 1st
ed. published 1929*

## Weaverham

1809 **Weaverham Cricket & Hockey Club**
■ New pavilion scheme. Weaverham, the
Club, 1972. 10p. illus. plan
*with brief history of the club*

## CHESHIRE C.C.C.

1810 **Cheshire County Cricket Club**
□ Annual report and statement of accounts for the season. Chester, the Club. scores, stats.
*?/1959 . . . 1974/to date*

## CORNWALL

1810 **Cornwall Cricket Association**
–1 Journal. The Assoc. *typescript*
□ No. 1. Sept. 1979 to date
*formed Feb. 1979*

1811 **Cornwall Cricket League**
□ Handbook. Redruth, the League. *annual.*
stats.
*?/1905–14, ?1920–38, 1946?/1953–73/– ?*
*contd. as:* Cornwall Cricket League and Association. Handbook. *?/1978/to date*

1811 **Crossing, William,** *compiler*
–1 Cricket averages: a record of the batting & bowling analyses of the cricket clubs of Devonshire and Cornwall in 1894. Plymouth, *printed by* Hoyten and Cole, 1895. [ix],1–59p? stats.
*intended as annual, but the only issue?*

1811 **Douch, Henry Leslie**
–2 Old Cornish inns and their place in the social history of the county. Truro, D. Bradford Barton, 1966. 219p. illus.
*cricket pp. 59 (reference to a single wicket game in 1781) and 138*

### Falmouth

1812 **Dorning, W.N.**
■ Falmouth Cricket Club, 1910–1959. Falmouth, the Club, [1959]. [28]p. incl. adverts. 1 illus. ports. stats.

### Launceston

1812 **Robbins, Alfred F.**
–1 Launceston, past and present. Launceston, W. Weighell, 1888. 450p. illus.
*cricket pp. 306–7, 373*

### Newquay

1813 **Trist, J. Fincher**
■ Reminiscences of a grand tennis tournament, and of an equally grand cricket match, (bats versus broom-sticks) which were played at Newquay on the 13th, 14th, 16th, and 17th August, 1886. Truro, "Royal Cornwall Gazette", 1886. 59p.
*cricket pp. 20–33; in verse form*

### Tintagel

1814 **Caple, Samuel Canynge,** *compiler*
■ Tintagel Cricket Club year book, 1949. [Tintagel C.C., 1949]. 48p. ports. scores, stats.
*includes brief history of the club*

### Troon

1815 **Hughes Simon**
■ Kings of village cricket: the Troon story—from the beginning to their first trip to Lord's. Troon (Cornwall), Troon C.C., 1973. 24p. team ports.
*Troon were winners of The Haig National Village Cricket Championship, 1972*

## CORNWALL C.C.C.

1816 **Cornwall County Cricket Club**
Annual report. Truro, the Club. stats.
*1903? to date*

1817 Gillette Cup Competition 1970. First
■ round Saturday April 25th . . . at Boscawen Park, Truro: souvenir book, containing a brief history of Cornwall County Cricket Club by S. Canynge Caple and facts and figures about Cornwall and Glamorgan cricketers. [Truro, the Club, 1970]. [38]p. ports. stats.

1817 Gillette Cup Competition, 1977. First
–1 round Wednesday, June 29 . . . Cornwall
■ versus Lancashire at Boscawen Park, Truro: souvenir brochure containing A brief history of Cornwall County Cricket Club 1895–1977 by S. Canynge Caple. [St. Agnes, S.C. Caple, 1977]. [52]p. team port. scores, stats.
*pre-match; despite title, mostly S. Canynge Caple's history of Cornwall C.C.C.*

## CUMBERLAND

### Cockermouth

1818 **Cockermouth** Cricket Club, 1823–1973. Cockermouth, the Club, [1973]. 20p.
*members' handbook with history and rules of club*

### Penrith

1819 **Hurst, John Laurence**
■ Century of Penrith cricket. Penrith, the Club, 1967. 91p. illus. ports. scores, stats.

## DERBYSHIRE

1820 **Central Derbyshire Cricket League**
□ Yearbook. The League. stats.

*?–1956?, 1973 to date?*
*League disbanded 1956? but reformed 1970.*
*The yearbook resumed publication 1973*

1821 **Derbyshire and Cheshire Cricket League**
□ Annual report. The League. stats. (of same year)
*1952/1956 . . . 72/to date*

1822 **Derbyshire Cricket League**
□ [Handbook]. Chesterfield, the League. *annual*
*?/1955–8/to date*

1822 **North Derbyshire Cricket League**
–1 Handbook. Derby, the League. *annual*
*1974 to date*

1823 **Nottinghamshire and Derbyshire Border**
□ **Cricket League**
[Handbook]. The League. *annual. stats.*
*1920?/1955–58/to date*

1824 Rules. The League, 1972. 15p.
■

1825 **The Nottinghamshire** cricketers' handbook. Bury, Fletcher & Speight. *annual.*
*1881*
*1882–3 with title: "The Notts and Derby cricketers' handbook"*
*1884 with title: "The cricketers' handbook for Notts, Derby and Leicestershire"*

1826 **S.E. Derbyshire College of Further**
■ **Education.** *Dept. of Liberal Studies & Adult Education*
Derbyshire cricket 1870–1970: a short course on the history of the game in Derbyshire during the last 100 years. Ilkeston, the College, [1970]. 4p. of text on 6p fold.
*details of course*

1827 **The Victoria** history of the counties of
■ England: Derbyshire; ed. by William Page. Vol. 2. Constable, 1907
*cricket pp. 298–301*

## Belper

1828 **Dicken, Arthur,** *compiler*
■ Belper Meadows Cricket Club: short history and records 1880–1908. [Belper, the Club], 1908. 28p. ports. stats.

## Brassington

1828 **Life** and history of Brassington Village,
–1 Derbyshire. Brassington, W.E.A., 1967.
[ii],62p. maps
*cricket pp. 59–61*

## Chatsworth

1829 **Chatsworth Cricket Club**
Rules, also the Laws of the game of cricket. Bakewell, *printed for the Club,* 1859

## Chesterfield

1829 **Suttle, Charles Richard William**
–1 Junior cricket reborn in the seventies.
■ [Chesterfield, the Author, 1973]. 2–160p. illus. ports. facsims. stats. pbk.

## Clifton

1830 **[Corbishley, George J.]**
■ A history of Clifton Cricket Club 1867–1967. *Privately printed,* [1967]. 36p. ports. stats.

## Derby

1831 **Derby and District Cricket Association**
■ Official handbook. Derby, the Association. *annual*
*1946–53:*
*1946; edited by Charles Hewitt*
*1947–53; edited by A.F. Dawn*

1832 **Derby** Congregational Cricket Club
■ 1869–1969. [Derby, the Club, 1969]. [48]p. ports.

1833 **Derby Cricket Club**
Bazaar souvenir 1910. Derby, the Club, 1910

## Duffield

1833 **Gregory, K.V.,** *and* **Thorn, D.S.,** *compilers*
–1 Duffield C.C. 1878–1978. Duffield, the
■ Club, [1978]. 103p. illus. ports. facsims. stats.

## Glossop

1834 **Glossop and District Cricket League**
[Handbook]. Glossop, the League. *annual*
*?/1893–1915, 1919?–29*

1835 **Stapley, Harry,** *and* **Hodgett, H.O.**
■ History of the Glossop Cricket Club, established 1833: centenary souvenir. Glossop, the Club, 1933. 54p. scores

## Hathersage

1836 **Hathersage** Cricket Club celebrate a
■ Festival of Cricket to commemorate one hundred and twenty years participation in the village game: programme of events, Saturday 23 May to Sunday 31 May, 1970, together with an account of the history of the club and personalities compiled by members. Hathersage, the

Club, [1970]. 46p. incl. adverts. illus. ports.

## Hayfield

1837 **History** of the Hayfield Cricket Club.
■ Hayfield, [the Club], 1938. [56]p. incl. adverts. team ports.

## High Peak

1838 **High Peak Cricket League**
□ [Handbook]. Hayfield, the League
*1904? to date; 1963–with title: Fixtures and rules*

## Ilkeston

1838 **Blasdale, Frank**
–1 The story of Ilkeston Rutland Cricket
■ Club. Ilkeston, the Club, 1979. 36p. illus. ports. scores

1839 **Trueman, Edwin**
Ilkeston cricketers of the past. Ilkeston, J. Wombwell, 1881. 71p. scores
*rptd. from "Ilkeston Pioneer"*

## Stanton-by-Dale

1840 **Waller, Harold**
■ Echoes of Stanton cricket. [The Author], 1951. [vi],75p. ports.

## Sundiacre

1840 **Dunn, Joyce,** *compiler & editor*
–1 Sundiacre Town C.C. 1877–1977: a
■ miscellany of writings. [Sundiacre, the Club, 1977?]. 39p. ports. facsims. scores

## Wirksworth

1841 **Hilditch, Brian**
■ Wirksworth Cricket Club centenary, 1949; the history of the Club. Derby, The Author, 1949. [32]p. illus. ports. scores, stats.

# DERBYSHIRE C.C.C.

1842 **Ashley-Cooper, Frederick Samuel**
■ Derbyshire county cricket. George W. May, 1924. 32p. illus. ports.

1843 **The Daily Telegraph (Sheffield)**
Derby County boomerang; edited by E.M. Pike. Sheffield, Daily Telegraph, 1902
*a souvenir published daily during the Derbyshire C.C.C. Bazaar, April, 1902*

1844 **Derbyshire Advertiser**
■ Derbyshire County Cricket Club: winners

of 1936 championship. Derby, "Derbyshire Advertiser", 1936. [12]p. incl. adverts. ports. stats.
*supplement issued Sept. 11 and 12, 1936*

1845 **Derbyshire County Cricket Club**
□ List of members and subscribers. Derby, the Club
*for 1934. 150p.*
*1950. 84p.*
*1967. 88p*

1846 Year book; edited by F.G. Peach and A.F.
■ Dawn. Derby, Derbyshire C.C.C. Supporters' Club. illus. ports. scores, stats.
*1954 to date, including Centenary year book 1970. 266p.*

1847 Membership campaign. [Derby, the Club,
■ c.1961]. 12p. illus. ports. map

1848 Gillette Cup 1969 souvenir brochure;
■ edited by Michael Carey. [Derby, the Club, 1969]. [42]p. illus. ports.

1849 Centenary 1870–1970. Derby, the Club.
■ 2p. card in first day cover, 4th Nov. 1970

1850 Derbyshire's cover-drive: centenary cele-
■ brations 1870–1970. Derby, the Club, [1970]. 6p. fold. illus.
*a centenary drive to raise funds*

1851 **The Derbyshire** cricket annual; edited by E. Elliott and T. Thornhill. Derby. port. stats.
*1885–1891. Bowley & Rae*
*1892. Wilkins*
*1893; ed. by E. Elliott [only]. Simpson*
*contd. as: "The Derbyshire cricket guide"*

1852 **The Derbyshire** cricket guide; compiled by L.C. Wright and W.J. Piper. Derby. *annual. port. stats.*
*1896. Simpson.*
*1897–1914. Bacon and Hudson*
*1919–1939.*
*formerly: "The Derbyshire cricket annual"*

1853 **Piper, Walter J.,** *junior*
■ A history of the Derbyshire County Cricket Club. Derby, *printed by* Bacon & Hudson, 1897. 338p. port. scores, stats.
——2nd ed. Derby, "Daily Telegraph", 1899. 390p.
*covers history 1872 to date of publication*

1854 **Shawcroft, John**
■ A history of Derbyshire County Cricket Club, 1870–1970. [Derby, the Club, 1970]. xii,230p. stats. bibliog.
*limited to 250 copies*
——2nd ed. [1970]
*limited to 250 copies*

1855 **Simpson, Llewellyn Eardley**
■ The rise of Derbyshire cricket 1919–1935. Derby, G.C. Brittain, [1936]. 98p. ports. scores, stats.

# DEVON

1855 **Crossing, William,** *compiler*
–1 Cricket averages: a record of the batting
■ and bowling analyses of the cricket clubs of Devonshire and Cornwall in 1894. Plymouth, *printed by* Hoyten and Cole, 1895. [ix],59p. stats.
*intended as annual, but the only issue?*

1855 **Devon County Cricket Association**
–2 Newsletter. The Assoc. *monthly*
*Aug.(?) 1948 to date*
*editor to 1975(?) Francis Doidge*

1856 Rules; honorary secretaries of clubs in membership; annual report. *typescript*
*1948/1950/to date?*

## Axminster

1856 **Oakland, Ian,** *and* **Bird, Michael,**
–1 *compilers*
Axminster Town Cricket Club [1850–1975]: 125th anniversary souvenir. [Axminster, the Club], 1975 [40]p. incl. covers. & adverts. illus. team ports.

## Bideford

1856 **Bideford, Littleham & Westward Ho!**
–2 **Cricket Club**
□ Year book. Westward Ho!, the Club. illus. ports. scores, stats. *of prev. yr*
*?/1973/to date?*
*formed 1970*

## Bovey Tracey

1856 **Thomas, Eric**
–3 Bovey Tracey Cricket & Bowling Club
■ 125th anniversary year 1852–1977. [Bovey Tracey, the Club, 1977]. [16]p. team port. stats.

## Exmouth

1857 **Rodgers, Jack,** *and* **Rodgers, Marjorie**
■ Exmouth Cricket Club centenary festival brochure: 1860–1965. Exmouth, the Authors, 1965. 64p. ports.

1857 **Rodgers, Jack**
–1 Exmouth Cricket Club – ten years on 1966–75. Exmouth, the Author, 1976. 88p. team ports. stats.
*sequel to no. 1857*

## Newton Abbot

1858 **South Devon** Cricket Club, Newton
■ Abbot, 1851–1911: diamond jubilee souvenir; illustrated by Charles Lane Vicary. [Newton Abbot, the Club, 1911]. 36p. illus. scores

## Plymouth

1859 **The Mount Cricket Club**
■ List of members. [Plymouth, the Club]. *2-yearly? typescript*
*?/1969, 1974, 1976/to date*
——Amendments. *2-yearly? typescript*
*?/1975, 1977/to date*

1859 The Molehill: the record of the Mount
–1 Cricket Club. Plymouth, the Club. *annual*
*1962?/1975, 76/to date*
*founded in 1935*

1860 **Plymouth and District Cricket League**
□ Handbook and guide. Plymouth, the League, *annual*
*1939, 1946/1950 . . . 74/to date*

## Sidmouth

1860 **Dean, Martyn,** *editor*
–1 Sidmouth Cricket Club. Sidmouth, the
■ Club, 1978. 20p. incl. covers. illus. ports.
*founded 1823*

1861 **Sutton, Anna**
■ A story of Sidmouth. Sidmouth, [the Author], 1953. xi,148p. illus.
*cricket pp. 112–5*
——2nd revd. ed. 1959. 205p.
*cricket pp. 114–8*

## Tavistock

1862 **Tavistock Cricket Club**
List of rules, 1870. [Tavistock, the Club. 1870]. 8p.

1862 Tavistock Cricket Club proudly presents
–1 Tavistock v Gloucestershire, 1973 Gillette
■ Cup winners, at The Ring, Whitchurch Down, Tavistock Sunday 21 July 1974. Tavistock, the Club, [1974]. 36p. incl. covers & adverts. ports.

## Teignbridge

1863 **Davies, Edward William Lewis**
Memoir of the Rev. John Russell and his out-of-door life. New ed. rptd. with illustrations by N.H.J. Baird. Exeter, Commin; London, Chatto & Windus, 1902, xiii,352p. col. illus.
*limited ed. of 1000 copies, plus 75 copies on Japanese vellum; first published, Bentley, 1878; new ed. Bentley, 1883*
*cricket p. 89 refers to Teignbridge C.C.*

1864 **Ormerod, George Wareing,** *compiler*
■ Annals of the Teignbridge Cricket Club, 1823–1883. Plymouth, *privately printed by W. Brendon,* 1888. xii,103p. frontis. scores

### Torquay

1865 **Torquay** Cricket Club centenary 1951; ■ some notes on the history and development of the club since its formation in 1851. Torquay, [the Club, 1951]. 36p. illus. stats.

## DEVON C.C.C.

1866 **Devon County Cricket Club**
■ [Handbook]. Exeter, [the Club]. *annual.* illus. ports. scores, stats. in v.y.
*season 1951 to date*
*in later years* with title: Yearbook
1979 Championship yearbook, *with results of previous season*

## DORSET

1866 **Dorset Natural History and Archaeo-**
–1 **logical Society**
■ Proceedings . . . for 1971. Volume 93; edited by J. Stevens Cox. Dorchester, the Society, 1972. 260p. illus. port. maps, plans, diagrs.
*the Presidential address, pp. 247–251, "Notes on cricket history with references to Dorset cricket", by W. Stuart Best*

1866 **Southern Cricket League**
–2 Handbook. The League. illus. ports.
□ stats. *annual*
*1979?/1980/–*
*full title:* Town & Country Southern C.L. *Covers Hants and Dorset*

### Dorchester

1867 **Dorchester Cricket Club**
■ Centenary year book 1956. [Dorchester, the Club, 1956]. 12p. incl. adverts.

### Wimborne

1868 **Wimborne and District Cricket**
□ **Association**
Rules and fixtures. [Wimborne], the Association
*?/1952/–?*

## DORSET C.C.C.

1869 **Kingston Park and Dorset County Cricket Club**
Rules, with list of members and matches. Dorchester, the Club. *annual*
*1876–87*

1870 **Dorset County Cricket Club**
■ Report, statement of accounts, list of officers, list of members. Dorchester, the Club. *annual?*
*season?/1933/–?*

1871 Yearbook. Dorchester, the Club. illus.
■ ports. scores, stats. *in v.y.*
*1949 to date*

## DURHAM

1872 **Cleveland,** Durham, Northumberland and Yorkshire cricketers' handbook. Bury, Fletcher & Speight, 1882
*contd, as: The Durham and Yorkshire cricketers' handbook*

1873 **The cricketers'** handbook containing the match fixtures of the principal clubs in Northumberland, Durham and North Yorkshire. Bury, Fletcher & Speight. *annual.* illus.
*1891–3, 1897–1900*
*1891 issue entitled: Henry A. Murton's cricketers' companion*

1874 **The Durham** and Yorkshire cricketers' handbook. Bury, Fletcher & Speight. *annual*
*1883–1900;* formerly: *Cleveland, Durham, Northumberland and Yorkshire cricketers' handbook*

1875 **Durham Senior Cricket League**
□ Handbook. Sunderland, the League. *annual*
*1903–14, 1920–39, 1946 to date*
*formed 1902*

1876 **Durham Senior Cricket League (Eastern Division)**
Fixtures. Sunderland, the League. *annual*
*1904–14, 1919–31?*
*the designation of the League varies*

1877 Handbook. Sunderland, the League. *annual*
*1911–14, 1920–31?*

1878 Instructions to umpires. Sunderland, the League, *annual.*
*?/1925 . . . 1931/–?*

1879 **Lambert, Thomas,** *compiler*
□ Cricket annual for Northumberland and Durham, 1896. Newcastle-on-Tyne, Lambert, [1896]. 110p. stats.
*results of 1895, fixtures for 1896*

1880 **North Yorkshire and South Durham**
□ **Cricket League**
[Handbook]. Middlesbrough, the League
*?/1893–1914, ?1919 to date*

1881 Statistics 1893–1947; compiled by H. Tren-
■ holm. The League, [1948]. 184p. port.
scores, stats.
——Statistics 1948–1955; supplement.
The League, [1956]. 75p. score, stats.

## Bishop Auckland

1881 **Hunt, Brian**
–1 125 not out: Bishop Auckland Cricket
■ Club. History and records 1853–1978.
Newcastle upon Tyne, Paull & Goode,
[1978]. 96p. incl. adverts. 1 illus. ports.
scores, stats.

## Burnopfield

1881 **Baker, Tom** *compiler*
–2 Burnopfield Cricket Club: a review of the
■ post-war years. [Birtley (Durham), the
Compiler], 1974. [iv],76p. stats.

## Consett

1882 **The Consett** story, written and compiled
by the Consett Lions' Club. Consett,
Ramsden Williams, 1963. 180p. illus.
ports. diagrs. maps.
*contains articles on Jack Carr, Leadgate
C.C., Shotley Bridge C.C., H.L. Dales,
Consett C.C.*

1882 **Raw, John J.**
–1 The cricketers of Consett & District Club.
Newcastle upon Tyne, Mail and Leader
Ltd., 1907. 83p. illus. ports. scores, stats.

## Durham

1883 **Parsons, A.L.,** *compiler*
■ Durham City Cricket Club history.
Durham, the Club, 1972. 307p. incl.
adverts. illus. ports. scores, stats.

## Seaton Carew

1884 **Hornby, Derek**
■ The history of Seaton Carew Cricket Club
1829–1965. Seaton Carew, West Hartlepool, the Author, [1965]. 100p. illus.
ports. scores, stats.

1885 ————, *editor*
■ Five star year. Hartlepool, *printed by* W.
Barlow, 1969. 106p. illus. ports. scores,
stats.
*includes "Seaton Carew C.C." by D.
Hornby*

## South Shields

1885 **Hodgson, George B.**
–1 The borough of South Shields from the
earliest period to the close of the nine-

teenth century. Newcastle upon Tyne, A.
Reid, 1903. illus. x,510p.
*cricket pp. 126, 453, 483*

1886 **South Shields Cricket Club**
■ Souvenir of the centenary dinner,
Wednesday, 10th May, 1950. South
Shields, [the Club], 1950. 24p. ports.
stats.

## Stockton

1886 **Heavisides, Henry**
–1 The annals of Stockton-on-Tees with
biographical notices. Stockton-on-Tees,
[The Author], 1865. vi,224p. frontis.
*cricket pp. 134–8*

1887 **Stockton Cricket Club**
Member's booklet. Stockton, the Club.
*annual?* stats.
*?/1948/to date?*
*formed/1816*

1888 Stockton cricketers' grand bazaar:
souvenir. Stockton, [the Club], 1906.
illus.

## Sunderland

1889 **Moses, E. Watts,** *and others*
■ To Ashbrooke and beyond: the history of
the Sunderland Cricket and Rugby Football Club 1808–1962. [Sunderland, the
Club, 1962]. [xi],204p. illus. ports. map,
scores, stats.
*cricket section by D.G. Greig*

# DURHAM C.C.C.

1890 **Bell, William R.**
■ Fifty years history of the Durham County
Cricket Club 1882–1931 inclusive. Sunderland, *printed by* Sunderland Post Co.,
1932. 218p. scores, stats.

1891 **Durham County Cricket Club**
□ Annual report. Durham, the Club.
scores, stats.
*1882 to date*

1891 **Durham** versus New Zealand: photogra-
–1 phic souvenir and fixtures list.
■ Birmingham, E. Kavanagh, 1949. [4]p.
ports.

# ESSEX

1892 **Essex** cricket: a magazine on Essex cricket
■ at county and club level. illus. ports.
scores, stats.
*4 issues only*
*Spring 1973;* edited by Laurence
Mumford. County Cricket Publ. Ltd.

*Summer, Autumn 1973;* edited by Laurence Mumford. Sports Publications
*Spring 1974:* edited by Laurence Mumford & Dave Lawrence. Sports Publications

1892 **Essex Cricket Assocation**
–1 Directory & handbook. The Assoc.,
■ [1976?]. [33]p. *typescript*

1892 **Essex League**
–2 Official cricket handbook. The League.
□ *annual.* stats.
*1972–4*
*contd. as:* Truman Essex League. Official cricket handbook.
*1975 to date*

1893 **The Gentlemen of Essex Cricket Club**
□ [Rules, fixtures and list of members]. The Club. *annual*
*?/1927, 31, 55/to date?*

1893 **Greene King Essex Senior Competition**
–1 Handbook. *annual*
□ *season?/1976/to date?*
*contains officials, final placings of last season, fixtures, member clubs, constitution, match rules, etc.*

1894 **The Official** handbook of the bicycle, cricket and football clubs; edited by Robert Cook. Chelmsford, E. Durrant, Essex County Chronicle. *annual*
*at least 18 issues 1883–1900*

1895 **Romford, Hornchurch, Upminster and**
□ **District Cricket Association**
Rules and register of clubs. The Association. *annual*
*1953?/1964–70/*

1896 **Thompson, Leslie**
■ Cricketing in Essex then and now. [Orsett, nr. Grays, Essex, the Author, 1963]. [iii],42;[i],36p. scores, *typescript*
*"Then–1760–1800"; "Now–1900–1960"*

1897 **The Victoria** history of the counties of
■ England: Essex; edited by William Page and J. Horace Round. Vol. 2. Constable, 1907
*cricket pp. 599–612. stats.*

1898 **West Essex Gazette**
Cricket annual; edited by C.E. Waller, Epping, West Essex Printing Co., 1948. 88p. illus.
*the only issue?*

## Belhus

1898 **Belhus Cricket Club**
–1 Barbados tour November 15–30th, 1976.

■ [The Club, 1976]. [12]p. incl. adverts. ports.
*pre-tour*

1898 A brief account of the Belhus Cricket Club
–2 Barbados tour 1976; by Denis Reed, tour
■ organiser. Belhus, the Club, 1976. 16f. stats. *typescript*
*post tour; 8 copies distributed*

## Billericay

1898 **Billericay Cricket Club**
–3 Centenary 1875–1975. Billericay, the
■ Club, [1975]. 30p. incl. adverts. team ports. facsim.

## Brentwood

1899 **South Weald Cricket Club**
■ An appeal. Brentwood, the Club, [1972]. [24]p. illus. team port. plan, stats.
*an appeal for support for a new ground and pavilion*

## Buckhurst Hill

1900 **Buckhurst Hill Cricket Club**
60th anniversary, 1923. [Buckhurst Hill, the Club, 1923]

1901 **Buckhurst Hill Cricket and Lacrosse**
■ **Club**
One hundred years 1864–1964. [Buckhurst Hill, the Club, 1964]. 81p. illus. ports.

## Debden

1902 **Debden Cricket Club**
[Handbook]. Debden, the Club. *annual.* illus. *typescript*
*?/1951 . . . 54/to date?*

## Great Bentley

1903 **Great Bentley Cricket Club**
■ Cricket at Gt. Bentley 1771–1971. [Great Bentley (Essex), the Club, 1971]. 20p. incl. adverts. scores, stats.

1904 **Morton, Carl**
■ 200 years of sport on Gt. Bentley Green 1771–1971, celebrating the bicentenary of the Gt. Bentley Cricket Club. [The Author, 1971]. 12p. *typescript*

## Hornchurch

1904 **Perfect, Charles Thomas**
–1 Ye olde village of Hornchurch. Colchester, Benham & Co., 1917. illus. 154p.
*cricket pp. 135–42*

## Hutton

1905 **Hutton Cricket Club**
■ Centenary year 1864–1964; [edited by Peter Myall]. Hutton, the Club, [1964]. [16]p. illus. ports. scores, stats.

## Ilford

1906 **Clayhall Cricket Club**
■ 50 not out 1919–1969. [Ilford, the Club, 1969]. [36]p. illus. ports.

1907 **Ilford and District Cricket Association**
■ Handbook. [Ilford, the Assoc]. scores, map. *annual*
*1968 to date*

1907 **Ilford C.C.** & Essex C.C.C. present a
–1 double wicket competition sponsored by
■ Byron Shipping Ltd. on Sunday, 8th October 1978. Valentines Park, Cranbrook Road. Ray East benefit: souvenir programme. [The Clubs 1978]. [20]p. incl. adverts. ports. stats.
—— . . . 7 October 79. Stuart Turner's benefit: souvenir programme. [The Clubs, 1979]. [28]p. incl. adverts. ports. stats.

1907 **Polson, John S.**
–2 Ilford Cricket Club: a history of the first
■ 100 years and centenary souvenir [1879–1978]. [Ilford, the Club, 1979]. 140p. incl. adverts. ports.

## Leyton

1908 **Leyton** cricket festival 1968; souvenir
■ programme, August 10th to 19th. Godfrey Banks [for Festival Cttee., 1968]. 24p. incl. adverts. illus.
——1969, August 2nd to 12th. A.E. Sedgwick [for Festival Cttee., 1969]. 24p. incl. adverts. team port.

## Loughton

1909 **Loughton Cricket Club**
□ Report and balance sheet. Loughton, the Club. *annual*. stats.
*season ?/1968/to date*
*formed 1880*

## Maldon

1910 **Williams, E. Montague**
■ Cricket: let's look at the past. Maldon, [Maldon C.C., 1951]. 13p. illus. on cover. score
*historical souvenir issued for the Festival of Britain, 1951*

1911 Cricket: a bicentenary in an Essex setting. Maldon, the Author, 1955. 15p. illus.

## Orsett

1911 **Rowley, E.H.**
–1 133 years of cricket in Orsett and district. 1948

## Rickling

1912 **Bax, Clifford**
Highways and byways in Essex. Macmillan, 1939. xv,359p. illus.
*reference to "wild cricket" at Rickling Green*

## Romford

1913 **Romford Cricket Club**
■ Centenary year 1963; edited by Laurie Mumford. Romford, the Club, [1963]. [24]p. incl. adverts. port.

## Saffron Walden

1914 **Rowntree, Charles Brightwen**
More Saffron Walden then and now: Walden cricket 1841–1851. Saffron Walden, the Author, 1954. illus. ports.

## Shenfield

1914 **Sightscreen:** the Shenfield Cricket Club
–1 magazine. [Shenfield, the Club].
□ *typescript*

## South Woodford

1914 **South Woodford Cricket and Sports Club**
–2 Annual report. The Club. stats. *typescript*
□ *?/1973, 1974/*
*compiled by W.J.A. Hubbard; contd. by* Results and averages

1914 Results and averages; compiled by W.J.A.
–3 Hubbard. Leytonstone, the Compiler.
■ *annual*. stats. *typescript*
*season 1975 to date*
*formerly:* Annual report

## Tollesbury

1914 **Tollesbury C.C.** v. Essex C.C.C., Robin
–4 Hobbs' benefit match at Tollesbury
■ cricket ground . . . 14 September. Tollesbury, the Club, 1974. 36p. incl. covers & adverts. illus. ports. stats.

## Upminster

1915 **Upminster** Cricket Club, 1858–1958: history and centenary programme. Upminster, [the Club], 1958. 60p. illus.

## Walthamstow

1916 **Couzens, Sidney A.,** *compiler*
■ Walthamstow Cricket & Lawn Tennis Club: the first hundred years. Walthamstow, the Club, 1962. 13p.

## Wanstead

1917 **Berridge, Geoffrey**
■ "The first century": the history of the Wanstead Cricket Club 1866–1966. The Author, [1966]. [i],48p. incl. adverts. illus. ports.

## Westcliff-on-Sea

1918 **Thornton, V. John**
■ The Westcliff-on-Sea Cricket Club: the first fifty years. Westcliff-on-Sea, the Club, [1953]. 88p. illus. stats.

1919 **Westcliff-on-Sea Cricket Club**
■ Westcliff Cricket Club v. The Lord's Taverners, Chalkwell Park, Sunday, July 16th, [1972]. Westcliff-on-Sea, The Club, [1972]. 24p. incl. adverts.

## Woodford Green

1920 **Two** centuries of cricket at Woodford
■ Green 1735–1952: some notes and facts about the Woodford Green Club. Walthamstowe P., 1952. 32p. illus.

# ESSEX C.C.C.

1921 **Baily, Robin,** *editor*
■ Cricket: all about London's big four. John Smith, Lord's and Oval Bookstalls, [1928]. 16p. illus. ports. (on covers), stats.
*Kent, Surrey, Essex, Middlesex, giving averages for 1927 and fixtures for 1928*

1922 **Bray, Charles**
■ Essex county cricket. Convoy Publications, 1950. 106p. illus. ports. stats. (County cricket series)

1923 **County** cricket in Essex. [Chelmsford,
■ Essex C.C.C., 1959]. 32p. incl. adverts. illus. ports. stats.
*issued in aid of the Ken Preston benefit fund*

1924 **Essex County Cricket Club**
List of members 1908. [Chelmsford, the Club, 1908]. 102p.
——1912. 84p.

1925 Year book. Chelmsford, the Club, illus.
■ ports. stats.
*1927–1939*
*1948; edited by R.F.T. Paterson*
*contd. as: Essex C.C.C. Annual*

1926 Annual. Chelmsford, the Club, illus.
■ ports. scores, stats
*1949 to date*
*1949–51; ed. by R.F.T. Paterson*
*1952–66, including 1954 Diamond Jubilee edition; ed. by T.E. Bailey*

*1967–70; ed. by C.A. Brown*
*1971–?; ed. by John Thurman*
*1976: Centenary souvenir edition; ed. by G.J. Saville. 160p. incl. adverts. illus. ports. scores, stats.*
*formerly: Essex C.C.C. Year book; in later years: Handbook*

1927 Membership campaign. [Chelmsford,
■ Essex C.C.C., 1962]. 14p. illus. ports.

1928 The appeal. Chelmsford, the Club.
■ [1966]. [8]p. illus. ports. plan
*to equip the recently purchased County Cricket Ground, Chelmsford*

1929 Westcliff-on-Sea cricket festival.
☐ Southend, Southend News for Southend Cricket Festivals Committee. *annual*
*1970 to date*
*1970: July 11, 13, 14 & July 12 v. Middlesex. 20p. incl. adverts.*
*1971: July 10, 12 & 13 v. Hampshire; July 14, 15 & 16. v. Sussex; July 11 v. Somerset. 16p. incl. adverts.*
*1972: July 12, 13 & 14 v. Middlesex; July 15, 17 & 18 v. Gloucestershire, 16p. incl. adverts.*
*1973: July 14, 16,17 v. New Zealand: July 15 v. Middlesex; July 18–20 v. Northants, 16p. incl. adverts.*

1929 Essex & Cricket: the official journal of the
–1 Essex County Cricket Club. illus. ports.
☐ stats. *3x a year* and special members' issue at Christmas
*Spring 1975 to date*
*includes news etc. of club cricket in Essex; edited by Brian Meggison*
*from 1978, no. 1 has incorporated* The Essex supporter

1929 **Essex County Cricket Supporters'**
–2 **Association**
☐ Essex cricket magazine. The Assoc.
*Vol. 1, no.1 13 May 1972–? 1972*
*it was hoped that publication would be in each week in which we have a home match' – 'a minimum of 10 issues per season'*
*contd. as:*
The Essex supporter; edited by Brian Meggison. *irregular 1973–1977*
*incorporated 1978 in* Essex & cricket

1930 **Essex** cricket: a magazine on Essex cricket
■ at county and club level. illus. ports. scores, stats.
*4 issues only*
*Spring 1973;* edited by Laurence Mumford. County Cricket Publ. Ltd.
*Summer, Autumn 1973;* edited by Laurence Mumford. Sports Publications
*Spring 1974:* edited by Laurence Mumford & Dave Lawrence. Sports Publications

1931 **Foster, Denis**
■ Essex. Findon Publications, [1949]. 32p. ports. stats. ("Know Your Cricket County Series)

1932 **Gordon,** *Sir* **Home Seton Charles**
■ **Montagu,** *bart., compiler*
Essex County Cricket Club facts and figures 1894–1947. Chelmsford, the Club, 1948. 24p. stats.

1933 **Leprechauns Cricket Club**
■ Leprechauns Cricket Club v. Essex County Cricket Club, College Park, Dublin, July 6th and 7th, 1971: souvenir brochure. [Dublin], the Club, [1971]. 44p. incl. adverts. ports.

1933 **Newnham, Leslie**
–1 Essex County cricket 1876–1975: a brief
■ history. [Colchester, Essex C.C.C., 1975]. [v],93p. illus. ports. stats.
*includes a register of cricketers who have appeared for Essex since 1876*

# GLOUCESTERSHIRE

1933 **The Gloucestershire** coach: players
–2 welfare & benefit fund. [Bristol], Glouces-
■ tershire C.C.C., [1973]. [12]p. incl. adverts. illus. ports.

1934 **The Gloucestershire** cricketer: Glouces-
□ tershire cricket and cricket in Gloucester-shire. [Bristol], Gloucestershire C.C.C. 6 *monthly?* illus. ports. stats. *typescript*
*?/Feb. 1972 . . . May 1975/to date*

1934 **Howard, Colin**
–1 Cotswold days. Blackie, 1973. 277p. illus.
*cricket pp. 103–7;182–5*

1935 **The Victoria** history of the counties of
■ England: Gloucestershire; edited by William Page. Vol. 2. Constable, 1907
*cricket pp. 306–11. stats.*

## Almondsbury

1936 **Almondsbury Cricket Club**
■ Centenary season 1861–1961. Almondsbury, the Club, [1961]. [6]p.
*officers & fixtures*

## Apsley Park

1937 **Apsley Park Cricket Club**
■ Scores. Bristol, the Club. *annual.* scores, stats.
*seasons 1886–93. [?1887–94]*

## Blockley

1937 **Icely, Henry Edward McLaughlin**
–1 Blockley through three centuries: annals of a Cotswold parish. [Blockley Antiquarian Society], 1974. illus. (1 col.), ports. maps, facsims.
*cricket pp. 144–5, 148–9*

## Bristol

1937 **Arrowsmith's** dictionary of Bristol; edited
–2 by Henry J. Spear and J.W. Arrowsmith. Bristol, Arrowsmith, 1884. illus. map. 292p.
*cricket pp. 88–91: notes on date of formation, etc. of 40 local clubs*
——2nd ed. 1906. 448p. illus.
*cricket pp. 127, 375–6: rewritten sections on cricket and the county ground*

1938 **Bedminster Cricket Club**
■ Centenary book 1847–1947. [Bristol, the Club], 1947. 46p. 1 illus. ports.

1939 **Bristol and District Cricket Association**
□ [Handbook]. Bristol, the Association
*?/1954 . . . 1973/to date*
*formed 1896*

1940 **The Bristol** cricketers' annual
companion. Bristol, *printed by* Hemmons Central Printing Works
*?/1893, 1895/–?*

1941 **Bristol Evening World**
■ Cricket annual. Bristol, Bristol Evening World. illus. scores, stats. ports.
*1947, 1948*
cover title: *Pink 'Un cricket annual*
*cricket in general, but particularly reports of Gloucestershire and Somerset C.C.C.'s matches and Bristol club cricket*

1942 **The Schoolmasters' Cricket Club**
■ Centenary 1852–1952; compiled by J.D. Caines. Bristol, the Club, [1952]. 36p. incl. adverts. ports.

## Cheltenham

1942 **Pakenham, Simona Vere**
–1 Cheltenham: a biography. Macmillan, 1971. 192p. illus. maps
*cricket pp. 21, 134–5, 169*

1943 **Taylor, Alfred Daniel**
■ Cheltenham Cricket Week: a review of the games from 1878 to 1904, together with a brief outline of other important matches played in the district. Cheltenham Newspaper Co., 1905. [i],60p. illus. ports. scores
——2nd ed. 1906

## Chipping Sodbury

1944 **Guy, Peter,** and **King, John,** *editors*
■ Chipping Sodbury Cricket Club, 1860–1960: centenary handbook. [Chipping Sodbury, the Club, 1960]. 96p. illus. ports. scores

## Cirencester

1944 **Beecham, Kennett John**
-1 History of Cirencester and the Roman city Corinium. Cirencester, G. Harmer, [1887]. 314p. illus. map, plan
——facsimile rpt. [Dursley, Glos.], Sutton, 1978. v,314,30p.
*cricket p. 234*

## Downend

1945 **Downend Cricket Club**
□ Annual report. Downend, the Club. stats.
*?/1962/to date?*
*formed 1893*

## Frenchay

1946 **Lucena, John**
■ Victorian cricket on Frenchay Common, and other glimpses into Victorian Frenchay. Frenchay, Frenchay Preservation Society, [1972]. 8p. illus.

1947 **Reed. C.H.,** *editor*
■ Frenchay Cricket Club centenary book 1846–1946. Frenchay, the Club, [1946] 116p. illus. ports. scores, stats.

## Frocester

1947 **Frocester Cricket Club**
-1 [Handbook]. Frocester, the Club. *annual.*
□ stats.
*?/season 1975/to date?*

## Gloucester

1947 **Gloucester City Cricket Club**
-2 150th anniversary 1829–1979. Gloucester,
■ the Club, [1979]. 88p. incl. adverts. 1 illus. ports. stats.
*includes an account of the history of the Club by D.L. Howell*

## Hambrook

1947 **Hambrook Cricket Club**
-3 Centenary booklet. Hambrook, the Club, 1978

## Kingscote

1948 **Kingscote Cricket Club**
[Handbook]. Kingscote, the Club. *annual*
*1825–30*

## Knowle

1949 **Baker, George,** *editor*
■ Knowle Cricket Club centenary book 1852–1952. Bristol, the Club Centenary Committee, [1952]. 46p. illus. ports. stats.

## Lydney

1950 **Hart, Cyril E.**
■ 101 not out!: the story of Lydney Cricket Club 1862–1963. [Lydney, the Club], 1963. vi,68p. illus. ports. scores, stats.

## Stapleton

1951 **Stapleton** Cricket Club 1863–1963:
■ [centenary booklet]; edited by H.F.J. Watkins and others. [Stapleton, the Club, 1963]. 45p. illus. ports. scores, stats.

## Tetbury

1952 **Tetbury Cricket Club**
■ Sam Cook's benefit year: an appreciation written for the club by John Arlott. Tetbury, the Club, [1957]. [4]p.

## Thornbury

1953 **Caple, Samuel Canynge,** *editor*
■ Thornbury Cricket Club centenary handbook, 1871–1971. [Thornbury, the Club, 1971]. 47p. illus. ports.

## Westbury-on-Trym

1954 **Westbury-on-Trym Cricket Club**
■ Centenary handbook. [The Club, 1958]. 56p. incl. adverts. frontis. score, stats.

# GLOUCESTERSHIRE C.C.C.

1955 **Ashley-Cooper, Frederick Samuel**
■ Gloucestershire county cricket. George W. May, [1924]. 32p. illus. ports.

1955 **Association of Cricket Statisticians,**
-1 *compilers*
■ Gloucestershire cricketers 1870–1979. Cleethorpes, the Assoc., 1979. 36p. map, stats.

1956 **[Bermuda Cricket Association]**
■ Bermuda Clubs vs. Gloucestershire County Cricket Club 1962 . . . [Hamilton, the Assoc., 1962]. 40p. incl. adverts. ports.

1957 **Caple, Samuel Canynge**
■ A history of Gloucestershire County Cricket Club, 1870–1948. Worcester, Littlebury, 1949. 182p. illus. ports. scores, stats.

1958 **Craven, Nico**
■ To Gloucester with thanks: a tribute to Gloucestershire County Cricket Club on the occasion of its centenary 1970. Bristol, Gloucestershire C.C.C., 1969. 34p.

1959 Gloster's centenary cricket: the diary of a
■ supporter during the centenary season of Gloucestershire County Cricket Club 1970. [Bristol, Gloucestershire C.C.C., 1970]. 56p.

1960 From a window in Cumberland: the
■ views of a Gloucestershire exile during the cricket season of 1971. . . .West Cumberland, the Author, 1971. 66p. 1 illus. scores

1960 Best of both worlds. [Seascale, the
–1 Author, 1976]. 115p. frontis.
■ *subtitle on cover:* fun and games in The Lakes and The Cotswolds
*Gloucestershire cricket 1946–1975; some two-thirds reprinted from previous booklets*

1960 The festive season: 'happy hours'. Seas-
–2 cale, [the Author, 1976?]. 23p.
■ *subtitle on cover:* the year of the bat 1975

1960 Suddenly it was summer: lollipops and
–3 roses. [Seascale, the Author, 1977]. 99p.
■ 1 col. illus. scores.
*personal account of Gloucestershire cricket during 1976 season*

1960 A sign of the times. [Seascale (Cumbria)],
–4 the Author, 1978. 157p. col. frontis.,
■ scores
*a personal diary of the English season 1977, especially concerned with Gloucestershire*

1960 August occasions; with illustrations by
–5 Frank Fisher. [Seascale (Cumbria)], the
■ Author, 1979. 111p. illus. [1 col.). scores
*mostly Gloucestershire in 1978 season*

1961 **Dutton, Harry**
Poems and acrostics of Gloucestershire cricket and cricketers. Cheltenham, [the Author], 1900. [8]p. ports.

1962 **Gloucestershire County Cricket Club**
[List of members and balance sheet, April 30, 1874]. Bristol, the Club, [1874]. 3p.

1963 Rules and list of members. Bristol, the Club. *annual*
*?/1896,98,1900,01/–?*

1964 Year book. Bristol, the Club. illus. ports.
■ scores, stats.
*1920–24, 1928–39, 1947 to date*

1965 Membership campaign 1962. [Gloucester,
■ Gloucestershire C.C.C., 1962]. 13p. illus. ports.

1966 Newsletter. Gloucester, the Club. *occasional publication*
*Nov. 1964/Mar. 1967/to date?*

1966 [Facilities available for sponsorship/
–1 hosting with advertising rates]. Bristol,
■ the Club, [197–?]. [6] cards inserted in folder. *typescript*

1967 **Parker, W. Grahame**
■ 100 years of Gloucestershire cricket. Bristol, Gloucestershire C.C.C., 1970. 68p. illus. & ports. (some col.) stats.

1968 **Plenty, Claude M.,** *compiler*
■ The book of Gloucestershire county cricket records from 1919 to 1960. Bristol, the Compiler, 1960. 140p. illus. ports. score, stats.

1969 **Pogson, Rex**
■ Gloucestershire cricket and cricketers 1919–1939. Lytham St. Annes, the Author, [1944]. 36p.
*some copies have errata slip*

1970 **Scores** made in county matches by the
□ Gloucestershire County Cricket Club. Bristol, Arrowsmith. scores, stats. *annual*
*1874–1889*
*1900–1914* with title: Scores of the Gloucester C.C.C.
*also issued in single volumes:*
*1870–74. 1874*
*1870–77. 1878. 18p.*
*1870–89 with cover-title:* Twenty years of Glo'cestershire county cricket. [1890]

# HAMPSHIRE AND ISLE OF WIGHT

1971 **"Aesop",** *pseud.*
■ Sporting reminiscences of Hampshire from 1745 to 1862. Chapman & Hall, 1864. xx,380p.

1972 **Arnold, Ralph Crispain Marshall**
A yeoman of Kent: an account of Richard Hayes, 1725–1790, and of the village of Cobham in which he lived and farmed. Constable, 1949. xii,203p. illus. (1 col.), score
*includes an account of England v. Hampshire at Sevenoaks Vine 1776*

1973 **Eagar, Edward Desmond Russell**
■ Readers' guide to Hampshire cricket. Boscombe, Boscombe Printing Co. (1933) Ltd., 1964. [12]p.
*limited ed. of 25 copies*

Hampshire cricket: The Bat and Ball Inn, Hambledon, a water-colour by Goddard Frederick Gale,
1879, which shows the inn virtually unchanged from the great days of Hambledon cricket
*photo: M.C.C.*

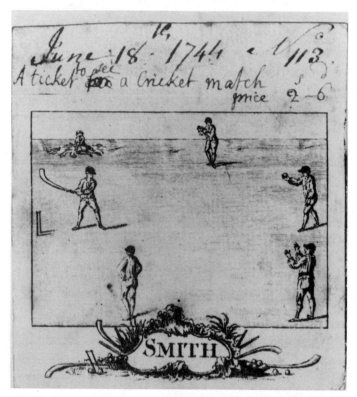

Kent cricket: A ticket of admission for the Kent v. All England match
1744, the design adapted from Louis Boitard's engraving "An Exact
Representation of a Game of Cricket" published 1743 *photo: M.C.C.*

Oxfordshire cricketer in front of his wicket and pavilion, 1787
*photo: BBC Hulton Picture Library*

1974 **Hampshire** cricket; edited by Laurence
■ Mumford. County Cricket Publications
Ltd. illus. ports.
*1973*
*intended to appear quarterly, but one issue*
*only*

1975 **Hampshire Cricket League**
■ Handbook. The League. *annual*. illus.
ports. diagrs. stats.
*1973 to date*

1976 **The Hampshire** cricketer's guide: edited
■ by George Bagshaw. Southampton, G.
Buxey. *annual*. scores, stats.
*1885–1890*
*includes club and county cricket*

1977 **May, John**
■ Cricket in North Hants: records and reminiscences. Basingstoke, Warren, 1906.
x,192p. illus. ports. scores
*includes a chapter on Hambledon by F.S.*
*Ashley-Cooper*

1978 **Parker, Eric**
■ Hesketh Prichard: hunter: explorer: natu-
ralist: cricketer: author: soldier: a memoir.
London, T. Fisher Unwin; New York,
Dutton, 1924. 272p. illus. ports.
*contains some Hampshire cricket interest*

1979 **Pope, L.T.**
■ A cup for cricket: fifty years of I'Anson
competition. Farnham, E.W. Langham,
1951. xi,101p. illus. ports. scores, stats.
*an account of the I'Anson competition*
*between village clubs along the Surrey-*
*Hampshire border*

1980 **Read, D.H. Moutray**
■ Highways and byways in Hampshire;
with illustrations by Arthur B. Connor.
Macmillan, 1908. xvii,444p. illus. map
——2nd ed. 1919
*cricket pp. 114, 371, 376–7*
——pocket ed. 1923

1980 **South Hants Cricket Club**
–1 Rules and list of members of the South
Hants Cricket Club, established May
1839. Southampton, *printed by* J.
Bennett & Son, 1849. 16p.

1980 **Southern Cricket League**
–2 Handbook. The League. illus. ports.
□ stats. *annual*
*1979?/1980/–*
*full title:* Town & Country Southern
C.L.
*covers Hants and Dorset*

1981 **The Victoria** history of the counties of
■ England: Hampshire and the Isle of

Wight; edited by William Page. Vol. 5.
Constable, 1912
*cricket pp. 574–76*

1982 **Woodley, H.**
■ Reminiscences of the South Hants Cricket
Club, between 1842 and 1859, by H.G.
Green (H. Woodley). Southampton, H.
King, Hants. Advertiser Co. Ltd., 1905.
30p.

## Andover

1982 **Andover Cricket Club**
–1 Rules. [Andover, the Club, *n.d.*]. [4]p.
■

1982 Statement of accounts for the year ended
–2 31st December. Andover, the Club.
□ *annual*
*?/1947, 1949/to date?*

## Basingstoke

1982 **Basingstoke & North Hants Cricket Club**
–3 Annual report. Basingstoke, the Club.
□ stats. *of prev. yr.*
*?/1978/to date*

1983 **Basingstoke** Cricket Club: a complete list
■ of scores and averages of the matches
played during the past season of 1877.
Basingstoke, C.J. Jacob, 1877. 12p. scores

1984 **Harrison, B.R.S.,** *and* **Bichard, P.M.**
■ Basingstoke and North Hants Cricket
Club 1865–1965. [Basingstoke, the Club,
1966]. 121p. illus. ports. scores, stats.

1984 **Ray, F.**
–1 The Mays of Basingstoke with special
reference to Lieut.-Colonel John May,
V.O., J.P. London, Simpkin; Basingstoke,
"Basingstoke News", 1904. x,60p. illus.
ports.
*cricket pp. 46–9 – contains brief history of*
*Basingstoke C.C.*

## Beaulieu

1984 **Norris, Anthony C.**
–2 Two centuries of Beaulieu cricket
■ 1775–1975. [1978]. 56p. incl. adverts. illus.
ports. facsims. scores

## Bournemouth

1985 **Bournemouth and District Cricket**
□ **Association**
Official handbook. Bournemouth, the
Association. *annual*. stats.
*?/1966/to date?*
*formed 1896*

1985 **Bournemouth and District Cricket**
−1 **League**
[Handbook]. Bournemouth, the League.
■ *annual?*
?/1946,47/−?

1985 **Bournemouth and South Hampshire**
−2 **Cricket Club**
■ Tour of Sri Lanka February 1977: souvenir
brochure. Bournemouth, the Club,
[1977?]. 28p. incl. adverts. ports.
*pre-tour*

1985 **Mate, Charles Henry,** *and* **Riddle,**
−3 **Charles**
Bournemouth 1810–1910. Bournemouth,
W. Mate & Sons, 1910. illus. iii,292p.
*cricket pp. 219–21*

## Bramshall

1985 **Bramshall Cricket Club**
−4 Centenary 1877–1977. [Bramshall, the
■ Club, 1977]. 62p. incl. adverts. illus.
ports. score

## Burley

1985 **Burley Cricket Club**
−5 Centenary year handbook 1875–1975;
edited by S.N.R. Burley, the Club, [1975].
64p. incl. adverts. illus. ports. stats.

## Crondall

1985 **Butterfield, Roland Potter**
−6 Monastery and manor: the history of
Crondall. Farnham, *printed by* E.W.
Langham, 1948. xi,138p. illus.
*cricket pp. 103–4*

## Froxfield

1985 **Burt, Ian R.**
−7 Froxfield Cricket Club: the history of a
■ cricket club in a Hampshire village. [The
Author], 1979. 40p. illus. ports. stats.

## Grayshott

1985 **Smith, J.H.**
−8 Grayshott: the story of a Hampshire
village. Petersfield, F. Westwood, 1978.
[xi],192p. illus. ports.
*cricket pp. 141, 167*

## Hambledon

1986 **Ashley-Cooper, Frederick Samuel**
■ The Hambledon cricket chronicle,
1772–1796, including the reproduction of
the minute and account books of the
Club. Herbert Jenkins, 1924 [1923],187p.
illus. ports. scores

1986 **Bicentenary** cricket match. Hambledon
−1 C.C. v. England (M.C.C.) on Broad-
■ halfpenny Down, Hambledon, Sunday
31st July 1977. Hambledon, the Club,
[1977]. 24p. incl. covers & adverts.
facsims.
*includes "A glimpse at Hambledon past"
by Irving Rosenwater*

1987 **Broadhalfpenny Down,** Hambledon,
■ Cricket match, New Year's Day, 1929.
Winchester, *printed by* Warren, [1929].
[4]p.
*Hampshire Eskimos v. Invalids. See also
no. 2004*

1988 **Bryant,** *Sir* **Arthur**
■ The years of endurance, 1793–1802.
Collins, 1942. xiv,370p.
*references to Hambledon pp. 28–30*

1989 **Collison-Morley, Lacy**
Companion into Hampshire. Methuen,
1940. ix,244p. illus.
——2nd ed. 1947
——3rd ed. 1948
*references of Hambledon and Thomas Lord*

1990 **[Cotton, D.,** *i.e.* **Reynell Cotton]**
■ Cricket, published by order of the
Hambledon Cricket Club, June 5th 1781.
bs.
*a song in honour of Hambledon, written
about 1767 and published in its original form
in the Canterbury Journal, October, 1773.
It had already appeared, with certain alterations in favour of Kent, in the Kentish
Gazette of August 1772. (D. Rait Kerr)*

1991 **Dean, Winton**
■ Hambledon v. Feathercombe 1928–1950:
the story of a village cricket match.
[Milford, Surrey, the Author], 1951. 32p.
scores, stats.

1992 **Egan, Pierce**
Pierce Egan's book of sports and mirror
of life. T.T. & J. Tegg, 1832. iv,414p. illus.
——*another ed.* W. Tegg, 1836
——*another ed.* 1840
——*another ed.* 1847
*originally issued in 25 pts., 1 pt. [pp.
337–352) being devoted entirely to cricket,
with an article on Hambledon cricket and John
Small*

1993 **Goldsmith, Dora**
■ Hambledon, Hants: past and present.
Bromley, *printed by* T. Martin, 1908. 31p.
illus.

1994 **Goldsmith, John**
■ Hambledon: the biography of a
Hampshire village. Winchester, Winton
Publications, 1971. 119p. illus. plan
*cricket pp. 73–94*

1995 **Grand** bi-centenary cricket match (1757–1957) on Broad Halfpenny Down, Sunday, 14th July 1957: Hambledon v. Dartford. Gosport, Kemp Bros. & Wootton, 1957. 8p. illus.
*scorecard of match, notes on Hambledon &*
*quotations from Nyren*

1996 **A grand** Coronation festival old-time
■ match at cricket on Broad Halfpenny Down, Saturday 30th May 1953: The Men of Hambledon versus the Ancient Firemen. Brentford, *printed by* Buckley P., [1953]. [8]p. illus.

1997 **Jeans, George Edward,** *editor*
■ Memorials of old Hampshire. Bemrose, 1906. xiv,288p. illus. (1 col.)
*contains "The Hambledon Cricket Club" by*
*Horace Hutchinson, pp. 274–82, with a poem*
*"On the game of cricket"*

1997 **Knight, Ronald D.**
–1 Hambledon's cricket glory. Weymouth,
■ The Author, Bat & Ball P., 1975–. illus. ports. facsims. diagrs. *typescript*
*to be completed in 26 vols: those published*
*to date:*
vol. 2. 1756. 1975. [iv],69p.
  3. 1757–1764. 1976. [iv],124p.
  4. 1765–1768. 1977. [iv],86p.
  5. 1769–1771. 1979. [iv],72p.
  6. The Hambledon cricket song of the Rev. Reynell Cotton; edited and annotated by Ronald D. Knight. 1975
——2nd (revd.) ed. 1977. [iv],28p.
  26. Supplement & index (1756–1771). 1979. [ii],86p.
*vol. 26 is intended to be published periodi-*
*cally with supplements and amendments until*
*the series is complete*

1998 **Lucas, Edward Verrall,** *editor*
■ The Hambledon men: being a new edition of John Nyren's 'Young cricketer's tutor', together with a collection of other matter drawn from various sources all bearing on the great batsmen and bowlers before round-arm came in. Frowde, 1907. xxviii,252p. illus. ports. scores
——*rptd.* Sportsman's Book Club, 1952
——*another ed.* Phoenix House, 1954. xxvii,252p.
see *no. 390*

1999 **"A match** at cricket", Hambledon v.
■ H.M.S. "Nelson", Broad-Halfpenny Down, 1st August 1931: souvenir programme. Portsmouth, *printed on board* H.M.S. Nelson, [1931]. 14p. illus.

2000 **Nyren, John**
■ The young cricketer's tutor; comprising full directions for playing . . . cricket; . . . to which is added "The cricketers of my

time," or, Recollections of the most famous old players. The whole collected and edited by Charles Cowden Clarke. Effingham Wilson, 1833. 126p. frontis.
*for full entry and later eds. see no. 390*

2001 **Rait Kerr, Diana Mary**
■ Hambledon cricket and the Bat and Ball Inn. Henty & Constable, 1951. [16]p. illus. ports. bibliog.
——3rd ed. *i.e. 2nd ed.* Friary Meux, 1963

2002 **The Reynell Cotton** memorial match:
■ Rudgwick C.C. versus Rev. David Sheppard's XI: souvenir programme, May 23, 1959. Rudgwick, the Club, [1959]. [5]p. port. on cover
*includes song composed by Reynell Cotton*
*for the Hambledon Club. c.1767*

2002 **Russell, Leonard,** *editor*
–1 Printers' pie: pocket miscellany; decora-
■ tions by Laurence Scarfe. Hutchinson, [1943]. 144p. incl. adverts. illus. ports. stats.
*includes pp. 114–136,140, "They played for*
*money" by Harold Hobson*

2003 **Smith, Thomas**
Sporting incidents in the life of another Tom Smith. Chapman & Hall, 1867. 224p. illus.
*cricket at Hambledon, pp. 26–29*

2004 **Warlock, Peter,** *pseud., composer [i.e.*
Philip Heseltine]
The cricketers of Hambledon: song with chorus for voice and piano; words by Bruce Blunt. Augener, [1929?] 6p.
*composed for the Hampshire Eskimos' New*
*Year's Day cricket match at Hambledon,*
*1929, see no. 1987*

2005 **[Wheeler, Gordon Lee]**
■ East of Itchen: the Hampshire of William Cobbett, Gilbert White and John Nyren, by Gordon Lee. Guildford, Wodeland Publications, [1932]. 120p. 1 illus. bibliog.
*includes, an account of Hambledon cricket*

2006 **[Wright W.R.]**
■ A peep into the past, by W.R. Weir. Ayres, 1902. 23p. illus.

2007 ————, and **Craig, Albert**
■ The cradle of cricket: a Hambledon souvenir. Wright, [1908]. 15p. illus. port.
——2nd ed. 1909. with additional illus.

2007 **Wymer, Norman George**
–1 A breath of England: the southern shires. Lutterworth P., 1948. 288p. illus. maps on end-papers
*Hambledon cricket pp. 172–4; illus. 'The*
*Bat and Ball at Hambledon' f.p. 137*

2008 **Young, Francis Brett**
■ The island. Heinemann, 1944. viii,451p.
*includes a description of a match at*
*Hambledon "On Windmill Down A.D.*
*1789", pp. 319–334*

## Hartley Wintney

2009 **Hartley Wintney Cricket Club**
■ 200 not out: cricket in Hartley Wintney
over two centuries: souvenir programme.
[Hartley Wintney, the Club], 1971. 7p.
illus. ports.

## Havant

2009 **Barnard, S.P.**, *compiler*
–1 Havant Cricket Club centenary
■ 1874–1974. [Havant], the Club, [1974].
[16]p. 1 illus. ports. score, stats.

2010 **Havant Cricket Club**
□ News letter. Havant, the Club. issued
pre-season and end of season, and from
1955 mid-season also
*?/1953–56/to date?*

## Kingsclere

2011 **Garrett, Charles, and Sanders, David,**
■ *editors*
A history of cricket in Kingsclere. [Kings-
clere, the Club], 1973. 20p. incl. adverts.
1 illus. ports.
——rev. and extended ed. *with title:* Two
hundred years of cricket in Kingsclere,
1774–1974. Kingsclere, The Club, 1974.
24p. incl. adverts. 1 illus. team ports.
stats.

## Liss

2012 **Bashford,** *Mrs.*
All about Lyss. Liss, D.H. Watney, 1922.
46p. illus.
*pp.44–6 gives details of the cricketers who*
*played at Hambledon from 1771*

## New Forest

2013 **New Forest Club Cricket Association**
□ Yearbook. The Association.
*1966?/1967 . . . 1974/to date*

## Odiham

2013 **The origins** of cricket: the history of two
–1 Hampshire Clubs. Odiham & Greywell
■ C.C., [1979?]. 29p. incl. adverts. illus.
ports. score

## Old Alresford

2013 **Old Alresford Cricket Club**
–2 Yearbook. Alresford, the Club. stats.
□ *typescript*
*?/1973/to date?*

## Portsmouth

2013 **Cricket** extraordinary. Portsmouth Town
–3 Council v. Havant Local Board [May
1890]. [4]p.
*report of the game, including the scorecard*
*and account of the speeches after the game at*
*a dinner in the pavilion*

## Selborne

2013 **White, Gilbert**
–4 Gilbert White's year: passages from The
■ Garden Kalendar and The Naturalist's
Journal 1751–1793; selected by John
Commander. Scolar P., 1979. 92p. col.
frontis. illus.
*cricket illustration p.26 [drawing done in*
*1776] by Samuel Hieronymus Grimm*

## Southampton

2013 **le Bas, Malcolm**
–5 The Trojans Club, Southampton
1874–1974: the first hundred years.
Southampton, the Club, [1974?] 60p.
illus.

2014 **Lee, Arthur F.,** *editor*
■ Souvenir of the diamond jubilee of the
Deanery Cricket Club, 1931: a short
history of the club from 1921 to 1931.
Southampton, Southern Newspapers
Ltd., 1931. 64p. illus. ports. scores, stats.

2015 **Montgomery, F.J.,** *editor*
■ History of the Deanery Cricket Club from
its birth in the Deanery grounds to the
present day. Southampton, *printed by*
Queensland Printing Works, 1921. 121p.
illus. ports. scores, stats.
*cover-title:* Deanery Cricket Club jubilee
1871–1921

## West Meon

2016 **Souvenir** programme of a cricket match
■ played at West Meon on Saturday August
6th 1955 between the West Meon and
Warnford Sports Club and the Marylebone Cricket Club to celebrate the two-
hundredth anniversary of the birth of
Thomas Lord. Petersfield, Hants,
Thwaites & Watts, [1955]. 8p. port. score

## Winchester

**2016** **[Fearon, William Andrewes]**
**–1** The passing of old Winchester by Fratibus
Wiccamicus [pseud.]. Winchester,
Warren, *printed for private circulation*,
1924. 97p. illus.
——reissued. Winchester, P. and G.
Wells, 1936. 93p. illus.
*cricket pp. 27–30*

**2016** **Furley, John Sampson**
**–2** Winchester in 1867. Winchester,
Warren & Son, [1936]. 45p.
*cricket pp. 24–8*

**2017** **Gard, R.M.**
■ The Castle Cricket Club, golden jubilee
1912–1962. Winchester, [the Club, 1962].
[ii],10p. ports. stats.

**2018** **Vesey-Fitzgerald, Brian Seymour**
■ Winchester. Phoenix House, 1953. 187p.
illus. map, plan
*cricket pp.15, 116–118 with plate*

## HAMPSHIRE: ISLE OF WIGHT

**2019** **Harlequin Cricket Club**
■ Rules and regulations. [Ryde, the Club].
3–6p.
*printed rules. Lord's copy has two addi-*
*tional rules 19 and 20 added in Ms. together*
*with separate MS list of members*
*formed 1837*

**2020** **Isle of Wight Cricket Club**
Rules and regulations. Newport (I. of
W.), the Club, 1839
*in Goldman*

### Calbourne

**2021** **Westover Park Cricket Club**
■ 1855 cricket 1973: last match at Westover
Park, Calbourne . . . Westover (Past and
Present) v. Vintage XI (Villages' Stal-
warts), September 16th. Calbourne, the
Club, [1973]. 8p. incl. adverts. 1 illus.
team port. plan

### Northwood

**2022** **Miell, Frank**
■ Northwood Cricket Club: a series of short
stories. Cowes, [the Author], 1959.
[iii],23p.

### Shanklin

**2023** **Shanklin Cricket Club**
Just for the record: 1871–1971 Shanklin
Cricket Club centenary. Shanklin, the
Club, 1971. 36p. illus. ports.

# HAMPSHIRE C.C.C.

**2024** **Altham, Harry Surtees,** *and others*
■ Hampshire county cricket: the official
history of the Hampshire County Cricket
Club, by H.S. Altham, John Arlott,
E.D.R. Eagar and Roy Webber. Phoenix
House, 1957. 240p. illus. ports. stats.
——*another ed.* Sportsman's Book Club,
1958

**2025** **Ashley-Cooper, Frederick Samuel**
■ Hampshire county cricket. George W.
May, 1924. 32p. illus. ports.

**2026** **Hampshire** County Cricket Club
■ 1863–1963: the centenary match
[Hampshire v. An England XI].
[Southampton, Hampshire C.C.C., 1963].
4p.
*contains "The centenary match" by H.S.*
*Altham, and "Such men as we are . . ." by*
*John Arlott; 1550 copies, the first 50 contai-*
*ning 4 aquatints by Kenneth New as a contri-*
*bution to the Hampshire C.C.C. Centenary*
*Fund*

**2027** **Hampshire County Cricket Club**
■ Illustrated handbook; edited [1961–1977]
by Desmond Eagar. *annual*
*1950.* Bournemouth, K. Peskett for
H.C.C.C. *illus. stats.*
*1951–3.* Sports Publications. *illus. scores,*
*stats.*
*1954. Not issued*
*1955–67.* Harrow (Mddx.), Pepper
Publicity for H.C.C.C. *illus. ports. scores,*
*stats.*
*1956 Diamond jubilee number. 136p. incl.*
*adverts. illus. ports. scores, stats.*
*1968 to date. [1978 edited by Peter*
*Marshall]* Southampton, the Club. *illus.*
*ports. scores, stats.*
*1962 [with] souvenir history of Hampshire*
*champion county*
*1974 souvenir edition to mark Hampshire*
*winning the championship in 1973. Together*
*with 1962 vol. brings up-to-date the history*
*of the Club publd. in 1957*

**2028** 1863–1963: [centenary appeal]. [South-
■ ampton, the Club, 1963]. [12]p. illus.
ports.

**2029** **Hampshire** County Cricket Club guide;
■ edited [to 1908] by Edward Lee Ede.
Southampton. *annual.* ports. scores, stats.
*1892–95. G. Buxey*
*1896–1910. H. King, "Hants Advertiser"*
*Office*
*1911–14, 1920–39 with title: Hampshire*
*county cricket guide. H. King, "Hants Adver-*
*tiser" Office*

2030 ■ **Hampshire** cricket; edited by Laurence Mumford. County Cricket Publications Ltd. illus. ports.
*1973*
*intended to be published quarterly, but one issue only*

2031 ■ **The Hampshire** cricketer's guide; edited by George Bagshaw. Southampton, G. Buxey. *annual.* scores, stats.
*1885–1890*
*includes club and county cricket*

2032 ■ **The Summer** of triumph: a four page 'Echo' tribute to the team which has made Hampshire cricket history by winning the Championship pennant for the first time. [Southampton], "Southern Daily Echo", 1961. 4p. illus. ports. stats.
*rptd. in miniature from issue of Sept. 6, 1961. Contributors include H.S. Altham, John Arlott, Desmond Eagar*

2033 ■ **Webber, Roy,** *compiler*
Hampshire in first-class cricket: county records 1895 to 1961. [Southampton, Hampshire C.C.C., 1962]. [48]f. illus. ports. stats.
*limited ed. of 50 copies; statistical record first published in Hampshire C.C.C. Handbook, 1962*

2034 ■ ————, and **Drake, Norman,** *compilers*
Hampshire cricket statistics 1895–1968; compiled by the late Roy Webber and brought up to date with additions by Norman Drake. Southampton, Hampshire C.C.C., 1969. 87p. ports. stats.
*limited ed. of 200 copies; kept up-to-date by each successive Hants C.C.C. "Handbook"*

## HEREFORDSHIRE

2035 ■ **The rise,** progress and vicissitudes of cricket in Herefordshire since its introduction to the county. Hereford Times, [1874]. 62p. scores, stats.
*previously printed in the "Hereford Times"*

## HEREFORDSHIRE C.C.C.

2036 ■ **Anthony, Edwyn**
Herefordshire cricket. Hereford, Anthony Bros., 1903. 211p. scores, stats.

## HERTFORDSHIRE

2037 □ **The Hertfordshire Cricket Competition**
Official handbook. Welwyn Garden City. scores, stats. *annual*
*1968/to date*

2038 ■ **The Victoria** history of the counties of England: Hertfordshire; edited by William Page. Vol. 1. Constable, 1902
*cricket pp. 372–81*

### Baldock

2038 ■ **Gazely, R.,** *compiler & editor*
–1 Baldock Town Cricket Club centenary year 1979. [Baldock, the Club, 1979]. [20]p. incl. adverts.

### Berkhamsted

2039 ■ **Todd, Herbert E.**
Berkhamsted Cricket Club 1875–1965. E. Finchley, Edgar Publ. Co., [1965]. 43p. incl. adverts. ports.

### Bishop's Stortford

2040 ■ **Bishop's Stortford Cricket Club**
Centenary souvenir 1825–1925. [Bishop's Stortford, the Club, 1925]. 46p. illus. ports. stats.

2041 ■ **Saul, T.G.**
Bishop's Stortford Cricket Club 1825–1950: a history. [Bishop's Stortford, the Club, 1950]. 55p. ports. scores

2041 ■ **The story** of the Bishop's Stortford
–1 Cricket Club 1825–1975. [Bishop's Stortford, the Club, 1975]. 80p. incl. adverts. illus. ports. scores

### Bushey

2042 ■ **Dutton, E.W.P.**
Bushey Cricket Club centenary, 1864–1964. East Finchley, Edgar Publishing Co., 1964. 44p. illus. ports.

### Colney Hatch

2043 ■ **Colney Hatch Cricket Club**
Rules and regulations of the Colney Hatch Cricket Club, held at the Orange Tree Inn, Colney Hatch, established the 30th day of August, 1853. Barnet, W. Baldock, 1856. 7p.

### Harpenden

2044 ■ **D[avenport], E.C., M[arsh], W.H.,** *and* **N[elson], R.**
A short history of the Harpenden Cricket Club. [Harpenden, The Club, 1951], 24p. stats.

### Hitchin

2045 ■ **Hine, Reginald Leslie**
The history of Hitchin. 2 vols. Allen & Unwin, 1927–9. illus. ports. maps
*cricket in vol. II, pp. 250, 265, 274, 489*

## King's Langley

2046 **Kings Langley Cricket Club**
■ Centenary souvenir 1830–1930. [Kings Langley, the Club, 1930]. 19p. illus. ports. score

## Potters Bar

2047 **Woolard, J.**
Potters Bar Cricket Club centenary year souvenir handbook, 1862–1962. East Finchley, Edgar Publishing Co. Ltd., 1962. 42p. 1 port. 1 illus.

## Royston

2048 **Perkins, Henry,** *compiler*
Matches of the Royston Cricket Club during the seasons 1855–63. Royston, Royston P., 1864

## St. Albans

2049 **Mackenzie, Harry W.**
■ Recollections of St. Albans cricket and cricketers fifty years ago. [St. Albans, the Author, 1915]. 24p.

## Watford

2050 **Watford Bridge Cricket Club**
[Handbook]. Watford, the Club, 1886
*in Taylor*

## Welwyn Garden City

2051 **Welwyn Garden City Cricket Club**
Twenty fifth anniversary cricket week: souvenir programme. Welwyn, [the Club], 1947. 32p.

2052 Fifty years of cricket by a club called
■ Welwyn Garden City. [Welwyn, the Club], 1971. [i],17p. illus. ports. stats.

## Wheathampstead

2052 **Wheathampstead Cricket Club**
–1 150th anniversary celebrity match Norm-
■ ansland Common Sunday July 28: Mike Edwards benefit year. Wheathampstead, the Club, [1974]. 12p. incl. adverts. illus. ports.

## HERTFORDSHIRE C.C.C.

2053 **Hertfordshire County Cricket Club**
□ Official handbook. Watford, the Club. *annual*. ports. scores, stats.
*?/1911, 1925 . . . 39, 1946/to date*

2054 Herts County Cricket Club 1876–1925:
■ souvenir programme for jubilee cricket week at Watford, Aug. 10th-15th, 1925. Watford, Herts C.C.C., 1925. 16p. ports. scores

## HUNTINGDONSHIRE C.C.C.

2055 **Huntingdon County Cricket Club**
Members' fixture card. Huntingdon, the Club. *annual*
*?/1963 . . . 68/to date?*

## St. Neots

2055 **Tebbutt, Charles Frederick**
–1 St. Neots: the history of a Huntingdon-shire town. Phillimore, 1978. xi,363p. illus. ports. facsims. map, plan
*cricket pp. 100–01, 116–7*

## KENT

2056 **Abell, Henry Francis**
■ History of Kent. Ashford, Kentish Express (Igglesdon & Co.), 1898. vii,328p. illus. ports. maps
*App. D, pp. 314–322 "Old Kent cricket" with portraits of Fuller Pilch & Alfred Mynn*

2057 **All** about Kent cricket 1911: coronation
■ souvenir and cricket handbook for the county of Kent. Watford, *printed by* Blower Bros., 1911. 128p. incl. adverts. illus. ports. stats.
——1914; 2nd ed. in commemoration of the county's 4th championship. 1914. 48p. incl. adverts. illus. ports. stats.

2058 **Association of Kent Cricket Clubs**
□ Cricket in Kent: the official handbook. Chislehurst, the Association. *annual*. illus. ports. scores, stats.
*/1954–60, 1966/to date*
*1954, 1955 compiled and edited by H.A.W. Daniels*
*1956–? compiled and edited by E.W. Duckett*
*1971–75 – to date? edited by J.G. Overy*

2059 White horse: the official journal of the
■ Association of Kent Cricket Clubs. Chislehurst, the Association
*3 issues only, July & Oct. 1951, Jan. 1952*

2060 **Bligh, Hon. Edward Vesey**
Former Kent cricket. Maidstone, *privately printed*, 1896. [7]p.

2061 **[Burney, John]**
■ The Kentish cricketers: a poem. By a Gentleman. Being a reply to a late publi-cation of a parody on the Ballad of Chevy Chase; intituled Surry triumphant; or, The Kentish Men's defeat. Canterbury,

printed by T. Smith & Son, and sold by them and W. Flackton; also, by B. Law, in Avemary Lane; Messrs Richardson and Urquhart, under the Royal Exchange . . . 1773. 22p.

2062 **Darton, Frederick Joseph Harvey**
■ A parcel of Kent. Nisbet, 1924. xiii,291p. illus.
   *cricket pp. 13–15, 55–56, 80, 152–53, 182, 212, 221–22*

2063 **De Vaynes, Julia H.L.,** *editor*
■ The Kentish garland; with additional notes, and pictorial illustrations copied from the rare originals by J.W. Ebsworth. 2 vols. Hertford, S. Austin, 1881–2. illus.
   *cricket in vol. 1. pp. 418–428*

2064 **[Duncombe, John]**
■ Surry triumphant: or the Kentish-mens defeat; a new ballad; being a parody on Chevy-Chace. Printed for J. Johnson, 1773. 24p. vignette on t.p. score
   *includes score of the match Surrey v Kent extracted from the Kentish Gazette of Saturday, July 24, 1773. See also no. 6387*

2065 **Goulstone, John**
■ Early Kent cricketers. International Research Publications, 1971. [48]p. *typescript*
   *limited ed. of 50 copies*
   ——[2nd edition]. 1972. 62p. *typescript limited ed.*

2066 Cricket in Kent. International Research
■ Publications, 1972. [iii],62p. scores. *typescript*
   *limited ed. of 50 copies. Covers 1750s to 1850s*

2067 **Igglesden,** *Sir* **Charles**
■ 66 years' memories of Kent cricket Ashford, Kentish Express Office, 1947. [ii],82p.

2067 **Jerrold, Walter Copeland**
–1 Highways and byways in Kent. Macmillan, 1907. xix,447p. illus. map.
   *cricket pp.61–4,376,417*
   ——*another ed.* 1920 (The Highways & Byways Series)
   ——*another ed.* 1933. (The Highways & Byways Series)
   ——1st pocket ed. 1923

2068 **Kent Archaeological Society**
■ Archaeologia Cantiana, vol. LXIII for 1950. The Society, 1951. illus.
   *includes "A note on early Kent cricket" by L.R.A. Grove, which refers to records of cricket in Kent in the 17th century from c.1610*

2069 **Kent Metropolitan Cricket League**
■ Official handbook. Bexley, the League. *annual*
   *1973 (no issue in 1974), 1975*

2070 **The Kentish** cricketer's guide. Maidstone, J. Burgiss Brown. *annual*. stats.
   *1883–90*

2071 **South Thames Cricket League**
■ Fixtures. The League. *annual*.
   *1973*
   *1974 to date with title Year book. team port. stats.*

2072 **Thomas, Percy Francis**
■ Cricket in the Weald . . . by H.P.-T. Nottingham, Richards, 1928 *i.e.* [1929]. 128p. 1 illus. (Old English Cricket)

2073 **The Victoria** history of the counties of England: Kent; edited by William Page. Vol. 1. Constable, 1908
   *cricket pp. 509–13. stats.*

2074 **[Winnifrith, A.]**
■ Men of Kent and Kentish men: biographical notices of 680 worthies of Kent, written by a Man of Kent. Folkestone, Parsons, 1913. 562p. illus. ports. map, stats.
   *includes review of 1913 season when Kent were county champions and a biographical notice of A. Mynn*

## Ashford

2075 **Ashford Cricket Club**
□ Fixtures. Ashford, the Club. *annual*
   *?/1960/–?*
   *1960 centenary year issue; contains history of the club*

## Bearsted Green

2076 **Daw, Walter A.**
■ Cricket on Bearsted Green 1850–1907. Maidstone, Kent Messenger, 1907. 16p. illus. ports. scores
   *includes details of Billenness & Weeks' Automatic Wicket*

## Beckenham

2077 **Beckenham** Cricket Club 1866–1966, centenary year. Beckenham, the Club, [1966]. 38p. illus. ports.
   *includes "100 years of cricket at Foxgrove" by Ronnie Bryan*

2077 **Borrowman, Robert**
–1 Beckenham past and present. Beckenham, *printed by* T.W. Thornton, 1910. xvii,307p. illus. (1 col.)
   *cricket pp. 65, 234, 250*

## Bexley

**2078  Bexley Cricket Club**
150th anniversary . . . 1805–1955:
souvenir handbook. [Bexley, the Club,]
1955. 32p. illus. ports. scores. stats.
*includes "History of Bexley C.C." by G.F.
Lovegrove*

**2079  Bexley Heath** Sports Club 1870–1970:
■  centenary brochure. [Bexley Heath, the
Club, 1970]. 24p.

## Bickley

**2080  Bickley Park Cricket Club**
■  Centenary year 1967; compiled by D.A.G.
Reid. [Bickley, the Club, 1967]. 24p. incl.
adverts. illus. ports.

## Bromley

**2081  Eames, Geoffrey L.,** *compiler & editor*
■  Bromley Cricket Club 1820–1970: a miscellany of writings. Bromley, the Compiler,
1970. 112p. illus. ports. map, scores,
stats.

**2082  Horsburgh, Edward Lee Stuart**
■  Bromley, Kent, from the earliest times to
the present century. . . . Hodder &
Stoughton, for the "History of Bromley"
Committee, 1929. xvi,463p. illus. (2 col.),
ports. map
*cricket pp. 315–324*

**2082  [Strong, Edward]**
**–1**  A history of Bromley in Kent and the
surrounding       neighbourhood       . . .
together with an account of the colleges,
their founders, benefactors, etc. E.
Strong, 1858. vi,146p. illus.
*cricket pp. 19–21*

## Canterbury

**2083  Canterbury** cricket festival, 1924: official
programme

**2084  The Canterbury** cricket week: an
■  authentic narrative of the origin and
career of the institution; including the
programmes of the Old Stagers' performances, with the original prologues, epilo-
gues, &c. spoken at each season. Vol.
1. Canterbury, W. Davey, 1865. ix,86p.
ports. scores
*covers period 1843–1851; vol. 2. not publd.*

**2084  Canterbury** Cricket Week centenary
**–1**  1842–1948: Kent v. Australia scorecard.
■  Canterbury, J.A. Jennings Ltd., [1948].
[4]p. folded card.
*with results of Kent v. Australia at Canter-
bury since 1882*

**2085  Church, Richard Thomas**
A portrait of Canterbury. Hutchinson,
1953. 234p. illus. bibliog.
*references to Canterbury cricket week, pp.
216–17*

**2086  [See no. 2084–1]**

**2087  Kentish Gazette**
Bridging three centuries. Canterbury,
Kentish Gazette, July 1929.
*includes "Canterbury week in 1842"*

**2088  St. Lawrence Cricket Club**
■  Centenary year 1864–1964. Canterbury,
the Club, [1964]. [4]p. fold. 1 illus.
*text comprises the history of the club*

**2089  Small, E. Milton**
■  The Canterbury cricket week: its origin,
career, and jubilee, 1842–1891. Canterbury, Jennings, for the Author, 1891.
viii,151p. frontis. scores
——*2nd issue.* 1891. viii,154p.
——*3rd issue.* [1892]. viii,155p.
*last issue has an insert leaf giving 1892
scores*

**2089  Taylor, Tom**
**–1**  A cricketer's prologue, spoken in the
■  Kentish dialect, before the play of "The
Poor Gentleman", at the Theatre, Canter-
bury, during the Great Cricket Match,
August 1st, 1842. 1p. of fold

**2089  Theatre Royal, Canterbury**
**–2**  Canterbury cricket week. Epilogue, 1923.
■  "C.U.R." (Canterbury's Universal
Remedy,") a Pilgrim's Tale of 1923 by
Lieut.-Col. C.P. Hawkes. Music arranged
by Major A. Clarke-Jervoise. Canterbury,
Theatre Royal, 1923. 12p.
*script of musical play*

**2090  Warner, Harold William**
■  A history of Beverley Cricket Club,
1835–1959. [Canterbury, the Author,
1959]. 22p. illus. port. scores

**2091**  The story of Canterbury cricket week.
■  Canterbury, Jennings, 1960. 78p. illus.
port. stats.

## Catford

**2092  Catford Wanderers Sports Club**
☐  Handbook. Catford, the Club. *annual.*
ports.
*?/1954–56, 1959–73/to date*
*formed 1906; the 1956 issue is entitled
"Jubilee Year Handbook"*

**2092**  Tour of Ceylon 14 December 1970–
**–1**  6 January 1971. The Club, [1970]. [4]p.
fold
*fixture list & names of tour party*

2092 **Panther Cricket Club**
-2 Report of Committee, statement of accounts, etc. to be presented at the General Meeting . . . [Catford], the Club. stats. *annual*
*1887?/1896,1897/–?*

## Chislehurst

2092 **Views** and scenery of Chislehurst.
-3 Rock & Co., [1871?]
*12 topographical prints including one captioned "Cricket Ground, Chislehurst, Kent, 1871"*

## Cobham

2093 **Arnold, Ralph Crispian Marshall**
■ A yeoman of Kent: an account of Richard Hayes, 1725–1790, and of the village of Cobham in which he lived and farmed. Constable, 1949. xii,203p. illus. (1 col.). score
*includes a history of Cobham cricket and an account of England v. Hampshire at Sevenoaks Vine 1776*

2094 **Baker, Thomas Henry**
■ History of the Cobham Cricket Club from its foundation in 1850 to the close of the season of 1898. Rochester, *printed by* W.T. Wildish, 1899. 102p. scores, stats.
*limited ed. of 100 copies*

2095 **Cobham Sports and Social Club**
■ Cobham playing fields, souvenir of the official opening and dedication, combined with cricket club centenary, May 1950. Chatham, Solus Arts Advertising for the Cobham Parish Council, 1950. 16p. scores

## Cranbrook

2096 **"A Critic"**, *pseud.*
The spy, or Mr. Speedwell's rambles during the Cranbrook cricket match of July 1851, by a Critic. Cranbrook, R. Waters, 1851. 34p.

2097 **"A Picture-Maker,"** *pseud.*
The search for pleasure, or Mr. Illspeed's trip to the Cranbrook cricket match, by a Picture-Maker. Cranbrook, R. Waters, 1850. 40p.

## Dartford

2097 **Dartford Historical and Antiquarian**
-1 **Society**
■ News-letter. Dartford, the Society. *annual.* illus. *typescript*
*1964 to date*
*No. 10, 1973 includes pp. 12–18, "The life and career of John Ring" and pp. 19–22,*

*"Early references to Dartford cricket", both by John Goulstone*
*No. 11, 1974 contains p. 14 "Addendum to Early references to Dartford cricket" by John Goulstone; pp. 31–9 "Some local sportsmen" [includes cricketers]*

2097 **Goulstone, John**
-2 The history of cricket in Dartford: 250
■ years; edited by R. Walter. [Dartford, the Club], 1978. 80p. illus. ports. facsims. scores

2098 **Keyes, Sidney Arthur Kilworth**
■ Dartford: some historical notes. Dartford, the Author, 1933. xiv,727p. illus. ports. scores
*cricket pp. 352–360*

2099 Dartford: further historical notes. Dart-
■ ford, the Author, 1938. xxii,984p. illus. ports. scores
*cricket pp. 504–540*

2100 **Sparvel-Bayly, John Anthony**
Some historical notes. Dartford Chronicle, [c.1880]. 100p.
*cricket pp. 3–7*

## Edenbridge

2100 **Somers-Cocks, Henry Lawrence,** *and*
-1 **Boyson, V.F.**
Edenbridge; with illustrations by J.E. Clutterbuck. Edenbridge, Edenbridge Chronicle, 1912. viii,296p. illus. map
*cricket pp. 166–7, mostly on A. Hoare who played for Sussex and Kent*

## Eynsford

2101 **Eynsford Cricket Club**
■ Souvenir programme issued on the occasion of the opening of the new pavilion by Sir Oliver Hart-Dyke on Saturday, 25 April, 1959. Eynsford, the Club, [1959]. [12]p. incl. covers
*includes "Notes on the history of the Club" compiled by G.C. Adams*

## Farningham

2102 **Drew, Bernard**
■ A hundred years of Farningham cricket: the story of how the greatest game in the world is played in a Kentish village, told in this, the club's centenary year. [Farningham, the Author], 1957. 28p. illus. ports. scores

## Gravesend

2103 **Chapman, Edward H.**
■ Bat and Ball memories: [reminiscences of cricket at the Bat & Ball Ground,

Gravesend]. Gravesend & Dartford Reporter, [1972]. [iv],48p. port. plan

## Folkestone

2104 **Folkestone** cricket festival 1925,
■ matches & players. Folkestone, *printed by* "Herald" Printing Works, [1925]. 8p. ports.

## Hayes

2104 **Thompson, P.A.**
–1 History of Hayes (Kent) Cricket Club
■ 1828–1978. [The Club?, 1978?]. (viii),71,LVp. illus. ports. map, scores. *spiral binding*

## Horsmonden

2105 **Horsmonden** Sports Club. [1955?] 8p. illus.

## Lee

2105 **Granville (Lee) Cricket Club**
–1 Scores & averages. Lee, the Club. *annual 11 issues 1892–1902*

## Maidstone

2105 **Boorman, Henry Roy Pratt**
–2 Pictures of Maidstone, the county town of Kent. Maidstone, Kent Messenger, 1965. 230p. illus. ports.
   *photographs of cricket and cricketers, pp. 95–9, 180*

2106 **Kent Messenger**
■ Cricket souvenir: a pictorial record of Maidstone's cricket week 1910. Kent Messenger, [1910]. 19p. illus. ports. scores
   ——1911. 19p
   ——1912?
   ——1913. 30p.
   ——1914. 28p.
   ——[cricket week brochure]. 1933

2107 Maidstone cricket week July 14th–21st,
■ Festival of Britain year 1951; official programme. Maidstone, Kent Messenger, [1951]. 24p.

2108 **Maidstone** cricket week July 19–25th
■ [1952]: [programme]. [Maidstone, the Cricket Week Committee, 1952]. 24p. incl. adverts. port.

2109 **[Ratcliffe, Alfred Edward]**
■ Look to your Mote, 1857–1967: the history of the Mote cricket ground, Maidstone, by "Aero". Maidstone, Kent Messenger, 1957. 32p. illus. ports. stats.

## Meopham

2109 **Gunyon, William**
–1 The history of Meopham Cricket Club.
■ Meopham, the Club, 1976. 66p. illus. ports. scores

## Otford

2109 **Clarke, Dennis,** *and* **Stoyel, Anthony**
–2 Otford in Kent: a history. Otford, Otford and District Historical Society, 1975. xiv,297p. illus.
   *cricket pp. 238, 254, 260*

## Petts Wood

2109 **Edwards, J.P.**
–3 History of the Petts Wood Sports Associ-
■ ation. *Printed by* Chas. F. Thorn & Son, Kent, [1976]. 92p. team ports. scores, stats.
   *limited ed. of 400 copies; mainly the history of the cricket club*

## Sevenoaks

2110 **Cheeseman, Dick,** *compiler*
   The Sennocke Cricket Club 1942–1963: a short history. [Sevenoaks, the Club, 1963]. 35p. stats. *typescript*

2110 **Dunlop,** *Sir* **John**
–1 The pleasant town of Sevenoaks: a
■ history. The Author, 1964. iv,238p. illus.
   *cricket pp. 134, 155, 142, 185, 199*

2111 **Sackville-West, Victoria Mary**
■ Knole and the Sackvilles. Heinemann, 1922. xvi,231p. illus. ports.
   *cricket pp.155, 181–3*
   ——*another ed.* Benn, 1958. 224p.

### Vine C.C.

2112 **Harrod, William**
■ Sevenoke: a poem. Humbly inscribed to His Grace the Duke of Dorset. Printed for J. Fuller, in Ave-Mary-Lane; and Bryan Holland, Sevenoke, 1753. 21p.
   *reference to cricket at The Vine, pp. 13–15*

2113 **Knocker, Herbert W.**
■ Notes as to the history and origin of the Vine Cricket Ground. *Typescript MS* in Sevenoaks Public Library. 10p.

2113 **Richards, F.**
–1 Old Sevenoaks. Illustrated by C.
■ Essenhigh Corke. Sevenoaks, J. Salmon, 1901. 132p. illus. scores
   *contains an account of the Vine C.C. in Chapter XII*

2114 **Richardson, J.S.**
■ Some notes on Sevenoaks cricket and the Vine cricket ground. Sevenoaks. J. Salmon, 1909. 28p. frontis.

2114 **Sevenoaks** bi-centenary cricket week July
–1 16th-21st, 1934: souvenir programme. [Sevenoaks, Sevenoaks Vine C.C.,] 1934. 11p. illus.

2115 **Sevenoaks Vine Cricket Club**
☐ Annual report. Sevenoaks, the Club
*?/1908, 09, 1921, 23, 1936–38, 1947 to date*

2116 **[Entry cancelled]**

2117 Club rules. Sevenoaks, the Club, 4p.
■ folded card
*1950, 1963*

2118 **Smart, Kenneth John**
■ Sevenoaks Vine cricket 1731–1959. Sevenoaks, Sevenoaks Vine C.C., 1959. 22p. frontis.

## Sidcup

2118 **Bennett, Walter,** *compiler*
–1 Sidcup Cricket Club 1877–1977: a history
■ and reference book. Sidcup, the Club, 1977. 380p. illus. ports. scores, stats.
*limited to 250 copies*

## Southborough

2119 **Southborough Cricket Club**
☐ Report and fixtures. Southborough, the Club. *annual*
*?/1957/to date*
*formed c.1800*

2120 Souvenir programme to commemorate
■ the official opening of the new pavilion. [Southborough, the Club], 1955. 4p. illus.
*contains brief history of the club*

2120 **History** of Southborough Cricket Club.
–1 [Southborough, the Club], 1975. 16p.
■ *typescript*
*extracts from Minutes of the Club*

2120 **Thurston, E. Paget**
–2 Southborough: its chalybeate springs, climate and attractions as a health resort. Tunbridge Wells, The "Corner Printing and Publishing Co.", 1885. 69p. illus.
*cricket pp. 28–9 and illus. p. 16*

## Sturry

2121 **Butler, Derek R.**
■ 100 years of Sturry cricket: the official history of the Sturry Cricket Club. [Sturry, the Club, 1963]. 38p. ports. scores

2121 **Sturry:** the changing scene. Ramsgate,
–1 K.H. McIntosh, 1972. 113p. illus. ports.
■ diagrs. maps
*limited ed.; pp. 83–4 "100 years of Sturry cricket" by Derek R. Butler*

## Sydenham

2121 **Sydenham Tradesmen's Cricket Club**
–2 [Year book]. Sydenham, the Club. scores, stats.
*Season 1929, 1930*
*with scores and results of previous years; the only two issues*

## Teston

2121 **Severn, Joan**
–3 The Teston story: Kent village life through the age. Teston, Rufus Fay Publications, 1975. 76p. illus.
*notes on Alfred Reader & Co., cricket ball makers, pp. 6, 62, 66–7*

## Thanet

2121 **Thanet Works Cricket League**
–4 Handbook. The League. *annual*
☐ *1969 season* to date; edited by John Websper
*founded 1968; includes rules, fixtures*

## Tunbridge Wells

2121 **Linden Park Cricket Club**
–5 Centenary year 1876–1976. [Tunbridge
■ Wells, the Club, 1976]. 48p. incl. adverts. ports. stats.
*with historical account by Mike Taylor*

2122 **Royal** Tunbridge Wells cricket week:
■ programme of events. Tunbridge Wells, Hepworth, 1911. 20p.
*also issued for other years, e.g. 1892*

2123 **Tunbridge Wells Cricket Club**
■ Year book. Tunbridge Wells, the Club. illus. stats.
*1950, 1951 only*

## West Kent

2124 **Norman, Philip**
■ Scores and annals of the West Kent Cricket Club, originally the Prince's Plain Club; with some account of the neighbourhoods of Chislehurst and Bromley and of the families residing there. Eyre & Spottiswoode, 1897. viii,387p. illus. ports. scores, stats.

2125 **[Rees, John]**
■ A short history of the West Kent Cricket Club. The Club, *for members only*, [1961]. 12p.

## West Kent Wanderers

2126 **Fear, Herbert**
■ "The W.K.W.C.C.: something of its story". *Printed by* Blackheath P., 1955. 34p. scores

## Wittersham

2127 **Centenary** cricket match at Wittersham
■ on Saturday 5th September, 1936 between an eleven of the Isle of Oxney and two players, W. Ashdown of Kent and A.F. Wensley of Sussex: souvenir programme. Canterbury, Jennings, [1936]. [4]p. folded card. ports. scores
*post match; on the centenary of the match between E.G. Wenman and Richard Mills of Benenden against Isle of Oxney XI, 1834*

# KENT C.C.C.

2128 **All** about Kent cricket 1911: coronation
■ souvenir and cricket handbook for the county of Kent. Watford, *printed by* Blower Bros., 1911. 128p. incl. adverts. illus. ports. stats.
——1914; 2nd ed. in commemoration of the county's 4th championship. 1914. 48p. incl. adverts. illus. ports. stats.

2129 **Arrowsmith, Robert Langford**
■ Kent. Barker, 1971. 165p. illus. ports. (A History of County Cricket)
——*another ed.* Sportsman's Book Club, 1972

2130 **Ashley-Cooper, Frederick Samuel**
■ John Wisden's cricket match histories. 1. Kent v. Surrey 1731–1921. Wisden, [1922]. 16p. stats.

2131 Kent county cricket. George W. May,
■ [1924]. 40p. illus. ports.

2132 Kent cricket, a few notes. The Author,
■ 1929. [16]p. stats.
*a Christmas card for private circulation*

2133 Kent cricket records. Canterbury, "Kent
■ Herald", 1929. 44p. stats.

2134 **Baily, Robin,** editor
■ Cricket: all about London's big four. John Smith, Lord's and Oval Bookstalls, 1928. 16p. illus.
*Kent, Surrey, Essex, Middlesex, giving averages for 1927 and fixtures for 1928*

2135 **Clair, Colin**
■ A Kentish garner. Watford, Friends of St. Lawrence College in assoc. with Bruce & Gawthorn, [1962]. 160p. illus. ports. (1 col.). map
*"From Cawte to Cowdrey", pp. 139–158*

2136 **Davey, H.N.**
■ Bat, ball and Cowdrey: some reminiscences of 50 years of cricket. Canterbury, Jennings, [1968]. 40p. illus. ports.

2137 **Descriptive** key to Mason's national print
■ of a cricket match between Sussex and Kent, 1849. Brighton, W.H. Mason; London, Gambert, 1849. 23p. 1 illus.
*issued only to purchasers of the artist's proof; see also no. 2151*

2137 **Evans, John,** editor
–1 Kent, the winning eleven. [Canterbury],
■ Kent C.C.C., 1978. 124p. incl. covers & adverts. illus. ports. (some col.), stats.

2138 **Fagg, Arthur Edward**
■ Arthur Fagg souvenir benefit book. Maidstone, the Author, [1951]. [12]p. ports.
*includes photographs of past Kent C.C.C. teams, 1904–50*

2139 **Foster, Denis**
Kent. Findon Publications, [1949]. 32p. ports. stats. ("Know Your Cricket County" Series)

2140 **Fowle, Dennis,** editor
■ Kent, the glory years. Everest Books Ltd., 1973. 68p. illus. ports. scores, stats.
*covers the period 1967–1973*

2140 Kent – the glorious years. The Author,
–1 Kentfern Ltd., 1979. 192p. illus. team
■ ports. scores
*limited to 1000 copies; covers period 1967–1979*

2141 **Harris, George Robert Canning Harris,**
■ *4th baron, editor*
The history of Kent county cricket; containing contributions by the several captains of the Kent team. Eyre & Spottiswoode, 1907. xvi,510p. illus. ports. stats.
*includes Appendices A-D*
——Appendix E. 1907–9 Eyre & Spottiswoode, 1910. 16p. 1 illus.
——Appendix F. 1910–23. Canterbury, Gibbs, 1924. 55p.
——Appendix G. 1924–45. Ashford, Geerings, 1946. 56p.
——Appendix H. 1946–63. Canterbury, Jennings, [1964]. [ii],70p.

2142 ————, *and* **Ashley-Cooper, Frederick**
■ **Samuel,** *editors*
Kent cricket matches, 1719–1880. Canterbury, Gibbs, 1929. 500p. scores

2143 **Kent County Cricket Club**
□ Rules, list of subscribers, balance sheet, matches, etc. Canterbury, the Club.
*annual*
*59 issues 1878–1946; ceased publication during both World Wars i.e. 1916–18, 1940–44; each issue contains review of season prior to year of publication. Pre-1919 the year*

*given in title is the year of publication; thereafter the year in title is the season reviewed. Known as the Kent "Blue books"*

2144 ■ Dinner to the Kent XI, Hotel Cecil, October 11th, 1906. [The Club, 1906]. 12p. illus. port. stats. [for 1906]
  *includes "A Canterbury Week ode" by Philip Trevor*

2144 -1 How Kent won the championship: complete record for 1906. (With a tribute to the Kent team, by George Marsham). Maidstone, "Kent Messenger", [1906]. 58p. illus.

2145 ■ Annual; edited by Sir Home Gordon. Canterbury, the Club. ports. scores, stats.
  *1933-36, 1939*

2146 Year book. [Canterbury, the Club]. illus. ports. scores, stats.
  *1947-50*
  *1948 commemorates the Centenary of the Canterbury Cricket Week with an historical account by R.L. Arrowsmith, and an article on "The Old Stagers 1842-1948" by Nigel de Grey*
  *1951 to date with title: "Kent County Cricket Club Annual"*

2147 ■ Centenary appeal 1870-1970. [Canterbury, the Club], 1969. 8p. illus. ports.

2148 ■ 1870-1970, one hundred years of Kent cricket; edited by Basil Curtis. Canterbury, [Kent C.C.C.], 1970. 53p. illus. ports. stats.

2148 -1 ■ **Kent** v. Australians 1882-1975: souvenir match card. *n.p.*, [1975]. [4]p. folded card, scores
  *'to mark the occasion of Kent's fine victory in June 1975'; full scores of Kent wins in 1899 & 1975, results 1882-1972*

2149 ■ **Marshall, F.E.**, *editor*
  Twenty years of Kent cricket: the full scores of all the matches played by Kent from 1879 to 1898; also batting & bowling averages of each year. Benenden, Cranbrook, the Editor, [1899]. viii,387p. scores, stats.

2149 -1 ■ **Milton, Howard**
  Several hundred years not out!: a history of Kent county cricket, first broadcast on B.B.C. Radio Medway, March 29/April 28, 1977. [i],23f. *typescript*
  *transcript in The Cricket Society's Library*

2150 ■ **"Senex"**, *pseud.*
  The tale of the Kent eleven. W.H. Smith, [c.1906]. 4p.

2151 ■ **Taylor, Alfred Daniel**
  The story of a cricket picture (Sussex and Kent). Hove, Emery, 1923. 61p. illus. scores
  *on the engraving by W.H. Mason of a match between Sussex and Kent at Brighton, 1849*
  ——*rptd.* Wakefield. S.R. Publishers Ltd., 1972. [iii],61p.
  See *no. 2137*

2152 ■ **Williams, Leroy ("Fathead")**, *editor*
  Kent v. Trinidad . . . January 1973. Port-of-Spain, [the Editor, 1973]. [16]p. incl. adverts. ports. stats.

# LANCASHIRE

2152 -1 ■ **Aspin, Christopher**
  Lancashire, the first industrial society. Helmshore, Helmshore Local History Society, 1969. 190p. illus. facsims.
  *cricket pp.108, 178-81*

2153 □ **Central Lancashire Cricket League** [Handbook]. Rochdale, the League. *annual.* stats.
  *1889?/1952 . . . 66/to date*
  *simultaneous issues in cloth & paper*

2154 **The cricketer's** handbook. Bury, Fletcher & Speight. *annual*
  *1880. 32p.*
  *contd. as: The Lancashire cricketers' handbook*

2155 ■ **Kay, John**
  "Fifty years of league cricket": the Central Lancashire Cricket League 1892-1946. Manchester, *printed by* Hilton Bros., [1946]. [ii],62p. 1 illus. ports. stats.

2156 □ **Lancashire and Cheshire Cricket League** [Handbook]. Levenshulme, Manchester, the League. *annual.* stats.
  *seasons 1919/1956 . . . 74/to date*
  *formed 1915*

2157 Hon. Secretary's report. Manchester, the League. *annual.* stats. *typescript*
  *1953 to date?*

2158 **Lancashire** cricket: county, league, club and Manchester District fixtures. Manchester, Eastwood Publ. Co.
  *1938. 32p.* stats.

2158 -1 ■ **Lancashire Cricket Association**
  League and club officials, fixtures and laws of cricket: handbook. The Assoc.
  *1978 to date*
  *incorporates L.C.A. Newsletter*

2159 **Lancashire Cricket Federation**
  The official annual handbook of club and league cricket in Lancashire and district;

ed. by Albert E. Hall. Bolton, the Federation. ports. diagrs. stats.
*1949–55*
*1956–74* with title *"Lancashire cricket annual"*
*1968–74 published by A.E. Hall*
*1969–74* with sub-title: *covering all grades of cricket in Lancashire & other North-West counties*
*final issue 1974: 24th ed. by Albert E. Hall*
[*1974*]. [*i*],*236p. illus. ports. stats.*

2160    Rules . . . and reports, as given at the fifth annual meeting, held on 20th February, 1952. Bolton, the Federation, 1952, 20p.

2161    **Lancashire Cricket League**
□    Official handbook. The League. *annual.* illus. ports. stats.
*?1893–1916, 1920?* to date

2162    **The Lancashire** cricketers' handbook;
□    containing match fixtures for the principal clubs in Lancashire, the Counties, etc. Bury, Fletcher and Speight. *annual.* stats.
*season 1882–1903*
formerly *The cricketers' handbook*

2163    **Lancashire** League professionals
■    1892–1939; League champions and Worsley Cup winners. [Accrington], the League, [1939]. 16p.
*chronological lists of club professionals*
——*1892–1961;* compiled by Ernest Brown. [1961]. 32p.
*publd. in aid of Colne C.C. new pavilion fund*

2164    **Merseyside** cricket handbook; edited by J. MacDowall. Liverpool, J. MacDowall. *annual*
*3 issues 1926–28*

2165    **North Lancashire and District Cricket**
□    **League**
Rules and fixtures. Dalton, the League. *annual*
*?1893–1914, 1920–39, 1945* to date
*formed 1892*

2166    **North-East Lancashire Amateur Cricket**
□    **League**
Official handbook. Blackburn, the League. *annual.* stats.
*?1891–1915, ?1920* to date
formerly: *The Blackburn and District C.L.*

2167    **North-Western Cricket League**
□    Officials, fixtures, rules, positions of grounds. Manchester, the League. *annual.* diagr. stats.
*1947?* to date

2168    **Northern Cricket League**
□    Official handbook. The League. *annual.* ports. stats.
*/1952–63, 1968/*to date

2169    **Northern Daily Telegraph**
□    Cricket annual. Northern Daily Telegraph. ports. scores, stats.
*1906/1911–15/*

2170    **Ormerod, Frank**
Lancashire life and character. Manchester, J. Heywood, [1910]. vii,231p.
——2nd ed. Rochdale, Edwards & Bryning, [1915]. vii,231p.

2171    **Pateman, T.W.**
Dunshaw: a Lancashire background. Museum P., 1948. 262p. illus.
*cricket in ch. 11. "Sport and recreations". The author describes an East Lancashire town (under the name of Dunshaw) and the district surrounding it*

2172    **Record** of Lancashire cricket 1881. Bury,
■    Fletcher & Speight, [1882]. 70p. scores, stats.
——[1882 season] *with title:* Record of Lancashire cricket during last season. 1883. 68p. scores, stats.

2173    **South Lancashire Cricket League**
[Handbook]. Manchester, the League. *annual*
*?1905–15, ?1920–29*
*formed 1904;* contd. as: *South Lancashire Industrial League*

2174    **South Lancashire Industrial League**
□    [Handbook]. Manchester, the League. annual. illus. ports.
*1947/1949 . . . 58/*to date?
formerly: *South Lancashire Cricket League*

2175    **South West Lancashire Cricket**
□    **Association**
[Handbook]. Wigan, the Association. annual. *stats.*
*1965?/1970/*to date

2176    **The Victoria** history of the counties of
■    England: Lancashire; edited by William Farrer and J. Brownbill. Vol. 2. Constable, 1908
*cricket pp. 489–93*

2177    **West Lancashire Cricket League**
□    [Handbook]. Wigan, the League. *annual*
*1920?–39, 1946* to date?
formerly: *Wigan and District Cricket League. See no. 2250*

## Accrington

**2178  Accrington and District League**
☐  Officials. [Accrington], the League. *annual*. folded card
   *?/1957/to date?*

**2179  Holden, S.M.**
■  History of Accrington Cricket Club, 1877–1927. Accrington, the Author, [1927]. 90p. illus. ports. scores, stats.

**2180  Pilkington, Samuel Turnell**
   Accrington cricket down the ages 1841–1960. [Accrington, the Author, 1961]. [ii],30f. port. stats.
   *first publd. in 7 articles in Accrington Observer & Times, 1960*

## Ashton-under-Lyne

**2181  Ashton-Under-Lyne Cricket, Bowling and Tennis Club**
   Centenary handbook 1857–1957; compiled by S. Oldham. Ashton-under-Lyne, the Club, 1957. 40p. illus.

**2182  [Cordingley, David]**
■  Forty-four years of Ashton cricket, 1857–1900, by 'D. C.' Ashton-under-Lyne, J. Andrew, 1901. xv,126p. scores, stats.

## Barrow in Furness

**2183  Furness Cricket Association**
☐  Handbook. Barrow-in-Furness, the Assoc. *annual*
   *1956? to date*

## Blackburn

**2184  Blackburn Mid-Week Cricket League**
☐  Official handbook of clubs and fixtures. Blackburn, the League. *annual*
   *1948?/1950 . . . 69/to date*

**2185  East Lancashire Cricket Club**
■  History and reminiscences of the East Lancashire Cricket Club [1864–1947]. Blackburn, the Club, [1947]. 60p. incl. adverts. ports. score
   cover-title: *History and memories*

**2186**  Centenary souvenir 1864–1964. Blackburn, the Club, [1964]. 44p. incl. adverts. illus. ports.

## Blackpool

**2187  The Alhambra** Shield Competition. Blackpool. *annual*
   *1902–07*
   contd. as: *The Palace (Blackpool) Shield Competition*

**2188  The Palace (Blackpool)** Shield Competition. Blackpool. *annual*. team ports.
   *?1907–15, ?1919 to date*
   *formerly:* The Alhambra Shield Competition

**2189  Blackpool Cricket League**
☐  Rules and fixtures. Blackpool, the League. *annual*. stats.
   *1932?/1968 . . . 70/1971?*
   *1972? to date with title: Official handbook*

## Bolton

**2190  Bolton and District Cricket Association**
☐  Rules and fixtures. Bolton, the Association. *annual*
   *?1889 to date*
   *formed 1888*

**2190  [Bolton Cricket Club]**
**–1**  Official handbook of the grand bazaar to be held in the Albert Hall, Town Hall, Bolton, on . . . April 20, 21, 22, 1899. [Bolton, the Club, 1899]. iv,80p. incl. adverts. illus.

**2191  Bolton Cricket League**
☐  Rules and fixtures. Bolton, the League. *annual*
   *1931?–1970*
   *1971? to date with title: Official handbook. team ports. stats.*

## Burnley

**2191  Bennett, Walter**
**–1**  The history of Burnley. 4 parts. Burnley,
■  Burnley Corporation, 1946–1951.
   Pt. 4. The history of Burnley from 1850. 1951. 300p. illus. plans
   *ch. xii Cricket and football, militia, etc.*
   (cricket pp. 221–5)

**2191  Burnley Cricket Club**
**–2**  Souvenir handbook of the centenary
■  bazaar . . . Feb. 21, 22 & 23, 1935, in The Mechanics' Institution, Burnley. Burnley, the Club, 1935. 96p. incl. adverts. 1 illus. ports. facsim. stats.
   *cover-title*: Centenary bazaar: history and souvenir 1834–1934
   *contains "A short history of Burnley Cricket Club 1833–1934" compiled by E. Whittaker*

## Bury

**2192  Bury and District Sunday Schools Cricket League**
☐  List of officers, matches, etc. Bury, the League. *annual*
   *?1906–15, ?1919–39, ?1947 to date*

## Castleton

**2192 Taylor, Frank**
**–1** A lifetime of cricket. [c.1925]. Ms.
*personal recollections of the Castleton C.C.*
*1874–1911. In Area Central Library, Roch-*
*dale; see also no. 2245–2*

## Chorley

**2193 Chorley and District Amateur Cricket**
☐ **League**
Rules and fixtures. Chorley, the League.
*annual.* stats.
*?1904–40, 1946?/1951 . . . 1971/to date*

## Clitheroe

**2193 Clarke, Stephen**
**–1** Clitheroe in its railway days. Clitheroe, J.
Robinson, 1900. vi,311p. illus.
*cricket pp. 265–72*

## Colne

**2194 Colne Cricket and Bowling Club**
■ Souvenir handbook of the Cricket Club
bazaar . . . 1933. Colne, [the Club, 1933].
96p. incl. adverts. illus. ports. scores
*contains history of the club*

## Darwen

**2195 Darwen Cricket League**
☐ Official handbook. Darwen, the League.
*annual*
*1950?/1950 . . . 58/to date*
*formed 1891*

## Droylsden

**2195 Speake, Robert, *and* Witty, Frank Roy**
**–1** A history of Droylsden. Stockport,
Cloister P., 1953. 268p. illus. maps
*cricket pp. 224–6*

## Edenfield

**2196 Edenfield Cricket Club**
[Handbook]. Edenfield, the Club. 1888
*issued to members only. (In Taylor)*
*?Edenfield, Lancs.*

## Eccles

**2197 Eccles and District Cricket League**
☐ [Handbook]. Eccles, the League. *annual*
*1949?/1954, 55/to date?*

## Fylde

**2198 Fylde Cricket League**
☐ Handbook and fixtures. The League.
*annual*
*1929?/1968 . . . 73/to date*
*formed 1928*

**2199** Rules and regulations for league and
■ knock-out competition matches. Fylde,
the League, [1972]. [8]p.

## Haslingden

**2200 Aspin, Christopher**
■ Haslingden 1800–1900: a history. Haslingden, Haslingden Printing Works Ltd.,
1962. viii,187p. illus. port.
——2nd ed. 1963
*cricket pp. 159–60*

**2200** Gone cricket mad: the Haslingden Club
**–1** in the Victorian era. [Helmshore],
■ Helmshore Local History Society, 1976.
[v],70pp. illus. facsim. scores

## Horwich

**2201 Horwich Churches Welfare Cricket**
■ **League**
50; edited by J.A. Hester [and others].
[Horwich, the Club, 1972]. 40p. illus.
*covers the years 1922–72*

## Huyton

**2202 Huyton Cricket and Bowling Club**
■ Centenary souvenir programme:
1860–1960. Huyton, the Club, [1960]. 36p.
incl. adverts. score, stats.

## Lancaster

**2203 Gilchrist, J.J.**
■ The Lancaster Cricket Club, 1841–1909.
Lancaster, Beeley Bros., 1910. viii,378p.
frontis. scores
*limited to 250 copies*

## Leyland

**2204 Kirby, Thomas, *compiler***
■ A record of the matches played by
Leyland Cricket Club from the year 1877
to 1897. Preston, *printed by* C.W.
Whitehead, 1898. xiv,280p. scores

**2205** A complete list of matches played by the
■ Leyland Cricket Club. Preston, *printed by*
C.W. Whitehead. scores. *annual*
*in 1898 (–1903). Publd. 1899 (–1904)*

**2205 Rogers, Norman Richard**
**–1** The story of Leyland (A.D. 1080–1950):
being an account of the ancient and
industrial history of Leyland, and the
progress of "The Town". Blackpool, the
Author, 1953. xi,124p. illus. ports. maps
*ch. x "The Leyland Cricket Club", pp.*
*95–106*

## Littleborough

2206 **Littleborough Cricket Club**
[Handbook]. The Club, *annual?*
*?/c.1880/–?*

2207 The village fair [bazaar handbook]. Little-
■ borough, the Club, 1932. 36p. incl.
adverts. ports. stats.
——1937. 48p. incl. adverts. ports. stats.

## Liverpool

2208 **Brooking, George A.,** *compiler*
■ The complete history of Liverpool &
District (including Gentlemen of Liverpool) versus colonial and foreign teams,
first class counties and Cambridge
University. Liverpool, [the Compiler],
1931. [vii],84p. scores. *typescript*
*match scores of Liverpool C.C. with brief*
*summaries*

2209 **Liverpool** cricket annual. Liverpool, W.
☐ Blevin. ports. stats.
*issues recorded: 1889–90. 1926–31, 1950*
*to date. All issues from 1926 state that 1st*
*issue was 1884, but publisher's preface to 1889*
*issue states it is the 3rd. Gaston and Taylor*
*give 1888 as 1st issue. No issues during 1st*
*World War nor 1939–49 inclusive. At some*
*time title changed to "Liverpool and District*
*cricket annual"*

2210 **Liverpool Cricket Club**
■ Matches 1847–1864. [Liverpool C.C.],
1865. iv,254p. scores

2211 L.C.C. public school tours, 1866 to 1896;
■ also Birkenhead Park 1865 to 1896. [Liver-
pool, the Club, 1896]. 142p. scores
*no title-page. Preface signed T.O. P[otter]*
——, 1866 to 1907. [1907]. [i],144p. scores
——, 1866 to 1912. [1912]. [i],179p. scores,
stats.
*no title-page. Preface signed E.C.*
*H[ornby]; A. L. M[elly]*

2212 **Lodge, P.Y.**
■ Liverpool Cricket Club: a sketch of the
historic continuity of the club: local
champions—season 1919. Liverpool,
*printed by* Ratcliffe, [c.1920]. 16p. stats.

2213 **A sketch** of the Liverpool Cricket Club.
■ [Liverpool C.C.], 1930. 4p.
*contains rules of the Mosslake Field Cricket*
*Society 1807, the origin of the Liverpool C.C.*
*For original see no: 2215*

### Anfield

2214 **"A Cricketer",** *pseud.*
■ A week's cricket: a rhyming record of the
doings of a Liverpool eleven in Shrop-

shire and neighbouring counties. Liverpool, printed by wish of the [Anfield]
Eleven, [c.1865]. 33p.

### Mosslake Field Cricket Society

2215 **Mosslake Field Cricket Society**
The original and unrivalled Mosslake
Field Cricket Society: we the undersigned
having become members of this Society
do hereby agree to stand to and observe
the following rules and regulations. The
Society, 1807. bs.
*rptd. in no. 2213*

### Sefton

2216 **Lynch, J.D.**
■ Sefton Cricket Club 1862–1925. Liverpool,
*printed by* W. Williams, 1926. 44p. illus.
ports. scores, stats.

2217 **Roper, Edward**
■ A sportsman's memories; edited by Fred
W. Wood. Liverpool, C. Tinling, 1921.
286p. illus. ports.

2218 **Sefton Cricket Club**
■ Centenary souvenir programme
1860–1960. Liverpool, the Club, [1960].
40p. incl. adverts. ports. scores, stats.

2218 **Whittington-Egan, Richard**
–1 Liverpool soundings. Liverpool, The
Gallery P., 1969. 191p.
*cricket pp. 174–5 "Cricket on the green"*
*(impressions of a match Sefton v. New*
*Brighton)*

### Waterloo Park

2219 **Matthews, Jack,** *and* **Davidson, Frederick**
■ **B.,** *compilers*
History of Waterloo Park Cricket Club
1890–1950: a diamond jubilee souvenir.
Liverpool, [the Club, 1951]. 74p. illus.
ports. stats.

## Manchester

2220 **Brindley, William Harrison,** *editor*
■ The soul of Manchester. Manchester,
Manchester Univ. P., 1929. xi,280p.
*cricket references by W.P. Crozier, pp.*
*250–52*

2220 **Hayes, Louis M.**
–1 Reminiscences of Manchester and some
of its local surroundings from the year
1840. Sherratt and Hughes, 1905. 349p.
illus.
*cricket pp. 55–8*

2221 **Kennedy, Michael**
■ Portrait of Manchester. Hale, 1970. 192p.
illus. ports. maps. (The Portrait Series)
*cricket pp. 117–122, etc.*

2222 **Manchester and District Cricket**
□ **Association**
[Handbook]. [Manchester], the Association. *annual.* stats. [from 1952]
*?1892–1914, ?1920–39, ?1946–47, 1948*
to date

2223 **Manchester Districts Works and**
□ **Commercial Sports Association**
[Handbook]. Manchester, the Association. *annual?*
*?/1947/–?*

2224 **The Manchester Sports Guild and**
**Cricket Club**
[Brochure]. Manchester, the Guild,
[1957]. [4]p.

2225 **North Manchester Cricket League**
□ Rules and fixtures. [Manchester], the
League. *annual.* stats.
*1956/1970/to date*
*formed 1955*

2226 **Swinton & District Amateur Cricket**
□ **League**
Rules and fixtures. Swinton, the League.
*annual*
*?1922–39, 1946–46 (1947 fixtures only)*
contd. as: *West Manchester Cricket League*

2227 **West Manchester Cricket League**
□ Rules and fixtures. Manchester, the
League. *annual*
*1948 to date?*
formerly: *Swinton & District Amateur*
*Cricket League*

**Blackley**

2228 **Blackley and District Amateur Cricket**
□ **League**
[Handbook]. The League. *annual*
*?/1955/to date?*

*Cheetham Hill*

2229 **House of Lords.** *Court of Appeal*
■ Between Harold Bolton and others [on
behalf of the Cheetham Cricket Club],
Appellants, and Bessie Stone (Spinster),
Respondent, 10th May 1951
*On August 9th, 1947, the Plaintiff was*
*standing in Beckenham Road, Cheetham Hill*
*Road, Manchester, outside her house when she*
*was struck by a cricket ball hit out of the*
*adjoining cricket ground; see also no. 7884-*
*1*

2230 **Kingham, G.P.,** *and* **Hall, F.**
■ The Cheetham Hill Cricket Club
1847–1947; edited by E.F. Chaney.
Manchester, Cheetham Hill C.C., 1947.
116p. ports. scores, stats.

*Longsight*

2231 **Longsight Cricket Club**
Memoirs. Manchester, Service Guild,
1928. 36p. illus.

**Middleton**

2232 **Middleton Cricket Club**
□ [Handbook]. Middleton, the Club
*?/1971/to date*

2233 100 years of cricket 1852–1952: fete and
■ gala, Saturday, 2nd August, 1952.
Middleton, [the Club, 1952]. 32p.
including adverts. ports.
*contributors include: F.R. Brown, E. Kay,*
*T. Ward, H. Hilton, N. Yardley, C. Barnet,*
*C. Washbrook*

**Milnrow**

2234 **Milnrow Cricket Club**
Centenary year 1857–1957 souvenir
brochure. Milnrow, the Club, 1957. 24p.

**Nelson**

2234 **Metcalfe, Derek**
–1 Nelson Cricket Club (at Seedhill)
■ 1878–1978: centenary brochure. [Nelson,
the Club, 1978]. 76p. incl. adverts. illus.
ports. scores, stats.

2235 **Nelson Cricket and Bowling Club**
Balance sheet. Nelson, the Club. *annual*
*?/1926/–?*

**Oldham**

2236 **Oldham and Ashton District Cricket**
□ **League**
[Handbook]. Oldham, the League.
*annual.* stats.
*?1898–1940, !1947/1955–58/to date?*

2237 **Oldham Cricket, Bowling and Tennis**
**Club**
Souvenir brochure; compiled by A.S.
Mellor. Oldham, the Club, 1934. 16p.
illus.

**Preston**

2238 **Church Lads Brigade Preston Cricket**
■ **Club**
Report and full score of every match,
season 1904. 21p. *typescript.* scores

2239 **Preston and District Cricket League**
□ Fixtures. Preston, the League. *annual.*
*1924?/1953 . . . 63/to date?*

**Radcliffe**

2239 **Hardman, S.**
–1 Reminiscences of Radcliffe Cricket Club.
*Priv. publd.,1924*

2240　**Masset, Joseph**
Radcliffe Cricket Club: jubilee handbook 1908–1958. Radcliffe, The Radcliffe Printing Co., 1958. 48p. illus.

## Ramsbottom

2241　**Ramsbottom Cricket Club**
[Handbook]. Ramsbottom, the Club, 1882
*in Taylor*

## Rawtenshall

2241　**Hamer, W. H.**
–1　A brief history of the Rawtenshall Cricket Club 1868–1925. 1926

## Rishton

2242　**Rishton Cricket and Tennis Club**
Report and balance sheet. Rishton, the Club. *annual*
*?/1927/–?*

## Rochdale

2243　**Beal, Clifford**
■　Parkin to Pepper: Rochdale cricket since World War I. Rochdale, "Observer" Office, 1947. 60p. incl. adverts. ports. stats.

2244　**Brierley, Henry**
Reminiscences of Rochdale. Rochdale, "Rochdale Times", [1923]. 148p. ports. scores
*includes ch. on "Games & Sport", pp. 86–92*

2244　**Buckley, George Bent,** *compiler*
–1　Rochdale cricket 1812–1953: a collection of cricket scores. 1958

2245　**Fothergill, J.**
■　History of the Rochdale Cricket Club, 1824–1902. Rochdale, Rochdale Observer, 1903. vi,192p. illus. ports. scores, stats.

2245　**Heywood, T.T.**
–1　New annals of Rochdale. Rochdale, Rochdale Times, 1931. 287p.
*cricket pp. 208–11*

2245　**Mattley, Robert Dawson**
–2　Annals of Rochdale: a chronological view from the earliest times to the end of the year 1898. Rochdale, *printed by* J. Clegg, the Aldine P., 1899. iv,178p. map
*cricket clubs: Castleton pp.51, 63, 67, 70, 85, 88*
*Rochdale pp.12, 41, 44, 69, 72, 112, 157*
*Union pp.55, 86*

2245　**Norden Cricket Club**
–3　Centenary brochure 1875–1975. Rochdale, the Club, [1975]

2246　**Rochdale and District Cricket League**
□　Handbook. Rochdale, the League. *annual*
*?/1957 . . . 69/to date*

2246　**Rochdale Cricket Club**
–1　Centenary 1926. Rochdale, the Club, 1926
*contains a history of the Club*

## Royton

2247　**Chapman, Frank**
Royton cricket: a condensation of the history of the club over 75 years. Royton, T. Varley & Co., 1947. 48p. illus.

## Southport

2247　**Porter, K.H.**
–1　A hundred years of cricket at Trafalgar
■　Road, 1874–1974; edited by C.J. Burgess. [Southport, Southport & Birkdale C.C., 1974]. 44p. incl. covers & adverts. illus. ports.

2248　**Southport and District Amateur Cricket**
□　**League**
[Handbook]. Southport, the League. *annual*
*?/1957, 58/to date?*

## Widnes

2249　**Widnes Cricket Club**
■　A souvenir of the Club's 50 years at Lowerhouse Lane 1874–1924. Garston, Garston Printing Works, [1924], 57p. ports.

2249　**Haigh Colliery Cricket Club**
–1　Rules. Haigh, the Club, 1849
*entry from* Bibliotheca Lindesiana, *vol. 1.*

## Wigan

2250　**Wigan and District Cricket League**
□　[Handbook]. Wigan, the League. *annual*
*1907–14*
contd. as: *West Lancashire Cricket League.* See *No. 2177*

2251　**Wigan** Cricket Club history: the centen-
■　ary 1848–1948. Wigan, the Club, 1948. 48p. incl. adverts. ports.

## Winton

2251　**Winton** Cricket Club 1878–1978: centen-
–1　ary brochure. [Winton, the Club, 1978].
■　36p. incl. adverts. illus. ports. scores

## Worsley

2252　**Jackson, W.W.**
Worsley Cricket Club over one hundred years. [Worsley, the Club, 1946]. 32p. illus. ports. score

**Wrea Green**

2252 **Wilson, Dick**
–1 1929–1979: fifty years with Wrea Green
Cricket Club. The Author, 1979

# LANCASHIRE C.C.C.

2253 **Addison, Vernon,** *and* **Bearshaw, Brian**
■ Lancashire cricket at the top. S. Paul,
1971. 128p. illus. ports. stats.

2254 **Ashley-Cooper, Frederick Samuel**
■ Lancashire cricket and cricketers: the
Lancashire team in 1897; together with a
synopsis of Lancashire cricket since the
formation of the County Club in 1864.
"Cricket P." 1898. 16p. incl. adverts. team
port. on cover, stats.

2255 **[Axon, Thomas]**
■ Annual record of Lancashire cricket, by
"Lancastrian": giving full score and
bowling analysis of all the county
matches in 1886. Manchester, T. Axon,
[1887]. 48p. scores

2256 **Craig, Albert**
■ Craig on the cricket champions of 1897.
The All England Athletic Publishing Co.,
[1898]. 44p. ports. stats.
——2nd ed. 1898
——3rd ed. 1898

2257 **Foster, Denis**
■ Lancashire. Findon Publications, [1949].
32p. ports. stats. ("Know Your Cricket
County" Series)

2258 **Kay, John**
■ Lancashire. Barker, 1972. 185p. illus.
ports. stats. (A History of County Cricket)
——*another ed.* Sportsman's Book Club,
1974

2259 **Lancashire County and Manchester**
■ **Cricket Club**
Testimonial to the Hon. Secretary, Mr.
S.H. Swire: report of dinner and presen-
tation, November 24th, 1888. [Manches-
ter, S.H. Swire, 1889]. 37p. port.

2260 Official handbook. Manchester, the Club.
■ *annual.* illus. ports. scores, stats.
*1930–38, 1947 to date*
editors: *1930–34 Sir Home Gordon*
*1935–38 J.A. Brierley*
*1947–48 J.A. Brierley & T.*
*Longworth*
*1949–50 T. Longworth*
*1951–56 not named*
*1957–62 C.G. Howard*
*1963–64 C.G. Howard & R.*
*Warburton*

*1965–67 R. Warburton & A.*
*Barrow*
*1968–? R. Warburton*
*from 1957 the statistics have been compiled*
*by Charles Oliver*

2261 **Lancashire County Cricket Club**
■ Diamond jubilee 1864–1924: official
souvenir. Manchester, Manchester
Guardian, in collaboration with the
Lancashire C.C.C., 1924. 40p. illus. ports.
stats.

2262 One hundred years of Old Trafford,
■ 1857–1957. Manchester, Lancashire
County & Manchester C.C., 1957. 32p.
illus.

2263 100 years of cricket, 1864–1964.
■ Manchester, Lancashire C.C.C., 1964.
[64]p. illus. ports. scores

2264 Introducing the new indoor sports centre.
■ Manchester, the Club, [1969]. [16]p. col.
illus. port.

2265 This is Lancashire: a souvenir brochure
■ for season 1972. [Manchester, the Club,
1972]. 44p. incl. adverts. illus. ports.

2265 Team up with us. Manchester, the Club,
–1 [1979]. [6]p. fold incl. advert. illus.
■ *membership facilities, etc. Sponsored by*
*Allied Oils and Fats Ltd*

2266 **Lancashire Youth Cricket Council**
A first report. Manchester, the Council,
1953. illus.
*the Council is the youth organisation of the*
*Lancashire County and Manchester Cricket*
*Club*

2267 **Lang, William**
■ The jubilee book of Lancashire cricket.
Manchester Weekly Times, [1914]. 22p.
illus. ports. stats.

2268 **Ledbrooke, Archibald William**
■ Lancashire county cricket: the official
history of the Lancashire County and
Manchester Cricket Club, 1864–1953; statistics compiled by Charles M. Oliver.
Phoenix House, 1954. 304p. illus. ports.
plan, stats.

2268 **Manchester Guardian**
–1 The bedside 'Guardian' 3: a selection by
■ Ivor Brown from The Manchester
Guardian 1953–1954. Collins, 1954. 255p.
illus.
*includes pp. 195–9 "Lancashire heroes" by*
*Neville Cardus, a review of* Lancashire
County cricket: the official history
1864–1953, *by A.W. Ledbrooke; pp. 191–4,*
*"Cricket on the hearth", by John R. Townsend*

2269 **Newnes, George,** *compiler*
Lancashire cricket: souvenir for 1881.
Manchester, *printed by* S. Blomeley, 1881.
26p. scores, stats.

2270 **Podgson, Rex**
■ Lancashire county cricket. Convoy Publications, 1952. [vi],108p. illus. ports.
(County Cricket Series)

2271 **Prittie, Terence Cornelius Farmer**
■ Lancashire hot-pot. Hutchinson, [1949].
232p. illus. ports. diagrs. scores. (Hutchinson's Library of Sports and Pastimes)
——*rptd. tog. w.* Mainly Middlesex *in*:
Cricket north and south. Sportsman's
Book Club, 1955. 237p.

2272 ————, and **Kay, John**
■ Second innings: the revival of Lancashire
cricket. Altrincham, J. Sherratt, 1947.
151p. illus. ports. stats.

2273 **Reynolds, Frederick Reginald**
■ Lancashire county cricket: a complete
record of the full scores and bowling
analyses of all matches played by the
county from . . . 1864 . . . up to the close
of the season 1880. Manchester,
Heywood, 1881. scores
——2nd ed. . . . 1881. 1882
——3rd ed. . . . 1882. 1883.

2274 **Swindells, Thomas**
■ Lancashire county cricket records 1865 to
1908. Altrincham, Artistic Printing Co.,
[1909]. 94p. port. stats.

2275 **Trew-Hay, John**
■ The match of the season: a lay of the
Oval. Wright, 1894. 26p. score
*a poem on the tied match, Surrey v. Lancashire, Aug. 1894*

2276 **W., G.T.**
□ Record of Lancashire county matches
from 1865 to 1881. Manchester, Capleton,
1882. 46p. stats.
——2nd ed. . . . 1865 to 1882 inclusive.
[1882]. 52p.
——3rd ed. . . . 1865 to 1883 inclusive.
1884

2277 **Ye Battel** of Middlesex versus Lancashire,
■ foughten at Old Trafford, July 14th, 15th
and 16th, 1892. Manchester, Ladies'
Pavilion, Old Trafford, 1892. 4p.
*poem*

# LANCASHIRE *v.* YORKSHIRE

2278 **Ashley-Cooper, Frederick Samuel**
■ Lancashire v. Yorkshire at the wicket,
1849–1923. Northampton, Lea and Co.,
[1923?]. 15p. stats.

2279 **Cook, R.F.W.,** *compiler*
Lancashire C.C.C. v. Yorkshire C.C.C.
1849–1964. Leeds, the Compiler, [1965].
12p. stats.
*limited ed. of 100 copies; statistical analysis
1st published in Vol. 3 No. 1 of Cricket Quarterly, Winter 1965*

2280 **Thomson, Arthur Alexander**
■ Cricket: the wars of the roses. Pelham,
1967. 219p. illus. ports. bibliog.
——*another ed.* Sportsman's Book Club,
1968

2281 **The war** of the roses 1849–1949: a dinner
■ to mark the centenary of Yorkshire-
Lancashire county cricket matches, 7th
October 1949, Grand Hotel, Sheffield,
Yorkshire. Mexborough, Times Printing
Co., 1949. 8p. illus.
*brief historical notes*

2282 **Wilson, E. Rockley,** *compiler*
■ Yorkshire v. Lancashire 1849–1949: outstanding performances and records during
one hundred years. Leeds, Yorkshire
C.C.C., [1949]. 6p folded. stats.

2283 **Yeomans, C. Ronald,** *compiler*
■ Roses for remembrance; collected by Ron
Yeomans. Leeds, the Author, 1960. 28p.
illus. ports. score
*extracts from newspaper reports of the Roses
match at Old Trafford Aug. 1960. Limited ed.
of 100 copies*

# LEICESTERSHIRE

2284 **The Gentlemen of Leicestershire Cricket**
□ **Club**
List of members and rules. The Club.
*quinquennially*
*?/1962/to date*
*with annual Addenda and Corrigenda*

2285 **Leicester** and county cricket annual;
edited by J.A. Mackley. Leicester,
Mackley, 1947. 64p. diagr. stats.
*the only issue?*

2286 **Leicester and County Cricket Association**
Official handbook. Leicester, the
Association
*1902/1903, 1926, 1929, 1940/*
contd. as: *Leicester Cricket Association.
Official handbook
formed 1873*

2287 **Leicestershire** cricket 1902. Leicester,
■ Gamble & Johnson, 1902. 8p. illus. ports.

2288 **Leicestershire** cricket annual. Leicester,
Hinckley, Walker. ports. stats.
*season 1898. 96p*
*1902. 88p*
*1903. 64p.*

2289 **Leicestershire Cricket Association**
☐ Official handbook. Leicester, the Association. *annual.*
   *season 1948/1948–51, 1954/to date?*
   formerly: *Leicester and County Cricket Association*

2289 Southern tour August 1948 for the Young
–1 Amateurs of Leicestershire (under eighteen). Team and Itinerary. Leicester, the Assoc., [1948]. [4]p. fold
   *1949 with title: Inter-county matches August 1949*
   *1950, 1952 with title: Southern tour August 1950 (1952)*
   *1966, 1968, 1970 with title: The Young Amateurs of Leicestershire. Tour. Team and itinerary*
   *1972, 1973, 1975–79 with title: The Young Amateurs of Leicestershire. Players and fixtures*

2290 Centenary year 1873–1973. Leicester, the
■ Assoc., [1973]. 68p. incl. adverts. port.

2291 **North Leicestershire Cricket League**
Handbook. The League. *annual.* stats.
   *1897 to date*
   *formed 1896; until 1910 issued in form of folded card with rules*

2292 **The Nottinghamshire** cricketers' handbook. Bury, Fletcher & Speight. *annual*
   *1881*
   *1882–3 with title: The Notts and Derby cricketers' handbook*
   *1884 with title: The cricketers' handbook for Notts, Derby and Leicestershire*

2292 **Pilgrims Cricket Club**
–1 Yearbook. Wigston Magna. *typescript.*
☐ stats.
   *1967 to date*
   *the 1st issue includes 8p. of club history; 1973 issue with title: Pilgrims cricket 1973; 1974 covers 1974 and 1975 seasons; now play at Barsby*

2293 **South Leicestershire Cricket League**
Official guide. Hinckley, Hancox, 1902. 55p. ports. stats.
   *cover title: Cricket–1902: Hancox's Pocket cricket guide*

2294 [Handbook]. The League. *annual*
☐ *?/1911, 20, 21/*
   *in folded card form giving officers and rules contd. as: Official handbook*
   *1922–41, 1946 to date*
   *1946 issue with title: Jubilee Roll of Honour victory handbook. 30p.*

2295 **The Victoria** history of the counties of
■ England: Leicestershire; edited by W.G.

Hoskins and R.A. McKinley. Vol. 3. O.U.P., 1955
   *cricket pp. 282–86*

## Billesdon

2296 **Billesdon** Cricket Club 1872–1972.
■ [Billesdon], the Club, [1972]. 32p. incl. adverts. illus. ports.

## Hathern

2297 **Hathern Old Cricket Club**
The story of Hathern Old Cricket Club: 1967 souvenir programme. Hathern, the Club, [1967]. [4]p. illus.

## Leicester

2297 **Gimson, C.**
–1 The Leicester Ivanhoe C.C.: the second fifty years 1923–1973. [Leicester, the Club, 1975]. 314p. scores. *typescript*
   *limited ed. of 150 copies*

2298 **Gimson, Josiah Russell,** *and others*
■ The Leicester Ivanhoe Cricket Club 1873–1923, by J[osiah] R[ussel] Gimson, B[enjamin] W[alter] N[eville] Russell and R[obert] G[uy] Waddington. Leicester, the Club, 1923. 230p. illus. ports. scores. stats.
   *private circulation*
   ——Index to the History of the Leicester Ivanhoe Cricket Club 1873–1923; compiled by Henry Grierson. Leicester, the Club, [1926]. ixp. stats.

2299 **Leicester Mutual Sunday School Cricket**
☐ **League**
Handbook and register of bone fide playing members. Leicester, the League, 1898. 28p.
   ——. *annual. 1919 to date?*
   *formed 1896*

2299 **The Leicester** record. Leicester. *annual*
–1 *1887/1887–1889/–?*
   *1887 and 1888 issues compiled by W. Major 1889 issue compiled by H.J. Pickard.*
Printed by *Pickard, Valentine & Co. 64p.*
   *sporting records of the previous year in the Leicester area; cricket in the 1889 issue pp. 6–12*

2300 **Leicester United Trades' Cricket League**
Handbook. Leicester, the League. *annual.*
   *–?/1928,1931–3,1939/–?*
   *formed 1899*

2301 **Mason, Alan J.**
The History of Trinity Methodist Cricket Club. 1959–1969. Leicester, the Club, 1969. 54p. stats. *typescript*

2302 **Oxford and Wycliffe Cricket Club**
Cricket in wartime. Leicester[?], The Club.

*3rd season 1942; edited by the Skipper.*
*[1942?]. 11p.*
*other annual issues?*

### Loughborough

2303 **Deakin, Joseph**
Loughborough in the XIXth century.
Loughborough, Echo P., 1927. 144p. illus.
maps
*rptd. from the "Loughborough Echo";*
*cricket pp. 50–51*

2304 **Loughborough and District Junior**
☐ **Cricket Association**
[Handbook]. Loughborough, the Association. *annual?*
*?/1952/–?*

### Lutterworth

2305 **Dyson, Arthur Henry**
Lutterworth: John Wycliffe's town; edited
by Hugh Goodacre. Methuen, 1913.
ix,195p. illus.
*ch. xxvii, "Cricket", pp. 164–9*

### Market Harborough

2305 **Bland, John**
–1 Bygone days in Market Harborough.
Market Harborough, Green, 1924. x,125p.
illus.
*cricket pp. 76–7*

### Shepshed Town

2306 **[Smalley, Ralph]**
■ A century of cricket: a history of Shepshed Town Cricket Club from 1869 to
1969. Shepshed, [the Author], 1969. 42p.
illus. ports.

2307 **[See no. 2292–1]**

# LEICESTERSHIRE C.C.C.

2307 **Association of Cricket Statisticians,**
–1 *compilers*
■ Leicestershire cricketers 1879–1977.
Hampton in Arden (Warks.), the Assoc.,
1977. 27p. stats.
*limited to 750 copies; contains errata and*
*addenda for the previously published*
*Warwickshire, Worcestershire, Somerset and*
*Middlesex vols.*

2308 **The Australians,** including photographs
■ and record of the Leicestershire v.
Australia match, 1921. Leicester, George
Johnson, [1921]. [16]p. illus. ports. score

2308 **Book** of the words and songs of More
–1 Stir Still; or, The Public Prevaricator of
Lycaster: a musical seizure in two fits.
Leicester, Tilley and Garner, 1910. 32p.
*specially written for the Leicestershire*
*County Cricket Bazaar of 1910*

2309 **Leicestershire County Cricket Club**
☐ Year book. Leicester, the Club. *annual.*
scores, stats.
*1900–1914* with title, *Officials, rules,*
*fixtures, report. . . .*
*1934* with title: *"Annual". ed. by A.G.G.*
*Webb. illus. ports. diagrs. scores, stats.*
*1949; ed. by G.O.J. Elliott*
*1951–57; ed. by C.H. Palmer*
*1958–59; ed. by R.A. Diment and E.E.*
*Snow*
*1960–75* with title *"Year book" ed. by E.E.*
*Snow and F.M. Turner*

2310 Official handbook of the County Cricket
☐ Bazaar. Leicester, Leicestershire C.C.C.,
1901. 62p. illus. port.
——1910. 64p. illus. port.
——[Balance sheet for the Bazaar]. 1911.
folded card
——1935. 48p. ports.
*includes 1p. on Leics. and County C.A.,*
*and 4p. of Leics. cricket memoirs*

2311 Annual report and statement of accounts.
☐ Leicester, the Club. illus. ports.
*?/1935 . . . 76/to date*

2312 The County journal: Leicestershire
☐ County Cricket Club's magazine for
members. Leicester, the Club. illus.
ports. *6-monthly*
*no. 1. Oct. 1965/Oct. 65. Mar. 66/–?; edited*
*by F.M. Turner*

2312 Championship year: official souvenir
–1 [1975]. Leicester, the Club, [1975]. 48p.
■ incl. adverts. illus. scores, stats.

2312 **Packer, Sydney Charles,** *compiler*
–2 Leicestershire County Cricket Club
■ jubilee souvenir 1879–1928; a record of
fifty years . . . [Leicester]; the Club,
[1928]. 84p. incl. adverts. illus. ports.
stats.

2313 **Snow, Edward Eric**
■ A history of Leicestershire cricket. Leicester, Backus, 1949. 380p. illus. ports.
diagr. scores, stats. bibliog.

2313 Leicestershire cricket 1949 to 1977. S.
–1 Paul, 1977. 240p. illus. ports. scores,
■ stats.

# LINCOLNSHIRE

2314 **[Entry cancelled]**

2315 **Grimsby & District and Lincolnshire**
☐ **County Cricket Leagues**
Rules and official guide. The Leagues.
*annual.* stats.
*season 1964–68*
*1969* with title: *Lincolnshire C.C.L. &*
*Grimsby & District C.L.*

*for later issues* see: *Grimsby and District C.L.; Lincolnshire C.C.L.*

2316 **Lincolnshire County Cricket League**
□ Handbook. The League. *annual. illus.. ports. stats.*
 *1970 to date*
 *for previous issues* see: *Grimsby & District and Lincolnshire C.C.Ls.*

### Gainsborough

2317 **Gainsborough and District Amateur**
□ **Cricket League**
 Official handbook. Gainsborough, the League. *annual?*
 *?/1966/to date?*
 *formed 1906*

### Grimsby

2318 **Grimsby & District Cricket League**
□ Handbook. Grimsby, the League. *annual.*
 *1970 to date (1970 in typescript)*
 *for previous issues* see: *Grimsby & District and Lincolnshire C.C.Ls.*

2319 **Grimsby Town Cricket Club**
□ Official year book. Grimsby, the Club. stats.
 *?/1973/to date*

2320 **Lincoln, Robert**
 Reminiscences of sport in Grimsby. Grimsby News, 1912. 411p. illus.
 *contains "Cricket from 1868 to 1912"*

### Lincoln

2321 **Lincoln & District Amateur Cricket**
□ **Association**
 Official handbook. Lincoln, the Association. *annual?* team port.
 *?/1912/–?*
 *formed 1904*

2322 **Lindum Cricket Club**
□ Annual report of the committee. Lindum, the Club. stats.
 *?/1953 . . . 58/to date?*
 *formed 1856*

2323 1856–1956 centenary dinner, County
■ Assembly Rooms, Lincoln, 18th January 1956. Lincoln, Lindum C.C., 1956. 6p. plus 1p. insert.
 *contains short history of the Club*

2324 The centenary. [Lincoln, the Club, 1957]
■ [3]p.

### Long Sutton

2325 **Long Sutton Cricket Club**
□ Year book & fixtures. Long Sutton, the Club, stats.
 *1934? to date. (1970 was 37th season)*

### Skegness

2325 **Kime, Winston**
–1 Skeggy!: the story of an East coast town. Skegness, Seashell Books, 1969. 171p. illus. map.
 *cricket pp. 147–9*

### Sleaford

2325 **Sleaford Cricket Club**
–2 Official handbook. Sleaford, the Club.
□ illus. ports. stats. *annual*
 *?/1979/to date*

## LINCOLNSHIRE C.C.C.

2326 **Charlton, R.J.**
■ The history of the Lincolnshire County Cricket Club 1853–1960. [Lincoln, the Club], 1960. 31p. ports.

2327 **Lincolnshire County Cricket Club**
■ Year book. Lincoln, the Club. ports. stats.
 *1937–39, 1946 to date*
 *volumes for 1959 and 1960 contain the history of the Club, 1853–1960*

2328 News sheet. Lincoln, the Club. *monthly*
□ *during Summer.* scores
 *1950/Sept. 1967, June 1972/to date?*
 *the 2 issues seen are in the form of broadsheets*

## LONDON

(only general London items are listed here; for individual clubs see under the respective adjoining counties)

2328 **Australia House (London) Cricket Club**
–1 Los Angeles tour 1978 (16th–30th
■ September). The Club, [1978]. [8]p. incl. covers. ports.
 *pre-tour*

2328 **Brown, Ivor John Carnegie**
–2 London; illustrated by Felix Kelly. Newnes, 1960. 250p. illus. ("Cities of Enchantment")
 *cricket pp. 17, 206–13, 215*

2328 **The Cricketers Club of London**
–3 Capital cities tour Australia & Far East
■ 1979, departing January 3rd 1979 and including Australian series. The Club, [1978]. [8]p. illus. ports.
 *pre-tour itinerary*

2329 **Cunningham, George Hamilton**
■ London: being a survey of the history, tradition & historical associations of buildings & monuments. Dent, 1927. xxviii,887p.
 *cricket pp. 26–27, 143, 191, 492, 565, 613*

2330 **Kent, William Richard Gladstone**
■ London in the news through three centuries. Staples P., [1954]. 242p. illus.
*pp.223–4 "Man who walked on at the Oval" extract from* Daily News, *Aug. 4, 1919; p.224 "A suicidal sparrow". [M.C.C. v. Camb. Univ., July 4, 1936], extract from* The Cricketer, *Aug. 8, 1953*

2331 **London County Council**
■ Parks and open spaces: cricket. L.C.C., 1951, *i.e.* [1952]. 7p.
*availability and regulations for the use of cricket pitches*

2332 **London New Zealand Cricket Club**
□ Annual report. The Club. *typescript ?/1970/to date?*

2332 **Lucas, Edward Verrall**
–1 A wanderer in London. Methuen, 1906.
■ xi,305p. illus. (some col.)
*cricket pp. 210, 218, 242, 245, 246 many subsequent editions, e.g.*
——16th ed. 1914. xii,276p.
*cricket pp. 178, 186, 211, 212*

2333 London. Methuen, 1926. 443p. illus.
■ *ch. xxxi "Two cricket grounds"*

2334 London afresh. Methuen, 1936. vi,330p.
■ *cricket references, pp. 41–45, 192, 240, 253, 264, 281*
——2nd ed. illus. 1937. vii,330p. illus.

2335 A wanderer's notebook: cricket in London. 21p.
*MS. now in M.C.C. Library at Lord's*

2335 **Massingham, Hugh,** *and* **Pauline**
–1 The London anthology. Phoenix House,
■ 1950. xiv,514p. illus. ports. facsims.
*cricket pp. 433–4*

2336 **Metropolitan Board of Works Cricket Club**
[Handbook]. The Club. *annual? in Taylor*

2337 **Morton, Henry Vollam**
■ The London year: a book of many moods; decorated from 'A London Sketch Book', by A.E. Horne. Methuen, 1926. xii,211p. illus.
——2nd ed. rev. 1933. xiii,213p.
*Eton v. Harrow pp. 134–137 and family cricket pp. 173–6*

2338 **South London Cricket Association**
□ Official handbook. The Association. *annual*
*1894/1898/–?*
*1898 ed. by E.A.C. Thomson*

2339 **The South London Cricket League**
Handbook of rules and fixtures. The Association. *annual*
*1909–14*
*formerly: Camberwell and District Cricket League*

2340 **West End Cricket Association**
□ [Handbook]. The Association. *annual ?1892–1914, ?1919–39, ?1946 to date formed 1881*

2341 **Whitaker-Wilson, Cecil**
■ Two thousand years of London. Methuen, 1933. ix,330p. illus.
*cricket pp. 100–102*

# MIDDLESEX

2341 **[Association of Middlesex Cricket Clubs]**
–1 Semi-finals and final Middlesex K.O. (20
■ overs) cricket competition . . . the Cricket Ground, Park Road, Uxbridge, Sunday, 7th October, 1973 at 11 a.m.: [souvenir programme]. [A.M.C.C., 1973]. 64p. incl. adverts. + xxxii p. insert. ports.
*in aid of funds for the British Red Cross Society*

2341 Benson and Hedges Middlesex Cricket
–2 League official handbook. The Assoc.
□ *annual*
*?/1977/to date*

2341 ——. *Harrow Committee*
–3 Harrow tour of Barbados 1975. Joint
■ organisers The Barbados Overseas Community and Friends Association. The Organisers, [1975]. 24p. incl. adverts. ports.

2342 **Brett-James, Norman George**
■ Middlesex. Hale, 1951. 432p. illus. map. bibliog. (The County Book Series)
*chap. xxii "Middlesex cricket" pp. 330–9*

2342 **Cricket** on the up: a miscellany of
–1 Middlesex cricket, sponsored by The
□ Seaxe Club & the Middlesex Cricket Union. illus. ports.
*June 1975/Spring 1976/to date?*

2342 **The Middlesex Colts Cricket Association**
–2 Official handbook. The Assoc. *annual*
□ *?/1975 . . . 1978/to date officers, fixtures, rules*

2342 **The Middlesex** Colts Cricket Association.
–3 The Association, [1972]. [4]p. fold
■ *information leaflet*

2342 **Middlesex Cricket League**
–4 M.C.L. news: news – views – reports –

☐ fixtures. The League. illus. ports. tabloid format
*May 1976?/June 1976/to date?*

2342 Trinidad & Tobago tour 1978 11 March
–5 – 29 March: official tour brochure. The
■ League, [1978]. [52]p. incl. adverts. ports.

2343 **The Middlesex Cricket Union**
☐ News bulletin. The Union. *typescript*
*No. 1. Nov. 1970/Apr., Aug., Nov. 1974/*
to date?

2344 **North Middlesex Cricket, Lawn Tennis**
☐ **and Bowls Club**
Report of the Committee, results, averages, etc. The Club. *annual.* stats.
*?/1969/to date?*
*formed 1875*

2345 Seventy-fifth anniversary 1875–1949:
■ souvenir. The Club, [1949]. [12]p.

2346 **Robbins, Richard Michael**
Middlesex. Collins, 1953. xxii,456p. illus.
map. (New Survey of England)
*cricket pp. 144, 145, 162, 328, 356*

2347 **The Victoria** history of the counties of
■ England: Middlesex; edited by William
Page. Vol. 2. Constable, 1911
*cricket pp. 270–75*

### Ashford

2348 **Hudson, D.L.,**
■ Ashford Cricket Club, 1855–1955.
Ashford, [the Club, 1955]. 71p. incl.
adverts. illus.

### Brondesbury

2349 **Brondesbury Cricket and Tennis Club**
Rules and bye-laws. Brondesbury, the
Club, 1953. 12p.

### Chelsea

2350 **Prince's** Cricket Club, Hans Place,
■ Belgrave Square: list of members, 1873.
[The Club, 1873]. 70p.
*formed 1870, closed 1886*

2350 **Upper Chelsea Institute**
–1 The Institute journal; edited by Bertram
W. Matz and John Fox. 1887. 200p. illus.
scores, stats. *typescript*
*Vol. 1, 1887–?*
*no more published? contains a running*
*record of the Sloane Park C.C. 1887 season,*
*with a folding sheet of averages*

### Cockfosters

2351 **[Lawman, Trevor]**
■ Cockfosters Cricket Club—a history of
the first 100 years: 1873–1972. [Cockfosters, the Club, 1973]. [iv],91p. illus. ports.
map, scores, stats.

### Cricklewood

2352 **Dexter, B.W.**
Cricklewood guide. Cricklewood, W.J.
Fowler, [c.1904]. 96p. illus. ports.
*cricket p. 93 with illus.*

### Crouch End

2352 **North London Cricket Club**
–1 The Shepherds Cot platform; produced
☐ by North London Cricket Club. The Club.
*monthly. typescript*
*Aug. 1979 to date*

### Ealing

2353 **The Ealing Cricket Club**
Rules. Ealing, the Club, 1889. [4]p.

2354 **Ealing** Cricket Club 1970: centenary
■ booklet. [Ealing, the Club, 1970]. 63p.
illus. ports. stats.

### Ealing Dean

2355 **Ealing Dean Cricket Club**
■ Compton handbook in aid of the Denis
Compton benefit fund; edited by W.
Stimpson. Ealing, the Club, [1949]. 16p.
illus. ports. stats.

2356 **Harris, Bruce,** *editor*
Ealing Dean Cricket Club 1846–1946
centenary dinner. [Ealing, the Club],
1946. 14p. illus. score
*contains brief history of the Club*

### Eastcote

2357 **Eastcote Cricket Club**
☐ Annual report. Eastcote, the Club. scores,
stats.
*?/1964/–?*
*the 1964 report was issued in centenary*
*year, the Club having been formed in 1865;*
*contains "The history of the Club" by Lionel*
*Cooke*

### Edmonton

2358 **[Eastwood, C.W.]**
■ Edmonton Cricket Club, 1872–1922.
[Edmonton, the Club, 1922]. 8p.
*rptd. from "Tottenham and Edmonton*
*Weekly Herald"*

2359 **Edmonton Cricket Club**
■ Season 1894. [Edmonton, the Club, 1894].
59p. stats.
*contains a review of the Club 1873–1893*

2360 Centenary 1872–1972. Edmonton, the
■ Club, [1972]. [20]p. ports.

## Enfield

2360 **Myddelton House Cricket Club**
–1 Centenary year 1879–1979: fixtures and
■ rules. [Enfield, the Club, 1979]. 8p.
*with 5pp. history of Club by Peter Deering*

## Finchley

2361 **Finchley Cricket Club**
■ [Pavilion appeal brochure. Finchley, the
Club, 1957]. 26p. illus.

2361 Newsletter. The Club. illus. ports. bs.
–1 *No. 1. Oct. 1975 to date?*

## Hampstead

2362 **Ashley-Cooper, Frederick Samuel**
■ Hampstead Cricket Club: a record of the
year 1901. [Hampstead, the Club], 1901.
71p. scores, stats.
*privately printed for Club members*

2363 **Baines, Frederic Ebenezer,** *editor*
■ Records of the manor, parish, and
borough of Hampstead. Whittaker, 1890.
xvi,575p. illus. ports. maps.
*cricket refs. pp. 30, 156–59, 297*

2364 **Hampstead Cricket Club**
■ Programme annual athletic meeting,
Saturday, September 25th, 1886.
[Hampstead, the Club, 1886]. [4]p.
*includes the record innings by Hampstead
v. Stoics, Aug. 4th 1886: Hampstead 814
(A.E. Stoddart 485)*

2365 Analysis of season. Hampstead, the
□ Club, *annual?* stats.
*?/1887/–?*
*1887 issue is in form of [4]p. folded card*

2366 A summary of results 1892. Hampstead,
□ the Club, for private circulation, 1892.
——A record of results for the season
1893. 1893. xi,89p. scores, stats.
——Season 1894. 1894. xi,75p. scores,
stats.

2367 Averages from 1879 to 1900, with the
■ exception of the years 1881 and 1882 of
which no record can be found.
Hampstead, the Club, [1900]. 41p. stats.

2368 Hampstead Cricket Club 1867–1967.
■ [Hampstead, the Club, 1967]. 7p.

2368 **Hawdon, Tony,** *and* **Audrey,** *compilers &*
–1 *editors*
■ South Hampstead Cricket Club
1875–1975. [The Club, 1975]. 44p. illus.
ports. stats.

2369 **Mackie, John**
Sixty-two years of club cricket. Castle
Cary, J.H. Roberts, 1948. 47p. ports.
stats.

2370 **Monro, Frederick Robert D'Oyly**
A history of the Hampstead Cricket Club.
Home & Van Thal, 1949. xi,194p. illus.
ports. scores, stats.

2371 **Potter, George William**
Random recollections of Hampstead.
Hampstead, Hewetson, 1907. 112p. illus.
*cricket pp. 90–92*

2372 **Waugh, Arthur**
One man's road: being a picture of life in
a passing generation. Chapman & Hall,
1931. xv,390p. illus. ports.
*references to Sydney Pawling and
Hampstead C.C.*

## Hampton Wick

2373 **Hampton Wick Royal Cricket Club**
Souvenir programme, centenary year
1963. [Hampton Wick, the Club, 1963].
[16]p. incl. adverts. illus. ports. map

## Harrow

2374 **Harrow Cricket Club**
■ Israel tour 12–29 October 1972. [Harrow,
the Club, 1972]. [6]p. fold. 1 illus. ports.
*pre-tour*

2375 **Israel** Cricket Association Northern Zone
■ versus Harrow Cricket Club, London,
18.10.72 at Kiryat Ata Hapoel Stadium;
and Israel Selectors XI versus Harrow
C.C., 19.10.72 at Haifa Municipal
Stadium: [souvenir programme]. [Haifa,
the Assoc., 1972]. [12]p. inc. adverts.
*pre-matches*

## Hendon

2376 **Hendon Buccaneers Cricket Club**
□ Fixtures handbook. Hendon, the Club.
*annual. stats.*
*1949 to date; issue for 1958 with title: A
10th anniversary booklet; edited by John C.
Harkness and G.K. Whitelock*

2377 Newsletter. The Club. *typescript. bi-
monthly*
*No. 1. July 1963–*

2378 **Whitelock, Geoffrey K.**
■ Hendon Buccaneers Cricket Club 1948–1973. [Hendon, the Club, 1973]. [i],47p. illus. ports. stats.

### Highgate

2379 **Chadwick, Arnold W.**
Fifty years of the Highgate Club 1879–1929. The Club, 1929. [iii],7p.

2380 **Lloyd, John H.**
The history, topography and antiquities of Highgate in the county of Middlesex, with notes on the surrounding neighbourhood. Printed by subscription on behalf of the Highgate Literary and Scientific Institution, 1888. xiv,519p. illus. map
*p. 428 refers to a match in 1802 between "Gentlemen of Marylebone and nine Gentlemen of Hampstead and Highgate"*

### Hornsey

2381 **Dey, Anthony,** *and* **Cox, David Burgess**
■ The history of the Hornsey Club, 1870–1970. [London, the Authors, 1970]. [4]iii,168. illus. ports. scores

2382 **[Nicholls, E.W.]**
■ History of Hornsey Cricket Club. "Hornsey Journal", 1908. 16p.
*rptd. from* Hornsey Journal *11th Sept., 1908*

### Hounslow

2383 **Pilley, Phil**
■ A century of cricket: a history of Hounslow Cricket & Sports Club 1868–1968. [Hounslow, the Club, 1968]. [ii],64p. illus. ports. stats.

### Indian Gymkhana Club

2384 **The Indian Gymkhana Club Ltd.**
■ Golden jubilee souvenir 1916–1966. Osterley, the Club, [1966]. [42]p. incl. adverts. illus. ports. scores

2384 60 and going strong. Diamond Jubilee
–1 dinner, Café Royal, London W.1., 16
■ December 1977. [The Club, 1977]. 25p. illus. ports. score
*includes historical account of the Club by Sunder Kabadi*

### Islington

2385 **Nelson, John**
■ History, topography and antiquities of the parish of St. Mary Islington . . . including biographical sketches of the most eminent and remarkable persons who have been born, or have resided there. Nichols, 1811. viii,416p. illus. plan
*Cricket Club at White Conduit House, p. 93*
——3rd ed. 1829. iv,375p. illus. plan
*reference to "a curious cricket match, between 11 women of Hants. against 11 of Surrey, and which lasted two days" in Oct. 1811, pp. 178–179*

2386 **Smith, John Thomas**
■ A book for a rainy day; or, Recollections of the events of the last sixty-five years. R. Bentley, 1845.
——2nd ed. iv,311p. 1845.
——3rd ed. rev. 1861
——. . . events of the years 1766–1833; ed. with an introduction and notes, by Wilfred Whitten. Methuen, 1905. xxiv,332p. illus. ports.
*cricket in White Conduit Fields in 1784, pp. 192–3, with notes*

### Kilburn

2387 **Taylor, William Henry**
■ History of Kilburn cricket: a verbatim report of a lecture delivered at the "Canterbury Arms", Kilburn, February 9th, 1886. Kilburn, Ford, 1886. 57p.
*rptd. from* The Kilburn Post

### Mill Hill

2388 **Mill Hill Village Sports Club.** *Cricket*
□ *section*
Handbook and fixtures. Edgware, the Club. *annual? illus. team port. stats.
1972/1972/–?*
*the only issue? formed 1868*

### Northwood

2389 **Kemp, William, Albert George**
The story of Northwood and Northwood Hills, Middlesex. [Northwood], the Author, 1955. illus.
——4th enl. ed. 1957. 128p.
*pp. 34–47 "Northwood Cricket Club"*

### Norwood Green

2390 **Norwood Green Cricket Club**
The elms: the magazine of the . . . Club; edited by Brian Styles. Norwood Green, the Club. *typescript
1958–?
2 issues in 1958*

2391 'One ton'—not out: centenary souvenir
■ programme. [Norwood Green, the club, 1967]. [20]p. incl. covers & adverts. illus.

## Paddington

2392 **Paddington Cricket League**
Handbook. Paddington, the League, 1895

## Shepherds Bush

2393 **Shepherds Bush Cricket Club**
□ 1931: fiftieth season. Shepherds Bush, the
Club, 1931. 52p. ports.
*contains history of the Club*
*formed 1882*

## Shepperton

2394 **Chipp, Maurice,** *compiler*
History of the Shepperton Cricket Club,
1905–1960. Shepperton, the Club, 1962.
90p. stats.

2394 **John Edrich** testimonial year 1975. Gala
–1 cricket match: Vic Lewis All Star XI versus
■ Shepperton C.C. . . . 18th May 1975:
souvenir programme. Woking, *printed by*
Unwin Bros. Ltd., [1975]. [24]p. incl.
adverts. ports.
*includes a brief note on Shepperton C.C.*

## Southgate

2395 **Southgate Adelaide Cricket Club**
■ A short history of the Southgate Adelaide
Cricket Club (1870–1970). Southgate, the
Club, [1970]. 20p. incl. covers & adverts.
team port.
*cover-title: Centenary 1870–1970*

2396 **Southgate Cricket Club**
□ Annual report. Southgate, N.14, the
Club.
*season?/1955/to date?*
*formed 1854*

## Stanmore

2397 **Stanmore Cricket Club**
■ 100 years of Stanmore cricket. Stanmore,
the Club, [1953]. 22p. illus. ports. score

## Sutton

2398 **Sutton Cricket Club**
□ "The Suttonian". Sutton, the Club. *types-*
*cript.* stats.
*1942 to date?*
*16 issues 1942–51; 1952–63 annually.*
*Christmas issue 1964 was postponed until*
*midsummer 1965*

## Teddington

2399 **Teddington Town Cricket Club**
Fixture list and handbook. Teddington,
the Club. *annual*
*?/1971,1972/to date*
*formed 1891*

## Turnham Green

2400 **Turnham Green Cricket Club**
□ Fixtures. Turnham Green, the Club.
*annual.* illus. ports. stats.
*1938–39, 1949 to date*
*prior to 1938 fixture lists only publd. 1953*
*issue with title: Centenary handbook*

## Twickenham

2401 **The Twickenham Cricket Club**
The first one hundred years 1833–1933.
Twickenham, the Club, 1933. 78p. illus.

## Uxbridge

2402 **Griffiths, Dennis M.**
■ A history of Uxbridge Cricket Club.
[Uxbridge, the Club], 1971. 75p. illus.
ports. scores
*limited ed. of 500 copies*

2403 **Uxbridge Cricket Club**
Year book. Uxbridge, the Club. illus.
stats.
*1972 to date*

## Walham Green

2404 **Walham Green Cricket Club**
□ Annual report. The Club. stats.
*1882/1898/–?*
*1898 was 17th season*

## Wembley

2404 **Wembley Cricket and Sports Association**
–1 Annual report and accounts for the year.
□ The Assoc.
*?/1974 . . . 1978/to date*

2405 **Wembley** Cricket Club 1860–1960.
■ [Wembley, the Club, 1960]. 40p. incl.
adverts. ports. scores, stats.

## West Drayton

2406 **Bayley, Peter C.**
100 years young: West Drayton Cricket
Club 1868–1968 centenary handbook. W.
Drayton, the Club, [1968]. 40p. illus.
ports.

## Wood Green

2407 **Wood Green Cricket Club**
■ Rules. 1870. [Wood Green, the Club,
1870]. 7p.

# MIDDLESEX C.C.C.

2408 **Ashley-Cooper, Frederick Samuel**
■ John Wisden's cricket match histories. III.

Middlesex v. Surrey 1730–1921. Wisden, [1922]. 16p. stats.

2408 **Association of Cricket Statisticians,**
–1 *compilers*
■ Middlesex cricketers 1850–1976. Hampton in Arden (Warks), The Assoc., [1976]. 51p. stats.
*limited ed. of 700 numbered copies*

2409 **Baily, Robin,** *editor*
■ Cricket: all about London's big four. John Smith, Lord's and Oval Bookstalls, 1928. 16p. illus.
*Kent, Surrey, Essex, Middlesex, giving averages for 1927 and fixtures for 1928*

2410 **Foster, Denis**
■ Middlesex. Findon Publications, [1949]. 32p. ports. stats. ("Know Your Cricket County" Series)

2411 **[Lane, John D.,** *compiler*]
Surrey v. Middlesex, 1730–1956. The Author, 1957. 22p. (Cricket match history)
*limited ed. of 100 copies*

2412 **Mason, Ronald**
■ Plum Warner's last season (1920). Epworth P., 1970. x,186p. illus. ports. scores

2413 **[Middlesex County Cricket Club]**
■ Middlesex club and colts' matches, 1905–6. [The Club, 1906]. 12p. scores

2414 Annual report and statement of accounts
□ for the year . . . The Club. illus. ports. stats.
*/1951–79/to date*

2415 Rules. The Club, 1953. 4p.

2416 Centenary youth campaign 1864–1964.
■ Middlesex C.C.C., [1964]. 8p. illus.
*enclosing a 4 page pamphlet with same title*

2417 Proceedings at the centenary dinner of
■ the Club, held at Grosvenor House, Park Lane, on Monday, the 20th day of July, 1964. [The Club, 1964]. 17f. *typescript*
*texts of speeches by the Duke of Edinburgh, G.C. Newman (the President), G.O. Allen, and Sir Alec Douglas-Home*

2417 Players' handbook and itinerary. The
–1 Club. *annual*
□ ?/1965–70/to date?
*pre-season*

2418 [Booklet of photographs reprinted from
■ the 1969 Yearbook]. The Club, [1969]. [12]p. illus. ports.

2418 Newsletter. The Club.
–1 *?/No. 2 (Nov. 1974), no. 3 (Jan. 1975), no. 4 (Mar. 1976)/–?*

2418 Middlesex County Cricket Club cham-
–2 pion county 1976. M.C.C.C, [1976]. 32p.
■ incl. adverts. illus. ports. stats.

2418 Benefit Middlesex souvenir brochure
–3 1979. Benefit Middlesex Cttee., [1979].
■ [48]p. incl. adverts. illus. ports.
*an appeal brochure*

2419 ————. *Junior Cricket Committee*
□ [Annual report]. Lord's, Middlesex C.C.C. stats.
*1952–58*
*later reports incorporated in Middlesex C.C.C. Annual reports*

2420 **Middlesex** County Cricket Club. 3 vols.
■ ports. scores, stats.
[Vol. 1]: 1864–1899 by W.J. Ford. Longmans, 1900, [v],547p.
Vol. 2: 1900–1920 by F.S. Ashley-Cooper. Heinemann, 1921. vii,486p.
Vol. 3: 1921–1947 by N.E. Haig & H.R. Murrell. Middlesex C.C.C., 1949. 673p.

2421 **Middlesex** cricket: the official journal of
■ the Middlesex County Cricket Club; edited by James Gleeson. Stuart Fraser Woodford & Partners [for the Club]. illus. ports. stats.
*[1972] containing record of 1972 season; Mar. 1973–?*

2422 **Middlesex** cricket handbook 1932

2423 **Middlesex** team 1896 souvenir

2424 **Prittie,** *the Hon.* **Terence Cornelius**
■ **Farmer**
Mainly Middlesex. Hutchinson, [1947]. 226p. illus. ports. (Hutchinson's Library of Sports and Pastimes)
————*rptd. tog. w.* "Lancashire hot-pot" *in:* Cricket north and south. Sportsman's Book Club, 1955. 237p.

2425 Middlesex County Cricket Club. Convoy
■ Publications, 1951. 179p. illus. ports. scores, stats. (County Cricket Series)

2426 **Wellings, Evelyn Maitland**
■ Middlesex. Barker, 1972. 176p. illus. ports. stats. (A History of County Cricket)
————*another ed.* Sportsman's Book Club, 1973

2427 **Ye battel** of Middlesex versus Lancashire,
■ foughten at Old Trafford, July 14th, 15th and 16th, 1892. Manchester, Ladies' Pavilion, Old Trafford, 1892. 4p.
*poem*

# NORFOLK

**2428 Mackie, Charles**
■ Norfolk annals: a chronological record of remarkable events in the nineteenth century (compiled from the files of the "Norfolk Chronicle"). 2 vols. Norwich, *printed at* the Office of the Norfolk Chronicle, 1901
*vol. 1, 1801–1850; vol. 2. 1851–1900*
*50 cricket references in vol. 1, including for 23rd May 1823: "A cricket match was played at Hockwold-cum-Wilton between 11 married and 11 single females for eleven pairs of gloves. The match terminated in favour of the former. 'The parties were dressed in jackets and trousers tastefully decorated with blue ribbands' "; 23 references in vol. 2*

**2429 Norfolk** cricket annual. London &
■ Norwich, Jarrold. port. scores
*season 1889; ed. by W.S. Barker & J.H. Hatch*
*1890; ed. by F.W. Watson*
*1891; ed. by R.H. Legge & F.W. Watson*
*1892–8; ed by Robin H. Legge*

**2430 Norfolk** cricket annual; edited by C.B.L.
■ Prior. Norwich, Prior. *annual.* illus. ports.
*season 1909–10*
*1910–11*

**2431 Norfolk** cricket annual; edited by Robert Barrett and R.G. Pilch. [Norwich], R.A. Sparke. illus.
*1926, 1927*

**2432 Norfolk Cricket Association**
Official handbook, directory and fixture list. Norwich, the Association. *annual*
*?/1953, 56, 67/to date?*

**2433 Norfolk Cricket Club**
Rules. Norwich, Bacon and Kinnebrook, 1827. 8p.

**2433 Penny, John Saffrell,** *compiler*
**–1** Cricketing references in Norwich newspapers, 1701 to 1800 arranged in chronological order. Norwich, the Compiler,
■ 1979. xvi,63f. *typescript*

**2434 Wilson, B. Knyvet**
Norfolk tales and memories. Norwich, Jarrold, 1930. xvi,71p. illus.
*cricket in ch. v.*

### East Dereham

**2435 Armstrong, Benjamin John**
A Norfolk diary: passages from the diary of the Rev. B.J. Armstrong; edited by Herbert B.J. Armstrong. Harrap, 1949. 288p. ports.
*author was vicar of East Dereham during latter half of 19th century; brief cricket references pp. 167, 180, 181, 286*

**2435 Boston, Noel,** *and* **Puddy, Eric**
**–1** Dereham: the biography of a country
■ town. Dereham, G. Arthur Coleby, 1952. xii,304p. illus. map
*cricket pp. 83–4*

### Hingham

**2436 [Driver, Thomas]**
■ The register of cricket for Hingham, by An Old Player. Norwich, *printed by* Matchett, Stevenson & Matchett, 1844. 36p. scores

### King's Lynn

**2436 Lynn Cricket Club**
**–1** Rules of the Lynn Cricket Club 1833. Lynn, the Club, [1833]. 12p.

### Letheringsett

**2436 Cozens-Hardy, Basil**
**–2** The history of Letheringsett in the county of Norfolk with extracts from the diary of Mary Hardy (1773 to 1809). Norwich, Jarrold and Sons, 1957. 172p. illus. folding map
*cricket pp. 74 (1789 reference), 134–7*

### Norwich

**2437 Nelson Cricket Club**
Rules and fixtures. Norwich, the Club. *annual*
*?/1884, 94, 1903, 05, 06, 08/–?*

**2438 Norfolk County Asylum Cricket Club**
Programmes. Norwich, the Club. *annual*
*?/1888 . . . 1906/–?*

**2439 Penny, John Saffrell,** *compiler*
The Norwich Mallard Cricket Club, formerly the Civil Service Cricket Club (Norwich): club records and statistics 1921–1970. [Norwich, the Compiler, 1970?]. scores, stats. *typescript*

**2439 Cricketing references in Norwich news-**
**–1** papers, 1701 to 1800 arranged in chrono-
■ logical order. Norwich, the Compiler, 1979. xvi,63f. *typescript*

**2440 Stanley Cricket Club**
Fixtures card and rules. Norwich, [the Club]. *annual*
*?/1896–98, 1902, 05, 08/–?*

### Thetford

2441 **Thetford Cricket Club**
Rules. Thetford, [the Club], *n.d.*

### Upper Sheringham

2442 **Upper Sheringham Cricket Club**
Programme. Holt, Arthur Preston, 1894
*other issues?*

## NORFOLK C.C.C.

2443 **Armstrong, David John Michael**
■ A short history of Norfolk county cricket.
Holt (Norfolk), the Author, 1958. 32p.

2444 **Norfolk County Cricket Club**
Handbook of the grand Venetian fête and
bazaar . . . 2–4 April, 1891. Norwich, [the
Club], 1891. 50p. incl. adverts.
*includes a history of the club by H.W.*
*Turner*

2445 Season 1905: souvenir of a record season.
■ Norwich, the Club, [1905]. 52p. port.
scores, stats.

2446 Annual report. Norwich, the Club. illus.
ports. scores, stats.
*?/1948 . . . 78/to date*
*1977 was 150th anniversary season*

## NORTHAMPTONSHIRE

2447 **Northamptonshire County Cricket**
□ **League**
Official handbook and list of fixtures for
season. [Northampton], the League.
*annual.* ports. scores, stats.
*1951–1955*
*1956–1972 with title: Year book*
*not issued 1973*

2448 **Northamptonshire** cricket annual 1890;
■ edited by Arthur E. Daniell. Northampton, Spence, 1890. 84p. port. scores, stats.
*the only issue; covers both county and club*
*cricket*

2449 **Northamptonshire** past and present.
■ Northampton, Northamptonshire Record
Society.
*Vol. II, no. 3 (1956)*
*pp. 131–7 "Early Northamptonshire*
*cricket" by James D. Coldham*
*Vol. IV, no. 4 (1970)*
*p. 214 "Ladies' cricket match at Courteen-*
*hall, 23rd July 1883" by Joan Wake*
*Vol. IV, no. 5 (1971)*
*pp. 321–3 "Cricket at Althorp, 1867" by*
*Stephen Green*
*Vol. V, no. 4 (1976)*
*pp. 363–5 "A Northamptonshire cricket*
*song": an article on the song composed by J.P.*
*Kingston by James D. Coldham with*
*biographical notices of the players*

2450 **The Victoria** history of the counties of
■ England: Northamptonshire; edited by
Rev. R.M. Serjeantson and W. Ryland D.
Adkins. Vol. 2. Constable, 1906.
*cricket pp. 388–93. stats.*

### Billing

2450 **Billing Cricket Club**
–1 Souvenir book. Billing, the Club. *annual.*
□ stats. of season
*?/1969, 1970/to date?*

### Boughton

2450 **Kimbell, Charles Eaton**
–2 Boughton, Northants, in the eighties. The
Mitre P., [1951]. 52p.
*cricket pp. 40–8*

### Great Oakley

2451 **Bagshaw, Harold,** *and* **Bagshaw, Edward**
■ Great Oakley cricket: the history of a
village club. [Corby, P.H.G. Bagshaw],
1964. 57p. ports.

### Kettering

2452 **Kettering and District Cricket League**
□ [Handbook]. Kettering, the League
*?/1936 . . . 57/to date?*

### Northampton

2453 **Nethercote, Henry Osmond**
■ The Pytchley hunt, past and present: its
history from its foundation with personal
anecdotes of the masters and principal
members . . . Sampson Low, 1888.
x,376p. 1 illus. ports.
——2nd ed. by Charles Edmonds. 1888.
*pp. 139–43 on Northampton C.C. and other*
*cricket references pp. 44, 94–95, 132*

2454 **Northampton Cricket League**
□ [Handbook]. Northampton, the League
*?1887/1956–67/to date?*
*formed 1886*

### Peterborough

2455 **Peterborough and District Cricket**
□ **League**
Official handbook. Peterborough. *annual*
*season?/1969/to date*
*formed 1908*

## Silverstone

2456 **Linnell, John Edward**
Old oak: the story of a forest village;
edited with a memoir of the author by
his sons [J.W. Linnell and C.D. Linnell].
Constable, 1932. xxxiii,195p. illus. ports.
map
*includes references to cricket at Silverstone,
pp. 132–43*

# NORTHAMPTONSHIRE C.C.C.

2457 **Brown, William C.,** *and* **Smith, Cyril**
■ Northamptonshire County Cricket Club
records 1905–1949; edited by A. St. G.
Coldwell. [Northampton, the Club,
1950.] 32p. stats.

2458 **Coldham, James Desmond**
■ Northamptonshire cricket: a history.
Heinemann, 1959. x,318p. illus. ports.
stats.

2459 ———, *compiler*
■ Northamptonshire v. Yorkshire at the
wicket 1908–1960. The Author, [1961].
16p. stats.
*limited ed. of 25 copies only, reptd. from
The Journal of the Cricket Society, Apr.
1961*

2460 **Northamptonshire County Cricket Club**
Annual dinner: song by the Captain (J.P.
Kingston, Esq.). Northampton, the Club.
bs.
*tune: "Bonny Dundee"*

2461 Year book. Northampton, the Club. illus.
□ ports. scores, stats.
*seasons 1925–39, 1946–65
1946 contains results & scores of 1939
contd. as: Annual report and statement of
accounts*

2461 Grand bazaar, Town Hall, Northampton,
–1 Wednesday March 15, 1939 . . . Thursday
■ March 16, 1939: official programme.
Northampton, the Club, [1939]. 24p. incl.
adverts.

2462 Membership campaign 1962. [North-
■ ampton, Northamptonshire C.C.C.,
1962]. 13p. illus. ports.

2462 Winter newsletter. Northampton, the
–1 Club. *annual*
□ *?/1964 . . . 1972/–?*

2463 Annual report and statement of accounts.
□ Northampton, the Club. illus. ports.
stats.
*seasons/1966 . . . 78/to date
formerly: Yearbook*

2464 **Northamptonshire** cricket annual 1890;
■ edited by Arthur E. Daniell. Northampton, Spence, 1890. 84p. ports. scores,
stats.
*the only issue; covers both county and club
cricket*

# NORTHUMBERLAND

2465 **Cleveland,** Durham, Northumberland
and Yorkshire cricketer's handbook.
Bury, Fletcher & Speight, 1882
*contd. as: The Durham and Yorkshire
cricketer's handbook*

2466 **The Cricketers'** handbook containing the
match fixtures of the principal clubs in
Northumberland, Durham and North
Yorkshire. Bury, Fletcher & Speight.
*annual. illus.
1891–3, 1897–1900
1891 issue with title: Henry A. Murton's
cricketers' companion*

2467 **Harbottle, George**
■ A century of cricket in south Northumberland, 1864–1969. Newcastle upon
Tyne, Fenwick & Wade, 1969. 87p. illus.
ports. map, plan, scores

2468 **Lambert, Thomas,** *compiler*
■ Cricket annual for Northumberland and
Durham, 1896. Newcastle-on-Tyne,
Lambert, [1896]. 110p. stats.
*results of 1895, fixtures for 1896*

2468 **North-Eastern Cricket Club**
–1 Rules & regulations. Newcastle, the Club,
[1860]. 8p.
*established 1859; contains officers of the
Club for 1860*

2468 **Stevens, B.D.R.**
–2 Northumberland's non-league cricket
■ clubs. Newcastle-upon-Tyne, Smith Print
Group, 1978. 180p. 1 illus. ports. stats.
*limited ed. of 120 copies*

## Newcastle

2468 **Middlebrook, Sydney**
–3 Newcastle upon Tyne: its growth and
■ achievement. Newcastle, Newcastle
Journal and Chronicle Ltd., 1950.
xii,361p. illus. maps, plans
———rptd. with revisions. Wakefield, S.R.
Publishers, 1968. xii,361,[25]p.
*with appendix 1950–1968
cricket pp. 223–4, 302–3*

## Tynemouth

2469 **The Borough of Tynemouth Cricket Club**
■ Souvenir of the centenary dinner

1847–1947 held at Grand Hotel, Tynemouth on Friday 25th April, 1947. [Tynemouth, the Club], 1947. 8p. illus. ports.
*with brief extracts from records*

## Tyneside

**2469** **Lawson, William D.**
**-1** Lawson's Tyneside celebrities: sketches of the lives and labours of famous men of the North. The Author, 1873. xii,387p. illus.
*cricket pp. 304–5*

**2470** **Tyneside Senior Cricket League**
[Handbook]. Newcastle, the League. *annual*
*?1902–14, ?1920 to date*

# NORTHUMBERLAND C.C.C.

**2471** **Northumberland County Cricket Club**
□ Annual report and financial statement. Newcastle, the Club. illus. ports. scores, stats.
*1947–55*
*1956 to date with title: Yearbook*

# NOTTINGHAMSHIRE

**2472** **Daft, Richard**
■ A cricketer's yarns; to which have been added a few genealogical tables of Nottinghamshire cricketing families; ed. with an introduction by F.S. Ashley-Cooper. Chapman & Hall, 1926. xix,201p. illus. ports.

**2472** **Howitt, William**
**-1** The rural life of England. 2 vols. Longman, etc., 1838. illus.
*Vol. II, ch. x, pp. 273–6 gives an account of a match played Sept., 1835 between the Sussex Club and the Nottingham Club. The extract is quoted in The language of cricket, by W.J. Lewis, pp. 315–6*

**2473** **Nottinghamshire Amateur Cricket**
□ **League**
Rules and fixtures. Nottingham, the Club. *annual*
*1953/1953 . . . 75/to date*

**2474** **Nottinghamshire and Derbyshire Border**
□ **Cricket League**
[Handbook]. The League
*1921?/1955–58/to date*
*formed 1920*

**2475** Rules. The League, 1972. 15p.
■

**2476** **Notts. Cricket Association**
□ Official handbook. Nottingham, the Association. *annual*. team ports. scores
*?/1951–79/ to date*
*formed 1900; earliest extant copy (1951) at Trent Bridge*

**2477** **The Nottinghamshire** cricketers' handbook. Bury, Fletcher & Speight. *annual*.
*1881*
*1882–3 with title: The Notts and Derby cricketers' handbook*
*1884 with title: The cricketers' handbook for Notts, Derby and Leicestershire*

**2478** **The Victoria** history of the counties of
■ England: Nottinghamshire; edited by William Page. Vol. 2. Constable, 1910
*cricket pp. 405–10. stats.*

**2479** **Wab's** cricket annual and who's who in Notts cricket; compiled by Walter A. Briscoe. Nottingham, Johnson
*1904. 44p.*
*1905. 112p.*

## Arnold

**2479** **A history** of Arnold, Nottinghamshire.
**-1** Nottingham, Saxton, 1913. xii,166p. illus. folding map
*cricket pp. 115–9 "Arnold cricketers" (mostly on the Oscrofts)*

## Bassetlaw

**2480** **Bassetlaw and District Cricket League**
□ Rules, fixtures, and list of registered players. The League
*3 issues 1904–14; 1920–1969*
*1970 to date with title: Official handbook. stats.*

**2480** **Langdale, George R.**
**-1** A history of the Bassetlaw & District
■ Cricket League 1904–1978. The Management Cttee. of the League, [1978]. [iii],85p. stats.

## Bothamsall

**2480** **Wynne-Thomas, Peter**
**-2** Bothamsall cricket and cricketers: a brief
■ essay to commemorate the 50th anniversary of the founding of the present village cricket club in 1926. Hampton in Arden (Warks.), Assoc. of Cricket Statisticians, 1976. 28p. ports. map, scores

## Calverton

**2480** **Turton, Amos**
**-3** Calverton Cricket Club 1869–1969. Newark, *printed by* F.H. Davage & Co., 1969. 16p. incl. adverts.

## Carlton

**2481 Carlton Cricket Club**
■ 1860–1960 centenary. Carlton, the Club. [6]p.
*officers & fixtures*

## Mansfield

**2481 Buxton, Albert Sorby**
**–1** Mansfield one hundred years ago. Mansfield, Linney, 1972. 98p. illus. (some col.), plans
*facsim. reprint of 1923 ed. Cricket pp. 63–5*

## Nottingham

**2482 Church, Roy A.**
■ Economic and social change in a Midland town: Victorian Nottingham 1815–1900. Cass, 1966. xxiv,409p. illus. maps, bibliog.
*cricket pp. 14–15, 210, 211–12, 376*

**2483 Gray, Duncan**
■ Nottingham: settlement to city. Nottingham, Nottingham Co-operative Society Ltd., 1953. [ix],127p. illus. (1 col.), map on end-papers
*cricket pp. 53, 64, 74, 86, 92, 109*

**2484 Hogarth, Robert George**
■ The Trent and I go wandering by: stories of over fifty years of my life in Nottingham. Nottingham, Cooke & Vowles, [1949]. xi,144p. illus. ports.
*Pres. of Notts. C.C.; cricket pp. 69–77 including account of Notts. Amateur C.C.*

**2484 A hundred** years at Bestwood Park
**–1** 1868–1968. Nottingham, 1968. 28p. incl. adverts.

**2485 Nottingham** and District cricket souvenir, 1899. Sheffield, Yorkshire Advertising Co., [1899]. 48p. ports.
*pen-portraits of the famous cricketers of the day*

**2485 Nottingham Evening Cricket League**
**–1** Annual; compiled by G.F. Hornbuckle. Nottingham, the League.
*1977 to date*

**2486 Sutton, John Frost**
The date book of remarkable and memorable events connected with Nottingham and its neighbourhood, 1750–1850. London, Simpkin & Marshall; Nottingham, R. Sutton, 1852. 512p.
*several cricket references*
——1750–1879, from authentic records. Nottingham, H. Field, 1880. [i],v,608p. frontis.
——*another ed.* 1884. v,628p.

*cricket 1880–1884 on pp. 611, 614, 619, 621, 627*

**2487** ————, *compiler*
■ Nottingham cricket matches, from 1771 to 1853; with an introductory chapter, descriptive of the local history of the game; and brief sketches of the principal players. Nottingham, the Author, 1853. 118p. scores
——2nd ed. . . . from 1771 to 1859. Sutton Brothers, 1859. 118,22p
——3rd ed. . . . from 1771 to 1865. A.K. Sutton, 1865. 118p.

### Forest Wanderers

**2488 Wynne-Thomas, Peter**
■ A history of Forest Wanderers Cricket Club. Haughton (Notts), the Author, 1973. 52p. ports. stats.

### Nottingham Castle

**2489 Notts Castle Cricket Club**
Grand bazaar 1895. [Nottingham, the Club], 1895. 96p. incl. adverts. illus. ports. stats.
*with history of the club*

### Nottingham Forest Amateur Cricket Club

**2489 Devereux, Bernard**
**–1** A century in cricket: Nottingham Forest Amateur Cricket Club. Nottingham, the Club, 1976. 31p. illus.

**2490 Nottingham Forest Amateur Cricket**
■ **Club**
Records 1877–1901; [compiled by H.H. Goodall]. Nottingham, *printed by* W.B. Cooke, Thoroton P., 1902. 207p. ports. scores, stats.

**2491** Jubilee dinner 1877–1926: verbatim report of the speeches. Nottingham, *printed by* "Trader" Office, 1926. 17p.

### Nottingham Old Cricket Club

**2492 North, William**
A correct account of all the cricket matches played by the Nottingham Old Cricket Club from 1771 to 1829 inclusive. Nottingham, R. Sutton, 1830. 52p. scores
——2nd ed. 1836

**2493 Wynne-Thomas, Peter,** *compiler*
■ A complete register of cricketers to represent Nottingham Old Club and Nottinghamshire County Cricket Club from 1821 to 1965. London, the Author, 1966. [14]f. *typescript*
*some copies have amendments by author dated July 1966*

## Wollaton Cricket Club

**2493 Wollaton Cricket Club**
**-1** Black & White Minstrels v. Wollaton C.C., June 2nd, 1968: souvenir programme. Nottingham, the Club, 1968. 38p. incl. adverts.

## Plumtree

**2494 Cover** point: a journal of Plumtree C.C.
☐ *annual? typescript*
*?/1970/to date?*
*issue Oct. 1970 was 6th; [edited by W.S. Smith]*

**2495 Plumtree Cricket Club**
■ Plumtree C.C. v. Nottinghamshire County Cricket Club, 5th Sept. 1971: Brian Bolus benefit; edited by W.S. Smith. Plumtree (Notts), the Club, [1971]. 36p. incl. adverts. ports.

## Retford

**2495 Hopkinson, C.W.,** *and* **Birkett, H.J.**
**-1** Retford cricket and cricketers 1850–1950. Retford, *printed by* Retford, Gainsborough & Worksop Times Co. Ltd., 1950. 32p. incl. adverts. illus. stats.

## Sutton-in-Ashfield

**2495 Bonser, George Gersham**
**-2** A history of Sutton-in-Ashfield. Nottingham, *printed by* Cooke and Vowles Ltd, *n.d.* vii,178p. illus.
*cricket pp. 91–2*

**2495 History** of Sutton-in-Ashfield, or, Past
**-3** links with the present. [Nottingham], L. Lindley, 1907. 40,80p. ports.
*pp. 33–4 contains a section "The nursery of cricket" with portraits of J.C. Shaw and T. Wass*

## Wiseton

**2495 Edwards, R.F.**
**-4** Wiseton Cricket Club: the centenary history 1877–1977. [Wiseton, the Club], 1977. 24p. illus.

# NOTTINGHAMSHIRE C.C.C.

**2496 Ashley-Cooper, Frederick Samuel**
■ Surrey v. Notts at the wicket. "Cricket" Office, 1899. 16p. ports. stats.
——*another issue* with an "Addendum" 1900

**2497** John Wisden's cricket match histories II.
■ Surrey v. Notts. 1851–1921. Wisden, [1922]. 16p. stats.

**2498** Nottinghamshire cricket and cricketers.
■ Nottingham, H.B. Saxton, 1923. vii,410p. stats. bibliog.

**2499** Nottinghamshire cricket in 1923; being a
■ continuation of "Notts. scores and biographies". Nottingham, Richards, 1923. 48p. scores, stats.

**2500** Nottinghamshire cricket records.
■ Nottingham, Richards, 1928. 20p. stats.

**2501** Nottinghamshire cricket championship
■ souvenir, 1929. Nottingham, Richards, 1929. 17p. stats.
——2nd ed. 1929

**2501 Association of Cricket Statisticians**
**-1** Nottingham cricketers 1835–1978; [compiled by Peter Wynne-Thomas]. The Assoc., 1978. 36p. stats.

**2502 Bayly, A. Eric,** *and* **Briscoe, Walter**
■ **Alwyn**
Chronicles of a country cricket club; being odd tales of the national game. Sands, 1900. 146p.

**2503 Browne, Edwin**
■ A short history of Nottinghamshire cricket, including the season of 1887. Nottingham, G. Richards, 1887. 56p. ports. scores, stats.

**2504 Hunter, T.R.**
Complete account and full statistics of all matches, Nottinghamshire v Australia 1878–1930. *MS*
*now in Notts C.C.C. library, Trent Bridge*

**2505 Lane, John D.,** *compiler*
■ Surrey v. Nottingham, 1851–1959. The Author, [1960]. [22]p. stats. (Cricket match history)

**2505 Lester, John Henry**
**-1** Nottinghamshire cricket 1789–1912: aggregate records of batting, bowling, wicket keeping and catches, made by every player taking part in Nottinghamshire cricket during the period . . . . London, 1912. 140p. stats.
*unpublished MS. In A.E. Winder's collection*

**2506 Lucas, Edward Verrall,** *editor*
■ A hundred years of Trent Bridge. Nottingham, *privately printed* for Sir Julien Cahn, 1938. xi,80p. illus. (1 col.). ports.

**2507 Mellors, Robert**
■ Men of Nottingham and Nottinghamshire. Nottingham, Bell, 1924. viii,351p.
——*rptd.* with suppl. (1925). Wakefield S.R. Publishers, 1969. viii,368p.
*cricketers pp. 107–08*

2508 **The Nottinghamshire** county cricket
■ annual: being a continuation of "Notts.
scores & biographies"; compiled by C.H.
Richards. Nottingham, the Compiler.
*annual. illus. scores, stats.*
*season 1901–4 and 1907 compiled by C.H.*
*Richards, 1913*

2509 **Nottinghamshire County Cricket Club**
Rules and list of members. Nottingham,
the Club, 1914. 118p.

2510 Annual report and balance sheet.
□ Nottingham, the Club.
*1891 to date*
*earliest extant issue, 1892, at Trent Bridge.*
*In 1980 combined with no. 2513, but sepa-*
*rated again in 1981*
——Supplement to Annual Report of the
Committee 1935. Nottingham, the Club,
[1935]. 10p.
*concerning Larwood, Voce and 'body-line'*

2511 Year book; edited by Sir Home Gordon.
Nottingham, the Club. illus.
*3 issues only 1932–4*

2512 Season 1946: a guide for the use of
patrons at Trent Bridge Ground. Nottingham, the Club, 1946. 8p.

2513 [Handbook]. Nottingham, the Club.
□ *annual. illus. ports. scores, stats. in v.y.*
*1948 to date*
*see no. 2510*

2514 Membership campaign 63. [Nottingham,
■ the Club, 1963]. 14p. illus. ports.

2515 Notts County Cricket Club and Trent
■ Bridge: [souvenir handbook]. Nottingham, the Club, 1946. illus. ports. stats.
*the forerunner of no. 2513, the first issue*
*of which, published 1948, covered 1947 season*

2515 Notts. cricket voice: official magazine of
–1 Nottinghamshire C.C.C. Nottingham,
the Club. *tabloid format*
*1st issue April 29, 1972*
*2nd issue May, 7, 1972*
*any more issued?*
*published before every home one-day game*

2515 A Silver Jubilee tribute to Her Majesty the
–2 Queen marking the Queen's visit to Trent
Bridge, July 28, 1977. Nottingham, the
Club, 1977. 28p. incl. adverts. illus. scores

2515 **Nottinghamshire** county cricket matches
–3 1881. Nottingham, Geo. Richards, 1881.
18p. scores
*"First year of publication" printed on cover*

2516 **Nottinghamshire** versus New Zealand:
pictures, fixtures and personalities, 1949.

Birmingham, E. Kavanagh, 1949. [4]p.
fold. ports.

2517 **Richards, Charles Henry,** *compiler*
■ Nottinghamshire cricket scores and biographies. Nottingham, G. Richards. ports.
scores, stats.
*Vol 1. from 1838 (Opening of the Trent*
*Bridge Ground), 1888. [iv],41,179,[2]p.*
*the 41 page sequence is biographical, the*
*179 contains match scores; contains mounted*
*team-portrait of Nottinghamshire XI of 1866*
*Vol. 2 1838–1890; compiled by C.H. Rich-*
*ards. 1890. pp.42–82; 183–388*
*the first pagination sequence follows the*
*biographical sequence of vol. 1, and the second*
*sequence continues the match scores*
——Vols. 1 and 2 were also issued with
title: *Fifty years of Nottinghamshire cricket,*
*1838–1887: being vols. 1 and 2 of "Notts.*
*cricket scores and biographies". Nottingham,*
*G. Richards, 1890. [iv],82,388p. ports. scores*
*Vol. 3. 1888–89–90 with other important*
*matches played in and around Nottingham.*
*Nottingham, C.H. Richards, 1891. [iii],*
*83–122, 389–492*
*the 2 pagination sequences follows those of*
*vol. 2.*
the 3 vols. were also issued bound tog.
with title: *Nottinghamshire cricket scores and*
*biographies 1838 to 1890 . . . Nottingham,*
*C.H. Richards, 1891. [iv],492p. ports. scores,*
*stats.*
*contains the mounted team-portrait of*
*Notts. XI of 1866*
——[continuation volumes]
*season 1891. iii,493–526p. scores, stats.*
*season 1892. iii,527–557p. scores, stats.*
——*Nottinghamshire cricket scores and biog-*
*raphies. Vol. 2. 1888 to 1900. 1903. [iii],*
*83–134,1–7,389–808*
*contd. as: The Nottinghamshire county*
*cricket annual*

2518 **Richards, Charles Henry**
□ Celebrated Nottinghamshire cricketers.
Nottingham, G. Richards, 1890
——*another ed. with title:* Nottinghamshire
cricketers: photographs and account of
the players. Nottingham, C.H. Richards,
1897. 22p. 1 illus. ports.

2518 Notts. C.C.C. souvenir championship
–1 year 1907–1908. Nottingham, C.H. Richards, 1908. 48p. ports. stats.

2519 **Richards'** Nottinghamshire cricket guide.
■ Nottingham, Richards. *annual.* ports.
stats.
*1903–07 edited by C.H. Richards,*
*1910–14, 1920*
*1921–31; edited by 'Incog', [F.S. Ashley-*
*Cooper]*

2520 **Sharman, A.,** *compiler*
■ Notts. cricket for the season 1883; full
scores of county matches, bowling

analysis, batting and bowling averages. Basford (Nottingham), F.R. Webb, 1883. 16p. scores, stats.

2521 **Shelton, A.W.**
Nottinghamshire County Cricket Club: complete list of members of the committee. 1936. *MS.*
*in Trent Bridge Library*

2522 **Nottinghamshire** county cricket, 1835–1935: a complete list of the 360 men who have played for the county. 1936. *MS.*
*in Trent Bridge Library*

2523 **Spybey, Francis George,** *compiler*
■ Nottingham county cricket matches, from 1865 to 1877 inclusive. Nottingham, Spybey, 1878. 127p. scores
contd. as: *Spybey's Annual register of Nottingham county cricket matches*

2524 Annual register of Nottingham county cricket matches, with bowling analysis and batting averages. Nottingham, Spybey. scores, stats.
*9 issues 1878–86; 2 issues of 1884*

2524 **Trent Bridge** journal. Nottingham,
–1 *printed by* R. Milward & Sons.
No. 1. June 1963. 12p. illus. scores (of matches played in May)
2. Nov.? 1963. 10p. *typescript.* (News items only)
*no more issued?*

2524 **Trent Bridge** monthly; edited by Terry
–2 Bowles and John Lawson. Trent Bridge,
□ Nottingham, the Editors. illus. ports. scores
*May 1979 to date*
*tabloid format, published in May, June, July, August*

2525 **"Underwood"**
■ Who's who in Nottinghamshire County Cricket Club: 20 caricatures and biographies drawn & compiled by Underwood. Nottingham, Barnes & Humby, [1946]. folded bs. illus.

2526 **Walker, Violet**
Nottinghamshire County Cricket Club: list of men who have played for the county from 1936 onwards. 1938. 3p. of text. *MS.*
*in Trent Bridge Library*

2527 **Wynne-Thomas, Peter,** *compiler*
■ A complete register of cricketers to represent Nottingham Old Club and Nottinghamshire County Cricket Club from 1821 to 1965. London, the Author, 1966. [14]f. *typescript*
*some copies have amendments by author dated July 1966*

2528 Nottinghamshire cricketers 1821–1914.
■ Haughton, Retford, Notts., The Author, 1971. 362p. ports. stats. bibliog.

2528 Nottinghamshire cricketers 1919–1939.
–1 Nottingham, Notts. C.C.C., 1979. 114p. ports.

2529 **Ye famous** battel of Trent Bridge, a most ancient ballad to ye tune of 'Ye bailiff's daughter of Islington'. [c.1880]. bs.
*celebrated Notts C.C.C. victory v. The Australians in 1880?*

2530 **Yorkshire** v. Notts. London, *n.d.* illus.
*in Taylor*

# OXFORDSHIRE

2531 **Oxfordshire Cricket Association**
□ [Handbook]. Oxford, the Association. *annual*
*1920?/1968/to date*
*formed 1919; no cricket 1940–45*

2532 **South Oxfordshire Amateurs**
■ Report for the season. The Club
*1934 and 1935. [1935]*
*1936, 1937, 1938*
*1939–47. [1948]*
*1948–52. [1953]*
*1960–71 with title* History of the years 1960–1971, *by Peter Frankenburg. [1972]. [iii],244p.*
*the years 1953–59 not published*

## Charlbury

2532 **Charlbury Cricket Club**
–1 In aid of 'The Primary Club' for blind
■ young cricketers: grand cricket match Gloucestershire XI versus Charlbury C.C. at Charlbury, 15 Sept. 1979. [Charlbury, the Club, 1979]. 32p. incl. covers & adverts. 1 illus.
*includes a brief history of cricket in Charlbury*

## Kidmore End

2533 **Townsend, W.E.**
A history of cricket in Kidmore End: Kidmore End Cricket Club 1863–1955. [Kidmore End, the Club], 1956. 8p. ports.
——[rev. ed.] *with title:* 100 not out: a history of cricket in Kidmore End since 1863. [Kidmore End, the Club], 1968. 14p. ports.

## Oxford

2534 **Oxford City Cricket Club**
Report, list of subscribers and balance sheet for 1892. Oxford, [the Club], 1893. 15p.

## Wheatley

**2535 Oxfordshire Record Society**
■ Wheatley records 956–1956; edited by W.O. Hassall. Vol.xxxvii. The Society, 1956. 199p. illus. maps
*cricket, pp.76, 77, 90 & 100, including a reference to "cricket batts' in an inventory of William Thoms of Wheatley dated 1750*

## OXFORDSHIRE C.C.C.

**2536 Frewer, Louis B.**
■ Oxfordshire county cricket 1945–1970 (with an epilogue, 1971, 1972). Oxford, [the Club], 1973. [i],40p. frontis. stats.

**2537 Oxfordshire County Cricket Club**
□ Report, balance sheet, list of subscribers, etc. Oxford, the Club. ports. stats.
*season1947/1947–78/todate*

**2538** Rules. Oxford, the Club, 1953. 8p.
■

## SHROPSHIRE

**2539 The Victoria** history of the counties of
■ England: Shropshire; edited by A.T. Gaydon. Vol. 2. O.U.P., 1973
*cricket pp.194–97*

### Ellesmere

**2540 Hall, P.A.,** *editor*
■ Fifty years of Ellesmere, 1884–1934. Eyre & Spottiswoode, 1934. xvi,199p. illus. ports.
*many cricket references and plates*

## SHROPSHIRE C.C.C.

**2541 Shropshire County Cricket Association**
□ Handbook. [Shrewsbury], the Association. *annual*. scores
*?/1952. . .54/1956?*

**2542 Shropshire County Cricket Club**
□ Handbook. Shrewsbury, the Club. *annual*. illus. scores, stats.
*1957?/1965. . . 74/todate*

**2543 Shropshire Cricket Club**
Statement of accounts, list of members, matches, scores, averages etc. for the year. Shrewsbury, the Club. *annual*.
*seasons 1865–70*

## SOMERSET

**2544 Somerset Stragglers Cricket Club**
□ [Handbook]. Taunton, the Club. *annual*. scores, stats.
*?/1931,32,35–38/–?*

formed 1900; 1931 issue contains a history of the club, and 1932 a supplement

**2545 Tate, William James**
■ Old Somersetshire cricketing days: a record of some matches played at Wells, Shepton Mallet, Glastonbury, Yeovil, Langport, Chewton Mendip, &c. from the years 1853 to 1865. London, Blackwood; Wells, J.M. Atkins, 1895. xii,71p. scores
——2nd ed. 1895. xii,73p.

**2546 The Victoria** history of the counties of
■ England: Somerset; edited by William Page. Vol. 2. Constable, 1911
*cricket pp.597–600. stats.*

## Bath

**2547 The Bath** and district cricketers' companion. Bury, Fletcher & Speight, 1891. 40p.

**2548 Bath** cricket: a weekly journal devoted to the game in Bath and neighbourhood. Bath, J.J. Goodwin, 8p. ports. scores, stats.
*20 issues 10 May–20 Sept. 1893*

**2549 Bath Cricket Club**
■ Centenary handbook, founded 1859. Bath, the Club, [1959]. 80p. illus. ports. scores, stats.

### Lansdown

**2550 Bradfield, Donald**
■ The Lansdown story: the history of Lansdown Cricket Club. [Bath], the Club, 1971. [xvi], 117p. illus. ports. scores, stats.

**2551 Lansdown** Cricket Club matches 1825–
■ 1851. Bath, R.E. Peach, *for priv. circulation*, 1852. [iv],120p. scores

## Clevedon

**2551 McBride, Piers J.**
**–1** Fools on the hill. Clevedon, Clevedon C.C., 1975. 28p. *typescript*

## Midsomer Norton

**2551 Taylor, R.C.,** *and* **Bell, Michael T.,**
**–2** *compilers and editors*
■ Not out 100: Midsomer Norton Cricket Club 1878–1978. [Midsomer Norton, the Club, 1978]. [vi], 105p. illus. ports. facsims.

## Weston-Super-Mare

**2551** **Buckley, George Bent**
**–3** Weston-super-Mare Cricket Club
1845–1891. 234p. *typescript*

**2552** **Weston-Super-Mare Cricket Club**
☐ Handbook. Weston-super-Mare C.C.
illus. *annual*
*1954?/1954 to date/*

## SOMERSET C.C.C.

**2553** **Ashley–Cooper, Frederick Samuel**
■ Somerset county cricket. George W. May,
1924. 36p. illus. ports.

**2553** **Association of Cricket Statisticians,**
**–1** *compilers*
■ Somerset cricketers 1875–1974. Hampton
in Arden (Warks.), the Assoc., 1974. 36p.
stats.
*limited ed. of 500 numbered copies*

**2554** **Davies, John,** *editor*
■ Up from Somerset for the cup: the story
of Somerset's fight to the final. The
Editor, for the Somerset Players Welfare
Fund, [1967]. [40]p. illus. ports. (1 col.),
score
*the Gillette Cup, 1967*

**2554** **Foot, David,** *editor*
**–1** Ton-up for Somerset 1875–1975. [Bristol,
■ Somerset C.C.C., 1975]. 64p. incl.
adverts. illus. ports. stats.

**2554** **The Guardian**
**–2** The bedside 'Guardian' 24: a selection
■ from The Guardian 1974–75; edited by
W.L. Webb. Collins, 1975. 263p. illus.
*includes "Close thing at Taunton", by
Frank Keating (on Somerset v. Northamptonshire) July' 75*

**2555** **Gustard, Frederick Joseph Charles,**
■ *compiler*
Somerset county cricket: facts and figures
from 1891 to 1924. Taunton, Barnicott &
Pearce, 1925. 64p. stats.

**2556** **Lane, John D.,** *compiler*
■ Surrey v. Somerset, 1879–1958. The
Author, 1959. [18]p. stats. (Cricket match
history)

**2557** **Roberts, Ronald Arthur**
■ Sixty years of Somerset cricket. Westaway, 1952. 208p. illus. ports. scores, stats.

**2558** **Somerset County Cricket Club**
☐ [Year book]. Taunton, the Club. ports.
scores, stats
*seasons 1890–1905*
*1906–08 not issued*
*1909–13, 1920–39*

*1940–46 issued in 1 vol.*
*1947–67*
contd. as *Cricket in Somerset*

**2559** Membership campaign. [Taunton,
■ Somerset C.C.C., 1962]. 13p. illus.

**2560** Cricket in Somerset: the handbook of the
■ Somerset C.C.C. & club cricket 1967/68.
[Taunton, the Club, 1968]. illus. ports.
scores, stats.

**2561** The Somerset dragon: the official maga-
☐ zine of the Somerset C.C.C. [Taunton,
the Club]. *annual.* illus. ports. scores
*1969*
"The Year book and The Dragon have
been merged"; report on 1968

**2561** Annual report and statement of accounts.
**–1** Taunton, the Club.
*1969*
*1970–78 with cricket tables & statistics*
contd. by Handbook (no. 2561–3)

**2561** Somerset v. Australian touring team,
**–2** 1977. Taunton, the Club, [1977]. 18p.
*commemorates Somerset's first victory over
an Australian team*

**2561** Handbook. [Taunton], the Club. illus.
**–3** ports. scores, stats. *annual*
■ *1979 to date*
*1979 issue edited by Eric Coombes; a contin-
uation of nos. 2558, 2560, 2561, and 2561–1*

**2562** **Somerset** County Cricket Club. Bristol,
Arrowsmith, 1878. 22p.

**2562** **Somerset Wyverns**
**–1** Newsletter. Taunton, the Club. *typescript*
☐ *no. 17, Spring 1979*
*the Somerset C.C.C. Supporters Club*

**2563** **Trump, R.F.,** *compiler*
■ Facts and figures of Somerset County
Cricket Club (including all players) from
1891–1946, published in aid of Frank
Lee's benefit. [Taunton, the Club, 1947].
36p. stats.

## STAFFORDSHIRE

**2564** **North Staffordshire and District Cricket**
☐ **League**
[Handbook]. The League. *annual.* ports.
stats. *in v.y.*
*?/1890–1914, ?1919–39, 1946? to date*
*formed 1889; in recent years with title:
Report*

**2565** **North Staffordshire and South Cheshire**
■ **Cricket League**
Annual report. The League. stats.

*1963, 1964*
1965 to date with title: *Official report*

2566 Official handbook. The League
■ 1963 to date

2567 **South Staffordshire Cricket League**
Handbook. The League. *annual?*
*?/1948/–?*

2568 **Staffordshire Cricket Association**
Newsletter: the voice of Staffordshire
cricket. The Association. *monthly*
*May–Sept. typescript*
*1973?–*

2569 **The Staffordshire Sentinel**
□ Cricket annual. Hanley, Staffordshire
Sentinel. ports. stats.
*1907–12*
*1913–14, 1922–24* with title: *Sentinel*
*cricket annual*

2570 **The Victoria** history of the counties of
■ England: Staffordshire: edited by M.W.
Greenslade and J.G. Jenkins. Vol. 2.
O.U.P., 1967
*cricket pp.368–70. illus.*

2571 **Watson, William Gatus**
■ Staffordshire cricket: records: reviews:
reminiscences from the earlier years of
the nineteenth century to 1923. Stafford,
Allison & Bowen, 1924. 246p. scores

## Aldridge

2572 **Matthews, Jack**
■ Aldridge cricket: a review. [The Author],
1948. 44p. illus. team ports.

## Aston

2573 **Patterson, T.M.,** *compiler*
■ Doings of the Aston C.C. 1896–1901. The
Compiler, 1901. 76p. scores

## Brewood

2573 **Brewood Cricket Club**
–1 Golden jubilee 1919–1969. Brewood, the
■ Club, [1969]. 32p. incl. adverts. illus.
ports. scores, stats.

## Cannock

2574 **Cannock Cricket Club**
■ Centenary, 1860–1960: souvenir. [Can-
nock, the Club, 1960]. [24]p. illus. stats.

## Dudley Kingswinford

2575 **[Dudley Kingswinford Cricket Club]**
■ Ladies v. men cricket match at Heath-

brook, Wall Heath, Sunday, 2 July, 1967:
Rachel Heyhoe International Ladies XI v.
Dudley Kingswinford C.C. [Dudley, the
Club, 1967]. [20p]. incl. adverts

## Enville

2576 **Enville Cricket Club**
■ Centenary festival 1850–1950. [Enville,
the Club, 1950]. 3p. illus. score

## Fordhouses

2576 **Fordhouses Cricket Club**
–1 The occasion of the official opening of
■ the new pavilion by E.R. Dexter, Esq.,
20 September 1964: souvenir programme.
[Fordhouses, the Club, 1964]. 8p. incl.
covers.
*includes brief history of the Club by J.T.*
*("Old Trafford")*

## Kidsgrove

2577 **Kidsgrove and District Junior Cricket**
□ **League**
Annual report. Kidsgrove, the League.
stats.
*season 1947?/1956 . . . 73/to date*

2578 [Handbook]. Kidsgrove, the League.
□ *annual.* port. stats.
*1948/1964–69/to date*

2579 **Trafford, H.S.**
An historical survey of Kidsgrove
(Clough Hall) Cricket Club since its incep-
tion. The Author, 1963. 32p. ports.

## Leek

2579 **Bailey, S.W.,** *compiler*
–1 A century of Leek cricket 1844–1944.
■ [Leek, the Club, 1944]. 48p. ports. stats.

2579 **Miller, Matthew Henry,** *editor*
–2 Olde Leeke, historical, biographical,
anecdotal, and archaeological. Reprinted
from the "Leek Times". Leek, Times
Office, 1891. xviii,350p. illus.
*cricket pp.124–31*

2580 **Tipper, Tom**
■ Records, recollections and reminiscences
of 80 years of Leek cricket 1844–1924.
[Leek, the Club, 1925?] 461p. ports. stats.

## Norton

2581 **Norton Cricket Club & Miners' Welfare**
□ **Institute**
Annual report. Norton, the Club. stats.
*?/1967/to date?*

## Tamworth

2582 **Lloyd, Bernard**
■ The story of Tamworth Cricket Club. [Tamworth, the Club, 1968]. 29p. ports. facsim.

## Trentham

2583 **Boullemier, Lucien,** *composer*
■ The Trentham Cricket Club song—"The good old has-beens". [The Club, c.1925]. 6p.

## Tutbury

2584 **Tutbury** Cricket Club 1872–1972:
■ centenary year; edited by T.L. Coxon and F.H. Wilson. Tutbury, the Club, [1972]. [40]p. team ports. scores, stats.

## Walsall

2585 **Cook, E.J.A.**
■ The Gorway story: the later history of Walsall Cricket Club. Walsall, the Club, 1959. 141p. illus. ports. stats.

2586 **Evans, Benjamin,** *and* **Griffin, John**
■ **Baldwin**
The history of the Walsall C.C. Walsall, J. & W. Griffin, "Observer" Office, 1904. 91p. illus. ports. scores, stats.
——*2nd edition,* by Benjamin Evans. Walsall, the Author, 1909. 86p. illus. ports. scores, stats.

## Wolverhampton

2587 **Smith, Irving W.**
■ Harborne Cricket Club versus Wolverhampton, 1901–1914: [a brief history of the matches]. The Author, [c.1915]. 20p.
*typescript*

# STAFFORDSHIRE C.C.C.

2588 **Staffordshire County Cricket Club**
□ Annual report, statement of accounts, full scores of matches, rules and list of members. Stoke-on-Trent, the Club. ports. scores, stats.
*?1891–1913, ?1919–1939, 1948 to date later issues with title "Year book"; until 1952 each issue contains record of the season's cricket indicated on cover, from 1954 each issue contains account of previous season, so no issue titled 1953*

2589 Staffordshire County Cricket Club,
■ winners of the Minor Counties' Cricket Championship 1920 & 1921: scores of matches, averages, and tables of results.

Stoke-on-Trent, the Club, 1922. 31p. port. scores, stats.

2590 [List of members, fixtures]. Stafford, the
□ Club
*?/1964/to date*
*1964 was centenary year*

# SUFFOLK

2591 **Suffolk County Cricket Association**
■ The Suffolk cricket annual; edited by R.L. Hodgson. Ipswich, the Association. scores, stats.
*3 issues 1903–05*

2591 Handbook. Ipswich, the Assoc. *annual.*
–1 team ports. scores, stats.
□ *?/1973/to date?*

## Eye

2592 **Jesse, Edward**
■ An angler's rambles. J. Van Voorst, 1836. vii,318p.
*"The Village Cricket Club" [Eye, Suffolk], pp.292–311*

## Ipswich

2592 **Ipswich & East Suffolk Cricket Club**
–1 125th anniversary cricket week, Chantry
■ Park, Ipswich, 22–28 July 1978: official handbook [edited by D.H. Freeman]. Ipswich, the Club, [1978]. 24p. incl. adverts. illus. ports. facsims. stats.

## Mildenhall

2592 **Mildenhall Cricket Club**
–2 Mildenhall cricket: centenary year
■ 1876–1976. Mildenhall, the Club, [1976?]. 33p. incl. adverts. illus. ports. stats.

## Newmarket

2593 **Hore, Herbert Francis**
Sporting and rural records of the Cleveley Estate. *Privately printed,* H. Cox, 1899. v,128p. illus.
*Newmarket cricket pp.69–75*

## Sudbury

2593 **Grimwood, C.G.,** *and* **Kay, S.A.**
–1 History of Sudbury, Suffolk. Sudbury, the Authors, 1952. 158p. illus. map
*cricket pp.17,133,135–6*

# SUFFOLK C.C.C.

2594 **Suffolk County Cricket Club**
■ Handbook. Ipswich, the Club. illus. *annual.* ports. scores, stats.
*1950 to date*

# SURREY

**2595 Alverstone, Richard Everard Webster,**
■ *viscount, and* **Alcock, Charles William,**
*editors*
Surrey cricket: its history and associations. Longmans, Green, 1902. xiii,539p.
illus. ports. scores, stats.
——*cheap edition.* 1905

**2596 Bonner, W.J.,** *editor*
■ Old Surrey cricketers. Dorking, Old
Dorkinian C.C., [1972]. [i],10p. *typescript.*
illus. on cover.
*early history of Surrey clubs and players*

**2597 [Duncombe, John]**
■ Surry triumphant: or the Kentish-mens
defeat; a new ballad; being a parody on
Chevy-Chace. Printed for J. Johnson,
1773. 24p. vignette on t.p.
*includes score of the match Surrey v. Kent
extracted from the Kentish Gazette of
Saturday, July 24, 1773*

**2598 Malden, Henry Elliot**
■ A history of Surrey. Elliot Stock, 1900.
viii,321p. (Popular County Histories)
*references to cricket in ch.23, "Social life
and customs" pp.304–6*

**2599 Montgomery, Henry Hutchinson**
■ Old cricket and cricketers. H. Stacey
Gold: Wright, 1890. [xiii],77p. illus. ports.
scores
*a reprint of the chs. on cricket from the
author's The History of Kennington. See
no. 2642*

**2600 Parker, Eric**
■ Highways and byways in Surrey: with
illustrations by Hugh Thomson. Macmillan, 1908. xix,452p. illus. map. (Highways and Byways Series)
——*2nd ed.* 1909
*scattered cricket references*

**2601** Surrey anthology. Museum P., 1952.
■ 248p. illus. ports.
*cricket pp.77–83*

**2602 Pope, L.T.**
■ A cup for cricket: fifty years of I'Anson
competition. Farnham, E.W. Langham,
1951. xi,101p. illus. ports. scores, stats.
*an account of the I'Anson competition
between village clubs along the Surrey-
Hampshire border*

**2603 South Thames Cricket League**
■ Fixtures. The League. *annual.*
*1973*
*1974 to date with title Year book. team
port. stats.*

**2604 [Sturt, George]**
■ The Bettesworth book: talks with a Surrey
peasant, by George Bourne [pseud.].
Lamley, 1901. 325p.
*another ed.* Duckworth, 1911. vi,325p.
(The Reader's Library)
——*rptd.* Duckworth, 1920. xiv,325p.
*cricket ch. xxvii,pp.237–39*
——facsimile rpt. of 2nd ed. [i.e. 2nd
imp.] 1902. Firle (Sx.), Caliban Books,
1978. [vii],280p.

**2605 Surrey Association of Cricket Clubs**
■ Illustrated handbook; edited by Louis
Palgrave. The Association. *annual.* illus.
ports. scores
*3 issues 1948–9, 1951*
*1st issue contains "brief histories of 200
cricket clubs in the county of Surrey'. No issue
for 1950, the 1951 issue entitled "Illustrated
annual"*

**2606 Surrey County Cricket League**
Official handbook and fixtures list.
Worcester Park, the League. *annual.*
*1971 to date*
*From 1974 known as Truman Surrey
County Cricket League*

**2606 The Surrey** magazine; edited by James
**–1** Cassidy. illus. *monthly*
*Vol. 1. Apr. 1899–Mar. 1900*
*includes pp. 40–44 "Surrey cricket
1773–1844" and pp. 73–77 "Surrey cricket –
second period", both by W.M. Wilcox*

**2607 Surrey Cricket Clubs Championship**
□ **Association**
Official handbook and fixtures programme. Cheam, The Assoc. *annual.*
illus. ports. scores, stats.
*1969–1977*
*covers previous season; title changed to
'Yearbook' 1973*
contd. as:
**Surrey Championship Association**
Official handbook 1978
contd. as:
**The Surrey Championship**
Yearbook 1979

**2607 Surrey Cricketers' League**
**–1** Handbook. The League. *annual.*
□ *1978 to date; edited by John Marriott
founded 1971*

**2608 The Victoria** history of the counties of
■ England: Surrey; edited by H.E. Malden.
Vol. 2. J. Street, 1905.
*cricket pp.526–49. illus. stats.*

**2609 [See no. 1289]**
■

**2610 [See no. 1290]**
■

## Addiscombe

2611 **Addiscombe** Cricket and Lawn Tennis
■ Club. East Croydon, the Club, [c.1950].
[8p]. 1 illus. port. map
*includes history of club*

## Ashtead

2611 **Jackson, Alan A.**, *editor*
–1 Ashtead: a village transformed. Leather-
■ head, Leatherhead & District Local
History Society, 1977. 237p. illus. ports.
maps, plans, bibliog.
*cricket pp.104–5*

2611 **[Robertson, R.A.]**
–2 Ashtead Cricket Club 1875–1954.
Ashtead, *printed by* Johnson, 1955. 14p.

## Banstead

2612 **Mason, Ronald Charles**
■ Batsman's paradise: an anatomy of cricketomania. Hollis & Carter, 1955. 167p.
illus. ports.
*includes a chapter on cricket at Banstead*

## Barnes

2613 **Old Barnes Cricket Club**
■ Centenary year 1860–1960; history and
fixture list; compiled by R.W.N. Simpson,
[Barnes, the Club, 1960]. 15p.

2614 **Turner, E.G.**, *editor*
■ Barnes Cricket Club, 1919/1969. [Barnes,
The Club, 1969]. [6]p.

## Beddington

2615 **Beddington Cricket Club**
■ Programme of a concert given by
Beddington Cricket Club, April 6th 1910,
Public Hall, Carshalton. [Beddington, the
Club, 1910. [4]p.

2616 **Bentham, Thomas**
■ A history of Beddington. Murray, 1923.
xiv,90p. illus. ports.
*cricket pp.65–6*

2617 **Bulfield, R.W.**
■ Beddington Cricket Club. Wallington,
*printed by* B. Johnson, [1949]. 28p. illus.
on cover, stats.

2618 **"Carolus"**, *pseud.*
■ The Beddington cricket week; reprinted
from the "Weekly Record". Wallington,
Weekly Record, 1911. 23p. scores, stats.

2619 **Scovell, Brian**
■ Beddington Cricket Club 1863–1963: a
history of the first hundred years.
[Beddington, the Club, 1963]. 40p. illus.
ports, score
*cover title: Bedders, 1863–1963*

## Blackheath

2619 **[Bryers, Tim]**
–1 A century at Blackheath: an illustrated
■ account of the development of a cricket
club in the life of a Surrey village from
1878 to 1978. Blackheath, the Club,
[1978]. 48p. incl. adverts. illus. ports.
facsims. stats.

## Brixton

2619 **Brixton West Indian Cricket Club**
–2 Fixture list. The Club. team port. stats.
□ *annual*
*?/1979/*
*founded 1967*

## Camberley

2620 **Camberley Cricket Club**
A short history of Camberley Cricket
Club. Reid-Hamilton, 1952. 24p.

## Carshalton

2620 **Barrett, Charles Raymond Booth**
–1 Surrey: highways, byways, and water-
■ ways. Written and illustrated by C.R.B.
Barrett. Bliss, Sands, & Foster, 1895.
xv,251p. illus.
*includes pp.30–31 description and illustra-
tions of the Carshalton cricket bowl one of the
"only two ceramic representations of eight-
eenth-century cricket . . . known to be in
existence."*

## Caterham

2621 **Caterham Cricket Club**
Bi-centenary cricket match v. Hambledon
C.C. at Queens Park, Caterham on
Sunday, 25th June, 1967: programme.
[Caterham, the Club, 1967]. 8p.
*contains 'History of Caterham C.C.' by
A.T. Braid*

2622 Caterham Cricket Club 1873–1973:
■ souvenir programme. [Caterham, the
Club, 1973]. [8]p. 1 illus. on cover. ports.
stats.
*programme of centenary match*

2623 **Turk, Nigel,** *and* **Charman, Geoffrey**
■ Cricket in Caterham: a brief history of the
present club and its predecessors
1767–1973. Caterham, the Club, 1973.
69p. ports. stats. bibliog.

## Cheam

**2624 Cheam Cricket Club**
■ Centenary year 1964. Cheam, the Club [1964]. [12]p.
*officers & fixtures*
n.b. *A booklet (not seen) was issued by the Club c.1932 on the occasion of the opening of a new pavilion*

## Cranleigh

**2624 Swinnerton, Frank**
**–1** Reflections from a village. Hutchinson,
■ 1969. 196p. illus.
——*another ed*. H. Hamilton, 1978. 196p. illus.
*cricket pp.127–34*

## Croydon

**2624 Bannerman, Ronald Robert Bruce**
**–2** Forgotten Croydon. Croydon Times,
■ 1933. [vii],56p. illus. ports.
*ch.vii, pp.34–40, "Cricket" [18th century matches]*

## Dorking

**2625 Cole, Kenneth J.**
■ Two hundred years of Dorking cricket 1766 to 1968. Putney Heath, the Author, 1969. 70p. illus. ports. scores, bibliog.

**2626 The Dorking** Cricket Club 1937; edited by
■ A.K. Kirk. Dorking, the Club, [1937]. 32p. incl. adverts.

**2627 Dorking** Cricket Club 1956: [annual
■ magazine]; edited by W.J. Bonner. Dorking, [the Club, 1956]. [i],21p. stats.
*other issues?*

## Dulwich

**2628 Dulwich Cricket Club**
■ Centenary 1867–1967. [Dulwich, the Club, 1967]. 48p. illus. ports. stats.

**2629 Marlborough (1870) Cricket Club**
■ M 1870–1970: centenary facts & fixtures. [Dulwich], the Club, [1970]. [24]p. stats.

## East Molesey

**2630 East Molesey Cricket Club**
■ East Molesey v. The Australians [1953]: match souvenir. [East Molesey, the Club], 1953. 44p. incl. adverts. illus. ports. scores, stats.
*includes history of the East Molesey Club*

**2631** East Molesey C.C. v. M.J. Stewart's XI: souvenir brochure. East Molesey, the Club

**2632 Nickolls, Louis Albert**
The crowning of Elizabeth II: a diary of coronation year. Macdonald, 1953. 127p. illus. ports.
*refers to Duke of Edinburgh's visit to East Molesey C.C. and to Lord's to open the Imperial Cricket Memorial Gallery*

## Englefield Green

**2632 Englefield Green Cricket Club**
**–1** Centenary handbook. The Club, [1979].
■ 32p. incl. adverts. illus. ports. facsims.

## Epsom

**2633 Epsom Cricket Club**
☐ Year book. Epsom, the Club. illus.
1950/1950 . . . 55/to date?
*1950 issue contains a resumé of the Club's history*

## Esher

**2634 Esher** Cricket Club centenary year: a
■ short history of one hundred years of cricket 1863–1963. [Esher, the Club, 1963]. 20p. illus. ports. stats.

**2634 Esher Cricket Club**
**–1** Barbados tour 1977. Esher, the Club, [1977]. 20p. illus. ports.

**2634 Stevens, Ian D.**
**–2** The story of Esher. Esher, Michael
■ Lancet, 1966. 128p. illus.
*cricket pp.110–11*

## Farnham

**2635 Lach, John Vincent**
■ A short history of the Farnham Cricket Club. Reid-Hamilton, for Farnham C.C., [1953]. 5–22p. illus. ports. score

## Godalming

**2635 Turner, Matthias Cathrow**
**–1** A saunter through Surrey. W. Walker, 1857. xi,234p. frontis.
*pp.194–5 "The cricket ground" which refers to a match played by Surrey on the Broadwater Ground, Godalming, against Notts.(?)*

## Godstone

**2636 Godstone Rover Scouts, 1st**
■ Glorious Godstone; edited by H. Fairall. Godstone & London, A. Coleman, *n.d.* 143p. illus. port. maps
*cricket pp.109–112, etc.*

## Hamsey Green

2637 **The Hamsey Green Cricket Club**
□ Year book. Hamsey Green, the Club.
stats.
*?/1972/to date?*
*formed 1952; 1972 issue compiled and edited by Alan Little*

## Haslemere

2638 **Swanton, Ernest William Brockton,** *and*
■ **Woods, Percy**
Bygone Haslemere: a short history of the ancient borough and . . . neighbourhood. West, 1914. xvi,394p. illus. maps
*cricket pp.296–304*

## Honor Oak

2639 **Alexander, Maurice Benjamin**
■ A history of the Honor Oak Cricket and Lawn Tennis Club, 1866–1965. Dulwich Common, the Club, [1965]. viii,121p. illus. ports. stats.

2640 **Honor Oak Cricket and Lawn Tennis**
□ **Club**
Honorary secretary's report. Dulwich Common, S.E.21. the Club. *annual. typescript*
*1949/1959–73/to date*

2640 **Honor Oak Cricket Club**
–1 [Club averages]. The Club. annual. stats.
□ *?/1904. . .1938/1938*
*founded 1866, from 1912 known as Honor Oak Cricket and Lawn Tennis Club*

## Horley

2641 **History** of the Horley Cricket Club;
■ compiled from notes supplied by one of the veteran members of the Club, Mr. W. Young. [Horley C.C., 1939]. 8p. scores

## Kennington

2642 **Montgomery, Henry Hutchinson**
■ The history of Kennington and its neighbourhood, with chapters on cricket past and present. H. Stacey Gold, 1889. 190,[2],iiip. frontis. illus. map, scores
*the cricket chs. were rptd. See no. 2599*

## Limpsfield

2642 **Mumford, W.F.**
–1 Pages from the past in Oxted, Limpsfield and Tandridge. Tunbridge Wells, printed by The Courier Printing and Publishing Co., 1949. 90p. frontis. map
*cricket pp.72–81 "Giants at Limpsfield" and p.82 "A memorable catch"*

## Malden

2642 **Burns, Michael**
–2 Malden Wanderers Cricket Club
■ 1879–1979. [Malden], the Club, 1979. 64p. illus. ports. facsims. stats.

2643 **The Malden** Wanderers gazette. Malden, Malden Wanderers C.C. *monthly*
*at least 39 issues Feb. 1927–Dec. 1930*

## Mitcham

2644 **Mitcham Cricket Club**
□ [Handbook]. Mitcham, the Club. *annual.* illus. ports. stats.
*?/1936,38/39,49/50. . .to date/*

## Norwood

2645 **Norwood Cricket Club**
■ A century of cricket 1871–1971; compiled by John Cracknell [and others]. The Club. [1971]. 52p. incl. adverts. illus. ports. scores, stats.

## Oatlands Park

2646 **Oatlands Park Cricket Club**
List of members, rules and fixtures for 1965. Oatlands Park, the Club, [1965]. 32p. illus.

2647 Oatlands Park Cricket Club 1867–1967.
■ Oatlands Park, the Club, [1967]. 32p. incl. adverts. illus. facsims.

2648 Handbook. Oatlands Park, the Club.
□ *annual.* illus. ports.
*?/1971–73/to date*

2649 Newsletter. Oatlands Park, the Club.
*?/Spring. 1971/–?*

## Old Coulsdon

2650 **Cooper, John Sydney**
■ The Old Coulsdon Cricket Club: a short history. Old Coulsdon, the Author, 1961. 9p.

## Outwood

2651 **Waller, L.C.**
■ Outwood Cricket Club, founded 1889: a brief history. Beckenham, Good, Hurst & Co., 1966. [iii],33p. illus. ports. score

## Putney

2652 **One** hundred years of Putney Cricket
■ Club 1870–1970. [Putney, the Club, 1970]. 64p. incl. adverts. illus. ports. stats.

## Redhill

2653 **Crawshaw, George**
■ A brief history of the Redhill Cricket Club. [Redhill, the Club, 1969]. [iii],9p. *typescript*
——Appx. List of Officers. [1969]. 3p.

## Richmond

2654 **Old Deer Park:** [being a history of the
■ royal and ancient park, and of the well-known sporting clubs associated with it]. Richmond, Richmond C.C., [1951]. 47p. illus. ports. map.
*includes history of Richmond C.C.*

2655 **Richmond Town Cricket Club**
■ [Appeal for a new ground; ed. by Kenneth J. Compton]. Richmond, the Club, [1960]. 9–22p. ports.
*contains 1 page biography of Tom Richardson and brief history of club*

2655 **White, Graham**
–1 The late George Lindsay Holt, Esq. Rich-
■ mond, Richmond C.C., 1964. [4]p. port.
*Life Patron of the Club*

## Ripley

2656 **Cricket** at Ripley. Ripley, Acme P., [c.1943]. 4p.

## Roehampton

2657 **Towards** the second century: a brief
□ history of Roehampton Cricket Club. Roehampton, the Club, 1946
——2nd ed. 1951. iv,28p. 1 illus. port.

## South Nutfield

2658 **Wilderspin, Reginald D.**
■ South Nutfield Cricket Club, 1893–1968. [The Author, 1968]. 12p. ports.

## Streatham

2659 **Streatham Cricket Club**
■ 150th anniversary dinner, 29th April, 1955: [menu]. [Streatham C.C., 1955]. 4p. illus.
*with insert single leaf reprint of the Rules of the Club as formulated at the Horse & Groom on Monday, 5th May, 1806 and revised at the London Tavern on Tuesday 27th January, 1807*

2660 **The Streatham** Cricket Club magazine.
□ Streatham, the Club
*?/1967/to date?*
*issue for July 31st, 1967 was vol. x, no.15*

## Surbiton

2660 **Surbiton Cricket Club**
–1 List of members and rules 1893. Surbiton, [The Club, 1893]. 22p.

## Sutton

2661 **Sutton Cricket Club**
■ Batting & bowling averages. Season 1906. [Sutton, the Club, 1906]. 15p. stats.
*other issues?*

2662 Handbook. Sutton, the Club. illus. stats.
■ *annual*
*3 issues 1951,52,54*
*the 1954 issue covers seasons 1952 and 1953*

## Thames Ditton

2662 **Thames Ditton** Cricket Club: the year of
–1 opportunity 1977. Thames Ditton, the
■ Club, [1977]. 16p. incl. adverts. illus. port.

## Thornton Heath

2662 **Penfold, Peter**
–2 Thornton Heath Cricket Club centenary
■ year 1876–1976: souvenir brochure. The Club, [1976]. 40p. incl. adverts. ports.

## Thorpe

2663 **Thorpe Cricket Club**
■ Annual report. Thorpe, the Club. stats.
*1896–1905*
*titles vary: 1896–98 Thorpe Juniors C.C. Annual report*
*1899 Reports of Thorpe St. Mary's and Thorpe Juniors C.C.*
*1900–04 Thorpe St. Mary's C.C. Second [–Sixth] annual report*
*1905 Thorpe C.C., late Thorpe St. Mary's. Seventh annual report.*

2664 **Thorpe Working Men's Club**
Year book. Thorpe, the Club
*1886–97*

## Walton-on-Thames

2665 **Walton-on-Thames Cricket Club**
□ Handbook. Walton-on-Thames, the Club. *annual?* illus. ports.
*1969/1969/–?*

## Wandsworth

2666 **[Gordon, John Thomas]**
■ The Spencer Cricket and Lawn Tennis Club: a souvenir of fifty years. Wandsworth Common, [the Club], 1921. 23p. illus.

2667 ■ "75 not out": the story of the Spencer Cricket and Lawn Tennis Club 1872–1946. Wandsworth Common, the Club, 1947. 24p. illus. port.

## Weybridge

2668 ■ **Weybridge** Cricket Club, 1924–1973. Weybridge, the Club, [1973?]. 48p. illus. ports. scores (facsims.), stats.

## Wimbledon

2669 "A Member of the Club". *pseud.* The matches of the Wimbledon Cricket Club from 1856 to 1861. [Wimbledon, the Club.] 1862. 8p. *author may have been F.W. Oliver*

2670 ■ **[Oliver, Frederick Wiliam]**, *compiler* The matches of the Wimbledon Cricket Club and averages of the members from 1854 to 1870, compiled by the secretary. *Printed by* Diprose & Bateman, 1871. iv,191p. scores, stats.

2671 ■ **[Reeves, E.W.]**, *compiler* The scores of matches played by the Wimbledon Cricket Club with a summary and table of the results from 1871 to the end of 1889, also the batting averages. Walsall, *printed by* W.H.H., [1890]. viii, 186p. scores, stats.

2672 ■ **Wakley, Bertram Joseph** The history of the Wimbledon Cricket Club, 1854–1953. Wimbledon, Wimbledon C.C., [1954]. 151p. illus. ports. stats.

2672 –1 ■ **Wimbledon Cricket Club** 125th season anniversary dinner. [Wimbledon, the Club, 1979]. [32]p. incl. covers and adverts. illus. team ports. *includes an account of the Club over the past 25 years by Bert Seaborn and John Spalton*

## Woking

2672 –2 ■ **Ellis, G.C.**, *compiler* Westfield & District Cricket & Sports Club 1875–1975. [Westfield], the Club, [1975]. 16p. illus. ports.

# SURREY C.C.C

2673 □ All about Surrey cricket: the Oval cricket guide. *annual.* ports. stats. 7 issues 1922–28 1922–23; *edited by Herbert J. Henley. & E.J. Larby* 1925–28; *edited by Robin Baily. C.E. Smith, Oval Bookstall*

2674 ■ **Ashley-Cooper, Frederick Samuel** Surrey v. Notts at the wicket. "Cricket" Office, 1899. 16p. ports. stats. ——*another issue* with an "Addendum". 1900

2675 ■ John Wisden's cricket match histories. Wisden, [1922]. 16p. stats. 1. *Kent v. Surrey 1731–1921* 2. *Surrey v. Notts. 1851–1921* 3. *Middlesex v. Surrey 1730–1921*

2676 ■ **Baily, Robin**, *editor* Cricket: all about London's big four. John Smith, Lord's and Oval Bookstalls, 1928. 16p. illus. *Kent, Surrey, Essex, Middlesex, giving averages for 1927 and fixtures for 1928*

2677 ■ **Christian, Edmund Brown Viney** The epic of the Oval. *Privately printed,* 1930. 36p. *prose and verse on Surrey cricket and the Oval*

2678 ■ **Colman, Sir Jeremiah** (1886–1961) Reminiscences of the Great War, 1914–1918. [Norwich, the Author], 1940, 104p. *chap. 16 "The Surrey County Cricket Club", pp.81–2*

2679 ■ **De Lugo, Anthony Benitez**, *Marquis de Santa Susana* Surrey at the wicket: a complete record of all the matches played by the county XI since the formation of the club. Yearly & general batting and bowling averages with all other informations [sic] interesting to Surrey cricketers. Madrid, the Author, *for private circulation,* 1888. iii,159p. stats.

2680 ■ A summary of Surrey cricket 1844–99. Madrid, the Author, *for private circulation,* 1900. 87p. stats.

2681 ■ **Foster, Denis** Surrey. Findon Publications, 1949. 32p. ports. stats. ("Know Your Cricket County" Series)

2682 ■ **Holmes, Robert Stratten** Surrey cricket and cricketers 1773 to 1895: a complete summary of every match played with various interesting tables. "Cricket" Office, 1896. [iii],80p. illus. ports. scores, stats.

2682 –1 ■ **Lane, John D.**, *compiler* Surrey v. Glamorgan 1923–1955. 1955. 34p. stats. *typescript not published; MS in the Cricket Society's Library*

2683 **[Lane, John D.**, *compiler*] Surrey v. Middlesex, 1730–1956. The

Author, 1957. 22p. (Cricket match history)
*limited ed. of 100 copies*

2684 Surrey v. Yorkshire, 1851–1957. [The
■ Author], 1958. [26]p. stats. (Cricket match history)
*limited ed. of 250 copies*

2685 Surrey v. Somerset, 1879–1958. The
■ Author, [1959]. [18]p. stats. (Cricket match history)

2686 Surrey v. Nottingham, 1851–1959. The
■ Author, [1960]. [22]p. stats. (Cricket match history)

2687 **McCance, James L.**
■ The Surrey eleven in 1895: a descriptive record of the matches played in that season. With batting and bowling averages, &c., and a photograph of the champion team. Merritt & Hatcher, [1896]. 60p. port. scores, stats.
——1896, 1897. 75p. port. scores, stats.

2688 **Palgrave, Louis**
■ The story of the Oval and the history of Surrey cricket 1902 to 1948. Birmingham, Cornish, 1949. [viii],215p. illus. ports. scores

2689 **Ross, Gordon**
■ The Surrey story. S. Paul, 1957. 208p. illus. ports. stats.
——*another ed.* Sportsman's Book Club, 1958

2690 Surrey. Barker, 1971. 175p. illus. ports.
■ stats. (A History of County Cricket)

2691 **Stanton, Henry Valentine Labron**
■ Surrey team of 1895. Cricket P., 1895. 16p. illus. stats.

2692 The Surrey team. Cricket P., 1897. 18p.
■ illus. stats.

2693 **Surrey County Cricket Club**
□ [Handbook]. The Club. *annual.* illus. ports. (in v.y.), scores, stats.
*1884–1914, 1915–20 (in 1 vol.), 1921–39, 1940–45 (in 1 vol.), 1946–53, 1955–65 1966 to date with title: Year book until 1953 each report contained record of current year, but handbook for 1955 contained record of 1954 season and this practice has continued*

2694 A souvenir of the centenary of Surrey
■ cricket 1845 to 1945. Croydon, Home Publishing Co., [1946]. 168p. incl. adverts. illus. ports. stats.

2695 Six golden years: the souvenir of Surrey's
■ six successive championships; ed. by Gordon Ross. Surrey C.C.C., [1958]. 36p. incl. adverts. illus. ports. stats.

2695 Extra cover: a publication of Surrey
–1 County Cricket Club. The Club. *quarterly.*
■ 4p. per issue. illus. ports.
*Vol. 1, no.1, Feb. 1968 to Vol.3, no.2, Nov. 1970*

2695 **Surrey County Cricket Club Supporters**
–2 **Association**
■ Around the Oval: official publication of the Surrey County Cricket Club Supporters Association. The Association. *quarterly.* illus. stats.
*No. 1. May 1978 to date; edited by T.M. Jones*

2696 **The Surrey** team in 1888: complete scores
■ of all matches played, with full page portraits and short biographical sketches of each member of the team. "Cricket" Office, [1889]. [ii],67p. ports. scores, stats.

2697 **Surrey** team 1891: biographical sketches
■ of each member of the team. "Cricket" Office, 1892. 16p. incl. adverts. mounted team port. on t.p.

2698 **Trew-Hay, John**
■ The match of the season: a lay of the Oval. Wright, 1894. 26p. score
*a poem on the tied match, Surrey v. Lancashire, Aug. 1894*

2699 **Williams J. Lincoln,** *editor*
■ Surrey county cricket handbook, season 1930. Imperial Publishing Co., [1930]. 32p. ports. stats. (Williams' Sports Handbooks)

# SUSSEX

2699 **Baker, Michael Henry Chadwick**
–1 Sussex scenes; with drawings by the author. Hale, 1978. 207p. illus.
*pp. 88–90 cricket with illus.*

2700 **Blaker, Nathaniel Paine**
■ Sussex in bygone days: reminiscences. New rev. ed. Hove, Combridge, 1919. xvi,199p. illus.
*cricket pp.61–3; 1st ed. published 1906 for private circulation only under the title of "Reminiscences of Nathaniel Paine Blaker"*

2700 **Bryden, Hedley A.R.**
–1 A cricket ballad; the ballad written . . . in
□ the year 1905, privately printed at his own expense, and like distributed in the year of its printing. The Author, 1905

——reprinted in 1973, with commentary based upon modern research facts, by E.A. Marsh. Eastbourne, Marsh, 1973. [ii],11p. bibliog. *typescript*
*on a match played at Selmeston, Sussex, between The Ladies of East Sussex and The Gentlemen of East Sussex*

**2701 Champion, Victor**
My Sussex. Brighton, Southern Publishing Co., 1947. 24p. illus.

**2702 Evening Argus**
■ Sussex cricket handbook; edited by James T. Hyslop and H. Jack Arlidge. Brighton, Southern Publishing Co. *annual.* illus. ports. scores, stats.
*1948–49*
*1950 jointly with the Sussex Cricket Association*

**2703 Fleet, Charles**
■ Glimpses of our ancestors in Sussex; and gleanings in East and West Sussex. 2nd series. Lewes, Farncombe, 1883. x,306p. illus.
*'Cricket in Sussex' pp.300–306*

**2704 Gaston, Alfred J.**
■ The history of cricket in Sussex, from the earliest records to the present time. London, Wright; Brighton, Friend, 1898. 73p. ports. stats.

**2704 Hopkins, Robert Thurston**
**–1** The lure of Sussex. Cecil Palmer, 1928. 176p. illus. ports.
*pp.84–95 'Some records of Sussex cricket'*

**2705 Hove Museum of Art**
■ Sussex cricket past and present: an exhibition of pictures, mementoes and photographs under the auspices of the Sussex County Cricket Club: [catalogue]. [Hove, Museum of Art], 1957. 24p. illus. ports.

**2705 Howitt, William**
**–1** The rural life of England. 2 vols. Longman, etc., 1838. illus.
*Vol. II, ch. x,pp.273–6 gives an account of a match played Sept., 1835 between the Sussex Club and the Nottingham Club. The extract is quoted in The language of cricket, by W.J. Lewis, pp.315–6*

**2705 Lucas, Edward Verrall**
**–2** Highways and byways in Sussex; with illustrations by F.L. Griggs. Macmillan, 1904. xx,424p. illus. map
*many times reprinted, also thin-paper edns. and pocket edns. (in 2 vols. – 'Highways and byways in East Sussex' and Highways and byways in West Sussex'); cricket pp. 74, 81, 103, 132, 165, 235, 268, 384*
——2nd ed. 1935. xix,469p.

*cricket pp. 51, 83, 93–4, 120–5, 128, 136–7, 149, 177–8, 192–3, 248, 302*

**2705 Mid Sussex** – highways and byways; with
**–3** illustrations by Frederick L. Griggs. Macmillan, 1937. xi-xviii,129–289p. illus. map on end-papers
*cricket pp.136–7,149,177–8,192–3,248; a re-issue of chs.12–25 of "Highways and byways in Sussex", 2nd ed., with different preliminary matter and index.*
*cover-title:* Highways and byways booklets

**2705 McCann, Timothy J.**
**–4** "Cricket and the Sussex County by-elec-
■ tion of 1741". *In* Sussex Archaeological Collections. Vol.114. 1976. pp.121–5

**2706 Meynell, Esther**
■ Sussex. Hale, 1947. x,260p. illus. map, bibliog. (County Books Series)
*cricket pp.248–51*

**2707 Squire, Henry Fremlin**
■ Sussex cricket 1837–1850, together with Addenda to "Pre-Victorian Sussex cricket". Henfield (Sx.), the Author, 1959. 94p. *typescript*
*notices of matches*

**2708** ——*,and* **Squire, A.P.**
■ Pre-Victorian Sussex cricket. Henfield, The Authors, 1951. 61p.

**2709 Sussex Archaeological Society**
■ Sussex archaeological collections, relating to the history and antiquities of the county: Vol. 28. Lewes, George P. Bacon for the Society, 1878. xix,215p. illus.
contains (pp.59–82): "On the archaeology of Sussex cricket", by the editor [Charles Francis Trower], with a lithograph of cottage at Westhampnett where Lillywhite was born
rptd. separately 1879. See no.2717

**2710** Sussex notes and queries. Vol. 11. 1946–47. Lewes, the Society, 1948
*p.133 a note by H.J. Glover on the burial at Chailey, in 1737, of one John Boots "killed at Newick by running against another man in crossing the wickets".*
——Vol. 12. 1948–49. 1950
*pp.42 and 65, early references to the use of the words 'cricket bat' at Selsey and Boxgrove. For full entry see no. 844*

**2710 Sussex** Championship League (for the
**–1** "Wiley" Trophy): officials, constitution,
■ rules, fixtures 1975 and 1976. The League, [1975]. [12]p. incl. covers
*later issues?; sponsored by John Wiley & Sons, publishers*

**2711 Sussex County Cricket Club,** *and* **Sussex**
■ **Cricket Association**
Sussex cricket: official handbook. Hove,
Sussex C.C.C. & Sussex C.A. illus. ports.
scores, stats.
*1953*
*1954 to date with title:* Official Sussex
*cricket handbook*
*formerly:* Sussex C.A. Official handbook

**2712 Sussex Cricket Association**
■ Official handbook. Eastbourne, the
Assoc. scores, stats. *annual*
*1945–52*
*1950 with title* Sussex cricket: official
*handbook; compiled by James T. Hyslop and
Jack Arlidge. The Assoc. and "Evening
Argus". illus. ports. scores, stats.*
*contd. as:* Sussex C.C.C. and Sussex C.A.
*Sussex cricket*

**2713 Sussex** sports annual; edited by Harold
Jack Arlidge. Southern Publishing Co.
*1948–49 to 1950–51*

**2714 The Sussex Youth Cricket Council**
■ A brief description of the constitution of
the Sussex Youth Cricket Council, its
purpose and aims, and the service it
offers towards creating an interest in the
game of cricket among young people, and
the training of cricket coaches. [Brighton],
the Council, [1962?]. [ii],12p. bibliog.

**2715 Taylor, Alfred Daniel**
■ Sussex cricket in the olden time, with
glances at the present. Hove, Hove Printing and Publishing Co., 1900. [ii],93p.
scores

**2716** Cricket siftings. Hove, Taylor Bros., 1922.
■ 31p.
*events and curiosities connected with
Sussex cricket and cricketers*

**2717 [Trower, Charles Francis]**
■ Sussex cricket past and present, by An
Old Sussex Cricketer. Lewes, A. Rivington, 1879. 60p.
*rptd. with additions, from the "Sussex
archaeological collections". See no. 2709*

**2718 [Entry cancelled]**

**2719 The Victoria** history of the counties of
■ England: Sussex; edited by William Page.
Vol. 2. Constable, 1907
*cricket pp.467–76. stats.*

**2720 Wymer, Norman George**
Companion into Sussex. Methuen, 1950.
x,284p. illus. maps (on end papers)
bibliog. (Methuen's Companion Books)
——rev. ed. Spur Books, 1972
*cricket pp.53,63,94,95,130,158,185*

## Bexhill

**2721 Bartley, L.J.**
■ The story of Bexhill. Bexhill-on-Sea, F.J.
Parsons, 1971. xx,212p. illus. ports.
maps, plans
*cricket pp.19,23,34,66,132,144,147,148*

## Boxgrove

**2721 McCann, Timothy J.,** *and* **Wilkinson,**
**–1 Peter M.**
■ "The cricket match at Boxgrove in 1622".
*In* Sussex Archaeological Collections. Vol.
110. 1972. pp.118–22
*25 offprints were printed. "The earliest
recorded instance so far discovered of a game
of cricket played by several named players"*

## Brighton

**2722 Bishop, John George**
□ Brighton in the olden times: a peep into
the past. Brighton, Brighton Herald
Office, 1880. 390p.
——New ed. *with title* "A peep into the
past": Brighton in the olden time. 1892.
[viii],22,434p. map, illus. ports. scores
*cricket pp.93–102*

**2723 Brighton** and Hove cricket week. Brighton, [Sussex C.C.C.] *annual.* illus. ports.
*3 issues 1908–10*

**2724 Gilbert, Edmund William**
■ Brighton, old ocean's bauble. Methuen,
1954. xvi,275p. illus. ports. maps, plans,
bibliog.
*cricket at Brighton and Hove, pp.89,
171–72,251*

**2725 Taylor, Alfred Daniel**
■ Ireland's Gardens and its cricket associations. *Privately printed*, 1899. 36p. scores
*limited to 50 uncorrected proof copies*

## Belvedere

**2725 Belvedere Cricket Club**
**–1** [Scorebook 1854–56]. 106p. MS.
*scores of 21 matches all played at Brighton;
in A.E. Winder's collection*

## Brighton

**2726 King, George William**
■ Matches played by the Brighton Cricket
Club during the seasons 1849 and 1850.
Brighton, *printed by* Cohen, 1851. 14p.
scores

*Brighton Brunswick*

2727 **Brighton** Brunswick Cricket Club:
■ centenary year 1870–1970. [Brighton, the
Club, 1970]. 15p. port.

*Clifton*

2728 **Stringer, Henry W.,** *ed.*
■ Clifton Cricket Club Brighton annual,
1904: [tour in the Isle of Wight, 1904]:
containing full scores and analysis, averages, remarks on the players and mems.
on the tour. Brighton, H. Crowhurst,
[1904]. 16p. scores, stats.

2729 Clifton Cricket Club tour in Kent, 1907:
■ containing everything of interest relative
to a most successful holiday. Words and
music by Henry W. Stringer. Brighton,
H. Crowhurst, [1907]. 18p. scores, stats.

*St. James*

2729 **Redbourn, Dick**
–1 The domestic cricketer: memoirs.
■ Tunbridge Wells, Midas Books, 1977.
128p. illus. ports. pbk.

**Burgess Hill**

2729 **Gregory, Albert H.**
–2 The story of Burgess Hill. Haywards
Heath, Clarke, 1933. 215p. folding map
*cricket pp.56–9*

**Dicker**

2729 **Dicker Cricket Club**
–3 Commemorative booklet 1977: 300 years
■ of cricket in Dicker. Dicker, the Club,
1977. [28]p. incl. adverts. ports. facsims.
*the historical account "Cricket at Dicker
1677–1977" by Jack Cocks*

**East Grinstead**

2729 **Hills, Wallace Henry**
–4 The history of East Grinstead. Lewes,
Farncombe, 1906. xv,288p.
*cricket pp.246–50*

**East Preston**

2730 **[Hurle-Hobbs, Charles Rienzi Hurle]**
■ History of the East Preston Cricket Club,
1860–1960. [The Author, 1960]. 24p.
ports.

**Eastbourne**

2731 **Chambers, George Frederick**
East Bourne memories of the Victorian
period 1845 to 1901, and some other
things of interest, divers and sundry.

East-Bourne, V.T. Sumfield, 1910. xv,
304p. illus.
*cricket pp.144–8*

2732 **Eastbourne Cricket and Football Club**
Reminiscences of Eastbourne cricket.
Eastbourne, the Club, [1950]. 8p.

2733 Sport at the Saffrons. Eastbourne [the
Club, 195–]. [8]p. illus.

2734 **Eastbourne Cricket Club**
□ Six-a-side-tournament: official programme. Eastbourne, the Club. *annual.*
*1965 to date*
*1973 issue with title: Brighter cricket six-
a-side tournament: official programme. [4]p.
of typescript inserted within printed covers*

2735 Cricket at the Saffrons . . . then and now.
Eastbourne, the Club. 1975. 4p.

2735 **Wright, J.C.**
–1 Bygone Eastbourne. Spottiswood, 1902.
xix,334p. illus. map
*cricket pp.228–30*

**Ebernoe**

2736 **Scott, Hardiman**
■ Secret Sussex. Photographs by John
Milner. Batchworth P., 1949. 125p. illus.
*ch. 1: "Cricket at Ebernoe", pp.11–15*

**Findon**

2737 **Higgins, Frank**
■ Findon Cricket Club, 1867–1967. Worthing, Allsport Programmes, [1967]. 48p.
incl. adverts. illus. ports. scores

**Goodwood**

2737 **Goodwood Cricket Club**
–1 Established rules of the Goodwood
Cricket Club, July 5, 1813. Chichester,
*printed by* William Mason, 1813. 8p.
*only copy known is among the Goodwood
MSS in the West Sussex Record Office,
Chichester*

2737 **250th anniversary** cricket match in the
–2 dress and under the laws of 1727, The
Duke of Richmond's XII v. The
Gentlemen of Pepperharrowe, the cricket
ground, Goodwood, Sussex, Sunday July
10, 1977: souvenir scorecard. Illustrated
London News, 1977. 12p. incl. covers &
adverts. illus. ports. facsim.
*explanatory article by Timothy J. McCann
and a facsimile of the Articles of Agreement
signed on July 11, 1727 by the 2nd Duke of
Richmond and the Captain of Peper Harow,
Mr. A. Brodrick*

## Hailsham

**2738** **Geering, Thomas**
■ Our Sussex parish. Methuen, 1925.
xviii,253p. illus. ports.
*cricket pp.70–76, based on Hailsham and neighbourhood. Originally publd. with title: Our parish: a medley, by T.G.H. 1884*

## Hastings

**2739** **Baines, J. Manwaring**
■ Historic Hastings. Hastings, Parsons, 1955. xv,433p. illus. ports. maps, plans
*cricket pp.66,340,349–54*

**2739** **Belt, Anthony,** *editor*
**–1** Hastings: a survey of times past and present by members of the Hastings Natural History Society and others. Hastings, Saville, 1937. 259p.
*cricket pp.233–41 by W.E.F. Cheesman*

**2739** **Hastings and St. Leonards Cricket Club**
**–2** Annual report and balance sheet. The Club
*1873/1873. . .1892/1893?*

**2740** A short review of local cricket 1840–1893.
■ Hastings, the Club, 1893. 28p. stats.
——*2nd ed.* with special reference to the doings of the above Club 1894. [1894]. 28p. stats.

**2740** Review of the season 1894. The Club.
**–1** 16p. scores, stats.
*the only issue?*

**2740** **Hastings Central Cricket Club**
**–2** Report for 1872. The Club. 4p.

**2741** **The Hastings** cricket festival view of the ground. Hastings, F.J. Parsons, 1895. folder

**2742** **How's zat!:** the Park Cricket Club maga-
■ zine; edited by W. Thurlow. Hastings, Park C.C. *typescript.* stats.
*3 issues only Spring & Oct., 1949, Spring 1950*

**2743** **Priory Cricket Club**
□ Year book. Hastings, the Club. ports. scores, stats.
*1949/1949–1956/–?*

**2744** **Ransom, W.J.**
■ Central Cricket Ground, Hastings: an address . .. at the Rotary Club, May 12th 1933. [The Author, 1933]. 8p.

**2745** **Taylor, Alfred Daniel**
■ A review of the Hastings & St. Leonards Cricket Festival from 1887 to 1903. Hastings, F.J. Parsons, "Observer" Office, 1903. [i].34p. scores

## Heathfield Park

**2745** **[Alexander, Leslie F.,** *and* **Ticehurst,**
**–1** **Hazel P.,** *compilers*]
■ Heathfield Park Cricket Club 1878–1978: souvenir centenary brochure. [Heathfield, the Club], 1978. 48p. incl. adverts. illus. ports.

## Henfield

**2745** **Bing, T.W.**
**–2** Henfield Cricket Club bicentenary 1971.
■ [Henfield, the Club, 1971]. 52p. ports. scores, stats.

**2746** **Henfield Cricket Club**
■ Centenary of the Henfield Cricket Club 1837–1937. [Henfield, the Club, 1937]. [4]p. fold. facsim of the original rules 1837

**2747** Report and accounts for the season Henfield, the Club. *annual. typescript*
*?/season1951/to date?*

**2748** **Squire, Henry Fremlin,** *and* **Squire, A.P.**
■ Henfield cricket and its Sussex cradle. Hove, Combridges, 1949. 268p. illus. ports. scores, stats.

## Horsham

**2749** **Horsham Cricket Club**
Scores. Horsham, the Club, 187–
*in Taylor ("Published in the seventies for several seasons")*

**2750** Horsham county cricket week festival.
□ Horsham, the Club.
1931. 64p incl. adverts. illus. ports.
1932. 56p. incl. adverts.
1933. 48p. incl. adverts.
1936. 56p. incl. adverts. 1 illus. stats.
1946. 32p. incl. adverts.
1948. 44p. incl. adverts. 1 illus. 1 team port.
1950. 44p. incl. adverts. 1 illus. ports. diagr. stats.
1952. 44p. incl. adverts. team ports.
1954. 44p. incl. adverts.
1956. 86p. incl. adverts. 1 illus. ports.
*the last county cricket week at Horsham; includes pp.6–12 an historical account 1908–56 by Bob Green, and pp.57–73, a record of matches played*

**2751** Bicentenary 1971; edited by B.J. Edwards.
■ [Horsham, the Club, 1971]. 32p. illus.

**2751** **Windrum, Anthony**
**–1** Horsham: an historical survey. Phillimore, 1978. xi,212p. illus.
*cricket pp.141–2*

## Ifield

2752 **[Stonehouse, Frank]**
■ Ifield Cricket Club 1804–1954: one hundred and fifty years of cricket on the village green. [Ifield, the Club], 1954. 16p. illus. score

## Lindfield

2752 **Hall, Helena**
–1 Lindfield past and present. Haywards Heath, C. Clarke, 1960. 238p. illus.
*cricket pp.29–30*

2753 **Lindfield Cricket Club**
■ Bi-centenary festival 1747–1947, Lindfield v. Sussex Club and Ground. [Lindfield C.C.], 1947. 8p.
*brief history and festival score-card*

## Mayfield

2753 **Bell-Irving, E.M.**
–1 Mayfield: the story of an old wealden village. Clowes, 1903. viii,204p. illus.
*cricket pp.191,192*

2754 **Bradfield R.**
■ Mayfield Cricket Club: a history 1866–1966: centenary souvenir. [Mayfield, the Club, 1966]. 44p. incl. adverts. illus. ports. score

2754 **Lester, Fred**
–1 Looking back, with additional narrative
■ of John Eldridge "Mayfield 70 to 130 years ago"; also the diary of Walter Gale (Mayfield schoolmaster 1750–1772). 2nd ed. Mayfield, Henry Thomas, 1953. 217p. illus. ports.
*cricket pp.42, 148, 173–4*

## Midhurst

2755 **Midhurst Cricket Club**
■ 1806–1956: souvenir fixture card. Midhurst, the Club, 1956. [8]p.
*with a brief history of the Club*

## Newick

2756 **[Powell, T.B.]**
■ 101 scores of cricket matches contested by players of Newick during the years 1893 to 1898. Lewes, *printed by* Farncombe, 1910. 100p. scores

## Ninfield

2756 **Ridel, Alfred T.**
–1 Ninfield in the nineties: reminiscences of village life in all its activities. [Ninfield, Ninfield Parish Council], 1979. [viii], 186p.
*cricket pp.122–6*

## Petworth

2756 **Greenfield, John Osborn**
–2 Tales of old Petworth. Petworth, The Window P., 1976. 112p.
*cricket pp.110–2*

## Ripe and Chalvington

2757 **Esdaile, Edmund**
■ Ripe and Chalvington 1762–1962. [The Author, 1962?]. [5]p. illus. on cover

## Rottingdean

2758 **Blyth, H.E.**
■ Rottingdean Cricket Club 1758–1967: the history of one of the oldest cricket clubs in the world. Rottingdean, the Club, [1967]. [8]p. 1 illus.

2758 **Moens, Seabourne May**
–1 Rottingdean: the story of a village; edited and arranged by H.E. Blyth. Brighton, John Beal and Son, 1952. 68p. illus.
——Coronation ed. 1953. 196p.
*ch. 12 "Rottingdean cricket"*

## Rudgwick

2759 **The Reynell Cotton** memorial match:
■ Rudgwick C.C. versus Rev. David Sheppard's XI: souvenir programme, 23rd May, 1959. Rudgwick, the Club, [1959]. [5]p. port. on cover.
*includes song composed by Reynell Cotton for the Hambledon Club, c.1767 and an article on him*

## Southbourne

2760 **Southbourne Cricket Club**
History of the Southbourne Cricket Club. Southbourne, the Club. 16p. *typescript*

## Storrington

2760 **Storrington Cricket Club**
–1 Year book. The Club.
■ 1974; edited by S.H. Welland. 20p. incl. covers & adverts.
*the only issue?*
*founded 1973*

## Worthing

2761 **Worthing and District Cricket League**
Handbook. Worthing, the League. *annual*
*?/1901–14*

# SUSSEX C.C.C.

**2762 Ashley-Cooper, Frederick Samuel**
■ Sussex cricket and cricketers. Merritt &
Hatcher, 1901. vii,106p. stats.
*limited edn. of 30 copies; reprinted from
"Cricket"*

**2763** Sussex cricket champions: a record of
■ their doings from 1815–1901. Brighton,
W.J. Towner, 1902. 155p. stats.

**2763 Barty-King, Hugh**
**–1** Sussex in 1839. Reading, Osprey, 1974.
■ 64p. illus. map. (The Landscape Histories)
*cricket pp. 55,57*

**2764 County** cricket festival souvenir, August
21–27, 1929. Eastbourne, [*n.p.*, 1929]. 32p.
illus. ports.

**2765 Descriptive** key to Mason's national print
■ of a cricket match between Sussex and
Kent, 1849. Brighton, W.H. Mason;
London, Gambert, 1849. 23p. 1 illus.
*issued only to purchasers of the artist's
proof; see also Taylor, A.D. The story of a
cricket picture, 1923*

**2765 Epps, Norman F.S.**, *compiler*
**–1** Sussex in first class cricket in 1975: some
notes. Hove, The Compiler, 1977. 12p.
scores, stats.
*limited to 100 signed and numbered copies*

**2766 [Ewbank, George]**
■ Sussex county cricket scores from
1855–1878. [India, privately printed,
1878?] ii,288p.
*limited ed. of 4 copies (Taylor). 2 copies in
M.C.C. Library, Lord's*

**2767 Foster, Denis**
■ Sussex. Findon Publications, [1949].
32p. ports. stats. ("Know Your Cricket
County" Series)

**2768 [Gaston, Alfred James]**, *compiler*
■ Pocket synopsis of Sussex county cricket,
containing highest batting averages since
1868, complete batting & bowling statistics, 1887, century innings since 1850 etc.
etc., compiled and arranged by A.J.G.
Brighton, Sussex Evening Times, [1888?].
7p. stats.

**2769 Gaston, Alfred James**, *compiler*
■ Sussex county cricket 1728–1923; compiled by "Leather Hunter" (A.J. Gaston).
Brighton, Southern Publishing Co., 1923.
70p. illus. ports. score, stats.
——autograph edition limited to 100
copies. 1923

——2nd ed. 1924. 74p.
——3rd ed. 1924. 65p.
——[4th ed.] 1925. 65 + [3],75–78 +
adverts.
*cover-title: Sussex county cricket 1728–
1923–5*

**2770 Gilligan, Arthur Edward Robert**
■ Sussex cricket. Chapman & Hall, 1933.
276p. illus. ports. stats.

**2771 Gordon, *Sir* Home Seton Charles**
■ **Montagu**, *bart*.
Sussex county cricket. Convoy Publica-
tions, 1950. 132p. illus. ports. stats.
(County Cricket Series)

**2771 Hill, Alan**
**–1** The family fortune: a saga of Sussex
■ cricket. Shoreham-by-Sea, Scan Books,
1978. xv,152p. illus. ports. score, bibliog.
*families connected with Sussex CCC,
including Lillywhite, Gilligan, Parks, Langridge, Buss, etc.*

**2772 Marshall, John**
■ Sussex cricket: a history. Heinemann,
1959. x,266p. illus. ports. stats.

**2773 The spectator's** Sussex county cricket
■ companion for 1901: containing last
season's scores and averages, and diary
for present season's matches. Brighton,
Mytton & Co., 1901. 32p. scores, stats.

**2773 Stapleton, Laetitia**
**–1** A Sussex cricket odyssey: over 50 years
■ of recollection and enjoyment. Havant,
Ian Harrap, Pelham Bookshop, 1979.
184p. illus. ports.
*a personal account of Sussex County cricket
since 1921*

**2774 Sussex** county cricket annual; edited
■ by "Willow Wielder" [A.D. Taylor].
Brighton, Nash. scores, stats.
*9 issues 1901–09; issues for 1903 and 1904
have portraits of the Sussex team*

**2775 Sussex** cricket companion and almanack;
■ edited by "A.J.G." [Gaston]. Brighton,
Wisden, 1889. [24]p. illus. ports. stats.
*only year of issue*

**2775 [Sussex County Cricket Club]**
**–1** Correspondence between the Sussex
C.C.C. and Mr Perkins relative to the
second Australian match with Sussex, on
August 21st, 22nd and 23rd 1882. [Hove,
the Club, c.1883]. 11p.

**2775 Sussex County Cricket Club**
**–2** Rules 1887. Brighton, *printed by* M.
Crowhurst, printer to Sussex C.C.C.,
[1887]. 11p.

——*another ed.* Brighton, Southern Publishing Co., for Sussex C.C.C., [1907]. 32p.
——*with 1p. insert of* alterations and additions to rules. [1908]

2776 Bazaar souvenir. Sussex cricket: historical
■ sketch, by Alfred D. Taylor. Brighton, Sussex C.C.C. Bazaar Committee, [1904]. 8p. illus. on cover

2776 Programme of entertainments at the
–1 grand bazaar in aid of the funds of the Sussex C.C.C., April, 6,7 & 8, 1904. [Hove, the Club, 1904]. 12p. incl. adverts. illus.

2777 **[See no. 2775–2]**

2778 Carnival week, August 21st–28th: official programme. Hove, the Club, 1920. 24p.

2779 Year book. Hove, the Club. port. stats.
■ *1927; ed. by 'Leather Hunter' ?[A.J. Gaston]*
*1928; ed. by 'Leather Hunter'*
*1929–39, 1949; ed. by Sir Home Gordon*
*1951–52 with title: Annual; ed. by A.W.T. Langford. illus. ports. score, stats.*
*cover-titles: 1927–29 Official handbook and guide*
*1930–37 Sussex cricket annual*
*1938–52 Sussex county cricket annual*
*For subsequent issues see no. 2781*

2780 Hove 1872–1972. Hove, the Club, 1972. 49p. illus. ports. scores, stats.
*issued to celebrate the centenary of the Hove cricket ground*

2780 ———, *and* **Hove Museum of Art**
–1 The golden ages of Sussex cricket: exhibi-
■ tion at Hove Museum of Art 3rd to 31st of May, 1978. Hove, Sussex C.C.C. & Hove Museum of Art, [1978]. 32p. ports. stats.
*compiled by H.A. Osborne, Hon. Librarian to the Club*

2781 ———, *and* **Sussex Cricket Association**
■ Sussex cricket official handbook. Hove, Sussex C.C.C. & Sussex C.A. illus. ports. scores, stats.
*1953*
*1954–76 with title: Official Sussex cricket handbook*
*1977–78 with title: Sussex County Cricket Club handbook*
*contd. as:*
**Sussex County Cricket Club**
Handbook
1979

2782 **Sussex Cricket Society**
■ Monthly news letter. The Society. *typescript*
*Nov. 1965 to date*

2783 **Taylor, Alfred Daniel**
■ Famous Sussex cricketers, past and present. Hove, Hove Gazette, 1898. [iv],49p.

2784 Sussex County Cricket Club: its diamond
■ jubilee 1839–1899. *Privately printed,* [1899]. 92p. scores, stats.
*limited ed. of 100 copies*

2785 Sussex cricket battles; reprinted from the
■ "Hove Gazette". Hove, Emery, 1903. [i],55p.

2786 Sussex cricket records (compiled to May
■ 1921). Hove, Taylor Bros., [1921]. 28p. stats.

2787 The story of a cricket picture (Sussex and
■ Kent). Hove, Emery, 1923. 61p. illus. scores
*on the engraving by W.H. Mason of a match between Sussex and Kent at Brighton, 1849*
——*rptd.* Wakefield, S.R. Publishers Ltd., 1972. [iii],61p.
*see no. 2765*

2788 **Washer, George,** *compiler*
■ A complete record of Sussex county cricket, 1728 to 1957. Hove, Sussex C.C.C.,1958. ix,150p. frontis. stats.

# WARWICKSHIRE

2789 **The Daily Gazette**
Warwickshire and Midland Counties cricket guide. Birmingham, Daily Gazette. *annual.* ports. stats.
*1893–99?*
*1900?–03 with title: The Birmingham Daily Gazette cricket guide*
*1904–06 with title: The Birmingham Gazette and Express cricket guide*

2790 **The Victoria** history of the counties
■ of England: Warwickshire; edited by William Page. Vol. 2. Constable, 1908
*cricket pp.395–410*

2791 **Warwickshire Cricket Association**
■ Yearbook. The Association. illus. ports. scores
*1970/1970–73/*
*final issue 1974 ed. by P.L. Hancock*

2792 **Warwickshire Pilgrims Cricket Club**
□ [Handbook]. The Club. *typescript.* scores
*?/1964/to date*
*formed 1934*

## Bedworth

2792   **Bedworth** Cricket Club 1861–1961. [Bed-
–1      worth, the Club, 1961]. 12p.
        *presented to subscribers to the Club's Score-
        box Appeal, 1961*

## Birmingham

2793   **Birmingham Cricket Club**
■      Rules. Birmingham, the Club, [1836]. 8p.

2794   **Pollard, Fred**
■      Cricketers' guide for Birmingham and
       District, containing names and addresses
       of secretaries, county, first-class and local
       fixtures, laws of cricket, etc., etc. Bir-
       mingham, *n.p. annual. stats.*
       *at least 5 issues 1892–6; title varies: Cricket
       guide . . .*

### Associations and Leagues

2795   **Birmingham and District Cricket League**
□      Rules, fixtures and instructions to
       umpires. Birmingham, the League. *annual*
       *?/1889–1914, 1920/to date*
       *formed 1888*

2796   Divisions I and II averages. Birmingham,
□      the League. *annual. bs. stats.*
       *season ?/1959,60/to date?*

2797   **Birmingham and District Works
       Amateur Cricket Association**
       Official handbook. Birmingham, the
       Assoc., 1914
       *the only issue?*

2798   **Birmingham Industrial Sports Leagues.**
□      *Cricket Section*
       [Handbook]. Birmingham, the Leagues.
       *annual*
       *?/1947/–?*

2799   **Birmingham Public Parks Cricket**
□      **Association**
       [Handbook]. Birmingham, the Assoc.
       *illus. stats.*
       *?/1968,1975/to date*
       *1968: 75th year. 72p. illus. stats.*

2800   **Hill, H. Grosvenor**
       Birmingham & District Cricket League: its
       history, and what it has done. [1898]
       *pamphlet*

### Ashfield

2801   **Butler, Leslie O.**
■      Ashfield Cricket Club: the story of fifty
       years, 1900–1950; statistician Arthur E.
       Bourne, edited by T.W. Hutton. [Ash-
       field, the Club, 1950]. [ii],41p. 1 illus.
       ports. stats.

### Harborne

2802   **Benson, Derek H.**
■      Harborne Cricket Club 1868–1968.
       Birmingham, the Author, [1968?] 73p.
       ports. scores

2803   **Harborne Cricket Club**
□      Souvenir chronicle. Birmingham, the
       Club.
       *vol. 1, no. 2. Spring 1943. 46p. illus.
       ports. scores*

2804   **Smith, Irving W.**
■      Harborne Cricket Club versus Wolver-
       hampton, 1901–1914: [a brief history of
       the matches]. The Author. [c.1915]. 20p.
       *typescript*

2805   Random reminiscences of the Harborne
       Cricket Club 1901–1914. The Author,
       [c.1915]. 79p. *typescript*

2806   ————, *and others*
■      Cricketing days: Harborne Cricket Club
       1884–1946, by I.W. Smith, O.R. White
       and P.G. Whitehouse. Birmingham,
       Stanford & Munn, 1946. 36p.

### Kings Heath

2807   **Jones, W. Leslie,** *editor*
■      Cricket memories: a history of the Kings
       Heath C.C. 1868–1947. *Privately printed*
       [1947]. 32p. illus. ports.

### Pickwick Athletic

2808   **Ewing, J. Elliot,** *editor*
■      Pickwick Athletic Club: 1858–1958
       centenary year handbook. [Birmingham,
       the Club, 1958]. 110p. illus. stats.

2809   **Pickwick Athletic Club.** *Cricket Section*
■      Visit of the South Australian cricket
       touring team, Aug. 31, Sept. 1,2, & 3,
       1956: programme of events. [Birming-
       ham], the Club, [1956]. 8p.

## Coventry

2810   **Dalton, Gilbert**
■      The making of a century: the history of
       Coventry and North Warwickshire C.C.,
       1851–1951. Coventry, Curtis & Beamish,
       1951. 40p. illus. scores, stats.

## Dudley

2811   **Dudley Cricket Club.** *Wayfarers Touring*
■      *Side*
       The way of the Wayfarers: an account of
       the . . . cricket tour of the Wayfarers (a
       band of strolling cricketers). Dudley, [the

Club]. *annual. illus. ports. scores, stats.*
*in v.y.*
　*1913, 1914, 1920–21; ed. by Cover-Point,*
*i.e. Joseph Lewis*
　*1922–23; ed. by J. Lewis & J.E. Cartwright*
　*1924–39; ed. by J.E. Cartwright*
　*1947; ed. by H. Mayhew*

## Earlswood

2811　**Earlswood Cricket Club**
–1　Centenary 1876–1976. [Earlswood, the
■　Club, 1976]. [24]p. illus. ports. facsims.
　score

## Kineton

2812　**Hanbury, Patience**
■　The story of Kineton Cricket Club.
　Kineton, Roundwood P., 1956. [4]p.

## Leamington

2813　**Leamington Cricket Club**
□　[Handbook]. Leamington Spa, the Club.
　*annual?*
　*?/1963/–?*
　*officers and fixtures*

2814　**Rayner, Kenneth,** *editor*
■　A history of the Leamington Cricket Club
　1900–1950. [Leamington, the Club], 1950,
　23p. ports.

## Rugby

2814　**Badger, F.R.**
–1　The four "F's" of local cricket: facts, feats,
　figures & fixtures of cricket in Rugby &
　District. Rugby, Adcock, 1946. 63p.

2815　**Buchanan, David**
■　The Rugby Cricket Club: its rise and
　progress, from 1844 to 1894; including an
　account of foreign matches played on the
　ground, also an article on slow bowling.
　Rugby, "Rugby Advertiser", 1894. 45p.
　ports. scores
　*—continued by W.H. Pridmore, from*
　*1886 to 1928. Rugby, "Rugby Advert-*
　*iser", 1928. 132p. ports. scores*

# WARWICKSHIRE C.C.C.

2816　**Brooke, Robert W.,** *compiler*
■　Warwickshire v. Worcestershire 1899–
　1968: a statistical survey. Hampton-in-
　Arden, the Author, 1969. 11p. stats.

2817　Warwickshire cricketers 1843–1973.
■　Hampton-in-Arden, Association of
　Cricket Statisticians, 1973. 36p. stats.
　*limited ed. of 350 copies*

2817　**Duckworth, Leslie Blakey**
–1　The story of Warwickshire cricket: a
■　history of the Warwickshire County
　Cricket Club and ground 1882–1972. S.
　Paul, 1974. xvi,691p. illus. (1 col.) ports.
　plan, scores, stats. bibliog.

2818　**Edgell, George W.,** *and* **Fraser, Michael**
■　**Forbes Keeling**
　Warwickshire County Cricket Club: a
　history. Birmingham, Cornish, 1946.
　xvii,153p. illus. ports. scores, stats.

2819　**Santall, Sydney**
　Fifty years of Warwickshire cricket. [4]p.
　folded card. stats.

2820　History of Warwickshire cricket. Cricket
■　& Sports Publishers, 1911. 216p. illus.
　scores, stats.
　*with contributions by R.V. Ryder and*
　*H.W. Bainbridge*

2821　————, *compiler*
■　Warwickshire as a first-class county: a
　complete record of the team's perform-
　ances in the County Championship and
　other matches 1894–1903. Birmingham,
　*printed by* White & Pike, [1904]. [ii],95p.
　ports. stats.

2822　**Warwickshire County Cricket Club**
□　Annual report [and statement of
　accounts]. Birmingham, the Club.
　*1889/1939*
　*1945 to date. illus. ports. scores, stats.*
　*seasons 1904–06, 1908–11, 1915–29,*
　*1938–39 in sheet form*

2823　The Warwickshire diary for cricket lovers:
■　an occasional publication; edited by
　M.F.K. Fraser. Birmingham, the Club.
　illus. ports.
　*nos. 1–9. 1947–49*

2824　The story of Warwickshire County
■　Cricket Club. [Birmingham, the Club,
　1950]. 24p. illus. ports. stats.

2825　Rules. Birmingham, the Club, [1955].
□　[8]p.
　*also subsequent issues*

2826　Membership drive brochure 1966.
　Birmingham, the Club, 1966. 12p. illus.
　(some col.), ports. diagrs.

2826　**The Warwick Pool** Under-25 county
–1　cricket competition: rules of competition
□　and fixtures. Birmingham, Warwickshire
　C.C.C. *annual*
　*1972/1973 . . . 78/to date*
　*1973 with title: under 25 county cricket*
　*competition*
　*limited to uncapped (first-class county or*

*country) players under 25 years of age who are identified with their respective first-class clubs*

2827 **Warwickshire** County Cricket Club photo
■ album. Nottingham, Le Butt, [1948]. [16]p. ports.

2828 **Warwickshire C.C.C. Supporters'**
■ **Association**
[Aims and objectives]. Birmingham, the Club, [1966]. 16p. illus. diagr.

2829 **Warwickshire** county cricket guide and handbook; compiled by Sydney Santall. Birmingham, Moody Bros. *annual.* team port. stats.
*3 issues 1924–26*

2830 **The Warwickshire** cricket handbook.
■ Birmingham.
*1936: a record of first class cricket in Warwickshire, 1895–1935; compiled by Claude L. Westell. C.W. Towers, [1936]. illus. ports. stats.*
*1949, 1950. Davies-Towers. illus. ports. stats.*
*1952: edited by W.E. Hall. Sparkhill Printing Co. illus. ports. scores, stats.*
*1953–1963; edited and compiled by W.G. Wanklyn and E.A. Davis*

# WESTMORLAND

2830 **Westmorland Cricket League**
–1 Official handbook. The League. *annual.*
□ stats.
*from ? to 1974 season*

### Kendal

2831 **Clarke, James,** *compiler*
■ History of cricket in Kendal from 1836–1905. Kendal, Thomson, *printer,* 1906. 426p. illus. scores, stats.

# WILTSHIRE

2832 **The Victoria** history of the county of
■ Wiltshire; edited by Elizabeth Crittall. Vol. 4. O.U.P., 1959
*cricket pp.377–379*

### Box

2833 **Box** Cricket Club 1870–1970: centenary
■ souvenir card. [Box C.C., 1970]. 16p.

2834 **Bradfield, Donald**
■ A century of village cricket: the history of the Box Cricket Club. [Box C.C.], 1964. 98p. incl. adverts. illus. ports. scores

### Corsham

2835 **Lakeman, H.S.**
■ Eighty years of cricket: a brief history of the Corsham Sports Club 1848–1928. Bristol, *printed by* Matthews, Cabot, P., 1929. 56p. ports. stats.
*contents include "Corsham Cricket": a sonnet by Clifford Bax*

### Devizes

2836 **Devizes Cricket Club**
■ Rules as approved . . . 1954 with amendments made . . . 1955 and 1957. Devizes, the Club, [1957]. 3f. *typescript*

2837 **Weeks, J.S.,** *compiler & editor*
■ Devizes Cricket Club, 1850–1950. Devizes, *printed by* Wiltshire Gazette, 1951. 82p. ports. scores

### Goatacre

2837 **The first** fifty: the story of Goatacre
–1 Cricket Club 1928 to 1978. [Goatacre, the
■ Club, 1978]. [viii], 58p. incl. adverts with centre insert pp.i–viii. illus. ports.

### Purton

2838 **[Bradford, J.E.G.]**
■ Purton Cricket Club: reminiscences. [Swindon, North Wilts Herald], 1911. 12p.
*reprinted from North Wilts Herald of 31st Dec., 1909*

2839 **[Gardner, J.]** *compiler*
■ Cricket and Purton: Purton Cricket Club 150th anniversary. [Purton C.C., 1970]. 24p. ports.

2840 **Purton** Cricket Club 1862. Cirencester,
■ *printed by* E. Baily, 1862. 15p.
*rules and list of members*

### Trowbridge

2841 **Wiltshire County Records Committee**
Wiltshire records in 1969: annual report of the . . . Committee. Trowbridge, the Cttee., 1970. 12p. illus.
*contains an illustration of a souvenir scorecard of a cricket match at Trowbridge, 1897—Rt. Hon. W.H. Long's XI v. W.G. Grace's XI*

# WILTSHIRE C.C.C.

2842 **Wiltshire County Cricket Club**
□ Annual report. [Swindon], the Club. scores, stats. (of same year)
*1930–39, 1946 to date*

The Worcestershire Cricket Ground viewed from the roof of the
Cathedral *photo: Patrick Eagar*

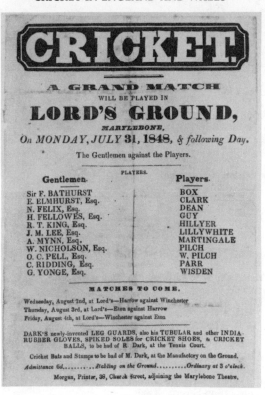

Gentlemen v. Players: A poster for the 1848 match
*photo: M.C.C.*

One-day cricket: Mike Denness holding
the Gillette Trophy after Kent's victory
over Lancashire, 1974 *photo: Patrick Eagar*

# WORCESTERSHIRE

**2843** The Victoria history of the counties of
■ England: Worcestershire; edited by J.W.
Willis-Bund and William Page. Vol. 2.
Constable, 1906
*cricket pp.340–46*

**2844** Worcestershire cricket annual for 1907.
■ Worcester, Worcester Daily Times, 1907.
126p. scores, stats.
*the only issue*

**2844** Worcestershire Cricket Association
**–1** Year book. Worcester, the Assoc. ports.
□ stats.
*1976/1976,78/to date*
*formed 1970*

## Barnt Green

**2844** Barnt Green Cricket Club
**–2** Jubilee Year 1889–1939. [Barnt Green, the
■ Club, 1939?]. [12]p. stats.

## Hagley

**2844** [Jackson, P.W.H., Spencer, A., *and*
**–3** Davies C.]
■ A history of Hagley Cricket Club
1834–1975. [Stourport-on-Severn, the
Club, 1975]. [iv],117p. illus. port. scores,
stats. *typescript*
*contains pp.7–9 an account of the match
played by the Lyttelton family team against
Bromsgrove School whom they defeated by 10
wickets*

## Kidderminster

**2844** Tomkinson, Ken, *and* Hall, George
**–4** Kidderminster since 1800. Kidderminster,
the Authors, 1975. xiii,236,xxvi,p.
*cricket pp.38–9,42–3,60,65–7*

## Malvern

**2844** Malvern Ramblers Cricket Club
**–5** Newsletter. Malvern, the Club. *typescript*
□ *?/1976/to date?*
*Vol. 9, no.1. Jan/Feb 1976; no.2 Mar/Apr
1976; nos.4 & 5 Jul/Oct 1976; edited by G.D.
Baxandall*

## Netherton

**2845** Rollason, F.
■ Netherton Cricket Club, 1866–1966: one
hundred years of cricket: a short story of
Netherton Cricket Club. Netherton, the
Club, [1966]. [ii],51p. illus. ports. scores,
stats.

## Stourbridge

**2846** Haden, Harry Jack
■ Stourbridge Cricket Club early days
recalled. Stourbridge, Mark & Moody,
1957. 20p.
*rptd. from the "County Express"*

## Tenbury

**2846** Tenbury Cricket Club 1851–1951:
**–1** centenary year. [Tenbury, the Club,
1951]. 56p. incl. covers & adverts. 1 illus.
ports.

# WORCESTERSHIRE C.C.C.

**2846** Association of Cricket Statisticians
**–2** Worcestershire cricketers 1899–1974;
■ compiled by Philip Thorn. Bottesford
(Notts.), the Assoc., 1974. 31p. stats.
*limited ed. of 500 numbered copies*

**2847** Brooke, Robert W., *compiler*
■ Warwickshire v. Worcestershire: a stat-
istical survey, 1899–1968. Hampton-in-
Arden, the Author, 1969. 11p. stats.

**2848** Chignell, Wilfred Rowland
■ A history of the Worcestershire County
Cricket Club, 1844–1950. Worcester,
Littlebury, [1951]. 443p. illus. ports. stats.

**2849** Worcestershire cricket, 1950–1968. Wor-
■ cester, Littlebury, [1969]. 305p. illus.
ports. scores, stats.

**2850** Ernest T. Potter's Worcestershire county
■ cricket guide. Worcester, Potter. *annual.*
ports.
*3 issues 1902–04*

**2851** Genders, Roy
■ Worcestershire county cricket. Convoy
Publications, 1952. 102p. illus. ports.
(County Cricket Series)

**2851** The Guardian
**–1** The bedside 'Guardian' 14: a selection
■ from The Guardian 1964–1965. Collins,
1965. 256p. illus.
*includes pp.16–8, "Worcestershire cham-
pions at last", by Henry Blofeld*

**2852** Payne, John Bertram, *compiler and editor*
■ Worcester County Cricket Club history
and guide 1928. Denny, 1928. 47p. illus.
ports. stats.
*covers 1927 season*

**2853** Worcestershire Cricket Club
Rules, bye-laws and members, 1891.
Worcester, the Club, 1891. 22p.
——1895. 22p.

2854 Programme of the grand bazaar organ-
■ ised by Mr. C.P. Green and exhibited in
aid of the Worcestershire C.C.C., the
Shirehall, Worcester . . . 1903. Worcester,
[Worcestershire C.C.C.], 1903. 72p. illus.
ports.

2855 Grand Fete, County Ground, Worcester,
■ Saturday, 27th July, 1929: official programme. Worcester, the Club, [1929].
[12]p. incl. adverts.

2856 Official year book. Worcester, the Club.
■ illus. ports. scores, stats. (in v.y.)
*1933*
*1936–39, 1947–52; compiled by the
Secretary*
*1953–56 edited & compiled by the Secre-
tary, [etc.]*
*1957 compiled by J. Lister & W.R. Chignell
1958 to date compiled by the Year Book
Sub-Committee.*
*1965 with title: Centenary year book
contains history of the Club*

*World tour 1965*

2857 **Calcutta Cricket Club**
■ Cricket: the English County Champions
of 1964: Worcestershire C.C.C. in
Calcutta 4th to 11th March, 1965: official
souvenir programme. Calcutta, the Club,
[1965]. 68p. incl. adverts. illus. ports.
scores
*pre-visit*

2857 **Malaysian Cricket Association**
–1 Visit of Worcestershire Cricket Club
■ (County Champions 1964) to Singapore,
Malaysia, 11–17 March 1965: souvenir
programme. Singapore, the Assoc.,
[1965]. [76]p. incl. adverts. ports.
*includes brief history of Worcs. C.C.C.
1865–1965 and pen sketches of opposing teams*

2858 **Midlands Cricket Association**
■ Worcestershire C.C.C. (English County
Champions 1964) vs. Rhodesia Country
Districts at the Que Que Sports Club,
24th, 25th February, 1965. [Que Que
(Rhodesia)], the Assoc., [1965]. 56p. incl.
adverts. ports.
*pre-visit*

2858 **Royal Bangkok Sports Club**
–1 Worcestershire County C.C. v. R.B.S.C.
■ at the R.B.S.C. Ground, Bangkok, March
24, 1965: souvenir programme. Bangkok,
the Club, [1965]. [36]p. mostly adverts.
ports.

2859 **Selangor** Cricket Association welcomes
Worcestershire: souvenir. Kuala Lumpur,
the Association, 1965. 88p. incl. adverts.
ports.

2860 **Worcestershire County Cricket Club**
■ World tour February/March/April 1965:
[itinerary and fixtures]. Worcester, the
Club, [1965]. 11p. map

*Jamaica tour 1966*

2861 **Jamaica tour** March/April 1966: [itinerary
■ and fixtures]. Worcester, the Club, [1966].
[8]p. map

# YORKSHIRE

2862 **Cleveland,** Durham, Northumberland
■ and Yorkshire cricketer's handbook.
Bury, Fletcher & Speight, 1882
contd. as: *The Durham and Yorkshire
cricketers' handbook*

2863 **The Cricketers'** handbook containing the
match fixtures of the principal clubs in
Northumberland, Durham and North
Yorkshire. Bury, Fletcher & Speight.
*annual. illus.*
*1891–3, 1897–1900*
*1891 issue with title: Henry A. Murton's
cricketers' companion*

2864 **Dales Council Cricket League**
□ Official handbook. The League. *annual.*
*stats.*
*1956 to date?*

2865 **The Durham** and Yorkshire cricketers'
handbook. Bury, Fletcher & Speight.
*annual*
*1883–1900; formerly: Cleveland, Durham,
Northumberland and Yorkshire cricketer's
handbook*

2866 **Duthoit, W.**
■ Yorkshire cricketers' guide for 1878.
Leeds, W. Duthoit, 1878. 118p. port.
scores, stats.
*the only year of issue. Portrait is mounted
photograph of Ephraim Lockwood*

2867 **East, Harry**
The heart of Yorkshire cricket: a story of
village cricket in Yorkshire; illustrations
by Brian Johnson. Driffield, Riding Publ.
Co., [1973]. 86p. illus.

2867 **Fletcher, Joseph Smith**
–1 A picturesque history of Yorkshire.
Founded on personal observations. 6
vols. Caxton Publishing Co., 1903–04
*cricket in Vol. V, ch.63, pp.237–248;
includes extended interview with George
Ulyett; first publd. in 3 vols. Dent, 1899*

2868 **Harrison, Thomas**
■ Yorkshire Cricket Council, 1899–1951.
Leeds, Yorkshire Post, 1952. [iv],119p.
illus. ports. scores, stats.

2868 **Hattersley, Roy**
-1 Goodbye to Yorkshire. Gollancz, 1976.
■ 163p. illus. map on endpapers
*cricket pp.19,24–5,109–14,137–8,151–3*

2869 **Mayhall, John,** *compiler*
■ The annals of Yorkshire from the earliest
period to the present time. Leeds, J.
Johnson, 1861. iv,768p. illus.
*details of cricket matches, pp. 390, 532,*
*549, 558, 567, 699*
——*another ed.* 2 vols. 1866
*cricket in vol. II*

2870 **North Yorkshire and South Durham**
□ **Cricket League**
[Handbook]. Middlesbrough, the League.
*annual*
*?/1893–1914, ?1919 to date*

2871 Statistics 1893–1947; compiled by H. Tren-
■ holm. The League, [1948]. 184p. port.
scores, stats.
——Statistics 1948–1955: supplement.
The League, [1956]. 75p. score, stats.

2872 **Overend, J.W.**
■ Some interesting links of Yorkshire
cricket. Eccleshill, Yorks., the Author,
[1918]. 16p. illus. ports. score
*rptd. from Yorkshire Weekly Post*

2873 **Rosenwater, Irving**
■ The story of a cricket playbill. The
Author, 1968. [4]p. facsim.
*limited ed. of 25 copies only; refers to a*
*playbill "At the Theatre, Leeds, 12th June,*
*1780" which contained an allusion to cricket*
*being played at that time in Yorkshire*

2874 **Sheffield Telegraph**
■ Cricket guide and annual: a club and
county chronicle; edited by "Looker-On".
Sheffield, Sheffield Telegraph. illus.
ports. stats.
*3 issues 1904–06; includes all English 1st*
*class cricket results*

2875 **The Victoria** history of the counties of
■ England: Yorkshire; edited by William
Page. Vol. 2. Constable, 1912
*cricket pp.537–41. stats.*

2876 **Yorkshire Central Cricket League**
□ Official handbook. The League. *annual*
*?/1895 to date*
*1970 incorporated with Barkston Ash C.L.,*
*to form The Barkston Ash and the Yorkshire*
*Central C.L.*
*formed 1894*

2877 **Yorkshire Cricket Association**
□ Newsletter. The Association. *irregular*
*May 1973–*
*list of officials, reports of league and schools*
*cricket in Yorkshire, coaching courses, etc.*

2878 **The Yorkshire** cricket chronicle. Sheffield, J.W. Northend by the authority of
the Yorkshire C.C.C., 1903. *weekly*
*15 issues 4th May to 17th Aug., 1903*

2879 **Yorkshire Cricket Council**
□ Official guide. Leeds, the Council. *annual.*
*1900–14*
*1920 to date with title: Rules and official*
*guide*

2880 Umpires appointments. Leeds, the
Council. *annual*
*?/1925,1927–31,1935/–?*

2881 **Yorkshire Cricket Federation**
□ Official handbook. The Federation.
*irregular.* ports. (v.y.)
*?/1936–48, 51, 54, 57, 60, 64, 68, 73/to*
*date?*
*1945 "Rules" only*
*formed 1929*

2882 **Yorkshire** cricket handbook: English,
■ Yorkshire and local records and fixtures.
Leeds, A. Wigley, the Waverley P.
*annual.* ports. stats.
*1926–9*

2883 **Yorkshire Cricket League**
□ Official handbook. The League. *annual.*
ports. stats.
*? 1936/1938-39, 1969-73/to date*

2884 **Yorkshire** cricketers' guide and diary.
□ *annual.* stats.
*9 issues 1882–90. Leeds, Briggs & Rochfort*
*1891; with which is incorporated The West*
*Riding cricketers' guide. Bradford, J.S.*
*Toothill. ports.*
See *no. 3014*

2885 **The Yorkshire** cricketers' handbook,
□ containing match fixtures for the principal clubs in Yorkshire, . . . Bury,
Fletcher & Speight. *annual.* ports, stats.
*12 issues season 1881–1902*

2886 **Yorkshire Owl**
■ Grand cricket annual: record of the championship county and league cricket.
Leeds, H. Burniston, 1896. 40p. illus.
ports. stats.
*only issue*

2887 **The Yorkshire** Post cricket record. Leeds,
Yorkshire Post Office, 1886. scores
*4 monthly issues, June-Sept., 1886*

2888 **Yorkshire Post and Evening Post**
■ Cricket annual; edited by "Old Ebor".
Leeds, Yorkshire Conservative Newspapers, 1906. 128p. team port. stats.
*only issue*

**2889  Yorkshire Sports**
■     Cricket annual: records, fixtures and
      guide to season. Bradford, Yorkshire
      Sports. scores, stats.
      *1922–26*

## Airedale and Wharfedale

**2890  Airedale and Wharfedale Senior Cricket**
□     **League**
      Official handbook. The League. *annual.*
      stats.
      *?1893–1916,1936/1957,58/to date*

## Barkston Ash

**2891  Barkston Ash Cricket League**
□     Handbook. Barkston Ash, the League.
      *annual.* stats.
      *?1891–1914, 1919?/1926 . . . 58/–1969*
      contd. as: *Barkston Ash and Yorkshire
      Central C.L. Handbook*

**2892  Barkston Ash and Yorkshire Central**
□     **Cricket League**
      Handbook. The League. *annual.* stats.
      *1970 to date*
      formerly: *Barkston Ash C.L. Handbook*

## Barnby Dun

**2893  Barnby Dun Cricket Club**
■     Centenary brochure 1870–1970. [Barnby
      Dun], the Club, [1970]. 32p. incl. adverts.
      score

## Barnsley

**2894  Barnsley and District Cricket League**
□     Rules and official handbook. Barnsley,
      the League. *annual.* ports.
      *1951/1951–58/to date*
      *formed 1894; see also West Riding cricket
      guide, no. 3014*

## Bingley

**2895  Dodd, E.E.**
■     Bingley, a Yorkshire town through nine
      centuries. [Bingley], Harrison, 1958. xvi,
      268p. illus. maps
      *cricket pp.112,164,186,212*

## Bradford

**2896  Bradford and District Amateur Cricket**
□     **Council**
      Official handbook. Bradford, the Council.
      *annual.* stats.
      *?1922–41, ?1946 to date*

**2897  Bradford & District Evening Cricket**
□     **League**
      Official handbook. Bradford, the League.
      stats.
      *1938–40?,1946/1969–72/to date*

**2898  Bradford Central Cricket League**
□     Official guide. Bradford, the League.
      *annual.* stats.
      *season 1908/1956–61, 1971–73/to date*

**2899  Bradford Cricket, Athletic and Football**
□     **Club Ltd**
      Official programme. Bradford, the Club.
      *annual*
      *?/season 1910–11/–?*

**2900  Bradford Cricket League**
□     Official guide. Bradford, the League.
      *annual.* ports. scores, stats.
      *1904?/1917 . . . 79/to date*
      *in 1950's changed title to* Official hand-
      book; *combined issues 1942/43 to 1953/54*

**2901  Bradford** cricketers' journal. Bradford,
      J.S. Toothill. *weekly. illus.*
      *4 issues 27th Apr.–19th May, 1877*

**2902  Bradford Mutual Sunday School Cricket**
□     **League**
      Official handbook. Bradford, the League.
      *annual.* stats.
      *?/1896–1916, ?1919 to date*
      *1956 issue with title:* Diamond jubilee
      handbook. 80p.

**2903  Burnley, James**
      West Riding sketches (Bradford District).
      Hodder & Stoughton, 1875. 408p.
      *includes "Cricket off the hearth", pp.165–
      181 concerning early Bradford cricketers*

**2904  South Bradford Evening Cricket League**
□     Official handbook. Bradford, the League,
      *annual.* stats.
      *?1933–42, ?1946 to date*

**2905  West Bradford Cricket League**
□     Official guide. Bradford, the League.
      *annual.* port. diagrs. stats.
      *1893?–1915, 1919?/1953–58, 1971,72,76/*
      to date
      *1953. Jubilee handbook 1893–1953; edited
      and compiled by Raymond Newiss and Percy
      Hardacre. 112p. illus. port. scores, stats.*

## Burton Leonard

**2905  Diggle, Henry Frederick**
–1    Burton Leonard past and present.
      [Harrogate, the Author], 1978. 124p. illus.
      ports.
      *1st publd. 1951*
      *pp.118–120 "The Cricket Club"*

## Calverley

**2906  Marshall, J.**
      History of Calverley cricket (1843–1920)

## Cawthorne

2907　**Cawthorne** Cricket Club welcomes you to the 1972 season. [Cawthorne, the Club, 1972]. 32p.
*includes brief history of the club*

## Craven

2908 □　**Craven Cricket League**
Handbook. Skipton, the League. *annual*
*1922–26*
*1935?* to date with title: *Craven and District C.L. Official handbook. annual. stats.*
*previously known as: Craven Cricket Union, 1890–1904*
*Skipton Junior C.L., 1904–1908*
*Skipton & District C.L. 1909–1921*

2909 ■　A history of the Craven and District Cricket League and its forerunners 1888–1958. Craven, the League, [1959]. 63p. stats.
——Summary of information submitted by member clubs of the Craven & District Cricket League and published as an addendum to the Official history of the League. The League, [1959]. 8f. *typescript.* stats.

2909 –1　**Williams, T. Russell**
Human documents: memories of the Craven Dales. Keighley, Wadsworth & Co., [c.1900]. 101p.
*pp.33–46 "The cricketers"*

## Denby Grange

2910 □　**Denby Grange & District Cricket League**
[Handbook]. Horbury Bridge, the League. *irregular*
*various years 1920/1958/to date?*

## Dewsbury

2911 □　**Dewsbury and District Cricket League**
Official handbook. Dewsbury, the League. *annual*
*1912?–16, 1920–40, 1946/1957, 58/to date?*

## Doncaster

2912 ■　**Baines, W. Eric,** *and* **Evans, Kenneth**
The first history of the Doncaster & District Cricket League. Doncaster, [the League], 1951. 40p. illus. ports. scores, stats.

2913 □　**Doncaster and District Cricket League**
Official guide. Doncaster, the League. *annual. stats.*
*?1914–15, 1918/1955–57, 1971–72/ to date*

## East Riding

2914　**East Riding Amateur Cricket League**
Official handbook. The League
*?/1956/–?*

## Eccleshill

2915 ■　**Overend, J.W.**
Eccleshill Cricket Club record and history book 1860–1916. Eccleshill, the Author, 1916. 64p. illus. ports. scores, stats.

## Gargrave

2916　**Gargrave Cricket Club**
Souvenir programme to commemorate the opening of the new pavilion, 18th May, 1957. Gargrave, the Club, [1957]. 4p. 1 illus.

## Halifax

2917 □　**Halifax and District Amateur Cricket Association**
Rules and fixtures, etc. [Halifax], the Association. *annual. stats.*
*?/1957, 58, 69/to date*

2918 □　**Halifax Cricket League**
Official handbook: rules, fixtures and umpires. Halifax, the League. *annual. stats.*
*seasons ?/1956–59, 1972/to date*

2919　**Halifax Nomads Cricket Club**
[Annual]. Halifax, the Club. stats. *typescript*
*season ?/1971/to date*

2920 ■　Halifax Nomads Cricket Club 1939 to 1962. [Halifax, the Club, 1962]. [22]p. illus. ports. stats. *typescript*

2921 ■　**King Cross Cricket and Bowling Club**
Jubilee bazaar . . . April 18th, 19th and 21st, 1928. Halifax, the Club, [1928]. 28p. incl. adverts. ports.
*includes brief history of the club*

2922 ■　**[Pearce, Kenneth]**
Illingworth St. Mary's C.C. 1884–1961. [Halifax, the Club, 1961]. 69p. illus. ports. scores

## Hallam

2922 –1 ■　**[Watt-Smith, Simon J.]**
Hallam C.C. 175th anniversary cricket festival 17–22 June, 1979, Sandygate Road: [souvenir programme]. [Sheffield], the Club, [1979]. 32p. incl. adverts. illus. team ports.

## Harrogate

**2922** **Greaves, George L.**
**-2** Over the summers again: a history of the Harrogate Cricket Club. Harrogate, the Club, 1976. 171p. illus. ports. scores, stats. bibliog.
*celebrates the centenary of the Club*

**2923** **Harrogate and District Amateur Cricket League**
Annual report and statement. Harrogate, the League.
*?/1946/-?*

**2924** Rules and fixtures. Harrogate, the League.
*?/1946,47/-?*

**2924** **Harrogate Cricket Club**
**-1** Harrogate Taverner; edited by Brian
■ Rotheray. Harrogate, the Club. *monthly*
*Vol. 1, no.1 April 1979 to date*

## Hebden Bridge

**2925** **Hebden Bridge and District Cricket**
■ **League**
Rules and byelaws. Hebden Bridge, the League, 1952. 8p.

## Heckmondwike

**2926** **Heckmondwike Cricket and Tennis Club**
■ Centenary brochure 1864–1964. Heckmondwike, the Club, [1964]. 24p. port. score, stats.

## Honley

**2926** **Jagger, Mary A.**
**-1** The history of Honley and its hamlets
■ from the earliest time to the present. Honley, *printed by* A. Judd, 1914. viii,338, viii,p. illus. ports. facsims.
*cricket pp.144–5*

## Huddersfield

**2927** **Brook, Roy**
■ The story of Huddersfield, MacGibbon & Kee, 1968. xxi,394p. illus. (1 col.), ports. maps
*cricket pp.263,267–69*

**2928** **Ellam, Ben,** *compiler*
Huddersfield cricket feats through the years. Huddersfield, *printed by* E. Woffenden, [1950]. 68p. ports.

**2928** **Fieldhouse, Harry**
**-1** Huddersfield sportsmen of then and now. Harry Fieldhouse's cartoons from the Saturday Evening "Examiner". [Huddersfield, the "Examiner", c.1935]. 47f.
*46 full page cartoons*

**2929** **Huddersfield and District Cricket**
□ **Association**
Annual handbook. Huddersfield, the Association. stats.
*?/1953–8,1969–73/to date*
*formed 1886*

**2930** **Huddersfield and District Cricket League**
[Handbook]. Huddersfield, the League. *annual.* ports. stats.
*1892?/1922. . . .60,1969–71/*
*titles vary, e.g. Official handbook, Guide.*
contd. as: *Huddersfield Cricket League -*
See *no. 2934*

**2931** Diamond jubilee 1891–1951: 60 years of
■ glorious cricket!; edited by J.P. Hanson. Huddersfield, the League Council, [1951]. 51p. illus. port.

**2932** **Huddersfield and District Evening**
□ **Cricket League**
Fixtures. Huddersfield, the League. *annual.* stats.
*1937?/1956–58,1969–72/to date*
*1969 with title: Official yearbook*

**2933** **Huddersfield Central Cricket League**
□ [Handbook]. Huddersfield, the League. *annual.*
*1914?/1969,72/to date*
*formed in 1914*

**2934** **Huddersfield Cricket League**
□ Official guide. Huddersfield, the League. *annual.* stats.
*1972 to date*
*formerly: Huddersfield & District C.L.*
See *no.2930*

**2935** **Lockwood, Ernest**
Colne Valley folk. Heath, Cranton, 1936. 190p.
*ch. "Sporting reminiscences" includes several pages on Huddersfield area professionals and other cricketers*

**2936** **Moriarty, Brian,** *and* **Cooper, John,**
■ *compilers*
A brief history of the Golcar Cricket & Athletic Club. 1871–1971. Huddersfield, [the Club, 1971]. 40p. ports. scores

**2936** **Primrose Hill Cricket and Athletic Club**
**-1** Centenary year 1875–1975. [Primrose
■ Hill], the Club, [1975]. [52]p. incl. adverts. illus. ports. facsim. scores, stats.

2937 **Thompson, Alan G.**
■ Cradle of cricket: the story of Huddersfield's cricketers who have brought
honour and glory to the town throughout
the years. Huddersfield, Union Publishing, [c.1955]. 72p. ports. scores

2937 **"Umpire"**, *pseud.*
-1 Huddersfield cricket 50 years ago. . .
interesting reminiscences of Mr. C.H.
Bradley: a novel single wicket match.
Reprinted from the "Huddersfield Daily
Chronicle", October 14th, 1908. [4]p. fold

2938 **Whitehead, B.D.**
Huddersfield and District Cricket Associ-
ation 1886–1961. Huddersfield, the
Assoc., [1961]. 56p. illus. port.

## Ilkley

2939 **Cobley, Frederick**
■ Black hats and white hats, or, Ilkley
tradesmen at the wickets and around the
festive board. Otley, W. Walker, 1895.
148p. illus. ports. scores

## Keighley

2940 **Keighley Cricket Club**
■ Keighley cricket: the jubilee of the Lawk-
holme ground, with records of leading
players. Keighley, the Club, 1919. 31p.
illus. ports. scores, stats.

## Kingston-upon-Hull

2941 **Hull** cricket yearbook; compiled by
■ Norman J. Pogson. Hull, the Compiler.
illus. team ports. scores, stats.
*1945–51*
*the 1945 issue contains details of the years*
*1834,44,54,64,74,84,94,1904,14,24,34.*
typescript

2942 **Ulyatt, Mike**, *compiler*
■ Hull Railway Clerks Cricket Club
centenary, 1873–1973. Hull, *printed by* J.A.
Sellars, [1973]. [68]p. incl. adverts. illus.
ports.

## Kirkburton

2943 **Kirkburton Cricket Club**
■ Souvenir handbook of the bazaar held on
March 1st, 1930. Kirkburton, the Club,
1930. 20p. incl. adverts. ports. score

2944 100 years of glorious circket. Kirkburton,
■ the Club, [1961]. [48]p. incl. adverts. illus.
ports. stats

## Knaresborough

2945 **Knaresborough Cricket Club**
■ Souvenir brochure to commemorate the
official opening of the New Pavilion and
Ground, Aspin Lane, Knaresborough on
Sunday 22nd May, 1966 by A. Brian
Sellers Esq. Knaresborough, the Club,
[1966]. 20p. incl. adverts. 1 illus.

## Lascelles Hall

2946 **Lodge, Harry**
■ Lascelles Hall Cricket Club centenary
1825–1925. Huddersfield, the Author,
1925. 24p. ports. scores
——*single leaf addendum:* History continued January 1944

2947 **Wood, Edward Allen**, *editor*
■ The History of Lascelles Hall Cricket
Club: a famous nursery of Yorkshire
cricket, 1825–1968. [The Editor, 1969].
34p. illus. ports. scores

## Leeds

2948 **Champion, C.L.**
■ The Leeds Zingari Cricket Club. *n.p.,*
[1945]. [42]p. ports.
*a chronicle covering 1932–1944*

2949 **Leeds** and district cricket annual. Arnley,
G. Dawson. illus.
*at least 3 issues, 1922–24*

2950 **Leeds and District Cricket League**
□ [Handbook]. Leeds, the League. *annual.*
stats.
*?/1893–1914,1919?/1956–58,1969–73/*to
date
*Presidential year 1971. 64p. incl. adverts.*
stats. *[of 1970]*

2951 **Leeds and District Printing Trades**
**Cricket League**
Coming of age souvenir year book
1905–25. Leeds, the League, 1925. 48p.
illus.

2952 **Leeds and District Sunday Schools**
□ **Cricket League**
[Handbook]. Leeds, the League. *annual*
*?/1956/*to date?

2953 **Leeds Combination Cricket League**
□ [Handbook]. Leeds, the League. *annual*
*?/1953-57/*to date?

2954 **Leeds Cricket Club**
Annual report. Leeds, the Club. stats.
*?/1925–27/–?*
*formed 1890*

**2955 Leeds Cricket, Football and Athletic Co. Ltd.**
Official programme, 1914–15. Leeds, the Company, [1914]. 48p. stats.
*cricket 28pp.*

**2956** Official souvenir, 1928. Leeds, the
■ Company. 1928. 80p. illus. ports.
*cricket section 5 pages only with brief history and illus.*

**2957 Leeds Cricket League**
□ Official guide. [Leeds], the League. *annual. port. stats.*
*?/1935,38/–?*
*1938 with title: Official handbook formed 1892; reorganized 1924*

**2958 Leeds Evening Cricket League**
Official rules and fixtures. Leeds, the League. *annual.*
*?1920/1938/–?*

**2959 Leeds Junior Cricket League**
□ Official fixture list. Leeds, the League. *annual*
*?/1972,75/to date*

**2960 Leeds Non-Conformist Cricket League**
Rules and fixtures. Leeds, the League. *annual?*
*?/1926/–?*
*formed 1893*

**2961 Leeds Second Cricket League**
□ Official handbook. Leeds, the League. *annual*
*?/1933. . .57/todate?*
*formed 1892*

**2962 Leeds Springfield Cricket Club**
□ Annual. Leeds, the Club. *illus.*
*?/1903. . .1970/to date?*
*later issues with title "Fixtures" including lists of officers and playing members*

**2963 North Leeds Cricket Club**
□ Sightboard. Leeds, the Club. *occasional*
*?/May 149 . . . July 1971/to date?*

**2964** Newsletter. Leeds, the Club. *typescript*
□ *1973 to date?*

**2965 Thompson, Brian**
■ Portrait of Leeds. Hale, 1971. 191p. illus. map. (Portrait Series)
*cricket pp.84,85,88–91*

## Linthwaite

**2966 Linthwaite Cricket Club**
[Handbook]. Linthwaite, the Club, 1884
*in Taylor*

## Lofthouse

**2967 Wraith, William**
■ Lofthouse Cricket Club, 1857–1957; souvenir brochure. Wakefield, [the Club, 1957]. [32]p. incl. adverts. illus. ports.

## Malton

**2968 Spiegelhalter, Cecil**
Local cricket history: the annals of the Malton Cricket Club, 1862–1906
*a collection of newspaper cuttings*

## Marske-by-the-Sea

**2969 Marske-by-the-Sea Cricket Club**
■ Centenary, 1869–1969. [Marske-By-The-Sea, the Club, 1969]. 108p. incl. adverts. illus. ports. scores

## Mexborough

**2969 Grand** cricket match. Geoff Boycott's XI
**–1** versus Mexborough and District XI,
■ Mexborough Athletic Club Ground, Thursday 1st August 1974. [Mexborough, the XI, 1974]. 16p. incl. adverts. team port.
*the match was postponed to Thursday Sept. 10, 1974*

**2970 Mexborough and District Evening**
□ **Cricket League**
Official guide. Mexborough, the League.
*1949?–1964*
*1965?–1969 with title: Official handbook*
*1970, 1971 with title: Mexborough and District Cricket Leagues. Official handbook*
*1972 to date: Mexborough & District Evening C.L. Official handbook*

## Middlesbrough

**2971 Lillie, William**
■ The history of Middlesbrough: an illustration of the evolution of English industry. Middlesbrough, The Middlesbrough Corporation, 1968. xiv,492p. illus. ports. map, plan
*cricket pp.351–54*

**2972 Middlesbrough Cricket Club**
■ The first—. Middlesbrough, the Club, [1956]. 32p. incl. adverts. ports.
*souvenir programme of the first county championship match played at Middlesbrough (Yorkshire v. Glamorgan). Contains brief history of Middlesbrough C.C.*

## Mirfield

**2973** **Mirfield and District Evening Cricket**
☐ **League and Kilner Cup Knockout Competition**
Official handbook. Mirfield, the League. *annual*
*1950/1956,58/*to date?

## Morley

**2973** **Smith, William**
**-1** Morley: ancient and modern. Longmans, Green, 1886. xv,322p. illus.
*cricket pp.129-30*

## Nidderdale

**2974** **Nidderdale & District Amateur Cricket**
☐ **League**
Rules and fixtures. The League. stats.
*?/1970-72/*to date
*formed 1895*

## Otley

**2975** **Beadle, Ray,** *editor*
■ Otley Cricket Club 1820-1970: [anniversary booklet]. [Otley, the Club, 1970]. 28p. illus. ports. score

## Pontefract

**2976** **Pontefract & District Cricket League**
☐ Official handbook. Pontefract, the League. *annual*
*1960?/1970-73/*to date

## Pudsey

**2977** **Pudsey Sunday School and District**
☐ **Cricket League**
[Handbook]. Pudsey, the League. *annual*
*?/1970/*to date
*formed 1895*

**2977** **Rayner, Simeon**
**-1** The history and antiquities of Pudsey; edited by William Smith. Longmans, Green, 1887. illus. xvi,313,xxi,p. illus.
*cricket pp.197-8*

## Rastrick

**2978** **Rastrick Cricket and Athletic Club**
■ Centenary year 1863-1963: a hundred years of glorious cricket. Rastrick, the Club, [1963]. [16]p. incl. adverts.

## Ribblesdale

**2979** **Ribblesdale Cricket League**
☐ Official handbook. Clitheroe, the League. *annual*. stats.
*?/1893-1914,1919/1958,68,71/*to date

## Ripon

**2980** **Gatenby, George,** *comp.*
■ A correct account of all the cricket matches played by the Ripon Cricket Club 1813-36. Ripon, *printed by* T. Proctor, 1837. 36p. scores
*the only two known copies are in the M.C.C. Library, Lord's*

## Rotherham

**2981** **Rotherham and District Cricket League**
☐ [Handbook]. Rotherham, the League. *annual?*
*?/1958/*to date?

## Saddleworth

**2982** **Delph and Dobcross Cricket Club**
■ Centenary year brochure, 1873-1973. Saddleworth, Yorks., the Club, 1973. 48p. incl. adverts. illus. ports. scores, stats.

**2983** **Friarmere** Cricket Club 1864-1964: one
■ hundred glorious years. [Saddleworth, the Club, 1964]. [8]p.

**2984** **Saddleworth and District Cricket League**
☐ [Handbook]. Saddleworth, the League. *annual*. stats.
*?/1899-1915,1919?/1958,1968-73/*to date

**2985** **Saddleworth Cricket, Bowling & Tennis**
■ **Club**
Centenary 1868-1968. Saddleworth, the Club, [1968]. [24]p. incl. adverts. ports. facsim.

## Saltaire

**2986** **Saltaire** Cricket Club, 1869-1969: sou-
■ venir centenary booklet. [Saltaire, Shipley, the Club, 1969]. 33p. illus. ports. stats.

## Saltburn

**2986** **Gray, Robin**
**-1** Saltburn Cricket Club: one hundred years of cricket 1876-1976. Saltburn, the Club, 1976. 76p. incl. adverts. team ports. scores, stats.

## Scarborough

**2986** **Baker, Joseph Brogden**
**-2** The history of Scarborough from the earliest date; edited by W. Smith. Longmans,
■ Green, 1882. xiv,527p. illus. ports. maps
*cricket pp.402-3*

**2987** **Kilburn, James Maurice**
■ The Scarborough Cricket Festival. Scarborough, Scarborough C.C., 1948. 86p. illus. ports. scores

2988 **Mayfair,** *Supplement*
Scarborough Cricket Festival: supplement to "Mayfair", September 1921. 8p. illus.
*the illustrations are 2 cartoons by "Spy" of C.I. Thornton and H.D.G. Leveson Gower*

2989 **Rowntree, Arthur,** *editor*
■ The history of Scarborough. Dent, 1931. xvii,456p. illus. (1 col.). ports. maps on end-papers
*cricket pp.290–2*

2990 **Scarborough Cricket Club**
□ Annual report and statement of accounts. Scarborough, the Club. illus. ports. [in v.y.] stats.
*1873?/1919–77/to date*

2991 **Scarborough** cricket festival: official
■ souvenir. Scarborough C.C. *annual.* illus. ports. scores
*6 issues 1951–56*

2992 **Sitwell,** *Sir* **Osbert**
■ Before the bombardment. Duckworth, 1926. 320p.
——*another ed.* Harmondsworth, Penguin, 1938. 310p.
*fiction: references to Scarborough Festival*

2993 **Watson, William Gatus**
Carnival cricket at Scarborough: twenty years of local cricket 1877–1897. Scarborough, 1897

## Sheffield

2994 **Farnsworth, Keith**
100 not out: the story of a century of cricket at Shiregreen C.C. Sheffield, *printed by* F. Melling, [1969]. 30p. team port. scores

2995 **Morley, L.A.**
■ The "Old" Sheffield Wednesday Cricket Club established 1820: copy of a paper read Feb 5, 1896. Sheffield, J. Robertshaw, 1896. 24p. score
*limited to 100 copies*

2996 **Neville's** handy cricket guide for Sheffield and district. Sheffield, Jas. Neville, 1896. 44p.

2997 **Sheffield Alliance Midweek Cricket**
□ **League**
Rules and fixtures. Sheffield, the League. *annual*
*1950/1950–58/to date?*

2998 **Sheffield and District Works' Sports**
□ **Association**
Official handbook for cricket. Sheffield, the Association. *annual*
*?1920/1955,57/to date?*
*formed 1919*

2999 Golden jubilee 1919–1969. Sheffield, the Association, [1969]. 8p.
*a short history, including cricket*

3000 **Sheffield Cricket League**
□ Official handbook. Sheffield, the League. *annual*
*1938/1949–59/to date*

3001 **[See no. 4992–1]**

3002 **Sheffield United Cricket and Football**
□ **Club**
Cricket fixtures. Sheffield, the Club. *annual.* ports. stats.
*season ?/1907 . . . 1911/–?*
*statistics, etc. of Yorkshire Cricket Council*

3003 **Sparling, Richard A.**
The romance of the [Sheffield] Wednesday 1867–1926. Sheffield, Leng, 1926. 274p. illus. ports.
*with ch. on the Cricket Club*

3004 **Sugg Thursday Cricket League**
□ Handbook of rules and fixtures. Sheffield, the League. *annual*
*?/1954–8/to date?*

3004 **Woodhead, Don M.**
–1 Three ducks on the trot. Sheffield, the
■ Author, 1979. [iv],96p. illus. team ports. facsims. map, stats.
*post-war account of a South Riding/Derbyshire club which after amalgamation ran teams with three different names: Sheffield Lombards, Eckington and Eckington St. Peters*

## Slaithwaite

3005 **Sugden, John**
Slaithwaite notes—past and present. Huddersfield, the Author, 1902
——*3rd. ed. enl.* Manchester, Heywood, 1905. xv,264. illus. ports.
*several chs. contain cricket references*

## South Riding

3006 **South Riding Cricket League**
Handbook. The League. *annual.* stats.
*1972? to date*

## Stocksbridge

3007 **Stocksbridge and District Cricket League**
Official guide. Stocksbridge, the League. *annual?*
*?/1912/–?*

## Thurstonland

3007 **Pearson, Andrew**
–1 Thurstonland Cricket Club 1874–1974.

Women's cricket: Lady cricketers: a good catch, 1889, by Lucien Davis *photo: M.C.C.*

Cricket in Wales. Glamorgan v. Gloucestershire at St. Helens, Swansea *photo: Patrick Eagar*

Women's cricket. Rachel Heyhoe (now Rachel Heyhoe-Flint), captain of the English Women's team in the nets, 1960 *photo: Sport and General*

■ Thurstonland, nr. Huddersfield, the Club, [1974]. [32]p. incl. adverts. ports. scores

## Wakefield

3008 **Wakefield** and district cricket and cycling guide. Wakefield Advertising Agency. *annual*
*1902–10*

3009 **Wakefield and District Cricket Union**
Rules and fixtures. Wakefield, the Union. *annual*
*?1893/1954 . . . 68/to date*

3010 **Wakefield Cricket Club**
■ Rules. [Wakefield C.C.], 1895. 8p.

3011 **Wakefield Cricket and Bowling Club**
■ Official handbook of the Wakefield Cricket and Bowling Club bazaar, with history of the club 1872–1906 . . . Wakefield, [the Club], 1906. 60p. ports.

3012 **Wakefield Cricket, Bowling and Tennis**
■ **Club**
Ye olde Wakefield fayre . . . Oct.23rd. 24th & 25th, 1929. Wakefield, the Club, [1929]. 44p. incl. adverts.
*includes short history of the club*

### West Riding

3013 **Cooper, Lettice**
■ Yorkshire West Riding. Hale, 1950. xi,305p. illus. ports. map. (County Book Series)
*cricket pp. 166–67, 209, 261–62*

3014 **West Riding** cricket guide; edited by F. Lodge. Barnsley, F. Lodge. *annual*
*1895–1901*
*1898–99 with title: Barnsley and district cricket guide; also in 1898 as: Yorkshire West Riding cricket guide*

3015 **West Riding Cricket League**
□ Handbook. Pontefract, the League. *annual*
*?1922/1957 . . . 72/to date*

3016 **The West Riding** cricketers' guide and diary. Bingley, T. Briggs. *annual. stats.*
*1881–85*
*later incorporated with: Yorkshire cricketers' guide and diary. See no. 2884*

### Wetherby

3017 **Wetherby and District Cricket League**
□ Handbook. Wetherby, the League. *annual. stats.*
*?1920–40, 1946?/1955, 56, 1970, 72/to date*
*formed 1919*

## Whitby

3018 **The Whitby District Cricket League**
□ [Handbook]. Whitby, the League. *annual season – ?/1968/to date?*

## Wombwell
*(see also:* **Wombwell Cricket Lovers' Society)**

3019 **Woodhouse, Anthony,** *and others*
■ Cricketers of Wombwell, by A. Woodhouse, R. D. Wilkinson, J. Sokell. Wombwell, Wombwell Cricket Lovers' Society, 1965. [x],39p. illus. ports. stats. (Wombwell Cricket Lovers' Society Publications)
*on Irving Washington, Roy and Norman Kilner*

## Wortley

3019 **Benn, William**
–1 Wortley-de-Leeds: history of an ancient township. Leeds, the Author, 1926. 118p. illus.
*cricket pp. 107–9*

## York

3020 **York and District Senior Cricket League**
□ [Handbook]. York, the League. *annual. stats.*
*1912?–14, 1920–39, 1946/1956–58, 72, 73/ to date*

# YORKSHIRE C.C.C.

(for Yorkshire v. Lancashire matches see nos. 2278–2283)

3020 **Bailey, Les.**
–1 Legends of Yorkshire cricket. [Rotherham, *privately circulated*], 1974. [v],43f.
■ *typescript. illus. ports.*
*a collection of poems*

3021 **The British Columbia Cricket**
■ **Association**
Yorkshire C.C.C. vs. British Columbia on Saturday, September 26, 1964, at Brockton Point. Vancouver, B.C.: programme. Vancouver, the Assoc., [1964]. [4]p. folded card
*pre-match*

3022 **Brooke, Frederick A.**
■ Yorkshire county cricket matches 1733–1891. 3 vols.
*unpublished typescript in M.C.C. Library, Lord's*

**3022 Brown, Alfred John**
**–1** Broad acres: a Yorkshire· miscellany. Country Life, 1948. x,210p. illus. map on end-papers
*pp. 170–4, 'Watching Yorkshire'*

**3023 Coldham, James Desmond,** *compiler*
■ Northamptonshire v. Yorkshire at the wicket 1908–1960. The Author, [1961], 16p. stats.
*limited ed. of 25 copies only, rptd. from The Journal of the Cricket Society, Apr. 1961*

**3024 Foster, Denis**
■ Yorkshire. Findon Publications, [1949]. 32p. ports. stats. ("Know Your Cricket County" Series)

**3025 Holmes, Robert Stratten**
■ The history of Yorkshire county cricket 1833–1903. Constable, 1904. viii,298p. illus. ports. scores, stats.
*for later volumes, see 3037 and 3028*

**3026 Irish Cricket Union**
■ Ireland versus Yorkshire, 22nd and 23rd July, 1959 at N.I.C.C. Grounds, Ormeau: souvenir programme and score card. Belfast, the Union. [1959]. 36p. ports.
*pre-match*

**3027 Kilburn, James Maurice**
■ Play! Leeds, Yorkshire Conservative Newspaper Co., [1937]. [15]p. illus. ports.

**3028** History of Yorkshire county cricket, 1924–1949, by J. M. Kilburn in collaboration with J. H. Nash. Leeds, Yorkshire C.C.C., 1950. [x],344p. illus. (1 col.), ports. stats.
see also *nos. 3025 and 3037*

**3029** Yorkshire county cricket. Convoy Publications, 1950. 116p. illus. ports stats. (County Cricket Series)

**3030** A century of Yorkshire county cricket. Doncaster, Yorkshire Post, [1963], 67p. illus. ports.

**3031** A history of Yorkshire cricket. S. Paul, 1970. 192p. illus. ports.
——*another ed.* Sportsman's Book Club, 1971

**3032 Lane, John, D.,** *compiler*
■ Surrey v. Yorkshire, 1851–1957. [The Author], 1958. [26]p. stats. (Cricket match history)
*limited ed. of 250 copies*

**3033 Middlesbrough Cricket Club**
■ The first——. Middlesbrough, the Club, 1956]. 32p. incl. adverts. ports.

*souvenir programme for the first county championship match played at Middlesbrough (Yorkshire v. Glamorgan)*

**3034 Moore, David**
About Yorkshire. Cheltenham, Shenton's Printing Works, [1947]. [4]p. illus.

**3035 National Playing Fields Association**
Yorkshire Present XI v. Yorkshire Past XI, June 20, 21, 1951 at Headingley. Leeds, *printed by* Balsham Bros., [1951]. 48p. incl. adverts. ports.
*organised by Leeds Sportsmen's Committee as part of the City of Leeds effort on behalf of N.P.F.A. appeal*

**3036 Pullin, Alfred William**
■ Talks with old Yorkshire cricketers. Leeds, Yorkshire Post, 1898. 239p. ports. score, stats.
——2nd ed. 1898
*rptd. from the* Yorkshire Evening Post

**3037** History of Yorkshire county cricket, 1903–1923. Leeds, Chorley & Pickersgill, 1924. 337p. illus. ports. stats.
*see also nos. 3025 and 3028*

**3037 Rayner, G.H.**
**–1** After the golden age: some thoughts on 60 years of cricket – especially Yorkshire cricket – since 1919. [The Author], 1979. [viii],63p. illus. ports.

**3038 Record** of Yorkshire cricket. Bury, Fletcher & Speight. *annual*
*in 1881. 1882*
*in 1882. 1883*

**3039 Reeves, Robert**
How Yorkshire won the great cricket match in 1906. Leeds, Yorkshire Oval Printing Press, 1906

**3040 Roberts, Edward Lamplough**
■ 100 Yorkshire records. Leeds, Yorkshire C.C.C., [1946]. 24p.

**3041** Yorkshire's 22 championships, 1893–1946; including Yorkshire profiles by J. M. Kilburn. Arnold, 1949. 275p. illus. ports. scores, stats.

**3042 Sharpe, Philip J.,** *compiler*
■ American tour. Leeds, Martin Black Publications Ltd., [1965]. ii,66p. incl. adverts. illus. ports. scores
*Yorkshire C.C.C. tour to U.S.A., Canada & Bermuda, 1964*

**3042 Sheffield Daily Telegraph**
**–1** Cricket guide and annual: a club and county chronicle; edited by "Looker-On".

Sheffield, Daily Telegraph. illus. ports.
stats.
*3 issues 1904–06; includes all English 1st
class cricket results*

3043 **Sheffield Telegraph**
■ Yorkshire's glorious century; 100 years of
Yorkshire cricket 1863–1963; Sheffield
Telegraph supplement, May 1963.
Sheffield, Sheffield Telegraph & Star
Ltd., 1963. 24p. illus. ports. stats.

3044 **Somers Isles Cricket League**
■ Yorkshire County Cricket Club tour
Bermuda 1969: official tour souvenir.
[Hamilton, the League, 1969]. [16]p. incl.
adverts. ports.
*pre-tour*

3045 **Stevenson, Mike**
■ Yorkshire. Barker, 1972. 176p. illus.
ports. stats. (A History of County Cricket)

3046 **Tate, Harold Aubrey**
■ Yorkshire team, 1897. Cricket P., [1897].
16p. incl. adverts. mounted team port. on
cover, stats.

3047 **Thomas, Peter**
■ Yorkshire cricketers, 1839–1939. Manchester, D. Hodgson, 1973. [vi],244p.
ports. stats. bibliog.

3048 **[Whitkirk Cricket Club]**
■ Grand cricket match in aid of the Yorkshire C.C.C. centenary appeal on the
Whitkirk Ground . . . Leeds: Whitkirk
and District XI v. Ron Yeomans' Yorkshire XI, July 7th, [1963]. [The Club,
1963]. 16p. incl. adverts.
*contains "Cricket in Yorkshire in 1863"
by Anthony Woodhouse. It rained so another
match was held in 1964:*

3049 Cricket match in aid of the Yorkshire
■ C.C.C. centenary appeal on the ground
of the Whitkirk C.C. Leeds, Sunday July
19th, [1964]: a Whitkirk XI v. A Yorkshire
XI. [The Club, 1964]. 16p. incl. adverts.
*contains 'The good old days?' by Anthony
Woodhouse*

3049 **Woodhouse, Anthony,** *and* **Yeomans, C.**
–1 **Ronald,** *compilers*
■ Yorkshire cricket: a pictorial survey.
Clapham, (Yorkshire), Dalesman, 1974.
80p. of illus. facsims. ports. (A Dalesman
Pictorial History). pbk.

3050 **Yeomans, C. Ronald**
■ "Yorkshire cricketers in Wintertime".
Leeds, Yorkshire Evening Post, [c.1959].
32p. ports.
*reprint of 13 articles originally appearing
in Yorkshire Evening Post*

——reissued. *The Author, [1967]. [14]f.
ports.* ·
*the articles mounted and issued in paper
covers*

3051 **Yorkshire County Cricket Club**
■ [Annual]: rules, list of subscribers, report,
balance sheet. Leeds, the Club. ports. *in
v.y.* scores, stats.
*1893–1940, 1947 to date
1894–8 ed. & compiled by Joseph Beckett
Wostinholm
1899–1903 ed. & compiled by J. B. Wostinholm & H. H. Stones
1904–30 ed. by F. C. Toone (1930 by Sir
Frederick Toone)
1931–40, 1947–73 ed. by J. H. Nash
1974 ed. by J. Lister
1975–79 ed. by J. Lister and R. D.
Wilkinson*

3052 Season 1914. Leeds, the Club, 1914. 8p.
■ 1 illus.

3053 Centenary appeal, by A.A. Thomson.
■ Leeds, the Club, [1963]. [8]p. illus. (1 col).
ports.
*for new dressing rooms and County Club
offices at Headingley*

3054 **Yorkshire** cricket album: photos of the
■ team. A book of records. Sheffield, W.
Whitham, [1902]. 17p. ports.

3055 **Yorkshire Post**
■ Yorkshire: a century of championship
cricket. Leeds, Yorkshire Post, [1973].
28p. incl. adverts. illus. & ports. (some
col.). score

3056 **Yorkshire Sports**
■ Cricket annual: records, fixtures and
guide to season. Bradford, Yorkshire
Sports. scores, stats.
*1922–26*

3057 **Yorkshire** county cricket team—season
■ 1964 and tour details for America-
Canada-Bermuda. Leeds, Martin Black
Publications, [1964]. 24p. incl. adverts. 1
illus. ports.

3058 **Yorkshire** team of 1896: souvenir.
'Cricket Office, [1896]. port.
*in Taylor*

3059 **Yor_shire** v. Notts. London, *n.d.* illus.
*in Taylor*

3060 **Yorkshire's** visit to Bermuda, October
1964. *n.p.,* [1964]. 24p. illus. ports.
*pre-tour*

# GENTLEMEN v. PLAYERS

3061 **Ashley-Cooper, Frederick Samuel,** *editor*
■ Gentlemen v. Players. Bristol, Arrowsmith; London, Simpkin, Marshall, 1900. 175p. scores, stats.

3062 **Buckley, George Bent,** *compiler*
■ Gentlemen v. Players at Lord's, 1806–1959: an alphabetical list of the Gentlemen and another of the Players who have taken part in these matches, with the years in which they did so and the numbers of their matches. 1959. *MS. typescript*
*in M.C.C. Library, Lord's*

3063 **Standing, Percy Cross**
■ Gentlemen v. Players, with an introduction and history of the contest since its origin in 1806. Wright, 1892. [ii],137p. incl. adverts. scores
——2nd rev. ed.: full scores of all reported matches to 1893. [1894]. xxxviii,134p. ports. scores

3064 **Warner,** *Sir* **Pelham Francis**
■ Gentlemen v. Players, 1806–1949. Harrap, 1950. 516p. illus. ports. scores

# ONE DAY CRICKET

3065 **A complete** guide to one day cricket, season 1969: featuring Player's County League, Gillette Cup, Bass/Charrington's Single Wicket Competition. [n.p., 1969]. 48p. illus. ports. scores, stats.

3065 **Laker, James Charles**
–1 One-day cricket. Batsford, 1977. 158p.
■ illus. ports.

## BENSON AND HEDGES CUP

### 1972

3066 **Benson & Hedges** cup semi-final. Yorkshire v. Gloucestershire, Wednesday, 28 June 1972: souvenir programme. Starkey, (1972). [8]p. 1 illus. ports.

3067 **Benson and Hedges** Cup Final 1972, Lord's Cricket Ground, 22nd July: official souvenir programme. Gallaher Ltd., [1972]. [24]p. illus. ports. stats.
*extensive pen-portraits and statistics by Irving Rosenwater*

3068 **Cricket** cup final. Yorkshire v. Leicestershire, Lord's, Saturday, 22 July 1972: souvenir programme. Starkey, [1972]. [8]p. 1 illus. ports.

### 1973

3069 **Benson and Hedges** Cup: the 1973 final at Lord's, Saturday 21st July; official souvenir. [Kent v. Worcs.]. Gallaher Ltd., [1973]. 24p. illus. ports. scores, stats.
*extensive pen portraits and statistics by Irving Rosenwater*

3070 **Times, The**
■ Advertisement feature [Benson and Hedges]. July 20th, 1973. 4p. incl. adverts. 1 illus. ports.
*articles on 'One-day cricket' and 'Benson and Hedges Cup-Final: Kent vs. Worcestershire'*

### 1974

3070 **Benson and Hedges** Cup: the 1974 final
–1 at Lord's, Saturday 20th July: official
■ souvenir programme. Gallaher Ltd., 1974. 24p. illus. (some col.), ports. scores, stats.
*Surrey v. Leics.*

### 1975

3070 **Benson and Hedges** Cup: the final at
–2 Lord's Cricket Ground, Saturday 19 July
■ 1975: official souvenir programme. Gallaher Ltd., 1975. 24p. illus. (some col.), ports. scores, stats.
*Leics. v. Middlesex*

### 1976

3070 **Benson and Hedges** Cup Final at Lord's
–3 Cricket Ground, Saturday, 17th July 1976:
■ official souvenir programme. Benson & Hedges, 1976. 24p. illus. ports. scores, stats.
*Kent v. Worcestershire*

### 1977

3070 **Benson & Hedges** Cup Final at Lord's
–4 Cricket Ground, Saturday 16 July 1977:
■ official souvenir programme. Benson &

Hedges, [1977]. 28p. incl. adverts. illus. & ports. (some col.), scores, stats.
*Gloucestershire v. Kent*

### 1978

3070 **Benson and Hedges** Cup Final at Lord's
–5 Cricket Ground, Saturday 22nd July 1978:
■ official souvenir programme. Benson & Hedges, [1978]. 28p. illus. ports. scores, stats.
*Derbyshire v. Kent*

### 1979

3070 **Benson and Hedges** Cup Final at Lord's
–6 Cricket Ground, Saturday 21st July 1979:
■ official souvenir programme. [Benson & Hedges, 1979]. 32p. incl. covers & adverts. illus. (some col.), ports. scores, stats.
*Essex v. Surrey*

## GILLETTE CUP

3070 **Fordham, Michael**
–7 The Gillette Cricket Cup 1976: a statistical
■ survey of the competition. The Compiler, [1976]. 13f.
*from 1963–1976 inclusive*

3071 **Gillette Safety Razor Co.**
■ The county cricket competition for the Gillette Cup: playing conditions for the competition (as laid down by the M.C.C.). [1963]. 2f. *typescript*

3072 **Ross, Gordon**
■ The first XI: a history of the Gillette Cricket Cup. [Gillette Industries Ltd., 1973]. 32p. illus. ports. stats.

### 1963

3073 **[Gillette Industries Ltd.]**
■ The final of the County Cricket Knock-Out Competition for the Gillette Cup. Lord's, 7 September. Sussex v. Worcestershire. [Gillette, 1963]. [6]p. fold

### 1964

3074 **Baker, Robert H.,** *compiler*
■ Cricket spotlight 1964: special 'Gillette' Cup Final souvenir. Sussex v. Warwickshire. Northampton, the Compiler, [1964]. 28p. incl. adverts. illus. ports. scores, stats.

3075 **[Gillette Industries Ltd.]**
■ The 2nd Gillette Cricket Cup Final: Sussex v. Warwickshire at Lord's September 5th, 1964. [Gillette, 1964]. [6]p. fold. 1 illus. ports.

### 1965

3076 **Cricket Society**
■ Gillette Cup statistics 1965; compiled by E. Solomon. The Society, [1965]. [4]p. stats.

### 1967

3077 **Davies, John,** *editor*
■ Up from Somerset for the cup: the story of Somerset's fight to the final. The Editor, for the Somerset Players Welfare Fund, [1967]. [40]p. illus. ports. (1 col.), score

3078 **[Gillette Industries Ltd.]**
■ The Gillette cricket cup final, Kent v. Somerset at Lord's, 2nd Sept. 1967: official souvenir programme. [Gillette Industries, 1967]. [24]p. illus. ports. scores, stats.

### 1968

3079 **[Gillette Industries Ltd.]**
■ The Gillette cricket cup final; Sussex v. Warwickshire at Lord's Saturday 7th September 1968: official souvenir programme. [Gillette Industries, 1968]. 24p. illus. ports. scores

### 1969

3080 **Derbyshire County Cricket Club**
■ Gillette Cup 1969 souvenir brochure edited by Michael Carey. [Derby, the Club, 1969]. [42]p. illus. ports.

3081 **[Gillette Industries Ltd.]**
■ The Gillette cricket cup final: Derbyshire v. Yorkshire at Lord's, Saturday 6th September 1969: official souvenir programme; edited by Gordon Ross. [Gillette Industries, 1969]. illus. ports. scores, stats.

### 1970

3082 **[Cornwall County Cricket Club]**
■ Gillette Cup Competition 1970. ·First round Saturday April 25th . . .at Boscawen Park, Truro: souvenir book. [Truro, the Club, 1970]. [38]p. ports. stats.
*Cornwall v. Glamorgan*

3083 **Fordham, Michael**
■ The Gillette cricket cup 1970: a statistical survey of the competition. The Author, 1970. 11p. stats. *typescript*

3084 **[Gillette Industries Ltd.]**
■ The Gillette Cup Final: Sussex v. Lancashire at Lord's, Saturday 5th September, 1970: official souvenir programme. Gillette Industries Ltd., [1970]. [28]p. illus. ports. stats.

## 1971

3085 **[Gillette Industries Ltd.]**
■ The Gillette Cup Final: Kent v. Lancashire at Lord's Saturday, 4th September, 1971: official souvenir programme. Gillette Industries Ltd., [1971]. [28]p. illus. ports. stats.

3086 **Gillette** Cup Final 1971: Kent cricketers
■ souvenir programme. Canterbury, the Kent players, [1971]. 24p. incl. adverts. ports. score

3086 **The Guardian**
–1 The bedside 'Guardian' 21: a selection
■ from The Guardian 1971–72; edited by W. L. Webb. Collins, 1972. 255p. illus.
*includes pp. 173–5 "A happy band of one-day wonders", by Neville Cardus on the Lancashire team which won the Gillette Cup*

## 1972

3087 **[Gillette Industries Ltd.]**
■ The Gillette Cup Final: Lancashire v. Warwickshire at Lord's, Saturday 2nd September, 1972: official souvenir programme. [Gillette Industries Ltd., 1972]. [28]p. incl. adverts. illus. ports. scores, stats.

## 1973

3088 **[Gillette Industries Ltd.]**
■ The Gillette Cup Final: Sussex v. Gloucestershire at Lord's, Saturday, 1st September, 1973: official souvenir programme. [Gillette Industries Ltd., 1973]. [28]p. incl. adverts. illus. ports. scores, stats.

3088 **Perry, Bruce**
–1 Road to glory: the story of Gloucester-
■ shire County Cricket Club's Gillette Cup win 1973; statistics by A.G. Avery. Bristol, the Club, [1973]. 48p. incl. adverts. illus. ports. scores, stats.

## 1974

3088 **[Gillette Industries Ltd.]**
–2 The twelfth Gillette Cup Final, Saturday
■ 7th September 1974 at Lord's: official programme. Gillette Industries Ltd., [1974]. [28]p. incl. adverts. illus. ports. scores, stats.
*Kent v. Lancashire*

## 1975

3088 **[Gillette Industries Ltd.]**
–3 The thirteenth Gillette Cup Final,
■ Saturday 6th September 1975 at Lord's: official programme edited by Gordon Ross. Gillette Industries Ltd., [1975]. 28p.

incl. adverts. illus. ports. scores, stats.
*Lancashire v. Middlesex*

## 1976

3088 **[Gillette Industries Ltd.]**
–4 The fourteenth Gillette Cup Final
■ Saturday 4th September 1976 at Lord's: official programme. Gillette Industries Ltd., 1976. 28p. incl. adverts. illus. ports. scores, stats.
*with a survey by Gordon Ross. Lancashire v. Northants*

## 1977

3088 **Gillette** Cup Competition, 1977. First
–5 round Wednesday, June 29 . . . Cornwall
■ versus Lancashire at Boscawen Park, Truro: souvenir brochure containing A brief history of Cornwall County Cricket Club 1895–1977 by S. Canynge Caple. [St. Agnes, S.C. Caple, 1977]. [52]p. team port. scores, stats.
*pre-match: despite title, mostly S. Canynge Caple's history of Cornwall C.C.C.*

3088 **[Gillette Industries Ltd.]**
–6 The fifteenth Gillette Cup Final Saturday
■ 3rd September 1977 at Lord's: official programme edited by Gordon Ross. Gillette Industries Ltd., 1977. 28p. incl. adverts. illus. ports. scores, stats.
*Middlesex v. Glamorgan*

## 1978

3088 **[Gillette Industries Ltd.]**
–7 The sixteenth Gillette Cup Final, Satur-
■ day 2nd September 1978 at Lord's. Gillette Industries Ltd., [1978]. 28p. incl. adverts. illus. ports. scores, stats.
*Somerset v. Sussex*

## 1979

3088 **[Gillette Industries Ltd.]**
–8 Seventeenth Gillette Cup Final Saturday
■ 8th September 1979 at Lord's: official programme [edited by] Gordon Ross. Gillette Industries Ltd., 1979. 28p. incl. adverts. illus. ports. scores, stats.
*Somerset v. Northants*

# JOHN PLAYER LEAGUE

3088 **John Player** cricket: John Player League
–9 information bulletin. Hayters Ltd; John Player & Sons. *weekly during season.* typescript
*–?/1979/–*

3089 **The John Player** Sunday League annual:
■ edited by Terry Harris, statistics by Bill Frindall. illus. ports. stats.

1971 *Wigston, Leicester, East Midland Press Services, [1971]*
1972. *Sales Link Ltd., [1972]*
1973. *Sales Link Ltd., [1973]*

3090　**Kallaway, Bill,** *editor*
■　Sports spectacular. Queen Anne P., 1972. 160p. illus. ports.
*includes "The John Player Sunday League cricket", by Peter C. Taylor, pp. 54–69*

3090　**The Limited Overs Cricket Information**
–1　**Group**
■　John Player League 1976. The Group, [1976?]. [124]p. incl. covers. score, stats.
*full scores with brief synopsis of every match*

## BRYLCREAM INTERNATIONAL INDOOR DOUBLE WICKET CHAMPIONSHIP

3090　**Brylcream** top of the world cricket. Inter-
–2　national indoor double wicket cham-
■　pionship. Twyford (Berks.), Sportsline, [1978]. 18p. incl. adverts. illus. ports.

## CHARRINGTON SINGLE-WICKET TROPHY

3091　**Charrington United Breweries Ltd.**
■　Charrington cricket trophy, Lord's 15–16 July 1965. Charringtons, [1965]. [4]p. folded card
*rules & players*

3092　**Bass Charrington Ltd**
■　Bass Charrington cricket trophy, single wicket championship. 1969 championship finals at Lords, July 31st,

August 1st. Bass Charrington Ltd. [1969]. [4]p. fold
*includes "Single wicket—a glance at history" by Irving Rosenwater*

## CHUBB DOUBLE WICKET CHAMPIONSHIP

3092　**Chubb** Double Wicket Championship,
–1　played at Wembley, April 19, 1979. *n.p.,* [1979]. 20p. illus. ports.
*pre-matches*

## COURAGE INTERNATIONAL BATSMAN OF THE YEAR

3092　**Courage** Challenge Cup International
–2　Batsman of the Year 1979. The Oval,
■　September 15 and 16: souvenir pro-gramme edited by Roger Thompson and Christopher Bazalgette. Wessex-Mede Marketing Ltd., [1979]. 48p. incl. adverts. illus. & ports. (some col.), stats.

3092　**International** batsman of the year 1979,
–3　15–16 September: souvenir programme.
■　*n.p.,* [1979]. [8]p. illus. ports.

## UNDER-25 COUNTY CRICKET COMPETITION

3092　**The Warwick Pool** Under-25 county
–4　cricket competition: rules of competition
□　and fixtures. Birmingham, Warwickshire C.C.C. *annual*
*1972/1973 . . . 78/to date*
*1973 with title: Under 25 county cricket competition*

# WOMEN'S CRICKET

3093　**The annals** of sporting and fancy gazette:
■　a magazine . . . Sherwood, Neely and Jones. *monthly.* illus.
*1822–8: 13 bi-annual vols. Vol. 2, 1822, contains a report of two ladies' matches*

3093　**Buckinghamshire Women's Cricket**
–1　**Association**
Women's cricket notes. the Assoc. *typescript*
*?/May 1950/–?*
*the May 1950 issue consisted of 12pp.*

3094　**Chesterfield Cricket Lovers' Society** *and*
■　**The Women's Cricket Association**
An England Women's XI versus A Selected Women's XI at Queen's Park, Chesterfield on Sunday, 21st June, 1970:

souvenir programme. [Chesterfield, the Society, 1970]. [8]p. port.

3094　**D'Esterre-Keeling, Elsa**
–1　Sir Joshua Reynolds, P.R.A. Scott, 1902. xii,232p. illus. ports.
*contains, p. 66, Mrs. Piozzi's comment concerning Reynolds' painting of "Lady Sarah Bunbury sacrificing to the Graces": "She never did . . . sacrifice to the Graces. Her face was gloriously handsome, but she used to play cricket and eat beefsteaks on the Steyne at Brighton".*

3095　**[Dudley Kingswinford Cricket Club]**
■　Ladies v. men, cricket match at Heath-brook, Wall Heath, Sunday, 2 July 1967: Rachel Heyhoe International Ladies XI v.

Dudley Kingswinford C.C. [Dudley, the Club, 1967]. [20]p. incl. adverts.

**3095** **Flint, Rachael Heyhoe,** *and* **Rheinberg,**
**–1** **Netta**
■ Fair play: the story of women's cricket. Angus & Robertson, 1976. 192p. illus. ports. stats.

**3096** **Jardine, Douglas Robert**
■ Cricket: how to succeed; with a chapter on women's cricket by Marjorie Pollard. Evans, for the National Union of Teachers, [1936]. 32p. illus. diagr.

**3097** **Joy, Nancy**
■ Maiden over: a short history of women's cricket and a diary of the 1948–49 Test tour to Australia. Sporting Handbooks, 1950. 168p. illus. ports. scores, stats.

**3098** **Noel, Susan,** *editor*
■ Sportswoman's manual. Hutchinson, 1950. 251p. illus. (Hutchinson's Library of Sports and Pastimes)
"Cricket" by Molly Hide, pp. 88–99

**3099** **Pollard, Marjorie**
■ Cricket for women and girls. Hutchinson, [1934]. 158p. illus. ports. scores
——another ed. 1935

**3099** **[Rheinberg, Netta],** *editor*
**–1** Gunnersbury: the first 50 years 1925–
■ 1975. [The Club?, 1975]. 9p. *typescript*
*the history of a women's cricket club*

**3100** **Rothmans**
■ Exhibition of women's cricketana, 1745–1963 at the Qantas Gallery . . . 13–25 May, 1963, to mark the third tour of England by the Australian Women's cricket team. Women's C.A., [1963]. 10p. illus.

**3101** **Women's Cricket Association**
■ Women's cricket: the official organ of the Women's Cricket Association. *monthly.* illus. ports. scores, stats.
*May 1930–Dec. 1967*
*for editors see no. 1214*

**3102** A handbook on women's cricket includ-
■ ing the laws of cricket and notes for players, umpires and scorers. The Association, [c.1935]. 47p. diagrs.

**3103** Report. The Association. *annual.* stats.
□ *1939–45 (in 1 vol. publd. 1946)*
*1946 to date*
*founded 1926*

**3104** Affiliation clubs and schools. The Associ-
□ ation. *annual?*
*season ?1940/–?*

**3105** Fixtures and information 1956. W.C.A.,
■ 1956. [4]p. 1 illus.

**3106** An England XI versus the Rest, 26 and 28
■ July 1958: souvenir official programme. The Assoc., [1958]. [24]p. incl. adverts, illus.

**3107** What's on in 1961. The Assoc., [1961].
■ [4]p. 1 illus.
*brief notes on 'players you may see' and fixtures*

**3108** Bulletin. The Association. *monthly. type-*
□ *script*
*Apr. 1970 to date?*

**3108** 1926–1976 Golden Jubilee, England v.
**–1** Australia: souvenir brochure. [The
■ Assoc., 1976]. 28p. incl. covers & adverts. illus. ports. stats.
*–includes Australian itinerary 1976*

### 1958 to Australia

**3018** **Australian Women's Cricket Council**
**–2** 1958 Australian tour of the English Women cricketers: programme of matches, photos of players, cricket records, items of interest, etc. The Council, [1958]. 48p. incl. adverts. illus. ports. stats.
*cover-title*: Official souvenir English Women cricketers 1958 Australian tour

### 1960–61 to South Africa and Rhodesia

**3108** **South Africa and Rhodesia Women's**
**–3** **Cricket Association**
Official souvenir programme of the inaugural visit by an English women's team 1960–61. [The Assoc., 1960?]. 64p. ports.

### 1968–69 to Australia and New Zealand

**3109** **Women's Cricket Association**
■ Report of the tour of Australia and New Zealand, 1968–69; edited by Netta Rheinberg. Frittenden (Kent), the Assoc., 1969. 20p. illus. scores, stats.

### 1970 to Jamaica

**3110** **Jamaica Women's Cricket Association**
■ Inaugural International Women's Cricket Series: souvenir programme. English Women's XI vs. Jamaica, Jan. 13-Feb. 2, 1970. Kingston, the Assoc., [1970]. 40p. incl. adverts. ports.

### 1971 to Bahamas, West Indies, Bermuda

**3111** **The Trinidad & Tobago** Women's Cricket
■ Association presents international cricket

from February 11–26, [1971]. [Diego Martin], the Assoc., [1971]. [12]p. ports.
*pre-tour*

3112  **Women's Cricket Association**
■     England Women's Cricket Association tour of the Bahamas, West Indies and Bermuda, 1971. The Assoc., [1971]. [12]p. team port. stats.
*pre-tour*

3113  West Indies tour 1971: official report. [The
■     Assoc., 1971]. 9p. port. stats.
*post-tour*

### World Cup Competition 1973

3114  **Women's Cricket Association**
■     Women's cricket: world cup 1973. The Assoc., [1973]. 3–18p. incl. adverts. illus. ports.
*pre-series*

3115  World Cup Competition 1973: official report. The Assoc., [1973]. 22p. illus. scores, stats.
*account of the competition held in England, June & July, 1973*

# CHARITY TEAMS AND MATCHES

3116  **Charity** cricket match in aid of Freedom
■     from Hunger Campaign: Tony Pawson's XI playing the Association of Kent Cricket Club's [sic] XI at the Garrison Ground (County Ground) Gillingham. Sunday May 24th: souvenir programme. *n.p.*, [1964]. 8p. incl. adverts. illus.

3116  **Charlbury Cricket Club**
–1    In aid of 'The Primary Club' for blind
■     young cricketers: grand cricket match Gloucestershire XI versus Charlbury C.C. at Charlbury, 15 Sept., 1979. [Charlbury, the Club, 1979]. 32p. incl. covers & adverts. 1 illus.

3116  **A grand** charity cricket match in aid of
–2    The Royal London Society for the Blind:
■     Tate & Lyle v. West Indies, Sunday, 3 July, 1955 at the Tate & Lyle Sports Ground, Manorway, East Ham: souvenir programme. Tate & Lyle C.Cs., [1955]. 24p. incl. covers & adverts.

3117  **Kent Playing Fields Association**
■     Grand charity match: Prime Minister's XI v. Kent on Sunday, May 4th . . . at Bickley Park. [The Association, 1958]. 16p. incl. adverts. port.

3117  **Middlesex K.O. (20 overs) cricket compe-**
–1    tition in aid of funds for the British Red
■     Cross Society. The Cricket Ground, Park Road, Uxbridge, Sunday, 7th October, 1973. [Assoc. of Middlesex C.Cs., 1973]. 64p. incl. adverts. illus. ports.
——Sunday, 5th October, 1975. 44p. incl. adverts. illus. ports.

3118  **The 'Two Freds'** cricket match. Fleet St.
□     Column Club. Cricket Sub-Cttee. illus. ports.
*?/1954 . . . 57/–?*
*1954 was 20th match of series*

### Duke of Edinburgh's XI

3118  **H.R.H.** the Duke of Edinburgh's team
–1    versus His Grace the Duke of Norfolk's team, Arundel Castle, Sussex, Sunday August 2nd, 1953: souvenir programme. [National Playing Fields Association, 1953]. [32]p. incl. adverts. ports.
*pre-match*

3119  **Cricket** match: H.R.H. the Duke of Edin-
■     burgh's team versus His Grace the Duke of Norfolk's team. Arundel Castle, Sussex, Sunday 4th August 1957. [National Playing Fields Association, 1957]. [32]p. incl. adverts. illus. ports. score

3120  **H.R.H.** the Duke of Edinburgh's team
■     versus Lord Porchester's team, Highclere Park, Hampshire, Sunday 3rd August 1958. National Playing Fields Association, [1958]. 18p. 1 illus. port. score

### International Cavaliers

3121  **The International** Cavaliers' cricket book;
■     ed. by Ian Wooldridge. Purnell, 1969. 157p. illus. ports.
*1970 with title: The International Caval-iers' world of cricket; ed. by Ian Wooldridge and Ted Dexter, 1970. 142p. illus. ports. (World of Sports Library)*
*1971: ed. by Ian Wooldridge. 93p. illus. ports. (World of Sport Library)*

### International Cricket Crusaders

3122  **The International** Cricket Crusaders tour
■     of Devon & Cornwall, September 1967: souvenir match brochure. Plymouth, *printed by E. J. Rickard Ltd.*, [1967]. [12]p. ports.

**3123** The International Cricket Crusaders tour
■ of the West Country, September 17 to
23, 1969: Weston-super-Mare, printed by
Allens (Weston) Ltd., [1969]. [16]p. illus.
ports. map

## Lord's Taverners

**3123** **Carmichael, Ian**
**–1** Will the real Ian Carmichael . . . : an auto-
■ biography. Macmillan, 1979. 400p. illus.
ports.
*includes an account of the formation of The
Lord's Taverners*

**3124** **Cricket** with the Lord's Taverners versus
■ The Cricket Society of Scotland, Sunday,
28th June, 1964 at Hamilton Crescent,
Glasgow. Newton Stewart, printed by
The Galloway Gazette P., [1964]. 28p.
incl. adverts. port.

**3125** **[Fatstock Marketing Corporation]**
■ F.M.C. XI versus the Lord's Taverners:
brochure of a charity cricket match.
Sunday 18th May, 1969 at the Marsh and
Baxter Sports Ground . . . Brierly Hill,
Staffs, in aid of the National Playing
Fields Association. [F.M.C., 1969]. 12p.
ports.

**3126** **Frewin, Leslie [Ronald],** *editor*
■ The boundary book: a Lord's Taverners'
miscellany of cricket: designs by Jack
Wood. Macdonald, 1962. 320p. illus.
ports.

**3127** **The Licensed Victuallers XI** v. The Lord's
Taverners, 10 May, 1970. P. & C. A.
Press, 1970

**3128** **Lord's Taverners**
■ [List of members 1954/5]. The Club,
[1955]. [24]p.
——1959. [12]p.
——*with title:* Rules and list of members,
1969. [40]p.

**3129** **The Lord's Taverners** versus an Old
□ England XI: souvenir programme. The
Club. illus. ports.
1962 . . . at Lord's, 16 June
1963 . . . at Lord's, 15 June
1964 . . . at Lord's, 13 June
1965 . . .
1966 . . . at Lord's, 11 June
1967 . . .

1968 . . . at Trent Bridge, 14 July
1969 . . . at Headingley, Leeds, 25 May
1970 . . . at Southport, 5 July
1971 . . . at Lord's, 31 July

**3130** The Lord's Taverners versus A Northern
■ XI, 22 July 1962 at Crosby. [The Club,
1962]. 24p. incl. adverts. port.

**3130** The Lord's Taverner: published for the
**–1** information and interest of all Lord's
□ Taverners; edited by Jack Rayfield. illus.
ports. *tabloid format*
*Vol. 1, no. 1. Jan. 1963, every two months
to May/June, 1964: then irregularly? to Spring
1973, possibly later*

**3131** The Lord's Taverners versus Lillywhite's
■ Centenary XI, Sunday, 5th May, 1963, at
Arundel Castle. The Club. [1963]. 28p.
incl. adverts. with [16]p. inset of
adverts. & scorecard. 1 illus. port.

**3131** The Lord's Taverners versus An All-
**–1** Edrich XI, Ingham, Norfolk, 15
■ September. [Lord's Taverners, 1963]. 28p.
incl. covers & adverts. port.
*with inset of [12]p. incl. adverts which
includes a brief note on 'The Edrich XI in the
cricket field'*

**3131** Cricket with the Lord's Taverners 1967 v.
**–2** Sussex County Cricket Club, the County
■ Ground, Hove, Sussex, 2nd July. [Lord's
Taverners, 1967]. 24p. incl. adverts. port.

**3132** The Lord's Taverners, 1968: [brochure].
■ The Club, [1968]. [32]p. ports. illus.
*published in aid of the National Playing
Fields Association*

**3133** The Lord's Taverners: edited by Jack
■ Rayfield and Gee Geeson. The Club,
[1971]. 40p. incl. adverts. illus. ports.

**3133** **Rice, Tim,** *editor*
**–1** The Lord's Taverners sticky wicket book;
■ edited by Tim Rice, aided and abetted by
William Rushton. Queen Anne P.,
Macdonald and Jane's, 1979. 159p. illus.
ports. diagr.

**3134** **Westcliff-on-Sea Cricket Club**
■ Westcliff Cricket Club v. The Lord's
Taverners, Chalkwell Park, Sunday, July
16th, [1972]. Westcliff-on-Sea, the Club,
[1972]. 24p. incl. adverts.

# CRICKET SOCIETIES AND NON-PLAYING CLUBS

3135  **The Council of Cricket Societies**
■     Constitution; revised 24 January 1970. The Council, [1970]. bs. *typescript*

### Association of Cricket Statisticians

3136  **The cricket** statistician: newsletter of the
■     Association of Cricket Statisticians; edited by Robert Brooke. Hampton-in-Arden, the Editor. *irregular, later quarterly.* scores, stats.
      No. 1, Jun. 1973/to date
      Nos. 3–9 with sub-title: the journal & newsletter . . .
      No. 10 *to date* with sub-title: the official journal . . .
      *typescript to issue 20, Dec. 1977, then format changed and cold type used issue 21, March 1978 to date. Issue 28 appeared Dec. 1979*

### Chesterfield Cricket Lovers' Society

3137  **Chesterfield Cricket Lovers' Society**
□     Newsletter. Chesterfield, the Society. *quarterly (now 2x a year, Apr. & Sept.)*
      *May 1963 to date*

3137  Handbook. Chesterfield, the Society.
–1    *annual. illus. ports.*
■     *1978 to date; ed. by F. G. Robinson*

3138  Annual report. Chesterfield, the Society.
□     *typescript*
      *1964 to date*

3139  ————, *and* **The Women's Cricket**
■     **Association**
      An England Women's XI versus A Selected Women's XI at Queen's Park, Chesterfield on Sunday, 21st June, 1970: souvenir programme. [Chesterfield, the Society, 1970]. [8]p. port.
      *includes "History of the Chesterfield Cricket Lovers' Society"*

### Cricket Book Society

3140  **The Cricket Book Society**
■     The Cricket Book Society: [membership and publications for 1948]. Hunstanton, the Society, [1947]. [4]p. fold

3141  Secretary's report. Hunstanton, Cricket
■     Book Society, [1947]. [8]p.

### The Cricket Society

3142  **The Cricket Society**
□     Newsletter. The Society. *occasional public-ation.* scores, stats.

      *Nos. 1–60, 1948–60*
      *superseded by: The journal of the Cricket Society. See no. 3145*

3143  Year book. The Society
□     *1948–49 to 1950–51, 1952–60*
      *issue for 1950–51 misdated 1951–52*
      *editor: A Weigall 1958–51, L. E. S. Gutteridge 1952–59, G. K. Whitelock 1960*
      *formerly: The Society of Cricket Statis-ticians. Year book*

3144  Monthly bulletin. The Society. *typescript*
□     *July 1954–June 1972*
      ————*contd. as: News Bulletin. irregular. illus.*
      *Aug. 1972 to date*

3145  Journal. The Society. ½ *yearly.* illus.
■     ports. scores, stats.
      *Vol. 1. no. 1, April 1961 to date*
      *editor: Vol. I, no. 1 to Vol. II no. 4, Irving Rosenwater (1961–65).*
      *Vol III, no. I to Vol. IV. no. 4, Cdr H. Emmet (1965–70)*
      *Vol. V. no. 1 to date, J. D. Coldham [1970–).*

3146  Rules. The Society, [1962]. [8]p.
■

3147  The library of the Cricket Society: [cata-
■     logue]. The Society, 1963. 12p. *typescript*

3148  Jubilee year 1970. Part 1: Officers and
■     members 1969/70; Part 2: The library of the Society: (catalogue). The Society, 1969. 52p.

3149  Tour to Corfu 1972. The Society, 1972.
■     pp.2–77. illus. port. map, plans. *typescript*
      *with glossary of Corfu cricketing terms*

3149  Library catalogue. December 1975. The
–1    Society, [1975]. [i,90]p. *typescript*
      *Librarian: Peter Ellis*

### Cricket Writers' Club

3150  **The Cricket Writers' Club**
■     [Handbook]. The Club. *annual*
      *?/1966 to date/*
      *largely a list of members*

### Cricketana Society

3150  **The Cricketana** Society, formed in 1929 –
–1    revived in 1933. List of members. [The Society, 1933]. *typescript*

3151 **Willow** leaves: the magazine of the
■ Cricketana Society. Pool-in-Wharfedale
(Yorks), the Society. *annual*. stats.
*typescript*
*3 issues, 1933–5*

## Hampshire Cricket Society

3151 **Hampshire Cricket Society**
–1 Newsletter. Basingstoke, the Society.
*monthly September to April*. scores, stats.
*typescript*
*No. 1. Jan. 1976 to date*
*issue no. 10 misnumbered as 9*
*12          11*
*13          38*
Editors: *No. 1. to No. 26 (Jan. 1976 to
Feb. 1979) Phil Bichard
No. 27 to date (Mar. 1979 – ) Tony
Mitchener*

## Hampshire Exiles

3151 **News from** Hampshire Exiles: bi-monthly
–2 newsletter. London. *typescript*. stats.
□ Jan. 1969 to date

## Lancashire and Cheshire Cricket Society

3152 **Jones, Eric G.,** *and others*
■ The Lancashire and Cheshire Cricket
Society 1953–1963. The Society, [1963].
[24]p. incl. adverts, illus. ports.

3152 [Twenty-first anniversary booklet]
–1 1953–74: 21st year. The Soc., [1974]. [28]p.
■ incl. adverts. ports.
*includes brief history of the Society*

## Lincolnshire Cricket Lovers' Society

3153 **Lincolnshire** Cricket Lovers' Society
■ [Yearbook]. Grimsby, the Society
*season 1965–66/to date*

## Northern Cricket Society

3154 **The Cricket Society,** *Northern Section*
■ Booklet; edited by C. R. Yeomans. Leeds,
the Society. *annual*. illus. ports. scores (in
v.y.)
*1949–51*
contd. as: *The Northern Cricket Society.
Booklet*

3155 A Catalogue of books. [Leeds, the
■ Society, 1950]. 20p.

3156 **The Northern Cricket Society**
□ Booklet. Leeds, the Society. *annual*. illus.
ports. scores (in. v.y.).
*1952–59 ed. by C.R. Yeomans
1960–68 ed. by L.C. Horton
1969 to date ed. by A. Woodhouse
1969 "21st anniversary number"; 1973
"Silver jubilee edition"*
formerly: *The Cricket Society*. Northern
Section. *Booklet*

3157 Cricket on Boxing Day; [compiled by
■ Arnold Whipp]. Leeds. Northern Cricket
Soc., [1964]. [ii],44p. illus. port. scores,
stats.
*limited ed. of 100 copies: recounts series of
matches played on Boxing Day 1949–63 by
N.C.S.*

3157 **The Seed Pod Club**
–1 Members' roll. The Club. *annual?*
□ *typescript*
*?/1975,79/to date
1979 issue with title: Induellaris roll
founded 1958*

## Sheffield Cricket Lovers' Society

3158 **Sheffield Cricket Lovers' Society**
■ Year book. [Sheffield, the Society]. illus.
ports. scores, stats.
*1969–70 to date*

## Society of Cricket Statisticians

3159 **The Society of Cricket Statisticians**
■ Year book. Leeds, W.A. Smith
*1946–47. 1947. 27p.
1947–48. 1948. 27p.*
contd. as: *The Cricket Society year book*

3160 The field of cricket; the official journal of
■ the Society of Cricket Statisticians.
Hunstanton, the Society, ports. stats.
*only one issue, July 1947*

## Sussex Cricket Society

3161 **Sussex Cricket Society**
■ Monthly news letter. The Society.
*typescript*
*Nov. 1965 to date*

## Wombwell Cricket Lovers' Society

3162 **The twelfth man:** the voice of Wombwell
□ Cricket Lovers' Society. Wombwell, the
Society. *annual*. illus. ports. (from 1959)
*1954/1954–1969/to date
21st anniversary edition publd. Sept. 1972;
25th anniversary 1976*

# CRICKET IN WALES

3162 **North Wales Cricket League**
-1 Official handbook. The League. *annual.*
□ *typescript*
  *season 1976 to date*

3163 **South Wales and Monmouthshire**
□ **Cricket Association**
  Official handbook. The Association.
  *annual.* ports. stats.
  *?1926–40,?1946/1951–8/to date*

3164 **South Wales Cricket Association**
□ Official handbook. The Association.
  *annual.* ports. scores, stats.
  *?/1966,67/to date*

3165 **South Wales** cricketers magazine.
■ Newport, R. H. Jones. ports. scores,
  stats.
  *Vol. I. 1948, 3 issues: July, Sept., and annual*
  *Vol II, 1949, 6 issues: May, June, July, Aug., Sept., Nov.*
  *Vol III. 1950, 6 issues: May, June, July, Aug., Sept., and annual*
  *Vol IV. 1951, 7 issues: May, June, July, Aug., Sept., Oct., and annual*
  *Vol V. 1952, 5 issues: May, June, July, Aug., Sept.*
  *Vol VI. 1953, I issue: Apr.-May.*
  *in July 1950 title changed to* The cricketers' magazine; *editors: 1948–51 Harold H. Jarrett; 1952 J. W. Speight; 1953 Tim Saunders*

3165 **Welsh Club Cricket Conference.** *Abacus*
-1 *Office Equipment League*
□ Rules, fixtures and club directory
  *?/season 1978/ to date*

3165 **Welsh Cricket Association**
-2 Year book. the Assoc. illus. ports. scores,
□ stats.
  *1969 to date*
  *founded 1969*

# CAERNARVONSHIRE

### Bangor

3166 **Cowell, J. R.**
■ Bangor, Cricket Club, 1856–1956. Bangor,
  [the Club], 1956. 8p. illus. on cover

3167 A history of the Bangor Cricket Club.
■ 1856–1964. Bangor, the Author. [1965].
  58p. illus. [on cover], ports. score

# DENBIGHSHIRE

### Colwyn Bay

3167 **Colwyn Bay and District Cricket League**
-1 [Handbook]. Colwyn Bay, the League.
  *annual*
  *?/1968/to date?*

# DENBIGHSHIRE C.C.C

3167 **Denbighshire County Cricket Club**
-2 [Handbook]. The Club. *annual*
  *season ?/1951/to date?*

# FLINTSHIRE

### Hawarden

3167 **Hawarden Park Cricket Club**
-3 Centenary souvenir 1966. Hawarden, the
■ Club, [1966]. 20p. incl. adverts. ports.
  *includes a brief history of the Club by Nigel Wright*

# GLAMORGAN

### Cardiff

3168 **The Cardiff** and District cricketers'
  companion; edited by W. Page Wood.
  Bury, Fletcher & Speight. *annual*
  *3 issues 1889–91*

3169 **Thomas, W. Alan**
■ Cardiff Cricket Club, 1867–1967. Cardiff,
  Penmark Publishers, 1967. 114p. incl.
  adverts. illus. ports. scores, stats.

### Maesteg

3170 **Maesteg Celtic Cricket Club**
■ Championship celebration presentation
  dinner, Friday, November 26, 1965.
  Maesteg, the Club, [1965]. [8]p. incl.
  covers, illus. port.
  *includes brief history and record of achievements*

### Pontardulais

3170 **Evans, Gerald,** *editor*
-1 Pontardulais Cricket Club centenary
■ 1876–1976. The Club, [1976?] 171p. incl.
  adverts. illus. ports. facsims.

## Pontypridd

**3171** **Williams, Brian**
■ Pontypridd Cricket Club 1870–1970. [Pontypridd, the Club, 1970]. 80p. illus. ports. score

## Swansea

**3171** **Griffiths, Ron,** *editor*
**–1** Swansea Cricket and Football Club
■ 1874–1974: 100 glorious years. [Swansea, the Club, 1974]. 100p. incl. covers and adverts. illus. (some col.), ports.
*mostly rugby football but cricket pp.79–81*

**3172** **Swansea Cricket and Football Club**
■ Cricket Section 100th anniversary 1850–1950 . . . centenary cricket match, Saturday, July 22nd 1950, Llanelly 1st XI v. Swansea 1st XI. Swansea, the Club, [1950]. [12]p.
*includes articles on Swansea and Llanelly cricket*

# GLAMORGAN C.C.C.

**3173** **Foster, Denis**
■ Glamorgan. Findon Publications. [1949]. 32p. ports. stats. ("Know Your Cricket County" Series)

**3174** **Gillette** Cup Competition 1970. First
■ round Saturday, April 25th . . . at Boscawen Park, Truro: souvenir book, containing a brief history of Cornwall County Cricket Club by S. Canynge Caple and facts and figures about Cornwall and Glamorgan cricketers. [Cornwall C.C.C., 1970]. [38]p. ports. stats.

**3175** **Glamorgan County Cricket Club**
■ Year book. Cardiff, the Club. illus. ports. scores, stats.
*1933–1939 [with] Survey, 1921–1932 [–1938]; ed. by J. C. Clay and M. J. Turnbull
1946 and records 1921–1939; ed. by J. C. Clay and A. E. Brown
1947; ed. by J. C. Clay and W. Wooller
1948; ed. by W. Wooller
1949 to date; 1979 ed. by M. Morgan and P. B. Clift*

**3176** Cricket in Wales; membership campaign
■ 1963. [Cardiff], the Club, 1963. [12]p. illus. ports. map

**3177** Glamorgan cricket news: Glamorgan
□ County Cricket Club members newsletter. The Club. bs. illus. stats.
*?/Dec. 1966/to date?
Dec. 1966 issue was no. 8*

**3177** **Lane, John D.**
**–1** Surrey v. Glamorgan 1923–1955. 1955. 34p. stats. *typescript*

*not published: MS in The Cricket Society's Library*

**3178** **Morgan, John Hinds**
■ Glamorgan county cricket. Convoy Publications, 1952. 117p. illus, ports. scores, stats. (County Cricket Series)

**3178** **Thomas, Wayne,** *compiler*
**–1** Glamorgan C.C.C. book of cricket records
■ (1921–1976). Woking, Davies & Sons (Publishers) Ltd., [1977]. [iv],87p. incl. adverts. ports. stats.
*to commemorate the Club's 50th first-class season in 1976; with amendment to the end of 1977 season*

**3179** **Webber, Roy,** *and* **Arnott, Kenneth M.**
■ Glamorgan C.C.C., 1921–1947. Hunstanton, Cricket Book Society, [1948]. 176p. illus. ports. scores, stats. (Blue Books of Cricket)
——*cheap ed.*, with supplement for 1948. [1949]. 183p. ports. scores, stats.

**3180** **Wooller, Wilfred**
■ Glamorgan. Barker, 1971. 172p. illus. ports. diagrs. scores, stats. (The History of County Cricket)

**3181** **Wynne-Jones, G.V.**
Sports commentary. Hutchinson, 1951. 191p. frontis. illus. (Hutchinson's Library of Sports and Pastimes Series)
*includes many references to Glamorgan cricket*

# MONMOUTHSHIRE

## Chepstow

**3182** **Waters, Ivor** ●
Chepstow miscellany. Chepstow, Chepstow Society, 1958. xii,134p. illus. maps
*pp. 42–54 ch. on Victorian sport including cricket*

**3182** The town of Chepstow. Chepstow,
**–1** Waters, 1975. 254p. illus. maps, plans
*originally published in 10 parts by the Chepstow Society: cricket pp. 45, 193, 200 and 215*

## Newport

**3183** **Collins, William John Townsend,**
■ *compiler and editor*
Newport Athletic Club: the record of half a century, 1875–1925. Newport, the Club, [c.1925]. 206p. illus, ports.
*cricket pp. 102–144*

**3184** **(Entry cancelled)**

**3185** **(Entry cancelled)**

# CRICKET IN SCOTLAND

3186 **Aspinall-Oglander, Cecil Faber**
Freshly remembered: the story of Thomas Graham, Lord Lynedoch. Hogarth P., 1956. ix,309p. illus. ports.
*contains a reference to the 1785 match at Shaw Park, Alloa, pp. 27–28.*

3187 **Bone, David Drummond**
■ Fifty years' reminiscences of Scottish cricket. Glasgow, Aird & Coghill, 1898. 290p. illus. ports.

3188 **Carruthers, John S.**
Story of cricket in Scotland. Dunlop C.C., 1950. 38p. illus. ports. stats.
*produced for 20th anniversary of the Dunlop C.C. in order to improve their ground at Netherhouses, Perthshire*

3189 **Douglas, Robert**
■ Reminiscences of cricket on the Borders, Selkirk, the Author, 1909. 48p. team port.

3190 **[East of Scotland Cricket Association]**
■ East of Scotland Cricket League: fixtures handbook; edited by A. M. C. Thorburn. The Association. *annual*
*2 issues only, 1960 and 1961*
*forerunners of* The Scottish cricket annual

3191 **[Entry cancelled]**

3192 **Fittis, Robert Scott**
■ Sports and pastimes of Scotland, historically illustrated. Paisley, Alexander Gardner, 1891. 212p. illus.
*cricket pp. 209–12*

3193 **Fleming, James M.**
■ "Welsh wanderings": or "Thro' Wales with bat and bottle". *Privately printed*, [c.1946]. 44p. illus. ports. scores, stats.
*an account of a tour by "A Scottish XI" organised by J.M.F.*

3194 **Gordon, Thomas Crouther**
David Allan of Alloa, 1744–1796: the Scottish Hogarth. [The Manse, Clackmannan, Gordon], 1951. xi,100p. col. frontis. illus.
*contains a reference to the first recorded game in Scotland in 1785, which was painted by Allan. The painting is reproduced*

3195 **Horne, Cyril D., *and* Harris, John L. F.**
■ History of the West of Scotland Cricket Club founded 1862. Glasgow, privately printed by R. Maclehose, the University P., 1962, 82p. illus. ports. scores

3196 **Northern Counties Cricket Club**
Constitution and rules. Inverness, the Club, *n.d.* 14p.

3197 **Umpire** and notcher: a journal devoted to East Scotland cricket; edited by M. Patterson and J. S. Cochrane. Edinburgh, [*n.p.*, c.1866]. *weekly*
*3 issues only*

3198 **West of Scotland Cricket Club**
Official handbook. The Club. *annual?* illus.
*?/1925/–?*

## Cricket Society of Scotland

3199 **The Summer** echo and news-letter: the
■ official publication of the Cricket Society of Scotland. The Society. illus.
*Vol 1. No. 1. Nov. 1953*
*2. Feb.(?) 1954*
*3. May 1954*
*no more issued*

# ANNUALS

3200 **Aitken & Niven** Scottish cricket guide;
■ edited by A. M. C. Thorburn. Edinburgh, Aitken & Niven. port. scores, stats.
*Season 1971 to date*
*gives record of previous year and fixtures for season for club cricket and the Scottish national team; superseded Scottish cricket annual*

3201 **The North** of Scotland cricketer's
■ companion; edited by Joe Anderson. Perth, J. Anderson. *annual.* stats.
*four issues 1900–03*

3202 **The Northern** cricket annual and direc-
■ tory of sports and pastimes. Aberdeen,
John Avery. ports. stats.
*for 1889–90. 1889. (April). 102p.*
*——2nd issue. 1889 (May)*
*for 1890–91. 1890*
*for 1891–92. 1891*
*for 1892–93 with title: Northern cricket*
*and football annual. 1893*
*for 1893–94 with title: Northern cricket*
*annual and cyclists guide. 1893*

3203 **Rowan's** cricket guide. Glasgow, Rowan.
■ *annual.* team ports. stats.
*1922–35*
*basically a fixtures list for Scottish clubs;*
formerly: *Scottish athletic guide*

3204 **Scottish** athletic guide; summer edition:
■ [fixture lists]. Glasgow, Rowan. *annual.*
illus. ports.
*1905-14; 1919?–21; contd. as: Rowan's*
*cricket guide*

3205 **The Scottish** cricket annual; edited by Joe
■ Anderson. Perth, J. Anderson
*1904–14*

3206 **The Scottish** cricket annual. Edinburgh.
■ illus. ports. scores, stats.
*7 issues 1962–68*
*1962, 1963 seasons: ed. by James Cowe &*
*A. M. C. Thorburn. J. Cowe [1962, 63].*
*1964 season: ed. by James Cowe &*
*A. M. C. Thorburn. Charlotte Publicity*
*Service, [1965]*
*1965. 1966 seasons: ed. by A. M. C. Thor-*
*burn & George G. Lawrie, Charlotte Publicity*
*Service, [1965, 66]*
*1967, 1968 seasons: ed. by A. M. C. Thor-*
*burn & George G. Lawrie. Interavon P.,*
*[1967, 68]*
*1969 exists in printer's proof state*

3207 **Scottish** cricket calendar. Edinburgh,
Stark.
*issues 1883, 1887*

3208 **Scottish** cricket record. *annual.* stats.
■ *1889–1906. Glasgow, R. W. Forsyth*
*1907–1914, 1922–1960. Glasgow & Edin-*
*burgh, R. W. Forsyth*
*fixtures, averages and outstanding results;*
*1940–45 for schools only*

3209 **Scottish** cricketers' annual and guide;
■ edited by Percival King. Edinburgh, P.
King. *annual.* ports.
*18 vols. 1870–71 to 1888–89; vol. V.*
*covered 1874–75–76*

3210 **Stewart's** cricket calendar: compiled by
J. C. Stewart. Edinburgh & Manchester,
Stewart. *annual*
*1875–99*

# PRIVATE CLUBS

## Capercailzies

3210 **The Capercailzies** Hong Kong tour 1978.
–1 [The Club, 1978]. 26p. illus. port.
■ *pre-tour; with article on cricket in Hong*
*Kong*

## The Centurions

3210 **Season 1975:** programme. [East Kilbride,
–2 the Club, 1975]. [36]p. incl. covers &
■ adverts. col. port. of touring party on
back cover
*sponsored by Lyle Barclay Ltd.*

# SCHOOLS AND UNIVERSITIES

3211 **Grange** schools cricket festival 28 July–1st
■ August, 1969: programme. Edinburgh,
Grange C.C., [1969]. [8]p.
*——1970*

## Edinburgh: Daniel Stewart's College

3212 **Thompson, John**
■ A history of Daniel Stewart's College
1855–1955. Edinburgh, the College, 1955.
119p. illus. ports.
*cricket pp.100–106, etc.*

## Edinburgh: Edinburgh Institution

3213 **Young, J. R. S.,** *editor*
Edinburgh Institution, 1832–1932. Edinburgh, the Institution, 1933. xix.443p.
illus.
*with references to the Former Pupils' C.C.*

## Edinburgh: Edinburgh University

3214 **Usher, C.M.,** *editor*
The story of the Edinburgh University
Athletic Club. Edinburgh. The Club,
1966. 439p. illus.
*contains a ch. on the E.U.C.C., pp.*
*138–156*

## Edinburgh: George Watson's College

3215 **Waugh, Hector Liston,** *editor*
George Watson's College: history and
record 1724–1970. Edinburgh, the
College, 1970. viii,264p. illus. ports. map
on end-papers
*contains chs. on Present Pupils' and Former*
*Pupils' cricket*

## Edinburgh: Fettes College

3216 **The Fettesian-Lorettonian Club,**
■ 1881–1931. Edinburgh, *priv. printed,* 1931.
vii,100p. ports.
*cricket pp. 56–78, 81*

3217 **Fifty** years of Fettes: memories of Old
■ Fettesians, 1870–1920. [Edinburgh, Fettes
College], 1931. ix,284p. illus & ports.
(some col.)
*references to cricket*

## Edinburgh: Merchiston Castle

3218 **Murray, David**
■ Merchiston Castle School 1855–58.
Glasgow, Maclehose, 1915. xi,194p. illus.
ports, map
*cricket pp.101–104*

## Edinburgh: Royal High School

3219 **Ross, William Charles Angus**
The Royal High School. 2nd. ed. Edinburgh, Oliver & Boyd, 1949. viii,165p.
illus. ports.
*1st publd. 1934*

3220 **Steven, William**
History of the High School of Edinburgh.
Edinburgh, 1849.

3221 **Trotter, James Jeffrey**
The Royal High School, Edinburgh.
Pitman & Sons, 1911. xii,195p. illus.
*cricket pp. 82–95 with illus. Contains a
reproduction of the etching "High School
1777" by Storer, dated 1819. This is one of
the few illustrations showing cricket in Scotland in 18th century*

## Glenalmond: Trinity College

3222 **St. Quintin, Guy**
The history of Glenalmond: the story of
a hundred years. Glenalmond, Trinity
College Council, 1956. xv,319p. illus.
ports. diagr., map on end-papers
*contains frequent references to cricket in the
School*

## Musselburgh: Loretto

3223 **The Fettesian-Lorettonian Club,**
■ 1881–1931. Edinburgh, *priv. printed,* 1931.
vii,100p. ports.
*cricket pp. 56–78, 81*

3224 **Loretto's** 100 years 1827–1927. The
School, 1928. 186p. illus. ports.
*issued as a special supplement to "The
Lorettonian" cricket references and port. of R.
Tomlinson, cricket pro. 1867–1908.*

3225 **Tristram, Henry Barrington**
■ Loretto School past and present. T. Fisher
Unwin, 1911. 320p. illus. port.
*chap. XI "Cricket" pp. 187–205*

# TOURNAMENTS

3226 **Scottish** national single wicket competi-
■ tion for the 'Father William' trophy at
Raeburn Place, Edinburgh on 28 June
1970 and 5 July 1970. Edinburgh, Grange
C.C., [1970]. [4]p. fold

# SCOTTISH CLUBS

## ABERDEENSHIRE

3227 **Aberdeenshire Cricket Association**
■ Official handbook. Aberdeen, [Aberdeen-
shire C.A.] *annual.* ports. stats.
*?/1945–52/–?*

3228 **Aberdeenshire Cricket Club**
■ Bazaar to aid the purchase of the new
cricket ground at Mannofield . . .
October, 1888: [souvenir programme].
[Aberdeen], the Club, [1888]. 66p. illus.
scores, stats.

3229 Official handbook. Aberdeen, the Club.
*annual.* illus. ports. stats.
*?/1924, 25, 26, 35/–?*

3230 Bazaar in Music Hall Buildings, Aber-
■ deen, on Saturday, 18th June, 1927. Aberdeen, the Club, [1927]. 20p. ports.

3231 Aberdeenshire Cricket Club centenary
■ 1857–1957: a historical survey; edited by
Richard C. Kelman. Aberdeen, published
for the Club by Northern Publishers,
1957. 87p. illus. ports. stats.

## Aberdeen: Stoneywood

3232 **Stoneywood Cricket Club**
Centenary, 1850–1950. Aberdeen, the
Club, [1950]. [iv],10p. illus. ports.

# ANGUS

## Arbroath

3233 **Arbroath United Cricket Club**
■ Grand bazaar in aid of the funds of the

Arbroath United Cricket Club on 11th, 12th, 13th April, 1889: album of bazaar; compiled by James Hood. [Arbroath, the Club, 1889]. [56]p. illus.

### Brechin

3234 **Brechin Cricket Club**
■ Bazaar book souvenir, September 23 & 24, 1927. Brechin, the Club, 1927. 36p. incl. adverts. illus. ports.

3235 1949 centenary year: a short history of the
■ Brechin Cricket Club 1849–1949. Perth, Robert K. Smith, [1949]. 44p. incl. adverts. illus. ports.

3235 125th anniversary year brochure
–1 1849–1974. Brechin, the Club, [1974].
■ [60]p. incl. adverts. illus. ports. stats.
*includes a history of the Club*

3236 **O'Neil, Alfred**
■ Annals of Brechin cricket, 1849–1927. Brechin, Black & Johnston, 1927. xvi,313p. illus. ports. scores, stats.

## ARGYLESHIRE

3237 **Maclagan, Robert Craig,** *compiler*
■ The games & diversions of Argyleshire. D. Nutt for the Folk Lore Society, 1901. vii,270p. illus.
*contains a photograph of equipment closely resembling cricket bat and stumps*

## AYRSHIRE

### Ayr

3238 **Ayr Cricket Club**
Official handbook. [Ayr, the Club]. *annual?* illus. port. scores
*?1926/–?*

3239 **Donaldson, H. C.**
■ Ayr Cricket Club 1859–1959. Alloway, [the Club], 1960. 139p. illus. ports. scores, stats.

### Kilmarnock

3240 **Aitchison, James**
■ Kilmarnock Cricket Club, one hundred not out. Kilmarnock, the Club, 1952. iv,90p. illus. ports. score, stats.

3240 **Farmer, John G.,** *editor*
–1 The golden years 1952–1976: Kilmarnock
■ Cricket Club 125th anniversary 1977. Kilmarnock, the Club, 1977. [vi],68p. incl. adverts. illus. team ports. stats.

## BERWICKSHIRE

### Manderston

3241 **Heatlie, Thomas,** *compiler*
■ Manderston Cricket Club 1899–1949: a record of the Club's activities during the past 50 years. Berwick, *printed by* Advertiser Printing Works, [1949]. 24p.

## CLACKMANNAN C.C.C.

3242 **Clackmannan County Cricket Club**
Official handbook. The Club. *annual*
*?/1925,26/–?*

3243 Centenary 1868–1968. Alloa, the Club,
■ 1968. 13–47p. illus. ports.

## FIFE

### Dunfermline

3244 **Dunfermline Cricket Club**
Bazaar album, Saint Margaret's Hall, Dunfermline, March 29, 30 & 31, 1900; compiled by A. S. Cunningham. Dunfermline, the Club, [1900]. 128p. incl. adverts. illus. ports.

3245 Official handbook. Dunfermline, the Club. *annual?* illus. ports.
*?/1926/–?*

3246 **Dunfermline Rugby Club and Dunfermline Cricket Club**
Donkey derby 16 May, 1970. Dunfermline, the Clubs, [1970]. 48p. incl. adverts.
*contains brief histories of both clubs*

3247 **Notes** on Dumfermline & Fife cricket, 1906–07. [1907]. 20p. scores

### Kirkcaldy

3248 **Kirkcaldy Cricket Club**
Official handbook. Kirkcaldy, the Club. *annual.* illus.
*?/1925, 26, 27/–?*

3249 **Kirkcaldy Cricket Club** [1872–1927].
■ Kirkcaldy, the Club, (1927). 12p. ports.

## FORFARSHIRE

3250 **Forfarshire Cricket Club**
Official handbook. Forfar, the Club. 2-*yearly.* illus. ports.
*?/1924, 26, 28/–?*

## Strathmore

3251 **Strathmore Cricket Club**
■ Centenary year souvenir brochure: a
short history of Strathmore Cricket Club
1854–1954. [Forfar, the Club, 1954]. 8p.

# LANARKSHIRE

## Calderbank

3252 **Neil, James W.**
■ Sixty years of cricket in Calderbank;
published in connection with the
diamond jubilee of Woodhall Cricket
Club. [Calderbank, the Author, 1948].
[10]p. team ports.
 rptd. *from* Airdrie and Coatbridge
*Advertiser, 29 May, 1948.*

## Clydesdale

3253 **Clydesdale Cricket Club**
A scrapbook, which has been micro-
filmed, exists containing press cuttings
1848–94. Originally compiled by A.
Campbell and used by D.D. Bone while
preparing his *Fifty years' reminiscences of
Scottish cricket.* The collection also
contains original posters and Lillywhite
scorecards for several of the All England
XI games in Edinburgh. I am indebted to
Mr. A.M.C. Thorburn for this
information.

3254 **Courtney, Samuel**
■ As centuries blend: one hundred and six
years of Clydesdale Cricket Club.
Glasgow, Clydesdale C.C., 1954. 99p.
illus. ports. scores

## Drumpellier

3255 **Drumpellier Cricket Club**
Centenary year 1963. Drumpellier, the
Club, [1963]. 16p.
 *fixtures, officers, etc.*

3256 Constitution, 1972. Drumpellier, the
Club, [1972]. [10]p.

3257 **Hamilton, William**
Portrait of a cricket club: Drumpellier,
1850–1950. The Club, 1950. 80p. ports.
scores

3258 **Thomson, John**
■ Drumpellier Cricket Club 1850–1906.
Airdrie, Baird & Hamilton, 1908.
viii,444p. illus. ports. scores

## Glasgow

3259 **"Peakodde, Bailzie"**, *pseud.*
The pump: ane righte lamentable dirge
composit be Bailzie Peakodde, poet laureate to ye Cricket Club; rendered into
modern verse by Dr. Minch. 1835. [8]p.
 *comic verses relating to Glasgow C.C., only
23 copies printed*

### Cartha

3260 **Cunningham, John**, *and* **Wylie, John**
■ Cartha 1889–1905: a retrospect: being a
short history of the Club since its inception. Glasgow, Kerr, 1905. 99p. illus.
ports.

### Poloc

3260 **Poloc Cricket Club**
–1 Centenary 1878–1978. [Glasgow, the
■ Club, 1978?]. 64p. illus. ports.

## Motherwell

3261 **Motherwell Cricket Club**
■ Centenary brochure 1873–1973; compiled
by M. K. Bonnar, W. B. Jardine, R.C.B.
Stirling. Motherwell, the Club, [1973].
48p. ports. stats.

## Uddingston

3262 **MacGill, James S.**
Uddingston Cricket Club, 1883–1933; fifty
years of cricket. [Uddingston, the Club],
1934. 102p. ports. scores

# MIDLOTHIAN

## Addiewell

3263 **King, A. A.**
Addiewell Cricket Club. (1870–1932).
[1932?]

## Edinburgh

### Carlton

3264 **Carlton Cricket Club**
■ Grand fancy fair and carnival, June 1912:
[souvenir programme]. [Edinburgh], the
Club, [1912]. 36p. incl. adverts. ports.
stats.
 *on the occasion of the Club's 50th
anniversary*

3265 Carlton redivivus 1919. Edinburgh, the
■ Club, 1920. 48p. illus. ports. scores, stats.

3266 The northern offensive 1921. Edinburgh,
■ [the Club, 1921]. 36p. illus. ports. scores,
stats.
*account of the season's play signed
N.L.S[tevenson]*

3267 The Morayshire manoeuvres: the doings
■ of the Carlton C.C. in 1922. [Edinburgh,
the Club, 1922]. 60p. illus.
*account of the season's play signed
C.S.P[aterson]*

3268 Shreds and patches, 1923. [Edinburgh,
■ the Club, 1923]. 79p. illus. ports. scores
*main part of text signed C.S.P[aterson]*

3269 Abstracts and chronicles, 1924. [Edin-
■ burgh, the Club, 1924]. 61p. illus. ports.
score, stats.
*main part of text signed C.S.P[aterson]*

3270 Bazaar in the Music Hall, George St., Oct.
15th & 16th, 1926: programme. [Edin-
burgh, the Club, 1926]. 40p. incl. adverts.
illus. ports. scores
*includes history of the Club, 1863–1926*

3271 Dr. N.L. Stevenson's northern tour 1927.
■ Edinburgh, *privately printed* by Lindsay &
Co., [1927]. 23p. illus. scores

3272 Outings and innings at inns, links and
■ castles. Edinburgh, [the Club], 1934. 72p.
illus. ports. scores, stats.
*review of the season*

3273 **Christie, Robert H.**
■ Carlton Cricket Club retrospect 1904.
Edinburgh, the Club, [1904]. 40p. ports.
scores, stats.

3274 **Stevenson, Norman Lang**
■ "Play!" the story of the Carlton Cricket
Club and a personal record of over 50
years' Scottish cricket. Edinburgh, C. J.
Cousland, 1946, viii,320p. illus. ports.
scores, stats.

*Crustaceans'*

3275 **Crustaceans' Cricket Club**
First annual report. Edinburgh, *printed by*
Sherwell Service P., 1933. 8p.
*compiled by N. L. Stevenson; the only
issue?*

*Edinburgh Academical*

3276 **Edinburgh Academical Club**
■ One hundred years at Raeburn Place
1854–1954: a short history of the Edinburgh Academy's playing field. Edinburgh, the Club, 1954. 48p. illus. ports.
scores

3277 **Edinburgh Academical Cricket Club**
■ Canadian tour 1969. Edinburgh, the
Club, [1969]. [24]p. incl. adverts. illus.
team ports.

*Grange*

3278 **Grange Cricket Club**
Rules and list of members. Edinburgh,
the Club, 1912. 20p.
*several issues published*

3279 Centenary of ground, Raeburn Place,
■ Edinburgh, 1872–1972; edited by A.M.C.
Thorburn. Edinburgh, the Club, [1972].
[48]p. incl. adverts. illus. ports. maps,
scores
*the historical material was written by
A.M.C.T.*

3280 **[Moncrieff, W,]**
■ Reminiscences of the Grange Cricket
Club Edinburgh with selected matches
1832–1862. Edinburgh, David Douglas,
1891, viii,115p. frontis. illus. scores

*Royal High School Former Pupils*

3281 **Royal High School Former Pupils**
■ **Cricket Club**
1861 Cricket Club centenary 1861–1961;
edited by A. M. C. Thorburn. [Edin-
burgh, the Club, 1961]. ports. stats.
*25 weekly pamphlets, each of 20p. issued 29
April-28 Sept. 1961. 16p. of text and adverts,
common to each, but 4p of weekly notes, and
details of teams changed each week*

**Leith**

3282 **Leith** cricket handbook 1898. Leith, Leith
Herald Office, 1898. 60p.
*contains notes on the Leith clubs; other
issues?*

**Penicuik**

3283 **One** hundred summers 1844–1944. Edinburgh, *printed by* Pillans & Wilson, 1946.
64p. illus.

3283 **Penicuik Cricket Club**
–1 Kirkhill 1875–1975 Ground centenary.
■ [Penicuik, the Club, 1975]. 28p. incl.
adverts. team ports. map, stats.

# PERTHSHIRE

3283 **Perth County Cricket Club**
–2 In the middle: the magazine and
□ programme of Perth County Cricket
Club. Perth, the Club. *weekly during season
?/1977,78/to date?*

**3284 Perthshire Cricket Club**
☐ Handbook. Perth, the Club. illus. ports.
?/1924 . . . 1949/to date

## Perth

**3285 Barlas, James**
■ Cricket in Perth 1827 to 1920; being the records of the Perth City and Perth County Cricket Clubs. Perth, Milne, Tannahill & Methven, 1921. 36p. illus. ports. scores, stats.

**3285 Halley, R.**
**–1** History of cricket in Perth, 1812–1894.
*mentioned in Barlas*

**3286 Perthshire Cricket Club**
Grand bazaar in aid of the Perthshire Cricket Club, to be held on . . . 12, 13, and 14 October, 1893: guide-book of Bazaar (arranged by Dr. Robertson). Perth, [the Club], 1893. 64p. ports. scores, stats.
*contains pp.14–32 "A history of the Club" by William Sievwright*

**3287 Sievwright, William**
■ Historical sketch of the Perth Cricket Club (the premier club of Scotland) from its origin in 1826–27 till 1879. Perth, James Barlas, 1880. viii,120p. scores, stats.

## RENFREWSHIRE

### Greenock

**3288 Greenock Cricket Club**
Official handbook. Greenock, the Club.
*annual*
?/1926/–?

**3289** Greenock Cricket Club, established 1862.
■ [Greenock, the Club, 1956]. [64]p. incl. adverts. 1 illus. ports.

**3290 Riddell, T. C.,** *compiler*
■ Greenock Cricket Club records 1887–1937. Greenock, McKelvie, [1937]. 275p. ports. stats.
——*Supplement. [1954]. 135p. stats.*
*contains 1885–86, 1938–39, 1946–53*
——*Supplement number two, 1954–59.* [1960]. 105p. stats

**3291** Greenock Cricket Club 1862–1962. Gourock, McKelvie & Sons, Cardwell Bay P., [1962]. [84]p. ports. stats.

**3292 Steven, John**
■ The book of Greenock cricket scores from 1862 to 1874, compiled from official score sheets and news reports with tables of averages, and explanatory and biographical notes, prefaced by the history of cricket in Greenock prior to 1862. Greenock, J. McKelvie, 1875. 518p. frontis. scores, stats.

## ROXBURGHSHIRE

### Hawick

**3293 Edgar, James**
■ Fifty years' cricket in Hawick, with portraits and sketches of prominent players, etc. Hawick, *privately printed* "Express" Office, 1910. 204p. illus. ports. stats.

**3294 Scott, John**
History of the game of cricket in Hawick. Hawick, Express Office, 1889. 144p.

**3295 [Wallis, I. Gray]**
Hawick & Wilton Cricket Club, 1849–1949: one hundred years of cricket. [Hawick, the Club], 1950. 11p.
*a reprint of the address made by the Club President at the centenary dinner, June 1949*

### St. Boswells

**3296 Ballantyne, J. K.**
■ A record of cricket in St. Boswells, 1895–1945. Galashiels, A. Walker, [c.1946]. 46p.

## SELKIRKSHIRE

### Galashiels

**3297 Anderson, R. A.**
■ History of Gala Cricket Club 1853–1939. Galashiels, *printed by* John McQueen, 1944. 51p.

### Selkirk

**3298 Anderson, William**
■ Selkirk Cricket Club: fifty years play at Philiphaugh, records & averages 1872–1922. Selkirk, James Lewis, [1922]. 83p. ports. scores, stats.

**3299** Selkirk Cricket Club centenary, 1851–1951: history-records-averages. Galashiels, A. Walker, 1954. ix,120p. ports. stats.

**3300 Selkirk Cricket Club**
Selkirk bazaar album: jubilee October, 1900 Selkirk, the Club, [1900]. 74p. incl. adverts, illus, team ports.
*contains articles by Andrew Lang and others*

3301 Philiphaugh centenary match programme, June 1972. Selkirk, the Club, [1972]. facsim. team port.
*with historical notes by W. B. Henderson and A. M. C. Thorburn*

## STIRLINGSHIRE

3302 **Stirling County Cricket Club**
Official handbook. Stirling, the Club. *annual*. ports, stats.
*?/1925, 26/–?*

3302 The Williamfield centenary 1877–1977.
–1 Stirling, [the Club, 1977]. 52p. incl.
■ adverts. illus. ports. score

### Falkirk

3303 **Hobson, W.**
■ Castings Cricket Club, 1899–1949: jubilee souvenir. [Falkirk, the Club, 1949]. 32p. team ports. stats.
"Castings C.C. was originally confined to employees of The Falkirk Iron Co. and now absorbed as a section of Allied Ironfounders' Social and Sports Club although still retaining the club name"

### Stenhousemuir

3303 **Stenhousemuir** Cricket Club 1876–1976;
–1 compiled by Duncan Walker, Morison Zuill and Alan Smith. Stenhousemuir, the Club, 1976

## WEST LOTHIAN

3303 **Wilson, James B.**
–2 West Lothian Cricket Association: 50
■ years of cricket 1929–1979. [The Assoc., 1979?]. 143p. 1 illus. ports. scores, stats.

# CRICKET IN IRELAND

3304 **Dermot** and Cicely; or, the Irish gimblet,
■ a tale in three canto's [sic], in the manner
of Hudibras. Printed for W. Trow,
without Temple-Bar, 1742. 23p.
*describes cricket in Munster, pp. 14–16*

3305 **Hone, William Patrick**
■ Cricket in Ireland. Tralee. The Kerryman,
1955. [xii],200p. illus. ports. scores, stats.
——another ed. *Sportsman's Book Club,
1958.*

3306 **[See no. 3313–2]**

3307 **[See no. 3313–3]**

3308 **Samuels, Arthur**
■ Early cricket in Ireland: a paper read
before the Kingstown Literary and Debat-
ing Society on the 22nd Feb., 1888.
Dublin, W. McGee for the Society, 1888.
34p.

## Irish Cricket Society

3309 **Irish** cricket: the official journal of the
■ Irish Cricket Society. Dublin, the Society,
*quarterly. illus. ports.*
*4 issues only Nov. 1973–Autumn 1974*
*Nov. 1973 ed. by Laurence Mumford*
*Spring 1974 ed. by Laurence Mumford and
Dave Lawrence*
*Summer and Autumn 1974 ed. by Michael
Brennan*

## Irish Cricket Union

3310 **Irish Cricket Union**
Hon. Secretary's report for the season.
Dublin, The Union. *annual*
*season ?/1950, 51/ to date*
*later issues with title: Yearbook. illus.
scores, stats.*

3311 Newsletter. Dublin, the Union. *annual*
*1953 to date?*

3312 [Officers, fixtures, members]. [Dublin],
the Union. *annual?*
*?/1961/to date?*

3313 **[Scott, Derek],** *compiler*
Irish Cricket Union statistics, 1920–51.
Dublin, 1952

## North West Cricket Union

3313 **North West Cricket Union**
–1 Tour to the West Indies 1975: official
■ brochure. Londonderry, the Union,
[1975]. 100p. incl. adverts. illus. ports.
stats.
*pre-tour*

3313 **Platt, William Henry Walker**
–2 North-West senior cricket 1888–1968.
■ Londonderry, [the Author, 1968]. 67p.
incl. adverts. illus. ports. stats.

3313 The greatest years in North-West cricket:
–3 1919–1941. Coleraine, the Author, 1971.
■ 94p. incl. adverts. ports.

3313 Cricket in the North-West, 1943–1963.
–4 Coleraine, the Author, [1976]. 104p. incl.
■ adverts. team ports.

## Northern Cricket Union of Ireland

3314 **Northern Cricket Union of Ireland**
Fixtures. Belfast, the Union.
*?/1965/to date*
*formed 1886*

# ANNUALS

3315 **Lawrence, John,** *publisher*
■ John Lawrence's handbook of cricket in
Ireland; compiled and edited by J. T.
H[urford]. Dublin, Lawrence. *annual*
*16 issues covering seasons, 1865–81, the
last volume published in 1882 covering both
1880 and 1881*

# IRISH CLUBS

## Bangor

3315 **Bangor** Cricket Club souvenir brochure
–1 1977: Ward Park re-opening special

■ matches. [Bangor], the Club, [1977]. [56]p. incl. adverts. scores
*includes "Cricket in Bangor 1933–1977" by Michael Rea*

## Clontarf

3316 **Clontarf Cricket Club**
■ Souvenir brochure May 1958. Clontarf, the Club, 1958. 88p. incl. adverts. illus. ports. scores
*includes brief history of the club*

3316 Centenary 1876–1976. [Clontarf, the
–1 Club, 1876]. [128]p. incl. adverts. illus.
■ ports. stats.

## Cork

3316 **Clusky, Jim,** *editor*
–2 Cork County Cricket Club centenary
■ 1874–1974. [Cork, the Club, 1974]. 112p. incl. adverts. illus. team ports.

## Instonians

3317 **White, W. Brownlow,** *editor*
■ Instonians 1919–69: "50 years of fun and games". Belfast, [the Club?, 1969]. 58p. illus. port.

## Kilkenny

3318 **Butler, James,** *Marquess of Ormonde*
■ A short account of the origin of the Kilkenny Cricket Club and of its proceedings, in the years 1830–1831. *Printed by* Poulter, 1832. 22f. scores

## Laurelvale

3318 **Kennedy, Billy,** *editor*
–1 Laurelvale Cricket Club centenary year
■ 1875–1975. Portadown (N.I.), the Club, [1975]. 64p. incl. adverts. illus. ports. stats.

## Leinster

3319 **Leinster Cricket Club**
Fifth Rose and White Ball, Jury's Hotel, 3rd March, 1967. Dublin, [the Club 1967]. 20p. incl. adverts.

3319 Leinster Cricket Club 1852–1977. [Dublin,
–1 the Club, 1977?]. [156]p. incl. adverts.
■ illus. ports. stats.

3319 **Leinster Cricket Union**
–2 Fixture handbook. Dublin, the Union.
□ *annual*
*?/season 1974/to date*
*regulations and fixtures*

## Leprechauns

3320 **Leprechauns Cricket Club**
■ Membership and fixtures 1949. Bray, [the Club, 1949]. [6]p.

3321 Handbook. Dublin, the Club. *annual.*
□ ports. *in v.y.* scores
*?/1970–73/to date*
*formed 1948; 1973 issue with title: Silver jubilee edition*

3322 Leprechauns Cricket Club v. Essex
■ County Cricket Club, College Park, Dublin, July 6th and 7th, 1971: souvenir brochure. [Dublin], the Club. [1971]. 44p. incl. adverts. ports.
*contains a brief history of the Leprechauns C.C.*

## Limavady

3323 **Limavady Cricket and Rugby Football Club**
Souvenir programme, Friday, 28th April, 1972. Limavady, [the Club, 1972]. 28p. illus. ports.
*cricket and rugby matches played on 28th April*

## Muckamore

3323 **Campbell, Peter L.,** *editor*
–1 Muckamore Cricket and Lawn Tennis
■ Club 1874–1974: centenary brochure. Muckamore(Antrim), [the Club, 1974?]. 96p. incl. adverts. illus. ports. score, stats.

## North of Ireland

3324 **Fry, P. P.**
■ The North of Ireland Cricket and Football Club, 1859–1959. Belfast, Brough, Cox & Dunn, 1959. 176p. incl. adverts, illus. ports. scores

## Old Belvedere

3324 **Old Belvedere Cricket Club**
–1 Silver jubilee, 1950–1974. The Club, 1974.
■ 49p. illus. ports. score, stats.
*Old Boys of Belvedere College, Leinster*

## Pembroke

3325 **Pembroke** Cricket Club 1868–1968:
■ centenary handbook. [Dublin, the Club 1968]. 116p. incl. adverts. illus. ports. scores

## Phoenix

3326 **Phoenix Cricket Club**
■ Festival Week Saturday, 31st July to

Saturday, 7th August: souvenir programme & score card. Dublin, the Club, [1943]. 16p. incl. adverts. ports.
*contains brief history of the club*

at Hibernian Hotel, Maryborough, on 26 March, 1895. Maryborough, the Club, [1895]. 24p. incl. covers

## Portlaoise (formerly Maryborough)

3327 **Maryborough & Queen's County Cricket Club**
Rules adopted at a General Adjourned Meeting of the members of the Club, held

## Waringstown

3327 **Maultsaid, Michael**
-1 Waringstown Cricket Club 1851–1974.
■ [Waringstown, the Club, 1974?]. [v],34p. illus. ports.

Cricket at Phoenix Park, Dublin, c. 1837. A drawing by John Powell *photo: M.C.C.*

Cricket in Australia. Sydney Cricket Ground *photo: Patrick Eagar*

# CRICKET IN AUSTRALIA

**3327** **Allan, James Alexander**
**–2** Men and manners in Australia: being a social and economic sketch history. Melbourne, Cheshire, 1945. 176p. illus.
*cricket pp. 137, 145–7, 156*

**3327** The Ampol book of Australiana, annals
**–3** and oddities; edited by Sidney J. Baker; with sports section by Geoff Allan; line drawings by Lindsay Parker. Sydney, Currawong Publishing Co., 1963. xvi,223p. illus.
*cricket pp. 127, 147–53*

**3328** **Ashley-Cooper, Frederick Samuel**
■ The Australian cricket guide, 1926: a book of records. Nottingham, Richards, 1926. 22p. stats.
——*another ed.* 1930. Nottingham, Richards, 1930. 32p. stats.
*mainly Australia v. England Test records*

**3328** **Association of Cricket Statisticians**
**–1** 16 unpublished Australian scores:
■ [compiled by Roger Page and A.H. Wagg]. Hampton in Arden (Warks)., the Assoc., 1976. [2],16p. *of duplicated typescript.* scores
*"friendly, but first-class matches" played in Australia 1873–1915*

**3328** A guide to first-class cricket matches
**–2** played in Australia. Hampton in Arden,
■ the Assoc., 1978. 31p. scores, stats.
*covers period 1850/51 to 1975/76; compiled by Ken Williams*

**3329** **Australian** Cricket Council, 1895

**3330** **Australian** cricket souvenir, sanctioned
■ by Australian Cricket Board of Control and N.S.W. Cricket Association. Sydney, the Assoc., [1909]. 84p. incl. adverts. illus. ports. scores, stats.

**3330** **Australia's** yesterdays: a look at our
**–1** recent past; edited and designed by Reader's Digest Services Pty. Ltd. Sydney, Reader's Digest, 1974. 360p. col. illus.
*cricket pp. 174, 175, 176, 177, 199, 340*

**3331** **[Bett, H. Drysdale]**
■ Who's who in Australian cricket 1932–33, by the editor of "the Australian Cricketer". Melbourne, Australian Cricketer, [1932]. 16p.

**3332** **Bevan, Ian,** *editor*
■ The sunburnt country. Collins, 1953. 256p. illus. port.
*cricket pp. 160, 164, 169, 172–80*

**3332** **Butler, Keith**
**–1** Howzat!: sixteen Australian cricketers
■ talk to Keith Butler. Sydney, Collins, 1979. 260p. illus. ports. stats.

**3333** **Campbell, R. H.**
■ Cricket records: a book of Test match statistics and a record of all centuries made in representative cricket in Australia previous to the season 1928–1929. Melbourne, The Speciality P., [1928]. 40p. ports. diagrs. stats.

**3333** **Comes, James William C.**
**–1** Their chastity was not too rigid: leisure times in early Australia. Melbourne, Longmans Cheshire; Sydney, Reed, 1979. xi,378p. illus. (1 col.)
*cricket pp. 17, 18, 40, 41, 49, 121, 171, 254, 299–303, with col. frontis. of cricket at Melbourne, 1841*

**3333** **Dunstan, Keith**
**–2** Knockers. Melbourne, Cassell Australia, 1973. xvi,335p. illus. pbk.
*many cricket and Bradman references*

**3334** Sports. N. Melbourne, Cassell Australia,
■ 1973. xiv,367p. illus. ports. diagr.
*on the Australian passion for certain sports including "The cricket passion" pp. 80–122*

**3335** **Fitzpatrick, J.**
■ Australian cricket record, 1894–5. Sydney & Melbourne, Gordon & Gotch, [1895]. 132p. scores, stats.

**3336** **Giffen, George**
■ With bat and ball: twenty-five years' reminiscences of Australian and Anglo-Australian cricket; with hints to young

cricketers on batting, bowling & fielding. Ward, Lock, 1898. xv.240p. illus. ports. stats.
——2nd ed. 1898
——3rd ed. [1899]

3336 **Great** Australian cricket pictures, intro-
−1 duced by Ian Johnson: photographs and
■ notes compiled by Jack Wilkinson. Melbourne, Sun Books, 1975. 96p. illus. ports.

3336 **Howard, Bruce**
−2 A nostalgic look at Australian sport. Adelaide, Rigby, 1978. 208p. illus. ports.
*many cricket refs.*

3337 **Illustrated News**
■ Australian cricket supplement. Vol. 10, no. 23. Calcutta, Illustrated News, 25 Nov., 1945. 88p. incl. adverts. ports. scores

3338 **Inglis, Gordon**
■ Sport and pastime in Australia. Methuen, 1912. xix,308p. illus.
*cricket pp. 104–130 and scattered references*
——2nd ed. 1912

3339 **Ironside, Frederick James**
□ Ironside's Australasian cricketing hand-book. Sydney, Ironside.
——New & rev. ed. 1880. [iv],v,80p. stats.

3339 **Jaques, T. D., and Pavia, G. R.**
−1 Sport in Australia: selected readings in physical activity. Sydney, McGraw-Hill, 1976. viii,171p.
*contains pp. 46–72 "Cricket and Australian nationalism in the nineteenth century" by William F. Mandle, rptd. from Journal of Royal Australian Historical Society, vol. 59, pp. 225–46 (1973)*

3340 **Jasdenvala, A. A.**
■ The "Cornstalks". Bombay, the Author, [1964]. [8]p. illus. ports.
*the development of cricket in Australia published in commemoration of the Australian tour of India 1964*

3340 **Larkins, John, and Howard, Bruce**
−1 Australian pubs. Adelaide, Rigby, 1973. 280p.
*pp. 141–3 "The cricket match" (Katherine v. Mataranka)*

3340 **Great** Australian book of nostalgia.
−2 Adelaide, Rigby, 1975. 295p. illus. ports.
*cricket pp. 13–5 with illus. on pp. 156–60 including Alan McGilvray in a school team, 'Yabba'—the famous barracker, a bush cricket team, etc.*

3340 **Lord, David,** *editor*
−3 The best of the last 10 years in Australian sport. Adelaide, H. K. Frost Holdings Pty. Ltd. in association with Lions International and Australian Guarantee Corp. Ltd., 1978. 224p. illus. & ports. (some col.)
*cricket pp. 19–28 by Peter McFarline*

3341 **McMahon's** cricket and sports manual; edited by Peter C. Curtis. Sydney, McMahon, 1910. 134p.

3341 **Mandle, William Frederick**
−1 "Cricket and Australian nationalism in the nineteenth century." In Journal of Royal Australian Historical Society. Vol. 59, part 4 (Dec. 1973), pp. 225–46

3341 Going it alone: Australia's national iden-
−2 tity in the twentieth century. Allen Lane,
■ the Penguin P., 1978. [vii],264p. bibliog.
*cricket pp. 24–36, 114*

3342 **Monfries, John Elliott**
■ Not Test cricket: happy reminiscences of every other kind of cricket in Adelaide, Melbourne, Sydney and Hobart. Adelaide, Gillingham, 1950. [v],106p. port.

3343 **Moody, Clarence Percival**
■ Australian cricket and cricketers 1856–1893/4: contains a brief resumé of intercolonial and international matches. Complete batting and bowling averages of Australians in eleven-a-side matches. Australian cricket records and curiosities. Melbourne, Thompson, 1894. [vi],98p. illus. ports. stats.

3344 Cricket album [of] noted Australian crick-
■ eters, past and present. Adelaide, Hussey & Gillingham, 1898. [74]p. illus. ports.
*issued in six monthly parts*

3345 **Moyes, Alban George**
■ Australian bowlers from Spofforth to Lindwall. London, Harrap; Sydney, Angus and Robertson, 1953. 192p. ports. stats.

3346 Australian batsmen from Charles
■ Bannerman to Neil Harvey. London, Harrap; Sydney, Angus and Robertson, 1954. 203p. ports. stats.

3347 Australian cricket: a history. Angus &
■ Robertson, 1959. xvi,615p. illus. ports. scores

3347 **Old times:** a unique illustrated history of
−1 the early days . . . Sydney, the Commer-
□ cial Publishing Co. illus. ports. *issued*

*in monthly parts*
4 issues only, April – July, 1903
*Apr. includes pp. 29–34 "The birth of cricket" and "Cricket and cricketers I: from Hyde Park to the Sydney Cricket Ground", by F. J. Ironside*
*May includes pp. 147–9 "Cricket and cricketers II – reminiscences of Mr. Harry Hilliard, the oldest exponent of the game"*
*June includes pp. 207–10 "Cricket and cricketers III – reminiscences of Mr. A. L. Park"*

3347 **Pearl, Irma,** *compiler*
–2 Our yesterdays: Australian life since 1853 in photographs; arranged by Irma Pearl with a commentary by Cyril Pearl. Angus & Robertson, 1954. [iv],164p. illus.
——*another ed.* 1963. 164p.
*cricket pp. 18, 19, 62, 63, 96, 127*

3347 **Phillipson, Neill**
–3 Cricket cavalcade: great Australian crick-
■ eters past and present. Melbourne, the Craftsman, P., 1977. iv,188p. illus. ports. stats.
——*another ed. with title:* The Australian cricket hall of fame. Melbourne, Outback P., 1979. [iv],212p. illus. ports. stats.

3348 **Pollard, Jack,** *compiler*
■ Six and out: the legend of Australian cricket. Wollstonecraft, N.S.W. Pollard Publishing Co., 1964; London, Angus & Robertson, 1965. [xiii],306p. illus. ports.
——*rptd. with subtitle: the legend of Australian and New Zealand cricket.* 1970. 366p.

3348 **Ritchie, John Douglas**
–1 Australia as once we were. Melbourne, Heinemann, 1975. 279p. illus.
*cricket pp. 145, 163–5, 199, 227–9, 243*

3349 **Samuels, Cyril**
The big game in Australia. Sydney, Publicity Press, 1925. 32p. illus.

3350 **Serjeant,** *Sir* **David Maurice**
Australia, its cricket bat, its kangaroo, its field for emigration. King & Jarrett, [1923?]. 77p. port.
*14pp. on cricket*

3350 **Shaw, Alan George Lewers**
–1 The story of Australia. Faber, 1955. 308p. illus. map, bibliog.
——*2nd. ed. revd.* 1961. 320p.
*cricket pp. 101, 252, 279–81*

3350 **Unstead, Robert John,** *and* **Henderson,**
–2 **W. F.**
■ Sport & entertainment in Australia. Black, 1976. 77p. illus. ports. facsims. (Black's Australia Social Studies)
*cricket pp. 8, 9, 20, 26–31, 51*

3351 **Walters, G.**
The general interest in cricket. Sydney, 1891

3352 **Whitington, Richard Smallpeice**
■ An illustrated history of Australian cricket. Melbourne, Lansdowne P., 1972; London, Pelham Books, 1974. 166p. illus. ports. stats.

3352 Great moments in Australian sport.
–1 Melbourne, Macmillan Co. of Australia, 1974. 144p. illus. ports.
——rptd. Melbourne, Sun Books, 1975. *pbk.*
*cricket pp. 12–17, 28–33, 46–57*

3353 **Zeigler, Oswald**
Australia 1788–1938. Sydney, Simmons, 1938
*contains Arthur Mailey on cricket*

## Australian Country Cricket Team

3354 **Australian Country Cricket Team**
■ A.C.C. XI United Kingdom tour April–September, 1965: souvenir tour programme. Naracoorte (S. Aust.), the Team, [1965]. [8]p. ports.

## Governor-General's Team

3355 **Levin, J.**
Cricket matches played in Australia by the Governor-General's teams, 1908/9–1910/11. MS.
*in M.C.C. library, Lord's*

# ANNUALS

3355 The Ampol book of Australian sporting
–1 records; edited by Jack Pollard. Sydney, Pollard Publishing Co., 1968. 325p. stats.
——*cricket pp. 1–2, 95–106*
——2nd ed. *with title* Ampol book of sporting records. 1969. x,556p. stats.
*cricket pp. 160–96*
——3rd ed. 1971. xi,716p. illus. stats.
*cricket pp. 3–63*
——4th ed. 1973
——revised 5th ed. by John Birch. 1978. 482pp. illus. ports. stats.
*cricket pp. 118–34: statistical records by David Roylance*

3356 The Argus cricket guide: compiled by Old
□ Boy, of the Argus and the Australasian [*i.e.* R. W. E. Wilmot]. Melbourne, the Argus and the Australian, v.y., 1928–31. illus. ports.
*1928 16p.*
*1930 16p.*
*1931 with title The Argus and Australasian cricket guide: issue for 1931–32. 16p.*
published in connection with various tours to & from Australia

*1928. The M.C.C. tour in Australia 1928–29*
*1930. Australia in England 1930*
*1931. S. Africa in Australia 1931–2*

3356 **Australia** 1949: the Courier-Mail year book;
–1 edited by J. A. Alexander. Brisbane, Queensland Newspapers Pty. Ltd., [1949?]. 800p. illus. ports. maps, stats.
——*also published with sub-title*: the Herald year book. Melbourne, Herald & Weekly Times Ltd.
*cricket pp. 692–704 including "The English tour – undefeated record of 1948" by Alan D. McGilvray*
*Australia 1950 [1950]. 800p. illus. ports. maps, stats.*
*cricket pp. 730–35*

3357 **Australian** cricket annual; a complete
■ record of Australian cricket. Edited by John C. Davis, Sydney. G. Robertson.
*3 issues: 1895–6. 1896. 190p. scores, stats.*
*1896–7. 1897. 250p. scores, stats.*
*1897–8. 1898. 200p. port. scores, stats.*
*contains 74p. account of M.C.C. tour to Australia, 1897–8*

3357 **Australian** cricket annual; edited by Phil
–1 Tresidder. Sydney, Modern Magazines Pty. Ltd. illus. & ports. (some col.), scores, stats.
*1979–*
*covers season 1978–79; formerly: Australian cricket yearbook*

3358 **Australian** cricket yearbook. Sydney,
■ Modern Magazines Pty. Ltd. illus. & ports. (some col.), scores, stats.
*1970–1978*
*1970–73; ed. by Eric Beecher*
*1974–78; ed. by Phil Tresidder*
*contd. as: Australian cricket annual*

3359 **The Australian Cricketer**
■ Annual; edited by H. Drysdale Bett. Sydney & Melbourne. illus. ports. scores, stats.
*1930–31; consisting of 6 issues of "The Australian cricketer", Nov. 1930–Apr. 1931 with suppl. giving full statistics covering the season*
*Autumn 1932; consisting of 7 issues Oct. 1931–May 1932 with index*
*Christmas annual 1932–33; consisting of 6 issues June–Nov. 1932 with index*
*1932–33 covering the whole tour of Jardine's eleven in Australia 1932–33; consisting of 5 issues Dec. 1932–Apr. 1933 with index*
*1933–34; consisting of 6 issues Oct. 1933–Apr. 1934*

3360 **The Australian** cricketer's guide.
■ Melbourne, Fairfax, *annual*. scores, stats.
*1856–7; ed. by H. Biers and William Fairfax. 72p.*

*1857–8 with title: Cricketer's guide for Australasia; ed. by William Fairfax. 72p.*
*1858–9 with title Australian cricketer's guide; ed. by William Fairfax. 94p.*

3361 **The Australian** cricketers' guide: edited
■ by T. W. Wills, Melbourne, J. & A. M'Kinley. scores, stats.
*1870–71, 1871. 120p.*
*according to Taylor there was another issue for 1874–75 – restated by Ken Piesse in The journal of The Cricket Society, vol. 10, no. 1. Autumn, 1980, p. 12, but no details given*

3362 **Australian** cricketers' guide; edited by
■ Henry F. Boyle and David Scott. Melbourne, Boyle & Scott. diagrs. score, stats.
*seasons 1879–80 to 1883–84. 1880–4*
*issue for 1879–80 has mounted port.*

3362 **Benson and Hedges** international cricket;
–1 edited by Frank Tyson. Melbourne,
■ Australian Cricket Board, Publications Sub-Cttee. *annual*. illus. & ports. (some col.), scores, stats.
*1976 to date*

3363 **Conway, John,** *editor*
■ Conway's Australian cricketer's annual.
*1876–7. Melbourne, Bailliere, 1877. 236p.*
*1877–8, with title: "The tour of the Australian XI through England, America and the Colonies". Melbourne, Ferguson & Moore, 1879. 400p.*

3363 **Cricket** in Australia. Melbourne, Garry
–1 Sparke & Associates. illus. & ports. (some
■ col.), diagrs. scores, stats.
*No. 1. 1979. 112p.*
*the 1978–79 Australian season, including 2 Test series, Australia v. England and Australia v. Pakistan*

3363 **Cricket scene** annual. Melbourne, Lav-
–2 ardin Pty. Ltd.
■ *[1978]. 108p. incl. covers. illus. scores, stats.*
*the only issue; coverage of Australia v. England 1977, and v. India 1977–78*

3364 **The cricketer**
□ 1968; ed. by P. F. A. Coffey. Adelaide, Willow Publications. illus.
1969; ed. by Ross L. Noble. Adelaide, Commercial Publications of S.A. Pty. Ltd. illus. ports. stats.

3364 **Cricketer** annual. Melbourne, Newspress
–1 Pty. Ltd. illus. & ports. (some col.),
■ scores, stats.
*1974–77; edited by Eric Beecher*
*1978 with title: Cricket close-up; edited by Eric Beecher*

*1979 with title: Cricket digest; edited by Ken Piesse*
*covers previous season*

**3365** **The cricketer's** guide and souvenir; season 1907–8. Melbourne, printed by J. J. Miller, [1907]. 48p. illus.
*the only issue*

**3366** **Cricketer's** register for Australasia; edited
☐ by W.J. Hammersley. Melbourne, Sands & McDougall. *annual*. scores, stats.
1862–63. 1863. c.170p.
*only known copy is in the Victorian State Library, Melbourne*
1863–64 *with title:* The cricketers' register: containing the scores of the principal matches played in Victoria during the season 1863–64; also, an account of the second visit of the All England Eleven. 1864. 178p. illus. diagrs. scores, stats.
*formerly:* Victorian cricketer's guide

**3366** **Daily Telegraph (Sydney)**
**–1** Sports year book; edited by W. Adam. Sydney, Consolidated Press Ltd. stats.
1948–?
[No. 1]. 1948. 1948. 256p.
    *cricket pp. 131–49*
No. 2. 1949. 1949. 320p.
    *cricket pp. 182–218*
No. 3. 1950–51. 1951. 320p.
    *cricket pp. 198–226*

**3367** **Frearson's** cricketers' guide and annual for season 1876–7. Adelaide, Frearson, 1876. 52p. illus. mounted ports.
*title-page reads: "Cricket: its rules, laws and regulations. Published under the auspices of the S.A. Cricketing Association; with hints on batting, bowling, fielding and wicket-keeping."*
*the only issue, reviews 1875–6 season.*

**3368** **Goodfellow** & **Hele's** cricketers'
■ almanack. Adelaide, Goodfellow & Hele. *annual*. mounted port. scores, stats.
1878–9. 1879. 124p.
1879–80. 1880. 148p.
1880–81 *published?*

**3369** **Ironside, Frederick James,** *compiler*
☐ Ironside's A.B.C. of cricketing engagements. Sydney, A. Hordern. *annual*
14 *issues, Season 1898–99 to Season 1911–12, published 1898–1911, under varying titles, e.g. "Ironside's cricket programme", "Ironside's cricket fixtures"*

**3370** **The Kookaburra** guide; edited by Eric
■ Beecher. Melbourne, Newspress Pty. Ltd. *annual*. illus. ports. stats.
Cricket '73–'74
Cricket '74–'75

**3370** **J.J. Miller's** sporting annual and athletic
**–1** record. Melbourne, The Herald and Weekly Times Ltd. stats.
1876 to date
*usually contains a section of Australian cricket statistics, which in recent years have been compiled by David Roylance*

**3371** **New** South Wales cricket annual for 1907:
■ full scores & bowling analyses of all grade and interstate matches played in 1906–7; edited by Neville J. Davis. Sydney, N.S.W. Bookstall Co., [1907]. 300p. ports. scores, stats.
*the only issue*

**3372** **New** South Wales cricketer's guide and
■ annual for season 1877–8; edited by Sidney Cohen. Sydney, Cohen, Harris, 1878. 312p. incl. adverts. diagr. scores, stats.
*the only issue*

**3373** **New** South Wales sporting annual 1883–4; edited by P. H. Gilbert. Sydney, C. E. Fuller, 1884. 158p.
*90p. on cricket*

**3373** **Pals annual** for the boys of Australia;
**–1** edited by Charles Barrett. Melbourne, The Herald and Weekly Times, 1921. 705p. illus. ports.
*cricket pp. 24–5, 35, 72, 168–9, 295, 393, 535, 627*
*originally issued as a series of fortnightly magazine parts 1–26, 28 Aug. 1920–13 Aug. 1921*

**3373** **Piesse, Ken**
**–2** A history of Australian cricket annuals and magazines. The Author, 1977. 66p. typescript
*5 copies only; a thesis submitted for a degree in journalism at the Royal Melbourne Institute of Technology; extracts published in* The journal of The Cricket Society, *vol. 9. no. 4; vol. 10. no. 1; vol. 10. no.2*

**3374** **Queensland** cricketers' guide and annual 1884–5; edited by D.G. Forbes. Brisbane, Trimble, [1885]. 120p.
*the only issue*

**3374** **Shepherd, Jim,** *compiler*
**–1** Australian sporting almanac. Sydney, Hamlyn, 1974. 304p,
*the only issue? Cricket pp. 90–102 and pp.16–23 "Australian sporting slang and famous nicknames"*

**3375** **The South** Australian cricketers' guide;
■ edited by W.O. Whitridge. Adelaide. *annual*
1876–7. E.S. Wigg, 1877. vi,60p. scores, stats.

1877–8, with title:——and footballers' companion. E.S. Wigg. 1878. [iv], 101p. stats. 1884–5. Whitridge. 1885. 50p. port. scores, stats.

3376 **The Sporting Globe** cricket annual
■ Melbourne, Sporting Globe. illus. ports. stats.
1924–5: a book of averages and records, Test and interstate matches surveyed; compiled by E.H.M. Baillie ("Bail") and R.H. Campbell. [1924]. 96p. incl. adverts.
subsequent issues with title: *The Sporting Globe cricket book; compiled by E.H.M. Baillie*
*1928–9. [1928]. 130p. incl. adverts.*
*1932–3. [1932]. 98p. incl. adverts.*
*1936–7. [1936]. 114p. incl. adverts.*
*1946–7. [1946]. 64p. incl. adverts.*
*1950–1. [1950]. 48p. incl. adverts.*
*pre-tours*

3376 **The Victorian** cricket annual; edited by
–1 Peter Curtis. illus.
*1969–70. 1970.*
*only 2 copies known (Ken Piesse 3373–2)*

3377 **Victorian** cricketer's guide. Melbourne,
□ Sands & Kenny. annual. scores, stats.
*1858–59 with cover title: "Sands & Kenny's cricketer's guide: ed. by J.B. Thompson. 1859. 150p.*
*1859–60 with title: "Sands & Kenny's cricketer's guide". 1860. 112p. diagrs. scores, stats.*
*1860–61. ed by. J.C. Brodie. 1861. 112p.*
*1861–62; ed. by W. J. Hammersley. Melbourne, Sands & McDougall, 1862. 169p.*
contd. as: *Cricketer's register for Australasia*

3378 **West** Australian cricket annual; edited by "Willow", Perth, [1902]. 131p. illus. ports.
*the only issue?*

## PERIODICALS

3379 **Australian** cricket: a weekly record of the
■ game; edited by C.T.B. Turner and J.A. Dobbie. Sydney, 1896–97. illus. ports. scores, stats.
*18 issues, 10th Sept., 1896 to 7th Jan., 1897*

3380 **Australian** cricket. Sydney, Modern
□ Magazines Pty. Ltd. *monthly during season, i.e. 6 issues per year.* illus. & ports. (some col.), scores, stats.
*Nov. 1968–Apr. 1973; edited by Eric Beecher*
*Nov. 1973 to date; edited by Phil Tresidder*

3381 **The Australian** cricketer. Sydney, 1924–
25. *monthly*
*Oct., 1924 to Mar., 1925 with extra issue Dec., 1924*

3382 **The Australian** cricketer; edited by H.
□ Drysdale Bett. Sydney & Melbourne. *monthly, later weekly, incorporating* The Australian footballer
*vol. 1, no. 1: 14th Nov. 1930 to vol. 7, no. 8, 7th July 1934*
*published as* The Australian cricketer *in the summer and* The Australian footballer *in the winter*

3383 **Australian** cricketer; edited by Ginty Lush. Sydney, 1947
*6 weekly issues 14th Nov. to 19th Dec., 1947*

3384 **The Brisbane** cricketer: a journal published in the interests of Brisbane cricketers and devoted to the advancement of the game. Editor . . . G. Augustus Ross. Brisbane, A.J. Ross. *monthly*
*Vol. 1, no. 1 Sept. 1892 to vol. 2. no. 8. Apr. 1894 (20 issues)*
*issue no. 4 (Dec. 1892) with title: The Queensland cricketer and general athlete. Brisbane, Ross's Weekly*
*issues nos. 5–7 (Jan.–Mar. 1893) with title: The Queensland cricketer and footballer*
*issues nos. 8–10 (Apr.–June 1893) with title: The Queensland footballer & cricketer*
*issues vol. 1. no. 11–vol. 2, no. 8 (July 1893–Apr. 1894) with title: The Queensland footballer & cricketer and general athlete*

3384 **The cricketer.** Brisbane. illus. ports. stats.
–1 *fortnightly*
*Vol. 1, no. 1. Sept. 22, 1962 to no. 6, Dec. 1, 1962, no. 7, Jan. 19, 1963*
*in tabloid newspaper format, the last issue smaller*

3384 **Cricketer.** Melbourne, Newspress Pty.
–2 Ltd. *monthly during season, i.e. 6 issues per*
□ *year.* illus. ports. scores, stats.
*Vol. 1, no. 1 Nov. 1973–Vol.5, no. 7. Apr. 1978; ed. by Eric Beecher*
*Vol. 6, no. 1. Nov. 1978 to date; ed. by Ken Piesse*
*Vol. 1. consisted of 11 monthly issues (no. 10 was the first Cricketer annual), Nov. 1973–Oct.1974*

3385 **David Lord's** world of cricket. Sydney,
□ David Lord Publishing Pty. Ltd. *monthly during season.* illus. ports. scores, stats.
*Vol. 1, no. 1. 1973 – Dec. 1977*
*5 issues in 1973, 1974; 9 issues in 1975 from vol. 4, no. 1. Jan. 1976 monthly with combined Apr.–May issue*
*from vol. 5. no. 1. Jan. 1977 publd. in*

*Sydney by Management Development Publishers*
contd. as:
**World of cricket.** Sydney, Management Development Publishers. monthly. illus. & ports. (some col.), scores, stats.
*vol. 6, no. 1. Jan 1978–no. 10 Feb. 1979(?)*
*editors successively Frank Bohlsen, Malcolm Andrews, Kevin Jones*

3385 **New cricket** reporter: a one day cricket
–1 monthly: contributing editor Brian Bavin.
□ Sydney, David Moeller & John Buchanan, CP Publishing. illus. ports. scores, stats.
*No. 1. Jan. 1979–*

3385 **Old times:** a unique illustrated history of
–2 the early days . . . Sydney, the Commer-
□ cial Publishing Co. illus. ports. *issued in monthly parts*
*4 issues only April–July, 1903*
*Apr. includes pp. 29–34 "The birth of cricket" and "Cricket and cricketers I: from Hyde Park to the Sydney Cricket Ground", by F.J. Ironside*
*May includes pp. 147–9 "Cricket and crick-eters II – reminiscences of Mr. Harry Hilliard, the oldest exponent of the game"*
*June includes pp. 207–10 "Cricket and cricketers III – reminiscences of Mr. A.L. Park"*

3385 **The parade.** Melbourne, Southdown
–3 Press. *monthly*
*Dec. 1950 to date*
*contains regular cricket articles*

3385 **Piesse, Ken**
–4 A history of Australian cricket annuals and magazines. The Author, 1977. 66p. *typescript*
*5 copies only: a thesis submitted for a degree in journalism at the Royal Melbourne Institute of Technology: extracts published in* The Journal of The Cricket Society, *vol. 9. no. 4; vol. 10, no. 1; vol. 10, no. 2*

3385 **Sport** magazine. Sydney, Ken G. Murray.
–5 *monthly*
*Vol. 1, no. 1 June 1954–(at least) June 1964*
contd. with title: *Australian sport and surfriding*
*in latter period edited by Jack Pollard; reasonable cricket coverage*

3385 **Sporting life.** Sydney, Australian News-
–6 papers Ltd. illus. & ports. (some col.)
*1947–Feb. 1957*
*good cricket coverage from A.G. Moyes, Ray Robinson, R.S. Whitington, Keith Miller, etc.*

3385 **Sports** fan. Sydney, P.M. Outteridge.
–7 monthly. illus & ports.

*Vol. 1, no. 1 no. 8 (Apr.-Nov. 1972) plus no. 9 Summer edition*
*regular cricket coverage*

3385 **Sports** novel. Sydney, Thorn Publica-
–8 tions. *monthly*
*Dec. 1946?/1947 . . . July 1964/–?*
*cricket coverage*

# PRIVATE CLUBS

## Australian Old Collegians

*1959 World tour*

3386 **Australian Old Collegians' Cricket Team**
■ World tour 1959. [The Club, 1959].[16]p. illus. port.
*prospects for prospective applicants for tour*

3387 Bermuda tour August 4–9, 1959: souvenir
■ programme. *Printed by Bermuda P.,* [1959]. 28p. incl. adverts. ports.
*pre-tour*

3388 World tour 1959: souvenir programme.
■ The Club, [1959]. [12]p. illus. ports.
*tour itinerary and fixtures*

3389 **De Carvalho, David,** and **Pearson, Tony**
Cricket cocktail: a world tour with the 1959 Australian Old Collegians, incorporating "The story of the 1960 A.O.C. tour" by Tony Pearson. Sydney, A.O.C., [1960]. 174p. illus. ports.

*1960 World tour*

3390 **Australian Old Collegians' Cricket Team**
■ World tour 1960: souvenir programme. [The Club, 1960]. [14]p. illus. ports.
see also *no. 3389*

*1964 World tour*

3391 **Australian Old Collegians' Cricket**
■ **Association**
1964 world tour programme; 1968 world tour plans. Wagga Wagga, the Assoc., 1964. illus. ports. map

3392 **Sandford, Sue**
The Merry wives of cricket. Adelaide, Griffin P., 1967. 148p. scores
*account of tour by Australian Old Colleg-ians around the world in 1964*

*1968 World tour*

3393 **Australian Old Collegians' Cricket**
■ **Association**
1968 world tour programme. [Sydney, the Assoc., 1968]. 16p. illus. ports.
——*supplement with same title.* 4p. [covers U.K. tour only]

## 1970 World tour

3394 **Hyderabad Blues Cricket Club**
■ Australian Old Collegians' Cricket Association v. Hyderabad Blues Cricket Club on 11th and 12th Jan. 1970. Hyderabad, the Club, 1970. [46]p. incl. adverts.

## 1972 World tour

3395 **Australian Old Collegians' Cricket**
■ **Association**
1972 world tour programme. The Assoc., [1972]. [16]p. ports.

3396 1972 world tour programme: programme
■ of matches for the tour in the U.K. The Assoc., [1972]. [4]p. fold (3pp. of text)

## 1976 World tour

3396 **Australian Old Collegians' Cricket**
–1 **Association**
■ World tour 1976. The Assoc., [1976]. [20]p. incl. covers & adverts. ports.
*pre-tour itinerary with pen-portraits*

## 1977 Tour of England and Wales

3396 **Australian Old Collegians' Cricket**
–2 **Association**
■ 1977 tour of England and Wales: programme. The Assoc., [1977]. [20]p. incl. covers & adverts. ports.
*pre-tour itinerary with pen-portraits*

## 1978/79 Tour of India, etc.

3396 **Australian Old Collegians' Cricket**
–3 **Association**
1978/79 tour of India, Sri Lanka & Singapore: programme. The Assoc., [1978]. 12p.
*pre-tour itinerary with pen-portraits*

## Bohemians

3397 **Bohemians Cricket Club**
[Handbook]. The Club. *annual?*
*season–?/1877–8/–?*

## Emus

3398 **The Emu Club**
□ [Annual report]. Tamworth (N.S.W.), the Club. illus. ports. stats.
*?/1968 . . . 72/to date*

## 1959 Tour of Singapore & Malaya

3399 **The Emu Club**
■ The Emu Club's tour of Singapore and Malaya, 1959: compiled by Ross Scott, Stan Gilchrist and John Henderson.

Muswellbrook, N.S.W., the Club, [1959]. [28]p.
*post-tour*

## 1961 World tour

3400 **The Emu Club**
■ The Emu Club cricket team world tour, 1961: souvenir programme. [Tamworth [N.S.W.], the Club, [1961]. 15p. ports.
*includes brief history of the Club: pre-tour*

## 1970 World tour

3400 **The Emu Club**
–1 The Emu Club world tour, 1970: [programme]. [Tamworth (N.S.W.)], the Club, [1970]. 16p. ports.
■ *pre-tour*

3400 The Emu Club world tour, 1970: [tour
–2 report compiled by various players].
■ [Tamworth (N.S.W.)], the Club, [1970]. 48p. illus. ports. score
*post-tour; contains President's report for 1970, reports of Colt tour 1970, etc.*

## 1972 Tour of Malaysia & Singapore

3400 **The Emu Club**
–3 The Emu Club Malaysia and Singapore,
■ 1972: [report]. [Tamworth (N.S.W.)], the Club, [1972]. 32p. illus. ports. scores, stats.
*post-tour*

## 1974 World tour

3400 **The Emu Club**
–4 The Emu Club world tour, 1974:
■ [programme]. [Tamworth (N.S.W.)], the Club, [1974]. [16]p. incl. covers, illus. ports.
*pre-tour; includes short reports to Northern N.S.W. by Singapore National XI and Malaysian Schoolboys*

## 1979 World tour

3400 **The Emu Club**
–5 The Emu Club world tour, 1979:
■ [programme]. [Tamworth (N.S.W.)], the Club, [1979]. [12]p. illus. ports.
*pre-tour*

## I Zingari Australia

3401 **Douglass, W. B.**
■ I Zingari Australia: 75 years of cricket 1888–1963. Point Piper, [the Author, 1963]. 79p. illus. ports. stats.

3402 **I Zingari Australia**
Annual report. Sydney, [the Club], stats.
*1888 to date*

## Wanderers (Q)

**3402** **Wanderers (Q) Cricket Club**
**-1** Annual report and financial statement. Brisbane, the Club. stats. *typescript*
*season 1935–36 to date*
*formed 1935*

**3402** 1977 Central Queensland tour. Brisbane,
**-2** the Club, [1977]. 32p. incl. adverts. illus. ports. scores, stats. *typescript*

**3402** New South Wales tour 1978. Brisbane.
**-3** The Club, [1978]. 26p. incl. adverts. ports. stats. *typescript*

## SCHOOL CRICKET

**3402** **Australian Schools Cricket Club**
**-4** Overseas cricket tour South Africa &
■ Rhodesia, Dec. 1967–Jan. 1968. The Club, [1967]. 12p. ports.
*pre-tour; includes a brief history of the Club by A.A.K. Gifford*

**3402** **Australian Schools Cricket Council**
**-5** 11th Australian schools cricket championship 3rd–10th January 1980, Adelaide. The Council, [1979]. 16p. ports.
*presumably earlier souvenir programmes were issued*

**3403** **Board of Control for Cricket in India**
Programme of tour in India by Australian Schools cricket team, 1966–67. The Board, [1966]

**3404** **Madras Cricket Association**
■ Australian Schools versus Indian Schools, first cricket Test, Dec. 20, 21, 22, 1966, Chepauk, Madras: official souvenir; edited by V. Pattabhiraman. Madras, the Assoc., [1966]. ii,60p. incl. adverts. ports.

**3405** **Ceylon Schools Cricket Association**
■ Australian Schoolboys Cricket Council tour of Ceylon 1972. Colombo, [the Assoc., [1972]. [38]p. incl. adverts. ports.
*pre-tour*

**3405** **Curtis, J. W.**, *and others*
**-1** 100 years of intercollegiate cricket
■ 1878–1978: a brief history of a century of cricket matches played between Prince Alfred College and the Collegiate School of St. Peter, Adelaide, South Australia. Adelaide, *printed by* Lutheran Publishing House, [1978]. 63p. illus. ports. stats.
*includes players such as Joe Darling, Clem Hill, C.E. (Nip) Pellew, the Chappells*

## St. Peter's College, Adelaide

**3406** **Foenander, Samuel Peter**
Souvenir of the visit of the St. Peter's College Adelaide cricket team to Ceylon, January 1928. Colombo, Ceylon Observer, [1928]. 6p. ports.

## Brisbane Grammar School

**3407** **Stephenson, Stuart**
Annals of the Brisbane Grammar School 1869–1922. Brisbane, A.J. Cumming, [1923]. xvi,280p. illus, ports.
*cricket pp. 64–77*

## UNIVERSITY CRICKET

**3407** **The Australian National University**
**-1** **Cricket Club**
Annual report. The Club. *typescript*
*season 1962–3/1972–3/to date?*

**3407** Year book. The Club. illus. ports. scores,
**-2** stats.
□ *season 1973–74. 1974*
*1974–75. 1975*
*1975–77. 1977*
*1977–79. 1979*
*editor: Julian Oakley*

**3407** Souvenir 1000th match (6th January
**-3** 1979); compiled and edited by Julian Oakley. The Club, [1979]. 8p. incl. covers. illus. stats.

**3407** **Sydney University Cricket Club**
**-4** Annual report and financial statement. Sydney, the Club. illus. ports. stats.
*season 1865–66 to date*

**3407** **University of New South Wales Cricket**
**-5** **Club**
Annual report and financial statement. Sydney, the Club. stats. *typescript*
*season 1950–51 to date*

**3407** **University of Queensland Cricket Club**
**-6** Annual report. Brisbane, the Club. illus. & ports. (in later years), scores, stats.
*season 1911–12 to date*
*formed 1911*

## SERVICES CRICKET

**3408** **Board of Control for Cricket in India**
■ Australian Services XI tour—1945: official souvenir; compiled by H.N. Contractor. Bombay, the Compiler for C.C. of India, [1945]. 42p. incl. adverts. ports. stats.
*pre-tour*

3409 **[Cricket Association of Bengal]**
■ Australian visit in Calcutta, 1945: official
programme. [Calcutta, the Assoc., *n.p.*,
1945], 46p. incl. adverts. illus. ports.
*pre-visit*

3409 **Cricketers Club of New South Wales**
–1 Commemorative dinner in honour of the
Australian Imperial Force and the Australian Services cricket team, Friday, July
9, 1971. Sydney, the Club, [1971]. [4]p. 2
team ports.

3409 **Foenander, Samuel Peter**
–2 Souvenir of the visit to Ceylon of the
Australian Services cricket team,
December 1945. Colombo, Ceylon
Observer, [1945]. 12p.

3409 **Madras Cricket Association**
–3 Australian Services XI vs. All-India XI,
unofficial Test, December 1945. [Madras,
the Assoc., 1945]. 30p. ports.

3410 **Queensland Cricket News**
■ Souvenir of cricket match Queensland
versus Australian Services team, Brisbane
Cricket Ground, January 18th, 1946. Brisbane, Queensland Cricket News, [1946].
32p. incl. adverts. illus. ports. scores,
stats.
*pre-match*

# TOURNAMENTS

3411 **Coca-Cola Bottlers**
■ Coca-Cola knockout cup including scoresheets. Sydney, Coca-Cola Bottlers,
[1971]. 12p. incl. covers. 1 illus. ports
——1972/73. [1972]. [4]p. team port. stats.

3411 **Fortitude Valley Junior Chamber of**
–1 **Commerce**
Australia's first Interstate single wicket
cricket competition, Sunday, 24 January
1965: programme. Brisbane, the Chamber
of Commerce, [1965]. 8p. incl. covers &
adverts. ports. stats.

3411 ——, and **Brisbane Cricket Ground Trust**
–2 International single wicket cricket, Bris-
■ bane Cricket Ground, 6th March 1966:
souvenir programme. [Brisbane, the
Chamber of Commerce, 1966]. [8]p. illus.
ports.

3411 **The Gillette** Cup Finals, Feb. 2 & 3, 1974:
–3 souvenir programme. Gillette (Aust.) Pty.
■ Ltd., [1973?]. 12p. incl. covers & adverts.
illus. ports.
*in 1969 ACB started a knockout competi-
tion, including New Zealand, and Gillette
took up sponsorship in 1973/74*

3411 **Queensland Junior Cricket Association.**
–4 *Brisbane Division*
Inter-state carnival, Brisbane, Dec. 11 to
Dec. 16, 1977: official programme. [Bris-
bane, the Assoc., 1977]. 18p. incl.
adverts. ports.

3411 **Richie Benaud's** international 'knockout'
–5 single wicket cricket match. Sunday, 21st
■ November, 1965 at St. Kilda Cricket
Ground. Melbourne, Junior Chamber of
Commerce, [1965]. [8]p. incl. covers,
ports.

3411 **Sportsmen in Action**
–6 The third annual cricket fixture: the
■ Australian XI, Ian Chappell (Capt.) v. A
World XI, Barry Richards (Capt.) South
Africa, Drummoyne Oval, October 6,
1974: official programme. Sportsmen in
Action, [1974]. 12p. incl. adverts.
*typescript*
*to aid of The Spastic Centre of New South
Wales*

3411 **The Sportsmen's Association of Austr-**
–7 **alia.** *South Australian Division*
■ Cricket carnival. Single wicket cricket,
Richmond Oval, October 2, 1966:
souvenir program. The Assoc., [1966].
[8]p. illus. ports.
*'A farewell to the Australian touring team's
visit to S. Africa'*

3412 **Vehicle and General Group of**
□ **Companies**
V & G. knockout cup [1969–70]: official
souvenir program. Sydney, the Group,
[1969]. 16p. incl. adverts. illus. ports.
scores
——1970–71 in conjunction with Inter-
state Cricket Conference. Sydney, the
Group, [1970]. 16p. incl. adverts. ports.

3413 **World** championship cricket—Australian
■ tour—1968. Sydney, N.L.T. Artists Pty.
Ltd. and K. & D. Wong, [1968]. 36p. incl.
adverts. illus.
*a double wicket championship, succeeding
rounds being played at Brisbane, Sydney,
Melbourne, Adelaide, Perth.*

# INTER-STATE AND SHEFFIELD
# SHIELD CRICKET

3414 **Australian Broadcasting Commission**
A.B.C. Sheffield Shield and testimonial
matches 1933–34. Sydney, A.B.C., 1933.
20p.

3414 **Australian Cricket Society.** *Canberra*
–1 *Branch*
■ 200th Sheffield Shield souvenir; edited by

Julian Oakley. Canberra, the Branch, [1975]. [12]p. illus. ports.

*contains accounts of the 1st [1892] and 200th [1974] Sheffield Shield matches both between Victoria and N.S.W., and list of Sheffield Shield holders. Limited ed. of 300 copies*

3415 **Campbell, R. H.**
■ Inter-state cricket guide: a complete record of games between Victoria and New South Wales [1856–1921] and Victoria and South Australia [1880–1920]. Melbourne, *printed at "Punch" Office*, [1921]. 48p. incl. adverts. stats.

3416 **Cricket** carnival: Western Australia v. Victoria 10th, 11th, 13th march, 1922 at W.A.C.A. Ground, Perth: souvenir. Perth, Bryans, [1922]. 32p. incl. adverts. ports. scores, stats.
*pre-match*

3416 **Far North Coast Cricket Council**
–1 "Centenary" Sheffield Shield cricket,
■ Lismore, N.S.W.: N.S.W. v. Qld., 15–18 Dec. 1979: souvenir programme. [The Council, 1979]. 16p. incl. covers & adverts. team port. stats.
*pre-match: to mark the playing of the first Sheffield Shield match in a country area of N.S.W.*

3417 **Hedley, Harry W.**
■ At the wicket: N.S.W. v. Victoria [1856–1888]. Melbourne, Centennial Publishing Co., 1888. 94p. scores, stats.

3418 **Ironside, Frederick James**
■ The laws of cricket as revised by the Marylebone Club with explanatory notes; together with the scores of all the inter-colonial matches, Victoria v. N.S. Wales . . . 1856 up to 1875. Sydney, Gibbs, Shallard, 1875. viii,63p. scores, stats.

3419 World of cricket: England v. Australia;
■ colony v. colony. 1856–1895. 3rd ed. Sydney, Dymock, 1895. 82p. diagr. scores, stats.

3420 **Kearney, Laurie, H.,** *compiler & editor*
Official souvenir of Queensland's entry into the Sheffield Shield: 1876–1926 Q.C.A. jubilee year . . . New South Wales versus Queensland. Brisbane, Q.C.A., 1926. 47p. incl. adverts. illus. ports. stats.

3421 **Lewis, Thomas H.**
Lines on the inter-colonial cricket match played in Sydney 1882. Sydney, Sands, 1887. 7p.

3421 **New South Wales Cricket Association**
–1 Cricket news: New South Wales v. Queensland at Sydney Cricket Ground, 31, December 1938—2, 3 & 4 January 1939. Sydney, the Assoc., [1938]. 12p. incl. adverts. ports. stats.

3422 Cricket news and score sheet. New South
■ Wales v. South Australia, January 14, 16, 17 & 18, 1939. Sydney, the Assoc., [1939]. 12p. ports.

3423 New South Wales v. South Australia [Jan.
■ 8, 9, 11, 12, 1960]. Crows Nest (N.S.W.), V. C. Davis, [1960]. [8]p. ports.

3424 **Queensland Cricket Association**
■ Cricket news: souvenir of cricket match: Queensland versus New South Wales, Brisbane Cricket Ground, 23rd November, 1945. Brisbane, Queensland Cricket News, [1945]. 32p. incl. adverts. ports.
——Queensland v. South Australia, February 1st, 1946. [1946]. 24p. incl. adverts.
——Queensland v. Victoria, February 15th, 1946. [1946]

3424 Official Q.C.A. magazine: Sheffield
–1 Shield Competition 1947–48; [match programmes]. Brisbane Cricket Ground. Brisbane, the Assoc., [1947–48]. 24p. incl. adverts. ports. stats.
*Queensland v. New South Wales, October 24, 1947*
*v. Victoria, November 14, 1947*
*v. Western Australia, February 6, 1948*

3424 Sheffield Shield Competition 1948–49,
–2 Queensland v. South Australia at Brisbane Cricket Ground, February 18, 1949: souvenir programme. Brisbane, The Assoc., [1949]. 18p. incl. adverts. illus. ports. stats.

3424 Official Q.C.A magazine: Sheffield Shield
–3 Series 1949–50: [match programmes]. Brisbane Cricket Ground. Brisbane, the Assoc., [1949–1950]. 20p. incl. adverts. ports. stats.
*Queensland v. Western Australia, November 11, 1949*
*v. South Australia, January 6, 1950*
*v. Victoria, February 3, 1950*

3424 Q.C.A. cricket magazine. Sheffield Shield
–4 Competition 1951–52: [match programmes]. Brisbane Cricket Ground. Brisbane, the Assoc., [1951–52]. 12p. incl. adverts. ports. stats.
*Queensland v. New South Wales, October 19, 1951*

3424   Queensland cricket magazine. 1954–5
–5      Sheffield Shield Series, Queensland v.
         Victoria, Brisbane Cricket Ground,
         January 21 to January 25, 1955. Brisbane,
         the Assoc., [1955]. 18p. incl. adverts.
         ports. stats.

3424   Queensland cricket magazine. 1957–8
–6      Sheffield Shield Series, Brisbane Cricket
         Ground, Qld. v. South Aust., January 17
         to January 21. Brisbane, the Assoc.,
         [1958]. 14p. incl. adverts. ports. stats.

3424   Sheffield Shield: [match programmes].
–7      Brisbane Cricket Ground. Brisbane, the
         Assoc., [1964–65]. ports. stats.
         Queensland v. New South Wales, 4, 5, 7,
              8, Dec., 1964. 24p. incl.
              adverts. ports. stats.
         v. Victoria, 5, 6, 8, 9, Feb.,
              1965. 24p. incl. adverts,
              ports, stats.

3425   Sheffield Shield official programmes
□       1965–1966 season. Brisbane cricket
         ground. Brisbane, the Assoc.,
         [1965–1966]. ports. stats.
         Queensland v. New South Wales, 29
              Oct.–2 Nov., [1965]. 24p.
              incl. adverts.
         v. Victoria, 4 Feb.–7 Feb.
              [1966]. 24p. incl. adverts.
         v. South Australia, 11
              Feb.–15 Feb. [1966]. 16p.
              incl. adverts.

3425   Sheffield Shield: [match programmes].
–1      Brisbane Cricket Ground. Brisbane, the
         Assoc., [1967–68]. ports. stats.
         Queensland v. New South Wales, Oct. 20,
              21, 23, 24, 1967. 24p. incl.
              adverts.
         v. South Australia, Dec. 22,
              23, 24, 25, 1967. 12p. incl.
              adverts.
         v. Western Australia, Feb.
              16–19, 1968. 10p. incl.
              adverts.

3425   Sheffield Shield cricket: official program.
–2      Brisbane Cricket Ground. Queensland v.
         South Australia, Feb. 22–Feb. 25. Bris-
         bane, the Assoc., [1969]. 12p. incl.
         adverts. illus. port. stats.

3425   Cricket news. Sheffield Shield Series:
–3      [match programmes]. Brisbane Cricket
         Ground. Brisbane, the Assoc., [1969–70].
         16p. incl. adverts. ports. stats.
         Queensland v. Western Australia, Oct.
              31, Nov. 1, 2, 3, 1969
         v. New South Wales, Nov. 28,
              29, 30, Dec. 1, 1969
         v. Victoria, Jan. 30, 31, Feb.
              1, 2, 1970

         v. South Australia, [Jan
              16–19, 1970]

3426   Cricket news: Sheffield Shield Series
         [1970–71]: [match programmes]. Brisbane
         Cricket Ground. Brisbane, the Assoc.,
         [1970–71]. 16p. incl. adverts. stats.
         Queensland v. New South Wales, Oct. 23,
              24, 25, 26, 1970
         v. Western Australia, Nov.
              13, 14, 15, 16, 1970
         v. South Australia, Jan. 16,
              17,18,19, 1971
         v. Victoria, Jan. 30, 31, Feb.
              1, 2, 1971

3427   Cricket news. Sheffield Shield Series
■       [1971–72]: [match programmes]. Brisbane
         Cricket Ground, Brisbane, the Assoc.,
         [1971–72]. 16p. incl. adverts. stats.
         Queensland v. New South Wales, Oct. 15,
              16, 17, 18, 1971
         v. Western Australia, Dec.
              24, 26, 27, 28
         v. South Australia, Jan. 21,
              22, 23, 24
         v. Victoria, Feb. 11, 12, 13, 14

3428   Cricket news. Sheffield Shield Series
■       1972: [match programmes]. Brisbane
         Cricket Ground. Brisbane, the Assoc.,
         [1972]. 16p. incl. adverts. stats.
         Queensland v. Victoria, Nov. 3, 4, 5, 6
         v. South Australia, Nov. 17,
              18, 19 & 20
         v. Western Australia, Nov.
              24, 25, 26 & 27.
         n.b. no programme publd. for match v.
         N.S.W.

3429   Cricket news. Sheffield Shield Series
■       1973–74: [match programmes]. Brisbane
         Cricket Ground. Brisbane, the Assoc.,
         [1973–74]. 20p. incl. adverts. stats.
         Queensland v. New South Wales, Oct. 19,
              20, 21, 22
         v. Victoria Oct, 26, 27, 28, 29
         v. South Australia, Nov. 16,
              17, 18, 19
         v. Western Australia, Nov.
              23, 24, 25, 26

3429   'Gabba cricket. '74–'75 Sheffield Shield:
–1      [match programmes]. 'Gabba Cricket
□       Ground. Brisbane, the Assoc., [1974–5].
         24p. incl. covers & adverts. illus. ports.
         stats.
         Queensland v. New South Wales, Oct.
              25–Oct. 28, 1974
         v. Western Australia, Nov.
              15–Nov. 19, 1974
         v. South Australia, Jan.
              17–Jan. 20, 1975
         v. Victoria Mar. 8–Mar. 11,
              1975

3429 'Gabba cricket – '75–'76 Sheffield Shield:
-2 [match programmes]. 'Gabba Cricket
□ Ground. Brisbane, the Assoc., [1975–76].
illus. ports. score
Queensland v. New South Wales, Nov.
24–Nov. 27, 1975. 36p.
incl. adverts.
v. Victoria, Jan. 16–Jan. 19,
1976. 48p. incl. adverts.
v. Western Australia, Feb. 27
– Mar 1, 1976. 38p. incl.
covers & adverts.
v. South Australia, Mar. 5 –
Mar. 8, 1976. 38p. incl.
covers & adverts.

3429 'Gabba cricket. '76–'77 Sheffield Shield:
-3 [match programmes]. 'Gabba Cricket
Ground. Brisbane, the Assoc., [1976–77].
illus. ports. stats.
Queensland v. Victoria, Oct.29–Nov.1,
[1976]. 32p. incl. adverts.
v. Western Australia, Nov.
5–8, [1976]. 24p. incl.
adverts.
v. South Australia, Nov.
12–15, [1976]. 24p. incl.
adverts.
v. New South Wales, Nov.
26–29, [1976]. 32p. incl.
adverts

3429 'Gabba cricket – '77–'78 Sheffield Shield:
-4 [match programmes]. Brisbane, the
Assoc., [1977–78]. illus. ports. stats.
Queensland v. Victoria, Nov. 4–7. 24p.
incl. adverts.
v. New South Wales, Jan.
13–16. 24p. incl. adverts.
v. Western Australia, Feb.
10–13. 28p. incl. adverts.
v. South Australia, Mar. 3–6.
24p. incl. adverts.

3429 'Gabba cricket – '77–'78 Sheffield Shield:
-4 [match programmes]. Brisbane, the
Assoc., [1977–78]. illus. ports. stats.
Queensland v. Victoria, Nov. 4–7. 24p.
incl. adverts.
v. New South Wales, Jan.
13–16. 24p. incl. adverts.
v. Western Australia, Feb.
10–13. 28p. incl. adverts.
v. South Australia, Mar. 3–6.
24p. incl. adverts.
v. South Australia, Jan.
19–22. 24p. incl. adverts.

3430 **Sheffield Shield Competition.** *Interstate*
■ *Cricket Conference*
Constitution, rules and conditions
[adopted 30 Dec., 1953]. [Melbourne], the
Conference, [1954]. 19p.
——rptd. with amendments, 1966. 19p.
interleaved

3430 **Shorley, Ezra Thomas**
-1 Poetic reflections in rhyme and reason.
Rockhampton (Qld), Record Printing Co.,
1925. 51p.
——rptd. Brisbane, Pole Print, [1937].
52p.
*includes poem pp. 10–13, "Inter-state
cricket, Queensland v. N.S.W. at Brisbane
1922–23 season"*

3430 **South Australia Cricket Association**
-2 A. J. Richardson benefit fund souvenir
programme. Sheffield Shield match,
South Australia v. Victoria, 4 to 8 March
1949. Adelaide, the Assoc., [1949]. 20p.
incl. adverts. illus. ports. stats.

3430 Sheffield Shield. South Australia v.
-3 Queensland, Adelaide Oval, 23–27
December, 1966. Adelaide, the Assoc.,
1966. 24p. diagr. stats.

3431 **Souvenir** cricket scoring-book: New
■ South Wales v. South Australia at Sydney
1898–9. 60p. incl. adverts. 1 illus. ports.
*pre-match*

3431 **Tasmanian Cricket Council**
-1 Jack's giant killers: Sheffield Shield
souvenir: official programme. Hobart, the
Council, [1977?]. 20p. incl. covers and
adverts. illus. ports. stats.
*a composite pre-match programme for the 3
home games in Tasmania's first season in the
Sheffield Shield Competition: versus S. Australia, Queensland and New South Wales*

3432 **[Victoria Cricket Association]**
■ Sheffield Shield match Victoria v. New
South Wales, December, 24, 27, 28 & 29,
1926: [commemorative scorecard]. bs.
*records match including Victoria's world
record innings of 1107*

3432 Victoria v. New South Wales: souvenir
-1 programme. All about English and
Australian players. Melbourne, [1936].
16p. ports. stats.
*1936–37 season*

3432 Shield souvenir: [1974–75]. Melbourne,
-2 the Assoc., [1974]
■ *Victoria v. Western Australia, November
1–4. 28p. incl. adverts. illus. ports. scores,
stats.
England special issue. Victoria v. England,
November 8–11. 24p. incl. adverts. illus.
ports. scores, stats.
Victoria v. Queensland, December 6–9.
22p. incl. adverts. illus. ports. score
Special 200th match edition. Victoria v.
New South Wales, December 20–23. 22p.
incl. adverts. illus. ports. score, stats.*

3433 **Western Australian Cricketing**
■ **Association**
Visit of the Victorian XI to Western Australia, 25th Feb to 6th March, 1928: official
souvenir; editorial matter compiled by
Leo Ryan. [Perth], the Association,
[1928]. 48p. illus. ports. scores, stats.
*pre-visit*

3433 **Western Australia Cricket Association**
–1 Interstate cricket: official programme.
South Australia v. Western Australia, 2
matches at W.A.C.A. Oval, 10, 12, 13
Feb. & 16, 17, 19 Feb., 1940. Perth, the
Assoc., [1940]. 24p. incl. adverts. illus.
ports. scores, stats.

# CRICKET STATE BY STATE

## AUSTRALIAN CAPITAL TERRITORY

3434 **Australian Capital Territory Cricket**
■ **Association**
Year book together with annual report
and financial statement. Deakin, the
Assoc. team ports. scores, stats. *typescript*
1972–73 to date
*the first issue included the 52nd annual
report; the second covered both 1973–74 and
1974–75 seasons, then annually*

3434 Competition handbook. Canberra, the
–1 Assoc.
*?/1979–80/ to date*
*fixtures and competition rules*

3435 **East Canberra District Cricket Club**
Annual report. Canberra, the Club
*season 1969–70 to date*

3436 **Western District Cricket Club**
Annual report. Canberra, the Club
1970 to date

3436 **Weston Creek Cricket Club**
–1 Weston Creek C.C. President's XI vs. An
■ Invitation XI . . . 26th February 1978 to
mark official opening of the Club's home
ground, Stirling Oval; compiled and
edited by Percy Samara-Wickrama.
[Weston Creek, the Club, 1978]. [8]p. 1
illus.
*contains pen-portrait of C. S. Cowdrey*

3436 Cover point: Weston Creek Cricket Club
–2 news magazine; edited by Percy Samara-
■ Wickrama. Weston (A.C.T.), the Club.
illus. and stats. in v.i. *typescript. Monthly
during season*
*Vol. 1, no. 1 Sept. 78 to date*
*published Sept. Oct. Nov. Dec. Jan–Feb.*

3436 Annual report and year book; edited by
–3 Percy Samara-Wickrama. Weston
□ (A.C.T.), the Club. illus. ports. scores,
stats. *typescript*
*–/1979–80/ to date*

## NEW SOUTH WALES

3437 **About** Trumper's team: (Queensland tour
■ 1906): official souvenir. Brisbane, R. S.
Hews, [1906]. 24p. incl. adverts. illus.
ports.

3438 **The Australian Cricketer.** *Supplement*
■ New South Wales team souvenir.
Sydney, the Australian Cricketer, 1932.
16p. ports. stats.

3438 **Bowd, Douglas Gordon**
–1 Macquarie country: a history of the
Hawkesbury. Melbourne, Cheshire,
1969. 242p. illus.
*pp. 149–50 early cricket*

3439 **Cricketers Club of New South Wales**
□ Annual repcrt of the Committee and
statement of accounts. Sydney, the Club.
illus.
*Season 1939–40, /1972–73/ to date*

3439 Silver jubilee 1940–1965: a brief history of
–1 the Cricketers Club of New South Wales.
Sydney, the Club, [1965]. 16p. illus.
ports.

3440 Between overs: journal of the Cricketers
Club of New South Wales. Sydney, the
Club. *occasional.* illus. ports.
*Vol. 1, no. 1 (Dec. 1970) to vol.1, no. 8
(Dec. 1973)*

3440 **James, John Stanley**
–1 The vagabond papers. 5 vols. Melbourne,
G. Robertson, 1877–8
*originally appeared in the Sydney Morning
Herald. The 5th series "Sketches in New
South Wales and Queensland" (1878)
contains cricket references; an extract "Cricket
in Queensland" appeared in* The Cricket
Quarterly *vol. VII (1969), pp. 12–15*
——abridged ed. edited with an introduction by Michael Cannon. Melbourne
Univ. Press, 1969. xi,274p. illus.

3441 **New South Wales Churches Cricket Union**
Annual report. Sydney, the Union
*season 1902–3 to date?*

3442 New South Wales cricket annual for 1907:
■ full scores & bowling analyses of all grade and interstate matches played in 1906–7; edited by Neville J. Davis. Sydney, N.S.W. Bookstall Co., [1907]. 300p. ports. scores, stats.
*the only issue*

3443 **New South Wales Cricket Association**
□ Annual report and balance sheet. Sydney, the Association
*season 1857–58 to date*
*also printed in* Year book

3444 Rules, bylaws and local competition
□ rules. Sydney, the Association, *annual*
*season ?1899–1900 . . . 1970 to date*
*16 issues at Lord's 1899–1970; titles vary, in recent years 'Rules and programmes'*

3445 Year book together with annual report
□ and balance sheet. Sydney, the Association. scores, stats.
*season 1927–28 to date*
*issue for 1948–49 covered seasons 1940–41 and 1945–46 to 1947–48*
*15th ed. covered seasons, 1949–50 and 1950–51*
*16th ed. covered seasons, 1951–52 and 1952–53*
*40th ed. covered seasons, 1976–77 and 1977–78*
*From 1949–50? with title: Cricket year book*

3446 Coaching magazine for the benefit of
■ sportsmasters and coaches; edited by G. L. Garnsey. Sydney, the Assoc. illus. diagrs. *monthly*
*7 issues, vol. 1, no. 1 Aug. 1930–Mar. 1931 (no issue Jan. 1931)*

3447 New South Wales cricketer's guide and
■ annual for season 1877–8; edited by Sidney Cohen. Sydney, Cohen, Harris, 1878. 312p. incl. adverts. diagr. scores, stats.
*the only issue*

3448 **New South Wales Junior Cricket Union**
□ Annual report and financial statement. Sydney, the Union. illus. ports. scores, stats. (in v.y.)
*season 1903–4 to 1914–15, 1919–20 to date; 70th annual report 1976–77*

3448 75th anniversary dinner held in Crick-
–1 eters' Club, Saturday, 8th April, 1978.
■ [Sydney], The Union, [1978]. [8]p.
*includes "A short history of the N.S.W. Junior Cricket Union" compiled by Alf James*

3449 **The New** South Wales sporting annual
■ 1884, containing a full account of the past season's cricket, football . . . , edited by Percival H. Gilbert. Sydney, C. E. Fuller, 1884. 158p.
*90p. on cricket season 1883–4*

3450 **The New** South Wales Teachers on tour,
■ North Island, New Zealand, Xmas, 1912. Sydney, *printed by* McMillan & Goddard, [1913]. 32p. illus. ports. scores, stats.
*post-tour*

3451 **New South Wales Wednesday Cricket Association**
Rules and fixtures. Sydney, the Association. *annual*
*?/1901/–?*

3452 **O'Hearn, James J.**
■ Summary of touring English cricket teams in the Hunter Valley, 1876–1971. [Newcastle, the Author, 1971]. 83f. stats.
*typescript*

3453 **Richards, Thomas**
New South Wales in 1881: being a brief statistical and descriptive account of the colony up to the end of the year. Sydney, Richards. 1882. v,144p. illus.
*cricket with illus. pp. 112–3*

## Bowral

3453 **Highlands District Cricket Association**
–1 Official re-opening of Bradman Oval by
■ Sir Donald Bradman, Saturday 4th September 1976: souvenir programme. [Bowral], the Assoc., [1976]. [8]p. stats.

## Illawarra

3454 **Fleming, Alexander Patrick**
■ The International Aboriginal Cricketers v. Illawarra; a record of "The Grand Cricket Matches" played at Wollongong, N.S.W., April and November, 1867. Illawarra, Illawarra Historical Society Museum, 1968. 16p. scores, stats.
*limited ed. of 300 copies*

## Newcastle

3454 **Manuel, David L.**
–1 Men and machines, the Brambles story. Sydney, Ure Smith, 1970. xxiv,147p. illus.
*contains pp. 45–51 "Brambles and cricket" covering some facets of early cricket in Newcastle*

3455 **Newcastle City and Suburban Cricket**
□ **Association**
Cricket annual: edited by N. T. McCaffery and D. H. Blackley. Newcastle, the Association. illus. ports. stats.
*season 1948–49/ 1948–49, 1949–50/—?*

3455 ————. *Charleston C.C.*
-1 Annual report. illus. ports. stats.
*1971 to date*

3456 **Newcastle District Cricket Association**
□ Annual report and statement of account.
Hamilton, the Association
*1889/90 to date*
*87th annual report 1975-6. ports. score,*
*stats.*

## Parramatta

3456 **Jervis, James**
-1 The cradle city of Australia – a history of
Parramatta 1788–1961; edited by George
Mackaness. Parramatta, (N.S.W.), the
City Council, 1961. xii,234p. illus. ports.
maps
*pp. 152-3 contains reference to early cricket*
*in the area*

## Sutherland Shire

3457 **Edson, Mort E.**, *editor*
Gateway to cricket. Sydney, Sutherland
Shire Cricket Association Boys' Competition, 1968. 28p.
*history of boys' cricket in Sutherland Shire*

## Sydney

3458 **Birch, Alan,** *and* **Macmillan, David S.**,
■ *editors*
The Sydney scene, 1788–1960. [Parkville,
Victoria], Melbourne Univ. P., 1962.
xix,387p. illus.
*cricket pp. 21, 62, 326–7, 333*

3458 **Pearl, Cyril Altson**
-1 Wild men of Sydney: a turbulent era in
Australian social and political life. W. H.
Allen, 1958. 255p. illus. ports.
————*later edns.*
*ch. 9, pp. 135–58 "Interlude; cricketer*
*versus priest"—on the Coningham conspiracy*

3458 **Scott, Geoffrey**
-2 Sydney's highways of history.
Melbourne, Georgian House, 1958. 263p.
illus.
*reference in ch. 11 "Hyde Park and its*
*surroundings" to early cricket*

### Sydney Grade Clubs

3459 **Balmain District Cricket Club**
□ Annual report and balance sheet.
Sydney, the Club, illus. stats. (in v.y.)
*1897–98 to date*
*75th issue for season 1971–72 includes a*
*brief history of the Club 1897–1972, by Clif-*
*ford Winning, President; later years with*
*title: Cricket year book*

3460 **Bankstown-Canterbury District Cricket
Club**
Annual report. Sydney, the Club. stats.
*season 1951–52/1973–74/to date*

3461 **Burwood District Cricket Club**
Annual report. Sydney, the Club
*season 1895-6 to 1912–13*
*contd. as: Western Suburbs D.C.C. See*
*no. 3484*

3462 **Central Cumberland District Cricket
Club**
Annual report and balance sheet.
Sydney. The Club
*season ?/1903–04/to date*

3463 **Glebe District Cricket Club**
□ Annual report. Sydney, the Club, stats.
*1892–93 to?*
*now defunct*

3464 **Gordon District Cricket Club**
□ Annual report & balance sheet. Sydney,
the Club. ports. stats.
*1905–06 to date*
*formed 1905*

3465 Jubilee 1905–1955. Sydney, [the Club,
1955]. illus. ports.

3466 **Manly-Warringah District Cricket Club**
Annual report and balance sheet.
Sydney, the Club. illus. ports. stats.
*season 1878–9 to date*
*originally known as: The Manly C.C.*

3466 Manly cricketers chronicle: newsletter of
-1 the Manly Warringah District Cricket
□ Club and the Manly Warringah Cricket
Association. illus. ports. *typescript*
*Nov. 1976 to date?*
*edited by Paul Stephenson*

3466 **Spencer, Tom,** *compiler*
-2 A history of the Manly-Warringah District
■ Cricket Club 1878–1978. Chatswood
(N.S.W.), Management Development
Publishers, 1978. 136p. illus. ports. score,
stats.

3467 **Marrickville District Cricket Club**
□ Annual report. Sydney, the Club. illus.
port. stats. (in v.y.)
*season 1920–21/1928–29 to 1934–35/–?*
*in 1951–52? amalgamated with Petersham*
*District C.C. and known as "Petersham-*
*Marrickville"*

3468 **Middle Harbour Cricket Club**
Annual report. Sydney, the Club
*season?/1905–6/–?*
*combined with Mosman District C.C. See*
*no. 3469–1*

**3469 Mosman District Cricket Club**
□ Annual report and financial statement. Sydney, the Club. illus. ports. stats. *in v.y.*
*season 1908–09–?*
——50th annual report 1957–58 includes a history and statistical record of the Club, 1908–58
*combined with Middle Harbour District C.C. See no. 3469–1*

**3469 Mosman-Middle Harbour District**
**–1 Cricket Club**
Annual report. Sydney, the Club
*?/1966–67 . . . 1976–71/to date*

**3470 Nepean District Cricket Club**
□ Annual report and financial statement. Sydney, the Club. stats. *typescript*
*season 1973–74 to date*

**3471 North Sydney District Cricket Club**
Annual report and balance sheet. Sydney, the Club. stats.
*season 1893–94 to date*

**3472** Illustrated souvenir. Sydney, the Club, 1905

**3473 Northern District Cricket Club**
Annual report and balance sheet. Sydney, the Club. stats.
*season 1925–26 to date*

**3474 Paddington District Cricket Club**
□ Annual report and balance sheet. Sydney, the Club. stats.
*season 1892–93 to 1965?*
*incorporates the old Paddington and Sydney District C.Cs; now defunct*

**3475 Petersham Electorate Cricket Club**
Annual report, Sydney, the Club
*season 1899–1900 to 1905–06*
*1906–07–? with title: Petersham District C.C. Annual report*
*in 1951–52? amalgamated with Marrickville District C.C. and known as "Petersham-Marrickville"*

**3476 Randwick District Cricket Club**
□ Annual report and balance sheet. Sydney, the Club. ports. stats. (*in v.y.*)
*season 1901–02/1916–17 to 1934–35/to date*
*formed 1900*

**3476 Jubilee year book 1900–75. Sydney, the**
**–1** Club, [1975?]. 64p. incl. adverts. illus. ports. stats.

**3477 St. George District Cricket Club**
■ Annual report and balance sheet. Sydney, Kogarah, the Club. ports. stats.
*season 1910–11 to date*
*season 1960–61 includes "Golden anniver-*

*sary: history and statistical records of the Club, 50 years, 1911–1961"*

**3478 Sutherland District Cricket Club**
Annual report and balance sheet. Sydney, the Club. stats.
*season 1965–66 to date*

**3479 Sydney Cricket Club**
Annual report and financial statement. Sydney, the Club. stats.
*season 1965–66 to date*

**3480 Sydney District Cricket Club**
Annual report. Sydney, the Club
*season 1900–01 to 1904–05*
*later incorporated with Paddington District C.C. See no. 3474*

**3481 Sydney University Cricket Club**
□ Annual report and financial statement. Sydney, the Club. illus. ports. stats.
*season 1865–66 to date*

**3482 University of New South Wales Cricket Club**
Annual report and financial statement. Sydney, the Club. stats. *typescript*
*season 1950–51 to date*

**3483 Waverley District Cricket Club**
□ Annual report and financial statement. Sydney, the Club
*season 1894–95 to date*
*79th season 1972–73 port. stats.*

**3484 Western Suburbs District Cricket Club**
Annual report, Sydney, the Club
*1913–14 to date*
*formerly: Burwood District C.C. See no. 3461*

**3485** 50 years of cricket: a brief history of the
■ first 50 years . . . 1895 to 1945. Sydney, the Club, 1946. [ii],126,xxiv,p. illus. ports. stats.

**3485** Anniversary 75 years of cricket
**–1** 1895–1970. [Sydney, the Club, 1970?].
■ 36p. team ports. stats.

*Sydney Shires' Clubs*

**3486 Bexley District Cricket Club**
□ Annual report. Bexley, N.S.W., the Club. *typescript*. stats.
*season 1929–30/1929–30 to 1931–32/to date?*

**3487 Epping District Cricket Club**
Annual report and balance sheet. Epping, the Club. ports. stats.
*season 1933–34 to date*

**3488 Lane Cove District Cricket Club**
Annual report and balance sheet. Sydney, the Club. illus. stats. (*in v.y.*)
season 1899–1900/1928–9 to 1934–5/to date?

*Other Sydney Clubs and Associations*

**3489 Albert Cricket Club**
[Handbook] Sydney, the Club, *annual*
?/1863–65/–?

**3490 Bullen, F. J.,** *compiler*
■ Historical record of the Newtown Congregational Cricket Club, 1882–1953. [Sydney, the Compiler, 1953]. 7p.

**3491 Centennial Park Cricket Association**
Rules. Sydney, the Association. *annual*
at least 5 issues, season, 1907–08 to 1911–12

**3492 City and Suburban Cricket Association**
Annual report. Sydney, the Association
season 1902–03 to date

**3493 Manly-Warringah Cricket Association**
Annual report and financial statement. [Manly-Warringah, the Assoc.]
season 1920/21 to date

**3494** Annual report of the Boys' Saturday Morning Competition. Manly-Warringah, the Assoc.
season 1957/58 to date?

**3495 Moore Park Cricket Association**
List of engagements. Sydney, the Association. *annual*
?/1920–1 to 1923–4/–?

**3496** Rules and regulations. Sydney, the Association. *annual*
at least 3 issues 1921–3

**3497 Plan** of cricket pitches and football grounds. Moore Park, Sydney, N.S.W. Murdoch, *n.d.*

**3498 Newtown District Cricket Club**
Annual report and balance sheet. Sydney, the Club
1905–19
t.p. of 1st issue is dated 1995 [sic]

**3499 Northbridge Cricket Club**
Annual report and financial statement. Northbridge, the Club. stats.
season 1918–19 to date?

**3500 St. George Cricket Association**
□ Annual. Kogarah, the Association
season 1903–04. 1904. 32p.
season 1904–5, 1905–6 with title: *Illawarra Suburbs Cricket Association. annual*

**3501 Western Suburbs Cricket Association**
□ Annual report. Sydney, the Association. stats.
season 1895–6/1920–21, 1927–28 to 1934–35, 1959–50/to date

**3502** Rules, conditions, fixtures. Sydney, the Association, 1905. 32p.

**Tamworth**

**3502 Tamworth District Cricket Association**
**–1** Official handbook. Tamworth (N.S.W.),
□ the Assoc. ports. *annual*
?/1979–80/–

**Wagga Wagga**

**3503 Swan, Keith**
■ A history of Wagga Wagga. City of Wagga Wagga, 1970. xxiii,218p. illus. ports. map, bibliog.
cricket pp.66, 72–73, 133, 154, 172

# NORTHERN TERRITORY

**3504 Northern Territory Cricket Association**
Annual report. Darwin, the Association
?/1964/todate?

# QUEENSLAND

**3504 Association of Cricket Statisticians,**
**–1** *compilers*
■ Queensland cricketers 1892–1979; [compiled by] Warwick Torrens. Cleethorpes, the Assoc., 1979. 38p. maps, stats.

**3505 The Australian Cricketer.** *Supplement*
■ Queensland cricket souvenir: Queensland team . . . . full match scoring sheet and programme [1932–33]. Melbourne, "The Australian Cricketer", [1932]. 16p. incl. adverts. ports. stats.

**3505 Bartley, Nehemiah**
**–1** Australian pioneers and reminiscences. . .; edited by J.J. Knight. Brisbane, Gordon & Gotch, [1896]. vii,424p. ports.
——facsimile rpt. Sydney, John Ferguson in assoc. with The Royal Australian Historical Soc., 1978. [6],vii,424p.
contains pp. 351–4 "Early Queensland cricket"

**3506 The Brisbane** cricketer: a journal published in the interests of Brisbane cricketers and devoted to the advancement of the game. Editor. . .G. Augustus Ross. Brisbane, A.J. Ross. *monthly*

*Vol. 1,no.1 Sept. 1892 to vol.2,no.8 Apr. 1894 (20 issues)*
*issue no.4 (Dec. 1892) with title The Queensland cricketer and general athlete. Brisbane, Ross's Weekly*
*issues nos.5–7 (Jan.–Mar. 1893) with title: The Queensland cricketer and footballer*
*issues nos.8–10 (Apr.–June 1893) with title: the Queensland footballer & cricketer*
*issues vol. 1, no.11–vol. 2, no.8 (July 1893–Apr. 1894) with title: The Queensland footballer & cricketer and general athlete*

**3506** **The cricketer.** Brisbane. illus. ports. stats.
**–1** *fortnightly*
*Vol. 1, no.1. Sept. 22, 1962 to no.6, Dec. 1, 1962, no.7, Jan. 19, 1963 in tabloid newspaper format, the last issue smaller*

**3506** **Francis, Alexander**
**–2** Then and now – the story of a Queenslander. Chapman & Hall, 1936. xii,227p. illus. ports.
*pp.140–1 cricket in Western Queensland*

**3507** **Hutcheon, E.H.**, *and others*
■ A history of Queensland cricket; edited by V.G. Honour. Brisbane, Queensland C.A., [1946]. [ix],342p. illus. ports. scores
*contd. by T.J. Bale and V.G. Honour from 1933–4 season to 1945–6*

**3507** **James, John Stanley**
**–1** The vagabond papers. 5 vols. Melbourne, G. Robertson, 1877–8
*originally appeared in the Sydney Morning Herald. The 5th series "Sketches in New South Wales and Queensland" (1878) contains cricket references; an extract "Cricket in Queensland" appeared in The Cricket Quarterly vol. VII (1969), pp.12–15*
——abridged ed. edited with an introduction by Michael Cannon. Melbourne Univ. Press, 1969. xi,274p. illus.

**3508** **Kearney, Laurie H.**, *compiler & editor*
Official souvenir of Queensland's entry into the Sheffield Shield: 1876–1926 Q.C.A. jubilee year. . .New South Wales versus Queensland. Brisbane, Q.C.A., 1926. 47p. incl. adverts. illus. ports. stats.

**3508** **Mullins, Patrick J.**, *and* **Spence, R.**,
**–1** *compilers*
Statistics of players who have played in first class matches for Queensland 1892–93 to 1976–77 (inclusive). Brisbane, the Compilers, 1977.

**3509** **National Cricket Union of Queensland**
Year book; edited by R.S. Ross. Brisbane, Ross. illus.
*3 issues 1895–6, 1897–8, 1898–9*
*contd. as: Queensland C.A. Constitution and rules*

**3509** **Queensland Church Cricket Union**
**–1** Annual report. Brisbane, the Union. stats.
*season 1903–04 to 1945–46*
*formed 1897; contd. as Queensland C.A. Church Union Division*

**3509** Fixture book. Brisbane, the Union. *annual*
**–2** *?/1936–37/–?*
*rules, officials and fixtures*

**3509** **The Queensland Country Cricket**
**–3** **Association**
Annual report and financial statement. Brisbane, the Assoc. stats.
*season 1972–73 to date*
*formed 1972; formerly Queensland C.A. Country Division*

**3509** Constitution and rules. Brisbane, the
**–4** Assoc., 1972. 99p. incl. adverts.

**3510** **Queensland Cricket Association**
□ Annual report and financial statement. Brisbane, the Association. scores, stats.
*season 1876–7 to date*

**3511** Constitution and rules. Brisbane, the
□ Association. *annual*
*1896–7, 1899–1900 to 1904–5*
*formerly: National Cricket Union of Queensland. Year book*
*contd. as: Queensland C.A. Annual*

**3512** Annual. Brisbane, the Association. scores, stats.
*1905–6 to 1913–14*
*title varies: "Annual" was adopted on wrappers from 1905 but appears on t.p. in 1913 only. 1908 & 1909 issues entitled 'Annual report'; 1910–1912, 'Report and balance sheet'; 1914, 'Annual report and balance sheet 1914–15' [i.e. 1913–14]*
*formerly: Queensland C.A. Constitution and rules*

**3512** Rules & by-laws. Brisbane, the Assoc.,
**–1** 1931. 23p.
*later editions in typescript*

**3513** Official programme. Brisbane, the Assoc., 1945. 31p. illus.
*the only issue?*

**3513** Handbook. Brisbane, the Assoc.
**–1** *1973/74 to date*
*regulations and fixtures*

**3513** Centenary of the formation of Queens-
**–2** land Cricket Association. Queensland vs.
■ Invitation XI, Gabba Cricket Ground, October 10, 1976: official programme. Brisbane, the Assoc., [1976]. 48p. incl. covers & adverts. illus. ports. stats.
*includes an historical survey "100 not out" by P.J. Mullins*

3513 ————. *Church Union Division*
-3 Annual report. Brisbane, the Division. stats. *typescript*
    *1946–47 to date*
    formerly: *Queensland Church Cricket Union*

3513 ————. *County Cricket Committee*
-4 1939–40 Carnival, Brisbane, December 27,
■ 1939 to January 4, 1940: official souvenir programme. Brisbane, the Assoc., [1939]. 33p incl. adverts. illus. ports. diagr. stats.

3513 1940–41 patriotic carnival, Brisbane,
-5 December 26, 1940 to January 3, 1941:
■ official souvenir programme. Brisbane, the Assoc., [1940]. 32p. incl. adverts. illus. ports. diagr. stats.

3513 ————. *Country Division*
-6 Annual report and financial statement. Brisbane, the Division.
    *season 1963–64 to 1971–72*
    formerly *Q.C.A. Country Committee;* contd. as *The Queensland Country C.A.*

3513 ————. *2nd Division*
-7 Annual report. Brisbane, the Assoc. scores, stats.
    *season 1923–24 to date*
    *formed 1923–24 as Junior Division. Name changed in 1953*

3513 ————. *Warehouse Division*
-8 Annual report. Brisbane, the Assoc. illus. (in later yrs.). scores, stats.
    *1921–22 to date*
    *formed in 1921 as Warehouse C.A.; amalgamated with Q.C.A. in 1923*

3513 **Queensland** cricket news. Brisbane,
-9 Martins Publications. ports. *irregular*
    */Vol. 1., no.1, Sept. 22, 1945 – no.16, Feb. 9, 1946/–?*

3514 **Queensland Cricket News**
■ Souvenir of cricket match Queensland versus Australian Services team, Brisbane Cricket Ground, January 18th, 1946. Brisbane, Queensland Cricket News, [1946]. 32p. incl. adverts. illus. ports. scores, stats.
    *pre-match*

3514 **Queensland Cricketer's Club**
-1 Annual report and financial report. Bris-
□ bane, the Club.
    *1960–61 to date*
    *with list of current members; formed 1959*

3514 Cricklet. Brisbane, the Club. illus. ports.
-2 *varying formats. irregular. typescript to no.*
□ *5*
    *?/no.7, Dec. 1965, Nov. 1979/ to date*
    *issue Nov. 1979 features interview with*

*G.S. Chappell; insert of coloured poster of Geoff Thomson and Dennis Lillee*

3515 **Queensland** cricketers' guide and annual 1884–5; edited by D.G. Forbes. Brisbane, Trimble, [1885]
    *the only issue*

3515 **Queensland Junior Cricket Association**
-1 Annual report. Brisbane, the Assoc. illus. ports. stats.
    *1974–75 to date*
    *formed 1974*

3515 ————. *Brisbane Division*
-2 Annual report. Brisbane. illus. ports. stats. *typescript*
    *1973–4 to date*
    *formed 1973*

3515 "Junior cricketer": the official publication
-3 of the Queensland Junior Cricket Association (Brisbane Division). *twice yearly?* illus. ports. stats.
    *Jan. 1976? to date*

3515 **Queensland Schoolboys Cricket**
-4 **Association**
Annual report. Brisbane, the Assoc. stats. *typescript*
    *1972–73 to date*

3515 **University of Queensland Cricket Club**
-5 Annual report. Brisbane, the Club. illus. & ports. (in later years), scores, stats.
    *season 1911–12 to date*
    *formed 1911*

## Brisbane

3515 **Lawson, Ronald**
-6 Brisbane in the 1890s: a study of an
■ Australian urban society. Brisbane, Univ. of Queensland P., 1973. xxxv,373p. illus. maps
    *cricket pp.193,198,199,201–3,211,240*

3515 **Mullins, Patrick J.,** *and* **Ogden, Tony**
-7 Early cricket in the Brisbane and Darling
■ Downs Districts 1846–1859. The Authors, 1979. 21p. *typescript*
    *limited to 9 copies only*

## Brisbane Metropolitan Clubs

3515 **Eastern Suburbs District Cricket Club**
-8 Annual report. Brisbane, the Club. ports. (in v.y.). stats.
    *season 1926–27 to date*
    *Originally from 1897–98 onwards known as the Woolloongabba C.C.; formed as Eastern Suburbs Electorate C.C. 1926–27 and changed to present name 1931–32.*

**3515** **Northern Suburbs District Cricket Club**
**–9** Annual report and financial statement.
Brisbane, the Club. illus. ports. stats.
*season 1927–28 to date*
*formed 1927 as Kelvin Grove Electorate*
*C.C., changed to Northern Suburbs C.C. in*
*1928 and to present name in 1931*
——twenty-fifth annual Silver Jubilee
report 1951–52 *includes a history of the Club*
*1927–52 by Q.F. Rice.*
——fiftieth annual Golden Jubilee report
1976–77 *includes a history of the Club*
*1927–77 by A.C. Pettigrew*

**3515** **Sandgate-Redcliffe District Cricket Club**
**–10** Annual report and financial statement.
Brisbane, the Club. ports.(in v.y.). stats.
*season 1924–25 to date*
*formed 1924 as Sandgate Turf C.C., subse-*
*quently known as Toombul-Sandgate C.C.*
*and given District Club status under present*
*name 1961–62. Reports re-numbered 1967–68*
*from 43rd to 7th to date*

**3515** **South Brisbane District Cricket Club**
**–11** Annual report and financial statement.
Brisbane, the Club. ports.(in v.y.). stats.
*season 1897–98 to date*
*formed 1897–98; report in typescript to*
*1958–59*

**3515** **Toombul District Cricket Club**
**–12** Annual report and financial statement.
Brisbane, the Club. stats.
*season 1921–22 to date*
*formed 1921 by an amalgamation of*
*Nundah and Toombul Cricket Clubs as*
*Toombul Electorate C.C. Changed to present*
*name in 1931–32*

**3515** **Valley District Cricket Club**
**–13** Annual report and financial statement.
Brisbane, the Club. illus. (in v.y.), stats.
*season 1897–98 to date, except for*
*1916–17, 1917–18; 50th Golden Jubilee*
*annual report 1949–50*
*formed 1897–98 as Valley Electorate C.C.*
*Changed to present name 1931–32*

**3515** **Western Suburbs District Cricket Club**
**–14** Annual report and financial statements.
Brisbane, the Club. port.(in v.y.), stats.
*season 1921–22 to date*
*formed 1921 as Western Suburbs Electorate*
*C.C. Changed to present name 1931–32*

**3515** **Wynnum-Manly District Cricket Club**
**–15** Annual report and financial statement.
Brisbane, the Club. ports. (in v.y.), stats.
*season 1961–62 to date*
*formed 1961–62 as a District Club*

## Cairns

**3515** **Collinson, James Warren**
**–16** More about Cairns, the second decade.
Brisbane, Smith & Paterson, 1942. 194p.
illus. facsim.
*limited ed. of 500 copies; cricket p.119*

**3515** More about Cairns, echoes of the past.
**–17** Brisbane, Smith & Paterson, 1945. 134p.
illus. facsim.
*limited ed. of 500 copies; cricket pp.60–2*

## Clermont

**3515** **Hill, William Richard Onslow**
**–18** Forty-five years' experience in North
Queensland, 1861 to 1905, with a few
incidents in England, 1844 to 1861. Brisbane, *printed by* H. Pole & Co., 1907.
153p. ports.
*cricket pp.41,118,119*

## Ipswich

**3516** **Chubb, Charles Frederick**
Fugitive pieces; prologues, etc. Brisbane,
Warwick & Sapsford, 1881. 113p.
*references to Ipswich cricket*

**3516** **Ipswich and West Moreton Cricket**
**–1** **Association**
Annual report and financial statement.
Ipswich, the Assoc. stats.
*season 1963–64? to date*

**3516** **Slaughter, Leslie Edgar**
**–2** Ipswich municipal centenary. Brisbane,
the Author, for the Council of the City of
Ipswich, 1960. 104p. illus.
*cricket pp.48–9*

## Mackay

**3516** **Mackay Cricket Association**
**–3** Souvenir programme and official scoring
card of the visit of Jack Chegwyn's New
South Wales team of international and
interstate cricketers, Queen's Park,
Mackay, 16 and 17 April – Easter 1949.
Mackay, the Assoc., [1949]. 28p. incl
adverts. ports. stats.

## Maryborough

**3517** **Mahoney, J.R.D.**
■ Wide Bay and Burnett cricket, 1864–1908.
[Maryborough, Maryborough C.A.,
1908]. [ii],119p. ports. scores

**3518** **[See no. 3515–10]**

## Townsville

**3518** **Townsville C.A.** presents the F.A.I.
**–1** sponsored Queensland Sheffield Shield
Team versus North Queensland,

Endeavour Park, Townsville, 18–19 November 1978: official programme incorporating a history of Townsville cricket, "The golden years". [Townsville, the Assoc., 1978]. 64p. incl. adverts. illus. ports. scores, stats.

*the history, pp.8–63, by Ken McElligott covers the period 1919–49*

## SOUTH AUSTRALIA

3519 **The Australian Cricketer.** *Supplement*
■ South Australian cricket souvenir; South Aust. team . . . full match scoring sheet and programme [1932–33]. Melbourne, "The Australian Cricketer", [1932]. 16p incl. adverts. ports. stats.

3520 **Country Carnival Cricket Association**
□ **Inc.**
Souvenir carnival programme. Adelaide, the Assoc.
*Feb./Mar. 1938*
*Feb. 26 to Mar. 7, 1940. 40p. incl. adverts, ports. stats.*
*8–18 March, 1954. 40p. incl. adverts. ports. map*
*with a history of the Country cricket carnival*
*4–14 March, 1957. 48p. incl. adverts. ports. diagr. stats.*

3521 **Lamshed, Max**
The South Australian story. Adelaide, Advertiser Newspapers, [1958]. 112p. illus. ports.
*published to mark centenary of the Advertiser, 1858–1958; includes reference to early cricket in S. Australia with illustration of Adelaide Oval*

3522 **Moody, Clarence Percival**
South Australian cricket. Reminiscences of fifty years. Adelaide, W.K. Thomas, 1898. 162p. illus.

3523 **O'Reilly, Charles Bernard**
■ South Australian cricket 1880–1930: a jubilee record. Adelaide, the Author, [1930]. 256p. port. scores, stats.

3524 **Pickwick Athletic Club.** *Cricket Section*
■ Visit of the South Australian cricket touring team, Aug. 31, Sept 1, 2 & 3, 1956; programme of events. [Birmingham], the Club, [1956]. 8p.
*pre-tour*

3525 **2nd South** Australian touring cricket
■ team, season, 1956. United Kingdom: souvenir programme. Adelaide, Publishers Ltd., [1956]. 16p. illus.
*pre-tour of South Australian club cricketers*

3526 **South Australian Cricket Association**
□ Report and statement of accounts. Adelaide, the Association. *annual*
*1871–1931*
*1932–38? with title: Year book with annual report . . . scores, stats.*
*1939?–45 with title: Annual report. . .*
*1946 to date: Year book. . .*

3527 Official handbook. Adelaide, the Associ-
□ ation. *annual.* plans
*season ?/1970–71/ to date*
*fixtures and by-laws*

3528 Centenary souvenir 1871–1971: one
■ hundred years of cricket plus South Australia versus Victoria, Sunday, October 24, 1971; editorial by Alan Shiell. Adelaide, the Assoc., [1971]. 32p. incl. adverts. illus. ports.

3529 **The South** Australian cricketers' guide;
■ edited by W.O. Whitridge. Adelaide. *annual*
*1876–77. E.S. Wigg, 1877. vi,60p. score, stats.*
*1877–78 with title: ——and footballers' companion. E.S. Wigg, 1878. [iv],101p. stats.*
*1884–85. Whitridge, 1885. 50p. port. scores, stats.*
*1884–85 issue contains the revised Laws and a complete record of matches played by the Norwood C.C. during their 22nd season*

3530 **Souvenir** programme: South Australian
■ touring cricket team, season 1954. Adelaide, 1954. 8p.

### Adelaide

3530 **The Adelaide and Suburban Cricket**
–1 **Association**
□ Official handbook. Adelaide, the Assoc. *annual*
*?/1975–76/to date*
*season 1975–76 contained the 76th annual report*

3531 **Adelaide Turf Cricket Association**
Constitution and rules and bylaws. Adelaide, the Assoc., 1938. 32p.

3532 **Downer, Sidney**
■ 100 not out: a century of cricket on the Adelaide Oval. Adelaide, Rigby, 1972. [ix],183p. illus. ports.

3533 **Norwood Cricket Club**
■ [Memento giving the records of the Club]. Adelaide, [the Club], 1879. bs.
*the Club was established in 1865 and disbanded in 1897 on the adoption of the electorate cricket system; see also no.3529*

**3533 Sutton, Ray W.**
**–1** "Great prospects": a half century of
■ cricket with the Prospect District Cricket
Club 1928–29—1978–79. Prospect (S.
Aust.), the Club, 1978. xiii,166p. ports.
diagr. scores, stats.

**3534 West Torrens District Cricket Club**
□ Annual report. West Torrens, the Club.
*typescript.* stats.
*?/1931–32—1933–34/–?*

# VICTORIA

**3534 Association of Cricket Statisticians**
**–1** Victorian cricketers 1850–1978; [compiled
■ by] Roger Page. Hampden in Arden
(Warks.), the Assoc., 1978. 64p. maps,
stats.

**3535 The Australian Cricketer.** *Supplement*
Victorian cricket souvenir. Sydney, The
Australian Cricketer, 1932. 16p. illus.

**3535 Cranfield, Louis Radnor**
**–1** Epics from Victorian history. Ilfracombe,
Stockwell, 1965. 94p.
——2nd (enl.) ed. 1969. 145p.
*cricket pp.76,93,127*

**3536 Cricket Union of Victoria**
■ Constitution, rules & by-laws. Melbourne, the Union, 1971. [24]p.

**3536 Hamilton, James C.**
**–1** Pioneering days in Western Victoria: a
narrative of early station life. Melbourne,
Exchange P., 1914. 112p. illus.
*pp.81–2 reference to aboriginal cricket team*
——*another ed.* Melbourne, Macmillan,
1923. 110p.
*the above reference appears on pp.76–7*

**3536 Mandle, William Frederick**
**–2** Games people played: cricket and football
in England and Victoria in the late nineteenth century. Melbourne, Univ. of
Melbourne P., [1973?]. [28]p.
*off-print from Historical Studies, vol.15,
no.60, April, 1973, pp.511–38*

**3536 Victorian Country Cricket League**
**–3** Rules governing the Country Cricketers'
□ Premierships. The League. *annual*
*?/1974–5/to date?*

**3537 Victorian Cricket Association**
□ Annual report. Melbourne, the Assoc.
illus. ports. scores, stats. *in v.y.*
*1895/6–1938/9,1945/6 to date*
*1949/50 and 1950/51 issued in 1 vol.*
*formerly: Victorian Cricketers' Associ-
ation. Annual report*

**3538** Objects, constitution and rules, revised
■ 12th Oct., 1906. Melbourne, the Assoc.,
[1906]. 18p.

**3539** Jubilee of international cricket: Victorian
■ Cricket Association invitation smoke
concert 30th Dec. 1911. Melbourne, the
Assoc., 1911. [12p]. illus. ports. scores,
stats.

**3540** Rules for the V.C.A. matches: district
■ clubs, first, second and third elevens.
[Melbourne], the Association
*season 1955–56. 47p.*

**3541 Victorian Cricketers' Association**
■ Annual report. Melbourne, the Assoc.
illus. ports. scores, stats. *in v.y.*
*season 1876–77 to 1894–95*
contd as: *Victorian Cricket Association.
Annual report*

**3542 Victorian** cricketer's guide. Melbourne,
□ Sands & Kenny. *annual.* scores, stats.
*1858–59 with cover-title: "Sands &
Kenny's cricketer's guide"; ed. by J.B.
Thompson. 1859. 150p.*
*1859–60 with title: "Sands & Kenny's
cricketer's guide". 1860. 112p. diagrs. scores,
stats.*
*1860–61; ed. by J.C. Brodie. 1861. 112p.*
*1861–62; ed. W.J. Hammersley. Mel-
bourne, Sands & Mcdougall, 1862, 169p.*

**3543 Victorian Junior Cricket Association**
Book of rules. [Melbourne], the Assoc.,
[c.1906]

**3544 Victorian Junior Cricket Union**
□ Annual report and balance sheet.
Melbourne, Victorian Junior C.U.
*season 1913–14?/1954–55/to date*

**3545** Objects, constitution and rules. [Mel-
■ bourne, the Union], 1954. 18p.
——*with title:* Constitution, rules and by-
laws. 1958. 16p.

**3546 Victorian Sub-District Cricket
Association**
Annual report. The Association
*season ?/1908–09/–?*

**3547 Wilmot, R.W.E.,** *editor*
■ The Victorian sporting record 1903.
Melbourne, McCarron, Bird, 1903. ix,
369p. ports. score, stats.
*cricket pp.1–110*

## Bendigo

**3548 Mackay, George,** *compiler*
■ Bendigo United Cricket Club 1861–1911:
jubilee souvenir. Bendigo, Cambridge &
Leaney, 1911. 39p. ports. stats.

## Brighton

**3549   Bate, Weston**
■   A history of Brighton. Melbourne Univ.
P., 1962. xi,425p. illus. ports. maps
*cricket 57–58,74,83,139–41,247,308*

**3549   Brighton Cricket Club**
**–1**   Annual report. Brighton (Vic.), the Club.
*?/1929–30/*to date?
*formed 1842*

## Geelong

**3549   Geelong Cricket Association**
**–2**   Rule and fixture book incorporating
□   annual report and financial statement.
Geelong, the Assoc. *annual*
*?/1973–74/*to date

## Melbourne

**3550   Dunstan, Keith**
■   The paddock that grew: the story of the
Melbourne Cricket Club; research by
Hugh Field. Melbourne, Cassell, 1962,
[i.e. 1963]. xv,304p. illus. ports. scores,
stats.
——rev. and enl. ed. Melbourne, Cassell,
1974. 286p. illus. ports. scores, stats.

**3550   Finn, Edmund ("Garryowen", *pseud.*)**
**–1**   Garryowen's Melbourne: a selection from
"The chronicles of early Melbourne,
1835–1852"; edited by Margaret Weiden-
hofer. Melbourne, Nelson, 1967. 198p.
illus.
*pp.148–9 Intercolonial cricket*; The chronicles . . . *were originally published in 2 vols.*
*1888*

**3551   Grant, James, *and* Serle, Geoffrey, *editors***
■   The Melbourne scene 1803–1956. Mel-
bourne, Melbourne Univ. P.; Cambridge,
Cambridge Univ. P., 1958. xviii,308p.
illus. (some col.)
*cricket pp.10,31,79,111,144,205,254*

**3552   Melbourne Cricket Club**
Annual report for the season. Melbourne,
the Club. stats.
*season 1875–6 to date*

**3553   Centenary celebrations: souvenir and**
■   programme, Saturday, December 10,
1938. Melbourne, the Club, [1938]. [8]p.
illus. ports. facsims.

**3554   Rules and bye-laws, altered and revised.**
□   Melbourne, the Club
*22nd July, 1952. 1952*
*18th March, 1954. 1954.36p.*

**3555   Newsletter. Melbourne, the Club. illus.**
□   ports.
*No. 1. June, 1957/Dec. 57 (no. 2), Mar. 71*
*(no.44), Jun. 71(no.45)/*to date

**3555   The M.C.G. story: the home of the**
**–1**   Melbourne Cricket Club. [Melbourne, the
■   Club], 1976. [16]p. incl. covers. illus.
(some col.)

**3555   Melbourne Cricket Club. *XXIX Club***
**–2**   Annual report. Melbourne, the Club.
scores, stats.
*1956–57 to date*
*a social non-playing club*

**3556   Mickle, Alan Durward**
■   After the ball: a book of sporting
memories. Melbourne, Cheshire, 1959.
x,106p. illus.

**3557   Shell Company of Australia Ltd.**
■   International cricket. Centenary occasion:
this booklet commemorates the first international cricket match played on the
Melbourne Cricket Ground on January
1st, 1862. The Co., [1962]. 8p. 1 illus.
score
*between Melbourne & Districts XVIII and*
*H.H. Stephenson's XI*

**3557   Taylor, E.C.H.**
**–1**   100 years of football: the story of the
Melbourne Football Club 1858–1958;
written and edited by E.C.H. Taylor
(research by Hugh Field). Melbourne,
(the Club), 1957. 183p. illus.
*cricket pp.ix,15–19 with illustrations on the*
*early history of the Melbourne Cricket Ground*

## *Camberwell*

**3558   Grace, Radcliffe**
■   A century to Camberwell: a history of
Camberwell Cricket Club, 1864–1964.
[Melbourne, the Club, 1964]. 30p. ports.
stats.

## *Carlton*

**3559   Cooke, T.F.**
■   Carlton Cricket Club jubilee history
1864–1914 . . . and Annual Report,
1913–14. Melbourne, the Club, 1914.
126p. illus. ports. stats.

**3560   Taylor, George Cyril Percival ("Percy")**
■   Carlton Cricket Club: 100 years of cricket
1864–1964. Melbourne, the Club, [1964].
89p. illus. ports. stats.
*the Annual report and balance sheet*
*1963–64*

## Collingwood

**3561**  **Collingwood Cricket Club**
Annual report and financial statement.
Melbourne, the Club
*1907? to date?*

## East Melbourne

**3562**  **[Clarke, Alfred E.]**
■   East Melbourne Cricket Club: its history,
1860–1910, jubilee year. Melbourne,
Robertson, [1910]. 162p. illus. ports.
stats.

**3563**  **East Melbourne Cricket Club**
Annual report. Melbourne, the Club
*season ?/1910–11 to 1920–1/*
contd. as: *Hawthorn and East Melbourne
C.C. Annual report*
*club originally formed 1860*

**3564**  **Hawthorn and East Melbourne Cricket
Club**
Annual report. Melbourne, the Club
*1921–2 to date?*
formerly: *East Melbourne C.C. Annual
report*

## East Suburban Churches' C.A.

**3564**  **East   Suburban   Churches'   Cricket**
**–1**  **Association**
■   Constitution and rules as at 25 August,
1975. [Melbourne, the Assoc., 1975]. 32p.

**3564**  Fixture book. Melbourne, the Assoc.
**–2**  *season–?/1975–76/to date?*
■

**3564**  **Shaw, Mervyn J.C.**
**–3**  Cricket in the park: a history of the East
■   Suburban Churches' Cricket Association.
Melbourne, the Assoc., 1975. [ix],85p.
stats.

## Fitzroy

**3565**  **Fitzroy Cricket Club**
Annual report. The Club
*season 1863–64 to?*
*Lord's has only 1911–12 and 1922–23*

## Heidelberg

**3566**  **Cranfield, Louis Radnor**
■   A century of cricket: centenary souvenir
of the Heidelberg Cricket Club. Heidelberg, The Cttee. of the Club, 1957. 16p.
incl. adverts. ports. score, stats.

## La Mascotte

**3567**  **La Mascotte Cricket Club**
■   Souvenir: the history of the club since its
inception. Melbourne, [the Club], 1906.
20p. stats.
*presented to members of the Club to mark
the occasion of the Club's entry into senior
cricket*

## North Melbourne

**3568**  **North Melbourne Cricket Club**
Annual report. Melbourne, the Club
*season 1868–69?/1922–23/to date?*

## Oakleigh

**3569**  **Oakleigh District Cricket Association**
■   Rules   and   constitution,   1957–58.
Oakleigh, the Assoc., 1957. 17p.
——Objectives, rules and constitution.
[Oakleigh], the Assoc., 1975. 24p.

## Prahan

**3569**  **Piesse, Ken**
**–1**  Prahan Cricket Club's centenary history.
■   Seaford, Melbourne, [the Author], 1979.
184p. illus. ports. score, stats.
*originally known as Hawksburn C.C. before
start of District cricket in 1906*

## Richmond

**3570**  **Richmond Cricket Club**
□   Annual report and balance sheet. S.
Melbourne, the Club
*season 1854–55/1911–12/to date*

**3571**  **Taylor, George Cyril Percival ("Percy")**
■   Richmond's 100 years of cricket: the story
of the Richmond Cricket Club 1854–1954.
S. Melbourne, Meehan, 1954. [vii],126p.
illus. ports. score, stats.

## St Kilda

**3572**  **St. Kilda Cricket Club**
Annual report of the Committee for the
season. Melbourne, the Club
*1856–57 to date?*

**3573**  Handbook. Melbourne, the Club. *annual*
*?/1956/to date?*

## South Melbourne

**3574**  **South Melbourne Cricket Club**
Annual report. Melbourne, the Club
*1863?/1876/to date?*

## Mildura

**3575**  **Mildura District Cricket Association**
Annual report. Mildura, the Association
*season?/1951–2/to date?*

## Mornington

3575 **Mornington Peninsula Cricket**
−1 **Association**
□ Directory: rules and fixtures. Mornington (Vic.), the Club. *annual*
*?/1973–74/*to date
*formed 1963*

### Warrnambool

3576 **Warrnambool and District Cricket**
□ **Association**
Annual report & financial statement. Warrnambool, the Association. illus. ports.
*season ?1946–47/1963–64/*to date

# WESTERN AUSTRALIA

3576 **Brayshaw, Ian**
−1 Cricket West. West Perth (W. Aust.),
■ Perth Building Soc., [1979]. 60p. illus. ports. facsims, diagr. scores, stats.
*produced by Perth Building Society in the interest of West Australian cricket; history of cricket in Western Australia*

3576 **Weekend magazine**
−2 Cricket, lovely cricket. Perth, Weekend News, December 12, 1970. 16p. illus. ports.
*cover and 4pp. devoted to cricket, including "WA cricket is a big boy now", by Ted Joll; and "How the Test was won" by David Brewtnally commemorating the first ever Test in Perth*

3577 **West** Australian cricket annual; edited by "Willow". Perth, [1902]. 131p. illus. ports.
*the only issue?*

3578 **Western Australian Cricketing**
□ **Association**
Annual report and balance sheet. Perth, the Assocation. ports, scores, stats. *in v.y.*
*season ?/1899–1900 to 1928–29*
*in Sept. 1929 title of Association changed to Western Australia Cricket Association*

3579 **Western Australia Cricket Association**
□ Annual report and balance sheet. Perth, the Association. ports. scores, stats. *in v.y.*
*season 1929–30 to 1947–48*
*1948–49 to date with title: Year book*
*formerly: Western Australian Cricketing Association*

3579 Fixtures. Perth, the Assoc. *annual. diagrs.*
−1 *?/season 1974–75/*to date
□ *includes official list of clubs, rules, etc.*

## Fremantle

3580 **Fremantle District Cricket Club**
□ Annual report. Fremantle, the Club. *typescript. stats.*
*?/1957–8/*to date?

### Perth

3580 **Rowe, Jack,** *and others, compilers and*
−1 *editors*
History of Nedlands Cricket Club 1928–1978. Perth, the Club, 1978. 16p. stats.

3580 **South Perth Cricket Club**
−2 Year book. Perth (W.A.), the Club. stats.
□ *typescript*
*?/1973–74/*to date
*the Club was admitted to W.A.C.A. 1st Grade status in 1945–46 season*

# TASMANIA

3580 **Noel Bergin's** Touring Cricket XI initial
−3 tour: Sydney, Wollongong, Goulburn, Canberra, Cooma, Wangaratta, Melbourne . . . Sunday 4 Feb., 1968 to Sunday 18 Feb. 1968 inclusive. [N. Bergin, 1968]. 6p.
*a team of Tasmanian cricketers privately organised by N.B.*

3581 **Northern Tasmanian Cricket Association**
□ Annual report and balance sheet. Launceston, the Assocation
*season ?1886–87/1910–11, 1930–31, 32–33/*to date

3582 **Page, Roger**
■ A history of Tasmanian cricket. Tasmania. L.G. Shea, [1958]. 143p. illus. ports. diagrs. scores, stats.

3583 **Southern Tasmanian Cricket Association**
Report. Hobart, the Association. *annual.* scores, stats.
*season 1866–67/1880–81, 1904–05/ to date*
*in early years with title: Annual circular*

3584 **Tasmanian Cricket Association**
■ Annual report and financial statement. Hobart, the Assoc. scores, stats. *in v.y.*
*1866–67 to date*

3585 History of the Tasmanian Cricket Association. [Hobart], the Assoc., [1969]. 54p.

3585 **Tasmanian** cricket yearbook. Hobart,
−1 Tasmanian Sporting Publications
■ *1979–80; edited by Allan Leeson. 1979. 96p. incl. adverts. illus. ports. score, stats.*

# WOMEN'S CRICKET

3585 **Womens Cricket Association**
–2 Report of the Australian Women's cricket
■ tour in England, Golden Jubilee Year,
1976; edited by N. Rheinberg. The
Assoc., [1976?]. 20p. incl. covers. team
ports. scores, stats.

# AUSTRALIAN CRICKET SOCIETY

3585 **Australian Cricket Scoiety**
–3 World tour 1979: souvenir tour brochure;
■ editor: Ronald L. Cardwell. The Society,
[1979]. 40p. incl. covers & adverts. ports.
*pre-tour*

## A.C.T. Branch, later Canberra Branch

3586 **Cricket** quadrant: official journal of the
■ Australian Cricket Society (A.C.T.
Branch). The Society. *quarterly.* illus.
ports. score, *typescript*
*vol. 1, no. 1 Sept 1973 to date*
*editor: Julian Oakley*
*vol.3, no.1 (1975) was the first issue of the
journal of the newly-titled Canberra Branch*

3586 Year Book. Canberra, the Branch. illus.
–1 scores
□ *season 1973–74 to date*
*edited by Julian Oakley. The Branch
founded 29 Dec. 1972*

3586 Constitution as at August 2, 1974.
–2 [Canberra, the Branch, 1974]. 19p. *type-*
■ *script*

3586 Cricket companion: [official annual
–3 journal]; compiled and edited by Julian
□ Oakley. The Branch. illus. ports. scores,
stats.
*'74 to date*

## Adelaide Branch

3586 **Cathedral** end: official journal of the
–4 Australian Cricket Society, Adelaide
□ Branch. *6-monthly. typescript. stats.*
*vol. 1, no.1. Dec. 1977 or Jan. 1978 to
date*
*formed July 1977*

3586 Newsletter. The Branch. *typescript*
–5 *Jan. 1978 to date*
□

## Melbourne Branch

3587 **Extra** cover: a winter journal of the
■ Australian Cricket Society. The Society.
*annual.* illus. ports. (in later yrs.), stats.
*1971–1976, 1978*
*edited by Derek Leong and Bruce
Sivewright, from 1975? by Sivewright only;
contains first-class Australian averages of
previous year*

3588 **Pavilion:** a journal of the Australian
■ Cricket Society. The Society. illus. ports.
stats. *3 times a year*
*Vol. 1 no. 1. Oct. 1968*
*2. Feb. 1969*
*3. Summer 1969–70 (Dec. 1969)*
*Vol. 2 no. 1. Winter 1970 (June 1970)* then
changed to annual:
*Pavilion '71: official journal of the Australian
Cricket Society. Dec. 1970*
*'72: Dec. 1971*
*'73: Jan. 1973*
*'74, '75, '79*
*Not published '76,'77,'78*

3589 **"Scoresheet":** [newsletter of] the Austra-
□ lian Cricket Society. Melbourne, The
Society. *quarterly.* stats. *typescript*
*1967 to date*

## Newcastle (N.S.W) Branch

3590 **"Straight** drive". Newcastle (N.S.W.).
*irregular. typescript*
*7 issues Feb. 1973 – Sept. 1974*
*the newsletter of the Branch*

## Sydney Branch

3590 **Hill** chatter: official journal of the Sydney
–1 Branch of the Australian Cricket Society.
□ *typescript. occasional during season*
*Vol.1, no.1. Apr. 1974 to date*

3590 New Zealand tour 1978. Sydney, the
–2 Branch, [1978]. 28p. incl. covers. *typescript*
■ *contains pp.5–6 "Recollections of N.Z.
cricket" by W.J. O'Reilly*

# ELECTRIC LIGHT CRICKET

3591 **Australian Electric Light Cricket Council**
■ Electric light cricket: book of rules.
Adelaide, the Council, 1936. 32p. incl.
adverts. illus. diagrs.

3592 **The South Australian Electric Light**
■ **Cricket Assocation**
Playing rules. Port Adelaide, the Associ-
ation, *n.d.* [12]p.

# CRICKET IN SOUTH AFRICA AND ZIMBABWE RHODESIA

**3593** **Ashley-Cooper, Frederick Samuel**
■ The South African cricket guide: a book of records. Nottingham, Richards, 1929. 34p. stats.
*mainly records of S.A. v. England Tests*

**3593** **The Cape Times**
**–1** Sports and sportsmen, South Africa. Cape Town, Atkinson, [1911?]. xiii,526p. illus.
*pp.87–101, Early cricket; pp.105–20, Cricket 1900–1910*

**3593** Sports and sportsmen, South Africa and
**–2** Rhodesia. 2 vols. Cape Town, The Cape Times, 1929. illus. ports.
*limited ed. of 500 copies; includes a ch. on cricket and short features on cricketers*

**3594** **Compton, Herbert Eastwick**
■ Semi-tropical trifles. Washbourne, 1875. 168p.
*"A colonial cricket match", pp.7–29*

**3595** **Duffus, Louis George**
■ Cricketers of the Veld; illustrated by Leyden. Sampson Low, Marston, [1947]. vii,182p. illus. score

**3596** South African cricket, 1927–1947. Johan-
■ nesburg, South African C.A., 1948. 625p. illus. ports. scores, stats.

**3597** **Giants** of South African cricket. [Cape
■ Town], Don Nelson Enterprises, 1971. 173p. illus. ports.

**3598** **Goldman, Arthur**
■ My greatest match. Johannesburg, Central News Agency, 1956. xiii,194p. ports. scores
*essays on South African sport including "Dudley Nourse, the Churchill of cricket", pp.37–53; "Jack Cheetham, leader of South African cricket renaissance", pp.78–99; "Bruce Mitchell, the 'quiet man' of cricket", pp.128–140*

**3598** **Lapchick, Richard Edward**
**–1** The politics of race and international
■ sport: the case of South Africa. Westport (Conn.), Greenwood P., 1975. xxx,268p.

bibliog. (Center on International Race Relations, Univ. of Denver. Studies in Human Rights. No. 1)
*many cricket references to the d'Oliviera Affair, Stop the Seventy Tour, Fair Cricket Campaign, etc.*

**3598** **Leek, Neville Ivor James**
**–2** South African sport. Cape Town, Macdonald South Africa, 1977. 63p. illus. (chiefly col.), bibliog. (Macdonald Heritage Library)
——*Afrikaans ed. with title:* Suid-Afrikaanse sport

**3599** **Litchfield, Eric**
■ The Springbok story from the inside. Cape Town, Timmins, 1960. 231p. illus. ports.
*South African sport generally, cricket pp.23–77*

**3600** **Luckin, Maurice William,** *editor and*
■ *compiler*
The history of South African cricket, including the full scores of all important matches since 1876. Johannesburg, Hortor, 1915. 848p. illus. ports. scores, stats.

**3601** South African cricket 1919–1927; a
■ complete record of all first-class South African cricket since the war. Johannesburg, the Author, [1928]. 494p. illus. ports. scores, stats.

**3601** **Odendaal, André,** *editor*
**–2** God's forgotten cricketers: profiles of
■ leading South African players. Cape Town, South African Cricketer, 1976. 150p. illus. ports. pbk.

**3601** Cricket in isolation: the politics of race
**–3** and cricket in South Africa. Cape Town,
■ the Author, 1977. xvii,384p. illus. ports.
*limited ed. of 1000 copies signed and numbered*

**3602** **Outspan.** *Supplement*
■ Cricket in South Africa: a history of the game, by Louis Duffus. Outspan,

December 14, 1956. 32p. incl. adverts. illus. ports.
*sponsored by the makers of Lifebuoy soap*

3603 **Parker, G.A.**, *editor*
■ South African sports: cricket, football, athletics, cycling . . .: an official handbook with portraits of leading athletes and officials. 1897 edition. Sampson Low, 1897. xxiv,234p. illus. ports. scores, stats.
*cricket pp.9–56*

3603 **Pickard, Abraham Benjamin de Villiers**
–1 Vanmelewe se rugby 1880 en vanmelewe se krieket 1874. Pretoria, the Author, 1943. 12p. port.
*-Afrikaans text; trs.: "Rugby formerly of 1880 and cricket of 1874"*

3604 **South African Cricket Association**
■ Annual report. Johannesburg, the Association. scores, stats.
*season ?1891–92/1906–07 . . . 1974–75/to date*
*contains full scores of Currie Cup matches formed 1891; not issued 1912 (1913 contains reports of 1911–12 and 1912–13)*

3605 Currie cup rules, articles of constitution, Oct. 1914. Johannesburg, the Assoc., 1914. 12p.
——*with title:* Constitution, boundaries and Currie Cup rules. 1950. 24p.

3606 **S.A. Cricketers'** war memorial: record of unveiling ceremony, 31st December 1948. Cape Town, Edson P., 1948. 4p. illus.

3607 **South African Olympic and British Empire Games Association**
Springboks . . . past and present: a record of men and women who have represented South Africa in international amateur sport, 1888–1947; compiled by J.A.T. Morris and Ira G. Emery. Johannesburg, the Assoc., 1948. [208]p. ports.

3607 **Sports** personalities: South Africa, 1971.
–1 Johannesburg, Perskor, 1971. xxvii,361p. illus.
*text in Afrikaans and English; cricket pp.75–94*

3608 **Stent, R.K.**
■ Green and gold: a sporting miscellany. Longmans, Green, 1954. [vi],188p. illus. ports. scores, stats.
*S. African cricket and rugby*

3608 **Swaffer, H.P.**, *editor*
–1 South African sport 1914. Johannesburg, "The Transvaal Leader", 1914. 174p. illus.
*cricket pp.27–49*

3609 **Who's** who in the sporting world, Witwatersrand and Pretoria. Johannesburg, Central News Agency, 1933. 92p. ports.

# ANNUALS

3610 **Cricket** annual; edited by S.J. Reddy.
■ Athlone (Cape), South African Cricketer. illus. ports. scores, stats.
*'73–'74/'73–'74, '76–'77/to date?*
*'76–'77 published by South African Cricket Almanack*

3611 **Natal** cricketers' annual: a record of
■ cricket clubs in the colony . . .
*edited by "Cover-point" [J.T. Henderson]*
*1884–5. Pietermaritzburg, Vause, Slatter & Co., 1885. iv,77p. stats.*
*edited by J.T. Henderson*
*1885–6. Natal Printing & Publishing Co., 1886. vii,129p.*
*1886–7. Times of Natal Steam Printing Works, 1887. ix,98p.*
*1887–8. Times of Natal Office, 1888, viii,121p.*
*contd. as: South African cricketers' annual*

3611 **The Protea** cricket annual of South Africa;
–1 edited by Denys Heesom. Cape Town, Protea Assurance Co. illus. ports. scores, stats.
*1976 to date*
*formerly: South African cricket annual; ceased publication 1981*

3611 **Rand Daily Mail**
–2 The South African 1967 sports annual; managing editor: Bode Wegerif. Johannesburg, Rand Daily Mail, [1967?]. 136p. illus. (some col.)
*the only issue*

3612 **The South African** cricket almanack,
■ 1949–50; compiled by G.C. Baker. Pietermaritzburg, Shuter and Shooter, [1949]. x,182p. illus. ports. scores, stats.
*the only issue*

3613 **South African** cricket almanack 1969;
■ edited by S.J. Reddy and D.N. Bansda. Cape Town. S.A. Cricket Board of Control, [1969]. 140p. ports. scores, stats.

3614 **South African** cricket annual; edited by
■ Geoffrey A. Chettle. Durban. illus. ports. scores, stats.
*1951–2, 1952–3, 1954–7, 1959–60. Knox Printing Co.*
*1961–62, 1963–75. S.A. Cricket Assoc.*
*21 issues over 23 yrs. No issues for 1953–54 and 1958*
*contd. as: The Protea cricket annual of South Africa*

3615 **South African** cricketers' annual. illus.
■ ports. scores, stats.
*edited by J.T. Henderson*
*1888–9. Durban, Robinson, Vause, 1889.*
*xii,134p.*
*1889–90. Durban, Robinson, Vause, 1890.*
*xix,144p.*
*1890–91. Durban, Robinson, Vause, 1891.*
*xvii,182p.*
*edited by Sir William Milton*
*1891–92. Cape Town, Richards, 1892.*
*ix,93p.*
*edited by J.T. Henderson*
*1905–6. Pietermaritzburg, Times Prin-*
*ting & Publ. Co., 1906. xvii,211p.*
*1906–7. Pietermaritzburg, Times Prin-*
*ting & Publ. Co., 1907, xix,191p.*
*formerly: Natal cricketers' annual*

3616 **South African** cricketing guide, 1871–2.
Cape Town. 24p.

3617 **South African** non-European cricket
■ almanack: edited by S.J. Reddy and D.N.
• Bansda. Port Elizabeth & Cape Town,
S.A. Non-European Cricket Publications.
ports. scores, stats.
*1953–54. 1953. 148p.*
*1954–55. 1954. 85p.*

## PERIODICALS

3618 **Cricket** and football and other popular
pastimes; edited by Frederick Yates.
Durban, 1914.
*3 monthly issues, Feb., Mar. & April 1914*

3618 **Cricket** digest. bs.
–1 *No. 1. 1978; edited by Sydney J. Reddy*
*deals with multi-racial cricket in South*
*Africa*

3618 **S.A.** cricket. East London. illus. ports.
–2 scores, stats. *monthly?*
☐ *Dec. 1979 to date*
*edited by Brian Bassano*

3619 **The South African** cricket review. Cape
■ Town, Howell & Rogers. illus. ports.
scores, stats.
*16 issues. Nov. 1956—Vol. 2, no. 7 Nov.*
*1958; monthly in winter months 2-monthly*
*Apr/May, and Aug/Sept. 1957*

3620 **The South African** cricketer: the national
■ cricket journal of Southern Africa; edited
by S.J. Reddy. Port Elizabeth, the Editor.
illus. ports. diagr. stats.
*vol. 1 no. 1, 1959 the only issue until*
*vol. 2 no. 2, Nov.–Dec. 1970*
*no. 3, 1971*

3620 **South African** cricketer; managing editor
–1 John Hetherington. Cape Town. illus.
☐ ports. scores, stats. *6 issues per year*

*Vol. 1, no.1 Nov. 1974 – Vol. 3, no.6 Nov./*
*Dec. 1977*

3620 **S.A.** sports illustrated. Capetown.
–2 illus. & ports. (some col.) *monthly*
*Vol.1, no.1. Aug. 1969 – ?*
*managing editor: Don Nelson; associate*
*editors Chris Greyvenstein, Neville Leck; good*
*cricket coverage*

3620 **The South African** sportsman
–3 *Vol. 1, no.1, 1892 – vol.2, no.47, 1893*
*contains regular cricket notes, scores, etc.*
Listed in Hart

3620 **Sport** spectacular. Cape Town, Don
–4 Nelson Enterprises. illus. & ports.
No. 1 Winter 1971
2. Summer 1971
3. Summer 1972–73
*managing editor: Don Nelson*

## PRIVATE CLUBS

3620 **Penguin Cricket Club**
–5 Rules, fixtures and list of members. Port
Elizabeth, the Club. *annual*
*?/1969–70/to date*
*founded 1946*

### Wilfred Isaacs XI

3621 **Wilfred Isaacs XI** overseas tour—July
■ 1966, Denmark, England & Holland.
Johannesburg, the Club, [1966]. 12p.
ports.
*pre-tour, includes a history of the club by*
*Eric Litchfield*

3622 **Litchfield, Eric**
■ Wilfred Isaacs XI England-Ireland tour
1969. Johannesburg, the Club, [1969].
11p. ports.
*pre-tour*

## SCHOOL AND UNIVERSITY CRICKET

3623 **Pichanick, Harry,** *compiler*
South African Schools Nuffield tournament: souvenir programme, 1949. 40p.

3624 **South African Universities Cricket**
**Association** ·
Cricket week December 1–5. 1969,
Durban. The Association, [1969]. 16p.
*fixtures, programmes, past results, etc.*

### Diocesan College

3624 **Taylor, Malcolm**
–1 A history of rugby football and cricket at
the Diocesan College. Cape Town, the
College, [1964?]. [iv],23p. illus. ports.

## Treverton School

**3624** **Treverton School**
**–2** Off the bat . . . compiled and edited by Treverton, with comment and advice to young cricketers by a cross-section of South Africa's leading cricketers. . . . Mooi River, (Natal), the School, 1968. [38]p. illus.

*published to co-incide with the exhibition match between Wilfred Isaacs' XI and Jackie McGlew's XI, Durban, 1968*

## University of Cape Town

**3624** **University of Cape Town**
**–3** The Sabres England tour 1975. West
■ Bromwich, *printed by* Peerless P., [1975]. [8]p. ports.

*pre-tour itinerary; pen-pictures of team*

# OLD SCHOOL CLUBS

## The Christian Brothers College Old Boys

**3624** **C.B.C.O.B. Cricket Club**
**–4** Tour of England and Holland 1977.
■ [Groenkloof, the Club, 1977]. [32]p. incl. adverts. ports.

# TOURNAMENTS

## Barnato Tournament

**3625** **South African Coloured Cricket Board**
Barnato tournament, Port Elizabeth, 26 December 1959–4 January 1960: programme. [Port Elizabeth, the Board, 1959]. [4]p.

## Bulawayo

**3625** **Bulawayo Athletic Club**
**–1** 1957 cricket festival at B.A.C. Ground, Sunday, 24 March, 1957. Bulawayo, the Club, 1957. 16p. incl. adverts. port.

## Datsun Shield

**3625** **Datsun Shield** cricket 1977–78. Semi final
**–2** – Rhodesia vs. Transvaal, 14 January,
■ Police Grounds. [Salisbury], *printed by* Barker, McCormac, [1978]. [16]p. incl. covers & adverts. illus. ports. stats.

## Gillette Cup cricket

**3626** **Gillette** cricket cup 1970: programme.
■ Gillette South Africa (Pty.) Ltd., [1970]. [16]p. incl. covers & adverts. ports.

*In English & Afrikaans:* Gillette-krieket-beker 1970

**3626** **[Rhodesia Cricket Union]**
**–1** Gillette Cup cricket 1976–77. Rhodesia vs.
■ Natal, 29 January, Police Grounds, Salisbury. [Salisbury, the Union, 1977]. [12]p. incl. adverts. ports. diagr.

## The Newlands Tournament

**3627** **Cape Times**
Special cricket edition. The Newlands Tournament, Christmas 1890 and New Year 1891: Western Province v. Eastern Province; [compiled by H.G. Cadwallader]. Cape Town, Cape Times, 1891. 43p.

## Nuffield Cricket Week

**3628** **Theobald, L.C.W.**
Nuffield Cricket Week: rules and conditions. South African Cricket Association, 1961. 16p.

**3628** **The thirty-sixth** Nuffield Cricket Week,
**–1** Bloemfontein, 18 to 23 December, 1978. The Nuffield Week Standing Cttee., [1978]. 40p. stats. The thirty-seventh Nuffield Cricket Week, Port Elizabeth, 17 to 22 December, 1979. The Nuffield Week Standing Cttee, [1979]. 40p. stats.

*sponsored by Coca-Cola Bottlers; includes an account of the origin & development of the Nuffield Cricket Week*

## Port Elizabeth Tournament

**3629** **The Tournament** chronicle. Port Eliz-
■ abeth, Advertiser Office. *daily.* team ports. scores, stats.

*9 issues 23rd Dec. 1884 to 2nd Jan 1885. Subsequently issued in 1 vol.*

*record of cricket tournament held at Port Elizabeth between Port Elizabeth (the winners), Cape Town, King William's Town and Kimberley*

## South African Country Districts Festival

**3630** **Chettle, Geoffrey A.,** *editor*
■ Fifth South African Country Districts Festival 1958 (including) Australia versus a S.A. Country Districts XI, played at Pretoria, January 1–8, 1958: official souvenir brochure. Durban, [the Editor, 1957]. 16p. incl. adverts. ports. stats.

**3631** **8th S.A. Country Districts** cricket festival at Vereeniging. Transvaal, 1961: souvenir programme. 28p.

*probably other souvenirs published*

## South African Cricket Board of Control: Biennial

3632 **South African Cricket Board of Control**
■ Second Biennial tournament, Johannesburg—Easter 1953: official souvenir programme. Johannesburg, the Board, [1953]. 76p. incl. adverts. ports.
——Third . . ., Johannesburg—Easter 1955. [1955]. [8]p. incl. adverts. ports.
——Fourth . . ., Cape Town, 25 Jan.–1st Feb. 1958; compiled by A. Quaise. [1958]. [40]p. incl. adverts. ports.
*the First tournament was held at Johannesburg, March 1951*

## South African Cricket Board of Control: Interprovincial

3633 First Inter-Provincial Cricket Tournament: souvenir programme. 27 December
□ '61–7 January '62, Johannesburg. Johannesburg, the Board, [1961]. [60]p. incl. adverts. illus. ports. stats.
Second——: souvenir programme. 26 Dec. 1963–10 Jan. 1964. Port Elizabeth, The Board, [1963]. [28]p. incl. adverts. ports.
3rd——: Durban-1966. Durban, [Natal Cricket Bd. of Control, 1966]. 16p. incl. adverts. ports.
Fourth ——: souvenir programme. Cape Town 9 to 19 January 1968. Athlone, [W. Province Cricket Bd., 1968]. 52p incl. adverts. ports.
Fifth——: Kimberley, 27 December, 1969 to 7 January, 1970: souvenir programme; edited by V.J. Naidoo. Cape Town, the Board, [1969]. 52p. incl. adverts. ports.

## South African Indian Cricket Union

3634 **South African Indian Cricket Union**
■ 5th Inter-Provincial tournament at Port Elizabeth: official brochure 1949. Port Elizabeth, [E. Province C.U., 1949]. 34p. incl. adverts. ports.
——6th . . . at Durban 1951. Durban, [Natal C.U., 1951]. 48p. incl. adverts. illus. ports.
——7th . . . at Cape Town 1953. Cape Town. [W. Province C.U., 1953]. 52p. incl. adverts. ports.
——9th . . . Port Elizabeth, January 1958; compiled by R. Bhana and S. Reddy. Port Elizabeth, [E. Province C.U., 1957]. 72p. incl. adverts. 1 illus. ports. diagr. stats.
——Zonal inter-provincial cricket 26 December 1973 – 1st January 1974, Mossel Bay: souvenir programme edited and compiled by S.J. Reddy. [Mossel Bay, S.W. Districts Cricket Bd., 1973]. [12]p. incl. adverts. ports.
*1st tournament was held at Durban, 1941*

*2nd tournament was held at Johannesburg, 1942*
*3rd tournament was held at Durban, 1945*
*4th tournament was held at Johannesburg, 1947*

## Western Districts Indian C.A. Tournament

3634 **Western Districts Indian Cricket**
–1 **Association**
□ Lenasia cricket tournament. The Assoc., 1967. 54p. illus.
——5th annual Easter tournament, 9,10,11,12 April 1971. The Assoc., [1971]. 76p. incl. covers & adverts. illus. ports.

# CURRIE CUP CRICKET

3635 **Crowley, Brian Mathew**
Currie Cup story; with contributions by Louis Duffus and A.C. Parker. Cape Town, Nelson, 1973. 199p. illus. ports. scores, stats.

## (In chronological order)

3636 **The Currie Cup** tournament of 1898: full scores of the matches. [Cape Town], *printed by* H.P. Warren, [1898]. 15p. scores, stats.

3637 **Difford, Ivor Denis**
The Currie Cup Tournament 1906–7: all about the teams and principal players; the history of the Cup and complete records. Johannesburg, Ben Wallach, 1906. 64p. ports.

3638 **South African Cricket Association**
Currie Cup rules, articles of constitution, Oct. 1914. Johannesburg, the Association, 1914. 12p.
——*with title:* Constitution, boundaries and Currie Cup rules, 1950. 24p.

3638 **Rhodesia Cricket Union**
–1 Currie Cup cricket, Transvaal versus Rhodesia, at Raylton Ground, Bulawayo, 1st, 3rd and 4th March 1947. The Union, [1947]. 32p. incl. adverts. ports. stats.

3639 **Curnow, N.S.**
[Scores of all Currie Cup matches]. *Privately printed*, [1951?]
*a brochure mentioned in* Cricket quarterly, *vol. 6, no.2, p.102*

3640 **[Rhodesia Cricket Union]**
Currie Cup cricket 1973, Rhodesia v. Transvaal, Police Ground, Salisbury, November 3,4,5: souvenir programme. [Salisbury, the Union, 1973]. 8p. incl. advert. illus. stats.

3640 **Currie Cup** cricket 1974: Rhodesia v.
-1 Eastern Province, Police Ground, Salis-
■ bury, February 2,3,4: souvenir programme. [Salisbury, Brewers of Castle
Lager, 1974]. 12p. incl. adverts. 1 port.
stats.

3640 **Currie Cup** cricket 1975: Rhodesia v.
-2 Eastern Province, Queens Ground, Bula-
■ wayo, February 22,23,24. [Bulawayo,
Brewers of Castle Lager, 1975]. 24p. incl.
adverts. ports. stats.

3640 **Currie Cup** cricket 1975: Rhodesia v.
-3 Natal, Queens Ground, Bulawayo,
■ November, 8,9,10: souvenir programme.
[Bulawayo, Brewers of Castle Lager,
1975]. 16p. incl. adverts. ports. stats.

3640 **Currie Cup** cricket 1975/1976 season:
-4 Rhodesia v. Eastern Province, Queens
■ Ground, Bulawayo, February, 21,22,
23: souvenir programme. [Bulawayo,
Brewers of Castle Lager, 1976]. 16p. incl.
adverts. ports. stats.

3640 **Currie Cup** cricket 1976/1977 season:
-5 Rhodesia v. Western Province, Queens
■ Ground, Bulawayo, 6/8 November 1976:
souvenir programme. [Bulawayo, Brewers of Castle Lager, 1976]. 16p. incl.
adverts. stats.

3640 **Currie Cup** cricket 1977/1978 season.
-6 Rhodesia v. E. Province, Queens
■ Ground, Bulawayo, 5/7 November 1977.
[Brewers of Castle Lager, 1977]. 8p. diagr.
stats.

3640 **Castle Currie Cup** cricket 1977–78. Police
-7 Ground, Salisbury. [Salisbury], *printed by*
■ Barker, McCormac. [16]p. incl. covers &
adverts.
*Rhodesia vs. Western Province. November
11,12 and 13, [1977]. illus. port. diagr.*
*Rhodesia vs. Natal. February 11,12 and 13,
[1978]. illus. port. stats.*

3640 **Castle Currie Cup** cricket 1978–79. Police
-8 Ground, Salisbury. [Salisbury], *printed by*
■ Barker, McCormac. [16]p. incl. covers &
adverts. stats. illus. on cover
*Rhodesia vs. Transvaal. November 11,12
and 13, 1978*
*vs. Eastern Province. February
3,4 and 5, 1979*
*vs. Western Province. March, 3,4
and 5, 1979*

3640 **Matabeleland Cricket Association**
-9 Zimbabwe Rhodesia versus Transvaal,
■ Queens Ground, Bulawayo, 3,4 and 5
November 1979: official souvenir programme. [Bulawayo, the Assoc., 1979].
[32]p. stats.

# BORDER

3641 **Border Cricket Union**
□ Annual report and balance sheet. East
London, the Union, *typescript*
*?/1929–30 to 1932–33/to date?*

3642 Bye-laws. East London, the Union, 1923

3643 Diamond jubilee: souvenir brochure 1896/
■ 7–1956/7. Incorporating 1956–7 M.C.C.
tour of South Africa; edited and compiled
by Geoffrey A. Chettle. [East London, the
Union, 1956]. 48p. incl. adverts. illus.
ports. stats.

# EASTERN PROVINCE

## Burghersdorp

3644 **Eastern Province Cricket Union**
Handbook. Port Elizabeth, the Union
*season –?/1921–2/–?*

3645 **Albert Athletic Association**
■ Facts and figures. Burghersdorp (Cape
Province), Burghersdorp C.C., 1908. bs.

## Grahamstown

3645 **Fort England** mirror. Grahamstown.
-1 *1891–1897?*
*references to cricket in Grahamstown.
Listed in Hart*

## Port Elizabeth

3646 **Levey, Sydney H.W.**
■ The hundred years: 1859–1959. Port Elizabeth, the Author, 1959. illus. ports.
*history of Port Elizabeth C.C. and Crusader
Rugby Football Club*

3647 **Port Elizabeth and District Cricket
Association and Eastern Province Cricket
Umpires Association**
Handbook. Port Elizabeth, the Assocs.
*annual?*
*season –?/1923–24/–?*

3648 **Port Elizabeth Cricket Club**
■ Handbook. Port Elizabeth, the Club.
*annual?*
*season –?/1968–69/to date?*
*fixtures, list of members, rules*

3649 **The Port Elizabeth** Cricket Club
■ 1843–1946: centenary souvenir. Port Elizabeth, the Club, [1946]. 24p. ports. score

3649 **Redgrave, J.J.**
-1 Port Elizabeth in byegone days. Cape
Town, the Author, 1947. 574p. illus.
*pp.273–4 early cricket in Port Elizabeth*

## NATAL

3649 **Hattersley, Alan F.**
-2 The British settlement in Natal.
Cambridge Univ. P., 1950. vii,351p.
*early cricket pp.333-4*

3650 **Natal Cricket Association**
Annual report, revenue and expenditure
account and balance sheet. Durban, the
Assoc. stats.
*1909?/1929/to date*
*1929 was 21st A/R.*

### Durban

3651 **Barn, H.,** *compiler and editor*
■ The Berea Rovers story. Durban, [Berea
Rovers Club, 1964]. 117p. illus. ports.
scores

3651 **Russell, George**
-1 The history of old Durban and reminiscences of an immigrant of 1850. Durban,
P. Davis, 1899. xi,512p. illus.
*cricket pp.493-5*

## TRANSVAAL

3652 **Platnauer, E.J.L.,** *editor*
Sport and pastime in the Transvaal. G.
Wunderlich, 1908. 256p. illus.
*72p and 8 illus. on cricket*

3653 **Transvaal Cricket Union**
□ Annual report. Johannesburg, the Union.
scores, stats.
*?/1906-16 . . . 1965-66/to date*

### Johannesburg

3654 **Gutsche, Thelma**
■ Old gold: the history of the Wanderers'
Club; with decorations by A.A. Telford.
Cape Town, Timmins, 1966. ix,206p.
illus. (1 col.). ports. plan

3654 **Sanitary Board Cricket Club,**
-1 *Johannesburg*
Rules. [Johannesburg, the Club., 189-?].
[4]p. fold.

3655 **The Wanderers' Club** magazine: official
organ of the Wanderers' Club, Johannesburg. *monthly*. illus. ports.
*?/1943 . . . 1959/to date?*

## WESTERN PROVINCE

3656 **Reddy, S.J.,** *editor*
■ Cricket: Western Province v. S.A. Invitation XI, March 3,4,5, 1973 Cape Town.
The Editor, [1973]. [16]p. incl. adverts.
ports. diagr.
*pre-match*

3657 **West, Stewart Ellis Lawrence,** *compiler*
■ Century at Newlands 1864-1964: a history
of the Western Province Cricket Club;
editor, W.J. Luker. [Cape Town, Western
Province C.C.], 1965. xiv,159p. illus. (1
col.). ports. plans, score, bibliog.

3658 **Western Province Cricket Board**
■ The match of the century: Basil D'Oliveira's South Africa Invitation XI vs.
Western Province (South Africa) Invitation XI at Green Point Track on 21 and
22 January 1967; edited by D.N. Bansda.
Cape Town, [the Board, 1967]. 16p. ports.
stats.
*pre-match*

3658 **Western Province Cricket Club**
-1 Annual report and statement of accounts.
□ Cape Town, the Club. illus. ports. plan,
stats.
*?/1964-65/to date*
*1964-65 was the centenary year*

### Cape Town

3659 **Green Point Cricket Club**
Report. Green Point, Cape Town, the
Club. *annual*
*?/1907-08/-?*

3659 **Slater, Francis Carey**
-1 Settler's heritage. Lovedale P., 1954.
261p.
*cricket pp.67,96,104,108-9,118-9*

## ZIMBABWE RHODESIA

3660 **Mashonaland Country Cricket Districts**
□ **Winter Cricket Association**
Cricket annual; edited by Charles Hill.
Salisbury, the Association. illus. ports.
scores, stats.
*?/1955 . . . 66/to date?*

3661 Cricket tour [of England] 1964. Salisbury,
■ [the Assoc., 1964]. 16p. incl. covers. illus.
ports. map
*pre-tour*

3662 Mashonaland Country Districts cricket
tour, 1964: programme. Salisbury, Mobil
Oil Southern Rhodesia, 1964. illus. ports.
*pre-tour*

3663 Record of a tour in England 1964. Salis-
■ bury, Rhodesia, the Assoc., [1964]. 31p.
illus. ports. scores, stats.
*post-tour*

3664 **Mashonaland Cricket Association,** *and*
□ **Brewers of Castle Lager**
The 1971 Castle Double Wicket Cricket
Competition, Police Ground, Salisbury 25

and 26 Sept: souvenir programme. [Salisbury, the Assoc., 1971]. 12p. illus. ports.
——1972 . . . 16 and 17 September: souvenir programme. Salisbury, the Assoc., [1972]. [8]p. illus.
——1973 . . . Police Ground, Salisbury. 22 and 23 September 1973. [Salisbury], the Assoc . . . with the Brewers of Castle Lager, [1973]. [12]p. incl. adverts. illus.

3665 **Rhodesia Cricket Union**
Annual report and accounts and balance sheet. Salisbury, the Union. *typescript*
*?/1968/*to date

3666 News sheet. Salisbury, the Union. *monthly.* stats. *typescript*
*No.39 Jan. 1968*
*No.41 Mar. 1968*

3667 **Rhodesian** cricket and tennis annual; ed. by D.R. Hayter
*1957 88p.*
*the only issue*

3667 **Stragglers Cricket Club**
–1 Promotion of African cricket. Salisbury.
□ bs. *weekly. typescript*

*30 Nov. 1977/ – 139th week 20 & 21 Sept. 1980/*todate?
*produced by R. Spencer Parker, President of the Club*

3668 **Thompson, John de Lano**
■ A history of sport in Southern Rhodesia 1889–1935. Bulawayo, The Rhodesian Printing & Publishing Co., 1935. 435p. illus. ports.
*cricket pp.12–84*

# WOMEN'S CRICKET

3668 **The Natal Women's Cricket Association,**
–1 *and* **The South African and Rhodesian Women's Cricket Association**
Welcome to Pietermaritzburg cricket week . . . Alexandra Park, Pietermaritzburg, 30th December 1966 to 7th January 1967. [Durban? the Assocs., 1966]. 12p. ports.

3668 **The Unicorns:** ladies cricket team, South
–2 Africa, 1974–75. *n.p.*, [1974?]. [12]p. ports.

# CRICKET IN THE WEST INDIES

**3669** **Ashley-Cooper, Frederick Samuel**
■ The West Indies cricket guide, 1928: a book of records. Nottingham, C.H. Richards, 1928. 28p. stats.
*a brief chronology with notes on the West Indies team of 1928*

**3670** **Birkett, T. Sidney**
■ A resumé of big cricket in the West Indies & British Guiana since the West Indies tour of 1923 to England, Barbados, Advocate Co. Ltd., 1927. 61p. scores, stats.

**3671** **Constantine, Learie Nicholas,** *Lord Constantine,* **and Batchelor, Denzil**
■ The changing face of cricket. Eyre & Spottiswoode, 1966. xii,178p. illus. ports. diagr.
*pp.71–140 is an autobiographical review of cricket in the West Indies by L.C.*

**3671** **Gibbes, Michael**
**–1** Testing time: the West Indies vs England 1974: an account of the M.C.C. tour of the Caribbean with essays on contemporary West Indian cricket. Trinidad, Unique Services, [1974]. 116p. illus.

**3672** **Hardy, W.A.S.,** *editor*
■ They live for cricket: a booklet containing the full story of West Indian cricket & featuring the West Indies tour 1950. The Author, [1950]. 32p. ports. stats.

**3672** **James, Cyril Lionel Robert**
**–1** Beyond a boundary. Hutchinson, 1963.
■ 256p.
——*another ed.* Sportsman's Book Club, 1964
——*rptd.* 1969. pbk.

**3672** **Jones, Brunell**
**–2** "Cricket? XI". Champs Fleur, Curepe
■ P.O. (Trinidad), the Author, 1976. 120p. incl. adverts. illus. ports. scores, stats.
*includes account of the 1975–76 series W.I. v. India*

**3673** **Nicole, Christopher**
■ West Indian cricket: the story of cricket in the West Indies with complete records.

Phoenix House, 1957. 256p. illus. ports. stats. bibliog. (Sports Books)
——*another ed.* Sportsman's Book Club, 1960

**3673** **Ross, Gordon**
**–1** A history of West Indies cricket. Barker,
■ 1976. [vii],175p. illus. ports. stats.

**3674** **[Smith, Lloyd S.]**
West Indies cricket history and cricket tours to England, 1900, 1906, 1923, including matches in Scotland, Ireland and Wales; by the Editor of "The Sporting Chronicle". Port of Spain, Yuille's Printerie, 1922, *i.e.* 1923. [iv],240p. illus. ports. scores

**3675** **Sobers, Gary,** *i.e.* **Garfield St. Aubrun**
■ **Sobers, and Barker, John Sydney,** *editors*
Cricket in the sun: a history of West Indies cricket; [Test match] statistics compiled by Ross Salmon. Barker, 1967. 128p. illus. ports. scores, stats.

**3676** **West Indies Cricket Board of Control**
Rules; also, Rules of the Intercolonial Cricket Tournaments. Amended October, 1950. Jamaica, [the Board, 1950]. 23p.
——*another issue with title:* Constitution and rules ... (amended September 1955). [1955]. 24p.

## ANNUALS

**3677** **Barbados** cricketers' annual; edited and
■ compiled by J. Wynfred Gibbons. Barbados. scores, stats.
*20 issues 1894–5 to 1913–14*
*1894–5, 1895–6. West Indian Guardian*
*1896–7/1913–14. Globe Office*

**3678** **Beckford, George W.,** *compiler*
■ Beckford's cricket annual. Kingston, Jamaica
*1953–54. The Compiler, [1954]. illus. ports. scores, stats.*
*1956. The Gleaner Co., [1956]. ports. stats.*

**3679** **Beecher, J. Colman,** *compiler*
Beecher's official cricket score book 1928;

8th annual. Kingston, Jamaica, Beecher, [1928]. illus. ports.

3679 **Caribbean** cricket; edited by Tony Cozier.
–1 Bridgetown (Barbados). illus. ports.
□ scores, stats. *irregular*
　　'73. *Australia v. West Indies. Literary Features (Caribbean) Ltd, [1973]. 48p. incl. adverts.*
　　'74. *Literary Features (Caribbean) Ltd, [1973]. 44p. incl. adverts. stats.*
　　*publd. for 1973–74 M.C.C. tour of West Indies*
　　'77. *The West Indies Cricket Annual, [1977]. 48p. incl. adverts*

3680 **The Jamaica** cricket annual for 1897; compiled by F.L. Pearce, and T.L. Roxburgh. Kingston, 1897
　　*the only issue?*

3680 **The players.** [Port of Spain (Trinidad)],
–1 Allied Printers Ltd. illus. ports. stats.
■ *annual*
　　*?/1975,76/–?*

3680 **South Trinidad** cricketers' almanack. San
–2 Fernando, Southern Printing.
　　*1932. 1932. 190p.*
　　*the only issue?*

3681 **The Sporting** Chronicle annual; edited by Lloyd S. Smith. Trinidad, "Sporting Chronicle". illus. ports.
　　*1921–35 under varying titles: 1st issued* with title: The Sporting Chronicle Christmas annual

3682 **The West Indies** cricket annual; edited by
■ Tony Cozier. Bridgetown Literary Features (Caribbean) Ltd. illus. ports. scores, stats.
　　*1970 to date*
　　*from 1979 with title: Benson & Hedges West Indies Cricket annual*

## PERIODICALS

3683 **The West Indian** sportsman. Kingston,
□ West Indian Sports Publishing Co. Ltd.
*monthly.* illus. ports. scores, stats.
　　*Vol. 1, no. 1 July 1947/1947 . . . 1960/–?*

## TOURNAMENTS

3683 **[Machado Sports Foundation]**
–1 Machado cricket festival, Sabina Park,
■ September 24 to October 1, 1963: souvenir programme. [Kingston, the Foundation, 1963]. 37p. incl. adverts. illus. ports. score, stats.
　　*mostly concerned with West Indies tour to England 1963*

## INTER-COLONIAL AND SHELL SHIELD

(in chronological sequence)

3684 **Georgetown Cricket Club**
British Guiana v. Jamaica, Sept. 1896: [scorebook]. Demerara, [the Club, 1896]. [8]p.

3685 **Intercolonial** cricket contest, 1897. Barbados, Cole, 1897. 41p.

3686 **Daily Argosy**
■ Intercolonial cricket tournament 1907: Trinidad v. British Guiana and Trinidad v. Barbados. Georgetown, Demerara, "The Argosy" Co., 1907. [ii],108p. scores, port.
　　*post-tournament*

3687 **The Intercolonial** cricket tournament: British Guiana versus Trinidad, Trinidad versus Barbados. Georgetown, Jardine, 1907. 29p.

3688 **Daily Chronicle**
■ The International cricket tournament: Barbados versus British Guiana, Trinidad versus Barbados. September 19th and 20th, 26th and 27th, 1910. Georgetown, Demerara, Daily Chronicle, 1910. 30p. scores
　　*post-tournament account reprinted from the "Daily Chronicle"*

3689 **Sporting Chronicle**
Intercolonial cricket tournament: Demerara versus Trinidad, Trinidad versus Barbados. Trinidad, Sporting Chronicle, 1910. 17p.

3690 **Barbados Advocate**
■ The revival of sport in Barbados: a complete chronicle of the Intercolonial cricket tournament, 1920. Barbados vs. Trinidad . . . Bridgetown, Advocate Co. Ltd., [1920]. [ii],60p. scores
　　*cover title: The revival of sport in the West Indies*
　　*43p. of cricket; post-tournament record*

3691 **Daily Chronicle**
Intercolonial cricket tournament, 1922. Georgetown, Daily Chronicle, 1922. 66p. illus.
　　*post-tournament*

3692 **Barbados Herald**
■ Intercolonial cricket tournament: fifteenth contest between Barbados, Trinidad and Demerara at Kensington, February 1924. Bridgetown, "Herald", 1924, 40p. scores
　　*post-tournament*

**3693 Daily Argosy**
International cricket tournament, 1925: British Guiana v. Barbados and Trinidad v. British Guiana. Georgetown, Argosy, 1925. 158p.
*post-tournament*

**3694 Yearwood, L.T.**
■ Cricket tour Antigua vs. Barbados and Leeward Islands vs. Barbados with commentary. Antigua, Browne, 1926. [iv],18p. scores
*post-Barbadian tour*

**3695 Daily Chronicle**
■ Intercolonial cricket after the war edited by " 'Daily Chronicle' cricket correspondent" (H.R. Harewood). Georgetown, Daily Chronicle, 1927. xii,103p. illus. ports. scores, stats.
*with insert supplement dated 1st Oct. 1927. 4p*

**3696 Gibbons, J. Wynfred,** *compiler*
■ Intercolonial cricket tournament 1927: 18th contest played at Kensington Oval, Barbados, Jany.–Feby. 1927. Bridgetown, Globe Office, [1927]. 20p. scores, stats.
*post-tournament*

**3697 Daily Argosy**
■ Intercolonial cricket tournament, 1929: British Guiana v. Barbados, and British Guiana v. Trinidad. Georgetown, "Argosy", 1929. 161p. scores, stats.
*post-tournament account reprinted from the "Daily Argosy"*

**3698 Daily Chronicle**
Intercolonial cricket tournament, 1929, played at Bourda, Georgetown, B.G. Georgetown, Daily Chronicle, 1929. 112p. illus.
*post-tournament*

**3699 Barbados Advocate**
■ Intercolonial cricket tournament, January, 1932, Kensington, Barbados. Who's who? Trinidad v. Barbados, January 16; British Guiana v. Challengers, January 23: record score book. [Bridgetown], Advocate Co., [1932]. [36]p. 1 illus. ports.

**3700** Intercolonial cricket tournament 1936:
■ twenty-fourth contest, being a record of the games played at Kensington Oval, Barbados, January–February 1936; compiled by J.M. Hewitt and W.B. Millar. [Barbados, Advocate Co. Ltd., 1936]. [vi],22p. scores, stats.
*post-tournament*

**3701 Daily Chronicle**
■ Intercolonial cricket tournament 1937, played at Bourda, Georgetown. British

Guiana, Sept.–Oct., 1937. Georgetown, Daily Chronicle, [1937]. 127p. ports. scores, stats.
*post-tournament*

**3702 Kingston Cricket Club**
■ Official programme Jamaica vs. Trinidad, June–July 1946; edited and compiled by C.A.O. Jack Anderson. Kingston, the Club, [1946]. 64p. incl. adverts. ports. stats.

**3703 Daily Chronicle**
Goodwill cricket tournament: Jamaica vs. British Guiana. Georgetown, Daily Chronicle, 1947. 124p.

**3704 Jamaica Cricket Association**
■ Jamaica v. Barbados, played at Sabina Park & Melbourne Park, Kingston, March 19–April 3, 1947: souvenir programme. Kingston, the Assoc., [1947]. 50p. incl. adverts. ports.
*celebrates Jamaica's entry in the Inter-Colonial tournament*

**3705 Queen's Park Cricket Club**
■ Trinidad vs. Jamaica 1950: official souvenir programme. Port-of-Spain, the Club, [1950]. 32p. incl. covers. illus. ports. stats.

# BARBADOS

**3706 Barbados Cricket Association**
□ Report and statement of accounts. Bridgetown, the Association. *annual.* scores
*?/1957–58 . . . 1979/80 to date*
*formed 1933*

**3707** Constitution and general rules . . . amended and consolidated on 21st December, 1973. [Bridgetown], the Assoc., [1974?]. 36p.

**3708 Barbados** cricketers' annual; edited and
■ compiled by J. Wynfred Gibbons, Barbados. scores, stats.
*1894–5 to 1913–14*
*1894–5, 1895–6. West Indian Guardian*
*1896–7 to 1913–14. Globe Office*

**3708 The Barbados Wanderers**
**–1** UK 1977 tour: team brochure. [The Club,
■ 1977]. [20]p. incl. covers & adverts. ports.
*itinerary and pen-portraits of team*

**3708** Centenary 1877–1977. Christ Church,
**–2** Barbados, the Club, [1977]. 120p. incl.
■ adverts. illus. ports. scores

3709 **Hamilton, Bruce**
■ Cricket in Barbados. Bridgetown, *printed at* the Advocate P., 1947. 168,viii,p. ports. scores

3709 **Lindo, Hugh**
-1 The social history of cricket in Barbados (1800–1970). University of East Indies Barbados, [c. 1970]. 14p. *typescript*
*thesis*

3710 **Lynch, Louis**
The Barbados book. Deutsch, 1964. 256p. illus. map
——2nd ed. revised by E.L. Cozier. 1972. 274p. illus. maps
*cricket pp.110,166–74*

3710 **Walcott, Leroy**
-1 The Barbados Cricket League: 40 years of service. Thesis. 1978. *typescript*
*a photocopy is in A.E. Winder's collection*

3711 **Winton, John**
We joined the Navy. M. Joseph, 1959. 254p.
*includes "Cricket in Barbados"*

## DOMINICA

3712 **Dominica Cricket Association**
■ Annual report. Dominica, the Association. *typescript*
*1973–*

3713 **Dominica Cricket Umpires Association**
■ How's that? 8th anniversary magazine 1965–1973. Dominica, the Association, [1973]. [i],33p. illus. diagrs.

## GUYANA

3714 **Birkett, T. Sidney**
■ A resumé of big cricket in the West Indies & British Guiana since the West Indies tour of 1923 to England. Barbados, Advocate Co. Ltd., 1927. 61p. scores, stats.

3715 **The Daily Argosy**
■ The cricket carnival: being an account of Sheppard's third tour in British Guiana. George Town, "The Argosy" Co., 1909. 106p. scores
*post-tour; rptd. from "The Daily Argosy"*

3715 **Ramsay, Alva**
-1 Souvenir programme: 1968 Guyana Sugar Producers' Association cricket tour of Jamaica. Kingston, Sugar Manufacturers' Association of Jamaica, 1968. 64p.
*see also 3725–1*

**Georgetown**

3716 **Georgetown Cricket Club**
Annual report. Georgetown, the Club ?/1885–1901, 1905/–?
*1905 report was composite volume covering 1901–4*

## JAMAICA

3717 **Beecher, J. Coleman,** *compiler*
■ Jamaica cricket 1863–1926; a book of information on cricket in Jamaica, the West Indies, England and Australia. Kingston, *printed by* The Gleaner, 1926. 96p. illus. ports. stats.

3718 **Fraser, Alexander**
Cricket in the West Indies: notes on the game at Trinidad and Kingston, Jamaica. Inverness, Northern Chronicle, [1929]

3719 **The Jamaica** cricket annual for 1897; compiled by F.L. Pearce, and T.L. Roxburgh. Kingston, [1897]
*the only issue?*

3720 **Jamaica Cricket Association**
Rules [of the] Senior, Junior and Minor Competitions. Kingston, [the Association], 1926

3721 Minutes of the annual general meeting.
□ Kingston, the Association
*1927/1930/to date*

3722 Report for the year ended 31st December.
□ Kingston, the Association. stats.
*1927 to date*

3723 **[The Jamaica]** Junior Challenge Cup
■ Competition: full text of the regulations. Kingston, [the Challenge Cup Cttee.], *n.d.* 4p.

3724 **Jamaica** v. Carreras, January 6th–25th,
■ 1964, under the auspices of the Jamaica Cricket Board of Control. Kingston, [Carreras Ltd., 1964]. 48p. incl. adverts. illus. ports. stats.
——Jan. 27–Feb. 17, 1965. [1965]. 36p. incl. adverts. illus. ports. scores, stats.
*two tours sponsored by Carreras Jamaica Ltd. of English teams to Jamaica*

3725 **Jamaica Women's Cricket Association**
■ Inaugural International Women's Cricket Series: souvenir programme. English Women's XI vs. Jamaica, Jan. 13–Feb. 2, 1970. Kingston, the Assoc. [1970]. 40p. incl. adverts. ports.
*pre-tour; includes history of Jamaica Women's cricket*

3725 **Sugar Manufacturers' Association of**
-1 **Jamaica**
Sugar Manufacturers' Association tour of
Guyana, 1967. Kingston, the Assoc.,
1968. 20p.
*see also 3715-1*

### Kingston

3726 **Kingston Cricket Club**
Report of the annual general meeting.
Kingston, the Club. stats.
*?/1890-1914/*
*issue published 1914 was "Jubilee year,*
*1863-1913." team port. scores, stats. There-*
*after publication lapsed*

3727 **Macdonald, Herbert G. de L.,** *compiler*
■ History of the Kingston Cricket Club,
1863-1938. Kingston, *printed by* Gleaner
Co., 1938. 122p. illus. ports. stats.

*Kensington*

3728 **Kensington Cricket Club**
Report of the annual general meeting.
Kingston, the Club
*?/1881-1905/-?*

## LEEWARD ISLANDS

3729 **Browne, Beresford,** *compiler*
■ Leeward Islands Cricket Tournament,
1927: Antigua v. St. Kitts, Dominica v.
Montserrat, Antigua v. Dominica.
Antigua, Browne for the Antigua Cricket
Tournament, [1927]. [iv],41p. scores
*post-tournament*

3730 Leeward Islands Cricket Tournament,
1928: Antigua v. Montserrat; Dominica v.
St. Kitts, played in St. Kitts, June 18-26,
1928. Antigua Cricket Tournament Publications Association, 1928
*post-tournament*

## TRINIDAD

3730 **Australian Schools Cricket Council**
-1 Trinidad & Tobago Secondary Schools
Association Under 19 cricket tour of
Australia 1979-80. The Council, [1979].
28p. illus. ports. stats.
*pre-tour with itinerary and pen-pictures*

3731 **Fraser, Alexander**
Cricket in the West Indies; notes on the
game at Trinidad and Kingston, Jamaica.
Inverness, Northern Chronicle, [1929]

3732 **Junior Chamber of Commerce of**
**Trinidad**
Trinidad v. Tobago: pictorial diary. Port
of Spain, J.C.C., 1964

3733 **The sporting** chronicle. Port of Spain.
*weekly.*
*Jan. 1921/Feb. 1925/-?*

3733 **Trinidad & Tobago Secondary Schools'**
-1 **Cricket Assocation**
■ Tour of England July – August 1977:
souvenir brochure compiled by Charles
Tuck. [The Assoc., 1977]. 64p. incl. adverts. illus. ports.
*pre-tour*

3734 **The Trinidad & Tobago Women's**
■ **Cricket Association**
Constitution & rules. [Diego Martin], the
Assoc., [196-?]. [12]p.

3735 **Trinidad** centenary cricketing souvenir
album. Trinidad, W.H. Whiteman, 1897.
illus.

3736 **Trinidad Cricket Council**
■ Year book. Port of Spain, the Council.
ports, scores, stats.
*1964 to date*
*Tenth year special edition 1964-1974;*
*edited by Stephen Almandoz and Karim Khan*

*Oriental C.C.*

3737 **Oriental Cricket Club**
Banquet to commemorate the diamond
jubilee of the Oriental Cricket Club . . .
13th June 1959: menu. [Trinidad, the
Club, 1959]. 8p.
*includes historical sketch of the Club*

*Queen's Park*

3738 **Queen's Park Cricket Club**
Diamond jubilee "The Oval is Sixty".
1896-1956. Trinidad, the Club, 1957.
148p. ports. plan

3739 Q.P.C.C. 7th anniversary 1896-1971.
■ Trinidad, [Port of Spain, the Club, 1971].
[80]p. incl. adverts. illus. ports.

# CRICKET IN NEW ZEALAND

**3740 Ashley-Cooper, Frederick Samuel**
■ The New Zealand cricket guide, 1927: a book of records. Nottingham, Richards, 1927. 28p. stats.
——, 1931, 1931. 23p. stats.
*mainly records of N.Z. v. England matches*

**3741 Brittenden, Richard Trevor**
■ Great days in New Zealand cricket. Wellington, N.Z., Reed; London, Bailey Bros. & Swinfen, 1958. 195p. illus. ports. diagr. scores

**3742** New Zealand cricketers. Wellington,
■ Reed, 1961. xii,180p. illus. ports.

**3743 Caple, Samuel Canynge**
■ The All Blacks at cricket: the story of New Zealand cricket, 1860–1958. Worcester, Littlebury, 1958. 260p. illus. ports. scores, stats.

**3744 Darwin Charles**
■ Diary of the voyage of H.M.S. "Beagle"; edited from the MS by Nora Barlow. Cambridge, C.U.P., 1933. xxx,443p. port. maps
*the first reference to cricket being played in New Zealand is found in the entry for 23rd Dec. 1835 when Darwin relates his arrival at Waimate where on a farm owned by British missionaries he saw farm employees playing cricket: "These young men & boys appeared very merry & good-humoured; in the evening I saw a party of them playing at cricket; when I thought of the Austerity of which the Missionaries have been accused, I was amused at seeing one of their sons taking an active part in the game".*

**3745 An encyclopaedia** of New Zealand;
■ edited by A.H. McLintock. 3 vols. Wellington, R.E. Owen, Government Printer, 1966. illus. maps. diagrs.
*cricket vol. 1, pp. 407–14*

**3746 May, Percy Robert**
■ With the M.C.C. to New Zealand. Eyre & Spottiswoode, 1907. vii,133p. illus. ports. scores, stats.
*includes "A short history of New Zealand cricket" by John F. Macpherson*

**3747 New Zealand Cricket Council**
■ Annual report and balance sheet for the season. Christchurch, the Council. ports. scores, stats. *in v.y.*
*season 1894–95 to date. Not issued 1916–17, 1917–18*
*titles vary*

**3748** Rules and roll of honour. Christchurch,
■ the Council
*1895 to 1906. [1906]. 32p. stats.*
*1895 to 1908. [1908]. 43p. stats.*
*1895 to 1909. [1909]. 47p. stats.*
*1895 to 1911. [1911]. 56p. stats.*
——also rules for the Plunket Challenge Shield . . . [1913]. 61p. stats.

**3748 Newton, Peter**
**–1** High country days. Wellington (N.Z.), Reed, 1949. 198p. illus.
*cricket ch.vi, pp.58–64, "Cricket match"*

**3749 Peake, John Frederick,** *compiler*
■ Statistics of New Zealand cricket and roll of honour. Christchurch, Whitcombe & Tombs, 1924. 63p. ports. scores, stats.

**3750 Pollard, Jack,** *compiler*
■ Six and out: the legend of Australian cricket. Wollstonecraft, N.S.W., Pollard Publishing Co., 1964; London, Angus & Robertson, 1965. [xiii],306p. illus. ports.
——*rptd. with subtitle:* the legend of Australian and New Zealand cricket. 1970. 366p.

**3751 Reese, T.W.**
■ New Zealand cricket 1841–1933. 2 vols. 1927–36. illus. ports. scores, stats.
*vol. 1: 1841–1914. Christchurch, Simpson & Williams, 1927*
*vol. 2: 1914–1933. Auckland, Whitcombe & Tombs, 1936*

**3751 Smith, Carl V.**
**–1** From N. to Z.; illustrated by G.E. Minhinnick. 5th ed. Wellington, Hicks, 1949. 157p. illus.
*ch. 21: Cricket and Hunting*

## ANNUALS

**3752 Brittain, F.E.,** *compiler*
■ A record of the past cricket season 1889–90. Wellington, [the Compiler], 1890. 54p. frontis. stats.
contd. as: *Wellington Cricketers' Association. Cricket annual*

**3753 The cricket** almanack of New Zealand.
■ Wellington, Sporting Publications. illus. ports. scores, stats.
*1948–1957; ed. by Arthur H. Carman and Noel S. Macdonald*
*1958 to date ed. by Arthur H. Carman*
*1965 to date with title: The Shell cricket almanack of New Zealand, sponsored by Shell Oil New Zealand Limited. Linden, Tawa, Sporting Publications*

**3754 The DB** cricket annual; edited by D.O.
■ Neely. Auckland, Moa Publications in association with Dominion Breweries Ltd. illus. ports. scores, stats. (Moa Sporting Library)
*1973 to date*
formerly: *The New Zealand cricket annual*

**3755 New Zealand** cricket annual for 1930–31; edited and compiled by E.G. Garbutt. Christchurch, N.Z., Simpson & Williams, 1930. 124p.
*the only issue. Includes 1929–30 M.C.C. tour*

**3756 The New Zealand** cricket annual; edited
■ by R. J. Howitt. Auckland, Moa publications. illus. ports. scores, stats.
*1972. 173p.*
contd. as: *The DB cricket annual*

**3757 New Zealand** cricketers' annual; edited
■ by "Trundler" Thames [*i.e.* William H. Newton]. Auckland, Abel, Dykes. ports. scores, stats.
*1895–98*

**3757 Payne, Francis,** *compiler & editor*
**–1** New Zealand first class cricket. Auckland
□ West, Cricket Publications. illus. scores, stats. *typescript. annual*
*1977–78. 1978. 106p.*
*1978–79 with title: Rothmans New Zealand first class cricket. 1979. 96p.*

**3758 Wellington Cricketers' Association**
■ Cricket annual; edited by F.E. Brittain. Wellington, the Assoc. mounted team port. scores, stats.
*1890–91. 1891. 106p.*
*1891–92 & 1892–93. 1893. 110p.*
*for previous year see no. 3752*

## PERIODICALS

**3758 The cricket** player. Remuera (Auckland),
**–1** Marlborough House. *monthly.* illus. ports. scores, stats.
*May 1974 to date*
*initially 6 issues per year; successor to New Zealand cricketer;*
*editors successively R.T. Brittenden, Robin St. C. Craze, D.J. Cameron, Richard Becht*

**3759 N.Z. cricketer;** edited by R.T. Brittenden.
□ Christchurch, Bowden Publicity Associates Ltd. illus. ports. scores, stats. 10 issues per year for 1st 2 years, then 6 issues Nov.-May
*Vol. 1. no. 1. Nov. 1967–vol. 6. no. 6 Sept. 1973*
contd. as: *The cricket player*

## SCHOOLS

**3759 Anderson, Walter Patterson**
**–1** Cricket in the Palmerston North Boys' High School 1902–1946, and Manawatu's Hawke Cup record. Dunedin, "Otago Daily Times", 1947. 88p. illus.

## TOURNAMENTS

**3760 Auckland Cricket Association**
■ "Guinness" Single Wicket Competition, Eden Park, 25 January, 1970. Auckland, the Assoc., [1970]. [8]p. incl. adverts.

**3761** Rothmans National under 23 Tournament
■ 1971: a statistical history of the 9 tournaments to date and the programme for this, the 10th tournament held at Auckland in its centennial year, January, 1971. Auckland, the Association, [1971]. 16p. stats.

## PLUNKET SHIELD MATCHES

(in chronological order)

**3762 [Wellington Cricket Association]**
■ Cricket: Wellington v. Auckland (Plunket Shield) Basin Reserve, 23rd, 25th and 26th December, 1922. Wellington, [the Assoc., 1922]. 16p. incl. adverts. port.

**3763 [Canterbury Cricket Association]**
Wellington v. Canterbury, Lancaster Park, Dec. 31, 1930, Jan. 1, 2 and 3, 1931: official score card. Christchurch, [the Assoc.], 1930. ports.
*similar publications issued 1924, 1927, 1928 and no doubt in other years*

**3764 Northern Districts Cricket Association**
■ Plunket Shield cricket: Northern Districts v. Auckland, 26, 28 & 29 December 1964, Seddon Park, Hamilton: official programme. Hamilton, the Assoc., [1964]. [16]p. incl. covers & adverts.

**3765 Central Districts Cricket Association**
■ Canterbury v. Central Districts, Pukekura Park, New Plymouth. New Plymouth, the Assoc., [1966]. 8p. stats.

**3765 Plunket Shield cricket: Northern Districts**
**–1** versus Central Districts, Pukekura Park, New Plymouth [Jan. 2, 3, 4, 1967]: programme. [New Plymouth], the Assoc., [1966?]. [12]p. incl. adverts. 1 illus. ports. stats.

**3766 Auckland Cricket Association**
■ Northern Districts v. Auckland, Eden Park—Auckland, January 8, 9, 10, 1970: official programme. Auckland, the Assoc., [1970]. 16p. incl. adverts. stats.

**3767** Wellington v. Auckland, Eden Park—
■ Auckland, January 16, 17, 18, 1970: official programme. Auckland, the Assoc., [1970]. 16p. incl. adverts. stats.

**3768** Canterbury v. Auckland, Eden Park—
■ Auckland, January 15, 16, 17, 1971: official programme. Auckland, the Assoc., [1971]. 16p. incl. adverts. stats.

**3769** Otago v. Auckland, Eden Park—Auckland, Jan. 4, 5, 6, 1971: official programme. Auckland, the Assoc., [1971]. 16p. incl. adverts. stats.

# AUCKLAND

**3769 Auckland Cricket Association**
**–1** Annual report & balance sheet. The
□ Assoc. scores, stats.
*season 1883–4? to date*

**3769** Official handbook. Auckland, the Assoc.,
**–2** *annual*
□ *?/1978–79/to date*

**3770** Rothmans N.Z. under 23 team v. Auckland, Cornwall Park, Auckland, February 7, 8, 9, 1971: official programme. Auckland, the Association, [1971]. 16p. incl. adverts. stats.

**3771 Pavilion** echoes from the South, 1884–5.
■ By the Twelve. Auckland, *printed by* Cecil Gardner, 1885. 36p. scores, stats.

**Parnell**

**3772 Parnell Cricket Club Inc.**
■ 75th jubilee 1884–85—1958–59. Auckland, [the Club], 1959. 32p. illus. ports. stats.

# CANTERBURY

**3772 Brittenden, Richard Trevor**
**–1** 100 years of cricket: a history of the
■ Canterbury Cricket Association 1877–1977. Christchurch (N.Z.), [the Assoc,, 1978?]. 96p illus. ports. stats.

**3773 Canterbury Cricket Association (Inc.)**
□ Annual report and balance sheet. [Christchurch], the Association. scores, stats.
*season 1877–78 to date*

**3774 Canterbury Cricket Supporters' Club**
□ **(Inc.)**
Year book. Christchurch, the Club. team port. stats.
*1918?/1965,68/to date*

**3775 "Not-Out"**, *pseud.*
■ Cricket notes: interprovincial matches. Christchurch, "The Press" Co., 1879. 31p. scores, stats.
*Otago v. Canterbury matches 1864–1879*

**3775 Tothill, Thomas Webb Compton**
**–1** Canterbury Boys' Cricket Association golden jubilee 1918–1968. Christchurch (N.Z.), the Assoc., 1968. 28p. ports.

**Christchurch**

**3776 Christchurch Cinemas Cricket Club**
■ "The valley of peace". [The Club, 1939]. [16]p. illus. port.

**3776 Slatter, Gordon**
**–1** Great days at Lancaster Park. [Christchurch (N.Z.) ], Whitcombe & Tombs, 1974. 234p. illus. ports.
*ch. 18 Victor Trumper; ch. 26 Women's cricket test; ch. 34 The cricketers*

**3777 Sydenham Cricket Club**
Annual report. Christchurch N.Z., the Club
*?/1912/—?*

# CENTRAL DISTRICTS

**3777 Central Districts Cricket Supporters**
**–1 Club**
□ Member's pass. Dannevirke (N.Z.), the Club. stats. *annual*
*?/1975–76/to date?*
*includes annual report of Central Districts Cricket Association*

## Hawke's Bay

3778 **Cane, F.F.**
■ Cricket in Hawke's Bay; containing a complete history of the game's progress in this district since 1886 [sic], and all records and averages during the past twenty-two years. Napier, *printed by* G.W. Venables, 1921. 90p. stats.
*should read 1866*

3779 Cricket centenary: the story of cricket in
■ Hawke's Bay, 1855–1955. Napier, N.Z., the Author, 1959. 319p. illus. ports. stats.

3780 **Hawke's Bay Cricket Association**
Annual report and balance sheet. Napier, the Association.
*1882–3/1921–22 . . . 1933–34/to date?*

## Nelson

3781 **Nelson** and Golden Bay cricketers handbook and guide. Nelson, N.Z., J.E. Hounsell, 1893
*in Taylor*

# NORTHERN DISTRICTS

3782 **Cricket N.Z.** Rothman's team versus Northern Districts, Seddon Park, Hamilton, 22, 23, 25 March, 1963: souvenir programme

3783 **Northern Districts Cricket Association**
□ Annual report. The Association
*season ?/1962–63 to 1965–66/to date*

3783 Shell series Northern Districts: official
–1 programme. The Association. *annual* ?/1976–77/to date
*season 1976–77; edited & compiled by Robin Craze. 36p. incl. adverts. illus. ports.*

# OTAGO

3784 **Bannerman, J.W.H.**, *compiler*
■ History of Otago representative cricket 1863–1906, with a chapter on the "Pre-rep" period, 1848–1863. Dunedin, Crown Printing Co., 1907. 63p. ports. scores, stats.

3785 **Griffiths, George J.**
■ Notes on some early arrivals in Otago. Dunedin, the Author
*No. 1 James Fulton and his family. 1969. 16p. illus. port. map, bibliog.*
*limited ed. of c.105 copies*
*2. The Maces of Macetown. 1969. 16p. illus. ports. map, bibliog.*
*limited ed. of c.225 copies*

3. *W.G. Rees and his cricketing cousins. 1971. 40p. illus. ports. map, bibliog.*
*limited ed. of c.150 copies. Later expanded into "King Wakatip"*
4. *Sale, Bradshaw, Manning, Wills and the "Little Enemy". 1971. 24p.*
*limited ed. of 75 copies*

3786 King Wakatip: how William Gilbert Rees,
■ cousin and cricketing godfather of the incomparable W.G. Grace, emigrated to the colonies and founded the most beautiful township in New Zealand. Dunedin, McIndoe, 1971. 156p. illus. ports. maps

3786 Otago University at cricket: its history,
–1 records and statistics. Dunedin (N.Z.),
■ Otago Heritage Books, 1978. 80p. illus. ports. stats. *typescript*

3787 **"Not-Out"**, *pseud.*
■ Cricket notes: interprovincial matches. Christchurch, "The Press" Co., 1879. 31p. scores, stats.
*Otago v. Canterbury matches 1864–1879*

3788 **Otago Cricket Association**
□ Annual report and balance sheet. Otago, the Association
*season ?/1919–20 . . . 1977–78/to date*

3788 Diamond jubilee celebrations, 1876–1936.
–1 [Dunedin, Evening Star Co. Ltd., 1936]. 31p. ports.

3788 Centennial souvenir programme 1876–
–2 1976. [Dunedin], the Assoc., [1976]. 64p.
■ incl. adverts. illus. ports. diagr. plan, score, stats.

## Dunedin

3788 **Albion Cricket Club**
–3 Jubilee souvenir programme, October 28th, 1912. Dunedin, Star Print, 1912. 4p. ports.

3789 **Albion** 1862–1962. Dunedin, [1962]. 18p.
■ illus. ports.

## Oamaru

3790 **Oamaru** Cricket Club—centennial history
■ 1864–1964. [Oamaru, the Club, 1964]. 14p. facsim. ports.

# SOUTHLAND

3791 **Bannerman, J.W.H.**, *compiler*
■ Early cricket in Southland from 1860 and right up to 1908. Invercargill (N.Z.), *printed by* W. Smith, 1908. 46p. incl. adverts. ports. stats.

3792 **Southland Cricket Association**
Annual report and balance sheet. The
Association. *folded sheet*
*?/1921–22/–?*

3793 Rules (revised 1921–22). [The Associ-
■ ation, 1922]. 32p.

# WELLINGTON

3794 **Brittain, F.E.,** *compiler*
■ A record of the past cricket season
1889–90. Wellington, the Compiler, 1890.
54p. frontis. stats.
*contd. as: Wellington Cricketers' Associ-
ation. Cricket annual*

3794 **Carman, Arthur H.**
–1 Wellington cricket centenary 1875–1975.
■ Linden, Tawa, (N.Z.), Sporting Publications, 1975. 148p. illus. ports. scores,
stats.

3795 **The cricketer:** official organ of the
□ Wellington Mercantile Cricket League
Inc. Wellington, the League. *monthly Oct.
to Apr.* illus. ports. scores, stats.
*Vol. 1, no. 1. 15 Oct. 1949/1949–54/to
date?*

3795 **Neely, Don O.**
–1 100 summers: the history of Wellington
■ cricket. Auckland, Moa Publications for
the Wellington C.A., 1975. 229p. illus.
ports. facsims. scores, stats.

3796 **Wellington Cricket Association**
□ Annual report and balance sheet.
Wellington, the Association
*season ?/1910–11, 1920–21 to 1930–31/to
date*
*1969–70 issue* with title: *Handbook*

3796 Objects, constitution and general rules.
–1 Wellington, the [Assoc.], 1930. 20p.
——*another ed.* [c.1950]. 31,[5]p.

3797 **Wellington Cricketers' Association**
■ Cricket annual; edited by F.E. Brittain.
Wellington, the Association. Mounted
team port. score, stats.
*1890–91. 1891. 106p.
1891–92 & 1892–93. 1893. 110p.
for previous year see no. 3794*

3798 **Wellington XI** v. President's XI, Basin
■ Reserve, Wellington, Oct. 24–26, 1964:
Atlantic Festival of Cricket programme.

Wellington, Atlantic Union Oil Co. (N.Z.)
Ltd., [1964]. 18p. ports. diagr. stats.
*President's XI: New Zealand Cricket
Council President's XI*

3798 **Wellington Mercantile Cricket League**
–1 Rules and bye-laws. [Wellington, the
League, 1939?]. 28p.

3798 50 years of cricket, 1921–1971: a history.
–2 [Wellington, the League, 1971]. 80p. illus.
ports.
*see also no. 3795*

## Hutt Valley

3799 **Hutt Valley Cricket Association Inc.**
Annual report & statement of accounts.
Hutt, Wellington
*season ?/1928–29 . . . 1965–66/to date*

3800 The Hutt Valley cricketer: official magazine of the Hutt Valley Cricket Association Inc. 4 issues Nov.-Mar.
*Vol. 1, no. 1, Nov. 1955?—Vol. 10, no.
4, Nov. 1965*

## Wairarapa

3801 **Wairarapa Cricket Association**
■ Seventy five years of cricket: a history
. . . 1894–1969. Masterton, Management
Committee of the Association, [1969].
51p. illus. ports. scores, stats.

## Wellington

*Kilbirnie*

3801 **Kilbirnie Cricket Club**
–1 The Kilbirnie crier. Wellington, the Club.
*?/issue for 20 Nov. 1936/–?*
*gives details of Committee with news items*

3802 **Ross, Walter A.**
Aquatic cricket. Wellington (N.Z.), the
Author, 1956. 59p. illus. *typescript*
*account of tour by Kilbirnie Club,
Wellington to Fiji in 1956*

*Onslow*

3803 **Onslow Cricket Club**
■ The Onslow cricketer. Wellington, the
Club. *monthly during season. scores, stats.
typescript*
*Vol. 1 nos. 1–5 Nov. 1939–Mar. 1940
Vol. 2 nos. 1– Nov. 1940–?*

Cricket in India. Eden Gardens, Calcutta, during the second test India v. England, 1977 *photo: Patrick Eagar*

# CRICKET IN INDIA

3804 **Aflalo, Frederick George,** *editor*
The sportsman's book for India. Horace Marshall, 1904. xvi,567p. illus. maps, plan
*cricket pp.478, 486–92*

3805 **Ashley-Cooper, Frederick Samuel**
■ Indian cricket chronology and memorabilia. Merritt & Hatcher, 1911. 16p.
*limited ed. of 30 copies; annals of the game*

3806 **Basu, Sankariprasad**
Kriket sundar kriket. Calcutta, Karuna, 1963. viii,142p. illus.
*in Bengali; trs. "Cricket lovely cricket"*

3807 **Begg, W.D.**
■ Cricket and cricketers in India. Ajmer, [the Author], 1929. [xiv],312p. incl. adverts. illus. ports. scores. stats.

3808 **[Bhattacharya, Rakhal]**
■ Indian cricket cavalcade, by Arbi. Calcutta, Eastlight Book House, 1957. [vi],252p. stats. ports. scores

3808 **Cashman, Richard,** *and* **McKernan,**
–1 **Michael,** *editors*
■ Sport in history: the making of modern sport history. Brisbane, Univ. of Queensland P., 1979. xii,368p. bibliog.
*papers delivered at a conference of historians, etc. at Univ. of N.S.W. in July, 1977.*
*Contains:*
*pp.180–204 "The phenomenon of Indian cricket" by Richard Cashman. See also nos. 4365–1, 4470–2*

3809 **Davar, F.J.**
Cameos of sport. Bombay, the Author, [c.1941]. 130p. illus.
*3 cricket chapters*

3810 **De Mello, Anthony S.**
■ Portrait of Indian sport. Macmillan, [1959]. x,342p. illus. ports. stats.
*cricket, chs. 2, 3, 5, 8, 9*

3811 **Deodhar, D.B.**
■ March of Indian cricket. Calcutta, S.K. Roy, Illustrated News, 1948. 140p. illus. ports.

3812 I look back: an autobiography. [Madras],
■ Sport & Pastime; London, "The Hindu", [1966]. 96p. illus. ports.
*originally issued with Sport and Pastime 9–14th June, 1966*

3812 **Desai, Kumarpal**
–1 Indian cricketers; artist Raynee Vyas.
■ Ahmedabad and Bombay, A.R. Sheth, [197–?]. [36]p. incl. covers. col. illus.
*Test cricketers*

3812 **Docker, Edward Wybergh**
–2 History of Indian cricket. Delhi, etc., S.G. Wasani for the Macmillan Co. of India, 1976. [vii],288p. illus. ports.

3812 **Dossa, Anandji**
–3 Cricket ties India – Pakistan. Calcutta,
■ etc., Rupa, 1978. [ix],191p. illus. ports. scores
*Indo-Pakistani Test cricketers of the 1950's*

3813 **Downing, Clement**
A compendious history of the Indian wars. . . . Printed for T. Cooper, 1737. iv,238p.
——*another ed. with title:* A history of the Indian wars; edited by William Foster. Oxford Univ. P., 1924. xxxii,206p. port. maps
*reference to mariners of the East India Company playing cricket at Cambay, India in 1721, pp.228–29 (1737); pp.188–89 (1924)*

3814 **Gurdeep Singh**
■ Cricket in northern India. Ludhiana, Cosmo Publications, 1966. viii,148p. illus. ports.

3815 **Hans, K.G.,** *and* **Modi, Rusi**
■ [Bharatiya cricket]. Lounder, Surat District, Hans, [1971?]. 155p. stats.
*in Gujarati*

3815 **Indian** cricketscene; edited by Jayant
–1 Nene. Bombay, Jayashree Publications, [1979]. 60p. incl. adverts. illus. ports.

3815 **Kadye, Nandu**
–2 Bhāratīya kriketce mānkani. Poona, Prestigi Prakashan, 1971. viii,142p.

*Marathi text; biographical sketches of 27 Indian cricketers*

3816 **Khadilkar, G.V.**
Kriketcī duniyā. Bombay, Sahitya Sahakar Sangha, 1970. vi,103p. illus.
*in Marathi; trs. "The world of cricket"*

3817 **Kincaid, Charles Augustus**
■ The land of 'Ranji' and 'Duleep'. Blackwood, 1931. xvii,138p. illus. ports.
——L.P. ed. limited to 250 copies signed by 'Ranji'. 1931
*cricket in ch. 12, pp.110–113*

3818 **Maitra, Jagadish Chandra**
■ Indian sports flashback. Bombay, the Author, [1965]. [viii],272p. 1 illus. port.
*cricket pp.1–88*
——2. Revised & enlarged ed. 1975
*cricket pp.25–67*

3818 **Mani, P.S.**
–1 Vilayāttu mannarkal kirikket. Madras, Kumaravel, 1964. 84p. illus.
*in Tamil*

3819 **Maqsood, Syed M.H.,** *compiler*
□ Who's who in Indian cricket. New Delhi, *printed at* Caxton P., 1940. [vii],132p. illus. ports.
——2nd ed. 1942. [v],116p. ports.
——3rd ed. 1943. 69p.
——4th ed. New Delhi, *printed at* Model P., 1945. [vi],96p. illus. ports. scores
——5th ed. 1946. [xvi],71p. ports. scores
——6th ed. 1947. 78p.

3820 **Mathur, L.N.**
■ The encyclopaedia of Indian cricket, 1965. Udaipur, Rajhans Prakashan, 1966. xvi,515p. illus. ports. scores, stats.
*also published in Hindi with title:* Bharatiya cricket ka vishvagya kosh. Ajmer, Krishan Bros., 1970. 576p.

3821 **Modi, Rusi**
■ Some Indian cricketers. New Delhi, National Book Trust, India, 1972. xii, 103p. illus. ports. (Young India Library)
——2nd revd. ed. 1974
——3rd revd. ed. 1977. xii,103p.

3822 **Moraes, Dom F.**
■ Green is the grass. Bombay & Calcutta, Asia Publishing House, 1951. vii,142p. illus.

3823 **Mukherjee, Sujit**
■ The romance of Indian cricket. Delhi, Hind Pocket Books, 1968. 168p. illus. ports.
——rptd. 1970

3824 **Northern India Cricket Association**
Cricket in Northern India: official year book. Lahore, the Association
*?/1931–32/–?*

3824 **Pandit, Bāl Jagannāth**
–1 Kriket cavkār satkar. Poona, Nilkantha Prakashan.
Pt. 1. 1971. xii,140p.
     2. 1971. xii,138p.
*in Marathi*

3825 **Patel, J.M. Framjee**
■ Stray thoughts on Indian cricket. Bombay, Times P., 1905. xvi,175p. illus. ports.

3826 **Polishwalla, Ponchaji Nussarwanji**
■ A brief history of the past 50 years of Indian cricket. Bombay, the Author, 1914. 111p. scores, stats.
*mostly Gujarati text*

3827 Representative matches in India from
■ 1892 to 1919. Bombay, the Author, 1919. 90p. incl. adverts. port. stats.

3828 Complete, unique and marvellous
■ records of cricket in India and Ceylon for the past 75 years. Bombay, [the Author], 1931. 164p. illus. ports. stats.
*issued in boards and in pbk.*

3829 ————, *compiler*
■ Cricketers' almanac for 1928: a standard book of reference on "Indian cricket". Bombay, the Compiler, 1928. 125p. stats.

3830 **Prashad, Krishnanandan**
Bharatiya cricket. Enlarged ed. Allahabad, Tarun Karyalaya, [1952]. 92p. illus. ports.
*in Hindi*

3831 **Prithvi Raj**
■ Cricket, Indian and universities. Amritsar, M.M. Bhardwaja, 1938. [4], v,200p. illus. ports.

3832 **Ramaswami, N.S.**
■ Indian willow: a short history of Indian cricket. Madras, Uma Books, 1971. iii, 264p. ports.

3832 From Porbandar to Wadekar. New Delhi,
–1 Abhinav Publications, 1975. [iv],224p.
■ illus. ports.
*a survey of first-class cricket in India*

3832 Indian cricket: a complete history. New
–2 Delhi, Abhinav Publications, 1976.
■ [vii],146p. illus. ports. pbk.
*first-class cricket in India; includes Test matches and the Ranjitsinhji and Duleepsinhji Championships*

3832 **Ramchand, Partab**
–3 Great Indian cricketers. Sahibabad,
■ Vikas, 1979. viii,205p. ports. stats.
*pen-portraits of 21 cricketers*

3833 **Roy, S.K.**
□ Indian cricketers: Indian cricket's who's
who. Calcutta, Illustrated News, 1941.
136p. ports. stats.
——2nd ed. 1944. 175p.
——3rd ed. 1946. 176p. incl. adverts.

3834 **Sahasrabuddhe, V.G.**
Kriket tantra āni mantra. Poona, S.G.
Kulkani, [1965/6?]. vi,146p. illus. diagrs.
*in Marathi; trs. "Cricket tradition"*

3834 **Saradesai, Raghunath Govinda**
–1 Mahān kriket karṇadhār. Poona, Y.G.
Joshi Prakashan, 1970. 112p.
*Marathi text; biographies of 11 Indian
captains*

3835 **Saraph, Dattā**
Bharatiya kriket (crickt) [sic] 1961–62 sālcā
dhāmutā palamarsa. Bombay, Anupam
Prakshan, 1962. 160p. illus. stats.
*in Marathi: Indian cricket 1961–62*

3836 **Sarbadhikary, Berry**
■ Indian cricket uncovered: "Inside story of
Indian cricket". Calcutta, S.K. Roy, Illus-
trated News, 1945. 162p.

3837 Amār dekhā kriket, Calcutta, Anandad-
hara, [196–]. vi,176p. illus. diagr.
*in Bengali; trs. "Cricket as seen by me"*

3838 ————, *editor & compiler*
■ Presenting Indian cricket: an introduction
to the 1946 Indian tourists. Calcutta,
Mukherjee, for Sporting Publications
(India), 1946. [xii],55p. illus. ports. stats.

3839 **Seervai, P.H.**
■ Cricket comments. Bombay, the Author,
1938. 114p. ports.
*essays and verses mostly on Indian cricket*

3839 **Sengupta, Acintyakumar**
–1 Mṛga nei mṛgayā. Calcutta, Anandad-
hara, 1966. vi,160p.
*in Bengali*

3840 **Setalvāo, Anant Venkatrāv**
Kriketno chello dāyako. Bombay, Parichay Trust, 1972. 32p.
*in Gujarati; trs. "Let us see cricket"*

3841 **Sport and Pastime**
■ Special cricket number; edited by K. Srini-
vasan. Madras, Kasturi, 2nd May 1959.
30p. illus.

3842 **Talyarkhan, A.F.S. ("Bobby")**
■ On with the game! Bombay, Hind Kitabs,
1945. 67p. illus.

## Board of Control for Cricket in India

3843 **Board of Control for Cricket in India**
□ Annual report. Delhi, the Board
*1929?/ season 1966–67 to date*
——Annexure to the Annual report. *v.y.*
*gives results of the season; later issues enti-
tled Statistical annual. See no. 3850–1*

3844 Constitution and rules. Delhi, the Board,
1930. 13p.

3845 Cricket diary. New Delhi, the Board.
illus. ports. stats. *annual?*
*?/1972/–?*

3846 **Ghose, A.N.**, *editor*
■ The Board of Control for Cricket in India
1928–53; edited by A.N. Ghose. [Cal-
cutta], Ghose, for the Board, 1954. 94p.-
illus. ports.

## Cricket Club of India

3847 **Cricket Club of India**
■ Official souvenir of the opening of
the Brabourne Stadium. Bombay, The
Stadium Publicity Co., [1937]. [74]p. incl.
adverts. illus. ports. (2 col.), score

3848 Indian cricket: the official organ of the
■ Cricket Club of India Ltd. Bombay, F.J.
Collins. illus. ports. scores, stats.
*63 issues from 15 Oct., 1934 to Jan., 1940
when incorporated with "The Sporting
Times"*

3849 Cricket tour to Australia and Far East
■ 1967. Bombay, the Club, [1967]. 24p. incl.
adverts. illus. ports.
*pre-tour*

3850 Cricket tour to Australia 1972. Bombay,
■ the Club, [1972]. 32p. incl. adverts. illus.
ports.
*pre-tour*

# ANNUALS

3850 **Board of Control for Cricket in India**
–1 Statistical annual: (Annexure to the
□ Annual Report). The Board. scores, stats.
*1974–75 to 1976–77; edited by P.N.
Sundaresan
with title: Cricontrol statistical annual.*
illus. ports. scores, stats.
*1977–78 to date; edited by P.N.
Sundaresan*

3851 **Cricket** annual; edited by A.J. Francis and Frank Pereira. Bombay. illus.
*1936. 1936. 48p.*
*1937–8*

3852 **The Crickinia** Indian cricketers' annual;
■ edited by Muni Lal. Lahore, Muni Lal. ports. scores, stats.
*six issues 1939–40 to 1944–45. 1939–44*

3853 **Illustrated News**
□ Annual cricket number. Calcutta, Illustrated News Office. illus. ports. scores, stats. *in v.y.*
*1935?/1945. . .1961/–?*
*publd. in Dec. or Jan.; Jan. 1961 issue was vol. 26, no, 1; ed. by Pearson Surita. 64p. illus.*

3854 **Indian Cricket**
■ All-India sports annual 1939. Bombay, F.J. Collins, [1939]. 94p. illus. ports. stats.
*includes survey of cricket in India 1938/9: the only issue*

3855 **Indian** cricket. Madras, Kasturi. illus.
■ ports. scores, stats. *annual*
*1946–47 to 1965; ed. by S.K. Gurunāthan. 1948–65. (19 issues; from 1962 onwards dated by years of publication, not as before by season covered, e.g. 1960–61)*
*1966/1966–1969/to date; ed. [–1974], by P.N. Sundaresan; editor not given in later years*

3856 **Indian** cricket annual; edited by P.N.
■ Polishwalla. Bombay, Polishwalla.
*1917. 122p. scores, stats.*
*1923–4. 1924. 102p. scores, stats.*
*1926. 144p. scores, stats.*
*1928. 125p. illus. scores, stats.*

3857 **The Indian** cricket-field annual; edited by
■ Dicky Rutnagur; statistics editor: Anandji Dossa. Bombay, the Editor. illus. ports. scores, stats.
*1957–58 to 1964–5. 1957–64.*
*6th issue 1962–63 includes an "Who's who of Indian cricketers" by Anandji Dossa*

3858 **Indian** cricketer annual: a digest of cricket
■ affairs in India and the world; edited by B. Sarbadhikary. Calcutta, S.G. Publications. illus. ports. scores, stats. *in v.y.*
*1954–58*

3859 **The "Indian Field"** athletic handbook for
■ 1896: a book of records of outdoor sports and athletics. Calcutta, ["Indian Field"], 1896. [iii],257p. ports. scores, stats.
*cricket pp.105–126; the only issue?*

3860 **The Indian** illustrated sports annual. Calcutta, C. Cyril, 1928. illus.

3861 **Polishwalla, Ponchaji Nussarwanji**
□ All India cricket. Bombay, the Author, 1923. 144p. port. scores, stats.
——*with title:* All India cricket annual 1933. 1933. 168p. illus. ports. diagrs. scores, stats.
——All India cricket annual 1934. "Special souvenir edition". Published in token of the compiler's journalistic career of over 30 years. 1934. 128p. illus. ports. stats.

3862 **Sport and Pastime**
□ Annual. Madras, Kasturi. illus. ports.
*?/1953. . .1966/–?*
*later issues also publd. by The Hindu, London; about 1/3 devoted to cricket*

3863 **Sports Guide**
□ Annual cricket number. Calcutta, Sports Guide. ports. stats.
*1954?/1956/–?*
*1956 issue was compiled by Sanu Basu and contained pen portraits of the Australian team in India, 1956*

3863 **Sportscine:** cricket special 1976; edited by
–1 P.N. Sundaresan. Bangalore, Manesh
■ Das for Sportscine and Publications, [1976]. 84p. incl. covers & adverts. illus. ports. stats.

3864 **Sportsweek**
□ Annual. Bombay, Inqilab Publications (Private) Ltd. illus. ports. (some col.), stats.
*?/1969. . .1974/–?*
*general sports annual, including cricket*

# PERIODICALS

3864 **Bengal monthly** sporting magazine.
–1 Calcutta. *monthly*
*1833*
contd. by
**Bengal sporting** magazine. Calcutta, William Rushton. *monthly*
*1834–36. New series 1–7 (no. 30) Feb. 1834–Dec. 1836*
*part numbering continuous, but vol. numbering inconsistent;*
contd. by
**Bengal sporting** and general magazine. Calcutta. *monthly*
*1837. New series 9 (no. 37) – 10 (no. 48) Jan.-Dec. 1837*
contd. by
**Bengal sporting** magazine and Eastern miscellany; edited by J.H. Stocqueler. Calcutta. *monthly*
*1838–42. New series 11 (no. 59) – 19 (no. 118) Jan. 1838-Dec. 1842*
contd. by

**Bengal quarterly** sporting magazine; edited by R. Macdonald Stephenson. Calcutta. *quarterly*
> *1843–44. New series 20 (no. 118) – Second new series 1 (no. 4) Apr. 1843–Dec. 1844*
> contd. by

**Bengal sporting** magazine. Calcutta. *monthly*
> *1845. ?Third new series 1 (no. 1) – 2 (no. 11) Jan.-Dec. 1845*
> *of the volumes seen and checked, vols. 7 (1836) and 17 (1841) contain no cricket, but vols. 11 and 12 (1838), vol. 15 (1840) and vol. 18 (1842) gives scores and reports mostly of Army matches*

3864
-2
■ **Cricket, India;** edited by Robert S. Aloysius. Bombay, R.S. Aloysius for Rosita Publications.
> *the only issue 26 Jan. 1975. 76p. incl. adverts. illus. ports. stats.*

3864
-3
□ **Cricket** quarterly; edited by Anandji Dossa. Bombay, Anandji Dossa/Ava Publications. illus. & ports. (in later issues some col.), scores, stats.
> *Vol. 1, no. 1. Jan. 1975/1975 . . . 1978/to date*
> *Vol. 4. no. 2, 1978 to date. Anan Setalvad editor*

3865 **The cricket** times. Bombay, S.G. Narwane. *weekly*
> *issued Aug.-Oct. 1933 and Aug.-Oct. 1934*

3866
□ **The illustrated** cricket and sporting news: and independent journal devoted to the interests of Indian cricket . . . ; edited by I.M. Mansukhani. Karachi, Mansukhani. *monthly.* ports. scores, stats.
> *Vol. 1, no. 1 Apr. 1931–no. 8 Nov. 1931?*
> contd. as: Indian cricketer

3867
■ **Indian** cricket: the official organ of the Cricket Club of India Ltd. Bombay, F.J. Collins. illus. ports. scores, stats.
> *63 issues from 15 Oct., 1934 to Jan., 1940 when incorporated with The Sporting Times*

3868
□ **The Indian** cricketer illustrated, with which the Illustrated Cricket and Sporting News is incorporated. Karachi, M.A. Wadhwani. *monthly.* illus. ports. scores
> *Aug. 1932?–?*
> *vol. II, no. 1 is dated Aug. 1933; edited by I.M. Mansukhani*

3869
□ **Sport** and pastime. Madras, Kasturi. *weekly.* illus. ports.
> *1947–?*

3870
□ **Sports**—Indian: national sports and cine weekly. Madras. illus. ports.
> *12 July, 1970–?*

3870
-1
□ **Sportsweek**. Bombay, Inquilab Publications (Pvt.) Ltd. *weekly.* illus. ports.
> *no. 1, 13 Oct. 1968/Nov. 16, 1975/to date?*

3870
-2
□ **Sportsweek** cricket quarterly; managing editor Khalid Ansari. Bombay, Inquilab Publications. illus. ports. scores, stats.
> *Vol. 1, no. 1. Jan.-Mar. 1974 – Vol. 2, no. 4 Oct.-Dec. 1975*
> contd. as:

**Sportsweek's** world of cricket
> *Vol. III, no. 1, Jan-Mar. 1976 to date*

# PARSI CRICKET

3871 **Baluchistan Gazette**
Cricket extra, 4th August, 1921. Quetta, Baluchistan Gazette. *single sheet*
——another issue dated 6th August 1921
> *contains scores of matches, Parsees v. Quetta Garrison and Parsees v. Staff College*

3872 **Darukhanawala, Hormusji Dhunjishaw**
■ Parsis and sports and kindred subjects. Bombay, the Author, 1935. 488p. incl. adverts. illus. ports.
> *cricket pp.55–99*

3873 **Master, Peshtanji Jeevanji**
An entertaining account of the Parsi Cricket Club's tours. Bombay, The Rising Star Printing P., 1892. 64p.
> *Gujarati text*

3874 **Parsee Gymkhana Bombay**
Annual report and balance sheet for the year ending 31st December. Bombay, the Gymkhana
> *1922. 1923. 18p.*
> *1923. 1924. 18p.*

3874
-1
■ Golden jubilee souvenir 1885–1935. [Bombay, the Gymkhana, 1935]. 28p. illus. ports.

3874 **Patel, J.M. Framjee**
-2 Stray thoughts on Indian cricket. Bombay, Times P., 1905. xvi,175p. illus. ports.
> *several chs. on Parsi cricket including an account of the 1886 Parsi tour in England*

3875 **Patel, Manekji Kavasji**
■ History of Parsee cricket, (being a lecture delivered at the Framji Cowasji Institute. . .) on the 10th December, 1892. Bombay [the Author], 1892. viii,101p. scores

3876 **Pavri, Mehrvanji Erachji**
■ Parsi cricket, with hints on bowling, batting, fielding, captaincy, explanation of laws of cricket, &c., &c. Bombay, J.B. Marzban, 1901. xvi,196p. ports. diagrs. score, stats.

3877 **Sorabjee, Shapoorjee**
■ A chronicle of cricket amongst Parsees and the struggle polo versus cricket. Bombay, the Author, [c.1898]. [iii],124p.

## SCHOOLS AND UNIVERSITIES

3878 **Antia, Jamshed Dinshaw**
■ Elphinstone College tours. Bandra, the Author, 1913. xxiv,219p. illus. ports. map on cover, scores
*tours in India 1901–12*

3879 **Ceylon Universities' Sports Association**
■ Indian Universities' cricket tour of Ceylon, 19 Oct. to 7 Nov. 1970. [Colombo], the Assoc., [1970]. [13]p. stats.
*pre-tour souvenir; contains account of the visit of the Indian University Occasionals Team 1935, by S.S. Perera*

3879 **English Schools Cricket Association**
–1 Indian Schools' tour in England 1973. The
■ Assoc., 1973. 8p. stats. *typescript*
*post-tour*

3880 **Inter university** cricket championship of
■ India: the Rohinton Baria Trophy. Bombay, *printed by* The Times of India P., [1935]. 12p. illus. port. map
*origin, rules, etc.*

3881 **London Schools Cricket Association**
■ All-India Schools' cricket tour of U.K., 1967: official souvenir. The Assoc., 1967. 12p. ports.

3882 **Polishwalla, Ponchaji Nussarwanji**
■ School and college cricket in India with 14 various important and interesting subjects on cricket. Bombay, the Author, 1921. 107p. diagr.

3883 **Prithvi Raj**
■ Cricket, Indian and universities. Amritsar, M.M. Bhardwaja, 1938. [4], v,200p. illus. ports.

3884 **R., J.**
■ An account of a cricket match: "Public Schools," (Eton, Harrow, and Winchester) versus "Private Schools," ("Miss Tims's Pupils") played at Calcutta, on the 4th and 5th February, 1870. Calcutta, [the Author], 1870. 19p.
*in verse form*

3885 **Sherring, Herbert**
The Mayo College: the Eton of India: a record of twenty years 1875–1895. Calcutta, Thacker Spink, 1897. 318p. illus.
*chapter XIII "Cricket" pp.226–289*

## FIRMS AND PROFESSIONS

### All India State Bank

3886 **Mercantile Cricket Association**
Visit of All India State Bank cricket team, 1966. Colombo, [the Assoc., 1966]. 86p. incl. 40 of adverts. ports.

3887 **Southern Gujarat Cricket Association**
■ Silver Jubilee Festival match: the Southern Gujarat Cricket Association XI vs. All India State Bank XI at Athwa Lines, Surat, 17, 18 & 19 October, 1970. Surat, the Assoc., [1970]. 92p. incl. adverts. illus. ports.
*in Gujarati; pre-match*

3888 **Tamil Union Cricket and Athletic Club**
■ Visit of All-India State Bank cricket team. Colombo, [the Club, 1968]. [40]p. incl. adverts. port.
*pre-tour*

## DULEEP AND IRANI TROPHY

3888 **Board of Control for Cricket in India**
–1 Duleep and Irani Trophy to 1979. Golden Jubilee edition, edited by P.N. Sundaresan. Bombay, the Board, 1979. 222p. illus.

## RANJI TROPHY

3889 **Gurunathan, S.K.**
■ Twelve years of Ranji trophy 1934–1945. Madras, The Hindu, 1946. xxvi, 294p. ports. scores, stats.

3890 **Railway Sports Control Board**
■ Ranji Trophy silver jubilee cricket souvenir: Bombay v. Rest of India . . . 18, 19, 20, March, 1960. New Delhi, the Board, [1960]. [74]p. incl. adverts. ports. stats.
*includes history of the Ranji Trophy by S.K. Guranathan*

## TOURNAMENTS

3891 **All-India Gwynne Cricket Tounament**
■ Rules of the . . . Tournament, Lucknow, 1926. Lucknow, Lucknow Steam Printing P., 1926. [i],5p.

3892 **All India** Sheesh Mahal cricket tournament, Lucknow: souvenir. Lucknow, [the Tournament Cttee.]. port. illus.
*22nd. Edited by Agha Rizvi. 1972. 124p.*
*23rd. Edited by Agha Rizvi. 1973. 130p.*

3892 **Illustrated News (Sports)**
-1 Exhibition cricket match: Prime Minister's
■ XI v. Governor's XI. Calcutta, Illustrated
News (Sports), [1962]. 32p. illus. ports.

3893 **Karachi Cricket Association**
History of the Sind cricket tournament
1919–1924. Karachi, the Association,
[1924?]

3894 **The Quadrangular** cricket tournament
souvenir. Bombay, New Indian Publicity,
1936. 18p. illus.

3895 **Rajputana Cricket Club**
■ The All-India cricket tournament, Ajmer
(192–) for "H.H. The Maharaja of Alwar's
Challenge Cup": [rules]. Ajmer, the
Club, [1923?]. 4p. fold
*the tournament has been held annually since
1923*

3896 **Rubie, Claude Blake,** *and* **Shanker, B.D.**
■ A history of the Sind Cricket Tournament
and Karachi cricket in general. Karachi,
E. Forster, 1928. [viii],100p. ports. scores,
stats.
——Appendix (records 1928 and early
1929). [1929]. 24p. incl. adverts. port.
scores, stats.

3896 **The Times of India** Challenge Shield
-1 cricket tournament: silver jubilee
souvenir 1931–56. Bombay, "The Times
of India", [1956]. 49p. incl. adverts. ports.
stats.

## ANDHRA PRADESH

3897 **Andhra Pradesh Sports Council**
Sports journal: Hyderabad, the Council.
ports. *quarterly*
*Vol. 1, no. 1, 26th Aug. 1973 to date*
Editor—B.C. Khanna
*includes cricket*

### Hyderabad

3898 **Deccan Blues Cricket Club**
Silver jubilee celebrations 1972: souvenir.
Secunderabad, the Club, [1972]. 50p. incl.
adverts.
*includes history of Club*

3898 Souvenir 1978 tour of Australia, Hong
-1 Kong, Phillipines, Malaysia, Singapore,
■ Thailand, Bangladesh. Hyderabad, the
Club, [1978]. [214]p. mostly adverts.
ports.

3899 **Hyderabad Blues Cricket Club**
□ Founder's Day celebration souvenir.
Hyderabad, the Club.
*1963? to date?*

*1966. 64p. incl. adverts. illus. ports.*
*1967. 128p. incl. adverts. illus. ports.*
*1970 8th Founder's Day celebrations. 38p.*
*incl. adverts*

3900 Tours of Malaysia, Singapore & Ceylon:
■ souvenir 1968. Hyderabad, the Club,
[1968]. [194]p. incl. adverts. illus. ports.
stats.
*pre-tour*

3901 Tour of Johore Bahru, June 1968: souvenir
programme. Hyderabad, the Club,
[1968]. 24p.
*pre-tour*

3902 Tour of Aden, Uganda, Kenya, Tanzania,
■ Kuwait: souvenir 1971. Hyderabad, the
Club. [1971]. [290]p. incl. adverts. illus.
ports.
*pre-tour*

3903 Tour of Australia, Malaysia, Singapore,
Hong Kong, Bangkok & Fiji: souvenir
1973. Hyderabad, the Club, [1973]. 246p.
incl. adverts. ports.
*pre-tour*

3904 **Hyderabad Union Cricket Club**
Silver jubilee celebration 1973: souvenir.
[Hyderabad], the Club, [1973]. 86p. incl.
adverts. ports.

3904 **Shyamnagar Cricket Club**
-1 6th annual celebrations: souvenir 1972.
■ Hyderabad, the Club, [1972]. [38]p. incl.
adverts. port.

## BENGAL

3904 **Bengal Sporting Club**
-2 Souvenir published on the occasion of
■ diamond jubilee celebration of Bengal
Sporting Club at Rungmahal Theatre Hall
on February twenty and twentyfirst 1978;
edited by Rabisekhar Sengupta. [The
Club, 1978]. 80p. incl. adverts. ports.

3905 **Cricket Association of Bengal**
Silver jubilee 1929–1954; edited by
Pearson Surita and P.D. Dutt. Calcutta,
A.N. Ghose, on behalf of the Association,
[1956]. 234p. illus. ports.
*published on the occasion of the visit of C.G.*
*Howard's team to Bengal 1956–7, when 'a*
*commemorative match was played against Dr.*
*B.C. Roy's XI*

3906 **Illustrated News**
■ C.A.B. silver jubilee souvenir. Calcutta,
Illustrated News, vol. 22, no. 2, Jan. 1957.
40p. incl. adverts. illus. ports.

### Calcutta

3907 **Ballygunge** Cricket Club and Ground,
■ 1864–1964: centenary souvenir. Calcutta,
the Club, [1964]. 136p. illus. ports. scores

3908 **Calcutta Cricket Club**
■ Matches 1844–1854. Calcutta, Free School
P., 1854. [3],v,119p. scores

3909 **Excelsiors Club**
Our news: bulletin of the Excelsiors Club.
Calcutta, the Club. *occasional publication.*
illus. ports.
*?/Oct.1965/*to date?

3910 **Ganguly, Narendranath**
■ The Calcutta Cricket Club: its origin and
development. Calcutta, the Author, 1936.
[i],35p. illus. plans, score

3911 **Longfield, Thomas C.**
Calcutta Cricket Club. 1950. 4p.
*a printed letter from the President of the
Calcutta C.C. to all members concerning the
disposal of the Eden Gardens ground*

3912 **Mohun Bagan Sports Club**
■ Mohun Bagan platinum jubilee cricket
souvenir: Chief Minister's XI vs. Commonwealth XI. Calcutta, Sports News Publication, [1964]. 32p. illus. ports.
*includes a note on the history of the club;
pre-match*

3912 **Rajkot Sports Association**
–1 Souvenir 10th anniversary (1960–1970).
■ Rajkot, Shri Velji Master, Hon. Sec. the
Assoc., [1970]. [100]p. incl. adverts.
ports.

## GUJARAT

3913 **Southern Gujarat Cricket Association**
■ Silver jubilee festival match: the Southern
Gujarat Cricket Association XI vs. All
India State Bank XI at Athwa Lines,
Surat, 17, 18 & 19 October, 1970. Surat,
the Assoc., [1970]. 92p. incl. adverts.
illus. ports.
*in Gujarati; pre-match*

## MAHARASHTRA

### Bombay

3913 **Bombay** Cavaliers: cricket in Sri Lanka,
–1 7th May-22nd May 1973; sponsored by
National Cricket Club of India, Bombay.
Bombay, printed by Sanjay P., [1973].
60p. incl. 48p. of adverts. illus.

3914 **Bombay Cricket Association**
Dr. H.D. Kanga Cricket League. Bombay,
the Association. *annual?*
*?/1950/–?*
*fixtures*

3915 The silver jubilee official souvenir
1930–1954. Bombay, the Assoc., [1954].
44p. illus. ports. stats.

3916 **Fifty** years of Bombay cricket: being an
■ authoritative compilation of the scores,
etc., of the Presidency matches, and the
Triangular, the Quadrangular and the
Pentagular Tournaments, 1895–1944;
compiled by A.A.A. Fyzee [and others].
Bombay, Thacker, 1946. [vi],116p. scores

3917 **Green Leaf.** *Special number*
■ Film star cricket festival. Bombay, Green
Leaf, vol. 1, no. 2–3, April-May 1951. 36p.
incl. adverts. illus. ports.

3918 **Mixers' Cricket Club**
Rules. Bombay, [the Club, 1944?]. 12p.

3918 **MV(Modh Vanik) Sports Club**
–1 Souvenir [brochure] 1955–64. Bombay,
■ the Club, [1964]. [76]p. incl. adverts. illus.
ports. stats.

3919 **Parmanddas Jivandas Hindu Gymkhana**
Annual report. Bombay, the Gymkhana
*?/1923. . .1930/–?*

3920 Diamond jubilee 1894–1954. Bombay, the
Gymkhana, 1954

3921 **Parsee Gymkhana Bombay**
Annual report and balance sheet for the
year ending 31st December. Bombay, the
Gymkhana
*1922. 1923. 18p.*
*1923. 1924. 18p.*

3922 **Roy, S.K.,** *editor*
■ Bombay Pentangular. Calcutta, Illustrated
News, 1945. 125p. illus. ports. scores, stats.
*Quadrangular and Pentangular cricket in
Bombay to date*

3923 **Shivaji Park Gymkhana**
■ Diamond jubilee souvenir 1909–1969.
Bombay, the Club, [1969]. 82p. incl.
adverts. illus. ports.

3924 **Sportsweek**
■ N.D.F. match special. [Bombay, Apr. 14,
15, 16, 17, 1972]. Bombay, Inqilab Publications (Private) Ltd., [1972]. 68p. incl.
adverts. illus. ports.
*match in aid of National Defence Fund; pre-
match*

3925 **Young Zoroastrian Cricket Club.** *Managing Committee*
Report read on the celebration of the golden jubilee. Bombay, Vartarnan, 1920. 6p.

**Poona**

3925 **The Guardian**
–1 The bedside 'Guardian' 19: a selection
■ from The Guardian 1969–70; edited by W.L. Webb. Collins, 1970. 256p. illus.
*includes pp.221–4, "The life and times of a Poona number nine", by Omar Kureishi*

# RAJASTHAN

3926 **Begg, W.D.**
Rajputana Cricket Club. Ajmer: souvenir of the private tour of Indian cricketers in England, 1938. Delhi, Hindustan Times, 1938. [ii],66p. illus. ports.

3927 **Rajputana** Cricket Club, Ajmer, in a nutshell. Ajmer, R.P. Works, [c.1938]. 4p.

# TAMIL NADU

3928 **Madras Cricket Association**
□ Annual report. Madras, the Association. illus. ports. stats.
*season ?/1958–59 . . . 1969–70/*
contd. as: *Tamil Nadu C.A. Annual report*
*formed 1930*

3929 Cricket fixtures, league & other tourna-
□ ments. Madras, the Association. *annual*
*season ?/1964–5 to 1969–70/*
*for later issues see: Tamil Nadu C.A.*

3930 Silver jubilee souvenir 1930–1955; edited by S.A. Govindarajan. Madras, Commercial Publishing House, 1956. 200p. incl. adverts. illus.

3931 Memorandum of Association and the
■ rules as and from the 26th April 1957. Madras, the Assoc., [1957]. 56p.

3931 **Madras Cricket Club**
–1 Silver jubilee 1978. Madras, the Club,
■ [1978]. [74]p. incl. adverts. illus. ports. diagrs.

3932 **Madras** sports annual; edited by S.K.
□ Gurunathan. Madras, Thompson. port. scores, stats.
*8 issues 1940–1950*
*each contains 60–90 pp. of cricket*

3933 **Tamil Nadu Cricket Association**
■ Annual report. Madras, the Association. illus. ports. stats.
*season/1970–71/to date*

——*Addenda. 1972–73*
formerly: *Madras C.A. Annual report*

3934 Cricket fixtures, league & other tourna-
■ ments. Madras, the Association. *annual*
*season/1970–71* to date/
formerly: *Madras C.A. Cricket fixtures. . . .*

## Gopalan Trophy: Madras to Ceylon

3935 **[See no. 4879–1]**

3936 **Board of Control for Cricket in Ceylon**
■ Gopalan Trophy, 1966: Madras C.A. v. President's XI: official souvenir. Colombo, the Board, [1966]. [24]p. incl. adverts. port.
*contains review of Gopalan Trophy matches 1953–1964; pre-match*

3937 Official souvenir of the visit of Madras Cricket Association to Ceylon, 1st–11th April, 1966. Colombo, the Board, 1966. ports.

3937 **Galle Cricket Club**
–1 Galle District Combined XI v. Madras Cricket Association – at Galle Esplanade, 9 & 10 April, 1966; compiled by S.S. Perera. Galle, the Club, [1966]

3938 **Perera, S.S.,** *compiler*
■ Souvenir of the visit of the Madras Cricket Association team to Ceylon, 11 to 22 April 1968. Galle (Ceylon), Galle C.C., [1968]. 14p. illus. port. stats.
*pre-visit*

## Coimbatore

3938 **Cosmic Recreation Club**
–1 Third anniversary celebrations 26 January
■ 1967: souvenir. Ramnagar, Coimbatore-9, Madras, the Club, [1967]. [80]p. incl. adverts. illus. ports.

3939 **Friends Cricket Club**
■ Souvenir: first anniversary celebrations on 26th January, 1969. Coimbatore, the Club, [1969]. [56]p. incl. adverts. ports.

## Madras

3940 **The Madras** Cricket Club 1848–1968.
■ Madras, the Club, [1968]. 68p. illus. ports.

3940 **Madras Occasionals Cricket Club**
–1 Souvenir '74. Madras, [the Club, 1974].
■ 12p. of text, ports.

3941 **Madras United Club.** *Executive Committee*
Report for the year. Madras, the Club.
*annual*
*?/1912/–?*

3942 **Netaji Cricket Club**
Silver jubilee celebrations (1947–72): souvenir. Madras, the Club, 1972. 186p. incl. adverts. illus. ports. stats.

3943 **Starlets Cricket Club**
Tour of Malaysia and Singapore: souvenir 1973. Madras, the Club, [1973]. 268p. incl. adverts.
   *mostly advertisements, but with list of members and some articles. There appears to be nothing about the tour.*
   *pre-tour*

# UTTAR PRADESH

## Lucknow

3944 **Sunil Misra,** *editor*
Morning Star Cricket Club: souvenir 1960. Lucknow, Beni Madho Ram Nath, 1960. 68p. incl. adverts. illus. ports.

"Going in" and "Coming out": Cricket in India as depicted in "The Graphic", 10 Aug. 1878 *photo: BBC Hulton Picture Library*

Cricket in Pakistan. Local cricket in Karachi *photo: Patrick Eagar*

# CRICKET IN PAKISTAN

**3945 Abdul Alim, Qazi**
Ball chotey bat uthey. Dacca, Sports
Publications, 1964. vi,179,v,p. illus.
*in Bengali; literal trs.: "The ball is bowled,
the bat is raised."*

**3946 Butt, Qamaruddin**
■ Pakistan cricket on the march (containing
complete eye-witness accounts of the
tours of New Zealand, M.C.C. "A" and
Australian teams to Pakistan, Quaid-e-
Azam Trophy 1956–57 and averages of all
the previous official series). Karachi, the
Author, 1957. 258p. illus. ports. scores,
stats.

**3947 Cricketers Guild of Pakistan**
■ Cricketers Guild's annual awards 1969;
edited by Syed Sirajul Islam Bukhari.
Karachi, the Guild, [1970]. [76]p. incl.
adverts. illus. ports.
*awards to the 5 best Pakistani cricketers*

**3947 Dossa, Anandji**
**–1** Cricket ties India – Pakistan. Calcutta,
■ etc., Rupa, 1978. [ix],191p. illus. ports.
scores
*Indo-Pakistani Test cricketers of the 1950's*

**3948 Ghulam Mustafa Khan,** *compiler*
■ Pakistan's book of cricket records. Chak-
lala, the Author, 1971. vii,56p. stats.

**3949 Maqsood, Syed M.H.,** *compiler*
□ Cricket in Pakistan. Karachi, Universal
C.C., 1948
——2nd ed. 1951. 108p. illus. ports. scores
——3rd ed. 1954. [xvi],100p. illus. ports.
scores
*contains an account of the 1952–53 Paki-
stan tour of India*

**3950** Twenty years of Pakistan cricket. Karachi,
■ Sporting Publications (Pakistan), 1968.
[xii],372p. ports. scores
*covers 1947–67*

**3951 Northern India Cricket Association**
Cricket in Northern India: official year
book. Lahore, the Association
*?/1931–32/–?*

## Pakistan Eaglets

**3952** Pakistan Eaglets cricket tour 1955: Paki-
■ stan Eaglets v. 'Evening Chronicle'
Lancashire Starlets, 30th August 1955 at
Rochdale C.C. Ground: official pro-
gramme. Manchester, Manchester Sports
Guild, [1955]. [8]p. ports.

**3953** Pakistan Eaglets cricket tour 1955: Paki-
■ stan Eaglets v. a Northern Cricket League
XI, 1st Sept. 1955 at Morecambe C.C.
Manchester, Manchester Sports Guild,
[1955]. [8]p. ports.

**3954** The Pakistan Eaglets cricket tour 1956.
■ Morecambe Festival: Pakistan Eaglets v.
A Commonwealth XI, 25, 26 July, 1956:
official programme. Manchester, Manchester Sports Guild, [1956]. [8]p.

**3955** Pakistan Eaglets cricket tour 1957: Paki-
■ stan Eaglets v. Hereford City C.C., 14th
July, 1957, the Racecourse, Hereford.
Manchester, Manchester Sports Guild,
[1957]. [16]p.

**3956 The Pakistan Eaglets Society**
■ Pakistan Eaglets 1959. Karachi, the
Society, [1959]. [100]p. incl. adverts.
ports. stats.
*produced for tour of England 1959; includes
survey of previous tours*

**3957 Pakistan International Airways**
■ Eaglets cricket tour of England 1963.
Karachi, P.I.A., [1963]. 12p. ports.
*pre-tour; pen-portraits of team with
itinerary*

**3958 The Pakistan Eaglets Society**
■ Pakistan Eaglets 1969: [tour of England].
The Society, [1969]. [14]p. incl. adverts.
ports.

## ANNUALS

**3959 Board of Control for Cricket in Pakistan**
□ Cricket annual. Lahore, illus. ports.
scores, stats.

1964–5; ed. by Bashir Ahmad, with statistics by Ghulam Mustafa Khan. 1966.
1966–7. 1968
1968–9. 1970
1970. 1971
1971–2; edited by Zafar Altaf, with statistics by G.M. Khan. 1972
1972–3; ed. by G.M. Khan. 1973
1974; ed. by G.M. Khan. 1974
*any more issued?*

3959 **Pakistan** book of cricket; edited by Qamar
–1 Ahmed. Karachi, Qamar Ahmed. *annual*.
□ illus. ports. scores, stats.
*1976, 1977, 1978–79, 1979–80—*
*a review of the previous season*

3960 **Pakistan Sports & Pastimes**
□ Annual number; ed. by M.H. Ghatala.
Karachi, the Editor. illus. ports.
*1954?/1956/–?*
*mostly cricket*

3960 **World cricket** annual; edited by A. Aziz
–1 Rehmatullah. Karachi, A. Aziz Rehmatullah.
■ matullah.
*1979–80. 160p. incl. adverts. illus. (some col.), ports. scores, stats.*

# PERIODICALS

3960 **Cricket world** quarterly; chief editor Haji
–2 Abdul Razzaque; editor A. Aziz Rehmatullah. Karachi, Haji Abdul Razzaque.
□ *quarterly. illus. ports. scores, stats.*
*publd. Jan., Apr., July, Oct. Vol. 1, no. 1. Jan. 1978 to date?*

3961 **The cricketer** (Pakistan); chief editor
□ Hanif Mohammed; editor Riaz Ahmed
Mansuri. Karachi, Umber Chughtai.
*monthly. illus. ports. scores, stats.*
*1972 to date*
*issue for Oct. 1977 was vol. 6, no. 7*

3962 **Sportimes:** the magazine for sportsmen.
□ Lahore, Mian Maqsood Ahmad. *monthly.*
illus. ports. scores, stats.
*Vol. 1, no. 1, Jan. 1956/Nov. 1960 . . . Aug. 1977/to date*
*includes cricket, with occasional special numbers; later issues publd. by Progressive Papers Ltd*

3962 **World of cricket** Pakistan. Karachi,
–1 Munir Hussain. *monthly.* illus. & ports.
(some col.), scores, stats.
*Mar. 1979 to date*
*managing editor: Munir Hussain*

# FIRMS, PROFESSIONS, etc.

## Pakistan International Airlines

3963 **Pakistan International Airlines**
■ PIA cricket team tour of Ireland 1969.
Karachi, PIA., [1969]. 32p. ports.
*pre-tour*

# TOURNAMENTS

## Bhutto Trophy

3963 **[Karachi Cricket Association]**
–1 Official souvenir for Premier Zulfikar Ali
■ Bhutto Trophy. Pakistan Under-19 vs. Sri
Lanka Under-19 played at Karachi
Gymkhana on 28 February 1976: organised by Karachi Cricket Association under
the auspices of Sind Cricket Association;
edited by S. Sirajul Islam Bukhari.
Karachi, [the Assoc.], 1976. [32]p. incl.
adverts. ports.
—— —— 1979. 14p.
*pre-match*

## Habib Sugar Mills Shield

3964 **The District Cricket Association,**
*Nawabshah*
Habib Sugar Mills Shield cricket tournament, Nawabshah 1965: opening
souvenir; edited by Aziz Ahmed Khan.
Nawabshah, the Assoc., [1965]. [14]p.
port.

## Multan

3964 **Multan Cricket Club**
–1 Souvenir: prize distribution ninth Multan
■ Cricket Tournament, March 3, 1963.
[Multan, the Club, 1963]. [40]p. illus.
ports.
*post-tournament with records of earlier tournaments*

## PTV Trophy

3965 **PTV** [Pakistan Television] cricket trophy
■ tournament 1972. [Lahore?, PTV, 1972].
[6]p. fold
*includes rules and results prior to final at Lahore*

## Sind Cricket Tournament

3966 **Karachi Cricket Association**
History of the Sind cricket tournament
1919–1924. Karachi, the Assoc., [1924?]

3967 **Rubie, Claude Blake,** *and* **Shanker, B.D.**
■ A history of the Sind Cricket Tournament
and Karachi cricket in general. Karachi,

E. Forster, 1928. [viii],100p. ports. scores, stats.
——Appendix (records 1928 and early 1929). [1929]. 24p. incl. adverts. port. scores, stats.

## PUNJAB

### Shahpur

3968 **Shapoor** Spencer cricket challenge cup: fixtures of 1923. [4]p.

## SIND

### Karachi

3969 **Karachi Cricket Association**
Rules. Karachi, the Association, 1928. 8p.

3970 **Story** of the Sind Club, 1871–1946. Karachi, Union P., 1946. 97p.

# CRICKET IN SRI LANKA

3971 **Foenander, Samuel Peter**
■ Sixty years of Ceylon cricket, containing in permanent form the history and authentic records of Ceylon cricket since 1860. Colombo, Ceylon Advertising & General Publicity Co., 1924. xi,268p. illus. ports. scores, stats.

3972 A short history of matches played by Dr.
■ John Rockwood's teams, 1918–25. [Colombo, Ceylon Independent, 1925]. [i],8p. ports. stats.

3973 **Jones-Bateman, R.**
■ A refugee from civilisation, and other trifles. E. Arnold, 1931. 191p. illus. map
*includes 2 chapters on cricket in the remote parts of Ceylon, pp.149–164*

3974 **Marambe, T.M.**
■ Pen pictures of "our cricketers;" (photographs by G. Powell). [Colombo], Times of Ceylon, [1949]. 48p. illus. ports. scores

3975 **Polishwalla, Ponchaji Nussarwanji**
■ Complete, unique and marvellous records of cricket in India and Ceylon for past 75 years. Bombay, the Author, 1931. 164p. illus. ports. stats.
*issued in boards and paperback*

3976 **[Entry cancelled]**

3977 **Wright, T.Y.**
Ceylon in my time 1889–1949. Colombo, Colombo Apothecaries Co., [1950].366p. illus. scores
*cricket pp.197–236*

## Board of Control for Cricket in Ceylon

3978 **Board of Control for Cricket in Ceylon**
□ Annual report of the Executive Committee. Colombo, the Board. *typescript later printed.* scores, stats.
*season 1949–50 to date*

3979 Constitution: revised May 1970. [Col-
■ ombo, the Board, 1970]. 39p.
——[1978]. 32p.

3979 **Board of Control** for Cricket in Sri Lanka
–1 1973. [Colombo, The Board, 1973]. [4]p. fold. team port. of Sri Lankan team

## Ceylon Cricket Association

3979 **Ceylon Cricket Association**
–2 Rules. [Colombo], the Assoc., 1922

3979 **(Foenander, Samuel Peter]**
–3 Ceylon Cricket Association golden jubilee souvenir 1907–1957. [Colombo, the Assoc., 1957?]. 114p. incl. adverts. illus.

3980 **Ismail, M.K.M., and Ondatje, Frank**
■ A souvenir of the 25th anniversary of the Ceylon Cricket Association. Colombo, the Assoc., 1947. 60p. incl. adverts. ports.

# ANNUALS

3981 **Bristol** book of cricket; compiled and
■ edited by D. Eardley and I. Perera. Colombo, Ceylon Tobacco Co. illus. ports. stats.
*season 1964–5. [1965?]. 64p.*
*the only issue?*

3982 **The Ceylon** cricket annual 1899. Col-
■ ombo, Ferguson, 1900. [v],108p. ports. scores, stats.
*the only issue; contd. as: Handbook to Ceylon cricket*

3982 **Ceylon** cricket annual; edited by B.A.
–1 Mendis. Colombo, *printed by* Laksilumma P., 1907. 70p.
*cricket in 1906*

3983 **The Ceylon** cricket annual 1922. Col-
■ ombo, Colombo Apothecaries Co., 1922. 75p. illus.
*the only issue*

3984 **Ceylon** cricketers' almanack; edited by
■ E.W. Foenander. Wellawatte, *printed by* Boys Industrial Home P. *annual.* ports. scores, stats.
*3 issues 1911–13*

**3985** **Ceylon** cricketers' companion; edited by
■ S.P. Foenander. Colombo, The Times of
Ceylon. ports. scores, stats. *annual*
*3 issues 1925–27*

**3986** **Ceylon** sport and pastime: an annual
record and review; edited by C.J.
Thompson. December 1887 to June 1888.
Colombo, Ceylon Sport and Pastime,
1888. 118p.
*the only issue*

**3987** **Ceylon** sports annual (incorporating The
■ Handbook to Ceylon cricket and other
field sports); edited by P.L. Bartholomeusz. ports. stats.
*1903–05, 1907–14*
*1903–10. Colombo, Capper*
*1911–14. Colombo, Times of Ceylon*
formerly: *Handbook to Ceylon cricket*

**3987** **The Ceylon** sports annual & directory
**–1** (1923–1924); edited and compiled by
Neville Piggott. Colombo, *printed by*
Frewin & Co., 1923. 124p.
*covers many sports*

**3987** **Ceylon** sportsmag; edited by Marathon.
**–2** Colombo, *printed by* St. Gerards Press.
illus.
*1917. 29p.*

**3988** **Handbook** to Ceylon cricket; edited by
P.L. Bartholomeusz. Colombo, Times of
Ceylon. *annual*
*1901–6*
formerly: *The Ceylon cricket annual* and
contd. as: *The Ceylon sports annual*

**3988** **Mercantile** cricket annual; edited by J.A.
**–1** Kambeek. Colombo, *printed by* The Independent P.
*1922*
*the only issue?*

**3989** **Sport** in Ceylon. Colombo, Plate Ltd.
*annual.* illus. ports.
*season 1922/1922, 1923, 1924/–?*

## PERIODICALS

**3989** **All sports**; edited by W.M. Colombo,
**–1** *printed at* City P.
*Vol. 1, no. 1. Jan. 1967*

**3990** **Camouflage**
Special cricket number, March 1921;
edited by "On-looker". Colombo, Daily
News.

**3990** **Ceylon** sports fortnightly; edited by M.
**–1** Lord-Price. Colombo, *printed by* Mercantile Stationers
*1962–?*
*ceased publication after about a year*

**3991** **Ceylon** sportsmag. Nugegoda, T.W.I.
□ Barrow. *monthly.* ports. scores, stats.
*Vol. 1, no. 1 March 1962–?*
*ceased publication after about a year*

**3991** **The Ceylon** sportsman: M.C.C. number.
**–1** Colombo, Monday, October 23, 1922
*newspaper supplement*

**3991** **Sportscene.** Colombo, Times of Ceylon.
**–2** *monthly.* illus. ports. scores, stats.
□ *Dec. 1966 to date?*

**3991** **Sportscope;** edited by Lawrence Heyn
**–3** and Ranjit Vethecan. Colombo, *printed by*
Spartacus P.
*Vol. 1, no. 1, April–May 1975–?*

**3991** **Sportsman.** Colombo, East West Agency
**–4** *Vol. 1, no. 1 Aug. 1976–?*

**3992** **Sri Lanka** cricket quarterly. Colombo,
□ Frewin. illus. ports. scores, stats. *irregular*
*ed. by Edward J. Melder*
*Vol. 1, no. 1 Jan.-Mar. 1973*
*2 Apr.-Jun. 1973*
*3 Jul.-Sept. 1973*
*4 undated*
contd. as
**The Sri Lanka** cricketer; ed. by Edward
J. Melder
*Vol. 2, no. 1 1974? – no. 7 1977? –?*

## TOURNAMENTS

**3993** **[see no. 3994–2]**

**3994** **Board of Control for Cricket in Ceylon**
■ Final 50 over knock-out cricket tourna-
ment sponsored by Browns Group and
conducted by the B.C.C.C. for the
Browns Group Challenge Trophy on
March 26, 1972 at N.C.C. grounds:
Nondescripts C.C. vs. Singalese S.C.
Colombo, the Board, [1972]. 6p. folded
card

**3994** Tournament cricket in Sri Lanka 1977–78.
**–1** [Colombo, the Board, 1978]. [60]p. incl.
■ adverts. scores, stats.
——1979–80. [1979]

**3994** **Burgher Recreational Club**
**–2** Annual six-a-side inter club cricket tournament; sponsored by the Ceylon
Observer and Maharaja Organisation:
[souvenir programme]. Colombo.
*1969 to date*

**3994** **Ceylon Daily News** 50 over cricket tour-
**–3** nament, April 19 – 6 May, 1968.
Colombo, Ceylon Daily News, [1968].
24p.

3994 **Colombo Colts Cricket Club**
-4 3rd annual double wicket tournament, 17 & 18 August; sponsored by N. Vaithalungam & Co. Ltd., for N. Vaithalungam Challenge Trophy. Colombo, the Club, [1974]. [4]p. fold
—— 6th annual . . . tournament, 20–21 August, 1977. [1977]. [4]p. fold
*rules, records, participating teams*

3995 **Colombo Cricket Club**
1967 single wicket cricket championship for the Times of Ceylon Trophy. Colombo, the Club, 1967. 12p.

3996 **Kandy Prison Department Recreation Club**
Single wicket cricket competition, 4 and 5 April, 1968. St. Anthony's College Grounds, Kandy. [Kandy, the Club, 1968]

3996 **Mercantile Cricket Association**
-1 Six-a-side tournament (35 over). Homa-
□ gama, the Assoc., 1973?
——2nd annual six-a-side tournament sponsored by Lever Brothers (Ceylon) Ltd. Final 10th May 1975, B.R.C. Grounds. Colombo, the Assoc., 1975. 52p. incl. adverts. illus. ports.
——3rd annual six-a-side tournament and M.C.A. Ball. 1976

3997 **[Ondatje, F.],** *compiler*
Handbook to inter-club tournament 1940–1941 for Daily News challenge cup, run under the aegis of the Ceylon Cricket Association; compiled by Wanderer. Colombo, Ceylon Observer P., [1940]. 40p.

**Europeans v. Ceylonese (in chronological order)**

3998 **Foenander, E.W.**
■ Test match cricket in Ceylon: Europeans vs. Ceylonese: an illustrated souvenir of the fourteenth struggle for supremacy . . . 1911. Wellawatte, [printed for the Author] by Industrial Home P., [1911]. 11p. ports. scores
——the fifteenth struggle . . . 1912. Colombo, Ceylon Sportsman, 1912. 16p. ports. scores

3998 **Wootler, S.T.,** *compiler*
-1 The cricket test: Europeans v. Ceylonese, 1912. Colombo, Independent P., [1912].

3998 **Foenander, E.W.**
-2 Test match cricket in Ceylon: a souvenir of the sixteenth struggle . . . 1913. Wellawatta, *printed by* Boys Industrial Home P., [1913]. 28p.

3999 **[Foenander, Samuel Peter]**
■ The European Ceylonese cricket match,

1913: the sixteenth struggle for supremacy. Colombo, "Amicus", [1913]. 12p. incl. adverts. ports. stats.
*pre-match*

3999 **Foenander, E.W.**
-1 Test match cricket in Ceylon: European vs. Ceylonese: a souvenir of the seventeenth struggle for supremacy. Colombo, *printed by* Frewin & Co., [1914]. 8p.

3999 **Wootler, S.T.,** *compiler*
-2 Test match cricket in Ceylon: Europeans vs. Ceylonese: eighteenth struggle for supremacy. Colombo, Independent P., [1915].

3999 **Foenander, Samuel Peter ("Onlooker",**
-3 *pseud.)*
Test match cricket in Ceylon: complete scores of all matches from 1887–1920, by "Onlooker". Colombo, Indpendent P., 1920

3999 **Wootler, S.T.,** *compiler*
-4 Test match cricket in Ceylon – Europeans vs. Ceylonese: an illustrated souvenir of the 20th struggle for supremacy. Colombo, Independent P., 1922. 12p.

4000 **Wootler, S.T.**
The cricket test: Europeans vs. Ceylonese . . . 1923. Colombo, Ceylon Independent P., 1923. 16p. ports.

4001 **Foenander, Samuel Peter**
Europeans v. Ceylonese at cricket. Colombo, Independent P., 1924. 9p. illus.

4002 **Lipton Ltd**
■ A souvenir of to-day's Test match Europeans vs. Ceylonese, 6th March, 1925. [Colombo, Lipton, 1925]. 24p. incl. adverts. ports. stats.

4003 **Foenander, Samuel Peter**
The struggle for supremacy: the twenty-third contest, Europeans vs. Ceylonese at cricket: March 6th & 7th 1925 . . . a complete record of the series of the Tests, 1887–1924: souvenir of the 23rd match. Colombo, Independent P., [1925]. 12p. ports.

4004 A complete history of Test cricket in
■ Ceylon: Europeans vs. Ceylonese 1887–1927. [Colombo], printed at C.A.C.P., [1929]. 48p. ports. scores

**FIRMS, PROFESSIONS, etc.**

4005 **Ceylon Combined Banks Cricket Association**
Festival cricket: Ceylon Combined Banks XI v. Ceylon Board of Control XI on 21st

March, 1968. at N.C.C. Grounds, Maitland Place. Colombo, the Assoc., 1968. 72p. incl. adverts. ports. stats.

**4006 Ceylon Daily Mirror**
The Mirrox XI vs. the C.C.A. President's XI at Colombo Oval on February 28, 1961: [souvenir programme]. [Colombo]. Ceylon Daily Mirror, [1961]. 10p. ports.
*The Mirror XI was captained by G.S. Sobers and included Conrad Hunte, R. Kanhai, W. Hall*

**4007 Ceylon Government Service Cricket**
■ **Association**
Golden jubilee 1907–1957; souvenir; [compiled by S.P. Foenander]. Colombo, the Assoc., [1958?]. 114p. illus. ports. stats.

**4007 Ceylon Tobacco Co. Ltd., Sports Club**
**–1** Cricket tour of South India Nov.–Dec., 1976. [Colombo, the Club, 1976]. 12p. incl. adverts. ports.

**4007 de Silva, W.M.K.,** *editor*
**–2** The Colombo Municipal C.C. tour of India 1959. [Colombo, the Club, 1959]. 40p. incl. adverts. ports.

**4007 Inter Banks** 50 over tournament: sou-
**–3** venir. The Combined Banks Souvenir Cttee., 1967

**4007 Nationalised Services Cricket**
**–4 Association**
First six-a-side cricket tournament and 2nd annual prize distribution 1969–70. Colombo, the Assoc., [1969].

**4007 The Post & Telegraph Library and Recre-**
**–5 ation Club**
Rules. The Club, 1891. 8p.
*issued free to members, 18 Feb. 1891*

**4007 The Railway Cricket Club**
**–6** Rules. The Club, 1891. 10p.
*issued free to members*

**4007 Railway Sports Club** souvenir 1961.
**–7** Colombo, the Club, [1961]. 82p. incl. adverts.
*includes a review of the cricket season*

# SCHOOLS AND COLLEGES

**4007 Ceylon Daily Mirror**
**–8** Schools 50 over tournament for Vaseline Trophy. [Colombo], Ceylon Daily Mirror.
*annual*
*1971/1971–75/to date?*

**4008 Ceylon Schools Cricket Association**
■ London Schools vs. Ceylon Schools, the Oval [Colombo], January 18th and 19th,

1966. Colombo, the Assoc., [1966]. [28]p. ports.
*pre-match*

**4008 Primary Schools Cricket Association**
**–1** Primary schools cricket championship March 1967: official, souvenir. The Assoc., [1967].

**4008 Sri Lanka Schools Cricket Association**
**–2** Sri Lanka Schools All Island U–12 cricket final: Ananda v. Nalanda. Colombo, the Assoc., [1976]

## Ananda v. Nalanda

**4008 Ananda-Nalanda** cricket encounter 1954,
**–3** the silver jubilee, 3rd and 4th April, at the Colombo Oval: souvenir edited by Fernando Laksman and Tilak Arthenayake. Colombo, [1954].
——Ananda–Nalanda golden jubilee: 50th Battle of the Maroons. Swaska P., [1979]. 90p. incl. adverts.
*cover printed in Sinhalese*
*annual matches, each with own pre-match souvenir*

## Law College v. Medical College

**4008 Law – Medical** 54th encounter, N.C.C.
**–4 ■** Grounds, 17 & 18 May. . . .Colombo, Law College Editorial Board, 1974. 68p. incl. adverts. ports.

## Mahinda College

**4008 Mahinda College** v. Mahinda College
**–5** Old Boys' Association, July 1978: souvenir to commemorate the Mahinda team when it was judged the best school team by S. Wijeratna & V. Vitharana. The College, [1978]. 28p. incl. adverts. scores

## Mahinda College v. Richmond College

**4009 Mahinda** vs. Richmond souvenir. Galle.
□ *annual.*
*1949 to date*
*1955 with title: Mahinda—Richmond golden jubilee souvenir; edited and compiled by M.A. Dharmasena De Silva. Galle, [Mahinda College], 1955. 126p. incl. adverts. ports. scores, stats.*
*1979 with title: Mahinda-Richmond 74th lovers quarrel 1979; edited by Chandana Gunawardin and Amanda Wijewicksema*

**4010 Richmond-Mahinda** souvenir. Galle.
□ *annual*
*1949 ? to date*
*1965 with title: Richmond-Mahinda diamond jubilee 1965; souvenir; editors, S. Wijeratna, T. Wijeratna, V. Vitharana.*

334

[1965]. 62p. incl. adverts. ports. score, stats.

**4010** **Richmond College** centenary (1876–
**-1** 1976). Colombo, *printed by* Aitken Spence Ltd., [1976]
   *cricket pp.94–100*

## Royal College v. St. Thomas' College

**4010** **Brooke Bond Ltd.**
**-2** Official score card of Royal-Thomian centenary match 1979. Colombo, Brooke Bond Ltd., 1979. ports.
   *portraits of players on both covers*

**4010** **Chetty, Mervyn Casie,** *and others*
**-3** A history of a hundred years of the Royal
■ – S. Thomas' cricket. Colombo, the Royal-Thomian Centenary Match Joint Central Committee of the Royal College Union and S. Thomas' College Old Boys Association, [1979]. 202p. illus. ports. scores, stats.

**4011** **Foenander, E.W.,** *editor*
■ Royal vs. St. Thomas': a complete record of all the matches played between the two colleges 1880 to 1917. Colombo, Ceylon Saturday Review, 1918. 62p. scores, stats.

**4012** **Foenander, Samuel Peter**
■ Royal vs. St. Thomas': an illustrated souvenir of the 46th match. A complete & authentic record of all matches 1880–1924. [Colombo], "Independent" P., [1924]. 21p. ports. scores, stats.
   *pre-match*

**4013** History of Royal—St. Thomas' cricket.
■ Colombo, *printed by* Times of Ceylon, 1949. [1],vi,112p. illus. ports. scores, stats.

**4014** **Morning Leader**
■ The great inter-collegiate match, Royal vs. St. Thomas', March 1911: souvenir; some reminiscences with this year's teams, past records and figures. [Colombo], Morning Leader, [1911]. [8]p. incl. adverts. team ports. stats.
   *pre-match*

**4015** **Perera, S.S.,** *compiler*
■ Four score & ten 1879–1969: history of the Royal-St. Thomas' match. Colombo, the Author, [1969]. 260p. ports. scores, stats.

**4016** **Royal** vs. S. Thomas: annual encounter.
□ team port. scores, stats.
   *issued in 2 series: Royal souvenir and Thomian souvenir with different text and illus.*

——Royal souvenir
  *season?/1911,13,16,18   . . .61. . .72/to date*
   *1979* with title: *Royal souvenir 1880–1979 centenary encounter; edited by Mrs. Indianee Seneiratne. Colombo, Royal College, [1979]. 158p. with adverts.*
——Thomian souvenir
  *season ?/1964,1977/to date*
   *match first played 1880; titles vary, e.g. Battle of the Blues*
   *1979* with title: *St. Thomas College, Mount Lavima, 8,9,10, March 1979 – 100 – S.S.C. Grounds. Centenary Battle of the Blues. 158p. incl. adverts.*

**4016** **Royal**–Thomian cricket centenary dinner,
**-1** Holiday Inn, Colombo, Friday, March 9, 1979: menu card
   *gives names of all past players from both schools attending the dinner*

## St. John's v. Central College

**4016** **St. Johns** – Central cricket match 1968:
**-2** the 70th match. Jaffna Central Grounds. Jaffna, *printed by* St. Joseph's Catholic P., for T.I. Abraham of Central College, [1968]

## St. Joseph's v. St. Peter's

**4017** **Josephian**–Peterite cricket encounter.
□ *annual*
   *1935?* to date
   *titles vary*
   *1979* with title: *Josephian-Peterite match 45th encounter 16 & 17 March 1979 at Saravanamuttu Stadium; edited by Daya Jayaswriya*

**4018** **Perera, C.E. Maurice,** *and* **Cooray,**
■ **Marius,** editors
Souvenir of the Josephian-Peterite cricket match, 23rd & 24th March 1956: twenty second encounter. Ratmalana, *printed by* Universal Printers, [1956]. 32p. ports.
   *pre-match*

## Thurstan v. Issipathana

**4018** **Thurstan** Issipathana 5[th] cricket en-
**-1** counter 1968, 3,4, April. S.S.C. Grounds.
■ Executive Cttee. of Thurstan College O.B.U., [1968]. [60]p. incl. adverts. illus. ports. stats.
   *annual encounters since 1964: 1979 with title:* Thurstan-Issipathana, 1979: 30 & 31 March 1979: 16th encounter at Colombo Oval; edited by Anura Dias, W.R.M. Abeysekera, & D.R.L. Ranaweera. Kelaniya, *printed by* Deepa Printers, [1979]. 82p. incl. adverts.

## OLD SCHOOL CLUBS

4019 **The Quadrangular** Cup Cricket Tourna-
■ ment. Old Antonians, Old Benedictines,
Old Josephians, Old Peterites: 5th annual
encounter, 27th August 1967, St. Joseph's
Grounds. Colombo. Colombo, *printed by*
Caxton Printing Works. [1967]. [36]p.
*contains results of previous matches and
historical accounts of clubs*

## CLUBS

### Badulla

4019 **Badulla Cricket Association**
–1 Souvenir & fixture card 1967; review of
previous years tournament. Badulla, the
Assoc., [1967]

4019 **Uva Club**
–2 Rules 1950. Badulla, the Club, [1950].
28p.
——1968

### Batticoloa

4019 **Batticoloa Cricket Club**
–3 Rules. Grounds – Batticoloa Esplanade.
Batticoloa, the Club, 1921. 8p.

### Colombo

4020 **Colombo Cricket Club**
Rules. Colombo, Times Office, 1893. 12p.

4020 Centenary year celebrations: 50 over tour-
–1 nament, Aug. 1973. Colombo, the Club,
[1973]. [4]p. fold

4021 **Foenander, Samuel Peter**
■ C[olombo] C.C. v. Up-country: a complete record of fifty years' cricket 1875–
1925. Colombo, C.A.C. Press, [1925]. [i],
92p. ports. scores, stats.

### *Bloomfield*

4021 **Bloomfield Cricket & Athletic Club**
–1 Souvenir XXVIth anniversary – 1919. The
Club, [1919]

4022 Diamond jubilee 1893–1953; compiled by
■ S.P. Foenander. Colombo, the Club,
1954. 58p. incl. adverts. illus. ports.
score, stats.

4023 75th jubilee souvenir, 1893–1968. Co-
■ lombo, the Club, 1968. 68p. incl. adverts.
illus. ports.

4023 Ceremonial opening of new grounds at
–1 Reid Avenue, 7 September '75. Colombo,
■ the Club, 1975. [96]p. incl. adverts. illus.
ports.

### *Colombo Colts*

4024 **Boer** prisoners in Ceylon: report of a
■ cricket match between an eleven selected
from the prisoners of war at Diyatalawa
and the Colombo Colts; played on the
ground of the Nondescript Cricket Club,
Victoria Park . . . July 5th and 6th, 1901.
Colombo, Independent P., 1901. 18p. 1
illus.
*rptd. from "The Ceylon Independent". The
title-page and much of the text were reproduced on pp.330–332 of "Cricket", 8th Aug.
1901*

4024 **Colombo Colts Cricket Club**
–1 Rules. Colombo, the Club, 1893
*reorganised July 1886*

4025 "Six wickets" Carnival in aid of Colombo
■ Colts Cricket Club ground fund, 2,3,4
December 1949. Havelock Park, Colombo. Colombo, [the Club], 1949. [40]p.
incl. adverts. ports.
*includes brief history of Club*

4026 Centenary 1873–1973: [edited by S.S.
■ Perera]. Colombo, the Club, [1973]. 134p.
incl. adverts. ports. scores, stats.

4027 Centenary year celebration: 2nd annual
■ double wicket tournament, 4th and 5th
August, 1973, sponsored by N. Vaitilingam & Co. Ltd., for the N. Vaitilingam
Challenge Trophy. [Colombo, the Club,
1973]. [6]p. stats.

4028 **Foenander, Samuel Peter**
History of the Colombo Colts Cricket
Club. Colombo, Caxton Printing Works,
1941. [xii],95p. ports.

### *Colombo Malay*

4029 **All Ceylon Malay Cricket Association**
■ The jubilee book of the Colombo Malay
Cricket Club. Colombo, Ceylon Ob-
server, 1924. vii,208p. illus. scores

4029 **Colombo Malay Cricket Club**
–1 Malay centenary book commemorating
the centenary of the Colombo Malay
Cricket Club (1872–1972), and the golden
jubilee of the All Malay Association
(1922–1972). Colombo, the Club, 1972.
53p.

### *Magpies*

4030 **The Magpies Cricket Club**
□ [Handbook]. [Colombo], the Club.
*annual?*
*season?/1962–63/–?*
*rules, officers, membership, fixtures*

*Moon Sports Club*

**4030** **Mashoor, S.M.H.**, *and others, compilers*
**-1** Moon Sports Club: golden jubilee souvenir 1908–1958. Colombo, *printed by* Rokeby P., [1958]

*Nondescripts*

**4031** **Nondescripts Cricket Club**
■ 75th anniversary souvenir, 1963. Colombo, the Club, [1963]. 84p. incl. adverts. ports. stats.

*Sinhalese Sports Club*

**4031** **de Silva, Henry A.**
**-1** Sinhalese Sports Club (1899–1940): memoirs and comments. Colombo, [the Club (?), 1940]. 27p.

**4032** **Sinhalese Sports Club**
■ S.S.C. souvenir 1899–1952; compiled by S.P. Foenander. Colombo, the Club, 1952. 94p. ports. scores, stats.

*Tamil Union*

**4033** **[Perumal, Joseph]**, *editor*
Tamil Union Cricket and Athletic Club 1899–1959: diamond jubilee souvenir. [Colombo, the Club, 1959]. 182p. incl. adverts. ports.

**4033** Tamil Union Cricket & Athletic Club
**-1** 1899–1974: seventy-fifth anniversary. Colombo, *printed by* Rajah P., 1974

**4034** **The Tamil** Union Cricket and Athletic Club. Colombo, H.W. Cave, 1926. 224p. illus. scores
*gives origin of Club, full score card of all matches 1903–1921, list of members, etc.*

**4034** **Tamil Union Cricket & Athletic Club**
**-1** Rules (reprint as amended) June 1964. Colombo, the Club, [1964]. 32p.

**4034** Seventy-fifth anniversary 1899–1974:
**-2** souvenir: edited by C.J. Gulasekharam.
■ Colombo, the Club, [1974]. [86]p. incl. adverts. ports.

*Dimbula*

**4034** **Jayewardene, Jayantha**, *editor*
**-3** A souvenir to commemorate the
■ centenary of the Dimbula Planters Association 1873–1973. Dimbula, the Assoc., [1973]. [136]p. incl. adverts. illus. ports.
*pp.62–7 'The Dimbula Athletic and Cricket Club'' by S.S. Perera*

**Galle**

**4034** **[Perera, S.S.]**, *compiler*
**-4** Pakistan v. Sri Lanka Board President's
■ XI . . . 11 & 12 January 1976, Galle Esplanade: souvenir to mark the above occasion and centenary celebrations of the Galle Cricket Club. Galle, the Club, [1976]. [40]p. incl. adverts.
*includes a brief history of Galle C.C.*

**Jaffna**

**4034** **Jaffna District Cricket Association**
**-5** Jaffna Combined XI vs. S.S. Perera's Sri
■ Lanka Schools Under 19 XI at St. John's College Grounds, Jaffna, 17 and 18 Sept. 1976. [20]p. incl. covers & adverts. ports.

**Kalutara**

**4035** **Kalutara Town Club**
■ Jubilee souvenir 1888–1963; edited by Peter de Zilva. [Kalutara, Ceylon, the Club, 1962]. [50]p. incl. adverts. illus. ports. stats.

**Kandy**

**4035** **Kandy Lake Club** presents cricket: Pala-
**-1** stan v. Up Country . . . August 25 & 26, 1964. Kandy, the Club, [1964]. 24p. incl. adverts.

**Matara**

**4036** **Matara Sports Club**
A souvenir in commemoration of the opening of the new pavilion . . . 1966. Matara, the Club, 1966
*includes an historical sketch of the Club by N.L. Rodrigo*

**4036** The constitution and rules, June 1967.
**-1** Matara, the Club, 1967. 18p.

**4036** Souvenir of Matara Combined XI vs. S.S.
**-2** Perera's Schools' U–19 XI played at Uyan-
■ watta Esplanade, Matara, on 3 & 4 July 1976. [Matara, the Club, 1976]. [12]p. incl. covers & adverts. team ports. score

**Panadura**

**4036** **Panadura Sports Club**
**-3** Rules and byelaws (revised). Panadura, the Club, 1964. 28p.

**4036** 50th anniversary (1924–1974): golden
**-4** jubilee souvenir. Panadura, the Club, [1974]

**Trincomalee**

4036
–5

■

**Trincomalee District Cricket & Athletic
Association**
Trincomalee District Cricket XI versus
S.S. Perera's Combined Schools U-19 XI
played at McHeyzer Stadium, Trincom-
alee, on 29 & 30 May 1977: souvenir.
[Trincomalee, the Assoc., 1977]. [12]p.
incl. adverts.

# CHARITY MATCH

4036
–6

**Cricket match** in aid of Ceylon War
Purposes Fund: Southern Province v.
Panadura & Kalutara District on Pana-
dura Sports Club Ground under the
patronage of His Excellency the Governor
Sir Andrew Caldecott, K.C.M.G., on 7th
September, 1940. [4]p. fold

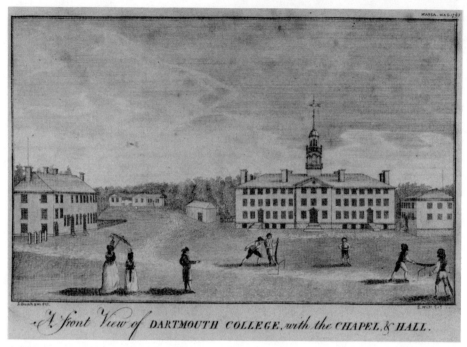

Cricket in the U.S.A. Cricket at Dartmouth College, an engraving published in the "Massachusetts Magazine", 1793 *photo: M.C.C.*

# CRICKET IN NORTH AMERICA AND BERMUDA

## CRICKET IN THE UNITED STATES

**4037 Chadwick, Henry**
■ Chadwick's American cricket manual, containing the revised laws of the game, with an explanatory appendix to each rule, instructions in bowling, batting, and fielding. Together with the averages of the leading clubs in America and the scores of the principal international contests of 1859, 1868, and 1872. New York, de Witt, 1873. 128p. illus. scores. (De Witt's Handbooks for the People)
——*another ed. with title:* De Witt's cricket guide, containing very full, plain and accurate information as to the best manner of bowling, batting and fielding . . . New York, de Witt, 1879. 105p. illus. diagrs. scores, stats.

**4038 Durant, John,** *and* **Bettmann, Otto**
Pictorial history of American sports from colonial times to the present. N.Y., Barnes, 1952. 280p. illus. ports.
*cricket pp.2,10,37 & 91*

**4039 Kelly, Frederick Fitzmaurice**
■ Centuries scored in the United States and Canada, 1844 to June 14th, 1902. Jersey City, Kelly, [1902]. 52p. stats.

**4039 Manchester, Herbert**
**–1** Four centuries of sport in America 1490–1890 illustrated from original sources. New York, The Derrydale P., 1931. xxiv,245p. illus. ports. facsims, bibliog.
——rptd. New York, Blom, 1968. 231 + 11p.
*cricket pp.120–23 with cricket illus. on p.126*

**4040 A new** book of sports; reprinted from the
■ "Saturday Review". Bentley, 1885. iv, 376p.
*includes "Cricket in America" pp.271–9*

**4041 Peverelly, Charles A.**
The book of American pastimes, containing a history of the principal base ball, cricket, rowing and yachting clubs of the United States. N.Y., the Author, 1866. 566p.
——2nd ed. 1868

**4042 Sayen, Henry**
■ A Yankee looks at cricket, as told to Gerald Brodribb. Putnam, 1956. viii,120p. illus. port. map, scores

### United States Cricket Association

**4043 United States Cricket Association**
Newsletter; edited by John Hayward. Los Angeles, the Association. *quarterly*
*No. 1. Dec. 1963/Feb. 1965/–?*
*restarted 1970 with title: Newsbrief; edited by Anthony Bathurst. monthly (8 months of yr.)*

**4044 England** tour 1968: souvenir edition. Los
■ Angeles, the Assoc., [1968]. [12]p. incl. adverts.
*pre-tour*

## ANNUALS

**4045 The American** cricket annual; compiled
■ and edited by Jerome Flannery. New York. scores, stats.
*1890. C.J. Sabiston*
*1891,92. The Week's Sport Co.*
*1893–1901. J. Flannery*
*1898–1901 with title: American cricket annual and golf guide*
*contd. as: Spalding's official cricket guide*

**4046 Cricket** schedule: edited by Jerome Flannery. New York. *annual*
*in Taylor: presumably a fixture list*

**4047 Spalding's** official cricket guide; compiled
■ and edited by Jerome Flannery. N.Y., American Sports Public Co. *annual. illus. ports. scores, stats.*
*1904–14*
*incorporated the American cricket annual after a lapse of 2 years, 1902–03*

**4048 Wright, George**
□ Cricket guide 1892. Boston, Mass., Wright & Dittson, 1892. 80p. port. diagrs. stats.
——*another ed.* N.Y., American Sports Publishing Co., 1894. 57p.

## PERIODICALS

4049 **American** cricket and kindred games:
■ devoted to the higher grade sport of
America. New York, The American
Cricket Office, 1890. ports. scores
*3 monthly issues, July, Aug., Sept., 1890*

4050 **The American** cricketer: a journal
□ devoted to the noble game of cricket.
Philadelphia (Pa.), Associated Cricket
Clubs of Philadelphia. *weekly* May to
Nov.; *monthly* Nov. to Apr. scores, stats.
*No. 1. 28 June, 1877 to April 1929*
*editors: F.H. Clarke, H.H. Cornish, Allen*
*J. King*

4051 **The American** cricketer: journal of the
□ United States Cricket Association. Los
Angeles, Calif., the Association. *2x a year*
(Spring & Fall). illus. ports. scores, stats.
*Vol. 1 No. 1. June, 1965 to date.*
*Editor–John Hayward*

4052 **Cricket** club life: a semi-monthly journal
□ devoted to the interests of the cricket
clubs. Philadelphia, Cricket Club Life
Publishing Co. illus. ports. scores, stats.
*Vol. 1 nos. 1–21 1st Sept. 1897 to 19 Aug.*
*1901*

4053 **The Mid-West** cricketer; edited by Robert
S. Blake. Bridgeton (Mo), Missouri C.A.
scores. *typescript*
*1964–?*
*Vol. 1. no. 1 Apr./May 1964*
*2 Jun./Jul.*
*3 Aug./Oct.*
*2. 1 Aug. 1965*
*2 Sep. 1965*
*3. 1 Aug. 1966*
*2 Dec. 1966*

## SCHOOLS AND UNIVERSITIES

### Concord. St. Paul's School

4054 **Pier, Arthur Stanwood**
St. Paul's School, 1855–1934. N.Y.,
Scribner, 1934. 385p. illus.
*cricket pp.24,79–82,85,142–7,187,188,*
*266,267; in Concord, New Hampshire*

### Pennsylvania University

4055 **Graham, Archibald Hunter**
Cricket at the University of Pennsylvania.
Burlington (Pa.), *privately printed*, 1930.
176p. illus. ports.

## TOURNAMENTS

4056 **Northwestern Cricket Association**
□ Souvenir of the sixth annual tournament
. . . August 17–24, 1901. Chicago, Ill.,
The Assoc., 1901. [16]p. illus. ports.
——tenth annual tournament . . . 1905.
Chicago, Ill., 1905. 4p.

## CALIFORNIA

4057 **California Cricket Association**
Year book. The Assoc., 1932. 64p.
*the only issue?*

4058 **Northern California Cricket Association**
Flannel. San Francisco, the Association.
*monthly*
*1967 to date*

4058 Fixtures. The Assoc. illus. *annual*
–1 *?/1979 to date*
□ *founded 1905; 1979 issue "featuring CCC*
*UK tour and how cricket is played"*

4059 **Southern California Cricket Association**
□ Official schedule. Los Angeles, the
Association
*?/1937/1960 . . . 1975/to date*
*later issues with title: Fixture schedule and*
*competition rules*

4060 Tour to Jamaica 1971. Los Angeles, the
■ Assoc., 1971. [8]p. incl. covers. ports.
*pre-tour*

4061 Year book. Los Angeles, the Association.
□ illus. ports. stats.
*1971 to date*
*editor: Anthony Bathurst*

## GEORGIA

### Savannah

4062 **The cricketer.** Savannah (Ga.), Savannah
□ C.C. *fortnightly.* illus. scores, stats.
*typescript*
*vol. 1, no. 1. June 1957–?*
*vol. 1, nos. 1,5 and 6 (June–Aug. 1957)*
*seen*

## ILLINOIS

4063 **Cricket** annual; edited by K.A. Auty.
■ Chicago, the Association. illus. scores,
stats.
*10 issues 1935–44 with varying titles:*
*1935–36: Cricket annual with supple-*
*mentary directory of allied clubs, societies*
*and associations*
*1937–39: Illinois C.A., and Illinois*
*Rugby Football Union. Cricket and rugby*

annual and directory of clubs and societies

1940–44: Illinois C.A. Illinois cricket annual (1940 with Rugby appendix; 1941–44 published by K.A. Auty)

**4064  Illinois Cricket Association**
Cricket festival; compiled by K.A. Auty. Chicago, the Assoc., 1933. 6p.

**4064**  Schedule and club secretaries. Chicago,
**–1**  the Assoc. *annual.* [4]p. folded card
□  *?/1943 . . . 1965/–?*

**4065  Illinois** sports review; edited by K.A. Auty. Chicago, the Editor. *occasional publication*
Vol. 1, no. 1. 17 May 1934/1934 . . .1941/ –?
*later issues with title: Illinois cricket review*

### Chicago

**4066  Chicago Cricket Club**
[Handbook]. Chicago, the Club. *annual.*
*?/1930–34/–?*
*1934 issue contains Club averages for 1933*

### Winnetka

**4066  Winnetka Cricket Club**
**–1**  [Fixture list]. Winnetka, the Club. *annual.*
□  [4]p. folded card
*?/1963,68,69/–?*
*founded 1928*

**4066**  Souvenir of the dinner dance held at Ferris
**–2**  Inn, Morton Grove, Ill. . . . Novem-
■  ber 29, 1940 . . . In celebration of their double achievement in winning the championship of the Illinois Cricket League and the K.A. Auty "Century of Progress Trophy". [Winnetka, the Club, 1940]. [4]p. illus.

**4066**  Souvenir of the dinner and entertainment
**–3**  held at Hearthstone House, Hubbard
■  Woods, Illinois . . . November 29, 1941. . . . In celebration of their double achievement in winning the championship of the Illinois Cricket League and the K.A. Auty "Century of Progress' Trophy for the second year in succession and the third time in four years. [Winnetka, the Club, 1941]. [4]p. with bs. supplement insert. illus.

## MASSACHUSETTS

**4067  Massachusetts State Cricket League**
Season of 1901. Needham Heights, Boston, the League, [1901]. 18p.
*annual?*

## MICHIGAN

### Detroit

**4068  Peninsular** Cricket Club. Detroit
*in Taylor (Appx. II)*

## NEW JERSEY

**4069  Leach, E.A.,** *compiler*
■  Union County Cricket Club handbook, season 1904, containing schedules of matches for the coming season, also summary of matches played in 1903, together with interesting items referring to the game of cricket. New Jersey, the Club, 1904. 22p. incl. adverts. illus. ports. diagr. stats.

**4070  New Jersey Athletic Cricket Club**
Souvenir. New Jersey, the Club, 1899
*in Taylor*

## NEW YORK

**4070  The Guardian**
**–1**  The bedside 'Guardian' 14: a selection
■  from The Guardian 1964–65. Collins, 1965. 256p. illus.
*includes pp.11–4, "Slip catchers in the rye", by Jim Markwick [on cricket in New York]*

**4071  Knickerbocker Club**
■  Knickerbocker Club [1859–62]. [New York], the Club, [1862]. 16p.
*formation, rules and list of members of the Club, 1859–62*

**4072  Knickerbocker Athletic Club**
The cherry diamond: [a newsletter] publi-shed for information of members of the . . . Club. New York, the Club.
*?/1898/1902/–*
*Lord's has Vol. V, no. 4, 15th Jan. 1902 8p.*

**4073**  Cricket schedule. New York, the Club. *annual?*
*?/1902/–?*

**4074  Manhattan Cricket Club**
Constitution and by-laws of the Manhattan Cricket Club of Brooklyn, N.Y.; incorporated 1866. As amended at annual meeting of the Club, October 15th, 1906. [Brooklyn, the Club, 1906]. 12p.

**4075  Metropolitan District Cricket League**
By-laws and constitution. New York, the League, 1906. 10p.
——Constitution and by-laws. Also the Laws of cricket . . . 1908. [1908]. 24p.

**4075** **New York & Metropolitan District**
**-1** **Cricket Association**
Constitution & by-laws. New York, the
Assoc., 1935. 16p.

**4075** **New York and New Jersey Cricket**
**-2** **Association**
Constitution and by-laws. New York, the
Assoc., 1910. 11p.
——*another issue.* 1914. 11p.

**4076** Schedule of matches. New York, the
Association. *annual*
*?/1923–25/–?*

**4076** **New York Cricket Association**
**-1** Constitution and by-laws. New York, the
Association, 1903. 11p.

**4077** **New York Veteran Cricketers'**
**Association**
Schedule of games. New York, the
Association. *annual?*
*season ?/1911/–?*

**4078** Constitution and by-laws. New York, the
Assoc., 1913. 11p.

**4078** **Staten Island Cricket and Lawn Tennis**
**-1** **Club**
Constitution and bylaws. New York, the
Club, *n.d.* 11p.

**4079** **Walker, Randolph St. George**
■ History of Staten Island Cricket and Lawn
Tennis Club 1872–1917, Livingston,
Staten Island. New York, the author,
[1917]. 24p. illus. ports.

# PENNSYLVANIA

**4080** **Bushnell, Edward Rogers**
Pennsylvania's athletic year of 1906–07.
Philadelphia, Winston, 1907

## Haverford

**4081** **[See no. 30–1]**

**4081** **Haverford College**
**-1** Athletic annual 1895–96. Published in the
interests of Haverford athletics by James
A. Babbitt . . . Philadelphia, Babbitt, for
the College, 1896. 80p. illus.
*cricket pp.39–70*

**4082** ——. *Alumni Association*
A history of Haverford College for the
first sixty years of its existence. Prepared
by a Committee of the Alumni Association. Philadelphia, Porter & Coates,
1892. 732p. illus. ports.
*contains numerous references to cricket in*
*Philadelphia*

## Philadelphia

**4083** **Associated Cricket Clubs of Philadelphia**
Rules adopted by the Associated Cricket
Clubs of Philadelphia to govern matches
in the Halifax, Philadelphia and A.C.C.
cup competitions. . . . Philadelphia, the
Clubs, 1915. 8p.

**4084** **International** cricket fete, 1872: official
■ handbook, containing the programme of
arrangements during the visit of the
English Gentlemen Eleven to Philadelphia. Philadelphia, Lippincott, 1872. 68p.
scores

**4085** **International Cricket Fetes Committee**
■ Official report on the international cricket
fetes at Philadelphia in 1868 and
1872. . . . together with a full account of
the visit of the English gentlemen cricketers, by R.A. Fitzgerald. . . .; also
"Cricket in America," "Cricket for
school-boys" . . . Philadelphia, Lippincott for the Committee, 1873. 38p. score

**4086** **Lester, John Ashby,** *editor*
■ A century of Philadelphia cricket. Philadelphia, Univ. of Pennsylvania P., 1951.
xviii,397p. illus. ports. diagr. map,
scores, stats. bibliog.

**4087** **Pleasants, Henry,** *junior*
From kilts to pantaloons. West Chester,
(Pa.), Horace F. Temple, 1945. 198p. illus.
*ch. xii "Green turf and white flannels"*
*pp.142–156 on cricket in Philadelphia*
*1890–1910*

**4088** **Taylor, Frank H.**
■ Youth and versatility. [Philadelphia], S.S.
White Dental Mfg. Co., 1919. 6p.
*report on Philadelphia cricket and the*
*author's performances in 1919*

**4089** **Wister, William Rotch**
■ Some reminiscences of cricket in Philadelphia before 1861. Philadelphia, Allen,
Lane and Scott, 1904. 144p. illus. port.
scores

## Chestnut Hill

**4090** **Chestnut Hill Cricket Club**
Reports and papers, 1878–1880
*collection in Philadelphia Library of the*
*Historical Society of Pennsylvania*

## Germantown

**4091** **Germantown Cricket Club**
Laws, instructions and record of matches
from 1855 to 1866. Philadelphia, Lippincott, 1867

4092 Roll of members and constitution; with the laws of cricket, etc. Philadelphia, Lippincott, 1867. 70p. illus.

4093 Annual report. Philadelphia, the Club.
*?/1911,1913–24/–?*
*not issued 1912*

4094 Charter, by-laws, rules, officers and
■ members. [Philadelphia, the Club], 1893. 105p.
——1901. 99p.
——1911. 99p.
——1914. 96p.

4095 **Newhall, George Morgan**
■ "The cricket grounds of Germantown and a plea for the game". *In* Papers read before the Site and Relic Society of Germantown. Germantown, the Society, 1910. illus. port. map
*an address delivered before the Society 11th March, 1910, pp.167–91*

4096 **100 years** of the Germantown Cricket Club. Philadelphia, the Club, 1954. 31p. illus.

*Merion*

4097 **Merion Cricket Club**
□ Charter, by-laws, house and ground rules, officers and members. Philadelphia, the Club, 1894. 90p. illus.
——*another ed.* 1902. 112p. illus. plan
——*another ed.* 1917

4098 Papers and reports, 1900–1907
*collection of papers in the Philadelphia Library of the Historical Society of Pennsylvania*

4099 Semi-centennial. Philadelphia, the Club, 1915. 8p

4100 Bulletin. Philadelphia, the Club
*?/1917/–?*
*the only issue recorded Sept. 1917. 12p.*

4101 **The Merion** Cricket Club, 1865–1965: being a brief history of the Club for the first hundred years of its existence, together with its roll of officers and members to 1965: [by Charles K.B. Wister]. Philadelphia, [the Club], 1965. [132]p. illus.

*Philadelphia C.C.*

4102 **Lippincott, Horace Mather**
■ A history of the Philadelphia Cricket Club, 1854 to 1954. [Philadelphia, the Club], 1954. 132p. illus. ports. score, stats.

4103 **Philadelphia Cricket Club**
Annual report. Philadelphia, the Club.
*1854/1886. . .1910/–?*

4104 Collection of papers, 1854–1929
*in the Philadelphia Library of the Historical Society of Pennsylvania*

4105 Circular. Philadelphia, the Club, 1858.3p.

4106 Constitution and by-laws, as revised
□ January 11, 1858: to which are added the Laws of cricket and some instructions for the young cricketer. Philadelphia, the Club, [1858]. 39p.
*'Instructions' by J. Pycroft*
*also issued 1883 [no instructions], 1886, 1890,1894,1897,1898,1902,1905 (Taylor); and 1911*

*Prior*

4107 **Prior** Cricket Club of Philadelphia tour of
■ England 1972. Philadelphia (Pa.), [1972]. [8]p.
*souvenir programme; pre-tour*

# RHODE ISLAND

4108 **Rhode Island and District Amateur Cricket League**
[Handbook]. Providence, the League.
*season ?/1912,1913/–?*

# VIRGINIA

4109 **Byrd, William**
The secret diary of William Byrd of Westover 1709–1712; edited by Louis B. Wright and Marion Tinling. Richmond (Va), the Dietz P., 1941. xxviii,622p. facsims.
*references to early cricket in Virginia, 1709–10*

# CRICKET IN CANADA

**4110 Canadian Cricket Association**
Revised constitution and by-laws.
[Toronto], the Assoc., 1909. 7p.

**4111 Hall, John E.,** *and* **McCulloch, R.O.**
■ Sixty years of Canadian cricket. Toronto,
Bryant Publishing Co., 1895. xvi,572p. 1
illus. ports. scores, stats.
*includes reminiscences by Colonel N.W.
Wallace and T.C. Patteson*

**4112 Hunter, Robert,** *junior*
■ Quebec to Carolina in 1785–6; being the
travel diary and observations of Robert
Hunter, jr., a young merchant of London;
edited by Louis B. Wright and Marion
Tinling. San Marino, (Calif.), The Huntingdon Library, 1943. ix,393p. map.
*entry for Sunday, 29th May, 1785 at
Montreal: "After tea we took a walk with Mr.
Lilly to a place called Vauxhall. They have a
very good assembly room and a pretty good
garden. The Canadians were playing at bowls,
cricket, and——. after having had their
consciences eased with the* grand fete *in the
morning."*

**4112 Kelly, Frederick Fitzmaurice**
**–1** Centuries scored in the United States and
■ Canada, 1844 to June 14th, 1902. Jersey
City, Kelly, [1902]. 52p. stats.

**4113 Whiting, Colin F.**
■ Cricket in Eastern Canada. Montreal,
Colmur, 1963. [vi],397p. illus. ports.
scores, stats.

## ANNUALS

**4114 Canadian Cricket Association**
□ Handbook. Toronto, the Association.
*annual.* scores, stats.
*1959/1959 . . . 69/to date*
*a record of Canadian cricket for the previous
season; 1959 issue edited by D. King and
Kenneth R. Bullock; 1969 issue by K.R.B.*

**4115 The Canadian** cricketer's guide and re-
□ view of the past season
*1858: by members of the St. Catherines
Cricket Club. St. Catherines, Constitution
Office. 74p.*
*1876. 1877; compiled by T.D. Phillipps and
H.J. Campbell. Ottawa, the Compilers. 133
+ 133p. mounted ports. scores, stats.*
*1877 = third year [on t.p.]*

**4116 The Daily News**
■ Cricket and football annual & sports-

man's almanac. St. John's, Newfound-
land, Daily News.
*1897. 103p. ports. scores, stats.
other issues?*

**4117 Toronto** cricket annual: edited by "Evan
■ Dale". Toronto. Toronto & Distriet
Cricket Council. illus. scores, stats.
*1921. 144p. illus.
1922 with title: Canadian cricket annual.
144p.
1923 with title: Canadian cricket annual.
142p.*

## PERIODICALS

**4118 The Canadian** cricket field: a journal
■ devoted to the interests of cricket in
Canada. Toronto. scores
*16 issues, 10th May to 17th Sept., 1882
A.G. Brown and G.G.S. Lindsey, editors
and proprietors*

**4119 The Canadian** cricketer; edited by E.H.M.
■ Burn. St. Catherines, Ontario. *monthly.
typescript. scores, stats.
Jan. 1952–Dec. 1964
Vol. 8, 1959 no issues July, Aug.
9, 1960 no issues June, July, Aug.
10, 1961 no issues July, Aug.
11, 1962 May/June combined issue,
July, Aug. not issued
12, 1963 May/June combined issue,
July, Aug. not issued
13, 1964 May/June was last issue
except for notice of termination Dec.
1964*

**4120 The Canadian** cricketer: the official maga-
□ zine of the Canadian Cricket Association;
edited by K.R. Bullock. Toronto, Sport
Federation of Canada. illus. ports. scores,
stats. *3x a year*
*Vol. 1, no.1 March 1972 to date
Vol.7, no.2 March 1979 World Cup '79
number*

**4121 The Canadian** cricketer: a petite journal
devoted to the weekly record of cricket in
Canada; edited by Arthur B. Morrison.
Toronto, Jackson-Davies P. illus. ports.
*19 issues, vol. 1, no. 1 (May 24, 1911) to
vol. 2, no. 4 (May 29, 1912)
vol. 2 with title: The Canadian cricketer
and amateur sports*

**4122 Cricket** and rugger times; edited by A.R.
Pryde. Montreal, St. Lawrence Rugger

and Cricket Association. Inc. *monthly*
*May–December*. illus. scores
*May 1961/June 1965/to date?*

4123　**Cricket** magazine; editor N.K. Vale.
■　Montreal, Cricket Magazine Co. illus.
ports. scores. stats.
*vol. 1 no. 1. March, 1934*
*2. April, 1934*
*3. May–June, 1934*
*other issues?*

## SCHOOLS AND COLLEGES

4124　**Trinity** College School Cricket Club:
■　records of matches, averages, analysis,
&c. from 1867 to 1887; compiled by Peter
Perry. Port Hope, Ontario, *printed by*
Guide Steam Book and Job Printing
Establishment, 1887. 13p. stats.
——*enlarged ed. with title:* The complete
records of the Trinity College School
Cricket Club 1867–1893; compiled by
E.M. Watson. Port Hope (Ontario), W.
Williamson, 1893. 54p. 1 illus. stats.

4125　**Upper Canada College,** *Toronto*
■　An invitation to observe the centenary of
Old Boys' cricket and the half-century of
Norval on June 1st. 1963. Toronto, the
College, [1963]. [8]p. folded card (5p. of
text)

## TOURNAMENTS

4126　**Ontario Cricket Association**
■　Junior interprovincial cricket tournament
1962, July 2 to July 7, at Ridley College,
St. Catherines and The Toronto Cricket,
Skating & Curling Club: souvenir programme. Toronto, the Assoc., [1962].
[20]p. incl. adverts.

4127　Senior inter-provincial cricket tourna-
ment programme [and] Canada vs.
M.C.C. Ottawa, 1967. [Ottawa], the
Assoc., [1967]. 8p. port.

*Western Canada*

4128　**British Columbia Cricket Association**
Souvenir programme Western Canada
tournament. Vancouver, the Assoc.,
1923. 16p. illus.

4129　**Manitoba Cricket Association**
Souvenir programme Western Canada
tournament. [Winnipeg, the Assoc.],
1924. 16p.

4130　**Western Canada Cricket Association**
Programme and scorecard, Western
Canada cricket tournament, Edmonton,
Alta. Edmonton, the Assoc., 1926. 4p.

4131　Cricket throughout the Empire souvenir
■　programme Alberta Tournament, Edmonton, Aug. 2nd to 7th, 1926; edited
by George Dewe. Edmonton, the Assoc.,
[1926]. iii,74p. incl. adverts. ports.

## ALBERTA

### Calgary

4132　**Calgary and District Cricket League**
Cricket handbook and fixtures. Calgary,
the League. *annual*
*?/1960,61/–?*

### Edmonton

4132　**The Edmonton** athlete: a journal devoted
–1　to all sport and pastime. Edmonton
(Alberta). illus.
*Vol. 1, no.2 (June 3rd, 1913) is devoted*
*mainly to the visit to Edmonton by the*
*Australians*

4133　**Edmonton Cricket League**
■　Smoking concert, Corona Hotel, March
21, '12: souvenir programme. Edmonton,
the League, 1912. 42p. incl. adverts. ports.
stats.
——Nov. 27, 1912. 64p. incl. adverts. illus.
ports. stats.
*with brief histories of League clubs*

4134　The Edmonton cricketer: an occasional
□　newsletter of the Edmonton Cricket
League. Edmonton (Alberta), the League.
illus. scores, *later issues typescript*
*1970/Vol. III, no. 1, Jan. 1977/to date?*

4134　**Edmonton's** sporting review and motor-
–1　ing journal. Edmonton (Alberta). *weekly*
□　*Vol. 1, no. 1 June 22, 1913/no.6 Aug.2,*
*1913/–?*
*includes cricket*

## BRITISH COLUMBIA

4135　**British Columbia Cricket Club**
Tour of England 1972. [The Club]. 4p.
illus.
*pre-tour*

4136　**British Columbia Mainland Cricket**
□　**League**
Official fixture list. Vancouver, the
League. *annual.* stats.
*1914?/1950 . . . 1977/to date*

4137　Cricket: fifty years of the game in
Vancouver, British Columbia, Canada,
1889 to 1938. Vancouver, the League,
[1938]. 24p. illus.

4138 British Columbia cricket festival 1939.
■ Vancouver, the League, [1939]. 28p. incl.
adverts.

4139 Canadian centennial cricket handbook.
■ Vancouver, the League, [1967]. 73p.
ports.
*yearbook of club cricket in B.C. for 1967
season*

**Vancouver**

4140 **Hann, Frank M.**
The Burrard story: 50 years of club
cricket, 1905–1954. Vancouver, Burrard
C.C., 1954. 20p. ports. scores

4141 **North Shore Cricket Club**
■ 6th annual North Shore cricket week,
August 24 to August 29, 1936 under the
auspices of The British Columbia Cricket
Association and the North Shore Cricket
Club. Vancouver, the Club, 1936. 28p.
incl. adverts.
*score book; pre-matches*

4141 **Vancouver Island Vagabonds Touring**
–1 **Cricket Club**
■ Club prospectus and membership application. [Victoria (B.C.), the Club, 1977].
[8]p.
*founded 1977 by Dave Barnicot*

4141 Who are the Vancouver Island Vaga-
–2 bonds? [Victoria (B.C.), the Club, 1978?].
■ [4]p. fold.

**Victoria**

4142 **Victoria and District Cricket Association**
□ [Handbook]. Victoria, the Association
*season ?/1958 . . . 1963/to date*
*1979 edited by David Barnicot*

## MANITOBA

4142 **Hargrave, Joseph James**
–1 Red River. Montreal, *printed for* the
Author, 1871. 506p.
*contains the earliest reference to the form-
ation of a cricket club in Manitoba (1864)*

4143 **Manitoba Cricket Association**
□ Official handbook, rules and fixtures.
Winnipeg, the Association. *annual.* illus.
port. stats. *in v.y.*
*?/1953 . . . 1965/to date*
*in 1958 title changed to: Official yearbook*
*Centennial yearbook issued 1965, edited by
Harry Davies, containing 12pp. of history*

4144 **Weighton, William**
■ Cricket . . . our weakness: a chronicle of
the many trials and few triumphs of
Manitoba's cricketers between 1948 and
1955. Winnipeg, Manitoba C.A., 1957.
93p. scores, stats.

4144 "The story of 100 years of cricket in Mani-
–1 toba". *In* Manitoba pageant; edited by
■ William J. Fraser. Vol. XX, no.1, Autumn
1974. pp.2–7

**Winnipeg**

4145 **Western Canada Cricket Association**
■ Welcome to Winnipeg, August 1st to 6th
inclusive, 1910. Winnipeg, the Assoc.,
[1910]. 12p. illus.
*the only cricket text, a brief account of the
Association, appears on the covers*

4146 **Winnipeg Cricket Club**
■ Cricket? Certainly! Winnipeg . . . of
course! (since 1864!): [appeal for
members]. Winnipeg, the Club, [1967].
[6]p. fold. illus.

## NEW BRUNSWICK

**Moncton**

4146 **Machum, Lloyd A.**
–1 A history of Moncton town and city
1855–1965. Moncton (New Brunswick),
the City Corporation, 1965. 447p. illus.
ports.
*cricket pp.142,192,196*

## NEWFOUNDLAND

4147 **Myler, P.J.**
■ Recollections of cricket. St. Johns, New-
foundland, Evening Herald, 1915. 86p.
stats.

## NOVA SCOTIA

4148 **Grand** cricket tournament at Halifax,
■ Nova Scotia . . . on August 18th and
following days. [1874]. [4]p. fold.
*fixtures, prizes, rules & conditions*

## ONTARIO

4149 **Ontario Cricket Association**
□ The annual record. The Association.
*1880–?*
*1880; compiled by the Honorary Secretary.
Philadelphia, the American Cricketer, 1881.
23p. scores. stats.*

4150 Constitution and by-laws. The Association, 1886

## Galt

4151　**Galt Cricket Club**
[Handbook]. Galt, the Club. *annual*. illus.
　*?/1958/*to date?

## Hamilton

4152　**Hamilton and District Cricket League**
[Handbook]. Hamilton, the League.
*annual*. scores, stats.
　*season ?/1937/–?*

## Ottawa

4153　**Ottawa Valley Cricket Council**
□　List of fixtures. Ottawa, the Council.
*annual*. stats.
　*?/1930 . . .1967/*to date?
　*includes report of previous season*

## Toronto

4154　**Grace Church Cricket Club**
□　"The tale end": the Grace Church Cricket
Club magazine. Toronto, the Club. *typescript*. stats.
　*?/1959/1962/–*
　*vol. 3, nos. 1 & 2 issued April, and
　Autumn, 1962*

4155　**Civic Employees Cricket Club**
□　Howz'at: a journal of the Civic Employees
Cricket Club; edited by Thomas Marshall.
Toronto, the Club. *irregular*. illus. ports.
diagrs. *typescript*
　*1962–?*
　*vol. 1, no. 1 March 1962
　　　　　2 April 1962
　　　　　3 November 1962*

4155　**Fillmore, Stanley**
–1　The pleasure of the game: the story of
■　the Toronto Cricket, Skating and Curling
Club: 1827–1977. Toronto, the Club, 1977.
176p. illus. ports. scores, bibliog.
　*cricket occupies the first 86p.*

4156　**King, Donald**
■　Our search for Canadian cricket: the story
of the Toronto Ramblers C.C. trans-
Canada tour 1954. Toronto, the Club,
1954. 32p. scores, stats.

4157　**Macpherson**
Toronto cricket guide souvenir 1905

4158　**"Stumps",** *pseud.*
■　How we raised the wind. Positively the
last edition. Toronto, Rolph Smith,
[1885?]. 8p. illus.
　*an account of how the Toronto C.C.
　acquired a gelding named "Economy" to pull
　the roller*

4159　**Toronto and District Cricket Council**
□　Toronto cricket annual; edited by "Evan
Dale". Toronto, the Council. illus. scores,
stats.
　*1921. 144p. illus.*
　*1922* with title: *Canadian cricket annual
　144p.*
　*1923* with title: *Canadian cricket annual.
　142p.*

4160　Manual. Toronto, the Council, 1931. 52p.

4161　A century of cricket. Toronto, the
Council, 1934. 24p. illus.
　*Toronto C.C. was formed 1834*

4162　Year book. Toronto, the Council
　*?/1958/*to date?

4162　**Toronto Cricket, Skating and Curling**
–1　**Club**
Papers, 1919–1970. Mss.
　*on deposit with Metropolitan Toronto
　Central Library*

4163　————. *Cricket Section*
[Handbook]. Toronto, the Club. *annual*
　*season ?/1967/*to date?
　*list of members and fixtures*

4164　Cricket tour England & Ireland, July 1969.
Toronto, the Club, [1969]. 32p. illus.
ports. map
　*pre-tour*

4165　Cricket tour England July 1972. Toronto,
the Club, [1972]. 40p. illus. ports. map
　*pre-tour*

4165　Fourth overseas cricket tour, England,
–1　July 1975. [Toronto, the Club, 1975]. 40p.
■　illus. ports.
　*cover-title:* Cricket tour England July
　1975
　*pre-tour*

4166　**Toronto** handbook of cricket. Toronto,
1845
　*in Taylor*

# QUEBEC

4167　**Quebec Cricket Association**
□　Handbook. Quebec, the Association.
stats.
　*season ?/1967/*to date
　*contains report of prev. season*

## Montreal

4168　**Montreal and District Amateur Cricket
League**
Handbook. Montreal, the League
　*season ?/1958/*to date?

## SASKATCHEWAN

4169 **Saskatchewan Cricket Association**
Saskatchewan v. New Zealanders, 14

June, 1964: souvenir. Moose Jaw, the
Assoc., 1964. 24p.
*includes historical notes on cricket in Saskatchewan*

# CRICKET IN BERMUDA

4170 **Bermuda Cricket Association**
□ Bermuda cricketer: an official publication
of the Bermuda Cricket Association.
*irregular*
1958 published as a souvenir and in
honour of the Ed Burn Canadian cricket
touring team to Bermuda June 14–29,
1958; ed. by "Jim" Murray. [32]p. incl.
adverts. ports.
1960 *with title:* Bermuda yachting and
cricket; ed. by Ed Burn. 40p. incl. adverts.
illus. ports.
*includes itinerary, fixtures, pen portraits of
the Association's tour of England 1960*
1961 to coincide with the visit of an
English touring team (S. Surridge) 1961.
[36]p. incl. adverts. ports.
1963 ed. by Ed Burn. 40p. incl. adverts.
port. stats.

4171 ————, *and* **Pond Hill Stars Cricket**
■ **Club**
Bermuda cricketers in England, June–July
1962; edited by Ed Burn. Bermuda, the
Assoc., & Club, [1962]. [9]p. ports.

4172 **Bermuda Cricket Board of Control**
■ European tour programme May–June
1969. [Hamilton, the Board, 1969]. [12]p.
ports.

4173 **Bermuda** cricketers in Canada, June–July
1966

4174 **Bermuda** cricketers in Canada, August 14
■ to 23, 1970. Bermuda Sportsman's Club,
[1970]. folded card, ports.
*pre-tour*

4174 **Bermuda Wanderers Touring Cricket**
–1 **Club**
■ Bermuda cricketers in Nassau, Bahamas,
February 24 – March 7, 1977. Bermuda,
[the Club 1977]. 4p. folded card, team
port.
*pre-tour*

4174 Bermuda cricketers in England, August
–2 10 to 30, 1978. Bermuda, the Club, [1978].
■ folded card, team port.
*6th tour by the Club: itinerary and pen
portraits of players*

4175 **The Cup** Match 1902–52: a brochure
commemorating the golden jubilee of the
match, July 31, August 1, 1952. Bermuda,
The Hamilton P., 1952. 76p.
*the annual match between Somerset and St.
George; a brochure is published for each match*

4176 **Hunt, Alma**
■ The Cup Match. Bermuda, Oleander
Book Club. [1942]. 15p. (Oleander Booklet no. 1]
*with 2 unnumbered pages in centre fold
[score-sheet]*

4177 **Simons, Arthur C.G.**
■ Bermuda cricket reminiscences; a brief
history of cricket in Bermuda 1902–1943.
Somerset, Bermuda, 1944. 72p. illus.
ports. diagr. score

4178 **Somerset Cricket Club,** *Bermuda*
Cricket tour, Scotland, England and
Wales; May, June, July, 1961. The Club,
1961. ports.
*pre-tour*

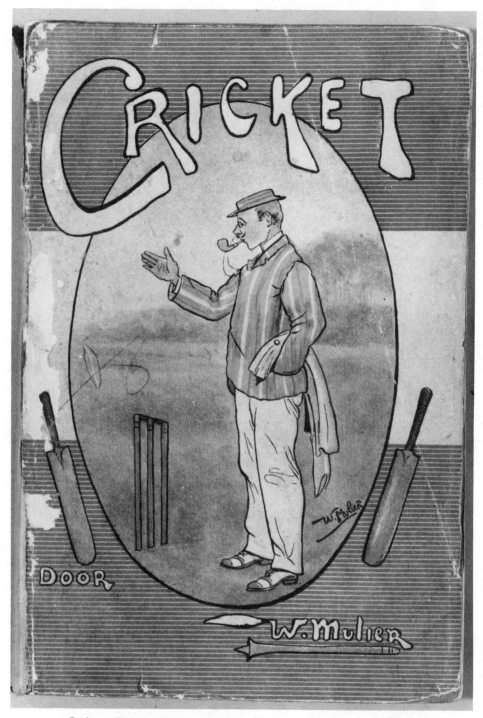

Cricket in Europe. The front cover of a Dutch manual of cricket (no. 457)

# CRICKET IN THE REST OF THE WORLD

## CRICKET IN EUROPE

4179 **Labouchere, Piet C.G., Provis, Tom A.J.,**
■ *and* **Hargreaves, Peter S.**
The story of continental cricket. Hutchinson, 1969. xiv,260p. illus. ports. map, scores, stats. bibliog.

4180 **Tattersall, Edmund Harry**
■ Europe at play. Heinemann, 1938. xiv, 358p. illus. port.
*cricket pp. 21,100,117,166,206,208,307*

### BELGIUM

4181 **Exposition Universelle et Internationale de Bruxelles**
Cricket: grandes epreuves internationales: 19–26 Juin, 1910. Brussels, L'Expansion Belge, 1910
*in French*

4182 **La Federation Belge de Cricket**
□ Annuaire. The Federation.
?/1912/–?
1912. [vi],86p. illus. diagr.

#### Brussels

4183 **Brussels Cricket Club**
Gazette and monthly record. Brussels, the Club
?/1926/–?

4184 Brussels cricket news. Brussels, the Club.
□ *occasional*
Feb. 1966–Feb.? 1967
*March 1967 to date with title: News letter*

4185 Hampshire C.C.C.–Brussels. C.C. 8–12
■ September 1967: souvenir programme. [Brussels, the Club, 1967]. 52p. illus.
*pre-visit*

### CHANNEL ISLANDS

4186 **Lewis, Victor A.**
Elizabeth College, Guernsey v. Victoria College, Jersey: full scores of all cricket matches 1899–1929, with a reference to early matches from the year of their inception 1862. Guernsey, Star & Gazette, 1930. 70p. scores
*a similar book was published in Jersey in 1898 by W. Renouf. A letter from V.A. Lewis to F.S. Ashley-Cooper dated 15th Sept. 1930 states that only 2 copies were known to exist—1 in possession of Lewis, the other in the Elizabeth College Library*

### CORFU

4187 **The Cricket Society**
■ Tour to Corfu 1972. The Society, 1972. pp. 2–77. illus. port. map, plans. *typescript*
*with glossary of Corfu cricketing terms*

4188 **Durrell, Lawrence George**
■ Prospero's cell: a guide to the landscape and manners of the island of Corcyra. Faber, 1945. 142p. illus. maps
*includes an account of cricket in Corfu*

4188 **Emmet, Heneage ("Bill")**
–1 Cricket in Corfu – future prospects.
■ [1970]. 8f. *typescript*
*a report prepared for the Anglo-Corfiot Cricket Association*

4189 **Forte, John,** *editor*
■ Corfu: Venus of the isles. Clacton-on-Sea, East Essex Gazette Ltd., 1963. 76p. illus.
——2nd ed. 1965. 96p. illus. map
*cricket, including account of the international tour, Autumn 1962 by R.A. Roberts, pp.68–73: also reference to Byron & Gymnastikos Clubs, p.85*

4190 **Luke,** *Sir* **Harry Charles**
Cities and men: an autobiography. 3 vols. Bles, 1953–54. illus. ports.
*references to cricket in Corfu in vol. III*

### DENMARK

4191 **Akademisk Boldklub**
Akademisk Boldklub 1939–1949. Copenhagen, the Club, 1949?

4192 Akademisk Boldklub 1889–1964; edited by P.W. Degner. Copenhagen, the Club, 1964?
*cricket section by T.A.J. Provis*

4193 **Bülow, K.**
Akademisk Boldklub gennem 50 aar. Copenhagen, the Club, 1939?

4194 **Dansk Boldspil-Union**
Dansk Boldspil-Unions 50 aars jubilaeum. Copenhagen, the Union
*cricket section by J. Cold*

4195 **Dansk Cricket Forbund**
□ Cricket: udgivet af Dansk Cricket For-bund. Aalborg, the Forbund. *fortnightly* June/July to November. illus. ports. stats.
*1930/1958 . . . 62/to date*
*vol. 1, no. 1, May 1930 with title: Kricket; edited by Harold Philipson. Later editors include Ole Breum, 1938–?, Ole Thomsen and Ole P. Larsen*

4195 Cricket '78: saernummer af "Cricket"
–1 udgivet af Dansk Cricket-Forbund. Viborg, Denmark, the Forbund
*special number of "Cricket" giving the laws of the game, addresses of clubs and officials, details of competitions, etc.*

4196 Cricket: turneringsplan. København, the
□ Forbund. *annual*
*?/1968, 69/to date?*
*tournament regulations and fixtures*

4197 **Kjøbenhavns Boldklub**
Kjøbenhavns Boldklub 1876–1926. Copenhagen, the Club, 1926?
*'Kricket' by L. Sylow*

4198 Kjøbenhavns Boldklub gennem 75 aar; edited by Ejner Middelboe. Copenhagen, the Club, 1951?

4199 Kjøbenhavns Boldklub eleven tour in England: itinerary, etc. Circularised by B. J. W. Hill, [1954]. *typescript*

4200 **Københavns Boldspil-Union**
Københavns Boldspil-Union 1903–1953. Copenhagen, the Union, 1953?
*'Cricket' by B. Pockendahl*

4200 **Pedersen, Axel Ivan**
–1 Kricket-sporten gennem 50 aar: Nykøbing Mors, 1885–1935. Nykøbing Mors, 1935. 24p.
*In Danish: trs. Cricket over the last 50 years: Nykøbing Mors [C.C.]. 1885–1935*

4200 **Prip, Poul**
–2 K.B. gennem 100 år: 1876–26 April·1976.
■ København, Kjøbenhavns Boldklub, 1976. 223p. incl. adverts. illus. ports.
*in Danish: with cricket section*

4201 **Werfel, J.**
[Newest collection of gymnastic games, party games and Christmas games, to pass the time and give enjoyment from Guthsuths]. Copenhagen, A. Soldin, 1801
——2nd. ed. *with title:* [Walter, and his pupils in their hours of leisure, or, Gymnastic games for young people . . . ]. 1802
*both eds. in Danish and contain first description of cricket in that language: a translation from the German*

# FRANCE

4202 **Jusserand, Jean Jules**
Les sports et jeux d'exercise dans l'ancienne France. Paris, Librairie Plon, 1901. [iv],474p. illus.
*ch. 6 includes sections on the history of jeu de paume and cricket, pp. 298–301*

## Arras

4202 **Arras and District Cricket Club**
–1 Fixture card. The Club. *annual.* folded
□ card
*season 1934*
*in M.C.C. Library, Lord's*

## Calais

4202 **Calais Cricket Club**
–2 Fixture card. Calais, the Club. *annual.* folded card
*?/season 1932/-?*

## Paris

4203 **Cricket** club. No. 1. Samedi, 11 Mars, 1961. Paris, 1961. bs. illus.
*an advertisement for a cigarette lighter, inviting membership of the Cricket Club de Paris*

4204 **"An Old Stump,"** *pseud.*
■ Le clef du cricket; ou, courte explication de la marche et des principales règles de ce jeu, par An Old Stump, M.P.C.C. [Paris, *private printed*, 1864?]. 23p.
*French text: with rules of the Paris C.C., pp. 21–23*

4205 **Paris Cricket Club**
□ [Annual]. Paris, the Club
*"several yearly issues" (Taylor); that for 1863 states that the Club was formed 1st July, 1863 and contains the Committee rules, revised 28 Sept. 1863, and a list of members. [i],29p.*

4206 **Saint-Albin, Albert de**
Les sports à Paris. Paris, Librarie Modern, 1889. 348p.
*le cricket pp. 283–5*

4207 **Walpole, Horace,** *4th earl of Orford*
■ Correspondence; edited by W. S. Lewis. 39 vols. London, Oxford Univ. P.; New Haven, Yale Univ. P., 1937–74. (The Yale edition)
*vol. 7, 1939, p. 307 the entry for 13 March, 1766 in "Paris Journals": "Dr. Smith and Gordon, Principal of the Scotch College came. To see a cricket match in the Plaine de Neuilly [now Neuilly-sur-Seine]. . . . '*

## GREECE

4208 **Bent, James Theodore**
■ The Cyclades: or, Life among the insular Greeks. Longmans, Green, 1885. xx,501p. map
*reference, p. 169, to the game 'sphaira', or ball, "which bears a closer relationship to cricket than anything I ever saw out of England."*

## ITALY

4209 **Maceroni, Francis**
Memoirs of the life and adventures of Colonel Maceroni, late Aide-de-Camp to Joachim Murat, King of Naples. 2 vols. Macrone, 1838
*references to cricket at Naples in 1811*

## THE NETHERLANDS

4210 **Eurosport**
■ "First class in cricket material". Eurosport, Meerle (Belgium), [197–]. 7 loose leaves in folder, port.
*advertisement brochure with batting averages of Dutch cricketers and portraits of Gary Sobers*

4210 **Mr. M. F. North's** tour in Holland. 1931
–1

4210 **Offerman, J.**
–2 50 jaar cricket 1910–60: productiever en aantrekkelijker actief cricket. Scheveningen, 1960. 36p.
*in Dutch: "50 years of cricket 1910–60: productive and attractive attacking cricket"*

4210 **Van Booven, Henri C.A.**
–3 Cricket. Propaganda Commissie van den
■ Nederlandschen Cricket Bond, [1912]. 16p.
——*another ed. with sub-title:* het propaganda boekje. The Bond, 1937. 18p.

**Nederlandsche Cricket Bond, Koninklijke**

4211 **Nederlandsche Cricket-Bond**
■ Geillustreerd jaarboekje. Den Haag, the Bond. illus. ports. scores, stats.

*2 issues 1916, 1917*
*1917 issue contains 'de Geschiedenis van den Bond van af zijne Oprichting in 1883' (a history of the Union since its foundation in 1883)*

4212 Jaarverslag. Den Haag, the Bond. type-
☐ script
*?/1939, 58/to date*
*formed 30th Sept. 1883; annual report*

4213 Cricket: officiële mededelingen van de
☐ Nederlandsche Cricket Bond. Den Haag, the Bond. *weekly* (May to Sept., with issue in Mar. or Apr. and in Dec.). illus. ports. scores, stats.
*22 April 1931 to date*
*originally described as the official organ of De Flamingo's and other clubs; now with sub-title: officieel orgaan van de Koninklijke Nederlandsche Cricket-Bond. Appeared 22 times in 1979*

4214 Gedenkboek uitgegeven ter gelegenheid
■ van het viftigjarig bestaan 1883–1933. [Den Haag], the Bond, [1933]. 317p. illus. ports. stats.
*souvenir book published for 50th anniversary*

4215 [Match scores]. Den Haag, printed by
☐ "Presto". *typescript. weekly during season*
*?/3 June–9 Sep. 1934/–?*

4216 Almanak van den Nederlandschen
■ Cricket-Bond: vijftig seizoenen eerste klas cricket, 1891–1940. Haarlem, the Bond, 1941. 69p. ports. stats.

4217 Gedenkboek uitgegeven ter gelegenheid
■ van het vijf en zeventigjarig bestaan van de Nederlandse Cricket-Bond 1883–30 September 1958. [Den Haag, the Bond, 1958]. 95p. illus. ports. stats.
*souvenir book published for 75th anniversary*

4218 ———, **Koninklijke**
■ Cricket: de ideale zomersport. [s'Gravenhage], the Bond, [1964]. 72p. illus. diagrs.
*brief history of cricket & the development of the game in the Netherlands. Description of game and guide to the laws. List of clubs*

4219 Jaarboekje. [den Haag, the Bond.] stats.
☐ *in v.y.*
*1968 to date*

4219 **Nederlandsche Dames Cricket Bond**
–1 Gedenkboek uitgegeven ter gelegenheid
■ van het vijf en twintigjarig bestaan van de Nederlandsche Dames Cricket Bond.

Cricket in Europe. Cricket on coconut matting in Corfu *photo: Douglas Dickens*

Cricket in the Middle East. An aerial view of the cricket ground, Sharjah, United Arab Emirates
*photo: Patrick Eagar*

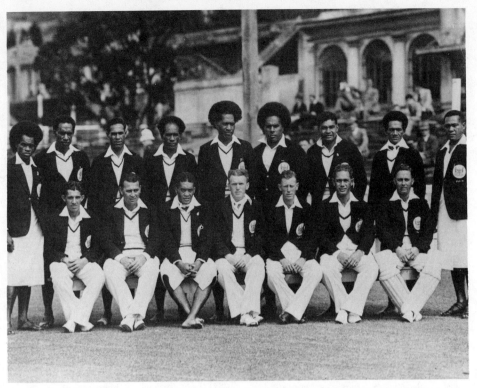

Cricket in the Pacific. The Fiji team which toured New Zealand, 1948, Philip Snow (in centre) captain *photo: courtesy of Philip Snow*

[Der Haag], The Bond, 1959. 43p. incl. adverts. stats. *typescript*
*cover-title:* Gedenkboek 1934–27 Januari–1959
*25th anniversary book*

## Amsterdam

4220 **Amsterdamsche Cricket Club**
■ Jubileumboek uitgegeven ter gelegenheid van het 25-jarig bestaan, 1921–1946. Amsterdam, the Club, 1946. 318p. ports. stats.

4221 Amsterdamsche Cricket Club 1921–5 maart 1961: jubileumboek. [Amsterdam, the Club, 1961]. illus.

4222 **Mulder, S. P.,** *editor*
■ V.R.A. jubileumboek, uitgegeven ter gelegenheid van het 50-jarig bestaan. [Amsterdam, V.R.A., 1964]. 108p. illus. port. stats.
*cover-title:* V.R.A. 1914–64
*an amalgamation of the Volharding (founded 20 June 1889), R.A.P. (14 Nov. 1887). and Amstels C.C. (April 1885)*

## De Flamingo's

4223 **De Flamingo's Cricket Club**
Cricket touring club De Flamingo's 1931. The Club, [1931]
*fixture list, list of members, etc. with a historical summary 1920–31*

4224 Twenty five tours with Free Foresters in
■ Holland 1921–1954. Presented by Flamingo's to Free Foresters during their 25th tour to Holland, 11th Aug. 1954. [The Club, 1954]. 12p.

4225 Gedenkboek uitgegeven ter gelegenheid
■ van het vijtig jarig bestaan van de cricket touring club 'de flamingo's' [1921–71]. The Club, [1971]. 127p. illus. ports. stats.
*souvenir book published for 50th anniversary*

## Haarlem

4226 **Haarlemsche Cricket Bond**
■ Gedenkboekje uitgegeven ter gelegenheid van het vijtigjarig bestaan de Haarlemsche Cricket Bond (opgericht in 1911). [Haarlem, the Club, 1961]. 83p. stats.
*cover title:* Een halve eeuw: Haarlemsche Cricket Bond (1911–1961)
*souvenir book for 50th anniversary*

4227 **Kleefstra, B.**
Haarlem 1920–1945

4228 **Rood en Wit**
Gedenkboek uitgegeven ter gelegenheid van het 50-jarig bestaan der Haarlemsche cricket club "Rood en Wit", 1881–1931. Haarlem, the Club, [1931]. 125p. illus. ports.
*souvenir book of 50th anniversary: similar souvenir books published covering 1881–1951: 1881–1956*

4229 De spriet: orgaan de Haarlemsche cricket club "Rood en Wit"; opgericht 22 Juni, 1881. Jubileumuitgave ter gelegenheid van het 80-jarig bestaan, 22 Juni, 1961. Haarlem, the Club, [1961]. *typescript*
*jubilee issue to celebrate 80th year of the Club*
—— . . . van het 85-jarig bestaan, 22 Juni, 1966. illus. *typescript*
*85th anniversary*

## The Hague

4230 **Haagsche Cricket Club**
Gedenkboek ter gelegenheid van het 50-jarig bestaan, 1878–1928; samengesteld door J. W. G. Coops, H. Van Manen, J. J. Koeleman. [Den Haag], the Club, 1928. [i],284p. illus. ports. stats.
*souvenir book on 50th anniversary*

4231 Gedenkboek ter gelegenheid van het 60-jarig bestaan, 1878–1938; samengesteld door J. W. G. Coops. etc. [Den Haag], the Club, [1938]. 197p. illus. ports. stats.
*souvenir book on 60th anniversary*

4232 Gedenkboek ter gelegenheid van het 80-
■ jarig bestaan, 1878–1958 . . . door R. Borgers, R. Colthoff and J. de Lavieter. [Den Haag], the Club, [1958]. 199p. illus. ports. stats.
*souvenir book on 80th anniversary*

4233 **Haagsche** Cricket Club, 1878–1968: jubilee issue. The Hague, Haagsche Cricket en Voetbalvereeniging, 1968. 126p. illus.

4233 **Haagsche** Cricket Club 1878–1978:
–1 eeuwboek; samengesteld door W. G. K.
■ Arendsen de Wolff, [and others]. [The Hague, the Club, 1978]. 160p. illus. ports. facsims. stats.

4234 **Der Haagsche Cricket en Voetbal**
□ **Vereeniging**
Clubblad. The Hague, the Club. *monthly,* illus. ports. stats.
1915?/Oct. 1933. Aug. 1953/*to date?*
*issue for 13th Oct. 1933 is 19th yr. no. 4*

4235 **De Krekels Cricket Club**
□ Krekels kroniek. Rijswijk (Z.H.), The Club. *typescript.* illus. ports. scores

*Kerstmis nummer 1954?/1962–4/–?*
the Christmas numbers of "Krekels kroniek", the journal of de Krekels C.C.
*Herfstnummer ?/1963/–?*
Autumn number; in 1963 gave survey of the season with stats.

4236 "De Krekels" 1941–66 [compiled by]
■ B. W. M. Hillenaar. Rijswijk, Z.H., the Club, 1966. 48p. illus. ports. diagrs. stats.
*Dutch text: jubilee issue of the official journal of De Krekels C.C. to celebrate its 25th year: issued Sept. 1966*

### Hilversum

4236 **"Dick,"** *pseud.*
–1 Gedenkboek, uitgegeven ter herdenking vat het 25-jarig bestaan der Hilversumsche Cricket en Footballclub "Victoria". [Hilversum, B.C. Rozenbeek], 1918. ports.

### Rotterdam

4237 **Rotterdamsche Cricket en Voetbalvereeniging**
Volharding-Olympia-Combinatie: 1 Januari 1895–1955: gedenkboek uitgegeven ter gelegenheid van het zestigjarig bestaan. Rotterdam, the Club, 1955. 288p. illus. ports. diagrs.
*trs.: Endurance-Olympia-Combination: . . . jubilee book published on the occasion of the 60th anniversary*
——*1895–1970. Rotterdam, the Club, 1970. 135p. illus. ports.*

### Schiedam

4237 **Nordlohne, J.,** *and others*
–1 Gedenkboek ter gelegenheid van het vijftigjarig bestaan van de cricket en footballclub "Hermes D.V.S." 1884, 8 April—1934. [Schiedam, Hermes D.V.S.], 1934. 61p. illus. ports.

### Still Going Strong C.C.

4238 **Still Going Strong Cricket Club**
[Handbook]. The Club. *annual*
*?/1959 . . . 69/to date*
*founded 1929; contains fixtures, lists of officials and members*

4239 Verslag. The Club. *annual*
*?/1961, 1965/to date*

4240 Itinerary of tour. The Club, 1964. 12p.

4241 Tour naar Engeland . . . 1968. The Club, [1968]. 4p.
*itinerary of tour*

4242 Gedenkboek 1929–1969. The Club, [1969].
■ 120p. illus. ports. scores, stats.

### Utrecht

4243 **De Herculaan:** officieel orgaan de U.C. en V.V. Hercules. Utrecht, the Club. illus.
*1921 ?/May 1964/to date?*
*issue for May 1964 was No. 10, 44th year*
——*80 lustrumnummer. 1962. 40p. illus. ports. stats.*
*80 years souvenir history of the Dutch cricket and football club 'Hercules', 1882–1962*

## PORTUGAL

4244 **Graham, Kenneth**　　　●
■ The noble game of cricket and how he should be played in Portugal described in "Pombo"—Português. Porto, the Author, 1958. 12p.
*humorous pamphlet*

4244 **Oporto Cricket and Lawn Tennis Club**
–1 List of members and rules. Oporto, the Club, [c.1914]

4245 Centenary 1855–1955. [Oporto], the Club,
■ [1955]. 15p.
*annals of the Club's history*

# CRICKET IN CENTRAL AND SOUTH AMERICA

4246 **South American Cricket Associations**
England tour 1932; [compiled by Hugh H. Spicer]. Chislehurst, *printed by* Waters, [1932]. 12p. stats.

## ARGENTINA

4247 **Holder, Arthur L.**
British and North American sports and pastimes in Argentina. Buenos Aires, the Author, 1923. 72p.
*cricket pp. 7–13*

4248 **McGough, James**
■ The book of hundreds; being a list of centuries made in Argentine cricket. Buenos Aires, the British Printery, 1921. 40p.

4249 Chronicles of cricket in Argentina, incor-
■ porating "The Year book of Argentine cricket". *In* The Argentine Magazine, No. 84. Apr. 1930, pp. 25–47. ports. stats.
*a review of the 1929–30 season with notes on Sir Julien Cahn team's visit*

4250 ———, and **Holder, Arthur L.**
■ A book of Argentine cricket: containing A retrospect of cricket in Argentina by [Arthur L. Holder]; The 1919 North v. South match; individual records of all players who have taken part in the game 1891–1919, compiled by James McGough; Returned Volunteers v. The Rest match [1919]. Buenos Aires, The British Printery, 1920. 36p. ports. scores, stats.

4251 **The Year Book** of Argentine cricket;
■ compiled by James McGough. Buenos Aires. ports. scores, stats.
    *8 issues, season 1919–20 to 1926–27. [1921–27], 1928*
    *seasons 1920–21 to 1922–23 with title: " . . . and other British sports".*
    *1919–20 to 1923–24 publd. by The British Printery*
    *1924–25 to 1926–27 by The Souvenir Publishing Co.*
    *see also no. 4249*

### Argentine Cricket Association

4252 **Argentine Cricket Association**
□ Fixtures. Buenos Aires, the Association. *annual*
    *season ?/1924–25 . . . 1947–48/to date*

4253 Report and accounts (Memoria y bal-
□ ance). Buenos Aires, the Association. *annual.* ports. scores, stats.
    *season ?/1945–46 . . . 1978–79/to date*

### North v. South

4254 **Argentine Cricket Association**
North v. South, 1891 to 1949: fifty not out. Buenos Aires, the Assoc., 1949. 12p.

4254 **Bridger, Kenneth E.**
–1 North and South: a history of the cricket
■ classic in Argentina. [Buenos Aires], *printed by* Talleres Graficos, 1976. 126p. illus. ports. stats.
    *covers period 1891–1974*

4255 **McGough, James,** *compiler*
■ The North v. South cricket match. Detailed scores of all matches 1891–1915 with individual records of all players . . . Buenos Aires, the British Printery, [1915]. 72p. incl. adverts. ports. scores, stats.

### Buenos Aires

4256 **Buenos Aires Cricket Club**
□ Report and accounts. Buenos Aires, the Club. *annual*
    *season ?/1906–07 . . . 1930–31/–?*
    *set at Lord's comprises seasons 1906–7, 1907–8, 1918–9 to 1920–1, 1922–3 to 1929–30*

4256 Club dinner to celebrate the winning of
–1 the First Division Championship [held at Strangers Club, Buenos Aires, April 7, 1925: menu]. Buenos Aires, the Club, [1925]. 6p. illus.
    *contains "A chapter of history: the first decade of the Buenos Aires Cricket Club 1861–1871", by J. McGough*

# BRAZIL

4257 **Argentine Cricket Association**
Brazilian tour December 1967. Buenos Aires, the Assoc., 1967
    *programme of matches played by Brazil team in Argentina*

4258 **State of São Paulo**
Cricket. São Paulo, *annual.* illus.
    *season ?/1943, 44/–?*

4259 **Wild, John James**
At anchor: a narrative of experiences afloat and ashore during the voyage of H.M.S. "Challenger" from 1872 to 1876. Illustrated by the Author. London & Belfast, Ward, 1878. 198p. illus. (some col.). port. map
    *contains a sketch by Wild of a team from "Challenger" playing against the Bahia C.C. in 1873; also reproduced in "The voyage of the Challenger", by Eric Linklater. Murray, 1972, p. 46*

# CHILE

4260 **Argentine Cricket Association**
■ Programme of the events to take place during the visit of the Chilean cricket team. December 1924–January, 1925. Buenos Aires, the Assoc., [1924]. [4]p.

# MEXICO

4261 **Mexican Union Cricket Club**
■ Rules and regulations . . . revised and corrected . . . at a general meeting held in February 1838 . . . together with the laws of the game. [Mexico City, the Club], 1838. 18p.
    *contains list of members of the Union Cricket Club 1827–1838*

4262 **Reforma** Athletic Club S.C.: a history and
■ description of the Club with the rules and records of its various sports, 1894 to 1910. Mexico City, printed by Imprenta Comercial, [c.1911]. 64p. stats.
    *cricket pp. 40–50*

## PANAMA REPUBLIC

4263 **Panama Tribune**
■ Cricket number, 23rd October 1930. Vol.

VI, No. 23. Panama, Panama Tribune.
24p. incl. adverts. illus. ports.
*to commemorate the visit of the West Indies
team on their way to tour Australia 1930/31*

# CRICKET IN EAST AFRICA

4264 **[East African Cricket Association]**
■ The East Africans. [Nairobi, the Assoc.,
1972]. [16]p. illus. ports.
*with programme of East Africans tour to
U.K. 1972*

4265 **East African Cricket Conference**
Articles of constitution. [Nairobi, the
Conference, [1960]. *typescript*

4266 **The history** of the Straggling Scallops
□ Cricket Club 1959–1963, *and* 1963–1965.
2 vols. Nairobi, *privately printed*, 1963–5.
team ports. typescripts.
*the Club originated within the Shell Co. of
E. Africa but membership has now widened*

4266 **Lillis, Kevin**
–1 The East Africans. Nairobi, the Author,
■ 1975. [80]p. incl. adverts. illus. ports.
scores, stats. *typescript*
*mostly on their participation in the World
Cup 1975*

4267 **Zambia Cricket Union**
■ The East African Cricket Conference
Combined XI Zambia tour: official
souvenir programme. The Union, [1966].
[12]p. incl. adverts. ports.
*sponsored by Northern Breweries Ltd.*

## KENYA

4267 **Africasports.** Nairobi, Kenya. illus. ports.
–1 *monthly*
*11 issues July 1974–May 1975*
*Incorporated June 1975 into* African
winner; *contains cricket articles*

4268 **Braimbridge, Clifford Viney,** *and*
■ **Downing, K. F. P.**
Kenya cricket records. Nairobi, [Kenya
Kongonis C.C.,] 1948. [iv],35p. team
port. stats.

4269 **The Kenya** cricketers' almanack 1958;
■ edited by J. L. Porter. Nairobi, the Editor,
[1958]. 68p. illus. ports. scores, stats.
*only issue?*

### Kenya Kongonis

4270 **Braimbridge, Clifford Viney**
■ Kenya Kongonis Cricket Club 1927 to
1946: with an appendix containing some

records of Kenya cricket. Nairobi, [the
Club], 1946. 42p. port. stats.

4271 **Kenya Kongonis Cricket Club**
Annual report and balance sheet.
Nairobi, the Club. *typescript*
*season ?/1956 . . . 1977–78/* to date

4272 Membership and fixture card. Nairobi,
the Club
*?/1964–5 to date*

4273 Officials v. Settlers. Nairobi, the Club,
[c.1963]. 25p. stats.
*a statistical record*

### Kenya Asian XI

4274 **Eastern Province Cricket Federation**
■ Kenya Asian cricket tour of South Africa,
1956: official souvenir. Port Elizabeth, the
Federation, [1956]. [12]p. incl. adverts.
ports.
*pre-tour*

4275 **South African Cricket Board of Control**
Kenya tour, November-December 1956,
Cape Town-Johannesburg-Durban: souvenir programme. The Board, [1956]. 72p.
incl. adverts. ports. stats.
*pre-tour*

### Pangani Sports Club

4275 **Pangani Sports Club**
–1 Cricket tour, England 1975. Nairobi,
Vaid, [1975?]. 98p. incl. adverts. illus.
*pre-tour*

## MALAWI

4276 **Nyasaland Cricket Club**
[Handbook]. The Club, 1951
*rules and list of life members*

## TANZANIA

4277 **Tanganyika** cricket annual. [Dar-es-
□ Salaam], Tanganyika Standard. ports.
scores, stats.
*?/1955, 1958/–?*

## UGANDA

4278 **The Uganda** cricket annual 1953. Uganda
■ Advisory Board for Cricket, 1953. 64p.
illus. ports. scores
*the only issue*
contd. as: *Uganda cricketer*

4279 **Uganda** cricketer. Entebbe, Uganda C.A.
□ *annual.* illus. ports. scores, stats.
*1954/1954–58. . .1961/–?*
*1960 & 1961 issues edited by C. J. Hall and
A. G. Petrie; formerly: The Uganda cricket
annual*

4280 **The Young** Uganda cricketer: the maga-
■ zine of the Uganda Schools Cricket
Association. illus. ports. diagrs. scores
*1968—the only issue?*

### Uganda Kobs

4281 **Uganda Kobs Cricket Club**
Report. Kampala, the Club. *annual*
*1921?/1962–63/–?*

4282 The Uganda Kobs: forty-fifth anniver-
■ sary, 1921–1966. Kampala, [the Club],
1966. 59p. port.
*history, list of members and rules*

4282 The Uganda Kobs: fiftieth anniversary
–1 1921–1971. Kampala, [the Club, 1971].
■ 47p. port.
*list of officers, nominal roll of members,
Roll of Honour and rules*

## ZAMBIA

4283 **Nondescripts Sports Club**
■ Annual dance, Hotel Inter-Continental 30
June 1973. [Lusaka, Zambia, The Club,
1973]. 40p. incl. adverts. illus. ports.
*text mostly on the history of the Club, with
lists of present officers; contd. as no. 4283.1*

4283 Nondes. Lusaka, the Club, ports. stats.
–1 1974/1974/to date?
□ *formerly no. 4283*

# CRICKET IN WEST AFRICA

## GAMBIA

4284 **Gambia Cricket Association**
■ Fourth Test match, The Gambia v.
Nigeria, Bathurst, 25th, 26, 27, 28 April,
1969: handbook and scorecard. [Bathurst,
the Assoc., 1969]. 28p. incl. covers &
adverts. scores

## NIGERIA

4285 **Butler, P. K.**
Cricket in Nigeria. Ibadan, Advert Press,
1946. 48p. illus.

# CRICKET IN ASIA

4285 **Asian** Cricket Conference, Lahore, Paki-
–1 stan, December, 1974: agenda. [Lahore,
■ the Conference, 1974]. 18p.

4285 **Asian** Cricket Conference, Sri Lanka,
–2 11th March, 1976: agenda. Colombo, [The
■ Conference, 1976]. 12p.
*with minutes of meeting held at Lahore, 14
Dec. 1974*

# CRICKET IN THE MIDDLE EAST

4285 **Gulf** international cricket tournament
–3 1979. (Participating states: Bahrain,
Kuwait, Qatar, Sharjah); edited by M. K.
Kazi and Khalid Mahmood. *n.p.*, [1979].
32p. incl. adverts. illus. ports.

## EGYPT

4286 **Davar, F. J.**
Cameos of sport. Bombay, the Author,
[1941?]. xii,130p. illus. ports.
*cricket, p. 29——cricket in the Sinai Desert*

### Alexandria

4287 **Alexandria Cricket Club**
■ Alexandria Cricket Club 1851–1951:
centenary match, 23rd & 24th May, 1953.
Alexandria, the Club, 1953. 12p. illus.

## ISRAEL

4288 **Israel Cricket Association**
■ Tour of England by the Israel cricket
team, August 23–September 17, 1970 at

the invitation of the Israel Cricket Supporters Association, London branch. The Assoc., [1970]. [8]p.

*includes details of cricket in Israel with fixture list of tour as insert*

4289 **Israel Cricket Supporters Association**
■ Israel National Cricket XI England tour 1970. The Assoc., 1970. [10]p. of text. ports.

*contains "The history and development of cricket in Israel" by Michael R. Mitzman rptd. from "Playfair cricket monthly"*

## KUWAIT

4290 **Hubara Cricket Club**
■ 1948–1973: 25th anniversary dinner dance, Ahmadi, 2 January 1974. [Kuwait], the Club, [1973]. 12p. illus.

*includes history of club 1948–73*

4291 **Tom Graveney's** International Cricket XI in Kuwait, 1969: souvenir programme. Kuwait, n.p., [1969]. 116p. incl. adverts. illus. ports.

*includes articles on cricket in Kuwait*

# CRICKET IN THE FAR EAST

## INTERPORT CRICKET
*(in chronological order)*

4292 **Hong Kong Telegraph**
The sportsman's pocket book: complete details of Hong Kong, Shanghai and coast port meetings, 1895, 1896. Hong Kong, "Hong Kong Telegraph" Office, 1895

4293 **Bains, J. W.,** *compiler*
■ Interport cricket, 1866–1908: a record of matches between Hong Kong, Singapore and Shanghai. Shanghai, Shanghai Times, [1908?]. 132p. stats.

*a record of cricket played by the Services and English residents in Shanghai; with errata slip*

4294 **Hong Kong Cricket Club**
Interport cricket programme: Hong Kong vs. Shanghai, Nov. 8, 10 & 11, 1947. Hong Kong, [the Club], 1947. 16p.

4295 **International Sporting Club of Shanghai**
Interport cricket programme, Shanghai v. Hong Kong. Shanghai, International Sporting Club of Shanghai, 1948. 16p.

4296 **Selangor Cricket Association**
Souvenir programme: Federation of Malay versus Hong Kong, played in Kuala Lumpur, Padang, on 23 and 24 June, 1948. Kuala Lumpur, the Assoc., [1948]. 12p.

4297 **Malayan Cricket Association**
■ Hong Kong v Malaya, 17–19 May, 1957, Selangor Club, Padang. The Association, [1957]. [36]p. incl. adverts. ports. stats.

4297 **Interport** souvenir programme Hong
–1 Kong v. Malaya, November 23, 24, 25,
■ 1963. Kong Kong, Hongkong C.L., [1963]. 51p. incl. adverts. illus. ports. score

4298 **Selangor Cricket Association**
Interport cricket series, Malaysia v. Hong Kong: souvenir. Kuala Lampur, Selangor C.A., 1965. 36p. illus.

## BRUNEI

4299 **Brunei State Cricket Association**
Davidson Trophy: Brunei v. Sarawak: souvenir programme. Brunei, the Association, n.d. 24p. illus. ports.

4300 1971–72: souvenir programme. The Asso-
■ ciation, [1971]. 32p. incl. adverts. illus. port.

## HONG KONG

4300 **The Capercailzies** Hong Kong tour 1978.
–1 [The Club, 1978]. 26p. illus. port.
■ *pre-tour; with article on cricket in Hong Kong*

4300 **Cathay Pacific** super stars. Hong Kong,
–2 Cathay Pacific, 1975. 20p. incl. adverts. illus. ports. scores
*post tour account of visit of team of former Australian Test players for series of 6 matches to commemorate the closure of Chater Road*

4300 **Cathay Pacific** Jumbo Superstars. Flash-
–3 back to 1975 Hong Kong – Australia match. Hong Kong, Cathay Pacific. 20p. incl. covers, illus. ports.
*includes account of early tours to Hong Kong by former Australian Test cricketers. This was the third tour*

4301 **Hong Kong** Garrison tour May 20–June
■ 28, 1909–Hong Kong, Shanghai, Japan. South China Morning Post, [1909]. 12f. scores, stats.
*post-tour*

4302 **Hong Kong** sporting annual. Hong
Kong.
*1909–10, 1910–11*

4302 **"Jin Slingsley,** and **Pot",** *pseuds.*
–1 S'what ho! Hong Kong, 1905. illus.
scores
*contains an account of a tour to Hong Kong
made presumably in 1905*

### Centaurs Cricket Club

4302 **Clark, Tony,** *and* **Fletcher, Graham**
–2 75 not out: seventy-five years of Civil
■ Service cricket in Hong Kong 1903–1978.
Hong Kong, Centaurs C.C., 1978. 44p.
incl. advert. illus. & ports. (some col.),
col. map

### Hong Kong Cricket Association

4303 **Board of Control for Cricket in Ceylon**
■ Hong Kong Cricket Association visit to
Ceylon, 19 to 29 March, 1971: official
souvenir. Colombo, [the Board, 1971].
[20]. incl. adverts. ports. score, stats.
*pre-tour*

4304 **Galle Cricket Club**
■ Visit of the Hong Kong Cricket Association to Galle, 21st March, 1971: souvenir;
compiled by S. S. Perera. Galle, the Club,
[1971]. [16]p. incl. covers
*pre-tour*

4304 **Hong Kong Cricket Association**
–1 Handbook. Hong Kong, the Association.
illus. ports. stats. *annual*
*season 1979–80; editor John Morgan. 118p.
incl. adverts.*

### Hong Kong Cricket Club

4305 **Hong Kong Cricket Club**
■ Centenary, 1851–1951. [Hong Kong, the
Club, 1951]. 99p. illus. ports.
——[Supplement]. Centenary celebration
report; edited by Arnold Graham. [1951].
22p. scores

4306 Report. Hong Kong, the Club. *annual*
□ *?/1953–54/to date?*

4307 Official handbook and league fixtures.
Hong Kong, the Club. *annual?* team
ports.
*season ?/1954–55/to date?*

4308 The pink 'un. Hong Kong, the Club.
*monthly*
*early 1960s to date*
*issue for August 1979, 24p. incl. adverts.
illus. ports. includes season 1978–79 and
Manila tour '79*

4308 Hong Kong Cricket Club. The Club,
–1 [1977?]. 28p. incl. adverts. illus. ports.
*covers 1976–77 season including "H.K.C.C.
in Singapore – a review of the 1977 match"*

4309 **Lemay, G. A.** *compiler*
■ A record of the first twenty post war
years [1948–1968] of the Hong Kong
Cricket Club 'Optimists' and 'Scorpions'
in the First Division of the Hong Kong
Cricket League. Hong Kong, the Author,
1968. [ii],vi, 201f. stats. *typescript*
*cover-title: The Hong Kong Cricket Club
1st Division League records 1948–1968*

# MALAYA

4310 **The Malacca** sports annual 1936; com-
■ piled and edited by P. G. Pamadasa. Malacca, *printed by* Wah Seong P., 1936.
[iv],205p. incl. adverts. ports. scores,
stats.
*the only issue? Cricket pp. 34–79 including
a history of the game in Malacca*

4310 **Malaysian Cricket Association**
–1 North vs. South annual cricket match,
■ Malacca Club, Padang, 27 August 1966
to 29 August 1966. Malacca, the Assoc.,
[1966]. [40]p. incl. adverts. ports.

4310 Malaysia in the I.C.C. Trophy 1979 at
–2 Birmingham, United Kingdom, 22nd
■ May–6th June 1979. The Assoc., [1979].
248p. incl. adverts. illus. ports.

4311 **Moreira, Allan E.**
The Malaya sports record: an illustrated
review of the past history of field sports
in Malaya. Kuala Lumpur, Huxley, Palmer, 1923. 2,iii,147p. illus.
*cricket pp. 1–43*

4311 **Selangor Club**
–1 90 up: the 90th anniversary of the
■ Selangor Club. Oct. 1974; edited by Felix
Abisheganaden. Kuala Lumpur, Com-
core Public Relations for the Selangor
Club, [1974]. 40p. incl. adverts. illus.
ports.

4311 Australian cricket tour 1976: souvenir
–2 programme. Kuala Lumpur, the Club,
■ [1976]. 76p. incl. adverts. illus. ports.
scores

4312 **Selangor** Cricket Association welcomes
Worcestershire: souvenir. Kuala Lumpur,
the Association, 1965. 88p. incl. adverts.
ports.
*summarises scores of the principal matches
played in Malaysia since the war*

4313 **Towers, A. C. J.**
Souvenir of the first all-Malay school cricket match played at Pasir Puteh, Ipoh, on Sunday, 2nd February, 1936. Ipoh, Charles Greiner, [1936]. 10p. illus.

## SINGAPORE

4313 **Colonials Cricket Club**
−1 Without prejudice. Singapore, the Club,
■ 1951. [i],13f. *typescript*
*correspondence between the Club and the Singapore C.A. concerning the relegation of the Club from the Senior Division. Presented . . . "to all cricket fans in Malaya"*

4314 **Malan, C. H.**
A soldiers' experience of God's love and of his faithfulness to his word . . . 4th ed. James Nisbet, 1875. xii,239p. col. frontis.
*folding frontis. shows a cricket match in progress at Tanglin Barracks, Singapore and pp. 118–121 contain description of the making of the cricket ground*

4314 **Malaysian Cricket Association**
−1 Visit of Worcestershire County Cricket
■ Club (County Champions 1964) to Singapore, Malaysia, 11–17 March 1965: souvenir programme. Singapore, the Assoc., [1965]. [76]p. incl. adverts. ports.

4315 **Malaysia Singapore Ligers**
First cricket tour of England, 1971. 8p. ports.
*pre-tour; 'Ligers' are a cross between a male lion and a female tiger*

4316 **Singapore Cricket Association**
■ Visit of Singapore Cricket Association Juniors team to Madras/Bangalore, December 1973. Singapore, the Assoc., [1973]. 40p. incl. adverts. ports.
*pre-tour*

4317 **Singapore Cricket Club**
■ Singapore cricket centenary 1837–1937: Malaya vs. Sir Julien Cahn's XI, March, 27, 28 and 29, 1937 at the Singapore Cricket Club. Singapore, the Club, 1937. 56p. incl. adverts. illus. ports. scores, stats.

4318 Report of the Committee and statements of accounts. Singapore, the Club, *annual ?/1947/–?*

4319 Tour of India and Sri Lanka 1973. [Singa-
■ pore, the Club, 1973]. [28]p. incl. adverts. illus. ports. score
*contains a historical note on the Club by Andrew Gilmour*

## TAIWAN

4320 **Souvenir** of University Cricket Group from Taiwan, Republic of China, to Manly, N.S.W., Australia, January 3 to February 7. 1970. ports.

4321 **Taiwan University Cricket Group**
■ [Instructional booklet on cricket produced to aid cricket in Formosa]. The Group, [1961]. 23p. illus. diagrs.
*in Chinese*

## THAILAND

4322 **Royal Bangkok Sports Club**
■ The Royal Bangkok Sports Club, sixth cycle commemorative book: Club's 6th cycle Sept. 6th. 1901–1973. Bangkok, the Club, [1973]. [84]p. incl. adverts. illus. ports. [some col.)
*72nd anniversary of Club: includes "Our Club's cricket through the year's [sic], by Ken Gregory. 6pp.*

4323 ————. *Cricket section*
□ [Annual report]. Bangkok, the Club. stats.
*season ?/1930–31, 1931–32, 1969/to date?*

4323 Worcestershire County C.C. v. R.B.S.C.
−1 at the R.B.S.C. Ground, Bangkok, March
■ 24, 1965: souvenir programme. Bangkok, the Club, [1965]. [36]p. mostly adverts. ports.

4324 R.B.S.C. cricket round-up 1972. Bangkok,
■ the Club, [1972]. 48p. incl. adverts. illus.

# CRICKET IN THE PACIFIC

**4324** Snow, Philip Albert, *and* Waine, Stefanie
**-1** The people from the horizon: an illustrated history of the Europeans among the South Sea Islanders. Oxford, Phaidon, 1979. 296p. illus. & ports. (some col.), maps, bibliog.
*cricket pp. 149, 165–6, 240*

## COOK ISLANDS

**4324** Shadbolt, Maurice, *and* Ruhen, Olaf
**-2** Isles of the South Pacific. Washington, National Geographic Magazine, 1968. 211p. illus.
*cricket pp. 40–1*

## FIJI ISLANDS

N.B. For a comprehensive bibliography of Fijian cricket *see* Snow, Philip A. Bibliography of Fiji, Tonga and Rotuma. Canberra, Australian National Univ. P.; Miami, Miami Univ. P., 1969; *and his* Cricket in the Fiji Islands, no. 4326

**4324** Arlott, [Leslie Thomas] John, *compiler*
**-3** Cricket. Burke, 1953. xiii,278p. illus. (some col.), ports. bibliog. ("Pleasures of Life")
*pp. 221–3*

**4324** Bowen, Rowland
**-4** Cricket: a history of its growth and development throughout the world. Eyre & Spottiswoode, 1970. 421p. illus. ports. map, bibliog.
*pp. 124, 155–6, 185, 223, 285, 302, 304, 316, 324, 353, 370, 372*

**4324** Bradman, *Sir* Donald George
**-5** My cricketing life. S. Paul, [1938]. 189p. illus. ports.
*pp. 76–7*

**4324** Cooper, H. Stonehewer
**-6** The coral lands. Bentley, 1880. 2 vols. illus. ports.
*cricket pp. 276–9*

**4324** Cricket Writers' Club
**-7** Cricket heroes, by members of the Cricket Writers' Club; edited by John Kay, cartoons by Roy Ullyett. Phoenix House, 1959. 191p. ports. stats. (Sports Books)
——*another ed.* Sportsman's Book Club, 1960
*pp. 72–82*

**4324** Des Voeux, *Sir* George William
**-8** My colonial service in British Guiana, St. Lucia . . . Fiji . . . Murray, 1903. 2 vols. illus. ports. map
*cricket pp. 88–9*

**4324** Donnelly, Terry A.
**-9** Fiji cricket 1950–1974. Suva, *printed by* Fiji
**■** Times & Herald, 1974. [iv],52p. illus. ports. scores, stats.

**4325** Fiji Cricket Association
Handbook. Suva, The Association. *typescript*
*?/1950/–?*
*1950 ed. by Philip A. Snow. 39p.*

**4325** The I.C.C. Trophy 1979: international
**-1** World Cup cricket: [calendar]. [I.C.C., 1979]. 40p. incl. adverts. illus. ports. map
*includes Fiji cricketers*

**4325** [Keyser, Arthur Louis]
**-2** People and places: a life in five continents. Murray, 1922. xii,337p. illus. map
*cricket p. 73*

**4325** Pacific saga: the personal chronicles of
**-3** the 37th Battalion and its part in the Third Division's campaign. Wellington (NZ), Reed, 1947. 115p.
*cricket pp. 20–21*

**4325** Snow, Philip Albert
**-4** "A century in the Fiji Islands'. *In* Wisden cricketers' almanack 1974
*pp. 123–9*

**4326** Cricket in the Fiji Islands. Christchurch,
**■** N.Z., Whitcombe & Tombs, 1949. xviii,250p. illus. ports. scores, stats. bibliog.

**4326** "Fiji". *In* The world of cricket: edited by
**-1** E. W. Swanton and Michael Melford. Joseph, 1966
*pp. 428–31*

**4326** Stock, Ralph
**-2** The confessions of a tenderfoot: being a true and unvarnished account of his world wanderings. Grant Richards, 1913. 260p. illus. ports.
*cricket pp. 167–71*

**4326** St. Johnston, *Sir* Thomas Reginald
**-3** South Sea reminiscences. T. Fisher Unwin, 1922. 213p. illus. port. maps
*cricket pp. 37–9*

**4326** Thomson, *Sir* Basil Home
**-4** The Fijians: a study in the decay of custom. Heinemann, 1908. xx,396p. illus.
*cricket p. 332*

## NEW CALEDONIA

4326 **Shadbolt, Maurice,** *and* **Ruhen, Olaf**
-5 Isles of the South Pacific. Washington, National Geographic Magazine, 1968. 211p. illus.
*cricket p. 143*

## OCEAN ISLAND

4326 **Grimble,** *Sir* **Arthur Francis**
-6 A pattern of islands. Murray, 1952. ix,250p. illus. map
*pp.48–52 "Cricket in the Blue (Pacific)"*

## PAPUA NEW GUINEA

4326 **Boroko Colts Cricket Club**
-7 Year book together with annual report and balance sheet. Boroko, the Club. *typescript.* scores, stats.
*1961–2/1962–3, 1963–4/–?*
*1962–3 and 1963–4 edited by L. Odgers formed 1949*

4327 **Entwistle, Mary,** *and* **Spriggs, Elsie H.**
■ The way and its heroes: stories illustrating some of the sayings of Jesus. Cargate P., 1945. 80p. illus.
*includes "Kilikity", a chapter on Charles W. Abel of Papua, pp. 13–19*

4327 **Murray,** *Sir* **John Herbert Plunket**
-1 Papua; or, British New Guinea. T. Fisher Unwin, 1912. 388p. illus. map

4327 **Papua New Guinea Board of Control**
-2 Papua New Guinea v. West Indies, world
■ champions at Lae, University Ground, 22 October 1975; Port Moresby, Sir Hubert Murray Stadium, 23 October 1975: souvenir programme. [The Board, 1975]. 24p. incl. adverts. illus. ports. stats.
*pre-visit; with brief history of cricket in Papua New Guinea compiled by L. B. Smart*

## PITCAIRN

4327 **Ball, Ian M.**
-3 Pitcairn – children of the 'Bounty'. Gollancz, 1973. xvi,380p. illus. ports. map
*cricket pp. 250–5*

## SAMOA

4327 **Churchward, William Brown**
-4 My consulate in Samoa: a record of four years' sojourn in the Navigators islands. Bentley, 1887. xii,403p.

4328 **Freeman, Lewis Ransome**
In the tracks of the trades: the account of a . . . yachting cruise to the Hawaiis, Marquesas, Societies, Samoas and Fijis, Heinemann, 1921. 380p. illus.
*chapter XIII 'Samoan cricket'*

4329 **Gibbings, Robert**
■ Over the reefs; illustrated by the author. Dent, 1948. [vi],240p. illus.
*cricket in Samoa pp. 52, 57, 77–81*

## TONGA

4329 **Diolé, Philippe**
-1 The forgotten people of the Pacific; [translated from the French]. Cassell, 1977. 303p. illus & ports. (some col.), maps
*cricket pp. 246, 249*

4329 **Snow, Philip Albert**
-2 Cricket in the Fiji Islands. N.Z. Christchurch (NZ), Whitcombe and Tombs, 1949. xviii,250p. illus. ports. scores, stats. bibliog.
*cricket in Tonga, pp. 8, 12, 17, 44, 141, 153*

# CRICKET IN OTHER COUNTRIES

## MAURITIUS

4330 **Barnwell, Patrick Joseph**
■ A century of cricket in Mauritius. *n.p.*, [c.1957]. 12p.

## NEPAL

4331 **Dikshit, Kumarmani A.,** *editor*
■ Madan Memorial Shield Tournament souvenier [sic]. Nepal, Cricket Association, [c.1953]. 30p. ports. stats.
*text in English and Nepalese; contains short biography of General Madam Shamsher*

## TENERIFFE

4332 **Port Oratova Cricket Club, Teneriffe**
■ Regulations 1826–28.
*MS minute book in M.C.C. Library, Lord's*

# INTERNATIONAL CRICKET

**4333** **Ashley-Cooper, Frederick Samuel**
■ Duke and Son's record of Test match cricket. Penshurst, Kent, Duke and Sons, 1912. 24p. ports. stats.

**4333** **Benson and Hedges** international cricket;
**–1** edited by Frank Tyson. Melbourne,
■ Australian Cricket Board, Publications Sub-Cttee. *annual*. illus. & ports. (some col.), scores, stats.
   *1976 to date*

**4334** **Browne, Frank,** *i.e.* **Francis Courtney**
■ **Browne**
   Some of it was cricket. Sydney, Murray, [1965]. 191p. illus. ports. bibliog.
   *Australian Test matches with England and West Indies*

**4335** **Buchanan, John,** *editor*
■ Cricket's greatest headlines. Lane Cove (N.S.W.), Project Publishing Pty., [1973]. 114p. illus. ports. scores
   *accounts of memorable Test matches*

**4336** **Campbell, R. H.**
■ The international cricket guide, season 1920–21. Melbourne, Farrow Falcon Press Pty., [1920]. 40p. incl. adverts. ports. stats.

**4337** Cricket records: a book of Test match stat-
■ istics and a record of all centuries made in representative cricket in Australia previous to the season 1928–1929. Melbourne, the Speciality P., [1928]. 40p. ports. diagrs. stats.

**4337** **Caro, Andrew**
**–1** With a straight bat. London, Springwood
■ Books; Hong Kong, The Sales Machine Ltd., 1979. 239p. illus. port.
   *on the present and future of world cricket*

**4337** **Cricket action:** [1978/79 pre-season
**–2** souvenir]. Garry Sparke & Associates,
■ 1978. 64p. illus. & ports. stats.

**4337** **Frindall, William H.,** *compiler & editor*
**–3** The Wisden book of Test cricket 1876–77

■ to 1977–78. Macdonald and Jane's, 1978. 1024p. scores, stats.
   ——Ltd. ed. of 300 copies. 1978
   *full scores, etc. of 824 official Test matches*

**4337** **Gibb, James,** *compiler*
**–4** Test cricket records from 1877. Collins,
■ 1979. 210p. stats.
   ——*another ed.* 1979. pbk.
   *gives brief scores of all Tests 1877 to 1978–79*

**4337** **Greig, Anthony William**
**–5** Test match cricket: a personal view.
■ Hamlyn, 1977. 176p. illus. & ports. (some col.), stats.

**4338** **International Cricket Conference**
   Rules. The Conference. *annual*
   *1966 to date*

**4339** **Kent, Cecil**
■ The story of the Tests in England, (1880–1934); containing information never before given in any publication. Hutchinson, [1934]. 127p. illus. scores, stats.
   ——new rev. and enlarged ed. [1935]. 152p. illus. scores, stats.
   *includes the 1934 Tests*

**4339** **Piesse, Ken**
**–1** Great triumphs in Test cricket. Sydney,
■ CP Publishing, [1979]. 84p. incl. covers. illus. ports. facsims. diagrs. scores, bibliog.
   *describes 18 'highlights' from 1902–1978*

**4340** **Pollard, Jack**
   Bumpers, boseys and brickbats. Sydney & Melbourne, Murray, [1971]. 192p. illus. ports. diagrs. score, bibliog.
   *accounts of controversial events, mostly in Test cricket*

**4341** **Roberts, Edward Lamplough**
■ Test cricket and cricketers 1877–1932. Williams, 1932. 145p. illus. scores, stats.
   ——new ed. 1877–1934. Hurst & Blackett, 1934. 240p. illus. ports. stats.
   ——revised & enlarged ed. Hurst & Blackett, 1935. 298p. illus. scores, stats.
   *a statistical record*

4342   Test cricket annual. Birmingham, Hudson
       *1938. 1938. 192p. stats. (complete to 1st
       Jan., 1938)
       1939. 1939. 201p. stats. (complete to 1st
       Nov., 1938)*

4343   Test cricket cavalcade, 1877–1946. E.
■      Arnold, 1947. 278p. illus. scores, stats.
       ——1877–1947. 2nd ed. 1948. xiii,304p.
       illus. scores, stats.

4344   **Robinson, Ray**
■      The wildest Tests. Pelham Books, 1972.
       186p. illus. scores
       ——*another ed.* Sportsman's Book Club,
       1973
       ——rev. & expanded ed. Cassell Aus-
       tralia, 1979. 223p. illus. ports. pbk.
       *accounts of Tests halted by riots and
       disturbances*

4344   **Sarbadhikari, Berry**
–1     My world of cricket: a century of Tests.
■      Calcutta, Cricket Library (India), 1964.
       340,viii,p. illus. ports.
       *essays & reminiscences giving a compar-
       ative study of cricket in many countries over
       last three decades*

4344   **Sichel, Peter,** *compiler*
–2     A century of Test cricket 1877–1977: a stat-
■      istical survey. Claremont, Cape (S.A.),
       the Compiler, 1977. 88p. illus. stats.

4345   **Simpson, A. W.**
■      Pictorial records of cricket tours
       1920–1950. I. M. Young, 1950. 32p. illus.
       ports.
       *team portraits of England, Australia, New
       Zealand, India, South Africa and West Indies*

4346   **Test** cricket. Burton-on-Trent, Allsop &
■      Sons, [1926]. 48p. incl. adverts. 1 illus.
       ports. stats.

4347   **Thomas, Anthony Alfred**
■      Test form at a glance. W. H. Allen, [1953].
       188p. ports. stats.
       ——*another issue.* 1953. pbk.

4347   **Tyler, Martin,** *editor*
–1     Test cricket: a pictorial history of the
■      world's greatest game. Marshall
       Cavendish, 1974. 128p. illus. & ports.
       (some col.), stats. (A 'Golden Hands'
       Book)
       *some of the material was first published in
       the part work 'The Game'. Statistics by Irving
       Rosenwater*
       ——updated and revised ed. 1976
       ——2nd ed. *with title:* The illustrated
       history of Test cricket: the first century.
       1977. 152p. illus. & ports. (some col.),
       stats.
       ——updated and revised ed. 1978
       ——*new ed;* edited by Martin Tyler and
       David Frith. 1979. 168p.

4348   **Vaidya, Sudhir**
■      Figures of cricket: statistics and records
       of Test cricket from 1876–77 to 1960–61.
       Asia Publishing House, 1962, xv,156p.
       illus. ports. stats.
       ——2nd and rev. ed. . . . to 1976. Bom-
       bay, Bombay, Cricket Assoc., 1976. [8],
       vi,436p. illus. stats.
       *statistics & records of 100 years of Test
       cricket from 1876–77 to 1976*

4349   **Webber, Roy**
■      Test match captains, 1876–1939. Hun-
       stanton, Cricket Book Society, 1947. 32p.
       stats. (Publications, Series 1, no. 6)
       *a statistical record*
       *re-issued in "Cricket omnibus, 1946",
       edited by Roy Webber. See no. 982*

4350   ——————, *compiler*
■      The Playfair book of Test cricket. 2 vols.
       Playfair Books, 1952–3. scores, stats.
       *vol. 1 [1877–1939]. 399p.*
       *vol. 2 [1946–1953]. 256p.*

4351   **Wrigley, Arthur,** *compiler*
■      The book of Test cricket, 1876–1964.
       Epworth, P., 1965. 752p. scores, stats.
       *scores of all Test matches*

England v. Australia. "Arrival of The All-England Eleven at Melbourne", 1861 *photo: M.C.C.*

Australia v. England. The Australia cricket team, 1886 *photo: BBC Hulton Picture Library*

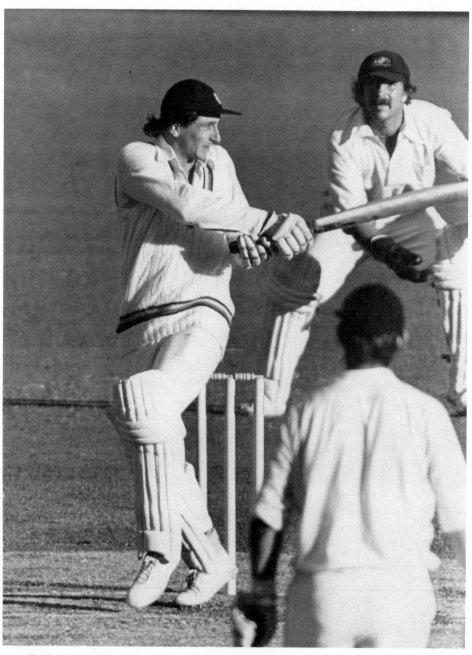

England v. Australia. Derek Randall batting in the Centenary Test, Melbourne, 1977
*photo: Patrick Eagar*

# ENGLAND

**4351** **Dalby, Ken**
**–1** Headingley Test cricket, 1899–1975.
■ Otley, Olicana Books, 1976. xi,158p. illus.
ports. facsims. scores, stats.
  *with full scores of all the Headingley Test matches*

**4352** **Rivers, James**
■ England versus South Africa, India, New Zealand, West Indies: complete Test match records. Boardman, 1950. [iv], 188p. illus. scores, stats.

**4353** **Ross, Gordon**
■ The testing years: the story of England's rise to the top in post-war cricket. S. Paul, 1958. 224p. illus. ports. stats.

**4353** **Victoria Sporting Club**
**–1** Champagne century award. [The Club,
■ 1979]. [16]p. incl. covers, illus. ports.
  *the award, first announced Nov. 1976, is presented to the England player who scores the first century in each Test series. Gives an account of the awards 1976/77–1978/79*

**4354** **Warner,** *Sir* **Pelham Francis**
■ Cricket in many climes. Heinemann, 1900, xiii,271p. illus. ports. scores, stats.
  *account of 5 cricket tours to West Indies, United States and Canada, Portugal, South Africa*

# ENGLAND v. AUSTRALIA

**4355** **[Ambridge, A. A.]**
■ Test matches between England and Australia 1877–1902, by Umpire. New Plymouth, N.Z., Ambridge, 1902. 60p. illus.

**4356** **Ashley-Cooper, Frederick Samuel**
England v. Australia: a synopsis of the Test matches. *Privately printed*, 1904. bs.

**4357** The Australian cricket guide, 1926: a book
■ of records. Nottingham, Richards, 1926. 22p. stats.
  ——*another ed.* 1930. Nottingham, Richards, 1930. 32p. stats.
  *mainly Australia v. England Test records*

**4357** **Australian Broadcasting Commission**
**–1** Bradman to Chappell: a history of Austr-
■ alia – England Test matches from 1946. Sydney, the Commission, 1974. 136p. illus. ports. scores
  ——new ed. 1976. 160p.
  *new ed. includes 1975 Australian tour of England*

**4358** **Baillie, E. H. M.,** *compiler*
■ Since eighteen hundred and seventy seven: comprehensive record of Anglo-Australian Test cricket 1877–1934. Pt. I.

The scoring board. The Compiler, [1934]. 179p. scores, stats.
  *Pt. II, due in 1935 was never published*

**4359** **Barker, Ralph,** *and* **Rosenwater, Irving**
■ England v. Australia: a compendium of Test cricket between the countries, 1877–1968. Batsford, 1969. vi,314p. ports. scores, stats.

**4360** **Bean, Ernest Edward**
Test cricket in England and Australia 1877–1921. Melbourne, *printed by* W. & J. Barr, 1924. 64p. illus. ports. scores, stats.

**4361** **Brumfitt, George,** *and* **Kirby, Joseph I.,**
■ *compilers*
England v. Australia at the wicket: a complete record of all cricket matches played between English and Australian elevens. Ilkley (Yorks.), Brumfitt & Kirby; London, Wright; Melbourne, Boyle & Scott, 1887. 293p. scores, stats.

**4361** **Buchanan, John,** *editor*
**–1** Great moments in England v. Australia
■ Test cricket. Lane Cove (N.S.W.), Project Publishing Pty. Ltd., [1975?]. 100p. incl. covers, illus. ports. stats.
  *mostly from 1932–33 to 1974–75*

4362 **Campbell, R. H.,** *compiler*
■ International cricket: England v. Australia, review of the fifty-one great Test matches . . . ; compiled by R.H.C., edited by 'Old Cricketer'. Melbourne, Edgerton & Moore, [1899]. [40]p. stats.

4363 **Caple, Samuel Canynge**
■ The Ashes at stake: memories of Anglo-Australian cricket. Worcester, Littlebury, 1961. 244p. illus. scores, stats.

4364 **Cardus,** *Sir* **Neville**
■ "The Ashes"; with background of the Tests and pen pictures of the 1948 Australian team. County & Sporting Publications, [1948]. 49p. ports. stats.
  *with summarized scores, results and statistics of all England v. Australia Tests*

4365 **Cary, Clif**
  Cricket Tests and records. Sydney, T. & H. Pty. Ltd., 1946. 202p. scores, stats.
  *scores of every England v. Australia match*

4365 **Cashman, Richard,** *and* **McKernan,**
-1 **Michael,** *editors*
■ Sport in history: the making of modern sport history. Brisbane, Univ. of Queensland P., 1979. xii,368p. bibliog.
  *Papers delivered at a conference of historians, etc. at Univ. of N.S.W. in July, 1977. Contains pp. 148–79 "Imperial cricket: Test matches between England and Australia 1877–1900", by K. S. Inglis. See also nos. 3808–1, 4470–2*

4366 **Catton, James Alfred Henry,** *"Tityrus",*
■ *pseud.*
  Wickets and goals: stories of play. Chapman & Hall, [1926]. ix,303p. illus. ports.
  *includes account of England v. Australia Tests, 1893–1909*

4366 **Centenary** of Australia & England Test
-1 cricket 1877–1977. Print folio. Sydney, 1977. 16p. col. illus. facsims. scores
  *with loose insert of 6 colour prints; limited ed.*

4367 **Davis, R. M.,** *editor*
■ Don Bradman's pictorial Test record: England—Australia cricket. Sydney, printed by Booth, [1932]. 100p. illus. ports. scores, stats.

4368 **Day, Cedric,** *and* **Mason, Michael**
■ The story of Test cricket: England v. Australia. Windsor, C. Day, [1948]. 27p. illus. ports. stats.
  ——*another ed.* Day, Mason & Ford, 1953. 32p. illus. ports. stats.

4369 **Dorey, H. V.,** *editor and compiler*
■ England v. Australia in the "Tests" from

1876–1909. Cricket and Sports Publishers, [1910], xvii,169p. incl. adverts. scores, stats.

4370 **Ellis, Jack L.,** *and* **Liddicut, Arthur E.**
□ Test match—Grace to Bradman: records of all games Australia v. England 1877–1938. West Melbourne (Vic.), Southdown P., [1946?]. 209p. scores, stats.
  ——suppl. 1947/48. [1948?]. [14]p.

4370 **Forsyth, Christopher**
-1 Pitched battles: the history of the Australia-England Test wars. Camberwell (Vic.),
■ Widescope International Publishers, 1977. 120p. illus. ports.
  ——rev. ed. 1978. xii,162p. pbk.

4370 **Foster, David,** *and* **Arnold, Peter**
-2 100 years of Test cricket England v. Austr-
■ alia. Hamlyn, 1977. 93p. illus. ports. facsims. stats.

4370 **Frith, David Edward John**
-3 England v. Australia: a pictorial history
■ of the Test matches since 1877. Guildford, Lutterworth P.; Adelaide, Rigby, 1977. 304p. illus. ports. facsims. scores, stats.

4371 **Ironside, Frederick James**
■ World of cricket: England v. Australia; colony v. colony, 1856–1895. 3rd ed. Sydney, Dymock, 1895. 82p. diagr. scores, stats.

4372 **Kilburn, James Maurice**
■ Cricket decade: England v. Australia 1946 to 1956. Heinemann, 1959. ix,170p. illus. scores
  ——*another ed.* Sportsman's Book Club, 1960

4373 **McCleary, George Frederick**
■ Cricket with the kangaroo: studies in Anglo-Australian cricket. Hollis & Carter, 1950. x,118p. illus. ports. stats.

4374 **Manchester Guardian**
■ Australia v. England 1877–1926: book of the Test matches. Manchester, Manchester Guardian, [1926]. 48p. incl. adverts. ports. scores
  *includes "A survey of Test cricket 1920–26 by 'Cricketer' ", (i.e. Neville Cardus)*

4375 **Marylebone Cricket Club**
■ The story of the Ashes. The Club, 1961. [4]p.
  ——*re-issued 1966*

4376 **Motels of Australia Ltd**
■ Test oddities: the 1965–6 M.C.C. cricket tour of Australia; compiled by L. J. Henderson. Motels of Australia Ltd., [1965]. 16p. incl. covers. illus. stats.

**4377 Pentelow, John Nix**
■ England v. Australia: the story of the Test matches; with full scores and bowling analyses of the matches, birth and death dates of men who have taken part in the games. Bristol, Arrowsmith, 1895. 180p. scores, stats. ("Bristol Library" Series)
——*paper ed.* 1895
——*2nd ed. with title:* England v. Australia: the story of the Test matches from 1877 to 1904. Bristol, Arrowsmith; London, Simpkin Marshall, 1904. 320p. scores, stats.

**4378 The pocket** book cricket guide, 1946–47:
■ story of 143 Test matches in facts and figures . . . Sydney, Associated News-papers Ltd., [1946]. 98p. illus. scores, stats.
*issued pre-1946/47 tour*

**4379 Qantas Gallery**
■ 100 years of cricket between England and Australia: [an exhibition] 27 April-1 July 1961. Qantas, 1961. 32p. illus. ports. stats.

**4380 Rivers, James,** *compiler*
■ England versus Australia: complete Test match records. Boardman, 1949. [vi], 233p. illus. port. scores, stats.

**4381 Roberts, Edward Lamplough,** *compiler*
■ Cricket careers at a glance. Horbury (Yorks.), Sykes, [1934]. 32p. incl. adverts. stats.
*England and Australia Test cricketers*

**4382** England v. Australia 1877–1934: a com-
■ plete record of the 134 test matches. Bir-mingham, Hudson, [1934]. 48p. scores, stats.
*includes 1934 Australian tour of England*
——*another ed.* 1877–1939. 1946. 112p. scores, stats.
*includes full scores of 49 Test matches 1919–39*
——*another ed.* 1877–1947. [1947]. 126p. scores, stats.

**4383** Cavalcade of Anglo-Australian Test
■ cricket 1877–1938. Birmingham, Hudson, 1938. 48p. incl. adverts. ports. stats.
*a statistical record*

**4384 Rothmans**
■ Test cricket almanack; compiled by Sydney Smith. London and Granville (N.S.W.), Rothmans of Pall Mall, [1958]. 64p. stats.
*statistical record of England v. Australia to 1956*
——[1961]. 64p. ports. stats.
*to 1958–59*

——1962–3 series. [1962]. 69p. ports. stats.
——England v. Australia 1964 [1964]. 68p. illus. (some col.) ports. stats.
*to 1963*
——1965–6 series. Sydney, Rothmans (Aust.) Ltd., 1965. 68p. ports. stats.
——M.C.C. cricket almanack: England v. Australia 1968. Rothmans of Pall Mall, [1968]. 32p. illus. ports. diagrs. stats.

**4385** Rothmans book of Test matches: England
■ v. Australia, 1946–1963; edited by Ted Dexter. Barker, 1964. 176p. illus. ports. scores, stats.

**4386 Smith, Sydney**
■ History of the Tests: a record of all Test cricket matches played between England and Australia, 1877–1946. Sydney, Australasian Publishing Co., 1946; London, Harrap, 1947. 359p. illus. ports. scores, stats.
——*2nd English ed.* 1947. 374p.

**4387 Sparks, William P. H.,** *compiler*
■ Test cricket: a unique record of England v. Australia matches (1877–1921). Ouse-ley, [1921]. xi,198p. scores, stats.
——*suppl.* 1924–25. Ouseley, 1925. 20p. scores, stats.
——*suppl.* 1924–26. Ouseley, [1926]. 32p. scores, stats.
——*3rd. ed., i.e. 2nd ed.* Old Royalty Book Publishers, [1929]. vii,223p. scores, stats.

**4388 The Sporting Globe**
■ The "Sporting Globe" Test cricket book; compiled by E. H. M. Baillie. Melbourne, 3DB and The Globe, 1930. 24p. incl. adverts. score, stats.
*records based on all Test matches to date between England and Australia; also includes scores of the first Test of 1930 Australian tour played at Nottingham*

**4389 Standing, Percy Cross**
■ Anglo-Australian cricket, 1862–1926. Faber & Gwyer, 1926. 205p. illus. ports. scores, stats.

**4390 The story** of the Tests. England v. Austr-
■ alia 1877–1920: official souvenir. Sydney, N.S.W., Carters, [1920]. 80p. incl. adverts. illus. ports. scores, stats.

**4391 Test** match cricket, England v. Australia:
■ a concise history of Anglo-Australian cricket. Leng, [1909]. 96p. ports. on cover, scores, stats.

**4392 Toms, T. Stanley,** *editor and compiler*
■ England v. Australia in the "Tests" from 1876 to 1908: being a complete record of

all Test matches between England and Australia, both on English and Australian grounds, with results of all other matches, batting and bowling averages of the touring sides, etc. Cricket & Sports Publishers, [1909]. [v],162p. scores, stats.

4393 **[Trowsdale, T. Broadbent]**
■ A complete history of the Test matches between England and Australia (1877–1905) . . . besides particulars, fixtures and latest averages of the Australian team of 1905, by "Cover-point". Routledge, [1905]. 110p. scores, stats.

4394 **Trumble, Robert**
■ The golden age of cricket. Melbourne, Melbourne C.C., 1968. 122p. illus.
*includes a memoir of Hugh Trumble*

4395 **Wakley, Bertram Joseph**
■ Classic centuries in the Test matches between England and Australia. Kaye, 1964. xxi,345p. stats.
*mostly statistical*
——another ed. Sportsman's Book Club, 1965

4396 **Warner,** *Sir* **Pelham Francis**
■ The story of the "Ashes." Morning Post, [1926]. 8p. illus. ports.
*rptd. in part from the chapter entitled "The Australians" in the Badminton "Cricket" 1920 ed.*

4397 **Wynne, Kenyon**
■ The story of the Tests. London Book Co. for Collins, 1929. 238p. (The Novel Library)

# ENGLISH TOURS TO AUSTRALIA

4398 **O'Hearn, James J.**
■ Summary of touring English cricket teams in the Hunter Valley 1876–1971. [Newcastle, the Author, 1971]. 83f. stats. *typescript*

4398 **Swanton, Ernest William**
–1 Swanton in Australia with M.C.C.
■ 1946–1975. Collins, 1975. xix,252p. illus. ports. scores, stats.
——rptd. Fontana, 1977. pbk.

## 1861–62 Tour (H. H. Stephenson)

4399 **The cabinet:** a repository of facts, figures
□ and fancies relating to the voyage of the "Great Britain" S.S. from Liverpool to Melbourne, with the Eleven of All England; edited by Alexander Reid. Melbourne, J. Reid, 1862
——photographic facsimile ed. S.S. Great

Britain Project, [197–]. [ii],46p.
*consists of 4 issues of The Cabinet, Nov. 9, Dec. 3, 13 and 19, 1861*

4400 **Great Britain** miscellany: ed. by G. H. Wayte. Melbourne, Masin & Firth, 1862. 172p.
*cricket pp. 2, 3, 15, 40–45, 57, 66–67, 68, 91–93, 110, 146–49, 164, 169 and 170–postscript "Result of the first cricket match"; mostly concerned with the voyage out but with pen-portraits of the England XI etc.*

4401 **Men** who have earned success: Messrs.
■ Spiers and Pond: how they took pity on the hungry travellers. Empire Hotels, [1950]. 15p. illus. ports.
*Spiers & Pond, the caterers, sponsored the first English team to tour Australia.*

4402 **Mount Alexander Mail**
The grand cricket match: All England Eleven v. Twenty-two of Castlemaine, March, 14, 15, 17, 1862.
*MS. transcription by H. J. Hill: photostat copy in M.C.C. Library, Lord's*

4403 **Shell Company of Australia Ltd**
■ International cricket. Centenary occasion: this booklet commemorates the first international cricket match played on the Melbourne Cricket Ground on January 1st, 1862. The Co., [1962]. 8p. 1 illus. score
*between Melbourne & Districts XVIII and H. H. Stephenson's XI*

## 1863–64 Tour (G. Parr)

4404 **Anderson, George**
Diary of a cricket tour to Australia in 1863–4
*Unpublished MS. in M.C.C. Library, Lord's*

4404 **The cricketers' register** 1863–4; contain-
–1 ing the scores of the principal matches played in Victoria during the season 1863–4; also, an account of the second visit of the All England Eleven. Melbourne, Sands & McDougall, 1864. 178p. illus. diagrs. scores, stats.
*the account of the tour occupies pp. 106–53*

4405 **[Grace, Edward Mills]**
■ The trip to Australia: scraps from the diary of one of the twelve. W. H. Knight, 1864. 20p.

## 1876–77 Test Tour (James Lillywhite, jun.)

4406 **Arlott, [Leslie Thomas] John,** *and*
■ **Brogden, Stanley**
The first Test Match: England v. Austr-

alia, 1877; The background by John Arlott, The story and account by Stanley Brogden. Phoenix House, 1950. 62p. frontis. (port). score
see also *next entry*

4407 **Brogden, Stanley [Marcel William]**
■ The first Test: the story of the first Test match played between England and Australia at Melbourne in March 1877. Melbourne, Hawthorn P., 1946. [iii],35p. score, stats.

4407 **Southerton, James**
–1 Diary [kept on 1876 England tour to Australia]. 5 notebooks. MS.
*in Trent Bridge Library*

## 1878–79 Test Tour [Lord Harris]

4407 **Bartley, Nehemiah**
–2 Opals and agates; or, Scenes under the Southern Cross and the Magellans: being memories of fifty years of Australia and Polynesia. Brisbane, Gordon & Gotch, 1892. xii,311p. illus. ports.
*pp. 243–47 "Lord Harris in Sydney 1879"*

## 1882–83 Test Tour (Hon. Ivo Bligh)

4407 **Bartley, Nehemiah**
–3 Opals and agates; or, Scenes under the Southern Cross and the Magellans: being memories of fifty years of Australia and Polynesia. Brisbane, Gordon & Gotch, 1892. xii,311p. illus. ports.
*pp. 252–57 "International cricket, January 26th, 1883, at Sydney – Ivo Bligh's Eleven v. Australia"*

4408 **Beeston, R.D.**
■ St. Ivo and the Ashes: a correct, true and particular history of the Hon. Ivo Bligh's crusade in Australia; illustrated by M.C.B. Massie, 1882–3. Melbourne, Australian Press Agency, [1883]. 23p. illus. scores, stats.
——rptd. with foreword by John Arlott. Together with a complete record of the tour of Australia by the English cricketers during 1882 and 1883, reprinted from John Wisden's Cricketers' almanack for 1884. [Ewell], J. W. McKenzie, 1978. [96]p. incl. adverts. with var. pagination. illus. scores, stats.
*limited ed. of 75 numbered copies*

## 1884–85 Test Tour (A. Shrewsbury)

4409 **Shaw, Alfred, *and* Shrewsbury, Arthur**
■ Cricket: Shaw and Shrewsbury's team in Australia 1884–5: the voyage out, descriptions of matches, description of players, the voyage home, batting and bowling averages, etc. Nottingham, Shaw & Shrewsbury, 1885. 181p. port. scores, stats.

## 1891–92 Test Tour (W. G. Grace)

4410 **"Catch-a-Catch"**, *pseud.*
■ Comical cricket in rhyme and picture. Melbourne, Marshall, [1891]. [42]p. illus.

## 1894–95 Test Tour (A. E. Stoddart)

4411 **A.E. Stoddart's** English eleven in Australia: souvenir of England v. Queensland. Brisbane, McCarron Stewart, 1894. 4p.

4412 **Cricket** souvenir: Mr. Stoddart's English eleven season 1894–1895. 1895. 8p. illus.

4413 **Record** of the tour of the All-England cricket team 1895 and scoring card of the last match in South Australia. Adelaide, A. & E. Lewis, 1895. 6p.
*post-tour*

4414 **Souvenir** of Stoddart's English cricket team 1894–5. Sydney, 1894. 14p. illus.

4415 **Stoddart's** English eleven versus combined Queensland and N.S.W. team: souvenir cricket scoring book. Brisbane, McCarron Stewart, 1895. 56p. illus.

4416 **Stoddart's** team in Australia, 1894–5.
■ Cricket P., 1895. 16p. incl. adverts. 1 mounted port. on cover, scores
*post-tour*

## 1897–98 Test Tour (A. E. Stoddart)

4417 **Ashley-Cooper, Frederick Samuel**
■ Stoddart's team in Australia 1897–98. Cricket P., [1898]. 48p. ports. scores, stats.
*post-tour*

4418 **Cabinet-sized** portraits (in position, at
■ the wicket) of A. E. Stoddart's English cricket team visiting Australia 1897–1898 with averages during the cricket season in England, 1897. Newspaper Distributing Agency for A. D. Jones, 1897. [16]p. ports. stats.
*cover-title: The English cricket team in Australia, 1897–98*

4419 **England** versus Combined Australia:
■ illustrated official souvenir. Sydney, [N.S.W. Fresh Food & Ice Company?], 1897. 88p. incl. adverts. ports. stats.

4420 **English** cricketers 1897–8: photographs,
■ performances, fixtures, records: scoring book and souvenir. Brisbane, *printed by* J. F. Searle, 1897. 36p. incl. adverts. ports. stats.

4421 **Illustrated** souvenir & official scoring
■ card: great cricket contest: English Eleven
v. N. S. Wales commencing November
12, 1897. [Sydney, *n.p.*, 1897]. 96p. incl.
adverts. ports.

4422 **Illustrated** official souvenir: cricket con-
■ test England v. N.S.W. commencing Saturday, Feb. 5, 1898. Sydney, *printed by* Builder
Printing Works, [1898]. 88p. incl. adverts.
ports.

4422 **Moody, Clarence Percival,** *editor*
–1 The English cricketers' tour in the
colonies; with portraits, scores, etc.
Adelaide, Hussey & Gillingham, [1898].
48p. incl. adverts. ports. scores
*post-tour*

4423 **Ranjitsinhji, Kumar Shri**
■ With Stoddart's team in Australia; with a
character sketch of the author by "Rover"
[Alfred Gibson]. Bowden, 1898. 288p.
illus. ports. stats.
——2nd ed. 1898
——3rd ed. 1898
——4th ed. 1898
*another ed.* Allenson, 1902. 290p.

### 1901–02 Test Tour (A. C. Maclaren) .

4424 **Cricket** sketches: with portrait of the
■ Yorkshire team. Also particulars of the
Test matches, etc. Leeds, Daisy Ltd.,
[1902]. 12p. port. stats.
*the 2nd issue of no. 7192*

4425 **Official** souvenir of Maclaren's English
cricket team in Australia, season 1901–2.
Sydney, Bookstall Co., [1901]. 44p. illus.
ports. stats.

### 1902–03 Lord Hawke's Team

4426 **Warner,** *Sir* **Pelham Francis**
■ Cricket across the seas: being an account
of the tour of Lord Hawke's team in New
Zealand and Australia. Longmans, 1903.
xiv,204p. illus. port. scores, stats.
*mainly in New Zealand*

### 1903–04 Test Tour (P. F. Warner)

4427 **Craig, Albert**
■ The Excelsior pictorial post card budget:
portraits of the complete English team
who brought home the "Ashes". [The
Oval, Albert Craig, 1904]. 4 postcards in
folder, ports.

4428 **Davis, John C.**
■ Official souvenir of Warner's English
cricket team in Australia. Sydney, N.S.W.

Bookstall Co., [1903]. 58p. incl. adverts.
illus. ports. stats.
*pre-tour*

4429 **My** guide: the English cricketers in Australia, season 1903–04. Melbourne,
Massina, [1903]. 71p. illus. ports. stats.
*pre-tour*

4430 **Queensland Cricket Association**
■ Official souvenir: cricket scoring book,
England v. Queensland, . . . November
27, 28 & 30, 1903, Brisbane Cricket
Ground, Woolloongabba. Brisbane,
[Q.C.A., 1903]. 48p. incl. adverts. ports.
stats.

4431 **Sinclair, Archibald**
■ The M.C.C. tour in Australia, 1903–4.
Warner's team. The Cricket P., 1904, 38p.
ports. scores, stats.
*post-tour*

4432 **[Stainton, James Hayton]**
■ Bringing back the Ashes: a complete and
accurate review of the M.C.C. tour in
Australia, 1903–1904, by "Looker-on".
Sheffield, "Sheffield Telegraph", 1904.
95p. illus. ports. scores, stats.
——2nd ed. 1904

4433 **Standing, Percy Cross**
■ Cricket of to-day and yesterday. Subscription illustrated ed. 2 vols. Caxton,
[1904].
*contains chapters on M.C.C. team in
Australia 1903–4*

4433 **The third** Test match, England v. Austr-
–1 alia, Adelaide Oval, commencing January
15, 1904: illustrated souvenir of the
English team, records of previous Test
matches and scoring sheet. Adelaide, J.
Gazard, 1904. 32p. incl. adverts. ports.
stats.

4434 **Warner,** *Sir* **Pelham Francis**
■ How we recovered the Ashes. Chapman & Hall, 1904. xxviii,340p. illus. ports.
scores, stats.
——2nd (paper ed.) Newnes, 1905. xvi,
208p.

### 1907–08 Test Tour (A. O. Jones)

4435 **Crawford, John Neville**
■ Trip to "Kangaroo" land; illustrated by
"Rip!" "Cricket" Offices, [1909]. 62p.
illus. ports. scores, stats.
*post-tour*

4436 **Davis, John C.**
■ Official souvenir of A. O. Jones' English
cricket team in Australia. Season 1907–

1908. Sydney, N.S.W. Bookstall Co., [1907]. 44p. illus. ports. stats.
*pre-tour*

4437 **Ironside, Frederick James**
■ Special souvenir in honour of the 18th visit of the English cricketers to Australia, 1907–8. Sydney, A. Hordern, [1907]. 24p. illus. ports. stats.
*pre-tour*

4438 **Trevor, Philip Christian William**
■ With the M.C.C. in Australia (1907–1908). A. Rivers, 1908. viii,290p. scores, stats.
*rptd. from the "Daily Telegraph"; post-tour*

## 1911–12 Test Tour (J. W. H. T. Douglas)

4439 **England** v. Australia: official souvenir. Melbourne, Lake & Cowell, by authority of the Victorian Cricket Association, 1911. 32p. illus.
*pre-tour*

4440 **Hobbs, Sir John Berry**
■ Recovering the "Ashes": an account of the cricket tour in Australia, 1911–12. Pitman, 1912. iv,146p. illus. scores, stats.

4441 **Piggott, F. Neville,** *editor*
■ The M.C.C. tour in Australia 1911–12. Warner's team! The Cricket P., 1912. 28p. incl. adverts. ports. scores, stats. (Cricket Press Series)
*the same text as no. 4443, but with more ports.*

4442 **Warner, Sir Pelham Francis**
■ England v. Australia: the record of a memorable tour. Mills & Boon, 1912. xiv,284p. illus. ports. scores, stats.
——L.P. *ed.* limited to 50 numbered copies. 1912
——*another ed.* Sportsman's Book Club, 1956

4443 **Wisden's** souvenir of the M.C.C. tour in Australia. Brighton, W. Wisden; London, Cricket P., 1912. 16p. ports. scores, stats. see *no. 4441*

## 1920–21 Test Tour (J. W. H. T. Douglas)

4444 **Campbell, R. H.**
■ The international cricket guide, season 1920–21. Melbourne, Farrow Falcon Press Pty., [1920]. 40p. incl. adverts. port. stats.

4445 **Fender, Percy George Herbert**
■ Defending the Ashes. Chapman & Hall, 1921. ix,203p. illus. stats. scores

4446 **Mailey, Arthur Alfred**
■ Who's who in Test cricket: England v. Australia, 1920–21; the caricatures by A. Mailey. Hutchinson, [1921]. [32]p. illus.

4447 **Marylebone Cricket Club**
■ M.C.C. tour in Australia 1920–21: [programme]. [M.C.C. 1920]. 5p.

4447 **Queensland Cricket Association**
–1 Mr. J. W. H. T. Douglas's M.C.C. English XI 1920–21 England v. Australia. B.C.G. Woolloongabba, December, 3, 4 and 6: official souvenir and scorebook. Brisbane, the Assoc., 1920. 16p. incl. adverts. illus. ports. stats.

4448 **Victorian Cricket Association**
■ Official souvenir programme illustrated: Australia versus England, Dec. 31st 1920, Jan. 1st, 3rd & 4th, 1921. V.C.A., [1920]. [36]p. incl. adverts. illus. ports. stats. score

## 1924–25 Test Tour (A. E. R. Gilligan)

4449 **Hartt, Cecil L.,** *artist*
■ Souvenir of the M.C.C. XI, 1924–25: sketches. Sydney, R. C. Switson, [1924]. [24]p. incl. adverts. illus.
*pre-tour*

4450 **Le Ros, T. E.,** *pseud.*
■ The tale of the Tests. Clapham Common, S.W.4, Ross Ltd., [1925]. 12p. illus.
*an advertising brochure for Ross's Teleros camera lenses*

4451 **Nickalls, Guy Oliver,** *editor*
■ With the skin of their teeth: memories of great sporting finishes in golf, cricket, . . . Country Life, 1951. 168p. illus.
*cricket section pp. 28–47, by Herbert Sutcliffe, contains account of England v. Australia Test at Adelaide, 1924–5*

4452 **Noble, Montague Alfred**
■ Gilligan's men: a critical review of the M.C.C. tour of Australia, 1924–25. Chapman & Hall, 1925. xii,280p. illus. port. scores, stats.
——*another ed.* Sportsman's Book Club, 1955

4452 **Queensland Cricket Association**
–1 Souvenir programme of the visit of Gilligan's English cricket team season 1924–25. Brisbane, P. J. Frawley, for the Assoc., 1924. 48p. incl. adverts. ports. stats.
*pre-tour*

4453 **Tasmanian Cricket Association**
England v. Tasmania, Hobart, 30 & 31 Jan, and 2 Feb., 1925: official souvenir

programme and scorecard. Hobart, the Assoc. [1925]

**4453** **Victorian Cricket Association**
**−1** [A magazine for the England v. Australia fourth Test at the Melbourne Cricket Ground, February 1925] ⁑
*noted by Ken Piesse in* The Journal of the Cricket Society, *vol. 10, no. 2 (Spring 1981)*

**4454** **Wright, W. R.,** *compiler*
Souvenir of English cricketers' visit to Adelaide. Adelaide, R. M. Osborne, 1925. 72p. incl. adverts.

## 1928–29 Test Tour (A. P. F. Chapman)

**4455** **Australia** v. England 1928–29; souvenir of the third Test at Melbourne. [1929]

**4456** **Fender, Percy George Herbert**
■ The turn of the wheel: M.C.C. team, Australia, 1928–1929. Faber, 1929. 384p. illus. stats. scores

**4457** **Mailey, Arthur Alfred**
■ Cricket sketches for the 1928–1929 Tests. Sydney, N.S.W. Bookstall Co., 1928. 24p. illus.

**4458** **Marylebone Cricket Club**
■ M.C.C. Australian tour 1928–29: itinerary . . . M.C.C., [1928]. 8p.

**4459** **Nickalls, Guy Oliver,** *editor*
■ With the skin of their teeth: memories of great sporting finishes in golf, cricket . . . Country Life, 1951. 168p. illus.
*cricket section pp. 28–47, by Herbert Sutcliffe, contains account of England v. Australia Test at Melbourne, 1928–9*

**4459** **Noble, Montague Alfred**
**−1** Test cricket certainties and possibilities for 1928–29: a review of the prospective players on both sides, the Australian attackers and the English defenders. Sydney, New Century P., 1928. 112p. ports. stats.
*pre-tour*

**4460** The fight for the Ashes, 1928–29: a critical
■ account of the English tour in Australia. Harrap, 1929. 316p. illus. port. diagrs. scores, stats.

**4461** **Official** souvenir and programme:
■ England v. Western Australia, 18 to 20 October, 1928. Perth, Country Publicity Co., [1928]. 48p. incl. adverts. illus. ports. stats.

**4462** **Orient** Line to Australia: visit of the
■ M.C.C. Test team to Australia 1928–9.

R.M.S. Otranto, Orient Line, [1928]. [12]p. 1 illus. ports.

**4462** **Queensland Cricket Association**
**−1** England v. Australia, first Test match 1928–29, played at Exhibition Ground, Brisbane: souvenir programme. [Brisbane, the Assoc., 1928]. 56p. 1 illus. ports. stats.

**4463** **Souvenir** of the England v. Australia Test
■ matches 1928–29; containing five complete score cards, batting averages and bowling analyses of both teams. Austin Rogers, [1929]. 8p. scores, stats.

**4463** **Souvenir** of the fifth Test match, Austr-
**−1** alia v. England, Melbourne, March 8 to 14, 1929. Melbourne, Spring, [1929]. 36p. illus.

**4464** **[Tasmanian Cricket Association]**
■ Visit of English cricket team to Hobart on 18, 19, 21 January, 1929: official souvenir programme and score card. Hobart, [the Assoc., 1929]. [4]p. team port. on cover

**4465** **Wright, W. R.,** *compiler*
■ Souvenir of English cricketers' visit to Adelaide, fourth Test match—Adelaide Oval, February 1st, 1929. Adelaide, Osborne, [1929]. [96]p. incl. adverts. illus. ports. scores, stats.

**4465** **Souvenir** of English cricketers' visit to
**−1** Melbourne, fifth Test match – Melbourne Cricket Ground, March 8, 1929. Adelaide, Osborne, 1929. [40]p. incl. adverts. illus. ports. scores, stats.

**4465** **Wynne, Kenyon**
**−2** The story of the Tests. London Book Co.
■ for Collins, 1929. 238p. (The Novel Library)
*contains 90 pages on 1928–29 tour to Australia*

## 1929–30 M.C.C. Visit (A. H. H. Gilligan)

**4466** **Orient** Line to Australia: visit of the
■ M.C.C. team to Australasia, 1929–30. R.M.S. Orford, Orient Line, [1929]. [12]p. ports.
*cover title: M.C.C. Australasian team 1929–30*
*pre-tour*

**4467** **Turnbull, Maurice Joseph,** *and* **Allom,**
■ **Maurice J. C.**
The book of the two Maurices: being some account of the tour of an M.C.C. team through Australia and New Zealand in the closing months of 1929 and the

beginning of 1930. E. Allom, 1930. 251p. illus. ports. scores. stats.
*deals mostly with tour of New Zealand*

## 1932–33 Test Tour (D. R. Jardine)

4468 **The Australian Cricketer**
■ Special Test souvenir, with careers of players to beginning of 1932–33 season. Melbourne, "The Australian Cricketer", [1932]. 16p. incl. adverts. ports. stats.
*pre-tour*

4469 Autumn annual covering the whole tour
■ of Jardine's eleven in Australia in 1932–33; edited by H. Drysdale Bett. Sydney & Melbourne, [1933]. iv,168p. illus. ports. scores, stats.
*consists of issues for Dec. 1932-Apr 1933 bound together and provided with index*

4469 **Barratt, A. H.**
–1 "Oh! those Ashes"; cartoon by Tom Fisher. Nottingham, *privately printed,* R. Milwood, 1933. [12]p.
*a humorous poem*

4470 **Blundell, R. W.,** *and* **Branson, V. M.**
■ Bodywhine: a treatise on the Jardinian theory; cartoons by R. W. Blundell with a few words by V. M. Branson. Adelaide, Rigby, 1933. 40p. incl. covers, illus.

4470 **The British** Empire. No. 68. B.B.C. TV/
–1 Time-Life Books, 1972. illus. (some col.)
■ *includes pp. 1900–03 "It's not cricket"*

4470 **Cashman, Richard,** *and* **McKernan,**
–2 **Michael,** *editors*
■ Sport in history: the making of modern sport history. Brisbane, Univ. of Queensland P., 1979. xii,368p. bibliog.
*papers delivered at a Conference of historians, etc. at Univ. of N.S.W. in July, 1977. Contains: pp. 127–47 "Cricket's imperial crisis: the 1932–33 M.C.C. tour of Australia", by Brian Stoddart. See also nos. 3808–1, 4365–1*

4471 **Connolly, Roy N.**
■ Contenders and defenders: the Ashes, 1932–33. *Printed by* Peverleys, [1932]. 56p. illus. ports. diagr. scores
*pre-tour*

4472 **Corrie, R. T.**
■ The barracker at bay: an outspoken reply to bodyliners. Melbourne. Keating-Wood, [1933]. 32p.

4472 **Docker, Edward Wybergh**
–1 Bradman and the bodyline series. Brigh-
■ ton, Sydney, etc., Angus & Robertson, 1978. [v],165p. illus. ports. bibliog.

4473 **Fingleton, Jack,** *i.e.* **John Henry Webb**
■ **Fingleton**
Cricket crisis. Cassell, 1946. 295p. illus. ports.
——*rptd.* 1947. 271p.
*"the rise and fall of bodyline"*

4474 **French, Edward Gerald**
The M.C.C. in Australia, 1932–33: a complete record of that sensational cricket tour. *MS typescript.* 1933. xiii,664f. illus.
*illustrated by cuttings from periodicals; in M.C.C. Library, Lord's*

4474 **Glover, Tom**
–1 Ow Zat!: souvenir of the 1932–3 Tests.
■ Sydney, Angus & Robertson, 1932. [20]p. illus.
*cartoons; pre-series*

4475 **Harris, [Stephen] Bruce**
■ Jardine justified: the truth about the Ashes. Chapman & Hall, 1933, xx,240p. illus. ports. diagrs. scores, stats.

4476 **Hobbs,** *Sir* **John Berry**
■ The fight for the Ashes 1932–33: a critical account of the English tour in Australia. Harrap, 1933. 300p. illus. port. diagrs. scores, stats.

4477 **Jardine, Douglas Robert**
■ In quest of the Ashes. Hutchinson, [1933]. 292p. illus. ports. scores, stats.

4478 **Kippax, Alan Falconer,** *and* **Barbour,**
■ **Eric P.**
Anti-bodyline. Sydney, Sydney & Melbourne Publishing Co., 1933. 85p. illus. diagr.
——*English ed.* Hurst & Blackett, 1933. 109p. illus. diagr.

4479 **Larwood, Harold**
■ Body-line?: an account of the Test matches between England and Australia, 1932–33. E. Matthews & Marrot, 1933. 220p. illus. port. diagrs. scores, stats.

4480 The Larwood story, by Harold Larwood
■ with Kevin Perkins. W. H. Allen, 1965. 232p. illus. ports.
——*another ed.* Sportsman's Book Club, 1967

4481 **Mailey, Arthur Alfred**
■ ——And then came Larwood: an account of the Test matches 1932–33; with numerous sketches by the author. Lane, 1933. 244p. illus. ports. scores, stats.
——*cheap ed.* 1934
——*another ed.* Sportsman's Book Club, 1951

4482 **"Man in The Street"**, *pseud.*
■ The "sporting" English?: a commentary. Sydney, MacQuarie Head P., [1933]. 90p.

4483 **Orient Line**
■ M.C.C. Australasian tour 1932–3. Orient Line, S.S. Orontes, [1932]. 16p. 1 illus. ports.
*itinerary and pen portraits of team*

4483 **Queensland Cricket Association**
–1 Official magazine and programme: fourth Test match, Brisbane 1933. [Brisbane, the Assoc., 1933]. 80p. incl. adverts. illus. ports. stats.

4484 **The Saturday** book: eleventh year; edited by Leonard Russell. Hutchinson, 1951. 280p. illus. & ports. (some col.)
*contains "The bowling called boyline" by John Arlott with illus.*

4484 **Shell Company Ltd. of Australia**
–1 A sixer!: cricket record and fixtures. The English team's visit to Australia 1932–33. The Co., [1932]. 12p. ports. stats.
*pre-tour*

4484 **The Tests** 1932–33. Australia v. England:
–2 series of photos illustrating the leading
■ cricketers of to-day, as well as champions of the past. Melbourne, Keating-Wood Pty. Ltd., [1932]. 63p. illus. ports. diagr.
*pre-tour*

4484 **Whitington, Richard Smallpeice,** *and*
–3 **Hele, George**
Bodyline umpire: an eyewitness account of a dramatic era in Test cricket. Adelaide, Rigby, 1974. [xiii],225p. illus. port. fac-sim.

4485 **The willow** test record and score book
■ 1932–33: Australia v. England program. Melbourne, Exchange Press Pty Ltd., [1932]. [24]p. incl. adverts. ports. diagrs.
*pre-tour*

4486 **Wilmot, R. W. E.**
■ Defending the Ashes 1932–1933. Melbourne, Robertson & Mullens, 1933. xvi, 222. illus. ports. diagrs. scores, stats.

4487 **Wright, W. R.,** *compiler*
■ Souvenir of English cricketers' visit to Adelaide, Third Test match January, 1933. Adelaide, R. M. Osborne, [1933]. [96]p. incl. adverts. illus. ports. scores, stats.

### 1936–37 Test Tour (G. O. Allen)

4488 **"The Argus",** *and* **"The Australasian"**
■ Cricket guide for the 1936–37 Test tour; compiled by Percy Taylor. Melbourne,

"Argus" & Australasian", [1936]. 32p. illus. ports. stats.
*pre-tour*

4489 **Australian Broadcasting Commission**
■ Cricket broadcasts 1936–37: Test matches, Sheffield Shield and Testimonial match. Sydney, the Commission, 1936. 8p. folded card, port.

4489 **The Australian cricketers** . . . Test
–1 souvenir 1936–7: photographs, score and resumés of four Tests. [Melbourne, The Australian Cricketer, 1937]. 12p. incl. covers & adverts. ports. score, stats.
*in format almost identical with* The Australian cricketer (see 3382). *Issued for the 5th Test at Melbourne*

4490 **Batchelor, Denzil Stanley**
■ The game goes on. Eyre & Spottiswoode, 1947. v,182p. scores

4491 **Cardus,** *Sir* **Neville**
■ Australian summer: the Test matches of 1936–37. Cape, 1937. 250p. scores
——*rptd.* Hart-Davis, 1949. 205p. scores

4492 **Federal Capital Territory Cricket Association**
M.C.C. visit Canberra, February, 1937: souvenir. Canberra, [the Assoc., 1937]. 16p. ports.
*pre-match*

4493 **Harris, [Stephen] Bruce**
■ 1937 Australian Test tour. Hutchinson, [1937]. 231p. illus. scores

4494 **Lee, Frank**
■ The Ashes?: cricketures of the Australian and English teams: souvenir 5th Test— 26th February, 1937. Melbourne, Magnet Publishing Co., [1937]. 36p. illus.
*pre-match: caricatures of the players*

4495 **Marylebone Cricket Club**
■ M.C.C. Australasian tour. 1936–1937: [itinerary]. [M.C.C., 1936]. [7]p.

4496 **New South Wales Cricket Association**
■ Souvenir Australian tour of the M.C.C. team 1936–37. Sydney, the Assoc., [1936]. [100]p. incl. adverts. illus. ports. stats.
*pre-tour*

4497 **Orient Line**
■ M.C.C. Australasian tour 1936–7. Orient Line, S.S. Orion, [1936]. [16]p. 1 illus. ports.
*itinerary and pen portraits of the team*

4498 **Pollock, William**
■ So this is Australia. Barker, 1937. 164p. illus. port. stats.

**4498  Queensland Cricket Association**
**–1**    Official programme for the Queensland
        visit of the English M.C.C. cricket team.
        England v. Queensland, November 27 to
        December 1, 1936; England v. Australia
        (first Test match) commencing 4 Decem-
        ber, 1936. Brisbane, the Assoc., [1936]. 80p.
        incl. adverts. ports. stats.

**4499  South Australia Cricket Association**
        4th Test match England v. Australia at
        Adelaide Jan. 1937: official cricket sou-
        venir. Adelaide, the Assoc., [1937]. 76p.
        illus. ports. scores, stats.
        *pre-test*

**4500  Western Australia Cricket Association**
        England v. Australia 1936–37: souvenir
        programme. Perth, the Assoc., [1936].
        44p. ports.
        *pre-tour*

**4501  Wrigleys (Aust.) Ltd**
■       The Ashes 1936–1937: the Wrigley sou-
        venir book and scoring records. Rose-
        bery, N.S.W. & Perth, W.A., [1936].
        [24]p. illus. ports. diagrs. stats.
        *pre-tour*

### 1946–47 Test Tour (W. R. Hammond)

**4502  Australian Broadcasting Commission**
        Cricket broadcast book: Test season
        1946–47: England [v]. Australia. Sydney,
        the Commission, 1946. 72p. illus.
        *pre-tour*

**4503  Cary, Clif**
■       Cricket controversy: Test matches in
        Australia 1946–1947. T. Werner Laurie,
        1948. xv,232p. illus.

**4504  Compton, Denis [Charles Scott]**
■       'Testing time' for England: the England
        and Middlesex batsman who here tells
        the story, and gives his personal view, of
        the M.C.C. tour of Australia in 1946–7. S.
        Paul, 1948. 233p. illus. ports. scores

**4505  Cricket Book Society**
■       The M.C.C. in Australia, 1946–47.
        Hunstanton, Cricket Book Society, 1947.
        31p. scores, stats. (Publications. Ser. 2.
        no. 2)
        ——re-issued in "Cricket omnibus 1947",
        edited by Roy Webber. *See* no. 982

**4506  Hammond, Walter Reginald**
■       M.C.C. tour of Australia and New
        Zealand, 1946–47: script of broadcast talk
        . . . Tuesday, 6th May, 1947. *typescript*
        *in M.C.C. Library, Lord's*

**4507  Harris, [Stephen] Bruce**
■       With England in Australia: the truth

about the Tests. Hutchinson, [1947].
204p. illus. scores, stats. (Hutchinson's
Library of Sports and Pastimes)
——2nd ed. with new "Prelude". 1948

**4507  Lee, Frank**
**–1**    The atomic cricket ball: the inside story
■       of the strange happenings of the 1946–47
        Test series. Adelaide, E. J. McAlister &
        Co., [1946?]. 32p. illus.
        *fiction in comic strip form*

**4508  Marylebone Cricket Club**
■       M.C.C. Australasian tour 1946–47: [fix-
        ture list]. [M.C.C., 1946]. 4p. folded card

**4509  Miller, S. G.,** *compiler*
        Ball by ball record together with averages
        and summary of 1946–47 series of Test
        matches England v. Australia in Aus-
        tralia. Ryde (N.S.W.), the Author, [1947].
        11p. scores, stats.

**4510  New South Wales Cricket Association**
■       Australian tour of the M.C.C. team,
        1946–47. Sydney, the Assoc., [1946]. 80p.
        incl. adverts. ports. stats.
        *pre-tour*

**4511  The pocket** book cricket guide, 1946–47:
        story of 143 Test matches in facts and
        figures . . . Sydney, Associated News-
        papers Ltd., [1946]. 98p. illus. scores,
        stats.
        *pre-tour*

**4512  Queensland Cricket Association**
■       England v. Queensland, Brisbane Cricket
        Ground, November 22 to 26, 1946: official
        programme. Brisbane, Queensland Publi-
        cations, [1946]. 54p. incl. adverts. ports.
        stats.

**4512  First Test, England v. Australia, Brisbane**
**–1**    Cricket Ground, November 29 to Decem-
        ber 5, 1946: official souvenir. Brisbane,
        the Assoc. [1946]. 54p. incl. adverts.
        ports. stats.

**4512  Sewell, N. E. J.,** *editor*
**–2**    1946–7 Test cricketers in caricature and
        digest of players records; caricatures by
        Lionel Coventry. Adelaide, Commercial
        Publications of Australia, [1946]. 32p.
        incl. adverts. stats.
        *pre-tour*

**4512  [South Australian Cricket Association]**
**–3**    The Tests: souvenir programme 1946–47.
        Adelaide, Star Publishing Co., [1946].
        32p. incl. adverts. ports. stats.
        *pre-tour*

**4512  [South Australian Cricket Association]**
**–4**    Fourth    Test:    illustrated    souvenir

programme and scoresheet, Adelaide Oval, 1947. Adelaide, [the Assoc., 1947]. [20]p. incl. covers & adverts. illus. ports. diagr. stats.

## 1950–51 Test Tour (F. R. Brown)

4513 **Australian Broadcasting Commission**
■ A.B.C. Cricket broadcast book: Test season 1950–51. Sydney, the Commission, 1950. 65p. illus. ports. diagrs. stats.
*pre-tour*

4514 **Compton, Denis [Charles Scott]**
■ In sun and shadow. S. Paul, 1952. 223p. illus. ports. scores

4515 **Fingleton, Jack,** *i.e.* **John Henry Webb**
■ **Fingleton**
Brown and company: the tour in Australia. Collins, 1951. 256p. illus. scores, stats.

4516 **First** Test match 1950–51 M.C.C. twenty-
■ fourth Australian cricket tour, Brisbane Cricket Ground, December 1–7, 1950: souvenir programme. [Brisbane, Amor Publications, 1950], 3–34p. ports. stats.

4517 **Harris, [Stephen] Bruce**
■ In quest of the Ashes, 1950–51. Hutchinson, 1951. 199p. illus. port. scores, stats. (Library of Sports and Pastimes)

4518 **Kay, John**
■ Ashes to Hassett: a review of the M.C.C. tour of Australia, 1950–51. Altrincham, Sherratt, 1951. 256p. illus. port. scores, stats.

4519 **Marylebone Cricket Club**
■ M.C.C. tour, Australia, New Zealand, 1950–51: [itinerary]. [M.C.C. 1950]. [16]p.

4520 **Marylebone** Cricket Club versus Northern New South Wales: souvenir programme. Lismore, 1950. illus.

4521 **Miller, Keith [Ross],** *and* **Whitington,**
■ **Richard Smallpeice**
Catch! An account of two cricket tours. Latimer House, 1951. 301p. illus. port. scores, stats.

4522 **Moyes, Alban George**
■ The fight for the Ashes, 1950–1951: a critical account of the English tour in Australia. London, Harrap: Sydney, Angus and Robertson, 1951. 260p. illus. scores, stats.

4523 **New South Wales Cricket Association**
■ Australian tour of the M.C.C. team, 1950–51; edited by E. W. Murphy. Syd-

ney, Dymock's Book Arcade, [1950]. 96p. incl. adverts. ports. stats.
*pre-tour*

4524 **Newcastle District Cricket Association**
M.C.C. v. N.S.W. Country: official souvenir booklet and score sheet. Newcastle, the Assoc., 1950. illus.

4525 **Official** programme for the Toowoomba visit of the Marylebone Cricket Club. Toowoomba, J. S. Pry, 1950. 24p. illus.
*pre-match*

4526 **O'Reilly, William Joseph**
■ Cricket task-force: the story of the 1950–1951 Australian tour. T. Werner Laurie, 1951. 192p. illus. ports. scores, stats.

4526 **Queensland Cricket Association**
–1 Q.C.A. cricket magazine. M.C.C. Australian tour 1950–51. M.C.C. v. Queensland, Brisbane Cricket Ground, November 24, 1950. Brisbane, the Assoc., [1950]. 16p. incl. adverts. ports. stats.

4527 **[Robertson-Glasgow, Raymond Charles]**
■ The story of the Test matches: the M.C.C. tour in Australia and New Zealand, 1950–51, by "The Times" Special Correspondent. The Times, 1951. [vi],105p. scores, stats.

4527 **[South Australian Cricket Association]**
–1 The Tests, 1950–51. Adelaide, [the Assoc., 1950]. 24p. incl. adverts. ports. stats.
*pre-tour*

4528 **Sporting Life**
■ Cricket book 1950–51: England v. Australia Tests. Sydney, Associated Newspapers, [1950]. 68p. incl. adverts. 1 illus. diagrs. stats.

4529 **Swanton, Ernest William**
■ Elusive victory: with F. R. Brown's M.C.C. team, 1950–51: an eyewitness account. Hodder & Stoughton, 1951. 256p. illus. ports. scores, stats.

4529 **Treasure** story book for boys. Beaver
–1 Books, [1966?]. 125p. illus. (The Bumper Book Series)
*contains "Sensation at Brisbane" (1950–51 Test)*

4530 **Warner, Rex,** *and* **Blair, Lyle**
■ Ashes to ashes: a post-mortem on the 1950–51 Tests. MacGibbon & Kee, 1951. viii,120p. illus. scores, stats.

4531 **Wellings, Evelyn Maitland**
■ No Ashes for England. Evans Bros., 1951. 256p. illus. scores, stats.

## 1954–55 Test Tour (L. Hutton)

4532 Arlott, [Leslie Thomas] John
■ Australian Test journal: a diary of the Test matches, Australia v. England, 1954–55. London, Phoenix House; Melbourne, Georgian House, 1955. 160p. illus. scores
——another ed. Sportsman's Book Club, 1956

4533 Australian Broadcasting Commission
■ A.B.C. cricket broadcast book: the M.C.C. tour of Australia 1954–55. Sydney, the Commmission, 1954. 64p. illus. ports. diagr. stats.
*pre-tour*

4534 Barnes, Sidney George
■ The Ashes ablaze: the M.C.C. Australian tour, 1954–55. Kimber, 1955. 192p. illus.

4535 Batchelor, Denzil Stanley
■ The Picture Post book of the Tests, 1954–5. Hulton P., [1955]. 48p. illus. scores, stats.
*post-tour*

4536 [Buggy, Hugh]
■ The battle for the Ashes, 1954–5. Melbourne, The Argus and Australasian Ltd., [1954]. 48p. incl. covers & adverts. illus. ports. stats.
*pre-tour*

4537 English Schools Cricket Association
■ 1954–55 "Ashes" Test album, by Robert H. Baker. The Assoc. [1955]. 24p. incl. covers, illus. ports. scores
*post-tour*
——2nd ed. [i.e. rptd., with erratum corrected]. [1955]

4538 Gilligan, Arthur Edward Robert
■ The urn returns: a diary of the 1954–55 M.C.C. tour of Australia. Deutsch, 1955. 207p. illus. scores, stats.

4539 Harris, [Stephen] Bruce
■ Ashes triumphant: Australia versus England, 1954–5. Hutchinson, 1955. 204p. illus. ports. scores, stats. (Library of Sports and Pastimes)

4540 Hughes, Margaret
■ The long hop. S. Paul, 1955. 176p. illus. ports.

4540 Manchester Guardian
–1 The bedside 'Guardian' 4: a selection by
■ Ivor Brown from The Manchester Guardian 1954–1955. Collins, 1955. 256p.
*includes pp. 111–8, "Why Australia lost", by Neville Cardus (on M.C.C. tour to Australia 1954–55)*

4541 Marylebone Cricket Club
■ M.C.C. tour Australia, New Zealand 1954–55: [itinerary]. [M.C.C., 1954]. [12p.]

4542 Mount Gambier and District Cricket
■ Association
English Test tour: M.C.C. v. South Australian Country XI at Vansittart Park, Mount Gambier, S.A., January 18 & 19, 1955: souvenir cricket programme. Mount Gambier, the Club. [1955]. [16]p. incl. adverts. illus.

4543 Moyes, Alban George
■ The fight for the Ashes, 1954–55: a critical account of the English tour in Australia. London, Harrap; Sydney, Angus and Robertson, 1955. 268p. illus. scores, stats.

4544 New South Wales Cricket Association
■ Australian tour of the M.C.C. team, 1954–55; edited by E. W. Murphy. Sydney, the Assoc., [1954]. 96p. incl. adverts. ports. stats.
*pre-tour*

4545 Peebles, Ian [Alexander Ross]
■ Ian Peebles on the Ashes, 1954–55. Hodder and Stoughton, 1955. 196p. illus. port. scores

4546 Picture Post
Cricket victory supplement. 9th April, 1955. Picture Post. 8p. illus.

4546 Queensland Cricket Association
–1 Test cricket magazine. Australia v. England Test series 1954–5. Brisbane, the Assoc., [1954]. 80p. incl. adverts. ports. stats.
*pre-Tests*

4547 Queensland Cricket Magazine
1954–5 cricket series: Qld. v. M.C.C., November 19 to November 23, 1954. Brisbane, Merchandising Services, [1954]. 48p. incl. adverts ports. stats.

4547 Rockhampton Cricket Association
–1 M.C.C. v's. Central Queensland, Rockhampton Agricultural Ground, December 4 and 6, 1954: souvenir programme. Rockhampton, the Assoc., [1954]. 40p. incl. adverts. illus. ports. stats.

4548 Ross, Alan
■ Australia 55: a journal of the M.C.C. tour. M. Joseph, 1955. 271p. illus. ports. scores, stats.

4548 [South Australian Cricket Association]
–1 The Tests: souvenir programme, 1954–55. Adelaide, *printed for* G. R. Lamprell at the Mail Newspapers Ltd., [1954]. 20p. incl. adverts. illus. ports. diagr. stats.

4549 **Swanton, Ernest William**
■ The Test matches of 1954/55. "Daily Telegraph", 1955. xxiii,172p. illus. scores, stats.

4550 **Wellings, Evelyn Maitland**
■ The Ashes retained. Evans Bros., 1955. 208p. illus. port. scores, stats.

4551 **White, Crawford,** *and* **Webber, Roy**
■ England keep the Ashes: the record of the England and M.C.C. tour of Australia, 1954–55. News Chronicle, 1955. [47]p. scores, stats.

4551 **Who's who** in Test cricket 1955. Adelaide,
–1 Dawn Publications (SA) Ltd., [1955]. 40p. incl. adverts. illus. ports. stats.
*pen portraits by Eric Gunton*

### 1958–59 Test Tour (P. B. H. May)

4552 **Australian Broadcasting Commission**
■ A.B.C. cricket book: M.C.C. tour 1958–59. Sydney, the Commission, [1958]. 64p. illus. ports. diagr. stats.
*pre-tour*

4553 **Bedser, Alec Victor**
■ May's men in Australia. S. Paul, 1959. [ix],214p. illus. scores

4554 **Fingleton, Jack,** *i.e.* **John Henry Webb Fingleton**
Four chukkas to Australia: the 1958–59 M.C.C. tour of Australia. Melbourne & London, Heinemann, 1960. [x],190p. illus. ports. scores, stats.

4555 **Kay, John**
■ England down under: the M.C.C. tour of Australia 1958–9. Sporting Handbooks, 1959. 192p. illus. ports. scores, stats.

4555 **Manchester Guardian**
–1 The bedside 'Guardian' 8: a selection
■ from The Manchester Guardian 1958–59. Collins, 1959. 256p. illus.
*includes pp. 119–21 "McDonald soon brings victory to Australia" by Denys Rowbotham on the final Test v. England in 1958–59 series*

4556 **Marylebone Cricket Club**
■ M.C.C. tour Australia and New Zealand: [itinerary]. M.C.C., [1958]. [12]p.

4557 **Miller, Keith [Ross]**
■ Cricket from the grandstand. Oldbourne P., 1959. 169p. illus. port. scores
——*another ed.* Sportsman's Book Club, 1960

4558 **Moyes, Alban George**
■ Benaud & Co.: the story of the Tests, 1958–1959. Angus & Robertson, 1959. [vii],200p. illus. scores, stats.

4559 **New South Wales Cricket Association**
■ Australian tour of the M.C.C. team, 1958–59: programme of matches, photos of players, score sheets, cricket records, items of interest, etc.; edited, compiled and distributed by V. C. Davis and Co. Sydney, the Assoc., [1958]. 80p. ports. stats.
*pre-tour*

4560 **Northern Tasmanian Cricket Association**
■ M.C.C. v. Combined XI, N.T.C.A. ground, Launceston, Dec. 18, 19 & 20, 1958. Launceston. The Assoc., [1958]. 16p. stats.

4561 **Peebles, Ian [Alexander Ross]**
■ The fight for the Ashes, 1958–1959: the English tour in Australia and New Zealand. London, Harrap; Sydney, Angus and Robertson, 1959. 228p. illus. scores, stats.

4561 **Queensland Cricket Association**
–1 Test cricket magazine. Australia v. England Test series. Brisbane, the Assoc., 1958. 36p.
*pre-tour*

4562 **Riverina Cricket Council**
■ M.C.C. v. A Southern N.S.W. XI, Bolton Park, Wagga Wagga, 9 February, 1959: souvenir programme and score card: compiled and edited by F. C. Butler. Wagga Wagga, the Council, [1959]. [24]p. 1 illus. team port. score

4563 **Rothmans** Test cricket almanack:
■ compiled by Sydney Smith. London & Granville (N.S.W.), Rothmans, [1958]. 64p. stats.
*gives statistical record of England v. Australia in 1956; pre-tour*

4563 **[South Australian Cricket Association]**
–1 4th Test 1959 Australia versus England: souvenir program. *n.p.,* [1959]. 20p. incl. adverts. illus. ports. stats.

4564 **Tasmanian Cricket Association**
International cricket at T.C.A. Ground, Hobart: M.C.C. v. Tasmania, Dec. 13, 15, 16, 1958: souvenir programme. Hobart, the Assoc., [1958]. [16]p. incl. adverts. ports.

4565 **[See no. 4561–1]**

4566 **Wangaratta and District Cricket**
■ **Association**
M.C.C. v. Victorian Country XI, Wangaratta 7th February, 1959: souvenir programme. Wangaratta, the Assoc., [1959].
[16]p. incl. adverts. ports. diagr.

4567 **Wellings, Evelyn Maitland**
■ The Ashes thrown away. Cape Town,
Timmins; Folkestone, Bailey Bros. &
Swinfen; Sydney, Dymock's, 1959. viii,
208p. illus. scores, stats.

4568 **Western Australian Cricket Association**
■ M.C.C. Australian tour 1958–59. Western
Australian fixtures, Perth, October 17–21,
24–28: official souvenir programme.
Perth, the Assoc., [1958]. [16]p. illus.
ports. scores

4569 M.C.C. Australian tour 1958–59: M.C.C.
■ v. Combined XI, W.A.C.A., Perth, 24–28
October, 1958: official souvenir programme; edited by John Lee. Perth, the
Assoc., [1958]. [16]p. ports. stats.

4570 **White, Crawford,** *and* **Webber, Roy**
■ The Ashes go home: the record of the
England and M.C.C. tour of Australia
1958–59. Illustrations by L. W. White.
News Chronicle, 1959. [47]p. scores,
stats.

### 1962–63 Test Tour (E. R. Dexter)

4571 **Australian Broadcasting Commission**
■ A.B.C. cricket book: M.C.C. tour of
Australia 1962–63. Sydney, the Commission, [1962]. 64p. illus. ports. stats. diagr.
*pre-tour*

4572 **Benaud, Richie**
■ Spin me a spinner. Hodder & Stoughton,
1963. 160p. illus.

4573 **Clarke, John [Campbell]**
■ Challenge renewed: the M.C.C. tour of
Australia 1962–3. S. Paul, 1963. 231p.
illus. scores

4574 **Commercial Banking Co.**
■ Souvenir cricket score book, Test season
1962–1963. Sydney, C.B.C. Savings
Bank & the C.B.C., [1962]. 31p. ports.
diagr. stats.
*pre-tour*

4575 **Eastern Goldfields Cricket Association**
■ M.C.C. v. Combined W.A. Country XI
. . . Kalgoorlie, 15th & 17th Oct. 1962:
official souvenir programme. Kalgoorlie,
the Assoc., [1962]. 16p. illus. ports.

4576 **Gray, Robert,** *editor*
■ Australian cricket handbook 1962-1963:
M.C.C. tour of Australia. Melbourne
(Vict.), Southdown P., [1962]. 95p. illus.
ports. scores, stats.
*pre-tour*

4576 **The Guardian**
–1 The bedside 'Guardian' 12: a selection
■ from The Guardian 1962–1963. Collins,
1963. 255p. illus.
*includes pp. 20–3 "Australia retain Ashes"
by Denys Rowbotham*

4577 **Lifebuoy**
Book of the Tests: England v. Australia
1962/63. Grosvenor P., [1963]. 20p. ports.
scores

4578 **Moyes, Alban George ("Johnnie"),** *and*
■ **Goodman, Tom,** *i.e.* **Thomas Lyall Good-**
**man**
With the M.C.C. in Australia, 1962–3:
a critical story of the tour. Angus &
Robertson, 1963. xvi,200p. illus. port.
scores, stats.
——*another ed.* Sportsman's Book Club,
1965

4579 **New South Wales Cricket Association**
■ Australian tour of the M.C.C. team
1962–63; edited, compiled & distributed
by V. C. Davis & Co. Sydney, the Assoc.,
[1962]. 80p. incl. adverts. ports. stats.
*pre-tour*

4580 **1962–63 the Tests in Australia: the full**
■ scores and averages: England under E. R.
Dexter v. Australia under R. Benaud.
Manchester, Tennant, [1963]. [7]p.
scores, stats.

4581 **Ross, Alan**
■ Australia '63: with drawings by Russell
Drysdale. Eyre & Spottiswoode, 1963.
223p. illus. scores, stats.
——*another ed.* Sportman's Book Club,
1964

4582 **Rothmans**
■ Test cricket almanack 1962–3 series;
compiled by Sydney Smith. Granville
(N.S.W.), Rothmans of Pall Mall (Australia), [1962]. 69p. ports. stats.
*statistics relate to all England v. Australia
Tests; pre-tour*

4583 **Swanton, Ernest William**
■ The Ashes in suspense: Test matches of
1962/63 . . . the series in figures by Arthur
Wrigley. Daily Telegraph, 1963. 176p.
illus. stats.

4584 **Test** cricket 1962–63: souvenir of the
■ 1962–63 England v. Australia Test series.

Adelaide, Associated Publishers, [1962]. 96p. incl. adverts. illus. ports. diagrs. stats.
*pre-tour*

4584 **Test cricket** magazine. Australia v.
–1 England first Test Brisbane 1962–3 series,
■ November 30 to December 5, 1962; incorporating M.C.C. v. Queensland programme. Brisbane, Merchandising Services, [1962]. 40p. incl. adverts. ports. stats.

4585 **Townsville Cricket Association**
■ M.C.C. v. Queensland Country at Townsville—7th and 8th December, 1962: souvenir programme. Townsville, the Association, [1962]. 24p. incl. adverts. ports. diagrs.

4585 **Wellings, Evelyn Maitland**
–1 Dexter versus Benaud. Bailey Bros. & Swinfen, 1963. x,182p. illus. ports. scores, stats.

4586 **Western Australia Cricket Association**
■ M.C.C. v. W.A. at the W.A.C.A. Ground, October 19–23 [1962]: official souvenir programme. Perth, the Assoc., [1962]. 24p. ports.

4587 **M.C.C.** v. Combined Side at the W.A.
■ C.A. Ground, October 26–30: official souvenir programme. Perth, the Assoc., [1962]. 24p. illus. port.

### 1965–66 Test Tour (M. J. K. Smith)

4587 **A.P.** Test cricket 1965–66. England v.
–1 Australia Test series. Adelaide, Associated Publishers, [1965]. 72p. incl. adverts.
■ illus. ports. diagr. stats.
*pre-tour*

4588 **Australian Broadcasting Commission**
■ A.B.C. cricket book: M.C.C. tour of Australia, 1965–66. Sydney, the Commission, [1965]. 64p. illus. ports. diagr. stats.
*pre-tour*

4589 **Bathurst District Cricket Association**
■ M.C.C. v. Western N.S.W. Country XI, Bathurst sports ground, December 18, 1965: souvenir programme. Bathurst, the Assoc., [1965]. 24p. incl. adverts. ports. diagr.

4590 **Beaudesert and District Cricket**
■ **Association**
M.C.C. versus South Queensland Country at Selwyn Park, Beaudesert, on 8 December, 1965. Beaudesert, the Assoc., [1965]. [20]p. incl. adverts. ports.

4591 **Central Midlands Cricket Council**
■ M.C.C. v. Combined W.A. Country XI, Moora Oval, October 27, 1965: official souvenir programme. Moora, the Council. [1965], 20p. incl. adverts.

4592 **Clarke, John [Campbell]**
■ With England in Australia: the M.C.C. tour 1965–66. S. Paul, 1966. 192p. illus. scores, stats.

4593 **Commercial Banking Co.**
■ Souvenir cricket score book: Test season 1965–1966. Sydney, C.B.C. Savings Bank & C.B.C., [1965]. 31p. ports. diagr. stats.
*pre-tour*

4594 **Euroa District Cricket Association**
■ M.C.C. England eleven, v. Victorian Country eleven. Memorial Oval, Euroa, November 24, 1965: souvenir programme. Euroa, the Assoc., [1965]. [8]p. incl. covers. 1 illus. ports.

4594 **The Guardian**
–1 The bedside 'Guardian' 15: a selection
■ from The Guardian 1965–1966. Collins, 1966. 255p. illus.
*includes pp. 232–4 "Test cricket in Australia", by Denys Rowbotham [on 3rd Test, 1965–66 series]*

4595 **The Hamilton Spectator**
■ Victorian Country XI versus M.C.C. XI, Melville Oval, Hamilton, 17 November, 1965: souvenir program. Hamilton, "Spectator" in conjunction with Hamilton & District C.A., [1965]. [12]p. ports.

4596 **[Henderson, L. J.],** *compiler*
The 29th tour: M.C.C. in Australia, 1965–6. Produced by "Cricket-figurs". Bondi Junction (N.S.W.), the Compiler, [1966]. 46p. scores, stats. *typescript*
*post-tour; a statistical review*

4597 **Mackay, Ken**
■ Quest for the Ashes, [by] Ken "Slasher" Mackay in collaboration with Frank O'Callaghan. Pelham, 1966. 196p. illus. ports. scores. (Cricketers' Library)
——*another ed.* Sportsman's Book Club, 1967

4598 **Marylebone Cricket Club**
M.C.C. tour Australia and New Zealand 1965–1966: [itinerary, match programme . . . ]. [M.C.C. 1965]

4599 **Motels of Australia Ltd.**
■ Test oddities: the 1965–6 M.C.C. cricket tour of Australia; compiled by L. J. Henderson. Motels of Australia, Ltd., [1965]. 16p. incl. covers, illus. stats.

**4600 Mount Gambier and District Cricket**
■ **Association**
English Test tour: M.C.C. v. South Austr-
alia Country XI at Vansittart Park, Mount
Gambier, S.A., December 22, 1965.
Mount Gambier, the Assoc., [1965].
[16]p. incl. adverts. illus.

**4601 New South Wales Cricket Association**
■ Australian tour of the M.C.C. team
1965–66; edited, compiled and distributed
by V. C. Davis & Co. Sydney, the Assoc.,
[1965]. 76p. incl. adverts. ports. stats.
*pre-tour*

**4602 Riverina Cricket Council**
■ M.C.C. v. A Southern N.S.W. Country
XI, Albury sportsground, 20 December,
1965: souvenir programme and score
sheet compiled and edited by W.
O'Loughlin. Riverina, the Council,
[1965]. 12p. incl. adverts. ports.

**4603 Rothmans**
■ Test Cricket almanack, 1965–66 series;
compiled by Sydney Smith. Sydney,
Rothmans of Pall Mall (Aust.) Ltd., 1965.
68p. ports. stats.
*pre-tour*

## 1968–69 Women's C.A. Tour

**4604 Women's Cricket Association**
■ Report of the tour of Australia & New
Zealand, 1968/69; edited by N[etta] Rheinberg. Frittenden, Nr. Cranbrook, Kent,
the Assoc., [1969]. 17p. port. (on cover),
scores, stats.

## 1970–71 Test Tour (R. Illingworth)

**4605 Australia** v. England, first Test 1970,
■ Nov. 27 to Dec. 2. Brisbane, Penpress,
[1970]. 24p. incl. adverts. 1 illus. port.
diagrs. stats.

**4606 Australian Broadcasting Commission**
■ ABC cricket book: M.C.C. tour of Australia 1970–71; edited by Alan McGilvray.
Sydney, the Commission, 1970. 88p.
illus. ports. diagr. stats.
*pre-tour*

**4607 The Cricketers' Club of London**
■ Australian tour 1971. [The Club, 1971]
[8]p. incl. covers, illus. map
*a social not a playing club; pre-tour*

**4608 The historic** Test: Australia v. England,
■ Perth, Western Australia, 11–16 December, 1970. Perth, Test Match Council,
[1970]. [48]p. illus. ports. stats.
*pre-match*

**4609 New South Wales Cricket Association**
■ M.C.C. team tour of Australia, 1970–71;
compiled and edited by Chris Ankin and
Julian Oakley. Sydney, Industrial Marketing & Printing Services, [1971]. 32p.
incl. adverts. illus. ports. scores. stats.
*post-tour*

**4610 Queensland Cricket Association**
■ Cricket News. International cricket
match, Brisbane Cricket Ground:
Queensland v. M.C.C., November 20, 21,
22, 23, 1970. Brisbane, the Assoc., [1970].
16p. incl. adverts.
*includes 'A portrait of T. R. Veivers' by
Irving Rosenwater*

**4610 First Test 1970. Australia v. England, Bris-
–1** bane Cricket Ground, 1970–71 series,
Nov. 27 to Dec. 2. Brisbane, the Assoc.,
[1970]. 24p. illus. ports. diagrs. stats.

**4610 Weekend magazine
–2** Cricket, lovely cricket. Perth, Weekend
News, December 19, 1970. 16p. illus.
ports.
*cover and 4pp devoted to cricket, including
"WA cricket is a big boy now", by Ted Jolly;
and "How the Test was won" by David
Brewtnally commemorating the first ever Test
in Perth*

**4611 Western Australian Cricket Association**
■ M.C.C. Australian tour, 1970–1971: 2nd
Test match: souvenir programme. Perth,
the Assoc., 1970. 40p. illus. ports. stats.

**4612 M.C.C. tour of Australia 1970–71: Aus-
tralia v. England, second Test match.
Appeal! Perth, the Assoc. [1970].
*pre-Test*

**4613 Whitington, Richard Smallpeice**
■ Captains outrageous?: cricket in the
seventies. S. Paul, 1972. 244p. illus. ports.
scores, stats.

## 1971 Club Cricket Conference Tour

**4614 Club Cricket Conference**
■ 1971 Australian tour: programme. The
Conference [1971]. [28]p. incl. adverts.
port.
——[Results]. [1971]. bs.

**4615 [Speakman, Arthur]**
■ The Club Cricket Conference tour of
Australia, Jan. 1st to Feb. 7th, 1971 as
seen, heard, and enjoyed by one of the
party. The Author, [1971]. [iii],12p.
*typescript*

## 1974–75 Test Tour (M. H. Denness)

**4615** **Australian Broadcasting Commission**
**–1** ABC cricket book 1974–75: MCC tour of
■ Australia; edited by Alan McGilvray.
Sydney, the Commission, 1974. 88p.
illus. ports. diagrs. stats.
*pre-tour*

**4615** **Australian cricket**
**–2** Ashes special; edited by Phil Tresidder.
■ Rushcutters Bay, Modern Magazines
(Holdings) Ltd., 1975. 72p. incl. covers &
adverts. illus. & ports. (some col.),
scores, stats.

**4615** **Australian Cricket Society.** *A.C.T. Branch*
**–3** M.C.C. team souvenir; profiles by Julian
■ Oakley, caricatures by Percy Samara-
Wickrama. Canberra, the Branch, [1974].
20p. incl. covers. illus. ports. score, stats.
*pre-tour*

**4615** **Buchanan, John,** *editor*
**–4** Australia v. England. The 10 Test
■ matches of 1975. Sydney, Project Publishing Pty. Ltd., [1975?]. 124p. incl. covers
+[4]p. insert. illus. ports. scores, stats.
*post-tours*

**4615** **Gold Coast and District Cricket**
**–5** **Association**
M.C.C. tourists versus South East
Queensland, George Jackman Oval,
Southport, Tuesday, November 26th,
1974. Southport, the Assoc., [1974]. 6p.
ports. stats.

**4615** **The Guardian**
**–6** The bedside 'Guardian' 24: a selection
■ from The Guardian 1974–75; edited by
W. L. Webb. Collins, 1975. 263p. illus.
*includes pp. 36–7, "Typhoon hits England
– latest", [a leader article on the 1st Test at
Brisbane]*

**4615** **Martin-Jenkins, Christopher**
**–7** Assault on the Ashes: M.C.C. in Austr-
■ alia and New Zealand 1974–75.
Macdonald and Jane's, 1975. viii,216p.
illus. scores, stats.
——*another ed.* Newton Abbot, Reader's
Union, 1975

**4615** **M.C.C. tour of Australia**: programme
**–8** 1974–75. T.A.A., [1974]. [6]p. folded card,
■ ports.

**4615** **New South Wales Cricket Association**
**–9** M.C.C. – Australia 1974–75: souvenir
■ programme. [Sydney], the Assoc., [1974].
40p. incl. covers & adverts. illus. (some
col.), ports.

**4615** **Newcastle District Cricket Association**
**–10** M.C.C. vs. Northern N.S.W. at New-
■ castle No. 1 Sports Ground, February 1,
2 and 3, 1975: souvenir programme.
[Hamilton, the Assoc., 1975]. 20p. incl.
adverts. illus. ports.

**4615** **Queensland Cricket Association**
**–11** 'Gabba cricket: – '74–75 M.C.C. tour.
■ International match: Queensland vs.
M.C.C., 'Gabba Cricket Ground, Nov.
22–Nov. 25, 1974. Brisbane, the Assoc.,
[1974]. 24p. incl. covers & adverts. illus.
ports. stats.

**4615** 'Gabba cricket. '74–75 M.C.C. tour. Nov.
**–12** 29 – Dec. 4, 1974. 'Gabba Cricket Ground.
■ 1st Test 1974–75, Australia versus
England: souvenir programme. Brisbane,
the Assoc., [1974]. 32p. incl. covers &
adverts. illus. ports. stats.

**4615** **South Australian Cricket Association**
**–13** 1974–75 M.C.C. tour – cricket. Australia
■ v. England, fifth Test 1974–75, Adelaide
Oval, January 25–30, 1975: souvenir
programme. Adelaide, the Assoc., [1975].
28p. illus. ports. scores

**4615** **Sunday Observer**
**–14** Ashes of terror: souvenir book of the
■ 1974–75 M.C.C. tour of Australia. Richmond (Vic.), Maxwell Newton, [1975].
[80]p. illus. & ports. (some col.), scores,
stats.
*post-tour*

**4615** **Sunshine Coast Cricket Association**
**–15** Qld. Country vs. M.C.C., Nambour,
November 20, 1974: souvenir programme. [Nambour, the Assoc., 1974].
20p. incl. adverts. ports. stats.
*pre-match which was abandoned*

**4615** **Tresidder, Phil,** *editor*
**–16** M.C.C. cricket tour guide 1974–75.
■ Sydney, Modern Magazines (Holdings)
Ltd., [1974]. 68p. incl. covers & adverts.
illus. ports. scores, stats.
*pre-tour*

**4615** **Tyson, Frank Holmes**
**–17** Test of nerves. Melbourne, Manark Pty.,
■ 1975. 256p. illus. scores, stats.
——*another ed.* 1975. pbk.

**4615** **Victorian Cricket Association**
**–18** Test souvenir England v. Australia [third
■ Test]. [Melbourne], the Assoc., [1975].
32p. incl. adverts. illus. ports. scores,
stats.

**4615** Test souvenir: official publication of the
**–19** Victorian Cricket Association. Australia
■ v. England, sixth Test. Jolimont, the

Assoc., [1975]. 32p. incl. adverts. illus. ports. scores, stats.

**4615** **The Western Australian Cricket**
**−20** **Association**
■ The second Test, Australia v. England, WACA Ground, Perth. December 13–18, 1974: souvenir programme. Perth, the Assoc., [1974]. 20p. incl. covers, illus. ports.

## 1975 Club Cricket Conference Tour

**4615** **Club Cricket Conference**
**−21** Australian tour 75. The Conference, ■ [1975]. [48]p. incl. adverts. 1 illus. ports.
*pre-tour*

## 1976–77 Centenary Test (A.W. Greig)

**4615** **The Australian**
**−22** Match of the century: a souvenir issue to ■ commemorate a century of Tests between Australia and England, March 15, 1877 – March 12, 1977: [compiled by] Murray Hedgcock and Phil Wilkins. Parramatta, (Vic.), Cumberland Newspapers, issue 11 Mar. 1977, no. 3938. 12p. incl. adverts. illus. ports. (some col.)

**4615** **Australian Broadcasting Commission**
**−23** ABC cricket book – Pakistan tour of ■ Australia 1976–77 – Australian tour of New Zealand 1977 – England Australia centenary match; edited by Alan McGilvray. Sydney, the Commission, [1976]. 65p. illus. (some col.), ports. diagr. stats.
*pre-tours*

**4615** **Australian cricket**
**−24** Centenary Test special. Sydney, Australian cricket, 1977. 70p. illus. ports. scores, stats.
*pre-match special issue March 1977*

**4615** **Australian Cricket Board**
**−25** Centenary Test, Melbourne, March 12– ■ 17, 1977: official souvenir. Melbourne, The Board, 1977. 100p. incl. adverts. illus. & ports. (some col.), stats.

**4615** **The centenary** & jubilee pair: a commem-
**−26** orative folder issued in honour of the Centenary Test . . . and the Jubilee Test . . . Test & County Cricket Board, [1977]. 8p. ports. facsims.
*contains team portraits, printed scorecards and Australian and G.P.O. first day covers; limited to 500 numbered copies*

**4615** **Chappell, Gregory Stephen**
**−27** The 100th summer: 76–77 season— ■ Pakistan – New Zealand – Centenary Test. Toorak (Vic.), Garry Sparke & Associates, 1977. iv,220p. illus. & ports. (some col.), scores, stats.

**4615** **Cricketer**
**−28** Test of the century. Special issue; edited by Eric Beecher. Melbourne, Newspress Pty. Ltd., March 1977. 74p. incl. adverts. illus. ports. scores, stats.
*pre-match; vol. 4, no. 6 of Cricketer*
The incredible Test; edited by Eric Beecher; colour photos by Garry Sparke. Melbourne, Newsweek Pty. Ltd., April, 1977. 74p. incl. adverts. illus. ports. scores, stats.
*post-match; vol. 4, no. 7 of Cricketer*

**4615** **Frindall, William H.**
**−29** Frindall's score book, Jubilee edition: the ■ Centenary Test at Melbourne and England versus Australia, 1977: edited by Howard Spencer. Birmingham, Lonsdale P., 1977. 129p. illus. diagr. scores, stats.
*in hardback and limp covers*

**4615** **National 0–10 Network Television**
**−30** Cricket scene [1976–77], edited by Rod ■ Nicholson. Hawthorn (Vic.), Craftsman Press Pty. Ltd., 1976. 64p. incl. adverts. illus. ports. stats.
*with inset colour poster of Greg Chappell*

**4615** **Phillipson, Neill**
**−31** The Jubilee Test series 1977: England ■ versus Australia. Toorak (Vic.), Garry Sparke, 1977; London, Pelham Books, 1978. 80p. illus. scores, stats.

**4615** **Time**
**−32** [Issue of March 14, 1977]. The best of enemies – Test of the century. Time Magazine
*the front cover, editorial and pp.58–64 were devoted to cricket*

**4615** **Tyson, Frank Holmes**
**−33** The centenary Test: official publication of ■ the Australian Cricket Board. Sydney, the Board; London, Pelham Books, 1977. 64p. illus. & ports. (some col.), score, stats.
*contains excerpt from the account of the 1877 Test match by John Arlott and Stanley Brogden (see 4406)*

**4615** **Victorian Cricket Association**
**−34** Test souvenir: Australia v. England. Jolimont, the Assoc., [1977]. 32p. incl. adverts. illus. ports. scores, stats.

## 1978–79 Test Tour (J. M. Brearley)

**4615** **Albany and District Cricket Association**
**−35** England vs. Western Australia Country ■ XI, Centennial Oval, Wednesday 13 December 1978. Albany (W.A.), the Assoc., [1978]. 32p. incl. adverts. diagr.

4615 **Australian Broadcasting Commission**
–36 England tour of Australia 1978–79; edited
■ by Alan McGilvray. Sydney, the Commission, 1978. 104p. illus. (some col.), ports.
diagr. stats.

4615 **Australian cricket**
–37 England cricket tour guide 1978–79;
■ [edited by] Phil Tresidder. [Sydney],
Magazines Pty. Ltd., [1978]. 70p. incl.
adverts. illus. & ports. (some col.), stats.
*pre-tour*

4615 **[Australian Cricket Board]**
–38 Test cricket. Australia vs. England: the
■ battle for the Ashes: official souvenir. The
Benson & Hedges Co. Pty. Ltd., 1978.
64p. incl. covers & adverts. illus. (some
col.), ports. diagr. stats.

4615 The Benson & Hedges Cup fixture: sou-
–39 venir programme . . . to commemorate
■ the 1978/79 tour by the England cricket
team. The Board Publications Sub-Cttee.,
[1978]. [32]p. incl. adverts. illus. & ports.
(some col.), diagr.

4615 Benson & Hedges World Series Cup:
–40 official souvenir programme. Pymble,
■ Playbill (Australia) Pty. Ltd., 1979. 36p.
incl. covers & adverts. illus. & ports.
(some col.), diagrs.

4615 **Boycott, Geoffrey**
–41 Put to the test – England in Australia
■ 1978–79. Barker, 1979. 200p. illus. scores,
stats.

4615 **Brearley, Mike,** *and* **Doust, Dudley**
–42 The Ashes retained. Hodder & Stough-
■ ton, 1979. 160p. illus. (some col.), ports.
scores, stats.

4615 **Bundaberg Cricket Association**
–43 Cricket: England v. Queensland Country,
played at Salter Oval, Bundaberg, 22
November 1978. Bundaberg (Qld.), the
Assoc., 1978. 15p. incl. adverts. illus.
ports.
*pre-match*

4615 **Cornhill Insurance**
–44 Tour digest. Facts, figures and photo-
■ graphs of England's Test cricketers in
Australia 1978/1979. Cornhill Insurance,
(1978]. 40p. ports. stats.
*pre-tour: biographies & statistics by Bill*
*Frindall: photographs by Patrick Eagar*

4615 **Cricket action:** [1978/79 pre-season
–45 souvenir]. Garry Sparke & Associates,
■ 1978. 64p. illus. ports. stats.

4615 **Cricket** in Australia. Melbourne, Garry
–46 Sparke & Associates. illus. & ports. (some
■ col.), diagrs. scores, stats.
*No. 1. 1979. 112p.*
*The 1978–79 Australia season, including 2*
*Test series, Australia v. England and Aus-*
*tralia v. Pakistan*

4615 **Cricketer**
–47 Cricket 1978–79: an Ashes special; edited
■ by Ken Piesse. Melbourne, Newspress
Pty. Ltd., [1978]. 74p. incl. covers and
adverts. illus. ports. stats.
*pre-tour*

4615 **Frindall, William H.**
–48 Frindall's score book Australia v. England
■ 1978–79. Macdonald & Jane's. 1979. 159p.
illus. scores, stats.
*post-tour*

4615 **Frith, David Edward John**
–49 The Ashes '79. Angus & Robertson, 1979.
■ 208p. illus. team port. scores, stats.

4615 **Lee, Alan**
–50 A pitch in both camps: England and
■ World Series Cricket in Australia 1978–79.
S. Paul, 1979. 188p. illus. ports. stats.

4615 **McFarline, Peter**
–51 A testing time. Richmond (Vic.), Hutch-
■ inson of Australia, 1979. [ix],176p. illus.
scores, stats.

4615 **Martin-Jenkins, Christopher**
–52 In defence of the Ashes: England's
■ victory, Packer's progress. Macdonald
and Jane's, 1979. x,218p. illus. ports.
scores, stats.
*mostly on Test series*

4615 **Meyer, John**
–53 From the outer: a view of the Ashes series
■ 1978–79. Wembley (Western Aust.), the
Author, 1979. viii,150p. illus. ports.
scores, stats.
*in a series of descriptive letters to a friend*
*in England*

4615 **Queensland Cricket Association**
–54 'Gabba cricket; '78–'79. Queensland v.
England, November 24–27: official programme. Brisbane, the Assoc., [1979].
32p. incl. adverts. illus. ports. stats.

4615 **Taylor, Robert William,** *and* **Gower,**
–55 **David Ivon**
■ Anyone for cricket?: a diary of an Australian tour; with the assistance of Patrick
Murphy. Pelham Books, 1979. 176p. illus.
scores, stats.
*with statistical summary of the tour by*
*Robert Brooke*

4615 **Yallop, Graham Neil**
–56 Lambs to the slaughter. Melbourne,
■ Outback P., 1979. [v],175p. illus. scores,
stats.
*personal account of the Australian 1978–79 season*

## 1979 Club Cricket Conference Tour

4615 **The Club Cricket Conference**
–57 Tour to Australasia 1979. The Confer-
■ ence, [1978]. [52]p. incl. adverts. 1 illus.
ports.
*pre-tour*
Tour of Australasia – Jan/Feb. 1979. The
Conference, [1979]. [44]f. facsims. scores
*post-tour*

## 1979–80 Tour (J. M. Brearley)

4615 **Australian Broadcasting Commission**
–58 ABC cricket book – England, West Indies
■ in Australia, 1979–80; edited by Alan
McGilvray. Sydney, the Commission,
1979. 96p. illus. (some col.). ports. diagrs.
stats.
*pre-tours*

4615 **Benson and Hedges Co.**
–59 Test programme 1979–80: Australia v.
West Indies – Australia v. England.
Sheffield Shield. Sydney, Playbill (Australia), 1979. 52p. incl. covers & adverts.
illus. & ports. (some col.)
*pre-series*

4615 **Cricketer**
–60 Cricketer's cricket guide 1979–80; edited
■ by Ken Piesse. Melbourne, Newspress
Pty. Ltd., [1979]. 76p. incl. covers &
adverts. illus. ports. stats.

4615 **The National Nine Network,** *and* **The**
–61 **Benson and Hedges Co.**
■ Cricket tour guide 1979/80; edited by Brad
Boxall. Sydney, Modern Magazines,
[1979]. 112p. incl. covers & adverts. illus.
(some col.), ports. stats.
*pre-tour*

## 1979–80 Universities Tour

4615 **Oxford** and Cambridge Universities
–62 cricket tour of Australia, December 1979
■ – January 1980. The Tour Management,
[1979]. [24]p. incl. adverts. ports.
*pre-tour itinerary with pen-portraits of team*

# ENGLAND v. SOUTH AFRICA

4616 **Ashley-Cooper, Frederick Samuel**
■ The South African cricket guide: a book
of records. Nottingham, Richards, 1929.
34p. stats.
*mainly records of South Africa v. England Tests*

4617 **Caple, Samuel Canynge**
■ The Springboks at cricket: England versus
South Africa, 1888–1960. Worcester,
Littlebury, 1960. 320p. illus. ports. scores,
stats.

4618 **Day, Cedric,** *and* **Mason, Michael**
■ The story of Test cricket: England v.
South Africa . . . tourists reviewed by
John B. Hughes. Windsor, W.D.S.,
[1948]. 15p. illus. ports.
——*another ed. with title:* Day & Mason
1951 Test book: England v. South Africa.
Windsor, Day, Mason & Ford, [1951].
23p. illus. ports. stats.

4618 **W., F. M.**
–1 England vs. South Africa, the Test
matches in a nutshell . . . Cape Town,
Central News Agency, [191–?]. 29p.
*cover-title:* A book of reference for cricketers: England vs. South Africa

## ENGLISH TOURS TO SOUTH AFRICA AND ZIMBABWE RHODESIA

### 1888–89 Test Tour (C. Aubrey Smith)

4619 **The cricketing** record of Major Warton's
■ tour 1888–89. Port Elizabeth, C. Cox,
1889. [viii],219p. ports. scores
*post-tour*

4620 **The visit** of Major Warton's team to
South Africa 1888-9. Port Elizabeth,
Walton, [1888]
*pre-tour*

4621 **Wright, W. R.**
■ Abel and Briggs: an amusing adventure
in South Africa. All England Athletic
Publishing Co., 1888. [4]p. folded card. 2
ports. on cover
*during the 1888–89 tour*

### 1891–92 Test Tour (W. W. Read)

4622 **Visit** of W. W. Read's 1891–1892 English
cricket team to South Africa. Port Elizabeth, Impey Walton, 1892. 108p. illus.

## 1895–96 Test Tour (Lord Hawke)

4623 **Cadwallader, H. G.,** *ed.*
■ Lord Hawke's team of English cricketers in South Africa, 1895–96. Cape Town, Country Life, [1895]. 88p. ports. stats.
*pre-tour*

## 1898–99 Test Tour (Lord Hawke)

4624 **Souvenir** of the visit of Lord Hawke's 2nd
■ English team to South Africa 1898–1899. Cape Town, W. A. Richards, [1899]. 71p. illus. ports. scores
*post-tour*

## 1905–06 Test Tour (P. F. Warner)

4625 **Difford, Ivor Denis**
The visit of the M.C.C. team 1905–1906, with biographical sketches. Johannesburg, Argus & Co., 1905. 64p. illus. ports.
*pre-tour*

4626 **M.C.C.** v. O.F.S.: souvenir book of match. Bloemfontein, Fraser, 1906. 32p. illus.
*match against Orange Free State*

4627 **The M.C.C.'s** South African tour 1905–1906. Cape Town, Hart, 1905. 20p.

4628 **Warner,** *Sir* **Pelham Francis**
■ The M.C.C. in South Africa. London, Chapman & Hall; Capetown, Juta, 1906. xiii,233p. illus. ports. scores, stats.

## 1909–10 Test Tour (H. D. G. Leveson Gower)

4629 **Difford, Ivor Denis**
■ The M.C.C. in South Africa, 1909–10: portraits and biographies of the M.C.C. team and of the South African team. Johannesburg, Transvaal Leader, 1909. 128p. incl. adverts. ports. scores, stats.
*pre-tour*

## 1913–14 Test Tour (J. W. H. T. Douglas)

4630 **Difford, Ivor Denis,** *editor*
■ The M.C.C. team in South Africa (1913–14); portraits and biographies of the visiting team and of the leading South African players. Cape Town, T.T.S., 1913. 128p. incl. adverts. illus. ports. stats.
——2nd ed. 1913. 131p. incl. adverts. illus. ports. stats.
*pre-tour*

4631 **England** v. South Africa: souvenir of
■ M.C.C. visit. First Test match, Lord's, Durban, 13, 15, 16 & 17 December 1913.
Durban, *printed by* R. C. Morris & Co., [1913]. [28]p. ports.

## 1922–23 Test Tour (F. T. Mann)

4632 **Cape Times**
■ The M.C.C. team in South Africa 1922–23, with special sketch of South Africa's international cricket history by I. D. Difford. Cape Town, Cape Times, 1922. 76p. incl. adverts. ports. scores, stats.
*2nd issue, 1922, and 3rd and 4th issues, 1923 were published during tour*

4633 **Paine, H. J. B.,** *compiler*
■ The five Test matches in figures: the following table constitutes a remarkable analysis in figures of the the five Tests, (by "South African"). [Cape Town, The Cape Argus, 1923]. bs. stats.
*rptd. from The Cape Argus, in column form 36¼" × 6"*

## 1927–28 Test Tour (Capt. R. T. Stanyforth]

4634 M.C.C. in South Africa 1927–28: photo-
■ graphs and snapshots. [Johannesburg], Walker & Snashall, [1927]. 56p. incl. covers & adverts. ports. stats.
*cover-title:* The 1927–28 M.C.C. in South Africa
*J. W. Goldman gives J. R. Perring as author*

## 1930–31 Test Tour (A. P. F. Chapman)

4635 **[Difford, Ivor Denis,** *editor*]
■ South African M.C.C. tour 1930–31: official handbook. Cape Town & Johannesburg, Central News Agency, [1930]. 64p. incl. adverts. illus. ports. stats.
*pre-tour*

4636 **O'Donogue, Terence P.**
The M.C.C. in South Africa, 1930–1931: official handbook golden jubilee number. Johannesburg, Transvaal C.U., 1930. 88p. illus.

4637 **Turnbull, Maurice Joseph,** *and* **Allom,**
■ **Maurice J. C.**
The two Maurices again: being some account of the tour of the M.C.C. team through South Africa in the closing months of 1930 and the beginning of 1931. E. Allom, 1931. 256p. illus. ports. scores, stats.

4638 **Union Castle Line**
■ Visit of the M.C.C. Test team to South Africa 1930–1. R.M.S. "Edinburgh Castle", The Union Castle Line, [1930]. [12]p. ports.
*pre-tour*

## 1938–39 Test Tour (W. R. Hammond)

**4639 Difford, Ivor Denis**
"Our cricket Springboks": official souvenir of the visit of the M.C.C. team to South Africa and Southern Rhodesia, 1938–39; a statistical record of all South Africa's cricket tours to Britain, Australia and New Zealand, 1894–1935, and of British & Australian teams to S. Africa, 1888–1936. Johannesburg, Central News Agency, 1939. 69p. stats.

**4640 Marylebone Cricket Club**
■ M.C.C. South African tour 1938–1939. M.C.C., [1938]. [8]p. map
*itinerary and programme*

**4640 Nelson, T. D.,** *compiler & editor*
**–1** Official souvenir programme of the M.C.C. visit to the Transvaal 1938–1939. Publicity Promotions with the permission of the Transvaal C.U., [1938?]. [40]p. ports.

**4640 Shell Company of South Africa Ltd.**
**–2** Fixture card of the M.C.C. cricket touring team 1938–39. [Capetown], the Co., [1938?]. folded card, illus. ports.

**4641 Union Castle Line**
■ Visit of the M.C.C. Test team to South Africa, 1938–39. R.M.V. "Athlone Castle", Union Castle Line, [1938]. [12]p. ports.
*pre-tour*

## 1948–49 Test Tour (F. G. Mann)

**4642 Arlott, [Leslie Thomas] John**
■ Gone with the cricketers. Longmans, Green, 1950. x,160p. illus. ports. scores
*includes N.Z. tour of England, 1949*

**4643** M.C.C. cricket tour of South Africa 1948.
■ Durban & Maritzburg, J. F. King, [1948]. [16]p. ports.
*pre-tour*

**4644 The M.C.C.** in South Africa: souvenir 1948–49. Cape Town, Stewart, 1948. 20p.
*pre-tour*

**4645 M.C.C.** vs. Rhodesia 1949. Bulawayo, S. Carver, 1949

**4646 Mashonaland Cricket Union**
■ M.C.C. v. Rhodesia at the Salisbury Sports Club Ground on 4th, 5th and 7th February, 1949, organised by the Mashonaland Cricket Association and compiled by Harry Pichanick: souvenir programme. Salisbury, [the Union, 1949]. 96p. incl. adverts. ports. stats.

**4647 South African Railways.** *Publicity and Travel Department*
Marylebone Cricket Club visit to Southern Africa 1948–1949. South African Railways, 1948
*pre-tour*

**4648 A souvenir** of the M.C.C. tour, 1948–9, to
■ South Africa & Rhodesia. Johannesburg, Donaldsons Publications (Pty) Ltd., [1948]. 40p. incl. adverts. ports. stats.
*pre-tour; with results of previous matches*

**4648 The Star**
**–1** M.C.C. tour of South Africa 1948–49 itinerary. Johannesburg, The Star, [1948]. [6]p. fold. ports.

**4648 Transvaal Cricket Union**
**–2** Official souvenir M.C.C. South African tour 1948–1949. Johannesburg, Selected Services, [1948]. 32p. ports.
*pre-tour*

**4648 United Tobacco Cos. (South) Ltd.**
**–3** M.C.C. cricket tour South Africa/M.C.C. krieket-tour Suid-Africa 1948–49. U.T.C., [1948]. 32p. ports. map
*in English & Afrikaans; contains details of Cricket Coach Scheme sponsored by U.T.C. and organised by the South African C.A.*

## 1956–57 Test Tour (P. B. H. May)

**4649 Border Cricket Union**
■ Diamond jubilee: souvenir brochure 1896/7–1956/7. Incorporating 1956–7 M.C.C. tour of South Africa: edited and compiled by Geoffrey A. Chettle. [East London, the Union, 1956]. 48p. incl. adverts. illus. ports. stats.

**4650 Chettle, Geoffrey A.,** *editor*
■ Cricketers from England (Test match edition): official souvenir brochure for the 1956–7 tour of South Africa. Durban, Knox Printing Co., [1956], 32p. incl. adverts. ports. diagr. stats.
cover title: *14th M.C.C. cricket tour of South Africa 1956/57*
*also 7 provincial editions with identical text except for details of home teams:*
*Eastern Province*
*Natal*
*North Eastern Transvaal*
*Orange Free State and Griqualand*
*Transvaal*
*Western Province*
*Western Province Country Districts*
*pre-tour*

**4651 Fortune, Charles**
■ The M.C.C. tour of South Africa, 1956–1957. Harrap, 1957. 262p. illus. scores, stats.

4652 **Maclean, Roy Alistair**
■ Pitch and toss. Hodder & Stoughton, 1957. xiv,170p. illus. ports. scores. stats.

4653 **Mashonaland Cricket Association**
■ Rhodesia versus M.C.C. 23–26 November, 1956, Salisbury Sports Club: official programme by Bill Kemmish; edited by Anne Buckley. Salisbury, A. Buckley, [1956]. 64p. incl. adverts. ports. stats.

4654 **Matabeleland Cricket Association**
■ M.C.C. and Rhodesia at Queens Ground, Bulawayo, 17, 18 and 19 November, 1956; compiled & edited by Stuart Manning. Bulawayo, the Assoc., [1956]. 60p. incl. adverts. ports. diagr. stats.

4655 **Outspan.** *Supplement*
■ M.C.C. tour in pictures. Outspan, 22nd March, 1957. 32p. incl. adverts. illus. ports. scores, stats.
*a record of the tour sponsored by the makers of Lifebuoy soap*

4656 **Ross, Alan**
■ Cape summer, and, The Australians in England. Hamilton, 1957. 255p. illus. scores, stats.

4657 **Shell South Africa Ltd.**
■ A Shell guide to the M.C.C. cricket tour of Southern Africa 1956–1957. Cape Town, Shell S.A. Ltd., 1956. [32]p. ports. diagr.
*in English & Afrikaans: pre-tour*

4658 **Swanton, Ernest William**
■ Report from South Africa: with P.B.H. May's M.C.C. team 1956/57. Hale, 1957. 253p. illus. port. diagrs. scores, stats.

4659 **United Paints Ltd**
■ 1956–1957 M.C.C. cricket tour of Southern Africa: itinerary-score card – pen sketches of the M.C.C. touring team . . . Durban, United Paints Ltd., [1956]. [12]p. ports.
*pre-tour*

### 1964–65 Test Tour (M. J. K. Smith)

4660 **Chettle, Geoffrey A.,** *editor*
■ M.C.C. in South Africa (1964–65). Durban, [the Editor, [1964]. [20]p. incl. adverts. ports. stats.
*also provincial editions with identical text except for details of home teams:*

*M.C.C. v. Eastern Province*
*M.C.C. at Newlands*
*M.C.C. in Natal*
*M.C.C. v. Transvaal*
*pre-tour*

4661 Test and career records and pen pictures
■ [M.C.C. tour of South Africa 1964–65]. Durban, [the Editor, 1964]. 24p. incl. adverts. ports. stats.
*similar text to editor's M.C.C. in South Africa (1964–65) series of brochures; pre-tour*

4662 **Fortune, Charles**
■ M.C.C. in South Africa, 1964–5. Hale, 1965. 176p. illus. scores, stats.

4663 **McGlew, Jackie,** *i.e.* **John Derrick**
■ **McGlew**
Cricket crisis. Cape Town, Timmins; London, Hodder & Stoughton, [1965]. xxiii, 168p. illus. port. stats.

4664 **Mashonaland Cricket Association**
■ Rhodesia vs. M.C.C., Police Ground, Salisbury, October 24th, 25th, 26th and 27th, 1964; official souvenir programme. Salisbury, the Assoc., [1964]. [44]p. ports.

### 1965 Worcestershire C.C.C. World Tour

4665 **Midlands Cricket Association**
■ Worcestershire C.C.C. (English County Champions 1964) vs. Rhodesia Country Districts at the Que Que Sports Club, 24th, 25th, February, 1965. [Que Que (Rhodesia)], the Assoc., [1965]. 56p. incl. adverts. ports.
*pre-visit*

### 1968–69 Intended M.C.C. Tour

4666 **Marylebone Cricket Club**
■ Special General meeting (notice of) in the Assembly Hall, Church House, Dean's Yard, Westminster, S.W.1. on Thursday, 5th Dec., 1968. 8p.

### 1969 A. J. McAlpine's XI

4667 **A. J. McAlpine's XI** tour of South Africa
■ and Rhodesia, 1969. Ellesmere Port, Cheshire, Sir Alfred McAlpine & Son Ltd., [1969]. 8p. 1 col. illus. on cover
*touring side based on those who have played in the Marchwiel Cricket Week—a country house cricket festival*

4668 **[See no. 5819]**

# ENGLAND v. WEST INDIES

**4669 Caple, Samuel Canynge**
■ England v. the West Indies, 1895–1957. Worcester, Littlebury, 1957. 206p. illus. ports. scores, stats.

**4670 Guinness** book of England v. West Indies
■ Test cricket records; statistics provided by Irving Rosenwater. Guinness Superlatives, 48p. ports. stats.
*1966, 1967*

**4671 Jamaica Cricket Board of Control**
■ Official souvenir programme: 50 years. M.C.C. visits to Jamaica; by Herbert G. de L. Macdonald. Kingston, Offset Printing Co., 1960. 64p. illus.

**4671 Jones, Brunell,** *editor*
**–1** "West Indies vs. England" 1895–1974.
■ Champs Fleurs, Curepe P.O., Trinidad, 1974. 213p. incl. adverts. illus. ports. scores, stats.

**4672 Rothmans**
■ Test cricket almanack: 1966 England—West Indies. Rothmans, [1966]. 56p. illus. ports. stats.
*records of matches 1928–1966*

## ENGLISH TOURS TO WEST INDIES

### 1894–95 R. S. Lucas's Team

**4673 Bowen, C. P.**
■ English cricketers in the West Indies: an account of the cricket matches played between Mr. R. Slade Lucas's English cricket team and the West Indian cricket teams during the season of 1895. Bridgetown, Barbados, "Herald" Office, 1895. [iii],144p. illus. ports. scores, stats.

**4674 The English** cricketers at Barbados, Jan. and Feb. 1895. Barbados, Agriculture Reporter, 1895. [i],54p. frontis.

**4675 English** cricketers in Trinidad. Port of Spain, 1895. 31p. scores
*post-tour*

### 1896–97 A. Priestley's and Lord Hawke's Teams

**4676 Cricket** tournament at Barbados, W.I. Lord Hawke's English XI v. Barbados. Bridgetown, "Bulletin" Office, 1897
*in Taylor*

**4677 Cricket** tournament at Barbados, W.I. Mr. Priestley's English XI v. Barbados (3 matches), and v. St. Vincent: complete details of a fortnight's cricket. Bridgetown, "Bulletin" Office, 1897
*in Taylor*

**4678 Price, A. B.**
■ English cricketers at Barbados . . . : an account of the cricket matches played by Mr. Arthur Priestley and Lord Hawke's English cricket teams at Barbados during the winter of 1896–'97. Barbados, The West Indian Guardian, 1897. [5], xvii,86p. illus. mounted team ports. scores, stats.

### 1905 Lord Brackley's Team

**4678 West Indian** cricket tour 1905: Lord
**–1** Brackley's XI to the West Indies. *n.p.,*[1906?]. [84]p. scores
*post-tour*

### 1910–11 M.C.C. Tour

**4679 Daily Mirror,** *Port of Spain*
■ Visit of the M.C.C. team, 1911. M.C.C. v. All Trinidad: detailed account of the matches from 7 to 13 March. Port of Spain, Daily Mirror, [1911]. 19p. scores
*rptd. from "The Daily Mirror"*

**4680 Davies, R. S.**
■ Score book England v. Barbados, Feb. 6th, 1911. Bridgetown, *printed by* Standard Print, [1911]. [30]p. ports.

**4681 Jamaica** v. M.C.C. team 1911: a souvenir score book. *n.p.,* 1911. 46p. illus.

### 1925–26 M.C.C. Tour

**4682 Daily Chronicle,** *Georgetown*
M.C.C. cricket tournament 1926. Georgetown, Daily Chronicle, 1926. 85p. illus.

**4683 [Georgetown Cricket Club]**
■ 1926 M.C.C. tour in The West Indies and British Guiana: record score book of matches played in the grounds of the Georgetown Cricket Club at Bourda. Demerara, [the Club, 1926]. [64]p. incl. adverts. illus. stats.
*contains brief history of the Georgetown C.C.*

**4684 Jamaica Cricket Association**
■ Official souvenir cricket score book: M.C.C. touring team v. All Jamaica, 1926; compiled by Archibald Morais. Kingston,

the Assoc., [1926]. [102]p. incl. adverts. ports. scores
*includes insert of blank score sheets and gives account of the earlier matches of the tour*

### 1926–27 Hon. L. H. Tennyson's Team

4685 **Beecher, J. Coleman**
Hon. Lionel Tennyson's cricket tour Jamaica: official souvenir cricket score book. Kingston, M.C. de Souza, 1927. 72p. illus.

4686 **Morais, Archibald**
Morais' cricket scorebook: the Hon. L. H. Tennyson's visiting team v. All Jamaica, 1927. Kingston, Mutual Printing Co., [1927]. illus. ports.

### 1927–28 Hon. L. H. Tennyson's Team

4687 **Jamaica Cricket Association**
■ Official programme of the 1928 tour of the Hon. Lionel Tennyson's touring team vs. All Jamaica. Kingston, [the Assoc.], 1928. [58]p. ports. scores, stats.
*pre-tour; scores and stats. are of Tennyson's tour of 1927*

### 1928–29 J. Cahn's Team

4688 **Beecher, J. Coleman**
■ Beecher's ninth annual 1928–1929: souvenir score book, and official revue of the matches vs. Mr. Julien Cahn's English touring team 1929; special cricket article by J. K. Holt. Kingston, Jamaica, National Printing Co., [1929]. 56p. incl. adverts. illus. ports.
*pre-tour*

4689 **Jamaica Cricket Association.** *Cricket Board*
■ *of Control*
Jamaica v. Mr. Julien Cahn's XI 1929: official programme: compiled by Herbert G. de L. Macdonald. Kingston, the Board, [1929]. [96]p. ports. stats.
*pre-tour*

4690 **Morais, Archibald**
■ Morais' cricket scorebook: Mr. J. Cahn's touring team v. All Jamaica 1929. Kingston, Mutual Printing Co., 1929. [69]p. incl. adverts. ports. scores, stats.
*pre-tour; contains scores of matches played by Tennyson's team of 1928*

### 1929–30 Test Tour (F. S. G. Calthorpe)

4691 **Barbados Advocate**
■ M.C.C. 1930 tour: cricket at Barbados: an account of the colony matches, the Test match and proceedings of the dinner to the cricketers. [Bridgetown, Barbados Advocate, 1930]. [iv],68p. ports. scores, stats.
*rptd. from the Barbados Advocate*

4692 **Daily Chronicle,** *Georgetown*
■ M.C.C. cricket tournament 1930, played at Bourda, Georgetown, B.G., Feb. 10–26. Georgetown, Daily Chronicle, [1930]. 120p. ports. scores, stats.
*post-tournament; rptd. from "The Daily Chronicle"*

4693 **Jamaica Cricket Board of Control**
■ Official souvenir cricket score book, West Indies & All Jamaica [vs] M.C.C. touring team, Sabina and Melbourne Parks, beginning Wednesday, 19th March 1930; edited by Archibald Morais. Kingston, the Board, [1930]. [120]p. inc. adverts. illus. ports. scores, stats.
*issued during tour*

### 1931–32 Hon. L. H. Tennyson's Team

4694 **Jamaica Cricket Board of Control**
■ Jamaica vs. Tennyson's team, Sabina and Melbourne Parks: official cricket score book; edited by R. St. G. Crawford. Kingston, [the Board, 1932]. [60]p. incl. adverts. ports. stats.

### 1947–48 Test Tour (G. O. Allen)

4695 **Cozier, E. L.,** *and* **Coppin, O. S.**
■ A pictorial souvenir of the visit of the Marylebone Cricket Club to the West Indies, January–April, 1948. Barbados, *printed by* Advocate Co. Ltd., 1948. [48]p. incl. adverts. illus. ports. scores, stats.

4696 **Garratt, Roland,** *editor*
■ M.C.C. v. West Indies cricket tournament 1948 played at Barbados, Trinidad, British Guiana and Jamaica. Georgetown, Daily Chronicle, 1948. 149p. illus. ports. scores, stats.
*post-tournament*

4697 **Jamaica Cricket Association**
■ Jamaica vs. the M.C.C.; West Indies vs. England 1948: official programme; edited by A. P. Ramsay. Kingston, the Assoc., [1948]. 64p. incl. adverts. ports. scores, stats.

4698 **M.C.C.** tour to the West Indies 1948:
■ souvenir programme. Port of Spain, *printed by* Guardian Commercial Printery, [1948]. 24p. incl. adverts. illus. ports. stats.
*pre-tour*

## 1953–54 Test Tour (L. Hutton)

4698
–1

"The Advocate's" pictorial souvenir of the visit of the M.C.C. team to the West Indies, December 1953–April 1954; edited by O. S. Coppin. Barbados, The Advocate, [1954]. 36p. incl. adverts. illus. ports. scores, stats.
*post-tour*

4699 ■ **Bannister, Alexander James**
Cricket cauldron: with Hutton in the Caribbean. S. Paul, 1954. 232p. illus. ports. scores, stats.

4700 ■ **Jamaica Cricket Board of Control**
Official programme of the Jamaican section of the M.C.C. tour of the West Indies, December 1953 to April 7, 1954; by Alva Ramsay. Kingston, the Board, [1953]. ii,66p. incl. adverts. illus. ports. scores, stats.
*issued during tour*

4701 ■ **Jamaica Gleaner.** *Overseas edition*
West Indies vs. England 1953–54: cricket souvenir, April 1954. Kingston, Jamaica Gleaner, 1954. 32p. illus. ports. scores, stats.
*post-tour*

4702 **The M.C.C.** tour of the West Indies 1954. Port of Spain, (Shell) Regent, [1954]. 28p. ports.
*pre-tour*

4703 ■ **Swanton, Ernest William**
West Indian adventure: with Hutton's M.C.C. team, 1953–54; edited by Michael Melford. Museum P., 1954. 205p. illus. port. scores, stats.
——*another ed.* Sportsman's Book Club, 1955
*an edited account of contributions to "The Daily Telegraph"*

## 1956–57 Duke of Norfolk's Team

4704 ■ **Jamaica Cricket Board of Control**
Cricket tour of Jamaica by the Duke of Norfolk: compiled by Alva Ramsay. Kingston, the Board, [1957]. 76p. incl. adverts. ports. stats.
*pre-tour*

## 1959–60 Test Tour (P. B. H. May)

4705 ■ **Barbados Advocate**
West Indies vs. M.C.C. 1st Test match at Kensington Oval on January 6, 7, 8, 9, 11 & 12, 1960. [Bridgetown], Barbados Advocate, [1960]. 4p. folded card

4706 ■ **Jamaica Cricket Board of Control**
Official souvenir programme, 50 years: M.C.C. visit to Jamaica—February, 1960; edited by Herbert G. Macdonald. Jamaica, the Board, [1960]. 64p. incl. adverts. illus. ports. scores, stats.
*issued during tour*

4706
–1

**Marylebone Cricket Club**
MCC tour of West Indies 1959–60. M.C.C., [1959]. 8p.
*itinerary, programme, etc.*

4707 ■ **Narain, C.,** *editor*
Welcome to cricketers from England 1960: the welcome souvenir number of the M.C.C. tour to British Guiana. Georgetown, Business Publications, 1960. 84p. incl. adverts. illus. ports.
*pre-visit*

4708 ■ **Peebles, Ian [Alexander Ross]**
Bowler's turn: a further ramble round the realm of cricket. Souvenir P., 1960. 195p. scores, stats.

4709 ■ **Ross, Alan**
Through the Caribbean: the M.C.C. tour of the West Indies, 1959–1960. Hamilton, 1960. 296p. illus. scores, stats.

4710 ■ **Swanton, Ernest William**
West Indies revisited: the M.C.C. tour 1959–60. Heinemann, 1960. 288p. illus. scores, stats.

4711 ■ **Visit** of Marylebone Cricket Club to British Honduras, April 1st–April 5th 1960: souvenir programme. [Belize], Central Committee, [1960]. [ii],56p. incl. adverts. ports. scores
*pre-visit; includes a "Short history of cricket in British Honduras"*

## 1966 Worcestershire C.C.C. Tour

4712 ■ **Worcestershire County Cricket Club**
Jamaica tour March/April 1966: [itinerary and fixtures]. Worcester, the Club, [1966]. [8]p. map

## 1967–68 Test Tour (M. C. Cowdrey)

4713 ■ **Barker, John Sydney**
In the Main: West Indies v. M.C.C. 1968. Pelham, 1968. 163p. illus. scores
——*another ed.* Sportsman's Book Club, 1969

4714 ■ **Blofeld, Henry Calthorpe**
Cricket in three moods: eighteen months of Test cricket and the ways of life behind it. Hodder & Stoughton, 1970. 192p. illus. scores on endpapers

*——another ed.* Sportsman's Book Club, 1971
*also contains account of West Indies tours of Australia 1968/69 and England 1969*

4715 **Close, Brian**
■ The M.C.C. tour of West Indies, 1968. S. Paul, 1968. viii,166p. illus. scores, stats.

4716 **Coca Cola Bottlers**
■ Cricket scorecard England v. West Indies '68. [Bridgetown, Coca Cola, 1968]. [8]p. illus. on cover, oblong
*pre-tour*

4717 **Daily News**
■ England in the West Indies: a Daily News souvenir edition; edited by Tony Cozier, Bridgetown, Barbados, Daily News, 1968. 24p. illus. ports. scores, stats.
*pre-tour*

4718 **Guinness** book of England v. West Indies Test cricket records; statistics provided by Irving Rosenwater. Guinness Superlatives, 1967. 48p. ports. stats.
*with pen portraits of M.C.C. team also by I.R.*

4719 **Guyana Cricket Board of Control**
■ M.C.C. tour 1968 played on the grounds of the Georgetown Cricket Club, Georgetown, Guyana, March 21–April 3: official souvenir programme. Georgetown, the Board, [1968]. [12]p. ports.

4720 **"Highlights of the Season"**
■ Souvenir scorebook West Indies vs. England Test cricket series: First Test Jan. 19–24; Fourth Test March 14–19, 1968 at Queen's Park Oval—Port-of-Spain. Port-of-Spain, "Highlights of the Season", [1968]. [36]p. ports.
*pre-Tests*

4721 **Jamaica Cricket Association**
■ 1968 M.C.C. tour: West Indies vs. England in Jamaica: official souvenir brochure. Kingston, the Assoc., [1968]. 88p. incl. adverts. ports. stats.
*pre-tour*

4722 **Marylebone Cricket Club**
M.C.C. tour West Indies, 1967–1968: itinerary, match programme . . . [M.C.C., 1967]

4723 **M.C.C.** vs. Jamaica Colt's [sic], Jarrett
■ Park, January 1968. [Montego Bay, *n.p.*, 1968]. [4]p. with single sheet insert. illus. ports. *newspaper format*

4724 **St. Lucia Cricket Association**
■ Windward Islands vs. M.C.C., March 8, 9, 11, 1968, Victoria Park, St. Lucia: sou-

venir programme. Castries, the Assoc., [1968]. [24]p. incl. adverts. ports.

4725 **West Indies Cricket Board of Control**
Fixture list: M.C.C. West Indies tour, 1967–68. The Board, [1967]

4726 **Williams, Leroy ("Fathead"),** *compiler*
■ M.C.C. tour of the West Indies 1967–1968. Port-of-Spain, [the Compiler, 1968]. 36p. incl. adverts. ports. stats.
*pre-tour*

## 1970 Duke of Norfolk's Team

4727 **Gillette Industries Ltd**
■ The Duke of Norfolk's West Indies tour February–March 1970; [compiled by E. W. Swanton and Irving Rosenwater]. Gillette Industries, [1970]. [8]p. ports. stats.
*for free distribution only in West Indies*

4728 **Williams, Leroy ("Fathead"),** *compiler*
■ Duke of Norfolk's XI vs. Trinidad & Tobago Queen's Park Oval, Port-of-Spain, March 6, 7, 8, 9, 1970; Shaw Park, Tobago, March 11. Port-of-Spain, [the Compiler, 1970]. 14p. incl. adverts. ports.

## 1970 Women's C.A. Tour to Jamaica

4729 **Jamaica Women's Cricket Association**
■ Inaugural International Women's Cricket Series: souvenir programme. English Women's XI vs. Jamaica, Jan.13–Feb. 2, 1970. Kingston, the Assoc., [1970]. 40p. incl. adverts. ports.
*pre-tour; includes history of Jamaican women's cricket*

## 1971 Women's C.A. Tour

4730 **The Trinidad** & Tobago Women Cricket
■ Association presents international cricket from February 11–26, [1971]. [Diego Martin], the Assoc., [1971]. [12]p. ports.
*pre-tour souvenir of English Women's C.A. tour to Jamaica, Trinidad & Tobago*

4731 **Women's Cricket Association**
■ England Women's Cricket Association tour of the Bahamas, West Indies and Bermuda, 1971. The Assoc., [1971]. [12]p. team port. stats.
*pre-tour*

4732 West Indies tour 1971: official report. [The
■ Assoc., 1971]. 9p. port. stats.
*post-tour*

## 1972 England Young Cricketers' Tour

4733 **National Cricket Association**
■ England Young Cricketers tour of the

West Indies 1972. The Association, [1972]. 16p. ports.
*pre-tour*

### 1973 Kent C.C.C. Tour

4734 **Williams, Leroy ("Fathead")**, *editor*
■ Kent v. Trinidad . . . January 1973. Port-of-Spain, [the Editor, 1973]. [16]p. incl. adverts. ports. stats.

### 1973–74 Test Tour (M. H. Denness)

4734 **Annamunthodo, W.**, *compiler*
–1 Cricket series 1974: M.C.C. tour of W.I. Shell Shield Series. Third Test, Kensington, Barbados, March 6, 7, 9, 10, 11, 1974. San Fernando, Trinidad, Unique Services, [1974]. [60]p. incl. adverts. illus. ports. scores, stats.

4734 **Australian cricket**
–2 1974 tour specials: Australians in New Zealand; England in West Indies; edited by Phil Tresidder. Rushcutters Bay, Modern Magazines (Holdings) Ltd., [1974]. 68p. incl. covers & adverts. illus. (some col.), ports. scores, stats.
*post-tours*

4734 **Cozier, Tony**, *editor*
–3 Caribbean cricket '74. Bridgetown, Barbados, Literary Features (Caribbean) Ltd., [1974]. 44p. incl. adverts. illus. ports. scores, stats.
*pre-series*

4734 **Gibbes, Michael**
–4 Testing time: the West Indies vs England 1974: an account of the M.C.C. tour of the Caribbean with essays on contemporary West Indian cricket. Trinidad, Unique Services, [1974]. 116p. illus.

4734 **[Guyana Cricket Board of Control]**
–5 The M.C.C. in Guyana. England vs. the West Indies 1974 tour; edited by Lance

Gibbs, Vic Insanally & Reds Perreira. [Georgetown, the Board, 1974]. 100p. incl. adverts. illus. ports. stats.

4734 **Guyana Cricket Board of Control**
–6 Tour '74: from Lord's to Bourda; edited
■ by Charles Chichester. Georgetown, the Board, [1974]. 64p. incl. adverts. illus. ports. score, stats.

4734 **Martin-Jenkins, Christopher**
–7 Testing time: M.C.C. in the West Indies,
■ 1974. Macdonald and Jane's, 1974. xiii,177p. illus. scores, stats.
——*another ed.* Newton Abbot, Readers Union, 1975

4734 **Spotlight** extra; edited by Robert Baker.
–8 Market Harborough, R. Baker, 1974.
■ ports. stats.
*includes review of 1973–74 tour of West Indies*

4734 **Williams, Leroy ("Fathead")**, *editor*
–9 5th Test: England v. West Indies,
■ Queen's Park Oval, March 30 – April 5, 1974. Port of Spain, the Editor, [1974]. [28]p. incl. adverts. ports. stats.
*pre-Test*

### 1976 England Young Cricketers' Tour

4734 **National Cricket Association**
–10 England Young Cricketers tour of the
■ West Indies 1976. The Assoc., [1976]. 8p. illus. ports.
*pre-tour*

### 1978 Middlesex Cricket League Tour

4734 **Middlesex Cricket League**
–11 Trinidad & Tobago tour 1978 11 March
■ – 29 March: official tour brochure. The League, [1978]. [52]p. incl. adverts. ports.
*pre-tour*

# ENGLAND v. NEW ZEALAND

4735 **Ashley-Cooper, Frederick Samuel**
■ The New Zealand cricket guide, 1927: a book of records. Nottingham, C. H. Richards, 1927. 28p. stats.
——1931. 1931. 23p. stats.
*mainly records of N.Z. v. England cricket*

4736 **Bedford, Alfred**, *compiler*
■ England versus New Zealand 1930–1949: a complete record of the Test matches. Findon Publications, [1949]. 47p. ports. scores, stats.

4737 **Caple, Samuel Canynge**
■ England v. New Zealand 1902–1949: a brief history of cricket between two countries. Falmouth, Barcliff Advertising & Publishing Co., [1949]. 72p. illus. ports. scores, stats.

4738 **Day, Cedric**, *and* **Mason, Michael**
■ The story of Test cricket: England v. New Zealand. Windsor, Day & Mason, [1949]. 22p. illus. ports. scores, stats.

**4739 Rothmans**
■ Test cricket almanack 1965: England–New Zealand. Rothmans, [1965]. 56p. illus. ports. stats.
*with summary of previous results and statistics*

**4739 The Times**
**−1** New Zealand against England: some
■ further reflections, by Alan Gibson. The Times, 1978. [4]p. fold. *offprint*

# ENGLISH TOURS TO NEW ZEALAND

(Accounts of English tours to New Zealand are generally included in the tours to Australia (*q.v.*), and only those which relate specifically to New Zealand are listed here)

## 1864 All-England Eleven Visit (G. Parr)

**4739 Grand match** between the All-England
**−2** Eleven and the Twenty-two of Canter-
■ bury, played at Hagley Park, Christ-church, 8, 9, & 10 February 1864. Christ-church, the Nag's Head P., 1976. 64p. score
*hand-set limited ed. of 225 numbered copies; match report rpdt. from the Lyttelton Times 'Summary for England', 13 February 1864*

## 1902–03 Lord Hawke's Team

**4740 Warner, Sir Pelham Francis**
■ Cricket across the seas: being an account of the tour of Lord Hawke's team in New Zealand and Australia. Longmans, 1903. xiv,204p. illus. port. scores, stats.
*mainly in New Zealand*

## 1906–07 M.C.C. Tour

**4741 May, Percy Robert**
■ With the M.C.C. to New Zealand. Eyre & Spottiswoode, 1907. viii,133p. illus. ports. scores, stats.
*includes "A short history of New Zealand cricket" by John F. Macpherson*

**4741 New Zealand** tour of the Marylebone
**−1** cricket team 1906–7: official programme. New Zealand (at Ch'ch.) March 1,2, and 4. Wellington, C.M. Banks, [1906]. 48p. incl. adverts. ports. stats.
*issued under the auspices of the New Zealand Cricket Council*

## 1922–23 M.C.C. Tour

**4742 [New Zealand Cricket Council]**
Cricket: New Zealand v. England: 1st Test, 31 Dec. 1922, 1 and 2 Jan, 1923, Basin Reserve, Wellington: official programme. Wellington, Warnes & Stephenson, [1922]. 32p. ports.

**4743 Wellington Cricket Association**
England v. Wellington, 26, 27, 29 January 1923. Wellington, the Assoc., [1923]. ports.

## 1929–30 Test Tour (A. H. H. Gilligan)

**4744 Nelson District Cricket Association**
■ M.C.C. Australasian tour 1929–30: souvenir programme of their visit to Nelson, N.Z., December 20th and 21st, 1929. Nelson, the Assoc., [1929]. [12]p. ports.

**4745 New Zealand** cricket annual for 1930–31; edited and compiled by E. G. Garbutt. Christchurch N.Z., Simpson & Williams, 1930. 124p.

**4746 Turnbull, Maurice Joseph, and Allom,**
■ **Maurice J. C.**
The book of the two Maurices: being some account of the tour of an M.C.C. team through Australia and New Zealand in the closing months of 1929 and the beginning of 1930. E. Allom, 1930. 251p. illus. ports. scores, stats.
*deals mostly with tour of New Zealand*

**4747 Wellington Cricket Association**
■ M.C.C. cricket team New Zealand tour 1929–30 M.C.C. v. Wellington Basin Reserve, December 13–17, 1929: official programme. Wellington, the Assoc., [1929]. 32p. incl. adverts. ports. stats.

**4748 M.C.C.** New Zealand tour 1929–30:
■ M.C.C. v. New Zealand (Second Test) official programme. Wellington, [the Assoc., 1930]. 36p. incl. adverts. ports.

## 1935–36 M.C.C. Tour (E. R. T. Holmes)

**4748 New Zealand Cricket Council**
**−1** M.C.C. New Zealand tour 1935–36: official programme. Wellington, the Council, 1936. 32p. illus. ports.

## 1936–37 M.C.C. Tour (G. O. Allen)

**4749 New Zealand Cricket Council**
■ Programme of matches for Marylebone Cricket Club team in New Zealand 1937. Christchurch, N.Z., N.Z.C.C., [1937]. 4p. folded card

## 1938–39 Sir J. Cahn's Team

4750 **Auckland Cricket Association**
■ Sir Julien Cahn's team v. Auckland, Eden Park, March 17, 18 and 20: official souvenir. Auckland, the Assoc., [1939]. 12p. incl. adverts. ports. stats.

4751 **Canterbury Cricket Association**
■ Sir Julien Cahn's team v. Canterbury, Lancaster, Park, February, 24, 25, 27. Christchurch, the Assoc., [1939]. [8]p. port.

4752 **New Zealand Cricket Council**
■ Sir Julien Cahn's team New Zealand tour 1939: [itinerary]. Christchurch, the Council, [1939]. [4]p. folded card

4753 New Zealand tour 1939: Sir Julien Cahn's
■ team v. New Zealand, Basin Reserve, Wellington 10–13 March, 1939: official programme. Wellington, the Council, [1939]. 32p. ports. score

## 1946–47 Test Tour (W. R. Hammond)

4754 **New Zealand Cricket Council**
Programme of matches for Marylebone Cricket Club in New Zealand 1947. Christchurch, N.Z., the Council, [1947]. 4p. folded card

## 1950–51 Test Tour (F. R. Brown)

4755 **New Zealand Cricket Council**
■ Programme of matches for Marylebone Cricket Club in New Zealand 1951. Christchurch, N.Z., the Council [1951]. [4]p. folded card

## 1954–55 Test Tour (L. Hutton)

4756 **Auckland Cricket Association**
■ International cricket, second Test England v. New Zealand, Eden Park, March 25th to 30th: souvenir programme. Auckland, the Assoc., [1955]. 50p. incl. adverts. illus. ports.

4757 **Canterbury Cricket Association**
■ M.C.C. v. Canterbury, Lancaster Park, March 5, 7 and 8, 1955: official souvenir programme. Christchurch, the Assoc., [1955]. 48p. incl. adverts. illus. ports. stats.

4758 **Evening Post**
M.C.C. versus Wellington. Wellington, Evening Post, 1955. 24p. illus.
*pre-match*

4759 **New Zealand Cricket Council**
Programme of matches for Marylebone Cricket Club in New Zealand 1955.
Christchurch, N.Z., the Council, [1955]. 4p. folded card

4760 **Otago Daily Times**
■ England v. New Zealand cricket—first Test match, Carisbrook Ground, Dunedin, March 11, 12, 14, 15, 16, 1955: official programme and score sheet. Dunedin, Otago Daily Times, [1955]. 48p. incl. adverts. illus. ports. diagr. stats.

## 1958–59 Test Tour (P. B. H. May)

4761 **Auckland Cricket Association**
■ International cricket: second Test M.C.C. v. New Zealand, Eden Park, March 14th to 18th, 1959: souvenir programme. Auckland, the Assoc., [1959]. 32p. incl. adverts. illus. ports. stats.

4762 **Canterbury Cricket Association**
■ England v. New Zealand. First cricket Test, Lancaster, Park, 27, 28, Feb. 2, 3, March 1959: official souvenir programme. Christchurch, the Assoc., [1959]. 52p. incl. adverts. illus. ports. stats.

4763 **M.C.C.** versus Northern & Central
■ District Combined Team, Seddon Park, Hamilton, March 10, 11, 12–1959: souvenir programme. Hamilton, A. Rice, [1959]. [16]p. stats.

4764 **Otago Cricket Association**
■ Cricket: Otago v. M.C.C., Carisbrook, February, 21, 23, 24, 1959. [Dunedin], the Assoc., [1959]. 12p. ports. stats.

4765 **Wellington Cricket Association**
■ M.C.C. versus Wellington at the Basin Reserve, Wellington, 6, 7 and 9 March: official programme. Wellington, the Assoc., [1959]. 38p. ports. diagr. stats.

## 1960–61 M.C.C. Tour (D. R. W. Silk)

4766 **Auckland Cricket Association**
■ His Excellency The Governor-General's Eleven v. M.C.C., Eden Park, Auckland . . . February, 24, 25, 27, 1961: souvenir programme. Auckland, the Assoc., [1961]. 32p. incl. adverts. ports. scores
*includes "A history of the Lyttelton Family and its contribution to cricket" by T. P. McLean*

4767 **Otago Cricket Association**
■ Otago v. M.C.C., Carisbrook, January 13, 14 and 16, 1961. Dunedin, the Assoc., [1961]. 12p. ports.

4768 **Wellington Cricket Association**
■ M.C.C. versus Wellington at the Basin Reserve, Wellington, Dec. 31, 1960, Jan. 2, 3, 1961: official programme. [Wellington, the Assoc., 1960]. 15p. illus. diagr.

4768 M.C.C. versus New Zealand: second
-1 unofficial Test at the Basin Reserve,
Wellington, February 3, 4, 6 and 7, 1961:
official programme. Wellington, the
Assoc., [1961]. 24p. incl. adverts. 1 illus.
ports. diagr.

## 1962–63 Test Tour (E. R. Dexter)

4769 **Auckland Cricket Association**
His Excellency The Governor General's
XI v. M.C.C., Eden Park, Auckland,
February, 1963. Auckland, the Assoc.,
[1963]

4770 First cricket Test England v. New
Zealand, Eden Park, Auckland, February
23, 25, 26, 27, 1963. Auckland, the Assoc.,
[1963]. 32p. incl. adverts. stats. score

4771 **[Otago Cricket Association]**
■ M.C.C. v. An Otago XI, Carisbrook,
March 8, 9 & 11, 1963 a souvenir of cricket
1863/64–1962/63. [Dunedin, the Assoc.,
1963]. 48p. incl. adverts. illus. ports.

4772 **Wellington Cricket Association**
■ England v. New Zealand, Basin Reserve,
March 1, 2, 4, 5, 1963: official programme.
Wellington, the Assoc., [1963]. 20p. incl.
adverts. ports. diagr. stats.

## 1965–66 Test Tour (M. J. K. Smith)

4773 **Auckland Cricket Association**
■ International cricket, third Test England
v. New Zealand, Eden Park, Auckland,
March, 11, 12, 14, 15, 1966: official
programme. Auckland, the Assoc.,
[1966]. ports, plan, scores

4774 **Canterbury Cricket Association**
■ International cricket—1st Test England v.
New Zealand, Lancaster Park, Christchurch, 1966, 25, 26, 28 Feb., 1st Mar.;
official souvenir programme. Christchurch, the Assoc., [1966]. 32p. incl.
adverts. illus. ports. stats.

4775 **Otago Cricket Association**
■ Cricket: England v. New Zealand, Carisbrook, March 4, 5, 7, 8, 1966: programme
score sheet. Dunedin, the Assoc., [1966].
[16]p. incl. adverts. ports. diagr.

4776 **[Wellington Cricket Association]**
■ President's XI v. M.C.C., Basin Reserve,
February, 19, 21, 22, 1966: official programme. [Wellington, the Assoc., 1966].
20p. incl. adverts. ports. diagr.

## 1970–71 Test Tour (R. Illingworth)

4777 **Auckland Cricket Association**
■ Test cricket: England's v. New Zealand at
Eden Park, Auckland on March 5, 6, 7, 8,
1971. Auckland, the Assoc., [1971]. 36p.
incl. adverts. ports, diagrs. stats.

4778 **Canterbury Cricket Association**
■ England v. New Zealand first cricket Test
1971, Lancaster Park, Christchurch:
official programme. [Christchurch, the
Assoc., 1971]. 32p. incl. adverts. illus.
ports. diagrs. stats.

4779 **Wellington Cricket Association**
■ M.C.C. v. Wellington 40 overs, Basin
Reserve, February 20, 1971: official
programme. Wellington, the Assoc.,
[1971]. 16p. incl. adverts. ports.

## 1974–75 Test Tour (M. H. Denness)

4779 **Auckland Cricket Association**
-1 Test cricket. England v. New Zealand,
■ February 20, 21, 22, 23, 25, 1975, Eden
Park, Auckland. Auckland, the Assoc.,
[1975]. 40p. incl. adverts. ports. plan,
diagr. stats.

4779 **Rothmans** international New Zealand vs.
-2 England, 9 March 1975, Basin Reserve,
■ Wellington. [Rothmans], 1975. [8]p. illus.
stats.

4779 **Wellington Cricket Association**
-3 Wellington v. M.C.C., Basin Reserve,
■ February 15, 16 and 17, 1975: official
programme, compiled by Don Neely.
Wellington, the Assoc., [1975]. 32p. incl.
covers & adverts. illus. diagr. score, stats.

## 1977–78 Test Tour (G. Boycott)

4779 **Auckland Cricket Association**
-4 Rothmans tour. International cricket:
■ England v. Auckland, Eden Park, Auckland, Jan. 27, 28, 29, 1978: official
souvenir programme. [Auckland, the
Assoc., 1978]. 48p. incl. adverts. illus.
ports. diagr. plan, stats.

4779 **Cricket** colour collection. Melbourne,
-5 Lavardin Pty. Ltd., [1978?]. 80p. col.
■ illus. & ports.
——pbk ed. [1978?].
*illustrations of Australia v. India, World
Series Cricket and New Zealand v. England*

4779 **Wellington Cricket Association**
-6 New Zealand v. England, first Test
match, February 10, 11, 12, 14, 15, 1978,
Basin Reserve, Wellington. The Assoc.,
[1978].

# ENGLAND v. INDIA

4780 **Caple, Samuel Canynge**
■ England versus India, 1886–1959.
Worcester, Littlebury, 1959. 163p. illus.
ports. scores, stats.

4781 **"Resdeb"**, *pseud.*
M.C.C. visits to India: story of a quarter
century. Windent Publications, 1951. 36p.
*author A. V. Bedser?; publd. in India*

4782 **Rothmans** 1967 cricket almanack:
■ England v. India; England v. Pakistan.
Rothmans, in conjunction with the
M.C.C., [1967]. 48p. illus. ports. stats.

## ENGLISH TOURS TO INDIA

### 1892–93 Lord Hawke's Team

4782 **Record** of Lord Hawke's cricket team in
–1 India 1892–93. Cambridge, Redin & Co.,
[1893?]. [28]p. team port. scores, stats.
*cover-title:* Lord Hawke's team in India
1892–'93
*post-tour*

### 1903 Oxford University Authentics' Tour

4783 **Headlam, Cecil**
■ Ten thousand miles through India and
Burma: an account of the Oxford Univer-
sity Authentics' cricket tour with Mr. K. J.
Key in the year of the Coronation Durbar.
Dent, 1903. xii,297p. illus. scores

### 1926–27 M.C.C. Tour (A. E. R. Gilligan)

4784 **Illustrated** autographed biography of the
M.C.C. cricket team's Eastern tour,
1926–1927. Bombay, F. Hebberd,
Publicity Ltd., 1926. 16p. illus.
*pre-tour*

4785 **M.C.C.** Bombay visit 1926: official
■ souvenir programme; compiled by Frank
Hebberd. Bombay, F. Hebberd, [1926].
[84]p. incl. adverts. ports.
*pre-visit*

4786 **Newham, Cyril Ernest**
■ The M.C.C. in Northern India. Lahore,
Civil and Military Gazette, [1927].
[v],48p. illus. ports. score, stats.

### 1933–34 Test Tour (D. R. Jardine)

4787 **Delhi and District Cricket Association**
Souvenir programme: M.C.C. visit to
Delhi. Delhi, the Association, 1933. 15p.
illus.
*pre-visit*

4788 **The Field** *(Madras)*
Souvenir of the M.C.C. visit to Madras,
1934. Madras, The Field, 1934. [iv],60p.
illus. ports.
*pre-visit*

4789 **[Karachi Cricket Association]**
Souvenir programme of the M.C.C. tour,
Karachi, Oct. 15 to 23, 1933. Karachi, [the
Assoc., 1933]. 28p. ports.
*pre-visit*

4790 **[Mysore State Cricket Club]**
Bangalore: M.C.C. souvenir programme.
January 28 and 29, 1934. Bangalore,
A. W. Smith, lessee for Mysore State
C.C, [1934]. 24p. ports.

### 1939–40 Intended Test Tour

4791 **Marylebone Cricket Club**
M.C.C. tour in India 1939–1940: [itin-
erary]. M.C.C. 1939. 8p.

### 1951–52 Test Tour (N. D. Howard)

4792 **Board of Control for Cricket in India**
■ Official souvenir of the M.C.C. tour of
India 1951–1952; compiled by B. D.
Panwelkar. [New Delhi], The Board,
[1951]. [64]p. incl. adverts. ports.
*pre-tour*

4793 **Cricket** prints. Series four: portrait gallery
■ of M.C.C. & All-India cricketers.
Calcutta, Netai Gopal Sen, [1951]. [48]p.
ports.

4794 **Kora, Kantilal**
Commemorative cricket souvenir:
M.C.C. visit, India 1951–52. Bombay,
Kora, Shah & Co., [1951]. 36p. ports.
*pre-tour*

4795 **Madras Cricket Association**
■ Fifth Test at Madras Chepauk Grounds
on February, 6, 7, 9, 10, 11: M.C.C. XI vs.
India XI: official souvenir. Madras, C. K.
Haridass, [1952]. 78p. incl. adverts. ports.
stats.

4796 **Mathur, L. N.**
■ M.C.C. in India: an account of the
M.C.C. tour to India 1951–52. Ajmer,
Rahjans Publications, 1952. [v],129p.
ports. scores, stats.
*post-tour*

4797 **National Council of Cultural Relations**
M.C.C. team's tour souvenir; compiled
by K. S. Bhatia. New Delhi, the Council,
1951. ports.
*pre-tour*

4798 **Phadke, Narayan Sitaram**
■ India vs. M.C.C. Tests, 1951–52. Bombay,
Anjali Prakashan, 1952. 116p. scores
*post-tour*

4799 **Rao, D. S. Gururaja,** *and* **Narayan, R. S.,**
■ *compilers and editors*
Welcome to Marylebone Cricket Club.
South Zone meet at Bangalore on Feb. 1,
2 & 3, 1952: souvenir. Bangalore, Kesari
Publishing House, [1952]. 54p. incl.
adverts. ports. score

4800 **Sport and Pastime**
■ Marylebone Cricket Club tour of India,
1951–52. Madras, Sport & Pastime,
[1951]. 9–84p. incl. adverts. ports. stats.
*pre-tour; contains an article by E. Hendren*

### 1961–62 Test Tour (E. R. Dexter)

4801 **Agarwal, Ramesh Chandra,** *editor*
■ Souvenir: M.C.C. vs. India: second
cricket Test match, Green Park, Kanpur.
Kanpur, Agarwal, [1961]. 65p. illus.
ports. map, plans, scores, stats.

4802 **Board of Control for Cricket in India**
■ Official souvenir of M.C.C. cricket tour of
India, 1961–62. [New Delhi], the Board,
[1961]. [120]p. incl. adverts. illus. ports.
stats.
*pre-tour*

4803 **Bombay** calling; edited by T. J. Mathew.
■ Bombay.
*Vol. 1, no. 5. Nov. 10, 1961. 49p.*
*tourist guide booklet to events in Bombay,*
*includes a pre-tour suppl. pp. 21–30 by Ron*
*Roberts of M.C.C. tour to India 1961–62.*
*illus. ports.*

4804 **Chaqrabutty, Paddy,** *editor*
Souvenir: fourth Test match, India v.
England, Calcutta, January, 1962.
Calcutta, Anna, [1961]. ports.

4805 **Cricket Association of Bengal**
■ M.C.C. and India 4th Test match, Dec.
30, 31, 1961, Jan. 1, 3, 4, 1962, Eden
Garden's Calcutta: official souvenir.
Calcutta, the Assoc., [1961]. [118]p. incl.
adverts. ports. stats.

4806 **Cricket** prints: M.C.C. visitors 1961.
■ Bombay, Lakhani Book Depot, [1961].
[32]p. illus. ports.
*pre-tour*

4807 **Cricket** prints: M.C.C. visitors and Indian
■ cricketers; introduced by Harish S.
Booch. Bombay, Lakhani Book Depot,
[1961]. 48p. illus. ports.
*pre-tour*

4808 **(Delhi and District Cricket Association]**
Official souvenir of third cricket Test
match. India v. M.C.C., December 13, 14,
16, 17 and 18, 1961. New Delhi, [the
Assoc., 1961]. ports.

4809 **Engee Sports**
M.C.C. in India 1961–62: cricket's in the
air. Bombay, Engee Sports, 1961. illus.
ports.
*pre-tour*

4810 **Haridass, C. K.**
■ India v. England 1961–62. Madras, Haridass, [1961]. 92p. incl. adverts. illus.
ports. stats.
*pre-tour*

4811 **Hyderabad Cricket Association**
■ Official souvenir: Board President's XI vs.
M.C.C. . . . on Nov. 18, 19, 20, 1961.
Hyderabad, the Assoc., [1961]. 92p. incl.
adverts. ports.

4812 **Illustrated News**
M.C.C. in India with elaborate statistics.
Calcutta, Illustrated News (Sports),
[1961]. 32p. illus.
*cover-title*

4813 **Jullundur District Cricket Association**
M.C.C. v. North Zone Cricket XI,
December 1961: official souvenir.
Jullundur, the Association, [1961]. ports.

4814 **M.C.C.** team's tour of India 1961–62.
■ Bombay, *printed by* Ashok Printing P.,
[1961]. 36p. incl. adverts. illus. ports.
stats.
*pre-tour*

4815 **M.C.C.** tour of India 1961–62: souvenir.
■ Lucknow, Dawar for Aryavart Agencies,
[1961]. [40]p. ports. score, stats.
*pre-tour*

4816 **Mason, R. F.,** *editor*
M.C.C. in India, 1961–62. Kanpur, Cawnpore Sports Club, [1961]. ports.
*pre-tour*

4817 **Misra, S.C.**
M.C.C. versus Services, Ranji Stadium,
Calcutta, 26 to 28 December, 1961:
[programme]. Calcutta, Bimal Chatterjee,
1961

4818 **Mysore State Cricket Association**
M.C.C. versus South Zone, Bangalore, 6,

7 and 8 January, 1962: souvenir; edited by K. S. Ramaswami. [Bangalore, the Assoc., 1962]. illus. ports.

**4819  Nava Bharat Staff Association**
Cricket souvenir: M.C.C. vs. Central Zone, Nagpur, 26, 27, 28, Nov., 1961. Nagpur, Maheshwari and Panchlothia, [1961]. ports. diagrs.
*partly in Hindi. Joint-editors D. P. Shukla and S. W. Dube*

**4820  Rajasthan Cricket Association**
■ Official souvenir M.C.C. vs. Rajasthan, Jaipur, November 22, 23, 24, 1961. [Jaipur], The Tournament Cttee., [1961]. [60]p. incl. adverts. ports. scores, stats.
*includes a brief history of Rajasthan cricket*

**4821  Sport & Pastime**
■ M.C.C. cricketers visit to India, 1961–62: souvenir. Madras, Sport & Pastime, [1961]. 3–82p. incl. adverts. ports. map, stats.
*pre-tour*

**4822  Uttar Pradesh Cricket Association**
■ England versus India, 2nd cricket Test, Dec. 1 to 6 Kanpur (U.P.), India, 1961: official souvenir programme. Kanpur, the Assoc., [1961]. 66p. illus. ports. map, plan, diagr. scores, stats,

### 1963–64 Test Tour (M. J. K. Smith)

**4823  Bhatia, C. P.**
■ Meet the M.C.C. & India. Bombay, *printed by* Ellora Printers, [1963]. [48]p. incl. adverts. ports. stats.
*pre-tour*

**4824  Bhupathy, D. R.,** *compiler*
■ England vs. India 1964. Madras, the Compiler, [1964]. 59p. incl. adverts. ports. stats.
*pre-tour*

**4825  Board of Control for Cricket in India**
M.C.C. tour in India: playing conditions. Bangalore, the Board, 1963

**4826**  Official souvenir of the M.C.C. cricket
■ tour of India, 1964. [New Delhi], the Board, [1964]. [96]p. incl. adverts. illus. ports. stats.
*pre-tour*

**4827  Haridass, C. K.**
■ M.C.C. v. India 1964. Madras, Haridass, [1964]. 100p. incl. adverts. illus. ports.
*pre-tour*

**4828  Hyderabad Cricket Association**
■ South Zone vs. M.C.C. on 6th, 7th and 8th January 1964: official souvenir.

[Hyderabad, the Association, 1963]. 34p. ports.

**4829  Indian Express**
■ M.C.C. visit to India, 1964: souvenir. Madras, Indian Express, [1964]. 96p. incl. adverts. illus. ports. stats.
*pre-tour; with insert scorecards*

**4830  Marylebone Cricket Club**
M.C.C. tour India 1963–64: itinerary, match programme, travel arrangements, postal arrangements, etc. [M.C.C., 1963]

**4831  Modi, Rusi**
■ Cricket forever. Bombay, the Author, 1964. [x],128p. illus. ports.

**4832  Sport & Pastime**
■ M.C.C. tour of India 1964: souvenir. Madras, Sport & Pastime, [1964?]. 82p. incl. adverts. ports. stats.
*pre-tour*

**4833  Uttar Pradesh Cricket Association**
■ England vs. India 1963–64 official souvenir 5th cricket Test. Kanpur (U.P.) India, February 15–20, 1964. Kanpur, the Assoc., [1963]. 74p. illus. ports. diagrs. map, stats.

### 1965 Worcestershire C.C.C. World Tour

**4834  Calcutta Cricket Club**
■ Cricket: the English County Champions of 1964: Worcestershire C.C.C. in Calcutta 4 to 11 March, 1965: official souvenir programme. Calcutta, the Club, [1965]. 68p. incl. adverts. illus. ports. scores

### 1972–73 Test Tour (A. R. Lewis)

**4835  Board of Control for Cricket in India**
■ Official souvenir of M.C.C. cricket tour of India 1972–73. New Delhi, the Board, [1972]. [96]p. incl. adverts. ports.
*pre-tour*

**4836  Cawnpore Colts Club**
■ Fourth Test January 25–30, 1973: M.C.C. meet India at Green Park, Kanpur. Kanpur, the Club, [1973]. [140]p. incl. adverts. illus. ports. diagr. scores

**4837  Cawnpore Sports Club**
■ M.C.C. v. India: souvenir; edited by Ashok Grover. Kanpur, the Club, [1973]. [76]p. incl. adverts. ports. diagrs.
*4th Test Jan. 1973*

**4838  Cricket Association of Bengal**
■ India vs. England second Test match, played at the Eden Gardens, Calcutta,

Dec. 30, 31st 1972, Jan 1, 3 and 4, 1973. Calcutta, the Assocation, [1972]. [64]p. ports. score
*pre-Test*

**4839 Delhi & District Cricket Association**
■ First Test match M.C.C. vs. India, Delhi, December 1972: souvenir. Delhi, the Assoc., [1972], 57p. incl. adverts. ports. score, stats.

**4840 Esso [India]**
■ Album of cricket stars: M.C.C. vs. India series 1972–73. Madras, Esso, [1972]. 48p. ports. stats.
*pre-tour*

**4841 Haridass, C. K.,** *compiler*
■ M.C.C. in Madras, 1973. Madras, Haridass for Shaw Wallace & Co., [1972]. [12]p. incl. adverts. illus. ports. diagrs.
*souvenir of 3rd Test*

**4842 The Hindu**
■ M.C.C. visit to India 1972–73: souvenir. Madras, the Hindu, [1972]. 100p. incl. adverts. illus. ports. stats.
*pre-tour*

**4843 Hyderabad Cricket Association**
■ M.C.C. vs. Board President's XI at Lal Bahadur Stadium, Hyderabad on December 5, 6 and 7, 1972. Hyderabad, the Assoc., [1972]. [200]p. incl. adverts. illus. ports.

**4844 Marylebone Cricket Club**
■ M.C.C. tour India, Pakistan and Ceylon 1972–73: itinerary. The Club, [1972].[16]p.

**4845 M.C.C.** in Madras 1973: [scorecard for the third Test played at Chepauk, Madras, Jan. 1973]. 12p. incl. adverts. ports. diagrs.
*with 2pp. of Madras Test history*

**4845 Rajan, Sunder,** *editor*
**–1** The hat-trick: M.C.C. tour of India, 1972–73. Bombay, Jaico, 1974. [vii],160p. illus. scores, stats. pbk.

**4846 Somaiya, A. V.,** *and* **Bhesania, P. S.**
■ MCC vs. India 1972–73 souvenir. Bombay, Trupti Publications, [1972]. 104p. incl. adverts. ports. stats.
*pre-tour*

**4847 Sportsweek**
■ M.C.C. special. Bombay, Inqilab Publications (Private) Ltd., [1972]. 76p. incl. adverts. illus. & ports. (some col.), stats.
*pre-tour*

**4848** Victory special. Bombay, Inqilab Publica-
■ tions (Private) Ltd., [1973]. [68]p. incl. adverts. illus. ports.
*post-tour*

**4849 Suresh Saraiya,** *editor*
■ M.C.C. 1972–73: a new challenge to Wadekar. Bombay, Neeta Publications, [1972]. [96]p. incl. adverts. ports. (some col.), stats.
*pre-tour*

**4850 Uttar Pradesh Cricket Association**
■ England vs. India 1972–73: official souvenir fourth cricket Test, Kanpur, 25–30 Jan. 1973. Kanpur, the Assoc., [1972]. 80p. illus. ports. diagrs. map, stats.

## 1976–77 Test Tour (A. W. Greig)

**4850 Bhupathy, D. P.,** *editor*
**–1** England vs. India: Test cricket souvenir
■ 1977. Madras, Bhupathy, [1977]. 68p. incl. adverts. ports. stats.

**4850 Board of Control for Cricket in India**
**–2** Official souvenir of M.C.C. tour of India
■ 1976–77. The Board, [1976]. [100]p. incl. adverts. ports. stats.
*pre-tour*

**4850 Delhi and District Cricket Association**
**–3** England vs. India, 1st cricket Test: official souvenir. Delhi, the Assoc., 1976

**4850 Haridass, C. K.,** *compiler*
**–4** M.C.C. in India 1976–77. Madras, C. K.
■ Haridass, 1976. 204p. incl. adverts. illus. ports. stats.
*pre-tour*

**4850 The Hindu**
**–5** M.C.C. in India 1976–77: souvenir.
■ [Madras], The Hindu, [1976]. 100p. incl. covers & adverts. ports. stats.
*pre-tour*

**4850 Martin-Jenkins, Christopher**
**–6** M.C.C. in India, 1976–77. Macdonald and Jane's, 1977. 190p. illus. scores, stats.
——*another ed.* Newton Abbot, Readers Union, 1977
*with statistical survey compiled by Patrick Allen*

**4850 Peerbhoy, A. E. M.**
**–7** M.C.C. in India 1977. Bombay, Peerbhoy, [1977]. 28p. illus. ports.
*issued during the tour*

**4850 Rana, H. J.**
**–8** [Cricket & cricketer: India vs. M.C.C.
■ 1976–77]. Nadiad, the Author, [1977?]. [146]p. incl. adverts. illus. ports. diagrs. stats.
*non-English text*

**4850** **Rutnagur, Dicky**
**–9** Test commentary: a diary of India vs.
■ England (1976–77). New Delhi, Vikas
Publishing House PVT Ltd., 1978. xi,
222p. illus. ports. scores, stats. (Bell
Books Paperbacks)

**4850** **Sharma, Ashok K.,** *editor*
**–10** M.C.C. vs. India 1976–77. New Delhi,
■ Young Sportwriters Co., [1976]. 76p. incl.
adverts. illus. ports. stats.
*pre-tour*

# ENGLAND v. PAKISTAN

**4851** **Rothmans**
■ 1967 cricket almanack: England v. India;
England v. Pakistan. Rothmans, in conjunction with the M.C.C., [1967]. 48p.
illus. ports. stats.
*includes record of matches England v. Paki-
stan 1954–1962*

## ENGLISH TOURS TO PAKISTAN

### 1955–56 M.C.C. Tour (D. B. Carr)

**4852** **Board of Control for Cricket in Pakistan**
Programme of the fourth unofficial Test,
Pakistan vs. M.C.C. "A", 9th March to
14th March, 1956. Karachi, the Board,
1956. ports.

**4853** **Butt, Qamaruddin**
■ Pakistan cricket on the march. Karachi,
the Author, 1957. 258p. illus. ports.
scores, stats.
*includes an account of M.C.C. 'A' team
tour of Pakistan 1955–6*

**4854** **East Pakistan Referees and Umpires'**
**Association**
Second unofficial Test match M.C.C. vs.
Pakistan at Dacca Stadium 3–8 February,
1956; compiled by Amiruddin Ahmed.
Dacca, the Assoc., 1956. illus. ports.

**4855** **Karachi Cricket Association**
Official souvenir of M.C.C. 'A' team vs.
the Governor General's XI. Karachi, the
Assoc., 1955. illus.

**4856** **Marylebone Cricket Club**
M.C.C. tour Pakistan 1955–6: team and
itinerary. [M.C.C., 1955]

**4856** **Pakistan Sports**
**–1** M.C.C. 'A' vs. Pakistan, first (unofficial)
■ Test match, Bagh-e-Jinnah, 20–26 January
1956: official souvenir; editors S. Naseer
Ahmed [and] Saleem Akbar. Lahore,
Pakistan Sports, [1956]. 64p. incl. covers
& adverts. illus. ports.

**4857** **Sind Cricket Association**
M.C.C.(A) vs. S.C.A., 6, 7 and 8 January,
1956: official souvenir. Hyderabad, The
Assoc., 1956. illus. ports.

### 1961–62 Test Tour (E. R. Dexter)

**4858** **Board of Control for Cricket in Pakistan**
■ England vs. Pakistan 1961, Lahore
Stadium, October 21, 22, 24, 25, 26, 1961.
The Board, [1961]. [68]p. incl. adverts. 1
illus. ports. stats.

**4859** **East Pakistan Sports Federation**
M.C.C. vs. Pakistan, 19–24 January, 1962:
official souvenir. Dacca, The Federation,
[1962]. illus. ports.

**4860** **Karachi Cricket Association**
■ Official souvenir of the third Test match,
Pakistan vs. England at the National
Stadium, Karachi, on 2, 3, 4, 6 & 7
February, 1962; edited by Munir Hussain.
Karachi, the Association, [1962]. [128]p.
incl. adverts. illus. ports. scores, stats.

**4861** **Lahore Division Cricket Association**
England v. Pakistan 1961, Lahore
Stadium, Oct. 21, 22, 24, 25 and 26:
souvenir. Lahore, Souvenir Committee of
the Association, [1961]. ports.

**4862** **M.C.C.** v. Governor's XI, Lyallpur
■ October, 1961, 17, 18, 19: [souvenir pro-
gramme]. Lyallpur, Rast Guftar P., 1961.
[20]p. incl. adverts. illus. ports.

**4863** **M.C.C.** v. Pakistan, Nov. 1961: official
souvenir

**4864** **Pakistan Wanderers Cricket Club**
■ M.C.C. Pakistan tour 1961–62. Lahore,
Taj Malik for the Club, [1961]. [42]p. incl.
adverts. illus. ports. stats.
*pre-tour*

**4865** **Rawalpindi Cricket Association**
■ President's XI vs. M.C.C., Pindi Club
Ground, October 13, 14, 15, 1961: souvenir. Rawalpindi, The Assoc., [1961].
[ii],73p. incl. adverts. illus. ports. diagrs.
stats.

**4866** **Sunday Telegraph**
■ England v. Pakistan: a record of the last
four Test matches. Sunday Telegraph,
[1962]. [6]p. fold. scores
*covers 3 Tests England in Pakistan
1961–62, and the first Test Pakistan in
England 1962*

*——2nd issue.* [1962]. [6]p. fold. scores
*covers 3rd and 4th Tests England in Pakistan 1961–62 and 1st and 2nd Tests Pakistan in England 1962*

### 1967 M.C.C. Under 25 Team (J. M. Brearley)

4867 **Board of Control for Cricket in Pakistan.**
■ *Souvenir Committee*
Souvenir of the cricket match: President's XI vs. M.C.C. XI, February 5, 6 & 7, 1967 at the Rawalpindi Club cricket ground, Rawalpindi. [Rawalpindi], Souvenir Committee, [1967]. 64p. incl. adverts. illus. ports.

### 1968–69 Test Tour (M. C. Cowdrey)

4868 **Butt, Qamarddin**
■ Sporting wickets: (eye-witness accounts of the tours of M.C.C. and New Zealand to Pakistan 1969). [Rawalpindi, the Author, 1970]. [vi],136p. illus. port. scores, stats.

4869 **Karachi Cricket Association**
■ Official souvenir of the third & final Test match, Pakistan vs. England at the

National Stadium, Karachi on 6, 7, 8, 9, 10 March 1969; edited by Munir Hussain. Karachi, the Assoc., [1969]. 64p. incl. adverts. illus. ports. diagrs. scores, stats.

4870 **Lahore Division Cricket Association**
■ 1st cricket Test England [v.] Pakistan at Lahore Stadium on Feb. 21–24, 1969. Lahore, the Assoc., [1969]. [48]p. incl. adverts. ports.

4871 **Multan Divisional Cricket Association**
■ Governor's XI v. England 15, 16, 17 February 1969 at Sahiwal: souvenir. Multan, the Assoc., [1969]. [64]p. incl. adverts. ports.

4872 **Sportimes**
■ Special cricket souvenir; edited by Sultan F. Husain. Lahore, Sheikh Aftab Ahmad, [1969]. 24p. illus. ports. stats.
*issued on the occasion of the M.C.C. visit to Pakistan: pre-tour*

### 1972–73 Test Tour (A. R. Lewis)

4873 **Punjab Cricket Association**
■ First cricket Test Pakistan vs. England, on March 2, 3, 4, 6 and 7 at Lahore 1973. Lahore, the Assoc., [1973]. [56]p. illus. ports. stats.

# M.C.C. v. SRI LANKA

## ENGLISH TOURS TO SRI LANKA

4874 **Foenander, Samuel Peter**
■ English cricket teams in Ceylon: a souvenir of the visit to Colombo of the M.C.C. team, October 4th, 1924. Colombo, Independent P., [1924]. [ii],29p. incl. adverts. ports. scores, stats.

### 1911–12 M.C.C. Visit (J. W. H. T. Douglas)

4875 **Amicus Illustrated Weekly**
The M.C.C. cricketers in Colombo: souvenir compiled by Ubique. Colombo, "Amicus," 1911. 10p. illus. ports.
*pre-visit*

4876 Special cricket number. Vol. 15, no. 171. Colombo, "Amicus", 21st March 1912. 38p. illus. ports.
*contains pp. 31–34 "The return of the all-conquering M.C.C. team", and pp. 35–38 "Test match cricket in Ceylon" by Ubique*

4877 **Foenander, E. W.**
■ Mr. P. F. Warner's team in Colombo: a souvenir of to-day's big match. Colombo,

"Ceylon Sportsman", [1911]. 10p. ports. scores, stats.
*M.C.C. v. Ceylon on their outward voyage to Australia 1911–12 tour*

### 1920–21 M.C.C. Visit (J. W. H. T. Douglas)

4878 **Plâté Ltd**
■ A souvenir of to-day's cricket match between "All Ceylon" and the M.C.C. team. Colombo, Plâté Ltd., [1920]. 10p. ports.

4878 **Wootler, S. T.,** *compiler*
–1 English cricketers in Ceylon: M.C.C. vs. All Ceylon, October 11th, 1920. Colombo, Independent P., [1920]. 12p.

### 1922–23 M.C.C. Visit

4878 **The Ceylon** sportsman: M.C.C. number.
–2 Colombo, Monday, October 23, 1922
*newspaper supplement*

### 1924–25 M.C.C. Visit (A. E. R. Gilligan)

4878 **Dunlop Rubber Co. Ltd., Ceylon**
–3 A souvenir of the visit of the M.C.C. team

to Ceylon, Saturday, October 4, 1924.
Dunlop, [1924]. 20p.

**4879 Foenander, Samuel Peter**
■ English cricket teams in Ceylon: a
souvenir of the visit to Colombo of the
M.C.C. team, October 4th, 1924. Colombo, Independent P., [1924]. [ii],29p.
incl. adverts. ports. scores. stats.

## 1926–27 M.C.C. Visit
## (A. E. R. Gilligan)

**4879 Foenander, Samuel Peter,** *editor and*
**–1** *compiler*
■ Official handbook of the visit of the
M.C.C. team to Ceylon, 1927. Colombo,
C.A.C. Press, [1927]. 44p. ports. scores.
stats.
*pre-visit*

## 1928–29 M.C.C. Visit
## (A. P. F. Chapman)

**4880 Foenander, Samuel Peter**
■ Official souvenir of the visit of the M.C.C.
team to Ceylon, 6th October, 1928.
Colombo, 1928. [i],48p. illus. ports.
scores
*pre-visit*

## 1929–30 M.C.C. Visit
## (A. H. H. Gilligan)

**4880 Foenander, Samuel Peter**
**–1** A souvenir of the visit of the M.C.C. team
to Ceylon, 19 October 1929: facts and
figures compiled by Onlooker of the
Ceylon Observer. Colombo, Ceylon
Observer, [1929]. 12p.

**4881 Turnbull, Maurice Joseph,** *and* **Allom,**
■ **Maurice J. C.**
The book of the two Maurices: being
some account of the tour of an M.C.C.
team through Australia and New Zealand
in the closing months of 1929 and the
beginning of 1930. E. Allom, 1930. 251p.
illus. ports. scores. stats.
*deals mostly with tour of New Zealand; v.
Ceylon on route out*

## 1932–33 M.C.C. Visit (D. R. Jardine)

**4882 Ceylon Cricket Association**
■ A souvenir of today's match between the
M.C.C. team and All Ceylon played on
Sinhalese S.C. Ground . . . October 8,
1932; [compiled by S. P. Foenander].
Colombo, the Association, [1932]. 36p.
incl. adverts. illus. ports. scores. stats.

## 1934 M.C.C. Visit

**4882 Times of Ceylon**
**–1** Official souvenir of the M.C.C. visit to
Ceylon, February 1934; review of
previous tours by Zingari. Colombo,
Times of Ceylon under the authority of
the Ceylon C.A., [1934]. 40p. incl.
adverts.

## 1936–37 M.C.C. Visit (G. O. Allen)

**4882 A souvenir** of today's match between the
**–2** M.C.C. team vs. All Ceylon played on the
C.C.C. Grounds, Saturday, 3rd October
1936. Colombo, Times of Ceylon, [1936].
26p.

## 1950–51 M.C.C. Visit (F. R. Brown)

**4883 Foenander, Samuel Peter**
■ Souvenir of visit to Ceylon the M.C.C.
team bound for Australia October 1, 1950.
Colombo, Ceylon Observer, [1950].
[iv],17p. ports.
*pre-visit*

## 1958–59 M.C.C. Visit (P. B. H. May)

**4884 Board of Control for Cricket in Ceylon**
■ Ceylon v. M.C.C., Oct. 5th; President's
XI v. M.C.C., Oct. 6th, played on the
Sinhalese Sports Club Ground, Maitland
Place: official souvenir. Colombo, the
Board, [1958]. 24p. incl. adverts. ports.

## 1962–63 M.C.C. Visit (E. R. Dexter)

**4885 Board of Control for Cricket in Ceylon**
■ Ceylon tour of the M.C.C. team, 1962:
official souvenir; edited by R. B. Wijesinha. Colombo, the Board, [1962]. 96p.
illus. ports. stats.
*pre-tour*

**4885 Perera, S. S.,** *editor*
**–1** A souvenir of the visit of the twentieth
M.C.C. team to Ceylon, 3rd October
1962. Telijjawila, *printed by* Singha Printers, [1962]

## 1965–66 M.C.C. Visit (M. J. K.
## Smith)

**4886 Board of Control for Cricket in Ceylon**
■ Official souvenir of the visit of the M.C.C.
Test team to Australia (1965–66): 18th
Oct., Ceylon XI vs M.C.C.; 19th Oct.,
Ceylon vs. M.C.C. . . . at the Oval,
Wanathamulla; compiled and edited by
R.B. Wijesinha. [Colombo], the Board,
[1965]. 64p. incl. adverts. ports. stats.
*pre-visit; contains "Milestones in the
growth of cricket in Ceylon" by S. S. Perera*

## 1968–69 M.C.C. Tour (M. C. Cowdrey)

4887 **Board of Control for Cricket in Ceylon**
■ M.C.C. tour for 1969 January 22nd—February 2nd: official souvenir compiled & edited by Eddie Melder & S. S. Perera. Colombo, the Board, [1969]. 76p. ports. stats.
*pre-tour*

4888 **Ceylon Tobacco Co. Ltd**
■ M.C.C. tour of Ceylon 1969, January 25, 26, 30, 31 & 1st February at the Colombo Oval, January 28 at Asgiriya Grounds, Kandy: itinerary. [Colombo], Ceylon Tobacco Co. Ltd., [1969]. 4p. folded card

4889 **Maharaja Organisation Ltd**
Scorecard, M.C.C. vs. Ceylon, 30th Jan.–1st Feb., 1969. Colombo, Maharaja Organisation Ltd., [1969]. 4p.
*pre-match*

## 1969–70 M.C.C. Tour (A. R. Lewis)

4890 **Board of Control for Cricket in Ceylon**
■ M.C.C. vs. Ceylon 20th to 23rd February, 1970: official souvenir compiled by S. S. Perera and E. J. Melder. Colombo, [the Board, 1970]. [32]p. ports. stats.
*contains review by S. S. Perera of previous tours to Ceylon by M.C.C.*

4890 **Ceylon Tobacco Co. Ltd.**
–1 M.C.C. tour of Ceylon 1970, 16 February–
■ 25 February, Colombo: official programme. [Colombo], the Co., [1970]. [4]p. folded card

4890 **Kathirgamathesan, C.**
–2 All time all world records, Ceylon—M.C.C. (1970): match souvenir. Jaffna, Rangi Publication, [1970]
*sponsored by Jolly Rovers Sports Club*

## 1972–73 M.C.C. Tour (A. R. Lewis)

4891 **Board of Control for Cricket in Ceylon**
■ M.C.C. tour 1973 of Sri Lanka, February 12th February 22nd: official souvenir, compiled and edited by S. S. Perera and E. J. Melder. [Colombo, the Board, 1973]. [56]p. incl. adverts. ports. stats.
*pre-tour*

4891 Sri Lanka vs. M.C.C. 1973, February 16,
–1 17, 18 and 19. The Board, [1973]. [4]p.
■ fold. ports. [of Sri Lankan team]

## 1976–77 M.C.C. Tour (A. W. Greig)

4891 **Board of Control for Cricket in Sri Lanka**
–2 M.C.C. tour 1977: playing conditions. Colombo, the Board, [1977]

4891 M.C.C. tour of Sri Lanka 19 Feb. to 3
–3 March 1977: official tour itinerary. [Col-
■ ombo, the Board, 1977]. [6]p. folded card

4891 M.C.C. tour of Sri Lanka 1977: official
–4 souvenir. [Colombo, the Board, 1977].
■ 28p. incl. adverts. ports.
*pre-tour*

4891 **Galle Cricket Club**
–5 Souvenir of the visit of the M.C.C. team
■ to Galle. Board of Control President's XI vs. M.C.C., 22 and 23 Feb. 1977. [Galle, the Club, 1977]. [8]p. 1 illus. ports.

# ENGLISH TEAMS v. CANADA AND THE UNITED STATES

## ENGLISH TOURS TO CANADA AND THE UNITED STATES

### 1859 G. Parr's Team

4892 **Irving, John B.**
■ The international cricket match played Oct. 1859, in the Elysian Fields at Hoboken, on the grounds of the St. George's Cricket Club. New York, *printed by* Vinten, 1859. x,31p.

4893 **Lillywhite, Frederick**
■ The English cricketers' trip to Canada and the United States. F. Lillywhite, 1860. viii,68p. illus. map, scores

4893 **Rhys, Horton ("Morton Price")**
–1 A theatrical trip for a wager through Canada and the United States. Charles Dudley (for the author), 1861. 140p. col. illus. ports.
*pp. 105–7 reference to English cricketers' trip to U.S. and Canada in 1859*

### 1868 Gentlemen of M.C.C. (E. Willsher)

4894 **International Cricket Fetes Committee**
■ Official report on the international cricket fetes at Philadelphia in 1868 and 1872 . . . together with a full account of the visit of the English gentlemen cricketers, by R. A. Fitzgerald . . . ; also "Cricket in

America," "Cricket for schoolboys" . . . Philadelphia, Lippincott for the Committee, 1873. 38p. score

## 1872 Gentlemen of M.C.C. (R. A. Fitzgerald)

4895 Fitzgerald, Robert Allan
■ Wickets in the west; or, The twelve in America. Tinsley, 1873, ix,335p. frontis. port. scores

4896 International cricket fete, 1872: official
■ handbook, containing the programme of arrangements during the visit of the English Gentlemen Eleven to Philadelphia. Philadelphia, Lippincott, 1872. 68p. scores
See also no. 4894

## 1879 R. Daft's Team

4897 Brown, Edwin
Richard Daft's English cricketers in Canada and the United States
unpublished MS. at Trent Bridge

## 1886 E. J. Sanders' Team

4898 Sim, William Clulow
■ The log of the "Old 'Un", from Liverpool to San Francisco [1886]. Exeter, H. S. Eland, for private circulation, [1887]. [i],30p. mounted port. as frontis. scores

## 1891 Lord Hawke's Team

4899 Crowhurst, Ernest H., and MacOwen,
■ Arthur H., editors
Souvenir volume of the visit of Lord Hawke's team of English amateur cricketers to America. Philadelphia, American Athletic Publishing Co., 1891. 96p. incl. adverts. illus. ports. plans, stats.
pre-tour

## 1895 Cambridge-Oxford Team

4900 International cricket match, Cambridge-
■ Oxford XI vs. Gentlemen of Philadelphia at Manheim September 20th, 21st & 23rd, 1895. Philadelphia, Dreka, 1895. 16p. illus.
pre-match; includes previous international matches at Philadelphia, 1859–1894

## 1898 P. F. Warner's Team

4901 Associated Cricket Clubs of Philadelphia
Official souvenir scorebook of the Gentlemen of Philadelphia vs. Gentlemen of England international cricket matches. Philadelphia, Frank V. Chambers, 1898. 48p. illus.

## 1899 K. S. Ranjitsinhji's Team

4902 Associated Cricket Clubs of Philadelphia
Official souvenir scorebook of the Gentlemen of Philadelphia vs. Prince Ranjitsinhji's eleven: international cricket matches. Philadelphia, Frank V. Chambers, 1899. 32p. ports.

## 1905 M.C.C. Tour

4903 American Cricketer
Official programme 1905 to commemorate the first visit of a Marylebone Cricket Club team to Philadelphia. Philadelphia, American Cricketer with authority of the Associated Cricket Clubs, 1905. illus.
pre-visit

4904 A souvenir score book of the match between Gentlemen of Toronto and Marylebone Cricket Club, Toronto, 1905. 16p. illus.

## 1907 M.C.C. Tour

4905 American Cricketer
Official programme 1907 commemorating the second visit of a team from the Marylebone Cricket Club to Philadelphia. Philadelphia, American Cricketer, by authority of the Associated Cricket Clubs, 1907. 20p. illus.
pre-visit

## 1913 Incogniti C.C. Tour

4906 Collins, Philip, and Falcon, Michael
■ Incogniti Cricket Club: an account of the American tour, 1913. Beckenham, T. W. Thornton, [1914]. 47p. illus. ports. scores, stats.

## 1920 Incogniti C.C. Tour

4907 England's Incogniti XI v. All New York,
■ Sept. 22, 23, 1920: souvenir programme. New York, Livingston, [1920]. 8p.

## 1933 Cambridge University Vandals Tour

4908 Illinois Cricket Association
Cambridge University Vandals on tour: U.S.A. and Canada, Chicago, the Assoc., 1933. 4p.

## 1933 Sir J. Cahn's Team to U.S.A., Bermuda and Canada

4909 Bermuda Cricket Association
Souvenir official score card: Sir Julien Cahn's touring team v. Bermuda Colts. Bermuda C.A., 1933. 16p.

4910 **Toronto and District Cricket Council**
■ Cricket matches at Toronto Cricket Club, Armour Heights . . . Sir Julien Cahn's XI v. Toronto Cricket Club . . . Toronto and District Council XI . . . All Toronto XI: souvenir programme. Toronto, the Council, [1933]. 12p. incl. adverts. ports.

### 1937 M.C.C. Tour to Canada

4911 **Alberta Cricket Association,** *and* **The**
■ **Calgary & District Cricket League**
Marylebone Cricket Club goodwill tour 1937: official souvenir programme, August 13 & 14, 1937, M.C.C. vs. Alberta played at Riley Park, Calgary, Alberta. Calgary, the League, [1937]. 16p. incl. adverts. diagr.

4912 **Marylebone Cricket Club**
M.C.C. Canadian tour 1937: [itinerary]. M.C.C., 1937. 4p.

4913 **Royal Society of St. George Cricket Club**
■ M.C.C. visit to Winnipeg, August 10 & 11, 1937: souvenir programme. Winnipeg, the Club, [1937]. [16]p. incl. adverts. ports. diagr.

4914 **Toronto and District Cricket Council,** *and*
■ **The Toronto Cricket Club**
Souvenir programme in honour of the M.C.C. team's 1937 tour. Toronto fixtures at Armour Heights, August 2, 3, 6 and 7. Toronto, [the Council, 1937]. 24p. incl. adverts.
*pre-visit; includes a brief history of the Toronto C.C.*

### 1951 M.C.C. Tour to Canada

4915 **Canadian Cricket Association**
Marylebone Cricket Club trans-Canada tour 1951: souvenir program. [Toronto], the Association, [1951]. 24p. illus. ports. diagrs.
*pre-tour*

### 1959 M.C.C. Tour

4916 **Calgary and District Cricket League**
■ Marylebone Cricket Club Canadian tour 1959; sponsored by Calgary & District Cricket League, Alberta Cricket Association, Canadian Cricket Association: official souvenir programme. August 26 . . . 30th, 1959, played at Riley Park, Calgary. Calgary, [the Assoc., 1959]. 12p. diagr.
*pre-tour*

4917 **Manitoba Cricket Association**
■ M.C.C. in Winnipeg 1959. Manitoba vs. M.C.C. at Assiniboine Park, 2nd Sep-

tember 1959: programme and score card. Winnipeg, the Assoc., [1959]. 12p. incl. covers, illus. port.

4918 **Victoria and District Cricket Association**
■ Marylebone Cricket Club trans-Canada tour 1959: souvenir program. Victoria, B.C., the Assoc., [1959]. 8p.
*pre-tour*

### 1964 Yorkshire C.C.C. Tour

4919 **The British Columbia Cricket**
■ **Association**
Yorkshire C.C.C. vs. British Columbia on Saturday, September 26, 1964, at Brockton Point, Vancouver, B.C.: programme. Vancouver, the Assoc., [1964]. [4]p. folded card

4920 **Sharpe, Philip, J.,** *compiler*
■ American tour. Leeds, Martin Black Publications Ltd., [1965]. ii,66p. incl. adverts. illus. ports. scores
*post-tour*

4921 **Yorkshire** county cricket team—season
■ 1964 and tour details for America—Canada–Bermuda. Leeds, Martin Black Publications Ltd., [1964]. 24p. incl. adverts. 1 illus. ports.
*pre-tour*

### 1967 M.C.C. Tour (D. R. W. Silk)

4922 **British Columbia Cricket Association**
■ Centennial cricket: the B.C.C.A. presents the M.C.C. on tour at Brockton Point, August 10th, 11th and 12th, 1967. Vancouver, the Assoc., [1967]. [8]p.
*pre-tour*

4923 **Marylebone Cricket Club**
■ M.C.C. tour, Canada and U.S.A., 1967: itinerary, match programme . . . M.C.C., [1967]. 13p.

4924 **Ontario Cricket Association**
■ Senior Inter-provincial Cricket Tournament: programme [and] Canada vs. M.C.C., Ottawa, 1967. [Ottawa], the Assoc., [1967]. 8p. port.

4925 **[Philadelphia Cricket Club]**
■ Marylebone Cricket Club visits Philadelphia, Saturday, September 2nd, 1967: souvenir programme. [Philadelphia, the Club, 1967]. 12p. incl. adverts.

4926 **Staten Island Cricket Club**
■ Staten Island C.C. [v] Marylebone Cricket Club. New York, the Club, [1967]. [20]p. incl. adverts. ports. stats.
*pre-match*

# OTHER ENGLISH TOURS

## TO EUROPE

### 1789 An English Team

4927 **Goulstone, John**
■ The 1789 tour. International Research Publications, 1972. [49]p. *typescript*
*limited ed. of 100 copies; an abortive attempt to send an English team to play in Paris immediately before the French Revolution*

### 1893 Yorkshire Wanderers

4927 **The Yorkshire** Wanderers Dutch tour,
–1 August 1893. 29p. stats. MS.
*post-tour; in A. E. Winder's collection*

### 1921–54 Free Foresters

4928 **De Flamingo's Cricket Club**
■ Twenty five tours with Free Foresters in Holland 1921–1954. Presented by Flamingo's to Free Foresters during their 25th tour to Holland, 11th Aug. 1954. [The Club, 1954]. 12p.

### 1938 Somerset Wanderers

4928 **Englische** Kricketer in Berlin. The
–1 Somerset Wanderers Kricket Club spielt
■ am 3. August 1938 gegen BFC. Preussen . . . am 5. August 1938 gegen BSV. 92 . . . am 7. August 1938 gegen einer Berliner Auswahlmannschaft . . . *n.p.*, [1938]. 12p. incl. adverts. 1 illus. 1 team port.
*includes an article on "How cricket is played"; German text*

### 1964 Buccaneers

4929 **Buccaneers Cricket Club**
Buccaneers' tour in France: Buccaneers v. Afcent C.C. at Fontainebleau; Buccaneers v. Combined Shape/Afcent XI at Versailles, June 13–14, 1964. The Club, [1964]. *typescript*

### 1967 Hampshire C.C.C.

4930 **Brussels Cricket Club**
■ Hampshire C.C.C.—Brussels C.C. 8–12 September 1967: souvenir programme. [Brussels, the Club, 1967]. 52p. illus.

### 1972 Cricket Society

4931 **The Cricket Society**
■ Tour to Corfu 1972. The Society, 1972. pp. 2–77. illus. port. map, plans, *typescript*
*post-tour*

## TO SOUTH AMERICA

### 1912 M.C.C. Tour to Argentina (Lord Hawke)

4932 **[Argentine Cricket Association]**
■ Tour of M.C.C. team in Argentina under the direction of Lord Hawke: programme February and March 1912. [Buenos Aires, the Assoc.,] 1912. [6]p.
*pre-tour*

4933 **McGough, James,** *compiler*
■ The M.C.C. tour in Argentine: detailed scores of all matches with individual records of the players who took part in the games. Buenos Aires, British Printery, [1912]. 24p. scores, stats.
*post-tour*

### 1926–27 M.C.C. Tour (P. F. Warner)

4934 **[Argentine Cricket Association]**
■ M.C.C. tour in Argentine, December 1926–January 1927: programme of fixtures and entertainments. Buenos Aires, [the Association, 1926]. 8p.

### 1937 Capt. Sir Theodore Brinckman's Team

4935 **Argentine Cricket Association**
Tour of Captain Sir Theodore Brinckman's English team. Buenos Aires, the Association, 1937. 16p. ports.

### 1958–59 M.C.C. Tour (G. H. G. Doggart)

4936 **Argentine Cricket Association**
■ M.C.C. tour 1958–59. Buenos Aires, the Assoc., [1958]. [64]p. incl. adverts. ports.
*pre-tour*

4937 **Brazil Cricket Association**
■ Souvenir programme of M.C.C. visit to Brazil, December 1958. [Sao Paulo], the Assoc., [1958]. [12]p. ports. stats.
*pre-visit*

### 1964–65 M.C.C. Tour (A. C. Smith)

4938 **Argentine Cricket Association**
■ M.C.C. tour 1964–65: official programme. Buenos Aires, the Assoc., [1964]. 84p. incl. adverts. illus. ports.
*pre-tour*

### 1966 Druids Tour

4939 **Argentine Cricket Association**
The Druids tour January 1966: official

programme. [Buenos Aires, the Assoc., 1966?]. 20p. illus. ports.
*pre-tour*

## TO BANGLADESH

### 1976–1977 M.C.C. Visit (E. A. Clark)

4939 **Bangladesh Cricket Control Board**
–1 M.C.C. vs. Bangladesh cricket match 7,
■ 8 & 9 January 1977: souvenir. Dacca, the
Board, [1977]. [64]p. incl. adverts. ports.
diagr. stats.

4939 **M.C.C. vs. Bangladesh East Zone, 3rd &**
–2 4th January 1977, Chittagong, Bangla-
■ desh. [Chittagong], Conception, [1977?].
[20]p. illus. ports. score, stats.
*sponsored by Rupali Bank*

## TO BERMUDA

### 1961 W. S. Surridge's Team

4940 **Bermuda Cricket Association**
■ Bermuda cricketer 1961. [Hamilton, the
Assoc., 1961]. [36]p. incl. adverts. ports.
*published to coincide with visit of W. S.
Surridge's touring team contains extensive
pen-portraits by Irving Rosenwater, the
manager*

### 1962 Gloucestershire C.C.C. to Bermuda

4941 **[Bermuda Cricket Association]**
■ Bermuda Clubs vs. Gloucestershire
County Cricket Club 1962 . . . [Hamilton,
the Assoc., 1962]. 40p. incl. adverts.
ports.

### 1964 Yorkshire C.C.C. Tour

4942 **Yorkshire** county cricket team—season
■ 1964 and tour details for America–
Canada–Bermuda. Leeds, Martin Black
Publications Ltd., [1964]. 24p. incl.
adverts. 1 illus. ports.
*pre-tour*

4943 **Yorkshire's** visit to Bermuda, October
1964. *n.p.*, [1964]. 24p. illus. ports.
*pre-tour*

### 1969 Yorkshire C.C.C. Tour

4944 **Somers Isles Cricket League**
■ Yorkshire County Cricket Club tour
Bermuda 1969: official tour souvenir.
[Hamilton, the League, 1969]. [16]p. incl.
adverts. ports.
*pre-tour*

## TO EAST AFRICA

### 1957–58 M.C.C. Tour (F. R. Brown)

4945 **Kenya Kongonis Cricket Club**
■ M.C.C. tour December 30, 1957–January
17, 1958: souvenir programme. Nairobi,
[the Club, 1957]. [20]p. incl. adverts.
ports. stats.
*pre-tour*

### 1961 F. R. Brown's Team

4946 **Kenya Kongonis Cricket Club**
■ Visit of F. R. Brown's touring team to East
Africa, October 19 to November 15, 1961:
programme. Nairobi, the Club, [1961].
[8]p. incl. covers. ports.
*pre-visit*

### 1963 M.C.C. Tour (M. J. K. Smith)

4947 **Marylebone Cricket Club**
■ M.C.C. tour, East Africa, 1963: itinerary,
match programme . . . M.C.C., [1963].
11p.

4948 **Sunday Post**
■ M.C.C. tour, East Africa, 1963: souvenir
programme. Nairobi, Sunday Post,
[1963]. 28p. incl. adverts. ports. stats.
*pre-tour*

4949 **Uganda Cricket Association**
M.C.C. tour in Uganda, October–
November 1963: official souvenir.
Kampala, the Assoc., 1963. ports.

## TO WEST AFRICA

4949 **Nigeria Cricket Association**
–1 M.C.C. maiden tour of West Africa,
■ Lagos, Nigeria 18–27 January 1976: official
programme. [Lagos, the Assoc., 1976].
20p. incl. covers. 1 illus. ports. score
*during tour: back cover carries score of 1st
match v. President's XI*

4949 **Sierra Leone Cricket Association**
–2 Cricket match: Sierra Leone team vs.
■ M.C.C. touring team, Cricket Oval,
Police Grounds, King Tom, January 3 to
13, 1976: official programme. The Assoc.,
[1976?]. [12]p. ports.

4949 **The West Africa Cricket Conference**
–3 First M.C.C. tour of West Africa 1975/76.
■ [Lagos, the Conference, 1976]. [24]p. incl.
adverts. score

## TO THE FAR EAST

### 1936–37 Sir J. Cahn's Team

4950 **Penang Gazette**
■ Souvenir of the visit of Sir Julien Cahn's eleven to Penang: a match played with Penang State on the Penang Esplanade, April 9 and 10, 1937. Penang, Penang Gazette P., [1937]. 20p. incl. adverts. ports.
*pre-visit*

4951 **Singapore Cricket Club**
■ Singapore cricket centenary, 1837–1937: Malaya vs. Sir Julien Cahn's XI, March 27, 28 and 29, 1937 at the Singapore Cricket Club. Singapore, the Club, 1937. 56p. incl. adverts. illus. ports. scores, stats.

4952 **Zilwa, Pat,** *compiler*
■ Visit of Sir Julien Cahn's cricket team, Malaya, 27th March–10th April, 1937; souvenir. Kuala Lumpur, the Compiler, [1937]. 96p. incl. adverts. illus. ports.
*pre-visit; contains article "History of Malayan cricket"*

### 1965 Worcestershire C.C.C. World Tour

4953 **Selangor** Cricket Association welcomes Worcestershire: souvenir. Kuala Lumpur, the Assoc., 1965. 88p. incl. adverts. ports.
*pre-visit*

### 1965–66 M.C.C. Visit to Hong Kong (M. J. K. Smith)

4954 **South China Morning Post**
M.C.C. tour of Hong Kong 1966: souvenir programme. Hong Kong, South China Morning Post, [1966]. 64p. illus. ports. scores
*pre-tour*

### 1970 M.C.C. Tour (A. R. Lewis)

4955 **[Marylebone Cricket Club]**
■ M.C.C. tour, Far East 1970: [itinerary, etc.]. M.C.C., 1970. 15p.

## TO IRELAND

### 1958 M.C.C. Visit

4956 **Irish Cricket Union**
■ Ireland v. M.C.C. 1858–1958 centenary year, College Park, Dublin, Sept. 6, 8, 9, 1958. Dublin, [the Union, 1958]. 80p. incl. adverts. illus. ports. stats.
*pre-match*

### 1959 Yorkshire C.C.C. Visit

4957 **Irish Cricket Union**
■ Ireland versus Yorkshire, 22nd and 23rd July 1959 at N.I.C.C. Grounds, Ormeau: souvenir programme and score card. Belfast, the Union, 1959. 36p. ports.
*pre-match*

Australia v. England. Armstrong and Trumper going out to bat, 27 May, 1909 at Edgbaston *photo:*
*BBC Hulton Picture Library*

# AUSTRALIA

4958 **Australian Board of Control for International Cricket Matches**
Objects, rules and by-laws. Sydney, the Board, 1905. 20p.
——*another ed.* 1922. 24p.
——*another ed.* with title: Constitution, rules and by-laws, 1924
——*another ed.* 1928. 20p.
——*another ed.* 1962. 40p.

4959 **[Entry cancelled]**

4960 **Browne, Frank,** *i.e.* **Francis Courtney**
■ **Browne**
Some of it was cricket. Sydney, Murray, [1965]. 191p. illus. ports. bibliog.
*Australian Test matches with England and West Indies*

4960 **Hill, Les R.**
–1 Australian cricketers on tour 1868–1974. Blackwood (S. Aust.), Lynton, 1974. 128p. illus. team ports. stats.
*a record of all Australian tours abroad*

4960 **Stokes, Edward**
–2 Australian Test cricket facts 1946–1978.
■ Sydney, Ure Smith, 1979. 576p. illus. ports. stats.

4960 **Swinstead, Gene,** *editor*
–3 Cricket action through the camera.
■ Toorak (Vic.), Garry Sparke for Allsport Publications, [1977]. 80p. illus. ports.
*illustrations of Australia v. England 1974–75; v. West Indies 1975–76; v. Pakistan 1976–77, and the Centenary Test*

4960 **Whitington, Richard Smallpeice**
–4 The Courage book of Australian Test
■ cricket 1877–1974. Melbourne, Wren Publishing, 1974. vii,336p. illus. ports. scores, stats.

## AUSTRALIAN TOURS TO ENGLAND

4961 **Baillie, E. H. M.**
■ Since eighteen hundred and seventy-seven. Part I. Australia. Melbourne & Adelaide, H. A. Morris, [1934]. 180p.
*part II due in 1935 was never published*

4962 **The Marvel.** *Supplement*
Australian cricket teams in England: a brief history of the 15 tours, by J. N. Pentelow. Amalgamated P., June 4, 1921. 16p. illus. ports.

4963 **Pogson, Rex**
■ Australia v. the counties (1878–1938). Birmingham, Hudson, [1938?]. 95p. stats.

4964 **Tate, William James**
Famous Anglo-Australian cricket matches played in England. Gregory, 1896
*unpublished owing to death of publisher. Proof copy now in M.C.C. Library at Lord's*

4965 **Test** matches played in England, 1880–1893. London, 1893
*in Taylor*

4966 **Webber, Roy**
■ The Australians in England: a record of the 21 Australian cricket tours of England, 1878–1953. Hodder & Stoughton, 1953. 256p. illus. ports. scores, stats.
——*another ed.* Sportsman's Book Club, 1956

## 1868 Australian Aboriginals (C. Lawrence)

4967 **Mulvaney, Derek John**
■ Cricket walkabout: the Australian Aboriginal cricketers on tour 1867–8. Melbourne, Melbourne U.P.; London, Cambridge U.P., 1967 [*i.e.* 1968]. xiv, 112p. illus. ports. facsims. map, stats.
*includes matches played by the team in Australia before and after the tour*

## 1878 Australian XI Tour (D. W. Gregory)

4967 **Blaikie, George**
–1 Scandals of Australia's strange past. Adelaide, Rigby; London, Angus & Robertson, 1963. 300p. illus.
*contains pp. 98–103 "Dust-up at Lord's", a description of the Australian match at Lord's on May 27, 1878*

4967 Great Australian scandals. Adelaide,
-2 Rigby, 1979. 214p. illus.
  *contains pp. 85–8 "The heiress and the
  trickey cricketer"; pp. 121–4 "Crook cricketer
  catches bank for millions"; pp. 151–3 "Revolt-
  ing cricketers bowl themselves out"*

4967 **Harrigan, Bob**
-3 Gerald Elkington. Offprint from the
■ Llanelli Star, August 1978. [4]f. score,
  *typescript*
    *an account of Elkington's role in the Austr-
    alia v. Gentlemen of S. Wales match at
    Swansea, 1878*

4968 **[Reynolds, P. E.]**
■ Tour of Australian cricketers through
  Australia, New Zealand, and Great
  Britain, by Argus. Sydney, Jarrett;
  Newcastle (N.S.W.), Sweet; Bathurst
  (N.S.W.), Rae, 1878. [ii],94p. illus. ports.
  scores
    *post-tour*

4969 **The tour** of the Australian eleven through
■ England, America and Colonies with
  Conway's Australian cricketers' annual
  for 1877–78. Melbourne, Fergusson &
  Moore, 1879. [iv],399p. scores, stats.
    *pre-tour*

### 1880 Test Tour (W. L. Murdoch)

4970 **The Australian** cricketers: account of
  their tour and matches in 1880. Shaw,
  1880. 8p. illus.

### 1882 Test Tour (W. L. Murdoch)

4971 **The Australian** cricketers: account of
  their tour and matches 1882. Etherington,
  1882. 8p. illus.

4972 **The Australian** eleven in England: the
  great match for the championship,
  England v. Australia at the Oval, 1882.
  Melbourne, Boyle & Scott, [1882]
    *"apparently printed for private distribu-
    tion" (Taylor)*

4973 **Masefield, John**
■ The bluebells, and other verse. Heinemann, 1961. [v],205p.
    *contains "Eighty-five to win", a narrative
    poem on England's second innings in the Test
    against Australia at the Oval, 1882, pp.
    73–81*

4974 **Pardon, Charles Frederick**
■ The Australians in England: a complete
  record of the cricket tour of 1882, with
  the batting and bowling averages of the
  Australians and the Englishmen who
  played against them. London, Bell's Life

Office; Manchester, Hutton; Melbourne,
Robertson, 1882, viii,192p. scores, stats.
  *rptd. with additions from "Bell's Life"*

4974 **[Sussex County Cricket Club]**
-1 Correspondence between the Sussex
  C.C.C. and Mr. Perkins relative to the
  second Australian match with Sussex, on
  August 21st, 22nd and 23rd 1882. [Hove,
  the Club, c.1883]. 11p.

4975 **The third** Australian team in England: a
■ complete record of all the matches with
  portrait & biography of each member.
  Cricket P., [1882]. vi,131p. illus. ports.
  scores, stats.
    *post-tour*

### 1884 Test Tour (W. L. Murdoch)

4975 **The Australian** cricketers: account of
-1 their tour and matches 1884. C.
  Humphreys, [1884]. 8p. incl. adverts.
  mounted team port.

4975 **Bax, Clifford**
-2 Members only. 8p.
■ *offprint from The New English Review,
  Sept. 1946, pp. 283–90; cricket in England
  1884 including the visit of the Australians*

4976 **The fourth** Australian cricket team: their
■ scores in the Colonies and in England,
  with portraits & biographies. "Cricket"
  Office, [1884]. vi,140p. ports. scores,
  stats.
    —*cover-title:* The doings of . . .
    *post-tour record rptd. from* Cricket

4977 **Pardon, Charles Frederick**
■ The Australians in England: a complete
  record of the cricket tour of 1884. London,
  Pardon; Melbourne, Robertson, 1884.
  viii,184p. scores, stats.

### 1886 Test Tour (H. J. H. Scott)

4978 **The Australian** cricketers: an account of
■ their tour and matches, 1886. F.
  Humphreys, [1886]. [8]p. mounted team
  port.

### 1890 Test Tour (W. L. Murdoch)

4979 **Moody, Clarence Percival**
■ The seventh Australian team in England,
  1890: biographical sketches. Wright &
  Co., [1890]. 16p. incl. adverts. mounted
  team port.

### 1893 Test Tour (J. McC. Blackham)

4980 **Stanton, Henry Valentine Labron**
■ The Australian cricket team of 1893:
  portraits, biographies, etc. London,

Wright; Birmingham, "Sport & Play" Office, [1893]. [ii],18p. ports. stats.
*pre-tour*

## 1896 Test Tour (G. H. S. Trott)

4981    **The Australian** cricketers' team for 1896, with biographies and portraits of the players, also full authentic report of Test match, Anglo-Australian team v. Rest of Australia. Howe, [1896]. [32]p. ports. score

4982    **The Australians** in England 1896.
■  London & Manchester, "Athletic News" Office, [1896]. 64p. 1 illus. scores, stats.
    *includes "An Australian opinion of the tour", by George Bull, and "A few jottings on the tour" by J.J.B.*

4983    **Cricket** match between the Australian eleven and the Earl of Sheffield's eleven, Sheffield Park, May 11th, 1896. *Printed by* John Beal, 1896. 4p.
    *a menu card and team list*

4983  **Netherway, E. S.,** *publisher*
–1  Album and guide of the 9th Australian team of cricketers. Adelaide, Netherway, [1896]. 16p. incl. adverts. ports. stats.
    *pre-tour*

4984  **The ninth** Australian tour, 1896: portraits
■  and biographies of all the players. "Cricket" Office, [1896]. 32p. incl. adverts. 1 illus. ports.
    *issued in both yellow covers with portrait of G. H. S. Trott and in pale green covers with portrait of H. Musgrove; pre-tour*

4985  **Pentelow, John Nix**
■  The Australian cricket team of 1896: complete biographies. London, [Wright]; Birmingham, "Sport & Play" Office, [1896]. 22p. ports. stats.
    *pre-tour*

4986  **Stanton, Henry Valentine Labron**
    The Australian team of 1896. Cricket P., 1896. 20p. ports. stats.
    *pre-tour*

## 1899 Test Tour (J. Darling)

4987  **Answers**
    Special cricket number, 8th July, 1899
    *in Taylor*

4988  **Billingham, Sidney,** *compiler*
■  The Australian team in England. Season, 1899. Toler Bros., [1899]. 50p. incl. adverts. illus. stats.

4989  **Ford, William Justice**
■  A cricketer on cricket. Sands, 1900. 171p.
    *includes the Australian team of 1899*

4990  **Laver, Frank**
■  An Australian cricketer on tour: reminiscences, impressions, and experiences of two trips; with records of matches and views on English cricket. Chapman & Hall; Bell, 1905. xiv,296p. illus. ports. scores, stats.
    *Australian tours of England, 1899 & 1905*

4991  **Pentelow, John Nix**
■  The Australian team of 1899. Cricket P., [1899]. 16p. incl. adverts. stats.
    *pre-tour*

4992  **Phillips, James**
■  The tenth Australian cricket team, with a note on unfair bowling. *Printed for* the Author, [1899]. [32]p. ports. stats.
    *pre-tour*

4992  **Sheffield** cricket souvenir. Sheffield, the
–1   Yorkshire Advt. Co., [1899]. 48p. incl.
■  adverts. ports.
    *potted biographies of the English and Australian teams 1899*

4993  **The tenth** Australian cricketers' team for 1899. Peckham, Howe, 1899. 15p. illus.
    *pre-tour*

4994  **The tenth** Australian tour 1899: portraits
■  and biographies of all the players. "Cricket" Office, [1899]. 32p. ports. stats.
    *pre-tour*

## 1902 Test Tour (J. Darling)

4995  **Cricket** sketches with portrait of the
■  Yorkshire team, also particulars of the Test matches, etc. Leeds, E. A. Tempest, [1902]. 12p. port. stats.

4996  **The eleventh** Australian tour, 1902:
■  portraits and biographies of the players. "Cricket" Office, [1902]. 32p. ports.
    *pre-tour*

4997  **Golden Penny**
■  Cricket album 1902; special photographic groups of the Australians and all the first-class counties; the story of each club illustrated. Golden Penny, [1902]. 28p. illus. ports.
    *pre-tour*

4998  **The kangaroo** in England. Sydney, Samuel Jones, 1902. 44p.
    *a review of the eleventh Australian XI's tour 1902*

## 1905 Test Tour (J. Darling)

4999  **Billingham, Sidney,** *compiler*
■  Australian team of 1905. Cricket P., [1905]. 16p. incl. adverts. ports. stats.
    *pre-tour*

5000 **Gibson, Alan**
■ Jackson's year: the Test matches of 1905. Cassell, 1965. [xi],155p. illus. ports. scores, stats. bibliog.
——*another ed.* Sportsman's Book Club, 1966

5001 **Laver, Frank**
■ An Australian cricketer on tour: reminiscences, impressions, and experiences of two trips; with records of matches and views on English cricket. Chapman & Hall; Bell, 1905. xiv,296p. illus. ports. scores, stats.
*Australian tours of England, 1899 & 1905*

5002 **Sketchy Bits.** *Special Number*
■ Australian & English cricketers of 1905. "Sketchy Bits" Co., [1905]. 24p. incl. adverts. ports. stats.
*pre-tour*

5003 **[Trowsdale, T. Broadbent]**
■ A complete history of the Test matches between England and Australia (1827–1905) . . . besides particulars, fixtures and latest averages of the Australian team of 1905, by "Cover-point". Routledge, [1905]. 110p. scores, stats.
*pre-tour*

5004 **The twelfth** Australian tour 1905: portraits and biographies of all the players. "Cricket" Office, [1905]. 32p. ports.
*pre-tour*

5005 **Twelfth** team of Australian cricketers. Birmingham, Hudson, 1905. bs.
*in Taylor*

**1909 Test Tour (M.A. Noble)**

5006 **Australian** cricket souvenir, sanctioned by Australian Cricket Board of Control and N.S.W. Cricket Association. [Sydney, N.S.W.C.A., 1909]. 84p. incl. adverts. illus. ports. scores, stats.
*includes account of 1909 Australian tour of England by L.O.S. Poidevin*

5007 **Jones, Arthur Owen,** *editor*
■ Official souvenir of the Australian cricket tour 1909. R. Empson, [1909]. 72p. incl. adverts. ports. stats.
*pre-tour*

5008 **[Stanton, Henry Valentine Labron]**
■ The Australian cricket team, 1909, by "Wanderer". "Sportsman" Offices, [1909]. 47p. ports. stats.
*pre-tour*

**1912 Test Tour (S.E. Gregory)**

5009 **Australia** and South Africa tour cricket sketches. Manchester, R. Scott, [1912]. 16p. ports.
*pre-tour*

5010 **The Daily Graphic**
■ Cricket number. H.R. Baines, 1912. 20p. incl. adverts. illus. ports. stats.
*pre-the Triangular Tests*

5011 **Dorey, H.V.,** *compiler*
■ The triangular Tests 1876–1912. Cricket & Sports Publishers, [1912]. [i],232p. scores, stats.

5012 **Sewell, Edward Humphrey Dalrymple**
■ Triangular cricket: a record of the greatest contest in the history of the game. Dent, 1912. x,211p. illus. ports. diagrs. scores
*account of the 1912 Tests between Australia, South Africa & England*

5013 **The year** 1912 illustrated. Headley Bros., 1913. 184p. illus.
*"The cricket season and Triangular Tests", pp. 155–162*

*The 1912 cricket dispute* (in order of publication)

5014 **Citizens' Cricket Committee**
■ Statement relative to matters arising out of the dispute between the Australian Board of Control and the leading players. Melbourne, the Committee, March, 1912. 8p.
*William Riggall, chairman*

5015 **Victorian Cricket Association**
■ Statement by the Victorian Cricket Association. Melbourne, the Assoc., 27th March, 1912. 24p.

5016 **Laver, Frank**
■ The cricket dispute: a reply to the V.C.A. Melbourne, [the Author], May, 1912. 16p.

5017 **M'Alister, Peter A.**
■ The cricket dispute: a reply to Mr. Frank Laver. Melbourne, [the Author], 29th June, 1912. [4]p.

5018 **Melbourne Cricket Club**
■ Reply to the "Statement by the Victorian Cricket Association". Melbourne, the Club, August, 1912. 31p.

5019 **Bean, Ernest Edward,** *and* **Rush, H.R.**
■ The 1912 Australian eleven in England: a few facts for fair-minded sportsmen.

Melbourne, the Authors, 7th September, 1912. [7]p. port. on cover, stats.

*a reply to the criticism by the Melbourne Press of the Australian team in England*

## 1919 Australian Services' Eleven

5019 **Goddard, George Hubert Denvers**
–1 Soldiers and sportsmen: an account of the sporting activities of the Australian Imperial Force during the period between November 1918 and September 1919. London, A.I.F., Sports Control Board, 1919. 118p. illus. scores
*includes account of the Australian Services Eleven's tour of England*

## 1921 Test Tour (W.W. Armstrong)

5020 **Armstrong, Warwick Windridge**
■ The art of cricket. Methuen, 1922. vii, 149p. illus.
*contains chapter on the Australian team in England, 1921*

5021 **Ashley-Cooper, Frederick Samuel**
■ England v. Australia: 100th Test-match souvenir. Nottingham, Richards, 1921. 21p. stats.
*pre-Test*

5022 **Australia** v. Cumberland (Mayor of
■ Whitehaven's team), September 12, 1921, Cricket field, Whitehaven: official programme. Whitehaven, *printed by* The Whitehaven News, [1921]. 4p.

5023 **The Australians,** including photographs
■ and record of the Leicestershire vs. Australia match, 1921. Leicester, George Johnson, [1921]. [16]p. illus. ports. score

5024 **Henley, Herbert J.,** *editor*
■ Test match souvenir. Welbecson P., [1921]. 32p. illus. (some col.), port.
*published in aid of St. Dunstan's Blinded Soldiers' and Sailors' Hostel; pre-tour*

5025 **Lynd, Robert**
■ The sporting life, and other trifles. Richards, 1922. 251p.
——*another ed.* Sportsman's Book Club, 1956
*chapters on 1921 Tests*

5026 **Mailey, Arthur Alfred**
The Australian fifteen for England . . . caricatured by . . . Arthur Mailey, with an appreciation by Warwick Armstrong and a note on Mailey's art by C.R. Bradish. Melbourne, McCubbin, [1921]. 16p. illus.

5027 Mailey's googlies: a series of sketches and
■ caricatures of English county and Test

match cricket. Graphic Publications, [1921], 32p. illus.

5028 Arthur Mailey's book: a series of sketches
■ illustrating the tour through England and Africa by the Australian slow bowler, Arthur Mailey. Sydney, *printed by* Goddard, 1922. 27p. illus.

5029 **Mason, Ronald**
■ Warwick Armstrong's Australians. Epworth P., 1971. 159p. ports. illus. scores, stats.
——*another ed.* Sportsman's Book Club, 1973

5030 **Smith, Sydney**
■ With the 15th Australian XI: (a complete record of the team's tour throughout Great Britain and South Africa). Sydney, E.T. Kibblewhite, 1922. 289p. illus. ports. scores, stats.

5031 **Trevor, Philip Christian William**
■ Cricket and cricketers. Chapman & Hall, 1921. viii,232p.

## 1926 Test Tour (H.L. Collins)

5032 **Australian Board of Control for Interna-**
■ **tional Cricket Matches**
Sixteenth Australian XI English tour, 1926: fixture card. Sydney, the Board, [1926]. 4p.

5033 **Baily, Robin,** *editor*
■ All about the Australians. Oval & Lord's, C.E. Smith, [1926]. 16p. port. stats.
*pre-tour*

5034 **British Australasian**
■ The Australian cricket team 1926: with notes on Anglo-Australian cricket from 1877. British Australasian, [1926]. 92p. incl. adverts. ports. stats.
*pre-tour*

5035 **Cricket 1926.** Barton, [1926]. [24]p. illus.
■ ports.
*photographs of Australian team, 30 leading English cricketers and the Test grounds; pre-tour*

5036 **Daily Mirror**
■ All about the Australians: fixtures, records, biographies, photographs. Daily Mirror, [1926]. [12]p. ports. stats.
*pre-tour*

5037 **East, Laurence,** *artist*
■ Australian cricketers 1926: portraits drawn from life and signed by each player [text by Frank Thorogood]. Fleetgate Publications, 1926. 34p. ports. stats.

5038 **Gilligan, Arthur Edward Robert**
■ Collins's men. Arrowsmith, 1926. 263p. illus. port. scores

5039 **Leicestershire** versus Australia, May 1, 3
■ and 4, 1926: souvenir. Leicester, G. Johnson, [1926]. [16]p. illus. ports. score

5040 **Mailey, Arthur Alfred**
■ The men from Australia: a souvenir in pen and pencil. Cassell, [1926]. [24]p. illus.
*cartoons by A.M., articles by H.L. Collins and J.M. Gregory*

5041 **Marchant, John,** *pseud. of* **Harold Lake**
■ The greatest Test match. Faber & Gwyer, 1926. 239p. illus. diagrs. scores, stats.
——*another ed.* Sportsman's Book Club, 1953. xvii,142p.
*with different illustrations*
*an account of 5th Test between England and Australia at the Oval in 1926*

5042 **Nickalls, Guy Oliver,** *editor*
■ With the skin of their teeth: memories of great sporting finishes in golf, cricket, . . . Country Life, 1951. 168p. illus.
*cricket section pp. 28–47, by Herbert Sutcliffe, contains account of England v. Australia Test at the Oval, 1926*

5043 **Noble, Montague Alfred**
■ Those "Ashes": the Australian tour of 1926. Cassell, 1927. xvi,272p. illus. port. diagrs. scores

5044 **Pickfords Ltd.**
■ Australian cricket team 1926: programme of journey, London to Sydney. Pickfords Ltd., [1926]. 41p. illus. team port. map

5045 **Scotland** v. Australia 1926: souvenir

5046 **Warner,** *Sir* **Pelham Francis**
■ The fight for the Ashes in 1926: being a critical account of the Australian tour in England. Harrap, 1926. 324p. illus. ports. scores, stats.

## 1930 Test Tour (W.M. Woodfull)

5047 **Baily, Robin,** *editor*
■ England v. Australia: special Test match edition of "Lord's and Oval annual". Lord's and Oval Bookstalls, 1930. 16p. ports. scores
*pre-tour*

5048 **Battersby Hats**
Programme of Australian matches. Battersby Hats, 1930. 4p.

5049 **East, Laurence,** *artist*
■ Autographed sketches of the 1930 Australian cricketers drawn from life . . . with biographical notes by G.C. Dixon. Jenkins, [1930]. 39p. ports. stats.

5050 **Fender, Percy George Herbert**
■ The Tests of 1930: the 17th Australian team in England. Faber, 1930. viii,259p. illus. ports. scores, stats.

5051 **"I was there"**: twenty exciting sporting events by sports writers of the "Daily Telegraph" and "Sunday Telegraph". Collins, 1966. [vii],152p. illus.
*includes an account of England v. Australia at Lord's, 1930, by E.W. Swanton*

5052 **Leicestershire County Cricket Club**
Souvenir Leicestershire v. Australia. Leicester, the Club, 1930. 12p. illus.

5052 **The Magnet** album of Test match cricke-
–1 ters, 1930 tour. Presented with "The Magnet", July 12th, 1930. [14]p. ports.
*with 28 photographic portraits mounted in*

5052 **Mailey, Arthur Alfred**
–2 The 1930 Australian XI and other caricatures. The Author, 1930. 20p. incl. adverts. illus.

5053 **1930 The Ashes:** Australian XI English tour: souvenir and scorer. Sydney, James Hill, [1930]. 34p. incl. adverts. ports.
*pre-tour*

5054 **Orient Line**
Australian XI 1930. Orient Line, 1930

5055 **Souvenir** of Australian cricket tour 1930.
■ Barton Pictorial Co., [1930]. 32p. illus. ports.
*pre-tour*

5055 **The Sydney Mail**
–1 Souvenir of the Australian cricketers – the 1930 team. Sydney, John Fairfax & Sons Ltd., 1930.
*a portfolio of 15 loose photographs of the team and team members issued weekly as supplements to The Sydney Mail from 5/2/1930 to 21/5/1930*

5056 **Tebbutt, Geoffrey**
■ With the 1930 Australians: behind the scenes in the fight for the Ashes. Hodder & Stoughton, 1930. 320p. illus. scores, stats.

5057 **Warner,** *Sir* **Pelham Francis**
■ The fight for the Ashes in 1930: being a critical account of the Australian tour in England. Harrap, 1930. xxix,288p. illus. ports. scores, stats.

## 1934 Test Tour (W.M. Woodfull)

**5057** **Australian Board of Control**
**−1** 18th Australian XI English tour 1934: [official itinerary]. The Board, [1934]. 4p. folded card
*team members and full fixture list*

**5057** **Australian Broadcasting Commission**
**−2** International cricket: the Australian team
■ in England 1934. Sydney, the Commission, [1934]. 52p. incl. covers & 20p. of blank score sheets. ports. diagrs. stats.
*pre-tour*

**5057** **The Australians** in England 1934: "The
**−3** Advertiser" record book giving a
■ complete review of the tour, with full scores and statistics. Adelaide, Advertiser Newspapers Ltd., [1934]. 56p. scores, stats.
*post-series*

**5058** **Cardus,** *Sir* **Neville**
■ Good days: a book of cricket. Cape, 1934. 288p. scores
——*another ed.* Cape, 1937. 288p. (New Library)
——*another ed.* Hart-Davis, 1948. 255p.
*includes account of England v. Australia Tests 1934*

**5059** **Donnelly, Ian**
■ The joyous pilgrimage: A New Zealander's impressions of 'Home'. Dent, 1935. xiii,224p.
*includes "A plain view of Test cricket"*

**5060** **Fender, Percy George Herbert**
■ Kissing the rod: the story of the Tests of 1934. Chapman & Hall, 1934. xvi,299p. illus. scores, stats.

**5061** **Gustard, Frederick Joseph Charles**
■ England v. Australia: a guide to the Tests, 1934. Joseph, [1934]. 158p. ports. scores, stats.
*a preview of the 1934 Tests with scores of 1930 and 1932–3 series*

**5062** **Hobbs,** *Sir* **John Berry**
■ The fight for the Ashes in 1934: a critical account of the Australian tour in England. Harrap, 1934. 350p. illus. diagrs. scores, stats.

**5063** **Jardine, Douglas Robert**
■ Ashes – and dust. Hutchinson, [1934]. 290p. illus. ports. scores, stats.

**5064** **Lynd, Robert**
■ Both sides of the road. Methuen, 1934. viii,184p.
*essays, including "Verity's Test match", pp. 124–30*

**5065** **Manchester Guardian**
■ The Australians in England, 1934. Manchester, Manchester Guardian, [1934]. 20p. scores, stats.
*includes "The Australians—who's who" by "Cricketer" [Neville Cardus], and scores of Test series 1932–3*

**5066** **Orient Line**
■ Australian XI English tour. Orient Line, R.M.S. Orford, [1934]. [12]p. 1 illus. ports.

**5067** **Simpson, A.W.,** *compiler & editor*
■ Australia's 18th cricket tour of England: souvenir. Nottingham, All Counties Publicity, [1934]. 40p. incl. adverts. illus. ports. diagrs.
*pre-tour*

**5068** **Wrigleys (Aust.) Ltd.**
■ The 1934 cricket tour. [Rosebery, N.S.W. & Perth, W.A., 1934]. [8]p. folded sheet
*pre-tour*

## 1938 Test Tour (D.G. Bradman)

**5069** **The Age,** *and* **The Leader**
■ Test cricket souvenir, 1938. Melbourne, Syme, [1938]. 20p. illus. ports. diagrs.

**5070** **Australian Board of Control for International Cricket**
1938 Australian XI tour in Great Britain: [official itinerary]. Sydney, the Board, 1938. 12p. maps

**5071** **Australian Broadcasting Commission**
Test cricket, 1938. Sydney, the Commission, 1938. 73p. illus. ports. diagrs.

**5071** **Higgins, Aidan**
**−1** Scenes from a receding past. Calder,
■ 1977. 204p.
*fiction; contains score of Oval Test, England v. Australia, 1938, and stroke diagram of Hutton's innings of 364*

**5072** **Irish Cricket Union**
Ireland v. the Australians 1938: official souvenir programme. The Union, [1938]. 16p. ports.

**5072** **The Jim Russell** cricket book of 1938
**−1** Australian XI: caricatures of the complete Australian team, itinerary of tour, general information. Sydney, Phillips, [1938]. 24p. incl. covers. illus.

**5073** **Lane, Trevor,** *editor*
■ The Ashes: the Australians are here. The England-Australia 1938 Cricket Tour Programme Co., 1938. 40p. incl. adverts. illus. ports. stats.
*pre-tour*

5074 **Manchester Guardian**
■ The Australians in England, 1938. Manchester, Manchester Guardian, [1938]. 32p. scores, stats.
*includes 2 articles by Neville Cardus and scores of Test series 1936–7*

5075 **Orient Line**
■ 1938—Australian XI tour in Great Britain. [Orient Line, R.M.S. "Orontes". 1938]. 12p. maps

5075 **The Returned Sailors', Soldiers' and**
–1 **Airmens' Imperial League of Australia.** *Mitcham Sub-Branch*
International cricket; follow the Tests with the radio. [Adelaide], R.S.S.-A.I.L.A., [1938]. [36]p. incl. covers & adverts. ports. stats.

5076 **Simpson, A.W.,** *editor*
■ Australian cricket tour 1938; edited by A.W. Simpson; statistics compiled by W. Ferguson. Canterbury, *printed by* Jennings, [1938]. 48p. incl. adverts. illus. ports. diagrs. stats.

## 1948 Test Tour (D.G. Bradman)

5077 **Aberdeenshire Cricket Club**
Scotland v. Australia: souvenir brochure. Mannofield, Aberdeen, Sept. 17, 18, 1948. Aberdeen, the Club, [1948]. 24p. incl. adverts. ports.

5078 **Arlott, [Leslie Thomas] John**
■ Gone to the Test match: primarily an account of the Test series of 1948. Longmans, Green, 1949. 192p. illus. scores

5079 Two summers at the Tests: England v.
■ South Africa 1947; England v. Australia 1948. Sportsman's Book Club, 1952. 320p. illus. ports. scores
*contents:* Gone to the cricket; Gone to the Test match

5080 **Australia.** Australian News & Informa-
■ tion Bureau. *quarterly.* illus. ports. stats.
*vol. 4, no. 6. Apr. 1948. 12p. includes pre-tour details of Australian tour of England 1948, pp. 3–5*

5080 **Australia 1949:** the Courier-Mail year
–1 book; edited by J.A. Alexander. Brisbane, Queensland Newspapers Pty Ltd., [1949?]. 800p. illus. ports. maps, stats.
——*also published with sub-title:* the Herald year book. Melbourne, Herald & Weekly Times Ltd.
*cricket pp. 692–704 including "The English tour – undefeated record of 1948" by Alan D. McGilvray*

5081 **Australian Board of Control**
■ 20th Australian XI tour in Great Britain 1948: [itinerary]. Sydney, the Board, 1948. 12p. maps

5082 **Australian Broadcasting Commission**
A.B.C. broadcast cricket book: the Australians in England: Test cricket 1948; [edited by Bernard Kerr]. Sydney, the Commission, 1948. 72p. illus. ports.
*pre-tour*

5083 **Australia's** 1948 Test team: . . . official
■ photographs, biographical notes of the team, tour fixtures. Manchester, Britannia P., 1948. 32p. ports.
*pre-tour*

5084 **Australia's** Test cricketers. Grant
■ Hughes, [1948]. 16p. ports.
*portraits only, no text*

5085 **Bannister, Alexander James**
■ "Here comes the Aussies": 1948 Test tour who's who, records, pictures. Batson's Sports Service, [1948]. 20p. illus. ports. stats.
*pre-tour*

5086 **Batchelor, Denzil Stanley**
■ Days without sunset. Eyre & Spottiswoode, 1949. 283p.
*includes account of Australian tour of England 1948*

5087 **Batson's Sports Service**
England versus Australians: third Test of 1948 tour, July 8th to 13th, at Manchester. Batson's Sports Service, 1948. 4p. illus.
*pre-Test*

5088 Lancashire versus Australians, played at
■ Old Trafford, August 7, 9, and 10, 1948: souvenir programme. Batson's Sports Service, 1948. [4]p. ports. stats.

5089 **Cardus,** *Sir* **Neville**
■ "The Ashes"; with background of the Tests and pen pictures of the 1948 Australian team. County & Sporting Publications, [1948]. 49p. ports. stats.
*pre-tour*

5090 **Day, Cedric,** *and* **Mason, Michael**
■ The story of Test cricket: England v. Australia. Windsor, C. Day, [1948]. 27p. illus. ports. stats.
*pre-tour*

5091 **England's** Test cricketers. Grant Hughes,
■ [1948]. [16]p. ports.
*portraits only, no text*

5091 **Fingleton, Jack,** *i.e.* **John Henry Webb**
-1 **Fingleton**
■ Brightly fades the Don. Collins, 1949.
256p. illus. ports. stats.
——*Australian ed.* Sydney, Collins, 1949.
[ii],277p. illus. ports. stats.

5092 **Flanagan, Andy**
On tour with Bradman. Sydney, Halstead
P., 1950. x,181p. illus.

5093 **"Haydn",** *pseud.*
Australian cricketers in cartoon. 1948

5094 **Kay, John**
■ Ducks and hundreds. Altrincham, Sherratt, 1949. ix,180p. illus. ports. scores,
stats.

5095 **Kevin, Dick,** *and* **Bird, Richard,** *pseud.,*
■ *i.e.* **Walter Barradell-Smith**
Cricket: the Ashes, 1948: fixtures, personalities, history, data, tables, records.
Devereaux Publications, [1948]. 96p. incl.
adverts. illus. ports. stats.
*pre-tour*

5096 Meet the Australians: extracts from
■ "Cricket: the Ashes, 1948". Devereaux
Publications, [1948]. 48p. illus. ports.

5097 **Ledbrooke, Archibald William**
■ The fight for the Ashes: a guide to the
1948 Test matches. London & Manchester, Withy Grove P., [1948]. 96p.
illus. ports. scores, stats. (Cherry Tree
Special)
*pre-tour*

5098 **Macartney, Charles Gordon,** *and* **Foster,**
■ **Denis**
Fight for the Ashes. Findon Publications,
[1948]. 100p. illus. ports.

5099 **O'Reilly, William Joseph**
■ Cricket conquest: the story of the 1948
Test tour. T. Werner Laurie, 1949. 224p.
illus. port. scores, stats.

5100 **Peninsular and Orient Line**
■ Australian XI's English tour 1948 Tests.
P. & O. Line, R.M.S. Straithaird, [1948].
[32]p. 1 illus. ports.
*pre-tour*

5101 **Rivett, Rohan Deakin,** *editor*
■ The Listener in Test cricket book: for the
fireside on Test match nights, June to
August, 1948; stories of Test matches,
grounds, and players. Records, averages
and other statistical information, [etc.].
Melbourne, United P., 1948. 52p. incl.
covers & adverts. illus. ports. stats. score
*pre-tour*

5102 Australia wins!: the illustrated story of
■ the Tests of 1948. Melbourne, United
Press, Herald & Weekly Times Ltd.,
[1948]. 52p. incl. covers. illus. ports.
scores, stats. (The Listener-In Cricket
Book, no. 2)
*post-tour*

5102 **Robinson, Ray**
-1 The greats of '48, as seen by Ray
■ Robinson who toured with the team.
Sydney, The Primary Club of Australia,
1979. 32p. illus. ports. scores, stats.

5103 **Simpson, A.W.,** *compiler & editor*
■ Cricket 1948: the Australian tour: fixtures,
records and photographs of players. I.M.
Young, 1948. 41p. illus. ports.
*pre-tour*

5104 **Test** record England [v.] Australia: sou-
■ venir programme. T. Ross [1948]. [4]p.
folded card. ports. stats.
*pre-tour*

## 1953 Test Tour (A.L. Hassett)

5105 **Alston, Rex,** *i.e.* **Arthur Reginald Alston**
■ Over to Rex Alston: a commentary on
the Australian tour 1953. Muller, 1953.
[ix],220p. illus. scores

5106 **Arlott, [Leslie Thomas] John**
■ Test match diary 1953: a personal, day-
by-day account of the Test series,
England–Australia. Barrie, 1953. xii,212p.
illus. scores
——*another ed.* Sportsman's Book Club,
1954
——[an extract appeared in]: Pleasure in
English for Australian schools; edited by
J.R.C. Yglesias and Joan Woodberry.
Longmans, 1965. pp. 129–30

5107 **The Ashes,** 1953: pictorial record of the
■ England v. Australia Test matches. Worcester, Littlebury, [1953]. [25]p. illus.
ports. scores, stats.
*post-tour*

5108 **Australia.** Australian News & Informa-
■ tion Bureau. *quarterly.* illus. ports. stats.
*Vol. 8, no. 5 Jan.-Feb. 1953. English Test
tour issue. 12p.*
*pre-tour*

5109 **Australia** coronation England tour 1953:
■ photographic souvenir. Birmingham, J.
Walker, [1953]. 4p. ports.
*pre-tour*

5110 **Australian Broadcasting Commission**
■ A.B.C. coronation cricket book: English
tour 1953. Sydney, the Commission,
1953. 64p. illus. ports. diagr. stats.
*pre-tour*

5111 **Australian** tour: souvenir programme.
■ Hammond News & Features Agency,
[1953]. 8p. ports. stats.
*pre-tour*

5112 **Bailey, Trevor Edward**
■ Playing to win. Hutchinson, 1954. 215p.
illus. ports. scores. (Library of Sports and
Pastimes)

5113 **Barnes, Sidney George**
■ Eyes on the Ashes. Kimber, 1953. 206p.
illus.
——2nd ed. 1953

5114 **Batchelor, Denzil Stanley**
■ The Picture Post book of the Tests, 1953.
Hulton P. [1953]. 48p. illus. scores, stats.
*post-tour*

5115 **Bedser, Alec Victor,** *editor*
■ Meet the Test stars: a souvenir of English
and Australian cricket in the coronation
summer of 1953. Charles Buchan's Publications, 1953. 51p. illus. ports. stats.
*pre-tour*

5116 **Buggy, Hugh**
The battle for the Ashes. Argus and
Australasian, 1953. 48p. illus.

5117 **Cricket** cavalcade, 1953: England v.
■ Australia Test match souvenir: the fight
for the Ashes in story, pictures and
records. Figurist P., [1953]. 64p. illus.
ports. scores, stats.
*post-tour*

5118 **Cutler, Norman**
■ Behind the Tests: the story behind the
1953 Test matches. Putnam, 1953. viii,
207p. illus. ports. scores

5119 **Day, Cedric,** *and* **Mason, Michael**
■ The story of Test cricket: England v.
Australia. Windsor, Day, Mason & Ford,
1953. 32p. illus. ports. stats.
*pre-tour*

5120 **East Molesey Cricket Club**
■ East Molesey v. The Australians [1953].:
match souvenir. [East Molesey, the
Club], 1953. 44p. incl. adverts. illus.
ports. scores, stats.

5121 **Fingleton, Jack,** *i.e.* **John Henry Webb**
■ **Fingleton**
The Ashes crown the year: a coronation
cricket diary. Collins, 1954. 320p. illus.
scores, stats.
——Sydney, Collins, 1954. 288p.

5122 **Harris, [Stephen] Bruce**
■ Cricket triumph: England versus Australia, 1953. Hutchinson, 1953. [ii],180p.

illus. scores, stats. (Library of Sports and
Pastimes)

5123 **Lester, Roy,** *ed.*
□ The fight for the Ashes in 1953: complete
account of the England v. Australia Tests
in words, pictures and records. Flagstaff
P., [1953]. 48p. ports. scores, stats.
——2nd ed. [1953]
——3rd., revised ed. [1953]

5124 **Mailey, Arthur Alfred**
■ Caricatures of the Australian XI English
tour 1953. Sydney, *printed by* Shepheard & Newman, 1953. [11]p. illus.

5124 **Manchester Guardian**
–1 The bedside 'Guardian' 2; a selection by
■ Ivor Brown from The Manchester
Guardian 1952–1953. Collins, 1953. 256p.
illus.
*includes pp. 208–31 Neville Cardus's re-
ports of the 1st, 2nd and 4th Tests, England
v. Australia, 1953*

5125 **Miller, Keith Ross,** *and* **Whitington,**
■ **Richard Smallpeice**
Gods or flannelled fools? MacDonald,
1954. xii,304p. illus. ports. scores

5126 **Simpson, A.W.**
■ Cricket 1953: the Australian tour to U.K.:
fixtures, descriptive records, individual
and group photographs of players.
Brighton, *printed by* Brighton Herald,
1953. 32p. ports.
*pre-tour*

5127 **Swanton, Ernest William**
■ The Test matches of 1953. Daily Telegraph, 1953. [iv],172p. illus. scores, stats.

5128 **Wellings, Evelyn Maitland,** *editor*
■ Meet the Australians. Associated Newspapers, [1953]. 64p. illus. ports. stats.
*pre-tour*

5129 **West, Peter**
■ The fight for the Ashes, 1953: a complete
account of the Australian tour; with a
statistical analysis by Roy Webber.
London, Harrap; Sydney, Australasian
Publ. Co., [1953]. 338p. illus. scores,
stats.

5130 ————, *editor*
■ Cricketers from Australia: the official
souvenir of the 1953 tour of England; . . .
statistics by Roy Webber. Playfair Books,
[1953]. 40p. illus. ports. stats.
*pre-tour*

5131 **White, Crawford**
■ The England victory: The Tests 1953 with
the actual scorebook and statistics of the

series by Roy Webber. News Chronicle, [1953]. [44]p. scores, stats.

## 1954 South Australian Club Cricketers Tour

5132 **Souvenir** programme: South Australian touring cricket team, season 1954. Adelaide, 1954. 8p.

## 1956 Test Tour (I.W. Johnson)

5133 **Alston, Rex,** *i.e.* **Arthur Reginald Alston**
■ Test commentary. S. Paul, 1956. 237p. illus. scores

5134 **Australia.** Australian News & Informa-
■ tion Bureau. *quarterly.* illus. ports.
*Vol. 11, no. 1. Jan.-Mar. 1956. Test tour of England, 1946. 12p*
*pre-tour*

5135 **Australia** souvenir tour programme:
■ pictures, fixtures and personalities 1956. M. Walker, [1956]. [4]p. ports.
*pre-tour*

5136 **Australian Board of Control for International Cricket**
Australian team on tour, 1956. Sydney, the Board, 1956. 4p.
*pre-tour*

5137 **Australian Broadcasting Commission**
■ ABC cricket book: tour of England 1956. Sydney, the Commission, 1956. 60p. illus. ports. diagr. map, stats.
*pre-tour*

5138 **The Australian** cricket tour 1956: sou-
■ venir programme. Cohen, [1956]. [4]p. fold. ports.
*pre-tour*

5139 **Batchelor, Denzil Stanley**
■ The Picture Post book of the Tests, 1956. Hulton P., [1956]. 48p. illus. stats.
*post-tour*

5140 **Cutler, Norman**
■ Behind the Australian Tests, 1956. Putnam, 1956. vii,237p. illus. scores, stats.
*post-tour*

5141 **The Duke** of Norfolk's XI v. The Austra-
■ lian touring team, Arundel Castle, Saturday, 28th April, 1956. Hove, Sussex County Cricket Welfare Assoc., [1956]. [24]p. incl. adverts. illus.

5142 **Gilligan, Arthur Edward Robert**
■ Australian challenge. London, Abelard-Schuman; Sydney, Ure Smith, 1956. 5–172p. illus. ports. scores
*post-tour*

5142 **Golden Fleece** souvenir score book,
–1 England v. Australia Test cricket series in
■ England 1956. H.C. Sleigh Ltd., [1956]. [16]p. stats.
*pre-tour; an Australian publication with records of Test cricket & pen pictures of the Australian team*

5143 **Harris, [Stephen] Bruce**
■ Defending the Ashes, 1956. Hutchinson, 1956. 192p. illus. scores, stats. (Library of Sports and Pastimes)

5143 **Institute of Journalists.** *London District*
–1 1926–1956 anniversary luncheon to the
■ Australian Test cricket team, Connaught Rooms, 27th April 1956. The Institute, [1956]. [8]p. incl. covers. 1 illus.

5144 **Johnson, Ian**
■ Cricket at the crossroads. Cassell, 1957. [viii],213p. illus. ports.

5145 **The kangaroo** hop. Vail, 1956. 20p.

5146 **London** calling: the overseas journal of
■ the B.B.C. Australian Test tour number. B.B.C., May 31, 1956. 36p. incl. adverts. illus. ports.

5147 **Meltonian**
■ Season 1956 Test matches, England v. Australia: souvenir scorecard and fixture list. Meltonian, [1956]. [6]p. folded card. stats.

5148 **Morris, Arthur,** *and* **Landsberg, Pat**
■ Operation Ashes. Hale, 1956. 189p. illus. ports. scores, stats. (Champion Sports Books Library)

5149 **The 1956 Australian** cricket tour: sou-
■ venir programme. Cohen, [1956]. 4p. ports.
*pre-tour*

5149 **Peninsular and Oriental Steam Navig-
–1 ation Company**
P. & O. souvenir tour programme 1956 Tests Australia v. England. Sydney, P. & O., [1956]. [16]p. 1 illus. ports.

5150 **Remington Rand Ltd.**
■ "Meet the Australian Test team". Remington, [1956]. [16]p. ports.
*advertising brochure; pre-tour*

5151 **Ross, Alan**
■ Cape summer, and The Australians in England. Hamilton, 1957. 255p. illus. scores, stats.

5152 **Ross, Gordon,** *editor*
■ Cricketers from Australia: the 1956 tour

official souvenir. Playfair Books, [1956]. 24p. illus. ports. stats.
*pre-tour*

**5153 Swanton, Ernest William**
■ The Test matches of 1956. Daily Telegraph, 1956. xix,164p. illus. scores, stats.

**5154 The Times**
■ The Ashes 1956: the story of the Test matches between England & Australia, by The Times Cricket Correspondent [John C. Woodcock]. Times Publishing Co., [1956]. [vi],122p. scores, stats.
*post-Tests* rptd. *from The Times*

**5155 West, Peter**
■ The fight for the Ashes, 1956: a complete account of the Australian tour; with statistical analysis by Roy Webber. Harrap, 1956. 310p. illus. scores, stats.
——*another ed.* Sportsman's Book Club, 1957

**5156 White, Crawford,** *and* **Webber, Roy**
■ The Ashes retained: the 1956 Tests, every ball, every run, every wicket by Crawford White . . . with Roy Webber's actual scorebook and statistics of the series including results of County matches. News Chronicle, 1956. 48p. scores, stats.

**5156 [Wrigleys Chewing Gum]**
**–1** Quest of the Ashes 1956. [Wrigleys
■ Chewing Gum 1956]. 24p. illus. ports. map, stats.
*pre-tour*

**1956 South Australian Club Cricketers Tour**

**5157 Pickwick Athletic Club.** *Cricket Section*
■ Visit of the South Australian cricket touring team, Aug. 31, Sept. 1, 2 & 3, 1956: programme of events. [Birmingham], the Club, [1956]. 8p.

**5158 2nd South** Australian touring cricket
■ team, season, 1956, United Kingdom: souvenir programme. Adelaide, Publishers Ltd., [1956]. 16p. illus.
*pre-tour of South Australian club cricketers*

**1961 Test Tour (R. Benaud)**

**5159 Arlott, [Leslie Thomas] John**
■ Cricket journal. Heinemann
4: The Australian challenge. 1961. 238p. illus. ports. scores
——*another ed.* Sportsman's Book Club, 1963

**5160 Australian Boradcasting Commission**
■ The A.B.C. cricket book: Australian tour

of the U.K., 1961. Sydney, the Commission, [1961]. illus. ports. diagr. stats.
*pre-tour*

**5161 Australia** souvenir tour programme:
■ 1961. M. Walker, [1961]. [4]p. ports.
*pre-tour*

**5162 Benaud, Richie**
■ A tale of two Tests: with some thoughts on captaincy. Hodder & Stoughton, 1962. 125p. illus. ports.
*Australia v. West Indies, Brisbane, 1960–61; England v. Australia, Manchester, 1961*

**5163 Bowes, Bill,** *i.e.* **William Eric Bowes**
■ Aussies and Ashes. S. Paul, 1961. [viii],184p. illus. scores

**5164 Fortune, Charles**
■ The Australians in England, 1961. Hale, 1961. xii,180p. illus. ports. scores, stats.

**5164 The Guardian**
**–1** The bedside 'Guardian' 10: a selection
■ from The Guardian 1960–61. Collins, 1961. 255p. illus.
*includes pp. 190–3, "Trueman destroys Australia", by Denys Rowbotham [on 3rd Test at Headingley, 1961]*

**5164 The bedside 'Guardian' 11:** a selection
**–2** from The Guardian 1961–62. Collins,
■ 1962. 255p. illus.
*includes pp. 231–4, "Benaud and his men", by Denys Rowbotham [on the Australian 1961 Test team]*

**5165 Irish Cricket Union**
■ Ireland v. Australians, College Park, Dublin, September 18 and 19, 1961. Dublin, the Union, [1961]. 96p. incl. adverts. illus. ports. stats.

**5166 Laker, Jim,** *i.e.* **James Charles Laker**
■ The Australian tour of 1961. Muller, 1961. xiii,207p. illus. ports. scores

**5167 Lester, Roy**
■ Fight for the Ashes: an historic account of the England v. Australia 1961 Test series. Flagstaff P., [1961]. 52p. illus. scores, stats.

**5168 Lindwall, Ray**
■ The challenging Tests. Pelham, 1961. 192p. illus. ports. scores

**5169 Morris, Peter,** *and* **Cumming, Malcolm,**
■ *editors*
Meet the Test stars: a souvenir of English and Australian cricket. Charles Buchan's Publications, [1961]. 48p. incl. adverts. illus. ports. stats.
*pre-tour*

5170 **Peninsular and Orient—Orient Lines**
■ Australian XI English tour 1961: souvenir programme. Sydney, P. & O.—Orient Lines, [1961]. [16]p. 1 illus. ports.
*pre-tour*

5171 **Roberts, Ronald Arthur**
■ The fight for the Ashes, 1961: with an account of the 1960–61 Australia—West Indies Tests. London, Harrap, 1961; Sydney, Australasian Pub. Co., [1962]. 286p. illus. scores, stats.

5172 **Ross, Gordon,** *editor*
■ Cricketers from Australia: the 1961 tour official souvenir, with statistics by Roy Webber. Playfair Books, [1961]. 24p. illus. ports. stats.
*pre-tour*

5173 **Rothmans**
■ Test cricket almanack; compiled by Sydney Smith. Rothmans, [1961]. 64p. ports. stats.
*pre-tour*

### 1964 Test Tour (R.B. Simpson)

5174 **Australia** souvenir tour programme: pictures, fixtures and personalities 1964. M. Walker, [1964]. [4]p. ports.
*pre-tour*

5175 **Australian Broadcasting Commission**
■ The A.B.C. cricket book: Australian tour of England, 1964. Sydney, the Commission, [1964]. 64p. illus. ports. diagrs. stats.
*pre-tour*

5176 **Batchelor, Denzil**
■ The Test matches of 1964: England v. Australia. Epworth P., 1964. vii,164p. illus. scores

5177 **Clarke, John [Campbell]**
■ The Australians in England, 1964. S. Paul, 1964. 192p. illus. scores, stats.

5178 **Compton, Denis [Charles Scott]**
■ Test diary 1964. London, Kaye; Adelaide, Rigby, 1964. 120p. illus. scores, stats.
——*another ed.* Sportsman's Book Club, 1965

5179 **Cricket 64:** Australian tour complete report. A Flamingo Production, [1964]. [40]p. illus. stats.
*a record of the English season including the Australian tour*

5180 **1964** Test tour of England: pen pictures, records, souvenir programme. Starkey, [1964]. [8]p. team port. stats.
*pre-tour*

5180 **Peninsular and Orient Lines**
–1 Australian XI English tour 1964. Australia v. England: souvenir programme. P. & O. Lines, [1964]. 20p. incl. covers. ports.
*itinerary, fixture list*

5181 **Ross, Gordon,** *editor*
■ The 1964 Australians: the 1964 tour official brochure. Dickens P., 1964. [i], 24p. illus. ports. stats. (Playfair Publication)
*pre-tour*

5181 **Rothmans**
–1 Test cricket almanack: England v. Australia 1964; compiled by Sydney Smith. London and Granville (N.S.W.), Rothmans of Pall Mall, [1964]. 68p. illus. (some col.), ports. stats.

5182 **Sport Pics:** Alan Davidson introduces the
■ Australians! 1964. Newnes, 1964. 16p. illus. & ports. (some col.)
*pre-tour action photos., introduced by Alan Davidson, with facts & information compiled by Gordon Jeffery*

5183 **Wellings, Evelyn Maitland**
■ Simpson's Australians: the England Tour, 1964. Hale, 1964. 160p. illus. scores, stats.

### 1965 Australian Country Cricket Team Tour

5184 **Australian Country Cricket Team**
■ A.C.C. XI United Kingdom tour April-September, 1965: souvenir tour programme. Naracoorte (S. Aust.), the Team, [1965]. [8]p. ports.

### 1968 Test Tour (W.M. Lawry)

5185 **Australia** tour programme, fixtures, pictures. M. Walker, [1968]. [8]p. ports.
*pre-tour*

5186 **Australian Broadcasting Commission**
■ The A.B.C. cricket book: the Australian tour of England. 1968: edited by Alan McGilvray. Sydney, the Commission, 1968. 72p. illus. ports. stats. diagr.
*pre-tour*

5187 **Irish Cricket Union**
■ Ireland v. Australians, Castle Avenue, Dublin, July 3, 1968. Dublin, the Union, [1968]. 80p. incl. adverts. ports. stats.

5188 Ireland v. The Australians, N.I.C.C.
■ Grounds, Ormeau, Belfast, 4th July 1968: souvenir programme. The Union, [1968]. 96p. incl. adverts. ports. stats.

5189 **Rothmans**
■ The Rothmans M.C.C. cricket almanack: England v. Australia, 1968. Rothmans of Pall Mall, [1968]. 32p. illus. ports. diagrs. stats.
*pre-tour*

5190 **Simpson, Robert Baddeley ("Bobby")**
■ The Australians in England, 1968. S. Paul, 1968. 192p. illus. ports. scores, stats.

## 1972 Test Tour (I.M. Chappell)

5191 **Arlott, [Leslie Thomas] John**
■ The Ashes, 1972; with photographs by Patrick Eagar and statistics by Bill Frindall. Pelham Books, 1972. 181p. illus. scores, stats.
——*another ed.* Sportsman's Book Club, 1973

5192 **Australia:** fixtures, tour programme, pictures. Walker, [1972]. [8]p. ports. scores, stats.
*pre-tour*

5193 **Australia** tour programme: pictures, fixtures, personalities 1972. Starkey, [1972]. [8]p. ports.
*pre-tour*

5194 **Australian Broadcasting Commission**
■ ABC cricket book: Australian tour of England, 1972; edited by Alan McGilvray. Sydney, the Commission, 1972. 88p. illus. ports. map, diagr. stats.
*pre-tour*

5195 **Chappell, Ian Michael**
■ Tigers among the Lions. Leabrook, S. Aust., Investigator P., 1972. 190p. illus. scores
——*another ed.* Adelaide, Lynton, 1974. 188p.

5196 **The Sun**
■ Test and county cricket book: complete guide to the 1972 Test series. The Sun, [1972]. 83p. illus. ports. plans, stats.
*with spaces for the insertion of 78 'cricket stickers' of individual players; pre-tour*

## 1975 Test Tour (I.M. Chappell)

5196 **Australian Broadcasting Commission**
-1 ABC cricket book. Australian tour of
■ England 1975; edited by Alan McGilvray. Sydney, the Commission, [1975]. 72p. illus. ports. (some col.), diagr. stats.
*pre-tour*

5196 **Australian** Test tour '75 – fixtures – tour
-2 programme – pictures. Starkey, [1975].
■ [8]p. incl. covers. illus. ports.

5196 **Buchanan, John,** *editor*
-3 Australia v. England. The 10 Test
■ matches of 1975. Sydney, Project Publishing Pty. Ltd., [1975?]. 124p. incl. covers + [4]p. insert. illus. ports. scores, stats.
*post-tours*

5196 **Cricketer**
-4 The 1975 Australians, written by Austra-
■ lia's Test cricket team; edited by Eric Beecher. Melbourne, Newspress Pty. Ltd., [1975]. 100p. incl. adverts. illus. ports.
*pre-tour*

5196 Australia in England 1975: a Cricketer
-5 special; edited by Eric Beecher, special
■ photographer Patrick Eagar. Melbourne, Newspress Pty. Ltd., [1975]. 88p. incl. covers & adverts. illus. & ports. (some col.), scores, stats.
*post-tour*

5196 **Frindall, William H.**
-6 Frindall's score book: England versus
■ Australia, 1975. Brentford, Lonsdale P., 1975. 3–95p. illus. scores, stats.

5196 **Kent** v. Australians 1882–1975: souvenir
-7 match card. *n.p.,* [1975]. [4]p. folded card.
■ scores
*'to mark the occasion of Kent's fine victory in June 1975'; full scores of Kent wins in 1899 & 1975, results 1882–1972*

5196 **Lewis, Tony (i.e. Anthony Robert Lewis)**
-8 A summer of cricket. Pelham Books,
■ 1976. 179p. illus. scores
——*another ed.* Newton Abbot, Readers Union, 1976
*the 1975 English cricket season; includes Prudential Cup matches and the short Test series with the Australians*

## 1977 Test Tour (G.S. Chappell)

5196 **Australian Broadcasting Commission**
-9 ABC cricket book: Australian tour of
■ England 1977; edited by Alan McGilvray. Sydney, the Commisssion, 1977. 80p. illus. ports. (some col.), diagr. stats.
*includes lift-out coloured poster; pre-tour*

5196 **Australian** cricket tour 1977: a souvenir
-10 programme & score card. *n.p.,* [1977]
■ [8]p. illus. ports.
*pre-tour*

5196 **Australian** Test tour '77 souvenir pro-
-11 gramme: pen pictures, records. Hammer-
■ smith, Starkey, 1977. [12]p. ports. stats.
*pre-tour*

5196 **Brearley, Mike,** *and* **Doust, Dudley**
-12 The return of the Ashes. Pelham Books,
■ 1978. 160p. illus. (some col.), ports. scores, stats.

5196 **The centenary** and jubilee pair: a
–13 commemorative folder issued in honour
of the Centenary Test . . . and the Jubilee
Test. . . . Test & County Cricket Board,
[1977]. 8p. ports. facsims.
*contains team portraits, printed scorecards
and Australian and G.P.O. first day covers;
limited to 500 numbered copies*

5196 **Chappell, Gregory Stephen,** *and* **Frith,**
–14 **David**
■ The Ashes '77; photographs by Patrick
Eagar. Angus and Robertson, 1977. 200p.
illus. ports. scores, stats.
——*another ed.* Newton Abbot, Readers
Union, 1978

5196 **Frindall, William H.**
–15 Frindall's scorebook, Jubilee edition: the
■ Centenary Test at Melbourne and England versus Australia, 1977; edited by
Howard Spencer. Birmingham, Lonsdale
P., 1977. 129p. illus. diagr. scores, stats.
*in hardback and limp covers*

5196 **Irish Cricket Union**
–16 Ireland v. Australia, sponsored by Roth-
■ mans of Pall Mall (Ireland) Ltd., Leinster
Cricket Club, Rathmines, Dublin, June
9–10, 1977. [Dublin, the Union, 1977].
80p. incl. adverts. ports. stats.

5196 **The Jubilee** cricket Tests. England v.
–17 Australia 1977. The five Test matches of
■ 1977; introduced by Alan Davidson. Lane
Cove, (N.S.W.), C.P. Publishing, [1977].
88p. incl. covers & adverts. illus. ports.
scores
*post-tour; day by day description of play*

5196 **McFarline, Peter**
–18 A game divided. Richmond (Vic.), Hutch-
■ inson of Australia, 1977. [iii],177p. illus.
ports. stats.

5196 **Martin-Jenkins, Christopher**
–19 The jubilee Tests, England v. Australia
■ 1977 and the Packer revolution. Macdonald and Jane's, 1977. [vii],207p. illus.
ports. scores, stats.

5196 **Phillipson, Neill**
–20 The Jubilee Test series 1977: England
■ versus Australia. Toorak (Vic.), Garry
Sparke, 1977; London, Pelham Books,
1978. 80p. illus. scores, stats.
*post-tour*

5196 **Somerset County Cricket Club**
–21 Somerset v. Australian touring team,
1977. Taunton, the Club, [1977]. 18p.
*commemorates Somerset's first victory over
an Australian team*

5196 **Tresidder, Phil,** *editor*
–22 England v. Australia Jubilee Test series.
■ Rushcutters Bay (N.S.W.), Modern
Magazines (Holdings) Ltd. for Tooth &
Co. Ltd., [1977]. 100p. incl. covers &
adverts. illus. & ports. [some col.), stats.
*pre-tour*

5196 **Yorkshire Evening Post**
–23 Test match special. "Go to it, Geoff."
Issue for 11th August, 1977. Leeds, Yorkshire Evening Post. 12p.
"It's magic!". Issue for 12th August 1977.
18p.

## 1977 Australia Young Cricketers Tour

5196 **Britain-Australia Society**
–24 Australia young cricketers tour of Eng-
■ land 1977 – the Queen's Silver Jubilee
1977 – at the invitation of The Britain-
Australia Society. The Society, [1977].
20p. incl. covers & adverts. illus. ports.
*pre-tour*

# AUSTRALIAN TOURS TO SOUTH AFRICA

5197 **Davis, R.M.,** *editor*
■ Don Bradman's pictorial Test record: S.
Africa—Australia cricket. Sydney, *printed
by* Evans, [1931]. 96p. illus. ports. scores,
stats.

### 1921–22 Test Tour (H.L. Collins)

5198 **Mailey, Arthur Alfred**
■ Arthur Mailey's book: a series of sketches
illustrating the tour through England and
Africa by the Australian slow bowler,
Arthur Mailey. Sydney, *printed by* God-
dard, 1922. 27p. illus.

5199 **Smith, Sydney**
■ With the 15th Australian XI: (a complete
record of the team's tour throughout
Great Britain and South Africa). Sydney,
E.T. Kibblewhite, 1922. 289p. illus. ports.
scores, stats.

### 1935–36 Test Tour (V.Y. Richardson)

5200 **Australian Cricket**
■ South African tour 1935–36: Christmas
card and fixture. 1935. folded card

5200 **Duffus, Louis**
–1 S. Africans in England 1935; Australians
in S. Africa 1935/36. Johannesburg, Gen.
Publishing Co., [1936]. 48p. illus. ports.
scores, stats.

**5200** "The Signaller", *pseud.*
**-2** The Australian cricket team, touring
■ South Africa 1935–36, told in verse &
lettered by "The Signaller" (1915–1920).
[The Author], 1936. [i],7p. *printed in script
signed "E.C." – a South African; originally
written as Greetings for Xmas 1935, revised &
lettered 26/2/36 for W.A.O. (W.A. Oldfield)
and published in South Africa*

**5200** **South African Cricket Association**
**-3** Australians in South Africa. Johannesburg, General Publishing Co., [1936].
23p. illus. ports.

**5201** **Vacuum Oil Company of South Africa**
■ **Ltd.**
Souvenir of the visit to South Africa of
the Australian cricket team 1935–36.
Capetown, the Co., [1935]. 24p. illus.
*with caricatures of the Australian team by
Arthur Mailey; pre-tour*

### 1949–50 Test Tour (A.L. Hassett)

**5202** **Allan, John,** *editor*
National brochure of Australian cricket
tour of South Africa and Rhodesia
1949–50. Johannesburg, Chettlow, [1949].
32p. ports. stats.
*pre-tour*

**5202** **Atlantic Refining Company of Africa**
**-1** **Ltd.**
■ Australian cricket tour: itinerary, diagrams of fields, etc. Cape Town, the Co.,
[1949]. [12]p. diagrs.
*includes pen pictures of Australian team*

**5202** **Caltex Map Service**
**-2** Australia versus South Africa, 1949–1950.
Caltex (Africa) Ltd., [1949?]. folder

**5203** **Miller, Keith [Ross],** *and* **Whitington,**
■ **Richard Smallpeice**
Catch! An account of two cricket tours.
Latimer House, 1951. 301p. illus. port.
scores, stats.
*pp. 13–109 Veld*

**5204** **Rhodesia Cricket Union**
■ Australia v. a South African XI, Salisbury
Sports Ground, 19, 21, 22 November,
1949: souvenir booklet; [compiled by
Harry Pichanick.] Salisbury, the Union,
[1949]. 104p. incl. adverts. ports.

**5205** **Shell South Africa Ltd.**
A Shell guide to the Australian cricket
tour 1949–50. Cape Town, Shell South
Africa Ltd., 1949. 8p. illus.
*a folder in English & Afrikaans; pre-tour*

**5205** **Transvaal Cricket Union**
**-1** Australian cricket tour South Africa
1949–1950; compiled by Selected Services.
Johannesburg, Selected Services, [1949].
32p. ports.
*title-page and part of text also in Afrikaans
with title:* Australiese krieket-toer 1949–
1950
*pre-tour*
——Supplement. [1950?]. bs. ports.
*post-tour*

**5205** **United Tobacco Companies**
**-2** Australian cricket tour South Africa
1949–50. . . . [Cape Town, the Companies, 1949?] 32p. ports. map
*text also in Afrikaans with title:* Australiese krieket-toer Suid-Afrika. . . .

### 1957–58 Test Tour (I.D. Craig)

**5206** The Australian cricket tour of South
Africa 1957–58: souvenir. "Charms"
American Candy, [1957]. [6]p. fold. ports.
*pre-tour*

**5206** Australian tour of S. Africa and Rhodesia
**-1** 1957–1958: Rhodesia v. Australian, 25, 26,
28, 29, October 1957, Police Ground:
official programme. [Salisbury], Anne
Buckley, under the authority of The
Mashonaland C.A., [1957]. 48p. incl.
adverts. ports. stats.

**5207** **Chettle, Geoffrey, A.,** *editor and compiler*
■ Cricketers from Australia (Pretoria edi-
tion): South African XI vs. Australian XI
at Loftus Versveld Ground: official
souvenir. Durban, [the Editor, 1957]. 20p.
incl. adverts. ports. stats.
*also 8 provincial brochures with identical
text apart from details of home teams:*
Australia vs. Transvaal. 16p.
Australians versus Natal. 20p.
Australians versus Eastern Province. 20p.
Australian versus Western Province. 16p.
Australians versus North Eastern Transvaal.
16p.
Australia versus Transvaal. 16p.
Australia versus Griqualand West. 16p.
Australia versus Orange Free State. 16p.

**5208** Fifth South African Country Districts
■ Festival 1958 (including) Australia versus
a S.A. Country Districts XI, played at
Pretoria, January 1–8, 1958; official souvenir brochure. Durban, [the Editor,
1957]. 16p. incl. adverts. ports. stats.

**5209** South Africa versus Australia, 1st Test
■ Johannesburg, December 23, 24, 26, 27,
28, 1957: official Test brochure. Durban,
[the Editor, 1957]. 20p. incl. adverts.
ports. stats.

5210 ——2nd Test, Cape Town, December
■ 31st, Jan, 1, 2, 3, 4, 1958: official Test
brochure. Durban, the Editor, [1957].
24p. incl. adverts. ports. stats.

5211 ——3rd Test, Durban, Jan, 24, 25, 27, 28,
■ 29, 1958: official Test brochure. Durban,
[the Editor, 1958]. 24p. incl. adverts.
ports. stats.

5212 ——4th Test, Johannesburg, Feb, 7, 8, 10,
■ 11, 12, 1958: official Test brochure.
Durban, [the Editor, 1958]. 24p. incl.
adverts. ports. stats.

5213 ——5th Test, Port Elizabeth, Feb. 28,
■ Mar. 1, 3, 4, 5, 1958: official Test brochure. Durban, [the Editor, 1958]. 24p.
incl. adverts. illus. ports. stats.

5213 **Coca-Cola Bottlers**
-1 Australians in South Africa & Rhodesia
1957–8. Johannesburg, Coca-Cola Bottlers, 1957. 36p. incl. adverts. ports. stats.
*pre-tour*

5214 **Maclean, Roy Alistair**
■ Sackcloth without ashes. Hodder &
Stoughton, 1958. ix.179p. illus. ports.
scores, stats.

5215 **Matabeleland Cricket Association**
■ Australia [v] Rhodesia at Queens
Ground, Bulawayo, 1st, 2nd and 4th
November, 1957: official souvenir; compiled & edited by Stuart Manning. Bulawayo, the Association, [1957]. 48p. incl.
adverts. ports. scores, stats.

5216 **Nkana Cricket Club**
■ The Australian tourists vs. Northern
Rhodesia Invitation XI, Harrison Oval,
Nkana, 19 & 21, October, 1957. Nkana-
Kitwe, the Club, [1957]. 21p. ports. diagr.
stats.

5216 **South African Railways**
-1 Australian cricket team tour of Southern
Africa 1957–58: souvenir itinerary. S.A.
Railways, [1957]. [16]p. incl. covers. illus.
*team names, travel itinerary and fixture list*

5216 **United Paints Ltd.**
-2 Australian cricket tour of Southern Africa
■ 1957–1958: fixture list. United Paints Ltd.,
[1957]. [16]p. incl. covers. ports. diagrs.
*pre-tour; pen-sketches of Australian team
and of possible S.A. players*

### 1966–67 Test Tour (R.B. Simpson)

5217 **Australia** vs. South Africa 1966–67 S.A.
■ cricket tour: Philips 75th anniversary

brochure. S.A. Philips (Pty.) Ltd., [1966].
[16]p. ports. diagrs. stats.
*statistics by G.A. Chettle; pre-tour*

5218 **Australian Broadcasting Commission**
■ The A.B.C. cricket book: Australian tour
of South Africa 1966–67. Sydney, the
Commission, [1966]. 56p. illus. ports.
map. diagr. stats.
*pre-tour*

5219 **Chettle, Geoffrey A.,** *editor*
■ The 1966–1967 Australians: official tour
brochure. Durban, [the Editor, 1966].
[24]p. incl. adverts. ports. stats.
——*N.E. Transvaal ed. with title:* Australian tour 1966–67.
——*Natal ed. with title:* 6th Australian tour
of South Africa, 1966–67
——*Border ed. with title:* Australian tour
1966–67
*these brochures have the same text and
portraits of the Australian team but with
different covers and articles on individual S.
African provincial teams*

5219 **Coca-Cola Bottlers**
-1 The Australian team in South Africa 1966.
Johannesburg, Coca-Cola Bottlers, [1966].
[32]p. illus. ports.
*in English and Afrikaans. Afrikaans title:*
Die Australiese span in Suid-Afrika 1966

5220 **McGlew, Jackie,** *i.e.* **Derrick John**
■ **McGlew**
Six for glory; with a section by Eric
Litchfield. Cape Town, Timmins; Wellington, N.Z., Reed, 1967. xx,215p. illus.
scores, stats.
*Pt. 1. "On tour with the Aussies", by E.L.,
pp. 1–71; Pt. 2. "Six for glory", by J. McG.,
pp. 73–187; statistical section, pp. 189–215*

5221 **Mashonaland Cricket Association**
Rhodesia vs. Australia at Police Ground,
Salisbury, November, 5th, 6th, 7th, 8th.
1966: official souvenir programme. Salisbury, the Association, [1966]. ports. stats.

5222 **Rand Daily Mail**
■ Book of the Tests: Test descriptions and
all statistics by Eric Litchfield. Johannesburg, Rand Daily Mail, 1967. 48p. illus.
ports. scores, stats.
*post-tour*

5223 **South African Broadcasting Corporation**
■ The S.A.B.C. English Service cricket
book: sixth Australian cricket tour to
South Africa, 1966–67; edited by Charles
Fortune. S.A.B.C., [1966]. 72p. illus.
ports. plan, diagr. stats.
*pre-tour*
——*Afrikaans ed.* [1966]

5224 **The Star**
■ Champagne cricket: the Australian tour of 1966–67; with summary by Louis Duffus. Johannesburg, The Star, [1967]. 52p. illus. ports. scores, stats.
*series of photographs publd. in 'The Star' recording the tour*

5225 **Steyn, Neil**
Sesse tot oorwinning: S.A. se Krieketsege 66–67. Johannesburg. Die Transvaler Boek handel, 1967. 220p. illus. scores, stats.
*in Afrikaans; trans. "Sixes for victory: South Africa's cricket triumph 66–67"*

5226 **Whitington, Richard Smallpeice**
■ Simpson's safari: South African Test series 1966–7. Heinemann, 1967. xviii, 235p. illus. scores, stats.

### 1969–70 Test Tour (W.M. Lawry)

5227 **Australian Broadcasting Commission**
■ The A.B.C. cricket book: Australian tour of South Africa 1969–70; edited by Alan McGilvray. Sydney, the Commission, 1969. 64p. illus. ports. stats.
*pre-tour*

5228 **Chettle, Geoffrey A.**, *editor*
■ Seventh Australia tour of South Africa, 1970: [a series of brochures]. Durban, [the Compiler, 1970]. ports. stats.
——Transvaal ed. 24p. incl. adverts.
——Natal ed. 24p. incl. adverts.
——N.E. Transvaal ed. 28p. incl. adverts.
——Western Province ed. 20p. incl. adverts.
——Eastern Province ed. 24p. incl. adverts.

5229 **Litchfield, Eric**
■ Cricket grand-slam. Cape Town, Timmins; Sydney, Reed; Folkestone, Bailey Bros. & Swinfen, 1970. 203p. illus. ports. scores, stats.

5230 **Rand Daily Mail**
■ Book of the Tests: S. Africa v. Australia, 1970: Test narratives and all statistics by Eric Litchfield. Johannesburg, Rand Daily Mail, 1970. 48p. illus. ports. scores, stats.
*post-tour*

5231 **South African Cricket Annual**
■ The 1970 Australians: official tour brochure; edited by Geoffrey A. Chettle. Durban, South African Cricket Annual, [1970]. 28p. incl. adverts. ports. stats.
*there are 2 versions of this brochure*

# AUSTRALIAN TOURS TO THE WEST INDIES

## 1954–55 Test Tour (I.W. Johnson)

5232 **The Daily Gleaner.** *Souvenir edition*
■ West Indies v. Australia 1955. Kingston, the Gleaner Co., June 1955. 20p. illus. ports. scores, stats.
*post-tour*

5233 **Jamaica Cricket Association**
■ Official programme of the Jamaica section of the Australian cricket tour; compiled by Gene Martinez and C.A.O. Jack Anderson. Kingston, the Assoc., [1955]. 56p. incl. adverts. ports.
*pre-tour*

5234 **Landsberg, Pat**
■ The kangaroo conquers: the West Indies v. Australia, 1955; [ed. by G. Ross]. Museum P., 1955. 224p. illus. ports. scores, stats.

5235 **Queen's Park Cricket Club**
■ Australia vs. West Indies 1955. Port of Spain, the Club, [1955]. 3–28p. ports. stats.
*pre-tour*

## 1964–65 Test Tour (R.B. Simpson)

5236 **Australian Broadcasting Commission**
■ The A.B.C. cricket book: Australian tour of West Indies, 1965. Sydney, the Commission, [1965]. 56p. illus. ports. diagr. map, stats.
*pre-tour*

5237 **Benaud, Richie**
■ The new champions: Australia in the West Indies, 1965. Hodder & Stoughton, 1965. 160p. illus. scores, stats.

5238 **[Henderson, L.J.]**, *compiler*
Australia in the West Indies 1965: a comprehensive and accurate statistical review of the tour with emphasis on the five Test matches . . . with records and achievements in the 25 Tests played to date. Bondi Junction, N.S.W., "Cricket figurs", [1965]. 42p. stats. *typescript*
*post-tour*

5239 **Jamaica Sports Association**
■ 1965 Australian tour. West Indies vs. Australia in Jamaica: official programme. Kingston, the Association, [1965]. 80p. incl. adverts. ports. scores, stats.
*pre-visit*

5240 **Rothmans**
■ Test cricket almanack: West Indies v. Australia 1965. [Kingston], Rothmans of Pall Mall (Jamaica), [1964]. 52p. illus. (some col.), ports. stats.
*pre-tour*

5241 **Williams, Leroy ("Fathead"),** *compiler*
■ Australia tour of the West Indies 1965. Port-of-Spain, [the Compiler, 1965]. 40p. incl. adverts. ports. score
*pre-tour*

## 1973 Test Tour (I.M. Chappell)

5241 **Annamunthodo, W.,** *compiler*
–1 Cricket series 1973: Australia vs. West
■ Indies. San Fernando, Trinidad, Unique Services, [1973]. [40]p. incl. adverts. port. scores, stats.
*pre-series*

5242 Cricket series 1973: Australia vs. West
■ Indies, 5th Test, Queen's Park Oval, April 21, 23, 24, 25 & 26. San Fernando, Trinidad, Unique Services, [1973]. [44]p. incl. adverts. ports. scores, stats.
*pre-Test*

5243 **Australian Broadcasting Commission**
■ A.B.C. cricket book: Australian tour of West Indies 1973; edited by Alan McGilvray. Sydney, the Commission, 1973. 72p. illus. ports. map, stats.
*pre-tour*

5244 **Australian Cricket**
■ Cricket tour guide: Pakistan in Australia 1972–73; Australia in West Indies 1973. Sydney, Australian Cricket, [1972]. 68p. incl. adverts. illus. ports. stats.
*pre-tour*

5245 **The Australians** in Guyana: Australia vs.
■ the West Indies 1973 tour. Georgetown, *printed by* Guyana Printers Ltd., [1973]. 80p. incl. adverts. illus. ports. score, stats.
*pre-visit*

5246 **Beecher, Eric,** *editor*
■ Australia in the West Indies 1973. Rushcutters Bay, Modern Magazines (Holdings) Ltd., [1973]. illus. & ports. (some col.), scores
*post-tour*

5247 **Chappell, Ian Michael**
■ Passing Tests. Coromandel Valley (S.A.), Lynton Publications, 1973. 191p. illus. ports. scores, stats.
*also includes account of Pakistan tour of Australia, 1972/3*

5248 **Cozier, Tony,** *editor*
■ The Australians in Barbados, 1973. Bridgetown, Literary Features (Caribbean) Ltd., [1973]. 32p. incl. adverts. illus. ports. score, stats.
*pre-tour*

5249 Caribbean cricket '73: Australia v. West
■ Indies. Bridgetown, Literary Features (Caribbean) Ltd., [1973]. 48p. incl. adverts. illus. ports. stats.
*pre-tour; largely statistical including Shell Shield statistics 1966–72*

5250 **Guyana Cricket Board of Control**
■ Tour '73 from Brisbane to Bourda; [edited by Charles J. Chichester]. Georgetown, the Board, [1973]. 80p. incl. adverts. illus. ports. stats.
*sponsored by The Demarara Tobacco Co. Ltd.*
*pre-visit*

5251 **Jamaica Cricket Association**
■ West Indies vs. Australia in Jamaica 1973: official souvenir programme; edited by Robert S. Dabdoub. Jamaica, the Assoc., [1973]. 72p. incl. adverts. ports. stats.
*pre-tour*

5252 **Jones, Brunell,** *editor*
■ Kangaroo invasion (the Australian cricket tour of West Indies, 1973). Curepe P.O. (Trinidad), the Editor, [1973]. 160p. incl. adverts. illus. ports. scores, stats.
*pre-tour, with scores, etc. of previous Australia v. West Indies Tests*

5253 **Williams, Leroy ("Fathead").** *compiler*
■ All fall down! Australia in the West Indies 1973. Port-of-Spain, [the Compiler, 1973]. [28]p. incl. adverts. ports. stats.
*mid-tour*

5254 Australia vs. West Indies, 3rd Test,
■ Queen's Park Oval, March 23–28, '73. Port-of-Spain, [the Editor, 1973]. [44]p. incl. adverts. illus. ports. stats.

## 1978 Test Tour (R.B. Simpson)

5254 **Australian Broadcasting Commission**
–1 A.B.C. cricket book: Australian tour of
■ West Indies 1978; edited by Alan McGilvray. Sydney, the Commission, 1978. 72p. illus. & ports. (some col.), diagr. stats.
*pre-tour*

5254 **Jamaica Cricket Association**
–2 West Indies vs. Australia in Jamaica,
■ 1978: official souvenir programme. Kingston, the Assoc., [1978]. 56p. incl. adverts. ports. stats.
*statistics and articles by Hubert Gray*

5254 **Jones, Brunell**
–3 Cricket confusion: a book on the 1978
■ W.I. – Australia series for the Sir Frank
Worrell Trophy. Trinidad, Sports News
Service, [1978]. 144p. incl. adverts. illus.
ports. scores, stats.
*post-series*

5254 **St. Lucia National Cricket Association**
–4 The Guinness international limited overs
■ game: Australia v. West Indies at Victoria
Park, Castries, St. Lucia, 12 April 1978:
souvenir brochure. Castries, the Assoc.,
[1978]. 48p. incl. adverts. illus. ports.

# AUSTRALIAN TOURS TO NEW ZEALAND

## 1877–78 Australian XI Tour

5254 **Demon Bowler:** Australian XI v. Canter-
–5 bury XV, played at Hagley Park,
■ Christchurch, 19, 23, 24 January 1878.
Christchurch, The Nag's Head P., 1980.
68p. score
*hand-set limited ed. of 225 numbered
copies; match report rptd. from The Lyttelton
Times, January 1878*

5255 **[Reynolds, P.E.]**
■ Tour of Australian cricketers through
Australia, New Zealand, and Great
Britain, by Argus. Sydney, Jarrett;
Newcastle (N.S.W.), Sweet; Bathurst
(N.S.W.), Rae, 1878. 94p. scores

## 1905 Australian XI Tour

5255 **New Zealand Cricket Council**
–1 Official souvenir and scoring book:
Australian cricket team in New Zealand,
1905; the official programme of the New
Zealand Cricket Council and the
Wellington and Canterbury Cricket
Associations. Wellington, C.M. Banks,
[1905]. 46p. ports.

## 1912–13 N.S.W. Teachers Tour

5256 **The New** South Wales Teachers on tour,
■ North Island, New Zealand, Xmas, 1912.
Sydney, *printed by* McMillan & Goddard,
[1913]. 32p. illus. ports. scores, stats.
*post-tour*

## 1913–14 A. Sims's Australian XI Tour

5256 **Great knock:** Sims's Australians v.
–1 Canterbury, played at Lancaster Park,
■ Christchurch, 27, 28 February, 2 March
1914. Christchurch (N.Z.), the Nag's
Head P., 1978. 68p. score, diagr.

*hand-set limited ed. of 225 numbered
copies; match report rptd. from The Sun
(Christchurch) issues of 28 Feb., 2 & 3 March,
1914*

## 1920–21 Australian XI Tour

5256 **Australia** v. Canterbury, Lancaster Park,
–2 March 11, 12 & 14, 1921: official scoring
■ card. [Christchurch], H.E. Lawrence,
[1921]. [8]p. incl. adverts. ports. diagr.

## 1923–24 New South Wales Team

5256 **[Otago Cricket Association]**
–3 Cricket: New South Wales v. Otago,
played on Carisbrook Ground on Feb. 15,
16, 18, 1924: official programme. [Dun-
edin], Otago Daily Times, 1924. 20p.

## 1924–25 Victorian Team

5257 **New Zealand Cricket Council**
Programme of matches for the tour of the
Victorian team through New Zealand
1925. Christchurch, the Council, [1925].
4p.

5258 International cricket: Victoria v. New
Zealand, the first Test . . . Wellington,
March . . . 1925: official programme.
[Wellington], Warnes & Stephenson,
[1925]. 32p. ports.

5259 **[Wellington Cricket Association]**
■ International cricket: Victoria v. Wellington, Basin Reserve, March 6th, 7th &
9th, 1925. Wellington, [the Assoc., 1925].
32p. incl. adverts. ports.

## 1927–28 Tour

5260 **[Wellington Cricket Association]**
International cricket: Australia v. Wellington, Basin Reserve, Wellington, February 17, 18, 20, 1928: official programme.
Wellington, [the Assoc., 1928].

## 1949–50 Tour

5261 **New Zealand Cricket Council**
Australian team, New Zealand tour,
1950. [Christchurch], the Council, 1950.
4p.

## 1959–60

5262 **Auckland Cricket Association**
■ International cricket: Australia v. Auckland, Eden Park, Auckland, February 12,
13, 15, 1960: official programme. Auckland, the Assoc., [1960]. 24p. diagr. plan,
stats.

5263 **Canterbury Cricket Association**
■ Australia v. New Zealand 2nd (Unofficial) Test match, 27, 29, Feb., 1, 2, March 1960: official souvenir. Canterbury, the Assoc., 1960. 48p. illus. ports. stats.

5264 **Otago Cricket Association**
■ New Zealand v. Australia, March 4, 5, 7 and 8, 1960: programme score sheet. [Dunedin], the Assoc., [1960]. 16p. ports.
  *cover title:* Australia v. New Zealand [at] Carisbrook

5265 **Wellington Cricket Association**
■ Australia versus New Zealand, first Test at the Basin Reserve, Wellington, February, 19, 20, 22 and 23, 1960: official programme. Wellington, the Assoc., [1960]. ports. diagr. stats.

### 1967 Tour

5265 **Auckland Cricket Association**
–1 International cricket. Fourth Test Aus-
■ tralia v. New Zealand, Eden Park, Auckland, March 25, 27, 28, 29, 1967: official programme. Auckland, the Assoc., [1967]. 24p. incl. adverts. ports. plan, diagr. stats.

5266 **Northern Districts Cricket Association**
Cricket—Australia v. Northern Districts 21–23 March 1967, Seddon Park, Hamilton: official programme. Hamilton, the Assoc., [1967]. 20p. incl. adverts.

5267 **Taranaki Cricket Association**
■ International cricket: 1st Test Australia v. New Zealand. Pukekura Park, New Plymouth, March 3, 4, 6, 7, 1967: official programme. New Plymouth, the Assoc., [1967]. [24]p. incl. adverts. ports.

### 1969–70 Tour of Australian 'B' Team

5268 **Auckland Cricket Association**
■ International cricket: Australia v. New Zealand, March 6, 7, 9, 10, 1970, Eden Park, Auckland: official programme. Auckland, the Assoc. [1970]. 32p. incl. adverts. ports. plan, diagr. stats.

5269 **Otago Cricket Association**
■ Australia v. Otago, Carisbrook, 26–28 February: souvenir programme & scoresheet. Dunedin, the Assoc., [1970]. [16]p. incl. adverts. ports. stats.

5270 **Wellington Cricket Association**
■ Australia v. New Zealand, Basin Reserve, March 28–April, 1970: official programme. [Wellington, the Assoc., 1970]. 24p. incl. adverts. ports. diagr. stats.

### 1973–74 Test Tour (I.M. Chappell)

5270 **Australian Cricket**
–1 1974 tour special: Australians in New
■ Zealand; England in West Indies; edited by Phil Tresidder. Rushcutters Bay, Modern Magazines (Holdings) Ltd., [1974]. 68p. incl. covers & adverts. illus. (some col.), ports. scores, stats.
*post-tours*

5270 **Canterbury Cricket Association**
–2 Australia versus Canterbury, 18, 19, 20,
■ February [1974]: official programme. Christchurch, the Assoc., [1974]. 24p. incl. adverts. port. stats.

5270 Australia v. New Zealand, second cricket
–3 Test, 1974, Lancaster Park, Christchurch,
■ 8, 9, 10, 12, 13 March: official souvenir programme. [Christchurch, the Assoc., 1974]. 28p. incl. adverts. illus. ports. diagr. stats.

5270 **Central Districts Cricket Association**
–4 International cricket: Australia v. Central Districts, McLean Park, Napier, March 18, 19, 20, 1974; official souvenir. Hawke's Bay C.A., [1974]. 28p. incl. adverts. stats.

5270 **Northern Districts Cricket Association**
–5 Cricket. Australia v. Northern Districts
■ 25–27 Feb. 1974, Seddon Park, Hamilton, N.Z.: official programme. Hamilton, the Assoc., [1974]. [16]p. incl. adverts. stats.

5270 **Wellington Cricket Association**
–6 New Zealand v. Australia [1st Test]
■ March 1, 2, 3, 5 and 6 [1974], Basin Reserve: official programme. Wellington, the Assoc., [1974]. 32p. incl. covers & adverts. illus. ports. diagr. stats.
*programme compiled by Don Neely and Ian Smith*

### 1976–77 Test Tour (G.S. Chappell)

5270 **Auckland Cricket Association**
–7 Rothmans tour: Test cricket, Australia v.
■ New Zealand, second Test, Feb. 25, 26, 27, March 1, 2, 1977, Eden Park, Auckland: official programme. [Auckland], the Assoc., [1977]. 52p. incl. adverts. illus. ports. plan, diagr. stats.

5270 **Australian Broadcasting Commission**
–8 A.B.C. cricket book – Pakistan tour of
■ Australia 1976–77 – Australian tour of New Zealand 1977 – England Australia centenary match; edited by Alan McGilvray. Sydney, the Commission, [1976]. 65p. illus. (some col.), ports. diagr. stats.
*pre-tours*

5270 **Chappell, Gregory Stephen**
–9 The 100th summer: 76–77 season-Pakis-
■ tan-New-Zealand-Centenary Test. Toorak
(Vic.), Garry Sparke & Associates, 1977.
iv,220p. illus. & ports. (some col.), scores,
stats.

5270 **National 9–10 Network Television**
–10 Cricket scene [1976–77]; edited by Rod
■ Nicholson. Hawthorn [Vic.], Craftsman
Press Pty. Ltd., 1976. 64p. incl. adverts.
illus. ports. stats.
*with inset colour poster of Greg Chap-
pell*

# AUSTRALIAN TOURS TO INDIA

5271 **Roy, S.K.**
■ Australian cricket tours to India. Calcutta,
Illustrated News, 1947. 81p. ports. scores,
stats.

## 1935–36 The Maharajadhiraj of Patiala's Team of Australians

5272 **Australian** cricketers' Calcutta visit: souvenir programme. Calcutta, R. Mukh-
erjee, 1935. 22p. illus.

5272 **H.H. The Maharaja** of Patiala's Austra-
–1 lian XI v. C.P. & Berar XI, December 20,
21 and 22: official score card and programme. Nagpur, C.P. & Berar C.A.,
[1935]. 8p. incl. adverts. illus.

5272 **Mandana, B.A.,** *compiler*
–2 Souvenir of the Australian cricketers' visit
■ to Mysore State. Bangalore, the Compiler, 1936. [xvi],90p. incl. adverts. illus.
ports. plan, stats.

5273 **Southern Punjab Cricket Association**
■ Official souvenir of the visit to Amritsar
of His Highness the Maharajadhiraj of
Patiala's team of Australian cricketers
1936; compiled by D.K. Kapur. Amritsar,
the Assoc., [1936]. 32p. incl. adverts.
ports.

## 1945–46 Australian Services' Team

5274 **Board of Control for Cricket in India**
■ Australian Services XI tour—1945: official
souvenir; compiled by H.N. Contractor.
Bombay, the Compiler for C.C. of India,
[1945]. 42p. incl. adverts. ports. stats.

5275 **[Cricket Association of Bengal]**
■ Australian visit in Calcutta, 1945: official
programme. [Calcutta, the Assoc., 1945].
46p. incl. adverts. illus. ports.

5275 **Madras Cricket Association**
–1 Australian Services XI vs. All-India XI,
unofficial Test, December 1945. [Madras,
the Assoc., 1945]. 30p. ports.

5276 **[See no. 5316–4]**

## 1956–57 Test Tour (I.W. Johnson)

5276 **Australians** in India, 1956: souvenir.
–1 Calcutta, V.R. Sarma, [1956]. [32]p. incl.
covers & adverts. illus. ports. diagrs.

5277 **Barman, S.K.,** *editor*
■ Cricket digdarshan: cricketers from Australia—the 1956 tour. Calcutta, the Editor,
[1956]. 42p. ports. diagr.
*pre-tour*

5278 **Board of Control for Cricket in India**
■ Official souvenir of Australian cricket
tour of India 1956; compiled by B.D.
Panwelkar. Madras, the Compiler for the
Board, [1956]. [94]p. incl. adverts. illus.
ports. score, stats.
*pre-tour*

5279 **Haridass, C.K.**
■ India vs. Australia, Madras, Bombay,
Calcutta, 1956. Madras, Haridass, [1956].
78p. incl. adverts. ports. stats.
*pre-tour*

5280 **"Kangaroos"** in India: India-Australia
■ Test series 1956. Calcutta, Sadhana,
[1956]. [32]p. incl. adverts, illus. ports.
*pre-tour*

5281 **Madras Cricket Association**
■ Official souvenir: India vs. Australia—
first Test—Oct. 1956; ed. by A.K. Pattabhiraman. Madras, the Assoc., [1956].
67p. incl. adverts. ports. stats.

5282 **Sport & Pastime**
■ Cricketers from Australia: tour of India,
1956. Madras, Sport & Pastime, [1956].
32p. incl. adverts. illus. ports. stats.
*pre-tour*

5282 **Sporting Times of India**
–1 Cricket number 1956. (Vol. 4, no. 5).
Calcutta, Mohon Chatterjee. 52p. incl.
adverts. illus. ports. stats.

5283 **Sports Guide**
■ Annual cricket number. Calcutta, Sports
Guide
*Vol. 3, no. 3. Nov. 1956; [compiled by]
Sanu Basu. 40p. ports. stats.*
*pre-tour, with pen portraits of Australian
team in India, 1956*

## 1959–60 Test Tour (R. Benaud)

5284 **Anand Ban;** edited by Shri Vijoy
■ Pansaray. Bombay, the Editor. illus. ports.
*Cricket special issue. Dec. 59–Jan. 60.*
*100p. incl. adverts.*
*Marathi text*

5285 **Australia XI** versus India XI: cricket
■ souvenir, Jan. 1, 2, 3, 5 & 6, Brabourne
Stadium. Bombay, Maya Publications,
1959. [40]p. ports. stats.

5286 **Board of Control for Cricket in India**
■ Official souvenir of Australian cricket
tour of India 1959–60. [New Delhi], the
Board, [1959]. [84]p. incl. adverts. ports.
stats.
*pre-tour*

5287 **Desai, R.N.,** *editor*
■ Australia vrs. India souvenir 1959–60.
Bombay, the Editor, [1959]. [30]p. ports.
*pre-tour*

5288 **Haridass, C.K.,** *compiler*
■ India vs. Australia, Madras 1960. Madras,
Jupiter P., [1960]. 106p. incl. adverts.
ports. stats.
*pre-tour*

5289 **Rangrekha:** edited by P.R. Joshi. Bombay, the Editor. *fortnightly.* illus. ports.
*[Cricket number]. Year 1, no. 6. 1st Jan.
1960. 32p.*
*Gujarati text*

5290 **Shishuranjan:** edited by P.R. Joshi. Bom-
■ bay, the Editor. *weekly.* ports.
*Cricket special issue. Year 1, no. 47. 13
Dec. 1959. 32p.*
*Marathi text*

5291 **Sport & Pastime**
■ Cricketers from Australia: tour of India,
1959–60. Madras, Sport & Pastime,
[1959]. [64]p. incl. adverts. ports. stats.
*pre-tour*

5292 **The Tide**
■ Souvenir of the Australian cricket team's
visit to India 1959–60; edited by
M.J.George. Bombay, the Editor for The
Tide Publications Private Ltd., [1959]. 8p.
incl.adverts. ports.
*pre-tour*

5293 **[Uttar Pradesh Test Management
Committee]**
Green Park greets you. . . . Visit of the
Australian and Indian cricket teams,
Kanpur (U.P), India, 1959, December
19–24 [Kanpur, U.P.C.A., 1959]. ports.
diagrs.
*pre-Test*

## 1964–65 Test Tour (R.B. Simpson)

5294 **Bhupathy, D.R..,** *compiler*
■ Australia vs. India, 1964. Madras, the
Compiler, [1964]. incl. adverts. ports.
stats.
*pre-tour*

5295 **Board of Control for Cricket in India**
■ Official souvenir of the Australian cricket
tour of India 1964. The Board, [1964].
[94]p. ports. stats.
*pre-tour*

5296 **Haridass, C.K.**
■ India vs. Australia: Test cricket souvenir
1964. Madras, Haridass, [1964]. 104p.
incl. adverts. illus. ports. diagr. stats.
*pre-tour*

5297 **Illustrated News**
■ Cricketers from Australia, with elaborate
statistics. Calcutta, Illustrated News,
[1964]. 32p. illus. ports. stats.
*pre-tour*

## 1969–70 Test Tour (W.M. Lawry)

5298 **Australia**—India 2nd cricket Test match
■ at Green Park, Kanpur: souvenir.
[Lucknow], [1969]. [38]p. ports. stats.

5299 **Bhupathy, D.R.,** *compiler*
Australia v. India 1969. Madras, the Compiler, [1969]. 48p. incl. adverts. ports.
stats.
*pre-tour*

5300 **Board of Control for Cricket in India**
■ Official souvenir of the Australian cricket
tour of India 1969. The Board, [1969].
[64]p. incl. adverts. ports. stats.
*pre-tour*

5301 **Burmah-Shell**
Between the kiwi and the kangaroo.
Bombay, M.K. Das for Burmah-shell,
1969. 14p. illus.
*pre-tour*

5302 **Cricket Club of India**
Australia-India Test series 1969. Bombay,
the Club, [1969]. 36p. ports. stats.
*pre-tour*

5302 **Cricket's** in the air. Australia in India
–1 (1969–70). Bombay, Onlooker P., [1969].
[136]p. incl. adverts. illus. ports. stats.
*pre-tour*

5303 **Haridass, C.K.**
Aussies in India, 1969. Madras, Haridass,
[1969]. 122p. incl. adverts. illus. ports.
stats.
*pre-tour*

**5304 The Hindu**
- Australians' tour of India 1969. The Hindu, 1969. 50p. incl. adverts. illus. ports. stats.
  *pre-tour*

**5305 Indian Oil Corporation**
Know your cricketers (Australians and Indians). Madras, the Corporation, 1969. 40p. illus. ports. scores, stats.
*pre-tour*

**5306 Rajan Bala**
- Kiwis and Kangaroos, India, 1969. Calcutta & New Delhi, The Statesman, 1970. v,176p. illus. scores, stats.
  *post-tour*

**5307 Saraiya, Suresh,** *editor*
- Australia vs. India 1969–70. [Bombay], The Author, [1970]. 88p. illus. ports. stats.
  *post-tour*

### 1970 Australian Old Collegians' Tour

**5308 Hyderabad Blues Cricket Club**
- Australian Old Collegians Cricket Association v. Hyderabad Blues Cricket Club on 11th and 12th Jan, 1970. Hyderabad, the Club, 1970. [46]p. incl. adverts.

### 1979–80 Test Tour (K.J. Hughes)

**5308 Board of Control for Cricket in India**
**–1** Official souvenir of Australian cricket team tour of India 1979. Hyderabad, the Masters Foundation on behalf of the Board, [1979]. [80]p. incl. adverts. illus. ports. stats.
*pre-tour*

**5308 Dossa, Anandji,** *editor*
**–2** India vs. Australia 1979. [Bombay], Trupti
- Publications, [1979]. 80p. incl. adverts. illus. ports. stats.
  *pre-tour*

**5308 Haridass, C.K.,** *editor*
**–3** Aussies in India 1979. Madras, C.K.
- Haridass & Sons, [1979]. 136p. incl. adverts. illus. ports.
  *pre-tour*

**5308 The Hindu**
**–4** Australian tour of India: the Hindu
- souvenir. [Madras], the Hindu, [1979]. 104p. incl. covers & adverts. illus. ports. stats.
  *pre-tour*

# AUSTRALIAN TOURS TO PAKISTAN

## 1956–57 Test Tour (I.W. Johnson)

**5309 Butt, Qamaruddin**
- Pakistan cricket on the march. Karachi, the Author, 1957. 258p. illus. ports. scores, stats.
  *includes an account of the only match of Australian visit to Pakistan in autumn 1956*

**5310 Pakistan Sports & Pastimes**
- Annual number and commemorative issue: ed. by M.H. Ghatala. Karachi, the Editor.
  *Vol. III, no. 1. Oct. 1956. illus. ports.*
  *mostly cricket; this issue welcomes the Australian touring team*

## 1959–60 Test Tour (R. Benaud)

**5311 Butt, Qamaruddin**
- Cricket cat and mouse: Australians' tour of Pakistan in 1959. Rawalpindi, the Author, 1961. [iv],113p. illus. ports. scores, stats.
  *post-tour*

**5312 East Pakistan Sports Federation**
- Official souvenir of the First Test, Australia vs. Pakistan at the Dacca Stadium on 13, 14, 15, 17 & 18, November, 1959; edited by Atiquzzaman Khan. Dacca, the Federation, [1959]. [82]p. incl. adverts. 1 illus. ports. scores, stats.

**5313 [Karachi Cricket Association]**
Official souvenir of the third Test, Pakistan v. Australia at the National Stadium, Karachi on 4, 5, 6, 8 and 9, December, 1959. [Karachi, the Assoc., 1959]. ports.

# AUSTRALIAN VISITS TO SRI LANKA

## 1912 Visit

**5314 Foenander, E.W.**
The Australian cricketers in Colombo: a souvenir of today's match: Australia vs. All Ceylon . . . April 4, 1912. Wellawatte, Boys Industrial Home P., [1912]. 10p. illus. ports.

## 1913 Rev. E.F. Waddy's Team

**5315 Foenander, Samuel Peter**
- Official souvenir of the visit of Rev. E.F. Waddy's team of New South Wales cricketers to Ceylon. Colombo, Ceylon Examiner, [1913]. 58p. ports. scores

## 1926 Visit

5316 **Foenander, Samuel Peter**
■ A souvenir of the visit of the 16th Australian cricket team to Ceylon, 24 March,
1926. [Colombo], C.A.C. Press, [1926].
16p. incl. adverts. scores
*pre-tour*

## 1934 Visit

5316 **Foenander, Samuel Peter,** *compiler*
–1 Australian cricketers in Ceylon, 1934.
11p.

## 1938 Visit

5316 **Foenander, Samuel Peter ("Onlooker",**
–2 *pseud.*)
Australian cricket team vs. All-Ceylon,
Wednesday, March 30, 1938 on S.S.C.
Ground, Colombo: official souvenir and
score card. Colombo, *printed by* Ceylon
Observer, [1938]. 12p. ports. stats.

## 1945 Visit of Australian Services Team

5316 **Foenander, Samuel Peter**
–3 Souvenir of the visit to Ceylon of the
Australian Services cricket team, December 1945. Colombo, Ceylon Observer, [1945]. 12p.

5316 **Sports and screen** weekly: Australian
–4 supplement. Vol. VIII, no. 42, 17th
November, 1945. 67p. incl. adverts. illus.
ports. scores, stats.
*includes "Who's who of the Australian visi-
tors" by S.P. Foenander*

## 1948 Visit

5317 **Foenander, Samuel Peter**
■ Souvenir of the visit of the Australian
cricket team to Colombo, March 27, 1948.
Colombo, "Ceylon Observer", [1948]. 8p.
ports.

## 1961 Visit

5318 **Ceylon Observer**
■ Ceylon v. Australian XI at the Oval,
Wanathamulla, April 4, 1961; edited by
R.B. Wijesinha. [Colombo], Associated
Newspapers of Ceylon, [1961]. 32p. incl.
adverts. ports. stats.

## 1964 Visit

5319 **Board of Control for Cricket in Ceylon**
■ Official souvenir of the visit of the Australian Test team, April 15, 1964: match
versus Ceylon played at The Oval, Wanathamulla; edited by R.B. Wijesinha.

Colombo, the Board, [1964]. 48p. incl.
adverts. ports. stats.
*includes an account of Australia v. Ceylon
matches 1884–1961 by Denzil L. Peiris*

## 1969 Tour

5320 **Board of Control for Cricket in Ceylon**
■ Australian tour 1969, Oct. 16–28: official
souvenir edited by E.J. Melder and S.S.
Perera. Colombo, the Board, 1969. 105p.
incl. adverts. illus. ports. diagr. stats.
*pre-tour; includes review of Ceylon v.
Australia 1884–1964 by S.S. Perera*

5321 **Ceylon Tobacco Cricket League**
Australian cricket tour of Ceylon, 1969:
itinerary. [Colombo], the League, [1969]

## 1978 Australian Under-19 Team Tour

5321 **Board of Control for Cricket in Sri Lanka**
–1 Australia under 19 tour of Sri Lanka 9
■ February to 6 March, 1978: official tour
programme. [Colombo, the Board, 1978].
[8]p. folded
*pre-tour*

# AUSTRALIAN TOURS TO CANADA AND THE UNITED STATES

## 1877–78 Tour

5322 **The tour** of the Australian eleven through
England, America and Colonies with
Conway's Australian cricketer's annual
for 1877–78. Melbourne, Fergusson &
Moore, 1879. [iv],399p. scores, stats.
*post-tour*

## 1912 Tour

5323 **Official** programme commemorating the
visit of the Australian cricketers to
America September and October 1912.
n.p., 1912. 16p. illus.
*pre-tour*

## 1913 Tour

5323 **The Edmonton athlete:** a journal devoted
–1 to all sport and pastime. Edmonton
(Alberta). illus.
*Vol. 1, no. 2. (June 3rd, 1913) is devoted
mainly to the visit to Edmonton by the
Australians*

5324 **International** cricket match: All New
York vs. Australia, Livingston, Staten
Island, Aug. 1st, 2nd, 1913. 1913
*scoring book*

5325 **Official** programme commemorating the
■ visit of the Australian cricketers to
America 1913. *n.p.*, [1913]. [8]p. ports.
*pre-tour*

**1926 Tour**

5325 **Australian** cricket team Canadian-
–1 American tour on the occasion of their
visit to the Westchester Biltmore Country
Club, Rye, New York: program October
10, 1926. [N.Y., the Club, 1926]. [8]p.
*apart from title only p.[5] bears any text,
giving the programme for the day*

5325 **Welcome** luncheon to the Australian
–2 cricket team. Westchester Biltmore
Country Club, Rye, New York. Oct. 10,
1926

**1932 Tour**

5326 **Australian** cricketers good will tour [of

■ Canada], 1932. [Vancouver, the Australian Team, 1932]. 16p. incl. adverts. illus.
ports.
*pre-tour*

5327 **Illinois Cricket Association Inc.**
■ Welcome! Australia, July 23, 24, 25, 26,
1932. Grant Park, Chicago, U.S.A.:
souvenir program in honour of the visit
of the Australian cricket team. Chicago,
the Assoc., 1932. [19]p. illus. ports.

**1975 Tour**

5327 **Canadian Cricket Association Board of**
–1 **Control**
■ Souvenir programme of the second
Australian cricket tour of Canada, May 19
– May 28, 1975. The Board, [1975]. [12]p.
ports. stats.

# OTHER AUSTRALIAN TOURS

## TO MALAYA

**1927 Tour**

5328 **Malayan Daily Express**
■ Souvenir of Australian cricketers' visit
May-June 1927. Kuala Lumpur, Malayan
Daily Express, [1927]. 44p. illus. ports.
scores
*issued during tour*

5329 **Souvenir:** Australians visit to Malaya
1927. Kuala Lumpur, *printed by* Kyle,
Palmer, [1927]. 56p. incl. adverts. illus.
ports.
*pre-tour*

**1959 Emu Club Tour**

5330 **The Emu Club**
■ The Emu Club's tour of Singapore and
Malaya, 1959; compiled by Ross Scott,
Stan Gilchrist and John Henderson.
Muswellbrook, N.S.W., the Club, [1959].
[28]p.
*post-tour*

5331 **Malayan Cricket Association**
Australian tour to Malaya souvenir 1959.
Singapore, the Assoc., [1959]. 40p. incl.
adverts. ports.
*pre-tour*

## TO TASMANIA

**1926 Visit**

5332 **[Tasmanian Cricket Association]**
■ Australian XI on tour: Australia v.
Tasmania, Hobart, March 4, 5 and 6,
1926. [Hobart, the Assoc., 1926]. [8]p.
ports. stats.

**1938 Visit**

5332 **Tasmanian Cricket Association**
–1 International cricket, Australian XI v.
Tasmania, to be played at Hobart, 3, 4, 5
March 1938. [Hobart, the Assoc., 1938].
16p. incl. covers & adverts. ports. stats.
*pre-match*

**1953 Visit**

5333 **Tasmanian Cricket Association**
Official souvenir programme: Australian
XI visit to Tasmania. Hobart, the Assoc.,
1953. 24p.

## AUSTRALIAN WOMEN'S TOURS

**1937 Tour to England**

5334 **Mitcham Cricket Club**
■ Australian Women's touring team v.

Surrey, Mitcham Green, Wednesday, July 28th, 1937; compiled by R.S. Culmer. Mitcham, the Club, [1937]. 15p. illus. ports.

5335 **Pollard, Marjorie**
■ A diary of the matches played by the Australian Women's cricket team in England, 1937. Letchworth, Pollard Publications, [1937]. 41p. illus. ports. scores, stats.
*reprinted from "Women's cricket"; post-tour*

5336 **Women's Cricket Association**
■ Programme of the tour and matches arranged for the first visit of the Australian Women's cricket team 1937. [The Assoc., 1937]. 16p. team port.

## 1951 Tour to England

5337 **Women's Cricket Association**
■ Australian Women's cricket tour 1951: souvenir programme. The Assoc., [1951]. 16p. incl. adverts. illus. ports. map
*pre-tour*

5338 Report of the Australian Women's cricket
■ tour in England 1951. [The Assoc., 1951]. 44p. team port. scores, stats.
*post-tour*

## 1963 Tour to England

5339 **Rothmans**
■ Exhibition of women's cricketana, 1745–1963 at the Qantas Gallery . . . 13–25 May, 1963, to mark the third tour of England by the Australian Women's Cricket team. Women's C.A., [1963]. 10p. illus.

5340 **Women's Cricket Association**
■ Australian Women's cricket tour [1963]: souvenir programme. [The Assoc., 1963]. 16p. incl. adverts. illus. ports.
*pre-tour*

5341 Report of The Australian Women's cricket
■ tour in England 1963. The Assoc., 1963. 31p. team port. scores, stats.
*post-tour*

Australia v. West Indies, third Test, Port of Spain, Trinidad, 1973 *photo: Patrick Eagar*

# SOUTH AFRICA

**5341 Bassano, Brian**
**–1** South Africa in international cricket
■ 1888–1970. East London, Chameleon Books, 1979. 208p. illus. ports. facsim.

**5342 Coleman, William H.,** *compiler*
■ South Africa v. England & Australia: Test cricket 1888–1924. Old Royalty Book Publishers, [1926]. 128p. scores, stats.
——2nd ed. 1888–1928. [1928]. 140p.

**5343 Duffus, Louis George**
■ Springbok glory. Capetown & London, Longmans, Green, 1955. [viii],206p. illus.
*on post-war S.A. cricket tours*

**5343 Greyvenstein, Chris**
**–1** Sprinkbok-seges in krieket en rugby. Kaapstad [Capetown], Buren-uitgewers, 1968. 116p. illus. ports.
*in Afrikaans; trs: Srpingbok triumphs in cricket and rugby*

**5343 Pollock, Peter MacLean**
**–2** The thirty Tests. Cape Town, Nelson, 1978. 136p. illus. ports.
■ *a pictorial history of South African Test cricket 1961–1970*

## SOUTH AFRICAN AND RHODESIAN TOURS TO ENGLAND

**5344 Difford, Ivor Denis**
"Our cricket Springboks": official souvenir of the visit of the M.C.C. team to South Africa and Southern Rhodesia, 1938–39; a statistical record of all South Africa's cricket tours to Britain, Australia and New Zealand, 1894–1935, and of British & Australian teams to S. Africa, 1888–1936. Johannesburg, Central News Agency, 1939. 69p. stats.

### 1904 Tour (F. Mitchell)

**5345 Wallach, Benjamin**
South African cricketers in England, 1904. Johannesburg, Wallach, [1905?]. [62]p. illus. scores, stats.

### 1907 Test Tour (P.W. Sherwell)

**5346 The Eventoscope** cricket souvenir: South Africans in England. Gale & Polden, [1907]. 38p. illus. ports.
*pre-tour*

**5346 Piggott, F. Neville**
**–1** The Springboks: history of the tour 1906–07. Cricket P., [1907]. 140p.

### 1912 Test Tour (F. Mitchell)

**5347 Australia** and South Africa tour cricket
■ sketches. Manchester, R. Scott, [1912]. 16p. ports.
*pre-tour*

**5348 The Daily Graphic**
■ Cricket number. H.R. Baines, 1912. 20p. incl. adverts. illus. ports. stats.
*pre-the Triangular Tests*

**5349 Dorey, H.V.,** *compiler*
■ The triangular Tests 1876–1912. Cricket & Sports Publishers, [1912]. [i],232p. scores, stats.

**5350 Sewell, Edward Humphrey Dalrymple**
■ Triangular cricket: a record of the greatest contest in the history of the game. Dent, 1912. x,211p. illus. ports. diagrs. scores
*account of the 1912 Tests between England, Australia & S. Africa*

**5351 Springbok** souvenir: triangular cricket Tests. 1912. 32p.
*pre-Tests*

**5352 The year** 1912 illustrated. Headly Bros., 1913. 184p. illus.
*"The cricket season and the Triangular Tests", pp. 155–162*

### 1929 Test Tour (H.G. Deane)

**5353 Leicestershire County Cricket Club**
Souvenir: Leicestershire v. South Africans. Leicester, the Club, 1929. ports.
*pre-match*

## 1935 Test Tour (H.F. Wade)

5353 **Duffus, Louis**
−1 S. Africans in England 1935; Australians in S. Africa 1935/36. Johannesburg, Gen. Publishing Co., [1936]. 48p. illus. ports. scores, stats.
*post-tours*

5354 **Simpson, A.W.,** *editor and compiler*
■ Souvenir book: South African cricket tour. Folkestone, "Day-by-Day" Publishing Co., [1935]. 40p. illus. ports.
*pre-tour*

5354 **South African Cricket Association**
−1 South Africans in England 1935. (The side that won the rubber). Johannesburg, General Publishing Co., 1936. 25p. illus. ports.
*post-tour*

## 1947 Test Tour (A. Melville)

5355 **Arlott, [Leslie Thomas] John**
■ Gone to the cricket. Longmans, Green, 1948. 206p. illus. ports. scores, stats.

5356 Two summers at the Tests: England v.
■ South Africa 1947; England v. Australia 1948. Sportsman's Book Club, 1952. 320p. illus. ports. scores
*contents:* Gone to the cricket; Gone to the Test match

5357 Vintage summer: 1947. Eyre & Spottis-
■ woode, 1967. 190p. illus. ports. scores, stats.
——*another ed*. Sportsman's Book Club, 1968

5358 **Cricket Book Society**
■ The Tests of 1947: England v. South Africa. Hunstanton, C.B.S., 1947. 32p. scores, stats. (Publications. Ser. 2, no. 5)
——*reissued in* "Cricket omnibus 1947", edited by Roy Webber. *See no.* 982.

5359 The South African team in England, 1947.
■ Hunstanton, C.B.S., 1947. 20p. scores, stats. (Publications. Ser. 2, no. 6)
——*reissued in* "Cricket omnibus 1947", edited by Roy Webber. *See no.* 982.

5359 **Cricket** fixtures South Africa tour Eng-
−1 land 1947. [South Africa], *printed by* W. & S., [1947]. [12]p.

5360 **Day, Cedric,** *and* **Mason, Michael**
■ The story of Test cricket: England v. South Africa. Windsor, W.D.S., [1947]. 15p. illus. ports.
*pre-tour*

5361 **Kay, John**
■ Cuts and glances. Altrincham, Sherratt, 1948. 144p. illus. ports. scores, stats.

5362 **Ledbrooke, Archibald William**
■ The Springboks here again: the story of the Test matches between England and South Africa, 1888–1939, with a who's who of the 1947 South African touring team. London & Manchester, Withy Grove P., [1947]. 94p. illus. ports. score, stats. (Cherry Tree Special)
*pre-tour*

5363 **Simpson, A.W.,** *compiler & editor*
■ South African cricket tour, 1947: fixtures, records and photographs of players. I.M. Young, [1947]. 32p. illus. ports.
*pre-tour*

5364 **Springbok** cricket and soccer tours 1947.
■ Pietermaritzburg, distributed by Central News Agency Ltd., [1947]. [84]p. incl. adverts. score, stats.
*cricket pp.[3–68]; pre-tour*

5364 **United Tobacco Companies**
−1 Springbok souvenir 1947: cricket tour: soccer tour, etc. Cape Town, the Companies, [1947?]. 24p. ports.

## 1951 Test Tour (A.D. Nourse)

5365 **Day, Cedric,** *and* **Mason, Michael**
■ Day & Mason 1951 Test book: England v. South Africa. Windsor, Day, Mason & Ford, [1951]. 23p. illus. ports. stats.
*pre-tour*

5366 **English** counties v. South Africa: programme, 1951. M. Walker, [1951]

5367 **Medworth, Cyril Oliver**
■ Noursemen in England: the South African cricket tour, 1951. T. Werner Laurie, 1952. 174p. illus. scores, stats.

5368 **Simpson, A.W.**
■ South African cricket tour 1951: photographs & pen pictures of South African players, fixtures, facts & averages. I.M. Young, [1951]. 24p. illus. ports. stats.
*pre-tour*

5369 **South Africa:** pictures, fixtures and
■ personalities, 1951. Sutton Coldfield, M. Walker, [1951]. [4]p. fold. ports.
*pre-tour*

5369 **South African** cricket tour 1951: souvenir
−1 programme. T. Ross, [1951]. [4]p. folded
■ card. ports.
*pre-tour*

5370 **West, Peter,** *editor*
■ Cricketers from South Africa: official souvenir for the 1951 tour of England. Playfair Books, [1951]. 24p. illus. ports. map, score, stats.
   *pre-tour*

## 1955 Test Tour (J.E. Cheetham)

5371 **Barnard, Werner**
   Amper krieketkampioene. Johannesburg, Nasionale Boekhandel, 1956. 124p. illus.
   *in Afrikaans; trs. Almost cricket champions*

5372 **Cheetham, Jack,** *i.e.* **John Erskine**
■ **Cheetham**
   I declare. Hodder & Stoughton, 1956. xi,227p. illus. scores, stats.

5373 **Cutler, Norman**
■ Behind the South African Tests. Putnam, 1955. ix,222p. illus. scores, stats.

5374 **Harris, [Stephen] Bruce**
■ England versus South Africa, 1955. Hutchinson, 1955. 184p. illus. ports. scores, stats. (Library of Sports and Pastimes)

5374 **Manchester Guardian**
–1 The bedside 'Guardian' 4: a selection by
■ Ivor Brown from The Manchester Guardian 1954–1955. Collins, 1955. 256p.
   *includes pp. 119–22, "Sway of battle", by Denys Rowbotham (on 2nd Test England v. S. Africa, 1955)*

5375 **Ross, Gordon,** *editor*
■ Cricketers from South Africa: the official souvenir of the 1955 tour of England. Playfair Books, [1955]. 24p. incl. adverts. ports. stats.
   *pre-tour*

5375 **Shell Company of South Africa Ltd**
–1 The Shell fixture card of the South African cricket tour of Great Britain 1955. . . . [Capetown, the Co., 1955]. folded card
   *title also in Afrikaans: Shell se wedstrydreeks van de Suid-Afrikaanse krieket toer van Groot Brittanje*

## 1960 Test Tour (D.J. McGlew)

5376 **Arlott, [Leslie Thomas] John**
■ Cricket journal—3: Cricket on trial. Heinemann, 1960. 256p. illus. ports. scores, stats.

5377 **Fortune, Charles**
■ Cricket overthrown. Cape Town, Timmins; London, Bailey Bros. & Swinfen, 1960. x,168p. illus. scores

5378 **Ross, Gordon,** *editor*
■ Cricketers from South Africa: the official souvenir of the 1960 tour of England. Playfair Books, [1960]. 24p. illus. ports. stats.
   *pre-tour*

5379 **South Africa** cricket tour of 1960: souvenir tour programme. 8p. illus.
   *pre-tour*

5380 **Waite, John**
■ Perchance to bowl (Test cricket today); edited and with chapters by R.S. (Dick) Whitington. Kaye, 1961. 176p. illus. scores

## 1964 Mashonaland Country Districts Winter C.A. Tour

5381 **Mashonaland Country Districts Winter**
■ **Cricket Association**
   Cricket tour of England. Salisbury, [the Assoc., 1964]. 16p. incl. covers. illus. ports. map
   *pre-tour*

5382 Record of a tour in England 1964. Salisbury, the Assoc., [1964]. 31p. illus. ports. scores, stats.
   *post-tour*

## 1965 Test Tour (P.L. Van Der Merwe)

5382 **1965** South Africa Test tour: souvenir pro-
–1 gramme. Hammersmith, Starkey, [1965].
□ [8]p. incl. covers. team port. stats.
   *pre-tour*

5383 **Ross, Gordon,** *editor*
■ The 1965 tourists: the official brochure for the 1965 tours of England. Dickens P., [1965]. [i],32p. illus. ports. stats. (Playfair Publication)
   *pre-tour*

5384 **Rothmans**
■ Test cricket almanack 1965: England v. South Africa. Rothmans of Pall Mall, [1965]. 56p. illus. (some col.), ports. stats.
   *pre-tour and records of matches England v. S. Africa 1888–1965*

5384 **South Africa** souvenir tour programme:
–1 pictures, fixtures and personalities 1965.
■ Wembley, Walker, [1965]. [4]p. fold. ports.

## 1966 Wilfred Isaacs XI Tour

5385 **Wilfred Isaacs XI** overseas tour—July
■ 1966, Denmark, England & Holland. Johannesburg, the Club, [1966]. 12p. ports.
   *pre-tour; includes a history of the club by Eric Litchfield*

## 1969 Wilfred Isaacs XI Tour

5386 **Litchfield, Eric**
■ Wilfred Isaacs XI England–Ireland tour 1969. [Johannesburg, the Club, 1969]. 11p. ports.
*pre-tour*

## 1970 Intended Test Tour

5387 **The Cricket Council**
■ Why the '70 tour?: The Cricket Council answer. The Council, 1970. 4p.

5387 **The Guardian**
–1 The bedside 'Guardian' 19: a selection
■ from The Guardian 1969–70; edited by W.L. Webb. Collins, 1970. 256p. illus.
*includes pp. 207–10, "The fury beyond cricket", by Patrick Keatley [on the proposed S. African tour, 1970]*

5388 **Hain, Peter**
■ Don't play with Apartheid: the background to the Stop the Seventy Tour Campaign. Allen & Unwin, 1971. 231p.

5388 **Humphry, Derek**
–1 The cricket conspiracy. National Council for Civil Liberties, 1975. 139p.
*concerning the private prosecution of Mr. Peter Hain for his part in the "Stop-the-Seventy-Tour" campaign*

5389 **1970 Cricket Fund**
The scene we must protect: appeal brochure. 1970 Cricket Fund, [1970]. 4p. illus. port.

## 1975 The Sabres Tour

5389 **University of Cape Town**
–1 The Sabres England tour 1975. West Bromwich, *printed by* Peerless P., [1975]. [8]p. ports.
*pre-tour*

# SOUTH AFRICAN TOURS TO AUSTRALIA

5390 **Crowley, Brian M.**
■ The Springbok and the Kangaroo: a complete history of South Africa versus Australia at cricket. Johannesburg, Blue Crane Books, [1968]. xiv,284p. ports. scores, stats. bibliog.

## 1931–32 Test Tour (H.B. Cameron)

5391 **The Argus,** *and* **The Australasian**
■ Cricket guide: records and personalities of the South African players, compiled by "Old Boy". Melbourne, the Argus and the Australasian, [1931]. 15p. ports. stats.

5392 **The Australian Cricketer.** *Program*
■ *supplement*
1931–32 South African season: pocket souvenir program and score sheet. Sydney, Australian Cricketer, 1931. [24]p. incl. adverts. ports. stats.

5392 **Queensland Cricket Association**
–1 South Africa v. Queensland, Nov. 20 to Nov. 24, [1931]; South Africa v. Australia, 1st Test match Nov. 27 to finish, Brisbane Cricket Ground: souvenir programme. Brisbane, the Assoc., [1931]. 32p. incl. adverts. illus. ports. stats.

## 1952–53 Test Tour (J.E. Cheetham)

5393 **Australian Broadcasting Commission**
■ A.B.C. cricket book: South Africans tour 1952–1953. Sydney, the Commission, [1952]. 65p. ports. diagrs. stats.
*pre-tour*

5393 **Bundaberg Cricket Association**
–1 South Africa v. Q'land Country, West Bundaberg Recreation Ground, 25 and 26 November 1952: [souvenir programme]. Bundaberg, the Assoc., [1952]. 11p. incl. adverts. illus. ports.

5394 **Cheetham, Jack,** *i.e.* **John Erskine**
■ **Cheetham**
Caught by the Springboks. Cape Town, Timmins; London, Hodder & Stoughton, 1954. 248p. illus. ports. scores, stats.

5394 **Miller, Keith [Ross],** *and* **Whitington,**
–1 **Richard Smallpeice**
Bumper. Latimer House, 1952. 256p. illus. port. scores
*pp. 163–235 'The Cheetham crusade'*

5395 **Moyes, Alban George ("Johnnie")**
■ The South Africans in Australia, 1952–1953. Harrap, 1953. xx,236p. illus. scores, stats.

5396 **Tasmanian Cricket Association**
South Africans visit to Tasmania: official souvenir programme. Hobart, the Assoc., 1953. 24p. incl. adverts.

## 1963–64 Test Tour (T.L. Goddard)

5397 **Australian Broadcasting Commission**
■ The A.B.C. cricket book: South African tour, 1963–64. Sydney, the Commission, [1963]. 64p. illus. ports. stats. diagr.
*pre-tour*

5397 **Central District Cricket Council**
–1 South Africa v. Western N.S.W. Country at Woodward Park, Parkes, Wednesday, January 8, 1964: [souvenir programme]. The Council, [1964]. [4]p.

**5398**    **New South Wales Cricket Association**
■    Australian tour of the South African team 1963–4; edited, compiled and distributed by V.C. Davis & Co. Sydney, the Assoc., [1963]. 64p. incl. adverts. ports. stats.
*pre-tour*

**5398**    **Queensland Cricket Association**
–1    Test cricket magazine. Australia v. South Africa, first Test Brisbane 1963–64 series December 6 to December 11, 1963, incorporating Sth Africa v. Q'ld programme. Brisbane, the Assoc., [1963]. 32p. incl. adverts. ports. stats.

**5398**    **South Africa Freedom Campaign.**
–2    *Melbourne*
Apartheid: a news sheet produced for the National Union of Australian University Students December 1963. Melbourne, [the Campaign, 1963?]. 4p. illus.
*published "on the occasion of the South African cricket tour of Australia"*

**5398**    **Western Australia Cricket Association**
–3    S. Africa vs. Western Australia at WACA Ground, Perth, 25–29 October, 1963: [programme]. Perth, the Assoc., [1963]. 20p. incl. adverts. ports. stats.

**5398**    S. Africa vs. Combined XI at the WACA
–4    Ground, Perth, 1–5 November 1963: [programme]. Perth, the Assoc., [1963]. 20p. incl. adverts. ports. stats.

**5399**    **Whitington, Richard Smallpeice**
■    Bradman, Benaud and Goddard's cinderellas. Cape Town, Timmins; Adelaide, Rigby; London, Bailey Bros. & Swinfen, 1964. 237p. illus. ports.

## 1971–72 Intended Test Tour

**5399**    **Personality**
–1    South African cricket tour of Australia 1971/72: "Personality" souvenir guide. [Sydney(?)], Personality, 1971. 12p. illus. & ports. (some col.)
*a "pull-out" souvenir in issue of 30th April, 1971*

# SOUTH AFRICAN TOURS TO NEW ZEALAND

## 1931–32 Test Tour (H.B. Cameron)

**5400**    **New Zealand Cricket Council**
South Africa v. New Zealand: official souvenir brochure. The Council, [1932]. 32p. incl. adverts. ports.
*pre-tour*

## 1963–64 Test Tour (T.L. Goddard)

**5401**    **Northern Districts Cricket Association**
Cricket—South Africa versus Northern Districts, 14 and 15 February, 1964. Hamilton, The Assoc., [1964].
*pre-match*

**5402**    **Wellington Cricket Association**
South Africa v. New Zealand, Basin Reserve, February 21, 22, 24, 25, 1964: official programme. Wellington, the Assoc., [1964]. 20p. incl. adverts. ports.
*pre-Test*

**5403**    **Whitington, Richard Smallpeice**
■    Bradman, Benaud and Goddard's cinderellas. Cape Town, Timmins; London, Bailey Bros. & Swinfen, 1964. 237p. illus. ports.

# WEST INDIES

5404 **Bajnath, Hiralal T.**, *compiler*
□ The West Indies Test cricketer, 1928–1959; second annual: a comprehensive detail of West Indies Test cricket from inception of Test status in 1928 to 1959. [Port-of-Spain, the Compiler, 1959]. 48p. illus. ports. stats.
——4th ed. 1964–5. 1965. [x],100p.
——5th ed. Port-of-Spain, Columbus Publishers, 1970. vii,98p. 1 illus. team port. stats.
*a statistical digest of West Indies Test cricket*

5404 **Cozier, Tony**
–1 The West Indies: fifty years of Test
■ cricket. Brighton, Angus & Robertson, 1978. xiv,223p. illus. ports. stats.
——*another ed.* Newton Abbot, Readers Union, 1978

5404 **West Indian** digest. London, Hansib
–2 Publishing Ltd. illus. ports.
■ *Vol. 5, no. 49 May/June 1978 contains special "Cricket feature to mark the 50th anniversary of West Indies Test cricket 1928–1978 from Constantine to Parry" by Clayton Goodwin, and others. 31p.*

5405 **West Indies Board of Control for International Cricket Matches**
Constitution, by-laws and rules. [The Board, 1928]. [15]p.

## WEST INDIES TOURS TO ENGLAND

5406 **[Smith, Lloyd S.]**
West Indies cricket history and cricket tours to England, 1900, 1906, 1923. Port-of-Spain, Yuille's Printerie, 1922, [*i.e.* 1923]. [iv],240p. illus. ports.

### 1900 Tour (R.S.A. Warner)

5407 **West** Indian cricket team: full report of
■ their first tour in England, June–August 1900. West Indian Club, [1900]. 50p. port. scores, stats.
*post-tour*

5408 **Reid, C.A.**, *compiler*
■ The tour of the West Indian cricketers in England, 1900. Georgetown, Baldwin, 1900. 40p. scores, stats.
*post-tour*

### 1906 Tour (H.B.G. Austin)

5409 **The West Indian** cricketers in England. Port-of-Spain, Pemberton's Printery, 1906. 46p.

### 1928 Test Tour (R.K. Nunes)

5410 **Ashley-Cooper, Frederick Samuel**
■ The West Indies cricket guide, 1928: a book of records. Nottingham, C.H. Richards, 1928. 28p. stats.
*a brief chronology with notes on the West Indies team of 1928*

5411 **The Barbados Advocate**
Xmas souvenir edition, 1928. Bridgetown, Barbados Advocate, 1928. 60p. illus.
*includes an account of the 1928 West Indies cricket tour with 6 plates illustrating the Tests, pp. 18–24*

5412 **Beecher, J. Coleman**, *compiler*
List of matches for W.I. cricket team in England. Kingston, [the Compiler], 1928. [4]p. fold

5413 **The sporting** chronicle: souvenir annual.
■ Manchester.
*vol. VIII, no. 8, Dec. 1928; edited by Lloyd S. Smith. 235p. incl. adverts. illus. ports. scores, stats.*
*cricket pp. 4–130 including 100 page account of West Indies tour of England, 1928*

### 1933 Test Tour (G.C. Grant)

5414 **Simpson, A.W.**, *compiler*
■ Souvenir West Indies cricket tour of England 1933: fixtures, photographs, descriptions of players and islands. Nottingham, All Counties Publicity, [1933]. 32p. incl. adverts. illus. ports.
*pre-tour*

## 1939 Test Tour (R.S. Grant)

5415 **The Ashes:** the West Indians are here.
■ English-West Indies 1939. Cricket Tour
Programme Co., [1939]. 32p. incl. adverts. illus. ports. stats.
*pre-tour*

5416 **Simpson, A.W.,** *editor*
■ West Indies cricket tour 1939: official
souvenir. Folkestone, F.J. Parsons, [1939].
36p. incl. adverts. illus. ports.
*pre-tour*

5417 **West** Indies cricket tour of England. 1939.
[4]p. fold

## 1950 Test Tour (J.D.C. Goddard)

5418 **Arlott, [Leslie Thomas] John**
■ Days at the cricket. Longmans, Green,
1951. viii,199p. illus. ports. scores

5419 **England** versus the West Indies: pictures,
■ fixtures and personalities 1950. Sutton
Coldfield, M. Walker, [1950]. [4]p. fold,
ports.
*pre-tour*

5420 **English** Counties versus the West Indies:
■ photographic souvenir and fixture list.
Sutton Coldfield, H. Johnson, 1950. 4p.
fold. ports.
*pre-tour*

5421 **Hardy, W.A.S.,** *editor*
■ They live for cricket: a booklet containing
the full story of West Indian cricket &
featuring the West Indies tour 1950. The
Author, [1950]. 32p. ports. stats.

5422 **Simpson, A.W.,** *compiler*
■ West Indies cricket tour England 1950:
souvenir. I.M. Young, [1950]. 12p. ports.
*pre-tour*

5423 **West, Peter**
■ Cricketers from the West Indies: official
souvenir for the 1950 tour of England.
Playfair Books, 1950. 32p. illus. ports.
map, stats.
*pre-tour*

## 1957 Test Tour (J.D.C. Goddard)

5424 **Birmingham Post**
■ Supplement in commemoration of Edgbaston Test match. Birmingham, Birmingham Post, May 30, 1957, viiip. illus. ports.
*issued in commemoration of the return of
Test cricket to Edgbaston after 28 years*

5425 **Hardy, W.A.S.,** *edtior*
■ They live for cricket: a souvenir programme featuring the West Indies cricket

tour, 1957. [The Editor, 1957]. 24p. illus.
ports. stats.
*contains single leaf insert "Words for a
1957 calypso" by Albert Mackie; pre-tour*

5426 **Harris, [Stephen] Bruce**
■ West Indies cricket challenge, 1957. S.
Paul, 1957. 182p. illus. port. scores, stats.

5427 **London** calling: the overseas journal of
■ the B.B.C. West Indies tour number.
B.B.C., Apr. 11; 1957. 36p. incl. adverts.
illus. ports.

5427 **Rogers, M.S.**
–1 Cricketers from the Caribbean. [The
■ Author, 1957]. [18]p. stats. *typescript*
*pre-tour*

5428 **Ross, Gordon,** *editor*
■ Cricketers from the West Indies: the
official souvenir of the 1957 tour of
England. Playfair Books, [1957]. 24p.
illus. ports. map, stats.
*pre-tour*

5429 **West** Indies souvenir tour programme:
■ pictures, fixtures and personalities 1957.
M. Walker, [1957]. [4]p. fold. ports.
*pre-tour*

## 1963 Test Tour (F.M. Worrell)

5430 **Barker, John Sydney**
■ Summer spectacular: the West Indies v.
England, 1963. Collins, 1963. 128p. illus.
port. scores, stats.
——*another ed*. Sportsman's Book Club,
1965

5431 **British Broadcasting Corporation**
■ Test match special: England v. West
Indies, 1963. B.B.C., 1963. 12p. illus.
plans, stats.
*pre-tour*

5432 **Clarke, John [Campbell]**
■ Cricket with a swing: the West Indies
tour, 1963. S. Paul, 1963. 200p. illus.
scores

5432 **The Guardian**
–1 The bedside 'Guardian' 13: a selection
■ from The Guardian 1963–1964. Collins,
1964. 255p. illus.
*includes pp. 21–4 "England's great fight"
by Denys Rowbotham [on 2nd Test at Lord's
v. West Indies, 1963]*

5433 **"I was there":** twenty exciting sporting
■ events by sports writers of the "Daily
Telegraph" and "Sunday Telegraph".
Collins, 1966. [viii],152p. illus.
*includes an account of England v. West
Indies at Lord's 1963, by Alan Gibson*

**5433** **[Machado Sports Foundation]**
**–1** Machado cricket festival, Sabina Park,
■ September 24 to October 1, 1963: souvenir
programme. [Kingston, the Foundation,
1963]. 37p. incl. adverts. illus. ports.
scores, stats.
*mostly concerned with West Indies tour to
England 1963*

**5433** **MacInnes, Colin**
**–2** Out of the way: later essays. Brian &
■ O'Keeffe, 1979. 344p. frontis.
*pp. 241–4, "Second Test, fifth day" [Eng.
v. W.I., Lord's, 1963] rptd. from* New Society *July 1963*

**5434** **Rosenwater, Irving**
■ West Indies cricket tour, 1963. Teletype-
setting, [1963]. [i], 32p. illus. ports.
scores, stats.
*pre-tour*

**5435** **Ross, Alan**
■ The West Indies at Lord's; drawings by
Lawrence Toynbee. Eyre & Spottiswoode, 1963. 104p. illus. diagrs. scores,
stats.
*centres on the Lord's Test*

**5436** **Ross, Gordon,** *editor*
■ Cricketers from the West Indies: the 1963
tour official brochure. Dickens P., [1963].
[i],24p. illus. ports. map, stats.
*pre-tour*

**5437** **Rothmans**
■ Test cricket almanack: West Indies [v.]
England 1963. Rothmans of Pall Mall,
[1963]. 68p. illus. ports. stats.
*pre-tour with records of matches 1928–1962
between W.I. and England*

**5438** **Standing Conference of Organisations**
■ **Concerned with West Indians in Britain**
**(London Region)**
West Indies touring team v. Sir Learie
Constantine's XI, the Oval, Kennington,
Saturday 14 September, 1963. The Con-
ference, [1963]. [16]p. incl. adverts. team
port.

**5438** **Sunday Telegraph**
**–1** England v. West Indies: a record of the
■ Test matches. Sunday Telegraph, [1963].
[6]p. fold. scores
*full scores of the first 4 Tests*

**5439** **West Indian** cricket tour 1963: a complete
■ report: souvenir book. "Flamingo", Chal-
ton Publ. Co., [1963]. 28p. incl. adverts.
illus. team port. stats.
*post-tour*

**5440** **West Indies** cricket tour of England 1963:
■ pen pictures, records, souvenir pro-

gramme. Starkey, [1963]. [8]p. team port.
stats.
*pre-tour*

**5441** **Wina Magazine**
West Indies—1963—England. London,
Wina Magazine, 1963. illus. ports.

**5442** **Wooldridge, Ian**
■ Cricket, lovely cricket: the West Indies
tour, 1963. Hale, 1963. 176p. illus. scores,
stats.

## 1964 Sir Frank Worrell's Team

**5443** **Rothmans of Pall Mall**
■ Sir Frank Worrell's West Indies XI tour
1964: souvenir programme. Rothmans,
[1964]. [12]p. illus. ports.
*pre-tour; an unofficial tour to play matches
against an England XI at Scarborough,
Edgbaston & Lord's*

**5444** Sir Frank Worrell's XI v. Yorkshire
League XI at Harrogate, Sept. 6th, 1964
in aid of General Porters Benevolent
Association: souvenir programme. Rothmans, [1964]. [12]p. illus. ports.

## 1966 Test Tour (G.S. Sobers)

**5445** **Clarke, John [Campbell],** *and* **Scovell**
■ **Brian**
Everything that's cricket: the West Indies
tour 1966. S. Paul, 1966. 192p. illus. ports.
scores, stats.
*post-tour*

**5446** **Cumming, Malcolm,** *editor*
■ Meet the Test stars 1966: a souvenir of
England and West Indies. Longacre P.,
[1966]. 50p. illus. ports. stats.
*pre-tour*

**5446** **The Guardian**
**–1** The bedside 'Guardian' 15: a selection
from the Guardian 1965–1966. Collins,
1966. 255p. illus.
*includes pp. 235–7, "Sussex beat West
Indians" by Christopher Ford*

**5447** **Guinness** book of England v. West Indies
■ Test cricket records; statistics provided by
Irving Rosenwater. Guinnness Superlatives, 1966. 48p. ports. stats.
*pre-tour*

**5448** **1966 West Indies** Test tour of England:
■ pen pictures, records, souvenir programme. Starkey, [1966]. 8p. stats.
*pre-tour*

**5449** **Ross, Gordon,** *editor*
■ Cricketers from the West Indies: the 1966
official tour brochure. Dickens P., 1966.

[i],24p. illus. ports. map, stats.
*pre-tour*

5450 **Rothmans**
■ Test cricket almanack: England—West
Indies, 1966. Rothmans of Pall Mall,
[1966]. 56p. illus. ports. stats.
*pre-tour and records of matches 1928–1966*
*England v. West Indies*

5451 **Sobers, Gary,** *i.e.* **Garfield St. Aubrun**
■ **Sobers**
King cricket, as told by Alan Bestic.
Pelham, 1967. 160p. illus. ports.
——*rptd.* Sphere, 1969

5451 **West Indies** souvenir tour programme:
–1 pictures, fixtures and personalities, 1966.
■ Wembley, Walker, [1966]. [4]p. fold.
ports.
*pre-tour*

### 1969 Test Tour (G.S. Sobers)

5452 **Blofeld, Henry**
■ Cricket in three moods: eighteen months
of Test cricket and the ways of life behind
it. Hodder & Stoughton, 1970. 192p. illus.
scores on endpapers
*also contains accounts of M.C.C. tour of*
*West Indies, 1967/68 and West Indies tour of*
*Australia 1968/69*

5453 **Rothmans**
■ Cricket almanack 1969: England v. West
Indies, England v. New Zealand. Rothmans of Pall Mall, [1969]. 32p. illus. ports.
diagrs. stats.
*pre-tour*

5454 **West** Indies tour programme, fixtures,
■ pictures. D. Walker, [1969]. [8]p. ports.
*pre-tour*

### 1970 West Indies Young Cricketers' Tour

5455 **West Indies** Young Cricketers' tour of
■ United Kingdom July/August, 1970, sponsored by the U.K. Committee of the Sir
Frank Worrell Commonwealth Memorial
Fund. *Printed by* Booker McConnell,
[1970]. [18]p. stats.
*pre-tour*

### 1973 Test Tour (R.B. Kanhai)

5455 **Birmingham Post**
–1 Test match special; compiled by Michael
Blair. Birmingham, Birmingham Post,
August 9, 1973. 4p. col. illus.

5456 **Lewis, Lester,** *editor*
■ Cricket 73. West Indies one up! a photographic and literary record of the Oval Test

match. The Editor, [1973]. 20p. illus.
ports. score
*mid-tour*

5457 **Sports review.** Rulmveldt, Guyana Prin-
■ ters Ltd.
*no. 4, July 1973 carried 26p. on the West*
*Indies victory v. England at the Oval 1973*
*and statistics of the West Indies in Test cricket*

5458 **West Indies** cricket souvenir 73 pro-
■ gramme: West Indies vs England 1973
cricket tour. *n.p.,* [1973]. 32p. incl. adverts. ports. stats.
*pre-tour*

5459 **West Indies** tour '73: pen pictures,
■ records, souvenir programme. Starkey,
[1973]. [8]p. ports.
*pre-tour*

5460 **Williams, Leroy ("Fathead"),** *compiler*
■ West Indies 1973 tour to England. [Port-
of-Spain, the Compiler, 1973]. [40]p. illus.
ports. scores
*pre-tour*

### 1973 West Indies Young Cricketers' Tour

5460 **National Cricket Association**
–1 West Indies Young Cricketers tour of
■ England, July-August 1974. The Assoc.,
[1974]. 16p. incl. adverts. ports.
*pre-tour. Sponsored by the U.K. Committee*
*of the Sir Frank Worrell Commonwealth*
*Memorial Fund and the National C.A.*

### 1976 Test Tour (C.H. Lloyd)

5460 **Frindall, William H.**
–2 Frindall's score book: England versus
■ West Indies, 1976; edited by Howard
Spencer. Birmingham, Lonsdale P., 1976.
111p. illus. port. facsims. diagr. scores,
stats.

5460 **Irish Cricket Union**
–3 Ireland v. West Indies, Leinster Cricket
■ Club, Rathmines, Dublin, July 14–15,
1976. [Dublin, the Union, 1976]. 92p. incl.
adverts. score, stats.
*pre-match; sponsored by Rothmans of Pall*
*Mall (Ireland) Ltd.*

5460 **Meet** the West Indians. Selwood P.,
–4 [1976]. col. illus.
*opens out into an 85cm. × 56cm. poster of*
*Anderson Roberts*

5460 **West Indies** tour '76 souvenir pro-
–5 gramme: pen pictures, records. *n.p.,*
■ [1976]. [8]p. ports.
*pre-tour*

### 1978 West Indies Under-19 Tour

5460 **National Cricket Association**
–6 Agatha Christie Under-19 Test series.
■ West Indies tour 1978, 12 July to 23
August. N.C.A., [1978]. [12]p. incl. covers. illus.
*pre-tour; sponsored by Agatha Christie Ltd.*

### 1979 West Indies Women's Tour

5460 **Women's Cricket Association**
–7 West Indies Women's cricket tour 1979:
■ souvenir programme; compiled by
Margaret Pascoe. The Assoc., [1979]. 20p.
incl. covers & adverts. illus. ports.
*pre-tour*

5460 Report of The West Indies Women's
–8 cricket tour in England; edited and
compiled by J.G. Hodges; statistics by M.
Collin, S. Hill. The Assoc., [1979]. illus.
team ports. scores, stats.
*post-tour*

# WEST INDIES TOURS TO AUSTRALIA

### 1930–31 Test Tour (G.C. Grant)

5461 **"Old Colour"**, *pseud., editor*
■ The West Indies in Australia: the 1930–31
cricket tour; edited by Old Colour with
the collaboration of The Judge. Port-of-
Spain (Trinidad), *printed by* The Trinidad
Publishing Co., [1931]. 140p. incl. adverts. ports. scores, stats.
*post-tour*

5462 **Panama Tribune**
■ Cricket number, 23rd October 1930. Vol.
VI, no. 23. Panama, Panama Tribune.
24p. incl. adverts. illus. ports.
*to commemorate the visit of the West Indies
team on their way to tour Australia 1930/31*

5463 **West Indies** cricket team: Australian tour
1930–31. Shaw, Savill & Albion, 1930.
10p.
*pre-tour*

### 1951–52 Test Tour (J.D.C. Goddard)

5464 **Australian Broadcasting Commission**
A.B.C. cricket book: West Indies tour
1951–1952. Sydney, the Commission,
1951. 65p. illus.
*pre-tour*

5465 **Dale, Harold**
■ Cricket crusaders. T. Werner Laurie,
1952. 239p. illus. stats. scores
——*another ed.* Sportsman's Book Club,
1953

5466 **Miller, Keith [Ross],** *and* **Whitington,**
■ **Richard Smallpeice**
Straight hit. Latimer House, 1952. 256p.
illus. port. scores

5467 **Moyes, Alban George ("Johnnie")**
■ With the West Indies in Australia,
1951–52: a critical account of the tour.
London, Harrap; Sydney, Angus and
Robertson, 1952. xi,180p. illus. port.
scores, stats.

5468 **New South Wales Cricket Association**
■ Australian tour of the West Indies team,
1951–52; edited by E.W. Murphy. Sydney, Dymock's Book Arcade, [1951]. 96p.
incl. adverts. ports. stats.
*pre-tour*

5468 **Queensland Cricket Association**
–1 West Indies v. Queensland. Brisbane
Cricket Ground, 3–7 November 1951:
[souvenir programme]. Brisbane, the
Assoc., [1951]. 18p. incl. adverts. ports.
stats.

5468 First Test match, 1951–52, West Indies
–2 second Australian cricket tour. Brisbane
Cricket Ground, November 9–14, 1951:
souvenir programme. Brisbane, the
Assoc., [1951]. 18p. incl. adverts. ports.
stats.

5469 **Rivett, Rohan Deakin,** *compiler*
■ Kings of cricket: Australia or West Indies?
a complete guide for 1951–52 Test series.
Melbourne, Sun News-Pictorial, [1951].
52p. illus. ports. scores, stats.
*pre-tour*

5469 **West Indies** Tests pictorial: souvenir pro-
–1 gramme 1951. Adelaide, *printed by* Sun-
■ rise P., [1951]. 24p. incl. adverts. illus.
ports. diagr. plan on back cover
*pre-tour*

5469 **Williams, Leroy ("Fathead")** *compiler*
–2 Operation Antipodes: a survey of the
West Indian tour of Australia and New
Zealand 1951–52. Port-of-Spain, [the
Compiler], 1952. 36p. incl. adverts. ports.
stats.
*post-tour*

### 1960–61 Test Tour (F.M. Worrell)

5470 **Australian Broadcasting Commission**
■ The A.B.C. cricket book: West Indies tour
1960–61. Sydney, the Commission,
[1960]. 64p. illus. ports. diagr. stats.
*pre-tour*

5470 Alan McGilvray recalls the tied Test
–1 (Australia v. West Indies Test match,
■ Brisbane, December 1960); edited by Mike

Kerr. Sydney, the Commission, 1976. 32p. illus. ports. scores

**5471 Benaud, Richie**
■ A tale of two Tests: with some thoughts on captaincy. Hodder & Stoughton, 1962. 125p. illus. ports.
  *Australia v. West Indies, Brisbane, 1960– 61; England v. Australia, Manchester, 1961*

**5472 Bunbury and District Cricket**
■ **Association**
West Indies touring XI versus W. Australian Country XI, Recreation Ground, Bunbury, October 25th and 26th, 1960. Bunbury, [1960]. 16p. incl. adverts. ports. score, stats.
  *pre-match*

**5473 Fingleton, Jack, i.e. John Henry Webb**
■ **Fingleton**
The greatest Test of all. Collins, 1961. 103,[24]p. illus. port. scores, stats.
  *at Brisbane, 9–14 Dec., 1960*

**5474 McGilvray, Alan**
Notes on the Test match, Australia v. West Indies; first Test, Brisbane, 1960–61. [Sydney, Australian Broadcasting Commission, 1970?]

**5474 McWhirter, Ross, and Norris**
**–1** Great moments in sport: a pictorial record of events that made headlines. Liverpool, Vernon Pools, 1962. 128p. illus. pbk.
  *cricket pp. 12–13 "The fantastic Test at Brisbane" by E.M. Wellings*

**5475 Moyes, Alban George ("Johnnie")**
■ With the West Indies in Australia, 1960–61: a critical story of the tour. Heinemann, 1961. xi,196p. illus. ports. scores, stats.

**5476 New South Wales Cricket Association**
■ West Indies tour of Australia 1960–61; edited, compiled and distributed by V.C. Davis & Co. Sydney, the Assoc., [1960]. 80p. incl. adverts. ports. stats.
  *pre-tour*

**5477 Queensland Country XI v. West Indies,**
■ cricket match, Albert Park, Gympie, December 16 & 17, 1960: souvenir programme. Gympie, Reid Printery with the authority of the Gympie C.A., [1960]. 24p. incl. adverts. illus. ports.

**5478 Roberts, L.D., ["Strebor"]**
■ Cricket's brightest summer. Kingston (Jamaica), the Author; London, Bailey Bros. & Swinfen, 1961. [xviii],158p. illus. ports. scores, stats.

**5479 Roberts, Ronald Arthur**
■ The fight for the Ashes, 1961; with an account of the 1960–61 Australia–West Indies Tests. London, Harrap, 1961; Sydney, Australasian Publ. Co., [1962]. 287p. illus. scores, stats.

**5479 Sport's** greatest headlines. Sydney,
**–1** Project Publishing, 1974. illus.
  *includes the Australia v. West Indies tied Test at Brisbane, 1960–61 series*

## 1968–69 Test Tour (G.S. Sobers)

**5480 Australian Broadcasting Commission**
■ The A.B.C. cricket book: West Indies tour of Australia 1968–69; edited by Alan McGilvray. Sydney, the Commission, [1968]. 80p. illus. ports. diagr. scores, stats.
  *pre-tour*

**5481 Blofeld, Henry**
■ Cricket in three moods: eighteen months of Test cricket and the ways of life behind it. Hodder & Stoughton, 1970. 192p. illus. scores on endpapers
  *also contains accounts of M.C.C. tour of West Indies, 1967/68 and West Indies tour of England, 1969*

**5482 Davidson, Alan Keith, editor**
■ Calypso cricket: the story of the West Indies on tour in Australia 1968–69. Rose Bay, M.G.A. Publications, [1968]. 48p. incl. adverts. ports. map, score, stats.
  *published during tour*

**5483 Henderson, L.J., compiler**
The West Indies in Australia, 1968–69: statistics. [Bondi Junction (N.S.W.), the Compiler, 1969?]. 8p. *typescript*

**5484 New South Wales Cricket Association**
■ West Indies tour of Australia 1968–69; edited, compiled & distributed by Chris Ankin, Industrial Marketing and Printing Service. Sydney, the Association, [1968]. 48p. incl. adverts. ports. stats.
  *pre-tour*

**5484 Queensland Cricket Association**
**–1** West Indies v. Queensland, Brisbane Cricket Ground, November 29 – December 4, 1968: [souvenir programme]. Brisbane, the Assoc., [1968]. 16p. incl. adverts. illus. ports. stats.

**5484** First Test, Brisbane Cricket Ground, West
**–2** Indies v. Australia, December 6–11, 1968: souvenir programme. Brisbane, the Assoc., [1968]. 16p. incl. adverts. illus. ports. stats.

**5485  Tresidder, Phil**
■   Captains on a see-saw: the West Indies tour of Australia, 1968–69. Souvenir P., 1969. 158p. illus. ports. scores, stats.

**5486  West Indies Cricket Board of Control**
Fixture list: the West Indies cricket team in Australia and New Zealand 1968–9. The Board, [1968]

**5486**   **West Indies** versus a N.S.W. Country XI
**–1**   at Kitchener Oval, Gunnedah, 11 Feb. 1969: souvenir programme. Gunnedah C.A., [1969]. 40p. incl. adverts. 1 illus. ports. stats.

**5487   Whitington, Richard Smallpeice,** *and*
■   **Miller, Keith [Ross]**
Fours galore: the West Indians and their tour of Australia, 1968–69. Sydney, Cassell Australia, 1969. viii,244p. illus. scores, stats.

### 1975–76 Test Tour (C.H. Lloyd)

**5487   Australian Broadcasting Commission**
**–1**   A.B.C. cricket book. West Indies tour of
■   Australia 1975–76; edited by Alan McGilvray. Sydney, the Commission, 1975. 72p. illus. (some col.) ports. diagrs. stats.
   *pre-tour*

**5487   Australian Capital Territory Cricket**
**–2   Association**
■   West Indies vs. A.C.T. & Southern N.S.W. XI, 13–14 Jan. 1975 [i.e. 1976], Manuka Oval: [souvenir programme] edited by Julian Oakley. Canberra, Australian Cricket Society (Canberra Branch) for the Assoc., [1976]. 24p. incl. covers & adverts. illus. ports.

**5487   Australian Cricket**
**–3**   West Indies cricket tour guide, 1975–76.
■   [Sydney, Modern Magazines (Holdings), Ltd., 1975]. 68p. incl. covers & adverts. illus. ports. scores, stats.
   *pre-tour*

**5487   Australian Cricket Board**
**–4**   Test souvenir: official publication of the
■   Australian Cricket Board to commemorate the 1975–76 West Indies tour of Australia. Melbourne, the Board, [1975]. 48p. incl. adverts. illus. ports. stats.
   *pre-tour; with colour poster insert*

**5487   Cricketer**
**–5**   Chappell's champions: West Indies in
■   Australia, 1975–76, a Cricketer special edited by Eric Beecher. Melbourne, Newspress Pty. Ltd., [1976]. 84p. incl. covers & adverts. illus. ports. scores, stats.
   *post-tour*

**5487   Frindall, William H.**
**–6**   Frindall's score book: Australia versus
■   West Indies 1975/76; edited by Howard Spencer. Brentford, Lonsdale P., 1976. 120p. illus. score, stats.
   *photographer: Patrick Eagar. The statistics for the first four matches were compiled by Geoffrey Saulez*

**5487   Newcastle    and    District    Cricket**
**–7   Association**
■   Newcastle cricket program. West Indies vs. Northern N.S.W., 10–11 January 1976. Newcastle (N.S.W.), The Assoc., [1976]. [12]p. incl. adverts. ports.
   *match sponsored by N.B.N. TV Newcastle*

**5487   Papua New Guinea Cricket Board of**
**–8   Control**
Papua New Guinea v. West Indies, world champions at Lae, University Ground, 22 October 1975; Port Moresby, Sir Hubert Murray Stadium, 23 October 1975: souvenir programme. [The Board, 1975]. 24p. incl. adverts. illus. ports. stats.
   *pre-visit*

**5487   Phillipson, Neill,** *editor*
**–9**   Cricket Caribbean: West Indies v. Aus-
■   tralia 1975–76. Hawthorn (Vic.), The Craftsman Press Pty. Ltd., [1975]. 52p. illus. (1 col.), ports. stats.

**5487   Queensland Cricket Association**
**–10**   Gabba cricket. Queensland vs. West
■   Indies, Gabba Cricket Ground, Nov. 21-Nov. 24, 1975: [souvenir programme]. Brisbane, the Assoc., [1975]. 40p. incl. adverts. illus. ports. score, stats.

**5487   Tyson, Frank**
**–11**   The hapless hookers. Toorak (Vic.),
■   Sparke, 1976. iv,316p. illus. scores, stats.

### 1979–80 Test Tour (C.H. Lloyd)

**5487   Australian Broadcasting Commission**
**–12**   A.B.C. cricket book – England, West
■   Indies in Australia, 1979–80; edited by Alan McGilvray. Sydney, the Commission, 1979. 96p. illus. (some col.), ports. diagrs. stats.
   *pre-tours*

**5487   Benson and Hedges Co.**
**–13**   Test programme 1979–80: Australia v.
■   West Indies – Australia v. England. Sheffield Shield. Sydney, Playbill (Australia), 1979. 52p. incl. covers & adverts. illus. & ports. (some col.)
   *pre-tours*

**5487   Cricketer**
**–14**   Cricketer's cricket guide 1979–80; edited
■   by Ken Piesse. Melbourne, Newspress

Pty. Ltd., [1979]. 76p. incl. covers & adverts. illus. ports. stats.
*pre-tour*

**5487** **Toowoomba** Cricket Association hosting
**–15** West Indies v. Q'ld Country, 19th
■ December 1979, Gold Park, Toowoomba: souvenir programme. [Toowoomba, the Assoc., 1979]. [12]p. incl. covers & adverts. ports. diagr. score

# WEST INDIES TOURS TO NEW ZEALAND

## 1930–31 Tour (G.C. Grant)

**5488** **Wellington Cricket Association**
West Indies versus Wellington: official programme. Wellington, the Assoc., 1930. 12p. ports.

## 1951–52 Test Tour (J.D.C. Goddard)

**5489** **Otago Cricket Association**
■ West Indies versus Otago, Feb. 2, 4 & 5, 1952 , Carisbrook, Dunedin: official souvenir programme and score sheet. Dunedin, the Assoc., [1952]. 16p. illus.

## 1955–56 Test Tour (D. Atkinson)

**5490** **Canterbury Cricket Association**
■ West Indies v. Canterbury [at] Lancaster Park: official programme. Christchurch, the Assoc., [1956]. 48p. incl. adverts. ports.

**5491** West Indies v. New Zealand, Lancaster
■ Park, 18, 20, 21, 22 February, 1956: souvenir programme. Christchurch, the Assoc., [1956]. 52p. incl. adverts. ports. diagr. stats.

**5492** **Wellington Cricket Association**
■ West Indies versus New Zealand third Test at the Basin Reserve, Wellington, 3, 5, 6 and 7 March, 1956: official programme. Wellington, the Assoc., 1956. 38p. ports. diagr. stats.

**5493** **West** Indies v. New Zealand: souvenir programme. Christchurch, Bullivant, 1956. 52p. illus.

## 1968–69 Test Tour (G.S. Sobers)

**5494** **Auckland Cricket Association**
West Indies v. New Zealand, first Test, Eden Park, February 27, 28, March 1, 3, 1969: souvenir programme. Auckland, the Assoc., [1969].

**5495** International cricket. Sir Frank Worrell
■ Memorial Match: His Excellency The Governor-General's Eleven v. West Indies touring team, Eden Park, Auckland, March 21, 22, 23, 1969. Auckland, the Assoc., [1969]. 28p. incl. adverts. illus. ports. map, plan, stats.

**5496** **Brittenden, Richard Trevor**
■ Scoreboard '69: an account of the West Indian cricket tour of New Zealand, and the New Zealand tour of Britain, India, and Pakistan. Wellington, Reed, 1970. 236p. illus. scores, stats.

**5497** **Wellington Cricket Association**
■ West Indies v. New Zealand, Basin Reserve, March 7–11, 1969. Wellington, the Assoc., [1969]. 28p. incl. adverts. 1 illus. ports. diagr. stats.

# WEST INDIES TOURS OF INDIA

**5497** **Chaturvedi, Ravi**
**–1** The complete book of West Indies–India
■ Test cricket. New Delhi, Orient Paperbacks, [1977?]. 200p. scores, stats.
*from 1948–49 to 1976*

**5497** **Jones, Brunell R.**
**–2** Gone with the Indians again! West Indies
■ v. India 1948–1976. Champs Fleur, Curepe P.O. (Trinidad), Sports News Service, 1976. 108p. incl. adverts. illus. ports. scores, stats.
*history of W.I. – India Test cricket 1948–1975, including a Who's Who of Indian players by Anandji Dossa and a report of the W.I. tour of India 1974–75*

**5497** **Sanyal, Saradindu**
**–3** India – West Indies Test cricket 1948–1971. Delhi, Macmillan, 1974. vii,194p. illus. scores, stats.

**5497** **Sarbadhikary, Berry,** *editor*
**–4** India v. West Indies Tests 1948–49 to
■ 1974–75: an eye-witness account of all 28 Tests up to 1971, with prospects of 1974–75 series. Bombay, V.R. Publications, [1974]. 72p. incl. adverts. illus. ports. stats.

## 1948–49 Test Tour (J.D.C. Goddard)

**5498** **Board of Control for Cricket in India**
■ Programme of the West Indies cricket team tour 1948–49. [New Delhi], the Board, [1948]. [8]p.
*cover-title: "West Indies v. India"; pre-tour*

**5499** **Haridass, C.K.**
West Indies cricket team visit to Madras,

January 1949: souvenir. Madras, Haridass, [1949]. 44p. ports. stats.
*pre-visit*

5500 **Sport & Pastime**
■ West Indies cricketers tour of India 1948–1949: a souvenir. Madras, Sport & Pastime, [1948]. 64p. incl. adverts. ports. map
*pre-tour*

## 1958–59 Test Tour (F.C.M. Alexander)

5501 **Board of Control for Cricket in India**
■ Official souvenir of West Indies cricket tour of India 1958–59. [New Delhi], the Board, [1958]. [68]p. incl. adverts. illus. ports. stats.
*pre-tour*

5502 **Delhi and District Cricket Association**
■ 5th Test match, Feb. 6, 7, 8, 10, 11, 1959, India vs. West Indies; official souvenir, edited by Om Narain, New Delhi, Chowdhri for the Assoc., [1959]. [28]p. incl. adverts. ports.
*pre-tour*

5503 **Hyderabad Cricket Association**
Hyderabad v. West Indies silver jubilee match Jan. 30, 31, Feb 1, 1959: official souvenir. Hyderabad, the Assoc., [1959]. 68p. ports. stats.
*silver jubilee of Sri E.B. Aibura's participation in the Ranji Trophy; pre-match*

5504 **Sport & Pastime**
Cricketers from the West Indies: tour of India 1958–59. Madras, Sport & Pastime, 1958. 32p. incl. adverts. illus. ports.
*pre-tour*

5505 **West Indies XI** vs. India XI, November
■ 28, 29, 30, December 2, 3, Brabourne Stadium. Bombay, *printed by* Fort Office Printing P., [1958]. [28]p. incl. adverts. ports.

## 1966–67 Test Tour (G.S. Sobers)

5506 **Bhatia, C.P.**
■ Meet the West Indies and India 1966–67. Bombay, Sevak P., [1966]. [60]p. ports. stats.
*pre-tour*

5507 **Bhupathy, D.R.,** *compiler*
West Indies v. India: Test cricket souvenir 1967. Madras, Bhupathy, [1966]. 68p. ports. stats.
*pre-tour*

5508 **Board of Control for Cricket in India**
■ Official souvenir of the West Indies

cricket tour of India 1966–67. The Board, [1966], [128]p. incl. adverts. ports.
*pre-tour*

5509 **Cricketers** from West Indies: souvenir.
■ New Delhi, R. Alung, [1966]. [56]p. including adverts. illus. ports. scores, stats.
*pre-tour*

5510 **Delhi and Districts Cricket Association**
■ West Indies v. Prime Minister's XI Dec. 20–23, 1966; official souvenir; edited by Ron Hendricks & K.R. Wadhwaney. New Delhi, the Assoc., [1966]. 90p. incl. adverts. illus. ports. stats.

5511 **Haridass, C.K.**
West Indies in India, 1966–67. Madras, Haridass, [1966]. 124p. incl. adverts. ports. stats.
*pre-tour*

5512 **Hyderabad Cricket Association**
■ West Indies vs. Indian Universities on 3, 4, and 5 December 1966 at Lal Bahadur Stadium. Hyderabad, the Assoc., [1966]. 48p. ports.

5513 **Madras Cricket Association**
The visit to Madras of the West Indies cricket team and the Indian Test team, January, 1967: programme. Madras, the Assoc., [1967].

5514 **Saraiya, Suresh,** *and* **Nene, Jayant,** *editors*
■ India vs. West Indies 1966–67: souvenir. Bombay, Trilochan Printing P., [1966]. 44p. illus. ports. stats.
*pre-tour*

5515 **Sport and Pastime**
■ West Indies tour of India 1966–67. Madras, Sport & Pastime, [1966]. 58p. incl. adverts. illus. ports. stats.

5516 **Vidarbha Cricket Association**
■ Hazare benefit match: West Indies v/s Board President's XI, 27, 28, 29 January, 1967. Nagpur, the Assoc., [1967]. 124p. incl. adverts. illus. ports. stats.

## 1974–75 Test Tour (C.H. Lloyd)

5516 **Board of Control for Cricket in India**
–1 Official souvenir of West Indies cricket
■ tour of India 1974–75. The Board, [1974]. [88]p. incl. adverts. ports. stats.
*pre-tour*

5516 **Haridass, C.K.,** *compiler*
–2 West Indies in India 1974–75. Madras,
■ Haridass, [1974]. 178p. incl. adverts. illus. ports. diagr. stats.
*pre-tour*

5516 **Himmat.** Bombay. *weekly.* illus. ports.
–3    Vol. 11, no.13; Jan. 1975: "Cricket
      special". 38p.
      *on the Bombay Test*

5516 **The Hindu**
–4   West Indies tour of India 1974–75: The
■    Hindu souvenir. Madras, the Hindu,
     [1974]. 100p. incl. covers & adverts. illus.
     ports. stats.
     *pre-tour*

5516 **Jones, Brunell R.**
–5   Gone with the Indians again! West Indies
■    v. India 1948–1976. Champs Fleur,
     Curepe P.O.(Trinidad), Sports News
     Service, 1976. 108p. incl. adverts. illus.
     ports. scores, stats.
     *history of W.I. – Indian Test cricket
     1948–1975, including a Who's Who of Indian
     players by Anandji Dossa, and a report of the
     W.I. tour of India 1974–75*

5515 **Rajan, Sunder**
–6   India vs. West Indies 1974–1975; statistics
■    by B.N. Nagaraja Rao. Bombay, Jaico,
     1975. [vii],205p. illus. scores, stats.
     *post-tour*

5516 **Salim, M.,** *editor*
–7   West Indies in India 1974–75. Bombay, M.
■    Salim, [1974]. [80]p. incl. adverts. ports.
     diagr. map, stats.
     *cover-title*: India v/s West Indies 1974–75
     *pre-tour*

5516 **Saraiya, Suresh,** *editor*
–8   West Indies in India 1974–75. Bombay,
■    Neeta Publications, [1974]. [86]p. incl.
     adverts. illus. ports. stats.
     *pre-tour*

5516 **Sarbadhikary, Berry,** *editor*
–9   India v. West Indies Tests 1948–49 to
■    1974–75: an eye-witness account of all 28
     Tests up to 1971, with prospects of
     1974–75 series. Bombay, V.R. Publica-
     tions, [1974]. 72p. incl. adverts. illus.
     ports. stats.

5516 **Somaiya, A.V.,** *and* **Bhesania, P.S.**
–10  1974–75 India v. West Indies. Bombay,
■    Trupti Publications, [1974]. 110p. incl.
     adverts. illus. ports. map
     *pre-tour*

5516 **Umrigar, Pahlan Ratanji,** *and* **Mantri,**
–11  **Madhav**
     India vs. West Indies 1974–75. Bombay,
     M. Salim, [1975]. [80]p. illus.
     *pre-tour*

### 1978–79 Test Tour (A.I. Kallicharran)

5516 **Haridass, C.K.,** *editor*
–12  West Indies in India 1978–79. Madras,
■    C.K. Haridass & Sons, [1979]. 148p. incl.
     adverts. illus. ports. stats.
     *pre-tour*

5516 **The Hindu**
–13  West Indies tour of India 1978–79:
■    souvenir. [Madras], The Hindu, [1978].
     100p. incl. adverts. & covers. illus. ports.
     *pre-tour*

5516 **Sharma, Ashok,** *editor*
–14  India-West Indies cricket special 1978–79.
■    New Delhi, 'The Young Sportswriters
     Co.', [1978]. 80p. incl. adverts. illus.
     ports. maps, stats.
     *pre-tour*

# WEST INDIES TOURS TO PAKISTAN

### 1958–59 Test Tour (F.C.M. Alexander)

5517 **Butt, Qamaruddin**
■    Cricket ups and downs: (containing a
     complete eye-witness account of West
     Indies tour of Pakistan in 1959). Karachi,
     Progressive Printers, 1960. xvii,132p.
     illus. ports. scores, stats.

### 1974–75 Test Tour (C.H. Lloyd)

5517 **Karachi Cricket Association**
–1   Pakistan v. West Indies, second Test
■    match, 1,2,3,5 and 6 March, 1975; edited
     by S. Sirajul Islam Bukhari. Karachi, the
     Assoc. Test Match Organising Cttee.,
     [1975]. [108]p. incl. adverts. ports. diagrs.
     scores, stats.

5517 **Punjab Cricket Association**
–2   Souvenir first Test Pakistan v. West In-
■    dies, Feb. 15–20, 1975. Lahore, the
     Assoc., [1975]. [116]p. incl. adverts.
     ports. stats.

# WEST INDIES TOURS TO SRI LANKA

### 1948–49 Tour (J.D.C. Goddard)

5518 **Board of Control for Cricket in Ceylon**
■    A souvenir of the West Indies tour in
     Ceylon Feb., 1949: compiled by M.K.M.
     Ismail & F. Ondatye. Colombo, the
     Board, [1949]. 74p. incl. adverts. ports.
     stats.
     *pre-tour*

### 1966–67 Tour (G.S. Sobers)

5519 **Board of Control for Cricket in Ceylon**
■ Bristol official souvenir: West Indies tour 1967; edited by R.B. Wijesinha. Colombo, Ceylon Tobacco Co. Ltd., [1967]. [48]p. incl. adverts. ports. stats.

### 1974–75 Tour (C.H. Lloyd)

5519 **Board of Control for Cricket in Sri Lanka**
–1 West Indies cricket tour to Sri Lanka 1st
■ to 12th Feb. 75: official souvenir; edited by S.S. Perera and Harold de Andrado. [Colombo, the Board, 1975]. [40]p. incl. adverts. ports. map, stats.
*pre-tour*

5519 West Indies tour of Sri Lanka: playing
–2 conditions 1975. Colombo, the Board, 1975

5519 **Ceylon Tobacco Co. Ltd.**
–3 Souvenir of West Indies cricket tour of Sri
■ Lanka, 1975. [Colombo, the Co., 1975]. 4p. folded card

### 1978–79 Tour (A.I. Kallicharran)

5519 **Board of Control for Cricket in Sri Lanka**
–4 West Indies tour of Sri Lanka 14–27 February 1979: official tour programme. Colombo, the Board, [1979]. [4]p. fold

5519 West Indies tour of Sri Lanka 1979:
–5 playing conditions. Colombo, the Board,
■ [1979]. 8p.

5519 West Indies tour of Sri Lanka 13 Feb. to
–6 27 Feb. 1979: official souvenir; edited by
■ S.S. Perera and Upali Mahanama. [Colombo, the Board, 1979]. [52]p. incl. adverts. illus. ports. maps, stats.

5519 **Galle Cricket Association**
–7 West Indies vs. Sri Lanka Board Presid-
■ ent's XI at Galle Esplanade on 20–2–79: [programme]; edited by Steven de Silva and Feisal Junaid. Galle, the Assoc., [1979]. [48]p. incl. adverts. ports.

5519 **Moratuwa Sports Club**
–8 Board President's XI v. West Indies, 15th
■ February 1979, Moratuwa Stadium: [sou-

venir programme]. Moratuwa, [the Club, 1979]. [30]p. ports.
*includes a 9-page "Historical sketch of cricket in Moratuwa 1865–1979"*

# WEST INDIES TOURS TO CANADA, UNITED STATES AND BERMUDA

## 1886 Tour of West Indian Gentlemen

5520 **[Wyatt, Charles Guy Austin,** *and* **Fyfe,**
■ **Lawrence R.]**
The tour of the West Indian cricketers, August & September, 1886, by One of them. Demerara, "Argosy" P., 1887. [i],92p. mounted team port. scores stats.
*post-tour*

## 1930 Tour

5521 **Caribbean Intercolonial Sporting Association**
Second tour of West Indies cricket team to America, 1930: a souvenir. New York, Hunt Print Co., 1930. illus. ports.

5522 **Souvenir** programme: welcome dance for the second visiting West Indian cricket team. New York, Hunt Printing Co., 1930. 32p. illus.

## B.R. Jones' Team

5522 **Jones, Brunell R.**
–1 Return to Bermuda: a souvenir booklet of the second visit to Bermuda by the B.R. Jones (West Indian) touring team. Port of Spain, the Author. 24p.

# OTHER WEST INDIES TOURS

## 1975–76 Visit (C.H. Lloyd)

5522 **Papua New Guinea Cricket Board of**
–2 **Control**
Papua New Guinea v. West Indies, world champions at Lae, University Ground, 22 October 1975; Port Moresby, Sir Hubert Murray Stadium, 23 October 1975: souvenir programme. [The Board, 1975]. 24p. incl. adverts. illus. ports. stats.

New Zealand v. England. The New Zealand cricket team 1975, captain G. M. Turner
*photo: Patrick Eagar*

# NEW ZEALAND

5522 **Brittenden, Richard Trevor**
-3 The finest years: twenty years of New
■ Zealand cricket. Wellington, Reed, 1977.
ix,190p. illus. ports. scores
*N.Z. cricket since 1956*

5523 **Caple, Samuel Canynge**
■ The All Blacks at cricket: the story of New
Zealand cricket, 1860–1958. Worcester,
Littlebury, 1958. 260p. illus. ports. scores,
stats.

5523 **Carman, Arthur H.,** *editor & compiler*
-1 New Zealand international cricket 1894–
■ 1974. Wellington, Reed, [1975]. 317p. ports.
facsims. scores, stats.
*gives full scores of 192 international
matches including Tests*

## NEW ZEALAND TOURS TO ENGLAND

### 1927 Tour (T.C. Lowry)

5524 **Leicestershire County Cricket Club**
Souvenir: Leicestershire v. New Zealand.
Leicester, the Club, 1927. 16p. ports.

5525 **N.Z. Cricket Ltd.**
■ Souvenir: summary of tour. N.Z. Cricket
Ltd., [1927]. 4p. fold, stats.
*list of tour results*

5525 **Souvenir** of the first New Zealand cricket
-1 team to visit Great Britain 1927. [*Privately
printed*, 1927]. 72p. ports. scores, stats.
*A copy was presented to each member of the
1927 touring team*

### 1931 Test Tour (T.C. Lowry)

5526 **Hintz, Orton Sutherland**
■ The New Zealanders in England, 1931.
Dent, 1931. xi,140p. illus. ports. scores,
stats.

5527 **New Zealand** cricket team in England,
1931. New Zealand Cricket Ltd., [1931].
[4]p. fold. team ports.
*pre-tour*

5528 **N.Z.** v. England 1931: fixtures, photog-
■ raphs and records of players. Thomas,
[1931]. 32p. incl. adverts. illus. ports.  ●
*pre-tour*

### 1937 Test Tour (M.L. Page)

5529 **Simpson, A.W.,** *compiler and editor*
■ New Zealand cricket tourists annual 1937.
Folkestone, Cheriton P., [1937]. 32p.
illus. ports.
*pre-tour*

### 1949 Test Tour (W.A. Hadlee)

5530 **Arlott, [Leslie Thomas] John**
■ Gone with the cricketers. Longmans,
Green, 1950. x,160p. illus. ports. scores
*also account of M.C.C. tour of S.A.,
1948–9*

5531 **Day, Cedric,** *and* **Mason, Michael**
■ The story of Test cricket: England v. New
Zealand. Windsor, Day & Mason, [1949].
22p. illus. ports. scores, stats.
*pre-tour*

5531 **Durham** versus New Zealand: photogra-
-1 phic souvenir and fixtures list. Bir-
■ mingham, E. Kavanagh, 1949. [4]p. ports.

5532 **Foster, Denis**
■ Welcome New Zealand! Background
Books, [1949]. 48p. ports.
*pre-tour*

5533 **Mitchell, Alan Williams**
■ Cricket companions. T. Werner Laurie,
1950. 223p. illus. port. scores, stats.

5534 **New Zealand Cricket Council**
English tour 1949: list of fixtures. Christchurch, the Council, 1949. [4]p. fold.

5535 **New Zealand** cricket tour 1949. Grant
■ Hughes. [1949]. [16]p. incl. covers. ports.
*pre-tour*

5536 **Nottinghamshire** versus New Zealand:
■ pictures, fixtures and personalities, 1949.
Birmingham, E. Kavanagh, [1949]. [4]p.
fold, ports.
*pre-match*

**5537  Simpson, A.W.,** *compiler*
■ Cricket 1949: New Zealand tour: a complete cricket handbook. I.M. Young, [1949]. 48p. incl. adverts. illus. ports.
*pre-tour*

**5538  West, Peter**
■ Cricketers from New Zealand 1949. Playfair Books, [1949]. 32p. illus. ports. map, scores, stats.
*pre-tour*

**5539  Wycherley, George Arthur**
■ Halo for Hadlee: a light-hearted history of the 1949 New Zealand cricket team. Dunedin (N.Z.), *printed by* Otago Daily Times, [1949]. 64p. stats.

### 1958 Test Tour (J.R. Reid)

**5540  Arlott, [Leslie Thomas] John**
■ Cricket journal. Heinemann, 1958. 255p. illus. ports. scores

**5541  Ross, Gordon,** *editor*
■ Cricketers from New Zealand: the official souvenir of the tour of England. Playfair Books, [1958]. 24p. illus. ports. stats.
*pre-tour*

**5542  Traill, Sinclair,** *editor*
■ The New Zealand touring team 1958: souvenir handbook. Wrotham, H.C. Dunkley, 1958. 30p. ports. scores, stats.
*pre-tour*

### 1965 Test Tour (J.R. Reid)

**5543  Brittenden, Richard Trevor**
■ Red leather silver fern. Wellington, Reed, 1965. 227p. illus. ports. scores, stats.

**5544  Ross, Gordon,** *editor*
■ The 1965 tourists: the official brochure for the 1965 tours of England. Dickens P., [1965]. [i],32p. illus. ports. stats. (Playfair Publication)
*pre-tour*

**5544  Rothmans**
**–1** Test cricket almanack 1965: England [v.] New Zealand. Rothmans of Pall Mall, [1965]. 56p. illus. ports. stats.
*pre-tour and records of matches England v. New Zealand 1930–1963*

### 1969 Test Tour (G.T. Dowling)

**5545  Brittenden, Richard Trevor**
■ Scoreboard '69: an account of the West Indian cricket tour of New Zealand, and the New Zealand tour of Britain, India, and Pakistan. Wellington, Reed, 1970. 236p. illus. scores, stats.

**5546  Rothmans**
■ Cricket almanack 1969: England v. West Indies, England v. New Zealand. Rothmans of Pall Mall, [1969]. 32p. illus. ports. diagrs. stats.
*pre-tour*

**5547  New Zealand** tour programme, fixtures, pictures. D. Walker, [1969]. [8]p. ports. stats.
*pre-tour*

### 1973 Test Tour (B.E. Congdon)

**5547  Air New Zealand**
**–1** New Zealand cricket tour of the British Isles 1973: itinerary. Air New Zealand, [1973]. [4]p. folded card

**5548  England** v. New Zealand, third Test match, Headingley, Thursday, 5th July 1973: souvenir programme. Starkey, [8]p. 1 illus. ports. stats.

### 1978 Test Tour (M.G. Burgess)

**5548  New Zealand Cricketers Partnership**
**–1** New Zealand cricket team tour of England 1978: official brochure; editors Christopher Bazalgette, Rodney Crang, David Broster. The Partnership, 1978. 48p. incl. adverts. illus. ports. stats.
*pre-tour*

**5548  White, Crawford**
**–2** Cornhill Insurance Test series 1978. England v. Pakistan; England v. New Zealand: a preview of the 1978 Test matches. Cornhill Insurance Group, [1978]. [16]p. col. illus. & ports.

**5548  Prudential Trophy '78:** England v. Pakistan, May 24 and 26; England v. New Zealand July 15 & 17. Prudential Assurance Co., [1978]. [8]p. fold, illus. stats.
*pre-matches*

## NEW ZEALAND TOURS TO AUSTRALIA

### 1967–68 Tour (B.W. Sinclair)

**5548  Queensland Cricket Association**
**–4** New Zealand versus Queensland, Brisbane Cricket Ground, December 1–4: souvenir programme. Brisbane, the Assoc., [1967]. 24p. incl. adverts. ports. stats.

### 1973–74 Test Tour (B.E. Congdon)

**5548  Beecher, Eric,** *editor*
**–5** Cricket '73–'74, the Kookaburra guide.

Melbourne, Newspress Pty. Ltd., [1973]. 66p. incl. adverts. illus. ports. stats.
*includes pre-view of New Zealand tour of Australia*

**5548** **Queensland Cricket Association**
**–6** Cricket news. International cricket match
■ 1973–74. Queensland v. New Zealand, Brisbane Cricket Ground, December 14, 15, 16 and 17: [souvenir programme]. Brisbane, the Assoc., [1973]. 32p. incl. adverts. scores, stats.

# NEW ZEALAND TOURS TO SOUTH AFRICA

## 1953–54 Test Tour (G.O. Rabone)

**5549** **Brittenden, Richard Trevor**
■ Silver fern on the veld: New Zealand cricketers in South Africa 1953–54. Wellington, N.Z., Reed; Cape Town, Timmins, 1954. x,223p. illus. port. diagrs. scores, stats.

**5550** **Chettle, Geoffrey A.**, *editor and compiler*
■ New Zealand tour of South Africa 1953/54; official souvenir brochure. Durban, [the Editor, 1953]. 48p. ports. stats.
*pre-tour*

**5550** **Nelson, T.D.**, *compiler*
**–1** Official souvenir New Zealand South African tour 1953–4. Johannesburg, *printed by* Electric Printing Works, [1953?]. [24]p. ports.
*pre-tour*

## 1961–62 Test Tour (J.R. Reid)

**5550** **Board of Control of the Rhodesian**
**–2** **Cricket Union**
■ New Zealand cricketers Rhodesian tour 1961: souvenir brochure. [Salisbury], the Board, [1961]. 28p. incl. adverts. ports. stats.
*pre-tour*

**5551** **Chettle, Geoffrey A.**, *editor*
■ New Zealand tour 1961–1962: [a series of brochures]. Durban, [the Editor, 1961–62]. [20]p. incl. adverts. ports. stats.
*v. Transvaal at Johannesburg; v. Transvaal Districts XI at Krugersdorp*
*v. Natal Districts XI at Umzinto; v. Natal at Durban*
*v. Griqualand West at Kimberley; v. S.A. Country Districts XI at Kimberley; v. Orange Free State at Bloemfontein*
*v. Western Province at Newlands; v. Country Districts XI at Oudtshoorn*
*v. Eastern Province at Port Elizabeth*
*v. Universities XI at Pretoria; v. N.E. Transvaal at Benoni*

*v. S.A. Colts XI at East London; v. Border at East London*

**5552** New Zealand tour 1961–62: New Zealand
■ v. South Africa—1st Test, Kingsmead, Durban, December 8, 9, 11 & 12: official souvenir brochure. Durban, [the Editor, 1961]. [28]p. incl. adverts. ports. stats.

**5553** ——: New Zealand v. South Africa,
■ second Test, Wanderers, Johannesburg, December 26, 27, 28, 29. Durban, [the Editor, 1961]. [20]p. incl. adverts. ports. stats.

**5554** ——: New Zealand vs. South Africa, third
■ Test, Newlands, Cape Town, January 1, 2, 3 and 4: official souvenir brochure. [Durban, the Editor, 1961]. ports. stats.
*pre-Test*

**5555** [see no. 5550–2]

**5556** **Reid, John Richard**
■ Sword of willow; including an account of the 1961–62 New Zealand cricket tour of South Africa. Wellington (N.Z.), Reed, 1962; London, Jenkins, 1963. 265p. illus. ports. diagrs. stats. scores

**5556** **South African Railways**
**–1** New Zealand cricket team tour of
■ Southern Africa 1961–62: souvenir itinerary. Johannesburg, S.A. Rlys., [1961]. [16]p. illus.

**5557** **Thompson, Richard**
■ Race and sport. O.U.P. (under the auspices of the Institute of Race Relations), 1964. [vii],73p.
*ch. v. 'Colour bar cricket' reviews the New Zealand tour of South Africa 1961–62*

**5558** **Whitington, Richard Smallpeice**
■ John Reid's Kiwis: New Zealand cricketers in South Africa 1961–62; with a tour summary by Gordon Leggat. Christchurch (N.Z.), etc., Whitcombe & Tombs, 1962. 216p. illus. ports. scores, stats.

# NEW ZEALAND TOURS TO WEST INDIES

## 1971–72 Test Tour (G.T. Dowling)

**5559** **Cameron, Don J.**
■ Caribbean crusade: the New Zealand cricketers in the West Indies 1972. Auckland, Hodder & Stoughton, 1972. viii, 166p. illus. scores, stats.
——*another ed.* Newton Abbot, Readers Union, 1974

**5560** First tour of the West Indies by a New
■ Zealand cricket team 1972: edited by W.
Annamunthodo, articles and statistics by
Michael Gibbes. Pleasantville, San Fernando, Unique Services, [1972]. [40]p.
incl. adverts. illus. ports. scores. stats.
——Barbados ed. [40]p. incl. adverts.
——Windward Islands ed. Unique Services for the St. Vincent C.A. [64]p. incl.
adverts.
*cover titles: Kiwis cricket tour 1972*
*all editions exhibit some variations in text,*
*illus. etc.*

**5561** Guyana Cricket Board of Control
■ Tour '72 from Wellington to Georgetown;
edited by Charles J. Chichester. Georgetown, the Board, [1972]. 60p. incl. adverts. illus. ports. stats.
*pre-visit; sponsored by the Demarara Tob-*
*acco Co. Ltd.*

**5562** Jamaica Cricket Association
■ West Indies vs. New Zealand in Jamaica
1972: official souvenir programme; edited
by Robert S. Dabdoub; statistics by Ron
Jones. Jamaica, [the Assoc., 1972]. 56p.
illus. ports. scores. stats.

**5563** Jones, Brunell
■ Gone with the Kiwis: a book on the New
Zealand tour of West Indies, 1972.
Champs Fleurs, Curepe P.O. (Trinidad),
the Author, 1972. 152p. illus. port. scores

**5564** Williams, Leroy ("Fathead"), *compiler*
■ New Zealand vs. West Indies, 5th Test,
Queen's Park Oval, April 20–26, 1972:
souvenir brochure. Port-of-Spain, [the
Compiler, 1972]. [24]p. incl. adverts.
ports. stats.

# NEW ZEALAND TOURS TO INDIA

## 1955–56 Test Tour (H.B. Cave)

**5565** Board of Control for Cricket in India
■ Official souvenir of New Zealand cricke-
ters tour of India 1955. New Delhi, the
Board, [1955]. [44]p. incl. adverts. ports.

**5565** Haridass, C.K.
**–1** Welcome to New Zealand cricketers: sou-
■ venir fifth Test [at Madras, Jan. 6, 7, 8, 10,
11, 1956]. Madras, C.K. Haridass, [1956].
50p. incl. adverts. ports. stats.
*pre-Test*

**5566** Sport & Pastime
■ Cricketers from New Zealand: tour of
India 1955–56. Madras, Sport & Pastime,
1955. 32p. incl. adverts. illus. ports. stats.
*pre-tour*

## 1964–65 Test Tour (J.R. Reid)

**5567** Bhupathy, D.R., *compiler*
New Zealand v. India: Test cricket souvenir. Madras, Bhupathy, [1964]. 42p.
ports. stats.
*pre-tour*

**5568** Board of Control for Cricket in India
■ Official souvenir of New Zealand cricket
tour of India 1965. The Board, [1965].
[50]p. incl. adverts. ports.
*pre-tour*

**5569** Madras Cricket Association
The visit to Madras of the New Zealand
cricket team and the Indian Test team,
February-March, 1965: programme. Madras, the Assoc., [1965]. ports.
*pre-visit*

## 1969–70 Test Tour (G.T. Dowling)

**5570** Brittenden, Richard Trevor
■ Scoreboard '69: an account of the West
Indian cricket tour of New Zealand, and
the New Zealand tour of Britain, India,
and Pakistan. Wellington, Reed, 1970.
236p. illus. scores. stats.

**5571** Burmah-Shell
Between the kiwi and the kangaroo.
Bombay, M. K. Das for Burmah-Shell,
1969. 14p. illus.
*pre-tour*

**5572** Hyderabad Cricket Association
■ New Zealand v. India, 3rd Test match,
Hyderabad: [souvenir programme]. Hyderabad, the Assoc., [1969]. [50]p. incl.
adverts. ports.

**5573** Rajan Bala
■ Kiwis and kangaroos, India, 1969. Calcutta & New Delhi, The Statesman, 1970.
v,176p. illus. scores. stats.

## 1976–77 Test Tour (G.M. Turner)

**5573** The Board of Control for Cricket in India
**–1** Official souvenir of New Zealand tour of
■ India 1976. The Board, [1976]. [80]p. incl.
adverts. ports. stats.
*pre-series*

**5573** Sharma, Ashok K., *editor*
**–2** New Zealand cricket tour of India 1976:
■ souvenir. New Delhi, Young Sportswriters Co., [1976]. 48p. incl. adverts. ports.
stats.
*pre-tour*

# NEW ZEALAND TOURS TO PAKISTAN

### 1955–56 Test Tour (H.B. Cave)

5574 **Butt, Qamaruddin**
■ Pakistan cricket on the march. Karachi, the Author, 1957. 258p. illus. ports. scores, stats.
*includes an account of the New Zealand tour to Pakistan, 1955–56*

### 1964–65 Test Tour (J.R. Reid)

5575 **Board of Control for Cricket in Pakistan**
■ Pakistan vs. New Zealand: souvenir of the first Test match, March 27, 28, 30 & 31, 1965 at the Rawalpindi Club Ground. Rawalpindi, the Board, [1965]. illus. ports. diagr.

5576 **Brittenden, Richard Trevor**
■ Red leather silver fern. Wellington, Reed, 1965, 227p. illus. ports. scores, stats.

### 1969–70 Test Tour (G.T. Dowling)

5577 **Brittenden, Richard Trevor**
■ Scoreboard '69: an account of the West Indian cricket tour of New Zealand, and the New Zealand tour of Britain, India and Pakistan. Wellington, N.Z., Reed, 1970. 236p. illus. scores, stats.

5578 **Butt, Qamaruddin**
■ Sporting wickets: (eye-witness accounts of the tours of M.C.C. and New Zealand to Pakistan 1969). [Rawalpindi, the Author, 1970]. [vi],136p. illus. ports. scores, stats.

# NEW ZEALAND VISIT TO SRI LANKA

5579· **Foenander, Samuel Peter,** *compiler*
■ A souvenir of the match between Ceylon and New Zealand, 8 October, 1927 on the C.C.C. Ground. Colombo, Ceylon Observer, [1927]. 12p. ports. stats.

# NEW ZEALAND VISIT TO CANADA

### 1964 New Zealand Cricket Council Team

5580 **Saskatchewan Cricket Association**
Saskatchewan v. New Zealanders, 14 June, 1964: souvenir. Moose Jaw, the Assoc., 1964. 24p.
*includes historical notes on cricket in Saskatchewan*

# NEW ZEALAND WOMEN'S TOURS TO ENGLAND

### 1954 Tour

5581 **Women's Cricket Association**
■ New Zealand Women's cricket tour 1954: souvenir programme. The Assoc., [1954]. [20]p. illus. ports. map
*pre-tour*

5582 Report of the New Zealand Women's
■ cricket tour in England, 1954. The Assoc., [1954]. 14p. scores, stats.
*post tour*

### 1966 Tour

5583 **Women's Cricket Association**
■ New Zealand Women's cricket tour, 1966: souvenir programme. [The Assoc., 1966]. 8p. illus. port.
*pre-tour*

5584 Report of the New Zealand Women's
■ cricket tour in England, 1966. The Assoc., [1966]. [16]p. port. scores, stats.
*post-tour*

# INDIA

5585 **Bacha, D.N.**
■ India in Test cricket, 1932–1952; illustrated by J.N. Srivastava. Bombay, Hind Kitabs, 1952. 199p. scores

5585 **Bala, Vijayan**
–1 Indian Test cricket: a statistical digest
□ 1932–1974. Delhi, Vikas, 1975. xi,142p. stats.
———2nd ed. 1975
———3rd ed. 1976. 142p.
*issued with a separate 32p supplement covering the Tests between India v. the West Indies in 1974–75 and India v. New Zealand in 1976, the book and supplement being held together with a paper wrapper bearing title and "updated to 1976"*
———4th rev. ed. 1932–1978. 1979. [v],180p. (Bell Books)

5585 **Bharatan, Raju**
–2 Indian cricket: the vital phase. New
■ Delhi, Vikas, 1977. x,385p. illus. ports. scores, stats. (Bell Books)
*covers period 1971–76*

5586 **Dutt, K. Iswara,** *and* **Ratnam, K.V.**
■ **Gopala**
Century of Tests. New Delhi, Sarada, 1968 [i.e. 1969]. [350]p. incl. adverts. ports. scores, stats.
*match scores of all Tests played by India to the completion of their tour of N.Z. 1968*

5587 **Gurunathan, S.K.**
■ The story of the Tests. 3 vols. Madras, Sport and Pastime, 1961?–1964. illus. ports. scores, stats.
*vol. 1. India v. England [1932–1959]. [1961?]. [vi],120p.
2. India v. Australia and West Indies, 1963. [vi],137p.
3. India v. Pakistan, New Zealand, and v. England 1961–64, 1964. [vi],126p*

5588 **Nagaraj Rao, B.N.,** *compiler*
■ India—England Test cricket 1932–1964: statistics. Madras, Sport & Pastime, [1964]. 32p. ports. stats.

5589 A century of Tests, 1932–67. Madras, "The Hindu", 1967. 32p. stats.

5589 **Puri, Narottam**
–1 Portrait of Indian captains. Calcutta,
■ [etc.], Rupa, 1978. [xiv],193p. illus. ports. stats. pbk.

5590 **Ramchand, Partab**
■ India in Test cricket: a statistical record. Madras, "Indian Express", 1972. [viii], 92p. stats.

5590 Great moments in Indian cricket. New
–1 Delhi, Vikas, 1977. ix,223p. illus. ports.
■ scores. (Bell Books). pbk.
*Indian Test cricket 1951/52 to 1976*

5591 **Rothmans**
■ 1967 cricket almanack: England v. India; England v. Pakistan. Rothmans, in association with the M.C.C., [1967]. 48p. illus. ports. stats.
*pre-tour with records of matches England v. India 1932–1964; England v. Pakistan 1954–1962*

5592 **Roy, S.K.,** *editor*
■ India-England cricket visits 1911–1946. Calcutta, Illustrated News, 1946. 392p. ports. scores, stats.

5593 **Sanyal, Saradindu**
■ 40 years of Test cricket: India—England (1932–1971). New Delhi, Thompson P., 1972, viii,192p. illus. ports. stats.
—revised ed. including 41st year: India–England (1932–1973). 1974. xii, 246p. illus. ports. scores, stats.

5594 **Sujit Mukherjee**
■ Playing for India. Madras, Orient Longman, 1972. [viii],240p. illus. pbk.
—*essays on Indian Test players*

5594 Between Indian wickets. New Delhi,
–1 Vision Books (Pvt.) Ltd., 1976. 208p. (Orient Paperbacks)

# INDIAN TOURS TO ENGLAND

### 1911 All Indian Team Tour (Maharajah of Patiala)

5595 [Mukerji, H.C.J.], *editor*
The Indian cricketers' tour of 1911, by "Extra Cover". Bombay, D.B. Taraporevala, 1911. [vi],183p. ports. scores

### 1932 Test Tour (Maharajah of Porbandar)

5596 **Board of Control for Cricket in India**
■ Indian cricket tour to England 1932. [New Delhi, the Board, 1932]. 48p. ports.
*pre-tour*

5597 **Simpson, A.W.,** *editor*
■ Souvenir of first All India cricket tour of England 1932. Hills & Lacy, [1932]. 32p. incl. adverts. illus. ports.
*pre-tour*

5598 **"Three-Stumps",** *pseud.*
■ All-India cricketers' tour 1932. Madras, Madras News Agency, 1932. [176]p. illus. ports. scores, stats.
*post-tour; includes "Test match day by day: 'Cricketer's tribute to the Indians", pp. 159– 70, by Neville Cardus*

### 1936 Test Tour (Maharajkumar of Vizianagram)

5599 **Seervai, P.H.**
■ Cricket comments. Bombay, the Author, 1938. 114p. ports.

5600 **Simpson, A.W.,** *compiler and editor*
■ Souvenir of All India tour of England 1936. Canterbury, Jennings, [1936]. 32p. illus. ports.
*pre-tour*

### 1938 Rajputana Cricket Club Team

5601 **Begg, W.D.**
Rajputana Cricket Club, Ajmer: souvenir of private tour of cricketers in England 1938. Delhi, Hindustan Times, 1938. [ii], 66p. illus. ports.

### 1946 Test Tour (Nawab of Pataudi)

5602 **Arlott, [Leslie Thomas] John**
■ Indian summer: an account of the cricket tour in England, 1946. Longmans, 1947. vi,141p. illus. scores, stats.

5603 **Gillette Industries**
India tour and first-class county cricket fixtures for 1946. Gillette Industries, 1946.
*pre-tour*

5604 **"Gully",** *pseud.*
■ The Indian team in England, 1946. Hunstanton, Cricket Book Society, 1946. 31p. scores, stats. (Publications. Ser. 1, no. 4)
*post-tour*
*re-issued in "Cricket omnibus 1946", edited by Roy Webber. See no. 982*

5605 **Mathur, L.N.**
■ The fight for the rubber. Ajmere, Newal Kishore P., [1946]. vii,266p. illus. ports. scores, stats.

5606 **Muni Lal**
■ Indian cricketers touring England: biographical sketches of the players together with complete record of England-India Test matches. Lahore, Hamidullah, [1946]. [ii],73p. scores, stats.
*pre-tour*

5607 Indian cricket tour in England 1946: a
■ complete record of all matches played by the Indian cricket team in England in 1946 together with an analytical survey in figures of the ten Test matches so far played between England and India since 1932 & summary results of previous Indian tours in England. Lahore, Press of the Civil & Military Gazette, [1947]. 75p. ports. scores, stats.

5608 **1946 Indian XI** tour in Great Britain. 1946. 12p. illus.
*pre-tour*

5609 **Parthasarthy, C.D.**
The Indian cricket touring team—1946 in England. Madras, P.V.K. Moorthy, 1946. 32p. illus.
*pre-tour*

5610 **Simpson, A.W.,** *compiler & editor*
■ All-India cricket tour of England 1946. I.M. Young, [1946]. 32p. incl. adverts. illus. ports. stats.
*pre-tour*

### 1952 Test Tour (V.S. Hazare)

5611 **Bharatan, Raju**
■ Rivals in the sun: a survey of the 1952 tour of England. Bombay, Popular Book Depot., [1952]. [xi],163p. illus. ports. scores, stats.

5612 **India** souvenir tour programme: 1952. M. Walker, [1952]. [4]p. ports.

5613 **Indian** cricket team versus Indian Gymkhana Club, 30 April and 1 May, 1952. London, N.W. 3, B.P. Press, 1952. [4]p.

**5614 Simpson, A.W.,** *compiler & editor*
- 1952 India cricket tour: fixtures, descriptive records, individual and group photographs of players. Brighton, *printed by* Brighton Herald, 1952. 32p. ports.
  *pre-tour*

**5615 West, Peter,** *editor*
- Cricketers from India: official souvenir of the 1952 tour of England: with statistics by Roy Webber. Playfair Books, [1952]. 24p. illus. ports. stats.
  *pre-tour*

### 1959 Test Tour (D.K. Gaekwad)

**5616 All** about the Indian tourists. Grelock P., 1959

**5617 Arlott, [Leslie Thomas] John**
- Cricket Journal—2. Heinemann, 1959. 260p. illus. ports. scores, stats.

**5618 British Sportsmans' Club**
Luncheon given to the India cricket touring team, Savoy Hotel. the Club, 1959. 8p.

**5619 Indian** cricket team's tour of England, 1959. Information Service of India, [1959]. 15p. *typescript*
  *pre-tour*

**5620 Meltonian**
Season 1959 Test matches England v. India: souvenir scorecard and fixture list. Meltonian, 1959. 6p.
  *pre-tour*

**5621 Ross, Gordon,** *editor*
- Cricketers from India: the official souvenir of the 1959 tour of England. Playfair Books, [1959]. 24p. illus. ports. stats.
  *pre-tour*

**5622 Sport & Pastime**
- Special cricket number, 2 May, 1959, Vol. XIII, no. 18. Madras, K. Gopalan for Kasturi & Sons. 32p. incl. adverts. illus. ports. (some col.)
  *pre-tour*

### 1967 Test Tour (Nawab of Pataudi)

**5623 India** 1967 tour programme: players, records, features, fixtures. Wembley, Walker, [1967]. [8]p. illus. stats.

**5624 Irish Cricket Union**
- Ireland v. the Indians, Castle Avenue, Dublin, July 21 & 22, 1967: souvenir brochure. Dublin, the Union, [1967]. 84p. incl. adverts. illus. ports. stats.

**5625 Rothmans**
- 1967 cricket almanack: England v. India; England v. Pakistan. Rothmans, in association with the M.C.C., [1967]. 48p. illus. ports. stats.
  *pre-tour with records of matches England v. India 1932–1964; England v. Pakistan 1954–1962*

### 1971 Test Tour (A.L. Wadekar)

**5626 India** tour programme, fixtures, pictures.
- D. Walker, [1971]. [8]p. ports.

**5627 Rajan, Sunder**
- India vs. England 1971: statistics by Nagaraja Rao. Bombay, Jaico, 1971. xiv,146p. illus. scores, stats.
  *pre-tour*

**5628 Sportsweek.** *Special issue*
- India in England 1971. Bombay, Inqilab Publications (Private) Ltd., [1971]. 52p. incl. adverts. illus. ports. (some col.), stats.

### 1974 Test Tour (A.L. Wadekar)

**5628 Board of Control for Cricket in India**
**–1** Indian cricket team's tour of United
- Kingdom 1974. The Board, [1974]. [28]p. incl. adverts. stats.
  *pre-tour programme with pen sketches of team*

### 1979 Test Tour (S. Venkataraghavan)

**5628 Cornhill** Test special, England v. India
**–2** 1979. Cornhill Insurance Test series. Cornhill Insurance, [1979]. 8p. illus.

**5628 Indian** tour 1979 souvenir programme.
**–3** *n.p.,* [1979]. [8]p. ports.
-

# INDIAN TOURS TO AUSTRALIA

### 1947–48 Test Tour (L. Amarnath)

**5629 Australian**— All India cricket tour 1947–
- 48: official magazine. Brisbane, Queensland Publications, [1947]. 40p. incl. adverts. ports. stats.
  *pre-tour*

**5630 Australian Broadcasting Commission**
- A.B.C. cricket broadcast book: Test season 1947–48, India—Australia; edited by Dudley Leggett. Sydney, the Commission, [1947]. 64p. illus. ports. diagrs. stats.
  *pre-tour*

**5631  Mathur, L.N.**
Indian cricketers in Australia (life sketches). Ajmere, Subhas Library, 1947. 84p. illus.

**5631  New South Wales Cricket Association**
**–1** All India Australia tour: India v. Australian XI at Sydney Cricket Ground, November 14, 15, 17, 18, 1947. Sydney, the Assoc., [1947]. 24p. incl. adverts. ports. stats.

**5632  Parthasarthy, C.D.**
All India cricket team in Australia. Madras, Sports Publications, 1947. 62p. illus.

**5632  Queensland Cricket Association**
**–1** Official magazine. Australia v. All-India Tests 1947–48. Brisbane, the Assoc., [1947]. 38p. incl. adverts. ports. stats.
*pre-tour*

**5632  Official magazine. All-India Australia**
**–2** tour, 1947–48, at Brisbane Cricket Ground. India v. Queensland, November 21, 22, 24, 25, 1947: [souvenir programme]. Brisbane, the Assoc., [1947]. 24p. incl. adverts. ports.

**5633** ————. *Country Committee*
Queensland Country v. India, Slade Park, Warwick, Dec. 6–8, 1947. Brisbane, Queensland Publications for the Assoc., [1947]. 24p. illus. ports.

**5634  Richardson, Victor York**
■ Indian cricketers in Australia 1947. Calcutta, Illustrated News, 1950. 72p. illus. ports. scores, stats.
*post-tour*

**5635  Taleyarkhan, Homi J.H.**
■ Cricket—United India in Australia. Bombay, Thacker, 1947. [3],vi,102p. incl. adverts. illus.
*pre-tour*

## 1967 Cricket Club of India Tour

**5636  Cricket Club of India Ltd.**
■ Cricket tour to Australia and Far East 1967. Bombay, the Club, [1967]. 24p. incl. adverts. illus. ports.
*pre-tour*

## 1967–68 Test Tour (Nawab of Pataudi)

**5637  Narayan, R.S.,** *editor*
■ The Indian cricket team's tour of Australia and New Zealand, 1967–68: review and record. Mysore, Pravin Prakashan, [1968]. 52p incl. adverts. ports. scores, stats.
*match scores and statistics only*

**5637  Queensland Cricket Association**
**–1** Australia versus India third Test Brisbane Cricket Ground, 19 January to 24 January 1968: souvenir programme. Brisbane, the Assoc., [1968]. 24p. incl. adverts. ports. stats.

## 1972 Cricket Club of India Tour

**5638  Cricket Club of India Ltd**
■ Cricket tour to Australia 1972. Bombay, the Club, [1972]. 32p. incl. adverts. illus. ports.
*pre-tour*

## 1977–78 Test Tour (B.S. Bedi)

**5638  Australian Broadcasting Commission**
**–1** ABC cricket book. India tour of Australia
■ 1977–78; edited by Alan McGilvray. Sydney, the Commission, [1977]. 67p. illus. & ports. (some col.), stats.
*pre-tour*

**5638  Australian Cricket Board**
**–2** Test souvenir: official publication of the
■ Australian Cricket Board to commemorate the 1977–78 Indian tour of Australia. Melbourne, the Board, [1977]. 48p. incl. adverts. illus. ports. (some col.), stats.
*pre-tour*

**5638  Cricket** colour collection. Melbourne,
**–3** Lavardin Pty. Ltd., [1978?]. 80p. col. illus.
■ & ports.
————pbk ed. [1978?]
*illustrations of Australia v. India, World Series Cricket and New Zealand v. England*

**5638  Cricket** scene: Australia v. India [and]
**–4** World Series Cricket 1977–78; edited by
■ Rod Nicholson. Toorak (Vic.), Garry Sparkes & Associates, [1977]. 64p. illus. ports. stats.
*a preview of the 1977–78 season in Australia. The 1st section is devoted to the official Test series; the 2nd an 8p. middle spread of colour poster and scoresheets; the 3rd (or 1st if turned upside down and round) World Series Cricket*

**5638  Gupta, Shivendra**
**–5** India's tour of Australia 1977–'78:
■ (souvenir) plus world Test records and World Cup cricket. Surat, the Author, 1977. 98p. incl. adverts. ports. stats.
*pre-tour*

**5638  Queensland Cricket Association**
**–6** 'Gabba cricket – '77–'78 India tour. Queensland v. India. Nov. 25–28: official programme. Brisbane, the Assoc., [1977]. 24p. incl. adverts. illus. ports. stats.

**5638** **Simpson, Robert Baddeley**
**–7** Bob Simpson's young Australians.
■ Melbourne, Lavardin, 1978. 64p. illus. &
ports. (some col.), diagr. scores, stats.
*post-tour*

# INDIAN TOURS TO WEST INDIES

(For India v. West Indies cricket generally *see
under* West Indies tours to India)

### 1952–53 Test Tour (V.S. Hazare)

**5639** **Jamaica Cricket Board of Control**
■ Official programme of the Jamaican
section of the Indian tour of the West
Indies, March 18 to April 7, 1953; [by]
Alva Ramsay. Kingston, the Board,
[1953]. 54p. incl. adverts. illus. ports.
plan, scores, stats.
*mid-tour*

**5640** **Sinha, Arun**
Cricket souvenir 1953. Calcutta, S.B.
Sinha, 1953. 20p. ports.
*pre-tour*

### 1961–62 Test Tour (N.J. Contractor)

**5640** **Illustrated News (Sports)**
**–1** Exhibition cricket match: Prime Minister's
XI v. Governor's XI. Calcutta, Illustrated
News (Sports), [1962]. 32p. illus. ports.
*includes 'Was Indian team "Manhandled"
in the Caribbean?' by Berry Sarbadhikary: an
analysis of India's defeat in their tour of West
Indies 1962*

**5641** India in West Indies with elaborate statis-
■ tics. Calcutta, Illustrated News, [1962].
32p. ports. stats.
*post-tour*

**5642** **Jamaica Cricket Association**
■ Indian tour West Indies in Jamaica, 1962:
official programme. Kingston, the Assoc.,
[1962]. 72p. incl. adverts. illus. ports.
scores, stats.
*mid-tour; includes p. 57 "Worrell as cap-
tain" by Neville Cardus*

### 1970–71 Test Tour (A.L. Wadekar)

**5642** **Chichester, Charles J.,** *editor*
**–1** Tour '71. From Bombay to Bourda.
■ Georgetown, Guyana Cricket Board
of Control, [1971]. [64]p. incl. adverts.
ports. stats.
*pre-tour*

**5643** **Jamaica Cricket Association**
■ 1971 Indian tour: West Indies vs. India
in Jamaica: official souvenir programme;

edited by Robert S. Dabdoub. Kingston,
the Assoc., [1971]. 60p. incl. adverts.
ports. scores, stats.
*mid-tour*

**5644** **Jones, Brunell**
■ "Gone with the Indians". San Juan, [The
Author, 1971]. [iii],54p. illus. ports.
scores, stats.
*post-tour*

**5645** **Misra, L.N.**
■ 'India wins series in Caribbeans'.
Lucknow, the Author, 1971. ix,57p. port.
scores, stats.

**5646** **Rajan, Sunder**
■ India v. West Indies 1971. Bombay, Jaico,
1971. [vi],133p. ports. scores, stats.
*post-tour*

**5647** **Welcome** ambassadors of sport: [souvenir
■ of India in West Indies, 1970–71]. [1971].
52p. incl. adverts. ports. stats.
*pre-tour*

### 1975–76 Test Tour (B.S. Bedi)

**5647** **Bhimani, Kishore**
**–1** West Indies '76: India's Caribbean ad-
■ venture. Calcutta, Nachiketa Publications
Ltd., 1976. [iv],162p. illus. scores, stats.
pbk.
*post-tour*

**5647** **Jones, Brunell**
**–2** "Cricket? XI". Champs Fleur, Curepe
■ P.O. (Trinidad), the Author, 1976. 120p.
incl. adverts. illus. ports. scores, stats.
*includes account of the 1975–76 series W.I.
v. India*

# INDIAN TOURS TO NEW ZEALAND

### 1967–68 Test Tour (Nawab of Pataudi)

**5648** **Auckland Cricket Association**
■ India. v. New Zealand, fourth Test, Eden
Park, Auckland, 7, 8, 9, 11 & 12 March,
1968. Auckland, the Assoc., [1968]. 24p.
incl. adverts. ports. plan, diagr. stats.

**5648** **Canterbury Cricket Association**
**–1** India v. New Zealand, second cricket
Test, 1968, Lancaster Park, Christchurch,
February 22, 23, 24, 26, 27: official
souvenir programme. [Christchurch, the
Assoc., 1968]. 32p. incl. adverts. ports.
diagr. stats.

**5648**   **Central District Cricket Association**
**-2**   International cricket. India v. Central Districts, Pukekura Park, New Plymouth: programme February 9, 10, 12, 1968. [Napier, the Assoc., 1968]. [16]p. incl. adverts. 1 illus. ports. stats.

**5649**   **Narayan, R.S.** *editor*
■   The Indian cricket team's tour of Australia and New Zealand, 1967–68: review and record. Mysore, Pravin Prakashan, [1968]. 52p. incl. adverts. ports. scores, stats.

### 1975–76 Test Tour (B.S. Bedi)

**5650**   **Auckland Cricket Association**
■   Test cricket. First Test, India v. New Zealand. . .January 24, 25, 26, 28, 29, Eden Park, Auckland: official souvenir programme. Auckland, the Assoc., [1976]. 48p. incl. adverts. ports. diagr. stats.

**5650**   **Canterbury Cricket Association**
**-1**   India v. New Zealand, second cricket
■   Test, 1976, Lancaster Park, Christchurch, February 5, 6, 7, 8, 10: official souvenir programme. [Christchurch, the Assoc., 1976]. 28p. incl. adverts. illus. ports. stats.

**5650**   Rothmans one day cricket international:
**-2**   New Zealand v. India, Lancaster Park, 21
■   February, 1976: programme. [Christchurch, the Assoc., 1976]. 20p. incl. adverts. ports. stats.

## INDIAN TOURS TO PAKISTAN

**5650**   **Dossa, Anandji**
**-3**   Cricket ties: India-Pakistan. Calcutta,
■   Rupa, 1978. [ix],191p. illus. ports. scores, typescript. pbk.
    *Test matches between India and Pakistan since 1952/53*

### 1954–55 Test Tour (A.V. Mankad)

**5651**   **Butt, Qamaruddin**
■   Cricket without challenge. Sialkot & Lahore, Maliksons, 1955. 302p. illus, ports. scores, stats.

**5652**   **Madras Cricket Association**
  Official souvenir: fourth Test; [compiled by] C.K. Haridass. Madras, the Assoc., 1954. 76p. incl. adverts. illus.
    *pre-Test*

## INDIAN TOURS TO SRI LANKA

### 1930 Visit of Maharaja Kumar of Vizianagram's Team

**5652**   **"Zingari",** *pseud.*
**-1**   A souvenir of the visit of the Maharaja Kumar of Vizianagram's team to Ceylon. Colombo, Times of Ceylon Ltd., 1930. 40p. incl. adverts.

### 1944–45 Tour

**5653**   **Ondatje, Frank,** *compiler*
■   C.C.A. souvenir of Indian tour to commemorate the inauguration of Indo-Ceylon series. Colombo, Ceylon C.A. [1945]. 16p. 1 illus. ports.
    *pre-tour*

### 1966 and 1968 All-India State Bank XI Tours

**5654**   **Mercantile Cricket Association**
■   Visit of All India State Bank cricket team, 1966. Colombo, [the Assoc. 1966]. [90]p. incl. 40 of adverts. ports.
    *includes a brief history of Mercantile cricket*

**5655**   **Tamil Union Cricket and Athletic Club**
■   Visit of All-India State Bank cricket team. Colombo, [the Club, 1968]. [40]p. incl. adverts. port.
    *pre-tour*

### 1970 Indian Universities Tour

**5656**   **Ceylon Universities' Sports Association**
■   Indian Universities cricket tour of Ceylon, 19 Oct. to 7 Nov. 1970. [Colombo), the Assoc., [1970]. [13]p. stats.
    *pre-tour souvenir: contains account of the visit of the Indian University Occasionals Team 1935, by S.S. Perera*

### 1973 Bombay Cavaliers' Tour

**5656**   **Bombay** Cavaliers': cricket tour of Sri
**-1**   Lanka, 7 May–23 May 1973; sponsored by
■   National Cricket Club of India, Bombay. Bombay, printed by Sanjay P., [1973]. 60p. incl. 48p. of adverts. illus. ports.

### 1973 National Cricket Club of India Tour

**5656**   **Colombo Cricket Club**
**-2**   Tour of Sri Lanka by National Cricket
■   Club of India, sponsored by Colombo Cricket Club: official programme; ed. by Nimal M. Gunasekera. Colombo, the Club, [1973]. 62p. incl. adverts. illus. ports.

**5656** **Galle Cricket Club**
**–3** Souvenir of the visit of the National
■ Cricket Club of India to Galle on 21 May
1973; [compiled by S.S. Perera]. Galle, the
Club, [1973]. [12]p. + insert of ports. of
Galle players.
*cover-title:* National Cricket Club of
India vs. Galle Combined XI

### 1973 Northern Railway Sports Association of New Delhi Tour

**5656** **Sri Lanka State Services Cricket**
**–4** **Association**
■ Northern Railway Sports Association of
New Delhi tour of Sri Lanka, sponsored
and organised by Sri Lanka State Services
Cricket Association, September 10 to
October 5, 1973. Colombo, the Assoc.,
[1973]. 54p. incl. adverts. ports.
*includes brief history of the State Services
C.A.*

### 1974 Tour

**5656** **Board of Control for Cricket in Sri Lanka**
**–5** Official souvenir of Indian tour to Sri
■ Lanka 17 January to 15 February 1974 and
25th anniversary of the Board. . .(formed
25th June 1948) 1948–1973. [Colombo],
the Board, [1974]. [108]p. incl. adverts.
ports. stats.

**5656** **Ceylon Tobacco Co. Ltd.**
**–6** Today's cricketers: printed autographs
and photographs of the Indian cricket
team in Sri Lanka. Colombo, the Co.,
[1974]. ports.

**5656** Today's cricketers: printed autographs
**–7** and photographs of the Sri Lankan team.
Colombo, the Co., [1974]. ports.

# OTHER INDIAN TOURS

### Hyderabad Blues Cricket Club
### 1968 Tour

**5657** **Hyderabad Blues Cricket Club**
Tour of Johore Bahru, June 1968: souvenir
programme. Hyderabad, the Club,
[1968]. 24p.
*pre-tour*

**5658** Tour of Malaysia, Singapore & Ceylon:
■ souvenir 1968. Hyderabad, the Club,
[1968]. [194]p. incl. adverts. illus. ports.
stats.
*pre-tour*

### 1971 Tour

**5658** **Coast Cricket Association**
**–1** Coast Cricket Association v/s Hyderabad
■ Blues (India) on 17 & 18 July 1971.
Mombasa, the Assoc., [1971]. [40]p. incl.
adverts. ports.
*pre-visit; mostly adverts*

**5659** **Hyderabad Blues Cricket Club**
■ Tour of Aden, Uganda, Kenya, Tanzania,
Kuwait: souvenir 1971. Hyderabad, the
Club, [1971]. [290]p. incl. adverts. illus.
ports.
*pre-tour*

### 1973 Tour

**5660** **Hyderabad Blues Cricket Club**
■ Tour of Australia, Malaysia, Singapore,
Hongkong, Bangkok & Fiji: souvenir
1973. Hyderabad, the Club, [1973]. 246p.
incl. adverts. ports.
*pre-tour*

### 1973 Starlets Cricket Club Tour

**5661** **Starlets Cricket Club**
Tour of Malaysia and Singapore: souvenir
1973. Madras, the Club, [1973]. 268p. incl.
adverts.
*mostly advertisements, but with a list of
members and some articles. There appears to
be nothing about the tour*

England v. Pakistan, third Test, Karachi, 1978. Gatting lbw Qadir, 5 *photo: Patrick Eagar*

# PAKISTAN

5661
-1
■
**Aziz Rehmatullah, A.,** *editor*
Cricket close-up. Karachi, the Editor,
[1979]. 104p. incl. adverts. illus. (1 col.),
ports. stats.

5661
-2
■
26 years of Pakistan Test cricket. Karachi,
the Editor, 1979. 224p. incl. adverts.
illus. & ports. (some col.), scores, stats.

5662
■
**Bashir-Ul-Haq,** *and* **Bhatti, Mukhtar**
Pakistan in Test cricket. Lahore, Bhatti
Publications, [1958]. 126p. illus. ports.
scores

5663
■
**Board of Control for Cricket in Pakistan**
Compendium of Pakistan Test cricket,
1947–1967; compiled by Bashir Ahmad.
Rawalpindi, the Board, [1968]. [ix],108p.
ports. scores, stats.

## PAKISTAN TOURS TO ENGLAND

### 1954 Test Tour (A.H. Kardar)

5664
■
**Butt, Qamaruddin**
Pakistan on cricket map (fully covering
Pakistan's cricket tour of England in
1954). Karachi, the Author, [1955].
[xviii],218p. illus. ports. scores, stats.

5665
**Husain, F.**
Shabash Pakistan. Lahore, Modern Papers Publicity, 1954. 139p.
*post-tour*

5666
■
**Kardar, Abdul Hafeez**
Test status on trial: the story of Pakistan's
cricket team's historic tour to England.
Karachi, National Publications, [1954].
[viii],151p. illus. ports. scores, stats.

5666
-1
■
**Manchester Guardian**
The bedside 'Guardian' 4: a selection by
Ivor Brown from The Manchester
Guardian 1954–1955. Collins, 1955. 256p.
*includes pp. 106–10, "Return of the
native" by Alistair Cooke (impressions of
England v. Pakistan Test at Old Trafford,
1954)*

5667
■
**Maqsood, Syed M.H.,** *and* **Merchant,
M.I.**
Pakistan vs. England: tour of 1954.
Karachi, Pakistan Printing Works, 1954.
194p. incl. adverts. illus. maps, scores

5668
■
**Ross, Gordon,** *editor*
Cricketers from Pakistan: the official
souvenir of the 1954 tour of England; with
statistics by Roy Webber. Playfair Books,
[1954]. 24p. illus. ports. stats.
*pre-tour*

### 1955 Pakistan Eaglets Tour

5669
■
**Pakistan** Eaglets cricket tour 1955: Pakistan Eaglets v. 'Evening Chronicle' Lancashire Starlets, 30th August 1955 at
Rochdale C.C. Ground: official
programme. Manchester, Manchester
Sports Guild, [1955]. [8]p. ports.

5670
■
**Pakistan** Eaglets cricket tour 1955: Paki-
stan Eaglets v. a Northern Cricket League
XI, 1st Sept. 1955 at Morecambe C.C.
Manchester, Manchester Sports Guild,
[1955]. [8]p. ports.

### 1956 Pakistan Eaglets Tour

5671
■
**The Pakistan** Eaglets cricket tour 1956.
Morecambe Festival: Pakistan Eaglets v.
A Commonwealth XI, 25, 26 July, 1956:
official programme. Manchester, Man-
chester Sports Guild, [1956]. [8]p.

### 1957 Pakistan Eaglets Tour

5672
■
**Pakistan** Eaglets cricket tour 1957: Paki-
stan Eaglets v. Hereford City C.C., 14
July 1957, the Racecourse, Hereford.
Manchester, Manchester Sports Guild,
[1957]. [16]p.

### 1959 Pakistan Eaglets Tour

5673
■
**The Pakistan Eaglets Society**
Pakistan Eaglets 1959. Karachi, the
Society, [1959]. [100]p. incl. adverts.
ports. stats.
*produced for tour of England 1959; includes
survey of previous tours*

## 1962 Test Tour (Javed Burki)

5674 **Bhatti, Mukhtar,** *editor*
■ Cricketers from Pakistan. Lahore, Bhatti
Publications, [1962]. 32p. incl. adverts.
illus. ports.

5675 **Board of Control for Cricket in Pakistan**
■ Pakistan England tour 1962. Karachi, the
Board, [1962]. [36]p. illus. ports. stats.
*pre-tour*

5676 **Pakistan** souvenir tour programme: 1962.
M. Walker, [1962]. [4]p. fold. ports.
*pre-tour*

5677 **Ross, Gordon,** *editor*
■ Cricketers from Pakistan; with statistics
by Roy Webber; the 1962 tour official
souvenir. Playfair Books, [1962]. 24p.
incl. adverts. illus. ports. stats.
*pre-tour*

5678 **Rothmans**
■ Pakistan Test cricket almanack. Rothmans of Pall Mall, [1962]. 16p. 1 illus.
ports. stats
*pre-tour, with 'A history of cricket in Paki-*
*stan' by Gordon Ross*

5679 **Sunday Telegraph**
■ England v. Pakistan: a record of the last
four Test matches. Sunday Telegraph,
[1962]. [6]p. fold. scores.
*covers 3 Tests England in Pakistan 1961–*
*62, and the first Test Pakistan in England*
*1962*

## 1963 Pakistan Eaglets Tour

5680 **Pakistan International Airways**
■ Eaglets cricket tour of England 1963.
Karachi, P.I.A., [1963]. 12p. ports.
*pre-tour; pen-portraits of team with*
*itinerary*

## 1967 Test Tour (Hanif Mohammad)

5681 **Board of Control for Cricket in Pakistan**
■ Pakistan tour in England 1967. [Karachi],
the Board, [1967]. 16p. illus. ports. stats.

5682 **Butt, Qamaruddin**
■ The Oval memories: (eye-witness accounts of the Pakistan cricket team's tour
of England 1967). [Rawalpindi, the
Author], 1968. [viii],301p. illus. ports.
scores, stats.

5683 **Pakistan,** cricketers in England, 1967.
1967. [4]p. fold. ports

5683 **Pakistan** 1967 tour programme: players,
–1 records, features, fixtures. Wembley,
■ Walker, [1967]. [8]p. illus. ports. stats.

5683 **Pakistan** Test tour of England 1967:
–2 programme. Hammersmith, Martin,
■ [1967]. [4]p. 1 team port. stats.

5684 **Rothmans**
■ 1967 cricket almanack: England v. India;
England v. Pakistan. Rothmans in association with the M.C.C., [1967]. 48p. illus.
ports. stats.
*pre-tour with records of matches England*
*v. India 1932–1964; England v. Pakistan*
*1954–1962*

## 1969 Pakistan Eaglets Tour

5685 **The Pakistan Eaglets Society**
■ Pakistan Eaglets 1969: [tour of England].
The Society, [1969]. [14]p. incl. adverts.
ports.

## 1971 Test Tour (Intikhab Alam)

5686 **Bangla Desh Students' Action**
■ **Committee in Great Britain**
Why the British people must boycott the
Pakistani cricket team's tour. The
Committee, [1971]. bs. *typescript*

5687 **Pakistan** tour programme, fixtures, pic-
■ tures. D. Walker, [1971]. [8]p. ports.
scores
*pre-tour*

5688 **Syed Zakir Hussain**
■ The young ones: a coverage of Pakistan
cricket team's tour of England 1971.
Lahore & Islamabad, West Pak Publishing Co., 1972. xii,152p. illus. scores,
stats.
*post-tour*

## 1974 Test Tour (Intikhab Alam)

5688 **[Board of Control for Cricket in Pakistan]**
–1 Pakistan tour to England 1974: itinerary.
■ [The Board, 1974]. [8]p.

5688 **Butt, Khalid**
–2 5th Pakistan cricket team to England 1974:
■ souvenir. [Karachi], Khalid Butt, [1974].
[64]p. incl. adverts. ports. stats. spiral
binding
*pre-tour*

5688 **Minor Counties** Cricket Association XI v.
–3 Pakistan Test touring XI, 20–22 July, 74,
■ Northumberland County Cricket Club,
Osborne Avenue, Jesmond, Newcastle
upon Tyne. Newcastle, [Northumberland
C.C.C., 1974]. folded card. 1 illus. 1 port.

## 1978 Test Tour (Wasim Bari)

5688 **Prudential** Trophy '78: England v. Paki-
–4 stan, May 24 and 26; England v. New

Zealand July 15 & 17. Prudential Assurance Co., [1978]. [8]p. fold, illus. stats.

5688 **White, Crawford**
–5 Cornhill Insurance Test series 1978.
■ England v. Pakistan; England v. New Zealand: a preview of the 1978 Test matches. Cornhill Insurance Group, [1978]. [16]p. col. illus. & ports.

# PAKISTAN TOURS TO AUSTRALIA

## 1972–73 Test Tour (Intikhab Alam)

5688 **Australian Capital Territory Cricket**
–6 **Association**
■ Pakistan visit to Canberra, 1972; compiled & edited by Julian Oakley. Canberra, the Assoc., [1972]. 28p. incl. covers & adverts. illus. ports. stats.
*cover title:* Pakistan v. Southern N.S.W. XI, Manuka Oval, Canberra, December 12, 13, 1972: official programme

5689 **Australian Cricket**
■ Cricket tour guide: Pakistan in Australia 1972–73; Australia in West Indies 1973. Sydney, Australian Cricket, [1972]. 68p. incl. adverts. illus. ports. stats.
*pre-tours*

5690 **Board of Control for Cricket in Pakistan**
■ Pakistan cricket team 1972–73. [Karachi], the Board, [1972]. [24]p. ports. stats.
*pre-tour*

5691 **Chappell, Ian Michael**
■ Passing Tests. Coromandel Valley (S.A.), Lynton Publications, 1973. 191p. illus. ports. scores, stats.
*deals mainly with Australia in West Indies, 1973*

5692 **Packages Ltd,** *Lahore*
■ Pakistan cricket team 1972–73. Karachi, Packages Ltd., [1972]. 24p. illus. ports. stats.
*pre-tour*

5693 **Queensland Cricket Association**
■ Cricket News. International cricket match 1972: Queensland v. Pakistan, Brisbane Cricket Ground, December 1, 2, 3 & 4. Brisbane, the Assoc., [1972]. 16p. incl. adverts. score

5694 **Syed Rashid Hussain,** *editor*
■ Ambassadors of goodwill: a match-by-match tour record of the 1972–73 Pakistan cricket team in Sri Lanka, Australia & New Zealand. Karachi, "The Cricketer", [1973]. 128p. illus. ports. scores, stats.

## 1976–77 Test Tour (Mushtaq Mohammad)

5694 **Australian Broadcasting Commission**
–1 ABC cricket book – Pakistan tour of
■ Australia 1976–77 – Australian tour of New Zealand 1977 – England Australia centenary match; edited by Alan McGilvray. Sydney, the Commission, [1976]. 65p. illus. (some col.), ports. diagr. stats.
*pre-tours*

5694 **Australian Cricket Board**
–2 Test souvenir: official publication of the
■ Australian Cricket Board to commemorate the 1976–77 Pakistan tour of Australia. Melbourne, the Board, [1976]. 32p. incl. adverts. illus. ports. score, stats.
*pre-tour*

5694 **Chappell, Gregory Stephen**
–3 The 100th summer: 76–77 season-Pakis-
■ tan-New Zealand-Centenary Test. Toorak (Vic.), Garry Sparke & Assocs., 1977. iv,220p. illus. & ports. (some col.), scores, stats.
*post-tour*

5694 **Kardar, Abdul Hafeez**
–4 "The cricket conspiracy". Lahore, the
■ Author, 1977. [ii],vi,116p.
*an answer to Australian press criticism in Nov/Dec. 1976 concerning the attitude of six Pakistan players on the issue of financial benefits from the tours of Australia and the West Indies*

5694 **National 0–10 Network Television**
–5 Cricket scene [1976–77]; edited by Rod
■ Nicholson. Hawthorn (Vic.), Craftsman Press Pty Ltd., 1976. 64p. incl. adverts. illus. ports. stats.
*with inset colour poster of Greg Chappell;*
*pre-tour*

5694 **Queensland Cricket Association**
–6 'Gabba cricket. Queensland vs. Pakistan,
■ January 8–10: [souvenir programme]. Brisbane, the Assoc., [1977]. 36p. incl. adverts. illus. ports. stats.

## 1978–79 Test Tour (Mushtaq Mohammad)

5694 **Australian Cricket Board**
–7 Test cricket. Australia vs Pakistan: official
■ souvenir. Melbourne, the Board, [1979]. 44p incl. covers. illus (1 col.), diagr. stats.

5694 **Cricket** in Australia. Melbourne, Garry
–8 Sparke & Associates. illus. & ports. (some
■ col.), diagrs. scores, stats.
No. 1. 1979. 112p.
*the 1978–79 Australian season, including 2 Test series, Australia v. England and Australia v. Pakistan*

5694 **Yallop, Graham Neil**
-9 Lambs to the slaughter. Melbourne,
■ Outback P., 1979; [v],175p. illus. scores,
stats.
*personal account of the Australian 1978–79
season*

## PAKISTAN TOURS TO WEST INDIES

### 1957–58 Test Tour (A.H. Kardar)

5695 **Butt, Qamaruddin**
■ Cricket wonders: (containing a complete
account of the Pakistan team's tour of the
West Indies in 1958). Karachi, the
Author, 1958. xii,132p. illus. ports. diagr.
scores, stats.

5696 **Kardar, Abdul Hafeez**
■ Green shadows. Karachi, the Author,
[1958]. xv,188p. illus. port. scores, stats.

5697 **Macdonald, Herbert G. de L.,** *editor*
■ Tour of Jamaica by the Pakistan cricket
team: official programme. Kingston (Jamaica), Gleaner Co., 1958. 92p. incl.
adverts. illus. ports. scores, stats.
*pre-visit*

5697 **Pakistan** v. West Indies 1958: souvenir
-1 programme. Georgetown, Arcade Publications, [1958]. [42]p. incl. covers & adverts. ports. stats.
*pre-tour*

### 1976–77 Test Tour (Mushtaq Mohammad)

5697 **Jones, Brunell,** *editor*
-2 What a tour! Cricket happenings of 1977:
■ a documentation of the West Indies –
Pakistan cricket series in the Caribbean
1977. . . .Champs Fleur, Curepe P.O.
(Trinidad), the Author, [1977]. 138p. incl.
adverts. illus. ports. scores, stats.

## PAKISTAN TOURS TO NEW ZEALAND

### 1964–65 Test Tour (Hanif Mohammad)

5698 **Auckland Cricket Association**
■ Pakistan v. New Zealand, second cricket
Test, Eden Park, Auckland. Jan. 29, 30,
Feb. 1, 2, 1965: souvenir programme.
Auckland, the Assoc., [1965]. 32p. incl.
adverts. illus. ports. stats.

5699 **Canterbury Cricket Association**
■ International cricket–third Test, Pakistan
versus New Zealand, Lancaster Park,
Christchurch, 1965, 12, 13, 15, 16 Feb.:
official souvenir programme. Christchurch, the Assoc., [1965]. 32p. incl.
adverts. ports. stats.

5700 **Northern District Cricket Association**
Cricket–Pakistan v. Northern Districts,
Seddon Park, Hamilton, 4, 5, 6 February,
1965: souvenir programme. Hamilton,
the Assoc., [1965].

5701 **Pakistan** v. N.Z. Basin Reserve. January
■ 22, 23, 25, 26, 1965: official programme.
[1965]. 20p. ports. diagr.

### 1972–73 Test Tour (Intikhab Alam)

5702 **Auckland Cricket Association**
■ Test cricket: Pakistan v. New Zealand,
Feb. 16, 17, 18 & 19, 1973, Eden Park,
Auckland: official programme. Auckland,
the Assoc., [1973]. 36p. incl. adverts.
ports. diagrs. stats.

5703 **Canterbury Cricket Association**
■ Canterbury versus Pakistan, Lancaster
Park, 13, 14, 15, Jan. Christchurch, the
Assoc., [1973]. 24p. incl. adverts. ports.

5703 **New Zealand Cricket Council**
-1 New Zealand – Pakistan 1st Test, Basin
Reserve, February 2, 3, 4, 5: official
programme. The Council, [1973]. 22p.
incl. adverts. illus. diagr. stats.

5703 **Wanganui Cricket Association**
-2 Central Districts versus Pakistan, Cooks
Gardens, Wanganui, January 16, 17 and
18: official programme. Wanganui, the
Assoc., [1973]. [12]p incl. adverts.

5703 **Wellington Cricket Association**
-3 Pakistan [v] Wellington, Basin Reserve,
Jan. 20, 21, 22, 1973: official programme.
Wellington, the Assoc., [1973]. 20p. incl.
covers. illus. ports. diagr. stats.

### 1978–79 Test Tour (Mushtaq Mohammad)

5703 **Central Districts Cricket Association**
-4 Rothmans tour, second cricket Test, Paki-
■ stan v. New Zealand, McLean Park,
Napier, 50th Test venue in world cricket
history. Feb. 16, 17, 18, 20, 21, 1979:
official souvenir programme. [Napier],
the Assoc., [1979]. [48]p. incl. adverts.
illus. ports. stats.

# PAKISTAN TOURS TO INDIA

## 1952–53 Test Tour (A.H. Kardar)

5704 **Board of Control for Cricket in India**
Official souvenir 1952 Pakistan vs. India;
compiled by B.D. Panwelkar. The Board,
[1952]. ports.
*pre-Test*

5705 **Chatterjee, A.C.**
Official souvenir: visit to Lucknow of
Pakistan cricket team 1952. Lucknow
Sports Association, 1952. 56p. incl. ad-
verts. ports.
*pre-visit*

5706 **Kardar, Abdul Hafeez**
■  Inaugural Test matches: an eye-witness
account of the Pakistan cricket team's
tour of India. Karachi, Asad Ali, [1954].
xiii,156p. illus. ports. scores, stats.

5707 **Madras Cricket Association**
■  India vs. Pakistan: fourth Test official
souvenir, Nov. 28, 29, 30 & Dec. 1. Madras, Haridass, [1952]. 68p. incl. adverts.
ports. stats.

5708 India vs. Pakistan: fifth Test official souvenir, Madras, Haridass, 1952. ports.
stats.

5708 **Maqsood, Syed M.H.**, *compiler*
–1  Cricket in Pakistan. 3rd ed. Karachi,
Universal C.C., 1954. [xvi],100p. illus.
ports. scores
*contains an account of the 1952–53 Paki-
stan tour of India*

5709 **Official** souvenir of the first official Test
match between India and Pakistan. New
Delhi, Services P., 1952. 40p. incl. adverts. illus.

5710 **Pakistan** v/s India: Test cricket players.
■  Bombay, A.L. Job, [1952]. ports.
*pull-out portraits of both teams*

## 1960–61 Test Tour (Fazal Mahmood)

5711 **Board of Control for Cricket in India**
■  Official souvenir of Pakistan cricket tour
of India 1960–61. The Board, [1960]. 100p.
incl. adverts. ports. stats.
*pre-tour*

5712 **Board of Control for Cricket in Pakistan**
■  Pakistan India tour 1960–61. Karachi, the
Board, [1961]. [56]p. incl. adverts. illus.
ports. scores, stats.
*pre-tour*

5713 **Butt, Qamaruddin**
■  Playing for a draw (containing a complete
eye-witness account of Pakistan's tour of
India in 1960–61). Karachi, Jahaniasons,
1962. [iii],295p. illus. ports. scores, stats.

5714 **Haridass, C.K.**
■  India vs. Pakistan 1960–61. Madras, Haridass, 1960. [98]p. incl. adverts. ports.
stats.
*pre-tour*

5715 **Hyderabad Cricket Association**
Pakistan v. South Zone, Jan. 21, 22, 23,
1961: official souvenir. Hyderabad, the
Assoc., [1961]. 80p. ports.

5716 **India**—Pakistan 2nd cricket Test match
■  at Kanpur: souvenir. Lucknow, Aryavart
Agencies, [1960]. 56p. incl. adverts. illus.
ports. stats.

5717 **India** Pakistan 5th cricket Test match at
■  Delhi, Feb. 8 to 13, [1961]. Lucknow,
Aryavart Agencies, [1961]. 48p. incl.
adverts. illus. ports. stats.

5717 **Monkey Brand Black Tooth Powder**
–1  "Meet the Pakistan Test team". [Bombay,
■  Monkey Brand, 1960]. [24]p. incl. covers.
ports. stats.

5718 **Sport & Pastime**
■  Pakistan cricketers tour of India 1960–61.
Madras, Sport & Pastime, [1960]. 58p.
incl. adverts. ports. stats.
*pre-tour*

5719 **Sportimes:** the magazine for sportsmen.
Lahore, Mian Maqsood Ahmad. *monthly.*
*Cricket number. vol. 5, no.11, November
1960. 64p. illus. ports. map, stats.*
*pre-tour*

5720 **Thackeray, S.K.**
■  Pakistan v/s India: cricketers in cartoon.
Bombay, S.K. Thackeray, [1960]. [36]p.
ports.

5721 **The Uttar Pradesh Cricket Association**
■  Pakistan versus India: second cricket
Test, Kanpur (U.P.), India, December
16–21, 1960: souvenir programme.
Kanpur (U.P.), the Assoc., [1960]. 52p.
illus. ports. map, plan, diagrs. stats.

## 1979–80 Test Tour (S.M. Gavaskar)

5721 **Board of Control for Cricket in India**
–1  Pakistan cricket team tour of India
■  1979–80: official souvenir. Hyderabad,
The Masters Foundation on behalf of the
Board, [1979]. [76]p. incl. adverts. illus.
ports. stats.
*pre-tour*

5721 **Gupta, Shivendra**
–2 Cricket series India vs. Pakistan 1979–80:
■ (souvenir). Surat, the Author, [1979].
64p. incl. adverts. (+[8]p. insert). ports.
stats.
*pre-tour*

5721 **Haridass, C.K.**, *editor*
–3 Pakistan in India 1979–80. Madras, C.K.
■ Haridass & Sons, [1979]. 134p. incl.
adverts. illus. ports. diagr. facsims.
scores
*pre-tour*

5721 **The Hindu**
–4 Pakistan tour of India 1979–80: the Hindu
■ souvenir. Madras, the Hindu, [1979].
100p. incl. covers & adverts. illus. ports.
stats.
*pre-tour*

# PAKISTAN TOURS TO SRI LANKA

## 1948–49 Tour

5722 **Board of Control for Cricket in Ceylon**
■ A souvenir of the Pakistan tour of Ceylon
March–April, 1949; edited & compiled by
Victor Lewis. [Colombo], the Board,
[1949]. 34p. incl. adverts. ports. scores
*pre-tour*

## 1964 Tour

5722 **Board of Control for Cricket in Ceylon**
–1 Ceylon v. Pakistan, played at Wanathamulla Oval, August 28, 29, 30, 31,
1964: [programme]. Colombo, the Board,
[1964]. 10p.

## 1972 Intended Tour

5723 **Board of Control for Cricket in Ceylon**
■ Pakistan tour 1972, 7–12 November;
edited by S.S. Perera & E. J. Melder.
Colombo, the Board, [1972]. [48]p. incl.
covers & adverts. ports. stats.
*pre-tour*

5724 **Colombo Cricket Club**
■ Tour of Sri Lanka by the Pakistan Test &
Provincial XI. Sponsored by the Colombo
Cricket Club: official programme. Col-
ombo, the Club, 1972. 48p. 1 illus. stats.
*the tour was cancelled at the last moment;
includes "A short history of the Colombo
C.C." by S.S. Perera*

## 1973 Pakistan Under 25 Team

5725 **Matara Sports Club**
■ Pakistan under 25 team in Sri Lanka: visit
of the . . . team to Matara: souvenir 19th
Nov. to 15th Dec., 1973. Colombo, the
Club, [1973]. [32]p. ports. score, stats.
*edited by S.S. Perera; includes history of
Matara Sports Club*

## 1975 Pakistan Under-19 Tour

5725 **Cricket** match Galle Esplanade. Pakistan
–1 U-19 v. Sri Lanka Southern Province U-
19 XI: [programme]. Galle, *printed by* Fort
Printers, [1975]. [4]p. fold

## 1976 Tour

5725 **Central Province Cricket Association**
–2 Pakistan vs Sri Lanka Board II, Trinity
■ College Grounds, Asgiriya, January 20,
21, 22, 1976: [programme]. [Kandy], the
Assoc., [1976]. [12]p.

5725 **[Perera, S.S.]**, *compiler*
–3 Pakistan v. Sri Lanka Board President's
■ XI . . . 11 & 12 January 1976, Galle
Esplanade: souvenir to mark the above
occasion and centenary celebrations of
the Galle Cricket Club. Galle, the Club,
[1976]. [40]p. incl. adverts.

## 1979 Tour

5725 **Board of Control for Cricket in Sri Lanka**
–4 Official tour programme of Pakistan team
■ to Sri Lanka 3rd to 5th April 1979.
[Colombo, the Board, 1979]. [6]p. folded

5725 Pakistan tour 1979: playing conditions.
–5 Colombo, the Board, [1979]. 8p.

# OTHER PAKISTAN TOURS

5726 **Bermuda Cricket Association**
■ The Bermuda Cricket Association presents to Bermuda the Pakistan cricket
team, April 12 to April 28, 1958. The
Assoc., [1958]. 32p. incl. adverts. illus.
ports.
*pre-tour*

5727 **Pakistan International Airlines**
■ PIA cricket team tour of Ireland 1969.
Karachi, PIA, [1969]. 32p. ports.
*pre-tour*

# SRI LANKA

**5727** **Board of Control for Cricket in Sri Lanka**
**-1** Summary of Sri Lanka in international
■ cricket presented at 2nd Asian Cricket
Conference, Colombo, Sri Lanka, 11th
March 1976, by the Board of Control for
Cricket in Sri Lanka; results of matches
played by Ceylon-Sri Lanka 1964–1976.
[Colombo, the Board, 1976]. 16p.

**5727** Sri Lanka in international cricket; com-
**-2** piled by S.S. Perera. Colombo, the Board,
1979. 25p.
*printed for distribution at the I.C.C. 1979*

**5727** **Boycott Racist Sri Lanka Cricket Team**
**-3** **Action Committee,** *Oxford*
■ Send brown racist Sri Lanka cricket team
to play white South Africa. Boycott racist
Sri Lanka team. . . [Oxford, the Cttee.],
1975. bs. *typescript*
*a dispute between Tamil minority and
Sinhala Sri Lanka*

## SRI LANKA TOURS TO INDIA

### 1932–33 Tour

**5727** **Ceylon** cricketers tour of India 1932/33.
**-4** Itinerary and fixtures list. Delhi, *printed
by Oxford Printing P.*, 1932

**5727** **Delhi Cricket Association**
**-5** Festival cricket. Ceylon XI v. an Indian XI
on the Ferozshah Kotla Grounds. Delhi,
the Assoc., 1932

### 1940–41 Tour

**5728** **Foenander, Samuel Peter**
■ Souvenir of the Ceylon cricketers' tour in
India, December 1940–January 1941.
Colombo, Ceylon Observer, [1940]. [ii],
8p. ports.stats.
*pre-tour*

### 1964–65 Tour

**5729** **Hyderabad Cricket Association**
■ India vs. Ceylon, 19, 20, 21, 22 Dec. '64:
official souvenir. Hyderabad, the Assoc.,
[1964]. [108]p. ports.

**5730** **Mysore State Cricket Association**
Ceylon vs. India, first Test, December 11,
12, 13, 14, 1964. Central College Grounds,
Bangalore: souvenir edited. . .by Shri
K.S. Ramaswami. Bangalore, the Assoc.,
1964. 60p. incl. adverts.

**5731** **Sports Writers' Club,** *Madras*
Ceylon cricket team's visit to Madras,
Tour of India, 1964–65. Madras, the Club.
[1964]. 24p. port. scores
*pre-tour*

### 1970–71 Tour

**5731** **Ceylon XI** vs. Andhra Pradesh Chief
**-1** Minister's XI at Bhramananda Reddy
Stadium, 16, 17, 18 January 1971: souvenir. [1971]. 100p. incl. adverts.

### 1975 Tour

**5731** **Hyderabad Cricket Association**
**-2** Sri Lanka vs. India first unofficial Test
■ Nov. 8, 9, 10, 11, 1975. Lal Bahadur
Stadium, Hyderabad: official souvenir.
Hyderabad, the Assoc., [1975]. [94]p.
incl. adverts. illus. ports.

**5731** **Sharma, Ashok K.,** *editor*
**-3** Sri Lanka tour 1975: guide. New Delhi,
The Young Sportswriters Co., [1975].
36p. incl. adverts. ports. stats.
*pre-tour*

### Gopalan Trophy Matches
### 1969

**5731** **Tiruchirapalli District Cricket**
**-4** **Association**
Exhibition match All Ceylon XI vs.
M.C.A. President's XI at Stadium
Grounds on 8, 9 & 10 March 1969. Tiruchirapalli, the Assoc., [1969]. 18p. incl.
adverts. ports.
*played during Gopalan Trophy visit of
Ceylon to Madras 1969*

### 1975

**5731** **Salem District Cricket Association**
**-5** Gopalan Trophy 1975. Salem (S. India),
the Assoc., 1975. 104p. incl. adverts.

# SRI LANKAN TOURS TO PAKISTAN

## 1950 Tour

5731 **Pakistan** v. Ceylon, 25 to 28 March 1950:
–6 souvenir of Test match. Lahore, *printed by* Civil & Military Gazette Ltd., [1950]

## 1966 Tour

5731 **East Pakistan Sports Federation**
–7 Ceylon v. Pakistan, second unofficial Test match, November 18, 19, 20 and 21 Dacca Stadium: official souvenir. Dacca, Raisuddin Ahmed, [1966]

5731 **Munu Hassan,** *editor*
–8 Pakistan v. Ceylon: third Test match, 25, 26, 27 & 28 November 1966 at National Stadium Karachi: souvenir. Karachi, Karachi C.A., 1966

5731 **Rawalpindi Cricket Association**
–9 President's XI v. Ceylon: souvenir of cricket match, Nov. 4, 5, 6, 1966. Rawalpindi, the Assoc., [1966]. 32p.

## 1974 Tour

5731 **Cricket match** Sri Lanka vs. Punjab
–10 Cricket Association team, 16, 17, 18
■ March 1974: souvenir. Lyallpur, Ijaz Hashmet Khan, [1974]. [36]p. incl. adverts. ports.
  *match organised by District Sports Association, Lyallpur*

5731 **Karachi Cricket Association**
–11 Second 'Test' match, Pakistan vs. Sri
■ Lanka, played at National Stadium, Karachi, 12, 13, 14, 15 April, 1974; edited by S. Sirajul Islam Bukhari. Karachi, the Assoc., 1974. [74]p. incl. adverts. ports. score, stats.

5731 **Multan District Cricket Association**
–12 Sri Lanka cricket team versus Pakistan
■ Under-19 cricket team played at Multan District Club Stadium, Multan, on April 7 to April 9, 1974: souveneir [sic.] Multan, [the Assoc., 1974]. [30]p. incl. adverts. ports.

5731 **Punjab Cricket Association**
–13 First unofficial cricket Test Pakistan v. Sri
■ Lanka on March 21, 22, 23 & 24, 1974 at Gaddafi Stadium, Lahore. [Lahore, the

Assoc., 1974]. [40]p. incl. adverts. ports. stats.

5731 **Sri Lanka** v. Pakistan Universities cricket
–14 match; Rawalpindi March 30, 31, 1st April. Lahore, *printed by* Caxton Printing P., [1974]. 24p.

5731 **Wirrasal Hussanin Rizir, Syed,** *editor*
–15 Sri Lanka vs. Sind Cricket Association. First class match at Mirpukhas on 10, 11, 12, March 1974. Mirpukhas, Tharpaikai Cricket Cttee., [1974]. 40p. incl. adverts.

# SRI LANKAN TOURS TO BANGLADESH

## 1978 Tour

5731 **Bangladesh Cricket Control Board**
–16 1st unofficial Test match: Sri Lanka v. Bangladesh, 13, 14, 15 January 1978, Dacca Stadium; edited by Mohinuddin Ahmed. Dacca, the Board, [1978]. 57p. incl. adverts.

5731 **Hyatt Hussein,** *editor*
–17 Sri Lanka v. Bangladesh 3rd unofficial Test match, 24, 25, 26 January 1978, Chittagong Stadium. [1978]

5731 **Sri Lanka** v. Bangladesh Central Zone
–18 cricket match, January 3 & 4, 1978. Momenshah Stadium, Mymensingh: official souvenir. Mymensingh, Organizing Cttee. of the Zonal Cricket Match, [1978?]. 88p. incl. adverts.

# OTHER SRI LANKAN TOURS

## 1957–58 Tour to Malaya

5732 **Gunaratam, M.,** *compiler*
■ Ceylon cricket team Malayan tour, Penang. [Singapore, Star P., 1957]. 36p. incl. adverts. ports.

## 1973 Tour to Kerala

5733 **Kerala Cricket Association**
■ Official souvenir of Sri Lanka cricket tour of Kerala 1973. Trivandrum, the Assoc., [1973]. [76]p. incl. 40p. of adverts. ports.
  *pre-tour*

5734 **[See no. 5731–4]**

THE

ENGLISH CRICKETERS

TRIP

TO

CANADA

AND THE

UNITED STATES

BY

FRED LILLYWHITE.

England v. Canada and the United States. The frontispiece to no. 4893 *photo: M.C.C.*

# UNITED STATES AND CANADA

**5735  Bowen, Rowland**
■    North America in international cricket.
     M.S. Morris Prints, 1960. [ii],21p. stats.
     *limited ed. of 100 copies in U.K., 50 copies
     in U.S.A.*
     *tours to and from U.S.A. and Canada*

**5736  Marder, John I.**
■    The international series: the story of the
     United States v. Canada at cricket.
     Kaye & Ward, 1968. 337p. illus. ports.
     scores, stats.
     *covers 1884–1967*

## UNITED STATES

### UNITED STATES TOURS TO ENGLAND

#### 1884 Gentlemen of Philadelphia

**5737  [Green, John Pugh]**
■    The tour of the "Gentlemen of Philadel-
     phia" in Great Britain in 1884. By One
     of the Committee. Philadelphia, Allen
     Lane & Scott, 1897. 89p. illus. scores,
     stats.

#### 1968 United States C.A. Tour

**5738  United States Cricket Association**
■    England tour 1968: souvenir edition. Los
     Angeles, the Assoc., [1968]. [12]p. incl.
     adverts. illus. ports.
     *pre-tour; forms no. 3 of vol. 3 of The
     American Cricketer (July 1968)*

#### 1972 Prior C.C. Tour

**5739  Prior** Cricket Club of Philadelphia tour of
■    England 1972. Philadelphia (Pa.), [1972].
     [8]p.
     *souvenir programme; pre-tour*

### UNITED STATES TOURS TO CANADA

#### 1874 American Twelve of Phila-delphia Tour

**5740  The Halifax** cricket tournament: an
■    account of the visit of the American
     Twelve of Philadelphia to Halifax, in
     August, 1874. Philadelphia, Lippincott
     for private circulation, 1874. 54p. diagr.
     scores, stats.

**5741  [Entry cancelled]**

#### 1965 Tour

**5742  Alberta Cricket Association**
■    International Test match between Canada
     and United States of America, Sunday,
     September 5th and Monday, September
     6th, 1965, Riley Park, Calgary, Alberta:
     official souvenir programme. Calgary, the
     Assoc., 1965. 12p. incl. adverts. diagr.

## OTHER AMERICAN TOURS

#### 1887–88 Tour of West Indies

**5742  Holmes, Henry Robert**
**–1**  The American cricketers in the West
■    Indies 1887–88. Lymington, the Author,
     1975. 16p. scores.
     *limited ed. of. 75 copies signed and num-
     bered*

#### 1971 Southern California C.A. Tour

**5743  Southern California Cricket Association**
■    Tour to Jamaica 1971. Los Angeles, the
     Assoc., 1971. [8]p. incl. covers. ports.
     *pre-tour*

# CANADA

## CANADIAN TOURS TO ENGLAND

### 1887 The Gentlemen of Canada Team

5744 ■ [Saunders, Dyce Willcocks, *and* Smith, George Goldwin Lindsay]
Cricket across the sea; or, The wanderings and matches of the Gentlemen of Canada, by Two of the Vagrants. Toronto, Murray, 1887. 223p. port. scores, stats.

### 1954 Tour

5745 ■ Canada: pictures, fixtures, personalities 1954: photographic souvenir. Manchester, W. Walker, [1954]. [4]p. fold, ports.
*pre-tour*

5746 The Canadian Cricketer
■ The Canadian tour of England 1954; edited by E.H.M. Burn. St. Catherines, Ridley College, The Canadian Cricketer, 1954. 35p. scores, stats. *typescript*
*post-tour*

5747 Canadian tour of England. 1954: autograph souvenir.1954. 4p. fold, illus.
*post-tour*

### 1969 Toronto C.C. Tour

5748 Toronto Cricket, Skating and Curling Club
Cricket tour England & Ireland, July 1969. Toronto, the Club, [1969]. 32p. illus. ports. map
*pre-tour*

### 1972 British Columbia C.C. Tour

5749 British Columbia Cricket Club
Tour of England 1972. [The Club]. 4p. fold, illus.
*pre-tour*

### 1972 Toronto C.C. Tour

5750 Toronto Cricket, Skating and Curling Club
Cricket tour England July 1972. Toronto, the Club, [1972]. 40p. illus. ports. map
*pre-tour*

### 1975 British Columbia C.C. Tour

5750 British Columbia Cricket Club
–1 Tour of England 1975. [The Club, 1975].
■ [4]p. fold
*pre-tour*

### 1975 Toronto C.C. Tour

5750 Toronto Cricket, Skating and Curling
–2 Club
■ Fourth overseas cricket tour, England, July 1975. [Toronto, the Club, 1975]. 40p. illus. ports.
*cover-title*: Cricket tour England July 1975
*pre-tour*

## CANADIAN TOURS TO UNITED STATES

### 1966 Tour

5751 Southern California Cricket Association
■ Official schedule, 1966. The Assoc., 1966. [24]p. incl. adverts. diagr.
*cover-title*: S.C.C.A. 1966. *United States v. Canada Test match 1966*

### 1972 Tour

5752 Cricket Club of Louisville, *and* United
■ States Cricket Association
U.S.A. v. Canada 1972 Test cricket, Louisville, Kentucky, Sept. 2, 3, 4: [souvenir programme]. [Louisville, the Club & Assoc., 1972]. 22p. incl. adverts. illus. ports.

## CANADIAN TOURS TO BERMUDA

### 1958 Ed Burn Canadian Team

5753 Bermuda Cricket Association
Bermuda cricketer, published as a souvenir & in honour of the Ed Burn Canadian cricket touring team to Bermuda, June 14–29, 1958; edited by Jim Murray. Bermuda, the Assoc., [1958]. 32p. incl. adverts. ports.

# TOURS OF OTHER COUNTRIES

## ARGENTINA

### 1922 Tour to Brazil

5754 **Anglo-Brazilian Chronicle**
■ Cricket: Brazil v. the Argentine, 1922. São Paulo, Anglo-Brazilian Chronicle, 1922. 45p. illus. ports. scores
*post-tour*

### 1953 Tour to Brazil

5755 **Nash, C.T.,** *editor*
■ Argentine cricket tour Brazil—1953. [Rio-de-Janeiro, Brazil C.A., 1953]; [40]p. ports. scores, stats.

### 1972 Tour to Great Britain

5756 **Argentine Cricket Association**
■ Great Britain tour 1972. [Buenos Aires], the Assoc., [1972]. 64p. incl. adverts. ports.
*pre-tour*

## BERMUDA

### 1961 Somerset C.C. Tour to U.K.

5757 **Somerset Cricket Club,** *Bermuda*
Cricket tour, Scotland, England and Wales; May, June, July, 1961. The Club, 1961. ports.
*pre-tour*

### 1962 Tour to England

5758 **Bermuda Cricket Association,** *and* **Pond**
■ **Hill Stars Cricket Club**
Bermuda cricketers in England, June-July 1962; edited by Ed Burn. Bermuda, the Assoc. & Club, [1962]. [9]p. ports.
*pre-tour*

### 1966 Tour to Canada

5759 **Bermuda** cricketers in Canada, June-July 1966

### 1969 Tour to Europe

5760 **Bermuda Cricket Board of Control**
■ European tour programme May-June 1969. [Hamilton, the Board, 1969]. [12]p. ports.
*pre-tour*

### 1970 Tour to Canada

5761 **Bermuda** cricketers in Canada, August
■ 14th to 23rd, 1970. Bermuda Sportsman's Club, [1970]. [4]p. folded card. ports.
*pre-tour*

### 1971 Somers Isles C.L. Tour

5761 **Somers Isles Cricket League**
–1 European cricket tour 1971: Bermuda-
■ England-Europe-America-Bermuda: official souvenir brochure. Bermuda, [the League, 1971]. 16p. incl. adverts. ports.
*pre-tour itinerary*

### 1977 Bermuda Wanderers Tour

5761 **Bermuda Wanderers Touring Cricket**
–2 **Club**
■ Bermuda cricketers in Nassau, Bahamas, February 24 – March 7, 1977. Bermuda, [the Club 1977]. 4p. folded card. team port.
*pre-tour*

### 1978 Bermuda Wanderers Tour

5761 **Bermuda Wanderers Touring Cricket**
–3 **Club**
■ Bermuda cricketers in England, Augst 10 to 30, 1978. Bermuda, the Club, [1978]. folded card. team port.
*6th tour by the Club; itinerary and pen portraits of players*

# BRAZIL

### 1954 Tour to Argentina

5761 **Brazil Cricket Association**
-4 B.C.A. cricket tour to Argentine November/December 1954. [The Assoc., 1954]. 8p. scores, stats.
*post-tour*

### 1967 Tour to Argentina

5762 **Argentine Cricket Association**
Brazilian tour December 1967. Buenos Aires, the Assoc., [1967].
*programme of matches played by Brazil in Argentina*

# CHILE

5763 **Argentine Cricket Association**
■ Programme of the events to take place during the visit of the Chilean cricket team. December 1924–January 1925. Buenos Aires, the Assoc., [1924]. [4]p. fold

# DENMARK

### 1954 Kjøbenhavns Boldklub XI

5764 **Kjøbenhavns** Boldklub eleven tour in England: itinerary, etc. Circularised by B.J.W. Hill, [1954]. *typescript*

### 1955 Tour to Holland

5765 **Nederlandsche Cricket Bond**
De landenwedstrijd 1955: Holland—Denemarken. The Hague, the Bond, 1955
*international match Holland v. Denmark*

# FIJI

### 1947–48 Tour to New Zealand

5766 **New Zealand Cricket Council**
Programme of matches arranged for the tour of the Fijian team through New Zealand, 1948. Christchurch, the Council, 1948. [4]p. folded card

### 1953–54 Tour to New Zealand

5767 **New Zealand Cricket Council**
Programme of matches arranged for the tour of the Fijian team through New Zealand, 1954. Christchurch, the Council, 1954. [4]p. folded card

# GOLD COAST

5767 **Nigeria Cricket Association**
-1 Nigeria v. Gold Coast, Lagos, April 1936: programme. Lagos, the Assoc., 1936

# HOLLAND

### 1968 Still Going Strong C.C. Tour

5768 **Still Going Strong Cricket Club**
Tour naar Engeland . . . 1968. The Club, [1968]. 4p. fold
*itinerary of tour*

### 1968–69 Netherlands Women's Tour to South Africa

5768 **South Africa and Rhodesia Women's**
-1 **Cricket Association**
Official souvenir programme of the inaugural visit by a Netherlands women's cricket team 1968/69. . . . [The Assoc., 1968?]. 44p. ports.

### 1971 Tour of England and Ireland

5769 **All Holland** tour England and Ireland, 1971. Rotterdam, *printed by* Van Leerdam's Drukkerij, [1971]. 12p. illus. ports.
*pre-tour*

# HONG KONG

## 1971 Tour to Ceylon

5770  **Board of Control for Cricket in Ceylon**
■      Hongkong Cricket Association visit to
       Ceylon, 19th to 29th March, 1971: official
       souvenir; edited by S.S. Perera. Colombo,
       [the Board, 1971]. [20]p. incl. adverts.
       port. score, stats.
       *pre-tour*

5771  **Galle Cricket Club**
■      Visit of the Hong Kong Cricket Associ-
       ation to Galle, 21 March, 1971: souvenir;
       compiled by S.S. Perera. Galle, the Club,
       [1971]. [16]p. incl. covers

5771  **Hong Kong Cricket Association**
–1     HK tour to Ceylon, Sabah & Singapore:
■      souvenir programme. Hong Kong, the
       Assoc., [1971]. 88p. incl. adverts. illus.
       ports. stats.
       *pre-tour*

## 1976 Tour to England

5771  **The Hong Kong** cricket tour of England
–2     July 1976. [n.p., 1976]. 72p. incl. adverts.
■      illus. ports.
       *pre-tour; sponsored by British-America
       Tobacco Co. (HK) Ltd.*

# IRELAND

## 1879 Gentlemen of Ireland to U.S.A.

5772  **Brougham, H.**
■      The Irish cricketers in the United States,
       1879, by One of Them. Dublin, Lawrence,
       Gill; London, Kent, 1880. [iv],103p.

Irish C.U., 1973. 96p. incl. adverts. illus.
ports.
*pre-tour*

## 1973 Tour to United States and Canada

5772  **Irish Cricket Union**
–1     Tour of U.S.A. and Canada. [Dublin],

5773  The tour to U.S.A. and Canada, Septem-
■      ber, 1973, [by] Derek Scott. The Union,
       [1973]. 27p. scores, stats. *typescript*
       *post-tour*

# ISRAEL

## 1970 Tour to England

5774  **Israel Cricket Association**
■      Tour of England by the Israel cricket
       team, August 23–September 17, 1970 at
       the invitation of the Israel Cricket Sup-
       porters Association, London branch. The
       Assoc., [1970]. [8]p.
       *includes details of cricket in Israel with
       fixture list of tour as inset*

5775  **Israel Cricket Supporters Association**
■      Israel National Cricket XI England tour
       1970. The Assoc., 1970. [10]p. of text.
       ports.
       *contains "The history and development of
       cricket in Israel" by Michael R. Mitzman
       rptd. from Playfair Cricket monthly*

## 1974 Tour to England and Eire

5775  **Israel Cricket Association**
–1     Tour of England by the Israel National
■      Cricket XI, August 22 – September 12,
       1974, at the invitation of the Israel Cricket
       Supporters Association. Tel Aviv, the
       Assoc., [1974]. [12]p. incl. adverts.
       *pre-tour*

5775  **Israel Cricket Supporters Association**
–2     1974 Israel National Cricket XI tour of
■      England and Eire. The Assoc., [1974].
       [40]p. incl. adverts.
       *pre-tour*

# KENYA

## 1956 Kenya Asian Team to South Africa

5776  **Eastern Province Cricket Federation**
■      Kenya Asian cricket tour of S. Africa 1956:
       official souvenir brochure. Port Elizabeth,
       the Federation, [1956]. [12]p. incl. ad-
       verts. ports.

5777  **South African Cricket Board of Control**
■      Kenya tour, November–December 1956,
       Cape Town–Johannesburg–Durban: sou-
       venir programme. The Board, [1956]. 72p.
       incl. adverts. ports. stats.
       *pre-tour*

# KUWAIT

5777 **Select Kuwait Wanderers**
−1 Souvenir cricket tour Denmark – United Kingdom – Switzerland, August/ September 1979. [The Club, 1979]. 40p. incl. adverts. illus. ports.

*pre-tour; co–editors: M.K. Kazi, K. Mahmood, V. Pereira; contains an earlier tour to India and Pakistan in January 1979*

# SINGAPORE

## 1971

5778 **Malaysia Singapore Ligers**
First cricket tour of England, 1971. 8p. ports.
*pre-tour*

## 1973

5779 **Singapore Cricket Association**
■ Visit of Singapore Cricket Association Juniors team to Madras/Bangalore, December 1973. Singapore, the Assoc., [1973]. 40p. incl. adverts. ports.
*pre-tour*

5780 **Singapore Cricket Club**
■ Tour of India and Sri Lanka 1973. [Singapore, the Club, 1973]. [28]p. incl. adverts. illus. ports. score
*contains an historical note on the Club by Andrew Gilmour*

## 1974

5780 **The Emu Club**
−1 The Emu Club world tour, 1974: [pro-
■ gramme]. [Tamworth (N.S.W.)], the Club, [1974]. [16]p. incl. covers. illus. ports.
*pre-tour; includes short reports of visit to Northern N.S.W. by Singapore National XI and Malaysian Schoolboys*

## 1976

5780 **Selangor Club**
−2 Australian cricket tour 1976: souvenir programme. Kuala Lumpur, the Club, [1976]. 76p. incl. adverts. illus. ports. scores

## 1977

5780 **Singapore Cricket Association**
−3 Singapore Colts tour of Queensland/New
■ South Wales 15 Jan.–4 Feb. 1977. Singapore, the Assoc., [1977?]. [100]p. incl. adverts. illus. ports. stats.
*pre-tour*

## 1979

5780 **Singapore Cricket Association**
−4 Souvenir brochure to commemorate visit
■ of Singapore team to England I.C.C. Trophy – 1979. [Singapore, the Assoc., 1979]. [120]p. incl. adverts. illus. & ports. (some col.)
*pre-tour*

5780 **Singapore Cricket Club**
−5 New Zealand '79: official journal of the Singapore Cricket Club tour of New Zealand 1979; edited by Peter Butler. Singapore, the Club, [1979]. 60p. incl. covers. illus. ports. scores

# SOUTH AMERICA

5781 **South American Cricket Associations** England tour 1932; [compiled by Hugh H. Spicer]. Chislehurst, *printed by* Waters, [1932]. 12p. stats.

5781 English tour 1932. The Assoc., [1932].
−1 [4]p. fold
■ *fixture list with names of players and officials representing the Argentine, Brazil & Chile*

# TAIWAN

5782 **Souvenir** of University Cricket Group from Taiwan, Republic of China to Manly, N.S.W., Australia, January 3 to February 7, 1970. ports.

# COMMONWEALTH AND INTERNATIONAL TEAMS

## 1949–50 Tour to India, Pakistan and Ceylon (George Duckworth's Team)

5783 **Board of Control for Cricket in Ceylon**
■ Commonwealth cricket pageant: a souvenir of the Commonwealth cricket team's tour of Ceylon, February–March, 1950. Colombo, "The Times of Ceylon" for the Board, [1950]. 40p. incl. adverts. ports. stats.
*pre-tour*

5784 **Board of Control for Cricket in India**
■ Official souvenir of visit to India of the Commonwealth cricket team 1949–50. [Bombay], the Board, [1949]. [68]p. incl. adverts. illus. ports.
*pre-tour*

5785 **Commonwealth** and India. Madras, N.S. Venkataraman, [1951?]. 96p. illus. ports.
*contains accounts of Commonwealth tours in India, 1949–50, 1950–51*

5786 **Commonwealth** tour 1949–50: a souvenir; ■ edited by R.J. Moses. Bombay, 'Trades' Publications, [1949]. [80]p. incl. adverts. illus. ports.

5786 **Haridass, C.K.**
–1 Welcome cricketers from the Common-
■ wealth: 5th Test at Madras [Feb. 17, 18, 19, 20 & 21, 1950]: souvenir. Madras, C.K. Haridass, 1950. 56p. incl. adverts. ports. stats.

5787 **The Hindu**
Commonwealth tour of India and Ceylon, 1949–50: articles reprinted from the Hindu, Madras, October 10, 1949–March 7, 1950. Madras, the Hindu, [1950].
*post-tour*

5788 **Sport & Pastime**
■ Commonwealth cricketers tour of India 1949–50. [Madras], Sport & Pastime, [1949]. 80p. incl. adverts.ports. map
*pre-tour*

## 1950–51 Tour to India (L.E.G. Ames)

5789 **Board of Control for Cricket in India**
■ Official souvenir of visit to India of a Commonwealth cricket team 1950–51. Bombay, the Board, 1950. [64]p. incl. adverts. illus. ports. stats.
*pre-tour*

5790 **Commonwealth** and India. Madras, N.S. Venkataraman, [1951?]. 96p. illus. ports.
*contains accounts of Commonwealth tours in India, 1949–50, 1950–51*

5791 **Delhi and District Cricket Association**
India versus Commonwealth: official souvenir; edited by A.N. Dhawan. Delhi, the Assoc., [1950]. 48p. incl. adverts. ports.

5792 **Dutt, P.D.**
Cricket souvenir: Commonwealth at the Eden Gardens. Calcutta, S.S. Dutta, 1950. 34p. illus.
*pre-match*

5793 **Haridass, C.K.**
■ Welcome to Commonwealth cricketers, fourth Test: illustrated souvenir. Madras, Haridass, [1951]. 70p. incl. adverts. ports. stats.

5794 **Phadke, Narayan Sitaram**
■ India vs. second Commonwealth unofficial Tests 1950–51. Bombay, Anjali Prakashan, 1951. [2],vi,80p.
*post-tour*

5795 **Sport & Pastime**
■ Commonwealth cricketers tour of India 1950–51. Madras, Sport & Pastime, [1950]. 80p. incl. adverts. ports.
*pre-tour*

## 1953–54 Tour to India (B.A. Barnett's Team)

5796 **Board of Control for Cricket in India**
■ Official souvenir of The Silver Jubilee Overseas Cricket team 1953–54; compiled by B.D. Panwelkar. [New Delhi], the Board, [1953]. [48]p. incl. adverts. ports. stats.
*pre-tour; to commemorate the Silver Jubilee of the Board*

5797 **Kamdar, Kantilal M.**
■ Indian cricket and jubilee team 1953–1954. Bombay, Art Avenue Duplicating Service, 1953. 32p. 1 illus. ports.
*pre-tour*

5798 **Madras Cricket Association**
■ Silver Jubilee overseas cricket team vs. India: 4th Test at Corporation Stadium, Madras, Jan. 13, 14, 15, 16 & 17, 1954: official souvenir. Madras, the Assoc., [1954]. 76p. incl. adverts. ports.

5799 **Sport & Pastime**
■ Commonwealth cricketers' tour of India 1953–54. Madras, Sport & Pastime, [1953]. 84p. incl. adverts. illus. ports. map, stats.
*pre-tour*

## 1959–60 Tour to South Africa (R.A. Roberts' Team)

5800 **Chettle, Geoffrey A.**, *editor*
■ Denis Compton's star-studded Commonwealth XI: official souvenir brochure. Durban, [the Editor, 1959]. 16p. incl. adverts. ports. stats.
*pre-tour*

## 1960–61 Tour to South Africa (R.A. Roberts' Team)

5801 **Chettle, Geoffrey A.**, *editor*
■ Transvaal v. Benaud's Cavaliers, September 24, 26, 27 . . . at Wanderers: official souvenir brochure. Durban, [the Editor, 1960]. [20]p. incl. adverts. ports. stats.
similar brochures:
*v. Natal, October 1, 2, 3 . . . at Kingsmead*
*v. Invitation XI, October 7, 8, 10 . . . at Wanderers*

## 1961–62 Tour to New Zealand (R.A. Roberts' Team)

5802 **Auckland Cricket Association**
■ Ron Roberts' Commonwealth Eleven v. The New Zealand Cricket Council President's Eleven, Eden Park, Auckland . . . March 22, 23, 24, 1962: souvenir programme. Auckland, the Assoc., [1962]. 24p. incl. adverts. ports.

5802 **Souvenir** programme commemorating
–1 the visit of the Commonwealth cricket
■ team to Hong Kong Mar. 27, 28, 29, 1962. Hong Kong, Hongkong C.L. [1962]. [60]p. incl. adverts. illus. ports. stats.
*pre-tour*

5802 **Wellington Cricket Association**
–2 Ron Roberts' Commonwealth team v.
■ Wellington: programme. Wellington, the Assoc., [1962]. [16]p. incl. covers. ports. diagr. stats.

## 1963 Tour to Pakistan (A.R. Gover's Team)

5803 **Butt, Qamaruddin**
■ Cricket reborn: (covering Commonwealth cricket team's tour in Pakistan, 1963). Rawalpindi, the Author, [1965]. vi,93p. illus. ports. scores. stats.
*post-tour*

5804 **Karachi Cricket Association**
■ Pakistan vs. Commonwealth first Test match, 15, 16, 17, 19 & 20, November 1963; edited by Munir Hussain. Karachi, the Assoc., [1963]. [116]p. incl. adverts. illus. ports. diagrs. stats.
*the extensive pen-portraits of the Commonwealth team are by Irving Rosenwater*

## 1964 Tour to Far East (E.W. Swanton's Team)

5805 **Malayan Cricket Association**
■ E.W. Swanton's Commonwealth XI visit to Singapore, March 20–25, 1964: souvenir programme. Singapore, the Assoc., [1964]. 56p. incl. adverts. illus. ports.
*pre-tour*

5806 **Penang Cricket Association**
■ E.W. Swanton's Commonwealth XI cricket tour, 18, 19 March 1964 at Penang Sports Club Ground. Penang, the Assoc., [1964]. [28]p. incl. adverts. illus. ports.
*pre-tour*

5807 **Royal Bangkok Sports Club**
■ E.W. Swanton's Commonwealth XI v. R.B.S.C., the R.B.S.C. Ground, Bangkok, 8th April, 1964: souvenir programme. Bangkok, the Club, [1964]. [32]p. incl. adverts. ports.

## 1968 Tour to Pakistan (Alex Bannister's Team)

5808 **Indus Advertising Co.**
■ Commonwealth XI vs. Pakistan XI, 1 to 4 March 196[8], Qasim Bagh Stadium, Multan. Multan, the Co., [1968]. [48]p. incl. adverts. illus. ports.
*includes the Constitution of the Multan Cricket Club*

5809 **Karachi Cricket Association**
■ Official souvenir of the match South Zone XI vs. Commonwealth XI at the National Stadium, Karachi, on 25, 26 & 27 February, 1968; edited by A.S. Bhagat. Karachi, the Assoc., [1968]. [50]p. incl. adverts. illus. ports.
*pen-portraits of C. team by Irving Rosenwater; pre-match*

5810 **B.C.C.P. XI vs. Commonwealth XI** at the
■ National Stadium on the 29, 30, 31 March & 1 April 1968: official souvenir; edited by Munir Hussain. Karachi, the Assoc., [1968]. [96]p. incl. adverts. illus. ports. scores, stats.
*extensive pen-portraits of the C. players by Irving Rosenwater; pre-match*

5811 **Lahore Division Cricket Association**
■ Pakistan vs. Commonwealth at the Lahore Stadium, 15–18 March 1968: souvenir. Lahore, the Assoc., [1968]. [44]p. incl. adverts. ports.

5812 **The Multan Divisional Cricket**
■ **Association**
Official brochure of the first Test Pakistan vs. Commonwealth at the Multan Stadium on 1, 2, 3 & 4 March 1968.

[Multan], the Assoc., [1968]. [54]p. incl. adverts. ports.

*pen-pictures of C. team by Irving Rosenwater; pre-match*

**5813 Rawalpindi Cricket Association**
■ President's XI vs. Commonwealth XI, March 24, 25 & 26, 1968 at the Rawalpindi Club ground: souvenir. Rawalpindi, the Assoc., [1968]. [28]p. illus. ports.

**5814 Sargodha Divisional Cricket Association**
■ Commonwealth cricket team v/s. Central Zone [at Sargodha, 6, 7, 8, March 1968]. [Sargodha], the Assoc., [1968]. [28]p. incl. adverts. ports.

## 1968 Tour to Ceylon and Malaysia (J. Lister's Team)

**5815 Board of Control for Cricket in Ceylon**
■ President's XI v. International Cricket XI, 5, 6 and 7 March '68: official souvenir; edited by R.B. Wijesinha. Colombo, the Board, [1968]. 48p. incl. adverts. ports. score, stats.

**5816 Ceylon Government Service Cricket**
■ **Association**
Joe Lister's International cricket XI vs. Ceylon Government Service Cricket Association XI, 9 & 10 March 1968, University Grounds, Peradeniya: souvenir. [Colombo], the Assoc., [1968]. [50]p. incl. adverts. ports.
*pre-match; includes brief history of C.G.S.C.A.*

**5817 Royal Bangkok Sports Club**
■ R.B.S.C. XI v. Joe Lister's International XI: souvenir programme. Bangkok, the Club, 1968. 24p. incl. adverts. ports.

## 1969 Tour to Kuwait (T.W. Graveney's Team)

**5818 Tom Graveney's** International Cricket XI
■ in Kuwait, 1969: souvenir programme. Kuwait, n.p., [1969]. 116p. incl. adverts. 1 illus. ports.
*includes article on cricket in Kuwait*

## 1970 Cyclone Disaster Relief Match

**5818 The Guardian**
**–1** The bedside 'Guardian' 21: a selection
■ from The Guardian 1971–72; edited by W.L. Webb. Collins, 1972. 255p. illus.
*includes pp. 164–7, "Who said the M.C.C. moved slowly?" by Omar Kureishi [on a World XI's exhibition match in Pakistan in aid of relief from cyclone devastation in East Pakistan]*

## 1972 International Wanderers' Tour

**5818 Rhodesia Cricket Union**
**–2** 1972 International Wanderers tour of Rhodesia, Bulawayo, 23, 24, 25 September, Gwelo, 27 September, Salisbury, 29, 30 September, 1, 2 October, 1972: souvenir programme. [Salisbury], the Union, [1972]. 16p. incl. adverts. ports. stats.
*pre-tour*

## 1973 Tour to South Africa (D.H. Robins' Team)

**5819 [Chettle, Geoffrey A.]**
■ Derrick Robins' XI tour of South Africa 1973: official souvenir brochure. Durban, [the Author, 1973]. [24]p. incl. adverts. ports. stats.
*pre-tour*
——*other brochures*: v. Provincial XI. [20]p. incl. adverts. ports. stats.
v. S.A. African XI at Moroka Jabara Stadium, Soweto, 20 October 1973. [8]p. ports. stats.
v. S.A. Invitation XI. [28]p. incl. covers & adverts. ports. stats.

**5819 Transvaal Cricket Union**
**–1** Derrick Robins' XI v. Transvaal XI, Jan.
■ 12, 13, 15, 1973, Wanderers Stadium, Johannesburg: official programme. Johannesburg, the Union, [1973]. [20]p. incl. adverts. ports.

## 1974 International Wanderers' Tour

**5819 Rhodesia Cricket Union**
**–2** International Wanderers tour of Rhodesia
■ September, 1974: souvenir programme. Salisbury, the Union, [1974]. 28p. incl. covers & adverts. illus. ports.
*pre-tour*

## 1976 International Wanderers' Tour

**5819 International Wanderers** tour South
**–3** Africa, March 12–April 13, 1976.
■ [Datsun–Nissan and Protea Assurance, 1976]. 24p. incl. covers. illus. ports.
*pre-tour; text in English and Afrikaans*

## 1977 Tour to Sri Lanka and Far East (D.H. Robins' Team)

**5819 Board of Control for Cricket in Sri Lanka**
**–4** Derrick Robins' tour of Sri Lanka 10 to 24
■ October, 1977: official tour programme. [Colombo, the Board, 1977]. [4]p. fold

**5819** Derrick Robins' tour of Sri Lanka 1977:
**–5** official souvenir. [Colombo, the Board,
■ 1977]. 32p. incl. adverts. ports. stats.

*pre-tour; with an account of privately spon-
sored English teams in Sri Lanka from 1889
by S.S. Perera*

5819 **Derrick Robins' XI** Far East tour 1977:
–6   programme. [1977]. [12]p. incl. covers.
■    ports.

# REST OF THE WORLD TEAMS

## 1965 Tour to England

5820 **Rothmans**
■    Rest of the World XI 1965: souvenir
     programme. Rothmans of Pall Mall,
     [1965]. [12]p. illus. port.

## 1966 Tour to England

5821 **Rothmans**
■    World Cup cricket tournament: An
     England XI v. A Rest of the World XI,
     Scarborough Festival September 7, 8 & 9;
     Lord's September 10, 12 & 13. Rothmans
     of Pall Mall, [1966]. [16]p. illus.

## 1967 Tour to Barbados

5822 **Barbados** versus Rest of the World at
■    Kensington [Oval, Bridgetown]: souvenir
     programme. Bridgetown, Banks
     Barbados Breweries Ltd., 1967. 20p. illus.
     ports.

## 1967 In England

5823 **Rothmans**
■    Rest of the World XI 1967. Rothmans of
     Pall Mall, [1967]. 16p. illus.

## 1968 In England

5824 **Rothmans**
■    Rest of the World XI 1968. Rothmans of
     Pall Mall, [1968]. 16p. illus. port.

## 1970 Tour of England

5825 **Rest** of the World fixtures: tour pro-
■    gramme: pictures. D. Walker, [1970].
     [8]p. ports.

## 1971–72 Tour of Australia

5825 **A.C.T. Cricket Association**
–1   Rest of the World versus Southern
■    N.S.W. XI at Manuka Oval, Canberra,
     January 18, 19, 1972: official programme
     edited by Julian Oakley. [Canberra], the
     Assoc., [1972]. 20p. incl. adverts. ports.
     stats.

5826 **Australian Cricket**
■    Rest of the World cricket tour guide
     1971–72 season; edited by Eric Beecher.
     Sydney, Modern Magazines (Holdings)
     Ltd., [1971]. 68p. incl. adverts. illus.
     diagr. stats.

5826 **Queensland Cricket Association**
–1   Cricket news. International cricket match,
     Brisbane Cricket Ground: Queensland v.
     The Rest of the World, 1971, Nov. 19, 20,
     21, 22. Brisbane, the Assoc., [1971]. 16p.
     incl. adverts. stats.

5827 Cricket news. International cricket match,
■    Brisbane Cricket Ground: Australia [v]
     The Rest of the World, November 26 to
     December 1, 1971. Brisbane, [the Assoc.,
     1971]. 16p. incl. adverts. port.

5828 **Western Australia Cricket Association**
■    Rest of the World v. Australia, WACA
     Ground, Perth, December 10–15, 1971:
     souvenir programme. Perth, the Assoc.,
     [1971]. 24p. incl. adverts. illus. ports.

# PRUDENTIAL WORLD CUP 1975

5828 **Australian Cricket Society.** *A.C.T. Branch*
–1   Cricket – World Cup 1975, England; edi-
■    torial Julian Oakley, caricatures Percy
     Samara–Wickrama. Canberra, the
     Branch, [1975]. 6p. of text. illus.
     *pre-tournament; contains itinerary, condi-
     tions of play, pen-pictures, and caricatures of
     Australian team printed on silk*

5828 **Cozier, Tony,** *editor*
–2   World Cup champions '75: a souvenir
■    tribute to the West Indies' triumph.

Bridgetown, Barbados, Literary Features
(Caribbean) Ltd., [1975]. 32p. incl. adverts. illus. ports. scores
*post-tournament*

5828 **Cricketer**
–3   World Cup special 1975; edited by Eric
■    Beecher. Special photographer Patrick
     Eagar. Melbourne, Newspress Pty. Ltd.,
     [1975]. 86p. incl. covers & adverts. illus.
     (some col.), ports. scores, stats.
     *post-tournament*

5828 **Lewis, Tony**
-4  A summer of cricket. Pelham Books,
■   1976. 179p. illus. scores
    ——*another ed.* Newton Abbot, Readers
    Union, 1976
        *the 1975 English cricket season; includes*
    *Prudential Cup matches and the short Test*
    *series with the Australians*

5828 **Lillis, Keith**
-5  The East Africans. Nairobi, the Author,
■   1975. [80]p. incl. adverts. illus. ports.
    scores, stats. *typescript*
        *mostly on their participation in the World*
    *Cup 1975*

5828 **Narasimhan, C.R.,** *editor*
-6  World Cup cricket vistas. Madras, T.V.
■   Ganesh Kumar, Pictorial Publications,
    [1975?]. [44]p. illus. & ports. (some col.),
    scores
        *post-tournament*

5828 **Pinto, Arthur,** *compiler*
-7  Sri Lanka, first tour: Prudential World
■   Cup: a souvenir. Twickenham, *printed by*
    White & Co., [1975]. ports.
        *pre-tournament; includes "Sri Lanka play-*
    *ers in overseas cricket" by S.S. Perera*

5828 **Prudential Cup '75:** international cham-
-8  pionship cricket. Prudential Assurance
■   Co., [1975]. 20p. incl. covers & adverts.
    illus. stats.
        *pre-tournament*

5828 **Ross, Gordon,** *editor*
-9  Prudential Cup review: international
■   championship cricket 1975. Ashurst
    (Kent), The Cricketer, 1975. 36p. incl.
    adverts. illus. ports. scores, stats. (A
    Cricketer Special)
        *post tournament*

5828 **World Cup** cricket championships: sou-
-10 venir programme and score card. Prog
■   Sports, [1975]. [8]p. illus.

# WOMEN'S WORLD CUP 1978

5828 **West Bengal Women's Cricket**
-11 **Association**
    [World Cup Competition: official sou-
    venir programme]; edited by Mrs. Nilima

Sen Gangopadhyay. Calcutta, the Association, [1977]
    *the second World Cup competition for*
*women's cricket held in India, January 1978*

# PRUDENTIAL WORLD CUP 1979

5828 **Dellor, Ralph**
-12 The 1979 Prudential Cup: the official
■   review. . . . Twyford (Berks), Ramcroft,
    [1979]. [40]p. illus. scores, stats.
        *cover-title*: The Prudential Cup Review
        *post-tournament*

5828 **Piesse, Ken,** *editor*
-13 National 0–10 network World Cup
■   cricket. Ashburton (Vic.), Sparke, 1979.
    60p. incl. covers and adverts. ports.
    scores, stats.
        *pre-tournament*

5828 **Prudential** Cup '79 official guide. Pruden-
-14 tial Assurance Co. Ltd., [1979]. 20p. incl.
■   covers & adverts. illus. score, stats.
        *pre-tournament*

5828 **Prudential** Cup 1979: souvenir pro-
-15 gramme. [1979]. [8]p. incl. covers. illus.
■   ports.

# I.C.C. TROPHY 1979

5828 **The I.C.C. Trophy** 1979: international
-16 World Cup cricket: [calendar]. [I.C.C.,
■   1979]. 40p. incl. adverts. illus. ports. map
        *the trophy is contested by Associate*
    *Members of the I.C.C.*

5828 **Malaysian Cricket Association**
-17 Malaysia in the I.C.C. Trophy 1979 at
■   Birmingham, United Kingdom, 22nd May

– 6th June 1979. The Assoc., [1979]. 248p.
incl. adverts. illus. ports.

5828 **Singapore Cricket Association**
-18 Souvenir brochure to commemorate visit
■   of Singapore team to England I.C.C.
    Trophy – 1979. [Singapore, the Assoc.,
    1979]. [120]p. incl. adverts. illus. & ports.
    (some col.)

# WORLD SERIES CRICKET

## 1977–78 Season

**5828 Ansett Airlines of Australia**
**–19** World Series cricket tour: itinerary 1977–78. [Melbourne], Ansett Airlines, [1977]. 40p.

**5828 Australian Cricket Board**
**–20** Statement made by R.J. Parish, O.B.E.,
■ Chairman of the Australian Cricket Board on behalf of the Board. Melbourne, 16 September 1977. 8p.
*concerns the Packer controversy re payments to Test players, the granting of television rights and sponsorships*

**5828 Beecher, Eric**
**–21** The cricket revolution: the inside story of
■ the great cricket crisis of 1977–78. Melbourne, Newspress Pty. Ltd., 1978. [vii],147p. illus. ports.

**5828 Blofeld, Henry**
**–22** The Packer affair. Collins, 1978. 256p.
■ illus. ports.
——*another ed.* Newton Abbot, Readers Union, 1979

**5828 Cricket** alive! World Series Cricket, the
**–23** first exciting year. Sydney, Golden Press
■ Pty. Ltd., in assoc. with World Series Cricket, 1978. 64p. illus. & ports. (some col.), scores, stats.

**5828 Cricket** colour collection. Melbourne,
**–24** Lavardin Pty. Ltd., [1978?]. 80p. col. illus.
■ & ports.
——pbk. ed. [1978?]
*illustrations of Australia v. India, World Series Cricket and New Zealand v. England*

**5828 Cricket** scene: Australia v. India and
**–25** World Series Cricket 1977–78; edited by
■ Rod Nicholson. Toorak (Vic.), Garry Sparkes & Associates, [1977]. 64p. illus. ports. stats.
*a preview of the 1977–78 season in Australia. The 1st section is devoted to the official Test series; the 2nd an 8p. middle spread of colour poster and scoresheets; the 3rd (or 1st if turned upside down and round) World Series Cricket*

**5828 Forsyth, Christopher**
**–26** The great cricket hijack. Camberwell
■ (Vic.), Widescope International Publications Ltd., 1978. [vii],273p. illus. scores, stats.
*also in pbk.*

**5828 McFarline, Peter**
**–27** A game divided. Richmond (Vic.), Hutch-
■ inson of Australia, 1977. [iii],177p. illus. ports. stats.

**5828 Martin–Jenkins, Christopher**
**–28** The jubilee Tests, England v. Australia 1977 and the Packer revolution. Macdonald and Jane's, 1977. vii,208p. illus. ports. stats.

**5828 World Series Cricket**
**–29** First World Series supertests. Sydney,
■ World Series Cricket, Dec. 1977. [16]p. fold. col. illus. & ports.
*one side (8p) shows Dennis Lillie in action*

**5828** Super Test series. International Cup.
**–30** Country Cup: merchandising and promotional opportunities. Neutral Bay, The Sales Machine Pty. Ltd., [1977?]. ports.
*folder containing promotional leaflets with portraits of W.S.C. players*

**5828** Super tests: the cricket revolution: official
**–31** programme. Sydney, WSC Pty. Ltd.,
■ [1977]. 32p. incl. adverts. illus. & ports. (some col.). diagr.

**5828** Supertest fun book: fun and games for
**–32** junior cricket fans. Sydney, Day &
■ Parsonage for World Series Cricket, [1978]. 64p. illus. ports. diagrs.

**5828** WSC International Country Cup matches:
**–33** [programme]. Kew, (Vic.), Tabulum
■ Holdings Pty. Ltd., [1977]. 32p. incl. adverts. illus. ports.
*itinerary*

**5828** World Series Cricket presents – Super
**–34** Test. [Sydney], World Series Cricket,
■ August 1977. 14p. illus. & ports. (some col.)

## 1978–79 Season

**5828 Cricket** action: [1978/79 pre-season sou-
**–35** venir]. Garry Sparke & Associates, 1978.
■ 64p. illus. ports. stats.

**5829 Cricket** alight! World Series Cricket in
**–36** Australia, New Zealand and the West
■ Indies. Sydney, Golden Press Pty. Ltd. in assoc. with World Series Cricket, 1979. 69p. illus. (some col.), scores, stats.

**5828 Lee, Alan**
**–37** A pitch in both camps: England and
■ World Series Cricket in Australia 1978–79. S. Paul, 1979. 188p. illus. ports. stats.

5828 **Martin–Jenkins, Christopher**
–38 In defence of the Ashes: England's
■ victory, Packer's progress. Macdonald
and Jane's, 1979. x,218p. illus. ports.
scores, stats.
*mostly on Test series*

5828 **World Series Cricket;** edited by Phil Tres-
–39 idder. Sydney, Modern Magazines (Hold-
■ ings) Ltd. for World Series Cricket. illus.
(some col.), scores
1978–79 (no. 1). 1978. 62p. incl. adverts.
1978–79 (no. 2). 1978. 62p. incl. adverts.

World Series Cricket. Australia v. West Indies, VFL Park, Melbourne, 1978 *photo: Patrick Eagar*

The Prudential World Cup, 1979. The competing teams – Sri Lanka, West Indies, England, Australia, New Zealand, India and Canada *photo: Patrick Eagar*

An illustration by Arrowsmith from "Cricket from the Hearth", by L. B. Duckworth (no. 7503)

# CRICKET IN LITERATURE

## ANTHOLOGIES

5829 **Agate, James Evershed,** *compiler*
■ Words I have lived with: a personal choice. Hutchinson, 1949. 224p.
*includes "The cricket match" from Our Village by Mary Russell Mitford, pp. 24–31; and "A great match" (Oxford v. Cambridge) from The Badminton book on cricket, by A. G. Steel and the Hon. R.H. Lyttelton, pp. 52–54*

5830 **Arkwright, J.S.,** *compiler*
■ Keate's Lane papers: an Eton miscellany, by J.K.S., J.R.C.R., H.J.S., K.E.C., W.F.S.D. and J.S.A. Eton, New, 1891. [viii],36p.
*cricket verses pp. 1 & 19*

5830 **Arlott, [Leslie Thomas] John,** *editor*
–1 My favourite cricket stories. Guildford &
■ London, Lutterworth P., 1974. 148p. illus. score. (My Favourite Stories Series)
——*another ed.* Sportsman's Book Club, 1975
*six factual and six fictional stories*

5830 **Arlott, [Leslie Thomas] John,** *and*
–2 **Trueman, Frederick Sewards**
■ Arlott and Trueman on cricket; edited by Gilbert Phelps. B.B.C., 1977. 280p. illus. & ports. (some col.), facsims. score, stats.
*accompanied the B.B.C. Further Education Television programmes of the same title, first shown on BBC 2 starting 11 April, 1977. Includes an anthology of cricket literature*

5831 **[Atkinson, John],** *compiler*
■ In praise of cricket: an anthology for all lovers of cricket, by John Aye. Muller, 1946. 64p. illus.

5831 **Baker, Denys Val,** *editor*
–1 Little reviews anthology 1945. Eyre & Spottiswoode, 1945. xix,236p.
*contains pp. 174–5 "Cricket at Worcester 1938" by John Arlott*

5832 **Black, Edward Loring,** *and* **Lawley, Alec**
■ **Henry,** *editors*
Sporting scenes. Methuen, 1956. xv,186p. (Methuen's Modern Classics)

cricket pp. 1–44; includes "The flower show match", by Siegfried Sassoon; "Jessop"; "The legendary Rhodes"; "Lancashire versus Yorkshire", by Neville Cardus; and "A village cricket match" by A.G. Macdonell

5833 ——, *and* **Parry, John Pearce,** *editors*
Starting work: a prose anthology. Pitman, 1957. viii,135p.
*an anthology for school use containing Neville Cardus on becoming a school cricket coach*

5834 **Blakeston, Oswell,** *editor*
■ Holidays and happy days. Phoenix House, 1949. 171p.
*includes "Packing my cricket bag"; and "A cricket watching holiday" by John Arlott*

5835 **Brodribb, [Arthur] Gerald [Norcott],**
■ *compiler*
The English game: a cricket anthology. Hollis & Carter, 1948. viii,234p. illus. ports. facsims.
——*cheap ed.* 1950

5836 **Buchan, John,** *1st baron Tweedsmuir,*
■ *compiler*
Great hours in sport: John Buchan's annual. Nelson, 1921. 288p. illus.
*includes "The finest match I ever played in" by P.F. Warner pp. 227–35*

5836 **Byrnes, Robert Steel,** *and* **Vallis, Val,**
–1 *editors*
The Queensland centenary anthology 1859–1959. Longmans, Green, 1959. 304p.
*p. 183 "A boy's cricket dream", a poem by John Henderson*

5836 **Cairncross, Andrew Scott,** *compiler &*
–2 *editor*
Fact & fiction. Macmillan, 1936. xiii,277p. (Scholar's Library)
*contains "The cricket match" from England, their England by A.G. Macdonell*

5837 **Catton, James Alfred Henry**
■ An excursion into cricket literature. London & Manchester, Sherratt & Hughes, 1911. 22p.
  *limited ed. of 25 copies; rptd. from* Manchester quarterly

5838 **Chapple, Fred James,** *compiler*
■ Some cover shots: a cricket anthology. Cape, 1924. 224p.

5838 **Christesen, Clement Byrne,** *compiler*
−1 On native grounds: Australian writing from Meanjin quarterly. Angus & Robertson, 1968. 483p. illus.
  *includes pp. 353–5 "The man who bowled Victor Trumper" by Dal Stivens*

5839 **Christian, Edmund Brown Viney,** *editor*
■ The light side of cricket: stories, sketches and verses, by Norman Gale [and others]. Bowden, 1898. 268p.

5840 **Cook, Hartley Trevor Kemball,** *editor*
Those happy days: an anthology of childhood; decorations by Nora S. Unwin. Allen & Unwin, 1945. 164p.
  *cricket pp. 139–40*

5841 **The Cricketer**
■ Pick of "The Cricketer"; edited by Michael Melford. Hutchinson & The Cricketer, 1967. 190p. illus. ports. scores, stats.

5842 Fresh pick of "The Cricketer"; edited by
■ Michael Melford. Hutchinson & The Cricketer, 1969. 198p. illus. ports. scores, stats.

5843 **Daily Telegraph and Sunday Telegraph**
❧ "I was there": twenty exciting sporting events by sports writers of the "Daily Telegraph" and "Sunday Telegraph". Collins, 1966. [viii],152p. illus.
  *includes accounts of England v. Australia at Lord's, 1930, by E.W. Swanton; and England v. West Indies at Lord's, 1963, by Alan Gibson*

5844 **Darwin, Bernard,** *editor*
■ The games afoot! a sporting anthology of sports, games, & the open air. Sidgwick & Jackson, 1926. xv,331p.
  *cricket pp. 120–42*

5845 At odd moments: an anthology. O.U.P.,
■ 1941. 352p.
  *includes extracts from* Days in the sun *by N. Cardus; "Farewell to Hambledon" by Rev. John Mitford, from* Gentleman's Magazine, 1833; *"The Downfall of Lumpy", and "Noah Mann" from* The Cricketers of my time *by John Nyren*

5845 **Duthie, Eric Edmonston,** *editor*
−1 Father's bedside book. Heinemann, 1960. xv,374p.
  *contains, pp. 350–65, "The cricket match", by A.G. Macdonell*

5846 **The Field**
One crowded hour. The Field, [1935]. 122p.
  *includes "The best innings I ever played", by Lord Tennyson*

5847 **Frewin, Leslie [Ronald],** *editor*
■ The boundary book: a Lord's Taverners' miscellany of cricket; designs by Jack Wood. Macdonald, 1962. 320p. illus. ports.

5848 Cricket bag: a miscellany for the twelfth
■ man. Macdonald, 1965. 320p. illus. ports. scores, stats.

5848 **Green, Benny,** *editor*
−1 The cricket addict's archive. Elm Tree
■ Books/Hamilton, 1977. xiii,241p. frontis. (The Addict's Archive Series)
  ——*another ed.* Newton Abbot, Readers Union, 1977

5848 **Gregory, Kenneth,** *compiler*
−2 In celebration of cricket. Granada Publishing, 1978. xv,336p. illus. ports. score, bibliog.
  *includes chs. on great cricketers by various authors, e.g. Cardus on Bradman, Tyson on Trueman, Swanton on Compton, etc.*

5848 **Horae** Sarisburienses. 2nd ed. Salisbury,
−3 *printed by K. Clapperton,* 1829. 345p.
  *pp. 17–19 "A scene in the cricket field" – poem*
  *a collection of miscellaneous pieces in prose and verse by the pupils of a college at Salisbury*

5849 **How's that?** including "A century of
■ Grace", by Harry Furniss, verses by E.J. Milliken and cricket sketches by E.B.V. Christian. Bristol, Arrowsmith, 1896. xii,163p. illus. (Arrowsmith's Bristol Library).
  ——*paper ed.* 1896

5850 **Ingelse, R.G.,** *compiler*
■ Cricket from here and there. *Typescript MS*
  *with cover title "Cricket van hier en daar". Cricket quotations, mainly in English, with some in Dutch. Presented to M.C.C. Library, Lord's, 1958*

5850 **Jenkins, Alan C.,** *compiler*
−1 The sporting life: an anthology. Blackie, 1974. 299p.
  *includes pp. 67–88 "Not at Lord's", an extract from* England, their England *by A.G. Macdonell*

5850 **Jepson, Rowland Walter,** *editor*
-2 Modern prose, a miscellany. Longman,
Green, 1949. 250p. frontis. (Clifford
Library)
*includes pp. 52–69, "The cricket festival"
by Osbert Sitwell from* Before the bombardment

5851 **Looker, Samuel Joseph,** *editor*
■ Cricket: a little book for lovers of the
game. Simpkin, Marshall, 1925. xxix,
225p. illus. ports. (Beechwood Books)

5852 **Lucas, Edward Verrall,** *compiler*
■ The open road: a little book for wayfarers.
Richards, 1899. xiv,310p.
*includes "The cricket ball sings", "Old
match days" by John Nyren and "William
Beldham's memories" by Rev. James Pycroft
many editions*

5852 **McGregor, Kenneth,** *compiler*
-1 Australian library – a prose selection.
Melbourne, Cheshire, 1963. 138p.
*includes pp. 117–23 "The miraculous
cricket bat" by Dal Stivens*

5853 **Moon, Arthur Reginald,** *and*
**Edmundson, Joseph,** *compilers*
Cavalcade of sport: a selection of
passages on sporting events. Univ of
London P., 1951. 160p. illus.
*includes extract from* England their
England *by A.G. Macdonell*

5853 **Moore, Tom Inglis,** *compiler*
-1 A book of Australia. Collins, 1961. 320p.
illus. map. (National anthologies)
*cricket pp. 247–53, "How M'Dougal
topped the score" by Thomas E. Spencer;
"Victor Trumper bats incognito" by Dal
Stivens; "The Scarlet Pimpernel" and
"Bradman versus bodyline" by Ray Robinson*

5854 **Moult, Thomas,** *editor*
■ Great stories of sport. L. Stein & V.
Gollancz, 1931. 602p.
*cricket pp. 431–82*

5855 Bat and ball: a new book of cricket, with
■ contributions by Neville Cardus [and
others]. Barker, 1935. [iv],283p. illus.
ports.
——*another ed.* 1938
——*another ed.* Sportsman's Book Club,
1960

5855 **Nash, Ian,** *editor*
-1 Images of Australian life: an anthology
for secondary schools. Melbourne, Pitman Publishing Pty. Ltd., 1979. vii,251p.
illus.
*contains pp. 151–62 "The match at Fyans
Creek" by Don Charlwood, and pp. 193–8
"Bradman"*

5856 **The new** forget-me-not: a calendar;
■ decorated by Rex Whistler. Cobden-Sanderson, [1929]. xii,143p. illus. (some
col.)
*calendar for 1930 and 1931 with essays and
poems including "Lord's" by Edward Shanks,
and "Cricket" by J.C. Squire*

5857 **Nickalls, Guy Oliver,** *editor*
With the skin of their teeth: memories of
great sporting finishes in golf, cricket. . . . Country Life, 1951. 168p. illus.
*includes Herbert Sutcliffe on cricket finishes, pp. 28–47*

5858 **The Oxford Magazine**
Echoes from the Oxford Magazine being
reprints of seven years. 2nd ed. Oxford,
H. Frowde, 1890. 159p.
——2nd ed. rptd. Frowde, 1908
*includes "The innings", pp. 56–59*

5859 **Parker, Eric,** *compiler*
■ Between the wickets: an anthology of
cricket. P. Allan, 1926. xvi,308p.

5860 The Lonsdale anthology of sporting prose
■ and verse. Seeley, Service, 1932. [vi],
376p. illus. (1 col.). ports. (Lonsdale Library)
——limited ed. of 100 copies signed and
numbered. 1932
*cricket pp. 183–211*

5861 The cricketer's week-end book; with illus-
■ trations by Cyril E. Rowell. Seeley,
Service, [1952]. 327p. illus. (Week-End
Library)

5862 **Pollard, Jack,** *compiler*
■ Six and out: the legend of Australian
cricket. Wollstonecraft, N.S.W., Pollard
Publishing Co., 1964; London, Angus &
Robertson, 1965. [xiii],306p. illus. ports.
rptd. with subtitle: *the legend of Australian and New Zealand cricket.* 1970. 366p.

5863 **Pringle, Patrick,** *editor*
■ The story of cricket. Harrap, 1952. 79p.
illus. (Harrap's Sports Readers Series)

5864 **Ray, Cyril,** *editor*
The compleat imbiber: an entertainment.
Putnam.
No. 1. designed by F.H.K. Henrion and
Jane Mackay. 1956. 256p. illus. (some
col.)
*contains pp. 68–72 "At the sign of the
Bat & Ball" by John Arlott, and pp. 218–22
"Spiers and Pond" by Philip Andrew*

5865 **Reynolds, Ernest Edwin,** *editor*
■ A book of sports and pastimes. Harrap,
1930. 215p. (Harrap's Junior Modern
English Series)

extracts from various authors including "Tillingfold bat" by Hugh de Selincourt, and "Ballade of cricket" by Andrew Lang

5866 **Roberts, Ronald Arthur,** compiler
■ The cricketer's bedside book. London, Batsford; Sydney, Angus & Robertson, 1966. 269p. illus. ports.

5867 **Ross, Alan,** compiler
■ The cricketer's companion. Eyre & Spottiswoode, 1960. xii,548p. illus.
——2nd ed. Eyre Methuen, 1979. xix,582p. illus.
*new material printed in two sections at the end, but less a story by H.A. Vachell, the section 'Great Matches', and a piece on Ranji by 'Country Vicar'*

5867 **Russell, Leonard,** editor
–1 Printers' pie: pocket miscellany; decora-
■ tions by Laurence Scarfe. Hutchinson, [1943]. 144p. incl. adverts. illus. ports. stats.
*includes pp. 114–36,140, "They played for money", by Harold Hobson*

5867 **Scott, Bill,** compiler
–2 Complete book of Australian folk lore. Sydney, Ure Smith, 1976. 429p. illus.
*contains "How McDougal topped the score"*

5868 **Sheppard, Hugh Richard Lawrie,** and **Marshall, H.P.,** compilers
Fiery grains: thoughts and sayings for some occasions. Longmans, 1928. 282p.
*cricket pp. 208–16*

5868 **Smith, Percy Raymond,** editor
–1 Australian pageant: an anthology of Australian prose. Sydney, Angus & Robertson, 1955. viii,216p.
*contains pp. 109–18 "The batting wizard from the City" by Dal Stivens, taken from Dal Stivens "The gambling ghost"*

5868 Australian cavalcade, an anthology of
–2 Australian prose. Melbourne & Sydney, Angus & Robertson, 1962. x,231p.
*contains pp. 215–31, "The match at Fyans Creek" by D.E. Charlwood, which first appeared in Blackwood's Magazine, Aug. 1955*

5869 **Smith, R.D.,** compiler
Not out: typescript. of an anthology compiled and produced by R.D. Smith on [B.B.C. Radio] Friday, 2 June 1950. [i]23f
*in M.C.C. Library, Lord's*

5870 **Sporting** stories and sketches. Paul, 1895
——2nd ed. 1896. 276p.

5870 **Stephens, Wilson,** edtior
–1 The Field bedside book; illustrated by B.S. Biro. Collins, 1967. 255p. illus.
*contains pp. 97–102 "Men in the middle", by Jeremy Alexander*

5871 **Summer** pie: miscellany for men and
■ women. Hutchinson, 1948. 112p. incl. adverts. illus. (some col.), ports. pbk. (Hutchinson Pocket Special)
*pp. 22–27 "The lure of cricket", by Robin Mangan*

5872 **Thomas, Samuel Evelyn,** compiler
■ Cricket fanfare and laughs around the wicket: a miscellany of stories, articles, items of cricketing history and cartoons, with a portrait gallery of England's stars in action. The Author, 1948. 64p. illus. ports.
——revised ed. 1949.

5872 **Thomson, Andrew Kilpatrick,** and
–1 **Hadcraft, Cecil Huddlestone,** editors
Essays and adventures, English and Australian prose selections. Brisbane, Jacaranda P., 1955. 169p.
*many reprints; contains "A country cricket match" by Mary Russell Mitford from "Our Village"*

5873 **Trewin, J.C.,** editor
■ West country book, number one; line illustrations by R.M. Lander. Westaway Books, 1949. 180p. illus.
*includes "Wickets in the West", by John Arlott, pp. 13–17; "Something of Somerset", by R.C. Robertson-Glasgow, pp. 128–31; "On Devon wickets", by Walter Taylor, pp. 147–51*

5874 **[Trowsdale, T. Broadbent]**
■ Coverpoint's cricket annual: facts, fun and fiction from the cricket field. R.A. Everett, 1905. 106p.
*the only issue?*

5874 **Trueman, Frederick Sewards**
–1 The thoughts of Trueman now: every
■ cricket maniac's anthology; thoughts by Fred Trueman, comments by Eric Morecambe, illustrations by William Rushton, compiled and edited by Fred Rumsey. Macdonald & Jane's, 1978. 144p. illus.

5874 **Wannan, Bill,** i.e. **William Fielding**
–2 **Wannan,** editor
The Australian: yarns, ballads, legends and traditions of the Australian people. Melbourne, Australasian Book Society, 1954. 290p.
——2nd ed. 1955.
——3rd ed. 1958. 233p.
*contains poem p. 40, "Spofforth, the demon bowler" from the East Charlton Tribune, Aug. 4, 1880*

5874 A treasury of Australian frontier tales.
-3 Melbourne, Lansdowne P., 1961. 256p.
illus. maps
——rptd. *with title:* Australian frontier
tales. Melbourne, Lansdownepp., 1971.
*contains poem pp. 215–6, "How McDougal
topped the score", by Thomas E. Spencer*

5874 The wearing of the green: the lore, litera-
-4 ture, legend and balladry of the Irish in
Australia. Melbourne, Lansdowne P.,
1965. 328p.
*contains pp. 248–52 "A cricket match at
Hogan's" by Edward S. Sorenson first published in* Quinton's Rouseabout *(1908); and
pp. 320–1 "Music Hall Song", with cricket
references, first published in* The Australian
theatrical, football, cricketers and general
sporting song book

5874 Australian folklore: a dictionary of lore,
-5 legends and popular allusions. Melbourne, Lansdowne P., 1970.
——2nd ed. 1972. xii,582p. illus.
*contains a number of cricket references
including pp. 1–2 "The Aboriginal Blacks of
Australia"; p. 76 "Bodyline tour"; pp. 152–5
"Cricket in the bush"; pp. 177–8 "The Demon
Bowler" (Spofforth); pp. 189–90 "The Don";
pp. 531–2 "Victor Trumper"*

5875 **Ward, Alfred Charles,** *compiler*
Grim and gay: an anthology, heroic,
dramatic, comic. O.U.P., 1942. 320p.
*includes "Hutton's match", pp. 45–48*

5875 Twentieth century prose 1940–1960.
-1 Longmans, 1962. xx,332p. (Heritage of
Literature Series)
*contains pp. 114–8 "An English cricketer"
by John Arlott from* Gone to the cricket

5876 **Watson, James,** *compiler*
Some historical and literary references to
English games. Stace, for private circulation, 1907. 123p.
*cricket pp. 72–78*

5877 **Watts,** *Mrs.* **Zilla Madonna**
The New Year's gift and juvenile souvenir. 2nd ed. Longmans, 1829. 240p.
illus.
*includes "The young cricketers" by Miss
Mitford, pp. 92–99*

5878 **Waugh, Alec,** *compiler*
■ These would I choose: a personal
anthology; with drawings by Laurence
Scarfe. Sampson Low, 1948. xvii,251p.
illus.
*cricket pp. 88–108*

5879 **Whitbread and Co., Ltd.**
■ Catalogue of the collection of pictures and
other items illustrating the history of
cricket at "The Yorker"; with an introduction and an anthology of quotations on
cricket by A. Lloyd-Taylor. Whitbread,
[1954]. 76p. illus. ports.
——*abridged ed.* Cranbourn P., *n.d.* 15p.
*a list of items in the full Catalogue without
the illustrations, introductory matter and
selection of writings on cricket*

5880 **Wilson, Andrew E.,** *compiler*
■ Stump high!!: cricket miscellany. Dursley,
*printed by* F. Bailey, 1953. 63p. incl.
adverts. illus. ports. score, stats.

5881 **Wood, Leonard Southerden,** *and* **Bur-**
■ **rows, Hubert Lionel,** *compilers and editors*
Sports and pastimes in English literature.
Nelson, 1925. xxi,256p. (Teaching of
English Series)
*scattered references to cricket*

5881 **World cricket** digest; contributing editors
-1 Jack Egan and Brian Bavin. Lane Cove
(N.S.W.), John Buchanan and David
Moeller, C.P. Publishing. illus. ports.
scores, stats. *6-monthly*
*No. 1. Summer 1978*
    *2. Winter 1978/79*
    *3. Summer 1979*
*an anthology of cricket writing*

# CRICKET AS PART OF THE ENGLISH SCENE

5882 **Agate, James Evershed,** *compiler*
■ Speak for England: an anthology of prose
and poetry for the forces. Hutchinson,
1939. 254p.
*cricket pp. 69–76*

5883 **Barker,** *Sir* **Ernest,** *editor*
The character of England. Oxford, Clar-
endon P., 1947. xii,595p. illus.
——*another ed.* Readers Union, 1950
*cricket refs. pp. 156, 210, 445, 446, 451,
454, 456 and 563*

5884 **Blunden, Edmund Charles**
■ The face of England in a series of occasional sketches. Longmans, Green, 1932.
xiv,178p. (English Heritage Series)
——*another ed.* Longmans, Green, 1949.
(Clifford Library)
*includes "An ancient holiday," pp. 66–82
a description of English village cricket*

5885 **Brogan, Denis William**
The English people: impressions and
observations 1880–1901. London, Hamil-

ton; New York, Knopf, 1943; Melbourne, Jaboor, 1945. 260p.
*cricket pp. 89–90,161,163*

5886 **Brown, Ivor John Carnegie**
□ The heart of England. Batsford, 1935. viii,120p. illus.
*cricket pp. 36, 47, 48, 64, 80, 81, 104–7; illus. of Trent Bridge*
——3rd ed. Batsford, 1951. 120p. (British Heritage Series)

5887 ——, *editor*
A book of England. Collins, 1958, 511p. illus. (Collins National Anthologies)
*cricket pp. 390–401*

5888 **Collier, Price**
England and the English from an American point of view. N.Y., Scribners; London, Duckworth, 1909. 434p.
——*another ed.* Duckworth, 1911. 360p.
*cricket in ch. 6*

5888 **Cowles, Virginia**
–1 No cause for alarm: a study of trends in
■ England to-day. H. Hamilton, 1949. x,333p.
*cricket pp. 22–3,24–6*

5889 **Egerton, Thomas,** *earl of Wilton*
On the sports and pursuits of the English, as bearing upon their national character. Harrison, 1868.
——2nd ed. 1869

5890 **[Entries cancelled]**
and
5891

5892 **Esquiros, Alphonse,** *i.e.* **Henri Francois Alphonse**
The English at home; translated and edited by Lascelles Wraxall. "Third series". Chapman & Hall, 1863. vi,370p.
*cricket ch. iv, pp. 79–106*
*originally published in the* Revue des deux mondes *under the title: 'L'Angleterre et la vie anglaise'*

5893 **Fearon, Ethelind**
■ Most happy husbandman; with decorations by Bernard Reynolds. Macdonald, 1946. 301p.
*cricket chs. xxix and xxx*

5893 **Ford, John**
–1 This sporting land, by John Ford in
■ association with Thames Television. New English Library/Times Mirror, 1977. 256p. illus. ports.
——pbk. ed. 1977
*historical account of English sports including cricket*

5894 **Gee, Herbert Leslie**
■ The shining highway: an account of a plain man's pilgrimage. Epworth P., 1935. vii,232p.
*cricket pp. 54–58*

5895 **Gibbs, J. Arthur**
□ A Cotswold village; or, Country life and pursuits in Gloucestershire. Murray, 1898. xvi,431p. illus.
——2nd ed. 1899. xx,431p.
——3rd ed. 1903.
——*another ed.* Cape, 1929. 315p. (Travellers' Library)
——*another ed. with title:* Cotswold countryman; ed. by John G. O'Leary. MacGibbon and Kee, 187p. (The Fitzroy Edition)
*cricket reference in ch. xi*

5895 **Gosse, Philip**
–1 Go to the country. Cassell, 1935. 282p.
*village cricket pp. 264–6*

5896 **Grisewood, Frederick Henry**
■ Our Bill-guide-counsellor-friend. Harrap, 1934. 111p.
*cricket pp. 52–67*

5897 **"Halsham, John",** *pseud.*
□ Idlehurst: a journal kept in the country. Smith, Elder, 1898. 272p.
——2nd ed. 1908. ix,263p.
*includes an account of a village cricket match in Sussex, pp. 229–36 (2nd ed.)*

5897 **Harrison, David**
–1 Along the South Downs. Cassell, 1958. xviii,277p. illus. maps
*cricket pp. 96,147,166–8,246,247,252*

5897 **Higham, Roger**
–2 The South country; with illustrations by the author. Dent, 1972. x,149p. illus. maps, bibliog.
*cricket pp. 77-9, 116-7*

5898 **Home, Michael**
■ Autumn fields. Methuen, 1944. vii,197p. illus.
——2nd ed. 1945
——3rd ed. 1946. vii,197p. illus. map
*ch. xiv. "Village cricket", pp. 165–77. (The Breckland area of Norfolk)*

5899 **Huber, Victor Aimé**
Reisebriefe aus Belgien, Frankreich u. England im Sommer 1854. 2 vols. Hamburg, 1855
*vol. 2, pp. 40–47 describes a cricket match played between Price's factory at Belmont and an eleven composed of Christian Socialists; in German*

5900 **Hughes, Mary Vivian**
About England. Dent, 1927. xvi,358p.
illus.
*cricket in ch. xxxii "Sport"*

5901 **Knox, Collie,** *editor*
For ever England: an anthology. Cassell,
1943. 244p.
*includes "A village cricket match", by A.G.*
*Gardiner, pp. 171–4*

5901 **The legacy** of England: an illustrated
–1 survey of the works of man in the English
country. Batsford, 1935. viii,248p. col.
frontis. illus. (The Pilgrims' Library)
*cricket pp. 1, 221–31, and part of an article*
*pp. 217–244, "Sport in the country" by*
*Bernard Darwin*

5901 **Longrigg, Roger**
–2 The English squire and his sport. M.
Joseph, 1977. 302p. illus. ports. plan
*cricket pp. 98,175–6,196,212–3,283–4*

5902 **McKenney, Ruth,** *and* **Bransten, Richard**
■ Here's England: a highly informal guide;
with illustrations by Osbert Lancaster.
Hart-Davis, 1951. 373p. illus. maps on
end-papers
*"Time out for cricket", pp. 64–77*

5903 **Mais, Stuart Petre Brodie**
■ Oh! to be in England: a book of the open
air. Richards, 1922. 312p. illus.
——*2nd ed.* 1933. 285p. illus.
*includes ch. xli, "Cricket on the green",*
*and ch. xlii, "Evil fairies of cricket"*

5903 England's character. Hutchinson, 1936.
–1 350p. illus.
*pp. 323–30 'The last match of the season'*

5904 **Middleton, Cecil Henry**
Village memories: a collection of short
stories & reminiscences of village life; illustrated by Jack Matthew. Cassell, 1941.
216p. illus.
*cricket pp. 181–8*

5905 **Middleton, Drew**
■ The British. Secker & Warburg, 1957.
284p.
——*rptd.* Pan Books, 1958
*cricket pp. 242,243,245–46*

5906 **Mitford, Mary Russell**
Our village: sketches of rural character
and scenery. 5 vols. Whittaker, 1824–32
*numerous later editions*
*includes "A country cricket match"*

5907 Children of the village; with illustrations
by F. Barnard [and others]. Routledge,
1880. 134p. illus.
*extracted from* Our village

5908 **Moore, John Cecil**
■ The countryman's England. Seeley Service, 1939. 255p. illus. diagrs.
*cricket pp. 53–7*

5909 Brensham village. Collins, 1946. 223p.
■ frontis.
——*another ed.* Harmondsworth, Penguin Books, 1952. 247p.
*"The cricket team", pp. 47–87, describing*
*village cricket in Gloucestershire*

5910 The blue field. Collins, 1948. 222p.
■ *"The umpire" pp. 164–173*

5911 The season of the year: some country
■ contentments; drawings by John Robinson. Collins, 1954. 254p. illus.
*cricket pp. 161–9*

5911 John Moore's England; chosen and edited
–1 by Eric Linklater. Collins, 1970. 192p.
*cricket pp. 37–45*

5912 **Mulgan, Alan Edward**
■ Home: a New Zealander's adventure;
with woodcuts by Clare Leighton. Longmans, 1927. xiii,226p. illus.
——*another ed. with title:* Home: a colonial's adventure. 1929
*cricket chs. xiv, xv, pp. 175–194*

5913 **Nicolson,** *Sir* **Harold George,** *compiler*
■ England: an anthology. Macmillan, for
the English Association, 1944. xxiv,296p.
*cricket pp. 85–89*

5914 **Our** way of life: twelve aspects of the
■ British heritage, by the Rt. Rev. J.W.C.
Wand, D.D., Bishop of London [and
others]. Country Life, 1951. 152p. illus.
*"Cricket" by Neville Cardus, pp. 141–152*

5915 **Parker, Ernest Walter,** *and* **Moon, Arthur**
**Reginald,** *editors*
England out of doors. Longmans, Green,
1934. vii,168p. frontis. (The Heritage of
Literature Series)
——*rptd.* 1934. vii,168p. (The Swan Library)
*contains pp. 154–62 "The spirit of cricket"*
*by Neville Cardus from his* Cricket, *1930*

5915 **Priestley, John Boynton**
–1 The English. Heinemann, 1973. 256p.
■ illus. & ports. (some col.)
*cricket pp. 33,109,110,135,236–8*

5916 **Quinain, Louis**
■ Country beat: a police constable's story.
Methuen, 1946. vii,247p.
*includes "The law and village cricket", pp.*
*184–7*

*'Cricket.'*

'Cricket'. From the Macmillan edition (1910) of "Our Village" by Mary Russell Mitford (no. 5906).

From "The Best of Cricket's Fiction", compiled by Leslie Frewin, illustrated by Jack Dunkley
(no. 5924)

Boys' stories: the cover to no. 6185–3

**5917** **Reading University.** *Museum of English*
■ *Rural Life*
The rural game of cricket: a loan exhibition illustrating scenes, personalities, and the making of the bat and ball. Reading, Univ. of Reading, [1957]. 9p.

**5918** **Redlich, Monica**
■ The pattern of England: some informal and everyday aspects. Kjøbenhavn, Busek, 1945. 317p. illus. maps
*cricket pp. 214, 219–21*

**5919** **[Remusat, Charles François Marie,** *comte*
■ *de]*
La vie de village en Angleterre, ou souvenirs d'un exile, par l'auteur de La vie de Channing. Paris, Librairie Academique Didier et Cie, 1862. vi,352p
——2nd ed. 1863. [4], vi,366p.
*ch. xvii "Le jeu de cricket"*

**5920** **Rhys, Ernest,** *editor*
□ The old country: a book of love and praise of England. Dent, 1917. 320p. illus.
——*revised ed.* 1922. 320p. illus. (some col.)
*includes pp. 218–22, "A country cricket match" by Mary Russell Mitford*

**5921** **Shanks, Edward Richard Buxton**
■ My England. Jarrolds, 1938. 320p. illus. port.
——*rptd.* The National Book Assoc., Hutchinson, 1939
*cricket in ch. 7 "Playing-fields", pp. 227–55*

**5922** **Silex, Karl**
■ John Bull at home: how he lives—amuses himself—dress—what he learns—does—earns and spends; translated from the German by Huntley Paterson. Harrap, 1931. 296p.
*cricket pp. 72, 116–22*

**5922** **Sproule, Anna**
**–1** The social calendar. Poole, Blandford P.,
■ 1978. 144p. illus. bibliog.
*cricket pp. 14,17,116 with an illustration "Boundary shot at the Eton and Harrow match"*

**5922** **Swinnerton, Frank**
**–2** Reflections from a village. Hutchinson,
■ 1969. 196p. illus.
——*another ed.* H. Hamilton, 1978. 196p. illus.
*cricket in Cranleigh, Surrey, pp. 127–34*

**5922** **Synge, Allen,** *editor*
**–3** Strangers' gallery: some foreign views of
■ English cricket. Lemon Tree Press, 1974. 174p. illus. facsim. ports.

**5923** **Timpson, George Frederick**
■ Kings and commoners: studies in British idealism. London & Cheltenham, Burrow, 1926. xvi,190p. illus. ports.
*chs. entitled "Cricketers all" and "C.T. Studd, cricketer and missionary"*

**5923** **Wingfield-Stratford, Esmé**
**–1** The squire and his relations. Cassell,
■ 1956. xii,424p. illus. ports. facsims.
*cricket pp. 248–51 (on the Duke of Dorset and the Vine), 271–2 (on George Osbaldeston), 273 (brief reference to Eton & Harrow match)*

# FICTION

**5924** **Frewin, Leslie [Ronald],** *compiler*
■ The best of cricket's fiction: an anthology; illustrated by Jack Dunkley. 2 vols. Macdonald, 1966–8. illus.

**5924** **Howarth, Patrick**
**–1** Play up and play the game: the heroes
■ of popular fiction. Eyre Methuen, 1973. xiii,178p. bibliog.
*many cricket fiction references*

## FICTION WITH A CRICKET THEME

**5925** **Alington, Adrian Richard**
■ The amazing Test match crime. Chatto & Windus, 1939. [viii],248p.

**5926** **Alington, Cyril Argentine**
■ Mr. Evans: a cricketo-detective story. Macmillan, 1922. viii,262p.

**5927** **Allen, Phoebe**
■ The cricket club; or, Warned just in time: a story for mothers' meetings; illustrated by W.J. Morgan. S.P.C.K., [1884]. [i], 160p. illus.

**5927** **[Bardswell, Emily]**
**–1** "Played on"; or, The troubles of a county
■ captain. Horace Marshall, [1898]. 60p. (Penny Popular Novels)
*See also:* 7297–1

**5928** **Batchelor, Denzil [Stanley]**
The Test match murder. Sydney, Angus & Robertson, 1936. 264p.

**5928 Bearshaw, Brian**
**–1** The order of death. Hale, 1979. 158p.
■ *members of a school cricket eleven of 25 years ago die in the batting order in which they played in the Old Boys' match*

**5929 Beresford, John Davys**
■ The Hampdenshire wonder. Sidgwick & Jackson, 1911. viii,295p.
——*another ed.* Martin Secker, 1926. 256p. (The New Adelphi Library)
——*another ed.* Penguin Books, 1937. 256p.
——*another ed.* Eyre & Spottiswoode, 1948. 234p. (Century Library)

**5930 Carew, Dudley Charles Hemington**
■ The son of grief. A Barker, 1936. 283p.

**5931 Carr, J.L.**
■ A season in Sinji: a novel. A. Ross, 1967. 192p.

**5931 Clark, Douglas**
**–1** The Libertines. Gollancz, 1978. 175p.
■ (Gollancz Detection)
*a murder investigation involving members of The Libertines C.C.*

**5932 De Selincourt, Hugh**
■ The cricket match. Cape, 1924. 253p.
——*another ed.* Readers Library Publishing Co., 1924. 254p.
——*another ed.* 1928. 253p. (Traveller's Library)
——*another ed.* Cape, 1932. 256p. (Florin Books)
——*another ed.* Readers Library Publishing Co., [1932]. 254p.
——concise ed. Longmans, Green, 1948. 190p. (Heritage of Literature Series)
——*another ed.* Hart-Davis, 1949. 201p.
——*another ed.*, illustrations by I. Armour-Chelu. Frewin, 1969. 223p. illus.
——*another ed.* Bath, Chivers, 1974. 204p.

**5933** The Saturday match; illustrated by James
■ Thorpe. Dent, 1937. 256p. (Tales of sports and games)

**5933 Dexter, Edward Ralph,** *and* **Makins,**
**–1 Clifford**
■ Testkill. Allen & Unwin, 1976. 3–187p.
——*another ed.* Penguin Books, 1977. 189p. pbk.

**5933 Dowling, Justin**
**–2** Clean bandage. Elek Books, [1963]. 191p.

**5933 East, Harry**
**–3** The heart of Yorkshire cricket: a story of village cricket in Yorkshire; illustrations by Brian Johnson. Driffield, Riding Publ. Co., [1973]. 86p. illus.

**5933 Fraser, George Macdonald**
**–4** Flashman's lady; from the Flashman
■ papers 1842–1845; edited and arranged by George Macdonald Fraser. Barrie and Jenkins, 1977. 328p.
*cricket pp. 1–4,15,20–32,34,50,71–80 and pp. 313–4 Appendix A: Cricket in the 1840s; also in pbk.*

**5933 Godfrey, William**
**–5** Malleson at Melbourne. Museum P., 1956. 205p.
——*another ed.* Sportsman's Book Club, 1958

**5934** The friendly game. M. Joseph, 1957.
■ 246p.
*the English captain 'Abdul Malleson' plays village cricket*

**5935 "Grant, Francesca",** *pseud.*
■ Caught and bowled: a romance of the cricket field. In seven "overs". Wright, 1888. 86p.
*the preface is signed Francesca Grant*

**5936 Hamilton, Bruce**
■ Pro: an English tragedy. Cresset P., 1946. [iv],240p.

**5937 Hatton, Charles**
■ Maiden over. Long, 1955. 192p.

**5938 Hobbs,** *Sir* **John Berry**
■ The Test match surprise: a romance of the cricket field. Readers Library Publishing Co., [1926]. 253p.
*for a critical resumé see: Sing all a green willow, by Ronald Mason, pp. 23–36*

**5939 Hobson, Harold**
■ The devil in Woodford Wells: a fantastic novel. Longmans, Green, 1946. 244p.

**5940 Hutchinson, Horace Gordon**
■ Peter Steele, the cricketer. Bristol, Arrowsmith; London, Simpkin, Marshall, 1895. 328p. (Arrowsmith's 3/6 Series)
——new ed. 1905. 126p.

**5941 Lyon, Malcolm Douglas**
■ A village match and after; illustrations by Aubrey Hammond. Nash & Grayson, 1929. 223p.
*the author played for Somerset*

**5942 Macdonell, Archibald Gordon**
■ The village cricket match. St. Hugh's P., [c.1950]. 56p.
*reprinted from England, their England; see no. 6025*

**5943 Miller, Alan**
■ Close of play; illustrated by Bip Pares. St. Hugh's P., 1949. 62p. illus.

**5944 Moiseiwitch, Maurice**
■ A sky-blue life. Heinemann, 1956. 239p.

**5945 Newman, Bernard Charles**
■ Death at Lord's. Gollancz, 1952. 221p.

**5946 Nixon, Christopher W.**
■ The tour: a novel. Sydney, Reed, 1973. 213p.
*fictional account of an M.C.C. tour to Australia*

**5947 "An Old Boy", *pseud.***
■ The adventures of a cricket ball, with the laws and practice of cricket. London, Ward, Lock & Tyler; Tunbridge Wells, H.S. Colbran, [1860]. 66p. illus.

**5947 Parker, John**
**-1** The village cricket match. Weidenfeld & Nicolson, 1977. [v],145p.
■ ——*rptd*. Penguin Books, 1978
*'replays' Hugh de Selincourt's" The cricket match"*

**5948 Pink, Hal**
■ The Test match mystery. Hutchinson, [1940]. 223p.

**5949 Raven, Simon**
■ Close of play. Blond, 1962. 192p.

**5950 Roberts, Denys**
■ The Elwood wager. Methuen, 1957. [vi], 198p.
——*rptd*. Ian Hendry Publications, 1975

**5951 Simons, Eric Norman**
■ Friendly eleven: a cricket chronicle; decorations by J. Quilter. T. Werner Laurie, 1950. 159p. illus.

**5952 Snaith, John Collis**
■ Willow the king: the story of a cricket match; with illustrations by Lucien Davis. Ward Lock, [1899]. 314p. illus.

**5953 Spain, Nancy**
■ Death before wicket. Hutchinson, 1946. 184p.

**5953 Stuart, Frank Stanley**
**-1** Never so young again. S. Paul, 1953. 208p.

**5954 Tack, Alfred**
■ The Test match murder. Jenkins, [1948]. 216p.

**5955 White, Graham**
■ Cricket at Benfield. S. Paul, 1960. 191p.

**5956 Worsley-Gough, Barbara**
■ Alibi innings. M. Joseph, 1954. 239p.

# FICTION WITH INCIDENTAL CRICKET

**5957 Adams, Henry Cadwallader**
■ College days at Oxford; or, Wilton of Cuthbert's; with illustrations by J. Lawson. Griffith & Farran, [1880]. viii,376p. illus.
*ch. xxiii "The cricket dinner"*
*1st publd. under title "Wilton of Cuthbert's"*

**5958 Alington, Cyril Argentine**
■ Blackmail in Blankshire. Faber, 1949. 192p.
*cricket in chs. iii, vi*

**5958 Amis, Kingsley**
**-1** Take a girl like you. Gollancz, 1960. 320p.
■ *cricket in chs. 21,22,23*

**5959 Askew, Alice, *and* Askew, Claude**
■ The Etonian. G. Bell, 1906. vi,430p. (Bell's Indian and Colonial Library)

**5960 Atkins, John**
■ Rain and the river. Putnam, 1954. [v], 202p.

**5961 Baker, Frank**
■ Embers: a winter's tale. Dakers, 1947. 232p.

**5962** My friend the enemy. Boardman, 1948.
■ 227p.
*cricket pp. 9,27-8, 43-4, 60-1*

**5963** [See no. 5927-1]

**5964 Barnes, Ronald Gorell, *3rd baron Gorell***
Warriors' way. Murray, 1945. 287p.

**5965 Barrie, *Sir* James Matthew**
■ The little white bird. Hodder & Stoughton, 1902. viii,312p.
*chap. xxv "The cricket match"*

**5966 [Beith, John Hay]**
■ "Pip": a romance of youth, by Ian Hay. Blackwood, 1907. 372p.
*chap. vii " A cricket week"*

**5967** A knight on wheels, by Ian Hay.
□ Hodder & Stoughton, 1914. 319p.
*cricket pp. 120–23*
——2nd ed. 1914. 319p.
——*another* ed. Nelson, 1916. 477p. (Nelson's Continental Library)
——*another ed*. Hodder & Stoughton, 1951. 256p.

**5968** The shallow end, by Ian Hay. Hodder & Stoughton, 1924. viii,276p. illus.

**5969** Housemaster, by Ian Hay. Hodder & Stoughton, 1936. 320p.

5970 **Bell, Josephine,** *i.e.* **Doris Bell Ball**
■ Death at half-term. Longmans, Green, 1939. 276p.
——*another ed.* Pan Books, 1955. 190p.

5971 **Bell, Vicars**
Death has two doors. Faber, 1950. 192p.

5972 Death walks by the river. Faber, 1959. 190p.

5973 **[Entry cancelled]**

5974 **Bradby, Godfrey Fox**
□ Dick: a story without a plot. Smith, Elder, 1906. 191p.
——*cheaper ed.* Murray. 1919. [vii],181p.
*cricket in chs. xv, xix*

5975 'For this I had borne him.' Smith, Elder, 1915. 196p.
□ ——2nd impression. Murray, 1915. [v],196p.
*ch. vii "Pot cricket-rumours"*

5976 **[Bradley, Edward]**
■ The adventures of Mr. Verdant Green, an Oxford freshman; with numerous illustrations designed and drawn on the wood by the author: 'a college joke to cure the dumps'. Blackwood, [1853]. iv,112p.
*cricket, with illus. pp. 100–102*
*the 1st of 3 pts. which have been frequently rptd. together as "Mr. Verdant Green", by Cuthbert Bede [pseud.]*

5977 **[Brooks, Vivian Collin]**
No match for the law, by Osmington Mills. Bles, 1957. v,247p.

5978 **Brown, Ivor [John Carnegie]**
■ Years of plenty. Secker, 1915. 339p.
*cricket pp. 157–65*

5979 Master Sanguine, who always believed what he was told. H. Hamilton, 1934. 341p.
■ *ch. v. "In which the hero plays the game and is misunderstood"*

5979 **Bruce, Leo**
–1 Case with ropes and rings. Nicholson & Watson, 1940. 273p.
——*rptd.* Hornchurch, Ian Henry Publications, 1975. 192p.

5980 **Bucknell, Edward**
Linden Lea. Williams & Norgate, 1925. 288p.
*the cricket excerpt is included in no. 5867*

5981 **Campbell, Michael**
Lord dismiss us. Heinemann, 1967. [iv], 378p.
——*another ed.* The Book Club, 1968. 306p.

5981 **Canning, Victor**
–1 Mr. Finchley discovers his England. Hodder & Stoughton, 1934. 352p. map on endpaper
■ *ch. 25 "How Mr. Finchley plays for a bed"*

5982 **Carstairs, John Paddy**
■ Solid! said the earl: a novel. Hurst & Blackett, [1948]. 224p.

5982 **Castle, Dennis**
–1 Run out the Raj: a novel. Billericay, Joanna Productions, 1974; Folkestone, Bailey Bros. & Swinfen, 1975. 283p.

5983 **Clutton-Brock, Alan Francis**
Murder at Liberty Hall. John Lane, 1941. 287p.

5984 **Collins, Sewell**
■ Take it from me: being an account of the emotions of one Dan Allerton of America during a year's sojourn in England; with illustrations by the author. G. Richards, 1921. 266p. illus.
*cricket pp. 32–37*

5985 **Collins, William Edmund Wood**
■ A scholar of his college. Edinburgh and London, Blackwood, 1900. viii,379p.
*cricket chs. xiii–xv, xxii*

5985 **Cook, [John] Lennox**
–1 Dark to the sun. Fortune P., 1952. 228p.
■ *cricket pp. 15–6,97–100,190–1*

5986 No language but a cry. H. Hamilton, 1958. 240p.

5987 **Creasey, John**
■ The mark of the crescent. Melrose, 1935. 288p.

5988 A six for the Toff. Hodder & Stoughton, 1955. 191p.

5989 **De Selincourt, Hugh**
Gauvinier takes to bowls. Longmans, 1949. 147p.

5990 **Dickens, Charles**
■ References to cricket are found in the following novels:
Barnaby Rudge. ch. 48
Bleak house. ch. 54
David Copperfield. ch. 17
Great expectations. ch. 27
Little Dorrit. Bk. II, ch. 6
Martin Chuzzlewit. chs. 4, 5, 27 & 36
The mystery of Edwin Drood. ch. 17
The old curiosity shop. chs. 24, 25
Pickwick papers. chs. 7, 24, 44, 52
see *no. 6761*

5991 The posthumous papers of the Pickwick
■ Club; with forty-three illustrations, by R.
Seymour and Phiz. Chapman & Hall,
1837. xvi,609p. illus.
  *contains the cricket plate facing p. 69 by*
  *R.W. Buss omitted from later edns.*

5992 **A** Pickwick portrait gallery; from the
■ pens of divers admirers of the illustrious
members of the Pickwick Club their
friends and enemies. Chapman & Hall,
1936. 243p.
  *contains 'Dingley Dell v. All-Muggleton*
  *cricket match' by A.G. Macdonell and the*
  *suppressed Buss plate*

5992 **Eddison, Eric Rücker**
–1 A fish dinner in Memison. N.Y., Dutton,
1941. xxx,349p. map
  *a cricket extract is rptd. in no 5848–1*

5993 **Farrar, F.W.**
Drie cricket spelers. Utrecht, Honig, 1896.
356p. illus.
  *Dutch text*

5994 **Fitzgerald, Percy Hetherington**
■ The second Mrs. Tillotson: a story . . .
reprinted from "All the year round". 3
vols. Tinsley, 1866

5994 **Fletcher, David,** *pseud.*
–1 Raffles: the Yorkshire Television series
■ based upon the stories of E.W. Hornung
adapted from the Yorkshire Television
series written by Philip Mackie. Macmillan, in association with Pan Books,
1977. [iv],217p.
  ——pbk. ed. Pan Books, 1977
  *cricket in chs. i, vi*

5994 **Forster, Edward Morgan**
–2 Maurice: a novel. E. Arnold, 1971. xi,
■ 241p.
  *cricket pp. 14,182,185–8,201*
  ——*another ed.* Harmondsworth, Penguin, 1975. 222p.

5995 **Foxell, Nigel**
Schoolboy rising: a novel. London,
Dobson; Canada, Oberon P., 1973. 220p.
1 illus.
  *cricket pp. 171–92*

5995 **Frankau, Pamela**
–1 A wreath for the enemy. Heinemann,
■ 1954. [vii],245p.
  *cricket pp. 84–9*

5996 **Fry, Beatrice,** *and* **Fry, Charles Burgess**
■ A mother's son. Methuen, 1907. vi, 304p.
  ——Cheap ed. Newnes, 1909. 150p.
  (Newnes' Sixpenny Copyright Novels)
  ——*another ed.* Methuen, 1916. 248p.
  frontis.

5997 **Fuller, Roy Broadbent**
■ The ruined boys. Deutsch, 1959. 248p.
  *cricket pp. 137–145*

5997 **Galsworthy, John**
–1 To let. Heinemann, 1921. viii,312p.
■ *other editions: cricket in Pt. II, xi "Timothy*
  *prophesies", and Pt.III, ch.i, "Old Jolyon*
  *walks"*

5997 **Gilbert, Michael**
–2 The night of the twelfth. Hodder &
Stoughton, 1976. 223p.
  *includes description of a school match*

5997 **Gould, Nathaniel**
–3 Thrown away; or, Basil Ray's mistake; an
ingenious racing story. Routledge, 1894.
300p.
  *ch. 1 "The winning hit"*

5998 A lad of mettle. Routledge, [1897]. 287p.
  ——*another ed.* Modern Publishing Co.,
[1935]. 254p.

5999 **Hadfield, John Charles Heywood**
■ Love on a branch line. Hutchinson, 1959.
291p.
  *contains an account of a comic cricket*
  *match, pp. 160–181*

6000 **Hartley, Leslie Poles**
■ The go-between. Hamilton, 1953. 296p.
  *describes cricket at Brandham*

6001 **Harvey, William Fryer**
■ Mr. Murray and the Boococks. Nelson,
1938. 280p.
  *cricket in chs. vii, xx, xxi*

6001 **Heygate,** *Sir* **John Edward Nourse,** *Bart.*
–1 Decent fellows: a new novel. Gollancz,
■ 1930. 317p.
  *ch.x, pp. 123–38, "Eton v. Harrow"*

6002 **Hickson, Mabel,** *afterwards* **Mrs. Sidney**
**Austin Paul Kitcat**
Concerning Teddy. Bowden, 1898. 304p.

6002 **Higgins, Aidan**
–1 Scenes from a receding past. Calder,
■ 1977. 204p.
  *contains score of Oval Test, England v.*
  *Australia, 1938, and stroke diagram of*
  *Hutton's innings of 364*

6002 **[Hilton, James]**
–2 Murder at school: a detective fantasia [by]
Glen Trevor [*pseud*]. Benn, 1931. 284p.

6003 **Hingley, Ronald**
■ Up Jenkins! Longmans, 1956. [v],226p.
  *cricket refs. pp. 178–200*

6004 **[Hogg, James]**
The private memoirs and confessions of a justified sinner; written by himself, with a detail of curious traditionary facts, and other evidence, by the editor. Longman, [etc.], 1824, 390p. frontis.
——rptd. Cresset P., 1947. xvi,230p. frontis. (The Cresset Library)
*refers to cricket being played in Edinburgh in 1704*

6005 **Hollis, [Maurice] Christopher**
■ Death of a gentleman: the letters of Robert Fossett. Burns & Oates, 1943. 208p.

6006 Fossett's memory. Hollis & Carter, 1944.
■ 251p.
*sequel to Death of a gentleman*

6007 Letters to a sister. Hollis & Carter, 1947.
■ vii,190p.

6008 **Hornung, Ernest William**
■ Tiny Luttrell. 2 vols. Cassell, 1893

6009 Young blood. Cassell, 1898. viii,332p.
——*another ed*. Cassell, 1912. 156p. (Cassell's Sixpenny Novels)

6010 A thief in the night. Chatto & Windus, 1905. 334p.
——*another ed*. Harrap, 1926. 340p.

6011 Mr. Justic Raffles. Smith, Elder, 1909. 315p.

6011 **Household, Geoffrey**
-1 Fellow passenger. M. Joseph, 1955. 255p.
*the hero/narrator "on the run" plays in a village cricket match and takes six wickets for nine runs bowling offbreaks*

6011 **Hudson, Liam**
-2 The nympholepts. Cape, 1978. 143p.
■ *cricket pp. 86–7*

6012 **Hutchinson, Horace Gordon**
Creatures of circumstance: a novel. 3 vols. Longmans, 1891

6013 **Hutchinson, Ray Coryton**
■ The unforgotten prisoner. Cassell, 1933. 529p.
*cricket pp. 84–100*

6014 **[Johnstone, Charles Frederick]**
■ Recollections of Eton, by an Etonian; with illustrations by Sydney P. Hall. Chapman & Hall, 1870. iv,362p. illus.
*contains an imaginary account of an Eton and Harrow match, pp. 313–332*

6015 **Joyce, James**
■ A portrait of the artist as a young man. Egoist P., 1916. 299p.
*cricket pp. 43–47*

6016 Ulysses. Paris, Shakespeare & Co.; Sylvia
■ Beach, 1922; London, Lane, 1937. 766p.
*reference to cricket p. 78*

6017 Finnegan's Wake. Faber, 1939. 628p.
■ *cricket, pp. 454, 583–84*
*see no. 6675 and also "Cricket in the writings of James Joyce" by Geoffrey K. Whitelock in the Journal of the Cricket Society, vol. 7, no. 2, Spring 1975; subsequently issued separately by the author in 1975 as a 4p. offprint in limited ed. of 20 numbered and signed copies*

6018 **Kennington, Alan**
■ Pastures new. A. Melrose, 1947. 223p.

6019 **King-Hall, Lou**
■ Fly, envious time. P. Davies, 1944. [iv], 176p.
*authoress's husband was Sec. of Hampshire C.C.C.; of considerable Hampshire interest (Eagar)*

6019 **Lang, William Henry**
-1 The thunder of the hoofs. Long, 1909. 376p.
*cricket chs v,vi and xii*

6019 **Le Fanu, Joseph Sheridan**
-2 All in the dark. 2 vols. Bentley, 1866
*cricket in vol. 1 ch. xxxiv*

6020 **Leslie, *Sir* [John Randolph] Shane**
■ The Oppidan: a novel of Eton. Chatto & Windus, 1922. [xvi],365p.
——*rptd*. 1969. (Landmark Library)

6021 The Cantab. Chatto & Windus, 1926. [viii],285p.
——2nd rev. ed. 1926. [xii],285p.
*the first ed. was withdrawn by the author*

6022 **[Lewis, Cecil Day]**
A question of proof, by Nicholas Blake. Collins, 1935. 286p.

6023 **Lucas, Edward Verrall**
■ Over Bemertons: an easy-going chronicle. Methuen, 1908. viii,282p.
*cricket references in ch. vii*

6024 Landmarks. Methuen, 1914. 316p.
■ *cricket in ch. viii "The wager"*

6024 **Lunn, Harold**
-1 The Harrovians. Methuen, 1919. 312p.
*cricket pp. 109–16*

**6024 Lushington, Franklin**
**-2** Pigeon hoo. Faber & Faber, 1935. 284p.
*ch.xxiii, pp. 230–47 "On village cricket"*

**6025 Macdonell, Archibald Gordon**
■ England, their England. Macmillan, 1933.
299p.
*ch. vii: "The village cricket match"*
——*another ed.* with a prefatory note by
Sir John Squire [on A.G. Macdonell]; illustrated by John Evans. Macmillan, 1942.
ix,299p.
——*another ed.* Macmillan, 1957. 250p.
(St. Martin's Library)

**6026** How like an angel! Macmillan, 1934.
297p.
——2nd ed. 1939. [iv],297p. (Cottage Library Series)

**6026** Autobiography of a cad. Macmillan, 1938.
**-1** 314p.
——*reissued.* 1951
*cricket pp. 30–31*

**6027 Mackail, Denis George**
■ We're here! or, The adventures of Milford
and Bailey. Hutchinson, [1947]. 240p.
*chs. 17 & 18 "The cricket match"*

**6027 McNeile, Herman Cyril**
**-1** Ronald Standish, by Sapper [pseud.].
Hodder & Stoughton, 1933. 319p.
*country-house cricket in the case of "The
second dog"*

**6028 Mankowitz, Wolf**
The biggest pig in Barbados: a fable; illustrated by Ron Sandford. Longmans, 1965.
91p. illus.
*cricket references and illus.*

**6028 Marric, J.J.**
**-1** Gideon's sport. Hodder and Stoughton,
1970. 192p. (King Crime)
*concerned more with tennis than cricket but
includes an account of an anti-apartheid
demonstration at Lord's*

**6029 Marshall, Bruce**
Prayer for the living. Gollancz, 1934.
284p.
*includes an account of an Old Boys match*

**6030** Girl in May: a novel. Constable, 1956.
■ ix,239p.
*cricket in ch. 7*

**6031 Mason, Ronald**
■ The gold garland. Sampson Low, Marston, [1939]. vi,408p.

**6032 Masterman, *Sir* John Cecil**
■ Fate cannot harm me. Gollancz, 1935.
285p.

——*another ed.* Penguin, 1940, 214p.
*describes the match between Fincham and
Besterton*

**6033 Mathers, Helen Buckingham**
□ Comin' thro' the rye. Bentley, 1875.
——*another ed.* Jenkins, n.d. 379p. illus.
*contains an account of cricket at a girls'
school, pp. 93–96*

**6034 Meredith, George**
*Several novels contain cricket references,
viz:*
The ordeal of Richard Feverel. 3 vols.
Chapman & Hall, 1859. chs. 1 & 12
Evan Harrington. 3 vols. Bradbury &
Evans, 1861. ch. 13
The adventures of Harry Richmond. 3
vols. Smith, Elder, 1871
Diana of the Crossways. 3 vols. Chapman & Hall, 1885. ch. 40

**6035 Mitchell, Gladys**
■ The echoing strangers. M. Joseph, 1952.
224p.
*cricket in ch. 4*

**6036 Monkhouse, Allan**
■ Farewell Manchester. Martin Secker,
1931. 320p.
*references to cricket at Old Trafford*

**6036 Montague, Charles Edward**
**-1** Rough justice: a novel. Chatto & Windus,
1926. 383p.
*cricket pp. 163–4*

**6036 Moore, John Cecil**
**-2** Dance and skylark, a novel. Collins, 1951.
256p.
*cricket pp. 51–2, 90, 93, 253*

**6037** The white sparrow. Collins, 1954. 256p.
■ ——*paper ed.* 1963

**6038 Morgan, Charles Longbridge**
■ Portrait in a mirror. Macmillan, 1929.
320p.
*cricket pp. 231–62*

**6039 Morris, David**
A name dishonoured. Leicester, Edmund
Ward, 1946. 184p.

**6039 Murdoch, Iris**
**-1** The sandcastle. Chatto & Windus, 1957.
318p.
*cricket in ch. 10*

**6040 [See no. 6295–1]**

**6041 Nicholson, John Gambril Francis**
In Carrington's duty-week: a private
school episode. Ouseley, 1910. 196p.

6041 The romance of a choir-boy. *Privately*
-1 *printed*, 1916. [ix],280p.
■   *ch. v. "The cricket match"*

6041 **Nicholson, Mary**
-2 These were the young. Longmans,
■ Green, 1938. v,314p.
  *cricket in ch. 1*

6042 **Norrie, Ian**
■ Quentin and the Bogomils. Dobson, 1966.
216p.

6043 **Odle, E.V.**
The history of Alfred Rudd: a novel.
Collins, 1922. 273p.

6044 The clockwork man. Heinemann, 1923.
213p.

6044 **Oppenheim, Edward Phillips**
-1 The missioner. Ward Lock, 1908. 320p.
illus.
——*another ed.* Ward, Lock, *n.d.* 253p.
frontis. (Ward, Lock & Co's. Sevenpenny
Net Novels)
  *cricket in ch. vi*

6044 **Pain, Barry Eric Odell**
-2 Robinson Crusoe's return. Hodder &
Stoughton, [1906]. 168p.
  *cricket ch. x*

6044 **Pleydell, Susan**
-3 Jethro's mill. Collins, 1974. 285p.
■

6045 **Portman, Lionel**
Hugh Rendal: a public school story. A.
Rivers, 1905. 310p.

6046 The progress of Hugh Rendal: a 'Varsity
story. Heinemann, 1907. 318p.

6046 **Pycroft, James**
-1 Elkerton Rectory: being part second of
"Twenty years in the Church", an autobiography. Booth, 1860
——*new and cheaper ed.* 1862
  *a religious novel*

6047 **Quinterley, Esmond**
Ushering interlude. Fortune P., 1936.
400p.

6048 **Radford, Edwin,** *and* **Radford, Mona**
■ **Augusta**
Murder isn't cricket. Melrose, [1946]. 168p.

6048 **Raven, Simon**
-1 Fielding Gray: the fourth novel of the
■ *Alms for Oblivion* sequence. Blond. 1967.
208p.
  *cricket pp. 34, 57–8, 60–7*

6049 **Raymond, Ernest**
Tell England: a study in a generation.
Cassell, 1922. viii,320p.

6050 To the wood no more. Cassell, 1954.
■ 314p.

6051 **Reade, Charles**
■ Hard cash: a matter-of-fact romance. 3
vols. Sampson Low, 1863

6052 **Richardson, Maurice**
■ The exploits of Engelbrecht, abstracted
from the Chronicles of the Surrealist
Sportsman's Club; with illustrations by
James Boswell. Phoenix House, 1950.
128p. illus.
  *ch. 7 "Engelbrecht and the demon bowler"*

6053 **Roberts,** *Sir* **Randal Howland**
■ Curb and snaffle. F.V. White, 1888.
v,242p.
  *ch.iii "Eton v. Harrow",pp. 30–54*

6054 **Sadleir, Michael**
■ Desolate splendour. Constable, 1923. xi,
315p.
——*popular ed.* Constable, 1925, xi,315p.
——*new ed., rewritten.* Constable, 1948.
vii,306p.
  *"contains an account of a scene at Lord's
during a 'Varsity match*

6055 **[Sassoon, Siegfried Lorraine]**
■ Memoirs of a fox-hunting man. Faber,
1928. 395p.
  *ch. 2: "The flower show match"*

6056 **Sassoon, Siegfried Lorraine**
The complete memoirs of George Sher-
ston. Faber, 1937. 804p.
——*another ed.* Reprint Society, 1940.
656p.
  *includes* Memoirs of a fox-hunting man

6057 **Sayers, Dorothy Leigh**
■ Murder must advertise: a detective story.
Gollancz, 1933. 352p.

6057 **Scott, Frederick George**
-1 Elton Hazlewood: a memoir by his friend
Henry Vane. Edinburgh, Oliphant, Anderson & Ferrier, 1893. 146p.

6058 **Sellar, Robert James Batchen**
■ They took the high road. Long, [1948].
224p.

6059 **Sitwell,** *Sir* **Osbert**
■ Before the bombardment. Duckworth,
1926. 320p.
——*another ed.* Harmondsworth, Penguin, 1938. 310p.
  *refs. to Scarborough Festival*

6060 **Sladen, Douglas**
■ The tragedy of the pyramids: a romance of army life in Egypt. Hurst & Blackett, 1909. xxiii,428p. col. frontis.
*ch. vi, "Introducing the Considines to the noble game of cricket"*

6061 **Smith, Vian Crocker**
■ Candles to the dawn. Hodder & Stoughton, 1946. 255p.

6061 **Smith, Wilbur**
–1 Shout at the Devil. Heinemann, 1968. [v],310p.
*cricket pp. 11, 235, 298*

6061 **Snow, Charles Percy,** *Lord Snow of Leices-*
–2 *ter*
Death under sail. Heinemann, 1932. 334p.
*contains mention of Lord's*

6061 The search. Gollancz, 1934. 429p.
–3 ——*another ed.* Macmillan, 1958. viii,343p.
——*another ed.* Penguin Books, 1965. 319p.
*scattered cricket references*

6061 The light and the dark: a novel. Faber,
–4 1947. 392p.
*references to Maus, a German cricketer*

6061 Last things. Macmillan, 1970. vi,346p.
–5 *cricket in ch. xxxiii*
■

6061 **Sprigg, Christopher St. John**
–6 The corpse with the sunburnt face. Nelson, 1935. viii,285p. (Nelson Thrillers)
—— *American ed. with title:* The corpse with the sunburned face. N.Y., Doubleday, Doran, 1935. 309p.
*cricket references*

6062 **Stevenson, Dorothy Emily**
Katherine Wentworth. Collins, 1964. 318p.

6062 **Strode, Ralph**
–1 Heart's mystery: being a story in three
■ periods. *Privately printed,* 1903. 315p.
*cricket in chs. ii,iii,iv,viii*

6063 **Symons, Julian Gustave**
Bland beginning: a detective story. Gollancz, 1949. 230p.

6064 **Thackeray, William Makepeace**
The Newcomes: memoirs of a most respectable family; edited by Arthur Pendennis, Esq,; with illustrations . . . by Richard Doyle. 2 vols. Bradbury, 1884–5

6065 **Thompson, Edward [John]**
■ Lament for Adonis. Benn, 1932. 315p.

*includes description of a cricket match on Mount Olivet*

6066 Introducing the Arnisons. Macmillan,
■ 1935. ix,268p.

6066 **[Thompson, Sir Henry]**
–1 "All but": a chronicle of Laxenford life, by Pen Oliver; with . . . illustrations by the author. K. Paul, 1886. 325p.

6066 **Thomson, Arthur Alexander**
–2 The records of Reggie. Herbert Jenkins, 1924 [i.e. 1923]. 312p.

6067 Trust Tilty. H. Jenkins, [1928]. 303p.
■

6068 The exquisite burden. H. Jenkins, 1935.
■ 312p.
——*another ed.* Epworth P., 1963. 312p.
*ch. 7: "The King of games"*

6069 Bijou Merle. Jenkins, 1936. 314p.
*sequel to* The exquisite burden

6070 **Trollope, Anthony**
The fixed period: a novel. 2 vols. Blackwood, 1882
*ch. v: "The cricket match". First publd. in "Blackwood's Edinburgh Magazine" 1881–82, it describes a match between England and Britannula in 1980*

6071 **Vachell, Horace Annesley**
■ The hill: a romance of friendship; illustrated by Percy Wadham. Murray, 1905. xii,319p.

6072 **Warner, Rex**
■ Escapade: a tale of Average. Bodley Head, 1953. 189p.
*describes a match between the Average XI and Fancy-under-Edge*

6073 **Watson, Edmund Henry Lacon**
■ In the days of his youth. Melrose, [1935]. 288p.

6074 **Waugh, Alec,** *i.e.* **Alexander Raban Waugh**
The loom of youth. G. Richards, 1917. 335p.
*the character of 'Lovelace' is based on A.W. Carr. See: A. Gibson "Cricket captains of England", p. 150*

6075 Kept: a story of post-war London. G. Richards, 1925. 320p

6075 Island in the sun. Cassell, 1956. 552p.
–1 *scattered cricket references*

6075 **Wells, Herbert George**
–2 You can't be too careful: a sample of life

■ 1901–1951. Secker & Warburg, 1941. 297p. diagrs.
*Book 2, ch. 2. pp. 47–55 "The cricket match"*

6076 **Whyte-Melville, George John**
■ Uncle John. 3 vols. Chapman & Hall, 1874

6077 **Willans, Geoffrey**
Crisis Cottage. M. Joseph, 1956. 207p.

6078 **[Willis, George Anthony Armstrong]**
■ Patrick, undergraduate, by Anthony Armstrong. S. Paul, 1926. 224p.

6078 **Winterton, Paul**
–1 Death and the sky above, by Andrew Garve [*pseud.*]. Collins, 1953. 192p.

6078 **Witting, Clifford**
–2 A bullet for Rhino: a novel of detection. Hodder & Stoughton, 1950. 255p. illus.

6079 **Wodehouse, *Sir* Pelham Grenville**
■ Mike: a public school story: with illustrations by T.M.R. Whitwell. A. & C. Black, 1909, xi,339p.
——*another ed.* Black, 1924. vii,339p. (Black's Boys' Library)
——*re-issued in 2 vols: (1)* Mike at Wrykyn. Jenkins, 1953. 189p.
*(2)* Mike and Psmith. Jenkins, 1953. 190p.
*both vols. rptd.* Armada Books. (Armada Paperbacks for Boys and Girls)
——Mike at Wrykyn. *Another ed.* May Fair Books Ltd. 1968
——Enter Psmith [a new ed. of chs. 30–59 of *Mike*]. Black, 1935. 247p.

6080 Psmith in the city: a sequel to "Mike"; 
■ with. . .illustrations by T.M.R. Whitwell. Black, 1910, x,266p. illus.
——new ed. Black 1923. iv,266p.
——*another ed.* Penguin Books, 1970. 158p.
*cricket in chs. i, xxvii, xxix*

6081 Piccadilly Jim. N.Y., Dodd, Mead & Co., 1917. 364p.
——. London, H. Jenkins, [1918]. 316p.
*cricket in ch. 2, pp. 35–51*
*for an appraisal of P.G. Wodehouse and cricket see essay in* Sing all a green willow, *by R. Mason, no. 6731*

6082 **[See no. 6133–1]**

6083 **Yates, Dornford**
■ The Berry scene. Ward, Lock, 1947. 286p.
*ch. iv "In which we play for the village . . ."*

6084 **Young, Francis Brett**
■ Portrait of a village: engravings on wood by Joan Hassall. Heinemann, 1937. [xi],3–180p.
*cricket in ch. 7 "The village at play"*

# SHORT STORIES

## Collections

6085 **Batchelor, Denzil,** *compiler*
■ Best cricket stories. Faber, 1967. 304p.

6086 **Bebbington, William George,** *editor*
■ Fancy free: a selection of short stories. Allen & Unwin, 1949. xi,131p.
*includes "How Jembu played for Cambridge", by Lord Dunsany, pp. 71–86*

6086 **Brissenden, Robert Francis,** *editor*
–1 Southern, harvest: an anthology of Australian short stories. Sydney & Melbourne, Macmillan, 1964. 288p.
*contains pp. 280–8 "The batting wizard from the city" by Dal Stivens*

6087 **Day, James Wentworth,** *editor*
■ Best sporting stories. Faber, 1942. 448p.
*includes pp. 147–85 J.S Fletcher "Won on the last wicket", and Lord Dunsany "How Jembu played for Cambridge"*

6088 **Edwards, Paul,** *compiler*
■ Best sports stories, edited with an introduction by Paul Edwards. Faber, 1966. 3–223p.
*includes pp. 82–7 'The cricket match' by Samuel Selvon, and pp. 209–22 'Prolegomena to W.G.' by C.L.R. James, a survey of changes in Victorian society leading to the growth of sport and the phenomenon of W.G. Grace*

6088 **Foster, John L.,** *compiler*
–1 Sports stories. Ward Lock Educational,
■ 1977. [ii],137p. (W.L.E. Short Stories 3)
*pp. 37–42 "The cricket match" by Samuel Selvon*

6088 **Hadgraft, Cecil,** *and* **Wilson, Richard,**
–2 *compilers*
A century of Australian short stories. Heinemann, 1963. xvi,336p.
*includes pp. 268–76, "That Barambah mob", by David Forrest (Denholm), a story about Eddie Gilbert, the former Queensland Aboriginal fast bowler of the 1930's.*

6088 **Hyne, Charles John Cutliffe Wright,**
–3 *editor*
For Britain's soldiers: a contribution to the needs of our fighting men and their fami-

lies. [Tales] by W.L. Alden, Sir W. Besant
. . .[edited by C.J.C.W. Hyne]. Methuen,
1900. iv,315p. (Methuen Colonial Library)
*contains pp. 87–102 "A bowler's innings"
by E.W. Hornung*

6089  **Lowe, R.H.,** *editor*
■  A cricket eleven: an anthology of cricket
short stories with verses. Howe, 1927.
350p. illus.

6090  **Marshall, Howerd Percival,** *editor*
■  Cricket stories. Putnam, 1933. xv,237p.
score
*short stories, essays and verses*

6090  **Murdoch, Walter,** *and* **Drake-Brockman,**
–1  **Henrietta,** *editors*
Australian short stories. O.U.P., 1951.
x,447p. (The World's Classics)
*contains pp. 393–7. "The man who bowled
Victor Trumper", by Dal Stivens*

6091  **Queen, Ellery,** *editor*
■  Sporting detective stories. Faber, 1946.
381p.
*includes "The Young God" by H.C. Bailey
from Mr Fortune's case book: Mr. Fortune
gets a cricketer out of trouble, pp. 244–68*

6091  **Russell, Alan K.,** *compiler*
–1  Rivals of Sherlock Holmes – two: forty-
■  six stories of crime and detection from
original illustrated magazines. Secaucus
(N.J.), Castle Books, 1979. xvii,502p. illus.
*includes pp. 274–83 "Gentlemen and
Players" and pp. 293–301 "The return
match" by E.W. Hornung*

6092  **Schwed, Peter,** *and* **Wind, Herbert War-**
■  **ren,** *editors*
Great stories from the world of sport.
Heinemann, 1960, xv,416p.
*includes "How our village beat the Austral-
ians" by Hugh de Selincourt, "A cup of cold
tea" by John Arlott, and "A bowler's innings"
by E.W. Hornung*

6093  **Swanton, Ernest William,** *compiler*
■  Best cricket stories. Faber, 1953. 318p.
——*another ed.* Sportsman's Book Club,
1963

6093  **Thiele, Colin Milton,** *compiler*
–1  Favourite Australian stories. Adelaide,
Rigby, 1963. 194p.
*contains, pp. 19–27. "The batting wizard
from the city" by Dal Stivens*

6094  **Twenty** five cricket stories. Newnes,
■  1909. 208p.

6095  **[Entry deleted]**

## By Individual Authors

6096  **Anthony, Michael**
■  Cricket in the road. Deutsch, 1973. 143p.
*includes "Cricket in the road", pp. 40–43*

6097  **Aumonier, Stacy**
■  Miss Bracegirdle and others. Hutchinson,
1923. 285p.
*includes "The match" pp. 173–87*

6098  Ups and downs: a collection of stories.
■  Heinemann, 1929. xii,644p.
*includes "The match", pp. 239–251*

6099  **Bennett, Eric**
■  "Four-in-one" sports crimes from the
case-book of Superintendent Aldgate.
Newservice Ltd., [1950?]. 39p.
*includes: "Murder at mid-wicket"*

6100  **Bleackley, Horace William**
■  Tales of the stumps: illustrated by Lucien
Davies and "Rip". Ward, Lock, 1901.
269p.

6101  More tales of the stumps; illustrated by
■  "Rip" and Arthur Rackham. Ward, Lock,
1902. 224p.

6102  **Bligh,** *Hon.* **Arthur**
■  Crotchets and foibles: stories of shooting,
cricket and golf. Bristol, Arrowsmith;
London, Simpkin, Marshall, 1903. 298p.
*includes "A draco of cricket"*

6102  **Bramah, Ernest,** *pseud. i.e.* **Ernest Bramah**
–1  **Smith**
■  Max Carrados mysteries. Hodder &
Stoughton, 1927. 318p.
——*rptd.* Remploy, 1978. 318p. (Deer-
stalker Series)
*includes pp. 135–73 "The curious circum-
stances of the two left shoes" with reference
to a game at Lord's pp. 162–3*

6103  **Clayton, William**
■  Tales and recollections of the southern
coast: series I. A. Hall, 1861. v,308,iiip.
illus.
*series 2 not published: includes pp. 294–308
"The cricketing Frenchman; a tale of the last
century"*

6104  **Clitheroe, Arthur,** *compiler*
■  Silly point: a book of cricketing stories;
illustrated by James Thorpe. Duckworth,
1939. 88p. illus.

6105  **Cochrane, Alfred John Henry**
■  Told in the pavilion: (stories of cricket
and other matters). Bristol, Arrowsmith,
1896. 192p. illus. (Arrowsmith's Bristol
Library)

6106 **Collins, William Edmund Wood**
■ Episodes of rural life. Edinburgh & London, Blackwood, 1902. [ix],371p.
*the first 4 stories, pp. 1–65, relate to cricket*

6107 **Daniels, Arthur J.**
■ Told out of school; or, Humorous stories of school life; illustrated by J. Prater and Gordon Browne. Cassell, 1894. vi,280p. illus.
——*another ed.* 1900

6108 **De Selincourt, Hugh**
■ The game of the season. Chapman & Hall, 1931. vii,213p.
——*reissued* Cape, 1935. (Florin Books)
——*reissued.* Cape, 1940. pbk.
——*another ed.* Hart-Davis, 1952. 127p.

6109 **Doyle,** *Sir* **Arthur Conan**
■ Adventures of Gerard. Newnes, 1903. x,394p.
*short stories originally published in* Strand Magazine *1900–3; cricket references in "How he triumphed in England"*

6110 Danger! and other stories. Murray, 1918.
■ ix,246p.
*includes "About cricket", pp. 216–27*

6111 The Maracot Deep, and other stories.
■ Murray, 1929. 310p.
*includes "The story of Spedegue's dropper", pp. 223–57*

6112 **Drury, William Price**
The petrified eye, and other naval stories as originally told to the Marines, by one of themselves. Portsmouth, Carpentier, 1896. 120p.

6112 **Gould, Nathaniel**
–1 On and off the turf in Australia. Routledge, 1895. vi,244p.
——*facsimile rpt.* Sandy Bay (Tasmania), Libra Books, 1973. 244p.
*cricket ch. xvi*

6112 **Graves, Robert**
–2 The shout. Mathews & Marrot, 1929. 31p.
■ (The Woburn Books, no. 16)
*a short story told against the background of a cricket match played in an Asylum, which has been identified as being at Littlemore, near Oxford. The story also appeared pp. 79–104 in R. Graves. But it still goes on: an accumulation. Cape, 1930; and his Occupation: writer. Cassell, 1951 (rptd. Chivers, Bath, 1974). pp. 62–79*

6112 **Hardy, Frank Joseph**
–3 The yarns of Billy Borker; illustrated by Vane. Sydney, etc., Reed, 1965. 153p.
*includes pp. 34–7 "How Sam Loxton was caught at square leg"*

6113 **Hillas, Norman**
■ Andrew Lees and the lion, and other stories. Derby, Pilgrim P., 1949. 205p.
*cricket pp. 51–74*

6114 **Hornung, Ernest William**
The amateur cracksman. Methuen, 1899. vii,257p.
*contains "Gentlemen and Players"*
——*later reprints with title:* Raffles: the amateur cracksman

6115 Old offenders and a few old scores.
■ Murray, 1923. ix,307p.
*includes "Chrystal's century", "The power of the game" and "A bowler's innings"*

6116 **Igglesden,** *Sir* **Charles**
■ The demon eleven, and other cricket stories. Ashford, Kentish Express Office, 1901. 146p.

6117 Those superstitions. Jarrolds, 1932. 240p.

6118 **Johnston, Robert Thomson**
■ Century of a lifetime; illustrated by the author. Macmillan, 1956. vii,151p. illus.

6119 **Macdonell, Archibald Gordon**
■ The Spanish pistol, and other stories. Macmillan, 1939. x,311p.
*contains "A love match", "Dingley Dell v. All-Muggleton cricket match", and "Those were the days"*

6120 The village cricket match. St. Hugh's P.,
■ [c.1950]. 56p.
*extract from "England, their England"; the match described is with J.C. Squires' 'The invalids Eleven'. See Alec Waugh in The Cricketer Winter Annual 1969/70*

6120 **McNeile, Herman Cyril**
–1 The Dinner Club, by Sapper, [pseud.]. Hodder & Stoughton, [1923]. 287p.
*pp. 98–111 "The soldier's story"*

6121 **Manning, Olivia**
My husband Cartwright; illustrations by Len Deighton. Heinemann, 1956. 125p. illus.
*includes "Cartwright on cricket", pp. 71–8*

6122 **[See no. 6733–1]**

6123 **Milne, Alan Alexander**
■ The day's play. Methuen, 1910. viii, 306p.
*short stories & poems reprinted from Punch*

6124 **Milner-Pugh, G.H.**
■ The bowler of a season and other cricket stories. Simpkin, Marshall, 1907. 136p.

6125 **Nelson, E. J.**
■ The story of the bat. Fratton, *printed by* Lloyd & Co., *n.d.* 16p.
*"the proceeds of the sale of this book will go to the new cricket ground of the White Company"*

6125 **Pater, Walter**
–1 Emerald Uthwart. [Canterbury?], *privately printed* for the King's School, 1905. 47p.
*brief references to cricket; originally printed in the* New Review, *June & July 1892 and reissued for the first time in book form in* 'Miscellaneous Studies', *1895*

o126 **Payn, James**
Stories and sketches. Smith Elder, 1857

6126 **Perowne, Barry**
–1 Raffles revisited: new adventures of a
■ famous gentleman crook; drawings by Richard Rosenblum. Hamilton, 1975. [viii],311p. illus.
*cricket in 'The Dartmoor hostage' and 'Six golden nymphs'*

6126 Raffles of the Albany: footprints of a
–2 famous gentleman crook in the times of
■ a great detective. Hamilton, 1976. [vii], 214p.
*cricket in 'The Victory match' and 'John L. Sullivan obliges'*

6126 Raffles of the M.C.C. Macmillan, 1979.
–3 ix,250p.
■ *a recreation of Raffles with cricket as a backdrop to the stories*

6126 **Sansom, William**
–4 Lord love us; with drawings by Lynton
■ Lamb. Hogarth P., 1954. 106p. illus.
*includes pp. 35–42 "Time gents please"*

6127 **Sassoon, Siegfried Lorraine**
The flower show match, and other pieces. Faber, 1941. 160p.
*the title piece pp. 26–53 from* Memoirs of a fox-hunting man

6127 **Stivens, Dal**
–1 The courtship of Uncle Henry: a collection of tales and stories. Melbourne, Reed & Harris, 1946. 199p.
*includes pp. 167–72 "When Trumper went for a blob"*

6127 The gambling ghost, and other tales;
–2 illustrated by H.J. Rothe. Angus & Robertson, 1954. 113p. illus.
*includes "The batting wizard from the city"*

6127 The demon bowler, and other cricket
–3 stories. Collingwood (Vic.), Outback P.,
■ 1979. [xi],113p.

6128 **Thomson, Arthur Alexander**
Bumbledinky. Mills and Boon, 1925. 188p.
*rptd: articles and stories from* Gaiety, London Opinion, *and* The Passing Show; *includes cricket story "The pride of the popping crease"*

6129 **The Umpire's** story told after a cricket match. *n.p.,* [c.1900]. 8p.

6130 **Waugh, Alec.** *i.e.* **Alexander Raban**
■ **Waugh**
Pleasure. G. Richards, 1921. 320p.
*cricket in "By way of prologue" pp. 11–29, and pp. 235–259*

6131 **Webber, Byron**
■ Pigskin and willow, with other sporting stories. 3 vols. Tinsley Bros., 1879
*cricket in vol. 1*
—— 1 vol. ed. Hogg. 1883. [ii],363p.

6132 **Wells, Arthur Walter**
■ All this is ended. A. Melrose, [1936]. 287p.
*includes "Last over"*

6133 **White, Graham**
■ Cricket on Saturday: cricket stories and essays. Sporting Handbooks, 1947. 170p.

6133 **Wodehouse,** *Sir* **Pelham Grenville**
–1 Nothing serious. Jenkins, [1950].254p.
■

# CHILDREN'S FICTION

## Collections

6133 **The boys'** school story omnibus. Collins,
–2 1939
*contains "The short term at Greyminster" by Hylton Cleaver, "Won for the school" by Harold Avery, and "Rivals at St. John's" by R.A.H. Goodyear, each with cricket content*

## By Individual Authors

6134 **Adams, Henry Cadwallader**
The first of June: or, Schoolboy rivalry: a tale of Charlton School. Routledge, 1856. 158p. illus.
*many later eds.; many illus. have cricket content*

6135 Barford Bridge; or, Schoolboy trials. Rout-
■ ledge, [1867]. 442p. illus.
*ch. xi. "The cricket match"*

6135 Wroxby College; or, the Luscombe Prize:
–1 a tale of boy life. Routledge, 1874. iv,380p. illus.

6136 **"Andrews, John"**, *pseud.*
■ Bodyline Bill the bowler. Amalgamated P., [1938]. 96p. frontis. (Boys' Friend Library)

6137 **Apps, Howard Llewellyn**
The making of Jerry Dickson. Blackie, 1950. 223p. illus.
*ch. xv "The Corbridge match"*

6138 **"Arnold, Frank"**, *pseud. [i.e.* **Fred W.**
■ **Young]**
Next man in. Amalgamated P., 1932. 64p. (Football and Sports Library)

6139 One for a win. Amalgamated P., 1932
■ 64p. (Football and Sports Library)

6140 One wicket to go. Amalgamated P., 1937.
■ 64p. (Football and Sports Library)

6141 **"Ascott, John"**, *pseud. [i.e.* **John William**
**Bobin]**
Boundary Billy. Amalgamated P., 1928. 64p. (Boys' Friend Library. New Series)

6142 **Avery, Harold**
The dormitory flag. Nelson, 1898. 444p.

6142 Stolen or strayed. Nelson, 1899. 126p.
–1 illus.
*ch. iii "Bagshaw the Great"*

6143 The triple alliance: its trials and triumphs.
■ Nelson, 1899. 326p. illus.
*ch. xii "The Wraxby match"*

6144 Head or tails: the story of a friendship.
Nelson, 1900. 496p. illus.

6144 Mobsley's Mohicans: a tale of two terms;
–1 with seven illustrations by J.H. Bacon.
■ Nelson, 1900. 318p. illus.
*cricket in chs. i, ii, iii, v, xx*

6145 Off the wicket: a school story. Nelson,
■ [1910]. 368p. col. illus.

6146 Not cricket!: a school story. Partridge, [1911]. 384p. col. frontis.

6147 Schoolboy pluck. Partridge, 1911
——*another ed.* Nisbet, [1921]. vi,295p. illus.

6148 Won for the school. Partridge, 1911.
——*another ed.* Collins, 1927. 320p.

6148 Head of the school. Partridge, [1912].
–1 384p. col. illus.
*cricket ch. xxiii*

6149 Talford's last term; with six illustrations by W.H. Groome. Partridge, [1912]. 300p. illus.
*cricket chs. ix, x, xv*

6149 The chartered company: a tale of Cails-
–1 thorpe College. Nelson, [1915]. 334p. illus.
*cricket ch. xix*

6150 A choice of chums. Nelson, 1922. 335p. illus.

6150 Between two schools. Nelson, [1923].
–1 446p. illus.
■ *cricket ch. xii*

6151 Who goes there? Nelson, [1927]. 190p. illus.
*cricket chs. vii, x, xii*

6152 The cock-house cup; illustrated by J. Phil-
■ lips Paterson. Nelson, 1933, 292p.

6153 The Marlcot mystery. Cheap ed. Ward, Lock, 1935. 255p.

6154 **Barker, Eric**
■ The watch hunt. Ward, Lock, 1933. 254p. illus.
*3 cricket chs.*

6155 **Barnard, Alfred**
■ The schoolfellows: or, Holidays at the Hall. Graham, 1845. 187p. illus.
*a cricket frontis. with incidental references*

6155 **[Barradell-Smith, Walter]**
–1 The liveliest term at Templeton, by
■ Richard Bird; illustrated by H.M. Brock. Blackie, 1924. 255p.
*cricket chs. iii, xiv, xix*

6156 **Barrow, Percy J.**
■ Cornered; illustrated by A. Talbot Smith. Wells, Gardner, Darton, [1910]. vii,221p.
*ch. vii "A cricket-match", pp. 56–63*

6157 **Batchelder, W.J.**
■ A born school captain: a tale of St. Poly-carp's. Blackie, [1915]. 256p. col. frontis.
*ch. xvi "The match with Tolliver's", pp. 141–49*

6158 **Bateman, Robert**
■ Young cricketer. Constable, 1959. 159p. (Sports Fiction Series)

6159 **Bell, Robert Stanley Warren**
■ The mystery of Markham; illustrations by H.M. Brock. Black, 1913. vii,238p. illus.
*2 cricket chs.*

6160 Smith's week: a school story. Newnes,
■ 1915. 253p.
——*another ed.* Black, 1923. 253p. (Black's Boys' Library)

6160 Greyhouse days; illustrated by T.M.R.
–1 Whitwell, Scott Calder, etc. Newnes,
■ 1918. 286p. illus.
*pp. 98–125 "Taking a trench"*

6161 **Bennett, Charles Moon,** *and* **Bennett, Harry Richard**
Camperdown captains: a yarn of a modern senior school. Blackie, 1937. 208p.
*2 cricket chs.*

6162 **Benson, Edward Frederic**
■ David Blaize. Hodder & Stoughton, 1916. 316p.
——*another ed.* N.Y. Doran, 1916. 365p.

6163 **Bevan, Tom**
One of the awkward squad. Nisbet, 1912. 320p.

6164 Rivals of the fourth; with illustrations by
■ A.S. Waye. Cassell, 1925. vi,216p. illus. (1 col.)

6165 **Biggs, Margaret**
Summer term at Mellings. Blackie, 1957. 204p.

6166 **[Bleakley, Horace William]**
A short innings: a public school episode, by "Tivoli". Digby Long, 1897. 247p. frontis.

6167 **Boyd, Edward**
■ Wanderlust's third innings; illustrated by Sam Fair. Collins, 1953. 256p. illus.

6167 **The boys** of Raven's Court; or, Be merry
-1 and wise. Warne, *n.d.* 88p. col. illus.
*cricket pp. 67–74 with illus.*

6168 **"Brearley, John",** *pseud. [i.e.* **John Gar-**
■ **butt]**
Allison of Avonshire. Amalgamated P., 1934. 96p. frontis. (Boys' Friend Library)
——*rptd.* [1938]

6169 **Brooks, Edwy Searles**
■ The schemer of St. Frank's. Amalgamated P., 1934. 96p. (Boys' Friend Library)

6170 The demon cricketer! Amalgamated P.,
■ 1938. 96p. (Schoolboys' Own Library)

6171 The schoolboy Test match player. Amal-
■ gamated P., 1938. 96p. (Schoolboys' Own Library)

6171 **Brown, John Howard**
-1 The master of the rebel First: a story of
■ a public school; with 6 illustrations by George Soper. Partridge, [1909]. 329p. illus.
*ch. xi "The St. Anne's match"*

6172 **"Browne, Reginald",** *pseud. [i.e.* **Edwy Searles Brooks]**
The rotter of Whitelands. Swan, 1947. 204p.

6173 **Bruce, Dorita Fairlie**
■ The best bat in the school. O.U.P., 1931. 95p. col. frontis.

6173 **Bruce, Mary Grant**
-1 Mates at Billabong; illustrated by J. MacFarlane. Ward, Lock, 1913. 252p. illus.
*ch. xiv "Cunjee v. Mulgoa" describes an Australian country match*

6174 **Buckeridge, Anthony**
■ According to Jennings. Collins, 1954. 255p. illus.
*ch. 6 "Indoor cricket"*

6174 Jennings abounding; illustrated by Mays.
-1 Collins, 1967. 160p.
■ *cricket in chs. 1 and 4*

6174 Jennings in particular; illustrated by
-2 Mays. Collins, 1968. 192p.
■ *cricket in chs. 1 and 14*

6175 **Burrage, Athol Harcourt**
■ The idol of Saint Moncreeth: a school story of mystery, humour, and sport. Nelson, [1925]. viii,11–319p.
*chap. xxiv "The great cricket match"*

6176 Three chums. Sampson Low, Marston,
■ [1929]. [vi], 250p. illus.
*cricket in chs. i, iii, viii, ix, x, xvii*

6177 For house and school: a school story. Low, 1937, vi,250p.

6177 Carry on Rippleton: a school story. Low,
-1 [1947]. vii, 248p.
■ *cricket in ch. xxvii*

6177 **Butcher, James Williams**
-2 Ray: the boy who lost and won. Culley,
■ 1908. 295p.
——*5th ed.* 1917. 295p.
*cricket Pt.1, ch. ii "Clevedale versus Southborne"*

6178 **Butler, Arthur Gray**
The three friends: a story of Rugby in the forties. Frowde, 1900. vi,127p.

6179 **Byrne, G.M.**
The Lower Fourth at Rimington. Gerald Swan, 1948. 208p. illus.
*2 cricket chs.*

6179 **Carr, Kent,** *pseud., i.e.* **Gertrude Kent**
-1 **Oliver**
Brought to heel; or, The breaking-in of St. Dunstan's; 8 drawings by Harold Copping. Chambers, 1904. vi,367p.

6179 Playing the game! Partridge, [1908]. 415p.
-2 *ch. xxiv "The match"*

6179 The shaping of Jephson's: a school story;
–3 illustrated by Harold Earnshaw. Cham-
■ bers, 1919. 383p.
    *cricket in chs. xiii, xxi*

6180 Caught out!: a public school story; illustrated by Percy Tarrant. Chambers, 1920.
350p.

6180 Dixie of the Cock House; a public school
–1 story; illustrated by J.R. Burgess. Cham-
■ bers, 1921. 352p.
    *cricket in ch. xxi*

6181 **Carr, Wallace**
■ Winning hit. Bognor Regis and London,
Crowther, [1944]. 120p.

6182 **Cartwright, John**
■ The chronicles of Durnford: a public
school story; illustrated by Leonard
Linsdell. S.P.C.K., 1901. 152p.

6183 **The case** of the colonial cricketer. The
Union Jack, 1912. 28p. illus. (The Union
Jack Library of High-class Fiction. New
Series)

6184 **Chandavarkar, R.P.**
■ A surprise for Allison. Arthur Stockwell,
[1936]. 62p.

6185 **Cleaver, Hylton [Reginald]**
■ The Harley first XI: illustrated in colour
by C.E. Brock. Oxford Univ. P., 1920
[1919]. 272p. illus.

6185 Brother o'mine: a school story; illustrated
–1 in colour by H.M. Brock. O.U.P., 1920.
■ 265p. illus.
    *cricket in ch. xxiii*

6185 Roscoe makes good – a story of Harley.
–2 O.U.P., 1921. 296p.
    *cricket in chs. xxv, xxvi*

6185 The old order; a public school story; illus-
–3 trated by C.E. Brock. O.U.P., 1922 [1921].
■ 296p. col. frontis.
    *largely cricket content*

6186 Leave it to Craddock. Warne, 1937. 288p.
(Treasure Library)

6186 The pilot prefect. Warne, 1937. 128p.
–1 frontis.

6186 Captain for a day. Collins, 1942. 256p.
–2 illus.

6186 Captains of Dukes. Warne, 1942. 196p.
–3 frontis.

6187 Dawnay leaves school. Warne, [1947].
■ 254p. col. frontis.
    *3 cricket chs.*

6188 Lawson for Lord's. Warne, 1950. 252p.
■ col. frontis. (Crown Library Series)

6189 Lucky break. Warne, 1950. 254p. col. frontis.
    *ch. x "The cricketers"*

6190 The forbidden study. Collins, 1955. 5–
188p. col. frontis.
    ——*another ed.* The Children's P., [1955].
188p. col. frontis. (The Boys' and Girls'
Library)
    *ch. 4 "Red cricket"*

6191 Caught in the slips. (Taken from "Cap-
■ tains of Greyminster"). Collins, n.d. 133p.
col. frontis.
    *28p of cricket*

6192 **Coatts, Rita,** *i.e.* **Mrs. Marguerite
Harcourt Coatts**
The wrong school!: a story for girls.
Redhill, Wells, Gardner, Darton, 1949.
253p. illus.
    *ch. xiv "The cricket match"*

6193 Breaking bounds. Redhill, Wells, Gardner,
Darton, 1951. 192p.

6193 **Coke, Desmond**
–1 The bending of a twig; with illustrations
from photographs. Chapman & Hall,
1906. 310p.
    ——new ed., rewritten & enlarged; with
illustrations in colour by H.M. Brock.
Henry Frowde; Hodder & Stoughton,
1909. 350p.
    ——rptd. Oxford, Cumberledge, 1949.
351p.

6194 The house prefect. O.U.P., 1907. 311p.
■     *cricket chs. 21 and 24*

6194 The chaps of Harton: a tale of frolic, sport
–1 and mystery at public school, by Belinda
■ Blinders [pseud.]; edited by Desmond
Coke. . .; illustrated. . .by the Authoress. Chapman & Hall, 1913. xvi,159p.
    *cricket in chs. xx,xxi*

6195 The worm. Chapman & Hall, 1927.
xii,304p.
    *cricket chs. x and xvi*

6195 **Conquest, Owen**
–1 The rivals of Rookwood. Spring Books,
[1960]. 228p. illus. (Halcyon Library)

6196 **Cooke, Beryl**
■ A fishy tale. Angus & Robertson, 1957.
5–69p illus. (some col.)
    *children's story about an underwater fish
cricket match*

**6197 Coombe, Florence**
■ Boys of the Priory School; illustrated by Harold Copping. Blackie, 1900 [i.e. 1899] 239p. illus.
  *ch. 1, pp. 7–20, "The challenge"*

**6198** A cricketer born: a thrilling story of sport and mystery. Aldine Publishing Co., [1908]. (The Boy's Own Library)

**6198 Cubitt, *Mrs.* Neville**
**–1** Two Tapleby boys; illustrations by Paul
■ Hardy. Wells, Gardner, Darton, 1909. vii,260p. illus.
  *cricket in ch. ix*

**6198 Cule, William Edward**
**–2** Baker secundus, and some other fellows.
■ The "Boy's Own Paper" Office, [1917]. 285p. frontis.
  *pp. 239–69 "The Atterbury Wanderers' C.C."*

**6199 "Dane, Donald", *pseud.* [*i.e.* Dugald**
■ **Matheson Cumming-Skinner]**
The cricketing Crusoes. Amalgamated P., 1933. 64p. (Champion Library)

**6199** Fireworks Flynn – and the secret six.
**–1** Amalgamated P., 1940. 64p. frontis. (Champion Library)

**6199 Daniels, Arthur J.**
**–2** Chums all through; illustrated by J.B.
■ Green. London, Nister; N.Y., Dutton, [1902]. 244p. illus.
  *ch. xv "The big match leads to a big 'flare-up' "*

**6200 Deadman, Ronald**
The happening; illustrated by Roger Payne. Leicester, Brockhampton P., 1968. 120p.
  *ch. 14 "The cricket match and after"*

**6201 "Drake, John", *pseud.***
■ One long run. Amalgamated P., 1931. 64p. (Football and Sports Library)

**6201** Hit for six! Amalgamated P., 1934. 64p.
**–1** frontis. (Football & Sports Library)

**6202** A wizard at the wicket. Amalgamated P.,
■ 1937. 64p. (Football and Sports Library)

**6202 Drake, Tony**
**–1** Playing it right. Collins, 1979. 123p.
  *junior school cricket*

**6203 Drew, Michael**
A menace to the school. Pyramid Productions, [c.1950]. 64p.

**6204 "Dundee, Douglas", *pseud.* [*i.e.* Dugald**
■ **Matheson Cumming-Skinner]**
Monty Mayne: the batsman who broke bowlers' hearts. Amalgamated P., 1939. 64p. (Champion Library)

**6205 Edgar, Alfred**
The Abbeygate cricket cup. Warne, 1929. 90p. (Warne's Welcome Books)

**6206** Lucky Jim. Amalgamated P., 1929. 64p. (Boys' Friend Library)

**6207 Elias, Frank**
The shadow on the school: a story of public school life. R.T.S., Lutterworth P., 1922. 192p.

**6208** The two captains of Tuxford: a story of public school life. "Boys' Own Paper", 1924. 254p. illus.
  *ch. vi. "Cricket practice"*

**6209** Captain's orders. Lutterworth P., 1947. 208p. illus.
  *ch. 12 "Body line bowling", pp. 107–123*

**6209 Elrington, Helen**
**–1** The Red House at Boville. Nelson, [1925]. 335p. illus.
  *cricket in ch. xxix*

**6209** The Manor School. Nelson, [1927]. 283p.
**–2** *cricket ch. xx*

**6209 Escott-Inman, Herbert**
**–3** David Chester's motto: "Honour bright":
■ a boy's adventures at school and at sea. Warne, [1904]. 371p. illus.
  *cricket in chs. xii,xiii; pictorial cricket binding*

**6210 Finnemore, John**
Three school chums; with illustrations by Harold Copping. Chambers, 1907. 318p.

**6211** Teddy Lester's chums. Chambers, 1910. 344p.

**6212** Teddy Lester's schooldays; illustrated by W. Rainey. London & Edinburgh, Chambers, 1914. 376p.

**6213** Teddy Lester—captain of cricket; with
■ . . . illustrations by W. Rainey. Chambers, 1916. vii,384p.

**6214** Teddy Lester in the Fifth; illustrated by
■ Percy Tarrant. Chambers, [1921]. 336p. illus.
  ——another ed. Latimer House, 1949
  ——another ed. Latimer House, 1953. 216p. illus. (The Teddy Lester Books, no. 5)
  *cricket in most chs.*

6215 **Flynn, Brian**
■ Tragedy at Trinket. Nelson, [1934]. viii, 301p. frontis.
*cricket in most chs.*

6215 **Forest, Antonia**
-1 The cricket team. Faber & Faber, 1974. 232p.
*a school story for girls*

6215 **Freeman, Robert Massie**
-2 Steady and strong; or, a friend in need:
■ a school story; illustrated by A. Foord-Hughes. Farran, Okeden & Welsh, [1891]. 379p. illus.
*cricket in chs. xxiv, xxvii*

6216 **[Gale, Frederick]**
■ Ups and downs of a public school. By a Wykehamist. Cash, 1856. viii,81p. frontis.

6216 **Gilchrist, Donald**
-1 Young Seeley-Bohn. Faber, 1956. 189p.

6216 **Gilson, Charles [James Louis]**
-2 The twelfth man. Warne, 1934. 288p.
*cricket in chs. iii,xv and xvi*

6216 The substitutes. Warne, 1935. 256p. illus.
-3 *many cricket references*

6216 **Goodwin, David**
-4 The cad of St. Corton's: a grand complete tale of school life. Amalgamated P., *n.d.* iv,122p. (The Boy's Friend Library)

6216 **Goodyear, Robert Arthur Hanson**
-5 The boys of Castle Cliff School; illustrated
■ by T.M.R. Whitwell. Blackie, [1921]. 288p. illus.
*cricket in chs. vi,vii,xxvi*

6217 The White House Boys. Harrap, 1921. 253p.
——*another ed.* The Children's P., *n.d.* 254p.

6217 Topsy-Turvy Academy. Harrap, 1922.
-1 239p. frontis.
■ *cricket in chs. xi,xix,xx*

6218 Jack o'Langsett: a public school story.
■ Nelson, [1923]. vi,9–364p. illus.

6218 Tom at Tollbar School; illustrated by
-1 T.M.R. Whitwell. Blackie, [1923]. 320p.
■ illus.
*cricket in ch. xxxi*

6218 The school's best man. Jarrolds, [1925].
-2 320p. illus.
■ *cricket in ch. iii*

6218 Boys of the mystery school. Sampson,
-3 Low, [1926]. [v],282p. illus.
■ *cricket in chs. xvii,xviii,xxii*

6219 The hope of his house. Nelson, [1926].
■ 341p. illus.

6219 His brother at St. Concord's. Jarrolds,
-1 [1927]. 252p. illus. (1 col.)
■ *cricket in ch. xx*

6220 Up against the school. Black, 1927. vi,247p. (Black's Boys Library)

6220 Rival schools at Schooner Bay. Ward,
-1 Lock, 1928. 250p. col. frontis.
■ *cricket in chs. xxix,xxx*

6220 The hardy Brockdale boys: a public school
-2 story. Sampson, Low, Marston & Co., [1929]. vi,250p. frontis.
*cricket in chs. vii,viii,ix*

6220 Something like a chum. Sampson, Low,
-3 [1932]. vi,282p.
■ *cricket in ch. xxvii*

6221 Rivals at St. John's. Collins. 1933. 288p.

6221 The school's airmen. Ward, Lock, 1936.
-1 256p. frontis.

6222 Tudorvale colours. Sampson, Low, 1936. vi,250p. illus.

6223 The broom and heather boys: a public school story. Ward, Lock, 1937. 256p. illus.

6224 **"Gordon Geoffrey"**, *pseud. [i.e.* **J.G.**
■ **Jones]**
The factory batsman. Amalgamated P., *n.d.* 120p. (Boys' Friend Library)

6225 **Gordon, Sir Home Seton Charles**
■ **Montagu**, *bart*
That Test match: a tale for boys and old boys. Duckworth, 1921. 183p.

6226 **Grant, Mrs. G. Forsyth**
■ The hero of Crampton School. Edinburgh, Nimmo, 1895. 176p.
*cricket in chs. i and ii*
——*another ed.* Sampson, Low, [1925]

6227 Chums at last: a tale of school life.
■ Nelson, 1898. 256p.
——*another ed.* 1915. 256p. frontis. (Nelson's Books for Boys)
*ch. iii, The great cricket match*

6228 The Beresford boys: a school story. Edin-
■ burgh, Nimmo, 1906. 294p. illus.
——*another ed.* Sampson, Low, Marston, [1924], illus.

6229 **"Grant, Howard"**, *pseud. [i.e.* **W.G.**
**Wright]**
Slogger Sam. Amalgamated P., 1926. (Boys' Friend Library New Series)

6230 **"Granville, Jeff,"** *pseud.*
■ The schoolboy Test cricketer. Patrick Johns, 1958. 224p.

6230 **Gray, Andrew**
–1 Honoured by the school: a grand complete school story. Amalgamated P., *n.d.* 64p. (The Boys' Friend Library)

6231 **Gray, Kay**
In final and Test match. Aldine Publishing Co., 1926. (Aldine Football Novels)

6231 **Green, Edith M.**
–1 The Dampier boys; a school story; illus-
■ trated by Harold Copping. Blackie, [1915]. 288p. illus.
*cricket in ch. xvii*

6231 **Grey, John**
–2 Captains of Claverhouse. Amalgamated P., 1933. 64p. (Boys Wonder Library)

6231 **Guy Rayner's** schooldays: a record of the
–3 doings of the worst boy ever known. Popular Publishing Co., [c.1880]. 223p.
*originally published in parts. cricket ch. xxx*

6232 **Gwynne, Reginald**
A cricketer cracksman. Aldine Publishing Co., [c.1908]. 64p. (Diamond Library Series)

6233 The last Test match. Aldine Publishing Co., [c.1908]. 64p. (Diamond Library Series)

6234 Cleverly caught!: a thrilling romance of
■ the cricket field. Aldine Publishing Co., [1909]. 64p. (Diamond Library Series)

6235 **Hadath, Gunby**
■ Schoolboy grit: a public school story; illustrated by Arthur Twidle. Nisbet, 1913. vi,296p. illus.
——*another ed.* 1942
*cricket in chs. xi, xviii, xix*

6235 Sheepy Wilson: a public school story.
–1 Nisbet, 1915. ix,304p. 1 col. illus.
■ *cricket in chs. ii,xxi*

6236 Against the clock: a public school story. Hodder & Stoughton, 1924. 318p.

6236 His Highness: a public school story.
–1 Nelson, [1924]. 428p. illus.
■ *cricket in chs. xvii,xviii,xxxiii,xxxv*

6236 Go-Bang Garry: a public school story.
–2 Hodder & Stoughton, [1926]. 318p.
■ *cricket in chs. xliv,xlv*

6236 Carey of Cobhouse. Oxford, Humphrey
–3 Milford, 1928. 287p.

——*reissued in* The new school omnibus. Oxford Univ. P., 1935.
*ch. xix "A Yorkshireman loses his prey"*

6236 The new school at Shropp: a public school
–4 story. O.U.P., 1930. 283p. col. frontis.
■ *cricket in ch. iv*

6236 Grim work at Bodlands: a public school
–5 story; illustrated by Reginald Mills.
■ O.U.P., 1935. 287p. illus. (1 col.)
*cricket in ch. xiii*

6237 Fight it out. Lutterworth P., 1944. 254p.

6238 The bridgehead. Oxford Univ. P., 1945. 192p.

6239 No robbery. Lutterworth P., 1950. 192p

6239 Playing the game. Latimer House, 1950.
–1 150p.
*cricket in chs. xxii, xxiii*

6239 Honours easy; illustrated by Drake
–2 Brookshaw. Nelson, 1953. vii,214p.

6240 **Hamilton, Charles Harold St. John**
■ King cricket. [Amalgamated P., c.1920], 120p. (Boys' Friend Library)

6241 The boy they couldn't trust by Martin Clifford [pseud.] Amalgamated P., 1939. (Schoolboys' Own Library)

6241 Cardew's catch; by Frank Richards.
–1 [pseud.]. Spring Books, [1960]. 302p. illus. (Fanfare Series)

6241 Down and out, by Frank Richards,
–2 [pseud.]. Spring Books, [1960]. 264p. illus. (Fanfare Series)

6242 **Hammond, Walter Reginald**
Cloyne of Claverhouse. Amalgamated P., 1939. 64p. (Boys' Friend Library)

6242 **"Hardy, Arthur S.,"** *pseud. [i.e.* **Arthur**
–2 **Skeffens]**
Sporting life: a new novel of school, of cricket & of adventure at home & abroad. Amalgamated P., [c.1914]. 120p. (Boys' Friend Library)

6243 The master batsman. Amalgamated P., [c.1924]. 64p. (Boys' Friend Library)

6244 The pride of the county. Amalgamated P., 1925. 64p. (Boys' Friend Library)

6244 **Harrison, Frederick**
–1 The boys of Spartan House School: a story of school and adventure; illustra-tions by Harold Piffard. S.P.C.K., [1902]. vi,383p.

6245 ■ The boys of Wynport College: a story of school life; illustrated by Harold Copping. Blackie, [1916], 351p. illus.
*ch. xii "The cricket match", pp. 109–114*

6246 **Havilton, Jeffrey**
■ Out of school; illustrated by H.M. Brock. Blackie, [1930]. 224p. illus.
*cricket in chs. 1 and 2*

6246 George pulls it off; illustrated by H.M.
–1 Brock. Blackie, [1932]. 240p. illus.
■ *cricket in ch. xiii*

6247 ■ The luck of study thirteen; illustrated by H.M. Brock. Blackie, [1934]. 223p. illus.

6247 **Hayens, Herbert**
–1 The Gayton scholarship: a school story.
■ Nelson, 1915. 204p.
*cricket in ch. ii*

6248 "Play up Blues!"; illustrated by Gordon Browne. Collins, 1920. 320p. illus.

6249 "Play up, Queens!"; illustrated by Gordon Browne. Collins, 1922. 320p. illus. (Boys' and Girls' Library)

6250 **[Entry cancelled]**

6251 "Play up Greys!" Collins, 1926. 318p.

6252 Jack, the merrymaker. Collins, [1930]. v,90p.
*cricket in chs. iv & v*

6252 Play up, Lions! Collins, [c.1930]. 318p.
–1 *cricket in chs. i, xxxiii*

6252 Play up Buffs! Collins, [c.1934]. 314p. col.
–2 frontis.
*cricket in chs. x, xi, xii*

6252 The inseparables (Play up, School!). Col-
–3 lins, *n.d.* 314p. col. frontis.

6252 'Play up, King's!' illustrated by Gordon
–4 Browne. Collins, *n.d.* 328p. col. frontis.
*cricket in chs. xx, xxvi*

6252 "Play up, Stag's!" illustrated by C.
–5 Morse. Collins, *n.d.* 320p. col. frontis.
■ *cricket in chs. xiii–xvi*

6252 **[Heldmann, Bernard]**
–6 Boxall School: a tale of schoolboy life.
■ Nisbet, [1881]. [vii],240p.
*cricket in ch. xi*

6253 **Heming, Jack**
■ Playing for the school. Purnell, 1961. viii,175p. frontis.

6253 **Henderson, W.R.**
–1 Tindertoken School. Blackie, 1934. 256p. (Horizon Library)
——rptd. 1941

6253 **Henty, George Alfred**
–2 With Kitchener in the Soudan, a story of Atbara and Omdurman. Blackie, 1903, [1902]. 384p. illus. maps
*cricket pp. 93–7*

6253 **Herbert, Charles**
–3 That boy Bert. John F. Shaw, [1928]. 184p.
■ col. frontis.
*cricket in chs. v, xvii*

6254 **Hincks, Cyril Malcolm**
The booming of Beachsea. Amalgamated P., 1924. 64p. (Football and Sports Library)

6255 A lad o' the village. Amalgamated P., 1929. 64p. (Boys' Friend Library)

6256 **Hobbs, *Sir* John Berry**
■ Between the wickets. A. & C. Black, 1926. viii,248p. col. frontis. (Black's Boys' and Girls' Library)

6256 **Holmes, Frederic Morell**
–1 Winning his laurels: the boys of St.
■ Raglan's. Nisbet, [1887]. vi,258p. illus.
*cricket chs. xx, xxi*

6257 **Home, Andrew**
■ From fag to monitor; or, Fighting to the front. A. & C. Black, 1896. ix,346p. col. illus.
*ch. 18 "Our match with 'Bryan's' "*

6258 The boys of Badminster: a school tale;
■ with illustrations by C.M. Sheldon. Chambers, 1905. vii,398p.
*cricket chs. ix and x*

6259 **Home-Gall, Edward R.**
■ The century-hitter from nowhere. Buck Bros. & Harding for Perry Colour Books, [1950]. 60p. (Boys Favourite Library)

6260 A prince of the willow. Hennel Locke,
■ 1950. 216p. col. frontis.

6261 Trailed by snake men. Buck Bros. & Harding, 1950. 60p. (Boys Favourite Library)

6262 **Hope, Graham Archibald**
Kerr of Castleburgh: a public school story. Shaw, 1913. 320p.

6262 **Hornung, Ernest William**
–1 Fathers of men. Smith, Elder, 1912. vi,
■ 371p.
*a school story*

6263 **Hough, Lewis**
■ Dr. Jolliffe's boys: a tale of Weston School. Blackie, [1883]. 288p. illus.

6264 **Houghton, Leighton**
■ Play up, Barnley! Collins, 1964. 188p.

6265 **"Howard, John M.,"** *pseud.* [*i.e.* **Cyril**
■ **Malcolm Hincks**]
Cricketer—cracksman. Amalgamated P., 1936. 64p. (Football and Sports Library)

6266 **[Hughes, Thomas]**
■ Tom Brown's school days, by an Old Boy. Cambridge, Macmillan, 1857. viii,420p.
*ch. viii "Tom Brown's last match"*

6267 **Hutcheson, John Conroy**
■ "Our scratch eleven": the story of a great victory. Blackie, [1896]. 48p. frontis.

6268 **Jessop, Gilbert Laird**
■ Arthur Peck's sacrifice: a tale of Leckenham School; illustrated by H.M. Brock. Nelson, [1920]. 377p. col. illus.

6269 Cresley of Cressingham; with illustra-
■ tions by Frank Gillett. Cassell, 1924. vii, 311p. col. illus.

6269 **Johnson, Joseph**
−1 The master's likeness: a school story for
■ boys. Religious Tract Society, [1885]. 215p. illus.
*cricket in ch. xi*

6270 **Judd, Alfred**
■ The luck of the Lennites: a public school story. Nelson, [1924]. 211p. illus.
*cricket chs. x, xi, xvii*

6271 The mystery of Meldon School. Jarrolds,
■ 1924. 307p. illus.
*cricket chs. xxviii–xxxi*

6272 Derry of Dunn's house. Blackie, 1925. 208p. illus.

6272 The school on the steep: a chronicle of
−1 happenings; illustrated by Brock. Nelson, [1926]. 198p. illus.
*ch. 10 "Fraser's biggest hit"*

6272 Pals at Allingham; with . . . illustrations
−2 . . . by H.M. Brock. Cassell, 1926.
■ [vii],216p. illus. (1 col.)
*ch. x, "The match of the season"*

6273 The riddle of Randley School. Blackie, 1927. 208p. illus.

6273 **Kenyon, Edith C.**
−1 The heroes of Moss Hall School: a public
■ school story. Religious Tract Society, [1905]. 384p. illus. (some col.)
*cricket in chs. xxiv, xxv*

6274 **Kenyon, James William**
■ Peter Trant, cricketer-detective; with illustrations by J. Abbey. Methuen, 1944. vi,186p. illus.

6274 Peter Trant: heavyweight champion.
−1 Methuen, 1946. 192p. illus.
*cricket in chs. i, ii, vii, xii, xxv*

6274 **Kilroy, Margaret**
−2 The little torment: a girl's school story
■ . . . with eight illustrations by Norman Ault. Chambers, 1909. 232p. illus.
*ch. x "The Dean, lunch and cricket"*

6274 **Kingston, William Henry Giles**
−3 Ernest Bracebridge; or, Schoolboy days.
■ Sampson Low, 1860. vii,328p. illus.
*cricket in ch. xvi*

6275 **[Knowles, Mabel Winifred]**
A term to remember: a girl's school story, by May Wynne. Aldine Publ. Co., 1930. 191p. frontis.
*ch. vi "The cricket match"*

6276 **Lea, Charlton**
Kettle's century: a rollicking story of Kettle and Co. at Wyeminster School. Aldine Publishing Co., 1909. 64p. (Diamond Library Series)

6277 The hope of his side. Aldine Publishing
■ Co., [c.1912]. 48p. (Diamond Library Series)

6277 **Leslie, Emma**
−1 Elleslie House: a book for boys. Partridge, n.d. 154p. illus.
*cricket ch. ix; 1st edition published 1867*

6278 **Leslie, Penelope**
Wetford Cricket Club; or, the story of a brave deed. Blackie, 1896. 32p. illus.

6279 **Lewis, J.H. Byron**
■ Molly's chance. Nelson, 1926. 191p. illus.

6280 **Leyland, Eric [Arthur]**
■ The cricket week mystery. Ward, Lock, 1950. [v],186p. frontis.

6281 Conspiracy at Abbey. Nelson, 1957. vii, 206p. col. frontis. illus.

6282 Going concern; illustrated by Robert Hodgson. Nelson, [1961]. vii,111p. illus.

6283 **Lind, Anton**
■ Leave it to Rags! Sampson Low, Marston, [1939]. [iii],252p. frontis.

6284 **Little, Sylvia**
■ Stanton's comes of age. Stanmore P., 1947. 200p.

6285 The twins at Castle School. Lutterworth, 1947 [i.e. 1948]. 208p.

6285 **The live doll**, or Ellen's new year's gift.
-1 Denton & Clark, [c.1840]. 50p. col. illus.
*with cricket illustrations*

6286 **Lyons, Ronald Samuel**
■ The school in the skies. Children's P., [1950]. 190p. col. frontis.

6286 **Maddock, Reginald**
-1 The willow wand; illustrated by Robert Hodgson. Nelson, 1962. 213p. illus.

6287 **Mant, Alicia Catherine**
□ Ellen and George; or, The game of cricket: a tale, calculated for the amusement and instruction of young persons. Holloway, 1825. illus. (Juvenile Library)
——another ed. Allmann, 1829. 3–60p. illus.
*frontis.: "Mrs. Danver's and Ellen's visit to the cricket-field"*

6287 **Marryat, Emilia**
-1 Harry at school: a story for boys; illustrated by John Absolon. Griffiths, Farran, [1883]. 157p.
*cricket in ch. ii*

6287 **Martin, Peter**
-2 Blake's fag. Cassell, 1929. [vi].186p. frontis.

6288 Miggs Minor: a school story. Cassell, 1930. 154p.

6288 **May, Emily Juliana**
-1 Louis' school days: a story for boys. Rout-
■ ledge, [c.1886]. viii,351p. illus.
*first published at Bath by Binns & Goodwin, 1851; cricket chs. viii, xvi*

6288 **Millington, Thomas Street**
-2 Some of our fellows: a school story. Hodder & Stoughton, 1886. vii,339p. illus.
*cricket in ch. vii*

6288 **Mills, George**
-3 Meredith and Co.: the story of a modern preparatory school. Oxford Univ. P., 1933. 288p. illus.
*cricket ch. xix*

6289 King willow; illustrated by H.M. Brock. Harrap, 1938. 221p. illus.
——another ed. Cambridge U.P., 1951. x,214p. frontis.
——another ed. Spring Books, n.d. 256p. col. frontis.

6290 **Morin, Maud**
That red-haired girl in Thorn's. Sampson Low, 1936. v,250p.
*two cricket chs.*

6291 **Mossop, Irene Maude**
Prunella plays the game. Sampson Low, 1929. vii,280p.

6292 Charm's last chance. Nisbet, 1931. 254p.

6292 **"Mowbray, John"**, *pseud.* [*i.e.* **John**
-1 **George Haslett Vahey**]
■ The way of the weasel: a public school story. Partridge, [1922]. 160p. illus.
*cricket in chs. ii, iii*

6292 Barkworth's last year: a school story.
-2 Cassell, 1925. 186p. frontis. (Cassell's
■ Popular Library for Boys and Girls)
*cricket chs. 1, 2 and 3*

6293 The black sheep of the school. Cassell,
■ 1926. [v],186p.
*ch. 11 "School v. Ashfield Valley"*

6294 Dismal Jimmy of the Fourth; with illustra-
■ tions by H.M. Brock. Cassell, 1928. [vii], 216p. illus. (1. col.)

6295 The feud at Fennell's; illustrated by H.M. Brock. Cassell, 1930. 216p. illus. (Cassell New Boys' Library)

6295 **Narayan, Rasipuram Krishnaswamy**
-1 Swami and friends. H. Hamilton, 1935.
■ 252p.
——another ed.; illustrated by R.K. Laxman. Oxford Univ. P., 1978. [v],184p. (Oxford Illustrated Classics)

6296 **Newman, Marjorie W.**
■ Scoring for the school; illustrated by S. Brier. Nelson, 1929. 231p.
*ch. xiv—"Jessica plays cricket"*

6296 **North, Jack**
-1 Birds of a feather: a splendid, long, com-
plete school yarn of Jack Jackson & Co. at Wycliffe. Amalgamated P., n.d. 64p. (Boy's Friend Library, no. 555)

6297 **Page, Richard St. Clair**
■ The three Merles: a boys' school story. S.P.C.K., [1926]. 128p. col. frontis.
*ch. iv "Unreformed cricket"*

6298 **Parker, Eric**
■ Playing fields; with eight drawings by J.D.M. Harvey. P. Allen, 1922. 383p.
——another ed. with sub-title: schooldays at Eton. Carroll & Nicholson, 1950. 352p.

6299 **Parker, Mary Louise**
Dormitory "Wistaria". Sampson Low, [1947]. vi,250p.
*2 cricket chs.*

6300 Suzette wins her way. Sampson Low, [1947]. v,246p.

6301 **Paull,** *Mrs.* **Henry B.**
■ Frank Merton's conquest; or, "Charity is not easily provoked". Jarrold, [1876]. 109p. col. frontis. [of cricket]
*cricket in ch. v*

6302 **Paull, M.A.,** *afterwards* **Mrs. John Ripley**
■ Dick's chum. Partridge. [c.1900]. [v],148p. frontis.
*ch. 1 "The Blue Boys' eleven"*

6303 **Pearce, St. John**
■ Off his own bat: a public school story. Ward, Lock, 1921. 320p. illus.

6304 The school Jonah: a public school story.
■ Ward, Lock, [1923]. 256p. frontis.

6305 "Slogger" and Co.: a public school story.
■ Ward, Lock, 1928. 256p. illus.

6306 **[Pentelow, John Nix]**
■ An uphill game: a school story by Harry Huntingdon; with original illustrations by Francis E. Hile. Warne, [1913]. vi,375p. col. frontis.
*large cricket content*

6307 The last choice, by Richard Randolph. Amalgamated P., 1922. 64p. (Boys' Friend Library)

6308 Young Yardley, by Richard Randolph. Amalgamated P., 1922. 64p. (Boys' Friend Library)

6309 Brother pros, by Richard Randolph. Amalgamated P., 1924. 64p. (Boys' Friend Library)

6310 Smith of Rocklandshire, a glorious long complete story of county cricket, by Richard Randolph. Amalgamated P., 1924. 64p. (Boys' Friend Library)

6311 For Carden and the county, by Richard Randolph. Amalgamated P., 1925. 64p. (Boys' Friend Library. New Series)

6312 Boy Bayley professional, by Richard Randolph. Amalgamated P., 1926. 64p. (Boys' Friend Library. New Series)

6313 The terror of the Tests, by Richard Randolph. Amalgamated P., 1926. 64p. (Boys' Friend Library. New Series)

6314 Good enough for England, by Richard Randolph. Amalgamated P., 1927. 64p. (Boys' Friend Library. New Series)

6315 The luck of the game, by Richard Randolph. Amalgamated P., 1930. 64p. (Boys' Friend Library. New Series)

6316 School and sport. Amalgamated P., [19–?]. (Boys' Friend Library)

6317 **Petersen, Christian**
■ Mystery comes to St. Christopher's. Sampson Low, Marston, [1950]. 256p. illus.

6317 **Pike, Lillian M.**
–1 Jack of St. Virgil's. Ward, Lock, 1917.
■ 319p. illus.
*cricket chs. viii, ix*

6318 **Plunket,** *Hon.* **Isabella Katherine**
■ "The cricket green"; or, "Malcolm's luck". Edinburgh & London, Gall & Inglis, [1876]. 127p. col. frontis.
——*another ed. with title:* Malcolm's luck; or The cricket green. Gall & Inglis, [1897]. [v],127p. col. frontis.

6319 **[Pollock, Edith Caroline]**
Captain Geoff., by Ismay Thorn. Wells, Gardner, Darton, 1892. viii,182p.
*cricket in chs. xxiii, xxiv*

6320 **Poole, Reginald Heber**
■ Dick never-say-die! Cassell, 1929. [v], 154p. frontis. (Cassell's Ludgate Library for Boys and Girls)

6321 "Well bowled, Grantley!" Blackie, 1929. 256p. illus.

6321 Under Ringwood's rule: a school story,
–1 by Michael Poole [pseud.] Sampson Low,
■ [1930]. [v],250p. frontis.
*cricket ch. x*

6322 Biddy's for ever, by Michael Poole [pseud.] Cassell, 1931. 216p. illus. (Cassell's New Boys' Library)

6322 The mystery of Cranston School, by
–1 Michael Poole [pseud.] Sampson Low,
■ [1935]. v,250p. frontis.
*cricket chs. ii, x*

6323 The hypnotised cricketer. Amalgamated
■ P., 1937. 96p. (The Boys' Friend Library)

6324 **Pringle, Patrick**
■ The missing cricketer. Evans Bros., 1952. 207p.

6325 **Probyn, Elise**
■ Joan's chance to play for England. Amalgamated P., 1958. 64p. (Schoolgirls' Own Library)

6325 **Protheroe, Ernest**
–1 Friar Tuck's first term. Epworth P., J.
■ Alfred Sharp, 1923. 256p. col. frontis.
*cricket ch. viii*

6326  From fag to hero. Epworth P., 1925. 272p. illus.

6326  **Pugh, S.S.**
–1  His masters: a story of school-life forty years ago. Religious Tract Society, [1887]. 256p.
*cricket ch. vi*

6327  **Reed, Talbot Baines**
■  The fifth form at St. Dominic's: a school story; illustrated by Gordon Browne. Religious Tract Society, [1887]. x,467p. illus. (The Boy's Own Bookshelf)
*1st appeared serially in the 4th vol. of the Boy's Own Paper, from Oct. 1, 1881 to June 24, 1882*

6328  The Willoughby captains; a school story. Hodder & Stoughton, 1887. iv,442p. frontis.
——*another ed.* Oxford Univ. P., 1924. vi,442p. illus.
——*another ed.* Latimer House, 1948. 312p.
*ch. xxiv. 'The Rockshire Match'*

6328  **Rhoades, Walter C.**
–1  Our fellows at St. Mark's: a school story.
■  Edinburgh, Nimmo, [1891]. 253p. illus.
*cricket ch. xiii*

6329  Two spacegraces: a school story. Constable, 1898. viii,340p.
——*another ed.;* illustrated by H. Copping. Blackie, 1908. ix,321p.

6329  The boy from Cuba: a school story; with
–1  six illustrations by J.R. Burgess.
■  Partridge, [1900]. 332p. illus.
*cricket chs. x, xi*

6330  For the sake of his chum: a school story; illustrated by N. Tenison. Blackie, 1909. 288p. illus.
*cricket chs. iv and v*

6330  "Quills": a tale of school-days at Beding-
–1  hurst; illustrated by Harold Copping.
■  Blackie, [1918]. 288p. illus.
*cricket ch. xviii*

6330  In the scrum: a school story; with illustra-
–2  tions by Gordon Browne. Oxford Univ.
■  P., 1922. 288p. illus.
*cricket chs. xviii, xxi*

6330  The last lap: a school story; illustrated by
–3  G.W. Goss. Oxford Univ. P., 1923. 288p. illus.

6331  The boys of Redcliff. Partridge, 1926. 332p.

6332  The whip hand: a school story. Blackie, 1940. 255p. illus.

6333  **Rice, Jo**
■  Mortimer Also; illustrated by David Knight. Kingswood (Sy.), The World's Work, 1968. 128p. illus.

6333  **Rittenberg, Max**
–1  The Cockatoo: a novel of public-school
■  life; illustrated by J.H. Dowd. Sidgwick & Jackson, 1913. viii,311p. illus.
*ch. xxvi "Not cricket!"*

6334  **Robinson, Hubert J.**
■  The impossible prefect; illustrated by Savile Lumley. Nelson, [1939]. 221p. illus. (Coronet Library)
——*reissued.* [1951]. (Apex Series)
*cricket chs. iv, v, viii, xiii, xiv*

6334  **Rowe, John Gabriel**
–1  The boys of Fellingham School; illustrated
■  by Percy Tarrant. Harrap, 1919. 240p. col. illus.
*cricket chs. xiv, xv, xxii, xxiii*

6335  The demon bowler of Hedingham. Aldine Publishing Co., [1921]. (Boys' Own Library)

6336  **The school** feud: a story of St. Christopher's School, by the Author of The mystery of Dangfield's House, etc. Henderson, [1911]. 56p. (The Nugget Library)

6337  **Scott, Michael George**
■  A modern Tom Brown's schooldays. Harrap, 1937. 297p. plan

6338  **Scott, T.H.**
■  A hit for six and what came of it. Warne, 1934. 256p. col. frontis.

6338  **Sewell, J.S.N.**
–1  Second innings. Sheldon P., [1933]. 160p.
■  col. frontis.
*cricket chs xi, xii, xiv, xxviii*

6339  **Shaw, Frank Hubert**
The champion of the school; illustrations by Ernest Prater. Cassell, 1911. 312p. col. illus.

6340  **[Smith, Charles Turley]**
■  Godfrey Marten, schoolboy, by Charles Turley. Heinemann, 1902. 256p.
*cricket in ch. ix*

6341  Godfrey Marten, undergraduate, by
■  Charles Turley. Heinemann, 1904. [iv], 358p.
*ch. xi: "A cricket match at Burtington"*

6342  Maitland Major and Minor, by Charles Turley; 6 illustrations by Gordon Browne. Heinemann, 1905. vii,319p. illus.

6342 The Minvern brothers, by Charles Turley.
–1 Nelson, [1909]. 448p. col. illus.
■    *cricket ch. xx*

6342 The new broom, by Charles Turley.
–2 Nelson, [1911]. 393p. col. frontis.
■    *cricket ch. xxvi*

6343 A band of brothers, by Charles Turley.
Heinemann, 1913. 356p.
——*rptd.* [1922]. 476p. (Nelson's Popular Novels Series)

6344 The left-hander, by Charles Turley.
Oxford U.P., 1930. 286p. illus.

6344 Tales of Lexham, by Charles Turley; illus-
–1 trated by Reginald Mills. Oxford Univ.
■ P., 1934. 288p.
   *cricket ch. x*

6345 **Sobers, Gary,** *i.e.* Sir **Garfield St.**
■ **Aubrun Sobers**
Bonaventure and the flashing blade.
Pelham Books, 1967. 160p. (Sportaces novels)

6346 **Spring, Howard**
■ Darkie and Co. Oxford U.P., 1932. 288p. illus.
——new ed. 1958
——*rptd.* 1969. (Oxford Children's Library)
*ch. xxiii "The cricket match"*

6347 **[Stagg, John Reynold]**
■ Skipper of the XI: a story of school life, [by] John Barnett; illustrated by T.M.R. Whitwell. Blackie, 1915. 255p. illus.
   *4 cricket chs.*

6348 **Sweet, John**
Bellamy comes back. Oxford U.P., 1930. 96p. frontis.
   *2 cricket chs.*

6349 Setting the pace. Oxford U.P., 1933. 96p.

6349 Barlow scores. Oxford Univ. P., 1935.
–1 96p. col. illus.

6350 **Tarrant, Elizabeth**
Crisis at Cardinal. Museum P., 1951. 190p. col. frontis.

6351 **Tempany, Greville H.**
■ The eight days' feud. Nelson, [1929]. 96p. frontis. (The Peerless Series)
   *ch. ii "LBW"*

6352 **Terrill, G. Appleby**
■ Out in the glare: a cricket story. Chambers, [1927]. 116p.
——re-issued. 1962

6353 **The Test** match kid. Amalgamated P., 1927. 64p. (The Boys' Friend Library. New Series)

6354 **"Thomas, Anthony",** *pseud.* [*i.e.* **Richard**
■ **Heber Poole]**
The mystery batsman. Amalgamated P., 1934. 96p. (The Boys' Friend Library)

6355 A pawn in the game. United P., *n.d.* 48p. (Lloyds Sports Library)

6356 The wicket swindlers. United P., *n.d.* 48p. (Lloyds Sports Library)

6357 **Tom** Garth of Hollowfield. Amalgamated P., *n.d.* 72p. (The Boys' Friend Library)

6358 **Tufty's** cricket triumph. James Henderson, [c.1910]. 56p. (Nugget Library)

6358 **Uncle Reg's** schooldays, by Himself.
–1 Kelly, 1912. 133p. illus. port.
■    *cricket in ch. iv*

6358 **Walker, Rowland**
–2 The fifth form detective. Partridge, [1924]. 255p.
——new ed. Black, 1938. 256p.
   *cricket ch. xi*

6359 Pepper's crack eleven: a book for boys.
■ Nelson, 1925. 198p. frontis.

6359 The Tiger's Cub at school. Partridge,
–1 [1934]. [vi],246p. col. frontis.
■    *cricket chs. xix, xxi, xxii, xxiii*

6359 **Wallace, William**
–2 Shunned by the school: how O'Mara
■ made good. Pilgrim P., *n.d.* 192p. col. frontis.
   *cricket ch. xiv*

6360 **[Watson, John]**
■ Young barbarians, [by] Ian Maclaren. Hodder & Stoughton, 1901. viii,316p.

6360 **Webster, William**
–1 Jack Stafford: a tale of the East coast. Religious Tract Society, [1911]. 278p. col. illus.
   *cricket ch. i*

6360 **West, Alfred**
–2 His first year at school: a book for boys and their parents. T. Fisher Unwin, 1896. xii,244p.

6360 **Whishaw, Fred**
–3 The competitors: a tale of Upton House School; illustrated by J. Ley Pethybridge. Wells Gardner, Darton & Co., 1906. vii, 208p. illus.
   *cricket chs. xi, xiv, xv*

6360 Gubbins minor and some other fellow: a
-4 story of school life. Griffith Farran, 1913.
315p. illus.
*cricket chs. xiii, xvi*

6360 **Whitehouse, Francis Cowley**
-5 Meltonians all! with coloured illustrations
■ by J. Finnemore. Religious Tract Society,
[1911]. 319p. col. illus.
*cricket ch. xvi*

6361 Rob Wylie of Jordan's: a story of public
■ school life; illustrated by T.M.R.
Whitwell. Blackie, [1914]. 288p. illus.
*cricket chs. vi, xii, xxviii, xxix, xxx*

6362 **Whiting, H.S.**
■ Just Percy: a tale of Dickton School.
Partridge, [1907]. 294p. illus.
*cricket in chs, vi and xviii*

6363 **Wodehouse,** *Sir* **Pelham Grenville**
■ A prefect's uncle; illustrations by R. Noel
Pocock. A. & C. Black, 1903. [vii],264p.
illus.
——new ed. 1924. (Black's Boy's Library)

6364 The gold bat; illustrations by T.M.R.
■ Whitwell. A. & C. Black, 1904. 286p.
——*another ed.* 1923. [vii],277p. col.
frontis. (Black's Boys' & Girls' Library)
*no cricket, but a school mystery concerning
the loss of a miniature gold bat*

6365 The head of Kay's; illustrated by T.M.R.
Whitwell. Black, 1905. 280p.
——*another ed.* 1922. vii,280p.

6366 **"A Wolvertonian"**, *pseud.*
Three years at Wolverton: a public school
story. Marcus Ward, 1877. 330p. illus.

6367 **Wyatt, Arthur**
■ The changeable twins. Nelson, [1910].
192p. col. frontis.
*cricket chs. x and xii*

6367 **Wyatt, G.E.**
-1 Lionel Harcourt, the Etonian; or, "Like
other fellows". Nelson, 1889 [1888]. 320p.
*cricket ch. xvi*

# CHILDREN'S SHORT STORIES

6367 **Turner, Ernest Sackville**
-2 Boys will be boys: the story of Sweeny
□ Todd, Deadwood Dick, Sexton Blake,
Billy Bunter, Dick Barton, et. al. M.
Joseph, 1948. 269p.
——new revised ed. 1957
——new revised ed. 3rd ed. 1975. 280p.
*ch. xvi "Vive le sport!" (sport including
cricket as appearing over the years in boys'
magazines)*

## Collections

6367 **Anerley, John,** *and others*
-3 Pilots of the Sixth (by J. Anerley), and
■ other stories of school and adventure [by
various authors]. Epworth P., 1938. 190p.
illus. (2 col.)
*ch. v. of title story "A hard fought match"*

6367 **Avery, Harold,** *and others*
-4 Gunpowder, treason and plot, and other
■ stories for boys. Nelson, 1907. 195p. illus.
*includes pp. 169–95 "The Cock-House Cup"*

6367 The A.C.B. schoolboys' story book, by
-5 Harold Avery, R.A.H. Goodyear, Herbert
Hayens, [and others]. Queensland,
A.C.B., [c.1933]. [196]p. illus.
*contains pp. 11–47 "Played to a finish" by
R.A.H. Goodyear*

6367 **Blackie's** boys' school story omnibus.
-6 Blackie, [1959]. 240,208,256p. frontis.
*contains 'George pulls it off' by J. Havilton*

6368 **Buckeridge, Anthony,** *editor*
Stories for boys. Faber, 1957. 272p.
*includes "The story of Spedegue's drop-
per", by Sir Arthur Conan Doyle*

6368 **Champion** book for boys. Dean & Son,
-1 n.d. 156p.
——*contains pp. 28–41 "Bone of contention"
by F. Dent*

6368 **Cole's** great boys' book no. 2. Melbourne,
-2 E.W. Cole, [1962]. 192p. illus.
*contains pp. 4–18 "The kidnapped crick-
eter" by Rex Grayson*

6368 **Dean's** favourite annual for boys. Dean,
-3 n.d. 125p. illus.
*contains pp. 119–25 "A Bank Holiday
match" by William Carr*

6368 **Dean's** supreme book for boys. Dean,
-4 1963. 125p. illus.
*contains pp. 36–9 "Straight bat Billings"
by Arthur Groom; in the form of a comic strip*

6368 **Dean's** super book for boys. Dean, 1965.
-5 125p. illus.
*contains pp. 81–91 "The interrupted cricket
match", by Arthur Waterhouse*

6369 **Dimmock, Frederick Haydn,** *compiler*
Stories for boys. Venture Books, 1948.
vii,190p. illus.
*includes "Dead keen' by H.J. Way*

6370 **Gribble, Leonard Reginald,** *compiler*
Fifty famous stories for boys. Burke, 1948.
450p.
——new ed. 1956
*contains a cricket chapter from The fifth
form at St. Dominic's by Talbot Baines Reed*

6371 **Lyons, Ronald Samuel,** *compiler*
■ Fifty-two sports stories for boys; illustrated by Julien. Hutchinson, 1935. 416p.
*includes "Safe hands" by Seeley Drane; "Darrow the dauntless' by A. Lowe*

6371 **Matthews, Leonard,** *compiler & editor*
-1 Super story book for boys. Hamlyn, 1976. 512p. illus.
*contains pp. 51–78 "Not cricket" by Rowland Yorke*

6371 **Schoolboys'** story book. Dean & Son, *n.d.*
-2 124p.
*contains pp. 29–32 "The duck that Drake made", by R.A. Moss*

6372 **Sports** stories for boys; illustrated by Reg Gray. Hamlyn, 1970. 360p. illus.
*includes "Mick's greatest innings", by Reg Clerk, pp. 267–84*

6372 **Strang, Herbert,** *editor*
-1 Gateway to adventure: stories for boys.
■ Oxford Univ. P., [1939]. 256p. col. frontis. illus. (Herbert Strang's Library)
*contains pp. 112–32, "Spikey's wicket" by J.C. Bristow-Noble*

6373 **Tarrant, W.G.,** *editor*
For girls and boys: stories from the "Inquirer". The Sunday School Association, 1924. 164p.
*includes "The miller talks cricket" pp. 25–30, and "The great mint match", pp. 31–36*

6373 **Treasure** story book for boys. Beaver
-1 Books, [1966?]. 125p. illus. (The Bumper Book Series)
*contains pp. 18–31, "A 'Stonewall' Jackson hits out" by George Mell, and "Sensation at Brisbane" (1950–51 Test)*

### By Individual Authors

6374 **Avery, Harold**
An old boy's yarns; or, School tales for past and present boys. Cassell, 1895. 279p.

6374 The school's honour and other stories.
-1 Sunday School Union, [1895]. 192p.
——*another ed.* Pilgrim's P., [1931]. 191p. illus.
*3 cricket chs. pp. 84–117*

6374 A toast fag, and other stories. Nelson,
-2 1901 [1900]. 176p. illus.
■ *includes pp. 96–119 "The enchanted bat"*

6375 **Barnard, Caroline**
The parent's offering; or, Tales for children. 2 vols. M.J. Godwin, 1813. 214p. illus.
——*improved ed.* 1823. 214p. illus.

6375 **[Barradell-Smith, Walter]**
-1 The third jump, and other stories [by] Richard Bird [pseud.]; illustrations by F. Gillett. Blackie, [1923]. 256p. illus.
*1 cricket story*

6376 Dawson's score, and other school stories,
■ by Richard Bird; illustrated by Frank Gillett. Blackie, [1924]. 255p. illus.

6376 **Bell, Robert Stanley Warren**
-1 Tales of Greyhouse; with sixteen illustra-
■ tions by T.M.R. Whitwell. Newnes, 1901. vii,294p. illus.
——*new ed.* 1907.
——*another ed.* Black, 1927
*contains a cricket story "Quits"*

6376 **Bowes, Joseph**
-2 Pals: young Australians in sport and adventure; with . . . illustrations by John Macfarlane. J. Glass, [19—?]. 311p. col. illus.
*contains pp. 17–24 "The great match"*

6377 **Butcher, J. Wilson**
The senior prefect, and other chronicles of Rossiter. C.H. Kelly, 1913. 356p.

6377 **Cleaver, Hylton**
-1 The Harley first XV. O.U.P., 1922. 288p.
■ illus.
*cricket in most stories*

6377 The test case. Collins, [1934]. 135p.
-2 *includes pp. 27–53 "A fool at the wicket"*

6378 **Coke, Desmond**
■ Youth, youth. . . ! with illustrations by H.M. Brock. Chapman & Hall, 1919. xi, 304p. illus.

6378 **Cule, William Edward**
-1 Barfield's blazer, and other school stories.
■ Andrew Melrose, [1900]. 235p. illus.
*title story*

6378 The black fifteen and other school stories.
-2 Melrose, [1906]. viii,280p. illus.
■ *pp. 51–70 "The great Grogan's bat"*
——*reissued.* Pilgrim's P., [1931]. v,268p.

6378 Rodborough School; with illustrations by
-3 Edgar Holloway. Pilgrim P., [1915]. xi,
■ 306p. illus.
*includes pp. 193–203 "Cox's century"*

6378 **[Fenn, Lady *Eleanor*]**
-4 Sketches of little boys and girls, by Solomon Lovechild. Dean, 1852

6378 **Hardcastle, Michael**
-5 The demon bowler; illustrated by Harry Bloom. Heinemann, 1974. [ii],38p. col. illus. (Red Apple Books)

6378 **Lee, Frank**
–6 The atomic cricket ball: the inside story
■ of the strange happenings of the 1946–47
Test series. Adelaide, E.J. McAlister &
Co., [1946?]. 32p. illus.
*in comic strip form*

6379 **Lucas, Edward Verrall**
Anne's terrible good nature, and other
stories for children. Chatto, 1908. 270p.

6380 **Lyster, Annette M.**
Oakhurst Manor. Chilworth & London,
Sunday School Union, 1879

6381 **Malan, Arthur Noel**
■ Schooldays at Highfield House. R.T.S.,
1898. 256p.

6382 **Mills, George**
Minor and Major; illustrated by John
Harris. Harrap, 1939. 256p.

6383 **Mowbray, John**
The strongest chap in the school; illustrated by H.M. Brock. Cassell, 1931. 216p.
illus. (Cassell's New Boys' Library)

6383 **Peach, Bill**
–1 Ginger Meggs meets the Test; created by
Bancks. Angus & Robertson, 1976. 28p.
(Young Australian Series)

*Ginger Meggs was a famous Australian
cartoon character created by Jimmy Bancks in
the 1920's*

6384 **Plant, K. Shirley**
■ The captain of the eleven, and other
school stories. R.T.S., 121p. col. frontis.
(The 'Golden Hour' Series)

6384 **Reed, Talbot Baines**
–1 Parkhurst boys, and other stories of
■ school life; with an introductory sketch
of the author as boy and man, by G.R.
Hutchison; with illustrations by Alfred
Pearse. Religious Tract Society, [1905].
[2]xx,9–375p. illus.
*pt. 1, ch. iv, "Parkhurst v. Westfield: a
cricket reminiscence"*

6384 **Tales** for Ellen. Vol. 1. Holloway, 1825
–2 *in Goldman*

6384 **Wodehouse, *Sir* Pelham Grenville**
–3 Tales of St. Austin's. Souvenir P., 1972.
■ 167p.
*short stories most of which appeared in* The
Captain *or* Public School Magazine.
*Cricket in "How Pillingshot scored", "The
odd trick", "L'affaire Uncle John", "Now,
talking about cricket – "*

# POETRY

## Collections

6384 **Alington, Cyril Argentine,** *compiler*
–4 Poets at play. Methuen, 1942. 206p.
*cricket pp. 113,200–03*

6384 **Amis, Kingsley,** *editor*
–5 The new Oxford book of light verse.
Oxford Univ. P., 1978. xxxiv,347p.
*includes pp. 292–3 poem by Roger Woddis
"Nothing sacred"*

6385 **Belcher, W.,** *and others*
The galaxy: consisting of a variety of
sacred and other poetry, the whole
original and new. Rochester, *printed by*
W. Gillman . . . *and sold by* James Evans,
Paternoster Row, London, 1790. var. pag.
*pp. 41–42, "Cricket: being a game peculiar
to Kent, and a few other countries, I subjoin
a short description of it, by way of episcode,
or rather detachment"*

6386 **Brodribb, [Arthur] Gerald [Norcott],**
■ *editor*
The book of cricket verse: an anthology.
Hart-Davis, 1953. 215p. illus.

6386 **The Bulletin**
–1 The old Bulletin book of verse: the best
verses from The Bulletin 1881–1901.
Melbourne, Lansdowne P., 1975. 204p.
illus.
*a reprint of* The Bulletin reciter, *compiled
by A.G. Stephens, 1901, and containing pp.
43–49 "How M'Dougal topped the score",
with illustration by A.J. Fischer*

6386 **Carmina** familiae. 11, Southwick Cres-
–2 cent, Hyde Park, London W., [1898]. 36p.
*a collection of poems by members of one
family: I.H.D., A.H.D., S.D., M.D., G.D.,
A.E. (ex A.D.). Includes p. 21 "The song of
the demon bowler"*

6386 **Daunt, Winifred Mary,** *compiler*
–3 Adventures into poetry. 8 books.
Macmillan, 1941–49. (Macmillan's Easy
Study Series)
*Book II (1943, repr. 1947, 1951, 1955), pp.
48–49 contains two poems: "Dreams that I
dream" by E.B.V. Christian, and "A cricket
triolet" by Coulson Kernahan*

6387 **Evans, Thomas,** *compiler*
Old ballads, historical and narrative, with some of modern date; now first collected and reprinted from rare copies and MSS. 4 vols. Printed for T. Evans in the Strand, 1777–1784
   *Vol. IV, pp. 323–335 contains "Surry triumphant; or, the Kentishmen's defeat"*

6387 **Finn, Frederick Edward Simpson,**
-1 *compiler*
The Albermarle book of modern verse for schools. Vol. 1. Murray, [1962]. xviii, 199p. (Albermarle Library for Schools)
   *includes "Cricket at Worcester, 1938", "Cricket at Swansea" and "To Sir John Berry Hobbs on his seventieth birthday", by John Arlott*

6387 **Freeman, Rowland,** *compiler*
-2 Kentish poets: a series of writers in English poetry, natives or residents in the county of Kent. . . . 2 vols. Canterbury, G. Wood, 1821
   *vol. ii, pp. 364–73 contains "Surry triumphant" by John Duncombe*

6388 **Frewin, Leslie [Ronald],** *compiler*
■ The poetry of cricket: an anthology. Macdonald, 1964. xxxiv,532p. illus.

6388 **Haileybury** verses. Hertford, Stephen
-1 Austin, 1882. viii,64p.
■    *pp. 51–60 "Ye anciente cricket match"*

6389 **Hamilton,** *Sir* **George Rostrevor,** *and*
■ **Arlott, [Leslie Thomas] John**
Landmarks: a book of topographical verse for England and Wales. Cambridge U.P., 1943. xv,236p.
   *includes "Cricket at Worcester (1938)", by John Arlott*

6389 **Haydon, Arthur Lincoln,** *editor*
-1 The boy's own reciter: a popular book of recitations for home, school and public platform. "The Boy's Own Paper" Office.
——revd. ed. 3 pts. [1921]. viii, 96, 96, 96p.
   *contains in Pt. III, pp. 36–8 "Our match with Amanda College", by A.N. Malan; pp. 50–2 "Our match with Fircombe", by Fred Edmonds; pp. 57–8 "Football and cricket – The King is dead; long live the King!" by Alfred Lindsay; pp. 86–7 "Our village eleven" by W.J. Hawkes, and an anonymous poem with the same title*

6389 **Hope, David**
-2 Fireside book: a picture and a poem for
■ every mood. Dundee & London, D.C. Thomson, 1974 [1973]. [102]p. col. illus.
   *contains the poem 'The game that's never done' by Eleanor and Herbert Farjeon*

6390 **Huddesford, George,** *editor*
■ The Wiccamical chaplet, a selection of original poetry. Leigh, Sotheby & Son, 1804. xv,225p.
   *p. 131 "Cricket-song: for the Hambledon Club, Hants, 1767" [by the Rev. Reynell Cotton]*

6390 **Hussey, Maurice Percival,** *editor*
-1 Poetry of the First World War: an anthology. Longmans, 1967. xvi,180p. (Longman's English Series)
   *contains "Three hills" by E.C.E. Owen*

6390 **Lamb, Geoffrey Frederick,** *compiler*
-2 Story and rhythm: an anthology of verse for secondary schools in three books. Book 3. Harrap, 1966. 158p.
   *includes "Cricket at Swansea" by John Arlott*

6391 **Leonard, Robert Maynard,** *compiler*
■ Poems on sport. O.U.P., 1914. 128p. (Oxford Garlands)
   *cricket pp. 70–77*

6391 **Lucas, Edward Verrall,** *compiler*
-1 A book of verses for children. Grant Richards, 1897. xii,348p.
   *pp. 57–8 "The cricket ball sings"*

6392 The joy of life: an anthology of lyrics
■ drawn chiefly from the works of living poets. Methuen, 1927. xv,288p.
   *cricket pp. 63–68*

6392 **Nichols, John,** *compiler*
-1 A select collection of poems; with notes,
■ biographical and historical, etc. 8 vols. J. Nichols, 1780–82. frontis.
   *vol. 8, pp. 45–55 contains "Surrey triumphant, or the Kentish-men's defeat" by John Duncombe*

6393 **Osborn, Edward Bolland,** *compiler*
■ Anthology of sporting verse. Collins, 1930. 288p.
   *cricket pp. 187–221*

6394 **Peek, Hedley,** *compiler & editor*
■ The poetry of sport, selected and edited by H. Peek, with a chapter on classical allusions to sport by Andrew Lang. Illustrated by A. Thorburn, L. Davis, C.E. Brock, etc. Longmans, 1896. xxxvi. 420p. illus. (The Badminton Library of Sports and Pastimes)
——L.P. ed. of 250 copies. 1896
   *cricket pp. 289–305 (333–352 L.P. ed.); for a review see no. 6680*

6395 **Ridout, Cyril James,** *compiler*
In poem-town. Book IV. Blackie, 1936. 104p.

*anthology of verse for children; includes*
*"The little man cricketer", pp. 56–7*

**6395** **Rose, Brian Waldron,** *and* **Jones, Regi-**
**–1** **nald Stranack,** *compilers*
Modern narrative poetry. Nelson, [1954].
x,182p. illus.
*includes pp. 117–9, "Cricket at Worcester,*
*1938", by John Arlott*

**6395** **Scott, Arthur Finley,** *compiler*
**–2** New paths to poetry; illustrated by Bert
Isaac. Book 4. Parrish, 1961. 120p. illus.
*includes "Cricket at Worcester, 1938", by*
*John Arlott*

**6395** **Skull, John,** *editor*
**–3** Sport and leisure. Heinemann Educational, 1970. viii,72p. illus. (Themes: a
series of poetry anthologies)
*includes "Cricket at Worcester, 1938", by*
*John Arlott*

**6395** **Thomson, Andrew Kilpatrick,** *editor*
**–4** Off the shelf. Brisbane, Jacaranda P.,
1961. [ix],212p.
*includes pp. 179–81, the poems "A cricket*
*bowler" by Edward Cracroft Lefroy, and*
*"Willow the king" by Edward Ernest Bowen*

**6396** **Tomlinson, William Weaver,** *editor*
■ Songs and ballads of sport and pastime.
Walter Scott, [1897]. xxiv,294p. frontis.
(Canterbury poets)
*cricket pp. 150–172*

**6397** **Wilkinson, C.H.,** *compiler*
Diversions. O.U.P., 1940. xvi,336p.
*poems of sport; cricket pp. 55–72*

**6398** **Williams (of Wadham College)**
■ The blunders of loyalty, and other miscellaneous poems; being a selection of
certain ancient poems, partly on subjects
of local history. Together with the
original notes and illustrations, &c. The
poems modernized by Ferdinando
Fungus, Gent. Printed for J. Murray,
1790. 44p.
*contains "The cryketeers: a gymnastic*
*poeme . . . by . . . Edmunde Byrk"*

**6399** Wit at a venture; or, Clio's privy-garden,
■ containing songs and poems on several
occasions never before in print. Printed
for Jonathan Edwin at the three Roses in
Ludgate Street, 1674
*one poem "The virtue of a hot-house"*
*contains the lines:*
*"Cricket or Gauff, which to some men is*
*As pretty a sport as Trap or Tennis"*
*the Epistle dedicatory is signed C.F. but "at*
*least three hands in this". (C.B.E.L.)*

## By Individual Authors

**6399** An adieu to the turf: a poetical epistle
**–1** from the E–L of A–N to his Grace the A–P
of Y–K. 2nd ed. London, printed for M.
Smith, 1778. [4],vii,24p.
*Scarce fourteen years had pass'd away*
*When first I thought of am'rous play*
*Of women not afraid:*
*For then I left more childish cricket;*
*I only strove to hit their* wicket,
*And* put out *every maid*

**6400** **Alington, Cyril Argentine**
■ Eton faces, old and young: [verses].
Murray, 1933. xix,199p.
*includes "Lord's, 1928"*

**6401** **"Amicus",** *pseud.*
■ A translation in verse of the mottos of
the English nobility and sixteen peers of
Scotland, in the year 1800. 2 vols. in 1.
Printed for the author by Robert Trip-
hook, 1822. [iii],127p.
*rptd. from The Morning Herald, 1801;*
*references to the Earl of Tankerville p. 24 and*
*Earl of Winchelsea, p. 15*

**6401** **Arkell, Reginald**
**–1** Playing the games; pictured by Robert S.
■ Sherriffs. Jenkins, 1935. 96p. illus.
*p. 34, "Body line bowling"*

**6402** **Arlott, [Leslie Thomas] John**
■ Of period and place. Cape, 1944. 45p.
*includes "On a great batsman", "Cricket*
*at Worcester, 1938" and "The old cricketer"*

**6403** **Ashley, Kenneth H.**
■ Up hill and down dale. Lane, 1924. x,88p.
*includes"Close of play" pp. 38–9*

**6404** **Baddeley, Richard Wheldon**
■ Cassandra, and other poems. Bell &
Daldy, 1869. viii,168p.
*includes "The stout cricketer" pp. 150–3*

**6405** **Bagshaw, William**
A cricket lullaby. London & Manchester,
Sherratt & Hughes, 1902. 8p.
*rptd. from Manchester Quarterly Oct.*
*1903 (sic!)*

**6405** **Bailey, Les**
**–1** Legends of Yorkshire cricket. [Rother-
■ ham, *privately circulated*], 1974. [v],43f.
*typescript. illus. ports.*
*a collection of poems*

**6405** A sporting smile. [Rotherham, *privately*
**–2** *circulated*], 1975. [iv],86f. *typescript*
■ *a collection of poems*

6405 When dreams come true – Geoff Boycott.
–3 [The Author, 1977?]. bs. card
   *a poem to commemorate Boycott's 100th century; limited edition of 250 copies*

6406 **Baker, W.W.**
■ Maurice Tompkin. [The Author], *n.d.* bs.

6407 **Bange, William**
   The happy village, and other poems. 1848
   *includes "Fair grove"*

6408 **Barnes, William**
■ Poems of rural life in the Dorset dialect.
   Third collection. J.R. Smith, 1862. viii,
   133p.
   *includes "Eclogue: Come and Zee us in the Zummer":*
   *"I'll goo, an' we'll zet up a wicket,*
   *An' have a good innens at cricket"*

6409 **Barratt, A.H.**
■ "Oh! those Ashes": [a poem]; cartoon by
   Tom Fisher. Nottingham, *privately printed,* R. Milwood, 1933. [12]p.

6410 **Bax, Clifford**
   Farewell my muse. Lovat Dickson, 1932.
   203p. port.
   *includes "Cricket days", pp. 41–2 and "A dead cricketer", p. 62*

6411 **Beavan, Edward**
■ Box Hill: a descriptive poem. J. Wilkie,
   1777. 34p.
   *reference to cricket p. 22 et seq. giving an account of a match on Cotman's Green*

6412 **Benson, Francis Colgate**
   Songs of the cricket field, and other
   verses. Philadelphia, The James Clark P.,
   1932

6412 **Betjeman, John**
–1 Collected poems; enlarged edition
■ compiled and with an introduction by
   The Earl of Birkenhead. 3rd ed. Murray,
   1970. xxxi,366p.
   *includes pp. 362–6 'Cricket master (an incident)' first published in* High and low
   *(1966)*

6412 High and low. Murray, 1966. 81p.
–2 *includes "Cricket master (an incident)"*

6413 **Blake, William**
   Poetry and prose; edited by Geoffrey
   Keynes. Nonesuch P., 1927. xi,1152p.
   *reference to cricket in "An island in the moon", p. 689. N.B. The plate for "The echoing green" in* Songs of Innocence
   *(1789) shows children playing cricket*

6414 **Blunden, Edmund Charles**
■ English poems. Cobden Sanderson, 1925.
   127p.
   ——new and revised ed. Duckworth,
   1929. 144p. (New Reader's Library)
   *includes "Pride of the village"*

6415 Poems 1914–30. Cobden-Sanderson,
■ 1930. xxvii,336p.
   ——Limited ed. *of 200 signed copies.* 1930
   *includes "Pride of the village", pp. 106–08*

6416 An elegy, and other poems. Cobden
■ Sanderson, 1937. 96p.
   *includes "Cricket, I confess", p. 80*

6417 After the bombing, and other short
■ poems. Macmillan, 1949. viii,51p.
   *includes "Hammond (England) a cricketer", pp. 43–45*

6418 Edmund Blunden: a selection of his
■ poetry and prose made by Kenneth
   Hopkins. Hart-Davis, 1950. 374p. port.
   *cricket pp. 183–218*

6419 Poems of many years. Collins, 1957.
■ 312p.
   *contains "Cricket, I confess", p. 211;*
   *"Hammond (England) a cricketer", pp.*
   *277–78; "H-bomb", pp. 288–89*

6420 **Bosanquet, Robert Carr**
■ Letters and light verse; edited by Ellen
   S. Bosanquet. Gloucester, *printed by* John
   Bellows, 1938. 270p. illus. port. map
   *poems include "The destruction of Eton,*
   *1889" [Eton v. Winchester]; "Eton v.*
   *Harrow, 1889" and "The prophecy of [Henry]*
   *Perkins"*

6421 **Bowen,** Hon. **William Edward**
■ Edward Bowen: a memoir. Longmans,
   1902. viii,417p. ports.
   *includes E. Bowen's cricket verses*

6422 **Bradby, Godfrey Fox**
   Parody and dust-shot. Oxford U.P., 1931.
   viii,42p.
   *includes "The black sheep"*

6423 **Brown, Alan Roderick Haig**
   Sporting sonnets, and other verses. G.
   Allen, 1903. viii,45p.

6423 **Bryden, Hedley A.R.**
–1 A cricket ballad; the ballad written . . . in
□ the year 1905, privately printed at his
   own expense, and like distributed in the
   year of its printing. The Author, 1905
   ——reprinted in 1973, with commentary
   based upon modern research facts by
   E.A. Marsh. Eastbourne, Marsh, 1973.
   [ii],11p. bibliog. *typescript*

*on a match played at Selmeston, Sussex,*
*between The Ladies of East Sussex and The*
*Gentlemen of East Sussex*

6424 **Bullett, Gerald William**
■ News from the village. Cambridge Univ.
P., 1952. 55p.
*includes "Saturday cricket", p. 40*

6425 **[Burnby, John]**
■ The Kentish cricketers: a poem. By a
Gentleman. Being a reply to a late publication of a parody on the Ballad of Chevy
Chase; intituled Surry triumphant; or,
The Kentish Men's defeat. Canterbury,
printed by T. Smith & Son, and sold by
them and W. Flackton; also, by B. Law,
in Avemary-Lane; Messrs Richardson
and Urquhart, under the Royal Exchange
. . . 1773. 22p.
*see no. 6450*

6426 Summer amusement; or, miscellaneous
■ poems inscribed to the frequenters of
Margate, Ramsgate. Printed for J.
Dodsley, 1772 [!] 94p.
*the copy at Lord's has date altered in ink to*
*1783 which on evidence of the fact that some*
*poems are dated 1779–81 is a more likely date*
*of publication. Includes "The Kentish cricke-*
*ters" (1st publd. 1773) pp. 40–52*

6427 **Byron, George Gordon Noel,** *6th Baron*
*Byron*
Hours of idleness, a series of poems,
original and translated. Newark, S. & J.
Ridge, 1807. xiii,187p.
*includes "Memories of Harrow" where he*
*played in the first match against Eton*

6428 **Calverley, Charles Stuart**
■ Verses and translations. Cambridge,
Deighton, Bell, 1861. vi,203p.
*includes "Hic vir, his est"*

6429 **Cameron, Ludovick Charles Richard**
■ **Duncombe-Jewell**
Rhymes of sport in old French verse
forms. Bungay, Suffolk, Benn, 1926. 71p.
*includes "Cricket—at Lord's", pp. 66*

6430 **Carnie, William**
■ Waifs of rhyme. Aberdeen, *privately*
*printed,* Edmond and Spark, 1887. viii,62p.
*limited ed. of 200 copies. Includes "Wicket,*
*bat and ball", pp. 60–1*

6431 **Carrick, Hartley McGregor**
■ The muse in motley. Cambridge,
Bowes & Bowes, 1907.xii,88p.
*includes "Cricketers all" p. 62*

6432 **Casson, Thomas Edmund**
A century of roundels: for the centenary
of the Oxford and Cambridge cricket

match, 1927. Ulverston, James Atkinson,
1927. 36p.

6433 **[Castleden, George]**
■ Woburn Park: a fragment in rural rhyme.
Woburn, S. Dodd, 1839. 66p.
*"Part the Second: Cricket" (pp. 14–28)*
*describes a match in some detail*
——2nd edition, with additions. T. Ward,
1840. xii,168p.

6434 **"Century",** *pseud.*
■ Cricket rhymes. Cricket P., 1899. 42p.
illus. ports. (Cricket Press Series)

6435 **Chadburn, Paul**
■ The cricket match. Coole Book Service,
1965. [vi],40p.
*limited ed. of 500 copies*

6436 **Chadwick, Archibald Eustace**
A modest score. Cambridge, *privately*
*printed,* W.P. Spalding, 1926. 19p.

6437 **Coates, Edward Groves**
■ The British Empire, and other poems.
Ilfracombe, Stockwell, 1954. 13p.
*"Cricket" p. 11*

6438 **Cochrane, Alfred John Henry**
■ The kestrel's nest, and other verses.
Longmans, Green, 1894. viii,75p.
*includes "Ballade of the corner stroke", pp.*
*47–8*

6438 Leviore plectro: occasional verses.
–1 Longman, Green, 1896. xi,82p.
*pp. 75–6 "The catch"*

6439 Collected verses. Longmans, Green,
■ 1903. xiv,199p. frontis.
*includes "England, past and present"; "To*
*Plancus"; "To A.J. Webbe"; "The enthusi-*
*ast's love song"; "Theory and practice";*
*"Monotonous ballade of ill-success"; "Ballade*
*of the corner stroke"; "The catch"; "To*
*Lucasta (on going to the wickets)"*

6440 Reptonian reprints: verses reprinted from
■ "The Reptonian", 1883–1907. Repton,
A.J. Lawrence, 1907. vi,63p.
*includes several of cricket interest*

6441 Later verses. Longmans, 1918. viii,111p.
■ frontis.
*includes "Verba non facta"; "Hambledon";*
*"The master's match (1889–1914)"*

6441 **Craig, Albert**
–1 A selection of original rhymes and anecdotes from our football and cricket
centres by A.C. Cricket Rhymester.
Hughes, 1906. 16p.
*includes poem dedicated to E.M. Grace "A*
*little hero" about A.E.J. Collins (mis-spelt*

*Collings) and anecdotes entitled "When Essex beat the Australians" and "Our return journey from Canterbury Cricket Week"*

6442 Cricket and football: rhymes, sketches,
■ anecdotes, etc. of Albert Craig; compiled, arranged and edited by Robert Abel and H.V. Dorey. Cricket & Sports Publishers, [1910]. iii.97p.

6443 Cricket rhymester's poems; edited by Robert Abel and H.V. Dorey. Cavendish P., 1914

6444 [Verses]. The author. bs.
□ *a series of verses written to commemorate memorable happenings on the cricket field, usually at The Oval*
The following have been recorded:—

Bravo! Shrewsbury: ninety-one runs (not out) in the first day's play in the England v. Australia match, at Lord's, June 19th, 1886

British grit triumphant: Sussex beat Australia at Hove, July 20th, 1888

Cambridge v. Australians. To Mr. Rock, the famous Cricketer, on his brilliant defence in batting for 5½ hours (for 75 n.o.) against the combined strength of the Australian bowling at Leyton, August 23rd 1886

The coming man: an old pro's opinion of George Lohmann, the famous Surrey cricketer. (July 30, 1886)

Composed on Kennington Oval on Dr. W.G. Grace's forty-first birthday, July 18th, 1888

"A credit to his country. Tom Richardson". [c.1895]
*printed on silk*

Cricket in Kent 118 years ago. [c.1891]
*reproduces the full scores, Kent v. Surrey, at Bishopsbourne Paddock, near Canterbury, June 24–26, 1773, and ends with a 4-line stanza extolling 'Kent's sturdy sons'*

Exciting Test match at Manchester, England v. Australia, July 26, 1902

First match between Surrey & Notts. c.1900
*on the first match between the two in 1851*

Fred Huish, the renowned Kentish wicket-keeper

George Lohmann, the brilliant Surrey cricketer: a true incident. Printed by J. & F. Wood, [c.1895]

Gloucestershire v. Surrey, Cheltenham week, 19th August 1889. Mr. Cranston played a magnificent innings and scored his century

A good day's work. (Surrey beat Lancashire by an innings and twenty-five runs in a single day at Manchester on August 2nd 1888)

Good old cricket. *n.d.*

A good sort: "Ted" Barrett, the veteran Surrey cricketer. Written on the occasion of his benefit, August 18th, 1887. Prima Printing Works, 1887

Great cricket match—Nelson v. Colne. Nelson 134 Colne 26. Nelson fairly settle Colne!

A hearty welcome home to Briggs, the famous Lancashire cricketer, on his return from the colonies, May, 1887
*see also another version "A welcome home to Briggs"*

In heartfelt remembrance of John West. For upwards of 20 years on the ground staff at Lord's

Kent final at Faversham, between Sittingbourne and Chatham, on Easter Monday, April 24th, 1905

Kent too good for Surrey at the Oval, 15th June 1906

The Kentish heroes, captained by Lord Harris, on their grand triumph against the Australians, at Canterbury, August 4th, 1886. Kent won by ten wickets
*see also another version "Victory of Kent"*

A Kentish veteran – Russell. *n.d.*

Lord Dalmeny, Surrey's noble captain. *n.d.* port.

A loving farewell to Frank Hearne, the famous Kentish cricketer, on his departure for South Africa, Sept. 1889

Loyal cricket worthies, & loyal cricket patrons. *n.d.*

Notts. v. Surrey, at Trent Bridge, on Bank Holiday, June 10, 1889. Old Notts. triumphant. "Buckle on the armour and have another try"

Old records thoroughly smashed by Fielder, the famous Kentish bowler who took 10 wickets for 90 runs in the

Gentlemen v. Players match, at Lords, July, 1906
  printed with "Seymour's splendid century"

On 'Bob' Abel, the famous Surrey favourite. *n.d.*

On the brilliant defence of Dr. W.G. Grace and Captain Shuter, against the Aust's. at Lord's, on May 28th, 1888

One of the most brilliant catches ever made, by Maurice Read at the Oval June 30th, 1887

Our glorious old summer pastime. Respectfully dedicated to George Weaver, Esq., "Green Man," Plumstead
——another issue. Respectfully dedicated to Tom Hearne, the old veteran cricketer

Our Grand Old Man, England v. Australian match, at the Oval, August 12th, 1886. (W.G. scored 170 in 4½ hours)

Oxford University v. Surrey (Walter Read's rare feat with the bat, June 26th 1888)

R. Abel, Surrey. 'Bob' Abel: on his remarkable innings at Lord's in the Middlesex v. Surrey match, when he scored 151 runs not out

A rare days work by Mr. Leslie Wilson, Thursday, 8th August, (Canterbury week). Mr. Wilson scored 132 against the renowned Gloucestershire eleven

The secret of an old cricketer's success. [c.1920]
  *poem on R. Abel*

Seymour's splendid century secured against Essex, during Tunbridge Wells cricket week, July, 1906
  *appended to "Old records thoroughly smashed by Fielder"*

A small tribute of admiration to Mr. W.W. Read and the Surrey County Team

"Strange but true". "The wasp that stung Tom Bowley". On the Hampshire County Cricket Ground, Sep. 3rd, 1886

The struggle in the dark [Surrey v. Yorkshire]

The sturdiest match of the year. *n.d.*
  *the Surrey v. Yorkshire match of ?*

Surrey defeated at Nottingham [May 1889]

Surrey still triumphant! The famous Lancashire eleven defeated by an innings with 134 runs to spare, June 18th, 1887

Surrey v. Sussex at Brighton: Quaife secured his century in fine style, Aug. 1887

Surrey victorious! Bank Holiday, Aug. 1st, 1887
  ——*another issue with on verso:* "Well-done Quaife"

Sussex beat Glo'ster, Whit-week, 1893. Brighton, *printed by* Trill & Sons, 1893
  see: *Sussex gallantly bring down Middlesex at Lord's, July 8, 1893*

Sussex gallantly bring down Middlesex at Lord's, July 8, 1893. Brighton, *printed by* Trill & Sons, 1893
  on verso: *Sussex beat Glo'ster, Whit-week, 1893*

Sussex triumph over Surrey, Kennington Oval, July 24, 1893. [1893].

Sussex v. Gloucestershire, Hove 10th June 1889. A magnificent performance by Major. He scores his first century. Bean plays a rare innings of 59

This day's struggle, at Kennington Oval, 5th Aug. 1889. May the best team win

To a true Yorkshire lad. On Ullyett's one handed catch at Lords on 7th July 1880

To Dr. Grace, on his 41st Birthday, July 18th, 1888

To George Brann, Esq., who secured a hard-earned sixty-eight runs against Glo'ster, at Brighton, Whit-week, 1897

To John Briggs – the brilliant Lancashire cricketer

To Lewis Hall, the rare old Yorkshire favourite. *Printed at* Scarborough, Sept. 1889
  on verso: *To Robert Peel*

To Mr. Murdoch, on his complimentary benefit, at Lord's, September 13, 1886

To Mr. Stoddart, on his brilliant achievement at Lord's in the centenary match, M.C.C. v. England, June 14, 1887

To Robert Henderson, one who did his duty [playing for Surrey v. Yorks]

To Robert Peel, the popular Yorkshire cricketer. Peel secured 79 runs in magnificent style against the pride of M.C.C., Scarboro' Week, Sept. 6th, 1889

To Tom Emmett, the veteran Yorkshire cricketer. *n.d.*

A tribute of. admiration to Mr. Walter Read and the Surrey County team. *n.d.*

A tribute of respect and admiration to Dr. W.G. Grace, written at the Middlesex match at Clifton, August 25th, 1885

University match. Oxford v. Cambridge. Eton v. Harrow, at Lords, 12th July 1889

Victory of Kent against the Australians, at Canterbury, August 4th, 1886. Kent won by ten wickets. To Lord Harris, Kentish captain

Vine's superb fielding. Always the same

We meet them again: what the Surrey champions say about the famous Australian team. July 30, 1888

Welcome Australia

Welcome home again. *n.d.*
*welcoming a new season and "our Colonial rivals back"*

A welcome home to Briggs, the brilliant Lancashire cricketer, on his recent return from the colonies

Well done! Mr. Pigg. Yorkshire v. Hastings and District at Hastings July28, 1887. (Mr. Pigg scored 180 in 4½ hours)

Well-done Quaife. Quaife secured 111 runs in brilliant style against the famous Surrey team, August 8th, 1887. In the second innings he got 46
*see also another issue on verso of "Surrey victorious!"*

Well done, Surrey! The Surrey champions beat the Nottingham Cracks, by 158 runs, June, 1887

A well earned century. Young Killick surprises the famous Australian eleven at Brighton, Thursday, July 27th, 1899

What the Surrey champions say about the famous Australian team. Wait till we meet 'em again! May 17th, 1888

Young Hobbs in his initiatory attempt in first-class county cricket secures 155 runs in the Surrey v. Essex match, at the Oval,

May 1905. Printed by T. Hughes & Son, [1905]

Young Strudwick has received, and accepted an invitation to join the M.C.C. eleven, as wicket-keeper, on their forthcoming visit to Australia

6445 **[Dance, James]**
■ Cricket: an heroic poem. Illustrated with the critical observations of Scriblerus Maximus. W. Bickerton, [1744]. [i],iv.25p.
——2nd ed. W. Bickerton, 1745. [i],iv, 25p.
——3rd ed. *In* "Poems on several occasions". Edinburgh, *printed by* R. Fleming, 1754. xvi,115p.
——4th ed. Printed for the author, 1770. [iv],30p.
*dedicated to 'Members of the Cricket Club at Richmond, Surrey'.*
——5th ed. T. Davies, 1771
——6th ed. by F.S. Ashley-Cooper. Nottingham, Richards, 1922. 29p. score
see: *The Journal of the Cricket Society. Vol. 4, no. 1 (1968/9)*

6446 **Dartmouth, William Heaneage Legge,**
■ *6th earl of*
'Thoughts': [verses]. *Privately printed,* [1925]. 23p.
*I Zingari Christmas card for Christmas 1925*

6447 Cricket more or less: [verses]. *Privately*
■ *printed,* [1926]. 55p.
*a Christmas "card" of poems for Christmas 1926*

6447 **Davie, Donald**
–1 Events and wisdoms: poems 1957–1963. Routledge and Kegan Paul, 1964. xi,52p.
*includes "Two dedications: 2. Barnsley Cricket Club"*

6447 Collected poems 1950–1970. Routledge &
–2 Kegan Paul, 1972. xvii,316p.
■ *includes pp. 133–4 "Two dedications: 2. Barnsley Cricket Club"*

6448 **Dermot** and Cicely; or, the Irish gimblet,
■ a tale in three canto's [sic], in the manner of Hudibras. Printed for W. Trow, without Temple-Bar, 1742. 23p.
*describes cricket in Munster, pp. 14–16*

6448 **Disney, Thomas**
–1 Cricket lyrics. Digby, Long, [1897]. 49p.
■

6449 **Doyle,** *Sir* **Arthur Conan**
■ The poems: collected ed. Murray, 1922. xii,242p.
*includes "A reminiscence of cricket", pp. 167–70*

6450 **[Duncombe, John]**
■ Surry triumphant: or the Kentish-mens defeat; a new ballad; being a parody on Chevy-Chace. Printed for J. Johnson, 1773. 24p. vignette on t.p. score

6451 **Dutton, Harry**
Poems and acrostics of Gloucestershire cricket and cricketers. Cheltenham, [the Author], 1900. [8]p. ports.

6452 **Eden, Guy**
Bush ballads, and other verses. Sisley, 1907. viii,152p.
*contains pp. 93–5 a poem on Victor Trumper*

6453 **Elliott, Mary**
The rose, containing original poems for young people, by their friend. W. Darton, [1824]. 36p. illus.
*includes "Cricket", pp. 24–25, and a frontis. depicting boys playing cricket*
——new ed., corrected and revised [1825?]
——*another ed.* Birmingham, Cornish, 1899. 62p.

6454 **Elphinston, James**
■ Education: [a poem] in four books. P. Vaillant, W. Owen and J. Richardson, 1763. [i],136p. frontis.
*cricket pp. 52–53 and frontis. engraving with boys playing cricket in foreground of Kensington House School founded by the author in 1753*

6455 **The Epi-log** of R.M.S.P. "Asturias": [a poem]. 3p.

6455 **Ewart, Gavin**
–1 No fool like an old fool: poems. Gollancz,
■ 1976. 76p. (Gollancz Poets)
*includes pp. 7–8 "An extended apostrophe to John Hatch Clark, a comrade both ancient and modern"; pp. 51–3 "The cricket of my friends"; pp. 61–2 "Valediction: to the cricket season"*

6455 **Field, Charlotte**
–2 Freddie Trueman: [a poem]. n.d. bs. port.
■

6455 The (1963) Test: [a poem]. [1963]. bs.
–3 ports.
■

6456 **Francis, Guy**
W.G.'s birthday, July 18th, 1888. 1888. bs.
*verses written on the occasion of a party in honour of W.G.'s 40th birthday*

6457 **Gale, Norman Rowland**
■ Messrs Bat and Ball. Rugby, the Author, 1930. [vi],55p.
*limited ed. of 250 copies*

6458 Close of play. Rugby, G. Over, 1936. [vi], 46p.

6458 **Gibney, James A.**
–1 Brisbane verses; edited by J.T. Fibney. Brisbane, the Gibney Family, 1977. 36p.
*limited edition of 200 copies; includes earlier published items: pp. 8–9 "Warwick Armstrong", and p. 32 "C.V. Grimmett"*

6458 **[Gibson, George Herbert]**
–2 Southerly busters [by] "Ironbark"; profusely illustrated by Alfred Clint, additional illustrations by Montagu Scott. Sydney, *printed by* John Sands, 1878. 210p. illus.
*contains poem, pp. 203–7 "The great cricket match, Brewers v. Publicans"*

6459 **Gill, Wilfred Austin**
■ Edward Cracroft Lefroy: his life and poems. John Lane, 1897. xiv,199p.
*includes 2 cricket poems—"A cricket-bowler" and "The new cricket ground"*

6459 **Gilmour, John S.L.**
–1 Some verses. *Privately printed*, 1977. v, 18p.
*p. 2 "Three wickets"*

6460 **Goldwin, William**
■ Musae juveniles. A. Baldwin, 1706. [i], 28p.
*Latin verses including pp. 9–12, "In certamen Pilae" which describes a game of cricket conforming almost entirely with the Code of Laws laid down in 1744. The earliest description of a match. A translation by Harold Perry appeared in Etoniana No. 31, Dec. 1922, and in The Cricketer, Feb, 1923*

6461 **Graham, Harry Joscelyn Clive**
■ Adam's apples; illustrated by John Reynolds. Methuen, 1930. [vii],92p. illus.
*includes "Lord's" pp. 71–3*

6461 **Graves, Alfred Perceval**
–1 More songs and snatches. Dunstable
■ (Beds.), Aperture Litho, 1977. [iii],21p.
*includes 3 cricket poems: "Phyllis at the wicket"; "When the meadows are aglow"; "Lancashire"*

6462 **Hamilton,** *Sir* **George Rostrevor**
The inner room: poems. Heinemann, 1947. vii,99p.
*includes "Ode to a cricketer"*

6463 The carved stone: small poems and epigrams. Heinemann, 1952. x,103p.
*includes "Cricket"*

**6464 Harrod, William**
■ Sevenoke: a poem. Humbly inscribed to His Grace the Duke of Dorset. Printed for J. Fuller, in Ave-Mary Lane; and Bryan Holland, Sevenoke, 1753. 21p.
*reference to cricket at The Vine, pp. 13–15*

**6465 Harvey, F.W.**
A Gloucestershire lad at home and abroad. Sidgwick & Jackson, 1916. xv, 63p.
*includes "The catch"*

**6465 Hill, Roland**
**–1** Songs in solitude and photographs in verse. Simpkin, Marshall, 1903. vii,166p.
*pp. 142–3 "The cricketer"*

**6465 Hodge, Hugh S. Vere**
**–2** Five overs & 2 wides; with illustrations
■ by Phillida Gili. *Privately printed*, 1975. xvii,72p.
*limited ed. of 500 copies. Tonbridge cricket verses*

**6466 Holloway, William**
Scenes of youth; or Rural recollections; with other poems. Vernor and Hood, 1803. 160p. frontis.

**6467 Hood, Thomas**
The dream of Eugene Aram, the murderer; with designs by W. Harvey. C. Tilt, 1831

**6468 Poems.** 8th ed. Moxon, 1855. xvii,388p. frontis.
*includes "The dream of Eugene Aram", pp. 1–8*

**6468 Humorous poems; with 130 line drawings**
**–1** by Charles E. Brock. Macmillan, 1893. xxxi,236p. illus.
*contains "Our village. By a villager" and an illustration "Right before the wicket" not Miss Mitford's village:*
*"Of course the green's cropt very close, and does famous for bowling when the little village boys play at cricket;*
*Only some horse, or pig, or cow, or great jackass, is sure to come and stand right before the wicket"*

**6469 Hurn, William**
Heath-Hill: a descriptive poem, in four cantos. Printed for the author and sold by W. Keymer, Colchester and G. Robinson, London, 1777. [ii],48p.
*five lines referring to cricketers, pp. 30–31*

**6470 Hutchinson, Thomas**
■ A little book of cricket rhymes. Morpeth, J. & J.S. Mackay, 1923. 19p.

**6471 James, Arthur C.**
■ Songs of sixpenny and pupil room rippings, etc. [Eton], Drake, College P., 1899. ii,88p. illus.
*some cricket references*

**6471 James, Edwin Stanley**
**–1** The little land: poems of Anglesey. Anglesey, the Author, 1958. 28p. col. illus.
*p. 19 "The village cricket field"*

**6472 Jephson, Digby Loder Armeroid**
■ A few overs. Cambridge, Heffer, 1913. [viii],38p.
*poems by the Surrey lob bowler*

**6473 Jolly, Charles**
■ An address and songs dedicated to the members of the City Charltonian Cricket Club. An address delivered by the author at the Annual General Meeting of the City Charltonian Club at the termination of the season, 1856. The Club, 1857. 26p.
——2nd ed. 1857
*in verse form*

**6474 Keigwin, Richard Prescott**
Lanyard lyrics; illustrated by P.L. Butt. London, Simpkin, Marshall; Portsmouth, W.H. Barrell, [1914]. 104p. illus.

**6475 Lyrics for sport.** Oxford, Blackwell, 1917.
■ viii,59p.
*includes "The Test", p. 27; "Run out O", p. 33; "To Anthea", p. 44; "The passport", p. 50*

**6475 Kelsey, James Moore**
**–1** A miscellany. *privately printed*, [c.1965]. 17p.
*includes p. 6 "Cricket"*

**6476 Kemp, William Albert George**
■ Men like these: sonnets. Chapman & Hall, 1946. 80p.
*includes "Cricket ground", p. 73, and "To Lord's again," p. 75*

**6477 [Kendall, John Kaye]**
■ A fool's paradise, by Dum-Dum. Constable, 1910. xi,128p.
*includes "The first catch"*

**6478 Dum-Dum, his selected verses.** Harrap,
■ 1947. 94p.
*includes "The first catch" pp. 72–73; "The ballad of a homeless bat", pp. 77–79*

**6479 Kent County Cricket Club**
Dinner to the Kent XI. Hotel Cecil, Oct. 11, 1906. [The Club, 1906]. 12p. illus. ports. stats.
*contains "A Canterbury Week Ode" by Philip Trevor*

**6480 Kerr, William**
The apple tree: poems. Leeds, Swan P.;
London, Gay & Hancock, 1927. 48p.
*includes "Past and present"*

**6481 [Kidd, Abel]**
The cricketer's alphabet for 1874, by Old
Stump. Printed and published by the
kind permission of the Mary-le-Bone
Cricket Club, for the benefit of the
author, [1874]. [3]p.

**6481 Kipling Rudyard**
**–1** Rudyard Kipling's verse. Definitive
■ edition. Hodder & Stoughton, 1940
*contains pp. 301–4 "The islanders" with*
*the lines*
*". . . then ye contented your souls*
*With the flannelled fools at the wicket or*
*the muddied oafs at the goals"*

**6482 Kitchen, Fred,** *i.e.* **William Frederick**
■ **Kitchen**
Songs of Sherwood; illustrated by Kenneth Beauchamp. Dent, 1948. vi,193p.
*verse and prose; includes "The Cricket*
*match" pp. 153–56*

**6483 Knox, Edmund George Valpy**
■ Blue feathers; illustrated by G.L. Stampa.
Chatto & Windus, 1929. x,147p.
*includes "A long day at Lord's", pp. 45–8*

**6484 [Knox, Ronald Arbuthnott]**
Signa severa, by R.A.K. Eton, Spottiswoode, 1906. vii,63p.
*includes "Again"*

**6485 Lang, Andrew**
■ Rhymes à la mode. Kegan Paul, Trench &
Trubner, 1884. x,139p.
*includes "Ballade of cricket", pp. 59–60;*
*five eds. by 1895*

**6486 New collected rhymes. Longmans,**
■ Green, 1905. ix,101p.
*contains "To Helen", "Ballade of dead*
*cricketers", "Brahma"*

**6487** The poetical works; edited by Mrs. Lang.
4 vols. Longmans, 1923. ports.
*includes "Brahma", "Ballade of dead crick-*
*eters", "Ballade of the three Graces", "A*
*ballade of mourning", "Ballade of cricket"*

**6488 [Lefroy, Edward Cracroft]**
Sketches and studies, and other sonnets,
by the author of "Echoes from Theo-
critus". Blackheath, Burnside, 1884
*includes "A cricket bowler" and "The new*
*cricket ground"*

**6489 Lucas, Edward Verrall**
■ The book of shops; verses by Edward
Verrall Lucas, illustrated by Francis D.

Bedford. Grant, Richards, [c.1899]. [vi],
24p. illus. (col.)
*includes a cricket verse and an illus.*
*"Athletic outfitter"*

**6490** Playtime & company: a book for children;
■ verses by E.V. Lucas, pictures by E.H.
Shepard. Methuen, 1925. 95p.
——limited ed. 1925
*limited to 15 copies on Japanese vellum*
*includes poem "Uncle Hugh"*

**6490** ————, and **Shepard, Ernest H.**
**–1** Mr. Punch's county songs. Methuen,
1928. 92p. illus.
*a poem on each odd numbered page*
*surrounded by a Shepard illustration, even*
*pages blank, pp. 1–85; notes pp. 87–92; pp.*
*25 (Gloucestershire), 27 (Hampshire), 39*
*(Lancashire), 75 (Warwickshire), 83 (The Two*
*Roses), 85 (Yorkshire) have either pictorial or*
*verse reference to cricket*

**6490 Martin, John**
**–2** Rhymes. Leicester, Tomkin and Shard-
low, 1878. 163p.
*p. 104 "The cricketer's song"*

**6491 Martineau, Gerard Durani**
The way of the South wind. Steyning
(Sussex), Vine P., 1925. ix,25p.
*limited to 330 copies, including 30 de Luxe;*
*includes "The village pitch"*

**6492** The epic of Hornden Green: a ballad of
■ village cricket. Cambridge, Heffer, 1926.
[vii],39p.

**6493** Teams of tomorrow. London, Dobell;
■ Steyning (Sussex), Vine P. 1926. xi,57p.
*limited ed. of 300 copies on toned antique*
*laid paper and 30 on handmade paper*

**6494** "A score, a score, and ten"; poems.
■ Methuen, 1927. ix,71p.
*includes "Songs of the crease", pp. 41–51*

**6495** Rhyme the rudder, swung by a service
man: verses of our age for lovers of plain
speech. British Authors' Press, 1944. 92p.

**6496** The game that is romance: cricket verses.
■ MS. 77p.
*in John Arlott's possession; a copy of the*
*typescript is held by The Library of the Cricket*
*Society*

**6497 Masefield, John**
■ The bluebells, and other verse. Heinemann, 1961. [v],205p.
*contains "Eighty-five to win", a narrative*
*poem on England's second innings in the Test*
*against Australia at the Oval, 1882, pp.*
*73–81; final version appeared in The Cricket*
*Quarterly (Vol. 3, no. 2, Spring 1965)*

**6498  Messing, S.**
■ Poems on various subjects: written in the years 1819 and 1820. Stamford, the Author, 1821. xi,60p.
  *includes "On a cricket match", pp. 13–14, "written after seeing a cricket match played at Burley, between the young gentlemen of the grammar school in Oakham and the Oakham old players, and won by the latter"*

**6499  Meynell, *Sir* Francis**
■ Fifteen poems. Nonesuch P.; Dent, 1945. 24p.
  *——a reissue incorporating the poem printed on the wrapper and one additional poem with title: Seventeen poems. Nonesuch P.; Dent, 1945. 25p.
  includes "Mirage at Mickleham", p. 19*

**6500  Milne, Alan Alexander**
■ For the luncheon interval: cricket and other verses. Methuen, 1925. 63p.
  ——2nd ed. 1925

**6501  Moffat, Douglas**
■ Crickety cricket; with illustrations by the author. Longmans, Green, 1897. 112p. illus.
  ——*2nd ed.* 1898

**6502  Moor, George**
Beauty and richness: poems. Glasgow, W. Maclellan, 1951. 46p.
  *includes "Club match"*

**6503  Moore, Ralph Westwood**
The trophy for an unknown soldier. Oxford Univ. P., 1952. ix,76p.
  *includes "The air is hushed"*

**6504  Moult, Thomas**
Willow pattern. 1936

**6505  Moultrie, John**
The dream of life, Lays of the English church, and other poems. W. Pickering, 1843. vii,368p.
  *references to cricket; author was Rector of Rugby*

**6505  Mullis, John H.**
**–1** All this and the hills: fifty poems. Ilfracome, Stockwell, 1970. 72p.
  *includes p. 13 "Village cricket"*

**6505  Murray, George**
**–2** Poems; edited with memoir by John Reade. Montreal, E. O'Connor, 1912. xxv,236p. port.
  *includes pp. 178–9 "The Gentlemen cricketers' team"*

**6506  New** universal magazine. February 1754
■ *contains a poem "Aestas: with a short description of the game at cricket (so much in favour with his Royal Highness the late Prince of Wales) address'd to boys at school"*

**6507  Newbolt, *Sir* Henry John**
■ Admirals all, and other verses. E. Mathews, 1897. 32p. (Elkin Mathews' Shilling Garland)
  *includes "Vitaï lampada"*

**6508** The island race. Elkin Mathews, 1898.
■ 119p.
  *includes "Vitaï lampada", pp. 81–82*

**6509** Collected poems 1897–1907. Nelson,
■ 1910. 266p. (Nelson's Shilling Library)
  *includes "Vitaï lampada", pp. 131–3*

**6510** Poems: new and old. Murray, 1912.
■ xi,232p.
  ——L.P. ed. 1912
  *limited edition of 100 copies*
  ——2nd ed. 1919. xv,268p.
  *includes "Vitaï lampada"*

**6511** A perpetual memory and other poems.
■ Murray, 1939. xix,40p. port.
  *includes "Cricket" p. 24*

**6511  O[ld] E[tonian], *pseud.***
**–1** Floreat Etona, Lord's 1910, by O. E. Windsor, Oxley & Son, 1910. [4]p.

**6511  Owen, Edward Charles Everard**
**–2** Three hills, and other poems. Sidgwick and Jackson, 1916. 14p.
  *the title poem has references to cricket*

**6512  Parker, Eric**
■ Sussex woods, and other verse. Eyre & Spottiswoode, 1936. vii,54p.
  *includes "Windmill Down", pp. 29–30*

**6513  "Peakodde, *Bailzie*", *pseud.***
The pump: ane righte lamentable dirge composit be Bailzie Peakodde, poet laureate to ye Cricket Club; rendered into modern verse by Dr. Minch. 1835. [8]p.
  *comic verse relating to Glasgow C.C.*

**6514  [Perfect, William]**
A bavin of bays: containing various original essays in poetry, by a Minor Poet. *Privately printed,* 1763. xiv,176p.

**6515  Phillips, Stephen**
Lyrics and dramas. Lane, 1913. vii,179p.
  *includes "Cricket I sing"*

**6516  Ponsonby, Frederick George Brabazon,**
*6th earl of Bessborough*
Cricket rhymes. 1877. 8p.

**6516  Prentice, Roger**
**–1** Devon born & Bristol bred: selected poems. Ilfracombe, Stockwell, 1975. 20p.

*includes p. 18 "Summer game" dedicated to Gilbert Jessop*

6517 **Priestcraft**, or the way to promotion: a poem addressed to the inferior clergy of England. Being wholesome advice, how to behave at the approaching election. Printed for J. Wilford, 1734. 10p.
*reference to cricket at Eton on p. 8*

6518 **Pugh, John Geoffrey**
■ Poems. The Author, 1962. 72p.
*limited ed. of 250 copies. Includes "Lines based upon John Keats' poem 'The Mermaid Tavern' ", pp. 14–15; "Two cricket verses", p. 22; "In memory of H. Rayner Esq.", p. 23*

6518 **A rod** for Tunbridge Beaus, bundl'd up
–1 at the request of the Tunbridge ladies, to jirk fools into more wit, and clowns into more manners. A burlesque poem. To be publish'd every summer, as long as the rakes continue their rudeness, and the gentry their vertue. London, Printed, and are to be sold by the booksellers of London and Westminster, 1701. [ii],30p.
*reference on p. 6:*
*It's true he can at* Cricket *play,*
*With any living at this day:*

6519 **Ross, Alan [John]**
■ To whom it may concern: poems 1952–57. H. Hamilton, 1958. x,84p.
*includes "Test match at Lord's", p. 48, and "Cricket at Oxford", p. 57*

6520 Poems 1942–67. Eyre & Spottiswoode,
■ 1967. 208p.
*includes "Cricket at Brighton", p. 74, and "A photograph of Hammond", p. 203*

6521 **Saint-Leger, Warham**
Ballads from "Punch", and other poems. Stott, 1890. viii,324p.
*includes "Cricket on the lawn", pp. 246–47*

6522 **Sammes, John**
Charterhouse cricket, June 1942. Reigate, the Author, [1942]. [4]p.

6523 **Sassoon, Siegfried Lorraine**
Satirical poems. Heinemann, 1926. 61p.
——New ed. [with 5 additional poems]. Heinemann, 1933. 69p.
*includes: "The Blues at Lord's"*

6523 Collected poems 1908–1956. Faber, 1961.
–1 xix,317p.
■ *includes pp. 138–9 "The Blues at Lord's"*

6524 **"Senex"**, *pseud.*
■ The tale of the Kent eleven. W. H. Smith, [c.1906]. [4]p.

6524 **Shorley, Ezra Thomas**
–1 Poetic reflections in rhyme and reason. Rockhampton (Qld.), Record Printing Co., 1925. 51p.
——rptd. Brisbane, Pole Print, [1937]. 52p.
*includes poem pp. 10–13 "Inter-state cricket, Queensland v. N.S.W. at Brisbane 1922–23 season"*

6525 **[Smith, Thomas]**
■ The cricket match: a poem in two cantos; by Copthall Chambers, Esq. J. Such, 1859. 31p.

6526 Poems. J. Such, 1867. 277p.
*includes "The cricket match" pp. 199–218, and "The origin of cricket" pp. 254–57*

6527 **Snow, John**
■ Contrasts: poems, Fuller d'Arch Smith, 1971. [19]p.
*limited ed. of 100 copies*
——*another ed. 1971. pbk.*

6528 Moments and thoughts: poems. Kaye &
■ Ward, in association with Michael de-Hartington, 1973. [24]p.
*1250 copies in hardback of which 50 specially bound, numbered & signed by author; also pbk. ed.*
*includes: "Lord's Test"*

6529 **Something** about a cricket match. n.p., 1830. 15p.
*a poem about Sunbury v. Hampton*

6530 **Sterry, Joseph Ashby**
■ The lazy minstrel. T. Fisher Unwin, 1886. xv,235p.
——L.P. ed. 1886
*includes "The kitten", pp. 54–55*

6531 **Stitch, Wilhelmina**
Through sunny windows. Methuen, 1931. 64p.

6532 **Tabor, Robert Montagu**
■ Odds and ends. Longmans, 1909. xvi, 224p.
*includes "At Lord's", "Eton and Harrow", "W.G., K.C.B.", "Cricket" and "Gentlemen v. Players, July 1906"*

6533 **[Thomas, Percy Francis]**
■ A daydream. [Signed] Pott. [The Author, 1910]. [4]p.

6534 **Thompson, Francis**
The collected poetry. Hodder & Stoughton, 1913. xix,413
——de luxe paper ed. 1913
*[the cricket writings of F.T., some unpublished elsewhere, are reprinted in the essay "A rhapsodist at Lord's, being pp. 199–215 of Lucas, E. V. One day and another. 1909]*

**6535 Thomson, Arthur Alexander**
■ Out of town; illustrated by Jenetta Vise. H. Jenkins, 1935. 96p.
*includes "The jolly cricketers", pp. 69–70, and "Almost cricket", p. 88.*

**6535 The torpedo,** a poem to the electrical eel.
**–1** Addressed to Mr. John Hunter, surgeon: and dedicated to the Right Honourable Lord Cholmondeley. Printed for Fielding and Walker, No. 20, Pater-Noster-Row, 1777. iv,17p.
*reference p. 14 to the Duke of Dorset, with footnote: "Every one knows the attachment of the Duke of D-rs-t to Cricket: The Following anecdote will prove it. Two Clergymen were candidates for a Living to hs Grace's presentation, which he bestowed on the best Batsman"*

**6536 Trew-Hay, John**
■ The match of the season: a lay of the Oval. Wright, 1894. 26p. score
*a poem on the tied match, Surrey v. Lancashire, Aug. 1894*

**6537 Vallins, George Henry**
■ After a manner: a book of parodies. Epworth P., 1956. 96p.
*cricket pp. 83–96*

**6538 Varty, J.**
■ The Cantian Olympia; or, allusion to cricket: an ode. Gravesend, *printed by* T. Caddel, [c.1814]. 8p.
*the only cricket reference is in the sub-title*

**6539 W., T.**
■ The little cricketer and other verses for children. [The Author], 1892. 70p.

**6540 Wall, Arnold**
■ The pioneers, and other poems. Wellington (N.Z.), Reed, 1948. 253p.
*includes "1916", p. 31; "A ball that is bowled", p. 130*

**6540 Wallace, George B.**
**–1** Reach for the higher. Kingston (Jamaica), *n.p.*, 1963. 52p. incl. adverts.
*includes p. 45 "Woman cricket"*

**6541 Waterfall, Henry**
Rivelin rhymes. Sheffield, *printed by* J. R. Robertshaw, 1880. xiii,128p. frontis.
*includes "Cricket" p. 114*

**6542 White, Francis de Lacy**
Poems. G. Philip, 1903. 32p.
*includes "On cricket"*

**6543 Whitney, Bevan**
■ Catch and farewell: a poem; with sketches by Joan Begbie. The Author, 1968. bs. in folder. col. illus.

**6544 Wilson, George Francis**
■ Cricket poems. London, Simpkin Marshall; Reigate, Reigate P., 1905. 65p.

**6545 Wilson, T.P. Cameron**
Sportsmen in paradise. [c.1948]
*unpublished MS in M.C.C. Library at Lord's*

**6545 Wolfe, Humbert**
**–1** Kensington Gardens. Benn, 1924. 81p.
■ *includes p. 45 "Cricket"*

**6546 Wyllarde, Dolf**
■ Verses. S. Paul, 1911. 114p. frontis.
*includes "Cricket", pp. 74–5*

**6547 Yeoman, George Dundas**
■ 2000 rhyming lines. Cambridge, Galloway & Porter, 1907. [v],71p.
*includes "The all round cricketer of the century" pp. 66–7 (George Hirst)*

**6548 Young, Francis Brett**
■ The island. Heinemann, 1944. vi,451p.
*includes a description of a match at Hambledon, "On Windmill Down A.D. 1789", pp. 319–334*

# SONGS

*(For a fuller bibliography of cricket songs, see: "A song for cricket", by David Rayvern Allen. Pelham Books, 1981)*

**6548 Haddon, Celia**
**–1** Great days and jolly days: the story of girls' school songs. Hodder & Stoughton, 1977. 128p. illus. facsims. ports.
*includes Roedean's cricket song*

## Collections

**6549 Armiger, Charles**
■ The sportsman's vocal cabinet: comprising an extensive collection of scarce, curious, and original songs and ballads, relative to field sports. T. Griffiths, 1830. iii,426p.
*includes "To live a life free from gout" pp. 157–8*
*other eds. in 1831, 1832 (Tegg), 1833 (Tegg), and 1834*

**6550 The cricketers'** pocket companion,
■ containing character & history of cricket, hints on batting, bowling and fielding,

M.C.C.'s revised rules, notabilities of cricket, original and other songs. J. Vincent, [c.1883]. 32p.

6551 **D'Urfey, Thomas**
Wit and mirth; or, Pills to purge melancholy: being a collection of the best merrry ballads and songs, old and new . . . 1699
*p. 311, "A Song", verse 3:*
*"Her was the prettiest Fellow*
*As Foot-ball, or at Cricket;*
*At Hunting Chace, or nimble Race,*
*Cots-plut how Her cou'd prick it"*
*for fuller entry see no. 853*

6551 **Farmer, John,** *editor*
–1 Gaudeamus: a selection of songs for colleges and schools. Cassell, 1890
——another ed. Cassell, 1905. 210p.
——another ed. Cassell, [1919]. 210p.
*no. 10: Willow the king: Harrow cricket song; words by E.E. Bowen*

6552 **Harman, Horace,** *and* **Campbell, Madeleine**
Three traditional folk songs of Buckinghamshire. Blandford P., 1954. 6p.
*includes "The Radnage cricket song"*

## By Individual Authors

6552 **Adams, Harry**
–1 Cricket after Grace; or Out! Out! Out!; written by Harry Adams, composed by Felix Dumas. Francis, Day & Hunter, 1895

6553 **Ainslie, Ralph St. John**
■ Sedburgh School songs, written and illustrated by R. St. J. Ainslie. Leeds, Jackson, 1896. 102p. illus.
*includes "A cricket song"*

6553 **[Baxter, John]?**
–1 My friends leave your work now to sport and play. Lewes, Baxter, [c.1839]. bs. decorated in colour

6553 **Book** of the words and songs of More
–2 Stir Still; or, The Public Prevaricator of Lycaster: a musical seizure in two fits. Leicester, Tilley and Garner, 1910. 32p.
*specially written for the Leicestershire County Cricket Bazaar of 1910*

6554 **Boullemier, Lucien,** *composer*
■ The Trentham Cricket Club song—"The good old has-beens". [The Club, c.1925]. 6p.

6555 **Bowen, Edward Ernest**
■ Harrow songs, and other verses. Longmans, 1886. viii,20p.

includes "Willow the king", "Lord's 1873," "Lord's 1878", "Giants", "R.G."., and "F.P."

6556 Willow the king: Harrow cricket song;
■ words by E. E. Bowen, music by John Farmer. Penshurst, Duke & Sons, [189–]. 4p. fold. (Harrow School Song, no. 7)

6556 **Brosang, Henry**
–1 1 Zingari galop. J. Wiseheart, for the Author, n.d.
*dedicated to the members of the I Zingari Club*

6557 **Bullock, W. J.**
The cricketer: a song; dedicated to the cricket clubs of the United Kingdom. Weippert & Co., [c.1869]. ports. and illus. on cover
*at least 4 editions. See: D.R. Allen, p. 59*

6557 **Burnby, John**
–1 See the cricketers of Kent; music by Samuel Porter; words by J. Burnby. W. Dale, [c.1825]

6558 **[Colborn, Rowland, and Colborn, A. G.]**
■ Down went the wicket! Humorous cricket song. Hart & Co., n.d.
*a MS copy at M.C.C. Library, Lord's; it was sung by T. H. Clark at League concert in Edmonton, Canada, March 1911 at the Corona Hotel. In previous edition erroneously attributed to T. H. Clark (See D. R. Allen, pp. 72–3)*

6559 **Cooper, A. B.**
King cricket: a song. J. Curwen, 1895.
*in Taylor*

6560 **[Cotton, D.,** *i.e.* **Reynell Cotton)**
■ Cricket, published by order of the Hambledon Cricket Club, June 5th 1781. bs.
*a song in honour of Hambledon, written about 1767 and published in its original form in the Canterbury Journal, October, 1773. It had already appeared, with certain alterations in favour of Kent, in the Kentish Gazette of August 1772. (D. Rait Kerr)*

6561 **The Reynell Cotton** memorial match:
■ Rudgwick C.C. versus Rev. David Sheppard's XI: souvenir programme, May 23, 1959. Rudgwick, the Club, [1959]. [5]p. port. on cover.
*includes song composed by Reynell Cotton for the Hambledon Club, 1761 (i.e. 1767?)*

6562 **Cricket** song: Eton v. Harrow. Swain, 1864
*in Taylor*

6562 **David, Worton**
-1 How's that?; written by Worton David, composed by Shirley Ilton. Reeder & Walsh, 1906. port. on cover

6562 **The death** of the Ashby-de-la Zouche
-2 Cricket Club: a song. Ashby, *printed by* Beadsmoores, [1827]. bs.

6561 **Denney, Charles**
-3 The cricketer's galop, with vocal chorus. Greenock, James Inglis & Sons, *n.d.*
*dedicated to the Greenock West End C.C.*

6563 **Eggar, William Douglas**
■ A song of Lord's and poems for the mag. Eton College, Spottiswoode, Ballantyne, 1942. 51p.
*includes "A Song of Lord's, July 8, 9, 1910", and the full score of Fowler's match (Eton v Harrow)*

6563 **"An Eton Boy"**, *pseud*
-1 Eton & Harrow valse. Eton, Ingalton & Drake, [1868]. illus. on cover.
*dedicated to C. I. Thornton captain of the Eton XI, 1868*

6564 **Eton** School songs. 2 series. Novello,
■ [c.1878].
*First series, no. 4: Cricket song; [words by] A.C. Ainger, composed by J. Barnby. [4]p. fold.*
——*with title:* Eton songs, written by Arthur Campbell Ainger, set to music by Joseph Barnby; illustrated by W. Marshall. First series. Novello, [c.1891]. [4]p. fold. illus.
*includes "Cricket is king"*

6565 **Ettling, Emile**
Cricket polka, pour piano. Robert Cocks, [18—]

6565 **Evans, George Essex**
-1 "Soldiers of the willow"; words by Geo. Essex Evans, music by Alberto Zelman. Melbourne, Allan & Co. for the Author, [c.1902]. [4]p. incl. covers, ports.
*with portraits of J. Darling and A. MacLaren on cover*

6565 **Frampton, Fred**
-2 The cricket-man: humorous song; written, composed & sung by Fred Frampton. Keith Prowse, 1904. illus. on cover

6566 **Gale, Norman Rowland**
■ Cricket songs and other trifling verses penned by one of the authors of "Thistledown". Rugby, Over, 1890. 55p.
*limited ed. of 80 copies*

6567 Advice gratis: a cricket song; words by
■ Norman Gale, music by Ellis J. Wynne. Wright, [1890?]. [i],5p.
*cover-title "Cricket songs" [sic]*

6568 Cricket songs. Methuen, 1894. xii,67p.
■ ——de luxe ed. 1894
*limited to 125 copies, on hand-made paper, and 15 copies on Japanese vellum*
——3rd ed. Constable, 1896. viii,76p.
*seven of these songs rptd. from no. 6566*

6569 More cricket songs. Alston Rivers, 1905.
■ 63p

6570 Two cricket songs. Old Bilton, Rugby.
■ [the Author, 1926]. [7]p.

6570 **Gifford, Harry,** *and* **Lawrence, Alf J.**
-1 The cricket and the bat: a natural history match in three innings and a musical score. Francis, Day & Hunter, 1914

6571 **Grange, A. Demain**
■ The cricketer's song; words by A. Demain Grange, music by Julian Wright. P. Derek, 1934. 3p.
*dedicated to the Blue Mantles C.C.*

6572 **[Graves, Alfred Perceval]**
■ Zummerzet versus Zurrey: cricket, Taunton, August 13th, 14th and 15th, 1891, [a song] by the author of "Father O'Flynn". Taunton, Woodley, [1891]. [7]p. team ports.
*rptd. from the Somerset County Gazette of Saturday, Aug. 22nd, 1891*

6573 **Hall, Frank**
Life is like a game of cricket; written & composed by Frank Hall. Duff & Stewart, [c.1870]

6573 **Harrow School**
-1 Churchill centenary songs. 30th October,
■ 1974, Royal Albert Hall. The School, [1974]. 24p. incl. covers
*includes p. 11 by E. E. Bowen, "Giants" and "A gentleman's a-bowling," dedicated to F. S. Jackson, Lord's 1888*

6574 Harrow School songs; edited by John
□ Farmer. London, Novello; Harrow, J. C. Wilbee, *n.d.* 147p.
*includes p. 16 "Willow the King", and p. 62 "Giants"*
——New Series; edited by Eaton Faning. London, Novello; Harrow, J. C. Wilbee, *n.d.*
——No. 2. The niner; a cricket song. Words by E.E.B. [Edward Ernest Bowen]; music by E.F. [Eaton Faning]. 3p.
*1st publd. 1887*

——No. 6. A gentleman's a-bowling. Words by E.E.B.; music by E.F. 3p.
*1st publd, 1888 to mark the Eton v. Harrow match of that year*
——No. 11. If time is up. Words by E.E.B.; music by E.F. 3p.
*1st publd. 1895*

6575 **Hartnell, Walter G.**
■ Cricket: a song; words by Walter G. Hartnell, music by Vincent Wilson. The Song Success Syndicate, 1923. [4]p. fold

6576 **Hicks, G. A.**
Cricket: a song. Williams, 1900

6577 **Hole, Samuel Reynolds**
■ A cricket song; edited by F. S. Ashley-Cooper. Nottingham, *privately printed by Richards*, [1922]. [4]p.

6578 **Hows** that?—Well caught!: a comic song. London, *n.d.*
*in Taylor*

6579 **Hughes, Donald Wynn,** *and* **Heywood,**
■ **Percy M.**
The batsman's bride: an operetta in one act; libretto by Donald Hughes; music by Percy M. Heywood. Oxford Univ. P., 1957. v,17p.

6580 **Jephson, Digby Loder Armeroid**
■ A song of cricket; words by D. L. A. Jephson (Ex-Captain of Surrey C.C.C.), music by A. H. Behrend. Weekes, 1919. 7p.

6580 **Jones, J. G.**
–1 The Domum galop, as performed at the Domum Ball, Winchester; composed and dedicated to superannuates of Winchester College . . . Winchester, J. G. Jones, [1877?]. illus. on cover

6580 **[Kidd, Abel]**
–2 A cricket song and elegy: John Smith . . .
■ by "Old Stump". Highgate, the Author, [1873]. [4]p. fold

6580 **Leo, Frank**
–3 "My cricket girl": (a vocal novelty); written & composed by Frank Leo. Francis, Day & Hunter, 1903. illus. on cover

6581 **Lucas, Edward Verrall**
■ Songs of the bat. [The Author], 1892. 7p.

6581 **Lumsdaine, Jack**
–1 Our eleven; words and music by Jack Lumsdaine. Sydney, D. Davis & Co., 1930. [4]p. ports.
*portraits of the 1930 Australian XI on front cover*

6582 **M., E. G.**
■ Cricketer's song; the words by E.G.M.; the music by G. A. MacFarren. Novello, *n.d.* 5–8p. (Novello's Part-Song Book)

6583 **M., P. T.**
Cricket song. J. Williams, 1888

6584 **Martineau, Gerard Durani**
■ Cricket spring song; words by G. D. Martineau, music by Edward St. Claire. Dix Ltd., [1927?] 3p.

6584 **Matheson, Greville Ewing**
–1 Songs of school life. Weekes & Co., 1914
*contains 'Up at Lord's'*

6584 **Meyder, Karl**
–2 Zingari galop. Chappell & Co., *n.d.* col. illus. on cover
*dedicated to the Zingari C.C.*

6585 **Mills, J. D.**
The tie match: a new comic song. Wandsworth, J. D. Mills, 1852
*in Taylor*

6585 The vexed bowler, a new comic song.
–1 Wandsworth, J. D. Mills, 1853

6585 **Nelson, Daniel H. C.**
–2 A cricketer's song, written by Daniel H. C. Nelson, and sung at one of the meetings of the East Surry [sic] Cricket Club, in the season of 1831. J. Chappell, [c.1831]. 16p.

6586 **"Noss Mayo",** *pseud.*
The umpire: a cricket song. Newton Ferrers (Devon), E. Donajowski, 1890
*dedicated to A. G. Steel*

6587 **Northamptonshire County Cricket Club**
Annual dinner: song by the Captain (J. P. Kingston, Esq.). Northampton, the Club. bs.
*tune: Bonny Dundee; first sung at the annual dinner in 1885*

6587 **Northamptonshire** past and present.
–1 Northampton, Northamptonshire Record
■ Society.
Vol. V, no. 4, 1976. illus. ports. maps
*contains pp. 363–5 "A Northamptonshire cricket song", an article on the song composed by J. P. Kingston with biographical notices of the players by J. D. Coldham*

6587 **O'Hagan, Jack**
–2 Our Don Bradman; words and music by Jack O'Hagan. Melbourne, Allan & Co., 1930. [4]p.

6588 **Perkins, Theron D.,** *composer*
■ "Zingari" march: two step. Boston

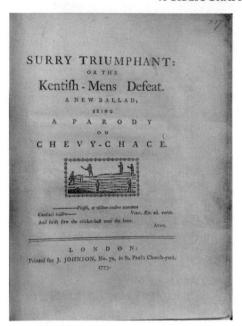

Poetry: the title-page of no. 6450
*photo: Patrick Eagar*

Cricket songs: the cover of the ~~piano score~~
"Cricket polka" by Emile Ettling (no. 6565)
*photo: M.C.C.*

Humour: from "Comic cricket" by "Alec
Nelson" illustrated by Chris Davis (no. 6831)

Humour: from "A royal road to cricket" by
W. A. Bettesworth (no. 6838)

It took two men and a boy to retrieve it.

Humour: from "Googlies" by H. V. Hordern,
illustrated by Tom Glover (no. 7721)
*photo: M.C.C.*

Humour: from Herbert Farjeon's "Cricket bag"
illustrated by Dennis Mallet (no. 6853)

Illustrations: the frontispiece to no. 6990, engraved by Edward Finden after a drawing by Captain
Lyon, R.N.

(Mass.), Jean White, 1897. 6p. incl. covers
*piano score*

**6588** **Porter, A. D.**
**–1** Valse I Zingari. Metzler & Co., *n.d.* col. illus. on cover

**6588** **Pratt, Charles E.**
**–2** The Australian eleven galop. Melbourne, W. H. Glen, [1878?]. team port. on cover
*dedicated to 1878 Australian eleven*

**6589** **Purry, A. A.**
■ A cricket song: vocal march with chorus; words by A. A. Purry; music by G. Lishman. London, Novello; Brighton, Chester, 1908. 3p. (The "Chester" Series of Unison Songs, no. 4)

**6590** **Robinson, Percy S.**
The cricketers' song; words and music by P. S. Robinson. Sylvester Music Co., 1934. [4]p.
*dedicated to Jack Hobbs*

**6591** **St. Clair, J.**
■ The hunt of the leather: a song of cricket; words by J. St. Clair, music by E. Harold Melling. Bach & Co., 1912. [4]p.
*dedicated to A. C. Oddie, Esq., and the Sussex C.C.C.*

**6592** **Scott-Gatty, Alfred**
Domestic ditties. Pearson, 1901

**6593** **Smith, J. Harcourt**
Cricket: a song dedicated to A. N. Hornby. Wolverhampton, [c.1882]

**6594** Cricket: the song of the "Centuries";
■ written and composed by J. Harcourt Smith. Howard & Co., [1895]. 5p. port.
*in honour of W. G. Grace's 100 hundreds*

**6595** **"A Spectator Esq.", *pseud.***
■ A digest of cricketing facts and feats appertaining to the year 1862, to which are added two new songs from the note-book of "Bat". F. Platts, 1863. iv,62p. frontis. scores, stats.
*the two songs are: "The cricketer's tent" and "The cricket bat an emblem of peace"*

**6596** **Stacey, Cyril**
■ Songs of sports and pastimes; with . . . illustrations by Finch Mason. Vinton, [1937]. 70p. illus. port.
*includes " 'Ow's that?", pp. 17–20; "Getting up a side", pp. 21–4; "To a chucker", pp. 25–7*

**6596** **Stephenson, E.**
**–1** The cricketers polka. Joseph Williams, *n.d.* 6p.

**6596** **Sutch, Henry A.**
**–2** The cricket pat polka. Charles Sheard & Co., *n.d.* port.
*dedicated to Dr. W. G. Grace (The Champion)*

**6596** **Sydney, Harry**
**–3** The cricketing songs, as sung by the author, Mr. Harry Sydney, at the Surrey Club dinner (Bridge-House Hotel), Thursday, 15th May, 1862. . . . The Author, [1862?]

**6596** **Thomson, Frank**
**–4** The cricketer's national song: a choral march, with words and music by Frank Thomson. J. Curwen, *n.d.*

**6597** **Thring, Edward**
■ Uppingham School songs and Borth lyrics. T. Fisher Unwin, 1887. [v],79p.
*includes "Uppingham cricket song, 1856", and "The Old Boys' match", pp. 21–27*

**6598** The Uppingham cricket & fives songs; the words by the Rev. E. Thring. The music composed & dedicated to his pupils by C. Reimers. J. J. Ewer, *n.d.* 9p.

**6599** **Timperley, H. W.**
■ Cricket songs; wood engravings by Jean Mills. Alan Dodson, 1941. [8]p. illus.
*they are: The beginning of the season; The end of the season; Sing a song of cricketers*

**6600** **Trevor, Harry, and Trevor, Leo.**
■ "Cricket"; words by Harry & Leo. Trevor; music by Alfred Scott-Gatty. Boosey, 1898. 9p. (Country House Ditties, no. 1)
*dedicated to I. Zingari*

**6601** **[Wanostrocht, Nicholas)**
■ A cricket song, by N. Felix; edited with an introduction by F. S. Ashley-Cooper. Nottingham, Richards, 1923. [ii],ii,12p.
*original MS in the M.C.C. Library at Lord's*

**6602** **"Warlock, Peter", *pseud., composer [i.e.* Philip Heseltine]**
The cricketers of Hambledon: song with chorus for voice and piano; words by Bruce Blunt. Augener, [1929?]. 6p.
*composed for the Hampshire Eskimos' New Year's Day cricket match at Hambledon, 1929*

**6603** **Warner, Robert Townsend**
■ Eton and Winchester: a song of the Eton & Winchester match; words by R. T. Warner, music by F. S. Kelly. Eton, College P., 1903. [i],7p.

6604 **Welman, C.**
■ The song of the Emeriti; song by Capt. C. Welman; music composed by L. Wheeler. Francis Bros. and Day, [1878]. 5p.

6605 **West, C. T.**
■ 'Ranji': new song. Words and music by C. T. West. Brighton and Hove, Lyon and Hall, [c.1895]. 5p. port. on cover

6605 Ranjitsinhji waltz. Weekes & Co., 1897.
–1 port. on cover

6605 **Wilmott, Charles**
–2 'Out', written by Charles Wilmott &

composed by Fred Eplett (sung with the greatest possible success by Fred Harvey). B. Mocatta & Co., *n.d.* 8p.

6606 **Wood, P. J.**
The Northern Congregational School cricket song; music by W. F. Kelvey. Wakefield, The School, 1902. [4]p. fold

6606 **Ye famous battel** of Trent Bridge, a most
–1 ancient ballad to ye tune of 'Ye bailiff's daughter of Islington'. [c.1885]. bs.
*celebrated a Notts C.C.C. victory over The Australians*

# ESSAYS

## Collections

6607 **Aldin, Cecil Charles Windsor,** *compiler*
■ *and illustrator*
The Cecil Aldin book. Eyre & Spottiswoode, 1932. 193p. port. illus. (some col.)
*an anthology of essays by C. C. W. Aldin & others, including "How to get into the eleven" by Jack Hobbs, pp. 47–53*

6608 **Arlott, [Leslie Thomas] John,** *compiler*
British sporting stories. News of the World, 1953. xi,223p.
*contains pp. 154–61 "The greatest Test match" by Neville Cardus from his A cricketer's book*

6609 ————, *editor*
■ Cricket. Burke, 1953. xiii,278p. illus. (some col.), ports. bibliog. ("Pleasures of Life")
*contains inter alia ch. xi, pp. 224–267 "The works of J. C. Clay" rptd. from Glamorgan C.C.C. Yearbooks 1935–47*

6609 **Aveling, Edward Bibbins,** *and others*
–1 The bookworm, and other sketches. Hamilton, Adams, 1879. 110p.
*includes "Old cricket match" pp. 43–59*

6609 **Boas, Guys** *editor*
–2 Modern English prose, third series. Macmillan, 1951. xiii,210p. (Scholar's Library Series)
*contains pp. 135–9 "Things that matter" by Neville Cardus, from Days in the sun*

6610 **Bullocke, John Greville,** *editor*
Narrative essays of today. Harrap, 1961. 192p. (Modern English Series)
*contains pp. 82–6. "On a fresh cricket season" by Neville Cardus from Days in the sun*

6611 **Carr, Richard Comyns,** *editor*
■ Red rags: essays of hate from Oxford. Chapman & Hall, 1933. 291p.
*includes "Frightfulness on the cricket field" by Ian Peebles, pp. 69–74, and "Cricket and the Cromwell cut" by Shamus Frazer, pp. 89–106*

6612 **Charlton, James M.,** *compiler*
Modern essays. Blackie, 1958. 182p.
*includes "The spirit of cricket" by Neville Cardus*

6613 **Daily Telegraph**
■ A Daily Telegraph miscellany; compiled by J. B. Firth. Hutchinson, 1940. 460p.
*cricket pp. 389–401*
——— . . . third miscellany; compiled by J. B. Firth. Hutchinson, 1942. xvi,422p.
*cricket pp. 313–331*
——— . . . fourth miscellany; compiled by G. C. Dixon. Hutchinson, [1947]. vii, 343p.
*cricket pp. 131–167*

6614 **English Association**
■ English essays of today. Oxford, O.U.P., 1936. viii,230p.
*contains pp. 30–34 "A sentimental journey" by Neville Cardus from Good days*

6615 **Essays** of the year; compiled by F. J.
■ Harvey Darton. Argonaut P.
*1931–1932. 1932. xix,255p.*
*includes E. V. Lucas "Three Kentish memorials", pp. 137–43*
*1933–1934. 1934. xxiv,420p.*
*includes N. Cardus "Blythe of Kent", pp. 95–101*

6616 **Flower, Margaret,** *editor*
A book of modern prose. Cassell, 1951. xii,290p.

——subsequent impressions *with title:* A second book of modern prose

*contains pp. 168–74 "Prelude" by Neville Cardus from* Cricket

6617 **Gough, Lionel,** *editor*
The Harrap book of modern essays. Harrap, 1952. 160p. illus. (Harrap's Modern English Series)

*includes "Oddly enough" by Paul Jennings and an extract from* Good days *by Neville Cardus*

6618 **The Guardian**
■ The bedside 'Guardian': a selection from The Guardian. Collins. illus.
10: a selection . . . 1960–61. 1961. 255p.
*pp. 190–3, "Trueman destroys Australia", by Denys Rowbotham [on third Test at Headingley, 1961]*
11: a selection . . . 1961–62. 1962. 255p.
*pp. 231–4, "Benaud and his men", by Denys Rowbotham [on the Australian 1961 Test team]*
12: a selection . . . 1962–63. 1963. 255p.
*pp. 20–3, "Australia retain Ashes", by Denys Rowbotham [on 1962–63 Tests]: and pp. 23–8, "J. B. Hobbs not out 80" by Neville Cardus*
13: a selection . . . 1963–64. 1964. 255p.
*pp. 21–4, "England's great fight", by Denys Rowbotham [on 2nd Test at Lord's v. West Indies, 1963]*
14: a selection . . . 1964–1965. 1965. 256p.
*pp. 11–4, "Slip catchers in the rye", by Jim Markwick [on cricket in New York]; pp. 16–8, "Worcestershire champions at last", by Henry Blofeld, and pp. 198–9 " 'Tich' Freeman", by Neville Cardus*
15: a selection . . . 1965–1966. 1966. 255p.
*pp. 232–4, "Test cricket in Australia", by Denys Rowbotham [on 3rd Test, 1965–66 series], and pp. 235–7, "Sussex beat West Indians", by Christopher Ford*
16: a selection . . . 1966–67; edited by W. L. Webb. 1967. 255p.
*pp. 208–12, "Miracle worker at the wicket", by Neville Cardus [on Frank Woolley]; and pp. 212–4, "Worrell – too soon for an era to end" by John Samuel*
17: a selection . . . 1967–68; edited by W. L. Webb. 1968. 254p.
*pp. 93–6, "An obsession with the new ball", by Neville Cardus; and pp. 96–8, "Batting for posterity", by Geoffrey Moorhouse*
18: a selection . . . 1968–69; edited by W. L. Webb. 1969. 240p.
*pp. 185–6, "The d'Oliveira decision"; and pp. 187–8, "Cricket still needs Colin Milburn", by John Arlott*
19: a selection . . . 1969–70; edited by W. L. Webb. 1970. 256p.

*pp. 207–10, "The fury beyond cricket", by Patrick Keatley [on the proposed 1970 M.C.C. tour to S. Africa]: and pp. 221–4, "The life and times of a Poona number nine", by Omar Kureishi*
21: a selection . . . 1971–72; edited by W. L. Webb. 1972. 255p.
*pp. 164–7, "Who said the M.C.C. moved slowly?", by Omar Kureishi; and pp. 173–5, "A happy band of one-day wonders", by Neville Cardus on the Lancashire team which won the Gillette Cup*
22: a selection . . . 1972–73; edited by W. L. Webb. 1973. 255p.
*pp. 174–7: "A test from the tee with Bradman", by Pat Ward-Thomas on Bradman as a golfer*
23: a selection . . . 1973–74; edited by W. L. Webb. 1974. 255p.
*pp. 126–9 "Bombay ducks", by Derek Malcolm [on The Guardian C.C.'s. tour of India]; pp. 230–45, "Queering the pitch", by Stanley Reynolds [a Northern view of Southern cricket]*
24: a selection . . . 1974–75; edited by W. L. Webb. 1975. 263p.
*pp. 36–7, "Typhoon hits England – latest", a Leader article on the 1st Test at Brisbane; pp. 212–5, "Latest rice-pudding man", by Neville Cardus [on bouncers]; pp. 215–7, "Thanksgiving for Neville Cardus", by J. B. Priestley; 217–9, "Close thing at Taunton", by Frank Keating [on Somerset v. Northamptonshire]*

■ The bedside "Guardian" 27: a selection from The "Guardian" 1977–78; edited by W. L. Webb. Collins, 1978. 252p. illus.
*includes pp. 245–6 "Primrose path to paradise" by Frank Keating on the start of the cricket season*
*for earlier issues see under: Manchester Guardian*

6619 **Hughes, Arthur George,** *and* **Parker, Ernest Walter,** *compilers*
Adventurers all; illustrated by H. M. Brock. Longmans, 1947. 288p. illus.
*"Village cricket" by Richard Binns, pp. 254–261*

6620 **Lamb, Geoffrey Frederick,** *editor*
Essays of action: a book of narrative essays and sketches. Macmillan, 1953. x,192p.
*contains pp. 66–72 "A boy's game" by Neville Cardus from* Cricket

6620 **Lord, David,** *editor*
-1 The glory of sport: indelible stories from ten of the world's best sportswriters. Adelaide, H. K. Frost Holdings in association with Lions Club International and Australian Guarantee Corporation, 1979. 224p. illus. ports.

includes pp. 26–31 Ian Wooldridge on Charlie Griffith, Ted Dexter, Ken Barrington; pp. 101–10 Peter McFarline "Tied Test"; pp. 189–97 Don Cameron "New Zealand Test cricket"

**6621  Lucas, Edward Verrall,** editor
■  Good company: a rally of men. Methuen, 1909. xii,362p.
*chap. iii "Two cricketers"—Alfred Mynn and Benjamin Aislabie*

**6622  Manchester Guardian**
■  The bedside "Guardian"; a selection by Ivor Brown from the Manchester Guardian 1951–1952. Collins, 1952. 256p.
*includes "Cricket goes west" by Alistair Cooke, pp. 147–151*
2: a selection by Ivor Brown . . . 1952–1953. 1953. 256p. illus.
*includes pp. 208–31 Neville Cardus's reports of the 1st, 2nd and 4th Tests, England v. Australia, 1953*
3: a selection by Ivor Brown . . . 1953–54. 1954. 255p. illus.
*includes pp. 195–9 "Lancashire heroes" by Neville Cardus, a review of Lancashire County cricket: the official history 1864–1953, by A. W. Ledbrooke; pp. 191–4 "Cricket on the hearth" by John R. Townsend*
4: a selection by Ivor Brown . . . 1954–1955. 1955. 256p.
*includes pp. 106–10 "Return of the native" by Alistair Cooke (impressions of England v. Pakistan Test at Old Trafford, 1954; pp. 111–4 "Cricket without art", and pp. 114–8 "Why Australia lost", by Neville Cardus (on M.C.C. tour to Australia 1954–55); pp. 119–22 "Sway of battle', by Denys Rowbotham (on 2nd Test, England v. S. Africa, 1955)*
5: a selection . . . 1955–1956. 1956. 256p. illus. map
*includes p. 110 "Innings declared" – a leading article on the retirement of Len Hutton from first-class cricket*
7: a selection . . . 1957–1958. 1958. 256p. illus.
*includes pp. 158–61 "Golden batting by an Old Master" by Denys Rowbotham on Len Hutton playing for M.C.C. at Old Trafford on the occasion of Lancashire's centenary*
8: a selection . . . 1958–1959. 1959. 256p. illus.
*includes pp. 118–9 a letter headed "The cricket face", and pp. 119–21 "McDonald soon brings victory to Australia" by Denys Rowbotham on the final Test v. England in 1958–59 series*
*for later issues see under: The Guardian*

**6623  Marriott, James William,** editor
■  Modern essays and sketches. Nelson, [1935]. xvi,198p. (Argosy Books)
——another ed. Nelson, 1935. xv,208p.

——another ed. Nelson, 1938. 198p. (Nelson Classics)
*contains "The greatest Test match" by Neville Cardus, pp. 121–29, from* Days in the sun

**6624  Millard, John,** editor
Late extra: a miscellany by "Evening News" writers, artists, and photographers. Associated Newspapers, 1952. 192p. illus.
*includes "The Chitty goes to cricket" by John Marshall, and "Cricket for thrills" by E. M. Wellings*

**6625  Moon, Arthur Reginald,** and **McKay,**
■  **George Harry,** editors
Leaders and pages. Longmans, 1938, [i.e. 1939]. xvi,272p. illus. (Heritage of Literature Series).
*an anthology of articles from newspapers and periodicals; includes "150 years of M.C.C. cricket" by Howard Marshall rptd. from the* Daily Telegraph

**6625  The Observer**
**–1**  'The Observer' re-visited 1963–64; compiled by Cyril Dunn. Hodder & Stoughton, 1964. 256p. illus.
*contains pp. 168–70 "Jack Hobbs, master batsman", by John Arlott*

**6626  Pink, Maurice Alderton,** editor
Modern portrait essays. Macmillan, 1954. xii,252p. (The Scholar's Library)
*contains pp. 88–96 "William Gilbert Grace" by Neville Cardus from* The great Victorians, *edited by H. J. & H. Massingham*

**6627  Pocock, Guy Noel,** editor
■  Junior modern essays. Dent, 1927. 253p. (King's Treasuries of Literature)
*includes "Cricket" by Charles Whibley, pp. 170–85 being his introduction to John Nyren's* Young cricketer's tutor, *and St. John Adcock on "The truth about sport"*

**6628  Ratcliff, Arthur James John,** editor
Prose of our time. Nelson, 1931. 279p. ("Teaching of English" Series)
*includes "Cricket and cricketers" by Neville Cardus, pp. 68–78, from* Cricket

**6629  Rhys, Ernest,** and **Vaughan, Lloyd,** editors
A century of English essays: an anthology ranging from Caxton to R. L. Stevenson & the writers of our own time. Dent, 1913. xiii,474p. (Everyman's Library)
*later eds. Includes p. 230–4 "Whitsun-Eve" by Mary Russell Mitford from "Our Village"*

**6629  Rodda, John,** and **Makins, Clifford,**
**–1**  editors
■  The sporting year: a selection of the best

sports writing of 1976–77. Collins, 1977. 256p. illus. ports. stats.

*a collection of 72 articles from British newspapers (excluding The Daily Mail) Sept. 1976 to Sept. 1977; 18 on cricket*

——2: a selection of the best sports writing of 1977–78. Collins, 1978. x,213p. illus.

*includes 10 cricket articles from English newspapers Sept. 1977–Aug. 1978*

**6629 The Saturday** book. Hutchinson. illus. &
**–2** ports. (some col.)
■     1941–42. edited by Leonard Russell. 1941. 446p.

*contains article on Lord Frederick Beauclerk by Harold Hobson*

3rd year; edited by Leonard Russell. 1943. 280p.

*includes pp. 267–80 "The Squire of England" by Bernard Darwin (on George Osbaldeston)*

5th year; edited by Leonard Russell. 1945. 288p.

*includes pp. 95–6 "Unforgettable days" by Bernard Darwin, and pp. 97–102 "From Herbert Farjeon's cricket bag" – an essay being prepared before his death in 1945*

8th year; edited by Leonard Russell. 1948. 288p.

*includes pp. 65–73 "The mathematician on cricket" by C. P. Snow (on G. H. Hardy)*

9th year; edited by Leonard Russell. 1949. 288p.

*includes pp. 275–80 "Cricket gadgets" by John Arlott*

11th year; edited by Leonard Russell. 1951. 280p.

*includes "The bowling called bodyline" by John Arlott*

12th year; edited by John Hadfield. 1952. 296p.

*includes pp. 247–57 "The Twenties – golden age of sport" by Howard Marshall*

17th year; edited by John Hadfield. 1957. 306p.

*includes "Poems of sport" by Alan Ross with "Cricket at Oxford" p. 14*

**6629 Smith, Frederick Edwin,** *earl of Birken-*
**–3** *head, compiler*
The hundred best English essays. Cassell, 1929. xxi,921p.

*contains "Cricket fields and cricketers" by N. Cardus*

**6630 The Spectator**
Spectator harvest. W. Hamilton, 1952. xii,234p.

*articles from The Spectator including: "The Englishman's cricket", by John Arlott; "C. B. Fry", by Neville Cardus; and "Season of mists", by J. P. W. Maclaren*

**6631 The Times**
Third leaders from the Times; compiled by George Gordon. E. Arnold, 1928. 288p.

*includes "A day's cricket" pp. 49–51*

**6632** Fifty years. Memories and contrasts. A composite picture of the period, 1882–1932 by twenty-seven contributors to The Times. Butterworth, 1932. 224p. illus.

*cricket pp. 202–10 in ch. "Games with a ball" by Bernard Darwin*

**6633** Through the eyes of "The Times"; compiled by H. S. Gordon and R. Bennett. Univ. of London P., 1937. 182p. illus.
*cricket pp. 123–39*

**6634** Fourth leaders from The Times, 1950.
□   Times Publishing Co., [1950]. [x],177p.
*cricket in "Good losers", "The sporting Rumanians", "Christian names" and "Thrown out"*

——, 1952. [1952]. [viii],175p.
*"C. B. Fry", "The village green" and "A caravan of bats"*

——, 1953. [1953]. [viii],168p.
*"With the gloves off", "Art for sports sake", "Sporting writers" and "Giants in those days"*

——, 1954. [1954]. 173p.
*"A dog looks at cricket"*

——, 1955. [1955]. 174p.
*"Where Angels fear to tread"*

——, 1956. [1956]. 175p.
*"Seamy side up", "Appealing" and "Any old piers"*

**6635 Williams,** *Sir* **Wiliam Emrys,** *editor*
A book of English essays. Harmondsworth, Penguin Books, 1942. 256p.
*contains pp. 246–50 "W. G." by Neville Cardus from A cricketer's book*

**6635 The Yorkshire Post**
**–1** The bed post: a miscellany of The Yorkshire Post; edited by Kenneth Young. MacDonald, 1962. 244p. illus.
*contains articles by J. M. Kilburn, pp. 75–7 "Golden dust and fairy dust: Yorkshire beat Worcester"; pp. 157–9 "Trueman's hour" (Yorkshire v. Lancs, Aug. 1961) and by Kenneth Gregory, pp. 219–21 "Marshall, burnt ball . . . O" (a soliloquy on a "Report" in the "Sheffield Iris" Aug. 2, 1842 of the singular mode of dismissal of J. Marshall)*

## By Individual Authors

**6636 Agate, James Evershed**
■ On an English screen. J. Lane, 1924. x,222p.
*"Cricket in the 'forties; . . . 'seventies; . . . 'eighties," pp. 60–81*

6637 The common touch. Chapman & Hall, 1926. x,247p.

6638 Kingdoms for horses; with decorations by
■ Rex Whistler. Gollancz, 1936. 150p. illus.
*cricket pp. 74–102*

6638 Here's richness, an anthology of and by
–1 James Agate. Harrap, 1942. 271p.
*cricket pp. 92–5*

6639 Noblesse oblige: another letter to another
■ son. Home & Van Thal, 1944. 32p.
*a reply to "A Letter to my son", by Sir Osbert Sitwell*

6640 **Allwood, Montagu Charles**
■ The nobodies who weave the fabric of civilisation; illustrated by Roland Wilkes. Wivelsfield Green (Sussex), the Author, 1950. 189p. illus.
*ch. 4 "Cricket, pp. 58–75 (on the philosophy of the game)*

6641 **Ames, Leslie**
■ Collected articles. [The Author, 1960]. 46p. incl. adverts.
*articles written during 1960 season*

6642 **Arlott, [Leslie Thomas] John**
■ Concerning cricket: studies of the play and players. Longmans, Green, 1949. vii,156p. bibliog.
*includes "The Old Man": a radio feature on the centenary of the birth of Dr. W. G. Grace*

6643 The echoing green: cricket studies. Long-
■ mans, Green, 1952. x,165p. illus.
——*another ed.* Sportsman's Book Club, 1957

6644 The works of J. C. Clay. Burke, 1953. 24p.
*offprint from the author's "Cricket" (1953).
See no. 6609*

6645 [Entry cancelled]

6646 **[Bagot, Arthur Greville]**
■ Sporting sketches at home and abroad, by Bagatelle. Swan, Sonnenschein & Allen, 1879, vii,166p.
——*2nd ed. 1881*
*includes "Cricket under difficulties" and "Frontier match", pp. 92–98*

6647 **Bagot, Arthur Greville**
■ Sport and travel in India and Central America. Chapman & Hall, 1897. viii,371p. illus.
*includes "An up-country cricket match"*

6648 **[Barron, Arthur Oswald]**
■ Day in and day out, by "The Londoner". Cassell, 1924. xv,255p.
*includes "The Bumpers", pp. 68–71, and "W. G." pp. 104–07*

6649 **Batchelor, Denzil Stanley**
■ The game goes on. Eyre & Spottiswoode, 1947. v,182p. scores
*includes account of England v. Australia Tests, 1936–7, and some fiction*

6650 Days without sunset. Eyre & Spottis-
■ woode, 1949. 283p.
*includes account of Australian tour of England 1948*

6651 Game of a lifetime. Laurie, 1953. 216p.
■ illus. scores
*the best matches of individual cricketers*

6652 **Bax, Clifford**
■ Inland far: a book of thoughts and impressions. Heinemann, 1925. 332p. ports.
*cricket in sections II and XII*

6652 Ideas and people. Lovat Dickinson, 1936.
–1 296p. illus. ports.
*2 chs. on cricket – "Little cricket" and "Great cricket"*

6653 **Beanland, Vincent Arthur Stanley**
■ Great games and great players: some thoughts and recollections of a sports journalist. W. H. Allen, [1946]. 151p. port.

6654 **Bennison, Ben**
■ Giants on parade: some sporting reminiscences. Rich & Cowan, 1936. v,290p. port.
*cricket ch. iii, pp. 128–146*

6655 **Binns, Richard**
■ Cricket in firelight: a cricketer's book for all the year round. Selwyn & Blount, [1935]. 255p. scores
——*another ed.* Sportsman's Book Club, 1955. v,182p. scores
*contains account of 1894–95 Australia v. M.C.C. Tests*

6656 **Blunden, Edmund Charles**
The mind's eye: essays. Cape, 1934. 284p.
——*re-issued* Cape. 1938. (Life and Letters Series)
*includes "Lord's, June 27th, 1930"*

6657 Cricket country. Collins, 1944. 224p.
■ ——*another ed.* Reprint Society, 1945
——*another ed.* Collins, 1951. (St. James's Library)

6658 **Bolland, William**
■ Cricket notes; with a letter containing

practical hints, by W. Clark. Trelawney Saunders, 1851. iv,155p.
*historical essays, reminiscences and commentary*

6659 **Brown, Ivor [John Carnegie]**
■ Masques and phases. Cobden-Sanderson, 1926. xv,229p.
*includes the essay "Those purple hours" pp. 38–52*

6660 Now on view. Methuen, 1929. vi,207p.
■ *cricket references in the 5 essays that form the section entitled "The sporting life", pp. 141–73*

6661 **Bryant, Sir Arthur**
□ Historian's holiday. Dropmore P., 1946. 84p. (Dropmore Essays)
*limited ed. of 500 copies*
——an enlarged ed. Collins, 1951. 127p. illus.
*includes "Cricketer's dreams" and "Harrow and Eton"*

6662 **Cardus, Sir Neville**
■ A cricketer's book. Grant Richards. 1922 x,256p. scores
——*re-issued.* Richards P., 1929

6663 Days in the sun: a cricketer's journal.
■ Grant Richards, 1924. 264p.
——*with sub-title: a cricketer's book.* Cape, 1929. 224p. (The Traveller's Library)
*contains items from A cricketer's book, 1922 and from Days in the sun*
——New ed. Hart-Davis, 1948. 184p.

6664 The summer game: a cricketer's journal.
■ Humphrey Toumlin at the Cayme P., 1929. 255p. diagr. scores
——*L.P. ed.* Grant Richards and Humphrey Toumlin at the Cayme P., 1929
*limited ed. of 120 copies signed and numbered*
——*another ed.* Cape, 1935. 256p. (The Traveller's Library)
——*another ed.* Cape, 1940. 256p. (St. Giles Library)
——*another ed.* Hart-Davis, 1948. 191p.

6665 Good days: a book of cricket. Cape, 1934,
■ 288p. scores
——*another ed.* Cape, 1937. 288p. (New Library)
——*another ed.* Hart Davis, 1948. 255p.
*includes account of Australia v. England Tests 1934*

6666 The essential Neville Cardus; selected,
■ with an introduction by Rupert Hart-Davis. Cape, 1949. 316p. scores
——*Pt. 1 rptd. with title:* Cardus on

cricket. Sportman's Book Club, 1951. 251p.
——Cardus on cricket. Souvenir P., 1977. 256p. 1 illus. scores
——Special ed. Souvenir P., 1977
*specially bound edition limited to 100 copies*

6667 Cricket all the year. Collins, 1952. 222p.
■ illus. ports. scores, stats.
——*another ed.* Sportsman's Book Club, 1953

6668 Close of play. Collins, 1956. 192p.
■ ——*another ed.* Sportsman's Book Club, 1957

6669 The Playfair Cardus: essays . . . first
■ published in 'Playfair Cricket Monthly'. Dickens P., 1963. 160p. ports.

6669 Cardus in the covers. Souvenir P., 1978.
–1 254p. frontis. scores
■ ——de luxe ed. limited to 100 numbered copies. 1978.
*an anthology of his writings including his reports to the Manchester Guardian of the England v. Australia Tests 1953*

6669 Play resumed with Cardus; [compiled by
–2 Margaret Hughes]. Souvenir P., 1979.
■ 293p. scores
——de luxe ed. of 100 numbered copies. 1979
*an anthology of his writings including his reports to the Manchester Guardian of the England v. Australia Tests, 1930*

6670 **Carew, Dudley Charles Hemington**
■ England over: a cricket book. M. Secker, 1927. 208p.

6671 **Catton, James Alfred Henry, "Tityrus",**
■ *pseud.*
Wickets and goals: stories of play. Chapman & Hall, [1926]. ix,303p. illus. ports.
*includes account of England v. Australia Tests, 1893–1909*

6672 **Christian, Edmund Brown Viney**
■ At the sign of the wicket: essays on the glorious game. Bristol, Arrowsmith, [1894]. 192p. (Arrowsmith's Bristol Library)

6673 **Cleaver, Hylton [Reginald]**
■ Sporting rhapsody. Hutchinson, 1951. 223p. illus. (Hutchinson's Library of Sports & Pastimes)
*cricket pp. 140–150 and scattered references*

6674 **Cobbett, Martin Richards,** *compiler*
■ Sporting notions of present days and past; selected from "The Referee", and

edited by A. Cobbett. Edinburgh, London, Sands, 1908. vii,366p.
*chap. viii "Cricket"; chap. ix "More cricket", pp. 134–67*

6675 **Dalton, Jack P.,** *and* **Hart, Clive,** *editors*
Twelve and a tilly: essays on the occasion of the 25th anniversary of "Finnegan's wake". Faber, 1966. 142p. port.
*"Sport and games in Finnegan's Wake", pp. 52–64*

6676 **Darwin, Bernard [Richard Meirion]**
Playing the like. Chapman & Hall, 1934. xii,246p.
*essays on golf, but cricket pp. 239–43*

6677 Every idle dream: with illustrations by
■ Elinor Darwin. Collins, 1948. 255p. illus.
*includes "Watching cricket", pp. 60–67; "Some writers on sport", pp. 97–106; "The boyhood of a hero" [W. G. Grace], pp. 122–130*

6677 Mostly golf: a Bernard Darwin anthology;
–1 edited by Peter Ryde. Black, 1976. xv,
■ 198p. illus. ports. facsims.
*cricket pp. 74–7, 126–30, 193–4*

6678 **Day, Harvey**
■ Luck of the toss. Pelham, 1970. 176p. illus. ports.

6679 **De Selincourt, Hugh**
■ Moreover: reflections on the game of cricket: with illustrations by J. H. Thorpe. G. Howe, 1934. 268p. illus.

6680 **Doyle, John Andrew**
■ Essays on various subjects; edited by W. P. Ker. Murray, 1911. xxviii,333p. port.
*includes a review of* The poetry of sport; *selected and edited by Hedley Peek, pp. 170–199. See no. 6394*

6680 **Edwards, Oliver**
–1 Talking of books. Heinemann, 1957. ix, 306p.
*a selection of articles which first appeared in* The Times *including one on E. W. Hornung and Raffles pp. 26–9*

6681 **Fingleton, Jack,** *i.e.* **John Henry Webb**
■ **Fingleton**
Fingleton on cricket. London & Sydney, Collins, 1972. xix,268p. illus. score

6681 **Fitzgerald, Percy Hetherington**
–1 Pickwickian studies. New Century P., 1899. [iv],114p.
*ch. vi "Muggleton and its cricket"*

6682 **Foenander, Samuel Peter**
■ A Ceylon schoolmaster abroad. [Colombo, the Author, 1928]. 53p.
*a collection of personal essays, some with cricket interest reprinted in pamphlet form*

6683 **Gale, Frederick**
■ The game of cricket. Swan, Sonnenschein, Lowrey, 1887. viii,270p. frontis. (port.)
——2nd ed. 1888

6684 **Game** for anything, by Alan Gibson,
■ Derek Robinson and David Foot. Bristol, printed by Electroprint, [1973?]. 3–41p. illus. ports.
*essays on a number of sports, including cricket, many with a West Country emphasis*

6685 **Gardiner, Alfred George**
■ Pillars of society. Nisbett, 1913. x,354p. ports.
——*another ed.* Dent, 1916. (Wayfarer's Library)
*biographical essays including "The Jam Sahib of Nawanagar"*

6686 **[Gardiner, Alfred George]**
■ Pebbles on the shore, [by] Alpha of the Plough. Dent, 1916. 255p. frontis.
*essays including "W.G.", pp. 27–31: reprinted from "The Star"*

6687 Leaves in the wind, by Alpha of the
■ Plough; illustrated by Clive Gardiner. Dent, 1918. xvi,270p.
——2nd ed. 1919
*includes "On a vision of Eden" pp. 68–72*

6688 Windfalls, by Alpha of the Plough; with illustrations by Clive Gardiner. Dent, 1920. xvi,270p.
——*another ed.* 1924. (Wayfarers Library)
*includes "The vanity of old age"*

6689 Many furrows, by Alpha of the Plough;
■ with illustrations by Clive Gardiner. Dent, 1924. x,275p. illus.
*essays including "Billitch at Lord's", pp. 25–8. "Billitch" was J. W. Hitch*

6690 Certain people of importance. Cape,
■ 1926. viii,311p. ports.
——*another ed.* Dent, 1929. 252p. (Wayfarer's Library)
——*American ed. with title:* Portraits and portents. N.Y., 1926
*biographical essays—includes "Jack Hobbs"*

6691 **Glanville, Brian [Lester]**
People in sport. Secker and Warburg, 1967. 255p.
*essays; cricket pp. 30, 35–38, 189, 190*

6692 **Gordon,** *Sir* **Home Seton Charles**
■ **Montagu,** *bart*
Background of cricket. Barker, 1939.
348p. illus. ports.

6692 **Habib, Gulamali**
–1 Cricket thrills. Bombay, Streamline, 1949.
16p. illus.

6693 **Hazlitt, William**
■ Sketches and essays: now first collected
and edited by his son. Templeman, 1839
——*another ed. with title* Men and
manners: sketches and essays, 1852
*refers to Robert Robinson ('Long Bob') in*
*"Merry England"*

6694 **Herklots, Hugh Gerrard Gibson**
Jack of all trades: a miscellany of prose
and verse. Benn, 1926. 111p.
——*paper ed.* 1926
*ch. 32 "Cricket", pp. 85–89*

6695 **Hoby, Alan**
■ One crowded hour. Museum P., 1954.
160p. illus.
*essays on famous contemporary sportsmen;*
*cricketers pp. 23, 40, 66, 105–07, 114, 115*

6696 **Hole, Samuel Reynolds**
■ Then and now. Hutchinson, 1901. viii,
333p. frontis.
*cricket pp. 113–7, etc.*

6697 **Hollowood, Bernard**
■ Cricket on the brain. Eyre & Spottiswoode, 1970. 224p. illus. ports. scores
——*another ed.* Sportsman's Book Club,
1972

6698 **Hornung, Ernest William**
The cricket on the green; illustrated by
R. E. Wethey. Middlesbrough, Jordison,
1895. illus.

6698 **Hudson, Derek**
–1 Talks with Fuddy and other papers.
Arundel (Sussex), Centaur, 1968. xvi,
112p.
*ch. xii 'Dr. Grace carries his bat' (a playlet)*

6699 **Hunt, [James Henry] Leigh**
The seer; or, Common-places refreshed.
2 vols. Moxon, 1840–41
*includes "Cricket and exercise in general"*

6700 **Inge, William Ralph**
More lay thoughts of a dean. Putnam,
1931. 320p.
*"Cricket past and present, pp. 173–78*

6701 **[Kendall, John Kaye]**
■ Says he, by Dum-Dum. Constable, 1932.
vii,119p.
*"The poor boaster", pp. 77–80*

6702 **Kilburn, James Maurice**
■ In search of cricket. Arthur Barker, 1937.
185p. illus. ports. scores

6702 Overthrows: a book of cricket. S. Paul,
–1 1975. 153p. illus. ports.
■

6703 **Knox, Edmund [George] Valpy**
■ An hour from Victoria and some other
excursions. Allen & Unwin, 1924, 156p.
*includes "Team-building", pp. 94–8;*
*sketches mostly reprinted from* Punch

6704 This other Eden. Methuen, 1929. vi,154p.
■ *includes "The prep. school comes to*
Lord's," pp. 113–18

6705 **Leighton, Clare**
Country matters, written and engraved
by Clare Leighton. Gollancz, 1937.
x,160p. illus.
*includes "The cricket match", pp. 93–98*

6706 **Lewin, Walter Henry**
■ Up stream. The Author, [1943]. viii,237p.
port.
*essays with references to cricket pp. 36–7,*
*96–109; limited to 100 copies*

6707 **Lucas, Edward Verrall**
■ Willow and leather: a book of praise.
Bristol, Arrowsmith; London, Simpkin,
Marshall, 1898. 142p. (Arrowsmith's
Bristol Library)
*verse and essays*

6708 Fireside and sunshine. Methuen, 1906.
■ vii,240p.
*essays, including "Cricket and the back-*
*ward look", pp. 180–196*

6709 Character and comedy. Methuen, 1907.
■ vii,240p.
*essays including "The cricket club concert",*
*pp. 233–240*

6710 One day and another. Methuen, 1909.
■ vii,251p.
*essays including "George Mariner",*
*pp. 145–151, "Winter solace", pp. 187–198,*
*and "A rhapsodist at Lord's", [Francis*
*Thompson]. pp. 199–215*

6711 A little of everything. Methuen, 1912.
■ 190p.
*essays including "The cricket club concert"*

6712 Loiterer's harvest: a book of essays.
■ Methuen, 1913. vii,255p. frontis.
*includes "The bats", pp. 144–147*

6713 Harvest home. Methuen, 1913. 180p.
*includes "Two amateurs—Alfred Mynn*
*and Mr. Aislabie", pp. 54–58*

6714 Variety lane. Methuen, 1916. 189p.
■ (Methuen's Shilling Books).
*essays and sketches including "The cricket match", pp. 170–189*

6715 A Boswell of Baghdad, with diversions.
■ Methuen, 1917. vii,245p.
*includes "The dark secret", pp. 176–179*

6716 The phantom journal and other essays
■ and diversions. Methuen, 1919. vii,207p.
illus.
——2nd ed. 1920
*includes "The visionary triumph" and "Enthusiasts"*

6716 Roving east and roving west. Methuen,
–1 1921. 144p. frontis.
*contains pp. 98–104 "The ball game" – on cricket and baseball*

6717 Giving and receiving: essays and
■ fantasies. Methuen, 1922. vi,213p. illus.
*includes "Another 'Young cricketers' tutor' ", pp. 117–21*

6718 Adventures and misgivings. Methuen,
1928. 146p.

6719 Turning things over: essays and fancies.
■ Methuen, 1929. vi,183p.
*includes "Cricket N.B." pp. 40–45*

6720 Reading writing and remembering: a
■ literary record. Methuen, 1932. xvii,339p.
illus. ports.
*cricket pp. 20, 45, 78, 147, 187, 188, 243, 303, 326, 327, 328*

6721 English leaves. Methuen, 1933. x,168p.
■ illus. ports.
*essays including "The English game", pp. 76–106, and "John Nyren", pp. 107–16*

6722 The old contemporaries. Methuen, 1935.
256p. illus.

6722 Pleasure trove. Methuen, 1935. vi,217p.
–1 frontis.
*cricket reference p. 31 to Gad's Hill cricket ground which is suggested as the inspiration of All Muggleton v. Dingley Dell*

6723 Only the other day: a volume of essays.
■ Methuen, 1936. vi,211p. frontis.
*includes "The incomparable game", pp. 178–86, and "A cricket poet" [James Dance], pp. 187–94*

6724 Cricket all his life: cricket writings in
■ prose and verse; assembled and arranged by Rupert Hart-Davis. Hart-Davis, 1950. 216p.

6724 Selected essays; arranged by H. N.
–1 Wethered. Methuen, 1954. 256p.
*cricket pp. 64–6*

6725 **Lynd, Robert**
■ Irish and English: portraits and impressions. Griffiths, 1908. 240p.
*includes "The Gentlemen of England batting", pp. 162–67*

6726 The sporting life, and other trifles. G.
■ Richards, 1922. 251p.
——another ed. Sportsman's Book Club, 1956
*chs. on the 1921 Eng. v. Aust. Tests*

6727 It's a fine world. Methuen, 1930. viii,
213p.
*includes "At Lord's"*

6728 Both sides of the road. Methuen, 1934.
■ vii,184p.
*essays: includes "Verity's Test match", pp. 124–30*

6728 **MacDonald, Donald**
–1 The brooks of morning: nature and reflective essays, selected by his daughter. Sydney, Angus & Robertson, 1933. vii,245p. port.
*contains pp. 17–21 "Conventions of cricket"*

6728 **MacInnes, Colin**
–2 Out of the way: later essays. Brian &
■ O'Keeffe, 1979. 344p. frontis.
*pp. 241–4, "Second Test, fifth day" [Eng. v. W.I., Lord's, 1963] rptd. from New Society, July 1963*

6729 **Mallalieu, Joseph Percival William**
■ Sporting days. Phoenix House, 1955. 190p. illus. (Phoenix Sports Books)
*cricket pp. 122–57, 162–90*
——another ed. Sportsman's Book Club, 1957

6729 **Marshall, Arthur**
–1 Girls will be girls. H. Hamilton, 1974.
■ x,180p.
*pp. 67–91 "The crooked bat" [on his youthful struggles on the cricket field]*

6730 **Mason, Ronald Charles**
■ Batsman's paradise: an anatomy of cricketomania. Hollis & Carter, 1955. 167p. illus. ports.
*includes a chapter on cricket at Banstead*

6731 Sing all a green willow, Epworth P., 1967.
■ 176p.

6732 **Masterman, Sir John C.**
Bits and pieces. Hodder & Stoughton, 1961. 192p. port.
*includes pp. 25–38 "W. E. W. Collins"*

**6733 Mickel, Alan Durward**
Appartement in Brussels, Melbourne,
Robertson & Mullins, 1939. 219p. frontis.
——2nd ed. 1940
——3rd ed. 1945
*"Cricket" pp. 160–66*

**6733 Middleton, Richard Barham**
**–1** The day before yesterday. T. Fisher
Unwin, 1912. viii,246p.

**6734 Milne, Alan Alexander**
■ Not that it matters. Methuen, 1919. viii,
240p.
*includes "A day at Lord's", pp. 124–28*

**6735** The sunny side. Methuen, 1921. x,246p.
*sketches and verses, mostly rptd. from*
*Punch*
*includes "Summer days"*

**6736** By way of introduction. Methuen, 1929.
■ viii,208p.
——L.P. ed. N.Y., Dutton, 1929. 202p.
*limited to 166 copies*
*a collection of prefaces, articles, etc.,*
*including "A village match", pp. 163–67, and*
*" 'A babbled of green fields"*

**6737** Those were the days: The days' play, The
■ holiday round, Once a week, The sunny
side. Methuen, 1929. xix,888p.
*an omnibus volume*

**6738 Moraes, Dom F.**
■ Green is the grass. Bombay & Calcutta,
Asia Publishing House, 1951. vii,142p.
illus.

**6739 Morgan, Charles [Langbridge]**
■ Reflections in a mirror. First series.
Macmillan, 1944. 225p.
*include "Nausicaa and the Pelicans", pp.*
*174–82*

**6740 Moyes, Alban George ('Johnnie')**
■ The changing face of cricket. Angus &
Robertson, 1964. viii,160p. illus. ports.
——*another ed.* Sportsman's Book Club,
1966

**6740 Napier, Sydney Elliott**
**–1** The magic carpet and other essays and
adventures. Sydney, Angus & Robertson,
1932. 237p.
*includes pp. 39–51 "Cricket and the poets"*
*and pp. 192–205, "The cricket of prose".*
*Reprinted in part from various periodicals*

**6740 [Neale, Erskine]**
**–2** The living and the dead, by a Country
Curate. C. Knight, 1827. vi,379p.
*cricket pp. 161–65*

**6741 [Nichols, George Herbert Fosdike]**
■ London town, by "Quex". Partridge,
1926. 190p.
*articles first published in Evening News;*
*ch. vi "Up at Lord's"*

**6742 Nicholson, Norman**
Provincial pleasures; illustrated by B.
Biro. Hale, 1959. 190p. illus.

**6742 Norman, Barry**
**–1** Tales of the Redundance Kid, or The
■ bedside Barry Norman. Van Nostrand
Reinhold, 1975. 180p. illus.
*a collection of the author's articles from The*
*Guardian, The Observer and Cosmopolitan;*
*cricket pp. 107–9, 113–5*

**6743 Peebles, Ian [Alexander Ross]**
■ Talking of cricket. Museum P., 1953.
207p. illus. ports. (The Sporting Scene
Series)
——*another ed.* Sportsman's Book Club,
1955

**6744** Batter's castle: a ramble round the realm
■ of cricket. Souvenir P., 1958. 191p. illus.
——*another ed.* Sportsman's Book Club,
1959

**6745** Bowler's turn: a further ramble round the
■ realm of cricket. Souvenir P., 1960. 195p.
illus. ports. scores, stats.
——*another ed.* Sportsman's Book Club,
1961
*includes an account of the M.C.C. tour of*
*the West Indies, 1959–60*

**6746 Phillpotts, Eden**
■ A mixed grill. Watts, 1940. viii,173p.
*includes "W. G. Grace 1848–1915" pp.*
*96–97*

**6747** One thing and another. Hutchinson,
■ 1954. 192p. port.
*includes "Ethiopian cricket match" pp.*
*164–175 [on St. Thomas Is., W.I.] first publd.*
*in The Idler, Vol. III, June 1893. pp.*
*512–525*

**6747 Pinter, Harold**
**–1** Poems and prose 1949–1977. Eyre
■ Methuen, 1978. ix,102p.
*includes pp. 85–90 "Hutton and the past",*
*a prose piece originally published as*
*"Memories of cricket" in the Daily Telegraph*
*Magazine, 16 May 1969*

**6748 Pollock, William**
■ The cream of cricket. Methuen, 1934.
xxvii,128p. illus. port.

**6749** Talking about cricket—. Gollancz, 1941.
167p. illus. stats.

**6750  Praed, Winthrop Mackworth**
■    Essays; collected and arranged by Sir George Young. Routledge, 1887. 279p.
    *includes: "The best bat in the school", pp. 273–79*

**6750  Prance, Claude Annett**
**–1**   The laughing philosopher: a further miscellany on books, booksellers and book collecting. Villiers Publications, 1976. 284p.
    *pp. 111–8 "A shelf of cricket books", and pp. 138–47 "Edward Verrall Lucas"*

**6751  Pridham, Charles Hawker Bruce**
■    The charm of cricket past and present. H. Jenkins, 1949. 256p. illus. ports. diagrs. scores

**6752  Priestley, John Boynton**
■    Open house: a book of essays. Heinemann, 1927. viii,197p.
    *includes "Sutcliffe and I"*

**6753**  Self-selected essays. Heinemann, 1932. vi,319p.
    *includes "Sutcliffe and I"*

**6754  Ramaswami, N. S.**
■    Winter of content. Madras, The Swadesamitran Ltd., 1967. [iv],109p.

**6755  Robertson,** *Sir* **Charles Grant**
■    Voces academicae. Methuen, 1898. viii, 266p. frontis.
    *sketches of Oxford life; includes "A cricket match", pp. 21–34*

**6756  Robertson-Glasgow, Raymond Charles**
■    Men only in sport; illustrations by Edgar Norfield Pearson, 1943. 96p. illus. (Men Only Series)
    ——2nd ed. 1945
    ——3rd ed. 1946
    *a reprint of author's articles in* Men Only; *cricket pp. 9–46, 52–60, 74–81, 88–91*

**6756**  Country talk: a miscellany. Blond, 1964.
**–1**   211p. illus.
    *includes pp. 9–10, "Cricket, pigs and fire"; pp. 68–70, "Deadlock in Parva"; pp. 154–5, "The scorer"; rptd. from* The Sunday Times

**6757**  Crusoe on cricket: the cricket writings of
■    R. C. Robertson-Glasgow; with an introduction by Alan Ross. A. Ross, 1966. 321p.

**6758  Robinson, Raymond John**
■    Between wickets. Collins, 1946. 192p. illus.
    ——*2nd* enlarged ed. 1946. illus.
    ——3rd ed. rev. 1948. 233,vi,p. illus.

——*4th* rev. ed. 256p. illus. (Fontana Books)
    *essays mainly about Australian players*

**6759**  From the boundary. Collins, 1951. 256p.
■    illus. diagrs. stats.

**6759**  "Writing about cricket". *In* The Austra-
**–1**   lian author: quarterly journal of the
■    Australian Society of Authors. Vol. 10, no. 2, Autumn issue – April 1978, pp. 27–9

**6760  Rogerson, Sidney**
■    The old enchantment; illustrated with woodcuts by J. E. Maunton. Nicholson & Watson, 1938. xiv,245p. illus.
    *includes "Characters at the crease", pp. 172–189*

**6761  Rosenwater, Irving**
    Charles Dickens and cricket. London, *priv. printed*, 1970. 12p.
    *limited ed. of 30 signed copies*

**6762  Russell, Charles James Fox,** *Lord*
■    Some recollections of cricket. Woburn, Fisher, 1879. 39p.
    *12 copies only (Taylor)*
    *contents: A dream of the past (rptd. from
        Baily's magazine)*
        *Round-arm recollections. (rptd.
        from Baily's magazine)*
        *Lord's and Prince's, 1872*
        *Bedfordshire cricket (rptd. from
        The Bedfordshire Mercury,
        Aug. 9, 1878)*
        *National testimonial to Mr. W.
        G. Grace: an address delivered
        on Lord's Cricket Ground. July
        22nd, 1879*
    ——rptd. [with] introduction by John Arlott. Ewell, J. W. McKenzie, 1979. [xvii],3–39p. port.
    *limited to 100 numbered copies*

**6763**  Woburn echoes. Woburn, Fisher, 1881.
■    262p.
    *essays, including cricket pp. 171–196*

**6764  Russell, George William Erskine**
■    A pocketful of sixpences. Richards, 1907. vii,344p.
    ——*another ed.* Nelson. [1911]. 371p. port. (Nelson's Shilling Library)
    *includes essay on Eton v. Harrow at Lord's*

**6765**  Some threepenny bits. Richards, 1908.
■    viii,322p.
    *includes "Sportsmanship", pp. 308–14
    [thoughts at an Eton v. Harrow match at Lord's]*

**6766  S[assoon], S[iegfried]**
■    An adjustment, by S.S. Royston, Herts,

The Golden Head P., 1955. [16]p. facsim.
*dialogue in Elizabethan style of how author
substituted one copy of 'The young cricketer's
tutor' for another as a gift to Edmund Blunden*

**6767 Scott, Clement William**
Among the apple orchards. Remington,
1895. 138p.

**6768 Sewell, Edward Humphrey Dalrymple**
■ Cricket up-to-date. Murray, 1931. xi,
295p. illus. ports. scores

6769 From a window at Lord's. Methuen,
■ 1937. v,234p. scores

6770 Cricket under fire. S. Paul, [1941]. 260p.
■ illus. ports.

6771 Overthrows. S. Paul, [1946]. 139p. illus.
■ ports. stats.

6772 Well hit! sir. S. Paul, [1947]. 200p. illus.
■ port. scores, stats.

**6773 Shuckburgh, Sir John Evelyn**
An ideal voyage, and other essays.
Chatto & Windus, 1946. 189p.
*includes "The Church at the wicket", pp.
17–21, and "A pre-war Test match", pp.
106–09*

**6774 Squire, Sir John Collings**
■ Sunday mornings. Heinemann, 1930.
x,338p.
*article, reprinted from* The Observer;
*cricket pp. 143–173*

**6774 Surr, Watson**
**–1** Daffodils. London & Melbourne, Ward,
Lock, 1925. 169p.
*cricket pp. 133–4*

**6775 Swanton, Ernest William**
■ Cricket from all angles. Joseph, 1968.
328p. illus. ports. scores
*selections from his writings for* The Daily
Telegraph *from 1946*

**6775 Thompson, Francis**
**–1** [Selected essays]. Harrap, 1927. 78p.
■ (Essays of To-day and Yesterday)
*includes pp. 70–8 "A prince of India on the
prince of games" (on Ranjitsinhji)*

**6776 Thomson, Arthur Alexander**
■ Strolling commentaries. H. Jenkins, 1938.
155p.
*reprinted from the* Radio Times: *including
"Willow, willow", pp. 62–3; "Summer
verdict", pp. 78–80*

6777 Cricket my pleasure. Museum P., 1953.
■ 192p. illus. ports, stats.
——*another ed.* Sportsman's Book Club,
1954

6778 Cricket my happiness. Museum P., 1954.
■ 192p. illus. ports.
——*another ed.* Sportsman's Book Club,
1956

6779 Pavilioned in splendour. Museum P.,
■ 1956. 199p. illus. ports.

**6780 Trevor, Philip [Christian William]**
■ The lighter side of cricket; edited by E. T.
Sachs. Methuen, 1901. xix,299p.

6781 Cricket and cricketers. Chapman & Hall,
■ 1921. viii,232p.
*includes an account of the Australian team,
1921*

6782 Cricket. Shell Oil and Petrol, [c.1930].
■ [12]p. col. illus.
*a series of articles published as an advertise-
ment brochure*

**6782 Tyson, Frank Holmes**
**–1** Cricket and other diversions. Melbourne,
■ Newspress Pty Ltd., 1978. xi,147p.
*'the best of more than 15 years of Tyson's
writings'*

**6783 Uttley, Alison**
■ Carts and candlesticks; with illustrations
by C. F. Tunnicliffe. Faber, 1948. 160p.
illus.
*cricket pp. 44–52*

6784 Something for nothing; illustrated by
■ C. F. Tunnicliffe. Faber, 1960. 128p. illus.
*includes "Cricket at Old Trafford", pp.
93–101*

**6785 [Vernon, John Richard]**
■ Poppies in the corn; or, Glad hours in the
grave years. Tinsley, 1872. [vii],318p.
*includes "Cricket generally, and a day at
Lord's Ground in particular", pp. 140–161;
rptd. from* London Society

**6786 Watson, Edmund Henry Lacon**
■ Notes and memories of a sports reporter.
M. Joseph, 1931. 288p. illus. port.
*has 3 chs. on cricket*

**6787 Waugh, Alec**
■ On doing what one likes. Cayme P., 1926.
158p.
*includes "The village heath" and 2 other
essays on cricket*

# SPEECHES AND BROADCASTS

6788 **Baldwin, Stanley,** 1st earl Baldwin of
■ Bewdley
Our inheritance: speeches and addresses. Hodder & Stoughton, 1928.
309p. frontis.
*reprints the introduction to "Eton v.
Harrow at Lord's" by Sir Home Gordon, pp.
301–03, and "Speech delivered at the luncheon
given to the Australian cricket team 20th
April, 1926", pp. 298–300*

6789 **Barrie, Sir James Matthew**
■ Cricket: being a speech delivered . . . on
the occasion of the luncheon given to the
Australian cricket eleven by the London
District of the Institute of Journalists,
April 20, 1926. *Privately printed* for
Clement Shorter, 1926. 8p.
*limited ed. of 25 copies*

6790 M'Connachie and J.M.B.: speeches. P.
■ Davies, 1938. xv,275p.
*contains 3 speeches given at dinners to
Australian touring teams of 1926, 1930 and
1934, pp. 110–114, 209–212 and 266–271*

6791 **The book** of ready-made speeches, con
■ taining examples . . . London, Reeves
and Turner; Halifax, Nicholson, 1867. xi,
244p.
*"Speeches and the business at a cricket club
dinner" pp. 122–4*

6792 **British Broadcasting Corporation**
■ Broadcast from Lord's cricket ground,
April 17th, 1936: speakers: R. H. Routledge, Derek McCulloch, a boy representative, R. Aird. 6p. *typescript*
*in M.C.C. Library, Lord's*

6793 **Cardus, Sir Neville**
■ Idle thoughts on cricket. Westminster P.,
1934. 8p.
*reprint of a broadcast talk, printed in The
Listener, 2nd May, 1934, presented to the
members of the Ditchling C.C. by G. T.
Meynell*

6794 **Ebbisham, Rowland Blades,** 1st baron
■ Speeches made at a dinner given by Lord
Ebbisham to the members of the Lords
and Commons cricket team on the occasion of the presentation by Rt. Hon.
Stanley Baldwin, M.P., to Sir Edward T.
Campbell at the House of Commons on
21st March, 1934. *Privately printed*, [1934].
19p.

6795 **[Frith, Henry]**
■ Speeches and toasts: how to make and
propose them. Ward, Lock, 1909. 190p.
*cricket pp. 84–90; many later editions*

6796 **Guise, John Lindsay**
■ Talking of cricket: the book of the broadcasts "Cricket for all." Methuen, 1952.
ix,117p. illus. port.

6797 **Hole, Samuel Reynolds**
Success to cricket. [1896]
*M.S. text of a speech 8th April, 1896; in
M.C.C. Library at Lord's*

6798 **The Listener**
The spoken word: a selection from 25
years of 'The Listener'; chosen and introduced by Richard Church. Collins, 1955.
318p.
*includes "The story of my people" by Learie
Constantine*

6799 **Lyttelton, Charles John,** 10th viscount
Cobham
Speeches: a selection from the speeches
made during his term of office as Governor-General of New Zealand; edited by
O. S. Hintz. Auckland, Wilson and
Horton, 1962. 216p. illus. ports.
*2 speeches on cricket pp. 6–12*

6800 **Mackenzie, Sir Compton**
■ Echoes. Chatto & Windus, 1954. 188p.
*broadcast talks including 'In praise of
cricket'*

6800 **Maclaren, Archibald Campbell**
–1 W. G. Grace: talk broadcast 25th October
1935. ("I knew a Man" Series, part four).
9p. *typescript*
*transcript of talk held in B.B.C. Written
Archives Centre, Reading*

6801 **Marylebone Cricket Club**
■ Speeches made at the 150th anniversary
dinner of the Marylebone Cricket Club
held on Thursday, 15th July, 1937 at the
Savoy Hotel, London. [M.C.C., 1937].
14p. *typescript*

6801 **Milton, Howard**
–1 Several hundred years not out!: a history
■ of Kent county cricket. first broadcast on
B.B.C. Radio Medway March 29/April 28,
1977. [i],23f *typescript*
*transcript in The Cricket Society's Library*

6801 Kent's greatest cricketer: a tribute to
-2 Frank Woolley on his ninetieth birthday,
■ broadcast on B.B.C. Radio Medway on 22
May 1977. 5f. *typescript*
*transcript in The Cricket Society's Library*

6802 **Pringle, John,** *editor*
■ The radio listener's week-end book: a
selection from notable broadcasts of the
past five years. Odhams, [1950]. 288p.
illus.
*includes "W. G. Grace—colossus and
legend" by Dudley Carew, pp. 245–250*

# PLAYS

6802 **Ayckbourn, Alan**
-1 Time and time again: a comedy. French,
■ 1973. [iii],67p.
*cricket and football play a large part in the
play which is set in the garden of a suburban
house adjoining a recreation ground*

6803 **Black, Jay,** *and* **Black, Stephen**
■ The atom bowler: typescript of play
produced by Ayton Whitaker on B.B.C.
Radio, Saturday, 17th July 1948. [2],31f.
*in M.C.C. Library, Lord's*

6804 **Colman, George,** *the younger*
The heir-at-law: a comedy in five acts, as
performed at the Theatres-Royal in
London and Dublin. Dublin, P. Byrne,
1797
——2nd ed. 1800. 66p.

6804 The poor gentleman: a comedy in five
-1 acts. T. N. Longman & O. Rees, 1802.
83p.
*1st performed at the Theatre Royal, Covent
Garden, Feb. 11, 1801. Ollapod in Act iv,
scene i, comments 'Stay – here's Kent, fertile
in pheasants, cherries, hops, yeomen,
codlings, and cricketers'.*

6805 **D'Urfey, Thomas**
■ The Richmond heiress; or, A woman in
the right: a comedy, acted at the Theatre
Roayl [sic], by their Majesties' servants.
Printed for Samuel Briscoe, over-against
Will's Coffee-House in Covent Garden,
1693. [vi],64p.
*reference to cricket in Shinken's 'Song of
the Harp', Act IV
"Hur was the prettiest Fellows, trum,
trum, etc.
At Bandy once and Cricket, trum, etc."*

6806 **Glover, C. Gordon**
■ Sticky wicket: typescript of a play
produced by Ayton Whitaker on B.B.C.
Radio. Wednesday, 27 February 1952.
[i],15p.
*in M.C.C. Library, Lord's*

6806 **Greene, Grahame**
-1 The return of A. J. Raffles: an Edwardian
■ comedy in three acts based somewhat

loosely on E. W. Hornung's characters in
'The Amateur Cracksman'. Bodley Head,
1975. 80p. pbk.
——Ltd. signed ed. of 250 copies, bound
in boards. 1975
——rptd. Penguin Books, 1978. 73p. pbk.
*many cricket references*

6807 **Hatton, Charles**
■ Maiden over: typescript of a play adapted
from author's own novel, produced by
R. D. Smith on B.B.C. Radio, and
recorded on Friday, 21 January, [1955?].
[i],33f.
*in M.C.C. Library, Lord's*

6807 **Keefe, Barrie**
-1 Gimme shelter: Gem, Gotcha, Getaway.
■ Eyre Methuen, 1977. 96p. (Methuen New
Theatre Scripts)
——rptd. 1978. (Methuen Modern Plays)
*a trilogy of short plays, the first and last of
which take place on the boundary of a cricket
pitch*

6808 **Morton, Thomas**
Speed the plough, a comedy in five acts.
Longman & Rees, 1800. 94p.
——*numerous eds., e.g.* Humphrey Milford, 1926. viii,93p. (English Comedies
of the Eighteenth Century)
*cricket reference, p. 16 " . . . we Hampshire
lads conceat we can bowl a bit . . . ' The
author was a member of the M.C.C.*

6808 **O'Keeffe, John**
-1 The farmer. In two acts. Performed at the
Theatre Royal, Covent Garden in 1787.
London, n.p., 1800. 48p.
*cricket references pp. 12, 13; 1st publd. in
Dublin, 1788*

6808 **Pinter, Harold**
-2 Five screenplays: The servant; The pump-
■ kin eater; The Quiller memorandum;
Accident; The go-between. Methuen, 1971.
[vi],367p.
*"Accident" and "The go-between" have
cricket scenes*

6808 No man's land. Eyre Methuen, 1975. 95p.
-3 (A Methuen Modern Play)
■ ——revd. pbk ed. 1975
*all four characters have names of famous cricketers with cricket references on pp. 30, 69*

6809 **Rattigan, Terence**
■ The final Test: typescript of a play adapted for radio by Cynthia Pughe, produced on B.B.C. Radio by Royston Morley and recorded on Friday, 2 December 1956. [i],59f.
*in M.C.C. Library, Lord's*

6810 **Sherriff, Robert Cedric**
■ Badger's green: a play in three acts. Gollancz, 1930. 112p.
——limited ed. *(of 50 signed copies).* 1930
——*another ed.* Badger's Green, followed by "The Cricketers of my time" by John Nyren. Dent, 1936. 190p.

6811 **Taylor, Tim**
■ A cricketer's prologue, spoken in the Kentish dialect, before the play of "The Poor Gentleman", at the Theatre, Canterbury, during the Great Cricket Match, August 1st, 1842. 1p. of fold

6811 **Theatre Royal, Canterbury**
-1 Canterbury cricket week. Epilogue, 1923.
■ "C.U.R." (Canterbury's Universal Remedy,") a Pilgrim's Tale of 1923 by Lieut.-Col. C.P. Hawkes. Music arranged by Major A. Clarke-Jervoise. Canterbury, Theatre Royal, 1923. 12p.
*script of musical play*

6812 **Travers, Ben**
A bit of a test. 1933

6813 **Vallings, Harold**
■ Three brace of lovers: a comedy-idyl. Bristol, Arrowsmith; London, Simpkin, Marshall, [1894]. 317p. illus. (Arrowsmith's 3/6 series)
*of cricket interest, with plate*

# ANECDOTES, HUMOUR AND SATIRE

## Collections

6814 **Barsley, Michael Henry,** *editor*
The Phoenix book of wit and humour. Phoenix House, 1949. 256p.
——*another ed.* Pan Books, 1954. 252p.
*includes "The cricket match" from* England, their England, *by A. G. Macdonell*

6815 **Boas, Guy,** *compiler*
■ A "Punch" anthology. Macmillan, 1932. xii,276p.
*includes "Ninth wicket" and "cricket in Russia" by A.P. Herbert; "Chant royal of cricket" by H. S. V. Lodge; "The Burden of days" by E. V. Knox*

6815 **Brayshaw, Ian**
-1 Round the wicket: a selection of cricket
■ stories; illustrated by Richard Gregory. Sydney, etc., Methuen of Australia, 1979. 128p. illus. pbk.

6815 **[Byerley, Thomas,** *and* **Robertson, Joseph**
-2 **Clinton,** *editors]*
The Percy anecdotes. Collected and edited by Reuben and Sholto Percy. A verbatim reprint of the original edition. Warne, n.d. 4 vols. (Chandos Library)
*cricket vol. 4, p. 372 in section entitled 'Anecdotes of Pastime'. Originally published in 41 monthly parts 1821–23*

6815 **Green, Jonathon,** *and* **Atyeo, Don,**
-3 *compilers*
■ The book of sports quotes. Omnibus P., 1979. 214p. illus. ports.
*includes cricket*

6815 **Hammerton,** *Sir* **John Alexander,** *editor*
-4 Sports and pastimes. Educational Book Co., n.d. viii,296p. illus. (The Fun Library, Vol. 5)
*cricket pp. 217–9, 233–46*

6815 **Hornadge, Bill,** *compiler*
-5 The ugly Australian: unkind quotes collected by Bill Hornadge. Sydney, Bacchus Books, 1976. 256p.
*cricket pp. 211–3*

6816 **Johnston, Brian Alexander,** *editor*
■ Stumped for a tale?: cricket stories from the stars; drawn by Tony Hart. The Cricketer Ltd., 1965. 80p. illus. pbk.
——new & revised ed. The Cricketer with S. Paul, 1966. 96p. illus.

6817 ——, *compiler*
■ The wit of cricket. Frewin, 1968. 96p. illus.

6817 **Keating, Frank,** *compiler*
-1 Caught by Keating: sporting quotations
■ from the seventies; cartoons by Les Gibbard. Deutsch, 1979. 112p. illus. pbk.

6817 **Mills, Frederick, J. ("The Twinkler")**
-2 Square dinkum: a volume of original
Australian wit and humour. Melbourne,
Melville and Mullen Pty. Ltd., 1917. 128p.
*ch. xiv "Old time cricket"*

6818 **My funniest** story: a collection of stories
■ chosen by their own authors. Faber &
Faber, 1932. 384p.
*includes "The guardian angel" by W. A.
Darlington, pp. 278–92*

6818 **New Statesman**
-1 This England: selections from the "New
Statesman" 1934–1968; edited by Michael
Bateman. Penguin, 1969. 128p. illus. pbk.
*cricket pp. 40–1*

6818 **Printer's** pie. The Sphere & Tatler, 1911.
-2 xlviii,112p. illus.
*pp. 110–2 "The lightest side of cricket" by
Sir Home Gordon, Bart.*

6819 **Pritchard, Francis Henry,** compiler
■ Humour of today. Harrap, 1927. 224p.
frontis.
*includes "The once-a-year cricketer" by
Basil Macdonald Hastings pp. 72–76*

6820 **Punch**
■ Mr. Punch's book of sports: the humours
of cricket football . . . ; edited by J. A.
Hammerton. Amalgamated P., by
arrangement with . . . "Punch", [1906?].
192p. illus. (Punch Library of Humour)
*cricket pp. 7–81*

6820 Mr. Punch's limerick book; selected by
-1 Langford Reed, with illustrations by G. S.
Sherwood. Cobden-Sanderson, [1934].
xv,140p. illus.
*section 8 "Limericks and sport" contains
pp. 77–80 "Songs of an Ovalite" by E. C.
Holt; p. 81 "Greysing at the Oval"; p. 82
"Pessimism" [on Arthur Gilligan regularly
losing the Toss]*

6821 **Russell, Leonard,** editor
Press gang!: Crazy World Chronicle.
Nicolas Bentley drew the pictures. Hutchinson, 1937. xv,299p. illus.
*parodies of press articles by various authors
including an article on cricket by Leonard
Russell*

6822 **Sporting** stories and jokes: the humour
■ of sports and pastimes. Foulsham, [1927].
91p. (Foulsham's Library of Humour)
*cricket pp. 7–12*

6823 **Williams, R. E.,** editor
A century of "Punch". Heinemann, 1956.
352p. illus.
*cricket pp. 129–36*

6824 **Wodehouse,** Sir **Pelham Grenville,** editor
A century of humour. Hutchinson,
[1934]. 1024p.

## By Individual Authors

6825 **Alcock, Charles William**
■ Cricket stories: wise and otherwise;
Bristol, Arrowsmith; London, Simpkin
Marshall, 1901. 174p. (Arrowsmith's
Bristol Library)

6825 **Alexandra** Palace, Muswell Hill. Whit
-1 Monday, June 5, 1876: book of words.
[1876]. 16p.
*a souvenir programme of events, including
"12 o'clock the celebrated clown cricketers on
the cricket ground"*

6826 **Anderson, Robert [George Grant],** editor
■ Heard in the slips: a light-hearted look
at the game of cricket; illustrated by Ray
Chesterton. S. Paul, 1967. 104p. illus.

6827 **[Arbuthnot, John]**
■ Lewis Baboon turned honest, and John
Bull, politician: being the fourth part of
"Law is a bottomless pit". Printed from
a manuscript found in the cabinet of the
famous Sir Humphrey Polesworth and
published by the Author of the New
Atlantis. John Morphew, 1712. [viii],37p.
*reference to a match of cricket, p. 18*

6828 **Arkell, Reginald**
■ Meet these people: [humorous verse];
caricatures by Bert Thomas. H. Jenkins,
1928. 151p. illus.
——rev. and enl. ed. 1930. 159p.
*includes "To Jack Hobbs" p. 5, and "Good
Old Perce", p. 79*

6829 **[Atkinson, John]**
■ Humour in sports, by John Aye.
Universal Publications, [1932]. 283p.
bibliog. (The Ideal Library)
*cricket pp. 13–40*

6830 **Attaboy,** pseud.
■ Cycling for fun with a dash of cricket for
makeweight and a preface for motorists.
Birmingham, Hetherington, 1936. 52p.
(Courier booklets)

6831 **[Aveling, Edward Bibbins]**
■ Comic cricket by the Cockney Sportsman
(Alec Nelson); with illustrations by Chris
Davis. Wright, [1891]. [iii],68p. illus.
*reprinted from Ariel (The London 'Puck')*

6831 **[Bagguley, G. A. F.]**
-1 Maiden over; or casual cracks for crick-
■ eters, by Caxtilian. Newcastle under
Lyme, the Author, 1948. 60p. illus.

6832 [Balchin, Nigel Martin]
■ Fun and games: how to win at almost
anything, [by] Mark Spade; illustrated by
W. M. Hendy. H. Hamilton, 1936. 156p.
illus.
*cricket pp. 54–61*

6833 Bayly, A. Eric, *and* Briscoe, Walter
■ Alwyn
Chronicles of a country cricket club: being
odd tales of the national game. Sands,
1900. 146p.

6634 Begley, J.
The block with the one holer: stories and
adventures concerning Bluey Jacks; with
illustrations by Paul Rigby. Adelaide,
Rigby, 1968. 212p.
*humorous short stories*

6835 [Beith, John Hay]
■ The lighter side of school life, by Ian Hay;
with illustrations . . . by Lewis Baumer.
Foulis, 1914. [x],227p. col. illus.
*scattered references*

6836 Bentley, Edmund Clerihew
■ Baseless biography: [humorous verses];
Nicolas Bentley drew the pictures.
Constable, 1939. 112p. illus.
*includes the clerihew "WG"*

6836 Bentley, Nicolas
–1 Le sport, by Nicolas Bentley, who also
drew the pictures. Gollancz, 1939. 191p.
illus.
*cricket pp. 93–101*

6837 How can you bear to be human? Deutsch,
1957. 120p. illus.
*humorous essays, with references to cricket*

6837 [Beresford, James]
–1 The miseries of human life: or, The
groans of Samuel Sensitive and Timothy
Testy. 3rd ed. W. Miller, 1806. viii,332p.
col. illus.
*p. 47: "At cricket—after a long and hard
service of watching out—bowled out at first
ball*

6838 [Bettesworth, Walter Ambrose]
■ A royal road to cricket, by An Old Sussex
Cricketer; with illustrations by the
author. Iliffe, [1891]. 24p. illus.

6839 Bodkin, Thomas
■ My uncle Frank. Hale, 1941. 149p. frontis.
*"The cricket match", pp. 125–135, (cricket
at Beaupare, near Newbridge, Co. Kildare)*
——New ed. Collins, 1947. 96p.

6840 Briscoe, Walter Alwyn, ("W.A.B.")
■ Cricket love and humour: tales told of
balls bowled. Grafton, 1921. 155p. illus.

*6 chapters originally appeared in Bayly, A.
E. & Briscoe, W. A. "Chronicles of a country
cricket club"*

6841 Broome, John Egerton, *and* Ross, John
■ Adrian
Keep your eye on the ball: a book of
sketches by J. E. Broome; with verse and
prose by John Adrian Ross. Collins, 1936.
48p. col. illus.
*"The googly", pp. 8–9: "The dropped
catch", pp. 14–15*

6842 "Catch-A-Catch", *pseud.*
■ Comical cricket in rhyme and picture.
Melbourne, Marshall, [1891]. [42]p. illus.

6842 Copeland, J. C.
–1 Watching Test cricket (1928–1954): what I
know about the game. [The Author]. *n.d.*
*blank pages only; In A. E. Winder's
collection*

6843 Craig, Albert
■ Cricket comicalities, and other trifles. All
England Athletic Publishing Co., 1899.
34p. incl. adverts.
——2nd ed. 1900
——3rd ed. 1901
*for later issues see no. 6926*

6843 Football funniosities & other trifles
–1 collected by A. Craig. 2nd ed. All
England Athletic Publishing Co., 1889.
19p. incl. adverts.
*includes cricket*

6844 Pleasant recollections and amusing inci-
■ dents: the outcome of personal experience on our cricket and football grounds.
Hughes & Son, 1900. [16]p.
——rev. ed. 1901. [16]p.

6845 The cricket enthusiast: a friendly satire.
Cricket Enthusiast. *weekly.* illus.
*7 issues 13th May to 24th June, 1922*

6846 Cricket sketches. Manchester, R. Scott.
1909. 12p. illus.

6847 Cricket sketches, grave and gay, old and
new. Leeds, E. A. Tempest, 1891. 8p.
illus.

6848 Cricket tit bits. Sheffield, Hurst, 1884
*in Taylor*

6848 Cruikshank, Percy
–1 Percy Cruikshank's comic almanac for
■ 1869. Read, Brooks, [1868]. [61]p. col.
illus.
*including p. 30 poem "The Cricket Club,
black-balling a member" accompanied by a
coloured illustration*

6848 **Cuddon, J. A.**
-2 "Cricket Russe". In Blackwood's maga-
■ zine, vol. 312, no. 1881 (July 1972). pp.
46–59
*a fanciful account of cricket in Russia*

6849 **Doyle, Richard,** *illustrator*
■ Manners & customs of ye Englyshe,
drawn from ye quick, by Richard Doyle;
with extracts from Mr. Pips his diary by
Percival Leigh. Bradbury, 1850. 98p. illus.
——*rptd.* London & Edinburgh, Foulis,
1911. viii,98p. illus. (The Cities Series)
*includes "A view of Mr. Lorde hys cryket
grounde" pp. 35–36*

6850 **[Dykes, T.]**
■ All round sport with fish, fur & feather
. . . , by "Rockwood". Fores, 1887. [xi],
302p. illus.
*"The Puddleton and Ground v. The Cotton
Spinners of Bobbinstown", pp. 41–7*

6851 **[Egan, Pierce]**
□ Sporting anecdotes, original and select;
including characteristic sketches of
eminent persons who have appeared on
the turf . . . By an Amateur Sportsman.
Sherwood. Jones, 1804. 592p. illus.
——*2nd ed.* [1808]. xv,579p.
——*3rd ed.* 1820. viii,497p.
——new ed., considerably enlarged and
improved. 1825. iv,592p.
*includes 5 references to cricket with
accounts of ladies' matches, and a match in
1796 at Montpelier Gardens, Walworth,
between eleven Greenwich pensioners each
with one leg, and another eleven each with
only one arm*
——*another edition with title*: Pierce Egan's
anecdotes, original and selected. 1827

6852 **[Esso (India)]**
■ Cricket gigglers. Madras, Imprint India,
[197–?]. [16]p. illus.
*free booklet of jokes*

6853 **Farjeon, Herbert**
■ Herbert Farjeon's cricket bag; illustrated
by Dennis Mallet. Macdonald, 1946,
159p. illus.
——*another ed.* Pelham Books, 1968. 160p.
illus.
——*another ed.* Sportsman's Book Club,
1969

6854 **Farjeon, Joseph Jefferson**
■ More little happenings. Methuen, 1928.
vi,185p.
*includes "Out for records", pp. 89–93*

6855 **[Fitzgerald, Robert Allan)**
■ Jerks in from short leg, by Quid; illustrated by W. H. du Bellew. Harrison,
1866. iii,137p. illus.
See: *Brodribb. Cricket in fiction. p. 30*

6856 **[Forrester, Alfred Henry]**
A bundle of crowquills, dropped by
Alfred Crowquill in his eccentric flights
over the field of literature. Routledge,
1854. 245p.
*contains "The demon bowler", pp. 147–153*

6857 **Freyberg, James**
Un-natural history not taught in bored
schools; illustrated by E. V. Campbell.
Simpkin Marshall, [1883]. 16p. illus.
*comic verse, includes "The Australian
cricket", p. 2*

6858 **"Fudge, Barnabas",** *pseud.*
■ Owzat? . . . the cricketers guyed; with
diagrams by A. N. Other. Blackwell,
1937. xiii,143p. diagrs.

6859 **Ganthony, Robert**
Bunkum entertainments: being a collection or original laughable skits on conjuring, physiognomy . . . to which are
added humorous sketches. Gill, 1895.
188p. illus.
*cricket pp. 131–34*

6860 **Gardiner, Arthur Stephen**
■ The autocrat of the cricket field and the
Old Crocks: being a record of the pro-
ceedings of the Rambling Wandering
C.C. The Office, 24, Mark Lane, E.C.3,
1917. x,104p. port.

6861 **Goldman, Arthur,** *compiler*
■ Try and stump me; (illustrations by
Sydney M. Moir). Johannesburg, Central
News Agency; Rhodesia, Kingstons,
1956. xii,171p. illus.

6862 Cricket capers; illustrations by Leyden.
Johannesburg, Afrikaanse Pers-Boek-
handel, 1964. 192p. illus.

6863 **Graham, Harry Joscelyn Clive**
■ Deportmental ditties, and other verses;
illustrated by Lewis Baumer. Mills &
Boon, 1909. 127p. illus.
*includes "Too old at thirty", pp. 174–6*

6864 Ruthless rhymes for heartless homes. E.
■ Arnold, [1909]. 80p. illus.
*includes "Obstruction", pp. 26–7*
——*set to music* by Victor Hely-Hutch-
inson. E. Arnold & Elkin, 1945. 40p. illus.

6865 Canned classics, and other verses; with
■ illustrations by Lewis Baumer. Mills &
Boon, 1911. 144p.

6866 The complete sportsman, (compiled from
■ the occasional papers at Reginald Drake
Biffin). E. Arnold, 1914. ix,300p. illus.
  *ch. vi "Village cricket", pp. 166–86*

6866 **Green, Michael**
–1 Even coarser rugby; or, What did you do
to Ronald?; illustrated by Haro. Hutchinson, 1963. 120p. illus.
——revised ed. Arrow, 1969.192p. illus.
pbk.
  *cricket pp. 75–87*

6867 Book of coarse sport; illustrated by Haro.
■ Hutchinson, 1965. 123p. illus.
  *cricket pp. 31–41, 97–99, etc.*

6868 **"Greendragon"**, *pseud.*, *and* **"Dande-
lion"**, *pseud.*
Sports spiced and pastimes peppered.
"Judy" Office, 1884. 120p. illus.
  *cricket pp. 42–6*

6868 **Heaton, Rose Henniker**
–1 The perfect hostess; decorated by Alfred
■ E. Taylor. Methuen, 1931. xv,160p. illus.
  *includes, with help from 'Plum' Warner,
  pp. 28–9, two luncheon menus, one for the
  local cricket team and one for the opposing
  team invited to lunch before the match*

6869 **Herbert**, *Sir* **Alan Patrick**
■ Mild and bitter. Methuen, 1936. ix.275p.
  *prose & verse including "Ninth wicket",
  pp. 42–44; "Cricket in the Caucasus, or the
  Volga Batmen", pp. 50–60; "Batter sweet: or
  'Not cricket' an operetta", pp. 142–55; "The
  fathers' match", pp. 208–24*

6869 General cargo. Methuen, 1939. ix,243p.
–1   *articles rptd. from "Punch"; cricket pp.
38–43*

6870 Look back and laugh. Methuen, 1960.
256p.
  *cricket pp. 105–07, 204–06, 225–28*

6870 **Hicks, Jeremy,** *compiler*
–1 Best cricket jokes. Wolfe Publishing Ltd.,
■ 1975. 64p. (The Wolfe Mini Ha-Ha-Books)

6871 **Hill, Merv**
■ Bats in the belfry; [illustrated by] Norm
Mitchell. Adelaide, Rigby, 1962. [32]p.
illus.

6871 **Hollands, Eileen**
–1 Never marry a cricketer. Fleet (Hants),
■ Quill Publications, 1974. 80p. illus. pbk.

6872 **Hughes, Cyrile E.,** *editor*
■ Sport in a nutshell, by the late Colonel
Bogey; [illustrated by] Fred Buchanan.
Jarrolds, [1921]. illus. diagrs.
  *cricket pp. 31–36*

6873 **Hughes, Spike,** *i.e.* **Patrick Cairns**
■ **Hughes**
The art of coarse cricket: a study of its
principles, traditions and practice; backed
up, pictorially by Antony Wysard.
Museum P., 1954. 123p. illus.
——*another ed.* Hutchinson, 1961

6874 **Hutchinson, Horace Gordon**
■ Cricketing saws and stories. Longmans,
1889. 51p. illus.

6875 **Jackson, Lawrence Nelson**
■ Lays from Lancashire; decorations by
Arthur Moreland. T. Werner Laurie,
1930. 60p. illus.
  *humorous verses;. includes "The cricket
match" pp. 42–4*

6876 **Jennings, Paul**
■ Even oddlier; illustrations by Haro
Hodson. Reinhardt, 1952. 160p. illus.
  *cricket pp. 42–45*

6876 **Johnston, Brian Alexander**
–1 It's a funny game . . . W. H. Allen, 1978.
■ 231p. illus. ports.

6876 Rain stops play; with cartoons by Bill
–2 Tidy; edited by Lynn Hughes. W. H.
■ Allen, 1979. xii,84p. illus.

6877 **Leacock, Stephen Butler**
■ My remarkable uncle, & other sketches.
John Lane, 1942. 218p.
  *humorous essays; cricket pp. 76–77, 144–50*

6877 **Lucas, Edward Verrall**
–1 If – a nightmare in conditional mood;
with illustrations by George Morrow.
Pitman, 1908. 100p. illus.
  *pp. 36–8 an account of a fictional match
  Yorkshire v. Middlesex*

6878 **"M.C.C.",** *pseud.*
■ Cricket on the brain; illustrated by "Gil."
T. Fisher Unwin, 1905. 80p. illus.

6879 Cricket at the breakfast table, by the
■ author of "Cricket on the brain"; illustrated by "Gil". Jarrold, 1909. 80p. illus.

6880 **Macleod, John**
The cricketer's dictionary [sic]. Sydney,
Dunvegan Publications, [1946?]. [112]p.
illus.
  *humorous definitions*

6881 **Mailey, Arthur Alfred**
■ Cricket sketches and short stories.
Sydney, *printed by* Simmons, [1933]. 31p.

6882 Cricket humour: stories and sketches.
■ Sydney, Market Printery Ltd., [1956].
19p. illus.

6883 **Mason, G. Finch**
■ Recollections of Finch Mason. Fores, 1885. xv,200p. illus.
——later eds. *with title: "Sporting recollections . . . ", e.g.:*
Sporting recollections: hunting, shooting, cricket, steeplechasing, racing, etc., etc.; illustrated by the Author. 5th ed. Fores, 1886. xv,200p. illus.
*includes 'Bowled out' by A. Humbug, Esq., pp. 9–19*

6884 **Melhuish, W. J.**
■ Mr. Biddle's cricket match. Simpkin, Marshall, 1884. [38]p. illus.

6885 **Meyrick, Arthur F.**
■ All in a day: coach, skittles and cricket by the Official Scorer; illustrated by Wallis Mackay. Simpkin, Marshall, etc., [1900]. 67p. illus.

6886 **Moir, James Whitehead**
■ Bran pie: a book of light verse. Harrow, School Bookshop, 1929. 52p.
*includes 2 humorous cricket poems*

6887 **Moreland, Arthur**
The comic history of sport. T. Werner Laurie, 1924. 64p. illus.
*rptd. from All Sports; cricket pp. 35–9*

6888 **The noble** cricketers: a poetical and
■ familiar epistle, address'd to two of the idlest Lords in his Majesty's Three Kingdoms. J. Bew, 1778. [iv],22p.
*a satire attacking the Duke of Dorset, the Earl of Tankerville and others*

6888 **Not yet** The Times. Stopeshill Ltd.
–1 *vol. 1, No. 1. August [i.e. July] 1979*
■ *the only issue: a spoof issue of "The Times" with various cricket articles including those on the final of the Prudential Cup, when Sri Lanka defeated the West Indies by 8 wickets and in which two Sri Lankan cricketers and a number of spectators were killed. Also the main news item announcing that Mr. Kerry Packer is to be granted exclusive rights to the televising of Parliament and control of all future television channels in return for £2 billion a year, thus allowing the Government to abolish income tax*

6889 **"An Old Cricketer"**, *pseud.*
■ A cricketer's notebook; containing original anecdotes, remarks, notes, reminiscences and other gossip. David Bogue, 1881. vii,94p.

6890 **Parkinson, Michael**
■ Cricket mad; drawings by Derek Alder. S. Paul, 1969. 119p. illus.
——*another ed.* Arrow Books, 1973. pbk.

6890 Bats in the pavilion: a follow-on from
–1 'Cricket mad'; drawings by Derek Alder.
■ S. Paul, 1977. [vi],114p. illus.
——*another ed.* Arrow Books, 1979. pbk.
*mostly based on contributions to Punch and The Sunday Times*

6891 **"Phipps"**, *pseud.*
■ Phipps' annual: essays by Phipps of the Daily Mail; illustrated by the Author. Methuen, 1933. x,182p. illus.
*cricket pp. 33–34, 73–74, 155–56*

6892 **Ponsonby-Fane, *Sir* Spencer Cecil**
■ **Brabazon**
Wise saws and modern instances; pursuits and pastimes, with some observations and cautions, by an Old Stager who has had experience "of moving accidents by flood and field". Railway Passengers Assurance Co., [c.1902]. [40]p. illus.

6893 **Potter, Stephen**
■ The theory and practice of gamesmanship; or, The art of winning games without actually cheating. Illustrated by Lt.-Col. F. Wilson. Hart-Davies, 1947. 128p. illus.
*cricket pp. 97–99, 110–111*

6894 Some notes on lifemanship: with a summary of recent researches in gamesmanship; illustrated by Frank Wilson. Hart-Davis, 1950. 126p. illus.
*a few cricket references*

6895 **Pratt, Art**
■ "Bally rot": versified reminiscences, many topical, some tropical, all diabolical. Ilfracombe, Stockwell, 1948. 96p.
*humorous verse; includes "Cricket" p. 24*

6895 **Pugh's** cricket stories
–1 *in Taylor*

6896 **Reedy, Wiliam Curran**
■ At the sign of the bat and ball: a cricket miscellany. Erskine Macdonald, 1926. 69p.
*verse and prose*

6897 Slip catches: a cricket miscellany; sketches
■ by W. R. Finch. Quality P., 1948. 95p. illus.
*humorous sketches in prose and verse*

6898 **Robertson-Glasgow, Raymond Charles**
■ The brighter side of cricket; illustrated by A. Savory. Barker, 1933. 191p. illus.
——*first cheap ed.* 1935
——*new and revised ed.* 1950. 128p.
*prose and verse sketches mostly rptd. from* The Cricketer

6899 How to become a Test cricketer. Blond,
■ 1962. 126p. illus.

6900 Rain stopped play; illustrated by
■ Wyndham Robinson. Dobson, 1948. 96p.
illus.
*articles reprinted from* The Observer

6901 All in the game; illustrated by Haro.
■ Dobson, 1952. 96p. illus.
*articles reprinted from* The Observer

6902 **Robinson, Raymond John**
■ Cricket's fun: sketches by D. Badior.
Sydney, Building Publishing Co., [1968].
20p. illus.
*50 humorous cricket stories*

6903 **Ryan, Patrick**
How I became a Yorkshireman: a short
guide to southern immigrants by a time-
serving apprentice Yorkshireman. Muller, 1967. [vi],98p. illus.
*ch. 7 "Learning about cricket": ch. 10
"Learning more about cricket"*

6904 **Sapte, William,** *junior*
■ Cricketers guyed for 1886; edited [or
rather written] by W. Sapte. Maxwell,
[1885]. 96p. illus.

6905 **Sellar, Robert James Batchen**
■ Sporting and dramatic yarns. T. Fisher
Unwin, 1925. 192p.
*sporting jokes, including cricket pp. 146–51*

6906 Play! the best sporting stories. Hamilton,
■ [1927]. 191p.
*"Comedies of cricket" pp. 34–41*

6907 Over the cocktails. Alston Rivers, 1931.
■ 159p.
*cricket pp. 27–36*

6907 **Spencer, Thomas E.**
–1 "How McDougall topped the score", and
other verses and sketches. Sydney,
Pollard Publishing Co., 1972. 174p. col.
illus. port.
*pp. 19–27 has the title-poem*

6908 **Sportive** snatches from playgrounds and
■ playhouses; compiled by Charles Plairre.
London; Wright, Manchester, Heywood.
illus. ports. *annual*
*5 issues 1889–93*
*contains biographical sketches with
portraits of leading sportsmen together with a
selection of anecdotes and verse relating to
various pastimes, culled from contemporary
literature*

6909 **Spurr, Harry A.**
■ A cockney in Arcadia; with illustrations
by Joan Hassall and Cecil Aldin. G. Allen,
1899. x,241p.
*cricket pp. 211–222*

6910 **Squire,** *Sir* **John Collings**
■ Weepings and wailings; drawings by Ian
Fenwick. Cobden-Sanderson, 1935. 90p.
illus.
*includes "The lament of a slow bat over the
new L.B.W. rule", pp. 57–61*

6911 **Sterndale Bennett, T. C.,** *and* **Hayes,
Cecil**
Games and how to play them: comic
sketches. S. French, *n.d.* 20p.
*cricket p. 18*

6912 **The Sun**
□ The Sun's cricket comic. W. C. Hall, the
Sun Office. *annual.* illus.
*2 issues: 1901: peing der remarks off Herr
Teufels on der kame mit many funny drawings
by Sol. 32p.*
*1902: with drawings by Sol and J. J. Proctor*

6913 **Taylor, Joseph**
The comic side of cricket; under the auspices of the Detroit Athletic Club. Chron-
icled by Joseph Taylor, illustrated by C.
Browne Calvert. Detroit, [the Club,
c.1891]. 21p. illus.
*see also no. 7009*

6913 **That's** cricket!: the funny side of cricket.
–1 Sydney, John Stuart, 1936. 12p. illus.
diagrs.

6914 **Thompson, Eric**
■ Mad about sport; illustrated by the
author. Hale, 1956. 128p. illus.
*ch. 3 "Mad about being behind the bowler",
pp. 21–26, etc.*

6915 **Thomson, Arthur Alexander**
■ Anatomy of laughter; drawings by R. G.
Phillips. Epworth P., 1966. 98p. illus.
*cricket humour pp. 74–80*

6915 **Trew, Maurice Frederick**
–1 Brighter cricket and other literary frolics.
Christchurch (N.Z.), Pegasus P., 1974.
64p.
*limited to 500 copies*

6915 **Trueman, Frederick Sewards,** *and* **Hardy,**
–2 **Frank**
■ 'You nearly had him that time . . . ' and
other cricket stories; illustrated by David
Langdon. S. Paul, 1978. 128p. illus.

6916 **Turner, Edward Francis**
■ More T leaves. Smith, Elder, 1888. iv,
284p.
*"An Old Bloke at cricket" pp. 95–99*

6917 **Turner, Tom**
■ Extra cover: light hearted hints for young cricketers. Regency P., 1972. 48p. illus.
*in humorous verse form*

6918 **Two-Game Cocks**, *pseud.*
Games made game of. J. Allen, 1857. 48p.
*cricket pp. 46–7*

6919 **Walton, W.**
■ Brother Muggins on cricket. Manchester, J. Heywood, [c.1886]. 8p.
——*cover title.* "The Punster's own": Watson and Pilling's comic sketch on cricket

6920 **Westmacott, Charles Molloy**
The English spy: an original work, characteristic, satirical and humorous. Comprising scenes and sketches in every rank of society, being portraits of the illustrious, eminent, eccentric, and notorious. Drawn from the life by B. Blackmantle. The illustrations designed by Robert Cruikshank. 2 vols. Sherwood, Jones, 1825–26. illus.
——*another ed.* Sherwood. 1852
——*rptd.* Methuen, 1907. 2 vols.

6920 **Willans, Geoffrey**, *and* **Searle, Ronald**
–1 How to be topp: a guide to sukcess for
■ tiny pupils, including all there is to kno about SPACE. Max Parrish, 1954. 106p. illus.
*cricket pp. 58–63*

6921 **[Willis, Anthony Armstrong]**
■ Warriors at ease, by Anthony Armstrong ("A.A."). Methuen, 1926. x,164p.
*includes "Our cricket match" pp. 56–59*
——*2nd ed.* 1928
——*3rd ed.* 1931

6922 Thoughts on things: humorous essays,
■ [by] Anthony Armstrong ("A.A."); illustrated by G. S. Sherwood. Methuen, 1935. 161p. illus.
*"On cricket", pp. 27–36*

6923 Warriors paraded. Methuen, 1938. 590p.

6924 **Wood, John J. ["I. Hickory Wood"]**, *pseud.*
Recitations, comic and otherwise. James Bowden, 1898. 116p.
*includes "The cricket club at Red Nose Flat: a yarn of "ole 'Frisco' "; this also appears in his "Merry thoughts for recitation or reading." Ward, Lock, 1912*

6925 **Wotherspoon, Ralph,** *and* **Jackson,**
■ **Lawrence Nelson**
Some sports and pastimes of the English; illustrated by Alison Fuller. Jenkins, 1937. 96p. illus.
*cricket pp. 89–95*

6926 **[Wright, W. R.]**
■ Cricket comicalities and other trifles, by W. R. Weir. Wright, 1902. 32p. incl. covers & adverts.
——*New ed. with title:* Cricket comicalities and football oddities, collected by W. R. Weir and A. Craig. [1906?]. 32p. incl. adverts. illus.
*for previous issues see no. 6843*

6927 Between the innings: cricket items—old
■ and new; collected by W. R. Weir. Wright, 1913. 30p. illus.
——*2nd. ed. i.e. reprint.* 1913. *with errata slip*
*contains "The cricket ball: something about its evolution" first published in American cricketer, March 1906.*

# DIARIES AND LETTERS

6928 **Armstrong, Benjamin John**
A Norfolk diary: passages from the diary of the Rev. B. J. Armstrong; edited by Herbert B. J. Armstrong. Harrap, 1949. 288p. ports.
*author was vicar of East Dereham during latter half of 19th century; brief cricket references pp. 167, 180, 181, 286*

6929 **Branch-Johnson, William**
The Carrington diary (1797–1810). C. Johnson, 1956. 184p. illus. diagr.
*contains scattered references to single wicket matches at Bramfield, Hertfordshire*

6929 "Memorandoms for. . . . ": the diary be-
–1 tween 1798 and 1810 of John Carrington. Phillimore, 1973. xiii,200p. illus.

6930 **Burney, Frances,** *afterwards* **Mrs. D'Arblay**
The early diary . . . 1768–1778; with a selection from her correspondence, and from the journals of her sisters Susan and Charlotte Burney; edited by Annie Raine Ellis. 2 vols. Bell, 1889
*quotes a letter (in vol. I) from Mrs. Rishton, dated 1773, requesting Miss Burney to obtain two cricket balls made by Pett of Sevenoaks*

6931 **Byrd, William**
The secret diary of Wiliam Byrd of Westover 1709–1712; edited by Louis B. Wright and Marion Tinling. Richmond (Va), the Dietz P., 1941. xxviii,622p. facsims.
*references to early cricket in Virginia 1709–10*

6932 **Chesterfield, Philip Dormer Stanhope,**
■ *4th earl of*
Letters . . . to his son, Philip Stanhope
. . . 11th ed. J. Nichols [and others], 1800.
4 vols.
*letter no. LXXI, dated Tuesday (May, 1741), first printed in this edition, urges his son 'to excell all boys of your age, at cricket . . .'*

6933 **Cutforth,** *Sir* **Arthur Edwin**
■ From other people's waste-paper baskets; with illustrations by C. Catherall. Elliot Stock, 1920. vii,69p. illus.
*includes "Many libels", pp. 41–45*

6933 **Farington, Joseph**
–1 The Farington diary; ed. by James Greig. 8 vols. Hutchinson, 1927. illus. ports.
*in vol. vii, pp. 53–4 (with footnote) the entry for October 21, 1811 concerns a visit paid to Duke the cricket ball maker*

6934 **Guest,** *Lady* **Charlotte Elizabeth**
■ Lady Charlotte Guest: extracts from her journal, 1833–1852; edited by the Earl of Bessborough. Murray, 1950. x,309p. illus. ports.
*cricket references*

6934 **Lowe, Bob**
–1 Letters to John. Christchurch (N.Z.). Whitcombe, 1976. 121p.
*cricket pp. 23, 27–8, 112*

6934 **Lyttelton, George,** *and* **Hart-Davis,**
–2 **Rupert**
■ The Lyttelton Hart-Davis letters: correspondence of George Lyttelton and Rupert Hart-Davis 1955–56; edited and introduced by Rupert Hart-Davis. Murray, 1978. xi,220p.
——Volume two 1956–57. 1979. x,226p.
*many cricket references; continuing*

6935 **Meredith, George**
■ The letters of George Meredith, collected and edited by his son William Maxse Meredith. 2 vols. Constable, 1912
*one letter describes a visit to Lord's, another dated July 4th 1863 gives an amusing account of the Prince of Wales who, having missed two*

*easy catches whilst fielding, was subsequently bowled first ball*

6936 **Parry,** *Sir* **William Edward**
■ Journal of a second voyage for the discovery of a north-west passage from the Atlantic to the Pacific; performed in the years 1821–22–23 in His Majesty's Ships Fury and Hecla under the orders of Captain William Edward Parry, R.N., F.R.S., and Commander of the Expedition. Murray, 1824. 572p. illus. folding charts
*frontis. engraved by Edward Finden after a drawing by Captain Lyon, R.N., depicts the crews playing cricket on the ice at Igloolik 1822–23*

6937 **Somers, Percival**
Pages from a country diary. E. Arnold, 1904. viii,280p.

6938 **Teonge, Henry**
The diary, anno 1675 to 1679 now first published. C. Knight, 1825. 327p.
——*another ed.* Edited by G. W. Mainwaring. Routledge, 1927
*reference to cricket at Aleppo in 1676; for full entry see no. 851*

6938 **The Times**
–1 The first cuckoo: a selection of the most
■ witty, amusing and memorable letters to The Times 1900–1975: chosen and introduced by Kenneth Gregory. Times Books/ Allen & Unwin, 1976. 3–350p.
*cricket pp. 25, 36–7, 71–3, 130, 143–6, 275–6, 307–8, 330*

6939 **Turner, Thomas**
■ The diary of Thomas Turner of East Hoathly (1754–1765); edited by Florence Maris Turner (Mrs. Charles Lamb); with an introduction by J. B. Priestley. Lane, 1925. xxxi,112p.
*references to cricket in 1763 and 1764, pp. 77, 85*
——*2nd ed. with title:* The diary of a Georgian shopkeeper; a selection by R. W. Blencowe and M. A. Lower edited with a new introduction by G. H. Jennings. Oxford Univ. P., 1979. 32; 95p. 1 illus.
*also pbk. ed.*

# RELIGIOUS TRACTS

6939 **Barbour. B. M'Call,** *editor*
–1 Bits for our boys. Edinburgh, The Boys' Purity Band. illus.
*vol. vi. pp. 33–4 "Cricket balls"*
*a description, with religious inferences, of how cricket balls are made; pictorial front cover with boy leaning on wall with cricket bat over his shoulder*

6940 **Bennett, Norman**
■ Our cricket match. Cambridge, Grey; Brighton, Friend; London, Simpkin, Marshall, [1893]. 16p.

6941 **Channon, Henry James**
■ A sportsman's parables. Epworth Press, 1936. 80p. frontis.

6942 **[Drummond, Henry]**
■ Baxter's second innings: specially reported for the —— school eleven. Hodder & Stoughton, 1892. 58p.
*bound in the form of a pair of pads, or as a blazer with author's initials and title incorporated on the badge; numerous later editions*

6943 **Duff, Gerald**
At the nets; or, Lessons from cricket. J.W. Butcher, 1909. 64p.

6944 **Entwistle, Mary,** *and* **Spriggs, Elsie H.**
■ The way and its heroes: stories illustrating some of the sayings of Jesus. Cargate P., 1945. 80p. illus.
*includes "Kilikity", a chapter on Charles W. Abel of Papua, pp. 13–19*

6945 **Everard, George**
■ "Your innings": a book for schoolboys. Nisbet, 1883. vii,145p.
*apart from pictorial cover and first page, little or no cricket interest*

6946 **Fleming, James**
William Saunders, the cricketer. Morgan & Scott, [1869]. 72p. frontis.

6947 **H[erschel], E. D.**
Mr. Yates' cricket club, by E.D.H. S.P.C.K., [1899]. 80p. frontis.

6947 **He did it for me:** or, The young cricketer
-1 and other stories. G. Morrish, [c.1888].
■ 45p. illus.
*title-story pp. 9–19*

6948 **"He's out".** Religious Tract Society, for
◘ the London City Mission, n.d. 12p. 1 illus. (Seek Me Early Series, no. 45)

6949 **Impulse** and principle. Monthly Tract Society, [c.1880]. 16p.

6949 **In school** and out of school; or, The
-1 history of William & John. An interesting
■ tale. By one who knows both. William Jones, 1825. [iv],131p.
cricket pp. 72–8
——First American ed. N.Y., William Burgess, jnr., 1827. 111p. frontis.
——*another ed.* Dean and Munday, 1827. [iii],131p. frontis.
*chs. 12, 13 and 14 and frontis. by S. Bellin after R. Seymour of a playground with cricket in progress*

6950 **Jones, J. D.**
The game of life: talks with boys and girls. T. Law, 1907. 148p.

6951 **Jones, Thomas Sherwood**
■ "The great Test match". Home Publishing Co., [c.1935]. 8p.

6952 **Lowe, Alfred Hardwick**
■ Sunlit fields: cricket and the greater game. [Seaton, 1929]. 136p. bibliog.

6953 **Menon, Sreecandath R.K.**
■ A philosophical reading of cricket. Lunawila, Ceylon, [the Author], n.d. 16p.
——*another ed.* Colombo, *printed for private circulation* by Harrisons & Crossfield Ltd., n.d. 12p.
*reprinted from the* Hibbert Journal, *vol. xxvii, no. 1, October, 1938*

6954 **Mogridge, George**
Sunny seasons of boyhood. Religious Tract Society, 1859

6955 **[Parcell, Norman Howe]**
■ The demon bowler, and other talks to schoolboys, by Norman Percival. Skeffington, 1945. 128p.
*religious talks, including 4 with a cricket background*

6956 **"A Picture-Maker",** *pseud.*
The search for pleasure, or Mr. Illspeed's trip to the Cranbrook cricket match, by a Picture-Maker. Cranbrook, R. Waters, 1850. 40p.
-

6956 **Pictures,** prose, and rhymes for children
-1 of all climes. Sunday School Union,
■ [1884]. 158p. illus.
*illustrations with moral captions; cricket pp. 8, 9, 56, 66*

6956 **Sandham, Elizabeth**
-2 The boys school; or, Traits of character in early life: a moral tale. 2nd ed. J. Souter, 1821. 152p. frontis.
*frontis. shows cricket being played, but no cricket in text; 1st publd. 1800*

6957 **T., L. A. M.**
Stories on the Commandments. S.P.C.K., 1865. 208p.
——*2nd ed.* 1869
*cricket references in "Robert Martindale: a story on the sixth Commandment", pp. 89–114*

6958 **Wallis, Reginald**
■ Life's cricket match. Pickering & Inglis, [1939]. 44p. illus.

6959 **Waugh, Thomas**
■ The cricket field of the Christian life. Stockport, the Author, n.d., [c.1900]. 148p. port.

6960 **Yapp,** *Sir* **Arthur Keysall**
Life's cricket. 2nd ed. Partridge, 1907. 16p.

The earliest book illustration of cricket being played (no. 6964): a reproduction book of a design by Hubert Gravelot originally published 7 May 1739 *photo: British Library*

# PICTORIAL RECORDS

## PRINTS, ILLUSTRATIONS AND CATALOGUES

(See also under Cricketana nos. 45–1 to 45–11)

**6961 Ackermann, Rudolph**
The history of Rugby School. R. Ackermann, 1816. illus.
*includes aquatint by J. Stadler after W. Westall of view of the Southern School and dormitories of Rugby School with cricket being played*

**6961 Adamson, Judith**
**–1** Australian film posters 1906–1960.
■ Sydney, Currency P./Australian Film Institute, 1978. 56p. illus. (some col.)
*cricket pp. 21, 22, 30 includes reference to the film "That's cricket" released at the State Theatre, Sydney in 1931. The poster features pictures of Woodfull, Bradman, Ponsford, Oldfield, McCabe, Grimmett and Kippax and is sub-titled "How to play cricket . . . as demonstrated by Australia's greatest players"*

**6962 Alken, Henry**
Illustrations for landscape scenery. Fuller, 1821. 26p. col. illus.
*1 plate on cricket*

**6962 Area Museums Services for South**
**–1 Eastern England**
■ The noble game of cricket. A.M.S.S.E.E., 1975. 6p. fold. 1 illus.
*brochure to accompany cricket exhibition circulated by the Service; text by Diana Rait Kerr*

**6963 Arlott, [Leslie Thomas] John**
■ The picture of cricket. Harmondsworth, Penguin Books, 1955. 32p. illus. & ports. (some col.). (King Penguin Books)

**6963 Arts Council of Great Britain**
**–1** British sporting painting, 1650–1850. The
■ Council, 1974. 160p. illus. & ports. (some col.), bibliog.
*in hardback and paperback: catalogue of an exhibition held at the Hayward Gallery, London, 13 Dec. 1974–23 Feb. 1975, Leicester Museum and Art Gallery, Leicester, 8 Mar.–6*

*Apr. 1975, Walker Art Gallery, Liverpool, 25 Apr.–25 May 1975. Cricket items pp. 91, 119, 121, 122, 229, 317, 332, 359*

**6964 Bickham, George,** *the elder*
■ The British monarchy; or, a New chorographical description of all the dominions subject to the King of Great Britain . . . with a short description of the American Colonies. G. Bickham, 1743. 188f. illus.
——*another ed.* 2 vols. G. Bickham, 1784. 190f. illus.
——*another ed.* G. Bickham, jun., 1749. 188f. illus.
*an illustration on f. 129 depicts children playing cricket, a reversed print of the first known depiction of cricket by the French artist Gravelot, issued in England in 1739. See Bowen (no. 62) pp. 32 and 36 (illus.)*

**6965 Birkett, William Norman,** *1st baron Birkett*
■ *of Ulverston*
The game of cricket; illustrated by a series of pictures in the museum of the Marylebone Cricket Club, principally from the collection of the late Sir Jeremiah Colman; with an introductory essay by Sir Norman Birkett and notes on the illustrations by Diana Rait Kerr. Batsford, 1955. 144p. illus. & ports. (some col.)

**6965 Blue Band Margarine**
**–1** Sportboek. Deel 1–10. Blue Band Margarine, [1954?]. col. paste-down illus.
*Dutch text. Each part contains a cricket article*

**6966 Blunden, Edmund Charles**
English villages. Collins, 1941. 48p. illus. (some col.). (Britain in Pictures)
*references to cricket and reproduction of "The cricketers" by Peter de Wint*

**6966 Boorman, Henry Roy Pratt**
**–1** Pictures of Maidstone, the county town of Kent. Maidstone, Kent Messenger, 1965. 230p. illus. ports.
*photographs of cricket and cricketers pp. 95–9, 180*

**6967 Cardus, Sir Neville, and Arlott, [Leslie**
■ **Thomas] John**
The noblest game: a book of fine cricket

589

prints. Harrap, 1969. 29[129]p. illus. & ports. (some col.)
——limited ed. of 100 copies signed and numbered. 1969

6967 **Carita, Roberto**
–1 Lo sport nell 'arte. Bergamo, Instituto Italiano D'Arti Grafiche, 1960. 114p. illus.
*includes pp. 86–7 two early cricket pictures, "Incontro di cricket, Londra" by Henry Hodgino, and "Lezione di cricket, Londra" by Arthur Davis*

6967 **The centenary** & jubilee pair: a commem-
–2 orative folder issued in honour of the Centenary Test . . . and the Jubilee Test . . . Test & County Cricket Board, [1977]. 8p. ports. facsims.
*contains team portraits, printed scorecards and Australian and G.P.O. first day covers; limited to 500 numbered copies*

6967 **Centenary** of Australia & England Test
–3 cricket 1877–1977. Print folio. Sydney, 1977. 16p. col. illus. facsims. scores
*with loose insert of 6 colour prints; limited ed.*

6967 **Christie's,** *auctioneers*
–4 The sale of pictures, etc., belonging to Sir Jeremiah Colman, Bt., September 18th, 1942
*31 of the 180 lots have a cricket theme*

6968 **Colman,** *Sir* **Jeremiah,** (1859–1942),
■ *compiler*
The noble game of cricket; illustrated and described from pictures, drawings and prints in the collection of Sir Jeremiah Colman, Bt., at Gatton Park, Surrey; with an introduction by Clifford Bax. Batsford, 1941. viii,434p. illus. & ports. (some col.)
*limited ed. of 150 copies*

6968 **Coombs, David**
–1 Sport and the countryside in English
■ paintings, watercolours and prints. Oxford, Phaidon, 1978. 192p. illus. (some col.)
*cricket pp. 84, 86, 87*

6969 **Cricket** calendar 1899. Marcus Ward,
■ [1898]. 12p. illus.
*the only issue; a calendar in book format, 2 months to a page, with background illustrations of cricket interest*

6969 **Cricket** colour collection. Melbourne,
–1 Lavardin Pty. Ltd., [1978?]. 80p. col. illus.
*illustrations of Australia v. India, World Series Cricket and New Zealand v. England*

6970 **Dagley, Richard,** *artist*
■ Death's doings; consisting of numerous original compositions, in prose and verse,

the friendly contributions of various writers; principally intended as illustrations of twenty-four plates designed and etched by R. Dagley. J. Andrews; W. Cole, 1826. xviii,369p. illus.
*contains 'The game of life; or, Death among the cricketers', a poem by S. Maunder, with an etching 'The cricketer' by R.D.; and a prose piece 'Death and the cricketer', by Barnard Batwell*
——2nd ed. with considerable additions. 1827. 2 vols.
*includes obituary on John Small the last survivor of the original members of the Hambledon C.C. in vol. 1 p. 69*

6971 **A descriptive** catalogue of the unique
■ collection of cricket trophies, curios, historic bats, balls, early cricket pictures, engravings, and prints; arranged by W. L. Murdoch, Esq. & Mr. Alfred J. Gaston. Exhibited in aid of the funds of the Sussex C.C.C. Brighton, Southern Publishing Co., [1894]. 16p. 1 illus. on cover

6972 **Descriptive** key to Mason's national print
■ of a cricket match between Sussex and Kent, 1849. Brighton, W. H. Mason; London, Gambert, 1849. 23p. 1 illus.
*issued only to purchasers of the artist's proof: see also no. 6998*

6973 **Dickens, Charles**
■ The posthumous papers of the Pickwick Club; with forty-three illustrations, by R. Seymour and Phiz. Chapman & Hall, 1837. xvi,609p. illus.
*contains the cricket plate facing p. 69 by R. W. Buss omitted from later edns.*

6973 **Eagar, Patrick,** *and* **Arlott, John**
–1 An eye for cricket. Hodder & Stoughton,
■ 1979. 208p. illus. & ports. (some in col.)
*index by Jim Coldham*

6974 **East, Laurence,** *artist*
■ Australian cricketers 1926: portraits drawn from life and signed by each player [text by Frank Thorogood]. Fleetgate Publications, 1926. 32p. ports. stats.

6975 Autographed sketches of the 1930 Austra-
■ lian cricketers drawn from life . . . , biographical notes by G. C. Dixon. Jenkins, [1930]. 39p. ports. stats.

6976 **Elliott, Mary**
The rose, containing original poems for young people. Darton, 1826. 36p. illus.
*cricket pp. 24–25; frontis. depicts boys playing cricket*

**6977 Elphinston, James**
■ Education: [a poem] in four books. P.
Vaillant, W. Owen and J. Richardson,
1763. [i],136p. folding illus.
*cricket pp. 52–53 and frontis. engraving*
*shows cricket in foreground of Kensington*
*House School, London, founded by the author*
*in 1753*

**6978 Fenning, Daniel**
The universal spelling book; or, A new
and easy guide to the English language.
1756. illus.
*numerous eds. e.g. 71st ed. 1823; with*
*cricket illustrations*

**6979 Fielding, Hugh**
■ The ABC of cricket: a black view of the
game. Chatto & Windus, 1903. [31]p.
illus.
*26 full-page silhouettes*

**6980 Freude** und Arbeit: offizielles Organ des
internationalen Zentrabüros Freude and
Arbeit. Berlin, Walter Kiel
*issue for Feb. 1939*
*contains pp. 4–5 double-spread reproduc-*
*tion of the painting 'Cricket at Moulsey*
*Hurst', wrongly captioned 'Cricketspiel: the*
*Pavilion at Lord's Cricket Ground"*

**6980 Frost and Reed Ltd**
**–1** Play the game: an exhibition of modern
■ sporting paintings. Bristol, Frost and
Reed, [1977]. 16p. incl. covers. illus.
ports.
*contains 6 reproductions of cricket pictures,*
*including the cover in colour, with a list of all*
*those exhibited December 1977 at Frost and*
*Reed's Gallery*

**6980 Geering & Colyer,** *auctioneers*
**–2** Fine art sale at the Spa Hotel, Tunbridge
■ Wells, Kent, Wednesday 28th March
1979. Tunbridge Wells, Geering & Colyer,
[1979]. 27p. illus.
*cricketana nos. 323–51*

**6980 Gillette**
**–3** Nostalgic moments of cricket: a special
■ collector's portfolio. [Camperdown,
N.S.W.], Gillette, [1975]. team ports. on
covers
*a portfolio containing 2 col. reproductions*
*of early cricket scenes in Australia and 1 of*
*'Famous English cricketers' (1880); a poster*
*of Victor Trumper and a 33 rpm record*
*narrated by Ian Chappell*

**6981 Graves Art Gallery,** *Sheffield*
■ Two centuries of cricket art: an exhibition
of paintings, drawings, prints, etc., in the
Graves Art Gallery, Sheffield, 1955.

Sheffield, City of Sheffield Printing and
Stationery Dept., 1955. 44p.
——Supplement. 2p.

**6981 Great** Australian cricket pictures, intro-
**–1** duced by Ian Johnson; photographs and
■ notes compiled by Jack Wilkinson.
Melbourne, Sun Books, 1975. 96p. illus.
ports.

**6981 Green, Stephen,** *editor*
**–2** Backward glances: an album of 60 early
■ cricket photographs, 1857–1917. Newport
(I. of Wight), Richards, [1976]. [64]p.
illus. ports.

**6981 Grundy Art Gallery,** *Blackpool*
**–3** Catalogue of an exhibition of cricket
pictures lent by Sir Jeremiah Colman . . .
June 1935. [Blackpool, the Gallery, 1935].
6p.

**6982 Hove Museum of Art**
Sussex cricket past and present: illustrated catalogue. Hove, Museum of Art,
1957. 24p. illus.

**6983 Laver, James**
■ English sporting prints. Ward, Lock,
1970. 96p. illus.
*contains 3 cricket prints*

**6984 The Laws** of the game of cricket. Cray-
ford, J. Ware
*a print on linen: the cricket scene is an*
*adaptation of Hayman's picture "Cricket in*
*Marylebone Fields" and the Laws (1744 Code)*
*are printed as a border (D. Rait Kerr)*

**6985 Leech, John,** *artist*
"Young troublesome": or, Master Jacky's
holidays; designed and etched by John
Leech. Bradbury & Evans, [1850]. col.
illus.
*a series of coloured engravings*

**6985 Lucas, Edward Verrall,** *and* **Shepard,**
**–1 Ernest H.**
Mr. Punch's county songs. Methuen,
1928. 92p. illus.
*a poem on each odd numbered page sur-*
*rounded by a Shepard illustration, even pages*
*blank, pp. 1–85; notes pp. 87–92; pp. 25*
*(Gloucestershire), 27 (Hampshire), 39 (Lanca-*
*shire), 75 (Warwickshire), 83 (The Two*
*Roses), 85 (Yorkshire) have either pictorial or*
*verse reference to cricket*

**6986 Manchester Art Gallery**
■ Cricket pictures from the collection of Sir
Jeremiah Colman, Bt. 3rd June to 25th
July 1937: [a catalogue]. Manchester, City
of Manchester Art Gallery, [1937]. 20p.
illus.

**6986** **Marsh, Roger,** *artist*
**-1** Exhibition of cricket paintings and prints, portraits and caricatures by Roger Marsh – July 20th–August 3rd, 1977. Cheltenham, Cheltenham & Gloucester Building Society, [1977]
*list of 30 exhibits*

**6987** **Marylebone Cricket Club.** *Imperial Cricket*
■ *Memorial Gallery*
Temporary catalogue. M.C.C., 1953. 9p. *typescript*
*a catalogue of the permanent collection has not been published*

**6987** **Muybridge, Eadweard**
**-1** The human figure in motion: an electric-photographic investigation of consecutive phases of muscular actions. Commenced 1872. Completed 1885. Chapman & Hall, 1901. 277p. illus. port.
*mostly illustrations; cricket sequences pp. 5, 9, 60, 69, 71, 209*

**6988** **National Gallery of British Sports and**
■ **Pastimes**
Cricket exhibition, July 17 to September 30; introduction by John Arlott. National Gallery of British Sports and Pastimes, [1950]. 84p. illus. on covers

**6988** The first 600 selected pictures: [catalogue
**-1** of an exhibition]. Hutchinson House, Stratford Place. The Gallery, *n.d.* 100p.
*includes 44 cricket paintings, drawings, prints, etc.*

**6989** **Nicholson, William,** *artist*
■ An almanac of twelve sports; words by Rudyard Kipling. Heinemann, 1898. 31p. 12 col. illus.
*1 col. plate of batsman with an 8-line verse; a few copies printed from original woodblocks, hand coloured and signed by artist. The cricket plate is reproduced as no. 64 in* Cardus & Arlott. The noblest game

**6990** **Parry,** *Sir* **William Edward**
■ Journal of a second voyage for the discovery of a north-west passage from the Atlantic to the Pacific; performed in the years 1821–22–23 in His Majesty's Ships Fury and Hecla under the orders of Captain William Edward Parry, R.N., F.R.S. and Commander of the Expedition. Murray, 1824. 572p. illus. folding charts
*frontis. engraved by Edward Finden after a drawing by Captain Lyon, R.N. depicts the crews playing cricket on the ice at Igloolik 1822–23*

**6990** **Pimlott, John Alfred Ralph**
**-1** Recreations; illustrations collected and
■ arranged by Arthur Lockwood. Studio

Vista, 1968. 155p. (incl. 80p. of plates). illus. facsims. bibliog. (A Visual History of Modern Britain)
*cricket pp. 11, 20, 33–5, 47–9, 51, 58, 62–4*

**6991** **Ponsonby-Fane,** *Sir* **Spencer Cecil Brab-**
■ **azon,** *and* **Eaton,** *Sir* **Frederick A.,**
*compilers*
Catalogue of the pictures, drawings, sculpture, prints, etc. belonging to the Marylebone Cricket Club. Clowes, 1902. 78p.
——2nd ed. rev. and enl. 1912. xvi,102p.

**6992** **Radclyffe, Charles Walter,** *artist*
■ Memorials of Rugby, from drawings by C. R. [sic] Radclyffe. Rugby, Crossley, 1841–2. illus.
*6 parts in 1. A series of lithographs including in pt. 5 "The school, from the close", showing cricket being played in the foreground*

**6993** Memorials of Charterhouse: a series of
■ original views . . . drawn on stone. Nutt, 1844. illus.
*includes one plate of cricket in the Charterhouse Fields*

**6993** **Reade, Eric**
**-1** The Australian screen: a pictorial history of Australian film making. Melbourne, Lansdowne P., 1975
*includes references to cricket newsreels, the filming in 1924 of "How McDougal topped the score" and in 1936 of "The Flying doctor", which includes Sir Donald Bradman in the cast*

**6994** **Rosenwater, Irving**
■ A portfolio of cricket prints: a nineteenth century miscellany; with an introduction and notes by Irving Rosenwater. Spearman; Holland P., 1962. 30p. illus. & ports. (col.) diagrs.

**6995** **Savillon's** elegies or poems, written by a gentleman, A.B. late of the University of Cambridge. T. Rickaby for Hookham and Carpenter, 1795. 155p. frontis.
*engraved frontis. by B. Reading after T. Cruikshank shows Harrow School with cricket in progress*

**6995** **Shell Ltd.**
**-1** Cricket. Shell Ltd., *n.d.* [12]p. col. illus.
■ *advertisement brochure of coloured posters by Drake Brookshaw showing the five 'Tests' of Shell petrol, with cricketing anecdotes by Philip Trevor*

**6995** **Swinstead, Gene,** *editor*
**-2** Cricket action through the camera.
■ Toorak (Vic.), Garry Sparke for Allsport

Publications, [1977]. 80p. illus. ports.
*illustrations of Australia v. England 1974–75: v. West Indies 1975–76; v. Pakistan 1976–77, and the Centenary Test*

6996 **Tate Gallery**
An exhibition of cricket pictures from the collection of Sir Jeremiah Colman, Bt. June 16th to September 30th, 1934: a catalogue. [Tate Gallery, 1934]. 16p. illus.

6997 **Tayler, Albert Chevalier**
■ The Empire's cricketers: famous players in their characteristic attitudes executed in crayon from drawings by Chevallier Tayler; biographies by G. W. Beldam. Fine Art Society, 1905. 97p. illus.
——de luxe ed. 1905
*originally issued in weekly parts; 48 plates with descriptive text*

6998 **Taylor, Alfred Daniel**
■ The story of a cricket picture (Sussex and Kent). Hove, Emery, 1923. 61p. illus. scores
*on the engraving by W. H. Mason of a match between Sussex and Kent at Brighton, 1849*

6998 **The Tests** 1932–33. Australia v. England:
–1 series of photos illustrating the leading
■ cricketers of to-day, as well as champions of the past. Melbourne, Keating-Wood Pty. Ltd., [1932]. 63p. illus. ports. diagr.

6999 **Tomkins, Charles,** *artist*
■ Views of Reading Abbey, with those of the churches originally connected with it in the County of Berks. 2 vols. printed by J. Whiting for J. Manson, 1805–10
*Vol. 1 contains two engraved plates, one "View of Caversham, through the gateway", the other "Warfield Church", both with cricket being played*

7000 **The Towner Art Gallery,** *Eastbourne*
The artist looks at cricket: exhibition catalogue, 1968. Eastbourne, the Gallery, [1968]
*the exhibition, sponsored by Rothmans of Pall Mall was shown at Taunton, Hove, Eastbourne, Portsmouth and Bournemouth*

7001 **Toynbee, Lawrence,** *artist*
Catalogue of an exhibition of cricketers and other recent paintings. The Leicester Galleries, Exhibition no. 1340, 29th September to 21 October, 1967. illus.

7001 **Tryon Gallery** cricketers series. The
–1 Moorland Gallery Ltd., [1979?]. [6]p. fold.
■ col. ports.
*folder advertising a set of coloured prints by Theodore Ramos of Mike Brearley, Derek Randall, Bob Willis, Alan Knott*

7002 **Usher Art Gallery,** *Lincoln*
■ Catalogue of an exhibition of pictures & mementoes of cricket: arranged in connection with the centenary celebrations of the Lindum Cricket Club and opened on July 30th, 1956, by Mr. R.E.S. Wyatt. Lincoln, Public Libraries, Museum and Art Gallery, 1956. 23p.
*272 items*

7002 **Victoria and Albert Museum**
–1 Charles Dickens: an exhibition to com-
■ memorate the centenary of his death June–Sept. 1970. The Museum, 1970. [xii],185p. illus. ports. facsims. plan
*item no. 78 shows the anonymous painting c.1868 of "Cricket at Gad's Hill", with Dickens bowling. See also note on p. 100*

7002 **Views** and scenery of Chiselhurst. Rock
–2 & Co., [1871?]
*12 topographical prints including one captioned "Cricket Ground, Chiselhurst, Kent, 1871"*

7002 **Views** and scenery of Harrow. J.E. Kay,
–3 [1871?]
*12 topographical prints including one of "The cricket ground, Harrow, 11th September 1860"*

7002 **Views** of Tonbridge School. Rock & Co.,
–4 1865
*six topographical prints, including one of the cricket ground*

7003 **Warner, Oliver**
■ Sport in art. Lighthouse Books, 1950. 31p. illus. (Zodiac Books)
*1 cricket plate with notes*

7004 **Whitbread and Co. Ltd.**
■ Catalogue of the collection of pictures and other items illustrating the history of cricket at "The Yorker"; with an introduction and an anthology of quotations on cricket by A. Lloyd-Taylor. Whitbread, [1954]. 76p. illus. ports.
——*abridged ed.* Cranborne, P., n.d. 15p.
*a list of items in the full Catalogue without the illustrations, introductory matter and selection of writings on cricket*

7004 **White, Gilbert**
–1 Gilbert White's year: passages from The
■ Garden Kalendar and The Naturalist's Journal 1751–1793; selected by John Commander. Scolar P., 1979. 92p. col. frontis. illus.
*cricket illustration p. 26 [drawing done in 1776] by Samuel Hieronymus Grimm*

7005 **Whitechapel Art Gallery**
Sports and pastimes: autumn exhibition 1912: [catalogue]. The Gallery, 1912

7005 Catalogue of an exhibition of cricket and
-1 sporting pictures, Friday Jan. 25 to
Saturday March 2, 1935. The Gallery,
[1935]. 16p.
*the cricket pictures were loaned from the
Jeremiah Colman collection*

7005 Catalogue of works of G.F. Watts, a 19th
-2 century phenomenon, 22 Jan–3 Mar. 1974
*exhibits chosen by John Gage; included
studies for lithographs of Felix, Pilch and
Mynn, the illustrations to* Felix on the bat
*and given by Watts to M.C.C. in 1895*

7006 **Wild, John James**
At anchor: a narrative of experiences
afloat and ashore during the voyage of
H.M.S. "Challenger" from 1872 to 1876.
Illustrated by the Author. London &
Belfast, Ward, 1878. 198p. illus. (some
col.). port. map
*contains a sketch by Wild of a team from
"Challenger" playing against the Bahia C.C.
in 1873; also reproduced in "The voyage of
the Challenger", by Eric Linklater. Murray,
1972. p. 46*

## CARTOONS AND CARICATURES

7007 **[Bird, Cyril Kenneth]**
A gallery of games, by Fougasse. Cape,
[1921]. 56p. illus.
*cartoons, including 4pp, on cricket*

7008 **Blundell, R.W., and Branson, V.M.**
■ Bodywhine: a treatise on the Jardinian
theory; cartoons by R.W. Blundell with a
few words by V.M. Branson. Adelaide,
Rigby, 1933. 40p. incl. covers, illus.

7009 **Calvert, C. Browne**
Comicalities of the cricket field; with the
compliments of the Peninsular Cricket
Club, Detroit, Michigan, 1878. bs. illus.
*series of 8 comic illustrations*
——*another ed.* Sheffield, Hurst, 1878.
illus.
*in Taylor*
——2nd [Eng.] ed. Sheffield, Hurst, 1884.
12p. illus.
*see also no 6913*

7010 **[Campbell, C. Bruce]**
■ The game's the thing! by Rodney. Link
House, 1946. x,122p. illus.
*humorous drawings with accompanying
text*

7011 **Cricket** terms. C.W. Faulkner, [c.1900].
illus.
*a set of comic cards*

7012 **Crombie, Charles E.**
■ Laws of cricket. Kegan Paul, Trench,
Trubner for "Perrier" Water, [1907]. 12p.
col. illus.
*humorous illustrations with captions*
——facsim. issue *of the 12 coloured prints
mounted on cards loose in folder.* Crombie
Illustrations Ltd., 1978

7012 **Fieldhouse, Harry**
-1 Huddersfield sportsmen of then and
now. Harry Fieldhouse's cartoons from
the Saturday Evening "Examiner".
[Huddersfield, the "Examiner", c. 1935].
47f.
*46 full page cartoons*

7012 **Glover, Tom**
-2 Ow Zat!: souvenir of the 1932-3 Tests.
■ Sydney, Angus & Robertson, 1932. [20]p.
illus.
*cartoons; pre-series*

7013 **[Graham, Alex]**
■ Please sir, I've broken my arm. . .: a spor-
ting commentary in cartoons, by
"Graham". N. Vane, 1959. 93p. illus.

7014 **Hargreaves, [Harry]**
■ How's that! H. Hammond, 1959. [48]p.
illus.

7015 Not out!; edited by Blos. Hammond,
■ Hammond, 1960. 46p. illus.

7016 Googlies. Macmillan, 1971. [64]p. illus.
■ *humorous cartoons*

7017 **Hartt, Cecil L.**
■ Souvenir of the M.C.C. XI, 1924-25:
sketches. Sydney, R.C. Switson, [1924].
[24]p. incl. adverts. illus.

7018 **"Haydn",** *pseud.*
Australian cricketers in cartoon. 1948

7019 **[Hill, Roland Pretty]**
■ Kricket karicatures from the Evening
News, season 1896, by Rip! [Evening
News, 1896]. [16]p. illus.

7020 Rip's kricket karicatures 1899!: souvenir
■ of the season. Evening News, [1899].
[28]p. illus.

7021 Rip's cricket caricatures! from "The
■ Weekly Dispatch": souvenir of the season
1907. Associated Newspapers, [1907].
[16]p. illus.

7021 **King, Jonathan**
-1 Stop laughing, this is serious: a social
history of Australia in cartoon. Cassell
Australia, 1978. 223p. illus.
*cricket pp. 60,61,73,108,210*

**7022 Lee, Frank**
■ The Ashes?: "cricket"ures of the Australian and English teams: souvenir 5th Test-26th February, 1937. Melbourne, Magnet Publishing Co., [1937]. 36p. illus.
*pre-match; caricatures of the players*

**7022 Maher, Rob**
−1 Cricket cartoons. Surrey Hills (N.S.W.),
■ Page Publications, [c.1975]. 48p. illus.

7022 Wacky Willow: a super collection of gags
−2 to titilate all cricket fans. Shelbourne P.,
■ n.d. [32]p. illus. (A Gresham Laugh-in)

**7023 Mailey, Arthur Alfred**
The Australian fifteen for England. . . caricatured by. . .Arthur Mailey, with an appreciation by Warwick Armstrong and a note on Mailey's art by C.R. Bradish. Melbourne, McCubbin, [1921]. 16p. illus.

7024 Mailey's googlies: a series of sketches and
■ caricatures of English county and Test match cricket. Graphic Publications, [1921]. 32p. illus.

7025 Who's who in Test cricket: England v.
■ Australia, 1920–21; the caricatures by A. Mailey. Hutchinson, [1921]. [32]p. illus.

7026 Arthur Mailey's book: a series of sketches
■ illustrating the tour through England and Africa by the Australian slow bowler, Arthur Mailey. Sydney, *printed by* Goddard, 1922. 27p. illus.

7027 The men from Australia: a souvenir in
■ pen and pencil. Cassell, [1926]. [24]p. illus.
*cartoons by A.M. articles by H.L. Collins and J.M. Gregory*

7028 Cricket sketches for the 1928–1929 Tests. Sydney, N.S.W. Bookstall Co., 1928. 24p. illus.

7028 The 1930 Australian XI and other caricat-
−1 ures. The Author, 1930. 20p. incl. adverts. illus.

7029 Caricatures of the Australian XI English
■ tour, 1953. Sydney, *printed by* Shepherd & Newman, 1953. [11]p. illus.

**7029 Ralston, W.**
−1 Sport for all ages and limited purses; drawings by W. Ralston. Glasgow, Bryce, [c.1899]. 32p. incl. adverts. illus. (some col.)
*humorous sporting scenes illustrating the "probable cost" of each sport. Cricket illus. on p. 10, recording "probable cost" to the wicket-keeper of two black eyes. (McKenzie Catalogue no. 48)*

**7029 Reed, Edward Tennyson**
−2 Prehistoric peeps from "Punch" drawn by E.T. Reed. Bradbury, Agnew & Co., [1896]. [vi],103p. illus.
*xiv–A cricket match*

**7030 Rowland, Ralph**
■ The humours of sport: 24 pen etchings of cricket, cycling and football. McCaw, Stevenson and Orr, n.d. 24 pages of illus.
*includes 6 cricket illus.*

**7030 Sewell, N.E.J.,** *editor*
−1 1946–7 Test cricketers in caricature and digest of players' records; caricatures by Lionel Coventry. Adelaide, Commercial Publications of South Australia, [1946]. 33p. incl. adverts. illus. stats.
*pre-tour*

**7031 Thackeray, S.K.**
■ Pakistan v/s India: cricketers in cartoon. Bombay, S.K. Thackeray, [1960]. [36]p. ports.

**7031 Tidy, Bill**
−1 Sporting chance. Hammond, Hammond & Co., 1961. 42p. illus.
*4 pages of cricket cartoons*

**7032 Ullyett, Roy**
□ Daily Express sports cartoons, Beaverbrook Newspapers, [1956]. [152]p. illus.
*cover-title: "Roy Ullyett's sports cartoon annual"*
*includes cartoons of England v. Australia 1956*
—— *annually with title:* Daily Express sports cartoon annual
*1958–1974?*

**7033 Watkins, Mike**
■ The funnier side of cricket: a collection of cricket cartoons. [Southampton], Shirley Press Ltd., [197–]. [36]p. incl. covers. illus.
*36 cartoons drawn by M.W.; proceeds in aid of the Hampshire Fighting Fund*

7033 Out in the middle: a book of cricket
−1 cartoons [in aid of] the Alan Ormrod
■ benefit fund. n.p., [1977]. 28p. incl. adverts. illus. port.

**7034 Webster, Tom**
Tom Webster of the "Daily Mail" among the sportsmen. Associated Newspapers, 1920. 96p. illus.

7035 Tom Webster's annual: cartoons from the
■ Daily Mail, Evening News, and Weekly Dispatch. Associated Newspapers. illus.
*1921–39*

A page from George Shepherd's sketch book, c. 1790 depicting, amongst others, the only representations we have of three Hambledon cricketers – David Harris, Tom Walker and William "Silver Billy" Beldam. (See no. 7228) *photo: M.C.C.*

# SPORTS AND GAMES
### (with references to cricket)

## FOR ADULTS

### 19th Century Works

**7036  Balck, Viktor Gustaf,** *editor*
■ Illustrerad idrottsbok handledning i olikar grenar af idrott och lekar. Parts I-III & Supplement. Stockholm, Fitze, 1886–88. illus. diagrs.
*cricket in Pt I, 1886, pp. 139–161; a handbook covering a number of sports in Swedish*

**7037  Beleze, Guillaume Louis Gustave**
Jeux des adolescents. Paris, Hachette, 1856, ii,355p. illus.
——2nd ed. 1858. viii,365p. illus.
——3rd ed. 1866. viii,367p. illus.
——5th ed. 1879. viii,352p. illus.
——6th ed. 1891. viii,352p. illus.

**7038  Bell, Ernest** *editor*
Handbook of athletic sports. 2 vols. Bell, 1890. illus. diagrs. (Bohn's Library of Sports and Games)
*"Cricket" by Edward Lyttelton, vol. 1., pp. 1–104*

**7039  Blaine, Delabere Pritchett**
□ An encyclopaedia of rural sports: or, A complete account, historical, practical, and descriptive, of hunting, shooting, fishing, racing and other field sports and athletic amusements of the present day. Longman, etc., 1840. xx,1240p. illus.
——new edition, revised and corrected. Longman, etc. 1848
——new ed. rev. & corr. by "Harry Hieover" pseud., A. Graham, esq., "Ephemera" pseud., etc. Longman, etc. 1852.
——new ed. rev. & corr. Longman, etc. 1858.
——new ed., rev. & corr. Longmans, Green, 1870
——new ed. rev. & corr. Longmans, Green, 1875
*cricket pp. 133–136a (5pp.)*

**7040  Burnand, Sir Francis Cowley**
■ Present pastimes of Merrie England interpreted from ancient Mss. and annotated by F.C. Burnand; with illustrations drawn

from ye quicke by J.E. Rogers. Cassell, Peter and Galpin, 1873. [iii]32p. col. illus.
*cricket pp. 30–32*

**7041  Cassell's** book of sports and pastimes.
□ Cassell, 1881. illus. port. diagrs.
*cricket pp. 1–28, 556–8*
——*another ed. issued in 15 parts.* [1886]
——new ed. 1888
——popular ed. *issued in 31 weekly parts.* [1896]
——new & revised ed. *with title:* Complete book. . .1896. 976p. illus. port. diagrs.

**7042  Chadwick, Henry**
■ The reliable book of outdoor games: containing official rules for playing base ball, foot ball, cricket, lacrosse, tennis, croquet, etc. New York, F.M. Lupton, 1893. 58p. illus. (The People's Handbook Series)

**7043  Cheer, John**
British angler's instructor, archer's guide, rules of cricket and catalogue of prices. Howlett, 1855. 120p.
*10p on cricket*

**7044  Egan, Pierce**
Pierce Egan's book of sports and mirror of life. T.T. & J. Tegg, 1832. iv,414p. illus. scores.
——*another ed.* 1836
——*another ed.* 1840
——*another ed.* 1847
*originally issued in 25pts., no. 22 (p. 337–352) being devoted entirely to cricket, with an article on Hambledon cricket, John Small, and the current Laws*

**7045  Fittis, Robert Scott**
■ Sports and pastimes of Scotland, historically illustrated. Paisley, Alexander Gardner, 1891. 212p. illus.
*cricket pp. 209–12*

**7046  Gale, Frederick**
■ Modern English sports: their use and their abuse. Sampson Low, 1885. xx, 201p. illus. ports.
——L.P. ed. of 100 copies. 1885
*cricket pp. 10–33*

7046 Sports and recreations in town and
-1 country. Swan Sonnenschein, 1888.
[viii],224p.
  *scattered cricket references but chapters
  "Bankruptcy in Arcadia" and "When we old
  Fogeys were boys" deal mainly with cricket*

7046 **Greville, Beatrice Violet,** *baroness Greville*
-2 The gentlewoman's book of sports. I.
Henry, [1892?]. 227p. ports. (The Victoria
Library for Gentlewomen)
  *pp. 161-76 'Cricket' by Lady Milner*

7046 **Hall, Henry,** *editor*
-3 The Tribune book of open-air sports
prepared by The New York Tribune with
the aid of acknowledged experts. N.Y.,
The Tribune Assoc., 1887. vii,500p.
  *cricket pp. 128-36. "This book is printed
  without type, being the first product in book
  form of the Mergenthaler machine (linotype)
  which wholly supersedes the use of moveable
  type".*

7047 **Harewood, Harry**
■ A dictionary of sports; or, companion to
the field, the forest and the riverside.
Tegg, 1835. vi,365p.
  *cricket pp. 91-2*

7048 **Heineken, Philipp**
Die beliebsten Rasenspiele: eine Zusam-
menstellung der hauptsachlichsten
Englischen Out Door Games zum zwecke
ihrer Einfuhrung in Deutschland. Stuttgart, Gustav Weise, 1893. illus.
  *includes section on cricket, which was
  reprinted separately. (See no. 438). Frontis
  shows cricket match at Cannstat in 1892. Also
  contains article, with an illustration, on
  ladies' cricket*

7049 **Howard, Henry Charles,** *earl of Suffolk &*
*Berkshire, and others, ed.*
The encyclopaedia of sport. 2 vols.
Lawrence & Bullen, 1897-8. illus.
  *cricket vol. 1. pp. 210-47*
——new and enlarged ed. 4 vols. Heinemann, 1911. illus.
  *cricket vol. 1. pp. 439-496*
  *see no. 430 and also no. 7159*

7049 **Howe, W.H.**
-1 Everybody's book of games (outdoor).
Howe, 1890. viii,167p. (Everybody's Series)
  *cricket pp. 53-61*

7050 **McGregor, Robert**
■ Pastimes and players. Chatto & Windus,
1881. 203p. (Mayfair Library)
  *"Early forms of cricket", pp. 1-10;
  "Cricketana", pp. 11-24*

7051 **Manly** exercises, sports and games, by
the Champion players of old England.
Dean, [1875]. 518p. illus. diagrs.

7052 **Maxwell, William Hamilton**
The field book: or, Sports and pastimes of
the United Kingdom. Effingham Wilson,
1833. viii,616p. illus.
  *cricket pp. 139-41*

7053 **A new** book of sports: reprinted from the
■ "Saturday Review". Bentley, 1885. iv,
376p.
  *includes "Cricket in America" pp. 271-79*

7053 **Palmer, Harry Clay,** *and others*
-1 Athletic sports in America, England and
Australia . . . Philadelphia (Pa.),
Hubbard Bros, 1889. 711p. illus. (some
col.), ports.
  *cricket played by U.S. baseball round-the-
  world team on ship and in Australia pp.
  228-30,234,249-50; 'Cricket' by J.A. Fynes,
  pp. 681-4 and portraits*

7054 **[Pardon, George Frederick]**
Games for all seasons, by G.F.P. Blackwood, 1858. 280p.
  *cricket pp. 9-23*
——another ed. 1868

7055 **Peverelly, Charles A.**
The book of American pastimes, containing a history of the principal base ball,
cricket, rowing and yachting clubs of the
United States. N.Y., Peverelly, 1866.
556p.
——2nd ed. 1868.

7056 **Strange, F.W.**
■ Outdoor games. Tokyo, Maruya, 1883.
[vii],55p. diagrs.
  *cricket pp. 30-37*

7057 **Strutt, Joseph**
□ Glig-gamena angel deod; or, The sports
and pastimes of the people of England.
T. Bensley for J. White, 1801. [2],lvi,301p.
illus.
  *cricket pp. 83-84*
  *many later eds. including:*
——much enlarged & corrected new
edition by J. Charles Cox. Methuen, 1903.
377p. illus.
——rptd. Detroit, Singing Tree P., 1968.
  *for fuller entry see no. 836*

7057 **Take** my advice on games & how to play
-1 them: and domestic pets, etc.: a book for
every home. Blackwood, [c.1864]. 56p.
(Take my advice series)
  *includes cricket*

7058 **Trollope, Anthony,** *editor*
■ British sports and pastimes. Virtue, 1868. [v],322p.
*"On cricket", pp. 290–322; rptd. from Saint Paul's Magazine*

7059 **Walker, Donald**
□ Games and sports; being an appendix to "Manly exercises" and "Exercises for Ladies". Hurst, 1837. xviii,369p. illus. diagrs.
*cricket pp. 214–236, includes the Laws as revised in 1835*
——new ed. Thomas, 1840. xii,230p. illus.
*cricket pp. 135–149*
——new ed. Orr, 1842

7060 **[Walsh, John Henry]**
Manual of British rural sports, by "Stonehenge". Routledge, 1856. xvi,720p. illus.
*cricket pp. 490–9*
——*numerous eds. e.g.* 16th ed. 1886

7061 ——, *and* **Wood, John George**
■ Athletic sports and manly exercises, by 'S.', J.G. Wood, etc. Routledge, 1864. 477p. illus. diagrs.
*cricket pp. 128–55*

7062 **W[heeler], C.A.,** *editor*
■ Sportascrapiana: cricket and shooting. . . by celebrated sportsmen; with hitherto unpublished anecdotes of the nineteenth century. . .; edited by CAW. Simpkin, Marshall, 1867. xvi,328p.
——*2nd ed. with title:* Sportascrapiana: facts in athletics. 1868. xvi,301p.
——cheap ed. 1870
*reminiscences of E.H. Budd*

7062 **Wilson, Tom**
–1 Illustrerad spelbok. Stockholm, Looström and Komps Forlag, 1888. 460p. illus.
*pp. 453–6 'I kricket'. Swedish text; trans.: Illustrated book of games*

## 20th Century Works

7063 **Adventures** in British sport. Murray, 1926. 184p. illus.
*cricket pp. 12–41*

7064 **Aflalo, Frederick George,** *editor*
■ The sports of the world. Cassell, 1903. viii,416p. illus.
*includes 'Australian cricket and cricketers' by W.J. Ford, pp. 305–09, and 'Cricket and cricketers' by Philip Trevor, pp. 340–43*
——2nd ed. 1905

7065 **The Aldin** book of outdoor games.
■ Eyre & Spottiswoode, 1933. xv,695p. illus. ports. diagrs.
*"Cricket" by M.D. Lyon, pp. 507–695*

7065 **Arlott, [Leslie Thomas] John,** *editor*
–1 The Oxford companion to sports and games; [line drawings by Carl James].
■ O.U.P., 1975. viii,1144p. illus. ports. diagrs.
——*pbk. ed.* St. Albans, Paladin, 1977. viii,1010p.

7065 **Atyeo, Don**
–2 Blood & guts: violence in sports. N.Y. & London, Paddington P., 1979. 384p. illus. bibliog.
*cricket pp. 293–5*

7065 **Australia's** sporting heritage. Melbourne,
–3 Southdown P., *n.d.* 56p. incl. covers.
■ illus. ports.
*includes articles on Don Bradman, Jardine & Larwood, Keith Miller*

7066 **Bade, Edwin**
■ The mechanics of sport: an elementary instructional handbook for all sportsmen, emphasizing the factors governing ball control with particular reference to fooball, cricket and golf . . . Kingswood (Surrey), Elliot, 1952. 107p. diagrs. (Right Way Books)
*Ch. v. "Cricket applications and tactics"*

7067 **Bass, Howard**
■ The sense in sport. Ilfracombe, Stockwell, [1945]. 96p. illus. port.
*concerning the value of sport; many cricket references*

7068 **Boldspil.** Køhbenhavn, Erichsen, [c.1908].
■ [iv],152p. illus. ports. diagrs.
*"Kricket" by H. Kalkan, pp. 49–79. In Danish*

7069 **Book** of rules of games and sports revised
■ and brought up-to-date. 16th ed. Calcutta, Y.M.C.A., [1962]. [viii],378p. diagrs.
*cricket pp. 74–95. The latest ed. seen*

7070 **Central Youth Employment Executive**
■ Choice of careers 120: professional sport. H.M.S.O., 1969. 40p. illus.
*cricket pp. 15–19*

7071 **Cerfberr, G.**
■ Les sports de plein air. Paris, Librarie de Paris, [1922–3]. [iv],283p. illus. ports. diagrs.
*in French. "Le cricket", pp. 93–97 with illus. 'Le batteur défend son "wicket" '*

7072 **Daily Express**
■ Book of popular sports; edited by Thomas Knowles Hodder. Daily Express, [1936]. 496p. illus. diagrs. stats.
*cricket pp. 144–74, with averages, etc. for 1935*

Illustrations: "The Cricketer", an etching by
Richard Dagley from his 'Death's Doings' (no.
6970) *photo: M.C.C.*

Sir Max Beerbohm's "Portrait of dear old
W. G. – to the left is the Grand Stand, to the
right, the funeral of one of his patients"
*photo:  M.C.C.*

Cartoons: "It's all in the game" by H. M. Bateman

LET'S HAVE A NICE GAME OF CRICKET
OR A POSSIBLE SCENE AT BRISBANE IN THE NEXT TEST MATCH.

Tom Webster's cartoon from the 1933 issue of no. 7035 commenting on the Body-line tour of 1932–33

**7073 Daish, C.B.**
■ The physics of ball games. English Univ. P., 1972. [v],180p. illus. diagrs. bibliog.

**7074 Darwin, Bernard [Richard Meirion]**
■ British sport and games. Longmans, Green, for the British Council, 1940. 42p. illus. (British Life and Thought)
——rev. ed. 1945. 39p.
*cricket pp. 16–20*

**7075 Eberbach, Kurt von**
Rasenspiele: erster Band: Golf, Krocket, Bowls, Kricket. Leipzig, Grethlein, [1901]. 160p. illus. diagrs. (Bibiliothek für Sport und Spiel)
*in German*

**7076 Encyclopaedia** of sports, games and pastimes. Amalgamated P., 1935. 768p. illus.
*cricket pp. 180–95*

**7076 Encyclopedia Britannica**
**–1** The book of sports and games [by] numerous eminent authorities, from their articles in the Encyclopedia Britannica. Encyclopedia Britannica, [1925?]. 69p. illus.
*cricket pp. 32–9*

**7077 Fenton, J. Vinten**
Games and sports by progressive practice: a handbook for training college students, teachers and youth leaders. Allen & Unwin, 1945. 184p. illus.

**7078 Francis, Philip Harwood**
The principles of missile games: field athletic sports, cricket, baseball, lawn tennis, football, bowls, etc. Liverpool, T. Brakell, 1948. 70p.

**7079** A study of targets in games. The Mitre
■ P., [1951]. 235p. illus. diagrs.
*cricket pp. 177–184*

**7080 The game:** The Marshall Cavendish encyclopedia of world sports. Marshall Cavendish, 1969–71. illus & ports. (some col.) diagrs. stats.
*issued in 126 weekly parts, each part having 28p., forming 8 vols. plus index*

**7080 Goulstone, John**
**–1** Modern sport: its origins and develop-
■ ment through two centuries. [Bexleyheath], the Author, 1974. 86p. *typescript*
*cricket pp. 25–38*

**7080 Grayson, Edward**
**–2** Sport and the law. Sunday Telegraph,
■ 1978. 78p. illus.

**7081 Harvey, Charles,** *editor*
■ Encyclopaedia of sport. Sampson Low. Marston, 1959. 328+16p. illus. ports. scores. stats.
*cricket pp. 105–126. with badges of county cricket clubs in colour, p. 11*
——another ed. with title: Encyclopaedia of sport and sportsmen. 1966. [viii],624p. illus. ports. diagrs. stats.
*cricket pp. 21–33,67–76,190–211,515–20, 580–7,612–3*

**7082** Sport international. Sampson Low, 1960. 416p. illus. ports. stats.
*contains "Cricket" compiled by Roy Webber, pp. 129–56: "Women's cricket" compiled by Netta Rheinberg, pp. 157–58*

**7082 Howard, Bruce**
**–1** A nostalgic look at Australian sport. Adelaide, Rigby, 1978. 208p. illus. ports.
*many cricket refs.*

**7082 Jaques, T.D., and Pavia, G.R.**
**–2** Sport in Australia: selected readings in physical activity. Sydney, McGraw-Hill, 1976. viii,171p.
*for full entry see no. 3339–1*

**7082 Jodey, J.M.**
**–3** Sportsmaths. Blond Educational, 1965. 118p. illus. ports.
*cricket pp. 5–7,76–7,81–3, 106–9,116–8*
——metricated ed. 1972. 92p. illus.

**7083 Joy, Bernard**
Forward Arsenal! a history of the Arsenal Football Club. Phoenix House, 1952. xvi,208p. illus.
——rev. ed. Panther Books, 1957. 191p.
*includes references to cricket*

**7084 Kircher, Rudolf**
■ Fair play: the games of merrie England; translated (from the German] by R.N. Bradley. Collins, 1928. ix,221p. illus.
*cricket pp. 57–64*

**7085 Knapp, Barbara**
Skill in sport: the attainment of proficiency. Routledge & K. Paul, 1963. xii,204p. illus. diagrs. bibliog.
*cricket pp. 31, 42, 60, 66, 67, 74, 81, 92, 99, 121, 163*

**7085 Leather, Herbert**
**–1** A book of national games: their value, organization and laws. Blackie & Son, 1914. 172p. diagrs.
*ch. ix, pp. 117–29, "Cricket and its rules"*

**7086 Ledbrooke, Archibald William, and Turner, Edgar**
Soccer from the press box. Kaye, 1950. 224p. illus.

*references to cricket pp. 155–63*
——new ed. Kaye, 1955. [vii],208p. illus.

**7086  Lord, David,** *editor*
**–1**  The best of the last 10 years in Australian sport. Adelaide, H.K. Frost Holdings Pty. Ltd. in association with Lions International and Australian Guarantee Corp. Ltd., 1978. 224p. illus. & ports. (some col.)
*cricket pp. 19–28 by Peter McFarline*

**7087  McBride, Peter**
The philosophy of sport. Heath Cranton, 1932. ix,190p.
*cricket pp. 6, 38, 51, 52*

**7088  McIntosh, Peter C.**
■  Games and sports. Educational Supply Association, 1962. [iv],90p. illus. diagrs. (How Things Developed)
*ch. iv "Stoolball, rounders and cricket", pp. 41–54*

**7089**  Sport in society, Watts, 1963. [i.e. 1964].
■  viii,208p. illus. bibliog.
*cricket pp. 52, 59, 61, 63–67, 70–74, 78, 82, 86, 89, 92, 135–137, 168, 178, 182, 190, 198–199*

**7090  Marples, Morris**
A history of football. Secker & Warburg, 1954. xi,276p. illus.
*scattered cricket references*

**7091  Menke, Frank Grant**
The encyclopedia of sports. N.Y., F.G. Menke, Inc., 1939. 319p. illus. ports.
——rev. and enl. ed. N.Y., Barnes, [1944]. xii, 628p.
——new. and rev. ed. N.Y., [1953]. ix. 1018p.
*cricket pp. 300–305*

**7092  Miles, Charles W.,** *editor*
■  They're off! a journalistic record of British sports by leading writers of the press. Archer, 1934. 278p. illus. ports.
*includes H.J. Henley on cricket, pp. 70–82*

**7093  Natan, Alex**
Sport and society. Cambridge, Bowes and Bowes, 1958. 208p.
*a symposium; slight scattered cricket references*

**7094  National Playing Fields Association**
■  Spotlight on British sport: edited by Louis Palgrave. Croydon, Home Publishing Co., [1952]. 216p. incl. adverts. illus.
*contributions by Sir Pelham Warner, pp. 41–44; Miss Molly Hide, pp. 95–97; Miss Marjorie Pollard, pp. 109–10; D.J. Knight, pp. 175–77; A.E.R. Gilligan, p. 189*

**7095  Noel, Susan,** *editor*
■  Sportswoman's manual. Hutchinson, 1950. 251p. illus. (Hutchinson's Library of Sports and Pastimes)
*"Cricket" by Molly Hide, pp. 88–99*

**7095  The official** world encyclopedia of sports
**–1**  and games: the rules, techniques of play
■  and equipment for over 400 sports and 1000 games; created by the Diagram Group. New York & London, Paddington P., 1979. 543p. col. diagrs.
*an abridged ed. of two works: Rules of the game (1974) and The way to play [c.1975]; cricket pp. 408–41*

**7096  Outdoor** sports: a complete guide to field and lawn games . . . giving the latest official regulations. Cassell, 1913. xi,336p. illus. diagrs.
*cricket p. 68–103*

**7097  Parker, Eric**
■  British sport. Collins for the Penns in the Rocks P., 1941. 48p. illus. (some col.). (Britain in Pictures)
*cricket pp. 30–36*

**7097  Patmore, Angela**
**–1**  Playing on their nerves: the sport experiment. S. Paul, 1979. 272p. illus.
*cricket pp. 29–51, 121–3, 131–2, 150–5, 189–90, 231, 235–6; the mental and physical pressures imposed by competitive sport*

**7098  Pick, John Barclay**
The Phoenix dictionary of games: outdoor, covered court and gymnasium, indoor: how to play 458 games. Phoenix House, 1952. 318p. diagrs.

**7099  The spectators'** handbook: an aid to the
■  appreciation of athletics, boxing, cricket, association and rugby football and lawn tennis. Phoenix House, 1956. 144p. illus. diagrs.
*cricket pp. 65–87*
——another ed. Sportsman's Book Club, 1958

**7100  Powell, Peter**
■  Good-bye games!: the modern degradation of sport. Search Publishing Co., 1932. 73p. (New Angle Books)
*scattered cricket references*

**7101  Presinksy, Franz**
□  Lawn tennis sowie zehn der beliebtesten englischen Kugel-und Ballspiele. Leipzig, Weber, 1907. viii,254p. illus. diagrs.
*ch. 8, Das Kricket (Torballspiel), pp. 129–161*

7101 **Scholtz, Gest Johannes Lindeque**
-1 Kompetisie en aggressie in spel en sport. Potchefstroom, Pro Rege-pers, 1977. vii,338p. bibliog.
*in Afrikaans: trs. "Competition and aggression in games and sport*

7102 **Sports** and games: official rules. N. Kaye, 1949. 488p. illus. diagrs.
——*subsequently issued with title*: Official rules of sports and games
——2nd ed. 1950–51. 1950. 500p.
——3rd ed. 1954–55. 1954. 539p.
——4th ed. 1957–58. 1957. 554p.
——5th ed. 1961–62. 1961. 596p.
——6th ed. 1964–65. 1964. 682p.
——7th ed. 1966–67. 1966. 675p.
——8th ed. 1968–69. 1968. 716p.
——9th ed. 1970–71. 1970. 778p.
——10th ed. 1972–73. 1972. 801p.
——[11th ed.] 1974–75. 1974. 806p.
——[12th ed.] 1976–77. 1976. 862p.
——[13th ed.] 1978–79. 1978. 870p.
*includes the Laws of cricket*

7102 **Sports facts 1979**: results, records,
-1 figures; edited by Graham Edge and
■ Keith Walmsley. Macdonald and Jane's, 1979. 345p. stats.
*cricket pp. 122–72*

7102 **Starmer-Smith, Nigel**
-2 The Barbarians: the official history of the
■ Barbarian Football Club. Macdonald & Jane's, 1977. 240p. illus. ports. facsims.
——*another ed.* Macdonald & Jane's in association with Futura Publications, 1978. 240p. illus. ports. facsims.
*cricket pp. 30–1 with team portrait of the Barbarian XI who played against the Corinthians at Queen's Club, 30 April, 1892*

7102 **The Sunday Times** sports book; edited
-3 by John Lovesey, Nicholas Mason and
■ Edwin Taylor. World's Work, 1979. 288p. illus. ports. diagrs.
*a selection of articles & photographs from* The Sunday Times *sports pages "over more than a decade"; many cricket references*

7103 **Thompson, Richard**
■ Race and sport. O.U.P. (under the auspices of the Institute of Race Relations), 1964. [vii], 73p.
*ch. v. 'Colour bar cricket' reviews the New Zealand tour of South Africa 1961–62*

7104 **Trembath, Hedley,** *editor*
■ British sport. Skelton Robinson, British Yearbooks, [1947]. 270p. illus.
*with biographical notes on contemporary sportsmen*

7104 **Ueberhorst, Horst,** *compiler*
-1 Geschichte der Leibesübungen. Band 4.
■ Berlin, Bartels & Wernitz K.G., 1972. 236p. illus. bibliog.
*the history of physical exercise: text mostly in English, cricket included in article "Sport in Britain" by Prof. H.A. Harris, pp. 134–81*

7105 **Vachell, Horace Annesley**
■ The best of England. Faber, 1930. [vii], 271p.
*cricket pp. 127–35*

7105 **Viney, Nigel,** *and* **Grant, Neil**
-1 An illustrated history of ball games.
■ Heinemann, 1978. [vi],201p. illus. facsims. bibliog.
*cricket pp. 73–86*

7106 **Wakelam, Henry Blythe Thornhill**
Harlequin story: the history of the Harlequin Football Club. Phoenix House, 1954. 172p. illus.
——*another ed.* Sportsman's Book Club, 1947
*scattered references to cricket*

7107 **[Warner,** *Sir* **Pelham Francis]**, *editor*
British sports and sportsmen past and present; compiled and edited by "The Sportsman". British Sports and Sportsmen, [1908–1936?]. 16 vols. illus. ports.
*Vol. 5. Cricket and football, 1917. xiii, 579p.*
*limited to 1,000 copies; cricket pp. 1–211*

7108 **Watson, Alfred Edward Thomas,** *editor*
■ English sport. Macmillan, 1903. xi, 361p. col. illus.
*includes "Cricket" by Lord Hawke, pp. 123–36*

7109 **Wheeler, Kenneth,** *editor*
■ Sports rules and records handbook. Hamlyn, 1962. 320p. illus. ports. diagrs. stats.
*contains ch., pp. 107–17, on cricket with stats. and summary of laws, etc.*

7110 **Whitcher, Alec E.**
■ Sportsman's club; illustrated by Reg Carter. Brighton, printed by Southern Publishing Co., [1948]. 229p. illus.
*cricket pp. 105–40; fact and fiction*

7110 **Whitington, Richard Smallpeice**
-1 Great moments in Australian sport. Melbourne, Macmillan Co. of Australia, 1974. 144p. illus. ports.
——*rptd.* Melbourne, Sun Books, 1975. *pbk.*
*cricket pp. 12–17, 28–33, 46–57*

7111 **Wolfenden Committee on Sport**
■ Sport and the community: report. Central

Council of Physical Education, 1960. vi,135p.
*cricket inter alia*

# FOR CHILDREN

## 18th Century Works

**7111** **[Johnson, Richard]**
**-1** Juvenile sports and pastimes. To which are prefixed, memoirs of the Author: including a new mode of infant education, by Master Michael Angelo. Printed for T. Carman, 177–?
——2nd ed. 1776
——3rd? ed. 1780
*has section on cricket; no copy of the first edition is known to survive; a copy of the 2nd ed. is in the Bodleian Library; two copies of the 3rd? ed. are recorded*

## 19th Century Works

**7111** **Aspin, Jehoshaphat**
**-2** A picture of the manners, customs, sports
■ and pastimes, of the inhabitants of England. . .down to the eighteenth century, selected from the ancient chronicles, and rendered into modern phraseology. J. Harris, 1825. iv,296p. illus.
*cricket pp. 246–9; based on Strutt's "Manners & customs". For children*

**7112** Ancient customs, sports and pastimes of
■ the English; explained from authentic sources, and in a familiar manner. John Harris, 1832. viii,256p. illus. (The Little Library)
——2nd ed. 1835.
*cricket pp. 221–3, for children*

**7112** **Atkinson, John Christopher**
**-1** Walks, talks, travels and exploits of two
□ schoolboys: a book for boys. Routledge, 1859. xi,433p.
——new ed. 1868. xi,433p. illus.
——new ed. Macmillan, 1892. xi,433p. illus.
——*another ed.* 1901
*ch. xiii, pp. 249–70, "The cricket match"*

**7113** **Ball** games. Routledge, [1867]. 64p. illus.
□ diagrs.
*cricket pp. 5–31*
——9th issue [1891?]

**7114** **Bertin, Théodore-Pierre,** *translator*
Les jeux de l'enfance, ou l'heure de récréation du premier et du second âges. . . traduction de l'anglais par T.-P. Bertin. 2 vols. Paris, Brunot-Labbe, 1811. illus.
——*another ed.* 2 vols. 1817. [4],xvi, 164+[iv],160p. illus.
——*another ed.* 1820

*ch. xi "Le jeu de criket" with engraved plates "Le battoir" and "Le cricket"*

**7115** **The book** of games; or, A history of the
□ juvenile sports, practised at the Kingston Academy. J. Adland for Tabart, 1805. [iv],156p. illus.
*cricket pp. 99–104*
——*another ed.* Philadelphia (Pa.), Johnson & Warner, 1811. 108p. illus.
——*another ed* ... . practised at a considerable academy near London. R. Phillips, 1812. 169p. illus.
——*another ed.* . . . . practised at the Kingston Academy. Philadelphia, (Pa.). Warner, 1821. 108p. illus.
——*another ed.* N.Y., G. Long, 1822
——*another ed.* N.Y., T. Illman, 1834
——*another ed.* . . . at the different academies. Philadelphia (Pa.), Crolius & Gladding, 1842

**7116** **Book** of games and sports. Nelson, 1856.
■ 17p. illus.
*cricket p. 8*

**7117** **Boys'** handy book of sports, pastimes,
■ games and amusements. Ward, Lock, [1863]. x,374p. illus. diagrs.
*cricket pp. 201–16; later edns.*

**7118** **The boy's** holiday book for all seasons: containing complete instructions for angling, swimming, conjuring, the making of fireworks, cricket, archery, gymnastics, and the various games for boys. . . Davidson, 1849. 240p. illus.
*cricket pp. 105–14*

**7119** **The boy's** own book: a complete encyclo-
□ pedia of all the diversions, athletic, scientific and recreative of boyhood and youth. Vizetelly, Branston, 1828. iv,448p. illus. diagrs.
*10 editions published by 1835; cricket pp. 19–24*
——20th ed. Longman, Brown, 1842. iv,462p. illus. diagrs.
*cricket pp. 51–6*
——*another ed.* D. Bogue, 1852, 611p. illus. diagrs.
*cricket pp. 67–88*
——new ed. thoroughly revised and partly rewritten. Crosby Lockwood, 1889. viii,726p. illus. diagrs.
*cricket pp. 101–26*

**7120** **Boys'** week-end book. Religious Tract Society, 1836.
——*another ed.* 1851

**7121** **Clarke, Charles Cowden,** *and* **Clarke,**
■ **Mary Victoria Cowden**
"Many happy returns of the day!": a birth-day book; with numerous engrav-

ings by the brothers Dalziel. Lockwood, 1860, viii,237p. illus. diagrs.
——new ed. Lockwood, [1869]. viii, 355p. illus. diagrs.
*cricket pp. 228–44*

7122 **Clarke, William**
Little boy's own book of sports and pastimes. D. Bogue, 1855. 222p. illus.
*a selection of portions of the "Boy's own book", see no. 7119*

7123 **The corner** cupboard: a family repository.
■ Houlston Wright, 1858. xii,368p. illus.
*cricket pp. 248–51*

7124 **Elliott, Alfred**
■ Out-of-doors: a handbook of games for the playground. Nelson, 1872. vii,225p. illus. diagrs.
*cricket pp. 137–51*

7124 **Every** boy's book: a complete encyclo-
-1 paedia of sports and amusements. Routledge, 1856. vi,636p. illus.
*many subsequent editions, e.g. 16th ed. 1889. 912p.*

7124 **Every** boy's book of games, sports, and
-2 diversions, or, The school-boys manual of amusement, instruction and health. Kendrick, 1852. vi,546p. illus.
*cricket pp. 237–54*
——*another ed.* Grieves, 1852. vi, 476p. illus. (1 col.)

7125 **Fuller, *Sir* Thomas Ekins**
■ The boy's holiday book. Tegg, 1865. [iii],544p. illus. diagrs.
*cricket pp. 4–19*

7126 **Games** for all seasons, consisting of
■ indoor and out-door sports. . .:a sequel to "Parlour pastime". Blackwood, 1858. 206p. illus. diagrs.
*cricket pp. 9–19*

7127 **Handbook** of outdoor games. Cassell,
■ Petter & Galpin, [1866]. 61p. illus. diagrs. (Cassell's Sixpenny Handbooks)
*cricket pp. 40–46*

7127 **Hoffman, Louis,** *pseud.,* [*i.e.* **Angelo John**
-1 **Lewis**], *editor*
Every boy's book of sport and pastime, by a large number of experts. London, Routledge; New York, Dutton, 1896. xix, 900p. illus. diagrs.
——2nd ed. revised and brought up to date by Frederick Bolton. Routledge, 1905. xii,918p. illus. diagrs.
*cricket pp. 397–425 by W.C.A. Blew*

7128 **Hutchison, George Andrew**
■ Outdoor games and recreations: a popular encyclopaedia for boys. Religious Tract Society, 1892. xvi,576p. illus. diagrs.
*3 cricket chs., pp. 1–41 including chs. i and ii "Cricket and how to excel in it" and "Cricket clubs: their formation and management" by W.G. Grace*

7129 **Martin, William**
■ The book of sports, athletic exercises and amusements. Darton & Clark, 1840. iv,238p. illus. diagr.
*cricket pp. 83–104*
——2nd ed. *with title:* The book of sports: containing out-door sports, amusements and recreations. . . for boys and girls. Darton & Co., 1852. 144p. illus. diagrs.
*cricket pp. 55–68*
*other editions with variant titles and contents*

7130 **Outdoor** sports. Darton & Clark, 1857. 144p. illus. (Darton's Holiday Library)

7131 **Miller, Thomas**
The boy's summer book, descriptive of the season, scenery, rural life and country amusements. London, Chapman & Hall, 1846: N.Y., Harper, 1847. 128p. illus. (The Boy's Own Library)

7132 **Modern** outdoor amusements. Warne, [c.1867]. viii,182p.
*cricket pp. 94–136*

7133 **[Pardon, George Frederick]**
■ The book of manly games for boys: a practical guide to the indoor and outdoor amusements of all seasons by Capt. Crawley: illustrated by John Proctor and others. Tegg, [1870]. xi,532p. illus. diagrs.
*cricket pp. 108–58*

7134 **Percival, Paul**
The youth's own book of healthful amusements. Otley, Walker; London, Longman's, 1845. 254p. illus.
*cricket pp. 63–66*

7135 **Richardson, H.D.**
■ Holiday sports and pastimes for boys. W.S. Orr, 1848. vi,112p. illus.
*cricket pp. 34–45*

7135 **Rural** sports: or amusement for infant
-1 minds. 4th ed. with improvements. J.T. Ward & Co., 1807. 47p. (Juvenile Library)
*illus. on t.p. of 2 boys with cricket bats*

7136 **School-boys'** diversions: describing many
■ new and popular sports; with proper directions for engaging in them. Dean & Munday, [1820?]. 54p. illus.
*cricket pp. 5–8*

**7137** **"Uncle Charles"**, *pseud.*
■ The boy's book of sports and games; containing rules and directions for the practice of the principal amusements of youth, with illustrations by Henry Sears. Allmann, 1850. viii,184p. col. illus.
*cricket pp. 28–51*
——*another ed. with title:* The little boy's own book; consisting of games and pastimes. . .Allman, 1850. viii,200p. illus.
*cricket pp. 33–46*

**7137** **[Wood, John George]**
**–1** The playground; or, The boy's book of games, by George Forrest, Esq., M.A. G. Routledge, 1858. x,265p.
——*reissued with title:* The playground: a series of games for boys. [1884]

**7138** **Wood, John George**
■ Athletic sports and recreations for boys. Routledge, 1861. iv,144p. illus.
——*another ed.* 1862
——*another ed.* 1864
*cricket pp. 1–17*

**7139** ————, *editor*
The modern playmate: a book of games, sports and diversions for boys of all ages. Warne, 1870. x,883p. illus.
—— new rev. ed. 1875
—— *another ed.* 1880
—— new rev. ed. *with title:* The Boy's modern playmate, 1891. x,816p.

## 20th Century Works

**7139** **Archer, Michael,** *and* **Leitch, Michael,**
**–1** *compilers & editors*
World of sport. Hamlyn, 1974. 128p. illus. & ports. (some col.), map
*pp. 62–5 "My heroes in cricket" by Rachael Heyhoe-Flint*

**7139** **Barnaby, Jane,** *editor*
**–2** Australians in sport; illustrated by John
■ Mason. N. Melbourne, Cassell Australia, 1974. 116p. illus. (some col.)
*includes pp. 31–41 "A quiet hero" by Anthony Davis [on Sir Donald Bradman]*

**7140** **Bateman, Robert,** *editor*
Bumper sports book. Spring Books, [1959]. 160p. illus. ports.
*cricket pp. 33–37, 45, 67–73, 117, 118, 153*

**7141** Sports world album. Spring Books. 160p. illus. (some col.), ports.
*cricket 16pp.*

**7141** **Bebbington, Jim**
**–1** Summer sports; illustrated by Stan Martin. Evans Bros., 1975. 61p. illus. pbk.
*26pp. on cricket*

**7142** **Benson, J.K.,** *editor*
The book of sports and pastimes. . . Pearson, [1906]. vii,344p. illus. diagrs.
*cricket pp. 102–09*

**7143** The big book of sports. Robinson, 1955. 94p. illus.
*cricket pp. 8–17 with illus.*
——*another ed.* 1956. 78p.
*cricket pp. 5–12*

**7143** **Buckland, Augustus Robert,** *editor*
**–1** The Empire annual for Australian boys. Religious Tract Society. illus. (some col.)
[c.1915]. 320p.
*includes pp. 231–5 "The future of cricket" by E.H.D. Sewell*
[c.1916]. 381p.
*includes pp. 30–35 "How to make a century" by R.R. Relf, and pp. 117–22 "What I think of South African cricket" by J. Hartigan*

**7144** **Chesterton, Thomas**
■ Organised playground games suitable for elementary and secondary schools. Educational Supply Association, [1901]. 115p. illus.
*centre cricket, pp. 79–81; cricket, pp. 82–84*
——2nd ed. rev. 1908. 119p.
*centre cricket pp. 87–90; cricket pp. 90–92*

**7145** **Daiken, Leslie Herbert**
■ Children's games throughout the year. Batsford, 1949. viii,216p. col. frontis. illus.
*refers to "stones" as an ancestor of cricket and to 'tip and run' pp. 24–26; col. frontis. of "The cricketer" c.1850 by W. Hunt*

**7146** **Games** for girls and boys. R. Tuck & Sons Ltd., [c.1930]. 62p. illus.

**7147** **Gardiner, William Chetwynd**
■ Team games for schoolgirls, or, How to win your matches. Tilling, [1932]. 80p.
*cricket pp. 21–33*

**7148** **Hayward, Charles Spencer**
■ The summer playground. G. Allen, 1902. xv,318p. illus. (some col.). (The Young England Library)
*cricket pp. 25–146, including chapters on batting by R.S. Nicholson*

**7149** **Jessop, Gilbert Laird,** *and* **Salmond, J.B.,**
■ *editors*
The book of school sports. Nelson, [1920], 288p. illus. diagrs.
*includes "Cricket" by Gilbert Jessop*

**7150** **Lucas, Edward Verrall,** *and* **Lucas,**
■ **Elizabeth**
Three hundred games & pastimes; or, What shall we do now?: a book of sugges-

tions for children's games and employments. Chatto & Windus, 1919. vii,354p. illus. diagrs.

> *stump and garden cricket, p. 108, paper cricket, p. 62. 1st publd, as: What shall we do now? 1900*

7151 **MacCuaig, Donald,** *and* **Clark, Grant Simpson**
Games worth playing for school, playground and playing field. Longmans, 1924. xii,116p. diagrs.
——new ed. 1932. xii,132p. diagrs.
——3rd ed. 1951. xiv,145p. diagrs.

7152 **Marshall, Francis James Charles**
■ Outdoor activities for boys' schools. Univ. of London P., 1951. 208p. diagrs.
> *cricket pp. 121–43*

7152 **Oldfield, William Albert Stanley**
–1 Oldfield's sports manual for 1935 – golf, tennis, cricket; introduced by W.A. Oldfield. Sydney, [1935]. 48p. incl. adverts. illus.
> *includes pp. 37–41 "Some hints on wicket-keeping" by W.A. Oldfield, and pp. 43–8 "Batting" by C.G. Macartney*

7153 **Phillips, Hubert,** *compiler*
The playtime omnibus: a miscellany for young people. Faber, 1933. xvi,264p.
> *"Stump cricket" and "Tip and run" pp. 158–59*

7153 **Smith, Bertie Webster,** *editor*
–1 The boy's companion. Glasgow, Blackie, 1947. 640p. illus. diagrs. (Centurions)
> *contains pp. 79–117, "Cricket, by the Editor"*

7154 **Spicer, Sir Howard Handley,** *and others*
■ Sports for boys. Melrose, [1900]. 137p. illus.
> *ch. 3 "How to prepare a wicket" by S. Apted, pp. 43–50*
> *ch. 4: "Hints to young cricketers" by M.A. Noble, pp. 51–9*

7155 **Sutherland, Euan,** *and* **Sutherland, Kate,**
■ *compilers and editors*
Complete book of sport. Ward, Lock, 1969. 256p. illus. diagrs.
> *cricket pp. 54–66*

7156 **Vredenburg, Edric,** *editor*
The book for boys; illustrated by C.E. Brock and others. R. Tuck, 1926. 160p. illus.

7157 **Wallace, Carlton**
The boy's book of sport. Ward, Lock, 1951. 352p. illus.
> *cricket, pp. 10–23*

7158 **Warner, Sir Pelham Francis**
The Boy's Own Book of outdoor games and pastimes. Boy's Own Paper Office, 1914. xiv,384p. illus. (The Recreation Series)
> *cricket pp. 1–36 by P.F.W. and J.B. Hobbs*

7159 **Watson, Alfred Edward Thomas,** *editor*
■ The young sportsman. Lawrence & Bullen, 1900. viii,663p. illus. diagrs. glossaries
> *the greater part rptd. from The Encyclopaedia of Sport, no. 7049; cricket pp. 131–85; contributors F.G.J. Ford (left-handed batsmen); W.J. Ford; M.C. Kemp (wicket keeping); K.S. Ranjitsinhji (batting); Tom Richardson (bowling)*

7160 **The Wembley** book of ball games: all
■ about major ball games. S. Paul, 1964. viii,266p. illus. diagrs.
> *cricket pp. 22–35*
> *1st published by Playcraft Toys Ltd., 1963*

7161 **Wheeler, Kenneth**
"Eagle" book of sport. Hulton P., 1958. 192p. illus. diagrs.
> *cricket pp. 65–96*

7162 **Williams, Archibald**
The boys' guide; illustrated by Howard Penton. Nelson, [1911]. 560p. illus.
——new ed. [1927]. 560p.
——rev. ed. 1937. 384p. (Nelsonian Library)

7163 **Wilson, Stanley**
■ The boy's book of sports and games; illustrated by R. MacGillivray. Allen & Unwin, 1949. 64p. illus.
> *ch. 4 "Cricket" pp. 28–38*

7164 The girl's book of sports and games; illus-
■ trated by R. MacGillivray. Allen & Unwin, 1952. 64p. illus. diagrs.
> *cricket pp. 27–37*

7165 **Wood, Walter,** *editor*
The boy's all-round book of stories, sports and hobbies. Nelson, 1926. 443p. illus.
> *"The making of a cricketer", pp. 18–30, by G.L. Jessop*

D^r. W. G. Grace

A Chevallier Tayler. 1905.

W. G. Grace

# REMINISCENCES AND BIOGRAPHY
(Including benefits and testimonials)

## COLLECTED BIOGRAPHY
(See also: Batsmen (713–19)
Bowlers (748–52)
Wicket-keepers (762–63)
Captains (767–769)

7166 **Alcock, Charles William,** *editor*
■ Famous cricketers and cricket grounds,
1895. Hudson & Kearns; "News of the
World", 1895. 292p. illus. ports.
*a photographic record originally published
in 18 weekly parts by* News of the World

7167 **Andrews,** *Sir* **William Linton**
Yorkshire folk; memories of a journalist.
Heath Cranton, 1935. viii,175p.
*references to George Hirst, Wilfred Rhodes
and Sir Stanley Jackson*

7167 **Arlott, [Leslie Thomas] John**
–1 John Arlott's book of cricketers. Guild-
■ ford & London, Lutterworth P.; Sydney,
Angus & Robertson, 1979. x,180p. illus.
ports.

7168 **Ashley-Cooper, Frederick Samuel**
Cricket and the church. Merritt & Hatcher, 1904. 15p.
*limited ed. of 30 copies; reprinted from*
Cricket

7169 Cricket veterans. *Privately printed,* 1928.
■ 8p.
*a Christmas card*

7170 **Bailey, Trevor Edward**
■ The greatest of my time; cartoons by Roy
Ullyett. Eyre & Spottiswoode, 1968. 216p.
illus. ports.
——*another ed.* Sportsman's Book Club,
1970

7171 **Batchelor, Denzil [Stanley]**
■ The book of cricket. Collins, 1952. 224p.
illus. ports.
——*another ed.* Sportsman's Book Club,
1953
*photographs, with biographical sketches, of
famous players*

7172 ——, *editor*
■ Great cricketers. Eyre & Spottiswoode,
1970. 368p. illus. ports. diagr.

7173 **Bateman, Robert**
■ 100 great sportsmen. Transworld Publishers Ltd., 1972. 208p. illus. ports.
(Carousel Books)
*includes 16 cricketers*

7174 **Betham, John Dover**
■ Oxford and Cambridge scores and biographies. London, Simpkin Marshall; Sedbergh, Jackson, 1905. 286p. scores

7174 **[Bett, H. Drysdale]**
–1 Who's who in Australian cricket 1932–33,
■ by the editor of "The Australian Cricketer". Melbourne, Australian Cricketer,
[1932]. 16p.

7175 **Bettesworth, Walter Ambrose**
■ Chats on the cricket field; with explana-
tory notes by F.S. Ashley-Cooper.
Merritt & Hatcher, 1910. xv,468,xxip.
*articles rptd. from* Cricket *and* The
Cricket Field

7176 The boy's book of cricket teams. Playfair
■ Books, [1949]. pp. 65–80. illus. ports.
*off-print of centre 16pp. of the "Playfair
Cricket Annual" 1949; portraits of national
and county teams*

7177 **Brasher, Christopher**
■ Sportsmen of our time. Gollancz, 1962.
144p. illus. ports.

7178 **Brittenden, R.T.**
■ New Zealand cricketers. Wellington,
Reed, 1961. xii,180p. illus. ports

7179 **Burke's** who's who in sport and sporting
■ records, 1922. The Burke Publishing Co.,
1922. [iv],378p. stats.
*2/3 biographical, 1/3 records (cricket records
pp. 295–302)*

7180 **Burrell, J.F.,** *compiler*
□ Who's who in the Minor Counties.
Bristol, the Compiler, [1960]. *typescript.*
stats.
*Pt. 1. Southern counties. [11]f.*
*Pt. 2. Northern counties plus Berkshire and
Hertfordshire. [8]f.*
—— *annual.* [Covering all Minor
Counties], *typescript. stats.*

1961–76
from 1962 with title: *Minor Countries
who's who*
   1976 issue published by Association of
Cricket Statisticians; ed. by R.W. Brooke
   *contd. as:*
   Minor Counties who's who & annual
1977; compiled by Brian Hunt, Jack
Burrell and Robert Brooke. Hampton-in-
Arden, Assoc. of Cricket Statisticians.
stats.
   *contd. as*
   Minor Countries annual. Assoc. of
Cricket Statisticians. stats. *1978 to date.*
   *editors: 1978–J.R. Burrell, B. Hunt, R.W.
      Brooke, P. Wynne-Thomas
      1979–R.W. Brooke, P. Wynne-
      Thomas*

7180  **Butler, Keith**
–1  Howzat!: sixteen Australian cricketers
■  talk to Keith Butler. Sydney, Collins,
1979. 260p. illus. ports. stats.

7181  **Cannon, R.J.,** *and others*
■  Selected for England, compiled by R.J.
Cannon, with L. Dodd and R. Wilcox. Ian
Allan, [1949]. 50p. ports.

7182  **Caple, Samuel Canynge,** *compiler*
■  The cricketers' who's who. Lincoln
Williams, 1934. 214p. ports. stats.

7183  The cricketers' who's who. Vol. 1. A–E.
■  Hunstanton, Cricket Book Society, 1947.
160p.
   *originally published in 5 parts 1946–47.
Cricket Book Society, Publication. Ser. 1, nos.
2, 8, 9; Ser. 2, nos. 3, 4. No more published*

7183  **Carr's** dictionary of extra-ordinary
–1  English cricketers. Kettering, J.L. Carr,
■  1977. [20]p. incl. covers. ports. on covers

7184  **Catton, James Alfred Henry**
■  Dictionary of cricketers. 13 vols.
   *unpublished MS at M.C.C. Library, Lord's*

7185  **Cole, Douglas,** *editor*
■  Stars of cricket; illustrated by Tom Kerr,
Perry Colour Books, [1948]. [32]p. col.
ports. (Signature Series)

7186  **Cook, Ray,** *editor*
■  More stars of cricket. Perry Colour Books,
[1949]..32p. col. ports. (Signature Series)

7187  **The County** of Surrey, with illustrated
biographies. St Albans, Truman, P., 1896.
87p. ports.
   *limited to 140 copies, published only for
subscribers. Includes Jeremiah Colman, Sir
Kingsmill Grove Key, bart., Rev. Edward
William Northey, Granville Charles Gresham*

*Leveson Gower, Walter Moresby Chinnery,
George C. Roller*

7188  **Craig, Albert**
□  Albert Craig, between 1887 and 1908,
produced a series of 4 page biographies
of individual players mostly published by
the All England Publishing Co. or by
Wright & Co. The following have been
traced, but there may be others:
   R. Abel
   W. Attewell
   W. Barnes
   J. Beaumont
   T. Bowley
   J. Briggs
   W. Brockwell
   J. Cranston
   J.N. Crawford
   J. Darling
   A. Fielder
   W. Flowers
   C.B. Fry
   W.G. Grace
   W. Gunn
   L. Hall
   Lord Harris
   Lord Hawke
   E.G. Hayes
   T. Hayward
   A. Hearne
   G.G. Hearne
   W. Hearne
   A. Hide
   J. Hide
   G. Rowland Hill
   A.N. Hornby
   K.L. Hutchings
   A.O. Jones
   H. Jupp
   W.S. Lees
   W. Lockwood
   G.A. Lohmann
   J.J. Lyons
   C.P. McGahey
   C.H.B. Marsham
   F. Martin
   J.R. Mason
   T.C. O'Brien
   W.H. Patterson
   R. Peel
   W. Quaife
   K.S. Ranjitsinhji
   J.T. Rawlin
   J.M. Read
   W.W. Read
   W. Rhodes
   T. Richardson
   W. Scotton
   J.W. Sharpe
   A. Shrewsbury
   J. Shuter
   A.E. Stoddart
   E.C. Streatfeild
   G.H.S. Trott

G. Ulyett
E. Wainwright
A.M. Waites
P.M. Waites
Sir Pelham Warner
A.J. Webbe
H. Wood
S.M.J. Woods
F.E. Woolley
*those seen are listed individually under
name of player*

7189 **The cricket** album: containing 36 artistic
□ photo postcards of all the first class
county teams. . . Gottschalk, Dreyfuss &
Davis, 1905. 6p. ports. (The Star Series of
Toy Books)
——2d ed. 1905
——3rd ed. 1905
*printed in Bavaria*

7190 **Cricket** chat: gleanings from "Cricket"
■ . . .: portraits and biographies of eminent
cricketers. "Cricket" Office. ports. *annual
1884–92, 1914 (2 issues by Archibald
Sinclair, May and July)*

7191 **Cricket** prints. Calcutta, S.K. Roy, Illus-
■ trated News, [1949?]. [48]p. illus.
——Series one. [1949?]. [48]p. illus.
——Series two. [1950?]. [48]p. illus.
——Series three. Calcutta, Bose P.,
[1950?]. [48]p. illus. ports.
—— Series four: portrait gallery of
M.C.C. & All-India cricketers. Calcutta,
Netai Gopal Sen, [1951]. [48]p. ports.

7192 **Cricket** sketches: interesting reading with
■ over 20 portraits. Leeds, Daisy Ltd., 1898.
[14]p. ports.
*head-title: Daisy cricket sketches
anecdotes, portraits and facts about contemporary cricketers*
——*another issue with title:* Cricket
sketches; with portrait of the Yorkshire
team, also particulars of the Test matches,
etc. [1902]. 12p. port. stats.

7193 **Cricket** stars – past-present-future. Fore
■ Publications. [32]p. ports.
*No. 1. [1948]
No. 3. [1949]
No. 2. was not published*

7193 **Cricket teams.** Maguire, n.d. illus.
–1 *in Taylor*

7194 **Cricket** who's who: the blue book of
■ cricket; edited by H.V. Dorey. Cricket &
Sports Publishing Co. *annual.* stats.
*1908?, 1909, 1910
1911–13 with title: Who's who in cricket*

7195 **Cricket Writers' Club**
■ Cricket heroes, by members of the Cricket

Writers' Club; edited by John Kay,
cartoons by Roy Ullyett. Phoenix House,
1959. 191p. ports. stats. (Sports books)
——*another ed.* Sportsman's Book Club,
1960

7195 **The Cricketer**
–1 Cricket gallery: fifty profiles of famous
■ players from 'The Cricketer'; edited by
David Frith; photographs by Patrick
Eagar. Guildford, Lutterworth P.;
Richard Smart Publishing for 'The Cricketer'; Adelaide, Rigby, 1976. 256p. ports.
——*another ed.* Newton Abbot, Readers
Union, 1977

7196 **Cricketers** of England: a descriptive
pamphlet, containing the names of cricketers to appear in *Scores and biographies.*
Greenwich, 1859
*in Taylor ("this little pamphlet, although
only issued for distribution. . .")*

7197 **The cricketers'** portrait gallery. Leeds,
■ printed by Tempest, [1903]. 16p. ports.
*3 separate issues with some variation of
portraits*

7198 **The cricketing** lives of W.G. Grace, C.B.
Fry, Maurice Tate and Don Bradman.
Sportsman's Book Club, 1953. 236p. illus.
ports. diagr. score
*originally published in 4 separate volumes
by Phoenix House*

7199 **Daft, Richard**
■ Kings of cricket: reminiscences and anecdotes with hints on the game. Bristol,
Arrowsmith; London, Simpkin, Marshall,
[1893], xiv, 274p. illus. ports. scores.
——Subscribers' ed. Bolton, Tillotson,
1893. xiv,274p.

7200 A cricketer's yarns: to which have been
■ added a few genealogical tables of
Nottinghamshire cricketing families; ed.
with an introduction by F.S. Ashley-
Cooper. Chapman & Hall, 1926. xix,210p.
illus. ports.

7201 **Denison, William**
■ Cricket: sketches of the players. Simpkin,
Marshall, [etc.], 1846. viii,76p. scores
——*rptd. in:* Chronicles of cricket:
facsimile reprints of Nyren's "Cricketer's
guide", Lillywhite's "Handbook of
cricket", Denison's "Sketches of the
players". Swann Sonnenschein, 1888.
iv,[6],101; 30; viii,76p. illus. ports. scores

7201 **Desai, Kumarpal**
–1 Indian cricketers; artist Rajnee Vyas.
■ Ahmedabad and Bombay, A.R. Sheth,
[197–?]. [36]p. incl. covers. col. illus.
*Test cricketers*

7202 **Dyer, Thomas Firminger Thiselton**
■ Great men at play. Remington, 1889. 2 vols.
  *cricket references in vol. 1. ch. 1. to Charles James Fox, Lord Byron, William Wilberforce, William Ward, Lord Frederick Beauclerk, Lord William Lennox, Sir Horace Mann, Lord Lyttelton, Lord Westbury, Bishop of Sodor and Man, etc.*

7203 **Elliott, Ernest C.**
Fifty leaders of British sport: a series of portraits by Ernest C. Elliott (of Elliott and Fry) with biographical notes. . .by F.G. Aflalo. John Lane, the Bodley Head, 1904. 148p. ports.
  *cricketers include: C.B. Fry, Lord Hawke, A.C. MacLaren, Ranjitsinhji, P.F. Warner, Major R.M. Poore, J. Daniell*

7204 **Famous** cricket teams. Manchester, R.
■ Scott. [16]p. ports.
  *at least 7 issues of photo albums:*
  *No. [1]. [1899]: principal county cricket teams and the Australians*
    *2. [1900]*
    *3. [1902]*
    *4. [1903?]*
    *[5]. [1904] with results of the tour in Australia*
    *6. [1905]*
    *[7]. [1907]*

7205 **Famous** cricketers. Manchester, R. Scott,
□ [c.1903]. [24]p. ports.
  ——[c.1905]. [16]p. ports.
  ——1907
  *portraits of leading players in each county; no text*

7206 **Fingleton, Jack,** i.e. **John Henry Webb**
■ **Fingleton**
Masters of cricket from Trumper to May. Heinemann, 1958. 260p. illus. ports. scores
  ——*another ed.* Sportsman's Book Club, 1959

7207 **Foenander, Samuel Peter**
■ Famous cricketers I have met. Colombo, Ceylon Observer P., [1933]. [iv],92p. ports.
  *many of the pen portraits first appeared in the Ceylon Sunday Observer*

7208 **Fry, Charles Burgess,** editor
■ The book of cricket: a gallery of famous players. Newnes, [1899]. 256p. illus. ports.
  *originally issued in 16 weekly parts; a pictorial record with commentary*

7209 **Glendenning, Raymond Carl,** and **Bateman, Robert**
Sportsman's who's who. Museum P., 1957. 256p.

——*another ed.* Sportsman's Book Club, 1958

7210 **Goldman, Joseph Wolfe**
■ Cricketers and the law. Egham, the Author, 1958. xx,138p. ports. bibliog.
  *a list of lawyer-cricketers with brief biographical details. Limited ed. of 350 signed and numbered copies*

7210 **Greig, Anthony William ("Tony")**
–1 Cricket: the men and the game; as told to
■ David Lord. London, Hamlyn; Sydney, Ure Smith, 1976. 128p. illus. & ports. (some col.)
  ——*rev. ed.* Hamlyn, 1977. 136p.

7211 **Haigh, F. Hanson**
■ Ashes and rubber: (great cricketers in Test and county cricket of the twentieth century). Canterbury, *printed by* J.A. Jennings, 1947. 143p. ports. stats.

7212 **Hayter, Reg,** editor
■ Cricket: stars of today. Pelham Books, 1970. 123p. illus. ports.

7212 **Hill, Alan**
–1 The family fortune: a saga of Sussex
■ cricket. Shoreham-by-Sea, Scan Books, 1978. xv,152p. illus. ports. score, bibliog.
  *families connected with Sussex CCC, including Lillywhite, Gilligan, Parks, Langridge, Buss, etc.*

7212 **Kadye, Nandu**
–2 Bhāratīya kriketce mānkani. Poona, Prestigi Prakashan, 1971. viii,142p.
  *Marathi text; biographical sketches of 27 Indian cricketers*

7213 **Kent, William Richard Gladstone**
■ London worthies. Heath Cranton, 1939. xiv,421p.
  ——*another ed.* Phoenix House, 1949. xiv,421p.
  *a biographical dictionary with notices of cricketers pp. 1, 63, 110, 111, 172, 173, 202–4, 226, 228, 258–61, 312, 377*

7213 **Laker, James Charles**
–1 A spell from Laker on cricket and crick-
■ eters past and present. Hamlyn, 1979. 160p. illus. ports.

7214 **Langford, Arthur William T.,** and **Roberts,**
■ **Edward Lamplough,** compilers
Who's who in county cricket 1937. Birmingham, Hudson, [1937]. 37p. stats.
  *a statistical record*

7215 **Leveson Gower,** Sir **Henry Dudley**
■ **Gresham**
Cricket personalities. Williams and Norgate, 1925. v,184p.

**7216  Lilley, Arthur Augustus**
■  Twenty-four years of cricket: recalling the most famous cricketers and their methods, together with some advice on the game. Popular ed. Mills & Boon, [1912]. viii,350p. illus. ports. diagrs.
——*pocket ed.* 1914. 303p.

**7217  Lyttelton, *the Hon.* Robert Henry, *and***
■  *others*
    Giants of the game; being reminiscences of the stars of cricket from Daft down to the present day, by the Hon. R.H. Lyttelton, W.J. Ford, C.B. Fry and G. Giffen. Ward, Lock, [1899]. 192p. ports.
——rptd. with a new introduction by John Arlott. Wakefield, EP Publishing, 1973. viii,5–192p. ports.
    *a facsimile reprint*

**7217  Manchester Guardian**
**–1**  The bedside 'Guardian' 9: a selection
■  from The Manchester Guardian 1959–1960. Collins, 1960. 256p. illus.
    *includes pp. 155–60 "Four great players" by Denys Rowbotham (on Laker, Evans, Washbrook, and O.G. Smith)*

**7218  Maqsood, Syed M.H., *compiler***
□  Who's who in Indian cricket. New Delhi, *printed at* Caxton P., 1940. [vii], 132p. illus. ports.
——2nd ed. 1942. [v],116p. ports.
——3rd ed. 1943. 69p.
——4th ed. New Delhi, *printed at* Model P., 1945. [vi],96p. illus. ports. scores
——5th ed. 1946. [xvi],71p. ports. scores
——6th ed. 1947. 78p.

**7219  Marambe, T.M.**
■  Pen pictures of "our cricketers". Colombo, Times of Ceylon, 1949. 48p.

**7220  Martineau, Gerard Durani**
■  The field is full of shades: historical portraits of men who helped to make the national game. Sporting Handbooks, 1946. 111p.
——*another ed.* Sportsman's Book Club, 1954
    *printed with* Bat, ball, wicket and all

**7221**  They made cricket. Museum P., 1956.
■  232p. illus. ports. bibliog.
——*another ed.* Sportsman's Book Club, 1957

**7222  The Marvel, *Supplement***
■  Who's who in the cricket world; compiled by J.N. Pentelow. Amalgamated P., June 18, 1921. 88p. ports.

**7223  Merchant, M.I.**
■  100 best cricketers. Karachi, "Union" P., [1960]. [xii],161p. illus. ports.

**7223  "Mid-On", *pseud.***
**–1**  Cricket & cricketers illustrated: "International cricket". Melbourne, J.T. Picket under the auspices of the Melbourne Cricket Club and the Victorian Cricket Association, [1901?]. [50]p. incl. adverts. ports. stats.

**7224  Modi, Rusi**
■  Some Indian cricketers. New Delhi, National Book Trust, India, 1972. xii, 103p. illus. ports. (Young India Library)

**7225  Moody, Clarence Percival, *editor***
■  Cricket album [of] noted Australian cricketers, past and present. Adelaide, Hussey & Gillingham, 1898. [74]p. illus. ports.
    *issued in six monthly parts*

**7226  Moyes, Alban George ("Johnnie")**
■  A century of cricketers. London, Harrap; Sydney, Angus & Robertson, 1950. 224p. illus. ports.
——*another ed.* Sportsman's Book Club, 1954

**7227  National Spastics Society**
■  Famous county cricketers. The Society, [1958]. [8]p. col. ports.
    *an album of 24 trade cards*

**7228  Nyren, John**
■  The young cricketer's tutor; comprising full directions for playing . . . cricket; . . . to which is added "The cricketers of my time," or Recollections of the most famous old players. The whole collected and edited by Charles Cowden Clarke. Effingham Wilson, 1833. 126p. frontis.
    *for full entry and later eds. see no. 390*

**7228  Odendaal, Andre, *editor***
**–1**  God's forgotten cricketers: profiles of
■  leading South African players. Cape Town, South African Cricketer, 1976. 150p. illus. ports. pbk.

**7229  Oliver, John, *compiler & editor***
■  Book of sports stars: an album of personalities from the world of sport. Tolgate P., 1962. 96p.
    *cricket pp. 40–48*

**7230  Our** cricketers past and present . . .
■  permanent photographs . . . and handy notes. 7 parts. A.D. Jones, [1896]. ports. stats.
    *parts I–VI contain 144 photographs of English county cricketers.*

*[part VII] with title:* Special Australian number
*with 24 photographs*

7230 **Pakistan** cricketers autographs 1961. Mad-
-1 ras, Sunder Bros., [1961]. [17f]. ports.
 *no text*

7230 **Pawson, Tony**
-2 The goalscorers from Bloomer to Keegan.
■ Cassell, 1978. xvi,240p. illus.
 *mentions a number of cricketers in their role as soccer players*

7231 **Pentelow, John Nix**
■ "Cricket's" guide to cricketers, giving information about all first-class English cricketers of the present day. Simpkin Marshall, 1911. 84p. ports.

7232 **The People**
 "The People's" gallery of celebrated cricketers. The People, 1895

7232 **Phillipson, Neill**
-1 Cricket cavalcade: great Australian crick-
■ eters past and present. Melbourne, The Craftsman P., 1977. iv,188p. illus. ports. stats.
 ——*another ed. with title:* The Australian cricket hall of fame. Melbourne, Outback P., 1979. [iv],212p. illus. ports. stats.

7233 **Photo** album of famous cricketers. E.
■ Maguire, [1902]. [20]p. ports.
 *no text; includes Australian team 1902*

7234 **Portraits** and sketches of noted players in the cricket field. Leeds, E.A. Tempest, 1893. 12p. ports.

7235 **Portraits** and sketches of England's cricketers. Leeds, E.A. Tempest, 1896. 16p. ports.

7236 **Portraits** and sketches of noted cricketers;
□ also, "In and out" doings in the cricket field. Leeds, E.A. Tempest, 1895. 16p. illus. ports.
 ——*another ed.* 1896
 *anecdotes and brief biographical notes*

7237 **Pugh, P.D. Gordon**
■ Staffordshire portrait figures. Barrie & Jenkins, 1970. xi,657p. illus. (some col.)
 *section F "Sport", pp. 530–46 includes illustrations of figures and brief biographical details of Thomas Box, Julius Caesar, William Clarke, Frederick William Lillywhite, George Parr and Fuller Pilch*

7238 **Pullin, Alfred William**
■ Talks with old Yorkshire cricketers. Leeds, Yorkshire Post, 1898. 239p. ports. score, stats.
 ——2nd ed. 1898
 *rptd. from the* Yorkshire Evening Post

7239 Talks with old English cricketers. Black-
■ wood, 1900. x,344p. illus. ports. scores

7239 **Puri, Narottam**
-1 Portrait of Indian captains. Calcutta,
■ [etc.], Rupa, 1978. [xiv],193p. illus. ports. stats. pbk.

7240 **[Pycroft, James]**
■ Cricket: reminiscences of the old players and observations on the young ones, by the author of 'The cricket field'. *n.p.,* [1868]. 22p. port.

7240 **Ramchand, Partab**
-1 Great Indian cricketers. Sahibabad, Vikas,
■ 1979. viii,205p. ports. stats.
 *pen-portraits of 21 cricketers*

7241 **Roberts, Edwards Lamplough,** *compiler*
■ Cricketography 1951. Nottingham, Gunn & Moore, [1951]. 34p. stats.
 *pen-portraits with statistics of leading cricketers*

7242 **Robertson-Glasgow, Raymond Charles**
■ Men only in sport; illustrations by Edgar Norfield. Pearson, 1943. 96p. illus. (Men Only Series)
 ——2nd ed. 1945
 ——3rd ed. 1946
 *a reprint of author's articles in* Men Only; *cricket pp. 9–46, 52–60, 74–81, 88–91*

7243 Cricket prints: some batsmen and
■ bowlers, 1920–1940. Laurie, 1943. 192p. frontis. (port.)
 ——*another ed.* Sportsmans' Book Club, 1951

7244 More cricket prints: some batsmen and
■ bowlers, 1920–1945. Laurie, 1948. 143p. frontis.

7245 **Robinson, Ray**
■ The glad season. Collins, 1955. 256p. illus. stats.
 ——*another ed.* Sportsman's Book Club, 1956
 ——*Australian ed. with title:* Green sprigs: cricket's age of youth. Sydney, Collins, 1954. 240p. illus. stats.
 *accounts of young first class and Test cricketers*

7245 On top down under: Australia's cricket
-1 captains. Stanmore (N.S.W.), Cassell
■ Australia, 1975. [xii],320p. illus. ports. bibliog.

the careers of 34 Australian captains from 1877 to 1975
——another ed. 1976. xiv,336p. illus. ports. pbk.
*updated to include Greg Chappell*

**7245 Ross, Gordon**
**–2** Cricket's great characters. [The Author],
■ 1977. 48p. ports.
*a series of essays on Cecil Parkin, George Gunn, "Patsy" Hendren, Arthur Mailey, Charlie Harris, Fred Trueman*
*limited to 300 copies signed and numbered*

**7246 Roy, S.K.**
□ Indian cricketers: Indian cricket's who's who. Calcutta, Illustrated News, 1941. 136p. ports. stats.
——2nd ed. 1944. 175p.
——3rd ed. 1946. 176p. incl. adverts.

**7246 Saradesai, Raghunath Govinda**
**–1** Mahān kriket karṇadhār. Poona, Y.G. Joshi Prakashan, 1970. 112p.
*Marathi text; biographies of 11 Indian captains*

**7247 Sewell, Edward Humphrey Dalrymple**
■ Who's won the toss? S. Paul, [1944]. 160p. illus. ports.
*"best ever" elevens of each of the counties, the Test playing countries, Gentlemen and Players & the universities, 1890–1939*

**7248 Sketchy Bits**
■ Cricket supplement. "Sketchy Bits" Co., August 7, 1899. [8]p. ports.
*photographs of the All England, Surrey, Somerset, Nottinghamshire teams, Maclaren, Ranjitsinhji, Hayward*

**7249 The sportfolio**: portraits and biographies of heroes and heroines of sports and pastimes. Newnes, 1896. 144p. ports.

**7250 Sportive** snatches from playgrounds and
■ playhouses: compiled by Charles Plairre. London, Wright; Manchester, Heywood. illus. ports. *annual*
*5 issues 1889–93*
*contains biographical sketches with portraits of leading sportsmen together with a selection of anecdotes and verse relating to various pastimes, culled from contemporary literature*

**7250 Sports** personalities: South African, 1971.
**–1** Johannesburg, Perskor, 1971. xxvii,361p. illus.
*text in Afrikaans and English*

**7251 Standing, Percy Cross,** editor
■ The cricketers' birthday book. Dent, 1898. 255p.
*birthdays of cricketers throughout the year*

**7252 Stoddart, Joseph**
■ Sports–pastimes: men I have met. 2 vols. ports.
*Vol. 1. Manchester, Athletic Journal Office, 1889*
*Vol. 2. Manchester & London, Heywood, [1890]*
*Vol. 3. projected but not published*

**7253 Tayler, Albert Chevallier**
■ The Empire's cricketers: famous players in their characteristic atitudes executed in crayon from drawings by Chevallier Tayler; biographies by G.W. Beldam. Fine Art Society, 1905. 97p. illus.
——de luxe ed. 1905
*originally issued in weekly parts*

**7253 Thomas, Peter**
**–1** Yorkshire cricketers, 1839–1939. Man-
■ chester, Derek Hodgson, 1973. [vi],244p. ports. stats. bibliog.

**7254 Thomson, Arthur Alexander**
■ Odd men in: a gallery of cricket eccentrics. Museum P., 1958. 184p. illus. ports.
—another ed. Sportsman's Book Club, 1959

**7255** Cricketers of my times. S. Paul, 1967.
■ 208p. ports. stats.
——another ed. Sportsman's Book Club, 1968

**7255 1000 famous** Australians. Adelaide, Rigby,
**–1** [1977]. 368p. ports.
*contains pp. 163–95 "The sporting arena" including concise biographies of Bannerman, Benaud, Bradman, the Chappells, Davidson, J.M. Gregory, Grimmett, Grout, Neil Harvey, Clem Hill, Macartney, Mailey, Miller, Oldfield, O'Reilly, V.Y. Richardson, Spofforth, Thomson, Trumper, Woodfull*

**7256 Timbs, John**
School-days of eminent men: or, Early lives of celebrated British authors, philosophers, and poets. . . . New ed. . . Lockwood, [1862]. viii,312p. ports.
*cricket p. 94 Dr Vaughan on games and athletics at Harrow*
*p. 146. Bishop Ken at Winchester*
*p. 194. Gray—"Urge the flying ball. . ."*
*p. 215. Cowper plays cricket at Westminster*
*p. 295. Byron at Harrow*

**7256 The Times**
**–1** Obituaries from The Times 1951–1960,
■ including an index to all obituaries and tributes appearing in The Times during the years 1951–1960; compiler: Frank C. Roberts. Newspaper Archive Developments, 1979. 896p.
*includes Warren Bardsley, L.C. Braund,*

Frank Chester, Prince Duleepsinhji, A.J. Evans, C.B. Fry, Sir Home Gordon, Sir H. Leveson Gower, George Hirst, D.R. Jardine, Gilbert Jessop, C.J. Kortright, C.J. Macartney, Philip Mead, Nawab of Pataudi, Hugh de Selincourt, Maurice Tate, Lord Tennyson
——1961–1970, including an index of all obituaries and tributes. . .1961–1970; compiler: Frank C. Roberts. Newspaper Archive Developments Ltd., 1975. 952p.
*includes Sydney Barnes, A.W. Carr, A.P.F. Chapman, A.P. Freeman, Walter Hammond, J.W. Hearne, Patsy Hendren, Sir Jack Hobbs, Maurice Leyland, Arthur Mailey, R.W.V. Robins, Emmott Robinson, R.H. Spooner, Herbert Strudwick, A.A. Thomson, Sir Pelham Warner, Sir Frank Worrell*
——1971–75 including an index of all obituaries and tributes. . .1971–1975; compiler: Frank C. Roberts. Newspaper Archive Developments Ltd., 1978. 647p.
*includes Sidney Barnes, Sir Neville Cardus, Leslie O'B. Fleetwood-Smith, J.M. Gregory, Percy Holmes, The Maharaja of Patiala, Wilfred Rhodes, Arthur Wood*

7256 **Titley, Uel A., and McWhirter, Ross**
–2  Centenary history of the Rugby Football Union. The Union, 1970. 312p. illus. (some col.), ports. maps, plans
*the biographical section contains detailed entries of many rugby players who were also cricketers*

7257 **Trowsdale, T. Broadbent**
■  The cricketer's autograph birthday book. W. Scott, 1906. xi,342p. illus.
*contains 130 facsimile autographs of famous cricketers*

7258 **Turner, Herbert Kyle,** *compiler*
The world's all sports who's who for 1950. Hove, Wex P., 1950, 380p. illus.

7259 **Varma, Arvind**
■  Eminent cricket left handers. Bombay, Jaico, 1972. x,128p. ports. stats.

7259 **"Vigilant",** *pseud., editor*
–1  Australian sporting celebrities with
■  biographical sketches of their career. Melbourne, A.H. Massina & Co., 1887. 4–67p. ports.
*includes pp. 34–5, Mr. G.E. Palmer; pp. 42–3, George Giffen*

7259 **Walker, Peter Michael**
–2  Cricket conversations: Peter Walker talks
■  with Gary Sobers, Ray Illingworth, Barry Richards, Tom Cartwright, Roy Fredericks, Greg Chappell, Mike Procter, Bishen Bedi, Alan Knott, Glenn Turner, Basil d'Oliveira, Majid Khan, Brian Close. Pelham Books, 1978. 191p. illus. ports.

——*another ed.* Newton Abbot, Readers Union, 1979

7260 **Walmsley, E.**
■  Cricket celebrities of 1890, with a complete resumé of the season's doings. Manchester & London, Heywood, 1890. xvii,76p. ports. stats.

7261 **[Warner, Sir Pelham Francis],** *editor*
■  British sports and sportsmen past and present; compiled and edited by "The Sportsman" British Sports and Sportsmen, [1908–1936?]. 16 vols. illus. ports.
*Vol. 5. Cricket and football, 1917. xiii,579p.*
*limited to 1,000 copies; cricket pp. 1–211*

7262 **Washbrook, Cyril**
■  Cyril Washbrook invites you to meet the players. Sportsguide Publications, 1949. 32p. illus. ports.

7263 **Webber, Roy**
■  Who's who in world cricket. Hodder & Stoughton, 1952. 192p. ports.
——new ed. all entries revised for 1954: 250 additional records. 1954. 192p. ports.
——*another ed.* Sportsman's Book Club, 1954

7263 **Whitington, Richard Smallpeice**
–1  The champions. Melbourne, Macmillan
■  Co. of Australia, 1976. [viii],135p. illus. ports.
*pen-portraits of the greatest Australian sportsmen; includes pp. 8–15, Dennis Lillee; pp. 25–31, Victor Trumper; pp. 64–9, Keith Miller; pp. 88–93, Victor Richardson; pp. 115–20, Sir Donald Bradman; pp. 129–35, Frederick Spofforth*

7264 **Who's** who in sport. Shaw Publishing Co., 1935. 322p.

7265 **Who's** who in the sporting world, Witwatersrand and Pretoria. Johannesburg, Central News Agency, 1933. 92p. ports.

7266 **Who's** who in world cricket: 700 biographies of world-famous players. Amalgamated P., 1934. 74p. ports.

# INDIVIDUAL BIOGRAPHY

## Abberley, Neal

7266 **Neal Abberley:** the official Neal Abberley
–1  benefit year brochure. [Benefit Cttee.,
■  1979]. 36p. incl. covers & adverts. illus. ports. stats.

## Abel, Charles W.

7267 **Entwistle, Mary,** *and* **Spriggs, Elsie H.**
■ The way and its heroes: stories illustra-
( ting some of the sayings of Jesus. Cargate
P., 1945. 80p. illus.
*includes "Kilikity", a chapter on Charles
W. Abel of Papua, pp. 13–19*

## Abel, Robert

7268 **Abel, Robert**
■ Life and reminiscences of Robert Abel in
the cricket field, told by himself and
edited by H.V. Dorey. Cricket & Sports
Publishers, 1910. [iv],118p. stats.
——*paper ed.* 1910

7269 **Benson, Edward Frederic,** *and* **Miles,**
■ **Eustace Hamilton,** *eds.*
The cricket of Abel, Hirst and Shrewsbury. Hurst & Blackett, 1903. xx,287p.
illus. (Athletic library)

7270 **[Craig, Albert]**
■ Robert Abel. [Cricket P.], 1898. [4]p.
folded card. port. (Second Series)

7271 **Wright, W.R.**
■ Abel and Briggs: an amusing adventure
in South Africa. All England Athletic
Publishing Co., 1898. [4]p. folded card. 2
ports on cover

7271 **Abse, Dannie**
–1 Ash on a young man's sleeve. Hutch-
■ inson, 1954. 200p.
——*rptd.* Vallentine, Mitchell & Co., 1971
——*rptd.* Corgi Books, 1972. 157p. pbk.
*a dream sequence of the author with J.C.
Clay batting for Glamorgan against Yorkshire,
with ten runs needed to win and Clay not out
9, Abse not out 92*

## "Aesop", *pseud.*

7272 **"Aesop",** *pseud.*
■ Sporting reminiscences in Hampshire
from 1745 to 1862. Chapman & Hall, 1864.
xx,380p.
*mainly hunting but some cricket*

## Agate, James Evershed

7272 **Agate, James Evershed**
–1 Ego: the autobiography of James Agate.
□ H. Hamilton, [1936]. 388p. frontis.
*contains reference to Neville Cardus and the
Manchester Guardian*

7273 Ego 6: once more the autobiography of
□ James Agate. Harrap, 1944. 307p. illus.
ports.

Ego 8: continuing the autobiography of
James Agate. Harrap, 1947. 269p. illus.
ports.

Ego 9: concluding the autobiography of
James Agate. Harrap, 1948. 352p. illus.
ports.
*all contain scattered references to cricket*

7273 A shorter ego: the autobiography of
–1 James Agate. Second selection. Reader's
■ Union/George G. Harrap, 1947. 230p.
frontis.
*cricket pp. 17, 19, 206, 207, 224*

## Aislabie, Benjamin

7274 **Lucas, Edward Verrall**
■ Harvest home. Methuen, 1913. 180p.
*includes "Two amateurs—Alfred Mynn
and Mr. Aislabie", pp. 54–58*

## Alderman, Albert Ernest

7275 **Derbyshire County Cricket Club**
■ A.E. Alderman's testimonial souvenir.
[Derby, the Club], 1948. 32p. incl. ad-
verts. ports. stats.

## Allen, Roland

7276 **Allen, Roland**
■ All in the day's sport. W.H. Allen, [1946].
186p.
*cricket in chs. 2, 22, 23*

## Alletson, Edwin Boaler

7277 **Arlott, [Leslie Thomas] John**
■ Alletson's innings. Epworth P., 1957.
40p. illus. port. score, stats. bibliog.
*Ltd. ed. of 200 numbered and signed copies*
——*2nd ed.* 1958
*an account of E.B. Alletson's 189 runs in
90 minutes in 1911*

## Alley, William Edward ('Bill')

7278 **Alley, William Edward (Bill)**
■ My incredible innings. Pelham Books,
1969. 160p. illus. ports. stats.

## Almond, Hely Hutchison

7279 **Mackenzie, Robert Jameson**
■ Almond of Loretto: being the life and a
selection from the letters of Hely Hutchison Almond. Constable, 1905. x,408p.
*scattered cricket references*

## Alston, Arthur Reginald ('Rex')

7280 **Alston, Rex,** *i.e.* **Arthur Reginald Alston**
■ Taking the air. S. Paul, 1951. 264p. illus.
ports.

## Altham, Harry Surtees

7281 **Altham, Harry Surtees**
■ The heart of cricket: a memoir of H.S. Altham; edited by Hubert Doggart. Hutchinson; 'The Cricketer', 1967. 216p. illus. ports. stats.
*includes essays by and about H.S. Altham*

7282 **Friends of Winchester Cathedral**
■ Winchester Cathedral record 1965. Winchester, the Friends, 1965. 40p. illus. port.
*contains pp. 7–8 an obituary of H.S. Altham, with port.; also on p. 3 an appreciation by the Dean of Winchester*

7283 **[Marylebone Cricket Club]**
■ H.S. Altham memorial. [M.C.C., 1965?] bs.
*an appeal for donations*

7284 **Swanton, Ernest William**
■ The compleat cricketer: a short sketch of H.S. Altham. [Southampton, Hampshire C.C.C.], 1960. [8]p. port.
*limited ed. of 25 copies only. First published in Hampshire C.C.C. Handbook, 1960*

## Armanath, Lala

7284 **Lala Amarnath** benefit match, Pakistan
–1 XI vs. President's XI played at The
■ Brabourne Stadium, Bombay, February 18, 19 and 20, 1961: official souvenir. Bombay Publicity Cttee., 1961. 52p. incl. adverts. ports. diagr. stats.

## Ames, Leslie Ethelbert George

7285 **Ames, Leslie [Ethelbert George]**
■ Close of play. S. Paul, 1953. 208p. illus. ports

## Amiss, Dennis Leslie

7285 **Amiss, Dennis [Leslie]**
–1 In search of runs: an autobiography; with
■ Michael Carey. S. Paul, 1976. 120p. illus. ports. stats.
*——another ed.* Newton Abbot, Readers Union, 1977

7285 **Dowell, Ian,** *editor*
–2 Dennis Amiss benefit year 1975. Bir-
■ mingham, Birmingham Evening Mail, [1975]. 48p. incl. adverts. illus. ports. stats.

## Andrews, Charles Freer

7285 **Chaturvedi, Benarsidas,** *and* **Sykes,**
–3 **Marjorie**
Charles Freer Andrews: a narrative. Allen & Unwin, 1949. xiv,334p. illus. ports.
*cricket pp. 10, 56, 296*

## Andrews, Frederick

7286 **Wallis, Isaac Henry**
■ Frederick Andrews of Ackworth. Longmans, 1924. ix,335p. illus. ports.
*cricket pp. 27, 167, 257*

## Andrews, William Harry Russell ('Bill')

7287 **Andrews, Bill,** *i.e.* **William Harry Russell**
■ **Andrews**
The hand that bowled Bradman: memories of a professional cricketer. Macdonald, 1973. 176p. illus. ports. score
*——another ed.* Sportsman's Book Club, 1974

## Archdale, Betty

7287 **Archdale, Betty**
–1 Indiscretions of a headmistress. Sydney, London, Angus & Robertson, 1972. [v], 226p.
*women's cricket pp. 6, 17–21, 32*

## Armstrong, Warwick Windridge

7287 **Grace, Radcliffe**
–2 Warwick Armstrong. Camberwell (Vic.),
■ the Author, 1975. [v],80p. illus. ports. stats.
*limited to 350 numbered & signed copies*

## Arnold, Geoffrey Graham

7287 **Geoff Arnold,** England & Surrey C.C.C.,
–3 benefit year 1976. Geoff Arnold All Star
■ XI versus Malden Wanderers C.C. gala cricket match. . .18 August 1976. [Benefit Cttee., 1976]. [44]p. incl. adverts. illus. ports. stats.

## Asche, Oscar

7288 **Asche, Oscar**
■ Oscar Asche; his life, by himself. Hurst & Blackett, 1929. 256p. illus. ports.
*cricket pp. 16–18, 212, 213, 246–248*

## Ashley-Cooper, Frederick Samuel

7289 **Rosenwater, Irving**
■ F.S. Ashley-Cooper: the Herodotus of cricket. The Author, 1964. 12p. port.
*limited ed. of 25 numbered and signed copies; rptd. from* Journal of the Cricket Society, *vol. II, no.3 (1963)*

## Astill, William Ewart

7290 **Leicestershire County Cricket Club**
■ W.E. Astill's benefit match. Leicestershire v. Sussex. Saturday, July 1st, 1922. Leicester, the Club, [1922]. 16p. illus. ports. stats.

## Astley, Sir John Dugdale

7290 **Astley**, *Sir* **John Dugdale**
–1 Fifty years of my life in the world of sport at home and abroad. 2 vols. Hurst and Blackett, 1894. ports.
——subscriber's limited ed. 1894
*scattered cricket references*

## Attewell, William

7291 **Richards, Charles Henry**
William Attewell: his cricket career. Nottingham, Richards, 1891. port.

## Austen-Leigh, Augustus

7292 **Austen-Leigh, William,** *editor*
- ■ Augustus Austen-Leigh. Provost of King's College, Cambridge: a record of college reform. Smith, Elder, 1906. xi, 306p. ports.
  *cricket pp. 18–20, 31, 32, 43–46, 73, 169–70, 212–13*

## Bader, Douglas

7293 **Brickhill, Paul**
■ Reach for the sky: the story of Douglas Bader. Collins, 1954. 384p. illus. ports.
  *cricket pp. 19, 21, 37, 38, 42, 104*

## Bagot, Arthur Greville

7294 **Bagot, Arthur Greville**
■ Sport and travel in India and Central America. Chapman & Hall, 1897. viii, 371p. illus.
  *ch. vii "An up-country cricket match", pp. 72–80*

## Bailey, Trevor Edward

7295 **Bailey, Trevor [Edward]**
■ Playing to win. Hutchinson, 1954. 215p. illus. ports. scores. (Library of Sports and Pastimes)
  *includes account of Australian tour of England, 1953*

7296 Cricket book. Muller, 1959. 127p. illus.
■ ports.

## Bannister, J.D.

7297 **Warwickshire County Cricket Club**
■ J.D. Bannister's benefit season 1964. [Birmingham], the Club, [1964]. 4p. fold. illus. port. stats.

## Bardswell Family

7297 **Deadman, Derek,** *and* **Sheppard,**
–1 **Christopher**
■ The Bardswells: fact and fiction, with a

reprint of "Played on" by Emily Bardswell. Leicester, *privately printed*, 1979. 41p. with inset of [ii],60,[vi]p. scores, stats. bibliog.
*limited to 50 copies numbered and signed*

## Barlow, Richard Gorton

7298 **Barlow, Richard Gorton**
■ Forty seasons of first-class cricket; being the autobiography and reminiscences of Richard Gorton Barlow during 40 consecutive seasons of first class cricket, playing and umpiring; together with many curious and interesting anecdotes incidental to cricket, and valuable advice to young cricketers on all points of the game. Manchester, Heywood, 1908, [8],xi,255p. illus. ports.
——2nd ed. 1908
*contains facsimiles of over 300 autographs of county cricketers*

## Barnes, Ronald Gorell, *3rd baron Gorell*

7299 **Barnes, Ronald Gorell,** *3rd baron Gorell*
■ One man . . . many parts. Odhams, 1956. 320p. ports.
  *cricket pp. 132–44 and other references*

## Barnes, Sidney George

7300 **Barnes, Sidney George**
■ It isn't cricket. Sydney, Collins, 1953. 222p. illus. ports.
——*1st English ed.* Kimber, 1953. 175p. illus. ports.
——*another ed.* Hamilton, 1955. 192p. (Panther Books)

## Barnes, Sydney Francis

7301 **Duckworth, Leslie**
■ S.F. Barnes—master bowler. The Cricketer; Hutchinson, 1967. 208p. illus. ports. diagrs. scores, stats. bibliog. ('The Cricketer' publications)
——*another ed.* Sportsman's Book Club, 1968

7302 **White, Wilfrid S.**
■ Sydney Barnes: the greatest bowler of all time; full story of his wonderful career. Birmingham, Hudson, [1937]. 56p. illus. port.

## Barnes, William

7302 **Hearl, Trevor William**
–1 William Barnes 1801–1886. The schoolmaster: a study of education in the life and work of the Dorset poet. Dorchester,

Friary P., 1966. xiv,355p. illus. ports. facsims. bibliog.
*cricket pp. 80, 185, 281*

### Barnes, William

7303 **William Barnes:** [a short biography].
■ [Nottingham, Richards, 1894]. 14p. port. stats.

### Barnett, Charles John

7304 **[Charles J. Barnett's** benefit souvenir].
■ Gloucestershire v. Yorkshire, the County Ground, Bristol, May 31, June 1 & 2, 1947. [4]p. folded card. port.
*contains article "About Yorkshire" by David Moore*

### Barrie, *Sir* James Matthew

7305 **Asquith,** *Lady* **Cynthia**
■ Portrait of Barrie. Barrie, 1954. vii, 230p. ports.
*scattered cricket references*

7306 **Chalmers, Patrick Reginald**
■ The Barrie inspiration. P. Davies, 1938. 271p. illus. ports.
*cricket pp. 41–53*

7307 **Darlington, William Aubrey Cecil**
■ J. M. Barrie. Blackie, 1938. xiv,158p. illus. ports.
*cricket pp. 64–6*

7308 **Darton, Frederick Joseph Harvey**
J.M. Barrie. Nisbet, [1929]. 127p. port. (Writers of the Day)
*cricket pp. 7–10, 116*

7309 **Dunbar, Janet**
■ J.M. Barrie: the man behind the image. Collins, 1970. 318p. illus. ports. bibliog.
*cricket pp. 70, 88, 99, 112, 123, 136*

7309 **Elder, Michael**
-1 The young James Barrie; illustrated by Susan Gibson. Macdonald, 1968. 128p. illus.
*cricket pp. 101–7*

7309 **Hammerton,** *Sir* **John Alexander**
-2 Barrie; the story of a genius. Sampson Low, 1929. viii,344p. illus. ports.
*cricket pp. 13, 220–23*

7309 **Mackail, Denis George**
-3 The story of J.M.B.: a biography. P. Davies, 1941. [v],736p. port.
*many references to the Allahakbarries*

7310 **Moult, Thomas**
Barrie: a critical estimate. Cape, 1928. 192p.

### Barrington, Kenneth Frank

7311 **Barrington, Ken,** *i.e.* **Kenneth Frank**
■ **Barrington**
Running into hundreds, [by] Ken Barrington as told to Phil Pilley. S. Paul, 1963. 191p. illus. ports. stats.

7312 Playing it straight, by Ken Barrington as
■ told to Phil Pilley. S. Paul, 1968. 153p. illus. ports.
——*another ed.* Sportsman's Book Club, 1969

7313 **Ken Barrington** benefit 1964: Sunday
■ fixture list & social arrangements. Mitcham, Ken Barrington Benefit, [1964]. fold with 3p. of text.

### Batchelor, Denzil Stanley

7314 **Batchelor, Denzil Stanley**
■ Babbled of green fields. Hutchinson, 1961. 224p.

### Bateman, Rowland

7315 **Maconachie, James Robert**
Rowland Bateman, nineteenth century apostle. C.M.S., 1917. x,208p. illus.
*cricket pp. 43, 70, 102 and 183*

### Bates, Donald Lawson

7316 **Don Bates** benefit year, 1968. [Benefit
■ Cttee., 1968]. 56p. incl. adverts. illus. ports.

### Bax, *Sir* Arnold Edward Trevor

7316 **Scott-Sutherland, Colin**
-1 Arnold Bax. Dent, 1973. xviii,214p. illus.
■ ports.
*cricket pp. 44–8*

### Bax, Clifford

7317 **Bax, Clifford**
■ Inland far: a book of thoughts and impressions. Heinemann, 1925. 332p. ports.
——*another ed.* Lovat Dickson, 1933. 332p.
*cricket references in chs. ii and xii*

7318 Evenings in Albany: [reminiscences].
■ Eyre & Spottiswoode, 1942, vi,153p.
*ch. iii "The happiest of all men"*

7319 Rosemary for remembrance; [autobiogra-
■ phical reminiscences], Muller, 1948. 207p. illus.
*cricket references chaps. 6 and 12 including "Members only" pp. 95–110, 1st published in the* New English Review, Sept. 1946

7320 **Waugh, Alec**
■ My brother Evelyn, and other profiles.
Cassell, 1967. [viii],340p.
*contains "Two poet cricketers" (Clifford
Bax, J.C. Squire), pp. 141–161*

## Bean, George

7321 **[George Bean's** benefit match. . .1898]
*contains pen-portrait of G.B. by "Leather
Hunter" [A.J. Gaston]*

## Beauclerk, Lord Frederick

7322 **Highmore, Nathaniel**
■ Jus ecclesiasticum Anglicanum; or, The
government of the Church of England
exemplified and illustrated. J. Budd,
1810. [7], xliii,160p. frontis.
*includes, pp. 50–58, correspondence
relating to the behaviour of the Rev. Lord
Frederick Beauclerk at Lord's*

7322 **The Saturday** book. Hutchinson
–1 1941–42; edited by Leonard Russell.
■ 1941. 446p. illus. ports.
*contains article pp. 80–98 on Lord Frederick
Beauclerk by Harold Hobson and includes statistical summary of his batting record, season
by season, 1791–1823*

7322 **Wilson, Harriette**
–2 Reminiscences of herself and others. P.
Davies, 1929. 671p.
*references to Lord Frederick Beauclerk, pp.
123, 126–30, 423*

## Beckett, Samuel

7322 **Bair, Deirdre**
–3 Samuel Beckett: a biography. Cape 1978.
■ xiv,736p.
*cricket pp. 27, 28–9, 30, 36, 37, 42
"Beckett probably. . .the only Nobel Prize
winner to be listed in Wisden"*

## Bedser Brothers

7323 **Bedser, Alec Victor,** *and* **Bedser, Eric**
■ **Arthur**
Our cricket story. Evans Bros., [1950].
240p. illus. ports.

7324 Following on. Evans Bros., 1954. 240p.
■ illus. ports.
*sequel to Our cricket story*

## Bedser, Alec Victor

7325 **Alec Bedser** benefit performance. Victoria
■ Palace, London, S.W.1. 10th May, 1953:
souvenir programme. Benefit Committee,
[1953]. [8]p. illus.

7326 **West, Peter,** *editor*
■ The Alec Bedser 1953 benefit book.
Surrey C.C.C., [1953]. 32p. ports. stats.

## Beldham, William ('Silver Billy')

7327 **Brown, Ivor [John Carnegie]**
■ Brown studies. Eyre & Spottiswoode,
1930. 201p.
*includes essay on "Silver Billy" Beldham*

## Benaud, Richie

7328 **Benaud, Richie**
■ Way of cricket. Hodder & Stoughton,
1961. 247p. illus. ports. scores
*includes chapters on techniques*

7329 Willow patterns. London & Sydney,
■ Hodder & Stoughton, 1969. 222p. illus.
ports.
——*another ed.* Sportsman's Book Club,
1970

7330 **Moyes, Alban George ("Johnnie")**
■ Benaud. Angus & Robertson, 1962.
[ix],205p. illus. ports. stats.
——*another ed.* Sportsman's Book Club,
1964

## Bennett, Donald

7331 **Middlesex County Cricket Club**
■ Don Bennett (Middlesex) benefit 1964:
Middlesex v. Sussex, Lords May 16th,
18th, 19th. Lord's, the Club, [1964]. 1
illus. fold.

## Binks, James Graham

7332 **Jimmy Binks** benefit matches, season
■ 1967. [Binks Benefit Cttee, 1967]. 8p. illus.
ports. stats.

7333 **Jimmy Binks** benefit 1967. Binks Benefit
Cttee, [1967]. 40p. illus. ports. stats.

## Bird, James Dennis

7333 **Bird, Dickie,** *i.e.* **James Dennis Bird**
–1 Not out. A. Barker, 1978. xii,161p. illus.
■ ports.
——*another ed.* Readers Union, 1979

## Birkenshaw, Jack

7333 **Lowe, Denis,** *editor*
–2 Jack Birkenshaw's testimonial brochure.
■ Benefit Cttee., 1974. [68]p. incl. adverts.
illus. ports. stats.

## Bligh, *Hon.* Edward Vesey

7334 **Wingfield-Stratford, Esmé Cecil**
■ This was a man: the biography of the

Ian Botham *photo: Patrick Eagar*

Geoffrey Boycott *photo: Patrick Eagar*

Don Bradman *photo: Keystone Press*

Dennis Compton *photo: Popperfoto*

Honourable Edward Vesey Bligh . . .
Hale, 1949. 288p. illus. ports.
*cricket pp. 173–175. etc.*

7335  The lords of Cobham Hall. Cassell, 1959.
▪    xii,451p. illus. ports. diagrs. maps, plan
     *cricket references mostly on John Bligh, 4th earl of Darnley, and Edward Bligh, pp. 291–2, 308, 319–21, 326, 334, 346, 368, 370, 422, 429, 432*

### Blunden, Edmund Charles

7335  **Prance, Claude Annett**
–1   "Edmund Blunden and cricket". *In* The
▪    Private Library, 3rd series. Vol. 1:4, Winter, 1978. pp. 142–7

7335  **University of Hong Kong.** *The English*
–2   *Society*
▪    Edmund Blunden sixty-five. November 1961; edited by Chau Wah Ching, Lo King Man, Yung Kai Kin. Hong Kong, Cultural Enterprise Co., for the Society, [1961]. 213p. illus. ports. facsims. bibliog.
     *many cricket references included p. 110 "To E.B. 65 not [out]" poem by Matthew Hodgart, and pp. 119–20 "A collection of words on E.B. the cricketer" poem by John R. Hung*

### Blythe, Colin ("Charlie")

7336  **Essays** of the year. 1933–34; compiled by
▪    F.J. Harvey Darton. Argonaut P., 1934. xxiv,420p.
     *includes N. Cardus "Blythe of Kent", pp. 95–101*

### Boger, Alnod John

7337  **Boger, Alnod John**
▪    The road I travelled. Bristol, Arrowsmith, 1936. 304p. illus. port.
     *chap. 3 "Country house and club cricket", pp. 39–53*

### Bolland, William

7338  **Bolland, William**
▪    Cricket notes; with a letter containing practical hints, by W. Clark. Trelawney Saunders, 1851. iv,155p.
     *historical essays, reminiscences and commentary*

### Bolus, John Brian

7339  **Plumtree Cricket Club**
▪    Plumtree C.C. v. Nottinghamshire County Cricket Club, 5th Sept. 1971: Brian Bolus benefit; edited by W.S. Smith. Plumtree (Notts.), the Club, [1971]. 36p. incl. adverts. ports.

### Bond, John David ('Jack')

7340  **Kay, John,** *editor*
▪    Jack Bond—the little giant: testimonial brochure. Testimonial Cttee., [1970]. [36]p. illus. ports. stats.

### Bone, David Drummond

7341  **Bone, David Drummond**
▪    Fifty years' reminiscences of Scottish cricket. Glasgow, Aird & Coghill, 1898. 290p. illus. ports.

### Booth, John Bennion

7342  **Booth, John Bennion**
▪    Old Pink 'un days. Richards, 1924. 413p. ports.
     *scattered cricket references*

7343  A "Pink 'un" remembers. T. Werner
▪    Laurie, 1937. xx,286pp.
     *ch. ix. "Some amateur cricketers", pp. 176–86*

### Botham, Ian Terence

7343  **Farmer, Bob**
–1   Ian Botham. Hamlyn, 1979. 160p. illus.
▪    ports. scores, stats.

### Bowen, William Edward

7344  **Bowen, Hon. William Edward**
▪    Edward Bowen: a memoir. Longmans, Green, 1902. viii,417p.
     *includes E. Bowen's cricket verses*

### Bowes, William Eric ('Bill')

7345  **Bowes, William Eric ('Bill')**
▪    Express deliveries. S. Paul, [1949]. 203p. illus. ports.
     ——*another ed.* Sportsman's Book Club, 1958

7346  **Yorkshire Evening News**
▪    Bill Bowes benefit 1947: souvenir brochure. [Leeds], Yorkshire Evening News, [1947]. [12]p. illus. ports. stats.

### Bowker, Archibald Edgar

7347  **Bowker, Archibald Edgar**
     Behind the bar. Staples P., 1947. 323p. illus. port.
     ——*2nd ed.* 1948
     *references to Sir Pelham Warner and Learie Constantine*

### Bowyer, John

7348  **[Gale, Frederick]**
▪    The Alabama claims. Supplementary

treaty between Her Most Gracious Majesty Queen Victoria on the one hand, and The Government of the United States on the other hand. By John Bowyer, cricketer of Mitcham, aetat 82. Mitcham, [the Author, 1872]. 4p. fold.

*"issued for a shilling subscription for John Bowyer, a worthy old cricketer, who played his first match for the County of Surrey, 62 years ago!"*

7349 Mr. Pepys on cricket: addition to Pepys'
■ Diary, discovered in the Mitcham Parish fire-engine, where it had been hidden for two centuries. Presented to both Houses of Parliament, by order of The Cricketers of England. Mitcham, [the Author], 1873. 4p. fold. illus.

*"proceeds to John Bowyer, the oldest Surrey cricketer alive, who will enter his 84th year on June 18th"*

## Boyce, Keith David

7349 **Copford C.C.** v. Essex C.C.C. Keith
–1 Boyce's benefit match, Copford Cricket
■ Club, 10 September. Copford, the Club, [1977]. [32]p. incl. adverts. ports.

7349 **Ilford Cricket Club**
–2 Keith Boyce benefit. Ilford C.C. & Essex
■ C.C.C. present a Double Wicket Competition on Saturday 2 October 1977, Valentines Park, Cranbrook Road: souvenir programme. Ilford, the Club, [1977]. [28]p. incl. adverts. ports. stats.

## Boycott, Geoffrey

7349 **Bailey, Les**
–3 When dreams come true – Geoff Boycott. The Author, [1977?]. bs. card
*a poem to commemorate Boycott's 100th century; limited edition of 250 copies*

7350 **Geoff Boycott**, Yorkshire & England, 10 years as no. 1. Pontefract, printed by Baker Bros., 1974. 36p. illus. ports. stats.

7350 **Yorkshire Evening Post**
–1 Test match special. "Go to it, Geoff." Issue for 11th August, 1977. Leeds, Yorkshire Evening Post. 12p.
"It's magic!" Issue for 12th August 1977. 18p.

## Bradley, Arthur Granville

7351 **Bradley, Arthur Granville**
■ Other days: recollections of rural England, and old Virginia, 1860–1880. Constable, 1913. xi,427p. port.
*ch. iv "Country cricket forty years ago", pp. 105–30, and pp. 410–20, Cricket v. Philadelphia*

7351 When squires and farmers thrived.
–1 Methuen, 1927. ix,244p.
■ *cricket pp. 10–16*

## Bradman, Sir Donald George

7351 **Barnaby, Jane,** *editor*
–2 Australians in sport; illustrated by John
■ Mason. N. Melbourne, Cassell Australia, 1974. 116p. illus. (some col.)
*includes pp. 31–41 "A quiet hero" by Anthony Davis on [Sir Donald Bradman]*

7352 **Bradman,** *Sir* Donald George
■ Don Bradman's book: the story of my cricketing life, with hints on batting, bowling and fielding. Hutchinson, 1930. 256p. illus. ports. scores, stats.
——de luxe ed. with additional chapters by Bruce Harris. 1938. 216p.
——paper ed. 1938

7353 My cricketing life. S. Paul, [1938]. 189p.
■ illus. ports.

7354 Farewell to cricket. Hodder & Stoughton,
■ 1950. 320p. illus. ports. stats.
——*limited ed.* Theodore Brun, 1950
*150 copies only*
——*another ed.* Sportsman's Book Club, 1953

7355 **Chitnis, Shankar Lakshmi**
Don Bradman. Bombay, Hindimata Prakashan, 1959. vi,128p. illus. ports.
*Marathi text*

7356 **[Entry cancelled]**

7357 **Davis, Anthony**
■ Sir Donald Bradman. Cassell, 1960. [v],122p. illus. (Red Lion Lives series)

7357 **Docker, Edward Wybergh**
–1 Bradman and the Bodyline Series.
■ Brighton, Sydney, etc., Angus & Robertson, 1978. [v],165p. illus. ports. bibliog.

7358 **Downer, Sidney**
■ Goodbye, Bradman. Shirakawa, 1944. [x], 3–224p. *unpublished MS*
*written from memory in a Japanese P.O.W. camp in Formosa and bound by a British soldier in Manchuria. At M.C.C. Library, Lord's.*

7359 **Fingleton, Jack,** *i.e.* **John Henry Webb**
■ **Fingleton**
Brightly fades the Don. Collins, 1949. 256p. illus. ports. stats.
——*Australian ed.* Sydney, Collins, 1949. [ii],277p. illus. ports. stats.

**7360 Flicker Productions Ltd**
□ Cricket: Don Bradman. Flicker Productions, [1930]. (Flickers. Sports Series)
  *No. 1. On drive and off drive*
  *2. Square cut and late cut*
  *3. Leg glance and pull*
  *cine-photographs in the form of a 'flicker-book'*

**7360 The Guardian**
**−1** The bedside 'Guardian' 22: a selection
■ from The Guardian 1972–73; edited by W.L. Webb. Collins, 1973. 255p. illus.
  *includes pp. 174–7, "A test from the tee with Bradman", by Pat Ward-Thomas [on Bradman as a golfer]*

**7361** The Guardian omnibus 1821–1971: an
■ anthology of 150 years of Guardian writing chosen and edited by David Ayerst. Collins, 1973. 768p.
  *includes: "Bradman, a problem everlastingly insoluble" by Cricketer [Neville Cardus], the article for Saturday, July 12, 1930*

**7362 Hoare, Robert J.**
■ Four-minute miler, *and* The boy from Bowral. Macmillan, 1962. 79p. illus. ports. (The Champion Library)
  *on Roger Bannister and Sir Don Bradman; for children*

**7363 Home and away:** a Contact book. Contact Publications, 1948. 112p. incl. adverts. illus. ports. diagrs.
  *includes "The phenomenal Bradman" by R.C. Robertson-Glasgow and other chapters containing cricket*

**7363 100 famous** Australian lives. Hamlyn,
**−1** 1969. 616p. ports.
  *contains pp. 482–8 "Sir Donald Bradman" by Stuart Reid*

**7364 Lindsay, Philip**
■ Don Bradman. Phoenix House, 1951. 64p. ports. (Cricketing Lives)

**7365 Moyes, Alban George ("Johnnie")**
■ Bradman. Harrap, 1948. 222p. illus. ports. stats.
  ——*also published*, Sydney, Angus & Robertson, 1948. xvi,216p.

**7366 Natu, G.N.**
  Bradman. Poona, R.B. Samudra, 1936. 96p. illus. bibliog.
  *in Marathi*

**7366 O'Hagan, Jack**
**−1** Our Don Bradman; words and music by Jack O'Hagan. Melbourne, Allan & Co., 1930. [4]p.

**7367 "Outfield",** *pseud.*
  The Bradman book: the story of the world's greatest cricketer; drawn by Will Mahony. [Melbourne], Atlas Publications, [1948]. [31]p. illus.

**7368 Roberts, Edward Lamplough**
■ Bradman 1927–1941: New South Wales, South Australia, Australia. Birmingham, Hudson, 1944. 64p. illus. ports. stats.

**7368 Rosenwater, Irving**
**−1** Sir Donald Bradman: a biography. Batsford, 1978. 416p. illus. ports. facsims.
■ ford, 1978. 416p. illus. ports. facsims. diagrs. stats.

**7369 Wakley, Bertram Joseph**
■ Bradman the great. Kaye, 1959. 317p. port. stats.
  ——*another ed.* Sportsman's Book Club, 1960

**7370 Walters, David William**
  Modern lives. Collins, 1954. 256p. illus.
  *includes Sir Donald Bradman*

**7371 Whitington, Richard Smallpeice**
■ Bradman, Benaud and Goddard's cinderellas. Cape Town, Timmins; London, Bailey Bros. & Swinfen, 1964. 237p. illus. ports.
  *includes an account of Sir Donald Bradman and of the South African matches in New Zealand, 1964*

## Brain, Brian

**7371 Triple** testimonial fund 1976: Brian Brain,
**−1** Jim Yardley, Rodney Cass. [Testimonial
■ Cttee., 1976]. 40p. incl. adverts. illus. stats.

## Braithwaite, Cecil

**7372 Braithwaite, Cecil**
■ Happy days with rod, gun and bat. Home Words Printing & Publishing Co., *for private circulation*, [1946]. 127p. frontis.
  *cricket pp. 115–27*

## Braithwaite, Charles H.

**7373 Pleasants, Henry**
■ Charles H. Braithwaite: one hundredth birthday, September 10th, 1945, 1845–1945. Philadelphia, Pa., Suburban & Wayne Times, 1945. [4]p. port

## Brayshaw, Alfred Neave

**7373 Brayshaw, Alfred Neave**
**−1** Memoir and selected writings. Birmingham. Woodbrooke Extension Committee

of the Society of Friends, [1941]. x,190p. illus. port.
*pp. 147–9 "Cricket days"*

## Brearley, John Michael

7373 Mike Brearley, O.B.E. benefit brochure
−2 1978. Benefit Cttee., [1978]. [40]p. incl.
■ adverts. illus. ports. (1 team port. in col.), stats.

## Bridges, John Affleck

7374 **Bridges, John Affleck**
A sportsman of limited income: recollections of fifty years. A. Melrose, 1910. vii,309p.

## Briggs, John

7375 **Craig, Albert**
■ John Briggs. Cricket P., 1897. [4]p. folded card. port.
*publd. anonymously*
——All England Publ. Co., 1898. [4]p. folded card. port.
*author's name given*

7376 **Swindells, Thomas**
■ John Briggs: a complete record of his performances in Lancashire county cricket ... Manchester, W.H. Smith, 1902. 24p. stats.

7377 **Turner, Herbert**
■ The life of John Briggs: humorous and pathetic anecdotes; astounding feats with bat and ball in England, Scotland, Australia and Africa; recollections of eminent cricketers; illustrated by "Rip". Manchester, T. Sowler, 1902. 44p. illus. port. stats.

7378 **Wright, W.R.**
■ Abel and Briggs: an amusing adventure in South Africa. All England Athletic Publishing Co., 1898. [4]p. folded card. 2 ports on cover
*during the 1888–89 tour*

## Brockwell, William

7379 **Coldham, James Desmond**
■ William Brockwell: his triumph and tragedy. *Privately printed*, 1970. [i],20p.
*100 signed and numbered copies; rptd. from* Journal of the Cricket Society

7380 **Craig, Albert**
■ William Brockwell. All England Athletic Publ. Co., 1898. [4]p. folded card. port.
——*another issue.* 1899

## Brookes, Dennis

7381 **Dennis Brookes** (Northamptonshire and
■ England) testimonial fund souvenir. [Northampton], Northampton Chronicle & Echo, [1948]. [4]p. fold. illus. port.

7382 **[Northamptonshire County Cricket**
■ **Club]**
Dennis Brookes benefit book. [Northampton, the Club, 1958]. 24p. incl. adverts. illus. ports. stats.

## Brooking, George A.

7383 **Brooking, George A.**
■ 55 years cricket memories. Liverpool, the Author, 1948. 156p. illus. ports. scores

## Brown, Anthony Stephen ("Tony")

7383 **Foot, David,** *editor*
−1 Tony Brown jubilee cricketer: souvenir
■ testimonial brochure 1953–1977. [Benefit Cttee. 1977]. 48p. incl. adverts. illus. ports. stats.

## Brown, David John

7384 **Warwickshire County Cricket Club**
■ David J. Brown's benefit 1973. [Birmingham], the Club, [1973]. [4]p. fold. illus. stats.

7385 David Brown benefit year 1973: souvenir
■ brochure. Birmingham, [the Club, 1973]. [68]p. incl. adverts. illus. ports.

## Brown, Frederick Richard

7386 **Brown, Frederick Richard**
■ Cricket musketeer. Kaye, 1954. 215p. illus. ports. stats.

## Brown, John Thomas

7387 **Interesting** facts about J.T. Brown
*chart; in Taylor*

## Brummell, George Bryan ('Beau')

7388 **[Benjamin, Lewis Saul]**
Beau Brummell: his life and letters, by Lewis Melville. Hutchinson, 1924. 313p. illus. ports.
*pp. 27–9 Brummell as a cricketer at Eton, with a list of his contemporaries in the Eton XI, 1793*

## Budd, Edward Hayward

7389 **Mr. Budd,** the cricketer
*only one copy seen by A.D. Taylor, bearing
no date, publisher or printer's name. Reprint
of magazine article?*

7390 **W[heeler] C.A.,** *editor*
■ Sportascrapiana; cricket and shooting . . .
by celebrated sportsmen; with hitherto
unpublished anecdotes of the nineteenth
century. . .; edited by CAW. Simpkin,
Marshall, 1867. xvi,328p.
——*2nd ed. with title:* Sportascrapiana:
facts in athletics. 1868. xvi,301p.
——*cheap ed.* 1870
*reminiscences of E.H. Budd*

## Burden, Mervyn

7391 **Arlott, [Leslie Thomas] John**
■ Mervyn Burden; a memoir. [Southamp-
ton, Hampshire C.C.C.], 1964. [8]p. port.
*limited ed. of 25 copies*

## Burgess, Graham

7391 **Graham Burgess** testimonial year 1977.
–1 [Testimonial Year Cttee., 1977]. 56p. incl.
■ adverts. illus. ports. stats.

## Burns, John

7392 **Kent, William Richard Gladstone**
■ John Burns: Labour's lost leader: a
biography. Williams & Norgate, 1950.
xv,389p. illus. ports.
*cricket pp. 349–56, etc.*

## Burrows, James Thomas

7392 **Burrows, James Thomas**
–1 Pathway among men. Adelaide, Whitcombe & Tombs, 1974. 212p. illus.
*pp. 61–7 "Cricket days"*

## Burstow, George Philip

7393 **Burstow, George Philip**
■ Cricket reminiscences 1923–1966; extracted from his diaries and journal.
Brighton, Brighton College, the Author,
1966. [iii],59p. *typescript*

## Burton, Geoffrey S.

7394 **Burton, Geoffrey S.**
■ Free gratis and for nothing. *Privately
printed,* 1948. 142p. frontis.
*cricket pp. 97–141*

## Buse, Herbert Thomas Francis

7395 **Moore, Bob,** *editor*
■ Bertie Buse benefit book. Bristol, Bristol

Evening Post, [1953]. [16]p. illus. ports.
stats.

## Buss, Michael Alan ("Mike")

7395 **Sussex County Cricket Club**
–1 Mike Buss benefit 1976. Hove, the Club,
■ [1976]. 6p. fold. illus.

## Butt, Harry

7396 [**Harry Butt's** benefit match. . .1900]
*contains pen-portrait of H.B. by "Leather
Hunter" [A.J. Gaston]; Sussex v. Yorkshire
match, Aug. 23, 24, 25, 1900*

## Butterworth, Hugh Montagu

7396 **Butterworth, Irene**
–1 He that has once been happy is, for aye,
out of destruction's reach. Bath, the
Mendip P., printed for pivate circulation,
1975. 53p. illus.
*includes ch. on ·Hugh Montagu Butter-
worth*

## Buxton, Ian

7397 **Mortimer, Gerald,** *editor*
■ All-rounder: Ian Buxton's testimonial
brochure. [Derby, Derbyshire C.C.C.,
1972]. 52p. illus. ports. stats.

## Caffyn, William

7398 **Caffyn, William**
■ Seventy-one not out: the reminiscences of
William Caffyn; edited by "Mid-on" [R.P.
Daft]. Blackwood, 1899. xiv,265p. illus.
ports. diagrs.
——*2nd rev. ed.* 1900. 284p.

## Campbell, Ian Maxwell

7399 **Campbell, Ian Maxwell**
■ Wayward tendrils of the vine. Chapman & Hall, 1947. viii,210p.
*limited to 750 copies*
——*another ed.* 1948
*cricket pp. 55, 109, 143–44, 159*

7400 Reminiscences of a vintner. Chapman &
■ Hall, 1950. xi,276p. illus. ports. score
*chap. 4 "The joy of cricket", pp. 35–48;
chap. 5 "W.G. Grace", pp. 49–66*

## Cannings, Victor Henry Douglas

7401 **Arlott [Leslie Thomas] John**
■ V.H.D. Cannings: an appreciation.
[Southampton, Hampshire C.C.C.,] 1958.
[8]p. port. stats.
*ltd. ed. of 50 signed copies; 1st publd. in
Hampshire C.C.C. Handbook, 1959*

## Cardus, *Sir* Neville

7402  **Cardus,** *Sir* **Neville**
■  Autobiography. London, Collins, 1947; Sydney, Collins, 1948. 288p. illus. ports.
——*rptd.* Collins in assoc. with the Book Society, 1947. 288p.
——*rptd.* Readers Union, 1949
——*rptd.* Collins, 1955. 252p. (Fontana Books)

7403  Second innings: more autobiography.
■  London & Sydney, Collins, 1950. 256p.

7403  My life: compiled from "Autobiography"
–1  and "Second innings" by H. G.
■  Earnshaw. Collins, 1965. 191p. (Modern Authors Series)

7404  Full score. Cassell, 1970. [vii],217p.
■  ——reissued. Quality Book Club, 1970. iii,217p.
    *cricket pp. 95–134; 161–89 and other scattered references*

7404  **Daniels, Robin**
–1  Conversations with Cardus. Gollancz,
■  1976. 288p. illus. ports. bibliog.
    *cricket pp. 55–69, 219, 221, 224–5, 226, 234–5, 246–7, 253–4, 256, 257*

7405  **Garvin, James Louis**
  Neville Cardus: an appreciation. The Observer, 1929. 3p.
    *reprint of author's review of "The Summer game" in* The Observer

7405  **The Guardian**
–1  The bedside "Guardian" 24: a selection
■  from The Guardian 1974–75; edited by W.L. Webb. Collins, 1975. 263p. illus.
    *includes pp. 215–7, "Thanksgiving for Neville Cardus", by J.B. Priestley*

## Carew, Dudley

7406  **Carew, Dudley**
■  The house is gone: a personal retrospect. Hale, 1949. 256p.
    *cricket in ch. 2*

## Carmichael, Ian

7406  **Carmichael, Ian**
–1  Will the real Ian Carmichael. . .; an auto-
■  biography. Macmillan, 1979. 400p. illus. ports.
    *many cricket references including an account of the formation of The Lord's Taverners*

## Carpenter, Robert

7407  **Spratt, A.W.**
  A short account of the career of the eminent cricketer Robert Carpenter. Cambridge, C.U.P., 1897. 15p.

## Carr, Arthur William

7408  **Carr, Arthur William**
■  Cricket with the lid off. Hutchinson, [1935]. 256p. illus. ports. stats.
——*rptd.* 1936
    see also: *no. 6074*

## Carson, W.N.

7409  **Carman, Arthur H.**
■  W.N. Carson, footballer and cricketer. Wellington (N.Z.), Sporting Publications, 1947. 66p. illus. ports. stats.

## Carter, Hanson

7409  **Atkins, Jack,** *compiler*
–1  Hanson Carter, "Australia's undertaker
■  wicketkeeper". Waverley (N.S.W.), Waverley Historical Society, 1976. 36p. ports. stats. ("Historical Waverley" Series 2)

## Carter, Robert George Mallaby

7410  **Worcestershire County Cricket Club**
■  Souvenir book to commemorate the testimonial year awarded to Bob Carter. [Worcester, the Club, 1973]. [42]p. incl. adverts. illus. ports. stats.

## Carter, Horatio Stratton ('Raich')

7411  **Carter, Raich,** *i.e.* **Horatio Stratton Carter**
■  Footballer's progress: edited by Edward Lanchbery. Sporting Handbooks, 1950. 237p. illus. ports.
    *ch. xv "Cricket against the Australians": chap. xxx "Cricket memories"*

## Cartwright, Thomas William

7412  **Warwickshire County Cricket Club**
■  T.W. Cartwright's benefit season, 1968. Birmingham, the Club, [1968]. [4]p. fold. ports. stats.

## Cass, Rodney

7412  Triple testimonial fund 1976: Brian Brain,
–1  Jim Yardley, Rodney Cass. [Testimonial
■  Cttee., 1976]. 40p. incl. adverts. illus. stats.

## Chappell, Ian Michael

7413  **Chappell, Ian Michael**
■  My world of cricket. N. Sydney (N.S.W.), Jack Pollard, 1973; Folkstone, Bailey Bros. & Swinfen, 1975. 144p. illus. and ports. (some col.)
    *a symposium built round I.C. apparently to the plan of Jack Pollard*

**7413** Cricket in our blood: an autobiography.
**–1** S. Paul, 1976 [i.e. 1977]. 206p. illus. ports.
■ stats.
  *originally published as "Chappelli: Ian Chappell's life story". Richmond (Vic.), Hutchinson of Australia, 1976*

### Cheetham, John Erskine ('Jack')

**7414** **Cheetham, Jack, *i.e.* John Erskine**
■ **Cheetham**
  Caught by the Springboks. Hodder & Stoughton, 1954. 248p. illus. ports. scores, stats.

**7415** I declare. Hodder & Stoughton, 1956.
■ xi,227p. illus. scores, stats.

### Chester, Frank

**7416** **Chester, Frank**
■ How's that! Hutchinson, 1956. 208p. illus. ports.

### Chipp, Herbert

**7417** **Chipp, Herbert**
  Lawn tennis recollections. Merritt & Hatcher, 1898. 144p.
  *contains references to A.E. Stoddart and other cricketers*

### Christian Victor, *Prince*

**7418** **Warren, *Sir* Thomas Herbert**
■ Christian Victor: the story of a young soldier. Murray, 1903. xviii,492p. illus. ports. maps
  ——*2nd ed. 1903*
  *ch. xiii: "The Prince as a cricketer"*

### Christopher, Alfred Millard William

**7419** **Reynolds, John Stewart**
■ Canon Christopher of St. Aldgate's. Oxford. Abingdon, Abbey P., 1967. xxiv,500p. ports.
  *cricket pp. 12–13, 23–25, 66, 101, 159, 187*

### Church, Alfred John

**7419** **Church, Alfred John**
**–1** Memories of men and books. Smith,
■ Elder, 1908. v,286p. port.
  *ch. xviii, "Seventy years of cricket", pp. 250–59*

### Clark, Norman

**7420** **Clark, Norman**
■ All in the game: memoirs of the ring and other sporting experiences. Methuen, 1935. xii,323p. illus. port.

### Clarke, Mary Cowden

**7421** **Clarke, Mary Cowden**
■ My long life: an autobiographical sketch. T. Fisher Unwin, 1896. [iii],264p. ports.
  ——2nd ed. 1896. 260p. ports.
  *references to Charles Cowden Clarke and Nyren*

### Clarke, Robert Wakefield

**7422** **The Bob Clarke** testimonial book.
■ Duston, Northampton, British Timken Ltd., [1957]. 24p. incl. adverts. ports. stats.

### Close, Dennis Brian

**7423** **Brian** Close benefit brochure. [1961]. 40p.
■ illus. ports. scores

**7424** **Close, Brian, *i.e.* Dennis Brian Close**
■ Close to cricket, as told to Frank Taylor. S. Paul, 1968. 152p. illus. ports. scores, stats.

**7424** ——, and **Mosey, Don**
**–1** I don't bruise easily: the autobiogra-
■ phy. . .written in association with Don Mosey. Macdonald and Jane's, 1978. [x],253p. illus. ports. stats.
  ——*another ed. Futura, 1979. 258p. pbk.*

**7424** **Fay, Peter,** *editor*
**–2** Souvenir testimonial brochure Brian
■ Close. Testimonial Cttee., 1976. 40p. incl. adverts. illus. & ports. (some col.), stats.

### Cobbett, Martin Richard

**7425** **Cobbett, Martin Richard**
■ The man on the march. Bliss, Sands, 1896. 370p.
  *"A game of cricket" pp. 335–40*

### Coe, Samuel

**7425** **Sam Coe's** benefit match: Leicestershire
**–1** v. Hampshire, July 6, 7 and 8, 1908. Leicester, Leicestershire C.C.C., [1908]. 22p. illus. ports. stats.

### Coldwell, Leonard John

**7426** **The Len Coldwell** souvenir book 1968.
■ Worcester, *printed by* Barneshall P., [1968]. 48p. incl. adverts. ports.
  *contains team portraits of the first-class counties*

### Collins, Arthur Edward Jeune

**7427** **Arlott, [Leslie Thomas] John**
■ The boy Collins: a biographical essay. [The Author, 1959]. [12]p. port.
  *limited ed. of 15 copies*

**7427 [Craig, Albert]**
**–1** A selection of original rhymes and anecdotes from our football and cricket centres by A.C. Cricket Rhymester. Hughes, 1906. 16p.
*includes* inter alia *poem dedicated to E.M. Grace "A little hero" about A.E.J. Collins (mis-spelt Collings)*

**7428 Unveiling** of a plaque commemorating
■ A.E.J. Collins' score of 628 runs not out in a Junior House cricket match played in June, 1899, by His Grace the Duke of Beaufort. 1962. [4]p. score
*with notes on A.E.J.C. by an O.C.*

## Collins, Thomas

**7429 Collins, Thomas**
■ School and sport: recollections of a busy life. Elliot Stock, 1905. xi,267p.
*cricket in ch. ii*

## Collins, William Edmund Wood

**7430 Collins, William Edmund Wood**
■ Leaves from an old country cricketer's diary. Edinburgh and London, Blackwood, 1908. [v],327p.
——paper ed. 1908

**7431 Masterman,** *Sir* **John Cecil**
Bits and pieces. Hodder & Stoughton, 1961. 192p. port.
*essays, including "W.E.W. Collins"*

## Colman, *Sir* Jeremiah (1886–1961)

**7432 Colman,** *Sir* **Jeremiah (1886–1961)**
■ Reminiscences of the Great War, 1914–1918. [Norwich, the Author]. 1940. 104p.
*ch. 16 "The Surrey County Cricket Club", pp. 81–2*

## Colman, Jeremiah James (1830–1898)

**7433 Colman, Helen Caroline**
Jeremiah James Colman: a memoir. *Privately printed*, the Chiswick P., 1905. xviii,464p. illus. ports. table
*cricket pp. 11, 98, 101, 438*

**7434 Colman, Jeremiah James,** *compiler*
■ Cricket records, 1845 to 1887. *Privately printed*, 1887. iv,125p. frontis. scores, stats.
*"collected chiefly from the reports of the matches, in which I have taken part, published by various newspapers"*

## Compton, Denis Charles Scott

**7435 Allen, John**
■ Denis Compton: our greatest all-round sportsman. Pitkin Pictorials, [1949]. 32p. illus. ports. stats.

**7436 Charles, Wyndham**
■ A great sportsman; illustrated by Hookway Cowles. Exeter, Haldon Books, 1967. 37p. illus. (They Reached the Top Series)
*for children*

**7437 Compton, Denis [Charles Scott]**
■ Playing for England: an autobiography. Sampson Low, 1948. xi,231p. illus. ports.
——2nd ed. 1949, xi,241p.

**7438** In sun and shadow. S. Paul, 1952. 223p.
■ illus. ports. scores

**7439** End of an innings. Oldbourne P., 1958.
■ 207p. illus. ports.
——another ed. Calcutta, Rupa, 1962. 180p. illus. ports.

**7439** ——, and **Edrich, William John**
**–1** Cricket and all that. Pelham Books, 1978.
■ 176p. illus. ports.
——rptd. Newton Abbot, Readers Union, 1979

**7440 Daily Graphic**
■ The Compton book: Daily Graphic souvenir. Daily Graphic, [1949]. 24p. incl. adverts. illus. ports. stats.

**7441 Ealing Dean Cricket Club**
■ Compton handbook in aid of the Denis Compton benefit fund: edited by W. Stimpson. Ealing, the Club, [1949]. 16p. illus. ports. stats.

**7442 Foster, Denis**
■ Focus on Denis Compton. Background Books, [1949]. 24p. illus. ports. (Background Sports-Photo Books)

**7443 Peebles, Ian [Alexander Ross]**
■ Denis Compton: the generous cricketer. Macmillan, 1971. 127p. illus. stats.

**7444 Swanton, Ernest William**
■ Denis Compton: a cricket sketch. Sporting Handbooks, 1948. 79p. illus. ports. stats.
——2nd ed. Playfair Books, 1949. 95p.

**7445 Whittaker, Tom**
■ Arsenal story: edited by Roy Peskett. Sporting Handbooks, 1957. 351p. illus. port.
——another ed. Sportman's Book Club, 1958
*numerous references to cricketers especially to Denis & Leslie Compton*

## Compton, Leslie Harry

**7446 Middlesex County Cricket Club**
■ L.H. Compton, Middlesex, benefit 1954;

Learie Constantine *photo: Popperfoto*

Colin Cowdrey *photo: Keystone Press*

George Headley *photo: Popperfoto*

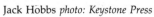

Jack Hobbs *photo: Keystone Press*

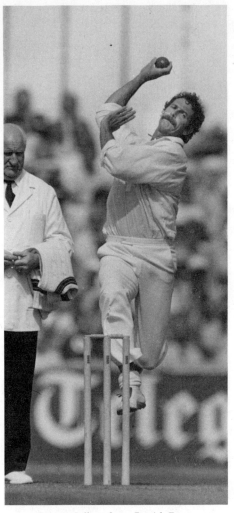

Dennis Lillee *photo: Patrick Eagar*

Middlesex v. Sussex, Lord's June 5th, 7th & 8th. Lord's the Club, [1954]. [4]p. fold

## Coningham, Arthur

**7446** **Clune, Frank**
**-1** Scandals of Sydney Town; illustrated by Virgil Reilly. Sydney, Angus & Robertson, 1957. [i.e. 1958]. xii,228p. illus.
   *ch. 30, pp. 176–9 "The Coningham Conspiracy"*

**7446** **Pearl, Cyril Altson**
**-2** Wild men of Sydney: a turbulent era in Australian social and political life. W.H. Allen, 1958. 255p. illus. ports.
   ——*later edns.*
   *ch. 9, pp. 135–58 "Interlude: cricketer versus priest" – on the Coningham conspiracy*

**7446** **"Zero", *pseud.***
**-3** The secret history of the Coningham case.
■ Sydney, *printed by* Finn Brothers, 1901. xvii,360p. illus. ports. facsims.
   *no cricket content, but of biographical interest*

## Constantine, Learie Nicholas, *Lord Constantine*

**7447** **Constantine, Learie Nicholas, *Lord***
■ *Constantine*
   Cricket and I. P. Allen, 1933. xv,252p. illus. ports. scores

**7448** Cricket in the sun. S. Paul, [1946]. 131p.
■ illus. ports.

**7449** Cricketers' carnival. S. Paul, [1948]. 192p.
■ illus. ports. scores
   *two photos. facing p. 81 listed as Tom Richardson and C.G. Maclaren are Albert Relf and J.W. Maclaren*

**7450** Cricket crackers. S. Paul, [1950]. 192p.
■ illus. ports.

**7450** **Giuseppi, Undine**
**-1** A look at Learie Constantine. Nelson, 1974. viii,144p. illus. ports. facsims. pbk.

**7450** **Howat, Gerald**
**-2** Learie Constantine. Allen & Unwin, 1975.
□ 250p. illus. ports. stats. bibliog.
   ——*another ed.* Readers Union, 1976
   ——*pbk. ed.* 1977

**7451** **Westminster Abbey**
■ Service of thanksgiving for the life and work of Learie Constantine (The Lord Constantine of Maraval and Nelson). Born 1901. Died 1971. Friday, 23 July 1971: (form of service). 12p.

## Cook, Cecil ("Sam")

**7452** **Tetbury Cricket Club**
■ Sam Cook's benefit year: an appreciation written for the club by John Arlott. Tetbury, the Club, [1957]. [4]p.

## Cordle, Anthony Elton ("Tony")

**7452** **Tony Cordle** benefit year 1977. [Benefit
**-1** Cttee., 1977]. 42p. incl. adverts. illus.
■ ports.

## Cornwallis, *Lord* Wykeham Stanley

**7453** **Boorman, H.R. Pratt**
   The spirit of Kent: the Rt. Hon Lord Cornwallis, K.C.V.O., K.B.E., M.C., D.C.L. Maidstone, "Kent Messenger", [1968]. 458p. illus. ports.
   *ch. 2 "Cricket", with references on other pages*

## Corrall, Percy ("Paddy")

**7453** **Leicestershire County Cricket Club**
**-1** Paddy Corrall's benefit. Leicestershire v. Middlesex, July 2, 4 and 5, 1949. [Leicester, the Club, 1949]. [3]p. port.

## Cotton, Reynell

**7454** **The Reynell Cotton** memorial match:
■ Rudgwick C.C. versus Rev. David Sheppard's XI: souvenir programme, May 23, 1959. Rudgwick, the Club, [1959]. [5]p. port. on cover
   *includes song composed by Reynell Cotton for the Hambledon Club, 1761 and an article on him*

## Cowdrey, Michael Colin

**7455** **Cowdrey, Michael Colin**
■ Cricket today. Barker, 1961. 127p. illus. port.

**7456** Time for reflection. Muller, 1962. 207p.
■ illus. ports.
   ——*another ed.* Sportsman's Book Club, 1963

**7457** The incomparable game. Hodder & 
■ Stoughton, 1970. 5–130p. illus. ports.

**7457** M.C.C.: the autobiography of a cricketer.
**-1** Hodder & Stoughton, 1975. 253p. illus.
■ ports. facsim.
   ——*another ed.* Sevenoaks, Coronet Books, 1977
   ——*another ed.* Newton Abbot, Reader's Union, 1977
   *with assistance from Ian Wooldridge and Tony Lewis*

7458 **Davey, H.N.**
■ Bat, ball and Cowdrey: some reminiscences of 50 years of cricket. Canterbury, Jennings, [1968]. 40p. illus. ports.

**Cox, George**

7459 **George Cox** benefit book 1951. [Hove],
■ Benefit Cttee., [1951]. 16p. port. stats.

**Cox, George Ruben**

7459 **George Cox's** benefit match, Sussex v.
–1 Surrey at Hove, September 3, 4 and 5, 1914. [4]p. fold. stats.
*above match was not played owing to outbreak of war. Cox took his benefit in 1920*

7459 **[G.R. Cox's** benefit match. . .1920]
–2 *contains pen-portrait of G.R.C. by "Leather Hunter" [A.J. Gaston]*

**Coxon, Stanley William**

7460 **Coxon, Stanley William**
■ And that reminds me: being incidents of a life spent at sea, and in the Andaman Islands, Burma, Australia and India. Lane, 1915. xvi,324p. illus. ports.
*cricket pp. 150–53, 197, 240, 242–43*

**Cozens-Hardy, Harry Theobald**

7461 **Cozens-Hardy, Harry Theobald**
■ The glorious years: random recollections. Hale, 1953. 255p. illus. ports.
*"Concerning cricket", pp. 125–136*

**Craig, Albert**

7462 **Craig, Albert**
■ Albert Craig: cricket and football rhymster. All England Athletic Co., 1900. [4]p. folded card. port.
*"to be contd. later on"*

7463 Pleasant recollections and amusing incid-
■ ents: the outcome of personal experience on our cricket and football grounds. Hughes & Son, 1900. [16]p.
——rev. ed. 1901. [16]p.

7463 **Intikhab Alam** benefit year 1978. [Benefit
–1 Cttee., 1978]. [48]p. incl. adverts. illus.
■ stats.
*includes "Poetry in motion" by John Arlott on Albert Craig*

7464 **Martin, Radcliffe**
The cricket jester: a study of Craig, cricket rhymster. 1904
*a "leaflet"*

**Crapp, John Frederick**

7465 **J.F. Crapp** benefit souvenir. [1951]. [4]p.
■ folded card. ports. stats.

**Crawford Family**

7465 **The Bourne Society**
–1 Local history records. [Caterham], the
■ Society. *annual*
Vol. XIII. 1974; edited by Mary Alderton. [1974]. 47p. incl. adverts. illus. maps
*includes pp. 10–4 "The Crawfords of Cane Hill" by Roger Packham. Rev. J.C. Crawford was chaplain of Cane Hill Asylum and ran the cricket club there. He and his three sons – V.F.S., R.T. and J.N. all played first-class cricket. J.N. also played for England*

**Crawford, John Neville**

7466 **Craig, Albert**
■ Mr. John Neville Crawford. Wright & Co., 1908. [4]p. folded card. port.

**Curteis, Herbert**

7466 **Curteis, Herbert**
–1 Cricket recollections. Hailsham (Sussex), Jenner, 1918. 12p.

**Daft, Richard**

7467 **Daft, Richard**
■ Kings of cricket: reminiscences and anecdotes with hints on the game. Bristol, Arrowsmith; London, Simpkin, Marshall, [1893]. xiv,274p. illus. ports. scores
——Subscribers' ed. of 150 signed copies. Bolton, Tillotson, 1893

7468 **Press** critiques: Cricket: past, present and
■ future, by W.G. Grace, with complete laws of cricket; also, Kings of cricket, by Richard Daft. Nottingham, Howe, [c.1893]. 32p. port.

7469 A cricketer's yarns: to which have been
■ added a few genealogical tables of Nottinghamshire cricketing families; ed. with an introduction by F.S. Ashley-Cooper. Chapman & Hall, 1926. xix,201p. illus. ports.

**Dance, James**

7470 **Lucas, Edward Verrall**
Only the other day: a volume of essays. Methuen 1936. vi,211p. frontis.
*includes "A cricket poet" [James Dance], pp. 187–94*

**Darling, Douglas K.**

7471 **Darling, Douglas K.**
■ Test tussles on and off the field. Hobart,

the Author, 1970. [6],v,74p. illus. ports. stats.

### Darling, Joseph

7472 **Craig, Albert**
Joseph Darling. All England Athletic Publ. Co., 1899. [4]p. folded card. port.

### Darwin, Bernard [Richard Meirion]

7473 **Darwin, Bernard [Richard Meirion]**
■ Green memories. Hodder & Stoughton, 1928. 333p. illus. ports.
*cricket pp. 38–39, 49–50*

7474 Life is sweet brother. Collins, 1940. 285p.
■ port.
*cricket pp. 21, 57–58, 62, 73, 198–99, 239–41*

7475 Pack clouds away: [autobiographical
■ reminiscences]. Collins, 1941. 288p.
*chap. 13 "A little cricket", pp. 205–18*

### Davey, H.N.

7476 **Davey, H.N.**
■ Bat, ball and Cowdrey: some reminiscences of 50 years of cricket. Canterbury, Jennings, [1968]. 40p. illus. ports.

### Davey, Jack

7476 **Jack Davey** [and] David Sheppard testi-
–1 monial souvenir. [1978]. 52p. incl. ad-
■ verts. illus. & ports. (some col.), stats.

### Davidson, Alan Keith

7477 **Davidson, Alan [Keith]**
■ Fifteen paces. Souvenir P., 1963. 190p. illus. ports. stats.
——*another ed.* Sportsman's Book Club, 1965
——*another ed.* [publd in India], 1969
——*another ed.* Richmond (Vic.), Hutchinson (Australia), 1977. (Marlin Edition). pbk.

### Davies, Dai

7477 **Davies, Dai**
–1 Dai Davies not out. . .78; talking to John
■ Edwards. Llanelli, Dyfed Publications, 1975. 152p. illus. ports. stats.

### Davies, Harry Donald

7478 **Cox, Jack**
Don Davies "an old international". S. Paul, 1962. 224p. illus. ports.
*references to cricket including a chapter on Old Trafford*

### De Mello, Anthony Stanislaus

7479 **National** sports: special Anthony de Mello number. Vol. 10, no. 1, August 1961. New Delhi, Services P., 1961. ports.

### De Selincourt, Hugh

7480 **De Selincourt, Hugh**
■ Young 'un. Methuen, 1927. viii,280p.
*chap. viii "Cricket and something more"*

7481 Studies from life. Unicorn P., 1934. 224p.
■

### Deane, Christopher

7482 **Watson, Edmund Henry Lacon**
Christopher Deane: a character study at school and college. E. Mathews, 1901. 317p. frontis.
——new and cheaper ed. Brown, Langham, 1906
*cricket chs. v and vi*

### Denness, Michael Henry

7482 **Denness, Michael Henry**
–1 I declare. Barker, 1977. 162p. illus. ports.
■ ——*another ed.* Newton Abbot, Readers Union, 1978

7482 **Mike Denness** benefit summer 1974:
–2 souvenir brochure. [Benefit Fund Cttee.,
■ 1974]. 48p. incl. covers & adverts. illus. ports. stats.

### Deodhar. D.B.

7483 **Deodhar, D.B.**
■ I look back: an autobiography. [Madras], Sport & Pastime; London, "The Hindu", [1966]. 96p. illus.
*originally issued with Sport and Pastime, 9–14th June, 1966*

### Dexter, Edward Ralph

7484 **Dexter, Ted,** *i.e.* **Edward Ralph Dexter**
■ Ted Dexter's cricket book. Barker, 1963. 128p. illus.

7485 Ted Dexter declares: an autobiography.
■ S. Paul, 1966. 126p. illus. ports.
——*another ed.* Sportsman's Book Club, 1967

7485 **Harris, Kenneth**
–1 Conversations. Hodder & Stoughton,
■ 1967. 286p.
*a series of interviews first broadcast on B.B.C. TV, or on B.B.C. radio or were first printed in* The Observer; *pp. 55–69 "Ted Dexter, 1964", then captain of the England cricket team*

7486 **Ted Dexter.** Bromley, Photofacts, [1963].
■ 36p. incl. adverts. illus. ports. stats.
(Photofacts no. 1)

## Dexter, Lawrence Victor

7487 **[Dexter Lawrence Victor]**
■ Your policeman are wondering, by Alec
J. Comryn. Gollancz, 1947. 200p.
*autobiography of a Nottingham policeman.*
*ch. 5 "The cricket match", pp. 85–137*

## Digby, Sir Kenelm Edward

7487 **Digby, Lettice**
–1 My ancestors, being the history of the
Digby & Strutt families. *Privately publi-*
*shed.* Spottiswoode, Ballantyne, 1928.
182p.
*cricket pp. 145, 148, 150, 151, 152*

## Dodds, Thomas Carter

7487 **Dodds, Thomas Carter (Dickie)**
–2 Hit hard and enjoy it. Ashurst, Tunbridge
■ Wells, The Cricketer Ltd., 1976. 120p.
illus. ports.
——*another ed.* 1976. pbk.

## D'Oliveira, Basil Lewis

7488 **D'Oliveira, Basil**
■ D'Oliveira: an autobiography. Collins,
1968. 176p. illus. ports. stats.
——*another ed.* Sportsman's Book Club,
1969

7489 The D'Oliveira affair. Collins, 1969. 183p.
■ port.

7489 **The Guardian**
–1 The bedside 'Guardian' 18: a selection
■ from The Guardian 1968–69; edited by
W.L. Webb. Collins, 1969. 240p. illus.
*includes pp. 185–6, "The d'Oliveira deci-*
*sion", by John Arlott*

7489 **Hayter, Reg,** *and* **Nicklin, Frank,** *editors*
–2 The Basil d'Oliviera benefit souvenir
■ book. Evesham, Journal P., 1975. 64p.
incl. adverts. illus. ports. stats.

## Dollery, Horace Edgar

7490 **Dollery, Horace Edgar, ("Tom")**
■ My life story. Birmingham, Birmingham
Gazette, [1950]. 23p. illus. ports.
*contains a section on earlier Warwickshire*
*cricket by Charles Harrold; 1st published as a*
*series of articles entitled "The Dollery Story"*
*in the* Birmingham Gazette

7491 Professional captain. S. Paul, 1952. 192p.
■ illus. port. diagrs.

7492 **"Tom" Dollery** benefit season souvenir
■ 1949. Birmingham, *printed by* Journal
Printing Office, [1949]. 18p. illus. ports.
stats.

7493 **Warwickshire County Cricket Club**
■ Tom Dollery's benefit. Birmingham, the
Club, 1949. 4p. fold. illus. ports. stats.

## Douglas, John William Henry Tyler

7494 **Craze, Michael**
■ A history of Felsted School, 1564–1947.
Ipswich, Cowell, 1955. 360p. illus. ports.
plans
*references to J.W.H.T. Douglas, pp. 233,*
*235, 238–9, 240, 271, 275, 283, 289*

7495 **[See no. 7717–3]**

## Doyle, Sir Arthur Conan

7496 **[Dickson, Carter]**
■ The life of Sir Arthur Conan Doyle, by
John Dickson Carr. Murray, 1949. 362p.
illus. ports.
——*rptd.* Pan Books, 1952
*cricket pp. 21, 75, 170*

7497 **Doyle,** *Sir* **Arthur Conan**
■ Three of them: a reminiscence. Murray,
1923. vii,99p. frontis.
*"About cricket", pp. 16–28*

7498 Memories and adventures. Hodder &
■ Stoughton, [1924]. 408p. illus. ports.
——*2nd ed.* Murray, 1930. 460p. illus.
ports.
*cricket pp. 325–332*

7498 **Higham, Charles**
–1 The adventures of Conan Doyle: the life
■ of the creator of Sherlock Holmes.
Hamilton, 1976. 368p. illus. ports. facsims. bibliog.
*many cricket references*

7498 **Nordon, Pierre**
–2 Sir Arthur Conan Doyle: l'homme et
■ l'oeuvre. Paris, [1964]. viii,481p. illus.
port. facsims. (Etudes anglaises)
*cricket pp. 21, 22, 33, 194, 195*

7498 **Pearsall, Ronald**
–3 Conan Doyle: a biographical solution.
■ Weidenfeld & Nicolson, 1977. vii,208p.
illus. ports. bibliog.
*cricket pp. 6–7, 69–70*

## Drinkwater, John

7499 **Drinkwater, John**
Discovery: being the second book of an
autobiography, 1897–1913. Benn, 1932.
235p. illus. ports.
*references to cricket in Nottingham*

## Druitt, Montague John

7500 **Cullen, Tom**
Autumn of terror: Jack the Ripper his
crimes and times. Bodley Head, 1965.
254p. illus. map, bibliog.
——*another ed.* Collins Fontana, 1966
——*rptd.* 1973
*names M.J. Druitt as Jack the Ripper*

7501 **Farson, Daniel**
■ Jack the Ripper. M. Joseph, 1972. 144p.
illus. ports. map on endpapers
——[rev. ed.] Sphere Books, 1973. 157p.
*pbk.*
*the rev. ed. incorporates the cricket material
on M.J. Druit by Irving Rosenwater first
published in* The Cricketer, *Jan. 1973*

7501 **Knight, Stephen**
–1 Jack the Ripper: the final solution.
■ Harrap, 1976. 284p. illus. ports. bibliog.
*Druitt's cricketing career pp. 135–6.
Author argues against M.J. Druitt being Jack
the Ripper*

7501 **McCormick, Donald**
–2 The identity of Jack the Ripper. Jarrolds,
1959. 192p. frontis. bibliog.
——*2nd rev. ed.* Long, 1970. 256p. illus.
ports. facsims. map, bibliog.
——*pbk. ed.* Arrow, 1970
*references to M.J. Druitt, pp. 178–9, 195,
197–202*

## Duckworth, Leslie Blakey

7502 **Duckworth, Leslie Blakey**
■ Cricket my love. Birmingham, Cornish,
1946. 50p. illus. ports.

7503 Cricket from the hearth; illustrations by
■ Arrowsmith. Birmingham, Cornish,
[1948]. [vi],98. illus.

## Duffus, Louis George

7504 **Duffus, Louis George**
■ Play abandoned: [an autobiography].
Cape Town, Timmins; Folkstone, Bailey
Bros. & Swinfen, 1969. 185p. illus. ports.

## Duleepsinhji, Kumar Shri

7505 **Merchant, Vijay,** *and others, editors*
■ Duleep, the man and his game: commemoration volume. Bombay, Vijay Merchant, for Commemoration Volume Committee, 1963. xvi,312p. illus. ports. stats.

## Eagar, Edward Desmond Russell

7506 **Arlott, [Leslie Thomas] John**
■ Desmond Eagar: a memoir on his retirement from first-class cricket. [Southamp-
ton, Hampshire C.C.C.], 1958. [6]p. port.
*limited ed. of 20 copies; first published in*
Hampshire C.C.C. Handbook, *1958*

## East, Ray

7506 **Ilford C.C. & Essex C.C.C.** present a
–1 double wicket competition sponsored by
■ Byron Shipping Ltd. on Sunday, 8th
October 1978, Valentines Park, Cranbrook Road. Ray East benefit: souvenir
programme. [The Clubs, 1978]. [20]p.
incl. adverts. ports. stats.

7506 **Ray East** benefit year 1978. Benefit Cttee.,
–2 [1978]. 52p. incl. covers & adverts. illus.
■ ports. stats.

## Edrich Family

7506 **Barker, Ralph**
–3 The cricketing family Edrich; with a stat-
■ istical summary by Irving Rosenwater.
Pelham Books, 1976. 190p. illus. ports.
stats.
——*another ed.* Readers Union, 1977

7506 **The Lord's Taverners** versus An All-
–4 Edrich XI, Ingham, Norfolk, 15 Septem-
■ ber. [Lord's Taverners, 1963]. 28p. incl.
covers & adverts. port.
*with inset of [12]p. incl. adverts., which
includes a brief note on 'The Edrich XI in the
cricket field'*

## Edrich, Geoffrey

7507 **Todd, Eric,** *editor*
■ The Geoff. Edrich benefit book 1955.
[Manchester], Kemsley Newspapers,
[1955]. 30p. incl. adverts. ports. stats.

## Edrich, John Hugh

7508 **Edrich, John [Hugh]**
■ Runs in the family; as told to David Frith.
S. Paul, 1969. 158p. illus. ports. stats.
——*another ed.* Sportsman's Book Club,
1970
——*another ed.* Bombay, Jaico, 1970. 160p.
illus. ports. stats.

7508 **John Edrich** testimonial year 1975. Gala
–1 cricket match: Vic Lewis All Star XI versus
■ Shepperton C.C. ... 18th May 1975:
souvenir programme. Woking, *printed by*
Unwin Bros. Ltd., [1975]. [24]p. incl.
adverts. ports.
*includes a brief note on Shepperton C.C.*

7508 **Martin, Tony,** *compiler*
–2 John Edrich testimonial year book 1975.
■ Old Woking, Unwin Bros., 1975. [32]p.
illus. port. stats.

**7509  Surrey County Cricket Club**
■ The John Edrich benefit brochure 1968. The Club, [1968]. 48p. incl. adverts. illus. ports. stats.

## Edrich, William John

**7510  Davis, D.S.**
■ Great batsmen photo-analysed: W.J. Edrich. Photo Instruction Books, [1949]. [31]p. illus. port.

**7511  Edrich, William John**
■ Cricket heritage. S. Paul, [1948]. 224p. illus. ports. scores

**7512** Cricketing days. S. Paul. [1950]. 231p.
■ illus. ports.

**7513** Round the wicket. Muller, 1959. viii,202p.
■ illus. ports. scores

## Edwards, Michael John ("Mike")

**7513  Surrey County Cricket Club**
**–1** Mike Edwards' benefit 1974. [The Club,
■ 1974]. [3]p.
    *with an appreciation by John Arlott*

## Elkington, Gerald

**7513  Harrigan, Bob**
**–2** Gerald Elkington. Offprint from the
■ Llanelli Star, August 1978. [4]f. score, *typescript*
    *an account of Elkington's role in the Australia v. Gentlemen of S. Wales match at Swansea, 1878*

## Elliott, Wallace Harold

**7513  Elliott, Wallace Harold**
**–3** Undiscovered ends: autobiography. P. Davies, [1951]. 281p.
    *cricket pp. 131,174–8*

## Engineer, Farokh Maneksha

**7513  Maddock, John,** *editor*
**–4** Farokh Engineer testimonial year book
■ 1976. Benefit Cttee., [1976]. 140p. incl. adverts. illus. ports. stats.

## Erskine, James Francis St. Clair, *earl of Rosslyn*

**7514  Erskine, James Francis St. Clair,** *earl of*
■ *Rosslyn*
    My gamble with life. Cassell, 1928. [x],309p. illus. ports.
    *references to cricket at Eton, Northants., etc. pp. 11–13*

## Evans, Alfred John

**7515  Evans, Alfred John**
■ Heir to adventure: notes for an autobiography. *Privately printed*, 1961. [vii], 157p. score

## Evans, Thomas Godfrey

**7516  Evans, [Thomas] Godfrey**
■ Behind the stumps. Hodder & Stoughton, 1951. 254p. illus. ports. diagrs.
    ——*another ed*. Hamilton, 1957. 208p. (Panther Books)

**7517** Action in cricket. Hodder & Stoughton,
■ 1956. 224p. illus.
    ——*another ed*. Sportsman's Book Club, 1957

**7518** The gloves are off. Hodder & Stoughton,
■ 1960. 253p. illus. ports.
    ——*another ed*. Sportsman's Book Club, 1961

**7519  Godfrey Evans** 1953 book of cricket:
■ [benefit fund brochure]. Canterbury (Kent), *printed by* Kentish Gazette, 1953. 16p. ports. stats.

## Fagg, Arthur Edward

**7520  Fagg, Arthur Edward**
■ Arthur Fagg souvenir benefit book. Maidstone, the Author, [1951]. [12]p. ports.
    *includes photographs of past Kent C.C.C. teams, 1904–50*

## Fairbairn, Stephen

**7521  Fairbairn, Stephen**
    Fairbairn of Jesus: being the personal reminiscences of Steve Fairbairn in Australia, Cambridge, and elsewhere. John Lane, 1931. xiii,293p. port.
    *cricket ch. 5, pp. 82–103*

## Farnes, Kenneth

**7522  Farnes, Kenneth**
■ Tours and Tests. R.T.S.–Lutterworth P., 1940. 203p. illus. ports.

## Favell, Leslie Ernest

**7523  Favell, Les,** *i.e. Leslie Ernest Favell*
■ By hook or by cut. Adelaide, Investigator P., 1970. [vi],238p. illus. ports.

## Fazal Mahmood

**7524  Fazal Mahmood**
    Fazal Mahmood and cricket. Lahore, 1959. 288p. illus.
    *in Urdu*

## Featherstone, Norman

7524 **Fowler, Bob,** *compiler*
-1 Norman Featherstone, Middlesex, testi-
■ monial 1979. [Middlesex C.C.C., 1979].
[40]p. incl. adverts. illus. ports.

## Fender, Percy George Herbert

7524 **Fender, Percy George Herbert**
-2 An A.B.C. of cricket. A. Barker, 1937.
■ 172p. illus. diagr.
*contains much autobiographical material*

## Ferguson, William Henry

7525 **Ferguson, William Henry**
■ Mr. Cricket: the autobiography of W.H.
Ferguson, B.E.M., as told to David R.
Jack. N. Kaye, 1957. 192p. illus. ports.
diagrs.
——*another ed.* Sportsman's Book Club,
1960

## Fielder, Arthur

7526 **Craig, Albert**
■ A. Fielder. Wright & Co., 1907. [4]p.
folded card. port.
——*another issue.* 1908

## Fingleton, John Henry Webb ('Jack')

7527 **Fingleton, Jack,** *i.e.* **John Henry Webb**
■ **Fingleton**
Cricket crisis. Cassell, 1946. 295p. illus.
ports.
——*rptd.* 1947. 271p.

## Fisher, Charles Dennis

7527 **Tennyson,** *Sir* **Charles Bruce Locker**
-1 Life's all a fragment. Cassell, 1953. xi,
■ 264p. ports.
*includes essay on C.D. Fisher*

## Fisher, Douglas

7528 **Fisher, Douglas**
■ Little world. Sylvan. P., 1948. [iv],198p.
*author's early life in a Cotswold village;*
*cricket pp. 135–42*

## Flemming, Leonard

7528 **Flemming, Leonard**
-1 A fool on the veld. Cape Town, Cape
Times Ltd., 1921. 142p.
*cricket pp. 40–6 "My native bowler, Hend-*
*riks"; 86–92 "On our cricket pitch"; pp.*
*114–7 "A Jessop on the veld"*

## Fletcher, Joseph Smith

7529 **Fletcher, Joseph Smith**
■ Memories of a spectator. Nash, 1912.
ix,298p.
*cricket pp. 63–78*

## Flint, Rachael Heyhoe

7529 **Flint, Rachael Heyhoe**
-1 Heyhoe!: the autobiography of Rachel
■ Heyhoe Flint. Pelham Books, 1978. 192p.
illus. ports. facsims.

## Flowers, Wilfred

7530 **Richards, Charles Henry**
W. Flowers the famous cricketer: full
account of his career. Nottingham, Richards, 1890. 12p.
*offprint from "Nottinghamshire cricket*
*scores and biographies", pp. 83–94 with*
*supplementary leaf covering the years 1891–4*

## Foley, Cyril Pelham

7531 **Foley, Cyril Pelham**
■ Autumn foliage. Methuen, 1935. x,281p.
illus. ports. diagrs.
*cricket at Eton, Cambridge & Middlesex*

## Ford, Lionel

7532 **Alington, Cyril Argentine**
■ Lionel Ford. S.P.C.K., 1934. ix,142p.
ports.

## Ford, William Justice

7533 **Ford, William Justice**
■ A cricketer on cricket. Sands, 1900. 171p.
*includes the Australian eleven of 1899*

## Foster, Frank Rowbotham

7534 **Foster, Frank Rowbotham**
■ Cricketing memories. London Publishing
Co., 1930. xxii,183p. illus. ports. diagrs.
——*limited ed.* of 50 copies. 1930

## Foster, Roland

7534 **Foster, Roland**
-1 Come listen to my song. Collins, 1949.
288p. ports.
*cricket pp. 17,18,34,38,65,82*

## Freeman, Alfred Percy

7534 **The Guardian**
-2 The bedside 'Guardian' 14; a selection
■ from The Guardian 1964–1965. Collins,
1965. 256p. illus.
*includes pp. 198–9, " 'Tich' Freeman", by*
*Neville Cardus*

## Fry, Charles Burgess

**7535 Batchelor, Denzil Stanley**
■ C.B. Fry. Phoenix House, 1951. 64p. illus. port. (Cricketing lives)

**7536 Bax, Clifford**
■ Some I knew well. Phoenix House, 1951. 192p. ports.
*biographical essays including "C.B. Fry" p. 110–14; "An author's eleven", pp. 168–76*

**7537 Fry, Charles Burgess**
Cricket (batsmanship); with thirty-two action photographs. Nash, 1912. 253p. illus. (National Library of Sports and Pastimes)

**7538 Life worth living: some phases of an**
■ Englishman. Eyre & Spottiswoode, 1939. 423p. illus. ports.
*later impressions, 1940, 1941, 1947 have fewer illus.*

**7539 Graham, Harry Joscelyn Clive**
■ The bolster book: a book for the bedside (compiled from the occasional writings of Reginald Drake Biffin). Mills & Boon, 1910. xii,306p. frontis.
*includes "C.B. Fry", pp. 71–74*

**7540 Myers, Arthur Wallis**
■ C.B. Fry: the man and his methods. Bristol, Arrowsmith; London, Simpkin, Marshall, [1912]. 190p.

**7541 St. Martin-in-the-Fields**
■ In memoriam Charles Burgess Fry 1872–1945, Tuesday, 18th September, 1956, 11.30 a.m.: order of service. [6]p.

**7542 The Spectator**
Spectator harvest. W. Hamilton, 1952. xii,234p.
*articles from The Spectator, including "C.B. Fry", by Neville Cardus*

## Furniss, Harry

**7543 Furniss, Harry**
■ Harry Furniss at home, written & illustrated by himself. T. Fisher Unwin, 1904. xvi,271p. illus.
*cricket references especially in chs. vii and x*

## Gabriel, Harold E.H.

**7543 Gabriel, Harold E.H.**
**–1** 76 not out – my cricketing life. *Privately*
■ *printed* for the Author, [1979]. [iv],49p. 1 illus. 1 port. *typescript*
*signed and numbered*

## Gardiner, Arthur Stephen

**7544 Gardiner, Arthur Stephen**
■ The autocrat of the cricket field and the Old Crocks: being a record of the proceedings of the Rambling Wandering C.C. The Office, 24, Mark Lane, E.C.3, 1917. x,104p. port.

## Gardner, Fred Charles

**7545 Warwickshire County Cricket Club**
F.C. Gardner benefit souvenir 1958. Birmingham, [the Club], 1958. 24p. illus.

## Garnier Family

**7546 Garnier, Arthur Edmund**
The chronicles of the Garniers of Hampshire during four centuries, 1530–1900. Norwich & London, Jarrold, 1900. xxviii,140p. illus.
*pp. 94–5 gives short account of the Eton v. Winchester match, 1858*

## Gaston, Alfred James

**7546 Rosenwater, Irving**
**–1** Alfred James Gaston: a study in enthus-
■ iasm. *privately printed*, 1975. [iv],11p.
*limited ed. of 50 copies, numbered and signed*

## Gavaskar, Sunil

**7546 Gavaskar, Sunil ("Sunny")**
**–2** Sunny days: an autobiography. Calcutta,
■ Rupa, 1976. [xvi],264p. illus. ports. stats.

## Geary, George

**7547 Leicestershire County Cricket Club**
■ George Geary's benefit. Leicestershire v. Warwicks. on Saturday, Monday and Tuesday, July 12, 14 and 15, 1924. Leicester, the Club, [1924]. [3]p. port. stats.

**7548 George Geary's benefit (Leicestershire v.**
■ Warwicks.) at Hinckley, Saturday, Monday and Tuesday, May 23, 25 and 26, 1936. Leicester, the Club, [1936]. [3]p. port. stats.

## Gee, Herbert Leslie

**7548 Gee, Herbert Leslie**
**–1** Nodding world: a friendly man's account of what he found there and the people he met. Epworth P., 1940. 251p.
*cricket in ch. xv*

## George III, *King*

**7549** **[Benjamin, Lewis Saul]**
Farmer George, by Lewis Melville. 2 vols.
Pitman, 1907. illus. ports.
*cricket p. 44*

## Gibbs, Lancelot Richard

**7549** **Kanhai-Gibbs:** a tribute to two outstand-
**–1** ing West Indians: [benefit brochure]. Port
■ of Spain, Trinidad, The Benefit Cttee.,
1974. [ii],82p. incl. adverts. illus. ports.
stats.

## Gibson, Alan

**7549** **Gibson, Alan**
**–2** A mingled yarn. Collins, 1976. 222p.
■ *many cricket references*

## Gibson, Archibald Lesley

**7550** **[Foenander, E.W.]**
■ A.L. Gibson's record in Ceylon cricket,
by "Onlooker". [Colombo], Ceylon Observer, [1931]. 6p. port. (on cover). stats.
*rptd. from the* Sunday Observer *of 25
Oct., 1931*

## Giffen, George

**7551** **Giffen, George**
■ With bat and ball: twenty-five years'
reminiscences of Australian and Anglo-
Australian cricket; with hints to young
cricketers on batting, bowling & fielding.
Ward, Lock, 1898. xv,240p. illus. ports.
stats.
——2nd ed. 1898
——3rd ed. [1899]

## Gilchrist, Roy

**7552** **Gilchrist, Roy**
■ Hit me for six. S. Paul, 1963. 126p. illus.
ports.

## Gilliat, Richard

**7552** **Richard Gilliat** beneft brochure 1978.
**–1** Southampton, Wessex-Mede Marketing
■ Ltd., [1978]. 64p. incl. adverts. illus.
ports. stats.

## Gilligan, Alfred Edward Robert

**7552** **A.E.R. Gilligan** 23rd December 1894 –
**–2** 5th September 1976: [order of memorial
■ service] St. Mary's Horsham, Thursday
21st October 1976 at 3pm. [3]p.

## Glendenning, Raymond Carl

**7553** **Glendenning, Raymond Carl**
Just a word in your ear. S. Paul, 1953.
192p. illus. ports.
*scattered cricket references*

## Glover, William

**7554** **Glover, William**
■ The memoirs of a Cambridge chorister. 2
vols. Hurst & Blackett, 1885
*references to mid-19th century cricket in
chs. xxvii–xxix, pp. 150–171*

**7555** Reminiscences of half a century. Reming-
■ ton, 1889. [2],xvi,360p.
*contains recollections of mid-19th century
cricket*

## Goddard, Thomas William John

**7556** **[T.W. Goddard** benefit souvenir. 1948].
[4]p. folded card. port.
*contains "Tom Goddard: an appreciation",
by David Moore*

## Goddard, Trevor Leslie

**7557** **Short, Graham**
■ The Trevor Goddard story. Durban,
Purfleet Productions, 1965; Folkestone,
Bailey Bros. & Swinfen, 1966. 215p. illus.
ports. scores

## Goldwin, William

**7558** **Oxford, Arnold Whitaker**
William Goldwin 1682–1747. Bristol,
Hemmons, 1911
*includes "In certamen Pilae" by William
Goldwin, pp. 10–13*

## Goodwin, Keith

**7559** **Kay, John,** *editor*
Lancashire's own loyalist: Keith Goodwin's testimonial brochure. Testimonial
match: Lancashire v. Yorkshire at Old
Trafford, May 26, 28, 29, 1973. Lancashire
C.C.C., [1973]. [28]p. incl. adverts. illus.
ports.

## Gopalan, M.J.

**7560** **Govindarajan, S.A.,** *editor*
■ 25 years of cricket & hockey. Madras,
M.J. Gopalan Silver Jubilee Working
Cttee., 1952. 40p. illus. ports. stats.
*the career of M.J. Gopalan; cricket pp. 1–37*

## Gordon, *Lord* Granville Armyne

7561 **Gordon,** *Lord* **Granville Armyne**
■ Sporting reminiscences; edited by F.G. Aflalo. Grant Richards, 1902. xii,209p. illus. port.
*cricket pp. 136–44*

## Gould, Nathaniel

7562 **Gould, Nathaniel**
The magic of sport, mainly autobiographical. John Long, 1909. x,365p. illus. port.

## Goulden, Mark

7563 **Goulden, Mark**
■ Mark my words! W.H. Allen, 1978. vii,256p. illus. ports. facsims.
*cricket pp. 162,250 concerning shining the ball*

## Grace Family

7564 **Jones, A. Emlyn**
History of Mangotsfield and Downend. Bristol, W.S. Mark, 1899
*references to the Grace family*

7565 **Powell, Archibald G.,** *and* **Caple, Samuel**
■ **Canynge**
The Graces (E.M., W.G. & G.F.). [Hunstanton], Cricket Book Society, 1948. 160p. illus. ports. scores, stats.
*limited ed. of 1,000 copies*
——rptd. with foreword by Patrick Morrah. Bath, Chivers, 1974. (New Portway Special)

## Grace, Edward Mills

7566 **Ashley-Cooper, Frederick Samuel**
■ Edward Mills Grace, cricketer. Chatto & Windus, 1916. xi,240p. ports. stats.

## Grace, William Gilbert

7567 **The Album:** a journal of photography of
■ men, women, and events of the day. Ingram Bros.
*Vol. 2. No. 22 contains Supplement: Dr. W.G. Grace: his family history and cricket career by G. Falconer-King. July 1, 1895. 16p. illus. ports.*

7568 **Arlott, [Leslie Thomas] John**
■ Concerning cricket: studies of the play and players. Longmans, Green, 1949. vii,156p. bibliog.
*includes "The Old Man": a radio feature on the centenary of the birth of Dr. W.G. Grace*

7569 The old man. Longmans, 1949. [34]p.
*off-print from* Concerning cricket, pp.- *123–56. 6 copies only*

7570 **Arrowsmith** 1854–1954. Bristol, Arrow-
■ smith, 1955. [vii],36p. illus.
*relations between W.G. Grace and J.W. Arrowsmith concerning the former's Cricket, pp. 9–10, and with reference to score-card printing with facsimile. p. 22*

7571 **Ashley-Cooper, Frederick Samuel**
■ W.G. Grace, cricketer: a record of his performances in first-class matches. J. Wisden & Co., 1916. vi,93p. front. stats.
*a year by year record*

7571 **Australian Broadcasting Commission**
–1 A.B.C. radio guide. The Commission. *monthly*
Vol. 9, no. 12. Sept. 1971 [last issue], *with sub-title*: the golden summers of W.G. Grace. 24p. port.
*features a radio programme on W.G. Grace, written by Norman Gear*

7572 **[Barron, Arthur Oswald]**
■ Day in and day out, by "The Londoner." Cassell, 1924. xv,255p.
*includes "The Bumpers", pp. 68–71, and "W.G.", pp. 104–07*

7573 **Bax, Clifford**
■ W.G. Grace. Phoenix House, 1952. 64p. ports. bibliog. (Cricketing lives)

7574 **Bentley, Edmund Clerihew**
Baseless biography: [humorous verses]; Nicolas Bentley drew the pictures. Constable, 1939. 112p. illus.
*includes the clerihew "WG"*

7575 **Brownlee, William Methven**
■ W.G. Grace: a biography with a "Treatise on cricket" contributed by W.G. Grace. Iliffe, 1887. 166p. port. diagrs. scores, stats.

7576 **Campbell, Ian Maxwell**
■ Reminiscences of a vintner. Chapman & Hall, 1950. xi,276p. illus. ports. score
*ch. 4 "The joy of cricket", pp. 35–48; ch. 5 "W.G. Grace", pp. 49–66*

7577 **[Craig, Albert]**
■ Dr. W.G. Grace. Cricket P., 1897. [4]p. folded card. port.
——All England Athletic Publ. Co., 1899. [4]p. folded card. port.

7578 **Cricket and Football Times**
Souvenir of the national testimonial to W.G. Grace. Cricket and Football Times, 22nd July 1879

7579 **Darwin, Bernard [Richard Meirion]**
■ W.G. Grace. Duckworth, 1934. 141p. bibliog. (Great lives series)
——rptd. 1948. 123p.

——new ed. with an introduction by John Arlott. Duckworth, 1978. 128p. illus. ports. stats. bibliog.

7580 **Francis, Guy**
W.G.'s birthday, July 18th, 1888. 1888. bs.
  *verses written on the occasion of a party in honour of W.G.'s 40th birthday*

7581 **[Gardiner, Alfred George]**
■ Pebbles on the shore, [by] Alpha of the Plough. Dent, [1916]. 255p. frontis.
  *essays, including "W.G." pp. 27–31 rptd. from* The Star

7582 **Grace, William Gilbert**
■ The history of a hundred centuries; edited by William Yardley. Gill, 1895. 135p. scores

7583 "W.G.": cricketing reminiscences and
■ personal recollections. J. Bowden. 1899. xx,524p. illus. ports. scores, stats.
  *ghosted by Arthur Porritt; see no. 7595*

7584 W.G.'s little book. Newnes, 1909. v,133p.
■ scores, stats.

7585 **Hannam-Clark, Theodore**
■ W.G. Grace and Gloucester. *n.d.* 8p. stats. *typescript*

7586 **Hawke, Martin Bladen Hawke,** *7th baron,*
■ **Harris, George Robert Canning Harris,** *4th baron, and* **Gordon,** *Sir* **Home,** *editors* The memorial biography of Dr. W.G. Grace; issued under the auspices of the Committee of the M.C.C. Constable, 1919. xv,388p. illus. ports. (1 col.), stats. bibliog.
  ——limited ed. 1919
  *150 copies only*

7587 **The hero** of cricket: an appreciation of
■ Mr. W.G. Grace together with some remarkable records. Iliffe, 1895. 16p. stats.

7588 **How's that?** including "A century of
■ Grace", by Harry Furniss, verses by E.J. Milliken and cricket sketches by E.B.V. Christian. Bristol, Arrowsmith, 1896. xii,163p. illus. (Arrowsmith's Bristol Library)
  ——*paper ed.* 1896

7589 **Hutchinson, Horace Gordon**
■ Portraits of the eighties. T. Fisher Unwin, 1920. xv,301p. ports.
  *ch. xxiii "W.G. Grace", pp. 279–286*

7590 **Lawton, Albert E.**
My W.G.: a collection of anecdotes relating to my own personal experiences

of and with that greatest of all cricketers, Dr. W.G. Grace, the centenary of whose birth will be reached on 18th July, 1948. [1947]. *MS typescript*
  *in M.C.C. Library, Lord's*

7591 **"Lesser Columbus",** *pseud.*
■ Greater Bristol. Pelham P., and Simpkin, Marshall, 1893. xi,300p. illus. ports.
  *"Dr. W.G. Grace", pp. 145–6*

7591 **Lewisham Local History Society**
–1 Transactions. Lewisham, London Bor-
■ ough of Lewisham.
  *1973 includes pp. 1–6 'W.G. Grace & Lewisham' by Stephen E.A. Green*

7591 **Maclaren, Archibald Campbell**
–2 W.G. Grace: talk broadcast 25th October 1935. ("I knew a Man" Series, part four). 9p. *typescript*
  *transcript of talk held in B.B.C. Written Archives Centre, Reading*

7592 **Massingham, Harold John,** *and*
■ **Massingham, Hugh,** *editors* The great Victorians. Nicholson & Watson, 1932. xx,556p.
  ——*another ed.* 2 vols. Penguin Books, 1937. (Pelican Books)
  *includes "William Gilbert Grace 1848–1915", by Neville Cardus, pp. 223–31*

7593 **Moore, David,** *and* **Powell, Archibald G.**
■ Dr. W.G. Grace 1848–1915: centenary souvenir booklet. Bristol, [Gloucestershire C.C.C., 1948]. [9]p. illus. port. stats.

7593 **The Penny Illustrated Paper**
–1 Cricket: gratis supplement June 22, 1895. 8p. *i.e.* pp. 409–16. illus.
  *cricket in general, but mostly on W.G. Grace*

7594 **Phillpotts, Eden**
■ A mixed grill. Watts, 1940. viii,173p.
  *includes "W.G. Grace 1848–1915" pp. 96–97*

7595 **Porritt, Arthur**
The best I remember. Cassell, 1922. x,253p.
  *ch. 5, pp. 31–35 refers to author's collaboration with W.G. Grace in the writing of* W.G.: cricketing reminiscences

7596 **Preston,** *Sir* **Harry John**
■ Memories. Constable, 1928. xvii,288p. illus. port.
  *cricket (W.G. Grace), pp. 51–55, and other references*

7597 **Pringle, John,** *editor*
■ The radio listener's week-end book: a selection from notable broadcasts of the

past five years. Odham, [1950]. 288p. illus.

*includes "W.G. Grace—colossus and legend" by Dudley Carew, pp. 245–50*

**7598 The Scots Observer**
Modern men from 'The Scots Observer'. E. Arnold, 1890. 123p.

*includes "W.G. Grace", pp. 86–91*

**7599 [Sidney, Thomas Stafford]**
■ "W.G." up-to-date: the doings of W.G. Grace from 1887 to 1895 inclusive, by King Willow. Ootacamund, Nilgiri News and South of India Observer P., 1896. [iv],100p. port. stats.

*1st published as weekly articles in the Nilgiri News and South of India Observer. A continuation of W. Methven Brownlee's biography*

**7600 Smith, J. Harcourt**
Cricket: the song of the "Centuries"; written and composed by J. Harcourt Smith. Howard & Co., [1895]. 5p. port.

*in honour of W.G. Grace's 100 hundreds*

**7601 Sugden, Andrew Neville Burn**
■ W.G. Grace 1848–1915: to mark the fiftieth anniversary of his death, 23 October 1965. Harrogate, the Author, 1965. [4]p. fold, port. illus.

*reprint of an address delivered at a service at Elmers End Cemetery when a plaque was unveiled on the grave*

**7602 Tate, Harold Aubrey,** *compiler*
■ Scores and mode of dismissal of "W.G." in first-class cricket, with summary of results, 1865–1895. "Cricket" P., 1895. [66]p. port. stats.
——2nd ed. *with title:* Life, scores and mode of dismissal . . . 1896. 148p. port. stats.

**7603 Thomson, Arthur Alexander**
■ The great cricketer. Hale, 1957. 224p. illus. ports. stats. bibliog.
——new edition. The Cricketer/Hutchinson, 1968. xv,216p. illus. ports. stats. bibliog.

**7604 Walker, William George**
■ A history of the Oundle Schools. The Grocers' Company, 1956. xviii,748p. illus. ports. plans, diagr.
*p. 514—account of the visits of W.G. Grace between 1897 and 1902 to play for the Masters XI, his son. W.G. jnr. being a master at the school*

**7605 Waring, Arthur J.**
■ "W.G.", or, The champion's career. Alexander & Shepheard, [1896]. 95p. stats.

**7606 Warne, Frederick G.**
■ Dr. W.G. Grace, the king of cricket. London & Manchester, Heywood; Bristol, H.A. Burleigh, [1899]. 53p. illus. ports. (Burleigh's Penny Biographies)

**7607 Weston, George Neville**
■ W.G. Grace, the great cricketer: a statistical record of his performances in minor cricket. Wymondham (Norfolk), the Author, 1973. xiii,180p. port. stats.
*limited ed. of 50 copies*

**7608 Wiltshire County Records Committee**
Wiltshire records in 1969: annual report of the . . . Committee. Trowbridge, the Cttee., 1970. 12p. illus.
*contains an illustration of a souvenir scorecard of a cricket match at Trowbridge, 1897—Rt. Hon. W.H. Long's XI v. W.G. Grace's XI*

**7609 The World**
■ Celebrities at home; reprinted from "The World". "World" Office, 1877. viii,342p.
*includes "Mr. W.G. Grace at Downend" pp. 119–127*

**7610 Wye, Acton**
■ Dr. W.G. Grace. H.J. Drane, 1901. 90p. port. stats. (Bijou Biographies)

## Graham, Norman

**7610 Norman Graham** benefit souvenir 1977.
**–1** [Benefit Cttee., 1977]. 60p. incl. adverts.
■ illus. ports. (some col.), stats.

## Graveney, Thomas William

**7611 Graveney, Tom,** *i.e.* **Thomas William**
■ **Graveney**
Cricket through the covers. Muller, 1958. 196p. illus. ports.

**7612** On cricket. Muller, 1965. 192p. illus. ports.
■ stats.

**7613** Cricket over forty. Pelham, 1970. 160p.
■ illus.

**7614 Tom Graveney** 1969 benefit brochure: Worcestershire v. Gloucestershire, 5, 7, 8 July, [1969]. Redditch, *printed by* Ideal P., [1969]. 12p. ports. stats.

**7615 [Worcestershire County Cricket Club]**
■ T.W. Graveney, O.B.E., England & Worcestershire benefit programme for 1969. [Worcester, the Club, 1969]. [4]p. folded card. 1 illus.

## Gray, James Roy

7616 **Arlott, [Leslie Thomas] John**
■ J.R. Gray: a biographical note. [South-ampton, Hampshire C.C.C.], 1960. [12]p. 1 illus. stats.
*ltd. ed. of 30 signed copies; 1st publd. in* Hampshire C.C.C. Handbook, *1960*

## Green, Michael Arthur

7617 **Green, Michael Arthur**
■ Sporting campaigner. S. Paul, 1956. 188p. illus. ports.

## Greenhough, Thomas

7618 **Kay, John,** *editor*
Tommy Greenhough benefit brochure. Bolton, Hopkins & Sons, "Central Press", [1964]. [24]p. illus. ports. stats.

7619 **Lancashire County Cricket Club**
■ T. Greenhough testimonial: Lancashire v. Hampshire at Old Trafford, June 13, 15 and 16, 1964. Manchester, the Club, 1964. [4]p. fold, port. stats.

## Grierson, Henry

7620 **Grierson, Henry**
■ The ramblings of a rabbit. Chapman & Hall, 1924. xi,238p. illus. ports.

## Grieves, Kenneth

7621 **Todd, Eric,** *editor*
■ The Ken Grieves benefit book 1956. [Manchester], Kemsley Newspapers, [1956]. 32p. incl. adverts. illus. ports. stats.

## Griffith, Charles Christopher

7622 **Griffith, Charlie,** *i.e.* **Charles Christo-**
■ **pher Griffith**
Chucked around, by Charlie Griffith in collaboration with David Simmons. Pelham, 1970. 160p. illus. ports.

## Grimston, Hon. Robert

7623 **Gale, Frederick**
■ The life of the Hon. Robert Grimston. Longmans, 1885. xii,322p. frontis. (port.)

7624 **R.G. [Robert Grimston].** 1884. bs.
■ *a poem in memory of Hon. Robert Grim-ston; almost certainly published at Harrow School*

## Grisewood, Frederick Henry

7625 **Grisewood, Frederick Henry**
■ The world goes by: autobiography. Secker & Warburg, 1952. 256p. port.
*cricket pp. 35–36, 39–40, 54, 55*

## Grout, Arthur Theodore Wallace ('Wally')

7626 **Grout, Wally,** *i.e.* **Arthur Theodore**
■ **Wallace Grout**
My country's 'keeper: Wally Grout talking to Frank O'Callaghan. Pelham, 1965. 212p. illus. ports.

7627 **Wally Grout** testimonial program:
■ Queensland v. West Australia, Brisbane Cricket Ground, November 22–25, 1968. [Brisbane], Mirror Print, [1968]. 8p. illus. ports. stats.

## Gunn, William

7628 **Craig, Albert**
■ William Gunn. All England Athletic Publ. Co., 1899. [4]p. folded card. port.

7629 **Richards, Charles Henry,** *compiler*
■ William Gunn the famous cricketer: full account of his cricket career. Nottingham, G. Richard, [1891]. pp. 95–108. port. stats.
*extracted from* Notts scores and biographies
——2nd ed. 1903. 12p.
——3rd ed. *with title:* The famous crick-eter William Gunn. Nottingham, C.H. Richards, 1921. 15p.

## Gwynn, Stephen Lucius

7629 **Gwynn, Stephen Lucius**
–1 Experiences of a literary man. Butter-worth, 1926. 312p. ports.
*cricket pp. 125–6*

## Haigh, Schofield

7629 **Yorkshire County Cricket Club**
–2 Schofield Haigh's benefit – Yorkshire v. Lancashire, August 2, 3 & 4, 1909, Park Avenue Cricket Ground, Bradford. Leeds, the Club, [1909]. bs. port. stats.

## Haines, Sir Frederick Paul

7629 **Rait, Robert S.**
–3 The life of Field-Marshal Sir Frederick
■ Paul Haines. Constable, 1911. xiii,366p. port. maps
*cricket pp. 36,41,42,197,346*

## Hall, Ian

7630 **Mortimer, Gerald,** *editor*
■ Cricket—the Derbyshire way: Ian Hall's testimonial brochure. [Derby, Derbyshire C.C.C.], 1971. 44p. illus. ports. stats.

## Hall, Wesley Winfield

7631 **Hall, Wes,** *i.e.* **Wesley Winfield Hall**
■ Pace like fire. Pelham, 1965. 140p. illus. ports.
——*another ed.* Sportsman's Book Club, 1966

## Hallam, Maurice

7632 **[Leicestershire County Cricket Club]**
■ Maurice Hallam benefit year (1962): souvenir. [Leicester, the Club, 1962]. 24p. incl. adverts. illus. port. stats.

## Hallows, Charles

7633 **Lancashire County Cricket Club**
■ Charles Hallows benefit, at Old Trafford, June 2, 4, 5, 1928. Manchester, the Club, 1928. 4p. fold. port. stats.

## Hamilton, *Lord* Ernest William

7634 **Hamilton,** *Lord* **Ernest William**
Forty years on. Hodder & Stoughton, [1922]. vii,311p. illus. ports.
*cricket pp. 114–122*

## Hammond, Walter Reginald

7635 **Blunden, Edmund Charles**
■ After the bombing, and other short poems. Macmillan, 1949. viii,51p.
*includes "Hammond (England) a cricketer', pp. 43–45*

7636 **Cambray Auction Galleries**
■ Cricketana: items, the property of the late W.R. "Wally" Hammond the famous Gloucestershire and England cricketer . . . Monday 24 March 1969 at Cambray Auction Galleries . . . Cheltenham, by order of Mrs. S. Hammond. Cheltenham, the Galleries, [1969]. *typescript.* [i],6p.
——Additions. *typescript.* single sheet foolscap

7637 **[Gloucestershire County Cricket Club]**
■ The W.R. Hammond benefit souvenir. Gloucestershire v. Hampshire, played at Bristol, August 4th, 6th & 7th, 1934. [Bristol, the Club, 1934]. 16p. port. stats.

7638 **Hammond, Walter Reginald**
■ Cricket my destiny. S. Paul, [1946]. 156p. illus. ports.

7639 Cricket my world. S. Paul, [1948]. 192p.
■ illus. ports.

7640 Cricket's secret history. S. Paul, [1952].
■ 191p. illus. ports.

7640 **Howard, Colin**
–1 Cotswold days. Blackie, 1937. 277p. illus.
*recollections of Hammond pp. 182–5*

7641 **Mason, Ronald [Charles]**
■ Walter Hammond: a biography. Hollis & Carter, 1962. 224p. illus. ports. bibliog.

7642 **Moore, David**
W.R. Hammond, cricketer: a complete record of his performances in first class cricket. Henbury, Bristol, Cricket Biographies, 1948. 136p. illus. stats.

## Hampshire, John Harry

7642 **John Hampshire** benefit brochure and
–1 Tribute to the Leagues. [Benefit Cttee.,
■ 1976]. 48p. illus. ports.
*contains "A tribute to the Leagues" edited by Keith Farnsworth*

## Hampson, William

7643 **Hampson, William**
■ The reminiscences of the career of William Hampson; written by himself from memory for the benefit of the Marsden Cricket Club. Slaithwaite (Yorks), F. Walker, *printer*, 1900? *MS typescript*
*never published?*

## Hardstaff, Joseph

7644 **Grimes, Arthur**
■ Joseph Hardstaff . . . statistics of his career up to and including 1954. Hollingworth, Manchester, the Author, 1954. 9f.
*typescript. stats.*

7645 **Nottinghamshire County Cricket Club**
■ Joe Hardstaff: a tribute to a champion. Nottingham, the Club, [1948]. [12]p. illus. ports. diagr. stats.

## Hardy, Godfrey Harold

7645 **The Saturday** book. 8th year; edited by
–1 Leonard Russell. Hutchinson, 1948. 288p. illus. & ports. (some col.)
*includes pp. 65–73 "The mathematician on cricket" by C.P. Snow*

7645 **Snow, Charles Percy,** *baron Snow*
–2 Variety of men. Macmillan, 1967. x,204p.
■ *includes "G.H. Hardy" pp. 15–46*

## Harris, Charles Bowmar

7646 **Nottinghamshire County Cricket Club**
■ Charles Harris' benefit. Nottinghamshire versus Yorkshire at Trent Bridge, Nottingham, July 16, 18 & 19, 1949. Nottingham, the Club, [1949]. [4]p. fold, port. stats.

## Harris, David

7647 **A book** of broadsheets, with an introduc-
■ tion by Geoffrey Dawson. Methuen, 1928. xvi,301p.
——2nd ed. 1928
——3rd ed. 1929
*contains "David Harris, cricketer", by John Nyren, from The Cricketers of my time, pp. 25–29*

7648 **Buckingham, Claude**
David Harris of Crookham. Hants and Berks Gazette, 1910. 11p. illus.
rptd. *from the* Hants and Berks Gazette, *29th Oct., 1910*

## Harris, George Robert Canning Harris, *Lord*

7649 **Craig, Albert**
■ Lord Harris. Wright & Co., 1908. [4]p. folded card. port.

7650 **Harris, George Robert Canning Harris,**
■ *4th baron*
A few short runs. Murray, 1921. vii,296p. port.

## Harris, Michael John

7650 **Smith, William S.,** *editor*
–1 The Mike "Pasty" Harris benefit 1977: a
■ souvenir brochure. [Notts. C.C.C., 1977]. 40p. incl. covers & adverts. illus. ports.

## Harrison, George Pickering

7651 **Northing, J.W.**
■ From "Last" to "Lords": incidents during the career of G.P. Harrison 'The Old County Cricketer'. [1934]. 33p.

## Harrison, Leo

7652 **Arlott, [Leslie Thomas] John**
■ Leo Harrison: an appreciation. [Southampton, Hampshire C.C.C.,] 1957. 6p. frontis.
*ltd. ed. of 70 signed copies*

## Harvey, Robert Neil

7653 **Harvey, Neil**
■ My world of cricket. Hodder & Stoughton, 1963. 160p. illus. ports. stats.

——*another ed.* Sportsman's Book Club, 1964

## Harvey, William Fryer

7654 **Harvey, William Fryer**
■ We were seven. Constable, 1936. viii,241p. illus. ports.
*childhood. memories; cricket pp. 171–75*

## Hassan, Sheikh Basharat

7654 **Smith, Frank,** *editor*
–1 Basher testimonial year book 1978. [Testi-
■ monial Cttee., 1978]. [64]p. incl. adverts. illus. ports. stats.

## Hassett, Arthur Lindsay

7655 **Whitington, Richard Smallpeice**
■ The quiet Australian: the Lindsay Hassett story. Melbourne & London, Heinemann, 1969. xvii,172p. illus. ports. scores, stats.

7656 **[Entry cancelled]**

## Hawke, Martin Bladen Hawke, *7th Baron*

7657 **Hawke, Martin Bladen Hawke,** *7th baron*
■ Recollections and reminiscences. Williams & Norgate, 1924. vii,336p. illus. ports.
——*2nd ed.* 1925

## Hawkes, Charles Pascoe

7658 **Hawkes, Charles Pascoe**
■ Heydays: a salad of memories and impressions; with drawings by the author. Methuen, 1933. ix,262p. illus. ports.
*cricket in ch. v*

7659 **[Entry cancelled]**

## Hawtrey, *Sir* Charles

7660 **Hawtrey, *Sir* Charles**
■ The truth at last; edited by W. Somerset Maugham. Butterworth, 1924. 352p. illus. ports.
*cricket in chs. iii and xxv*

## Haydon, Thomas

7661 **Haydon, Thomas**
Sporting reminiscences. Bliss, Sands, 1898. 282p.

## Hayes, Ernest George

7662 **Craig, Albert**
■ E.G. Hayes. Wright & Co., All England Publ. Co., 1908. [4]p. folded card. port.

## Hayes, Richard

**7663** **Arnold, Ralph Crispian Marshall**
■ A yeoman of Kent: an account of Richard Hayes, 1725–1790, and of the village of Cobham in which he lived and farmed. Constable, 1949. xii,203p. illus. (1 col.). score
*includes a history of Cobham cricket and an account of England v. Hampshire at Sevenoaks Vine 1776*

## Haygarth, Arthur

**7664** **Scores** of cricket matches in which A.
■ Haygarth distinguished himself, and other records, facts, deaths of cricketers, etc. 1842–73. [Unpublished MSS and scrapbooks of cuttings from *Bell's Life, The Sporting Life*, etc.] 4 vols.
*at Lord's. Vol. 3 covering years 1854–60 is missing*

## Hayward, Thomas Walter

**7665** **Craig, Albert**
■ Our hero: red letter day at Tom Hayward's happy home: [a poem], by A.C. 1906. bs.

**7666** Tom Hayward. Wright & Co., 1906. [4]p.
■ folded card. port.
——*another ed.* 1908

## Hazare, Vijay Samuel

**7667** **Hazare, Vijay Samuel**
■ My story. Bombay, Thacker, 1964. [vii],149p. illus. ports. stats.

**7667** ——, *and* **Naik, V.K.**
**–1** Cricket replayed. Calcutta, Rupa, 1974.
■ [x],157p. illus. ports.
——*another ed.* 1976. pbk.

**7668** **Vidarbha Cricket Association**
■ Hazare benefit match: West Indies v/s Board President's XI, 27, 28, 29 January, 1967. Nagpur, the Assoc., [1967]. [124]p. incl. adverts. illus. ports. stats.

## Hazel, Nigel

**7669** **Strathmore Cricket Club**
■ Nigel Hazel testimonial fund: souvenir brochure. Forfar, the Club, 1973. [12]p. illus. ports. stats.

## Headley, George Alphonso

**7670** **Burrowes, S.I.**, *and* **Carnegie, J.A.**
■ George Headley. Nelson, 1971. [x],80p. illus. ports.
*for children*

**7670** **Jamaica Cricket Association**
**–1** A tribute to George Headley: 70th
■ birthday testimonial dinner, Sheraton Kingston Ballroom, Friday, 1st June 1979: souvenir programme; edited by Robert S. Dabdoub. [Kingston, the Assoc., 1979]. 20p. incl. adverts. illus. ports. stats.

**7670** **James, Cyril Lionel Robert**
**–2** George Headley – batsman of the West Indies. [c.1964]. 20p. Ms.
*in the collection of A.E. Winder*

**7671** **Wallace, George B.**
■ "Immortal Headley G." Kingston, the Gleaner Co., [1948]. 12p. incl. adverts. port.
*mostly poems in praise of Headley*

**7671** **White, Noel,** *and* **Headley, George**
**–1** George 'Atlas' Headley. Kingston, Insti-
■ tute of Jamaica, 1974. [x],168p. illus. ports. stats. ("Jamaicans of Distinction")
——pbk. ed. 1974

## Headley, Ronald George Alphonso

**7672** **[Worcestershire County Cricket Club]**
■ Souvenir book to commemorate the benefit year awarded to Ron Headley. [Worcester, the Club, 1972]. 40p. incl. adverts. illus. ports. stats.

## Hearne, George Gibbons

**7673** **George** Gibbons Hearne. *Printed by* Blun-
■ dell, Taylor, 1890. 14p. port.

## Hedges, Bernard

**7674** **Bernard Hedges** benefit brochure on the occasion of Glamorgan v. Gloucestershire, July 6th, 8th and 9th, 1963, Ynysangharad Park, Pontypridd. illus. ports. stats.

## Hele, George

**7674** **Whitington, Richard Smallpeice,** *and*
**–1** **Hele, George**
■ Bodyline umpire: an eyewitness account of a dramatic era in Test cricket. Adelaide, Rigby, 1974. [xiii],225p. illus. port. facsim.

## Hendren, Elias Henry

**7675** **Hendren, "Patsy"**, *i.e.* **Elias Henry**
■ **Hendren**
My book of cricket and cricketers. Athletic Publications, [1927]. 141p. illus. port.

**7676** Big cricket. Hodder & Stoughton, 1934.
■ 160p. illus. ports.

7677 Cricket musings. Calcutta, Illustrated
■ News, 1947. 99p. illus. ports.

7678 **Peebles, Ian Alexander Ross**
■ 'Patsy' Hendren: the cricketer and his
times. Macmillan, 1969. 183p. illus. ports.
scores, stats.
——*another ed.* Sportsman's Book Club,
1971

**Heseltine, Christopher**

7679 **Press, Charles A. Manning**
■ Hampshire and Isle of Wight leaders:
social and political. Gaskill Jones, *for
private circulation,* 1903
*includes biography of Christopher Heseltine*

**Hide, Jesse**

7680 [Jesse Hide's benefit match . . . 1894].
[4]p. fold. stats.
*contains pen-portrait of J.H. by "Leather
Hunter"* [A.J. Gaston]

**Higgs. Kenneth**

7681 **The Ken Higgs** testimonial brochure: the
■ story of a cricket hero. "For Lancashire &
England." [Testimonial Committee,
1968]. [24]p. incl. adverts. illus. ports.
stats.

7682 **Lancashire County Cricket Club**
■ An appreciation of Ken Higgs. Manchester, the Club, [1968]. 4p. fold, 1 illus.

**Hilton, Malcolm J.**

7683 **Lancashire County Cricket Club**
■ M.J. Hilton & R. Tattersall joint benefit,
Lancashire v. Yorkshire at Old Trafford
on July 30, August 1 & 2, 1960.
Manchester, the Club, 1960. [4]p. fold,
ports. stats.

**Hirst, George Herbert**

7684 **Benson, Edward Frederic,** *and* **Miles,**
■ **Eustace Hamilton,** *eds.*
The cricket of Abel, Hirst and Shrewsbury. Hurst & Blackett, 1903. xx,287p.
illus. (Athletic library)

7685 **Humphrey, W.H.**
■ George Herbert Hirst and Wilfred
Rhodes, a record of cricket achievement.
Huddersfield, *printed by* Broadbent, 1937.
52p. illus. ports. stats.

7686 [Stainton, James Hayton]
■ George Hirst: recollections of his career,
by "Looker On". Sheffield, Sheffield
Telegraph, 1904. 16p. port.
*cover-title: "Snap shots of George Hirst's
career"*

7687 **Thomson, Arthur Alexander**
■ Hirst and Rhodes. Epworth P., 1959.
211p. illus. ports. stats. bibliog.
——*another ed.* Sportsman's Book Club,
1960

7688 **Yeoman, George Dundas**
■ 2000 rhyming lines. Cambridge, Galloway & Porter, 1907. [v],71p.
*includes "The all round cricketer of the
century" pp. 66–7 (George Hirst)*

**Hitch, John William**

7689 **Gardiner, Alfred George**
■ Many furrows, by Alpha of the Plough;
with illustrations by Clive Gardiner.
Dent, 1924. x,275p. illus.
*essays including "Billitch at Lord's", pp.
25–28. "Billitch" was J.W. Hitch*

**Hitchcock, Ray E.**

7690 **Warwickshire County Cricket Club**
■ R.E. Hitchcock's benefit season 1963.
Birmingham, the Club, [1963]. [4]p. fold,
illus. port. stats.

**Hoare, Arthur**

7690 **Somers-Cocke, Henry L.,** *and* **Boyson,**
–1 **V.F.**
Edenbridge; with illustrations by J.E.
Clutterbuck. Edenbridge, Edenbridge
Chronicle, 1912. viii,296p. illus. map
*cricket pp. 166–7, mostly on A. Hoare who
played for Sussex and Kent*

**Hobbs,** *Sir* **John Berry**

7691 **Arkell, Reginald**
■ Meet these people: [humorous verse];
caricatures by Bert Thomas. H. Jenkins,
1928. 151p. illus.
——*rev. and enl. ed.* 1930. 159p.
*includes "To Jack Hobbs", p. 5*

7691 **Arlott, [Leslie Thomas] John**
–1 The Master: an appreciation. *privately*
■ *printed,* [1979]. 8p.
*limited ed. of 20 signed copies; offprint from
John Arlott's Book of cricketers (1979)*

7692 **Baily, Robin,** *editor*
■ All Hobbs' centuries. C.E. Smith, Oval
Bookstall, [1925]. 16p. ports. stats.

7693 **Foenander, Samuel Peter,** *compiler*
■ A souvenir of Jack Jobbs' record number
of centuries: facts and figures. [Colombo],
Ceylon Independent P., [1925]. 6p.

7694 **Gardiner, Alfred George**
■ Certain people of importance. Cape,
1926. viii,311p. ports.

——*another ed*. Dent, 1929. 252p. (Way-farer's Library)
——*American ed. with title:* Portraits and portents. N.Y., 1926
*biographical essays—includes "Jack Hobbs"*

**7694** **The Guardian**
**–1** The bedside 'Guardian' 12: a selection
■ from The Guardian 1962–1963. Collins, 1963. 255p. illus.
*includes pp. 23–8, "J.B. Hobbs not out 80", by Neville Cardus*

**7695** **Hobbs,** *Sir* **John Berry**
■ My cricket memories. Heinemann, 1924. x.242p. illus. ports.

**7696** Playing for England!: my Test-cricket
■ story. Gollancz, 1931. 175p. illus. port.

**7697** My life story. "The Star" Publications
■ Dept., 1935. 320p. illus. ports. scores, stats.

**7698** **Kircher, Rudolf**
Englander, London, 1926. Frankfurt, Frankfurter Societats Druckerei, 1926. 351p. ports.
*includes pp. 253–263 "Panis et circensus—Mr. Hobbs"*
*in German*

**7699** **Landsberg, Pat**
■ Jack Hobbs, gentleman and player. Todd Publishing Group, 1953. 80p. illus. ports.

**7700** **Maclaren, Archibald Campbell**
■ The perfect batsman: J.B. Hobbs in action; with 98 cinema-photographs of J.B. Hobbs at the wicket. Cassell, 1926. [viii],138p. illus.

**7701** **Mason, Ronald [Charles]**
■ Jack Hobbs: a portrait of an artist as a great batsman. Hollis & Carter, 1960. xi,212p. illus.
——*another ed*. Sportsman's Book Club, 1961

**7702** **Memorial** service for Sir John Berry
■ Hobbs, Thursday, 20th February, 1964 at 12 noon. 4p.
*order of service*

**7702** **The Observer**
**–1** 'The Observer' re-visited 1963–64; compiled by Cyril Dunn. Hodder & Stoughton, 1964. 256p. illus.
*contains pp. 168–70 "Jack Hobbs, master bastman", by John Arlott*

**7703** **Sparks, William P.H.**
■ John Berry Hobbs (Surrey and England XI's): a complete record of all his performances in first-class cricket, 1905 to 1925

inclusive. Fleetgate Publications, [1926]. 64p. stats.

**7704** **The Star**
■ Farewell dinner to J.B. Hobbs to commemorate his retirement from county cricket, arranged by The Star, Wednesday, July 17, 1935, Dorchester Hotel, London. [The Star, 1935]. [14]p. 1 illus. 1 port.
*includes contribution by Neville Cardus*

**Hobbs, Robin**

**7704** **Tollesbury C.C.** v. Essex C.C.C., Robin
**–1** Hobbs' benefit match at Tollesbury
■ cricket ground . . . 14 September. Tollesbury, the Club, 1974. [36]p. incl. covers & adverts. illus. ports. stats.

**Hobson, Harold**

**7704** **Hobson, Harold**
**–2** Indirect journey: an autobiography.
■ Weidenfeld and Nicolson, 1978. [vii], 280p. illus. ports.
*cricket pp. 207–9,264*

**Hodgson, Randolph Llewellyn**

**7705** **[Hodgson, Randolph Llewellyn]**
■ Cricket memories, by a Country Vicar. Methuen, 1930. xii,248p. illus. ports.
——2nd ed. 1933
*contains list of first-class cricketers who died in 1st World War*

**7706** Second innings, by a Country Vicar.
■ Hutchinson, 1933. 288p. illus. ports.

**7707** The happy cricketer, by a Country Vicar.
■ Muller, 1946. 227p. ports.
——2nd ed. 1947

**Hogarth, Robert George**

**7708** **Hogarth, Robert George**
■ The Trent and I go wandering by: stories of over fifty years of my life in Nottingham. Nottingham, Cooke & Vowles, [1949]. xi,144p. illus. ports.
*Pres. of Notts. C.C.; cricket pp. 69–77, including account of Notts. Amateur C.C.*

**Hole, Samuel Reynolds**

**7709** **Hole, Samuel Reynolds**
■ The memories of Dean Hole. E. Arnold, 1892. xii,377p. illus. port.
*cricket pp. 108–27*
——new ed. 1893. xv,331p. illus. port.
——*new ed*. Nelson, [1908]. 378p. port.

**7710** The letters of Samuel Reynolds Hole,
■ Dean of Rochester; edited, with a mem-

oir, by George A.B. Dewar. G. Allen, 1907. lvi,279p. port.
*cricket pp. 145–46*

## Hollender, Bertie

7711 **Hollender, Bertie**
■ Before I forget. Grayson, 1935. 264p. illus.
*scattered cricket references*

## Hollies, William Eric

7712 **Hollies, [William] Eric**
■ I'll spin you a tale. Museum P., 1955. 147p. illus. ports.

7713 **Warwickshire County Cricket Club**
■ Eric Hollies' benefit. Birmingham, the Club, [1948]. [4]p. fold, illus. port. stats.

## Hollis, Maurice Christopher

7714 **Hollis, Maurice Christopher**
■ Along the road to Frome. Harrap, 1958. 256p. port.
*cricket pp. 11–13, 18, 19–20, 91, 105, 213–15*

## Holmes, Errol Reginald Thorold

7715 **Holmes, Errol Reginald Thorold**
■ Flannelled foolishness: a cricketing chronicle. Hollis & Carter, 1957. viii,192p. illus. ports. scores

## Holmes, Percy

7716 **Duckworth, Leslie**
■ Holmes and Sutcliffe: the run-stealers. The Cricketer; Hutchinson, 1970. 228p. illus. ports. stats. bibliog.

## Holt, Arthur

7717 **Arlott, [Leslie Thomas] John**
■ Arthur Holt, an appreciation. [Southampton, Hampshire C.C.C.], 1963. 8p.
*limited ed. of 50 copies. 1st published in Hampshire C.C.C. Handbook, 1963*

## Holt, George Lindsay

7717 **White, Graham**
–1 The late George Lindsay Holt, Esq. Rich-
■ mond, Richmond C.C., 1964. [4]p. port.
*Life Patron of the Club*

## Home, Alec Douglas, *baron Home of the Hirsel*

7717 **Home, Alec Douglas,** *baron Home of the*
–2 *Hirsel*
■ The way the wind blows: an autobiography. Collins, 1976. 320p. illus. ports.
*cricket pp. 25,31–4,39–40*

7717 **Young, Kenneth**
–3 Sir Alec Douglas-Home. Dent, 1970.
■ xii,282p. illus. ports.
*cricket pp. 19–20, 22–24, 257–58*

## Hooker, Ron

7718 **Middlesex County Cricket Club**
■ Ron Hooker benefit '68 at Lord's, Middlesex v. Sussex, June 1st, 3rd, 4th. Lord's, the Club, [1968]. illus. [4]p. fold

## Hope, Thomas

7719 **Mees and Zoonen** 1720–1970: history of R. Mees and Zoonen. Amsterdam, Mees & Zoonen, 1971. 84p. illus.
*The Amsterdam banking house of Hope & Co. merged with R. Mees and Zoonen in 1962*

7720 **National Art-Collections Fund**
65th annual report, 1968. The Fund, 1969. 52p. illus. ports.
*contains cover picture in colour of Mr. Hope of Amsterdam playing cricket with his friends and a black and white reproduction of the same*

## Hordern, Herbert Vivian

7721 **Hordern, Herbert Vivian**
■ Googlies: coals from a Test-cricketer's fireplace; illustrated by Tom Glover. Sydney, Angus & Robertson, 1932. xvii, 207p. illus.
——2nd ed. 1932

## Horner, Norman

7722 **Warwickshire County Cricket Club**
■ Norman Horner's benefit. Birmingham, the Club, [1962]. [4]p. fold. illus. port. stats.

## Horton, Henry

7723 **Arlott, [Leslie Thomas] John**
■ Henry Horton: a biographical note. [Southampton, Hampshire C.C.C.], 1964. 11p. illus. stats.
*limited ed. of 50 copies*

## Horton, Martin

7724 **[Worcestershire County Cricket Club]**
■ Martin Horton Worcestershire and England benefit fund 1965: benefit match Worcestershire v. Warwickshire 3, 5, 6 July. [Worcester, the Club, 1965]. [4]p. fold. 1 illus. stats.

## Howard, William E.

7725 **Howard, William E.**
■ Fifty years' of cricket reminiscences of a non-player. Manchester, the Author, 1928. x,141p. illus. ports. score

## Howarth, Richard

7726 **Perks, R. Geoffrey,** *compiler*
■ Dick Howarth benefit booklet. [1949]. 16p. ports. stats.

## Hughes, Margaret

7727 **Hughes, Margaret**
■ All on a summer's day. S. Paul, 1953. 191p. illus. ports. diagrs.

## Hughes, Thomas

7728 **Mack, Edward Clarence,** *and* **Armytage, Walter Harry Green**
Thomas Hughes: the life of the author of 'Tom Brown's Schooldays'. Benn, 1952. 302p. illus. ports.
*cricket pp. 19–20, 29, 39, 41, 57, 64, 81, 107, 188*

## Humphreys, Walter Alexander

7729 **[Gatson, Alfred J.]**
■ A short biography of Walter A. Humphreys, the famous Sussex cricketer, by "A.J.G." *n.p.,* [1888?]. 8p. stats.

7730 **[Walter Humphreys'** benefit match . . . 1891]
*contains pen-portrait of W.H. by "Leather Hunter" [A.J. Gaston]*

## Hunte, Conrad Cleophas

7731 **Hunte, Conrad [Cleophas]**
■ Playing to win. Hodder & Stoughton, 1971. 160p. illus. ports. scores

## Hunter, David

7732 **Reminiscences** of David Hunter the
■ genial Yorkshire stumper. Scarborough, W.H. Smith, [1909]. 46p. illus. port.
*author unknown*

## Hurley, Patrick

7732 **Lucas, Theophilus**
–1 Memoirs of the lives, intrigues and comical adventures of the most famous gamesters and celebrated sharpers. Printed for J. Brown, etc. 1714. xxiv,285p. frontis.
——*rptd.* in Games and gamesters of the Restoration: The compleat gamester, by Charles Cotton, 1674, and Lives of the gamesters, by Theophilus Lucas, 1714; with an introduction by Cyril Hughes Hartmann. Routledge, 1930. xxx,281p. illus. (English Library)
*contains an account of Patrick Hurley "very expert beyond the rest of his companions; as [sic] tipcat, cricket, skittles. . . .*

## Hutchings, Kenneth Lotherington

7733 **Craig, Albert**
■ Mr. K.L. Hutchings. Wright & Co., All England Publ. Co., 1908. [4]p. folded card. port.

## Hutton, *Sir* Leonard

7733 **Hartley, Marie,** *and* **Ingilby, Joan**
–1 Yorkshire portraits; with illustrations by M. Hartley. Dent, 1961. xxv,294p. illus. ports.
*pp. 274–8 "Sir Leonard Hutton"*

7734 **Hutton,** *Sir* **Leonard**
■ Cricket is my life. Hutchinson, 1949. 232p. illus. ports.

7735 Just my story. Hutchinson, 1956. 192p.
■ illus. ports.
——*another ed.* Sportsman's Book Club, 1957

7736 **Kilburn, James Maurice**
■ Len Hutton: the story of a great cricketer. Pitkin Pictorials, [1950]. 32p. illus. ports. score
——*rev. ed.* [1951]. 30p.
——*latest ed.* [1952] with stats. 1934–1951 inclusive

7737 **Kitchin, Laurence**
■ Len Hutton. Phoenix House, 1953. 64p. ports. (Cricketing Lives)

7738 **Len Hutton,** England and Yorkshire.
■ Facts & figures. L. Hutton's Benefit Fund, [1950]. 8p. stats.

7738 **Manchester Guardian**
–1 The bedside 'Guardian' 5: a selection
■ from The Manchester Guardian 1955–1956. Collins, 1956. 256p. illus. map
*includes p. 110 "Innings declared" – a leading article on the retirement of Len Hutton from first-class cricket*

7738 The bedside 'Guardian' 7: a selection
–2 from The Manchester Guardian 1957–1958. Collins, 1958. 256p. illus.
*includes pp. 158–61 "Golden batting by an Old Master" by Denys Rowbotham on Len Hutton playing for M.C.C. at Old Trafford on the occasion of Lancashire's centenary*

7739 **National Sporting Club**
■ A dinner to honour Len Hutton, Café Royal . . . 28th February, 1956. The Club, [1956]. 12p. score
*menu which reproduces the score book of the England v. Australia match at the Oval during which Len Hutton made his innings of 364*

Len Hutton *photo: Popperfoto*

K. S. Ranjitsinjhi *photo: M.C.C.*

Keith Miller *photo: Keystone Press*

7740 **Thomson, Arthur Alexander**
■ Hutton and Washbrook. Epworth P., 1963. 275p. illus. ports. stats. bibliog.
——*another ed.* Sportsman's Book Club, 1966

7741 **Trevor, Brian**
■ Len Hutton, the world's greatest batsman: the story of the Test career. Souvenir P., [1951]. 49p. illus. stats.

7742 **Ward, Alfred Charles,** *compiler*
Grim and gay: an anthology, heroic, dramatic, comic. O.U.P., 1942. 320p.
*includes "Hutton's match", pp. 45–48*

7743 **Yorkshire Evening News**
■ Len Hutton souvenir. Leeds, Yorkshire Evening News, [1950]. 12p. illus. ports.

7744 **Yorkshire Post**
■ Hutton benefit souvenir. Doncaster, Yorkshire Conservative Newspaper Co., [1950]. [36]p. illus. ports.
*includes series of "close-ups" of famous cricketers rptd. from the* Yorkshire Post *and* Yorkshire Evening Post

### Hyndman, Henry Mayers

7745 **Hyndman, Henry Mayers**
The record of an adventurous life. Macmillan, 1911. x,460p. illus.
*cricket pp. 21–23*

### Ibadulla, Khalid

7746 **Warwickshire County Cricket Club**
Khalid ('Billy') Ibadulla [benefit brochure] 1969. [Birmingham], the Club, [1969]. [4]p. fold. illus. stats.

### Ikin, John Thomas

7747 **Turner, Edgar,** *editor*
■ Jack Ikin's benefit book. [Manchester], Kemsley Newspapers, [1953]. 32p. incl. adverts. illus. ports. stats.

### Illingworth, Raymond

7747 **Fay, Peter,** *editor*
–1 'Illy': the Ray Illingworth souvenir testi-
■ monial brochure. Leicester, Testimonial Cttee., 1977. 40p. incl. adverts. illus. & ports. (some col.), stats.

7748 **Illingworth, Ray**
■ Spinner's wicket, as told to Peter Smith. S. Paul, 1969. 160p. illus. ports. stats.

7749 **Ray Illingworth** benefit brochure 1965. Driffield, *printed by* East Yorks Printers, [1965]. 44p. illus. ports. stats.

7749 **Stevenson, Mike**
–1 'Illy': a biography of Ray Illingworth.
■ Tunbridge Wells, Midas Books, 1978. xix,135p. illus. ports.
——*another ed. with title:* Illingworth: a biography. Ward, Lock, 1978. xix,135p. illus. ports. *pbk.*

### Ingleby-Mackenzie, Alexander Colin David

7750 **Arlott, [Leslie Thomas] John**
■ C. Ingleby-Mackenzie: a profile. [South-ampton, Hampshire C.C.C.], 1962. 12p. illus. stats.
*limited ed. of 50 copies. 1st published in* Hampshire C.C.C. Handbook, *1962*

7751 **Ingleby-Mackenzie, Colin**
■ Many a slip. Oldbourne, 1962. 190p. illus. ports.
——*another ed.* Sportsman's Book Club, 1963

### Insole, Douglas John

7752 **Insole, Douglas John**
■ Cricket from the middle. Heinemann, 1960. x,190p. illus. ports.
——*another ed.* Sportsman's Book Club, 1961

### Intikhab Alam

7752 **Intikhab Alam** benefit year 1978. [Benefit
–1 Cttee., 1978]. [48]p. incl. adverts. illus.
■ stats.
*includes "Poetry in motion" by John Arlott on Albert Craig*

### Iredale, Francis Adams

7753 **Iredale, Frank,** *i.e.* **Francis Adams Iredale**
■ 33 years of cricket. Sydney, Beatty, Rich-ardson, 1920. 168p. illus. port.

### Jackson, Archibald Alexander

7753 **Frith, David Edward John**
–1 The Archie Jackson story: a biography.
■ Ashurst, Tunbridge Wells, The Cricketer, 1974. 144p. illus. ports. scores, stats.
*limited ed. of 1000 numbered and signed copies*

### Jackson, *Sir* Francis Stanley

7754 **Standing, Percy Cross**
■ The Hon. F.S. Jackson. Cassell, 1906. xvi,164p. illus. ports. scores

### Jackson, Nicholas Lane

7755 **Jackson, Nicholas Lane**
■ Sporting days and sporting ways.

Hurst & Blackett, 1932. 288p. illus. ports.
*cricket, pp. 23, 27, 40–42, 69–70, 102–04, 116–17, 143, 144, 158–59, 171–72, 202*

### Jacob, Naomi

7755 **Jacob, Naomi**
–1 Me – again. Hutchinson, 1937. 280p. illus.
■ ports.
*cricket pp. 21–3*

7756 Me—yesterday and to-day. Hutchinson,
■ 1957. 263p. illus. ports.
*scattered cricket references, e.g. p. 61 on C. Aubrey Smith*

### Jai, Laxmidas Purshottamdas

7756 **Raiji, Vasant,** *editor*
–1 L.P. Jai: memories of a great batsman.
■ Bombay, Tyeby P., 1976. [xi],56p. illus.
ports. stats.
*a collection of tributes; scoring diagram on back cover*

### Jaisimha, Motganhalli Lakshminarsu

7756 **Jaisimha, M.L.**
–2 Benefit souvenir: International XI vs. An
■ Indian XI, Feb. 22, 23, 24, 1978 at Lal
Bahadur Stadium, Hyderabad. *n.p.*,
[1978]. [240]p. incl. covers & adverts.
stats. ports.
*54p. of text*

### James, Cyril Lionel Robert

7757 **James, Cyril Lionel Robert**
■ Beyond a boundary. Hutchinson, 1963.
256p.
——*another ed.* Sportsman's Book Club,
1964
——*rptd.* 1969. pbk.

### James, Sydney Rhodes

7758 **James, Sydney Rhodes**
■ Seventy years: random reminiscences
and reflections. Williams & Norgate,
1926. viii,285p. port.
*references to Eton and Cambridge cricket*

### Jameson, John Alexander

7758 **Warwickshire County Cricket Club**
–1 John A. Jameson's benefit season 1974.
■ [Birmingham, the Club, 1974]. [4]p. fold.
1 illus. 1 port. stats.

### Jayes, Thomas

7759 **Leicestershire County Cricket Club**
■ T. Jayes' benefit match. Leicestershire v.
Sussex July 8, 9 & 10, 1912. Leicester, the
Club, [1912]. 20p. ports. stats.

### Jepson, Arthur

7760 **Nottinghamshire County Cricket Club**
■ Arthur Jepson's benefit: Nottinghamshire
v. Yorkshire, Trent Bridge Ground,
Nottingham, July 21, 23 & 24, 1951.
[Nottingham, the Club, 1951]. 4p. port.
stats.

### Jessop, Gilbert Laird

7761 **Britton, Charles J.**
■ G.L. Jessop: a complete record of his
performances in first-class cricket;
amplified with anecdotes by some of his
greatest contemporaries. Birmingham,
Cornish, 1935. 143p. ports. stats.

7761 **Brodribb, Gerald**
–1 The Croucher: a biography of Gilbert
■ Jessop. London Magazine Editions, 1974.
[viii],239p. illus. ports. facsims. scores,
stats.

7762 **Jessop, Gilbert Laird**
■ A cricketer's log. Hodder & Stoughton,
[1922]. vii,264p. ports. scores
*previously serialised in* The Cricketer

### Joel, John

7763 **Joel, John**
■ Reminiscences. Eton, R.I. Drake, 1880.
22p.

### Jog, P.B.

7764 **Jog, P.B.**
■ Mehā ashā āhe. Poona, the Author, 1959.
256p. illus. ports.
*mostly in Marathi, some in English: trs. "I did it my way": [autobiography]*

### Johnson, Ian William

7765 **Johnson, Ian**
■ Cricket at the crossroads. Cassell, 1957.
[viii],213p. illus. ports.

### Johnson, Laurence Alan

7765 **Northamptonshire County Cricket Club**
–1 Laurie Johnson (Northamptonshire) bene-
■ fit 1973: benefit match John Player League
v. Yorkshire Sunday 3rd June 1973.
Northampton, the Club, 1973. [6]p. fold.
port.

### Johnston, Brian Alexander

7766 **Johnston, Brian Alexander**
■ Let's go somewhere. Cleaver-Hume P.,
1952. 172p. illus. ports.
*ch. viii: "Cricket in the office—television cricket commentating"*

7766 It's been a lot of fun: an autobiography.
−1 W.H. Allen, 1974. 310p. illus. ports.
■

## Jones, Arthur Owen

7767 **Craig, Albert**
■ Mr. Arthur Owen Jones. Wright & Co.,
1907. [4]p. folded card. port.

## Jones, *Sir* Lawrence Evelyn

7767 **Jones, *Sir* Lawrence Evelyn**
−1 A Victorian boyhood. Macmillan, 1956.
v,244p. frontis.
*cricket pp. 52, 166, 235–36*

7768 I forgot to tell you. Hart-Davies, 1959.
■ 234p.
*cricket pp. 28–29, 167–69*

## Kanhai, Rohan Babulal

7769 **Kanhai, Rohan [Babulal]**
■ Blasting for runs. London, Souvenir P.;
Toronto, The Ryerson P., 1966. 128p.
illus. ports.
——*another ed.* Blashing [sic] for runs.
Calcutta, Rupa, 1970. 118p.

7769 **Kanhai-Gibbs:** a tribute to two outstand-
−1 ing West Indians: [benefit brochure]. Port
■ of Spain, Trinidad, the Benefit Cttee.,
1974. [ii],82p. incl. adverts. illus. ports.
stats.

7769 **Rohan Kanhai:** a tribute to the "Little
−2 Master" in his benefit year: official benefit
■ brochure; edited and produced by J.
David Hogg & Associates. Rohan Kanhai
Benefit Cttee., 1977. [32]p. incl. covers &
adverts. illus. & ports. (some col.), stats.

## Kardar, Abdul Hafeez

7770 **Kardar, Abdul Hafeez**
■ Green shadows. Karachi, the Author,
[1958]. xv,188p. illus. port. scores, stats.

## Karloff, Boris, *pseud. i.e.* William Henry Pratt

7770 **Lindsay, Cynthia Hobart**
−1 Dear Boris: the life of William Henry
Pratt; a.k.a. Boris Karloff. N.Y. Knopf,
1975. xii,273p. illus. ports.
*ch. 14, pp. 88–99 "He had a great innings"
– B.K. and Hollywood C.C.*

7771 **Underwood, Peter**
Horror man: the life of Boris Karloff.
Frewin, 1972. 238p. illus. ports. bibliog.

## Kelaart, Thomas

7772 **[Bartholomeusz, P.L.]**
■ Ceylon's champion bowler: a sketch of
Tommy Kelaart, by "On-Looker". Colombo, Ceylon Sportsman, 1910. [4]p.
port. on cover, stats.

## Kennedy, Richard

7772 **Kennedy, Richard**
−1 A boy at the Hogarth Press; illustrated
■ by the author. The Whittington P., 1972.
xi,87p. illus.
——*limited ed. of 520 number and signed
copies*
——*another ed.* Heinemann Educational
Books, 1972. xi,86p. illus. (1 col.)
——*another ed.* Penguin Books, 1978.
104p. illus. pbk.
*contains brief observations of "A
Bloomsbury cricket match"*

## Kenny, Ramnath Bhaura

7772 **Ramnath Kenny** benefit match, Ahmed-
−2 nagar, 31 March & 1st April 1979:
■ [souvenir]. [Ahmednagar], Benefit Match
Cttee., [1979]. [130]p. incl. adverts. illus.
ports.
*mostly adverts*

## Kent, William Richard Gladstone

7773 **Kent, William Richard Gladstone**
■ The testament of a Victorian youth: an
autobiography. Heath Cranton, 1938.
296p. illus. ports.
*many cricket references*

7774 Fifty years a cricket watcher. Hunstanton,
■ Cricket Book Society, 1946. 31p. (Publications. Ser. 1, no. 5)

## Kenward, James

7774 **Kenward, James**
−1 Prep school; illustrated by Christopher
■ Brooker. M. Joseph, 1958. 202p.
*cricket pp. 71–81*

## Kenyon-Slaney, William

7775 **Durnford, *Sir* Walter,** *editor*
Memoir of Colonel the Right Hon.
William Kenyon-Slaney, M.P. Murray,
1909. viii,144p. illus. ports.
*chs. 3, 4, 6 & 7 by William Bridgeman; ch.
5 by Violet Kenyon-Slaney; scattered cricket
references*

## Kilburn, James Maurice

7776 **Kilburn, James Maurice**
■ Thanks to cricket. S. Paul, 1972. 204p.
illus. ports.
——*another ed.* Sportsman's Book Club,
1973

## Killick, Ernest Harry

7777 **Ernest H. Killick's** benefit match Sussex
■ v. Lancashire at Hove, August 8th, 9th
and 10th, 1910. [Sussex C.C.C., 1910].
[4]p. fold, score, stats.
*includes contribution by "Leather Hunter",
i.e. Alfred J. Gaston*

## Kilner, Norman and Roy

7778 **Woodhouse, Anthony,** *and others*
■ Cricketers of Wombwell, by A. Wood-
house, R.D. Wilkinson, J. Sokell. Leeds,
Wombwell Cricket Lovers' Society, 1965.
[10], 39p. illus. ports. stats. (Wombwell
Cricket Lovers' Society Publications)
*on Irving Washington, Roy and Norman
Kilner*

## King, John Herbert

7779 **Leicestershire County Cricket Club**
J.H. King's benefit match, Leicestershire
v. Kent, 1923. Leicester, the Club, 1923.
16p. illus.

## Kingscote, Henry Robert

7779 **Kingscote, Thomas A.F.**
–1 Henry Robert Kingscote 1802–1882:
memoir and autobiographical notes. Privately published, [c.1883]. 31p. ports.
*cricket pp. 5,9,13,20*

## Kinross, Albert

7780 **Kinross, Albert**
■ An unconventional cricketer. Shaylor,
1930. 212p.

## Kippax, Alan Falconer

7780 **Waverley District Cricket Club**
–1 Alan Kippax testimonial, Waverley Oval,
■ 9 September 1939, An International XI v.
Waverley: souvenir booklet. [Sydney],
the Club, [1939]. 28p. incl. adverts. illus.
*the illus. are caricatures by Arthur Mailey*

## Kitchen, Mervyn John

7781 **Souvenir** book 1973 to commemorate the
■ testimonial year awarded to Mervyn
Kitchen. [Testimonial Committee, 1973].
56p. incl. adverts. illus. ports. stats.

## Knott, Alan Philip Eric

7782 **Knott, Alan**
■ Stumper's view. S. Paul, 1972. [viii],238p.
illus. diagrs.
——*another ed.* Sportsman's Book Club,
1974

7782 **Rogers, Andy,** *editor*
–1 Alan Knott benefit 1976: souvenir.
[Benefit Cttee., 1976]. [44]p. illus. ports.
(1 team port. in col.), stats.

## Labuschagne, Frederick William Jacobus

7782 **Labuschagne, Frederick William Jacobus**
–2 Eye witness in sport. Cape Town,
■ Timmins, 1970. 168p. illus.
*cricket ch. x, pp. 120–38*

## Laker, James Charles

7782 **Arlott, [Leslie Thomas] John**
–3 Jim Laker. The Author, [c.1970]. 18p.
*limited ed. of 6 offprints*

7783 **Laker, Jim,** *i.e.* **James Charles Laker**
■ Spinning round the world. Muller, 1957.
220p. illus. ports. diagrs.
——*another ed.* Sportsman's Book Club,
1959

7784 Over to me. Muller, 1960. 238p. illus.
■ ports.

## Lambert, George E.

7785 **George E. Lambert,** Gloucestershire, bene-
■ fit souvenir card. 1955. [4]p. fold. ports.
stats.

## Lambton, Arthur

7786 **Lambton, Arthur**
■ My story: (being a full exposure of the
infamous legitimacy laws.) Hurst &
Blackett, [c.1925]. 296p. ports.
*scattered references*

7787 The galanty show. Hurst & Blackett,
■ 1933. 288p. frontis.
*cricket pp. 33–83*

## Lang, Andrew

7788 **Steward, Averil**
'Alicella': a memoir of Alice King Stewart
and Ella Christie. Murray, 1955. xxiv,
311p. illus. ports.
*reference to Andrew Lang, pp. 126–29*

## Langford, Arthur

7788 **Rosenwater, Irving**
–1 Arthur Langford: a memoir. *Privately*
■ *printed*, 1977. [8]p.
*limited ed. of 50 copies numbered and signed*

## Larwood, Harold

7789 **Larwood, Harold**
■ Body-line? an account of the Test matches between England and Australia, 1932–33. E. Mathews & Marrot, 1933. 220p. illus. port. diagrs. scores, stats.

7790 The Larwood story, by Harold Larwood
■ with Kevin Perkins. W.H. Allen, 1965. 232p. illus. ports.
——another ed. Sportsman's Book Club, 1967

7791 **Sutton-in-Ashfield Cricket Club**
Larwood benefit fund: souvenir programme June 10th, 1936. Sutton-in-Ashfield, Larwood Benefit Cttee., [1936]. 8p. port.

## Lawry, William Morris ("Bill")

7792 **Lawry, Bill,** *i.e.* **William Morris Lawry**
■ Run-digger: his own story; edited by Phil Tressider [i.e. Tresidder]. Souvenir P., 1966. 128p. illus. ports. stats.
——*another ed.* Sportsman's Book Club, 1968

## Lawton, Thomas

7793 **Lawton, Tommy**
■ Football is my business; edited by Roy Peskett. Sporting Handbooks, 1946. 229p.
*ch. iv "My cricket career"*

## Leary, Stuart

7794 **Stuart Leary** benefit brochure 1967

## Lee, Frank Stanley

7795 **Lee, Frank Stanley**
■ Cricket, lovely cricket. S. Paul, 1960. 196p. illus. ports.

7796 **Trump, R.F.,** *compiler*
■ Facts and figures of Somerset County Cricket Club (including all players) from 1891–1946, published in aid of Frank Lee's benefit. [Taunton, the Club, 1947]. 36p. stats.

## Lee, Harry William

7797 **Lee, Harry William**
■ Forty years of English cricket, with excur-
sions to India and South Africa, described by H.W. Lee; set down and edited by Laurence Thompson. Clerke & Cockeran, 1948. 191p. illus. ports.

## Lees, Walter Scott

7798 **Craig, Albert**
■ W.S. Lees. Wright & Co., 1906. [4]p. folded card. port.

7799 **Souvenir** of Lees' benefit, and Surrey v.
■ Notts, the Oval, August 6, 7 and 8. Souvenir Publishing Syndicate, [1906]. 48p. incl. adverts. illus. port. score

## Leigh, *Hon. Sir* Edward Chandos

7800 **Leigh,** *Hon. Sir* **Edward Chandos**
■ Bar, bat and bit: recollections and experiences; edited by F. Robert Bush. Murray, 1913. viii,232p. illus. ports.

## Leigh, *Hon.* James Wentworth

7801 **Leigh,** *Hon.* **James Wentworth**
■ Other days. T. Fisher Unwin, 1921. 255p. ports.
*cricket pp. 22, 85*

## Lennox, *Lord* William Pitt

7802 **Lennox,** *Lord* **William Pitt**
Pictures of sporting life and character. 2 vols. Hurst & Blackett, 1860. illus.
*cricket vol. 1, pp. 188–95, 234–5, 253–4, 280–2, 320*
*vol. 2, pp. 179–84*

## Lever, Peter

7803 **Kay, John,** *editor*
■ Peter Lever testimonial brochure: for Lancashire and England. [Manchester], Testimonial Committee, [1972]. [32]p. incl. adverts. illus. ports. stats.

## Leveson Gower, *Sir* George Granville

7804 **Leveson Gower,** *Sir* **George Granville**
■ Years of content 1858–1886. Murray, 1940. x,270p. ports.
*random cricket references*

## Leveson Gower, *Sir* Henry Dudley Gresham

7805 **Leveson Gower,** *Sir* **Henry Dudley**
■ **Gresham**
Off and on the field. S. Paul, 1953. 240p. illus. ports.

## Levy, Edward Lawrence

7806 **Levy, Edward Lawrence**
The autobiography of an athlete: essays.
Birmingham, Hammond, 1913. 272p.
ports.
*cricket pp. 80–85*

## Lewis, Cecil Day

7806 **Lewis, Cecil Day**
–1 The buried day. Chatto & Windus, 1960.
■ 244p. illus. ports.
*cricket pp. 72,126,144,197–8,230*

## Lillee, Dennis Keith

7806 **Lillee, Dennis [Keith]**
–2 Back to the mark, as told to Ian Brayshaw.
■ Richmond (Vic.), Hutchinson of Australia; London, S. Paul, 1974. 159p. illus.
ports.
——*another ed.* Newton Abbot, Readers
Union, 1975

## Lightfoot, Albert

7807 **Albert Lightfoot** benefit. Northampton-
■ shire XI v. Leighton Buzzard Town
Cricket Club, Sunday, August 30th, 1970.
[4]p. fold

## Lilley, Arthur Augustus

7808 **A.A. Lilley's** benefit 1903. Bourneville,
Bourneville Magazine

7809 **Lilley, Arthur Augustus**
■ Twenty-four years of cricket: recalling the
most famous cricketers and their methods, together with some advice on the
game. Popular ed. Mills & Boon, [1912].
viii,350p. illus. ports. diagrs.
——*pocket ed.* 1914. 303p.

## Lilley, Ben

7810 **Nottinghamshire County Cricket Club**
■ Ben Lilley's benefit, Nottinghamshire v.
Yorkshire, Trent Bridge Ground, July 20,
22, 23, 1935. Nottingham, the Club, 1935.
[4]p. folded card. port.

## Lillywhite, Frederick William

7811 **Rush, Philip**
Great men of Sussex. J. Lane, 1956. 128p.
illus. map. (Men of the Counties Series)
*includes ch. on F.W. Lillywhite*

## Lillywhite, James

7812 **Howe, W.H.**
Everybody's book of epitaphs. Howe,
1891. 192p.
*reference to James Lillywhite pp. 34–35*

## Lindwall, Raymond Russell ("Ray")

7813 **Lindwall, Ray,** *i.e.* **Raymond Russell**
■ **Lindwall**
Flying stumps. S. Paul, 1954. 184p. illus.
ports. stats.
——*another ed.* Arrow Books, 1957

## Livingston, Leonard ("Jock")

7814 **The Jock Livingston** testimonial hand-
■ book. Northampton, British Timken,
[1955]. 34p. illus. ports. stats.

## Lloyd, Clive Hubert

7814 **Maddock, John,** *editor*
–1 Clive Lloyd testimonial year book.
■ Manchester, [Benefit Cttee.], 1977. 80p.
incl. covers & adverts. illus. ports. (some
col.), stats.

## Lock, Graham Anthony Richard ("Tony")

7815 **Lock, Tony**
■ For Surrey and England. Hodder &
Stoughton, 1957. 192p. illus. ports.
diagrs.

7816 **Ward, [Bernard] Kirwan**
■ Put Lock on! Adelaide, Rigby; London,
Hale, 1972. [xiv],138p. illus. ports.

## Lockwood, William Henry

7817 **Craig, Albert**
■ William Henry Lockwood. All England
Publ. Co., 1898. [4]p. folded card. port.
—— *another issue.* 1899.

## Lohmann, George Alfred

7818 **[Craig, Albert]**
■ G.A. Lohmann. Cricket P., 1895. [4]p.
folded card. port.

7819 **George Lohmann's** benefit: souvenir,
portrait and biography. *n.p.,* 1896. port.

## Long, Arnold

7820 **Arnold Long** benefit year 1971: pro-
■ gramme. [16]p. incl. adverts. ports.

7820 **Surrey** v. Chelsea: 30 over cricket – 6-a-
–1 side football in aid of the Arnold Long
■ and Peter Bonetti benefits, Wednesday,
21st July, 1971: official programme.
*Printed by* King & Jarrett Ltd., [1971]. 16p.
incl. adverts. illus. ports.

Viv Richards *photo: Patrick Eagar*

Gary Sobers *photo: Patrick Eagar*

Fred Trueman *photo: Popperfoto*

Frank Worrell *photo: Keystone Press*

## Long, Walter, *1st viscount Long of Wraxall*

7821 **Long, Walter, *1st viscount Long of Wraxall***
■ Memories. Hutchinson, 1923. xv,380p. illus. ports.
   *cricket mainly at Harrow and Oxford in chs. iii, iv and xix*

## Lubbock, Alfred

7822 **Lubbock, Alfred**
■ Memories of Eton and Etonians; including my life at Eton, 1854–1863 and some reminiscences of some subsequent cricket, 1864–1874. Murray, 1899. xvi, 320p. illus. ports.

## Lucas, Edward Verrall

7823 **Blue Star Line**
■ Souvenir of . . . cricket match: Passengers versus Officers, played on board the Blue Star Liner "Avelona" at sea, voyage 4, February 4th 1928. 4p. stats.
   *E.V. Lucas made thirty runs for the Passengers*

7824 **Lucas, Audrey**
■ E.V. Lucas: a portrait. Methuen, 1939. xiii,159p. illus. ports. bibliog.
   ——2nd ed. 1939

7824 **Prance, Claude Annett**
–1 The laughing philosopher: a further miscellany on books, booksellers and book collecting. Villiers Publications, 1976. 284p.
   *pp. 111–8, "A shelf of cricket books", and pp. 138–47, "Edward Verrall Lucas"*

## Luckhurst, Brian William

7825 **Dimont, Charles,** *editor*
■ Brian Luckhurst benefit 1973. Canterbury, Benefit Cttee., [1973]. [44]p. incl. adverts. illus. ports. stats.

## Lyons, John James

7826 **[Craig, Albert]**
■ John James Lyons. Wright & Co., 1893. [4]p. folded card. port.

## Lyttelton Family

7826 **Askwith, Betty**
–1 The Lytteltons: a family chronicle of the
■ nineteenth century. Chatto & Windus, 1975. [x],214p. illus. ports. bibliog.
   *cricket pp. 47,48,49,156–8,160*

## Lyttelton, *Hon.* Alfred

7826 **Irwin, Clarke Huston**
–2 Alfred Lyttelton: statesman and cricketer. Religious Tract Society, *n.d.* 32p. (The Little Library of Biography)
   *cricket pp. 8–12*

7827 **Lyttelton, *Dame* Edith**
■ Alfred Lyttelton: an account of his life. Longmans, Green, 1917. xiv,431p. illus. ports.
   ——new edition, abridged. Longmans, 1923. xiv,287p.

7828 **Lyttelton, *Hon.* Edward**
Alfred Lytellton: his home-training & earlier life. [1916]. 62p.

7829 **[Thompson, Edward Raymond]**
■ Portraits of the new century (the first ten years), by E.T. Raymond. Benn, 1928. 336p.
   *"Alfred Lyttelton", pp. 150–63*

## Lyttelton, *Hon.* Edward

7830 **Alington, Cyril Argentine**
■ Edward Lyttelton: an appreciation. Murray, 1943. viii,72p. illus. ports.
   *cricket ch. v, pp. 19–21*

7831 **Lyttelton, *Hon.* Edward**
■ Memories and hopes. Murray, 1925. x,340p. illus. ports.
   *ch. v "Cricket", pp. 67–86 and other references*

## Lyttelton, *Sir* Neville

7831 **Lyttelton, *Sir* Neville**
–1 Eighty years: soldiering, politics, games. Hodder & Stoughton, [1927]. 312p. illus. ports.
   *cricket in ch. vii, and references in chs i and ii*

## Macadam, John

7832 **Macadam, John**
The Macadam road. Jarrolds, 1955. 192p. illus. ports.
   *cricket pp. 9, 44, 129, 183*

## Macartney, Charles George

7833 **Macartney, Charles George**
■ My cricketing days. Heinemann, 1930. ix,240p. illus. ports.

## McCool, Colin Leslie

7834 **McCool, Colin [Leslie]**
■ Cricket is a game. S. Paul, 1961. 144p. illus. ports.

## McGahey, Charles Percy

7835 **Craig, Albert**
■ Mr. Charles McGahey. Wright & Co., 1907. [4]p. folded card. port.

## McGlew, Derrick John ("Jackie")

7836 **McGlew, Jackie,** *i.e.* Derrick John
■ **McGlew**
Cricket for South Africa. Hodder & Stoughton, 1961. [ix],214p. illus. ports.

7837 Six for glory; with a section by Eric
■ Litchfield. Cape Town, Timmins; Wellington, N.Z., Reed, 1967. xx,215p. illus. scores, stats.
*Pt. 1. "On tour with the Aussies", by E.L., pp. 1–71; Pt. 2. "Six for glory", by J. McG., pp. 73–187; statistical section, pp. 189–215*

## McIntyre, Arthur John William

7837 **Surrey County Cricket Club**
–1 MRM '79 testimonial. 40 years at the
■ Oval, A.J. McIntyre, R.A. Radley, J.F. McQuirke. The Club, [1979]. 24p. incl. adverts.

## Mackay, Ian

7837 **Evans, Trevor,** *editor*
–2 The great Bohunkus: tributes to Ian Mackay. W.H. Allen, 1953. 208p. illus.
*includes pp. 182–5 "Willow and wine" by John Arlott*

## Mackay, Kenneth Donald

7838 **Mackay, Ken**
■ Slasher opens up. [by] Ken Mackay with Frank O'Callaghan. Pelham, 1964. 210p. illus. diagr.

## McKenzie, Graham Douglas

7838 **Graham McKenzie** testimonial book.
–1 [Perth] (W.A.), Denbar Sports Internat-
■ ional, 1978. 48p. incl. adverts. illus. ports. stats.

## Mackie, John

7839 **Mackie, John**
■ Sixty-two years of club cricket. Castle Cary, J.H. Roberts, 1947. 48p. ports. stats.

## Mackintosh, Harold Vincent, *1st viscount Mackintosh of Halifax*

7840 **Mackintosh, Harold Vincent,** *1st viscount*
■ *Mackintosh of Halifax*
By faith and work: the autobiography of the Rt. Hon, the first viscount Mackin-

tosh of Halifax, DL., LLD.; edited and arranged by A.A. Thomson. Hutchinson, 1966. 296p. illus. ports.
*cricket, pp. 29, 81–5; 173–5*

## McLaren, John William

7840 **Murphy, D.J.,** *and others, editors*
–1 Prelude to power: the rise of the Labor Party in Milton, Queensland 1885–1915; edited by D.J. Murphy, R.B. Joyce and Colin A. Hughes. Jacaranda P., 1970. xx,336p.
*contains p. 35 a reference to a threat of an industrial strike over the possible selection of J.W. McLaren to play for Australia*

## McQuirke, John Fergus

7840 **Surrey County Cricket Club**
–2 MRM '79 testimonial. 40 years at the
■ Oval, A.J. McIntyre, R.A. Radley, J.F. McQuirke. The Club, [1979]. 24p. incl. adverts.

## Mailey, Arthur Alfred

7841 **Mailey, Arthur Alfred**
■ 10 for 66 and all that; illustrated by the author. Phoenix House, 1958. 174p. illus. (1 col.). (Sports books)
*another ed.* Sportsman's Book Club, 1959

7842 **Ray, Cyril,** *editor*
■ The compleat imbiber 10: an entertainment edited by Cyril Ray and designed by Charles Hasler. Hutchinson, 1969. 224p. illus.
*includes "A bottle or so with Arthur" [Mailey], by Denzil Batchelor, pp. 32–37*

## Mais, Stuart Petre Brodie

7842 **Mais, Stuart Petre Brodie**
–1 All the days of my life. Hutchinson, 1937. 388p. illus. ports.
*ch. xvi, pp. 356–63 "Cricket"*

7843 Buffets and rewards: an autobiographical record (1937–1951). Hutchinson, 1952. 200p. port. illus.
*scattered cricket references*

## Malan, Charles Hamilton

7844 **Malan, Charles Hamilton**
A soldier's experience of God's love, and of his faithfulness to his word: being a few notes from military service. Nisbet, 1873. 239p. illus.
*cricket pp. 118–121. Frontis. shows cricket match at Singapore. Several editions by 1879*

## Mallalieu, Joseph Percival William

7845 **Mallalieu, Joseph Percival William**
■ Very ordinary sportsman. Routledge & K.
Paul, 1957. viii,168p. illus.
*ch. vii "Test match"*

## Mallett, Ashley Alexander

7846 **Mallett, Ashley**
■ Rowdy. Blackwood (S.A.), Lynton Publications, 1973. 140p. illus. ports. diagrs.

7846 Spin out. Toorak (Vic.), Garry Sparke &
−1 Associates, 1977. iv,172p. illus. ports.
■ stats.

## Manjrekar, Vijay Laxman

7847 **Hubli Sports Club**
■ Vijay Manjrekar benefit match, March 25,
26, 27, 1972 at Hubli. Hubli, the Club,
[1972]. [162]p. incl. adverts. illus. ports.
stats.

7848 **Shivaji Park Gymkhana**
■ Souvenir honouring Arjuna Award
winner Vijay Manjrekar and new Test cap
Ajit Wadekar, April 21, 1967. Bombay,
G.K. Menon for the S.P.G., [1967]. [82]p.
incl. adverts. illus. ports. stats.

## Mankad, Mulwantrai Himmatlal ("Vinoo")

7848 **Allahabad Cricket Association**
−1 Vinoo Mankad benefit cricket match at
■ Madan Mohan Malviya Stadium, Allahabad, on November 12, 13 and 14, 1971.
Allahabad, the Assoc., [1971]. [230]p.
mostly adverts. illus. ports.

7849 **Amrita Bazaar Patrika**
Vinoo Mankad souvenir. Amrita, Amrita
Bazaar Patrika, [c.1952]. 8p. illus.

7850 **Vaidya, Sudhir**
■ Vinoo Mankad. Bombay, Thacker, 1969.
xi,159p. illus. ports. stats.

7851 **[Entry cancelled]**

## Mariner, George

7852 **Lucas, Edward Verrall**
■ One day and another. Methuen, 1909.
vii,251p.
*essays including "George Mariner", pp.
145–151*

## Marlow, Francis William

7853 **[F.W. Marlow's** benefit match . . . 1904]
*contains pen-portrait of F.W.M. by
"Leather Hunter" [A.J. Gaston]*

## Marriott, *Sir* John Arthur Ransome

7854 **Marriott, *Sir* John Arthur Ransome**
■ Memories of four score years: the
autobiography. . . . London & Glasgow,
Blackie, 1946. 252p. ports.
*references to Repton, Oxford and Lancashire cricket*

## Marsh, Rodney William

7854 **Marsh, Rodney**
−1 You'll keep; as told to Ian Brayshaw.
■ Richmond (Vic.), Hutchinson of Australia; London, Hutchinson, 1975. 176p.
illus. ports. facsim.
——pbk. ed. 1976

## Marshall, John

7855 **Marshall, John**
■ The weaving willow; decorated by Gus.
Hodder & Stoughton, 1953. 190p. illus.

## Marshall, Roy Edwin

7856 **Arlott, [Leslie Thomas] John**
■ Roy Marshall: a biographical note.
[Southampton, Hampshire C.C.C., 1961].
14p. frontis. stats.
*limited ed. of 50 copies. 1st published in
Hampshire C.C.C. Handbook, 1961*

7857 **Marshall, Roy [Edwin]**
■ Test outcast. Pelham Books, 1970. 159p.
illus. ports.

## Marsham, Cloudesley Henry Bullock

7858 **Craig, Albert**
■ Mr. C.H.B. Marsham. Wright & Co.,
1907. [4]p. folded card. port.

## Martin, John

7859 **Johnny Martin** cricket testimonial: Richie
■ Benaud's "Thrashers" vs. New South
Wales, Newcastle . . . February 27, 1972.
[1972]. [4]p. fold. port.

## Martineau, Hubert Melville

7859 **Hubert** Melville Martineau, Welsh
−1 Guards: [memorial service]. The Royal
Military Chapel, Wellington Barracks,
Friday 24th Sept. 1976. [4]p.

7860 **Martineau, Hubert M.**
■ My life in sport. *Privately printed*, The
Water Martin P., 1970. viii,349p. illus. &
ports. (some col.). scores
*ch. 2 "Cricket story", pp. 25–206*

## Masefield, John

7860 **Masefield, John**
–1 So long to learn: chapters of an autobiog-
■ raphy. Heinemann, 1952. [v],242p.
   *cricket pp. 56–60 on the 1882 Australian
   team*

7860 Grace before ploughing: fragments of
–2 autobiography. Heinemann, 1966. vi,90p.
■ *cricket pp. 85–7*

## Mason, John Richard

7861 **Craig, Albert**
■ Mr. J.R. Mason. Cricket P., 1897. [4]p.
   folded card. port.
   *published anonymously*
   ——All England Athletic Publishing Co.,
   1899
   *signed*
   ——Wright & Co. 1906
   ——Wright & Co. 1908
   *both signed*

## Masterman, *Sir* John Cecil

7861 **Masterman, *Sir* John Cecil**
–1 On the chariot wheel: an autobiography.
■ Oxford Univ. P., 1975. x,384p. illus.
   ports.
   *cricket pp. 16–17, 59–60, 81–2, 154–63,
   198–9*

## May Family

7861 **Ray, F.**
–2 The Mays of Basingstoke with special
   reference to Lieut.-Colonel John May,
   V.O.,J.P. London, Simpkin; Basingstoke,
   "Basingstoke News", 1904. x,60p. illus.
   ports.
   *cricket pp. 46–9 – contains brief history of
   Basingstoke C.C.*

## May, Peter Barker Howard

7862 **May, Peter Barker Howard**
■ Peter May's book of cricket. Cassell, 1956.
   viii,119p. illus. ports. diagr.

7863 **Rodrigo, Robert**
■ Peter May. Phoenix House, 1960. 111p.
   illus. ports. ('Living Biographies' Series)

## Mead, Charles Philip

7864 **Arlott, [Leslie Thomas] John**
   Tribute to Philip Mead. 1958. 5p. MS.
   *typescript of a broadcast*

7865 **Ashley-Cooper, Frederick Samuel**
■ Mead's hundreds: a note. Milford
   (Surrey), [the Author], 1927. [4]p.
   *booklet designed as a Christmas card*

## Meckiff, Ian

7866 **Meckiff, Ian**
■ Thrown out, [by] Ian (Chucker) Meckiff,
   as told to Ian McDonald. S. Paul, 1961.
   191p. illus. ports. scores, stats.

## Menzies *Sir* Robert Gordon

7866 **Joske, *Sir* Percy˙**
–1 Sir Robert Menzies, 1894–1978: a new,
   informal memoir. Angus & Robertson,
   1978. 354p. illus. ports.

7866 **Menzies, *Sir* Robert Gordon**
–2 The wit of Sir Robert Menzies; compiled
   by Ray Robinson. Frewin, 1966. 127p.
   ports.
   *many cricket references*

7867 Afternoon light: some memories of men
■ and events. Cassell, 1967. [ix],384p.
   *ch. 16, "Cricket—a diversion," pp.
   341–360*

7868 The measure of the years. Cassell, 1970.
■ [viii],300p.
   *"Cricket and cricketers", pp. 267–300*

7868 **Perkins, Kevin**
–1 Menzies, last of the Queen's men.
■ London, Angus & Robertson; Adelaide,
   Rigby, 1968. [xi],264p. illus. ports.
   *cricket pp. 181–3*

## Merchant, Vijay Madharji

7869 **Knight, Edward,** *compiler*
■ Vijay Merchant. Calcutta, Illustrated
   News, 1950. 42p. illus. port. stats.

## Meynell, *Sir* Francis

7870 **Meynell, *Sir* Francis**
■ My lives. Bodley Head, 1971. 332p. illus.
   ports.
   *cricket in chs. 3 and 12*

## Mickle, Alan Durward

7871 **Mickle, Alan Durward**
■ After the ball: a book of sporting
   memories. Melbourne, Cheshire, 1959.
   x,106p. illus.

## Milburn, Colin

7871 **The Guardian**
–1 The bedside 'Guardian' 18: a selection
■ from The Guardian 1968–69; edited by
   W.L. Webb. Collins, 1969. 240p. illus.
   *includes pp. 187–8, "Cricket still needs
   Colin Milburn", by John Arlott*

**7872 Milburn, Colin**
■ Largely cricket. S. Paul, 1968. 136p. illus. ports.

**7873 Wooldridge, Ian,** *editor*
■ Colin Milburn testimonial. Bagenal Harvey Organisation, [1971]. 29p. incl. adverts. illus. ports. diagr. stats.

## Miller, Edward Darley

**7874 Miller, Edward Darley**
■ Fifty years of sport. Hurst & Blackett, [1925]. 350p. illus. ports.
*scattered cricket references*

## Miller, Keith Ross

**7874 Bose, Mihir**
**-1** Keith Miller: a cricketing biography.
■ Sydney, Allen & Unwin Australia Pty. Ltd., 1979. [xv],175p. illus. stats. bibliog.

**7875 Miller, Keith [Ross]**
■ Cricket crossfire. Oldbourne P., 1956. 174p. illus. ports.
——*another ed.* Calcutta, Rupa, 1962. 120p.

**7876** Cricket from the grandstand. Oldbourne
■ P., 1959. 165p. illus. port. scores
*includes an account of England in Australia 1958–59*
——*another ed.* Sportsman's Book Club, 1960

**7877 Miller, Keith [Ross],** *and* **Whitington,**
■ **Richard Smallpeice**
Cricket caravan. Latimer House, 1950. 207p. illus. port.

**7878** Straight hit. Latimer House, 1952. 256p.
■ illus. port. scores
*includes account of West Indies tour of Australia, 1951–2*

**7879** Bumper. Latimer House, 1953. 237p.
■ illus. diagr. scores

**7880** Gods or flanelled fools? MacDonald,
■ 1954. xii,304p. illus. ports. scores
*includes account of Australian tour of England, 1953*

**7881** Cricket typhoon; with a guest chapter by
■ C.B. Fry. Macdonald, 1955. 256p. illus. scores, stats.

**7881** Keith Miller companion: a selection from
**-1** 'Cricket caravan', 'Catch!' 'Straight hit' &
■ 'Bumper'. Sportsman's Book Club, 1955. 248p. illus. scores, stats.

## Milne, Alan Alexander

**7882 Milne, Alan Alexander**
■ It's too late now: the autobiography of a writer. Methuen, 1939. viii,248p. port.
*scattered cricket references*

## Mitford, John

**7883 Mitford, John**
The Rev. John Mitford on cricket; with a biographical note by F.S. Ashley-Cooper. Nottingham, Richards, 1921. 24p.
*reprints of articles reviewing Nyren's "Young Cricketer's Tutor" published in Gentleman's Magazine 1833*

## Modi, Rusi Sheriyar

**7884 Modi, Rusi**
■ Cricket forever. Bombay, the Author, 1964. [x],128p. illus. ports.
*includes account of MCC tour of India, 1963–4*

## Monckton, Walter, *Viscount Monckton of Brenchley*

**7884 Smith, Frederick Winston Furneaux,** *Earl*
**-1** *Birkenhead*
■ Walter Monckton: the life of Viscount Monckton of Brenchley. Weidenfeld & Nicolson, 1969. xii,388p. illus. ports.
*many cricket references, including pp. 264–7 on 'The Cricket Ball Case' (1951) Bolton v. Stone, concerning injury to a member of the public, struck by a cricket ball hit out of a private ground onto a public highway; see also no. 2229*

## Money, Walter Baptist

**7885 Money, Walter Baptist**
■ Humours of a parish, and other quaintnesses. Lane, [1920]. xiii,203p. ports.
——*2nd ed.* 1920
*cricket pp. 107–19*

## Monfries, John Elliott

**7886 Monfries, John Elliott**
■ Not Test cricket: happy reminiscences of every other kind of cricket in Adelaide, Melbourne, Sydney and Hobart. Adelaide, Gillingham, 1950. 106p. port.

## Montagu, Ivor

**7887 Montagu, Ivor**
The youngest son: autobiographical sketches. Lawrence & Wishart, 1970. 384p. illus. ports.
*cricket pp. 15, 55–61, 72, 106, 113, 218*

## Moraes, Dom F.

7888 **Moraes, Dom F.**
  My son's father: an autobiography. Secker & Warburg, 1968. 242p.

## Moran, Herbert Michael

7888 **Moran, Herbert Michael**
-1  Viewless winds – being the recollections and digressions of an Australian surgeon. P. Davies, 1939. 352p.
  *cricket pp. 25–6,48–9,60–1*

## Morrison, Pearse

7888 **Morrison, Pearse**
-2  Rambling recollections. Sonnenschein,
■  1905. iv,236p.
  *cricket pp. 5–8, 67–68*

## Mortimore, John

7888 **Gloucestershire County Cricket Club**
-3  John Mortimore's benefit. [Bristol, the
■  Club], 1965. 4p. fold, port. stats.

## Morton, Arthur

7889 **Derbyshire County Cricket Club**
■  Souvenir [of Arthur Morton's benefit]. Derby, the Club, 1924. 34p. incl. adverts. ports.
  *membership, rules and ports.—no text*

## Moseley, Hallam

7889 **[Somerset County Cricket Club]**
-1  Hallam Moseley testimonial book – 1979;
■  [edited by] Eric Hill. [Taunton, the Club, 1979]. 52p. incl. adverts. illus. ports.

## Moss, Alan

7890 **Middlesex County Cricket Club**
■  Alan Moss, Middlesex and England, benefit 1962: Middlesex v. Sussex, Lord's June 9–11–12th. Lord's, the Club, [1962]. [4]p. fold. 1 illus.

## Muncer, [Bernard] Leonard

7891 **[Thomas, J.B.G.]**, *compiler & editor*
■  Len Muncer benefit book; with special contributions by John Arlott and others. [Cardiff], Glamorgan C.C.C., [1954]. 32p. illus. ports. stats.

7892 **Len Muncer/Harry Sharp** testimonial,
■  1971: Len Muncer, an appreciation by Wilf Wooller; Harry Sharp, an appreciation by Bill Edrich. [1971]. illus. [4]p. folded card

## Murdoch, William Lloyd

7893 **[Craig, Albert]**
■  William Lloyd Murdoch. Wright & Co., [c.1890]. [4]p. folded card. port.

## Murray, John Thomas

7894 **John Murray,** Middlesex and England:
■  official benefit year souvenir. Organising Committee, 1966. 60p. incl. adverts. illus. ports.

7894 **John (J.T.) Murray,** Middlesex and Eng-
-1  land, 1975 benefit programme. Benefit
■  Cttee., [1975]. [4]p. fold

## Mushtaq Ali

7895 **Mushtaq Ali, Syed**
■  Cricket delightful. Calcutta, Rupa, 1967. [xii],272p. illus. ports. stats.

7896 **Uttar Pradesh Sports Writers' Club**
■  Exhibition cricket match in aid of S. Mushtaq Ali, 25, Oct. 1970: souvenir. Lucknow, the Club, [1970]. [52]p. incl. adverts. illus. ports. stats.

## Mushtaq Mohammed

7896 **Mustaq Mohammed** benefit year 1976.
-1  [Benefit Cttee., 1976]. 48p. incl. adverts.
■  illus. ports. stats.

## Myers, Arthur Wallis

7896 **Myers, Arthur Wallis**
-2  Memory's parade. Methuen, 1932. 211p. illus. ports.
  *cricket pp. 57,58,81,120,129*

## Mynn, Alfred

7897 **Lucas, Edward Verrall**
■  Harvest home. Methuen, 1913. 180p.
  *includes "Two amateurs—Alfred Mynn and Mr. Aislabie", pp. 54–58*

7898 **Morrah, Patrick**
■  Alfred Mynn and the cricketers of his time. Eyre & Spottiswoode, 1963. 224p. illus. ports. scores, stats. bibliog.

## Nash, William Gunner

7899 **Nash, William Gunner**
■  Not a bad innings: a few recollections of the last eighty-three years. [The Author], 1934. 64p. port.

## Nayudu, Cottari Kankaiya

7900 **[Sarbadhikary, Berry]**
■  C.K. Nayudu: "A cricketer of charm", by

"Eskari". Calcutta. Illustrated News, 1945. 110p. illus. ports. stats.

**7901 Vizianagram, Maharajkumar Vijaya of**
Colonel C.K. Nayudu Shastri-purti fund, sponsored by Vizzy . . . Delhi, Pearson's P., 1955. ports.

### Nelson, Robert Prynne

**7902 Nelson, Robert, [and Strickland, Hilda]**
■ R.P. Nelson: a memoir. Harpenden, privately published, [1955]. 28p. port.
*limited ed. of 300 copies*

### Newman, Leonard William

**7903 St. James's** Church, Piccadilly, Wednes-
■ day 22nd April, 1964. Leonard William Newman 1891–1964: [order of service]. [4]p. fold

### Nicholson, Anthony George

**7904 The Tony Nicholson** benefit 1973. [Leeds,
■ the Benefit Cttee., 1973]. 48p. incl. adverts. ports. stats.
*with full statistical survey by Roy D. Wilkinson*

### Noble, Montague Alfred

**7905 Noble, Montague Alfred**
■ The game's the thing: a record of cricket experience; with special chapters on the genius of Victor Trumper. Cassell, 1926. xv,248p. ports. diagrs.

### Noel Family

**7906 Noel, Emilia F.,** *compiler*
■ Some letters and records of the Noel family. The St. Catherine's P. and Nisbet, 1910. x,110p. illus. ports. tables
*cricket, p. 81 describes preparations for a game of cricket at Exton Park in 1772 in a letter from Lady Jane Edwards to her son Gerard N. Edwards (Sir Gerard Noel Noel) at Eton College, with the comment "but if Sir Robert Walpole does but improve as fast at cricket as he does . . . riding postillion, he will make a good figure on the cricket ground"; also pp. 86–87, in a letter from Sir G.N. Noel at Brighton to his sister "the Prince plays himself for an hour or two & he bowls very tolerably well"*

### Norman, Michael Eric John Charles

**7906 Mick Norman** benefit 1975. [Leicester],
**–1** Benefit Cttee., [1975]. 33p. illus. ports.
■ scores, stats.

### Nourse, Arthur Dudley

**7907 Nourse, Arthur Dudley**
■ Cricket in the blood. Hodder & Stoughton, 1949. x[ii],212p. illus. ports.
——2nd ed. 1950
——3rd ed. 1951

### Nutter, Albert Edward

**7908 The Nutter-Oldfield** testimonial book of
■ cricket. Northampton, British Timken Ltd., [1953]. 34p. illus. ports. stats.
*reminiscences of the two players chiefly during their Lancashire days*

### Nyren, John

**7909 Altick, Richard Daniel**
■ The Cowden Clarkes. Oxford Univ. P., 1948. xiii,268p. illus. ports.
*references to Nyren, pp. 95–99, etc*

**7910 Clarke, Mary Cowden**
■ My long life: an autobiographical sketch. T.F. Unwin, 1896. [iii],264p. ports.
——2nd ed. 1896. 260p. ports.
*references to Charles Cowden Clarke and Nyren*

**7911 [Entry cancelled]**

**7912 Esdaile, Edmund**
■ The Nyrens of Eartham and Hambledon: the facts and a reconstruction. Bournemouth, *printed by* The Boscombe Printing Co., 1967. [8]p.
*limited ed. of 25 copies; first published in Hampshire C.C.C. Handbook, 1967*

**7913 Lucas, Edward Verrall**
■ English leaves. Methuen, 1933. x,168p. illus. ports.
*essays including "John Nyren", pp. 107–16*

### Oakman, Alan Stanley Myles

**7914 Alan Oakman** benefit year, 1965. Benefit
■ Cttee., [1965]. 52p. incl. adverts. illus. ports. stats.
*contributions by John Arlott, E.W. Swanton, Ray Steele, etc.*

**7915 Oakman, Alan**
■ How I became a cricketer. Nelson, 1960. vii,88p. illus. port. (Enterprise Library)

### Old, Christopher Middleton

**7915 Carlisle Cricket Club**
**–1** Chris Old benefit: Yorkshire v. Cumbria
■ XI, Edenside, Carlisle, Sunday Sept. 16; ed. by Ted Roberts and Vernon Addison. Carlisle, the Club, [1979]. [20]p. incl. adverts. illus. ports. stats.

7915 **Fay, Peter,** *editor*
-2 Chris Old benefit year 1979: souvenir
■ benefit brochure. Benefit Cttee., 1979.
[28]p. incl. covers & adverts. illus. ports.
stats.

### "An Old Cricketer", *pseud.*

7916 **"An Old Cricketer",** *pseud.*
■ A cricketer's notebook; containing original anecdotes, remarks, notes,
reminiscences and other gossip. David
Bogue, 1881. vii,94p.

### Oldfield, Norman

7917 The **Nutter-Oldfield** testimonial book of
■ cricket. Northampton, British Timken
Ltd., [1953]. 34p. illus. ports. stats.
*reminiscences of the two players chiefly
during their Lancashire days*

### Oldfield, William Albert Stanley

7918 **Oldfield, William Albert Stanley**
■ Behind the wicket: my cricketing reminiscences. Hutchinson, 1938. 287p. illus.
ports. stats.

7919 The rattle of the stumps. Newnes, 1954.
■ 160p. illus. ports. stats.

### O'Neill, Norman Clifford

7920 **O'Neill, Norman [Clifford]**
■ Ins and outs. Pelham, 1964. 222p. illus.
ports.

### Ord, Hubert William

7921 **Ord, Hubert William**
The adventures of a schoolmaster: being
the autobiography of H.W. Ord, with
some account of the Blackheath Proprie-
tary School. Simpkin, Marshall, 1936.
237p. illus.

### Ord, James Simpson

7922 **Warwickshire County Cricket Club**
■ "Jimmy" Ord's benefit. Birmingham, the
Club, 1950. [4]p. fold, illus. port. stats.

### Ormrod, Alan

7922 **Watkins, Mike**
-1 Out in the middle: a book of cricket
■ cartoons [in aid of] the Alan Ormrod
benefit fund. *n.p.*, [1977]. 28p. incl.
adverts. illus.

### O'Reilly, William Joseph

7923 **Whitington, Richard Smallpeice**
■ Time of the Tiger: the Bill O'Reilly story.

Richmond (Vic.), Hutchinson; London, S.
Paul, 1970. 296p. illus. ports. stats.
——*another ed.* Sportsman's Book Club,
1972

### Osbaldeston, George

7924 **Nethercote, Henry Osmond**
■ The Pytchley hunt, past and present: its
history from its foundation with personal
anecdotes of the masters and principal
members. . . . Sampson Low, 1888. x,
376p. 1 illus. ports.
——2nd ed. by Charles Edmonds. 1888
*pp. 94–95 on 'Squire' Osbaldeston and
other cricket references pp. 44,132,139–43*

7925 **Osbaldeston, George**
■ Squire Osbaldeston: his autobiography;
edited with a commentary by E.D.
Cuming. London, Lane; New York,
Scribner, 1926. lvi,260p. illus. & ports.
(some col.)
——Limited ed. (100 copies). 1926
——*another ed.* 1927. xlix,331p. illus.
ports.

7925 The **Saturday book.** 3rd year; edited by
-1 Leonard Russell. Hutchinson, 1943. 280p.
illus. & ports.
*includes pp. 267–80, "The Squire of Eng-
land" by Bernard Darwin*

### Padgett, Douglas Ernest Vernon

7926 **Doug Padgett** benefit—1969. [48]p. incl.
■ adverts. illus. ports. stats.

7926 **Doug Padgett** testimonial year 1978:
-1 souvenir brochure with autographs.
■ Huddersfield, *printed by* E. Woffenden,
1978. [28]p. incl. covers & adverts. illus.
ports. stats.

### Pakington, Humphrey Arthur

7927 **Pakington, Humphrey Arthur**
■ Bid time return: an autobiography. Chatto & Windus, 1958. 218p.
*cricket pp. 39–40, 62*

### Pandit, Bāl Jagannāth

7928 **Pandit, Bāl Jagannāth**
Ek avismaranīya sāmana. Bombay, Vora,
1962. 44p.
*in Marathi; recollections*

### Parfitt, Peter Howard

7929 **Peter Parfitt** benefit: appreciation by Bill
Edrich. 1970

## Parker, John Frederick ("Jack")

7930 **Yorkshire Conservative Newspaper**
■ Jack Parker benefit souvenir. Doncaster, Yorkshire Conservative Newspaper, [1951]. [40]p. illus. ports.
*reprints the cricket strips by Ron Yeomans illustrated by Thack first published in York-shire Evening Post during 1949 and 1950 seasons*

## Parkin, Cecil Henry

7931 **The Cecil Parkin** benefit souvenir: benefit
■ match at Old Trafford, Lancashire versus Middlesex, July 18, 20, 21, 1925. Manchester, Whiteley & Wright, [1925]. 32p. incl. adverts. illus. ports. stats.

7932 **Parkin, Cecil Henry**
■ Cricket reminiscences, humorous and otherwise. Hodder & Stoughton, [1923]. 144p. illus.
*cover-title: Parkin on cricket*

7933 Parkin again: more cricket reminiscences.
■ Hodder & Stoughton, [1925]. 138p. illus. port. stats.

7934 Cricket triumphs and troubles. Manches-
■ ter, C. Nicholls, 1936. 207p. illus. ports. stats.

## Parkinson, Michael

7935 **Parkinson, Michael**
Cricket mad; drawings by Derek Alder. S. Paul, 1969. 119p. illus.
——rptd. Arrow Books, 1973. pbk.

7935 Sporting fever; drawings by Derek Alder.
-1 S. Paul, 1974. 184p. illus.
■ ——rptd. Arrow Books, 1976. pbk.
*cricket pp. 77–120, 132–3, 165–7*

## Parks, James Michael

7936 **Parks, Jim**
■ Runs in the sun. S. Paul, 1961. 143p. illus. ports.

7937 Time to hit out. S. Paul, 1967. 134p. illus.
■ ports.

7938 ———, *editor*
■ The book of cricket. S. Paul, 1962. 128p. illus. ports.

## Parnell, Charles Stewart

7939 **O'Brien, Richard Barry**
■ The life of Charles Stewart Parnell, 1846–1891. 2 vols. Smith, Elder, 1898.
——2nd ed. 2 vols. 1899
*cricket, vol. 1, p. 52*

## Parry-Okeden, William Edward

7939 **Perry, Harry C.**
-1 A son of Australia: memories of W.E. Parry-Okeden, 1840–1926. Brisbane, Watson, Ferguson, 1928. 341p. illus.
*cricket pp. 76–85, 94–99*

## Parsons, Edward

7939 **Parsons, Edward**
-2 Bible-back. The Author, [c.1976]. xviii, 233p. illus. ports.
*cricket pp. 17–8, 49, 71–2, 74–6, 87–9, 129–32, 156–9*

## Pataudi, Mohammed Mansur Ali Khan, *Nawab of*

7940 **Pataudi, Mohammed Mansur Ali Khan,**
■ *Nawab of*
Tiger's tale, as told to Kenneth Wheeler. S. Paul, 1969. 123p. illus. ports.
——*another ed.* Delhi, Hind Pocket Books, [1969]. 129p.

## Pawling, Sydney

7941 **Waugh, Arthur**
One man's road: being a picture of life in a passing generation. Chapman & Hall, 1931. xv,389p. illus. ports.
*references to Sydney Pawling and Hamp-stead C.C.*

## Paynter, Edward

7942 **Paynter, Eddie,** *i.e.* **Edward Paynter**
■ Cricket all the way; as told to Alan-Buckley. Leeds, Richardson, 1962. [vii], 115p. illus. ports. diagrs. stats.

## Peebles, Ian [Alexander Ross]

7943 **Peebles, Ian Alexander Ross**
■ Spinner's yarn. Collins, 1977. 222p. illus. ports.
——*another ed.* Sportsman's Book Club, 1978

## Peel, Albert

7944 **Peel, Albert**
■ Thirty-five to fifty. Independent P., 1938. 247p.
*cricket pp. 211–28*

## Peel, Robert

7945 **Morley Observer**
■ The cricketing career of Robert Peel, Y.C.C.: twelve years of county cricket, 1882 to 1893. Morley, "Observer" Office, 1894. 21p. ports. scores, stats.

## Pemberton, *Sir* Max

7946 **Pemberton,** *Sir* **Max**
■ Sixty years ago and after. Hutchinson, 1936. 282p. illus. ports.
*cricket pp. 63–66*

## Pentelow, John Nix

7947 **Rosenwater, Irving**
■ J.N. Pentelow: a biographical enquiry. *Privately printed*, 1969. [15]p. port.
*limited ed. of 50 copies numbered and signed; original published in* The Journal of the Cricket Society, *vol. iv, no. 2 (1969)*

## Phebey, Arthur

7948 **Phebey, Arthur,** *and others*
■ The Arthur Phebey benefit and coaching book. Canterbury, *printed by* "Kentish Gazette", [1960]. 32p. illus. ports.

## Philip, *Prince, duke of Edinburgh*

7948 **Baker, George**
–1 H.R.H. Prince Philip, Duke of Edinburgh. Cassell, 1961. [vi],122p. illus. ports. bibliog. (Red Lion Lives)
*for children; cricket pp. 70–71 with cricket team portrait at Gordonstoun School p. 42*

7949 **Boddey, Martin,** *editor*
■ The twelfth man: a book of original contributions brought together by The Lord's Taverners in honour of their patron H.R.H. Prince Philip, Duke of Edinburgh. Cassell, 1971. [x],285p. illus. (some col.)

7950 **Cathcart, Helen**
■ H.R.H. Prince Philip, sportsman. S. Paul, 1961. 208p. illus. ports.
*ch. 15 "Royal innings", pp. 177–183, and numerous other references*

## Phillip, Francis 'Mindoo'

7950 **French, Stanley**
–1 Francis 'Mindoo' Phillip: a portrait from
■ memory. St. Lucia, the Author, 1979. [vii],31p. port. on cover. *typescript*

## Phillips, Harry

7951 **[Harry Phillips'** benefit match . . . 1886]
*contains pen-portrait of H.P. by "Leather Hunter" [A.J. Gaston]*

## Piggott, Francis Stewart Gilderoy

7951 **Piggott, Francis Stewart Gilderoy**
–1 Broken thread: an autobiography. Alder-

shot, Gale & Polden, 1950. xx,424p. illus. ports. maps
*many cricket references*

## Pilling, Harry

7951 **Kay, John**
–2 Lancashire's little giant! Harry Pilling's
■ testimonial brochure. [Testimonial Cttee., 1974]. [32]p. incl. adverts. illus. ports. stats.

## Place, Winston

7952 **Ledbrooke, Archibald William,** *editor*
■ Winston Place benefit book. Manchester, *printed by* Withy Grove P., [1952]. 22p. illus. ports. stats.

## Pleasants, Henry

7953 **Pleasants, Henry,** *junior*
From kilts to pantaloons. West Chester [Pa.], Horace F. Temple, 1945. 198p.
*ch. xii "Green turf and white flannels"*

## Plumer, Herbert Charles Onslow Plumer, *1st viscount*

7954 **Harington,** *Sir* **Charles**
Plumer of Messines. Murray, 1935. xviii,351p. illus. ports. maps
*ch. xviii "His interest in cricket, President M.C.C."*

## Pocock, John

7954 **Ashworth, M.G.,** *compiler*
–1 The life and fortunes of John Pocock of Cape Town 1814–1876; compiled from his journals and letters by M.G. Ashworth. Cape Town, College Tutorial Press (Pty.) Ltd. for the Author, 1974. xii,165p. illus. ports.
*cricket pp. 8,53,62,77,87,96*

## Pocock, Patrick Ian

7954 **Pat Pocock,** England & Surrey C.C.C.,
–2 benefit year 1977. [Benefit Cttee., 1977].
■ 48p. incl. adverts. illus. ports. stats.

## Pollard, Richard

7955 **Kay, John,** *editor*
■ Dick Pollard testimonial fund: benefit match Lancashire v. Derbyshire, Old Trafford 6, 8 & 9, 1949. Manchester, Manchester Evening News, [1949]. 16p. illus. ports. stats.

## Pollock, Graeme

7956 **Pollock, Peter,** *and* **Pollock, Graeme**
Bouncers and boundaries. Johannesburg,

Sporting Enterprises; London, Bailey Bros. & Swinfen, 1968. 158p. illus. ports.
——2nd ed. 1968
——3rd ed. 1969

7957 **Pollock, Graeme**
■ Down the wicket; edited by Kenneth Wheeler. Pelham, 1968. 123p. illus. ports. stats.
——*another ed.* Sportsman's Book Club, 1969
——*Afrikaans ed. with title:* Grens toe. Johannesburg, Afrikaanse Pers, 1969. [viii], 131p. illus. ports. stats.

**Pollock, Peter**

7958 **Pollock, Peter,** *and* **Pollock, Graeme**
Bouncers and boundaries. Johannesburg, Sporting Enterprises; London, Bailey Bros. & Swinfen, 1968. 158p. illus. ports.
——2nd ed. 1968
——3rd ed. 1969

**Ponsonby-Fane, *Sir* Spencer Cecil Brabazon**

7958 **Ponsonby, *Sir* John**
–1 The Ponsonby family. The Medici Soc-
■ iety, 1929. xvi,263p. illus. ports.
*pp. 159–64 concerns Sir Spencer C.B. Ponsonby-Fane*

**Porritt, Arthur**

7959 **Porritt, Arthur**
The best I remember: [reminiscences]. Cassell, 1922. x,253p.
*ch. 5, pp. 31–35 refers to author's collaboration with W.G. Grace in the writing of "W.G.: cricketing reminiscences"*

7960 More and more of memories. Allen &
■ Unwin, 1947. 242p. port.
*ch. iv "Cricket and cricketers" pp. 49–57, and p. 71*

**Prasanna, Erapalli Anantharao Srinivasa**

7960 **Prasanna, Erapalli Anantharao Srinivasa**
–1 One more over: an autobiography.
■ Calcutta, Rupa, 1977. [xv],135p. illus. ports. stats.

**Pressdee, James Stuart**

7961 **Jim Pressdee** benefit [brochure]. [1964].
■ 56p. incl. adverts. illus. ports. stats.

**Preston, *Sir* Harry John**

7962 **Preston, *Sir* Harry John**
■ Memories. Constable, 1928. xvii,288p. illus. ports.

cricket (W.G. Grace) pp. 51–55, and other references

**Preston, Hubert**

7963 **In Memoriam:** Hubert Preston, 1868–
■ 1960. St. Bride's Church, Fleet St., Wednesday, 17th August, 1960 at 12.30 p.m. 7p.
*order of service*

**Preston, Kenneth**

7964 **County** cricket in Essex. [Chelmsford,
■ Essex C.C.C., 1959]. 32p. incl. adverts. illus. ports. stats.
*issued in aid of the Ken Preston benefit fund*

**Price, John Sidney Ernest**

7965 **John Price,** Middlesex & England, benefit
■ year, 1972: appreciations by Alec Bedser and John Arlott. [1972]. [4]p. 1 illus.

**Prichard, *afterwards* Hesketh-Prichard, Hesketh Vernon**

7966 **Parker, Eric**
■ Hesketh Prichard: hunter: explorer: naturalist: cricketer: author: soldier: a memoir. London, T. Fisher Unwin; New York, Dutton, 1924. 272p. illus. ports.
*contains some Hampshire cricket interest*

**Prittie, *Hon* Terence Cornelius Farmer**

7966 **Prittie, *Hon.* Terence Cornelius Farmer**
–1 Through Irish eyes. Bachman and
■ Turner, 1977. 309p. illus. ports.
*cricket pp. 40–1,48–9,162–3,177–9*

**Procter, Michael John**

7967 **Mike Procter** [benefit brochure]. [1971].
■ [4]p. folded card

7967 Cricket buccaneer. Cape Town, Nelson,
–1 1974. 162p. illus. ports. stats.
■

7967 **Procter:** the story of Gloucestershire's
–2 great all-rounder; edited by Bruce Perry
■ and John Davies. Bristol, Perry Russell Public Relations for Mike Procter, [1976]. [28]p. illus. ports. diagr. score, stats.

**Protheroe, Rowland Edmund, *1st* baron Ernle**

7968 **Protheroe, Rowland Edmund,** *1st baron*
■ Ernle
Whippingham to Westminster: reminiscences. Murray, 1938. xx,327p. illus. ports.
*cricket pp. 42, 46–8, 220–2*

### Pullar, Geoffrey

7969 **Kay, John,** *editor*
■ Geoff Pullar's testimonial book. [1967]. [24]p. incl. adverts. illus. ports. stats.

### Pycroft, James

7970 **Pycroft, James**
■ Oxford memories: a retrospect after fifty years. Bentley, 1886. 2 vols.
*cricket in vol. 2 only; extracts included in Arlott, John, ed. The middle ages of cricket.* [1949]. See no. 795

### Quick, Robert Herbert

7971 **Storr, Francis**
■ Life and remains of the Rev. R.H. Quick. Cambridge Univ. P., 1899. vii,544p. port.
*cricket pp. 38, 51, 522–23*

### Radley, Clive Thornton

7971 **Clive Radley** beneficiary souvenir pro-
–1 gramme, 1977. 36p. incl. adverts. illus.
■ ports. stats.

7971 **Clive Radley** in his benefit year 1977.
–2 Middlesex C.C.C., [1977]. [8]p. fold.
■ ports. stats.

### Radley, Reginald Alfred

7971 **Surrey County Cricket Club**
–3 MRM '79 testimonial. 40 years at the
■ Oval, A.J. McIntyre, R.A. Radley, J.F. McQuirke. The Club, [1979]. 24p. incl. adverts.

### Ramaswami, C.

7972 **Ramaswami, C.**
■ Ramblings of a games addict. Madras, the Author, [1966]. [x],211p. illus. ports. scores

### Ramsingh, A.G.

7973 **[Madras Cricket Association]**
■ A.G. Ramsingh testimonial souvenir. Madras, [the Assoc., 1956]. 44p. illus. ports. stats.

### Ranjitsinhji, Kumar Shri, H.H. Maharaja Jam Saheb of Nawanagar

7974 **[Craig, Albert]**
■ K.S. Ranjitsinhji. Cricket P., 1896. [4]p. folded card. port

7975 His Highness the Jam of Nawanagar.
■ Wright & Co., 1908. [4]p. folded card. port.

7976 **Gardiner, Alfred George**
■ Pillars of society. Nisbett, 1913. x,354p. ports.
——*another ed.* Dent, 1916. (Wayfarer's Library)
*biographical essays including "The Jam Sahib of Nawanagar"*

7977 **Graeme, Margaret**
■ Ranji's a-coming: a delightful 1903 reminiscence of the famous cricketer. Horsham, Price, 1903. 88p. illus. port.

7977 **Maneklal, H. Shah**
–1 Jam the great: sketches of life and administration of the late Jam Sahib of Nawanagar. Nadiad, "Gujrat Times", 1934. xiii, 192p. illus. ports.

7978 **Raiji, Vasant**
■ Ranji: the legend and the man. Bombay, the Author, [1963]. 95p. illus. ports.

7979 ——, *editor*
■ Ranji: a centenary album. Bombay, Seven Star Publications, 1972. 75p. illus. ports. (1 col.), stats.
*includes section on technique by Ranjitsinhji*

7980 **Reed, Edward Tennyson**
Mr. Punch's book of arms; drawn and written by E.T. Reed. Bradbury, Agnew, 1899. lxi f.
*references to Ranjitsinhji*

7981 **Standing, Percy Cross**
■ Ranjitsinhji, prince of cricket. Bristol, Arrowsmith; London, Simpkin, Marshall, 1903. 284p. illus. ports. scores, stats.
——*another ed.* 1903. 184p. pbk.

7981 **Thompson, Francis**
–1 [Selected essays]. Harrap, 1927. 78p.
■ (Essays of To-day and Yesterday)
*includes "A prince of India on the prince of games" (on Ranjitsinhji)*

7982 **West, C.T.**
■ 'Ranji': new song. Words and music by C.T. West. Brighton, Lyon and Hall, [c.1895]. 5p. port. on cover

7983 **Wild, Roland Gibson**
■ The biography of Colonel His Highness Shri Sir Ranjitsinhji Vibhaji, Maharaja Jam Sheb of Nawanagar. Rich & Cowan, 1934. xiv,330p. illus. ports. maps. stats.
——*de luxe ed.* 1934
*limited to 230 copies signed by the author*

## Rattigan, Frank

7983 **Rattigan, Frank**
−1 Diversions of a diplomat. Chapman &
Hall, 1924. xii,225p. illus.
*cricket pp. 4–11,18*

## Rawlin, John Thomas

7984 **[Craig, Albert]**
■ J.T. Rawlin. Wright & Co., [1892]. [4]p.
folded card. port.

## Read, John Maurice

7985 **[Craig, Albert]**
■ John Maurice Read. *n.p.*, [1889]. [4]p.
port.

## Read, Walter William

7986 **De Lugo, Anthony Benitez,** *Marquis de*
■ *Santa Susana*
The Surrey champion: a complete record
of Mr. Walter William Read's performances for Surrey and in representative
matches 1873–1897. Madrid, the Author,
1895. 98p. stats. scores
*private circulation limited to 100 copies*

7987 **Read, Walter William**
■ Annals of cricket: a record of the game
compiled from authentic sources, and my
own experiences during the last twenty-
three years. S. Low, 1896. 268p. illus.
port. map, scores, stats.
——de luxe ed. of 250 copies signed and
numbered. 1896
——2nd ed. 1896
——3rd ed. 1897

7988 **Sporting Sketches**
Special number on the occasion of W.W.
Read's complimentary benefit match in
1895
*entirely devoted to W.W. Read's perform-
ances; in Taylor*
Sporting sketches *was originally published under title:* Sporting bits, *6 Apr.
1892–March 1894; as* Sporting sketches, *2
Apr. 1894–10 Oct. 1907; and was contd. as:*
London sketches, *16 Oct. 1907–11 July,
1908*

## Redbourn, Richard

7988 **Redbourn, Dick**
−1 The domestic cricketer: memoirs. Tun-
■ bridge Wells, Midas Books, 1977. 128p.
illus. ports.

## Reddick, Tom Bokenham

7988 **Reddick, Tom Bokenham**
−2 Never a cross bat; illustrations by John

■ Jackson. Cape Town, Don Nelson, [1979].
141p. illus.

## Redpath, Ian Ritchie

7988 **Redpath, Ian,** *and* **Phillipson, Neill**
−3 Always Reddy. Toorak (Vic.), Garry
■ Sparke & Associates, 1976. [iv],204p.
illus. ports. stats.

## Rees, William Gilbert

7989 **Griffiths, George J.**
■ King Wakatip: how William Gilbert Rees,
cousin and cricketing godfather of the
incomparable W.G. Grace, emigrated to
the colonies and founded the most beautiful township in New Zealand. Dunedin
(N.Z.), McIndoe, 1971. 156p. illus. ports.
maps

## Reese, Daniel

7990 **Reese, Daniel**
■ Was it all cricket? Allen & Unwin, 1948.
568p. illus. ports. map on endpapers

## Reid, John Richard

7991 **Reid, John Richard**
■ Sword of willow; including an account of
the 1961–62 New Zealand cricket tour of
South Africa. Wellington (N.Z.), Reed,
1962; London, Jenkins, 1963. 265p. illus.
ports. diagrs. scores, stats.

7991 A million miles of cricket. Wellington,
−1 Reed, 1966. 174p. illus. ports. stats.
■

## Reynolds, Frederick

7992 **Reynolds, Frederick**
■ The life and times of Frederick Reynolds,
written by himself. 2 vols. Colburn, 1826,
frontis. (port.—vol. 1).
*extracts appeared in* Cricket, *13th Sept.,
1900, pp. 414–5*

## Rhodes, Harold J.

7993 **Carey, Mike,** *editor*
■ Harold Rhodes testimonial 1968. Derby,
Derbyshire C.C.C., 1968. [ii],108p. illus.
ports.

## Rhodes, Wilfred

7993 **Craig, Albert**
−1 W. Rhodes. Wright & Co., 1907. [4]p.
■ folded card. port.

7994 **Humphrey, W.H.**
■ George Herbert Hirst and Wilfred
Rhodes, a record of cricket achievement.

Huddersfield, *printed by* Broadbent, 1937. 52p. illus. ports. stats.

**7995 Northern Cricket Society**
■ The memorial service to Wilfred Rhodes, the great Yorkshire and England cricketer. [Leeds], the Society, [1973]. [4]p. fold, port. stats.

**7996 Rogerson, Sidney**
■ Wilfred Rhodes, professional and gentleman. Hollis & Carter, 1960. xiv,178p. illus. ports. stats.

**7997 Thomson, Arthur Alexander**
■ Hirst and Rhodes. Epworth P., 1959. 211p. illus. ports. stats. bibliog.

### Richards, Barry Anderson

**7997** **Barry Richards** benefit brochure. *n.p.*,
**–1** [1977]. 32p. incl. adverts. illus. & ports.
■ (some col.), stats.

**7997** **Richards, Barry**
**–2** The Barry Richards story. London,
■ Faber & Faber; Sydney, Angus & Robertson, 1978. 180p. illus. ports. facsim. stats.
——*another ed.* Newton Abbot, Readers Union, 1978

### Richards, Isaac Vivian Alexander

**7997** **Richards, Isaac Vivian Alexander,** *and*
**–3** **Foot, David**
■ Viv Richards. Kingswood (Sy.), World's Work, 1979. 160p. illus. ports.

### Richardson, Arthur John

**7998 Hill, Les R.**
■ Eighty not out: the story of Arthur Richardson, of Sevenhills, a former international cricketer . . . as told to and compiled by Les R. Hill. Mount Gambier, S. Aust., the Author, 1968. [i],44p. stats.
*typescript*
*limited ed. of 150 copies*

**7998 South Australia Cricket Association**
**–1** A.J. Richardson benefit fund souvenir programme. Sheffield Shield match, South Australia v. Victoria, 4 to 8 March 1949. Adelaide, the Assoc., [1949]. 20p. incl. adverts. illus. ports. stats.

### Richardson, John Maunsell

**7999 Richardson, Mary E.**
The life of a great sportsman—John Maunsell Richardson. Vinton, 1919. xxiii, 281p. illus. ports.
*cricket at Harrow and Cambridge*

### Richardson, Thomas

**8000 [Craig, Albert]**
■ Thomas Richardson. Cricket P., 1897. [4]p. folded card. port.

### Richardson, Victor York

**8001 Richardson, Victor York**
■ The Vic Richardson story: the autobiography of a versatile sportsman, [by] V.Y. Richardson in conjunction with R.S. Whitington. Adelaide, Rigby, 1967; London, Angus & Robertson, 1968. [xiii], 209p. illus. ports.

### Richmond, Charles Lennox, 2nd duke of

**8002 March, Charles Henry Gordon-Lennox,** *earl of*
A Duke and his friends: the life and letters of the second Duke of Richmond. 2 vols. Hutchinson, 1912. illus. ports.
*refers to the 'Articles of Agreement' between the Duke and Mr. Broderick of Peperharrow*

**8003 Marshall, John**
■ The duke who was cricket. Muller, 1961. x,193p. illus. ports. scores

### Ring, John

**8003 Goulstone, John**
**–1** "The life and career of John Ring". *In*
■ Dartford Historical and Antiquarian Society Newsletter. No.10, 1973. pp. 12–18 *See no. 2097–1*

### Roberts, Ronald

**8004 Ron Roberts:** [appeal fund brochure].
■ Appeal Fund Cttee., [1965]. [32]p. illus. ports. map

### Robertson, John David Benbow

**8005 Middlesex County Cricket Club**
■ Jack Robertson, Middlesex & England, benefit 1959: Middlesex v. Yorkshire, Aug. 15, 17, 18. Lord's, the Club, [1959]. [4]p. fold. stats.

**8006 West, Peter,** *editor*
■ Jack Robertson's benefit book. Armstrong P., [1951]. 24p. illus. ports. stats.

### Robertson-Glasgow, Raymond Charles

**8006 Hollis, Christopher**
**–1** Oxford in the twenties: recollections of
■ five friends. Heinemann, 1976. [v],136p.
*includes pp. 54–71 "R. C. Robertson-Glasgow"*

8007 **Robertson-Glasgow, Raymond Charles**
■ 46 not out. Hollis & Carter, 1948.
viii,206p. illus. ports.
——*another ed.* Sportsman's Book Club,
1954

### Robey, George

8008 **Cotes, Peter**
George Robey 'the darling of the halls'.
Cassell, 1972. xiv,212p. illus. ports.
bibliog.
*cricket pp. 138–39*

8008 **Robey, George**
–1 Looking back on life. Constable, 1933.
■ xviii,318p. illus. ports.
*cricket pp. 123–32 with illus.*

### Rogers, Neville

8009 **Arlott, [Leslie Thomas] John**
■ Neville Rogers: an appreciation.
[Southampton, Hampshire C.C.C.], 1956.
6p. port.
*limited ed. of 12 copies; 1st published in*
Hampshire C.C.C. Handbook, *1956*

### Root, Charles Frederick

8010 **Root, Fred,** *i.e.* **Charles Frederick Root**
■ A cricket pro's lot. E. Arnold, 1937. 224p.
illus. ports.
——*2nd ed.* 1938

### Roper, Edward

8011 **Roper, Edward**
■ A sportsman's memories; edited by Fred.
W. Wood. Liverpool, C. Tinling, 1921.
286p. illus. ports.
*cricket for Clifton, Yorkshire, Lancashire*
*and Sefton*

### Rowan, Athol Matthew Burchell

8012 **Arlott, [Leslie Thomas] John**
■ Athol Rowan: a memoir. The Author,
1952. [ii],9p. mounted port.
*limited ed. of 10 copies off-printed from The*
echoing green *and prepared for private*
*circulation*

### Rowan, Lou

8013 **Rowan, Lou**
■ The umpire's story, with an analysis of
the laws of cricket. North Sydney
(N.S.W), Jack Pollard Pty, 1972. [viii],
215p. illus.
——*pbk. ed.* 1973

### Russell, Charles James Fox, *Lord*

8014 **Russell, Charles James Fox,** *Lord*
■ Some recollections of cricket. Woburn,
Fisher, 1879. 39p.
*12 copies only (Taylor)*
contents: *A dream of the past.* (rptd. *from*
Baily's Magazine)
*Round-arm recollections* (rptd.
*from* Baily's Magazine)
*Lord's and Prince's, 1872*
*Bedfordshire cricket* (rptd. *from*
The Bedfordshire Mercury,
*Aug. 9, 1878)*
*National testimonial to Mr. W. G.*
*Grace; an address delivered on*
*Lord's Cricket Ground, July 22nd*
*1879*
——rptd. [with] introduction by John
Arlott. Ewell, J. W. McKenzie, 1979.
[xvii],3–39p. port.
*limited to 100 numbered copies*

### Russell, John

8015 **Davies, Edward Wiliam Lewis**
Memoir of the Rev. John Russell and his
out-of-door life. New ed. rptd. with illustrations by N. H. J. Baird. Exeter,
Commin; London, Chatto & Windus,
1902. xiii,352p. col. illus.
*limited ed. of 1000 copies, plus 75 copies*
*on Japanese vellum; first published, Bentley,*
*1878; new ed. Bentley, 1883.*
*cricket p. 89 refers to Teignbridge C.C.*

### Russell, William Eric

8016 **Middlesex County Cricket Club**
■ Eric Russell benefit year 1969. The Club,
[1969]. illus. [4]p. fold

### Rutter, Edward

8017 **Rutter, Edward**
■ Cricket memories: Rugby—Middlesex—
Free Foresters. Williams & Norgate, 1925.
[vii],214p. frontis. (port.)

### Sackville, John Frederick, 3rd Duke of Dorset

8017 **The torpedo,** a poem to the electrical eel.
–1 Addressed to Mr. John Hunter, surgeon:
and dedicated to the Right Honourable
Lord Cholmondeley. Printed for Fielding
and Walker, No. 20, Pater-Noster-Row,
1777. iv,17p.
*reference p. 14 to the Duke of Dorset, with*
*footnote: "Every one knows the attachment of*
*the Duke of D-rs-t to Cricket: The Following*
*anecdote will prove it. Two Clergymen were*
*candidates for a living in hs Grace's presenta-*
*tion, which he bestowed on the best Batsman"*

**8017** **The town** and country magazine, or,
**–2** Universal repository of knowledge,
instruction and entertainment. A.
Hamilton
> vol. 8. Oct. 1776. p. 513 *"Histories of the*
> *Téte-à-téte annexed, or Memoirs of the Noble*
> *Cricketer". Refers to John Frederick Sackville,*
> *3rd Duke of Dorset*

## Sainsbury, Peter James

**8018** **Arlott, [Leslie Thomas] John**
■ Peter Sainsbury: an appreciation.
[Southampton, Hampshire C.C.C.], 1961.
10p. frontis. stats.
> *limited ed. of 50 copies*

## Salter, John Henry

**8018** **Salter, John Henry**
**–1** Doctor Salter of Tolleshunt D'Arcy in the
County of Essex, medical man, free-
mason, sportsman, sporting-dog breeder
and horticulturalist: his diary and reminiscences from the year 1849 to the year
1932; compiled by J. O. Thompson. John
Lane, Bodley Head, 1933. xvii,404p. illus.
ports.
> *several cricket references*

## Sandham, Andrew

**8019** **A. Sandham's** benefit souvenir published
■ in connection with the famous Surrey &
All-England batsman's benefit Surrey v.
Kent at the Oval, July 27–29–30, 1935.
Fleetway, P., [1935]. 24p. incl. adverts.
illus. ports. stats.

## Saravanamuttu, Manicasothy

**8019** **Saravanamuttu, Manicasothy**
**–1** The Sara saga. Penang, [the Author],
■ 1970. viii,216p. illus. ports.
> *many cricket references*

## Sarbadhikari, Berry

**8019** **Sarbadhikari, Berry**
**–2** My world of cricket: a century of Tests.
■ Calcutta, Cricket Library (India), 1964.
340,viii,p. illus. ports.
> *essays & reminiscences giving a compar-*
> *ative study of cricket in many countries over*
> *last three decades*

## Sassoon, Siegfried Lorraine

**8019** **Sassoon, Siegfried [Lorraine]**
**–3** The old century and seven more years.
Faber & Faber, 1938. 293p.
> *contains 'The flower-show match' and a*
> *cricket poem 'The extra inch'*

**8020** The weald of youth: [autobiographical
■ reminiscences]. Faber, 1942. 278p. port.
> *scattered references*

**8020** **Silk, Dennis**
**–1** Siegfried Sassoon. Tisbury (Wilts.),
■ Compton Russell, 1975. 30p.
> *first delivered as the Guinness Lecture at*
> *the Salisbury Festival of the Arts, July 1974;*
> *cricket pp. 7, 27, 28, 29*

## Sayen, Henry

**8021** **Sayen, Henry**
■ A Yankee looks at cricket, as told to
Gerald Brodribb. Putnam, 1956. viii,120p.
illus. port. map, scores

## Scott, Clement William

**8022** **Scott, Clement William**
■ The wheel of life: a few memories and
recollections. Greening, 1897. vii,120p.
——new ed. 1898
> *includes "Cricket etiquette in India". pp.*
> *30–34*

## Scott, *Lord* George William Montagu Douglas

**8023** **Scott,** *Lord* **George William Montagu**
■ **Douglas**
The fleeting opportunity: [reminis-
cences]. Witherby, 1940. 286p. illus.
ports.
> *many references to cricket*

## Scott, Stanley Winckworth

**8024** **Scott, Stanley Winckworth**
Reminiscences of cricket 1863–1904.
*Private circulation*, 1928. *typescript*

## Scotton, William

**8025** **Richards, Charles Henry,** *compiler*
■ William Scotton: the celebrated Nottinghamshire cricketer; his cricket career from
commencement to the present time.
Nottingham, G. Richards, [1889]. 7p.
port.
> *rptd. from Notts. scores and biogra-*
> *phies*

## Sewell, Edward Humphrey Dalrymple

**8026** **Sewell, Edward Humphrey Dalrymple**
■ The log of a sportsman. T. Fisher Unwin,
1923. 247p. illus. ports. diagrs.

**8027** An outdoor wallah. S. Paul, 1945. 136p.
■ illus. ports.

## Shackleton, Derek

8028　**Arlott, [Leslie Thomas] John**
■　Derek Shackleton: an appreciation. [Southampton, Hampshire C.C.C.], 1958. [8]p. port.
　　*limited ed. of 50 copies. First publd. in* Hampshire C.C.C. Handbook, *1958*

8029　**Warr, J. J.,** *and* **Fordham, Michael**
■　Derek Shackleton. Boscombe, *printed by* Boscombe Printing Co., 1967. illus. stats.
　　*limited ed. of 25 copies*

## Shanker, B. D.

8030　**Shanker, B. D.**
■　40 years of active cricket. Lucknow, the Author, [1955]. viii,131p. ports. stats.

## Sharp, Harry

8031　**Len Muncer/Harry Sharp** testimonial,
■　1971: Len Muncer, an appreciation by Wilf Wooller; Harry Sharp, an appreciation by Bill Edrich. [1971]. illus. [4]p.
　　*folded card*

8032　**Middlesex County Cricket Club**
■　Alex Thompson & Harry Sharp, Middlesex, benefit 1955. Lord's, the Club, [1955]. [4]p. fold

## Sharpe, Philip John

8033　**Philip Sharpe** benefit 1971. Benefit
■　Committee, [1971]. 68p. incl. adverts. illus. ports. stats.

## Shaw, Alfred

8034　**Grundy, William Frederick**
■　A memento of two great Notts. cricketers, Arthur Shrewsbury and Alfred Shaw. Nottingham, Richards, 1907. 94p. ports. stats.

8035　Letters of acknowledgement of the Memento of Arthur Shrewsbury and Alfred Shaw, with a few notes and illustrations by W. F. Grundy. Nottingham, Richards, 1910. 18p. illus.

8036　**Shaw, Alfred**
■　Alfred Shaw, cricketer: his career and reminiscences; recorded by A. W. Pullin ("Old Ebor"), with a statistical chapter by Alfred Gaston. Cassell, 1902. vii,200p. port. scores, stats.

8036　**Shelmerdine, Jo**
–1　In remembrance of Jo Shelmerdine who
■　left us to join a greater multitude in peace

on 31st day of July 1967: [order of service]. [8]p.
　　*played for Cheltenham, Cambridge Univ. and Lancashire*

## Shepherd, David Robert

8036　**Jack Davey** [and] David Shepherd testi-
–2　monial souvenir. [1978]. 52p. incl.
■　adverts. illus. & ports. (some col.), stats.

## Shepherd, Donald John

8037　**The Don Shepherd** testimonial brochure
■　1968. Swansea, [Benefit Cttee., 1968]. 64p. incl. adverts. illus. port. stats.

## Sheppard, David Stuart

8038　**Sheppard, David [Stuart]**
■　Parson's pitch. Hodder & Stoughton, 1964. 253p. illus. ports.
　　——*another ed.* 1966. 220p. pbk.

## Sherwin, Mordecai

8039　**Richards, Charles Henry**
■　Mordecai Sherwin: (a short account of his cricket career). Nottingham, Richards, [189–]. 6p. port.
　　*rptd. from* Nottinghamshire cricket scores . . . *1890*

## Shipman, Alan

8040　**Leicestershire County Cricket Club**
■　Shipman's benefit. Leicestershire v. Derby, June 16th, 18th and 19th. Leicester, the Club. [1934]. [3]p. port. stats.

## Shrewsbury, Arthur

8041　**Benson, Edward Frederic,** *and* **Miles,**
■　**Eustace Hamilton,** *eds.*
　　The cricket of Abel, Hirst and Shrewsbury. Hurst & Blackett, 1903. xx,287p. illus. (Athletic library)

8042　**Craig, Albert**
■　Arthur Shrewsbury. [Wright & Co.?, 1889]. [4]p. folded card. port.

8043　**Grundy, William Frederick**
　　Memento of Arthur Shrewsbury's last match, with a few other notes. Nottingham, Richards, 1904. 22p. score, stats.

8044　A memento of two great Notts. cricketers,
■　Arthur Shrewsbury and Alfred Shaw. Nottingham, Richards, 1907. 94p. ports. stats.

8045　Letters of acknowledgement of the Memento of Arthur Shrewsbury and

Alfred Shaw, with a few notes and illustrations by W. F. Grundy. Nottingham, Richards, 1910. 18p. illus.

8046 **Hitchin, S.W.**, *compiler*
■ A biographical sketch of Arthur Shrewsbury the famous Notts. cricketer, with full details of his chief performances in England and Australia. Nottingham, Hitchin, 1890. [ii],42p. port. stats.

8047 **In Memoriam** Arthur Shrewsbury,
■ England's champion cricketer! Nottingham, Wilson, [1903]. [4]p. folded card
*a valedictory poem*

8048 **Richards, Charles Henry**
■ Arthur Shrewsbury, the great cricketer: a complete record of his cricket career. Nottingham, C.H. Richards, [c.1889]. 14p. port. stats.
——2nd ed. 1893. 17p.
——3rd ed. 1903. 12p.
*rptd. from* Notts. scores and biographies

### Shuter, John

8049 **Craig, Albert**
■ Mr. John Shuter. Wright & Co., [1890]. [4]p. folded card. port.

### Shuttleworth, Kenneth

8049 **Maddocks, John**, *editor*
–1 Ken Shuttleworth & John Sullivan official
■ joint testimonial brochure. [Manchester, Joint Testimonial Fund, 1975]. [36]p. incl. adverts. illus. ports. stats.

### Simpson, Robert Baddeley

8050 **Simpson, Bobby**, *i.e.* **Robert Baddeley**
■ **Simpson**
Captain's story. S. Paul, 1966. 191p. illus. port.
*withdrawn from circulation because of legal action*

8050 Simmo. Richmond (Vic.), Hutchinson of
–1 Australia, 1979. [v],169p. illus. ports.
■

### Sims, *Sir* Arthur

8051 Mitchell, Alan
■ 84 not out: the story of Sir Arthur Sims, Kt. Locke, in association with Harrap, 1962. 188p. ports.

### Sinfield, Reginald Albert

8052 **Gloucestershire County Cricket Club**
■ Sinfield's benefit: Gloucestershire v. Sussex, Wagon Works Ground, Glou-

cester, Sept, 3, 5 & 6, 1938. [Gloucester, the Club, 1938]. [4]p. port.
*with "An appreciation and an appeal" by C. B. Fry*

### Small, John

8053 **Dagley, Richard**, *artist*
■ Death's doings: consisting of numerous original compositions, in prose and verse . . . intended as illustrations of twenty-four plates designed and etched by R. Dagley. J. Andrews; W. Cole, 1826. xviii,369p. illus.
——2nd ed. with considerable additions, 1827. 2 vols.
*2nd ed. includes obituary on John Small, the last survivor of the original members of the Hambledon C.C. in vol. 1. p. 69.*
*for full entry see no. 6970*

8054 **Egan, Pierce**
Pierce Egan's book of sports and mirror of life. T. T. & J. Tegg, 1832. iv,414p. illus. scores
——*another ed.* 1836
——*another ed.* 1840
——*another ed.* 1847
*originally issued in 25 pts. 1 pt. (pp. 337–352) being devoted entirely to cricket, with an article on Hambledon cricket and John Small, and the current Laws*

### Smedley, Michael John ("Mike")

8054 **Mike Smedley** benefit official souvenir
–1 programme. *Printed by* Long Eaton
■ Advertiser, 1975. 12p. incl. covers & adverts. ports. stats.

### Smith, Charles Turley

8055 **Adlard, Eleanor**, *editor*
■ Dear Turley, contributed by Fougasse, [and others]. Muller, 1942. 136p. illus. ports.
*includes "Golf and cricket books", by H. N. Wethered, pp. 77–83 and "Friendship with J. M. Barrie", by Cynthia Asquith, pp. 3–30*

### Smith, Edwin

8056 **Edwin Smith** testimonial fund souvenir brochure. 1966

### Smith, Gilbert Oswald

8057 **Grayson, Edward**
■ Corinthians and cricketers. Naldrett P. in association with World's Work, 1955. 248p. illus. ports. scores
——*another ed.* Sportsman's Book Club, 1957
*on G.O. Smith*

## Smith, *Sir* Henry

8058   **Smith,** *Sir* **Henry**
From constable to commissioner: the
story of sixty years, most of them mis-
spent. Chatto & Windus, 1910. xii,236p.
port.
*cricket in ch. 9*

## Smith, John

8059   **[Kidd, Abel]**
■     A cricket song and elegy: John Smith . . .
by "Old Stump". Highgate, the Author,
[1873]. [4]p. fold

## Smith, Michael John ("Mike")

8059   **Middlesex County Cricket Club**
–1     Mike Smith in his benefit year 1976;
■     Middlesex & England 1 Day International. [The Club, 1976]. [8]p. fold. ports.
stats.

8059   **Mike Smith benefit 76: souvenir**
–2     programme. [Benefit Cttee., 1976]. [32]p.
■     incl. covers & adverts. illus. ports.

## Smith, Michael John Knight

8060   **Warwickshire County Cricket Club**
■     Presentation reception to Michael J. K.
Smith, Esq. . . . 26 March, 1968. Edgbaston, the Club, [1968]. [4]p. folded card.
illus. ports. stats.

## Smith, Raymond

8061   **Braintree Cricket Club**
■     Ray Smith's benefit fund: Essex County
XI v. Braintree C.C. . . . September 9,
1951; souvenir programme. Braintree, the
Club, [1951]. [4]p. fold. port. stats.

## Smith, Thomas

8062   **Smith, Thomas**
Sporting incidents in the life of another
Tom Smith. Chapman & Hall, 1867. 224p.
illus.
*cricket at Hambledon, pp. 26–29*

## Smith, Thomas Assheton

8063   **Eardley-Wilmot,** *Sir* **John,** *2nd Bart.*
□     Reminiscences of the late T. Assheton
Smith; or, the pursuits of an English
country gentleman. Routledge, 1860.
301p.
——2nd. ed. 1860, xvi,308p. ports. (1 col.)
——3rd ed. 1862. port.
——6th ed. Everest, 1902. xv,303p.
*references to cricket in chs. i and vii with
details of the matches in which he played in
App. I.*

## Smith, William Charles ("Razor")

8064   **Sewell, Edward Humphrey Dalrymple**
■     All about "Razor" Smith, Surrey XI. [The
Author], 1910. 6p.

## Smith-Turberville, Harry T.

8065   **[Smith-Turberville, Harry]**
■     Peeps into the past, by The Long 'Un.
Warwick, Evans, [1917]. 68p.

8066   Reprints: "Peeps into a mayor's parlour",
■     1914: "Peeps into the past", 1917; "When
golf came south", 1927; "Archery", 1928;
"If", by Rudyard Kipling. *Privately
printed*, [1929]. 171p. port.

## Snaith, John Collis

8066   **Tennyson,** *Sir* **Charles Bruce Locker**
–1     Life's all a fragment. Cassell, 1953.
■     xi,264p. ports.
*includes essay on J. C. Snaith*

## Snow Family

8066   **Johnson, Pamela Hansford,** *Lady* **Snow**
–2     Important to me: personalia. Macmillan,
■     1974. 254p.
*pp. 197–200 'Family cricket'*

## Snow, John Augustine

8066   **Snow, John**
–3     Cricket rebel: an autobiography. Hamlyn,
■     1976. [v],218p. illus. ports.
*includes poems*

## Sobers, *Sir* Garfield St. Aubrun

8066   **Bailey, Trevor**
–4     Sir Gary: a biography. Collins, 1976.
■     190p. illus. ports. stats.
——rptd. Fontana, 1977. pbk

8067   **Chalmers, Robert Erskine Shaw,** *and*
**Chalmers, Joan**
The world of sport. McGraw-Hill, 1968.
68p. illus.
*"Garfield Sobers", pp. 61 & 68*

8068   Gary Sobers benefit knockout cricket
■     tournament, Kensington Oval, [Bridge-
town], Barbados: souvenir programme
April 1973. Bridgetown, Crown Caribbean Publications Ltd., [1973]. 64p. incl.
adverts. illus. ports. stats.

8069   Gary Sobers benefit match: Gary Sobers'
■     XI v. Richie Benaud's XI, Aug. 6th 1972.
Trent Bridge Ground, Nottingham.
Nottingham, *printed by* Hickling &
Squires, [1972]. 20p. incl. adverts. ports.
stats.

8069 **Red Stripe** International Double Wicket
-1 Competition for the Gary Sobers benefit.
■ The Organising Cttee., [1972]. 48p. incl.
covers & adverts. illus. ports. stats.

8069 **Sobers, Sir Garfield St. Aubrun**
-2 Cricket crusader. London, Pelham Books;
■ Calcutta, Rupa, 1966. 172p. illus. ports.
stats.

8070 **West Bridgfordians Cricket Club**
■ Gary Sobers benefit match: West Bridgfordians v. Nottinghamshire, 24th Sept.
1972. West Bridgford, the Club, [1972].
40p. incl. covers and adverts. ports.

8071 **[See no. 8069–1]**

### Spencer, Charles Terry

8072 **Leicestershire County Cricket Club**
Terry Spencer benefit 1964: souvenir
brochure. Leicester, the Club, [1964]. 8p.
ports. stats.

### Squire, Sir John Collings

8073 **Howarth, Patrick**
■ Squire, 'most generous of men'. Hutchinson, 1963. 308p. frontis. bibliog.

8074 **Squire, Sir John Collings**
■ The honeysuckle and the bee: [autobio-
graphical reminiscences]. Heinemann,
1937. [v],282p.
*cricket pp. 43–45, 76–77, 144–45, and*
*other passing references*

8075 Solo and duet, including "The honey-
■ suckle and the bee" and "Water music".
Reprint Soc., 1943. 411p.

8076 **Waugh, Alec**
■ My brother Evelyn, and other profiles.
Cassell, 1967. viii,340p.
*contains "Two poet cricketers"—Clifford*
*Bax, J. C. Squire, pp. 141–61*

### Squires, Harry Stanley

8077 **Palgrave, Louis,** *editor*
■ Benefit souvenir of Stan Squires. F.C.
Dick, Oval Bookstall, [1948]. 24p. illus.
port. scores

### Stackpole, Keith Raymond

8077 **Stackpole, Keith [Raymond]**
-1 Not just for openers, with Alan Tren-
■ grove. Abbotsford (Vic.), Stockwell P.,
1974. 191p. illus. ports.

### Staples, Arthur

8078 **Arthur Staples'** benefit: Notts. County v.
■ Sutton & District . . . June 23rd, 1937.
Benefit Cttee., [1937]. [16]p. incl. adverts.
ports.

### Statham, John Brian

8079 **Kay, John,** *editor*
■ Brian Statham's benefit brochure. Bolton,
Hopkins, [1961]. [32]p. incl. adverts.
illus. ports. stats.

8080 **Lancashire County Cricket Club**
■ Brian Statham benefit, Lancashire v.
Australians at Old Trafford on July 1, 3,
and 4, 1961. Manchester, the Club,
[1961]. [4]p. fold. port. stats.
*with an appreciation by P. B. H. May*

8081 J.B. Statham: his retirement from first
■ class cricket, Lancashire v. Yorkshire,
August 3, 4 and 5, 1968. [Manchester, the
Club, 1968]. 4p. 1 illus. stats.

8082 **Statham, [John] Brian**
■ Cricket merry-go-round. S. Paul, 1956.
192p. illus. ports.

8083 Flying bails. S. Paul, 1961. 160p. illus.
■ ports. stats.

8084 A spell at the top: his own story; edited
■ by Peter Smith. Souvenir P., 1969. 141p.
illus. ports. stats.
——*another ed.* Sportsman's Book Club,
1970

### Stead, Barry

8084 **Nottinghamshire County Cricket Club**
-1 Barry Stead benefit official souvenir
■ programme. Nottingham, the Club,
[1976]. [16]p. incl. adverts. illus. ports.
stats.

### Steel, Alan Gibson

8085 **Lodge, P. Y.**
■ Cricketing sketch of Mr. A.G. Steel.
Liverpool, [the Author], 1895. 24p. port.

### Steele, David Stanley

8085 **Steele, David [Stanley]**
-1 Come in number 3, [by] David Steele with
■ John Morris. Pelham Books, 1977. 192p.
illus. ports. facsim. stats.

8085 **David Steele,** Staffordshire & Northamp-
-2 tonshire, benefit year souvenir autograph
■ brochure. Kettering, Preprint, [1975].
[40]p. incl. adverts. illus. ports.

## Stephenson, George Robert ("Bob")

8085
-3
■   Bob Stephenson benefit brochure 1979. Southampton, Wessex-Mede Marketing Ltd., [1979]. 48p. incl. adverts. illus. ports. stats.

## Stewart, William James

8086   **Warwickshire County Cricket Club**
■   W.J. Stewart's benefit season 1967. [Birmingham], the Club, [1967]. [4]p. fold. illus. port. stats.

## Stoddart, Andrew Ernest

8087   **Ashley-Cooper, Frederick Samuel**
■   Stoddart and Trumper in the cricket field. 1916. 11f.+11f.
   *an off-print from Wisden 1915 and 1916. Only known copy in M.C.C. Library, Lord's*

8088   **[Craig, Albert]**
■   Mr. A.E. Stoddart. Cricket P., 1897. [4]p. folded card. port.

8089   **Frith, David Edward John**
■   "My dear victorious Stod": a biography of A.E. Stoddart. New Malden, the Author, 1970. 199p. illus. ports. bibliog. stats.
   *limited ed. of 400 numbered and signed copies*
   ——new ed. Lutterworth, P., 1977. 199p. illus. ports. bibliog. stats.

## Storey, Stewart James

8090   **Booth, Alan,** *editor*
■   Stewart Storey benefit brochure 1973. Benefit Committee, [1973]. 32p. incl. adverts. illus. ports. stats.

## Streatfeild, Frank Newton

8091   **Streatfeild, Frank Newton**
■   Sporting recollections of an Old 'Un. Nash, 1913. xi,327p. illus. ports.
   *cricket in ch. vi, pp. 128–162*

## Strudwick, Herbert

8092   **Strudwick, Herbert**
■   Twenty five years behind the stumps. Hutchinson, [1926]. 254p. illus. ports.
   ——*cheap ed. 1927*

## Studd, Charles Thomas

8093   **Davey, Cyril James**
   Well played Sir!: [a biography of Charles T. Studd]. Edinburgh House P., 1950. 24p. (Eagle Books)

8094   **De Windt, Harry**
   From Pekin to Calais by land. Chapman & Hall, 1889. x,656p. illus. map
   *references to C. T. Studd*

8095   **Erskine, John T.**
   Millionaire for God: the story of C. T. Studd. Lutterworth P., 1968. 95p. col. port. (Stories of faith and fame)
   *based on* C. T. Studd, cricketer and pioneer *by Norman Grubb, 1933*

8096   **Grubb, Norman Percy**
■   C.T. Studd, cricketer and pioneer. Religious Tract Soc., 1933. 256p. illus. ports.
   ——1st pbk. ed. 1970
   ——*another ed.* 1972. 262p.
   ——*Afrikaans ed. with title:* C.T. Studd: die verhaal van in baanbreker in Afrikaans oovertel dur Susan Troskie. Johannesburg, Christlike Uitgewersmaatschappy, 1946. x,168p.

8097   C.T. Studd, cricketer and missionary.
■   Religious Tract Society, [1934]. 32p. (The Little Library of Biography)

8098   After C.T. Studd. R.T.S.-Lutterworth P., 1939. 185p.

8098
-1   C.T. Studd, cricketer & missionary illus-
■   trated; retold and drawn by Edmund Julian. Gerrards Cross, Worldwide Evangelisation Crusade, n.d.
   *in comic strip format; see no. 8097*

8099   **The life story** of an Eton, Cambridge and
□   All-England cricketer, Charles T. Studd. Belfast, [c.1926]. ports.
   ——*another ed.* Gerrards Cross (Bucks.), World Evangelisation Crusade, n.d. 32p. illus. ports. scores
   ——*another ed.* Christian Literature Crusade, [195–]

8100   **The life** story of C. T. Studd. Worldwide Evangelisation Crusade, [c.1928]. 35p. ports.
   ——*rptd.* [c.1939]

8101   **Pollock, John Charles**
   The Cambridge seven. Intervarsity Fellowship, 1955
   ——*rptd.* 1962. 112p. pbk.
   *ch. on C. T. Studd*

8102   **Timpson, George Frederick**
■   Kings and commoners: studies in British idealism. London & Cheltenham, Burrow, 1926. xvi,190p. illus. ports.
   *chs. entitled "Cricketers all" and "C. T. Studd, cricketer and missionary"*

**8103  Walters, Thomas B.**
■  Charles T. Studd, cricketer and missionary. Epworth P., 1930. 126p. port. stats. bibliog.
*cricket pp. 7–15*

### Studd, Kynaston

**8104  Hamilton, Alys Lilian Douglas**
■  Kynaston Studd, Baronet of Netheravon. London Polytechnic, 1953. xix,121p. port.
*cricket in ch. ii, pp. 11–20*

### Sullivan, John

**8104  Maddocks, John,** *editor*
**–1**  Ken Shuttleworth & John Sullivan official
■  joint testimonial brochure. [Manchester, Joint Testimonial Fund, 1975]. [36]p. incl. adverts. illus. ports. stats.

### Sutcliffe, Bert

**8105  Booth, Pat**
■  Bert Sutcliffe's book for boys, including "Meet Bert Sutcliffe' (his own story as told to Pat Booth). Christchurch (N.Z.), Whitcombe & Tombs, 1961. 112p. illus. ports. diagrs.

**8106  Sutcliffe, Bert**
■  Between overs: memoirs of a cricketing Kiwi. W. H. Allen, 1963. 190p. illus. ports. stats.

### Sutcliffe, Herbert

**8107  Duckworth, Leslie**
■  Holmes and Sutcliffe: the run-stealers. The Cricketer; Hutchinson, 1970. 228p. illus. ports. stats. bibliog.

**8108  Priestley, John Boynton**
■  Open house: a book of essays. Heinemann, 1927. viii,197p.
*includes "Sutcliffe and I"*

**8109  Roberts, Edward Lamplough,** *compiler*
■  Sutcliffe, Yorkshire, England, 1919–1939. Birmingham, Hudson, 1945. 78p. illus. stats.

**8110  Sutcliffe, Herbert**
■  Cricket memoirs and records, with advice to youths and others. Leeds, Storey Evans, [1928?]. 32p. illus. port. stats.

**8111  For England and Yorkshire. E. Arnold,**
■  1935. 192p. illus. ports. stats.
——paper ed. 1935
*reprints 1936, 1937, 1942, 1944 and 1946*

**8112  Herbert Stucliffe's cricket annual 1947.**
■  Programme Publications Ltd., [1947]. 112p. illus. ports. scores. stats.

### Suttle, Charles Richard William

**8113  Suttle, Charles Richard William**
■  The impact of junior and senior cricket. [Chesterfield, the Author, 1971]. 64p. illus. ports. stats.
*the author's club cricket in Barbados, London and Derbyshire and on his work with junior cricketers in the Chesterfield area*

### Swanton, Ernest William

**8114  Swanton, Ernest William**
■  Sort of a cricket person. Collins, 1972. 318p. illus. ports.
——*another ed.* Sportsman's Book Club, 1974
——pbk. ed. Fontana/Collins, 1974. 301p.

**8114  Follow on. Collins, 1977. 288p. illus.**
**–1**  ports.
■  ——*another ed.* Sportsman's Book Club, 1978
*sequel to no. 8114*

### Swire, Samuel Herbert

**8115  Lancashire County and Manchester**
■  **Cricket Club**
Testimonial to the Hon. Secretary, Mr. S.H. Swire: report of dinner and presentation, November 24th, 1888. [Manchester, S.H. Swire, 1889], 37p. port.

### Symonds, Calvin ("Bummy")

**8116  Calvin "Bummy" Symonds** benefit,
■  National Stadium [Hamilton, Bermuda], September 13–14, 1969. [Hamilton, the Benefit Cttee., 1969]. 8p. incl. adverts. illus. & port. on front cover

### Symons, Julian Gustave

**8116  Symons, Julian Gustave**
**–1**  Notes from another country. London
■  Magazine Editions, 1972. 147p.
*cricket in ch. 1, pp. 9–24 'Bonzo'*

### Talyarkhan, A. F. S.

**8116  A.F.S.T. testimonial souvenir. Bombay,**
**–2**  A.F.S.T. Felicitation Cttee., [1979]. 94p.
■  incl. adverts. illus. ports.

### Tate, Frederick William

**8117  [F.W. Tate's** benefit match . . . 1901].
*contains pen-portrait of F.W.T. by "Leather Hunter" [A.J. Gaston]*

### Tate, Maurice William

**8118  Arlott, [Leslie Thomas] John**
■  Maurice Tate. Phoenix House, 1951. 63p.

illus. ports. diagr. (Cricketing Lives)
——*another ed.* Sportsman's Book Club, 1961

**8118** **Brodribb, Gerald**
**-1** Maurice Tate: a biography. London
■ Magazine Editions, 1976. [vii],215p. illus. ports. facsims. stats. bibliog.
——*another ed.* Newton Abbott, Readers Union, 1977

**8119** **Tate, Maurice William**
■ My cricketing reminiscences. S. Paul, [1934]. 208p. illus. ports.

### Tattersall, Roy

**8120** **Lancashire County Cricket Club**
■ M. J. Hilton & Tattersall joint benefit, Lancashire v. Yorkshire at Old Trafford on July 30, August, 1 & 2, 1960. Manchester, the Club, 1960. [4]p. fold. ports. stats.

### Taylor, Brian

**8121** **Bexley United Football Club**
■ Brian Taylor benefit match v. Cricketers All Star XI. Monday, April 13th [1964]. The Club, [1964]. [12]p.

**8122** Brian Taylor souvenir brochure. [Benefit
■ Cttee., 1966]. [44]p. incl. covers & adverts. illus. ports.

### Taylor, Derek

**8122** Derek Taylor testimonial book 1978.
**-1** Wells, *printed by* Clare, Son & Co., [1978].
■ 56p. incl. adverts. illus. ports. stats.
*includes pp. 8–9 "Sammy Woods. A legend at Taunton", by John Arlott*

### Taylor, Frank H.

**8123** **Taylor, Frank H.**
■ Youth and versatility. [Philadelphia], S.S. White Dental Mfg. Co., 1919. 6p.
*report on Philadelphian cricket and the author's performances in 1919*

### Taylor, Gordon McLaren

**8124** **Lancashire County Cricket Club**
■ G.M. Taylor testimonial fund. Manchester, the Club, 1965. [4]p. fold. port.

### Taylor, Kenneth

**8125** **Yorkshire County Cricket Club**
■ Ken Taylor benefit—1968. [Leeds, Benefit Cttee., 1968]. [40]p. incl. adverts. illus. ports. stats.

### Taylor, Robert William

**8126** **Mortimer, Gerald,** *editor*
■ Bob Taylor testimonial brochure. Eckington (Derbyshire), *printed by* Raymond Walkley, [1973]. 40p. incl. adverts. illus. ports. stats.

### Tennyson, Lionel Hallam Tennyson, 3rd Baron

**8127** **Tennyson, Limited Hallam,** *3rd baron*
■ From verse to worse. Cassell, 1933. 277p. illus. ports.

**8128** Sticky wickets. C. Johnson, 1950. 173p.
■ illus. ports.
——*cheap ed.* 1951
*a sequel to* From verse to worse

### Tetley, James George

**8128** **Tetley, James George**
**-1** Old times and new. T. Fisher Unwin, 1904. viii,312p.
——2nd and revd. ed. 1904
*cricket pp. 153, 184–5, 215–7*

### Thomas, Edward

**8129** **Farjeon, Eleanor**
Memoirs. Book 1. Edward Thomas: the last four years. Oxford Univ. P. 1958. xv,271p. illus. ports.
*scattered cricket references*

### Thomas, Robert Dalzell Dillon

**8130** **Thomas, Robert Dalzell Dillon**
■ The note-book of a lieutenant in the Italian campaign. *Priv. printed,* [1944?]. 38p.
*references to cricket and a poem "Lament of the village groundsman"*

### Thompson, Alexander

**8131** **Middlesex County Cricket Club**
■ Alex Thompson & Harry Sharp, Middlesex, benefit 1955. Lord's, the Club, [1955]. [4]p. fold

### Thompson, Francis

**8132** **Lucas, Edward Verrall**
■ One day and another. Methuen, 1909. vii,251p.
*essays, including "A rhapsodist at Lord's",* [Francis Thompson] *pp. 199–215*

**8133** **Meynell, Everard**
□ The life of Francis Thompson. Burns Oates, 1913. xi,360p. illus.
*cricket pp. 13, 39–45, 326, 328*
——Fifth and revd. ed. 1926. vii,279p.

## Thomson, John

8133 **Thomson, John**
−1 Francis Thompson, poet & mystic. 3rd
ed. Simpkin Marshall, [1923]. 159p. ports.
*cricket pp. 22–4; 1st ed. (1912) and 2nd
ed. (1913) with title: Francis Thompson, the
Preston-born poet*

## Thomson, Arthur Alexander

8134 **Memorial** service for Arthur Alexander
■ Thomson, St. Mark's, Hamilton Terrace,
St. John's Wood, Wednesday, 24th July
1968. [4]p. fold

8135 **Thomson, Arthur Alexander**
When I was a lad. Epworth P., 1964. 60p.
illus.
*has a ch. on cricket*

## Thomson, Jeffrey Robert

8135 **Frith, David Edward John**
−1 Thommo: Jeff Thomson, the world's
fastest bowler tells his own story to David
Frith. Sydney, Angus & Robertson, 1980
[i.e. 1979]. 115p. illus. ports. stats.

## Thornton, Charles Inglis

8136 **Thornton, Charles Inglis**
East and West and back again. Ash, 1912.
68p.

8137 **Thornton, Percy Melville**
■ Some things we have remembered.
Samuel Thornton, Admiral, 1797–1859,
Percy Melville Thornton, 1841–1911.
Longmans, Green, 1912. xi,337p. illus.
ports.
*contains several references*

## Thorpe, James Henry

8138 **Thorpe, James Henry**
■ A cricket bag and some illustrations.
Wells, Gardner, Darton, [1929]. xvii,175p.
illus. bibliog.
——*2nd ed.* 1930
*has 2 chapters on cricket books*

8139 **Happy** days: recollections of an unrep-
■ entant Victorian. Howe, 1933. 318p. illus.
ports.

## Thurtle, Ernest

8140 **Thurtle, Ernest**
Time's winged chariot: memories and
comments. Chaterson, 1945. xii,190p.
illus. port.
*references to village green and Lords and
Commons cricket in ch. 2*

## Timms, John Edward

8141 **Speakman, F. S.,** *compiler*
■ Jack E. Timms' testimonial fund.
Northampton, Northampton Chronicle
and Echo, 1949. 16p. illus. ports. stats.

## Titmus, Frederick John

8142 **Middlesex County Cricket Club**
■ Fred Titmus (England and Middlesex)
benefit 1963: Middlesex v. Sussex, June
1, 3 & 4. Lord's, the Club, [1963]. [4]p.
fold. port.

8143 **Sunday Telegraph**
■ Benefit for Fred Titmus (England &
Middlesex): F. J. Titmus XI v. Cockfosters
C.C. programme, Aug. 18, 1963. Sunday
Telegraph, [1963]. [4]p. fold. port.

8144 **Titmus, Fred**
■ Talk of the double. S. Paul, 1964. 196p.
illus. ports. stats.
——*another ed.* Sportsman's Book Club,
1967

## Tolchard, Roger

8144 **Roger Tolchard** souvenir testimonial
−1 brochure. Leicester, [Benefit Cttee.,
■ 1979]. [44]p. incl. adverts. illus. ports.
(some col.), stats.

## Tompkin, Maurice

8145 **Baker, W. W.**
■ Maurice Tompkin: [a poem]. [The
Author]. *n.d.* bs.

## Townsend, Alan

8146 **Warwickshire County Cricket Club**
■ Alan Townsend's benefit. [Birmingham,
the Club, 1960]. [4]p. fold. illus. port.
stats.

## Travers, Ben

8147 **Travers, Ben**
■ Vale of laughter: an autobiography. Bles,
1957. xi,251p. illus. ports.

8147 A-sitting on a gate: autobiography. W. H.
−1 Allen, 1978. [ix],195p. illus. ports.
■ *cricket pp. 10, 11, 116–19, 126*

## Tribe, George Edward

8148 **[Tribe, George]**
■ Playing the game: the George Tribe testimonial book. Kettering, *printed by* Dalkeith P., 1956. 16p. 1 illus. diagrs.
*with articles by Dennis Brookes and F. R.
Brown*

## Trott, George Henry Stevens

8149　[Craig, Albert]
■　Mr. G. H. S. Trott. Cricket P., 1896. [4]p.
　　folded card. port.

## Troup, Walter

8150　Troup, Walter
■　Sporting memories: my life as a Glouces-
　　tershire county cricketer: rugby and
　　hockey player and member of Indian
　　police service. Hutchinson, 1924. x,312p.
　　illus. port.

## Trueman, Frederick Sewards

8151　Arlott, [Leslie Thomas] John
■　Fred: portrait of a fast bowler. Eyre &
　　Spottiswoode, 1971. 192p. illus. ports.
　　stats.
　　——another ed. Sportsman's Book Club,
　　1972
　　——pbk. ed. Coronet, 1974. 190p.

8152　Freddie Trueman benefit brochure, 1962.
■　Doncaster, printed by Yorkshire Evening
　　News, [1962]. 33p. incl. adverts. illus.
　　ports.

8153　The Star
■　Trueman special edition. August 29,
　　1964. Sheffield, Sheffield Newspapers
　　Ltd. 20p. illus. ports. stats.

8154　Trueman, Freddie, i.e. Frederick Sew-
■　ards Trueman
　　Fast fury. S. Paul, 1961. 192p. illus. ports.

8155　The Freddie Trueman story. S. Paul,
■　1965. 143p. illus. ports.

8155　Ball of fire: an autobiography. Dent, 1976.
－1　191p. illus. ports. facsims. stats.
■　——rptd. St. Albans, Mayflower, 1977
　　173p. pbk.

8156　Whitkirk Cricket Club
　　Charity match in aid of Freddie True-
　　man's benefit fund, Sunday, July 8th,
　　[1962] at Whitkirk: programme. [The
　　Club, 1962]. 12p. incl. adverts. ports.

## Trumble Family

8157　Trumble, Robert
■　The Trumble family in Australia.
　　Melbourne, the Author, 1972. [v],78f.
　　ports. scores, stats. bibliog.
　　limited ed. of 150 copies

## Trumble, Hugh

8158　Trumble, Robert
　　The golden age of cricket: a memorial
　　book of Hugh Trumble. Melbourne, The
　　Author, 1968. xiv,110p. illus.

## Trumper, Victor Thomas

8159　Ashley-Cooper, Frederick Samuel
　　Stoddart and Trumper in the cricket field.
　　1916
　　　an off-print from Wisden 1915 and 1916.
　　Only known copy in M.C.C. Library, Lord's

8160　Crown Street School Old Boys' Union
■　Official souvenir and programme of the
　　public reception and presentation Friday,
　　Dec. 12th 1902 tendered to Victor
　　Trumper. Sydney, C.H. Willmott for the
　　Union, 1902. 20p. incl. adverts. ports.
　　stats.

8160　Eden, Guy
－1　Bush ballads, and other verses. Sisley,
　　1907. viii,152p.
　　　contains pp. 93–5 a poem on Victor
　　Trumper

8160　Fingleton, Jack, i.e. John Henry Webb
－2　Fingleton
■　The immortal Victor Trumper. Collins,
　　1978. 208p. illus. ports. facsims. diagr.
　　stats.
　　——another ed. Sportsman's Book Club,
　　1979
　　　compares Trumper's record season by
　　season with that of Bradman

8161　Fletcher, J.W.
　　The greatest batsman. 1954. 5p. typescript
　　　article on Victor Trumper, part of which
　　was printed in the Sunday Mail, Brisbane,
　　21st Nov., 1954. Typescript in M.C.C.
　　Library, Lord's

8162　Glasson, —
　　School sport. Sydney, N.S.W., privately
　　printed, 1936. 62p.
　　　limited ed. of 5 copies. Deals mostly with
　　Victor Trumper

8163　Noble, Montague Alfred
■　The game's the thing: a record of cricket
　　experience; with special chapters on the
　　genius of Victor Trumper. Cassell, 1926.
　　xv,248p. ports. diagrs.

8164　Raiji, Vasant, editor
■　Victor Trumper: the beau ideal of a crick-
　　eter: an anthology. Bombay, Vivek Publi-
　　cations, 1964. xviii,96p. illus. ports. stats.
　　bibliog.

## Tunnicliffe, John

8165 [Tunnicliffe, John]
■ The story of my cricketing career. [Bradford, 1903]. 32p. illus.

## Turnbull, Maurice Jospeh

8166 Van Zeller, Claude Hubert
■ Willingly to school: a study in unceremonial practice. Sheed & Ward, 1952. x,262p. illus.
    *memories of cricket at Downside, particularly of Maurice Turnbull*

## Turner, Glenn Maitland

8166 Glenn Turner benefit souvenir book
-1 1978. [Benefit Cttee., 1978]. 32p. incl.
■ adverts. illus. ports. stats.

8166 Turner, Glenn Maitland
-2 My way. Auckland & London, Hodder &
■ Stoughton, 1975. 199p. illus. ports. diagrs. stats.
    ——*another ed.* Newton Abbot, Readers Union, 1976

## Turner, Henry

8167 [Turner, Henry]
■ Memories of club cricket, by a Nottingham Secretary. Nottingham, [the Author], 1890. 27p.

## Turner, Stuart

8167 Ilford Cricket Club, *and* Essex County
-1 Cricket Club
■ Double wicket competition . . . 7 October 79, Valentines Park, Cranbrook Rd., Ilford: souvenir programme. Ilford C.C., [1979]. [28]p. incl. adverts. ports. stats.
    *in support of Stuart Turner's benefit, with statistics of his career*

8167 Stuart Turner benefit year 1979. [Benefit
-2 Cttee., 1979]. 52p. incl. covers & adverts.
■ illus. ports. (1 col.), stats.

## Tyldesley, John Thomas

8168 Holmes, H.E.
■ J.T. Tyldesley in first class cricket: a detailed record and analysis of all his scores. Bury and Manchester. T. Crompton, 1912. 62p. frontis. (port). stats.

## Tyson, Frank Holmes

8169 Tyson, Frank (Holmes)
■ A typhoon called Tyson. Heinemann, 1961. 220p. illus. ports.

## Umrigar, Pahlan Ratanji ("Polly")

8170 Maharashtra Cricket Association
■ "Polly" Umrigar benefit match. Kolhapur. Poona, the Assoc., [1972]. [256]p. incl. adverts. illus. ports. stats.
    *about 20p. of text*

## Underwood, Derek Leslie

8170 Derek Underwood benefit year 1975:
-1 souvenir brochure. Benefit Fund Cttee.,
■ [1975]. 46p. incl. adverts. illus. ports. stats.

8170 Underwood, Derek [Leslie]
-2 Beating the bat: an autobiography. S.
■ Paul, 1975. 175p. illus. ports. stats.
    ——*another ed.* Newton Abbot, Readers Union, 1976

## Van Der Bijl, Vintcent

8170 Natal Cricket Association
-3 Vince Van der Bijl: benefit brochure. [Durban, the Assoc., 1979?]. 36p. incl. adverts. illus. ports. stats.

## Van Der Byl, Charles

8171 Van Der Byl, Charles
■ My fifty years of sport. Stockwell, [1937]. 202p. illus. port.
    *cricket in chs. 6 and 23*

## Venn, Henry

8171 Venn, Henry
-1 The life and a selection from the letters of the Rev. H. Venn. The memoir by J. Venn. Edited by the Rev. H. Venn. B.D. London, 1834
    ——2nd ed. 1835
    ——4th ed. xvi,594. 1836
    *includes references to Surrey v. England 1747*

## Verity, Hedley

8172 Davis, Sam
■ Hedley Verity: prince with a piece of leather. Epworth P., 1952. 64p. illus. ports. stats.

8173 Lynd, Robert
■ Both sides of the road. Methuen, 1934. viii,184p.
    *essays: includes "Verity's Test match", pp. 124–30*

8174 Roberts, Edward Lamplough, *compiler*
■ Hedley Verity, Yorkshire and England, 1930–1939. Birmingham, Hudson, [1943]. 46p. port. stats.

8175 [See no. 746–1]
■

8176 **Yorkshire Observer**
■ Hedley Verity, 18 May, 1905–31 July, 1943: the story of a gallant cricketer. Bradford, Yorkshire Observer, [1945]. [9]p. illus. port. stats.

## Vine, Joseph

8177 [Sussex County Cricket Club]
■ Joe Vine's benefit match: Sussex v. Yorkshire, at Hastings, August 28, 29 & 30. 1913. [Hove the Club, 1913]. [4]p. fold. stats.
  *contains "What he has done for Sussex" by "Leather Hunter" [A. J. Gaston]*

## Vizianagram, Shri Vijaya Anand, Maharajkumar of

8178 **Dutt, K. Iswara,** *and* **Ratnam, K.V.**
■ **Gopala,** *editors*
  Vizzy commemoration souvenir. New Delhi, Vishal P., 1966. 146p. incl. adverts. illus. ports.

## Waddy, Stacy

8179 **Waddy, Etheldred**
■ Stacy Waddy: cricket, travel and the church. Sheldon P., 1938. x,285p. illus. ports.
  *cricket in ch. iii, pp. 14–25*

## Wade, Thomas H.

8180 **Essex County Cricket Club**
■ T. H. Wade's benefit 1948. Chelmsford, the Club, [1948]. [4]p. fold. illus. ports. stats.

## Wadekar, Ajit L.

8181 **Shivaji Park Gymkhana**
  Souvenir honouring Arjuna Award winner Manjrekar and new Test cap Wadekar, April 21, 1967. Bombay, G.K. Menon for the S.P.G., [1967]. 82p. illus. ports. stats.

8182 **Wadekar, Ajit**
■ My cricketing years, as told to K.N. Prabhu. Delhi & London, Vikas, 1973. xii,159p. illus. port. scores, stats.

## Wainwright, Edward

8183 **Craig, Albert**
■ Edward Wainwright, [by] A.C. Cricket Rhymster. All England Athletic Publ. Co., 1898. [4]p. folded card. ports. stats.

## Waite, John Henry Bickford

8184 **Waite, John**
■ Perchance to bowl (Test cricket today); edited and with chapters by R.S. (Dick) Whitington. Kaye, 1961. 176p. illus. scores

## Wakelam, Henry Blythe Thornhill

8185 **Wakelam, Henry Blythe Thornhill**
■ Half-time: "the mike and me". Nelson, 1938. 344p. ports.
  *scattered cricket references*

## Walcott, Clyde Leopold

8186 **Walcott, Clyde Leopold**
■ Island cricketers. Hodder & Stoughton, 1958. 188p. illus. ports. scores

## Walker Family

8187 **Bettesworth, Walter Ambrose**
■ The Walkers of Southgate: a famous brotherhood of cricketers; ed. by E.T. Sachs. Methuen, 1900. xv,439p. illus. ports. diagr. scores, stats.

8188 **Taylor Walker and Company Limited**
■ Directors' report and statement of accounts for the year ended 31st December 1956. The Company, 1957. 12p. illus.
  *references to the Walkers of Southgate*

## Walker, Maxwell Henry Norman

8188 **Walker, Max,** *and* **Phillipson, Neill**
–1 Tangles. Toorak (Vic.), Gerry Sparke &
■ Associates, 1976. iv,204p. illus. ports.

8188 **Cricketer at the crossroads.** Toorak (Vic.),
–2 Garry Sparke & Associates, 1978. x,213p.
■ illus. & ports. (some col.), stats.

## Walker, Peter Michael

8189 **Peter Walker benefit souvenir brochure.**
■ Cardiff, [the Benefit Cttee.], 1966. 88p. incl. adverts. illus. ports.

## Walpole, Hugh

8190 **Hart-Davis, Rupert**
■ Hugh Walpole: a biography. Macmillan, 1952. xiv,503p. illus. ports. map, bibliog.
  *cricket pp. 252, 273, 303, 313, 315, 349, 358, 370, 393, 402*

## Walters, Kevin Douglas ("Doug")

8191 **Walters, Doug,** *i.e.* **Kevin Douglas**
■ **Walters**
  Looking for runs. Pelham Books, 1971. 175p. illus. ports.

## Wanostrocht, Nicholas

8192　Brodribb, [Arthur] Gerald [Norcott]
■　Felix on the bat: being a memoir of Nicholas Felix, together with the full text of
the 2nd ed. of 'Felix on the bat'. Eyre &
Spottiswoode, 1962. xiv,145;[4],viii,58p.
illus. (1 col.) ports. diagrs.
　　*Pt. 2 is a facsimile reprint of 2nd edn. 1850*

8192　Chapman, Ronald
−1　　The laurel and the thorn: a study of G.F.
■　Watts. Faber and Faber, 1945. 184p. illus.
ports. bibliog.
　　*references pp. 16, 21, to N.W. who was
schoolmaster to G.F.W.*

8193　Weston, George Neville
■　N. Felix, Esq.: the history of a portrait.
[*Privately printed*, The Author), 1937. 20p.
1 illus. port. scores
　　*limited ed.: 1st issue 10 copies, 2nd issue
3 copies, all signed and numbered*

## Ward, Sir Leslie

8193　Ward, Sir Leslie
−1　　Forty years of "Spy." Chatto & Windus,
1915. xvi,351p. illus. & ports. (some col.)
　　*cricket pp. 189, 216, 231*

## Wardle, John Henry

8194　Wardle, John Henry
■　Happy go Johnny: as told to A.A.
Thomson. Hale, 1957. 206p. illus. ports.
stats.

8195　Yorkshire Evening News
■　Johnny Wardle benefit brochure. Leeds,
Yorkshire Evening News, [1957]. [28]p.
incl. adverts. illus. ports.

## Warner, Sir Pelham Francis

8196　Ashley-Cooper, Frederick Samuel
P.F. Warner's cricket record 1888–1919.
233p. scores, stats. MS.
　　*compiled and bound by A–C for P.F.W.; in
A.E. Winder's collection*

8197　Craig, Albert
■　Mr. Pelham E. [sic] Warner, Wright & Co.,
1908. [4]p. folded card. port.

8198　Mason, Ronald Charles
■　Plum Warner's last season (1920).
Epworth P., 1970. x,186p. illus. ports.
scores

8199　Meynell, Laurence
■　'Plum' Warner. Phoenix House, 1951.
64p. illus. ports. (Cricketing Lives)

8200　Warner, Sir Pelham Francis
■　Cricket in many climes. Heinemann,
1900. xiii,271p. illus. ports. scores, stats.
　　*account of 5 cricket tours to West Indies,
United States and Canada, Portugal, South
Africa*

8201　Cricket reminiscences, with some review
■　of the 1919 season. G. Richards, 1920.
239p. illus. ports. scores
　　*rptd. from The Times*

8202　My cricketing life. Hodder & Stoughton,
■　[1921]. xi,336p. illus. ports. scores
　　——*limited ed.* of 200 copies. 1921

8203　Long innings: the autobiography . . .
■　Harrap, 1951. 240p. illus. ports. scores
　　——*de luxe ed.* limited to 260 signed
copies. 1951

## Warre, Edmond

8203　Fletcher, Charles Robert Leslie
−1　　Edmond Warre: sometime Headmaster
and Provost of Eton College. Murray,
1922. xii,323p. illus. ports.
　　*cricket pp. 19, 59, 61, 69, 201, 202, 217,
274*

## Washbrook, Cyril

8204　Lancashire County Cricket Club
■　C. Washbrook's testimonial. [Man-
chester], the Club. [1959]. [4]p. fold. port.
stats.

8205　Sharpe, Ivan, *editor*
■　Cyril Washbrook testimonial fund.
Manchester, Kemsley Newspapers,
[1948]. 16p. illus. ports. stats.

8206　Thomson, Arthur Alexander
■　Hutton and Washbrook. Epworth P.,
1963. 275p. illus. ports. bibliog. stats.
　　——*another ed.* Sportsman's Book Club,
1966

8207　Washbrook, Cyril
■　Cricket—the silver lining. Sportsguide
Publications. [1950]. 201p. illus. ports.
　　——*2nd ed.* [with chapter 20 re-written].
1950

## Washington, Irving

8208　Woodhouse, Anthony, *and others*
■　Cricketers of Wombwell, by A. Wood-
house, R.D. Wilkinson, J. Sokell. Leeds,
Wombwell Cricket Lovers' Society, 1965.
[10],39p. illus. ports. stats. [Wombwell
Cricket Lovers' Society Publications)
　　*on Irving Washington, Roy and Norman
Kilner*

## Watson, Alfred Edward Thomas

8209 **Watson, Alfred Edward Thomas**
A sporting and dramatic career. Macmillan, 1918. vi,390p.
*scattered cricket references*

## Watson, Edmund Henry Lacon

8210 **Watson, Edmund Henry Lacon**
■ Notes and memories of a sports reporter. H. Joseph, [1931]. 288p. illus. ports.
*cricket pp. 50–79*

## Watson, William ("Willie")

8211 **Watson, Willie**
■ Double international. S. Paul, 1956. 176p. illus. ports.

8212 **The Willie Watson** benefit book. Idle,
■ Bradford, *printed by* Watmoughs Ltd., [1956]. 16p. ports.

## Waugh, Alexander Raban ("Alec")

8213 **Waugh, Alec**
■ Myself when young: confessions. G. Richards, 1923. 259p.
*cricket mainly in chs. 5 and 6*

8214 The early years of Alec Waugh. Cassell,
■ 1962. xiii,313p. illus. ports.
*cricket pp. 15–16, 28–29, 30–31, 47–48, 56, 64, 67–69, 170–75*

8214 A year to remember: a reminiscence of
–1 1931. W. H. Allen, 1975. [v],191p. illus.
■ ports.
*cricket pp. 1, 78–81, 115–16, 117, 119–21*

8214 The best wine last: an autobiography
–2 through the years 1932–1969. W. H.
■ Allen, 1978. v,319p. illus. ports.
*many cricket references*

## Waugh, Arthur

8215 **Waugh, Arthur**
■ One man's road: being a picture of life in a passing generation. Chapman & Hall, 1931. xv,390p. illus. ports.
*references to Sydney Pawling and Hampstead C.C.*

## Wazir Ali

8216 **Tajammul Husan, Syed**
Late Major Wazir Ali: a life sketch. Karachi, October 1953. [Karachi, 1953]. [40]p. illus. ports.
*souvenir of an exhibition match played for the benefit of Wazir Ali's family, Karachi. Contains brief biography*

## Weigall, Antony

8216 **Antony Weigall.** 19 November, 1902–3rd
–1 July 1977. The Parish Church, St. John
■ the Baptist, Belmont, Wednesday, 20 July 1977: order of service. [4]p.

## Wellard, Arthur William

8217 **Andrews, William Harry Russell**
■ Arthur Wellard testimonial 1951: souvenir brochure. Paulton, *printed by* Purnell, [1951]. 12p. illus. ports.

## Wells, Herbert George

8218 **Wells, Herbert George**
■ Certain personal matters: a collection of material, mainly autobiographical. Lawrence & Bullen, 1898. viii,278p.
*"The veteran cricketer" pp. 104–11*
——*another ed.* T. Fisher Unwin, 1901. 184p. pbk.

8219 Experiment in autobiography: discoveries
■ and conclusions of a very ordinary brain (since 1866). 2 vols. Gollancz & the Cresset P., 1934. illus. ports.
*reference to his father Frederick Joseph Wells who played for Kent, pp. 62, 195*

## Wharton, Alan

8220 **Lancashire County Cricket Club**
■ A. Wharton's benefit, Lancashire v. Surrey at Old Trafford on May 28, 29 and 30, 1958. [Manchester], the Club, [1958]. [4]p. fold. port. stats.

8221 **Todd, Eric,** *editor*
The Alan Wharton benefit book 1958. Manchester, Kemsley Newspapers, 1958. 24p. incl. adverts. ports. stats.

## White, David William

8222 **Arlott, [Leslie Thomas] John**
■ David White. [Southampton, Hampshire C.C.C.], 1969. [8]p. stats.
*limited ed. of 25 copies*

## White, Edmund Yalden

8223 **White, Edmund Yalden**
■ Ordained in powder: the life and times of Parson White of Crondall from his diary, "A journal of domestic, and other events from August 1816 to August 1856"; edited by Roland P. Butterfield. Farnham, Herald P., 1966. viii,123p. illus. port. map on endpapers
*cricket pp. 83–86*

## Whitehead, Harry

8224 **Leicestershire County Cricket Club**
H. Whitehead's benefit: Leicestershire v.
Sussex, July 16, 17 & 18. Leicester, the
Club, [1914]. [4]p. fold. port. stats.

## Whiteside, John Parkinson

8225 **Leicestershire's** famous wicket-keeper [J.
P. Whiteside]. Leicester, Gamble &
Johnson, [1902]. 23p. port.

## Whitney, Caspar

8226 **Whitney, Caspar**
■ A sporting pilgrimage: . . . studies in
English sport, past and present. Osgood,
McIlvaine, 1894. xiii,397p. illus.
——2nd ed. 1895
*ch. xiii "Cricket" pp. 322–330*

## Whitty, William James

8227 **Hill, Les R.**
■ Eighty not out: the story of W. J. (Bill)
Whitty of Tantanoola, former international cricketer . . . as told to and
compiled by Les R. Hill. Mount Gambier,
S. Aust., the Author, 1966. 40p. illus.
ports. stats.

## Wight, Peter Bernard

8228 **Barnett, T.M.**, *editor*
■ Peter Wight benefit year 1963: souvenir
brochure. [Benefit Cttee., 1963]. 32p. incl.
adverts. illus. ports. stats.

## Wignall, Trevor

8228 **Wignall, Trevor**
–1 I knew them all. Hutchinson, [1938].
■ 340p. port.
*pp. 173–86 "The loveliest game"*

8229 Almost yesterday: [reminiscences].
■ Hutchinson, [1949]. 224p. illus. port.

## Wilding, Anthony

8230 **Myers, Arthur Wallis**
Captain Anthony Wilding. Hodder &
Stoughton, 1916. xii,306p. illus.
*cricket pp. 32–3, 37–8, 50, 59–60*

## Willis, Robert George Dylan ("Bob")

8230 **Willis, Bob**
–1 Diary of a cricket season. Pelham Books,
■ 1979. 157p. illus. team ports.
——*another ed.* Newton Abbot, Readers
Union, 1979
*the 1978 season*

## Wilson, Alan

8231 **Kay, John**, *editor*
■ Alan Wilson's benefit brochure. [Benefit
Cttee., 1962]. [24]p. incl. adverts. illus.
ports.

8232 **Lancashire County Cricket Club**
■ Alan Wilson testimonial Lancashire v.
Hampshire at Old Trafford . . . June 1962.
Manchester, the Club, [1962]. 3p. port.
stats.

## Wilson, Andrew E.

8233 **Wilson, Andrew**, *compiler*
■ Stump high!!! cricket miscellany. Andy
Wilson Benefit Fund, [1953]. 63p. incl.
adverts. illus. ports. scores, stats.

## Wilson, Clement Eustace Macro ("Clem")

8233 C.E.M. Wilson: some appreciations,
–1 notes and sketches. 30p. port.
■ *an 'In Memoriam' booklet*

## Wilson, Donald

8234 **Don Wilson** benefit 1972. [Leeds, Benefit
■ Cttee., 1972]. 44p. incl. adverts. illus.
ports. stats.

## Wilson, Evelyn Rockley

8235 **St. John's Wood** Church: [order of
■ service]. E.R.W. 1879–1957. 1st August
1957. [4]p. fold

## Wilson, Frederick Bonhote

8236 **Wilson, Frederick Bonhote**
■ Sporting pie. Chapman & Hall, 1922.
xv,287p. illus. ports.

## Wilson, John Victor

8237 **The Vic Wilson** benefit book. Malton,
■ *printed by* Brown's, [1958]. [28]p. illus.
port.

## Wilson, Peter

8237 **Wilson, Peter**
–1 The man they couldn't gag: an auto-
■ biography. Hutchinson/S. Paul, 1977.
387p. illus. ports.
*many cricket references*

## Wilson, Robert C.

8238 **[Kent County Cricket Club]**
■ Bob Wilson's benefit 1964. July 19 at
Staplehurst: Staplehurst v. Kent XI.
[Canterbury, the Club, 1964]. [4]p. fold.
ports. stats.

## Wingfield-Stratford, Esmé Cecil

8238  **Wingfield-Stratford, Esmé Cecil**
–1    Before the lamps went out. Hodder &
■     Stoughton, 1945. 256p. port.
      *cricket pp. 9, 21–22, 36–8, 208, 230, 244–8*

## Winton, John

8239  **Winton, John**
      We joined the Navy. M. Joseph, 1959.
      254p.
      *includes "Cricket in Barbados"*

## Wodehouse, *Sir* Pelham Grenville

8239  **Connolly, Joseph**
–1    P. G. Wodehouse: an illustrated biog-
■     raphy with complete bibliography and
      collector's guide. Orbis Publishing, 1979.
      160p. illus. ports. facsims. bibliog.
      *cricket pp. 16 (portrait of Wodehouse in the
      Dulwich College 2nd XI), 17, 19, 20–1, 30*

## Wolstenholme, Kenneth

8240  **Wolstenholme, Kenneth**
      Sports special. S. Paul, 1956. 160p. illus.
      ——*another ed.* Sportsman's Book Club,
      1958
      *scattered cricket references*

## Wood, Arthur

8241  **Briggs, A.,** *compiler*
■     For Arthur Wood's benefit. Yorkshire
      versus Middlesex . . . Bradford . . . 1939:
      commemorative programme. Bradford,
      Benefit Fund, [1939]. 24p. ports. stats.

## Wood, Barry

8241  **Higgs, Peter,** *editor*
–1    Barry Wood's testimonial year book 1979.
■     [Benefit Cttee., 1979]. [80]p. incl. adverts.
      illus. (some col.), ports. stats.

## Woodgate, Walter Bradford

8242  **Woodgate, Walter Bradford**
■     Reminiscences of an old sportsman; a
      gossip of memories and moods. Nash,
      1909. viii,499p. illus. ports.
      *cricket pp. 182–83*

## Woodhead, Francis Gerald ("Frank")

8242  **Frank Woodhead** testimonial year book,
–1    1979. Nottingham, Benefit Cttee., [1979].
■     [80]p. incl. adverts. illus. ports. score

## Woods, Samuel Moses James

8243  **Craig, Albert**
■     Mr. S.M.J. Woods. [The Cricket P.], 1897.

[4]p. folded card. mounted port.
——*another ed.* All England Publ. Co.,
1898. port.
——*another ed.* All England Publ. Co.,
1899. port.

8244  **Woods, Samuel Moses James**
■     My reminiscences: with personal appreci-
      ations by P.F. Warner and G.L. Jessop.
      Chapman & Hall, 1925. [v],211p. port.

## Woolley, Frank Edward

8245  **Craig, Albert**
■     Frank Woolley. Wright & Co., 1906. [4]p.
      folded card. port.

8246  **Flicker Productions Ltd.**
■     Cricket: Frank Woolley: square cut and
      walking shot. Flicker Productions,
      [c.1936]. illus.
      ——:——: pull to leg and forcing shot, off
      the back foot, to the off. [c.1936]. illus.
      *both are overprinted with "Frank Woolley's
      Cricket School"*

8246  **The Guardian**
–1    The bedside 'Guardian' 16: a selection
■     from The Guardian 1966–67; edited by
      W.L. Webb. Collins, 1967. 255p. illus.
      *includes pp. 208–12, "Miracle worker at
      the wicket" by Neville Cardus [on Frank
      Woolley]*

8247  **Haigh, F. Hanson**
■     The cricketing career of Frank Woolley.
      Canterbury, Jennings, 1927. 32p. illus.
      stats.
      ——2nd ed. 1928

8247  **Milton, Howard**
–1    Kent's greatest cricketer: a tribute to
■     Frank Woolley on his ninetieth birthday,
      broadcast on B.B.C. Radio Medway on 22
      May 1977. 5f. *typescript*
      *transcript in The Cricket Society's Library*

8247  **Nowll, A. K.**
–2    Cricket scores of Frank E. Woolley. Ms.
      *in M.C.C. Library, Lord's*

8248  **Peebles, Ian [Alexander Ross]**
■     Woolley—the pride of Kent. 'The Crick-
      eter'; Hutchinson, 1969. xi,152p. illus.
      ports. stats.

8249  **Thomson, Arthur Alexander**
■     Great men of Kent. Bodley Head, 1955.
      158p. ports. map. (Men of the Counties)
      *includes Frank Woolley, pp. 128–158*

8250  **Warner, Oliver**
■     Frank Woolley. Phoenix House, 1952.
      63p. ports. stats. (Cricketing Lives)

8251 **Woolley, Frank Edward**
■ The king of games. S. Paul, [1936]. 223p. illus. ports. stats.

8251 Early memoirs of Frank Woolley as told
−1 to Martha Wilson Woolley. Ashurst,
■ Tunbridge Wells, The Cricketer Ltd., 1976. 52p. illus. ports. stats.
*limited ed. of 1000 numbered and signed copies*

## Wordsworth, Charles

8252 **Wordsworth, Charles,** *bishop*
■ Annals of my early life 1806–1846; with occasional compositions in Latin and English verse. Longman, 1891. xvi,420p.
*cricket pp. 7, 55, 57, 86, 235*

8253 Annals of my life 1847–1856; edited by W.
■ Earl Hodgson. Longman, 1893. xxxvi,230p.
*ref to cricket at Glenalmond, p. 22*

## Wordsworth, Christopher

8254 **Overton, John Henry,** *and* **Wordsworth,**
■ **Elizabeth**
Christopher Wordsworth, Bishop of Lincoln. Rivingtons, 1888. xvi,542p. ports. score
*cricket references pp. 33–4, 46–50*
——new and cheaper ed. 1890. xvi,376p.

## Worrell, *Sir* Frank Mortimer Maglinne

8255 **Eytle, Ernest**
■ Frank Worrell; with . . . chapter commentaries by Frank Worrell. Hodder & Stoughton, 1963. 194p. illus. ports. stats.
——*another ed.* Sportsman's Book Club, 1965
——*another ed.* Calcutta, Rupa, 1976. xxiv,188p. illus. ports. stats.

8256 **Frank Worrell** of Barbados. 1924–1967.
■ Friday 7 April 1967 at 12 noon: [order of service]. [Westminster Abbey, 1967]. 9p.

8257 **Giuseppi, Undine**
■ Sir Frank Worrell; illustrated by John Patience. Nelson, 1969. [iv],92p. illus. ports. (Men of Greatness Series)
*for children*

8257 **The Guardian**
−1 The bedside 'Guardian' 16: a selection
■ from The Guardian 1966–67; edited by W. L. Webb. Collins, 1967. 255p. illus.
*includes pp. 212–4, "Worrell – too soon for an era to end", by John Samuel*

8258 **Sport & Pastime**
■ Worrell memorial match 1968: souvenir.

Madras, Sport & Pastime, 1968. 19p. ports. stats.
*the match, staged by Madras C.A. between "The Visitors" and Madras Chief Minister's XI, was held at Madras 29 Feb. 1968 in aid of the Sir Frank Worrell Memorial Fund; includes: "Knight errant of cricket" by P. N. Sundaresan*

8259 **Worrell,** *Sir* **Frank**
■ Cricket punch. S. Paul, 1959. 144p. illus. ports.

## Wright, Douglas Vivian Parson

8260 **Kentish Gazette**
■ D.V.P. Wright benefit souvenir. Canterbury, Kentish Gazette, [1957]. 32p. ports. diagr.

8261 **The Wright** book of cricket 1950: edited
■ by L.N. Bailey. The D.V.P. Wright Benefit Committee, [1950]. 16p. illus. ports. stats.

## Wyatt, Robert Elliott Storey

8262 **Wyatt, Robert Elliott Storey**
■ Three straight sticks. S. Paul, 1951. 192p. illus. ports.

## Wynyard, Edward G.

8262 **Masterman,** *Sir* **John Cecil**
−1 "A cricketer of the past". *In* Blackwood's
■ Magazine, vol. 315, no. 1904, June 1974. pp. 517–21

## Yardley, Norman Walter Dransfield

8263 **Yardley, Norman [Walter Dransfield]**
■ Cricket campaigns. S. Paul, [1950]. 232p. illus. ports.

## Yardley, Thomas James ("Jim")

8263 **Triple** testimonial fund 1976: Brian Brain,
−1 Jim Yardley, Rodney Cass. [Testimonial
■ Cttee., 1976]. 40p. incl. adverts. illus. stats.

## Young, Jack

8264 **Arsenal F.C.** v. Middlesex C.C.C.
■ Monday 11th August 1952, at 7.15 p.m. in aid of Jack Young's benefit fund: official programme. Programme Publications for Arsenal Football Club, [1952]. [4]p. fold. ports. stats.
*the first floodlit cricket match*

8265 **Middlesex County Cricket Club**
■ Jack Young, Middlesex and England, benefit 1952: Middlesex v. Sussex, Lord's May 31st, June 2nd & 3rd. Lord's, the Club, [1952]. [4]p. fold

# MISCELLANEOUS

8266 **Binstead, Arthur Morris**
■ More gal's gossip. Sands, 1901. ix,180p.
*cricket between Pentonville and an unnamed prison, pp. 98–9*

8267 **Castle, Dennis**
■ The pleasure of your company: how to give a party, make a speech, organise a wedding, dinner-dance, cricket match, garden fête, etc. Muller, 1969. xv,230p.
*"The charity cricket match" pp. 189–194*

8267 **Constantine, Learie Nicholas,** *Lord*
–1 *Constantine*
■ Colour bar. S. Paul, 1954. 193p. illus. ports.
*cricket pp. xvii,26–7,162–3,165–6*

8268 **The County Cricketers' Golfing Society**
□ Rules and list of members, 1939. 16p. Members' handbook and fixture list. 1963. 37p.
*probably other issues*

8269 **Day, James Wentworth**
■ Inns of sport. Naldrett P., for Whitbread & Co., 1949. 54p. illus. (some col.) ports. (Whitbread Library)
——2nd ed. 1949
*cricket inns, p. 40*

8270 **"De Doubleau",** *pseud.*
■ "Cricket patience" for one player: the new 1947 pastime. May be played when travelling or during leisure moments. Canterbury, *printed by* Jennings, [1947]. 19p.

8271 **"Dwarpa",** *pseud.*
■ Cricket as allied to the heavens; or, the astronomical interpretation of ball games. Stockwell, [1936]. 75p. illus.

8272 **Evans, Bertram James**
■ How to become a sporting journalist. W. H. Allen, 1946. 98p.
*cricket reporting pp. 51 & 61*

8273 **Goa** growler: a journal of no pretensions, no politics & no principles. Memento of a voyage per the B.I.S.N. Co.'s S.S. "Goa" from London to Karachi & Bombay.

Bombay, Duftur Ashkara P., Oct. 10th, 1883. 44p. scores
*several references to cricket matches on board*

8274 **Guirdham, Arthur**
A foot in both worlds: a doctor's autobiography of psychic experience. Jersey, N. Spearman, 1973. 221p.
*on p. 69 the author dreams about A.W. Carr and G.O.B. Allen*

8275 **Hine, Reginald Leslie**
■ Dreams and the way of dreams. London, Dent;N.Y.,Dutton,1913. xiv,281p. bibliog.
*includes an account of a dream of "A single-wicket cricket match", pp. 150–163*

8275 **Kaplan, Albert**
–1 Book-cricket: a fascinating game for
■ cricket lovers only. Dimona (Israel), the Author, n.d. [6]f.+[128]p. of scoresheets

8275 **McIntyre, Alasdair Chalmers,** *i.e.* **Alex-**
–2 **ander Chalmers**
A short history of ethics. N.Y., Macmillan 1966; London, Routledge & K. Paul, 1967. viii,280p.
*cricket pp. 88–9, 241–2*

8276 **Mahalaxmiwalla, Behram**
Debunking a critic on cricket: take it from A.F.S. Talyarkhan but with a pinch of salt. Bombay, B. Mahalaxmiwalla, *for private circulation.* 1948. 38p.

8277 **Mentz**
The cricketers' directory. Hovenden, 1863. 16p.
*this looks suspiciously like the entry in Taylor: Cricket directory. Mantz, London*

8278 **The National Cash Register Co. Ltd.**
■ 'The Test of the century': England v. Australia, September 20–24, 1971. The Banqueting Rooms, Lord's, [1971]. 5p. score
*match score of the 'computer test'*

8279 **Vockins, Michael D.**
■ Indoor cricket; edited by M.D. Vockins and K. Arch. Worcester, the Author, [1973]. 30p. incl. adverts. illus. score

# APPENDIX

Insufficient is known of the following items for them to be listed in the main sequence

8280 **Anthony, George**
A complete guide to cricket
——*new and rev. ed.* 30p.

8281 **[See no. 2814.1]**

8281 **Basu, Sankariprasād**
–2 Bal pade byāt nade. Calcutta, Kanura, 1962. iv,259p. ports.
*in Bengali; trs.: "The ball rolls, the bat is ready"*

8281 Nat āut. Calcutta. Ananda Publications,
–3 1965. x,224p. illus.
*in Bengali; trs.: "Not out"*

8282 **Cricket** extraordinary. Dean and Son, 1878
*in Taylor*

8283 **Criquet**. London, *n.d.*
*in Taylor*

8284 **[Entry cancelled]**

8285 **[See no. 2105–1]**

8286 **Kennedy, W. S.**
The quirks of cricket. 1971

8287 **Liddelow, Harold**
Cricket wisdoms; illustrated by C. Crampton. [c. 1950]. 32p. illus.

8287 **May Place** cricket seasons. Malvern,
–1 Malvern Advertiser, 1893. 42p.

8288 **Morris, C. A.**
Cricket isn't everything. 1970

8289 **The Moss Rose Cricket Club**
The Moss Rose annual: the official organ of the Moss Rose Cricket Club. The Club.
*No. 1. 1895*
*no more published*

8290 **Nichols, George Benjamin**
Moonlighter's cricket guide. 1897

8291 **Pabander, H.H.**, *and others*
Cricket 1948

8292 **[Entry cancelled]**

8293 **St. John's Cricket Club**
Rules and regulations. Simpkin, 1849. 18p.
*in Taylor*

8294 **Wallis**
Instructions to cricketers, both for double and single wicket

# INDEX

Amicus Illustrated Weekly. The M.C.C. cricketers in Colombo (1911)  4875
Special cricket number 21st Mar., 1912  4876
Amiruddin Ahmed. 2nd unofficial Test match M.C.C. v. Pakistan (1956)  4854
Amis, Kingsley. The new Oxford book of light verse  6384–5
Take a girl like you  5958–1
Amiss, Dennis. In search of runs  7285–1
*Amiss (Dennis) benefit year 1975.* I. Dowell  7285–2
*Among the apple orchards.* C.W. Scott  6767
*Amper krieketkampioene.* W. Barnard  5371
Amphlett, Edgar Montague. How to bat  685
*The Ampol book of Australian sporting records*  3355–1
*The Ampol book of Australiana*  3327–3
*Ampol book of sporting records*  3355–1
Amrita Bazaar Patrika. Vinoo Mankad souvenir  7849
Amsterdamsche C.C. Jubileumboek 1921–1946  4220
*Amsterdamsche C.C. 1921—5 maart 1961*  4221
*Anand ban*  5284
*Ananda-Nalanda cricket encounter*  4008–3
Anandji Dossa. *see* Dossa, Anandji
*Anatomy of laughter.* A.A. Thomson  6915
*Ancient customs, sports and pastimes for the English.* J. Aspin  7112
*"An ancient holiday."* E.C. Blunden  5884
*An ancient Kentish industry*  364
*The ancient ways.* W. Tuckwell  1577
*And that reminds me.* S.W. Coxon  7460
*—And then came Larwood.* A.A. Mailey  4481
Anderson, C.A.O. Jack. Jamaica v. Trinidad June–July 1946  3702
Anderson, George. Diary of a cricket tour to Australia in 1863–4  4404
Anderson, Joe. The North of Scotland cricketer's companion  3201
The Scottish cricket annual  3205
Anderson, R.A. History of Gala C.C. 1853–1939  3297
Anderson, Robert. Heard in the slips  6826
Anderson, Walter Patterson. Cricket in the Palmerston North Boys' High School  3759–1
Anderson, William. Selkirk C.C.. . .1872–1922  3298
Selkirk C.C. centenary  3299
Andhra Pradesh Sports Council. Sports journal  3897
Andover C.C. Rules  1982–1
Statement of accounts for the year  1982–2
Andrew, Edwyn Silverlock. Scores. . .between Rugby & Marlborough  1497, 1518
Andrew, Keith, & others. Cricket  554–1
Andrew, Philip. "Spiers and Pond"  5684
*Andrew Lees and the lion.* N. Hillas  6113
*Andrews, Charles Freer.* B. Chaturvedi & M. Sykes  7285–3
Andrews, Eamonn, *and* Mackay, Angus. Sports report  953
*Andrews (Frederick) of Ackworth.* I.H. Wallis  7286
Andrews, John. Bodyline Bill the bowler  6136
Andrews, William Harry Russell. Arthur Wellard testimonial 1951  8217
The hand that bowled Bradman  7287
Andrews, Sir William Linton. Yorkshire folk  7167
Anerley, John. Pilots of the Sixth  6367–3
*"Angelo, Master Michael,"* pseud. *see* Johnson, Richard
*An angler's rambles.* E. Jesse  2592
*Angliae notitia.* E. Chamberlayne  856
*Anglo-Australian cricket, 1862–1926.* P.C. Standing  4389
Anglo-Brazilian Chronicle. Cricket: Brazil v. the Argentine 1922  5754
Angus, J. Keith. The sportsman's year book for 1880  1032
Ankin, Chris. West Indies tour of Australia 1968–69  5484

—, *and* Oakley, Julian. M.C.C. team tour of Australia, 1970–71  4609
*Anleitung für des Lawn Tennis, Cricket, usw.* [–] Von Rauch  478
*Annals of an Eton House.* E. Gambier-Parry  1418
*Annals of Brechin cricket 1849–1927.* A. O'Neil  3236
*Annals of Brisbane Grammar School.* S. Stephenson  3407
*Annals of cricket.* W.W. Read  911, 7987
*Annals of Lord's and history of the M.C.C.* A.D. Taylor  1020, 1239
*Annals of my early life.* C. Wordsworth  8252
*Annals of my life.* C. Wordsworth  8253
*Annals of Rochdale.* R.D. Mattley  2245–2
*Annals of Sandhurst.* A.F. Mockler-Ferryman  1694
*Annals of Shrewsbury School.* G.W. Fisher  1536
*The annals of sporting and fancy gazette*  1179, 3093
*Annals of the Corinthian Football Club.* B.O. Corbett  1301–1
*Annals of the Free Foresters.* W.K.R. Bedford  1261
*Annals of the King's College. . .Eton.* Sir W. Sterry  1433
*Annals of the Teignbridge C.C., 1823–1883.* G.W. Ormerod  1864
*Annals of Westminster School.* J. Sargeaunt  1558
*The annals of Yorkshire.* J. Mayhall  2869
Annamunthodo, W. Cricket series 1973: Australia v. West Indies  5241–1
Australia v. West Indies 5th Test  5242
Cricket series 1974: M.C.C. tour of W.I.  4734–1
First tour of the West Indies by N.Z. 1972  5560
*Anne's terrible good nature.* E.V. Lucas  6379
*Annual record of Lancashire cricket.* T. Axon  2255
*Annual register of Nottingham county cricket matches.* F.G. Spybey  2524
*Annual six-a-side inter club cricket tournament. . .BRC Trophy*  3993
*"Anon, James",* pseud. *see* Barrie, Sir James Matthew
*Another look at the Leg Before Wicket law.* L.W.K. Martin  239–1
*"Another 'Young cricketers' tutor'".* E.V. Lucas  6717
Ansari, Khalid. Sportsweek cricket quarterly  3870–3
Sportsweek's world of cricket  3870–3
Ansett Airlines of Australia. World Series Cricket tour: itinerary 1977–78  5828–19
Answers. Special cricket number, 8th July, 1899  4987
*Anthology of sporting verse.* E.B. Osborn  6393
Anthony, Edwyn. Herefordshire cricket  2036
Anthony, George. A complete guide to cricket  8280
Anthony, Michael. Cricket in the road  6096
*Anti-bodyline.* A.F. Kippax & E.P. Barbour  4478
Antia, Jamshed Dinshaw. Elphinstone College tours  3878
*Anyone for cricket?* B. Taylor & D. Gower  4615–55
*Apartheid.* South Africa Freedom Campaign  5398–2
*Appartement in Brussels.* A.D. Mickle  6733
*The appeal.* Bristol and District Cricket Umpires Assoc.  254–1
*The appeal.* Essex C.C.C.  1928
*The apple tree.* W. Kerr  6480
Apps, Howard Llewellyn. The making of Jerry Dickson  6137
Apsley Park C.C. Scores 1886–93  1937
Apted, S. "How to prepare a wicket"  7154
*Aquatic cricket.* W.A. Ross  3802
*"Arbi",* pseud. *see* Bhattacharya, R.
Arbroath United C.C. Grand bazaar (1889)  3233
Arbuthnot, John. Lewis Baboon turned honest  858, 6827
*Archaeologia Cantiana.* Kent Archaeological Soc.  842, 2068
Archdale, Betty. Indiscretions of a headmistress  7287–1

Otago v. Auckland (1971) 3769
Pakistan v. New Zealand 2nd Test (1965) 5698
Ron Roberts' Commonwealth XI v. N.Z. C.C.
President's XI (1962) 5802
Rothmans National Under 23 Tournament
(1971) 3761
Rothmans N.Z. Under 23 team v. Auckland
(1971) 3770
Rothmans tour. Australia v. N.Z. 2nd Test
(1977) 5270–7
Rothmans tour. International cricket: England v.
Auckland. . .1978 4779–4
Sir Julien Cahn's team v. Auckland (1939) 4750
Test cricket: England v. New Zealand (1971) 4777
Test cricket: England v. New Zealand
(1975) 4779–1
Test cricket: India v. New Zealand 1st Test
(1976) 5650
Test cricket: Pakistan v. New Zealand (1973) 5702
Wellington v. Auckland (1970) 3767
West Indies v. New Zealand, 1st Test (1969) 5494
*Auction of cricketana.* Northern Cricket Society 45–3
*Audley End cricket book* 1315
*August occasions.* N. Craven 1960–5
*Augustus Austen-Leigh.* W. Austen-Leigh 7292
*Auld-Lang-Syne.* H.B. Neilson 1797–1
*Aumonier, Stacy. Miss Bracegirdle, and others* 6097
Ups and downs 6098
*Aussies and Ashes.* W.E. Bowes 5163
*Aussies in India, 1969.* C.K. Haridass 5303
*Aussies in India 1979.* C.K. Haridass 5308–3
*Austen-Leigh (Augustus).* W. Austen-Leigh 7292
Austen-Leigh, Richard Arthur. Eton records 1407–1
Eton v. Winchester 1826–1902 (–04) 1455
Austen-Leigh, William. Augustus Austen-
Leigh 7292
*Australia* 5080, 5108, 5134
*Australia 1788–1938.* O. Ziegler 3353
*Australia 1949* 5080–1
*Australia 1949, 1950: the Courier-Mail year book* 3356–1
*Australia 55.* A. Ross 4548
*Australia '63.* A. Ross 4581
*Australia (1972)* 5192
*Australia and Far East tour 1973.* Midlands Club Cricket
Conference 1722
*Australia and South Africa tour (1912)* 5009, 5347
*Australia as once we were.* J.D. Ritchie 3348–1
*Australia coronation England tour 1953* 5109
*Australia XI v. India XI (Bombay, 1959)* 5285
Australia House (London) C.C. Los Angeles tour
1978 2328–1
*Australia in England 1975.* Cricketer 5196–5
*Australia in the West Indies 1965.* L.J. Henderson 5238
*Australia in the West Indies 1973.* E. Beecher 5246
*Australia—India 2nd Test (1969)* 5298
*Australia—India Test series 1969.* Cricket Club of
India 5302
*Australia, its cricket bat. . .Sir D.M. Serjeant* 3350
"Australia retain Ashes". D. Rowbotham 4576–1
*Australia souvenir tour programme (1956)* 5135
*Australia souvenir tour programme (1961)* 5161
*Australia souvenir tour programme (1964)* 5174
*Australia Test tour of England 1956 number* 5134
*Australia tour of the West Indies 1965.* L. Williams 5241
*Australia tour programme (1968)* 5185
*Australia tour programme (1972)* 5193
*Australia under 19 tour of Sri Lanka.* Bd. of Control for
Cricket in Sri Lanka 5321–1
*Australia v. South African XI (1949).* Rhodesia
C.U. 5204
*Australia v. All-India Tests 1947–48.* Queensland
C.A. 5632–1
*Australia v. Auckland (1960).* Auckland C.A. 5262

*Australia v. Canterbury (1921)* 5256–2
*Australia v. Canterbury (1974).* Canterbury
C.A. 5270–2
*Australia v. Central Districts (1974).* Central Districts
C.A. 5270–4
*Australia v. Cumberland Sept. 1921* 5022
*Australia v. England 1877–1926.* Manchester
Guardian 4374
*Australia v. England (1920)*
*Australia v. England 1920–21.* Victorian C.A. 4448
*Australia v. England 1928–29, 3rd Test Melbourne* 4455
*Australia v. England, 5th Test (1929)* 4463–1
*Australia v. England Test series (1958–59).* Queensland
C.A.
*Australia v. England, 4th Test 1959.* S. Australian
C.A. 4563–1
*Australia v. England, 1st Test (1962–3)* 4584–1
*Australia v. England, 1st Test 1970* 4605
*Australia v. England, 1st Test (1974–75).* Queensland
C.A. 4615–12
*Australia v. England, 2nd Test (1974–75).* Western
Australian C.A. 4615–20
*Australia v. England, 5th Test (1974–75).* South
Australian C.A. 4615–13
*Australia v. England, 6th Test (1974–75).* Victorian
C.A. 4615–19
*Australia v. England (1977).* Victorian C.A. 4615–34
*Australia v. England (1978–79).* Australian Cricket
Bd. 4615–38
*Australia v. England: the 10. . .matches of 1975.* J.
Buchanan 4615–4, 5196–3
*Australia v. India 1959–60.* R.N. Desai 5287
*Australia v. India 1964.* D.R. Bhupathy 5294
*Australia v. India 3rd Test (1968).* Queensland
C.A. 5637–1
*Australia v. India 1969.* D.R. Bhupathy 5299
*Australia v. India 1969–70.* S. Saraiya 5307
*Australia v. India, 2nd Test match (1969)* 5298
*Australia v. New Zealand at Carisbrook (1960).* Otago
C.A. 5264
*Australia v. New Zealand, 1st Test 1960.* Wellington
C.A. 5265
*Australia v. New Zealand, 2nd Test 1960.* Canterbury
C.A. 5263
*Australia v. New Zealand, 1st Test. (Mar. 1967).* Taranaki
C.A. 5267
*Australia v. New Zealand, 4th Test (1967).* Auckland
C.A. 5265–1
*Australia v. New Zealand (1970).* Auckland C.A. 5268
*Australia v. New Zealand 1970.* Wellington C.A. 5270
*Australia v. New Zealand, 2nd Test (1974).* Canterbury
C.A. 5270–3
*Australia v. New Zealand, 2nd Test (1977).* Auckland
C.A. 5270–7
*Australia v. Northern Districts (1967).* Northern Districts
C.A. 5266
*Australia v. Northern Districts (1974).* Northern Districts
C.A. 5270–5
*Australia v. Otago 1970.* Otago C.A. 5269
*Australia v. Pakistan, First Test (1959).* East Pakistan
Sports Federation 5312
*Australia v. Pakistan (1979).* Australian Cricket
Bd. 5694–7
*Australia v. Rhodesia (1957).* Matabeleland C.A. 5215
*Australia v. South Africa, 1949–1950.* Caltex Map
Service 5202–2
*Australia v. S. Africa, 1st Test 1963–64.* Queensland
C.A. 5398–1
*Australia v. South Africa 1966/67.* S.A. cricket tour 5217
*Australia v. Tasmania (1926).* Tasmania C.A. 5332
*Australia v. the counties (1878–1938).* R. Pogson 4963
*Australia v. The Rest of the World (1971).* Queensland
C.A. 5827

Barlow, Richard Gorton. Batting and bowling 402
Forty seasons of first-class cricket 7298
*Barlow scores.* J. Sweet 6349–1
Barman, S.L. Cricket digdarshan 5277
Barn, H. The Berea Rovers story 3651
Barnaby, Jane. Australians in sport 7139–2, 7351–2
*Barnaby Rudge.* C. Dickens 5990
Barnard, Alfred. The Schoolfellows 6155
Barnard, Caroline. The parent's offering 6375
Barnard, S.P. Havant C.C. centenary
1874–1974 2009–1
Barnard, Werner. Amper krieketkampioene 5371
*Barnato tournament (1959–60).* S. African Coloured
Cricket Board 3625
Barnby, Joseph, *composer.* Eton songs 6564
Barnby Dun C.C. Centenary brochure
1870–1970 2893
Barnes, Ronald Gorell, *3rd baron Gorell.* One
man. . .many parts 7299
Warriors' way 5964
*Barnes (S.F.)—master bowler.* L. Duckworth 7301
Barnes, Sidney George. The Ashes ablaze 4534
Eyes on the Ashes 5113
It isn't cricket 7300
*Barnes (Sydney).* W.S. White 7302
Barnes, William. Poems of rural life in the Dorset
dialect 6408
*Barnes (William)* 7303
*Barnes (William) 1801–1886.* T.W. Hearl 7302–1
*Barnes C.C., 1919–1969.* E.G. Turner 2614
"Barnett, John," *pseud. See* Stagg, John Reynold
*Barnett (Charles J.) benefit souvenir* 7304
Barnett, T.M. Peter Wight benefit year 1963 8228
*Barnsley and district cricket guide* 3014
Barnsley & District C.L. Rules and official
handbook 2894
*"Barnsley Cricket Club."* D. Davie 6447–1, 6447–2
Barnt Green C.C. Jubilee year 1889–1939 2844–1
Barnwell, Patrick Joseph. A century of cricket in
Mauritius 4330
*The barracker at bay.* R.T. Corrie 4472
Barradell-Smith, Walter. Dawson's score 6376
The liveliest term at Templeton 6155–1
The third jump, etc. 6375–1
Barratt, A.H. "Oh! those Ashes" 4469–1, 6409
Barrett, Charles Leslie. Pals annual for the boys of
Australasia 3373–1
Barrett, Charles Raymond Booth. Surrey: highways,
byways & waterways 2620–1
*Barrett ("Ted"), the veteran Surrey cricketer, A good sort:*
A. Craig 6444
Barrett-Lennard, *Sir* Thomas. An account of the
families of Lennard & Barrett 851–1
Barrie, *Sir* James Matthew. The Allahakbarrie book of
Broadway cricket 1296
Allahakbarries C.C. 1295
Cricket . . . being a speech . . . 6789
The greenwood hat 1292
J.M. Barrie's Allahakbarries C.C. 1899 1296
The little white bird 5965
M'Connachie and J.M.B. 6790
*Barrie. Sir* J.A. Hammerton 7309–2
*Barrie.* T. Moult 7310
*Barrie, Portrait of. Lady* C. Asquith 7305
*Barrie (J.M.)* W.A.C. Darlington 7307
*Barrie (J.M.)* F.J.H. Darton 7308
*Barrie (J.M.)* J. Dunbar 7309
*B[arrie] (J.M.), The story of.* D. Mackail 1299, 7309–3
*The Barrie inspiration.* P. Chalmers 7306
*Barrier book of rules: cricket* 7313
Barrington, Ken. Playing it straight 7312
Running into hundreds 7311
*Barrington (Ken) benefit 1964* 7313

Barron, Arthur Oswald. Day in and day out 6648,
7572
Barrow, Percy J. Cornered 6156
*Barry Richards on cricket.* B. Richards 606
*The Barry Richards story.* B. Richards 7997–2
Barsley, Michael Henry. The Phoenix book of wit and
humour 6814
Bartholomeusz, P.L. Ceylon sports annual 3987
Ceylon's champion bowler . . . Tommy
Kelaart 7772
Handbook to Ceylon cricket (1901–6) 3988
Bartlett, Vernon. The past of pastimes 826
Bartley, L.J. The story of Bexhill 2721
Bartley, Nehemiah. Australian pioneers and
reminiscences 3505–1
Opals and agates 4407–2, 4407–3
Barty-King, Hugh. Quilt winders and pod
shavers 345–1, 364–2
Sussex in 1839 2763–1
Bas, Malcolm le. *See* le Bas, Malcolm
*Baseless biography.* E.C. Bentley 6836, 7574
*Basher testimonial year book 1978.* F. Smith 7654–1
Bashford, *Mrs.* All about Lyss 2012
Bashir, S.M. The forgotten factor 753
Bashir Ahmad. Compendium of Pakistan Test cricket,
1947–1967 5663
Cricket annual 3959
Bashir-Ul-Haq, *and* Bhatti, Mukhtar. Pakistan in Test
cricket 5662
*Basic cricket for South African schools.* N. & H.
Gordon 655–1
*Basingstoke & North Hants C.C. Annual
report 1982–3*
*Basingstoke and North Hants C.C. 1865–1965.* B.R.S.
Harrison & P.M. Bichard 1984
*Basingstoke C.C., 1877* 1983
Bass, Howard. The sense in sport 7067
Bass Charrington Ltd. Bass Charrington cricket trophy
(1969) 3092
Bassano, Brian. S.A. cricket 3618–2
South Africa in international cricket
1888–1970 5341–1
Bassetlaw & District C.L. Official handbook 2480
Rules, fixtures, etc. 2480
*Bassetlaw C.L., A history of the.* G.R.
Langdale 2480–1
Basu, Ajay. Akāśe kriket bani 773
Basu, Sānkarīprasād. Bal pade byāt nade 8281–1
Kriket sundar kriket 3806
Nat āut 8281–2
Basu, Sanu. 'Sports guide' annual cricket number
(1956) 3863, 5283
"Bat," *pseud. See* Box, Charles
*Bat and ball* 1181
*Bat and ball.* T. Moult 5855
*Bat and ball memories.* E.H. Chapman 2103
*Bat, ball and wheel* 1182
*Bat, ball and Cowdrey.* H.N. Davey 2136, 7458, 7476
*Bat, ball, wicket and all.* G.D. Martineau 333
*The bat of the Victorian era.* G.G. Bussey 350
*Bat v. ball.* G.R.K. Betham 560
*Bat v. ball.* J.H. Lester 118
Batchelder, W.J. A born school captain 6157
Batchelor, Denzil Stanley. Babbled of green
fields 7314
Best cricket stories 6085
The book of cricket 7171
"A bottle or so with Arthur" 7842
C.B. Fry 7535
Days without sunset 5086, 6650
The game goes on 4490, 6649
Game of a lifetime 6651
Great cricketers 7172

## —C—

Chetty, Mervyn Casie, *and others*. A history of a hundred years of the Royal-S. Thomas' cricket match  4010–3

Cheyne. George. An essay of health and long life  863–2

Chicago C.C. Handbook  4066

Chichester, Charles J. Tour '71 from Bombay to Bourda  5642–1

Tour '72 from Wellington to Georgetown  5561

Tour '73 from Brisbane to Bourda  5250

Chignell, Wilfred Rowland. A history of the Worcestershire C.C.C.  2848

Worcestershire cricket, 1950–1968  2849

*Chigwell School*. A history of. G. Stott  1392

*Children of the village*. M.R. Mitford  5907

*Children's games throughout the year*. L.H. Daiken  7145

*Chilean cricket team*, Programme . . . Argentine C.A.  4260, 5763

*Chinghoppers C.C. 1932–53*  1301

Chipp, Herbert. Lawn tennis recollections  7417

Chipp, Maurice. History of the Shepperton C.C.  2394

*Chipping Sodbury C.C., 1960–1960*. P. Guy & J. King  1944

Chisholm, Alexander Hugh. The incredible year  938–1

Chitnis, Shankar Lakshmi. Don Bradman  7355

*"The chitty goes to cricket,"* J. Marshall  6624

*Choice of careers 120: professional sport*. Central Youth Employment Executive  7070

*A choice of chums*. H. Avery  6150

Chorley & District Amateur C.L. Rules and fixtures  2193

*Chosen words*. I. Brown  49

Chris Coley's sportsquiz book. C. Coley  138–1

Christchurch Cinemas C.C. "The valley of peace"  3776

Christesen, Clement Byrne. On native grounds  5838–1

Christian, Edmund Brown Viney. At the sign of the wicket  6672

"Dreams that I dream"  6386–3

The epic of the Oval  1022, 2677

The light side of cricket  5839

Christian Victor. Sir. T.H. Warren  7418

Christie, Octavius Francis. Clifton School days  1393

A history of Clifton College, 1860–1934  1394

Christie, Robert H. Carlton C.C. retrospect  1904, 3273

Christie's. Sale of pictures . . . Sir Jeremiah Colman (1942)  6967–4

*Christopher, Canon, of St. Aldgate's, Oxford*. J.S. Reynolds  7419

*A chronicle of cricket amongst Parsees*. S. Sorabjee  3877

*Chronicles of a country cricket club*. A.E. Bayly & W. A. Briscoe  2502, 6833

*Chronicles of cricket*  873

*Chronicles of cricket in Argentina*. J. McGough  4249

*The chronicles of Durnford*. J. Cartwright  6182

*The chronicles of the Garniers of Hampshire*. A.E. Garnier  7546

*The chronicles of the United Though Untied F.F.* W.K.R. Bedford  1260

*"Chrystal's century."* E.W. Hornung  6115

Chubb. Charles Frederick. Fugitive pieces; prologues, etc.  3516

*Chubb Double Wicket Championship (1979)*  3092–1

*Chucked around*. C. Griffith  7622

Chums. The best of Chums  1182–2

*Chums all through*. A.J. Daniels  6199–2

*Chums at last*. Mrs. G.F. Grant  6227

Church, Alfred John. Memories of men and books  7419–1

Church, Richard Thomas. Kent  351

A portrait of Canterbury  2085

The spoken word  6798

Church, Roy A. Economic and social change in a Midland town  2482

*"The church at the wicket,"* Sir J.E. Shuckburgh  6773

Church Lads Brigade Preston C.C. Report and full score of every match, 1904  2238

*Churchill centenary songs*. Harrow School  1474–1, 6573–1

Churchward, William Brown. My consulate in Samoa  4327–4

Cillié, Christoffel, *and* Jordan, J.H. Krieketterme  50–1

*Cirencester*, History of. K.J. Beecham  1944–1

*Cities and men*. Sir H.C. Luke  4190

Citizen's Cricket Committee. Statement (1912)  5014

City & Suburban C.A. Annual report  3492

*City Charltonian Club*. An address and songs . . . C. Jolly  6473

Civil Service C.C. Rules and list of members . . . (1865)  1322

Clackmannan C.C.C. Centenary 1868–1968  3243

Official handbook  3242

Clair, Colin A. Kentish garner  2135

Clark, Douglas. The Libertines  5931–1

Clark, Norman. All in the game  7420

"Getting the best out of cricket"  1133–2

Clark. T. Theodore Hannam. See Hannam-Clark, Theodore

Clark, Tony, *and* Fletcher, Graham. 75 not out . . . Civil Service cricket in Hong Kong  4302–2

Clark, William Mark. The cricketer's handbook  378, 806

Clarke, Alfred E. East Melbourne C.C.  3562

Clarke, Basil. Cricket at preparatory schools  497

*Clark, (The Bob) testimonial book*  7422

Clarke, Charles Cowden, *and* Clarke, Mary Victoria Cowden. "Many happy returns of the day!"  7121

Clarke, Charlie C. "Cricket"  926

Clarke, Dennis, *and* Stoyel, Anthony. Otford in Kent  2109–2

Clarke, James. History of cricket in Kendal  2831

Clarke, John. The Australians in England 1964  5177

Challenge renewed  4573

Cricket with a swing  5432

With England in Australia (1965–66)  4592

—, *and* Scovell, Brian. Everything that's cricket  5445

Clarke, Mary Cowden. My long life  7421, 7910

Clarke, P.D. Cricket from the inside  65–1

Clarke, Stephen. Clitheroe in its railway days  2193–1

Clarke, William. Little boy's own book of sports and pastimes  7122

*Clark's companion to cricket*  374–1

*Clark's cricketer's handbook*. Member of the Marylebone Cricket Club  378, 806

*Classic centuries in the Test matches between England and Australia*. B.J. Wakley  719, 4395

*"Clava Recta", pseud. See* Rice, Tim

Claxton, William J. Journeys in industrial England  351–1

*"Clay (J.C.), The works of."* J. Arlott  6609, 6644

Clayhall C.C. 50 N.O. 1919–69  1906

Clayton, William. Tales & recollections of the Southern coast  6103

*Clean bandage*. J. Dowling  5933–2

Cleaver, Hylton. Brother o'mine  6185–1

Captain for a day  6186–2

Captains of Dukes  6186–3

Caught in the slips  6191

Dawnay leaves school  6187

"A fool at the wicket"  6377–2

The forbidden study  6190

Coppin, O.S. "The Advocate's" pictorial souvenir of . . . the M.C.C. to West Indies, 1953–1954  4698–1

*The coral lands.* H.S. Cooper  4324–6

Corbett, Bertie Oswald. Annals of the Corinthian Football Club  1301–1

Corbishley, George J. Clifton C.C. 1867–1967  1830

Cordingley, David. Forty-four years of Ashton cricket, 1857–1900  2182

*Cordle (Tony) benefit year 1977*  7452–1

*Corfu,* Tour to. Cricket Society  3149, 4187, 4931

*Corfu: Venus of the isles.* J. Forte  4189

*Corinthians and cricketers.* E. Grayson  8057

Cork County C.C. centenary 1874–1974. J. Clusky  3316–2

*The corner cupboard*  7123

*The corner stone of English cricket.* Hon. E.G.F. French  1218

*Cornered.* P.J. Barrow  6156

Cornhill Insurance. Tour digest . . . England's Test cricketers in Australia 1978/1979  4615–44

*Cornhill Insurance Test series 1978.* C. White  5548–2, 5688–5

*Cornhill Test special England v. India 1979*  5628–2

*The Cornish Choughs C.C. 1906–1976.* J.E. Prothero  1248–1

*The "Cornstalks."* A.A. Jasdenvala  3340

Cornwall C.A. Journal  1810–1

Cornwall C.C.C. Annual report  1816

Gillette Cup Competition 1970 (v. Glamorgan)  1817, 3082, 3174

"Cornwall C.C.C. Brief history of." S.C. Caple  1817, 1817–1

Cornwall C.L. Handbook  1811

Cornwall C.L. & Assoc. Handbook  1811

*Cornwall v. Lancashire, Gillette Cup 1977*  1817–1

*Coronation cricket book: English tour 1953.* Australian Broadcasting Commission  5110

*The corpse with the sunburnt face.* C. St. J. Sprigg  6061–6

*Corrall's (Paddy) benefit.* Leicestershire C.C.C.  7453–1

*A correct account of . . . cricket matches . . . played by the Mary-le-bone Club. . . .1786 to 1822.* H. Bentley  1221

*A correct account of . . . matches played by the Nottingham Old C.C. 1771–1829.* W. North  2492

*A correct account of . . . matches played by the Ripon C.C. 1813–36.* G. Gatenby  2980

*Correspondence between . . . and Mr. Perkins.* Sussex C.C.C.  2775–1

Corrie, R.T. The barracker at bay  4472

Cosmic Recreation Club. Third anniversary celebrations 1967  3938–1

*The cost of sport.* F.G. Aflalo  919

Cotes, Peter. George Robey "the darling of the halls"  8008

Cotgrave, Randle. A dictionarie of the French and English tongues  843

*Cotswold countryman.* J.A. Gibbs  5895

*Cotswold days.* C. Howard  1934–1, 7640–1

*A Cotswold village.* J.A. Gibbs  5895

Cotterell & Co. Sale lists A special collection of cricket books (1931)  9

Cotton, Reynell. Cricket  1990, 6390, 6560, 6561

*Cotton (The Reynell) memorial match (1959)*  2002, 2759, 6561, 7454

The Council of Cricket Societies. Constitution  3135

*The counties 1947.* Cricket Book Society  968

*Country beat.* L. Quinain  5916

Country Carnival C.A. Souvenir Carnival programme (1954, 1957)  3520

*Country crafts and craftsmen.* G. Hogg  357

*"A country cricket match,"* M.R. Mitford  5872–1, 5906, 5920

"A Country Curate," *pseud. See* Neale, Erskine

*Country matters.* C. Leighton  6705

*Country talk.* R.C. Robertson-Glasgow  6756–1

"Country Vicar," *pseud. See* Hodgson, Randolph Llewelyn

*The countryman's England.* J.C. Moore  5908

*County cricket 1873–1973.* J. Arlott  1732

*County cricket: a new and rational method. . . .* A Shrewsbury  1748

*County cricket championship.* A. Gibson  904, 1741

*The county cricket championship.* R. Webber  1755

*County cricket championship 1873–1896.* R.S. Holmes  907, 1742

*County cricket competion for the Gillette Cup.* Gillette Safety Razor Co.  3071

*County cricket festival souvenir* (Eastbourne)  2764

*County cricket in Essex*  1923, 7964

The County Cricketer's Golfing Society. Members' handbook  8268

Rules & list of members  8268

*County (first class) cricket diary*  1154

*The county of Surrey, with illustrated biographies*  7187

*The Courage book of Australian Test cricket 1877–1974.* R.S. Whitington  4960–4

*Courage Challenge Cup International Batsman of the Year 1979*  3092–2

*The Courier-Mail year book: Australia 1949, 1950*  3356–1

Courtney, Samuel. As centuries blend  3254

*The courtship of Uncle Henry.* D. Stivens  6127–1

Coutts' C.C. 1860–1960  1323

Couzens, Sidney A. Walthamstow Cricket & Lawn Tennis Club  1916

Coventry, Earl of. The cost of sport  919

Coventry, Lionel. 1946–7 Test cricketers in caricature  4512–2, 7030–1

"Cover Point," *pseud. See* Haydon, A.L.

"Cover Point," *pseud. See* Henderson, J.T.

"Cover Point," *pseud. See* Trowsdale, T. Broadbent

*Cover point* (Plumtree C.C.)  2494

*Cover point.* Weston Creek C.C.  3436–2

*Coverpoint's cricket annual.* T.B. Trowsdale  1122, 5874

Cowburn, Allen. Wykehamical scores  1565

*The Cowden Clarkes.* R.D. Altick  7909

Cowdrey, Michael Colin. Cricket today  964, 7455

The incomparable game  7457

M.C.C.  7457–1

Tackle cricket this way  568

Time for reflection  7456

Cowell, J.B. Bangor C.C.  1856–1956  3166

A history of the Bangor C.C. 1856–1964  3167

Cowles, Virginia. No cause for alarm  5888–1

*Cox (George) benefit book*  7459

Cox, Jack. Boy's own companion  1133–1

Cox, Jack. Don Davies "an old international"  7478

Coxhead, A.C. Cricket records  106

Coxon, Stanley William. And that reminds me  7460

Coxon, T.L., *and* Wilson, F.H. Tutbury C.C. 1872–1972  2584

*Cox's (G.R.) benefit match (1920).* A.J. Gaston  7459–2

*Cox's (George) benefit match . . . 1914*  7459–1

*"Cox's century".* W.E. Cule  6378–3

Cozens-Hardy, Basil. The history of Letheringsett  2436–2

Cozens-Hardy, Harry Theobold. The glorious years  7461

Cozier, E.L., *and* Coppin, O.S. A pictorial souvenir. . . of M.C.C. to West Indies, 1948  4695

Cozier, Tony. The Australians in Barbados, 1973  5248

Caribbean cricket  3679–1

Caribbean cricket '73  5249

—D—

Durham Senior C.L. (Eastern Division).
Fixtures 1876
Handbook 1877
Instructions to umpire 1878
*Durham University.* J.T. Fowler 1632
*Durham v. New Zealand (1949)* 1891–1, 5531–1
Durnford, *Sir* Walter. Memoir of Colonel the Right
Hon. William Kenyon-Slaney. M.P. 7775
Durrell, Lawrence George. Prospero's cell 4188
Duthie, Eric Edmonston. Father's bedside
book 5845–1
Duthoit, W. Yorkshire cricketers' guide for 1878 2866
*Duties, trials and troubles of a county cricket umpire.* A.
Skelding 278
Dutt, K. Iswara, *and* Ratnam, K.V. Gopala. Century
of Tests 5586
Vizzy commemoration souvenir 8178
Dutt, P.D. Commonwealth at the Eden Gardens
(1950) 5792
Dutton, E.W.P. Bushey C.C. centenary,
1864–1964 2042
Dutton, Harry. Poems and acrostics of
Gloucestershire cricket. . . 1961 6451
"Dux", *pseud. See* Trevor, P.
"Dwarpa", *pseud.* Cricket as allied to the
heavens 8271
Dyer, Thomas Firminger Thiselton. Great men at
play 7202
Dykes, T. All round sport with fish, fur &
feather 6850
*Dynamic cricket.* C. Bland 562
Dyson, Arthur Henry. Lutterworth 2305

—E—

E.G.M. *see* M., E.G.
"E.O.", *pseud. See* "Old Etonian," *pseud.*
Eagar, Desmond. Hampshire C.C.C. illustrated
handbook 2027
Readers' guide to Hampshire cricket 17, 1973
*Eagar (Desmond).* J. Arlott 7506
Eagar, Patrick, *and* Arlott, John. An eye for
cricket 6973–1
"*Eagle*" *book of sport.* K. Wheeler 7161
*Eaglets cricket tour of England 1963.* Pakistan
International Airways 3957, 5680
The Ealing C.C. Rules 2353
*Ealing C.C. 1970: centenary booklet* 2354
Ealing Dean C.C. Compton handbook 2355, 7441
*Ealing Dean C.C. 1846–1946.* B. Harris 2356
Eames, Geoffrey L. Bromley C.C. 1820–1970 2081
Eardley, D., *and* Perera, I. Bristol book of cricket 3981
Eardley-Wilmot, Edward Parry, *and* Streatfield,
Edmund Champion. Charterhouse old and
new 1381
Eardley-Wilmot, *Sir* John, *2nd bart.* Reminiscences of
the late T. Assheton Smith 8063
*Earlswood C.C. Centenary 1876–1976* 2811–1
*Early Birds C.C., A brief history of.* G.K. Reid 1255
*Early club & village cricket.* J. Goulstone 1705, 1725
*Early cricket.* P.F. Thomas 837
*Early cricket in Ireland.* A. Samuels 3308
*Early cricket in the Brisbane and Darling Downs Districts.*
P.J. Mullins & T. Ogden 3515–7
*Early days at Uppingham under Edward Thring.* "An Old
boy," *pseud.* 1548
*The early diary. . .1768–1778.* F. Burney 871, 6930
*"The early history of cricket".* S.M. Toyne 837–1
*Early Kent cricketers.* J. Goulstone 2065
*Early memoirs.* F. Woolley 8251–1
*"Early Northamptonshire cricket."* J.D. Coldham 2449
*"Early references to Dartford cricket".* J.
Goulstone 2097–1

*Early Victorian England.* G.M. Young 918–1
*The early years of Alec Waugh.* A. Waugh 8214
East, Harry. The heart of Yorkshire cricket 2867,
5933–3
East, Laurence. Australian cricketers 1926 5037, 6974
Autographed sketches of the 1930
Australians 5049, 6975
*East (Ray) benefit year 1978* 7506–2
East African C.A. The East Africans 4264
East African Cricket Conference. Articles of
constitution 4265
*The East African Cricket Conference Combined XI Zambia
tour.* Zambia C.U. 4267
*The East Africans.* K. Lillis 4266–1, 5828–5
*East and West and back again.* C.I. Thornton 8136
*East Bourne memories of the Victorian period.* G.F.
Chambers 2731
East Canberra District. C.C. Annual report 3435
*East Grinstead,* The history of. W.H. Hills 2729–4
East Lancashire C.C. Centenary souvenir
1864–1964 2186
History and reminiscences 2185
*East Lancs. C.C., History & reminiscences of* 2185
East Melbourne C.C. Annual report 3563
*East Melbourne C.C.* A.E. Clarke 3562
East Molesey C.C. East Molesey C.C. v. M.J. Stewart's
XI 2631
East Molesey v. The Australians 2630, 5120
*East of Itchen.* G.L. Wheeler 2005
East of Scotland C.A. East of Scotland C.L.: fixtures
handbook 3190
East Pakistan Referees' & Umpires' Assn. 2nd
unofficial Test, M.C.C. v. Pakistan (1956) 4854
East Pakistan Sports Federation. Ceylon v. Pakistan,
2nd Test (1966) 5731–7
First Test, Australia v. Pakistan (1959) 5312
M.C.C. v. Pakistan (1962) 4859
*East Preston C.C.,* History of. C.R.H. Hurle-
Hobbs 2730
East Riding Amateur C.L. Official handbook 2914
East Suburban Churches C.A. Constitution and
rules. . .1975 3564–1
Fixture book 3564–2
Eastbourne Cricket & Football Club. Reminiscences of
Eastbourne cricket 2732
Sport at the Saffrons 2733
Eastbourne C.C. Six-a-side tournament (1967,
1968) 2734
Eastbourne Saffrons C.C. Cricket at the
Saffrons 2735
Eastcote C.C. Annual report 2357
Eastern Goldfields C.A. M.C.C. v. Combined W.A.
Country XI (1962) 4575
Eastern Province Cricket Federation. Kenya Asian
tour of S. Africa 1956 4274, 5776
Eastern Province C.U. Handbook 3644
Eastern Suburbs District C.C. Annual report 3515–8
Eastwood, C.W. Edmonton C.C., 1872–1922 2358
Ebbisham, Rowland Blades, *1st baron.* Speeches made
at a dinner. . . 1307, 6794
Eberbach, Kurt von. Rasenspiele 7075
Eccles & District C.L. Handbook 2197
*Eccleshill C.C. record and history book 1860–1916.* J.W.
Overend 2915
*Echoes. Sir* C. Mackenzie 6800
*Echoes from old cricket fields.* F. Gale 809
*Echoes from the Oxford Magazine.* The Oxford
Magazine 5858
*Echoes of Stanton cricket.* H. Waller 1840
*The echoing green.* J. Arlott 6643
*The echoing strangers.* G. Mitchell 6035
*Economic and social change in a Midland town.* R.A.
Church 2482

Fay, Peter. Chris Old benefit year 1979  7915–2
'Illy': the Ray Illingworth testimonial
brochure  7747–1
Souvenir testimonial brochure Brian Close  7424–2
Fazal Mahmood. Fazal Mahmood and cricket  7524
Fear, Herbert. The West Kent Wanderers
C.C.  1313–1, 2126
Fearon, Ethelind. Most happy husbandman  5893
Fearon, William Andrewes. The passing of old
Winchester  2016–1
Featherstone, Donald F. Sports injuries  642
*Featherstone (Norman), Middlesex, testimonial 1979.* B.
Fowler  7524–1
*Feats, facts and figures.* F.S. Ashley-Cooper  920
Federal Capital Territory C.A. M.C.C. visit Canberra,
Feb. 1937  4492
Federasie Van Afrikaanse Kultuurvereninge. Engels-
Afrikaanse woordelys van Krieket  52
Krieketterme  50–1
La Federation Belge de Cricket. Annuaire  4182
Federation of Australian Cricket Umpires.
Over  257–2
*Federation of Malay v. Hong Kong (1948).* Selangor
C.A.  4296
"Felix" pseud. *see* Wanostrocht, Nicholas
*Felix (N.). Esq.: the history of a portrait.* G.N.
Weston  8193
*Felix on the bat.* G. Brodribb  688, 8192
*Felix on the bat.* N. Wanostrocht  397
*Fellow passenger.* G. Household  6011–1
Fellowes, Edmund Horace. A history of Winchester
cricket  1567
*Felstead School, A history of.* M. Craze  1458, 7494
Feltham, W. Feltham's cricket directory for 1883  1072
*Feltham's cricketer*  1073
Fender, Percy George Herbert. An ABC of
cricket  502, 7524–2
Defending the Ashes  4445
Kissing the rod  5060
The Tests of 1930  5050
The turn of the wheel  4456
Fenn, *Lady* Eleanor. Sketches of little boys and
girls  6378–4
Fenn, Eric Alfred Humphrey. Cricket for young
boys  503
*Fenner's.* P. Piggott  1628
Fenning, Daniel. Universal spelling book  6978
Fenton, J. Vinten. Games and sports by progressive
practice  7077
Fenton, S.J. Cricket fielding diagrams  755
Ferguson, John. Cricket at Bishop's Stortford College,
1868–1968  1371
Ferguson, W.H. Mr. Cricket  7525
Fernandes, C.W.L. The Crofton Wanderers' cricket
tours 1883–1893  1249
Ferryman, A.F. Mockler-. *see* Mockler-Ferryman, A.F.
*Festival cricket. Ceylon XI vs. An Indian XI (1932).* Delhi
C.A.  5727–5
*The Festival of Britain: exhibition of books.* National Book
League  32
*The festive season.* N. Craven  966–2, 1960–2
*The Fettesian-Lorettonian Club, 1881–1931*  3216,
3223
*The feud at Fennell's.* J. Mowbray  6295
*A few hints on cricket.* "An Etonian", pseud.  427–1
*A few hints on cricket.* R.A.H. Mitchell  455
*A few more memories.* M.A. de Navarro  1298
*A few overs.* D.L.A. Jephson  6472
*A few short runs.* Lord Harris  7650
*A few words to willow wielders.* A. Craig  689
Field, Charlotte. Freddie Trueman  6455–2
The (1963) Test  6455–3
The Field. One crowded hour  91, 5846

The Field (India). Souvenir of the M.C.C. visit to
Madras (1934)  4788
*The Field bedside book.* W. Stephens  5870–1
*The field book.* W.H. Maxwell  7052
*The field is full of shades.* G.D. Martineau  815, 7220
*The field of cricket*  3160
Fielden. R.G. Ingelse  756
*Het fielden.* H.C.A. van Booven  758–1
*Fielder (A).* A. Craig  7526
Fieldhouse, Harry. Huddersfield sportsmen of then
and now  2928–1, 7012–1
Fielding, Hugh. The ABC of cricket  6979
*Fielding.* M.J. Stewart  758
*Fielding Gray.* S. Raven  6048–1
*Fielding hints.* M.J. Procter  757–1
*The Fieldsman*  1314
*Fiery grains.* H.R.L. Sheppard & H.P. Marshall  5868
*Fifteen paces.* A.K. Davidson  7477
*Fifteen poems.* Sir F. Meynell  6499
*The fifth form detective.* R. Walker  6358–2
*The fifth form St. Dominic's.* T.B. Reed  6327
*5th Pakistan cricket team to England 1974.* K.
Butt  5688–2
*Fifth South African country districts festival 1958.* G.A.
Chettle  3630, 5208
*Fifty famous stories for boys.* L.R. Gribble  6370
*50 jaar cricket 1910–60.* J. Offerman  4210–2
*Fifty leaders of British sport.* E.C. Elliott  7203
*Fifty years. . .1882–1932.* The Times  6632
*Fifty years a cricket watcher.* W.R.G. Kent  7774
*Fifty years' cricket in Hawick.* J. Edgar  3293
*Fifty years' cricket reminiscences of a non-player.* W.E.
Howard  7725
*Fifty years history of the Durham C.C.C.* W.R. Bell  1890
*50 years M.C.C. visits to Jamaica.* Jamaica Cricket Board
of Control  4671
*Fifty years of Bombay cricket*  3916
*50 years of cricket, 1921–1971.* Wellington Mercantile
C.L.  3798–2
*Fifty years of cricket.* Welwyn Gardens City C.C.  2052
*50 years of cricket.* Western Suburbs District C.C.  3485
*Fifty years of Ellesmere.* P.A. Hall  2540
*Fifty years of Fettes*  3217
*Fifty years of league cricket.* J. Kay  2155
*Fifty years of my life in the world of sport.* Sir J.D.
Astley  7290–1
*Fifty years of Neston cricket.* J.H. Gilling  1805
*Fifty years of Nottinghamshire cricket.* C.H.
Richards  2517
*Fifty years of sport.* E.A. Bland  103
*Fifty years of sport.* E.D. Miller  7874
*Fifty years of sport at Oxford, Cambridge and the great
public schools.* Lord Desborough of
Taplow  1344, 1626, 1636
"*50 years of university sport,*" Universities Athletic
Union  1621
*A fifty years' record of the Bowdon C.C.* F.M. Jackson &
E.H. Longson  1798
*Fifty years' reminiscences of Scottish cricket.* D.D.
Bone  3187, 7341
*Fifty-two sports stories for boys.* R.S. Lyons  6371
*Fifty-two years of sport.* E.A. Bland  103
*55 years of cricket memories.* G.A. Brooking  7383
*The fight for the Ashes 1928–29.* M.A. Noble  4460
*The fight for the Ashes 1932–33.* Sir J.B Hobbs  4476
*The fight for the Ashes (1948).* A.W. Ledbrooke  5097
*Fight for the Ashes (1948).* C.G. Macartney & D.
Foster  5098
*The fight for the Ashes 1950–1951.* A.G. Moyes  4522
*The fight for the Ashes 1953.* P. West  5129
*The fight for the Ashes 1954–55.* A.G. Moyes  4543
*The fight for the Ashes 1956.* P. West  5155
*The fight for the Ashes 1958–1959.* I. Peebles  4561

Grace (W.G.), Souvenir of the national testimonial to. Cricket and Football Times 7578

"Grace (William Gilbert)." Sir N. Cardus 6626, 7592

Grace before ploughing. J. Masefield 7860–2

Grace Church C.C. "The tale end" 4154

The Graces. A.G. Powell and S.C. Caple 7565

Gradidge and Sons. How they made 1,000 runs in May! 355

How to make 1,000 runs in May! 354

Graeme, Margaret. Ranji's a-coming 7977

Graham, Alex. Please sir, I've broken my arm 7013

Graham, Archibald Hunter. Cricket at the University of Pennsylvania 405

Graham, Arnold. Hong Kong C.C. centenary celebration report 4305

Graham, Harry. Adam's apples 6461

The bolster book 7539

"C.B. Fry" 7539

Canned classics 6865

The complete sportsman 6866

Deportmental ditties 6863

Ruthless rhymes 6864

Graham, John Parkhurst. Forty years of Uppingham 1547

Graham, Kenneth. The noble game of cricket 4244

Graham (Norman) benefit souvenir 7610–1

Grand bi-centenary cricket match (1757–1957) Hambledon v. Dartford 1995

A grand charity cricket match in aid of The Royal London Society for the Blind. . .(1955) 3116–2

Grand Coronation festival old time match. . .on Broad Halfpenny Down (1953) 1996

Grand cricket match in aid of Yorkshire centenary (1963). Whitkirk C.C. 3048

Grand cricket tournament at Halifax, Nova Scotia (1874) 4148

Grand match between the All-England XI and the XXII of Canterbury (1864) 4739–2

Grandstand vol. 3: First class cricket. Texaco 1749

Grange, A. Demain. The cricketer's song 6571

The Grange C.C. Centenary of ground, 1872–1972 3279

Rules and list of members 3278

The Grange C.C. Edinburgh, Reminiscences of. W. Moncrieff 3280

Grange schools cricket festival (1969, 70) 3211

"Grant, Francesca," pseud. Caught and bowled 5935

Grant, Mrs. G. Forsyth. The Beresford boys 6228

Chums at last 6227

The hero of Crampton School 6226

Grant, Howard. Slogger Sam 6229

Grant, James, and Serle, Geoffrey. The Melbourne scene 1803–1956 3551

"Granville, Jeff," pseud. The schoolboy Test cricketer 6230

Granville (Lee) C.C. Scores & averages 2105–1

Graveney, Tom. Cricket over forty 7613

Cricket through the covers 7611

On cricket 7612

—, and Statham. Brian. Instructions to young cricketers 580

Graveney (T.W.) benefit programme for 1969. Worcestershire C.C.C. 7615

Graveney (Tom) 1969 benefit brochure 7614

Graveney's (Tom) International Cricket XI in Kuwait, 1969 4291, 5818

Graves, Alfred Perceval. More songs and snatches 6461–1

Graves, Percival. Zummerzet versus Zurrey 6572

Graves, Robert. But still it goes on 6112–2

Occupation writer 6112–2

The shout 6112–2

Graves Art Gallery, Sheffield. Two centuries of cricket art 6981

Gray, Andrew. Honoured by the school 6230–1

Gray, Arthur, and Brittain, Frederick. A history of Jesus College Cambridge 1631

Gray, Duncan. Nottingham: settlement to city 2483

Gray, George John. The Cambridge University cricket calendar 1625

Gray, Irvine Egerton, and Potter, William Edward. Ipswich School 1488

Gray, J.M. A history of Perse School, Cambridge 1504–1

Gray (J.R.). J. Arlott 7616

Gray, Kay. In final and Test match 6231

Gray, Robert. Australian cricket handbook 1962–63: M.C.C. tour 4576

Gray, Robin. Saltburn C.C. . . .1876–1976 2986–1

Graydon, John Allen. More never-to-be-forgotten sports thrills 93–1

Never-to-be-forgotten sports thrills 93

Still more never-to-be-forgotten sports thrills 94

Grayshott. J.H. Smith 1985–8

Grayson, Edward. Corinthians and cricketers 8057

Sport and the law 7080–2

Grayson, Rex. "The kidnapped cricketer" 6368–2

Great Australian book of nostalgia. J. Larkins & B. Howard 3340–2

Great Australian cricket pictures 3336–1, 6981–1

Great Australian scandals. G. Blaikie 4967–2

Great batsmen. G.W. Beldam & C.B. Fry 687

Great batsmen photo-analysed: W.J. Edrich. D.S. Davis 62, 7510

Great Bentley C.C. Cricket at Gt. Bentley 1771–1971 1903

The great Bohunkus. T. Evans 7837–2

Great bowlers and fielders. G.W. Beldam & C.B. Fry 721, 753–1

Great Britain miscellany 4400

Great Britain tour 1972. Argentine C.A. 5756

Great cricket contest: English XI v. New South Wales, 1897 4421

The great cricket hijack. C. Forsyth 5828–26

"The great cricket match, Brewers v. Publicans". G.H. Gibson 6458–2

Great cricket match—Nelson v. Colne. A. Craig 6444

Great cricket matches. E.H. Buchanan 89

The great cricketer. A.A. Thomson 7603

Great cricketers. D. Batchelor 7172

Great days and jolly days. C. Haddon 6548–1

Great days at Lancaster Park. G. Slatter 3776–1

Great days in New Zealand cricket. R.T. Brittenden 3741

Great days in sport. N. Fisher 92

Great expectations. C. Dickens 5990

The great French dictionary. G. Miege 851–2

Great games and great players. V.A.S. Beanland 6653

"The great Grogan's bat". W.E. Cule 6378–2

Great hours in sport. J. Buchan, 1st Baron Tweedsmuir 88, 5836

Great Indian cricketers. P. Ramchand 3832–3

Great knock: Sim's Australians v. Canterbury (1914) 5256–1

Great men at play. T.F.T. Dyer 7202

Great men of Kent. A.A. Thomson 8249

Great men of Sussex. P. Rush 7811

"The great mint match" 6373

Great moments in Australian sport. R.S. Whitington 3352–1

Great moments in cricket. G. Ross 97–1

Great moments in cricket. A. Thomas & N. Harris 97–3

Great moments in England v. Australia Test cricket. J. Buchanan 90–1, 4361–1

Great moments in Indian cricket. P. Ramchand 5590–1

Great moments in sport. A.W. Ledbrooke 96

Grundy, William Frederick. Letters of acknowledgement of the Memento of. . .Shrewsbury and. . .Shaw  8035, 8045
Memento of Arthur Shrewsbury's last match  8043
A memento of two great Notts cricketers. . . Shrewsbury and. . .Shaw  8034, 8044
Grundy Art Gallery, *Blackpool.* Catalogue of an exhibition of cricket pictures  6981–3
"Gryllus", *pseud. See* Symond, R.T.
The Guardian: The bedside "Guardian"  6618
The Guardian omnibus 1821–1971  7361
*Guardian.* D. Ayerst  1205–1
*Guardian cricket annual*  1080–1
Guardian Journal. Cricket handbook (1973–)  1046
*Gubbins minor and some other fellow.* F. Whishaw  6360–4
Guest, *Lady* Charlotte Elizabeth. Extracts from her journal, 1833–1852  878, 6934
Guggisberg. *Sir* Frederick Gordon. "The Shop"  1693
*The guide to cricketers.* F. Lillywhite  385, 1086
*A guide to first-class cricket matches played in Australia.* Assoc. of Cricket Statisticians  3328–2
*A guide to first class cricket matches played in the British Isle.* Assoc. of Cricket Statisticians  797–1
*Guide to the cricket ground.* G.H. Selkirk  470
*Guildford book of court*  840
Guillemard, Arthur George. Rugby School cricket scores 1831–1893  1521
*Guinness book of England v. West Indies test cricket records*  4670, 4718, 5447
*Guinness book of records*  113
*The Guinness international limited overs game: Australia v. W.I. (1978).* St. Lucia National C.A.  5254–4
*"Guinness" single wicket competition (1970).* Auckland C.A.  3760
Guirdham, Arthur. A foot in both worlds  8274
Guise, John Lindsay. Successful cricket  582
Talking of cricket  583, 6796
*Gulf international cricket tournament 1979*  4285–3
"Gully," *pseud.* The Indian team in England, 1946  5604
Gunaratham, M. Ceylon cricket team Malayan tour  5732
Gunasekara C.H. What every young cricketer should know  584
Gunn & Moore Ltd. Souvenir of the British Empire Exhibition, Wembley  356
The story of Gunn & Moore  325–1
Trade catalogue  325
*Gunn & Moore, The story of.* R. Kent  330
*Gunn (William).* A. Craig  7628
*Gunn (William) the famous cricketer.* C.H. Richards  7629
*Gunnersbury.* N. Rheinberg  3099–1
*Gunpowder, treason and plot.* H. Avery, *and others*  6367–4
Gunyon, William. The history of Meopham C.C.  2109–1
Gupta, Shivendra. Cricket series India vs. Pakistan 1979–80  5721–2
India's tour of Australia 1977–'78  5638–5
Gurdeep Singh. Cricket in northern India  3814
Gurunathan, S.K. Indian cricket  3855
Madras sports annual  3932
The story of the Tests  5587
Twelve years of Ranji trophy 1934–1945  3889
Gustard, Frederick Joseph Charles. England v. Australia. . .1934  5061
Somerset county cricket  2555
Gutsche, Thelma. Old gold: the history of the Wanderers' Club  3654
Guy, Peter, *and* King, John. Chipping Sodbury C.C., 1860–1960  1944

*Guy Rayner's schooldays*  6231–3
Guyana Cricket Board of Control. The M.C.C. in Guyana (1974)  4734–5
M.C.C. tour 1968  4719
Tour '72 from Wellington to Georgetown  5561
Tour '73 from Brisbane to Bourda  5250
Tour '74: from Lord's to Bourda  4734–6
*Guyana Sugar Producers' Assn. cricket tour of Jamaica (1968).* A. Ramsay  3715–1
Gwynn, Stephen Lucius. Experiences of a literary man  7629–1
Gwynne, Reginald. Cleverly caught!  6234
Cricketer cracksman  6232
The last Test match  6233

**—H—**

*"H-bomb".* E. Blunden  6419
H.E.D. *see* H[erschel], E.D.
*HK tour to Ceylon, Sabah & Singapore (1971).* Hong Kong C.A.  5771–1
*H.M.S. "Enterprise".* H.E. Stevens  1696–1
"H.P.T.," *pseud. see* Thomas, Percy Francis
*H.R.H. Prince Philip, Duke of Edinburgh.* G. Baker  7948–1
Haagsche C.C. Gedenkboek (1878–1928)  4230
Gedenkboek (1878–1938)  4231
Gedenkboek (1878–1958)  4232
*Haagsche C.C., 1878–1968*  4233
*Haagsche C.C. 1878–1978*  4233–1
Der Haagsche Cricket en Voetbal Vereeniging. Clubblad  4234
*Haandbog i cricket og langbold.* Den Kjøbenhavnske Boldspillklub  445
*Haarlem 1920–1945.* B. Kleefstra  4227
Haarlemsche Cricket Bond. Gedenkboekje (1961)  4226
Habib, Gulamali. Cricket thrills  6692–1
*Habib Sugar Mills Shield cricket tournament.* The District C.A.  3964
Hackwood, F.W. Old English sports  830
Hadath, Gunby. Against the clock  6236
The bridgehead  6238
Carey of Cobhouse  6236–3
Fight it out  6237
Go-Bang Garry  6236–2
Grim work at Bodlands  6236–5
His Highness  6236–1
Honours easy  6239–2
The new school at Shropp  6236–4
No robbery  6239
Playing the game  6239–1
Schoolboy grit  6235
Sheepy Wilson  6235–1
Haddon, Celia. Great days and jolly days  6548–1
Haden, Harry Jack. Stourbridge C.C. early days recalled  2846
Hadfield, John. The Saturday book  6629–2
Hadfield, John Charles Heywood. Love on a branch line  5999
A Wisden century  326
Hadgraft, Cecil, *and* Wilson, Richard. A century of Australian short stories  6088–2
*Hagley C.C. 1834–1975, A history of.* P.W.H. Jackson & *others*  2844–3
Haig, Nigel E., *and* Murrell, H.R. Middlesex C.C.C. Vol. 3: 1921–1947  2420
*The Haig book of village cricket.* J. Fogg  1729
Haig National Village Cricket Championship. Rules, etc.  1730
*The Haig village cricket annual*  1080–2, 1730–1
Haigh, F. Hanson. Ashes and rubber  7211
The cricketing career of Frank Woolley  8247

Indian cricketers. K. Desai 3812–1, 7201–1
Indian cricketers. S.K. Roy 3833, 7246
Indian cricketers in Australia (1947). L.N. Mathur 5631
Indian cricketers in Australia 1947. V.Y. Richardson 5634
The Indian cricketers' tour of 1911. H.C. Mukerji 5595
Indian cricketers touring England (1946). Muni Lal 5606
Indian cricketscene 3815–1
Indian Express. M.C.C. visit to India 1964 4829
"Indian field" athletic handbook for 1896 3859
The Indian Gymkhana Club Ltd. Golden jubilee souvenir 1916–1966 2384
60 and going strong 2384–1
The Indian illustrated sports annual (1928) 3860
Indian Oil Corporation. Know your cricketers 5305
Indian Schools' tour in England 1973. English Schools C.A. 3879–1
Indian sports flashback. J.C. Maitra 3818
Indian summer. J. Arlott 5602
The Indian team in England, 1946. "Gully," pseud. 5604
Indian Test cricket. V. Bala 5585–1
Indian tour 1979 souvenir programme 5628–3
Indian tour to Sri Lanka 1974. Bd. of Control for Cricket in Sri Lanka 5656–5
Indian tour West Indies; in Jamaica, 1962. Jamaica C.A. 5642
Indian Universities' tour of Ceylon, 1970. Ceylon Univs'. Sports A. 3879, 5656
Indian willow. N.S. Ramaswami 3832
India's tour of Australia 1977–'78. S. Gupta 5638–5
Indirect journey. H. Hobson 7704–2
Indiscretions of a headmistress. B. Archdale 7287–1
Individual batting analysis for cricket 288
Indoor cricket. M.D. Vockins 8279
Indoor cricket pitches, List of requirements of. National C.A. 311–1
Indus Advertising Co. Commonwealth XI v. Pakistan XI (1968) 5808
Inge, William Ralph. More lay thoughts of a dean 6700
Ingelse, D.L. Wicketkeepen 760
Ingelse, R.G. Cricket [the laws in Dutch] 222
Cricket, from here and there 5850
Fielden 756
Het batten 698
Ingleby-Mackenzie, Colin. Many a slip 7751
Ingleby-Mackenzie (C.) J. Arlott 7750
Inglis, Gordon. Sport and pastime in Australia 3338
Inglis, K.S. "Imperial Cricket" 4365–1
Inland far. C. Bax 6652, 7317
Inland Revenue, Board of. Reports of tax cases 942
Inman, Herbert Escott-. See Escott-Inman, Herbert
The inner room. Sir G.R. Hamilton 6462
"The innings" 5858
Inns of sport. J.W. Day 8269
Ins and outs. N. O'Neill 7920
The ins and outs of cricket. R.E.S. Wyatt 553
The Inseparables (Play up, School!). H. Hayens 6252–3
Insole, Douglas John. Batting 699
Cricket from the middle 971, 7752
Institute of Journalists, London District. 1926–1956 anniversary luncheon to the Australian . . . team . . . 1956 5143–1
Instonians 1919–69. W.B. White 3317
Instructions and advice upon the preparation of cricket pitches. Middlesex C.C.C. Junior Cricket Cttee. 308
Instructions and rules for playing . . . cricket. W. Lambert 383
Instructions for playing the game of cricket 382
Instructions to cricket coaches at Lord's. Sir F.E. Lacey 660
Instructions to cricketers. [–] Wallis 8294

Instructions to young cricketers. T. Graveney & B. Statham 580
Inter Banks 50–over tournament (1967) 4007–3
Intercolonial cricket after the war. Daily Chronicle 3695
Intercolonial cricket contest, 1897 3685
Intercolonial cricket tournament 1907. Daily Argosy 3686
The Intercolonial cricket tournament (1907): British Guiana v. Trinidad . . . 3687
Intercolonial cricket tournament (1910). Sporting Chronicle 3689
The Intercolonial cricket tournament (1910): Barbados v. British Guiana . . . 3688
Intercolonial cricket tournament 1922. Daily Chronicle 3691
Intercolonial cricket tournament (1924). Barbados Herald 3692
Intercolonial cricket tournament 1925. Daily Argosy 3693
Inter-colonial cricket tournament 1927. J.W. Gibbons 3696
Intercolonial cricket tournament 1929. Daily Argosy 3697
Intercolonial cricket tournament 1929. Daily Chronicle 3698
Intercolonial cricket tournament, January, 1932. Barbados Advocate 3699
Intercolonial cricket tournament 1936. Barbados Advocate 3700
Intercolonial cricket tournament 1937. Daily Chronicle 3701
Inter-county matches Aug. 1949. Leicestershire C.A. 2290–1
Interesting facts about J.T. Brown 7387
The International Aboriginal Cricketers v. Illawarra. A.P. Fleming 3454
International Batsman of the Year 1979 3092–2, 3092–3
The International Cavaliers' cricket book 1081, 3121
The International Cavaliers' world of cricket 1081, 3121
International County Cup matches. World Series Cricket 5828–33
International cricket: Australia v. Auckland (1960). Auckland C.A. 5262
International cricket. Australia v. N.Z. 4th Test (1967). Auckland C.A. 5265–1
International cricket: Australia v. New Zealand 1970. Auckland C.A. 5268
International cricket: Australia v. Wellington (1928). Wellington C.A. 5260
International cricket, Australian XI v. Tasmania (1938). Tasmanian C.A. 5332–1
International cricket. Centenary . . . Melbourne Cricket Ground. Shell 3557, 4403
International Cricket Conference. Rules 147, 4338
The International Cricket Crusaders tour of Devon & Cornwall 1967 3122
The International Cricket Crusaders tour of the West Country 1969 3123
International cricket: England v. Australia. R.H. Campbell 4362
International cricket fête, 1872, Official hand-book to the 4084, 4896
International Cricket Fetes Committee. Official report 4085, 4894
International cricket: 1st Test Australia v. N.Z. (1967). Taranaki C.A. 5267
International cricket; follow the Tests with the radio. R.S.S.A.I.L.A. Mitcham Sub-Branch 5075–1
International cricket guide. The Hon. E. Lyttelton 449
International cricket guide 1920–21. R.H. Campbell 4336, 4444
International cricket . . . M.C.C. v. Tasmania (1958). Tasmania C.A. 4564

*M.C.C. team souvenir (1974–5).* Australian Cricket Society. *A.C.T. Branch* 4615–3

*M.C.C. team to Ceylon (1924).* Dunlop Rubber Co. 4878–3

*M.C.C. team to Ceylon (1927).* S.P. Foenander 4879–1

*M.C.C. team to Ceylon (1928).* S.P. Foenander 4880

*M.C.C. team to Ceylon 1929.* S.P. Foenander 4880–1

*M.C.C. team to Philadelphia,* 1st visit of (1905). American Cricketer 4903

*M.C.C. team tour of Australia, 1970–71.* New South Wales C.A. 4609

*M.C.C. team v. All Ceylon (1936)* 4882–2

*M.C.C. team's 1937 tour.* Toronto & District Cricket Council & Toronto C.C. 4914

*M.C.C. team's tour of India 1961–62* 4814

*M.C.C. team's tour souvenir* (India, 1951). National Council of Cultural Relations 4797

*M.C.C. to the West Indies, Jan.–Apr. 1948.* E.L. Cozier & O.S. Coppin 4695

*M.C.C. tour,* Souvenir programme of (1933). Karachi C.A. 4789

*M.C.C. tour, 1948–9, to South Africa & Rhodesia* 4648

*M.C.C. tour (1957–8).* Kenya Kongonis C.C. 4945

*M.C.C. tour 1958–59.* Argentine C.A. 4936

*M.C.C. tour 1958–59.* Australian Broadcasting Commission 4552

*M.C.C. tour 1964–65.* Argentine C.A. 4938

*M.C.C. tour 1968.* Guyana Cricket Bd. of Control 4719

*M.C.C. tour 1969.* Bd. of Control for Cricket in Ceylon 4887

*M.C.C. tour 1973 of Sri Lanka.* Bd. of Control for Cricket in Ceylon 4891

*M.C.C. tour 1977: playing conditions.* Bd. of Control for Cricket in Sri Lanka 4891–2

*M.C.C. tour East Africa 1963.* Sunday Post 4948

*The M.C.C. tour in Argentine (1912).* J. McGough 4933

*M.C.C. tour in Argentine (1926–7).* Argentine C.A. 4934

*The M.C.C. tour in Australia, 1903–4.* A. Sinclair 4431

*The M.C.C. tour in Australia 1911–12.* F.N. Piggott 4441

*M.C.C. tour in India: playing conditions, 1963.* Bd. of Control for Cricket in India 4825

*M.C.C. tour in pictures* (S. Africa, 1957). Outspan 4655

*M.C.C. tour in Uganda (1963).* Uganda C.A. 4949

*M.C.C. tour Karachi (1933).* Karachi C.A. 4789

*M.C.C. tour of Australia 1954–55.* Australian Broadcasting Commission 4533

*M.C.C. tour of Australia 1962–63.* Australian Broadcasting Commission 4571

*M.C.C. tour of Australia 1965–66.* Australian Broadcasting Commission 4588

*M.C.C. tour of Australia 1970–71.* Australian Broadcasting Commission 4606

*M.C.C. tour of Australia 1970–71: 2nd Test. Appeal!* Western Australia C.A. 4612

*M.C.C. tour of Australia (1974–75).* Australian Broadcasting Commission 4615–1

*M.C.C. tour of Australia: programme 1974–75* 4615–8

*M.C.C. tour of Australia and New Zealand, 1946–7.* W.R. Hammond 4506

*M.C.C. tour of Ceylon 1969.* Ceylon Tobacco Co. Ltd. 4888

*M.C.C. tour of Ceylon 1970.* Ceylon Tobacco Co. Ltd. 4890–1

*M.C.C. tour of Hong Kong 1966.* South China Morning Post 4954

*M.C.C. tour of India 1951–1952.* Bd. of Control for Cricket in India 4792

*M.C.C. tour of India 1951–52.* Sport & Pastime 4800

*M.C.C. tour of India 1961–62* 4815

*M.C.C. tour of India 1964.* Sport & Pastime 4832

*M.C.C. tour of India 1976–77.* Bd. of Control for Cricket in India 4850–2

*M.C.C. tour of South Africa 1948–49 itinerary.* The Star 4648–1

*The M.C.C. tour of South Africa 1956–1957.* C. Fortune 4651

*M.C.C. tour of Sri Lanka 1977.* Bd. of Control for Cricket in Sri Lanka 4891–4

*M.C.C. tour of Sri Lanka (1977): itinerary.* Bd. of Control for Cricket in Sri Lanka 4891–3

*The M.C.C. tour of the West Indies 1954* 4702

*M.C.C. tour of the West Indies 1967–1968.* L. Williams 4726

*M.C.C. tour of West Africa 1975/76,* First. The West Africa Cricket Conference 4949–3

*M.C.C. tour of West Indies 1959–60.* Marylebone C.C. 4706–1

*The M.C.C. tour of West Indies 1968.* B. Close 4715

*M.C.C. tour to the West Indies 1948* 4698

*M.C.C. touring team v. all Jamaica (1926).* Jamaica C.A. 4684

*M.C.C. tourists v. S.E. Queensland (1974).* Gold Coast & District C.A. 4615–5

*M.C.C. trans-Canada tour 1951.* Canadian C.A. 4915

*M.C.C. trans-Canada tour 1959.* Victoria & District C.A. 4918

*M.C.C. 24th Australian cricket tour 1950–51* 4516

*M.C.C. v. A Southern N.S.W. XI (1959).* Riverina Cricket Council 4562

*M.C.C. v. A Southern N.S.W. Country XI (1965).* Riverina C.C. 4602

*M.C.C. v. All Trinidad (1911).* Daily Mirror 4679

*M.C.C. v. An Otago XI (1963).* Otago C.A. 4771

*M.C.C. v. Bangladesh (1977).* Bangladesh Cricket Control Bd. 4939–1

*M.C.C. v. Bangladesh East Zone 1977* 4939–2

*M.C.C. v. Board President's XI (Dec. 1972).* Hyderabad C.A. 4843

*M.C.C. v. Canterbury (1955).* Canterbury C.A. 4757

*M.C.C. v. Central Queensland (1954).* Rockhampton C.A. 4547–1

*M.C.C. v. Central Zone 1961.* Nava Bharat Staff Association 4819

*M.C.C. v. Ceylon 1969.* Maharaja Organisation Ltd 4889

*M.C.C. v. Ceylon 1970.* Bd. of Control for Cricket in Ceylon 4890

*M.C.C. v. Combined XI (Oct. 1958).* Western Australian C.A. 4569

*M.C.C. v. Combined XI . . . Launceston (1958).* Northern Tasmanian C.A. 4560

*M.C.C. v. Combined Side (1962).* Western Australian C.A. 4587

*M.C.C. v. Combined W.A. Country XI (1962).* Eastern Goldfields C.A. 4575

*M.C.C. v. Combined W.A. Country XI (1965).* Central Midlands C.C. 4591

*M.C.C. v. Eastern Province (1964–65).* G.A. Chettle 4660

*M.C.C. v. Governor's XI, Lyallpur (1961)* 4862

*M.C.C. v. India 1952,* 5th Test. Madras C.A. 4795

*M.C.C. v. India 1961,* 2nd Test. R.C. Agarwal 4801

*M.C.C. v. India 1964.* C.K. Haridass 4827

*M.C.C. v. India 1972,* 1st Test match. Delhi & District C.A. 4839

*M.C.C. v. India 1972–73.* A.V. Somaiya & P.S. Bhesania 4846

*M.C.C. v. India, (1973)* 4th Test. Cawnpore Sports Club 4837

*M.C.C. v. India 1976–77.* A.K. Sharma 4850–10

*M.C.C. v. Jamaica Colts (1968)* 4723

*My long life*. M.C. Clarke   7421, 7910
*My recollections of Wellington College*. G. F.-H. Berkeley   1553
*My remarkable uncle, etc*. S.B. Leacock   6877
*My reminiscences*. S.M.J. Woods   8244
*My son's father*. D.F. Moraes   7888
*My story*. V.S. Hazare   7667
*My story*. A. Lambton   7786
*My Sussex*. V. Champion   2701
*My uncle Frank*. T. Bodkin   6839
*My W.G.* A.E. Lawton   7590
*My way*. G.M. Turner   8166–2
*My world of cricket*. I.M. Chappell   7413
*My world of cricket*. N. Harvey   7653
*My world of cricket*. B. Sarbadhikari   4344–1, 8019–2
Myddelton House C.C. Centenary year 1879–1979   2360–1
Myers, Arthur Wallis. C.B. Fry   7540
  Captain Anthony Wilding   8230
  Memory's parade   7896–2
  The sportsman's year book (1905)   1091
Myler, P.J. Recollections of cricket   4147
"*Mynn (Alfred) and Mr. Aislabie*, Two amateurs—". E.V. Lucas   6713, 7274, 7897
*Mynn (Alfred) and the cricketers of his time*. P, Morrah   882, 7898
*Myself when young*. A. Waugh   8213
Mysore State C.A. Ceylon v. India 1st Test (1964)   5730
  M.C.C. v. South Zone (1962)   4818
Mysore State C.C. Bangalore: M.C.C. souvenir programme (1934)   4790
*The mysteries of love and eloquence*. E. Phillips   848
*The mystery batsman*. A. Thomas   6354
*Mystery comes to St. Christopher's*. C. Petersen   6317
*The mystery of B.B.* Band of Brothers C.C.   1242
*The mystery of Cranston School*. R.H. Poole   6322–1
*The mystery of Edwin Drood*. C. Dickens   5990
*The mystery of Markham*. R.S.W. Bell   6159
*The mystery of Meldon School*. A. Judd   6271

—N—

*N.D.F. match special*. Sportsweek   3924
Nagaraj Rao, B.N. A century of Tests 1932–67   5589
  India—England Test cricket 1932–1964   5588
Naish, Howard. Beaconsfield C.C. 150 not out   1777–2
*A name dishonoured*. D. Morris   6039
Nandy, Moti. *See* Moti Nandy
Napier, Sydney Elliott. The magic carpet and other essays. . .   6740–1
Narain, C. Welcome to cricketers from England 1960   4707
Narain, Om. India v. West Indies 5th Test match (1959)   5502
Narasimhan, C.R. World Cup cricket vistas   5828–6
Narayan, Rasipuram Krishnaswamy. Swami and friends   6295–1
Narayan, R.S. The Indian cricket team's tour of Australia and New Zealand 1967–68   5637, 5649
Narayan Sitaram Phadke. *See* Phadke, Narayan Sitaram
Narottam Puri, *see* Puri, Narottam
*Narrative essays of today*. J.G. Bullocke   6610
Nash, C.T. Argentine cricket tour Brazil—1953   5755
Nash, Ian. Images of Australian life   5855–1
Nash, William Gunner. Not a bad innings   7899
*Nat āut*. S. Basu   8281–2
Natal C.A. Annual report   3650
  Cricket teasers for junior umpires   271
  Vince Van der Bijil   8170–3

*Natal cricketers' annual*   3611
*Natal v. Benaud's Cavaliers* (1960). G.A. Chettle   5801
The Natal Women's C.A., *and* The South African and Rhodesian Women's C.A. Welcome to Pietermaritzburg cricket week (1967)   3668–1
Natan, Alex. Sport and society   7093
National Art-Collections Fund. 65th annual report   7720
National Association of Young Cricketers. Year book   789
National Book League. Cricket: a catalogue   31
  Cricket: an annotated book list   33
  The Festival of Britain: exhibition of books   32
  —. *Touring Exhibition*. Cricket books   34
*National brochure of Australian tour of S.A. & Rhodesia 1949–50*. J. Allan   5202
The National Cash Register Co. Ltd. 'The Test of the century'   8278
*National census of English cricket*. The Cricketer   970–1
National Club C.A. Rules   1708
National Council of Cultural Relations. M.C.C. souvenir (India 1961)   4797
*National cricket*. Canterbury C.A.   647
National C.A. Agatha Christie Under-19 Test series. West Indies tour 1978   5460–6
  Development of the coaching scheme   669
  England young cricketers tour of the West Indies 1972   4733
  England young cricketers tour of the West Indies 1976   4734–10
  Experimental laws   230
  Handbook   791–1
  An interim report of . . . census of cricket clubs   1709
  List of requirements of indoor cricket pitches   311–1
  Non-turf pitches: an assessment   309
  Regulations for junior cricket   791
  A summary of certain results from the interim report   1709
  'Test' cricket   670
  'Test' cricket in clubs and schools   670–1
  West Indies Young Cricketers tour of England, 1974   5460–1
  —, *and* The Wrigley Cricket Foundation. Report on school and youth cricket in the seventies   791–2, 1336
*The National Cricket Association*   790
*National C.C. of India* (1973), Tour of Sri Lanka by. Colombo C.C.   5656–2
*National C.C. of India v. Galle Combined XI (1973)*. Galle C.C.   5656–3
*National cricket coaching plan*. H.B. Taber   679–5
National Cricket Union of Queensland. Year book   3509
National Gallery of British Sports and Pastimes. Cricket exhibition   6988
  The first 600 selected pictures   6988–1
The National Nine Network, *and* The Benson & Hedges Co. Cricket tour guide 1979/80   4615–61
National 0–10 Network Television. Cricket scene [1976–77]   4615–30, 5270–10, 5694–5
*National 0–10 Network World Cup cricket*. K. Piesse   5828–13
National Opinion Polls. Major county cricket   1746
National Playing Fields Association. Sports ground maintenance   309–1
  Spotligĥt on British sport   7094
  Yorkshire Present XI v. Yorkshire Past XI (1951)   3035
  —, *and* Marylebone Cricket Club. *Standing Joint Committee*. Cricket on non-turf pitches   310
  On artificial cricket pitches   310

Phillips, Janet, *and* Peter. Victorians home and away  908–1

Phillips, Son & Neale. Cricketana (1979)  45–7
  English, continental and oriental ceramics and glass (1974)  45–5
  Oil paintings. . .; cricketana (1978)  45–6
  Sporting memorabilia (1979)  45–8

Phillips, Stephen. Lyrics and drama  6515

Phillipson, Neill. The Australian cricket hall of fame  3347–3
  Cricket Caribbean  5487–9
  Cricket cavalcade  3347–3, 7231–1
  The jubilee Test series 1977  4615–31, 5196–20

Phillpotts, Eden. A mixed grill  6746, 7594
  One thing and another  6747
  "W.G. Grace"  7594

*A philosophical reading of cricket.* S.R.K. Menon  6953

*The philosophy of sport.* P. McBride  7087

Philpott, Peter. Cricket fundamentals  603–1
  How to play cricket  603, 676

"Phipps," *pseud.* Phipps' annual  6891

*The Phoenix book of wit and humour.* M.H. Barsley  6814

Phoenix C.C. Festival Week (1943)  3326

*The Phoenix dictionary of games.* J.B. Pick  7098

*The Phoenix history of cricket.* R. Webber  84

*Photo album of famous cricketers*  7233

*"A photograph of Hammond."* A. Ross  6520

*Photographs of the teams, Sherborne School, 1901–1915*  1535

*"Phyllis at the wicket."* P. Graves  6461–1

*The physics of ball games.* C.B. Daish  7073

*Piccadilly Jim.* Sir P.G. Wodehouse  6081

Pichanick, Harry. Australia v. a South African XI (1949)  5204
  M.C.C. v. Rhodesia (1949)  4646
  South African Schools Nuffield Tournament (1949)  3623

Pick, John Barclay. The Phoenix dictionary of games  7098
  The spectator's handbook  7099

*Pick of "The Cricketer".* The Cricketer  5841

Pickard, Abraham Benjamin de Villiers. Vanmelewe se rugby 1980 en vanmelewe se krieket 1874  3603–1

Pickering, William Percival. Cricket "wrinkles"  464

Pickfords Ltd. Australian cricket team 1926: London to Sydney  5044

Pickwick Athletic Club. Visit of the S. Australian team (1956)  2809, 3524, 5157

*Pickwick Athletic Club 1858–1958.* J.E. Ewing  2808

*Pickwick Papers.* C. Dickens  5990, 5991, 6973

*A Pickwick portrait gallery*  5992

*Pickwickian studies.* P.H. Fitzgerald  6681–1

*Pictorial history of American sports.* J. Durant & O. Bettmann  4038

*The pictorial history of Lord's and the M.C.C.* H.S. Altham & J. Arlott  995, 1219

*Pictorial records of cricket tours 1920–1950.* A.W. Simpson  4345

"A Picture-Maker," *pseud.* The search for pleasure  2097, 6956

*The picture of cricket.* J. Arlott  6963

*A picture of the manners, customs, sports. . .* J. Aspin  825–1, 7111–2

Picture Post. Cricket victory supplement (1955)  4546

*The Picture Post book of the Tests, 1953.* D.S. Batchelor  5114

*The Picture Post book of the Tests, 1954–5.* D.S. Batchelor  4535

*The Picture Post book of the Tests, 1956.* D.S. Batchelor  5139

*Pictures of Maidstone.* H.R.P. Boorman  2105–2, 6966–1

*Pictures of sporting life and character.* Lord Lennox  7802

*Pictures, prose, and rhymes for children of all climes*  6956–1

*A picturesque history of Yorkshire.* J.S. Fletcher  2867–1

*Pierce Egan's anecdotes, original and selected*  6851

*Pierce Egan's book of sports and mirror of life.* P. Egan  1992, 7044, 8054

Pier, Arthur Stanwood. St. Paul's School  4054

Piesse, Ken. Great triumphs in Test cricket  4339–1
  A history of Australian cricket annuals and magazines  3373–2, 3385–4
  National 0-10 Network World Cup cricket  5828–13
  Prahan C.C.'s centenary history  3569–1

*Pigeon hoo.* F. Lushington  6024–2

*Pigg (Mr.), Well done!* A. Craig  6444

Piggott, F. Neville. The M.C.C. tour in Australia 1911–12  4441
  The Springboks: history of the tour 1906–07  5346–1

Piggott, Francis Stewart Gilderoy. Broken thread  7951–1

Piggott, Neville. The Ceylon sports annual & directory  3987–1

Piggott, Percy. Fenner's  1628
  Incidents in fifty years of Cambridge University cricket  1628

*Pigskin and willow.* B. Webber  6131

Pike, E.M. Derby County boomerang  1843

Pike, Lillian M. Jack of St. Virgil's  6317–1

Pilch, Fuller. Whole art of cricket  465

Pilgrims C.C. Yearbook (Leics.)  2292–1

Pilkington, Ernest Milbourne Swinnerton. An Eton playing field  1457

Pilkington, Samuel Turnell. Accrington cricket down the ages  2180

*Pillars of society.* A.G. Gardiner  6685, 7976

Pilley, Phil. A century of cricket. . .Hounslow  2383

Pilling, Richard. "Wicket-keeping"  402

*The pilot prefect.* H. Cleaver  6186–1

*Pilots of the Sixth.* J. Anerley  6367–3

Pimlott, John Alfred Ralph. Recreations  6990–1

Pink, Hal. The Test match mystery  5948

Pink, Maurice Alderton. Modern portrait essays  6626

*The Pink 'un.* Hong Kong C.C.  4308

*Pink 'un cricket annual*  1037

*A "Pink 'un" remembers.* J.B. Booth  7343

Pinter, Harold. Five screenplays  6808–2
  "Hutton and the past"  6747–1
  No man's land  6808–3
  Poems and prose 1949–1977  6747–1

Pinto, Arthur. Sri Lanka, first tour: Prudential World Cup  5828–7

Pioneer Catering Co. Cricket fixtures 1939  1170

*Pioneering days in Western Victoria.* J.C. Hamilton  3536–1

*The pioneers.* A. Wall  6540

*"Pip".* J.H. Beith  5966

Piper, Geoffrey. A history of S. Anselm's cricket 1888–1975  1530–1

Piper, Walter J., jun. A history of the Derbyshire C.C.C.  1853

*Pitcairn – children of the 'Bounty'.* I.M. Ball  4327–3

*Pitch and toss.* R.A. MacLean  4652

*A pitch in both camps.* A. Lee  4615–50, 5828–37

*Pitched battles.* C. Forsyth  4370–1

Pitt, William, *Lord* Lennox. *See* Lennox, William Pitt, *Lord*

*Place (Winston) benefit book.* A.W. Ledbrooke  7952

Plairre, Charles, *ed.* Sportive snatches  6908, 7250

*Plan of cricket pitches. . .Moore Park*  3497

Planché, Frederick d'Arros. Cricket as now played  466

Plant, K. Shirley. The captain of the eleven  6384

*Report of the Australian Women's cricket tour in England . . . 1976*. Womens C.A.   3585–2

*Report of the tour of Australia and New Zealand, 1968–69.* Women's C.A.   3109, 4604

Reporter, The. Cricket annual for 1910   1099

*Representative matches in India 1892–1919*. P.N. Polishwalla   3827

*Reprints*. H. Smith-Turberville   8066

*Reptiles, History of the.* B. Thomas   1284

*Repton, Records and reminiscences of.* G.S. Messiter   1512

*Repton, A short history of.* A. Macdonald   1511

*Repton 1557 to 1957.* B. Thomas   1514

*Repton cricket (1865–1905).* A.J.H. Cochrane   1510

*Repton cricket (1901–1951).* F.R.D. Monro   1513

*Repton sketches.* J. Bradstreet   1508

*Reptonian reprints.* A.J.H. Cochrane   1509, 6440

"Resdeb," pseud. M.C.C. visits to India   4781

*Rest of the World cricket tour guide 1971–72.* Australian Cricket   5826

*Rest of the World XI 1965.* Rothmans   5820

*Rest of the World XI 1967.* Rothmans   5823

*Rest of the World XI 1968.* Rothmans   5824

*Rest of the World fixtures; tour programme: pictures (1970)*   5825

*Rest of the World v. Australia 1971.* Western Australian C.A.   5828

*Rest of the World v. Southern N.S.W. XI (1972).* A.C.T.C.A.   5825–1

*Resumé of big cricket in the West Indies and British Guiana.* T.S. Birkett   3670, 3714

*Retford cricket and cricketers 1850–1950.* C.W. Hopkinson & H.J. Birkett   2495–1

"The return match". E.W. Hornung   6091–1

*The return of A.J. Raffles.* G. Greene   6806–1

*The return of the Ashes.* M. Brearley & D. Doust   5196–12

"Return of the native". A. Cooke   5666–1, 6622

*Return to Bermuda.* B.R. Jones   5522–1

*The Rev. John Mitford on cricket.* J. Mitford   389, 7883

"Reverie on cricket"   376, 427

*The revival of sport in Barbados.* Barbados Advocate   3690

Reynolds, Ernest Edwin. A book of sports and pastimes   5865

Reynolds, Frederick. The life and times   7992

Reynolds, Frederick Reginald. Lancashire county cricket   2273

Reynolds, John Stewart. Canon Christopher of St. Aldgate's, Oxford   7419

*Reynolds (Sir Joshua) P.R.A.* E. D'Esterre-Keeling   3094–1

Reynolds, P.E. Tour of Australian cricketers through Australia, New Zealand and Great Britain   4968, 5255

Reynolds, Stanley. "Queering the pitch"   1741–1

"A rhapsodist at Lord's." E.V. Lucas   6710, 7852, 8132

Rheinberg, Netta. Gunnersbury   3099–1
Report of the tour of Australia and New Zealand, 1968–69   3109, 4604
Women's cricket   7082

Rhoades, Walter C. The boy from Cuba   6329–1
The boys of Redcliff   6331
For the sake of his chum   6330
In the scrum   6330–2
The last lap   6330–3
Our fellows at St. Mark's   6328–1
"Quills"   6330–1
Two scapegraces   6329
"Umpires I have met"   278–3
The whip hand   6332

Rhode Island & District Amateur C.L. Handbook   4108

*Rhodes (Harold) testimonial 1968.* M. Carey   7993

*Rhodes (W.).* A. Craig   7993–1

*Rhodes (Wilfred).* S. Rogerson   7996

*Rhodes (Wilfred), The memorial service to.* Northern Cricket Society   7995

Rhodesia C.U. Annual report   3665
Australia v. a South African XI (1949)   5204
Currie Cup cricket 1973, Rhodesia v. Transvaal   3640
Currie Cup cricket, Transvaal v. Rhodesia (1947)   3638–1
International Wanderers tour of Rhodesia, Sept. 1974   5819–2
News sheet   3666
1972 International Wanderers tour of Rhodesia   5818–2
Rhodesia v. Natal (1977)   3636–1

Rhodesia Cricket Umpire's Association. Newsheet   277–1

*Rhodesia v. Australia (1957)*   5206–1

*Rhodesia v. Australia (1966).* Mashonaland C.A.   5221

*Rhodesia v. M.C.C. (1956).* Mashonaland C.A.   4653

*Rhodesia v. M.C.C. (1964).* Mashonaland C.A.   4664

*Rhodesia v. Natal (1977).* Rhodesia C.U.   3626–1

*Rhodesian cricket and tennis annual*   3667

*Rhyme the rudder.* G.D. Martineau   6495

*Rhymes.* J. Martin   6490–2

*Rhymes à la mode.* A. Lang   6485

*Rhymes of sport.* L.C.R. Cameron   6429

Rhys, Ernest. The old country   5920
—, and Vaughan, Lloyd. A century of English essays   6629

Rhys, Horton. A theatrical trip for a wager. . .   4893–1

Ribblesdale C.L. Official handbook   2979

Rice, Jo. Mortimer Also   6333

Rice, Tim. Heartaches cricketers' almanack   1302–3
The Lord's Taverners sticky wicket book   3133–1

Rich, Edward John George Henry. Recollections of the two St. Mary Winton colleges   1576

Richards, Barry. Barry Richards on cricket   606
The Barry Richards story   7997–2
Cricket   606–1

*Richards (Barry) benefit brochure (1977)*   7997–1

Richards, Charles Henry. Arthur Shrewsbury   8048
Celebrated Nottinghamshire cricketers   2518
Fifty years of Nottinghamshire cricket   2517
Mordecai Sherwin   8039
The Nottinghamshire county cricket annual   2508
Nottinghamshire cricket scores and biographies   2517
Nottinghamshire cricketers   2518
Notts. C.C.C. souvenir championship year 1907–08   2518–1
Richards' Nottinghamshire cricket guide   2519
W. Flowers the famous cricketer   7530
William Attewell   7291
William Gunn the famous cricketer   7629
William Scotton   8025

Richards, F. Old Sevenoaks   2113–1

Richards, Frank. See Hamilton, Charles

Richards, Isaac Vivian Alexander, and Foot, David. Viv Richards   7997–3

Richards, James Brinsley-. See Brinsley-Richards, James

Richards, Thomas. New South Wales in 1881   3453

*Richardson (A.J.) benefit fund souvenir programme (1949).* S. Australia C.A.   3430–2, 7998–1

Richardson, Sir Albert Edward. Georgian England   888

Richardson, Arthur J. Cricket coaching manual   679

Richardson, Eric C. Catford Wanderers Sports Club handbook   2092

Skull, John. Sport and leisure 6395–3

*A sky-blue life.* M. Moiseiwitsch 5944

Sladen, Douglas. The tragedy of the pyramids 6060

*Slaithwaite notes—past and present.* J. Sugden 3005

*Slasher opens up.* K. Mackay 7838

Slater, Francis Carey. Settler's heritage 3659–1

Slatter, Gordon. Great days at Lancaster Park 3776–1

Slatter, William H. Recollections of Lords and the Marylebone Cricket Club 1019, 1238

Slaughter, Leslie Edgar. Ipswich municipal centenary 3516–2

Slazengers Ltd. Cricket '70 340

Slazengers, Sykes, Gradidge, Ayres. 1810 to 1946 339

Sleaford C.C. Official handbook 2325–2

Slee, John. Ayres' (public schools) cricket companion 1343

*"Slip catchers in the rye".* J. Markwick 4070–1

*Slip catches.* W.C. Reedy 6897

*"Slogger" and Co.* St. J. Pearce 6305

*Slogger Sam.* H. Grant 6229

Slough Cricket & Bowls Club. Handbook and fixture list 1780

Slough Sports Club. Official handbook 1780

Sly, Christopher, *pseud. See* Davies, D.H.

Small, E. Milton. The Canterbury cricket week 2089

*A small tribute of admiration. . . .* A. Craig 6444

Smalley, Ralph. A century of cricket 2306

Smart, Kenneth John. Sevenoaks Vine cricket 1731–1959 2118

*Smedley (Mike) benefit souvenir programme* 8054–1

Smink, Pieter Johannes. Volledige handleiding bij het cricketspel 472

Smith, Bertie Webster. The boy's companion 7153–1

Smith, Carl V. From N. to Z 3751–1

Smith, Charles Turley. A band of brothers 6343

Godfrey Marten, schoolboy 6340

Godfrey Marten, undergraduate 6341

The left-hander 6344

Maitland Major and Minor 6342

The Minvern brothers 6342–1

The new broom 6342–2

Tales of Lexham 6344–1

Smith, David T., *and* Jonathan B. First-class cricketers from Christ College, Brecon 1392–1

Smith, E. Frank. Slough Cricket & Bowls Club handbook 1780

*Smith (Edwin) testimonial souvenir (1966)* 8056

Smith, Frank. Basher testimonial year book 1978 7654–1

Smith, Frederick Edwin, *earl of Birkenhead.* The hundred best English essays 6629–3

Smith, Frederick Winston Furneaux, *earl of Birkenhead.* Walter Monckton 7884–1

Smith, *Sir* Henry. From constable to commissioner 8058

Smith, Irving W. Harborne C.C. versus Wolverhampton, 1901–1914 2587, 2804

Random reminiscences of the Harborne C.C. 2805

—, *and others.* Cricketing days: Harborne C.C. 2806

Smith, J.H. Grayshott: the story of a Hampshire village 1985–8

Smith J. Harcourt. Cricket: a song 6593

Cricket, the song of the "Centuries" 6594, 7600

Smith, John Thomas. A book for a rainy day 2386

Smith, Lloyd S. The Sporting Chronicle annual 3681, 5413

West Indies cricket history 3674, 5406

Smith, Michael John Knight. Better cricket for boys 614

*Smith (Michael J.K.), presentation reception.* Warwickshire C.C.C. 8060

*Smith (Mike) benefit* 76

*Smith (Mike) in his benefit year 1976.* Middlesex C.C.C.

Smith, Nigel Starmer-. *See* Starmer-Smith, Nigel

Smith, Percy Raymond. Australian cavalcade 5868–2

Australian pageant 5868–1

Smith, Peter. Bowling 739

Smith, Peter. The observer's book of cricket 76–2

Smith, R.D. Not out 5869

*Smith ("Razor"), All about.* E.H.D. Sewell 8064

Smith, Ray. Bowling 739

Smith, Simon J. Watt-. *See* Watt-Smith, Simon J.

Smith, Simon Nowell-. *See* Nowell-Smith, Simon

Smith, Sydney. History of the Tests 4386

Test cricket almanack (Eng. v. Aust.) 4384, 4563, 4582, 4603, 5173

Test cricket almanack 1964 5181–1

With the 15th Australian XI 5030, 5199

*Smith (T. Assheton), Reminiscences of the late. Sir J.* Eardley-Wilmot 8063

Smith, T.E. Cricket umpiring and scoring 277, 290

Smith, Thomas. The cricket match 6525

Poems 6526

Sporting incidents in the life of another Tom Smith 2003, 8062

Smith, Vian Crocker. Candles to the dawn 6061

Smith, W.S. Brian Bolus benefit (1971) 7339

Smith, Walter Barradell. *See* Barradell-Smith, Walter

Smith, Wilbur. Shout at the Devil 6061–1

Smith, William. Morley: ancient and modern 2973–1

Smith, William S. The Mike "Pasty" Harris benefit 1977 7650–1

Smith & Sons (Tailors). First class cricket fixtures 1908 1170–1

Smith Meters Ltd. Cricket fixtures 1947 1171

*Smith of Rocklandshire.* J.N. Pentelow 6310

Smith-Turberville, Harry. Peeps into the past 8065

Reprints 8066

*Smith's (Ray) benefit fund.* Braintree C.C. 8061

*Smith's week.* R.S.W. Bell 6160

Snaith, John Collis. Willow the king 5952

*Snap shots of George Hirst's career.* J.H. Stainton 7686

Snow, Charles Percy, *Lord Snow.* Death under sail 6061–2

Last things 6061–5

The light and the dark 6061–4

"The mathematician on cricket" 7645–1

The search 6061–3

Variety of men 7645–2

Snow, Edward Eric. History of Leicestershire cricket 2313

Leicestershire cricket 1949 to 1977 2313–1

Sir Julien Cahn's XI 1300

Snow, John. The art of bowling 743

Contrasts 6527

Cricket: how to become a champion 614–1

Cricket rebel 8066–3

Moments and thoughts 6528

Snow, Philip Albert. "A century in the Fiji Islands" 4325–4

Cricket in the Fiji Islands 4326, 4329–2

"Fiji" 4326–1

Fiji C.A. handbook 4325

—, *and* Waine, Stefanie. The people from the horizon 4324–1

Snow, Terence Benedict. Sketches of old Downside 1401

*So long to learn.* J. Masefield 7860–1

*So this is Australia.* W. Pollock 4498

Sobers, *Sir* Garfield St. Aubrun. Bonaventure and the flashing blade 6345

Cricket advance! 615

Cricket crusader 8069–2

King cricket 5451

—, *and* Barker, John Sydney. Cricket in the sun 3675

Sparling, Richard A. The romance of the Wednesday 1867–1926   3003

Sparvel-Bayly, John Anthony. Some historical notes   2100

*Speak for England.* J. Agate   5882

Speake, Robert, *and* Witty, Frank Roy. A history of Droylsden   2195–1

Speakman, Arthur. The Club Cricket Conference tour of Australia 1971   1720, 4615

Speakman, F.S. Jack E. Timms' testimonial fund   8141

Spear, Henry J., *and* Arrowsmith, J.W. Arrowsmith's dictionary of Bristol   1937–2

*A special collection of cricket books* (1931). S.J.A. Cotterell   9

*Special souvenir . . . of the 18th visit of the English cricketers to Australia, 1907–8.* F.J. Ironside   4437

*Specification for . . . an artificial cricket pitch.* J.O. Tressider   314

The Spectator. Spectator harvest   6630, 7542

"A Spectator Esq.," *pseud.* A digest of cricketing facts . . . the year 1862   912, 6595

*The spectator's handbook.* J.B. Pick   7099

*The spectator's Sussex country cricket companion for 1901*   2773

*Speeches.* C.J. Lyttelton, 10th viscount Cobham   6799

*Speeches and toasts.* H. Frith   6795

*Speeches made at a dinner . . . Lord Ebbisham*   1307. 6794

*Speeches made at 150th anniversary dinner.* Marylebone C.C.   6801

*Speed the plough.* T. Morton   6808

*Speel krieket op die regte manier.* T. Reddick   605–1

*A spell from Laker. . . .* J.C. Laker   7213–1

*A spell at the top.* B. Statham   8084

*Spencer (Terry) benefit 1964.* Leicestershire C.C.C.   8072

Spencer, Thomas E. "How M'Dougal topped the score"   5853–1, 5874–3, 6386–1, 6907–1

Spencer, Tom. A history of the Manly-Warringah District C.C.   3466–2

*The Spencer Cricket & Lawn Tennis Club.* H.T. Gordon   2666

Spicer, *Sir* Howard Handley. Sports for boys   7154

Spicer, Hugh H. South American C.A.'s England tour 1932   5781

Spiegelhalter, Cecil. Local cricket history: annals of Malton C.C.   2968

"*Spiers and Pond*". P. Andrew   5864

*Spiers and Pond (Messrs): men who have earned success*   4401

"*Spikey's wicket*". J.C. Bristow-Noble   1146–1, 6372–1

*Spin bowling.* G. Goonesena   727

*Spin bowling.* R. Illingworth   729–3

*Spin me a spinner.* R. Benaud   4572

*Spin out.* A. Mallett   7846–1

*Spinner's wicket.* R. Illingworth   7748

*Spinner's yarn.* I. Peebles   7943

*Spinning round the world.* J.C. Laker   7783

"*The spirit of cricket.*" *Sir* N. Cardus   5915, 6612

*The spirit of Kent: Lord Cornwallis.* H.R.P. Boorman   7453

"*Spofforth, the demon bowler*"   5874–2

*The spoken word.* The Listener   6798

*Le sport.* N. Bentley   6836–1

*Sport and athletics in 1908*   1104

*Sport & entertainment in Australia.* R.J. Unstead & W.F. Henderson   3350–2

"*Sport and games in Finnegan's Wake*"   6675

*Sport and leisure.* J. Skull   6395–3

Sport and Pastime. Annual   3862

   Commonwealth cricketers' tour of India 1949–50   5788

   Commonwealth cricketers' tour of India 1950–51   5795

   Commonwealth cricketers' tour of India 1953–54   5799

   Cricketers from Australia 1956   5282

   Cricketers from Australia 1959–60   5291

   Cricketers from New Zealand 1955–56   5566

   Cricketers from the West Indies 1958–59   5504

   M.C.C. cricketers visit to India 1961–62   4821

   M.C.C. tour of India 1951–52   4800

   M.C.C. tour of India 1964   4832

   Pakistan cricketers tour of India 1960–61   5718

   Special cricket number, 2 May, 1959   3841, 5622

   West Indies cricketers tour of India 1948–49   5500

   West Indies tour of India 1966–67   5515

   Worrell memorial match 1968   8258

*Sport and pastime*   3869

*Sport and pastime in Australia.* G. Inglis   3338

*Sport and pastime in the Transvaal.* E.J.L. Platnauer   3652

*Sport and recreation in Britain.* Central Office of Information. *Reference Division*   963

*Sport and society.* A. Natan   7093

*Sport and society: Elizabeth to Anne.* D. Brailsford   827

*Sport and the community.* Wolfenden Committee on Sport   983, 7111

*Sport and the countryside in English paintings. . . .* D. Coombs   6968–1

*Sport and the law.* E. Grayson   7080–2

*Sport and travel in India and Central America.* A.G. Bagot   6647, 7294

*Sport at the Saffrons.* Eastbourne Cricket & Football Club   2733

*Sport for all ages and limited purses.* W. Ralston   7029–1

*Sport for fun.* P. Carpenter   137

*Sport in a nutshell.* C.E. Hughes   6872

*Sport in art.* O. Warner   7003

*Sport in Australia.* T.D. Jaques & G.R. Pavia   3339–1, 7082–2

*Sport in Britain.* Central Office of Information. *Ref. Div.*   963

*Sport in Britain.* H.A. Harris   810–1

"*Sport in Britain*". H.A. Harris   7104–1

*Sport in Ceylon*   3989

*Sport in England.* N.G. Wymer   825

*Sport in history.* R. Cashman & M. McKernan   3808–1, 4365–1, 4470–2

*Sport in silhouette.* W.W. Jelf   1444

*Sport in society.* P.C. McIntosh   7089

*Sport international.* C. Harvey   7082

*Sport magazine*   3385–5

*Lo sport nell'arte.* R. Carita   6967–1

*Sport pics 1964*   5182

*Sport pictures*   1209–1

*Sport problems.* H. Cleaver   138

*Sport spectacular*   3620–4

*Sportascrapiana.* C.A. Wheeler   897, 7062, 7390

*Sportboek.* Blue Band Margarine   6965–1

*The sportfolio*   7249

Sportimes. Special cricket souvenir (1969)   4872

*Sportimes*   3962, 5719

*Sporting almanack for 1900*   1075

*Sporting and athletic records.* H. Morgan-Browne   119

*Sporting and athletic register 1908*   1104

*A sporting and dramatic career.* A.E.T. Watson   8209

*Sporting and dramatic yarns.* R.J.B. Sellar   6905

*Sporting and rural records of the Cleveley Estate.* H.F. Hore   2593

*Sporting anecdotes.* P. Egan   6851

*The sporting annual 1878–79*   1105

*Sporting campaigner.* M.A. Green   7617

*Sporting chance.* B. Tidy   7031–1

Trincomalee District Cricket & Athletic Assoc. Trincomalee District XI v. S.S. Perera's Combined Schools U-19 XI . . . 1977  4036–5

*Trinidad & Tobago Secondary Schools Assoc. Under 19 tour of Australia 1979–80.* Australian Schools Cricket Council  3730–1

Trinidad & Tobago Secondary Schools' C.A. Tour of England 1977  3733–1

*Trinidad & Tobago tour 1978.* Middlesex C.L.  2342–5, 4734–11

The Trinidad & Tobago Women's C.A. Constitution & rules  3734

*The Trinidad & Tobago Women's C.A. presents international cricket* (1971)  3111, 4730

*Trinidad centenary cricketing souvenir album*  3735

Trinidad C.C. Year book (1964–)  3736

*Trinidad v. Jamaica 1950.* Queen's Park C.C.  3705

*Trinidad v. Tobago* (1964). Junior Chamber of Commerce of Trinidad  3732

*Trinity College School C.C.* P. Perry  4124

*Trinity College School C.C. 1867–1893.* The complete records of. E.M. Watson

*Trinity Methodist C.C. 1959–1969,* The history of. A.J. Mason  2301

*The trip to Australia.* E.M. Grace  4405

*Trip to "Kangaroo" land.* J.N. Crawford  4435

*The triple aliance.* H. Avery  6143

*Triple testimonial fund 1976*  7371–1, 7412–1, 8263–1

Trist, J. Fincher. Reminiscences of a grand tennis tournament. . .  1813

Tristram, Henry Barrington. Loretto School  3225

*The Trojans Club 1874–1974.* M. le Bas  2013–5

Trollope, Anthony. British sports and pastimes  7058
 The fixed period  6070

*The trophy for an unknown soldier.* R.W. Moore  6503

*Trott (Mr. G.H.S.)* A. Craig  8149

Trotter, James Jeffrey. The Royal High School, Edinburgh  3221

Troup, Walter. Sporting memories  8150

Trower, Charles Francis. "On the archaeology of Sussex cricket"  2709
 Sussex cricket past and present  2717

Trowsdale, T. Broadbent. A complete history of the Test matches between England and Australia 1877–1905  4393, 5003
 Coverpoint's cricket annual  1122, 5874
 The cricketer's autograph birthday book  7257

*The true book about cricket.* B. Harris  70

Truelove, Roger. The young cricketer  1217–1

Trueman, Edwin. Ilkeston cricketers of the past  1839

Trueman, Frederick Sewards. Ball of fire  8155–1
 Book of cricket  1147
 Cricket  622
 Fast fury  8154
 The Freddie Trueman story  8155
 The thoughts of Trueman now  5874–1
 —, and Hardy, Frank. 'You nearly had him that time. . .'  6915–2

*Trueman (Freddie).* C. Field  6455–2

*Trueman (Freddie) benefit brochure 1962*  8152

*"Trueman destroys Australia".* D. Rowbotham  5164–1

*Trueman's benefit* (1962), Charity match in aid of. Whitkirk C.C.  8156

*"Trueman's hour".* J.M. Kilburn  6635–1

Trueman Essex League. Official cricket handbook  1892–2

Trueman Surrey County C.L. Official handbook  2606

Trumble, Hugh Christian. Blades of grass  314–1

Trumble, Robert. The golden age of cricket  4394, 8158
 The Trumble family in Australia  8157

Trump, R.F. Facts and figures of Somerset C.C.C.  2563, 7796

*Trumper (Victor).* V. Raiji  8164

*Trumper (Victor),* Public reception to. Crown Street School Boys' Union  8160

"Trundler," *pseud. See* Newton, William H.

*Trust Tilty.* A.A. Thomson  6067

*"The truth about sport."* St. J. Adock  6627

*The truth at last.* Sir C. Hawtrey  7660

*Try and stump me.* A. Goldman  6861

*Tyron Gallery cricketers series*  7001–1

Tuck, Charles. Price's College C.C. tour of West Indies 1975  1504–2
 Trinidad & Tobago Secondary Schools' C.A. tour of England 1977  3733–1

Tucker, William Eldon, *and* Castle, Molly. Sportsmen and their injuries  643–1

Tucker, William Hill. Eton memories  1435
 Eton of old  1434

Tuckwell, William. The ancient ways  1577

*Tudorvale colours.* R.A.H. Goodyear  6222

Tuer, Andrew White, *and* Fagan, Charles Edward. The first year of a silken reign 1837–8  893

Tufnell, Carleton F. The cricketer's "form at a glance"  132

*Tufty's cricket triumph*  6358

Tunbridge Wells C.C. Year book  2123

Tunnicliffe, John. The story of my cricketing career  8165

Turberville, H. Smith-. *See* Smith-Turberville, H.

*Turf culture.* F. Hope  302–1

*Turf wickets, their overhaul, preparation and repair.* W.B. Watt  314–2

Turk, Nigel, *and* Charman, Geoffrey. Cricket in Caterham  2623

"Turley, Charles," *pseud. See* Smith, Charles Turley

*The turn of the wheel.* P.G.H. Fender  4456

Turnbull, Maurice Joseph, *and* Allom, Maurice J.C. The book of the two Maurices  4467, 4746, 4881
 The two Maurices again  4637

Turnbull, R.W. Cheltenham College cricket 1855–1900  1390

Turner, Charles Thomas Biass. The quest for bowlers  745
 —, *and* Dobbie, J.A. Australian cricket (1896–7)  3379

Turner, E.G. Barnes C.C., 1919/1969  2614

Turner, E.S. Boys will be boys  6367–2

Turner, Edgar. Jack Ikin's benefit book  7747
 Soccer from the press box  7086

Turner, Edward Francis. More T leaves  6916

Turner, F.M. The [Leicestershire] county journal  2312

Turner, Glenn Maitland. My way  8166–2

*Turner (Glenn) benefit souvenir book 1978*  8166–1

Turner, Henry. Memories of club cricket  1711, 8167

Turner, Herbert. The life of John Briggs  7377

Turner, Herber Kyle. The world's all sports who's who for 1950  7258

Turner, J.R.F. Cricket scheme for Oxford Elementary Schools  1611

Turner, Matthias Cathrow. A saunter through Surrey  2635–1

*Turner (Stuart) benefit year 1979*  8167–2

Turner, Thomas. The diary  894, 6939
 The diary of a Georgian shopkeeper  894, 6939

Turner, Tom. Extra cover  6917

*Turner's guide to county cricket*  1752

The Turnham Green C.C. Fixtures  2400

*Turning things over.* E.V. Lucas  6719

Turton, Amos. Calverton C.C. 1869–1969  2480–3

*Tutbury C.C. 1872–1972*  2584

Tweedsmuir, 1st Baron. *See* Buchan, John, 1st Baron Tweedsmuir

Underwood, Peter. Horror man  7771
*Undiscovered ends.* W.H. Elliott  7513–3
*"Unforgettable days".* B. Darwin  6629–2
*The unforgotten prisoner.* R.C. Hutchinson  6013
*The Unicorns: ladies cricket team, South Africa, 1974–75*  3668–2
Union Castle Line. Visit of M.C.C. . . . to South Africa 1930–1  4638
Visit of M.C.C. . . . to South Africa 1938–39  4641
*Union C.C.C. handbook.* E.A. Leach  4069
*United India in Australia (1947–48).* H.J.H. Taleyarkhan  5635
United London Banks C.A. Rules  1332
.Silver jubilee 1974  1332–1
United Paints Ltd. Australian cricket tour of S. Africa 1957–58  5216–2
1956–1957 M.C.C. cricket tour of Southern Africa  4659
United States C.A. The American cricketer  4051
England tour 1968  4044, 5738
Newsletter/Newsbrief  4043
*U.S.A. v. Canada 1972.* C.C. of Louisville & United States C.A.  5752
*United States v. Canada Test match 1966.* Southern California C.A.  5751
United Tobacco Companies. Australian cricket tour S. Africa 1949–50  5205–2
Springbok souvenir 1947  5364–1
United Tobacco Cos. (South) Ltd. M.C.C. cricket tour South Africa 1948–49  4648–3
*An universal etymological English dictionary.* N. Bailey  862
Universal Mat Co. Ltd. How's that?: Universal cricket mats  342
*Universal spelling book.* D. Fenning  6978
Universities Athletic Union. "50 years of university sport."  1621
*University match. Oxford v. Cambridge.* A. Craig  6444
University of Cape Town. The Sabres England tour 1975  3624–3, 5389–1
University of Hong Kong. *The English Society.* Edmund Blunden sixty-five  7335–2
University of New South Wales C.C. Annual report  3407–5, 3482
*University of Pennsylvania, Cricket at.* A.H. Graham  4055
University of Queensland C.C. Annual report  3407–6, 3515–5
*Un-natural history not taught in bored schools.* J. Freyberg  6857
*Unpublished scores 1.* Association of Cricket Statisticians  101
Unstead, Robert John, *and* Henderson, W.F. Sport & entertainment in Australia  3350–2
*Unveiling of a plaque commemorating A.E.J. Collins' score*  7428
*Up against the school.* R.A.H. Goodyear  6220
*'Up at Lord's'.* G.E. Matheson  6584–1
*"Up at Lord's."* G.H.F. Nichols  6741
*Up from Somerset for the cup.* J. Davies  2554, 3077
*Up hill and down dale.* K.H. Ashley  6403
*Up Jenkins!* R. Hingley  6003
*Up stream.* W.H. Lewin  6706
*An uphill game.* J.N. Pentelow  6306
*Upminster C.C., 1858–1958*  1915
Upper Canada College. Centenary of Old "Boys" cricket  4125
Upper Chelsea Institute. The Institute journal  2350–1
Upper Sheringham C.C. Programme  2442
*The Uppingham cricket & fives songs.* E. Thring  6598
*"Uppingham cricket song, 1856."* E. Thring  6597
Uppingham Rovers C.C. List of members  1687

*Uppingham School songs and Borth lyrics.* E. Thring  1551, 6597
*Ups and downs.* S. Aumonier  6098
*Ups and downs of a public school.* F. Gale  1345, 6216
*The urn returns.* A.E.R Gilligan  4538
Usborne, Richard. "The shadow of Tom Brown"  1362–1
Usher, C.M. The story of the Edinburgh University Athletic Club  3214
Usher Art Gallery, *Lincoln.* Catalogue of an exhibition of pictures. . .  7002
*Ushering interlude.* E. Quinterley  6047
*UTAH-QCA coaching manual*  861–2
Uttar Pradesh C.A. England v. India 2nd Test (1961)  4822
England v. India 1963–64: 5th Test  4833
England v. India 1972–73: 4th Test  4850
Pakistan v. India: 2nd Test, (1960)  5721
Uttar Pradesh Sports Writers' Club. Match in aid of S. Mushtaq Ali (1970)  7896
Uttar Pradesh Test Management Cttee. Green Park greets you. . .  5293
Uttley, Alison. Carts and candlesticks  6783
Something for nothing  6784
Uva Club. Rules 1950, 1968  4019–2
Uxbridge C.C. Year book  2403
*Uxbridge C.C., A history of.* D.M. Griffiths  2402

—V—

*V & G knockout cup (1969–70).* Vehicle and General Group  3412
*V.R.A. jubileumboek 1914–64.* S.P. Mulder  4222
Vachell, Horace Annesley. The best of England  7105
The hill  6071
Vacuum Oil Company of South Africa Ltd. Visit to South Africa of the Australian team 1935–36  5201
*The vagabond papers.* J.S. James  3440–1, 3507–1
Vaidya, Sudhir. Figures of cricket  4348
Vinoo Mankad  7850
Vaile, Philip A. Swerve or the flight of the ball  746
Vajiphdar, Homi J. How to play good cricket  623
Vale, N.K. Cricket magazine  4123
*Vale of laughter.* B. Travers  8147
*The valiant stumper.* G.D. Martineau  762
Valley District C.C. Annual report  3515–13
*"The Valley of peace."* Christchurch Cinemas C.C.  3776
Vallings, Harold. Three brace of lovers  6813
Vallins, George Henry. After a manner  6537
*Valse I Zingari.* A.D. Porter  6588–1
*Valuable cricket collection of . . . T. Padwick.* A.J. Gaston  19
Van Booven, Henri C.A. Cricket. Het propaganda boekje  4210–3
Cricket-spel  476–1
Het fielden  758–1
*Van der Bijl, Vince.* Natal C.A.  8170–3
Van der Byl, Charles. My fifty years of sport  8171
Van der Merwe, Peter. *See* Merwe, Peter van der
Van Manen, H. Veld-uitzetten  758–2
Van Zeller, Claude Hubert. Willingly to school  1402, 8166
Vancouver Island Vagabonds Touring C.C. Club prospectus  4141–1
Who are the Vancouver Island Vagabonds?  4141–2
*"The vanity of old age."* A.G. Gardiner  6688
*Vanmelewe se rugby 1880 en vanmelewe se krieket 1874* A.B. de V. Pickard  3603–1
*Variety lane.* E.V. Lucas  6714
*Variety of men.* C.P. Snow, *baron Snow*  7645–2

Wells, Herbert George. Certain personal matters 8218
Experiment in autobiography 8219
You can't be too careful 6075–2
Welman, C. The song of the Emeriti 1257, 6604
Welsh Club Cricket Conference. *Abacus Office Equipment League*. Rules, fixtures and club directory 3165–1
Welsh C.A. Year book 3165–2
Welsh Secondary Schools' C.A. Wales v. England (1959) 1614
*Welsh wanderings*. J.M. Fleming 3193
Welwyn Garden City C.C. Fifty years of cricket 2052
Twenty fifth anniversary cricket week 2051
*The Wembley book of ball games* 7160
*Wembley Cricket & Sports Assoc*. Annual report 2404–1
*Wembley C.C. 1860–1960* 2405
*Wenkrieket*. P. Van der Merwe 598
*We're here!* D.G. Mackail 6027
Werfel, J. Newest collection of gymnastic games 4201
Walter and his pupils 4201
Wesley, Reginald. Artificial cricket pitches 316
West, Alfred. His first year at school 6360–2
West, Charles T. "Ranji": a new song 6605, 7982
Ranjitsinhji waltz 6605–1
West, George. Feltham's cricketer 1073
*West (John), In heartfelt remembrance of*. A. Craig 6444
West, John Milns. Shrewsbury 1539
West, Peter. The Alec Bedser 1953 benefit book 7326
Cricketers from Australia (1953) 5130
Cricketers from India (1952) 5615
Cricketers from New Zealand (1949) 5538
Cricketers from South Africa (1951) 5370
Cricketers from the West Indies (1950) 5423
The fight for the Ashes, 1953 5129
The fight for the Ashes, 1956 5155
Jack Robertson's benefit book 8006
Playfair cricket annual (1948–53) 1098
West, Stewart Ellis Lawrence. Century at Newlands 1864–1964 3657
West, Victoria Mary Sackville-. *See* Sackville-West, Victoria Mary
The West Africa Cricket Conference. First M.C.C. tour of West Africa 1975/76 4949–3
*West Australia v. Victoria* (1922) 3416
*West Australian cricket annual* (1902) 3378, 3577
West Bengal Women's C.A. World Cup competition (1978) 5828–11
West Bradford C.L. Official guide 2905
*West Bridgford: then and now*. R. Mellors 1027–1
West Bridgfordians C.C. Sobers benefit match v. Notts. (1972) 8070
*West country book, number one*. J.C. Trewin 5873
*West Drayton C.C. 1868–1968*. P.C. Bayley 2406
West End C.A. Handbook 2340
West Essex Gazette. Cricket annual 1898
*West Indian adventure*. E.W. Swanton 4703
*West Indian cricket*. C. Nicole 3673
*West Indian cricket team: . . . first tour in England, 1900* 5407
*West Indian cricket tour 1905* 4678–1
*West Indian cricket tour 1963* 5439
*The West Indian cricketers in England* (1906) 5409
*West Indian digest* 5404–2
West Indian National Association. West Indies—1963—England 5441
*The West Indian sportsman* 3683
*The West Indies*. T. Cozier 5404–1
West Indies Bd. of Control for International Cricket Matches. Constitution, by-laws and rules (1928) 5405

West Indies Cricket Board of Control. First umpires' convention (1962) 281
M.C.C. West Indies tour, 1967–68: fixtures 4725
Red stripe 8071
Rules 3676
The West Indies in Australia and New Zealand 1968–9: fixtures 5486
*West Indies & All Jamaica v. M.C.C.* (1930). Jamaica Cricket Bd. of Control 4693
*The West Indies at Lord's*. A. Ross 5435
*The West Indies cricket annual* (1970–) 3682
*West Indies cricket challenge 1957*. B. Harris 5426
*The West Indies cricket guide 1928*. F.S. Ashley-Cooper 3669, 5410
*West Indies cricket history*. L.S. Smith.3674, 5406
*West Indies cricket souvenir 73 programme* 5458
*West Indies cricket team: Australian tour 1930–31* 5463
*The West Indies cricket team in Australia & N.Z., 1968–9*. West Indies Cricket Bd. of Control 5486
*West Indies cricket team visit to Madras 1949*. C.K. Haridass 5499
*West Indies cricket tour* (1939). A.W. Simpson 5416
*West Indies cricket tour 1963*. I. Rosenwater 5434
*West Indies cricket tour England* (1950). A.W. Simpson 5422
*West Indies cricket tour guide, 1975–76*. Australian cricket 5487–3
*West Indies cricket tour of England 1933*. A.W. Simpson 5414
*West Indies cricket tour of England* (1939) 5417
*West Indies cricket tour of England 1963* 5440
*West Indies cricket tour of India 1958–59*. Bd. of Control for Cricket in India 5501
*West Indies cricket tour of India 1966–67*. Bd. of Control for Cricket in India 5508
*West Indies cricket tour of India* (1974–75). Bd. of Control for Cricket in India 5516–1
*West Indies cricket tour of Sri Lanka 1975*. Ceylon Tobacco Co. Ltd. 5519–3
*West Indies cricket tour to Sri Lanka . . . 1975*. Bd. of Control for Cricket in Sri Lanka 5519–1
West Indies Cricket Umpires Association. Ninth biennial convention 1979 281–1
*West Indies cricketers tour of India 1948–49*. Sport & Pastime 5500
*West Indies XI v. India XI, Brabourne Stadium* (1958) 5505
*The West Indies in Australia* (1930–31). "Old Colour," pseud. 5461
*The West Indies in Australia 1968–69*. L.J. Henderson 5483
*West Indies in India 1966–67*. C.K. Haridass 5511
*West Indies in India 1974–75*. C.K. Haridass 5516–2
*West Indies in India 1974–75*. M. Salim 5516–7
*West Indies in India 1974–75*. S. Saraiya 5516–8
*West Indies in India 1978–79*. C.K. Haridass 5516–12
*West Indies—1963—England*. Wina Magazine 5441
*West Indies 1973 tour to England*. L. Williams 5460
*West Indies '76*. K. Bhimani 5647–1
*West Indies revisited*. E.W. Swanton 4710
*West Indies souvenir tour programme* (1957) 5429
*West Indies souvenir tour programme* (1966) 5451–1
*"West Indies Test cricket 1928–1978"*. C. Goodwin & others 5404–2
*The West Indies Test cricketer*. H.T. Bajnath 5404
*West Indies Tests pictorial* (1951) 5469–1
*West Indies : . . . tour 1948–49*, Programme of. . . . Bd. of Control for Cricket in India 5498
*West Indies tour 1951–1952*. Australian Broadcasting Commission 5464
*West Indies tour 1960–61*. Australian Broadcasting Commission 5470
*West Indies tour 1971*. Women's C.A. 3113, 4732